Art & Enterprise

American Decorative Art, 1825–1917
The Virginia Carroll Crawford Collection

Donald C. Peirce

High Museum of Art

in association with Antique Collectors' Club Ltd.

Art & Enterprise: American Decorative Art, 1825–1917, The Virginia Carroll Crawford Collection was organized by the High Museum of Art, Atlanta. The exhibition and catalogue are made possible by Virginia Carroll Crawford.

Generous support for the exhibition is also provided by Corporate Environments, The John Williams Family Foundation, and The Glover Family Foundation.

Frontispiece and page 12: *Cabinet,* ca. 1875 (detail), no. 107
Page 17: *Teapot,* 1830s (detail), no. 5
Page 31: *Window Pane,* ca. 1840 (detail), no. 11
Page 55: *Side Chair,* ca. 1850 (detail), no. 33
Page 73: *Sofa and Four Side Chairs,* ca. 1855 (detail), no. 44
Page 105: *Sofa,* 1865–1875 (detail), no. 66
Page 161: *Wooton Patent Office Cabinet Secretary,* 1880–1884 (detail), no. 87
Page 177: *Sideboard,* 1875–1885 (detail), no. 89
Page 193: *Bed,* ca. 1880 (detail), no. 108
Page 257: *Bowl,* 1900 (detail), no. 152
Page 281: *Pitcher,* patented 1911 (detail), no. 168
Page 297: *Side Chair,* designed 1903 (detail), no. 188
Page 361: *Elevator Grill with Decorative Plate,* 1893–1894 (detail), no. 221

Distributed by
Antique Collectors' Club Ltd.
Market Street Industrial Park
Wappingers Falls, NY 12590
www.antiquecc.com

For the High Museum of Art

Kelly Morris, Manager of Publications
Anna Bloomfield, Associate Editor
Melissa Duffes Wargo, Assistant Editor

Produced by Marquand Books, Inc., Seattle
Designed by Susan E. Kelly
Proofread by Sharon Vonasch
Index by Sigrid Asmus

High Museum of Art, Atlanta
June 12–September 12, 1999

Library of Congress Cataloging-in-Publication Data
Peirce, Donald C.
Art & enterprise : American decorative art, 1825–1917 : the Virginia Carroll Crawford collection / Donald C. Peirce.
p. cm.
Catalog of an exhibition held at the High Museum of Art, Atlanta, Ga., June 12–Sept. 12, 1999.
Includes bibliographical references and index.
ISBN 0-939802-87-2 (hardcover : alk. paper)
1. Decorative arts—United States—History—19th century Exhibitions. 2. Decorative arts—United States—History—20th century Exhibitions. 3. Crawford, Virginia Carroll—Art collections Exhibitions. 4. Decorative arts—Private collections—Georgia—Atlanta Exhibitions. 5. Decorative arts—Georgia—Atlanta Exhibitions. 6. High Museum of Art Exhibitions. I. High Museum of Art. II. Title. III. Title: Art and enterprise.
NK807.P44 1999
745'.0973'074758231—dc21 99-22014

PRINTED BY CS GRAPHICS PTE., LTD., SINGAPORE

Introduction

In December 1979, I had a job interview with Katharine Gross Farnham, curator of decorative art at the High Museum of Art, who was seeking a successor for her position. I was especially interested by Kitty's vision for a collection of nineteenth-century American decorative art and her enthusiastic description of a benevolent and enlightened patron, Virginia Carroll Crawford, who had endorsed the project. In the 1970s, general art museums were just beginning to collect nineteenth-century American decorative art, but few were focusing on this period. The Brooklyn Museum of Art, where I was then associate curator of decorative art, was an exception. It had begun to collect this material around 1940, and in 1953 it became the first art museum to install nineteenth-century American period rooms. When I returned to New York after the interview, I met with the Crawford Collection's consultant, David A. Hanks. I was impressed with the beginnings of the collection, which were being stored in a warehouse because the High lacked exhibition and storage space in its existing building. The promise of supervising the development of the Crawford Collection and the plan for a new museum building were key to my accepting the position when it was offered to me by Director Gudmund Vigtel, who shared Kitty's enthusiasm for both Mrs. Crawford and the collection.

When I came to Atlanta at the end of April 1980, I was delighted to find Mrs. Crawford as gracious and sensible as Kitty had described her. Mrs. Emory Cocke, a friend of Mrs. Crawford, was collecting English ceramics for the Museum, and my work with these ladies on their collections was a highlight of my first decade at the High. The Crawford Collection was first exhibited on much of the second floor of the new High Museum of Art building when it opened in 1983, in an installation by Richard Meier, the building's architect. The collection remained there with its many additions until 1996. Mrs. Crawford continues to develop the collection as new research evolves.

This catalogue covers the years between about 1830 and the First World War and is arranged chronologically by style. This orderly parade of styles is a bit of a distortion, of course. In reality, styles overlapped and often lasted thirty or more years after their introduction, but examples in the Crawford Collection are usually early and documented—many can be specifically placed and dated. Threading through the chronology, themes emerge in the Crawford Collection—for example, industrialism in the United States to the 1850s, and works designed and influenced by architects, from about 1850 to the First World War. Industrial technology had an amazing and far-reaching effect on nineteenth-century decorative art and consumer goods and habits in general. It helped new styles spread quickly and made them more affordable to a broad population. Industrialization also sparked such reactions against technology as the Aesthetic movement of the 1870s and the Arts and Crafts movement of the early twentieth century. In contrast to the mass-produced work made possible by industrialization, furniture designed by architects was generally intended for a specific interior.

Nineteenth-century innovations in transportation—steamboats, railroads, and canals—enabled more efficient distribution of manufactured goods and helped create national markets for work produced in New York and other eastern centers. Photography made it possible for the Gorham Manufacturing Company to produce illustrated notebooks that its wholesalers could show retailers. Such catalogues became standard in twentieth-century merchandising, and only now, at the end of the twentieth century, are they being replaced by the Internet.

World's fairs were another important nineteenth-century means of marketing. Manufacturers who displayed at the expositions gained prestige, particularly when they received an award of merit. A number of objects in the Crawford Collection were shown at international expositions. These world's fairs, beginning with the Great Exhibition at the Crystal Palace in London in 1851, were media events, and the extensive press coverage spread the latest taste and illustrated the most admired products of their times. At the Exposition Universelle in Paris in 1878, Tiffany and Company became the first American firm to receive international acclaim. The marketing skills of its founder, Charles Tiffany, and the silver creations of its chief designer, Edward C. Moore—a man of broad tastes and extraordinary skills—made the palatial Union Square store in Manhattan a destination for shoppers and tourists in New York.

On the eve of the American Revolution, Philadelphia was the second largest city in the British Empire and by far the largest and most sophisticated in the colonies. In the nineteenth century, New York emerged as the largest American city and the center of fashion and taste. The completion of the Erie Canal across the state of New York in 1828 linked the Hudson River and Manhattan with the Great Lakes and the rapidly expanding markets of the West, yet until the Civil War, affluent Americans in the South and West continued to shop along Philadelphia's Chestnut Street.

New York was the port of entry for many European craftsmen. Unrest in Germany led many to emigrate, and by 1850 furniture makers such as John Henry Belter and Gustave Herter were in New York. Parisian-trained furniture makers Alexander Roux and Leon Marcotte were among the city's most fashionable in the 1860s and 1870s. The European influence on American decorative art had begun with the English, Spanish, and French settlements in the New World, and European taste dominated the United States until the First World War. The continuing immigration of workers and designers increased the European influence in furniture, glass, metals, ceramics, textiles, and other decorative arts. Affluent Americans, manufacturers, and designers looked to both London and Paris for the latest in fashion, and European design periodicals and pattern books were readily available in the major cities of the United States soon after their publication.

The close relationships among merchants, managers, craftsmen, designers, and workers within each field, especially those with family ties, were vital to nineteenth-century American decorative art. For example, New York luxury goods dealer Baldwin Gardiner began his career working for his brother in the Boston silversmithing partnership of Fletcher and Gardiner. He moved with the firm to Philadelphia, where he and the two partners married the three Veron sisters. He then joined his brother-in-law Samuel Veron in establishing a luxury goods mercantile partnership before moving on his own to New York. Edwin Bennett, a successful pottery entrepreneur, grew up in a family of potters in England and joined his brothers in various ceramic enterprises before starting his own pottery in Baltimore. William L. Libbey revitalized the New England Glass Works in Massachusetts, while his son Edward Drummond Libbey later moved the glassworks to Toledo, Ohio, and changed the name to the Libbey Glass Company. Nineteenth-century American decorative art and business histories are filled with such family stories.

During the period covered by the Crawford Collection, the exploitation of natural resources, the Civil War, and the explosive growth of industry and commerce created enormous personal fortunes that were often spent lavishly on country estates, palatial town houses, suburban villas, and resort cottages. While industrial innovation was celebrated at international expositions, handcraftsmanship was still widely admired. Beautiful carving, exquisite marquetry, and luxurious and exotic materials characterize the finest American furniture before the Arts and Crafts movement put forth a simpler aesthetic.

The Virginia Carroll Crawford Collection at the High Museum of Art celebrates the achievements of diverse designers, workers, craftspeople, and technicians as the United States was beginning to mature as an industrial, enterprising, and artistic nation.

Donald C. Peirce
Curator of Decorative Art

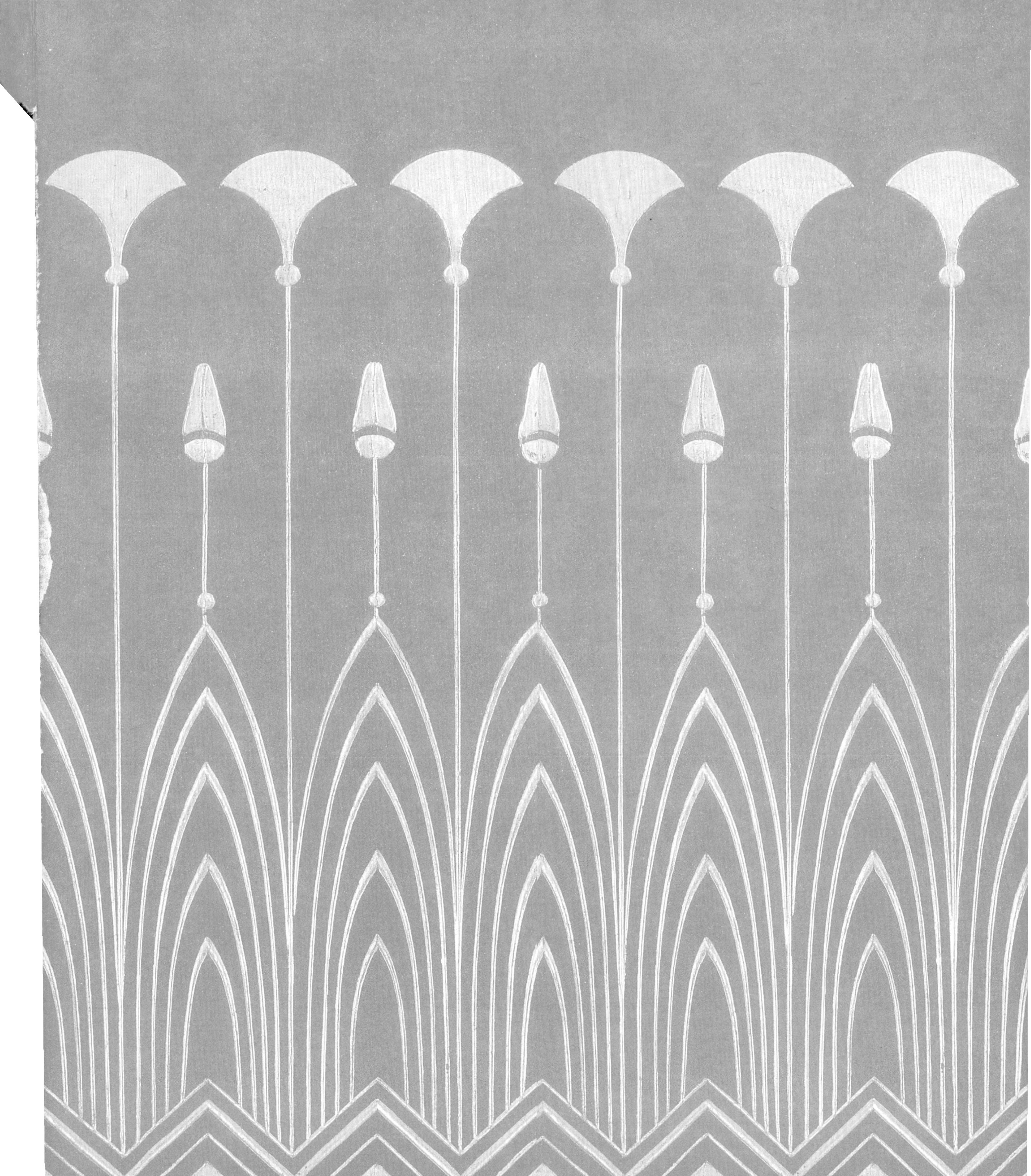

Art & Enterprise

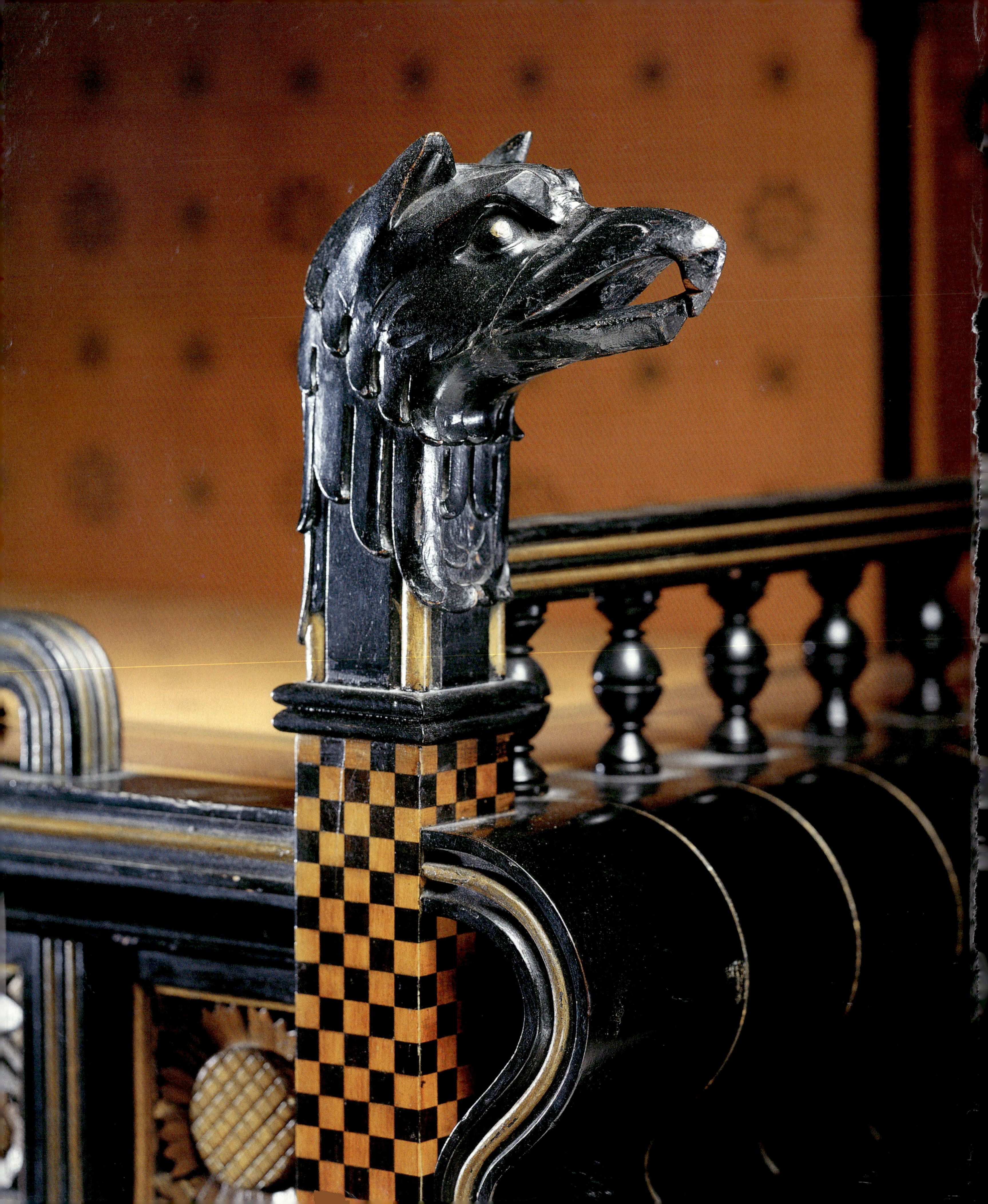

Contents

Foreword

THE HISTORY OF AN ART museum's collection almost always involves exceptional people who are either outstanding donors, astute private collectors, magnanimous philanthropists, or active scholars and agile curators. What is required to build excellence is the exquisite combination of funding, expertise, and, finally, the identification of the choice objects that are available at a particular moment. The High Museum of Art's premier collection of American decorative art has been an exemplar of just such a combination.

The patron, in this instance, is Virginia Carroll Crawford, whose involvement with this institution began more than thirty years ago, when, as a founding member of the Forward Arts Foundation, she and a dozen other visionary women began to raise critical funds for what was a fledgling museum in a growing southern city. At first, Mrs. Crawford, with the guidance of the High's director Gudmund Vigtel, purchased a couple of paintings as well as two choice examples of American furniture for the Museum. In the few years following the American Bicentennial, she had not yet determined a consistent direction for her collection. However, in 1978 Mrs. Crawford was elected to the Board of Directors of the High, eventually serving for two terms (four years) as the Vice President of the prestigious Acquisitions Committee, now the Collections Committee. It was at about this time that Mrs. Crawford, working closely with the Museum's curator of decorative art Kitty Farnham, determined what would become the ultimate direction of the Virginia Carroll Crawford Collection, which is the subject of this publication and the exhibition it accompanies.

Together they identified a time period of nearly one hundred years of American decorative art, 1825–1917—from just after the colonial and Federal periods to America's entry into the First World War—and with the support of generous grants from Mrs. Crawford, the High began purchasing important and major works from a period and area that were undervalued. Hence, the Museum was able to make significant acquisitions ahead of the trends that defined the decorative art market of that time, while compiling a survey of this period.

But Virginia Crawford is more than simply a patron and director of the High Museum of Art. She is one of those rare individual philanthropists who understand that building a collection of substance for a public that includes neophyte museum visitors as well as scholars and connoisseurs involves the study and documentation of the objects, not to mention their photography and conservation. Thus, as the High is the beneficiary of the splendid objects purchased and donated by Mrs. Crawford, we are also fortunate to be the recipient of generous grants given by this same outstanding patron to ensure proper care and recording of the material. Her support has allowed us to publish this catalogue, and it even provides support for the ongoing identification of important objects still in the market for potential purchase and donation. To this end, the High has retained the services of David Hanks, a specialist in this field, to be the Museum's "eyes" in New York galleries and auctions.

The Crawford Collection was revealed for the first time when the High's Richard Meier building opened in 1983. It is not unimportant to mention here that Mrs. Crawford made a significant contribution to the building campaign of the early 1980s, as she did again in 1991 for a collections endowment, and again in 1993 during a general operating endowment campaign. Simply said, the High Museum of Art has never had a patron whose focus on collection has had such a major impact, while at the same time someone who recognizes the totality of needs attending such an enterprise. Virginia Carroll Crawford is, as many have said for all of these years, a curator's dream patron.

It is to Donald C. Peirce, the High's curator of decorative art since 1980, that the special privilege of working with this magnificent patron falls. Donald has been a consummate professional from the beginning, as his entries and selections testify. He is a true lover of this splendid material and has worked closely with his colleagues and peers, and most of all with Mrs. Crawford, to enable the High to have one of the finest collections of American decorative art of this period in the world.

We rejoice in the partnership that is modeled in this catalogue and exhibition. However, while the combination mentioned above is essential to creating important and compelling collections, without the patron whose vision and standards drive the project, there is little, if anything, to celebrate. Hence, it is to Virginia Carroll Crawford, an elegant lady with an open mind, a determined spirit, and a public-minded generosity, that we owe the depth of our gratitude for this remarkable achievement. For it is through the objects that make up the Virginia Carroll Crawford Collection that the High Museum of Art is best known as a collecting institution. No museum could ask to be better represented.

Ned Rifkin
Nancy and Holcombe T. Green, Jr. Director

Preface

Katharine Gross Farnham, Curator of Decorative Art at the High Museum of Art from 1971 to 1980, was greatly impressed—as were many other curators—by the lavish and comprehensive 1970 exhibition at The Metropolitan Museum of Art, *19th-Century America: Furniture and Other Decorative Arts.* Other art institutions had acquired nineteenth-century objects earlier, notably the Philadelphia and Brooklyn Museums, but the Metropolitan's exhibition was the first to give widespread recognition to a full range of nineteenth-century decorative art.

Around this time, Mrs. Farnham was seeking a distinctive emphasis for decorative art at the High. In 1973, Mr. and Mrs. Emory Cocke began acquiring eighteenth-century English ceramics for the Museum, and their determined and passionate search assured the Museum of future strength in that area. In 1976, an anonymous donor made possible the acquisition of five key examples of eighteenth-century American furniture, but growth in that area was limited by the rarity and cost of museum-worthy objects. As a Bicentennial project, the Museum presented the exhibition and catalogue *Furniture of the Georgia Piedmont,* which gave southern regional emphasis to its decorative art program. But it seemed restrictive to limit the collection to regional objects. It was in *19th-Century America,* however, that Mrs. Farnham recognized an area that had been overlooked by many other American art museums, which generally stopped collecting at about 1825, when the Industrial Revolution expanded mass-market production.

In 1978, Virginia Carroll Crawford was elected to the Board of Directors of the High Museum of Art, and she expressed an interest to Director Gudmund Vigtel in developing a specific museum collection. Catherine Lynn, former curator at the Atlanta Historical Society, created a rationale for developing a nineteenth-century American decorative art collection at the High. She presented information on American designers, craftsmen, and opinion makers and on their European counterparts, who greatly influenced American taste. The great social, political, technological, and economic upheavals of the century provided rich interpretive background. Such a collection would be locally meaningful, since the century had seen Atlanta's transformation from a railroad crossing laid in 1837 to a major commercial city by World War I. With this rationale, Mrs. Farnham and Vigtel presented the idea of forming a nineteenth-century decorative art collection to Mrs. Crawford.

Virginia Crawford had enjoyed a longtime interest in decorative art, and even though this period was then outside her personal interest, she was attracted by the relative availability, the stylistic diversity, and the meticulous craftsmanship of nineteenth-century custom-made pieces. With rare wisdom, she understood the underlying needs and expenses of developing an important collection, and with a receptivity that was daring for the time and place, she endorsed the first systematic attempt to form a comprehensive art museum collection of American nineteenth-century decorative art of the highest quality.

In 1979, I came to Atlanta to lecture on an exhibition I had organized for the Smithsonian Institution, *The Decorative Designs of Frank Lloyd Wright,* which was on view at the High. In discussions with Mrs. Farnham, I found the idea of the Crawford Collection highly appealing, and I agreed to become a consultant based in New York. Manhattan dealers and auctions were then beginning to offer important works from the nineteenth century, and conservators and other services necessary for the new collection were readily available there.

In May 1979, we made our first acquisition for the Crawford Collection: an impressive cabinet of rosewood and marquetry with the label of the leading Baltimore furniture maker Thomas Godey (see no. 63). Its elaborate style, with exquisite gilt-bronze mountings, marquetry musical symbols, and porcelain plaque, related to New York examples by Alexander Roux (see nos. 46, 61) and other French-trained craftsmen. Godey's address on the label established that this high-style cabinet was made between 1867 and 1872 in Baltimore, a city with a post–Civil War furniture trade that was little known in 1979. The object testified to the broad appeal of elaborate Parisian-style furniture made outside New York in the 1860s and 1870s. The Godey cabinet was a landmark first acquisition for its extraordinary visual presence alone, but the label established contexts of a specific maker, time, and place, and gave it a historical background that greatly enhanced its importance.

The Godey purchase also established a procedure that would continue in the development of the collection. I discussed with Mrs. Farnham, and later with Donald C. Peirce, each potential acquisition, which was then presented to the Director for consideration. With the unanimous endorsement of the curatorial staff and administration, each object was then presented to Mrs. Crawford. With her final approval, objects were recommended for acquisition.

Today the Crawford Collection is internationally known not only for the quality of individual objects but also for its great breadth and depth, as illustrated in this catalogue and exhibition. Over the last two decades, the High Museum of Art has lent examples from it to major national exhibitions about nineteenth-century American art. Thus the Crawford Collection continues to enlarge scholarly knowledge as well as public appreciation of this now widely heralded period.

Mrs. Crawford's enthusiasm for nineteenth-century American material has increased along with the collection. Originally envisioned as a four-year project that would conclude when the new Museum building opened in 1983, the Crawford Collection continues to grow, and it now has over 227 objects. Its goal remains constant: to represent the period from 1825 to 1917 in American decorative art with masterpieces whose superior artistic quality is matched by their historical significance.

David A. Hanks
Consultant for the Virginia Carroll Crawford Collection

Acknowledgments

Katharine Gross Farnham, Curator of Decorative Art from 1971 to 1980, first envisioned a nineteenth-century American decorative art collection at the High Museum of Art. With Virginia Carroll Crawford as patron, she initiated it with consultant David A. Hanks. Hanks and I have discussed each possible acquisition at length, and we agreed to concentrate on objects of great quality and visual appeal, and whenever possible those that are documented. David has been enormously helpful not only in choosing objects, but also with many catalogue entries. I am also grateful to Ulysses Dietze, Curator of Decorative Arts at the Newark Museum, and Kenneth L. Ames of the Bard Center for Graduate Studies in the Decorative Arts, who provided two days of suggestions and insights into the organization of this exhibition.

The National Endowment for the Arts provided a generous grant for cataloguing the Museum's overall American decorative art collection, which enabled Kevin Stayton, Curator of Decorative Arts at the Brooklyn Museum of Art, and Alice Cooney Frelingheisen, Curator of American Decorative Arts at The Metropolitan Museum of Art, to examine and evaluate the silver and ceramic collections. Each provided valuable insights and made wonderful suggestions for further developments to the collections. These two scholars also reviewed drafts of the silver and ceramic catalogue entries. The Winterthur Museum, Libraries, and Gardens provided grants for two months of research at that remarkable scholarly resource. Under Eleanor Neville Thompson, Head of Printed Books and Periodicals, the research library staff has been enormously helpful in person, in correspondence, and over the telephone with research questions and photography inquiries.

Three curatorial assistants have significantly contributed to this catalogue over the last decade with conscientious good humor. For the last three years, Margaret Reneke has worked with entries and coordinated efforts of the publications and curatorial departments. She has secured photographs from individuals and institutions, and has supervised in-house photography with Peter Harholdt. Margaret also conducted invaluable research in the U.S. Patent Office record copies at the Georgia Institute of Technology, confirmed bibliography entries on the Internet, and pursued countless incidental research missions at Georgia Tech and Emory University. Linda Boyte began working with entries in their earliest forms in 1991 and supervised the first four years of photography. Colleen Callahan assembled photocopies of photographs and documentary information into five massive loose-leaf notebooks, making the collection somewhat portable during early research travels. Earlier decorative art assistants Rhetta Kilpatrick, Martha Sweeny, Elizabeth Bacchetti, Woodrow Mankin, Elizabeth Lang, Anne Woodworth, and Lynne Stradling coordinated developments of the Crawford Collection. Manager of Exhibitions Marjorie Harvey has sensitively reinstalled the collection over the years, and designed the special exhibition accompanying this publication. Technician Saskia Benjamin has prepared objects for the exhibition, and over the years preparators Mickey Clark and Evan Forfar carefully maintained the collections.

Gudmund Vigtel, Director of the Museum from 1963 to 1991, enthusiastically endorsed the collection from its inception, and Ned Rifkin has supported its development since his appointment as Director in 1991. Michael Shapiro, Deputy Director for Programs and Chief Curator, has thoughtfully and creatively weighed and discussed each acquisition as it was considered and has offered his excellent eye and expertise since 1994.

Documentary images have been provided by companies, institutions, and individuals, with special courtesies from Susan E. Perry, Library, Art Institute of Chicago; Michael Rose, Visual Arts Archivist, Atlanta History Center; Karen Tates Denton, Rights and Reproductions, The

Brooklyn Museum of Art; Dr. Mark N. Brown, Curator of Manuscripts, Brown University Library; Emily S. Rosen, Product Development Officer, Cleveland Museum of Art; Angela Giral, Director, Avery Architectural and Fine Arts Library, Columbia University, City of New York; Jill Bloomer, Department of Image Rights and Reproductions, Cooper-Hewitt National Design Museum, Smithsonian Institution; Michael K. Flanagan, Registrar, Everson Museum of Art; Margo Stipe, Registrar, Frank Lloyd Wright Archives, Frank Lloyd Wright Foundation; Laura Green, Library, Georgia Institute of Technology; Nina Gray; Barbara Hall, Archivist, Hagley Museum; Ellen Sulser, Iowa State Archives; Jeff Goldman, Photo Services, Maryland Historical Society; The Metropolitan Museum of Art; Wendy Rogers, Rights and Reproductions, Museum of the City of New York; Karen L. Otis, Office of Rights and Reproductions, Museum of Fine Arts, Boston; Paula Fleming, Anthropological Archives, National Museum of Natural History, Smithsonian Institution; Meg Haley, Library, Old Sturbridge Village; The Philadelphia Museum of Art; Lynn Horton, Curator of History, Sandwich Glass Museum; J. Duston Wees, Photograph and Slide Librarian, Sterling and Francine Clark Institute; Louisa Gann, Archives Coodinator, Tiffany and Company; Barbara Bezat, Northwest Architectural Archives, University of Minnesota Libraries; and Julia Moore Converse, Director, Architectural Archives of the University of Pennsylvania.

Many friends, colleagues, collectors, scholars, and students have shared their expertise, research, knowledge, and encouragement: James E. Allen; Anna D'Ambrosio, Curator of Decorative Arts, Munson-Williams-Proctor Arts Institute; Gary Baker, Curator of Glass, Chrysler Museum of Art; Dr. Crawford F. Barnett; David Brenneman, Frances B. Bunzl Family Curator of European Art, High Museum of Art; Charles E. Buckley; Bert Denker, Decorative Arts Photographic Collection, Winterthur Museum; Ellen Denker; Martin Eidelberg, Rutgers University; Anita Ellis, Curator of Decorative Arts, Cincinnati Art Museum; Donald L. Fennimore, Curator of Metals, Winterthur Museum; Dr. Lamar F. Fleming; Roy Frangiamore; Dr. Edward D. Frederickson; Nina Gray; Barry Harwood, Associate Curator of Decorative Arts, The Brooklyn Museum of Art; Sally Hawkins; Henry Hawley, Chief Curator of Later Western Art, Cleveland Museum of Art; Samuel J. Hough; Katherine Howe, Curator of Decorative Arts, The Museum of Fine Arts, Houston; Deanne Levison; Jack Linsey, Curator of American Decorative Arts, The Philadelphia Museum of Art; Millie B. McGehee; Dr. Richard Maxwell; Dr. Milton Mazo; Dr. David M. Moss; Susan Myers, Curator and Chair, Division of Social History, National Museum of American History, Smithsonian Institution; Dianne H. Pilgrim, Director, Cooper-Hewitt National Design Museum, Smithsonian Institution; Billy Poole; Lynn Springer Roberts; John C. Roesel; Arlene Palmer Schwind; Jane Spellman Shadel, Curator of American Glass and Chief Curator, Corning Museum of Glass; J. Garrison and Diana Stradling; Peter Strickland; Kenneth R. Trapp, Curator in Charge, Renwick Gallery, National Museum of American Art; Charles Venable, Chief Curator, Dallas Museum of Art; Katherine Hoover Voorsanger, Associate Curator of American Decorative Arts, The Metropolitan Museum of Art; Deborah Dependahl Waters, Curator of Decorative Arts, The Museum of the City of New York; Earl Webster; Gregory Weidman; Dr. John D. Whelchel; and Janet Zapata.

This handsome book, distributed by the Antique Collectors' Club, is the culmination of years of effort by the Museum's Publication Department, headed by Kelly Morris. Associate Editor Anna Bloomfield and Assistant Editor Melissa Wargo (and editors Amanda Woods and Margaret Wallace before them) have helped distill the mountain of research and thousands of words into the texts that finally appear in print. Marquand Books of Seattle, led by Ed Marquand, produced the book, which was deftly designed by Susan E. Kelly.

In the end, of course, greatest recognition should go to a remarkable and gracious patron, Virginia Carroll Crawford, who enthusiastically supported this project from its beginning.

Donald C. Peirce
Curator of Decorative Art
The High Museum of Art

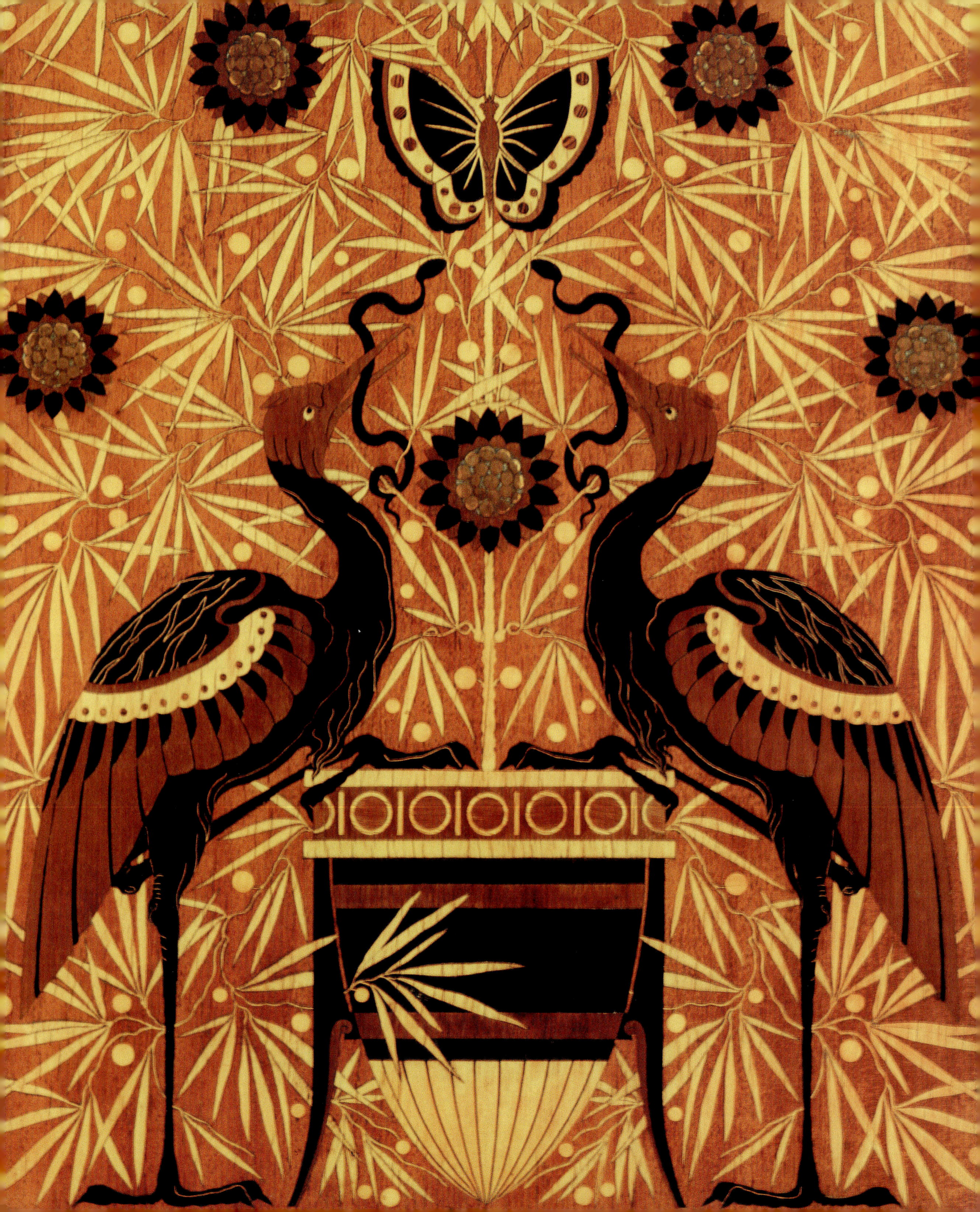

Catalogue of the Collection

Classicism, 1830s

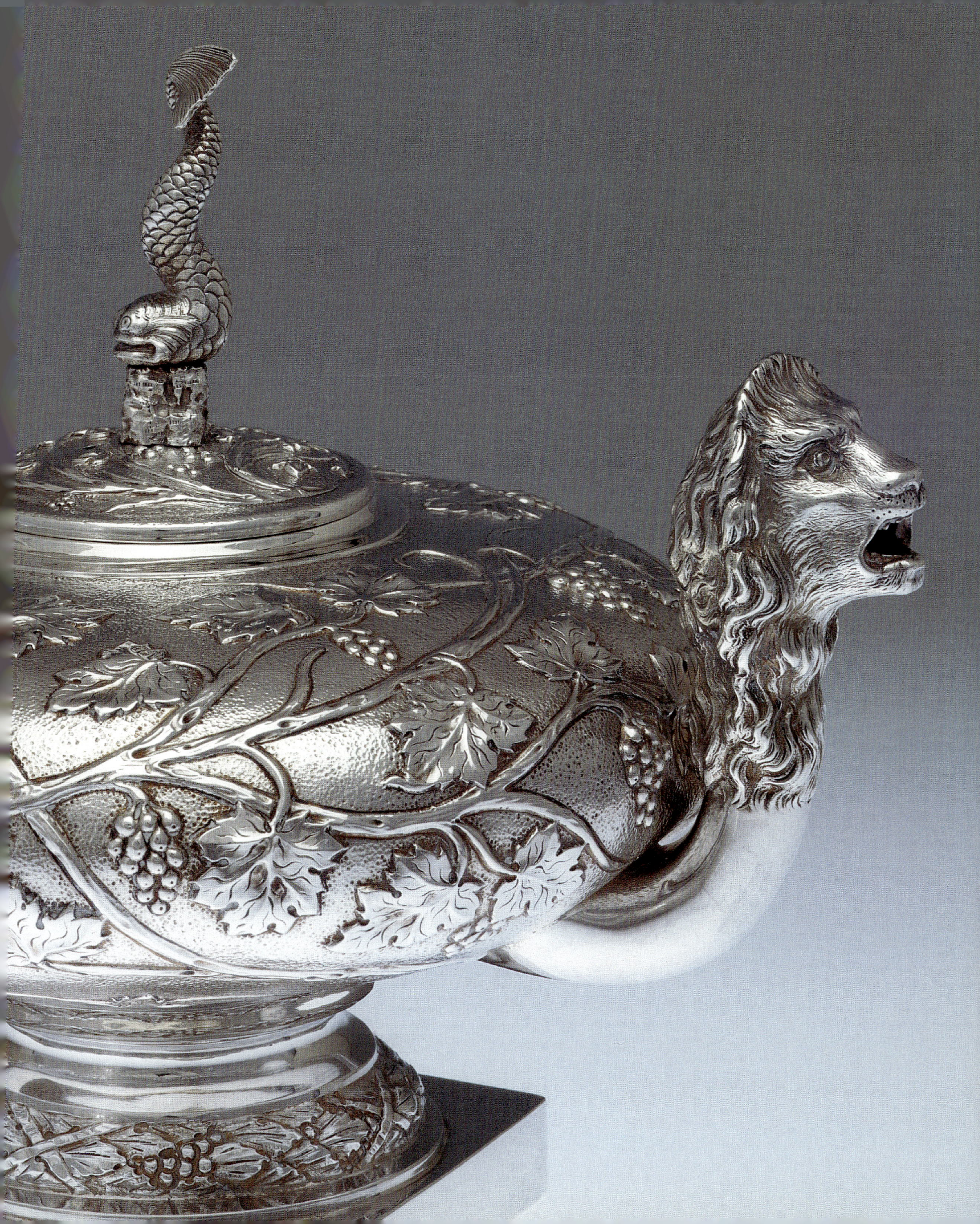

1.

Tea Set, dated 1832

Edward Lownes (1792–1834), Philadelphia
Silver
Hot water urn: 13¼ × 9¼ × 11 inches
Teapot: 12 × 11¼ × 6¼ inches
Teapot: 11½ × 11⅛ × 6 inches
Sugar bowl: 10½ × 9 × 9 inches
Cream pitcher: 9⅛ × 7¼ × 4½ inches
Marks: Stamped in each corner of the underside of square pedestal foot of each piece, *E. Lownes;* scratched on bottom of cream pitcher, *4*
Inscription: Engraved in script, partially enclosed within calligraphic eagle on side of each piece, *PRESENTED TO JOHN SWIFT ESQ./by his/Fellow Citizens/as a testimonial of their/Gratitude/ for his services at the/Arch Street Prison/on Sunday August 5, 1832/ during the prevalence of the MALIGNANT CHOLERA*
1982.301.1–.4, 1988.25

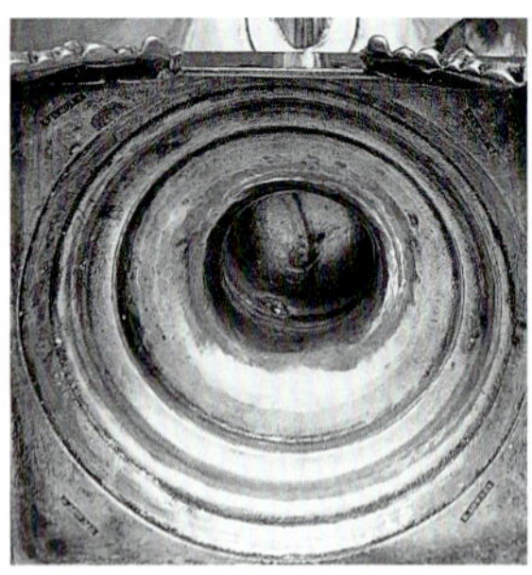

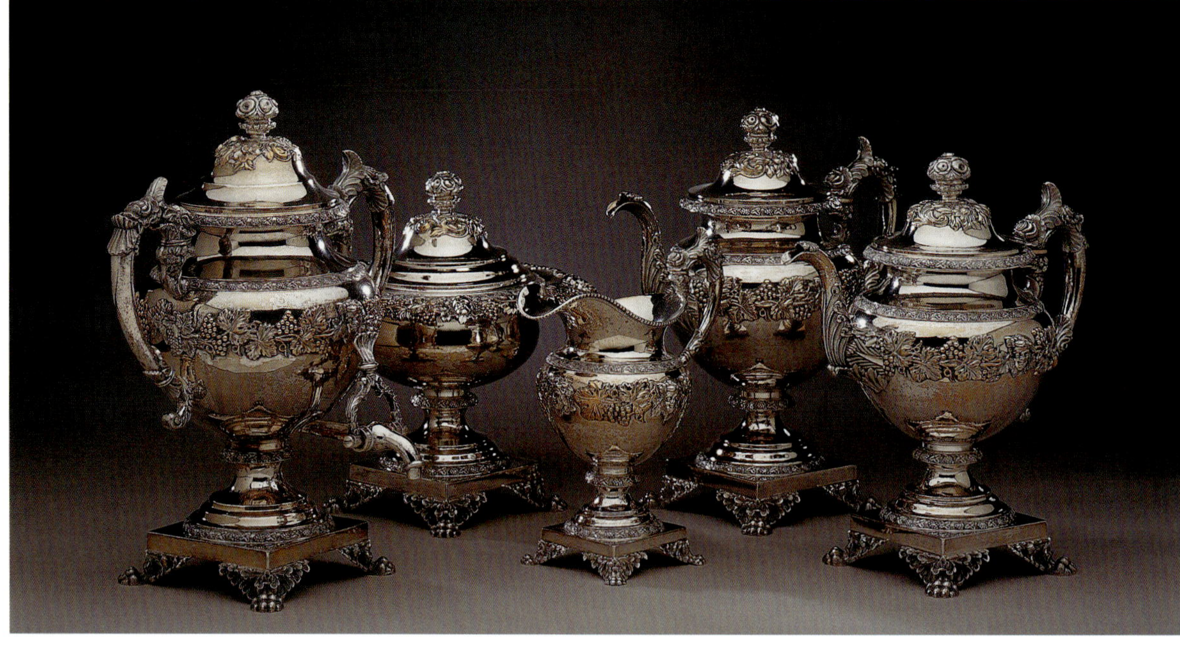

EDWARD LOWNES, maker of this monumental classical silver service, was born into a prominent silver-making family whose ancestors were Quaker settlers of Pennsylvania's Delaware County in the eighteenth century. His father, Philadelphia engraver Caleb Lownes, has been credited with designing the Commonwealth of Pennsylvania coat of arms in 1778. Perhaps as a result of his religion, Caleb Lownes was an early supporter of prison reform in Philadelphia in the late eighteenth century, which may have led to Edward Lownes receiving commissions from prison officials for works such as the Crawford service. It was presented to Philadelphia Mayor John Swift for his diligent work at the Arch Street Prison during a cholera outbreak in 1832.[1] As a young man, Edward Lownes may have worked with his father, which would explain the extraordinary engraving on this service. He may also have served an apprenticeship with his silversmith uncle, Joseph Lownes, in whose Philadelphia shop he was working as early as 1811. After Joseph retired in 1816, Edward worked in partnership with Henry Erwin at their silver manufactory at 191 South Second Street. A year later, he was listed in the city directory at his own shop at 10½ South Third Street. In 1821, Lownes moved to Chestnut Street, the major shopping thoroughfare in Philadelphia, where he worked until his death.[2]

In the 1820s and 1830s, Philadelphia was still the largest and most cosmopolitan city in the United States, although after the construction of the Erie Canal, which linked the Hudson River to the Great Lakes and the West, New York was rapidly gaining in population and sophistication. Chestnut Street, where Lownes maintained his store and manufactory near Fourth Street east of Independence Hall, was the most prestigious shopping district in the city. Until the Civil War, this area drew wealthy patrons from the South and the West, who traveled from as far as New Orleans and St. Louis to furnish luxurious new houses in the most up-to-date fashions available.[3] Lownes must have enjoyed prosperity as a silversmith and purveyor of imported silver and fancy goods, as reflected by his prominent location. Furthermore, around 1828 he bought out the business of another local silversmith, Harvey Lewis. Although it left him financially strapped, his confidence in making the purchase showed his high hopes and expectations in the late 1820s. Lownes's will, dated August 20, 1834—apparently when he knew he was dying—described his tight financial situation: "After a bond for ten thousand dollars to Harvey Lewis, and my other debts shall have been paid, there will remain but a small amount in my power to dispose of by will." The silversmith died September 9, 1834.[4]

Lownes not only made silver at his Chestnut Street shop, but also carried an extensive stock for retail. After his death, an inventory of the shop was compiled to settle his estate. Lists were drawn up and values assigned by local silversmith John Curry and Lownes's former partner, Henry Erwin, who was both a silversmith and watchmaker. Lownes dealt in silver vessels and flatware, as well as plated wares, watches, jewelry, and fancy articles. He sold his own work and probably the work of other local smiths. He also sold imported wares; a number of objects in the inventory were listed as French and English silver. The stock included plated wares, some described as "Birmingham," the major English center of manufacturing plated silver in the nineteenth century. The inventory also listed a wide assortment of fancy articles, including picture frames, thimbles, gold and silver spectacles, boxes, and gift items. Descriptions of Lownes's inventory are not extensive, but identifying elements provide clues to his design vocabulary and parallels with the Crawford service. In the listing of silver was a "Large Pitcher square foot & claws," which could have described the bases of the vessels in the Crawford service. "2 Table Pitchers with grape border" may have had decoration similar to that on the Crawford service.[5]

Elements of the service—the finely cast spouts and handles, the raised borders with grapevines and Bacchus heads, and the bold round shapes of the vessels contrasting with the square bases and claw feet—characterize the most sophisticated Philadelphia neoclassical silver of the 1820s and 1830s. The finely engraved and flamboyant spread-winged American eagle that frames the inscription to Swift would have seemed fitting to honor the service of a government official. Sumptuous and realistic repoussé grape borders show a growing interest in combining classical forms with naturalistic elements. Full-blown natural expressions in American design came to dominate at midcentury (see nos. 37–38).

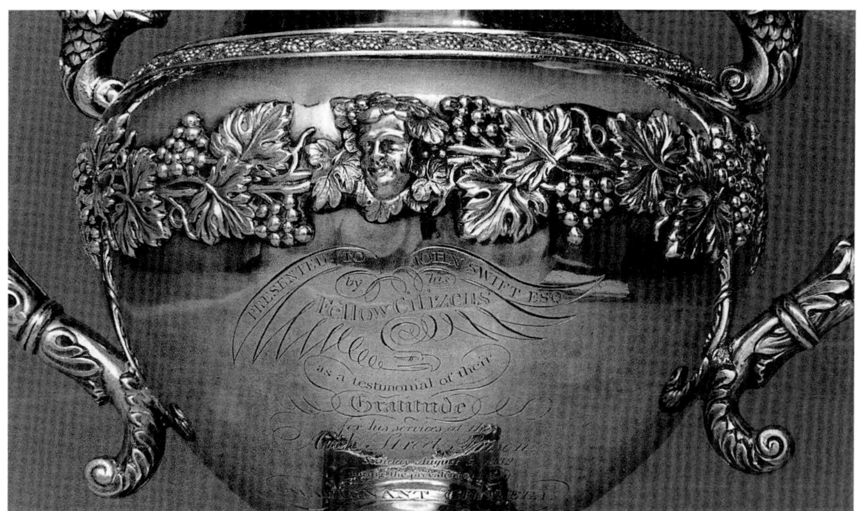

NOTES

1. For an account of the Lownes family in Delaware County, Pennsylvania, and a description of Caleb Lownes's work in prison reform, see Teeters 1963, pp. 1–10. Teeters credits Caleb Lownes with designing the Pennsylvania arms, pp. 2–3 n. 6. Waters 1981, p. 78, notes that in 1818 Edward Lownes was commissioned by the Philadelphia Walnut Street Prison Board of Inspectors to create a $200 pitcher for presentation to prison physician Dr. Thomas Hewson for service at the prison during a typhus epidemic in 1817. For an account of the 1832 cholera epidemic in Philadelphia and its effect on the Arch Street Prison and the 1833 presentation of the silver service to John Swift, see Scharf and Westcott 1884, pp. 1832–1834. For a biography of Swift, see p. 1539.

2. Waters 1981, pp. 45–47, outlines Edward Lownes's career in Philadelphia.

3. For an account of shopping for home furnishings in Philadelphia in 1855 by the affluent Mr. and Mrs. Robert Campbell of St. Louis, see Philadelphia Museum of Art 1976, pp. 346–347.

4. Philadelphia Registry of Wills, Will 138 (1834), Edward Lownes.

5. Ibid. The shop inventory was also filed with the will in the Philadelphia Registry of Wills. The inventory was organized according to types of merchandise: "Silver Plate," pp. 1–6; "Plated Wares," pp. 7–12; "Watches," p. 13; "Jewelry," pp. 14–24; and "Fancy Articles," pp. 25–29. It seems that Lownes's shop carried a range of inventory similar to that offered by the predecessor of Tiffany and Company in New York in the late 1840s (see no. 41).

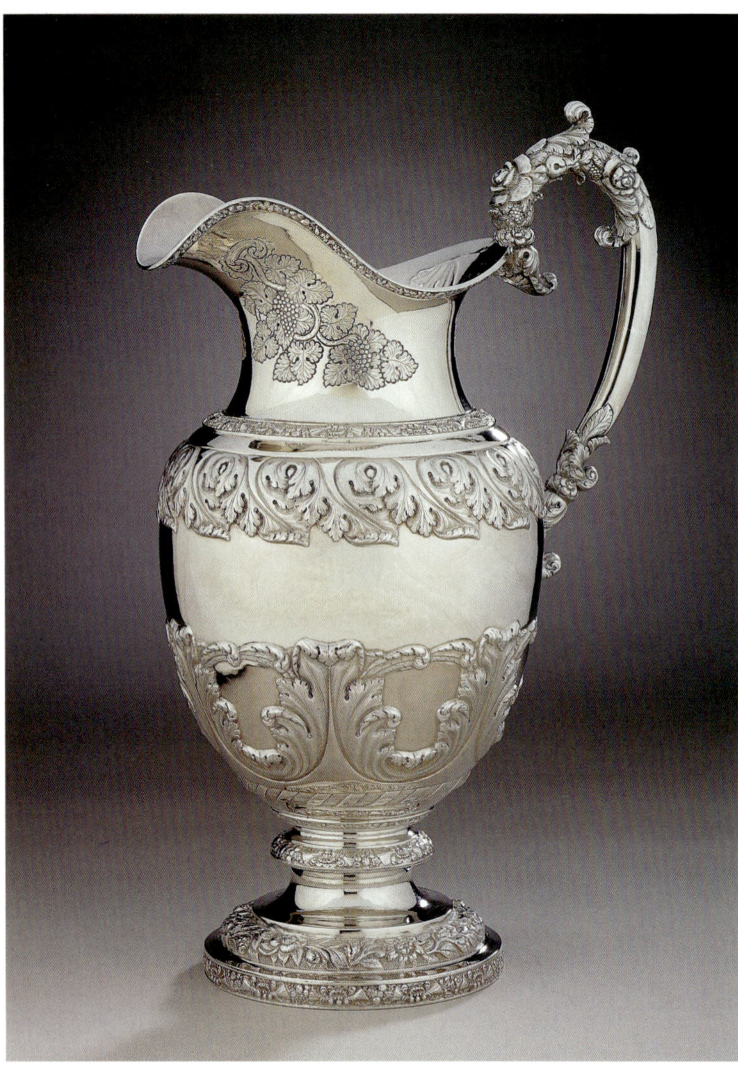

2.

Pitcher, ca. 1830

Stephen Richard (working 1802–1834), New York
Silver
14½ × 9⅜ × 6¼ inches
Marks: Impressed twice on bottom, *S.RICHARD*
1982.300

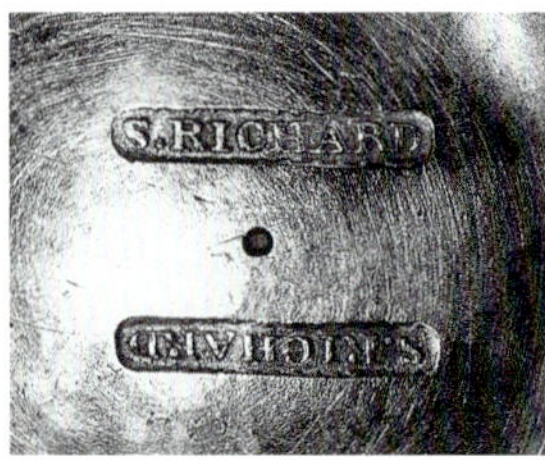

THIS SILVER PITCHER by Stephen Richard in New York dates to about the same time as the Edward Lownes tea service from Philadelphia. During the early nineteenth century, Richard's name appeared in New York directories as a jeweler and an enameler, while an 1802 newspaper advertisement described him as a jeweler, an enameler, and a hairworker. Examples of silver with his mark, *S.RICHARD/Maker* or *S.Richard fecit,* indicate that Richard was an accomplished silversmith working in both the early and mature classical styles between about 1802 and 1834. That he might have conducted business with other New York silversmiths is suggested by silver bearing both his mark and that of Hugh Wishart, who may have commissioned silver from Richard on behalf of clients.[1]

Richard executed this pitcher in the mature classical style of the mid-1820s to early 1830s. The design, a monumental vertical vase form with encircling repoussé acanthus decoration, is characteristic of this taste. These design elements, together with fruit and foliage repousséd around the base and cast into the handle, show an awareness of the latest styles in London, Paris, and Philadelphia. The repoussé fruits and leaves and the chased grapes and vines beneath the spout demonstrate a growing interest in natural motifs among American makers and clients in the middle of the nineteenth century. Popular styles often appeared first in expensive materials such as silver.

When the pitcher was first acquired for the Crawford Collection, it was thought to have descended in the family of New York governor De Witt Clinton, but subsequent communication with his descendants has not confirmed this provenance.[2]

NOTES

1. Quimby 1995, p. 277, discusses Richard's work for Wishart and outlines his listings in New York directories, including: 160 Broadway, 1802–12; 12 Maiden Lane, 1813–15; 10 Maiden Lane, 1816; 153 Broadway, 1817–26; and 169 Broadway, 1828. Hirschl & Adler Galleries 1991, p. 20, no. 2, and p. 35, no. 18, shows two examples of Richard's work. The term "hairworker" in Richard's advertisement may have referred to his making keepsake jewelry of human hair.

2. Correspondence, Marjorie Plunkett, Carriage House Antiques and Decorative Accessories, Poughkeepsie, New York, to R. T. Trump and Company, Philadelphia, November 6, 1969; Correspondence, Clinton B. D. Brown, Washington, D.C., to High Museum of Art, October 19, 1992, High Museum of Art document files.

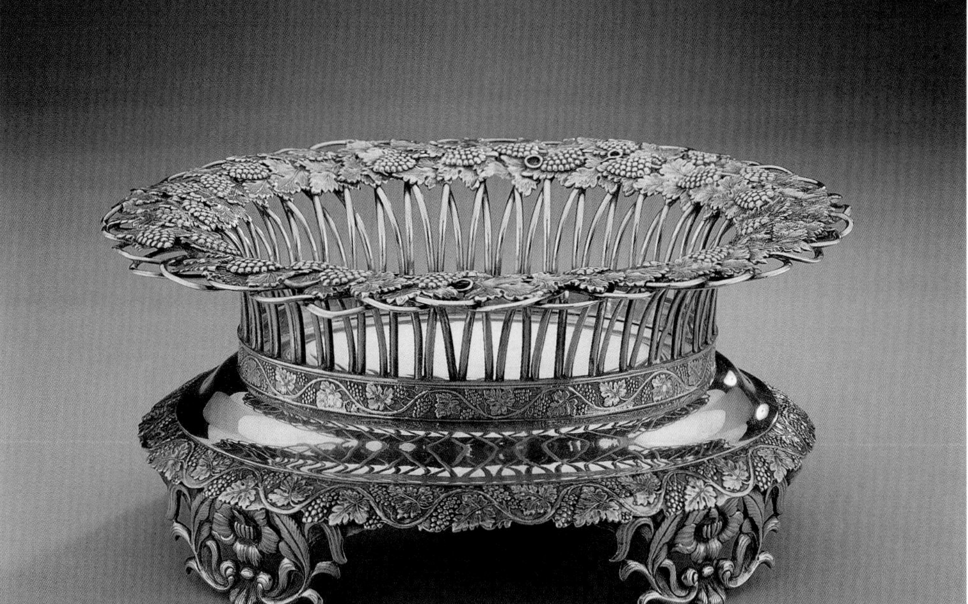

3.

Basket, ca. 1835

Retailed and possibly made by
Baldwin Gardiner and Company
(1827–1848), New York
Silver
5 × 11¼ × 9⅞ inches
Mark: Impressed on bottom,
B. GARDINER/profile *G* lion/
NEW YORK
EL 2.1998

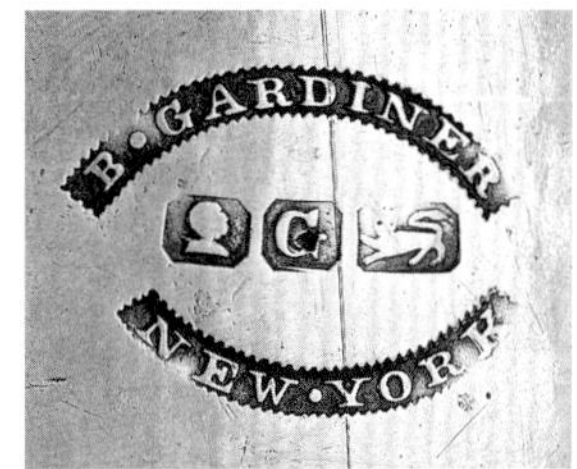

BALDWIN GARDINER worked in the Boston retail shop of his older brother, silversmith Sidney Gardiner, and Thomas Fletcher; he moved with the firm to Philadelphia in 1811. The company not only made silver, but also imported and sold luxury goods. Baldwin Gardiner married Louise Leroy Veron—whose sisters were married to the older Gardiner and Fletcher—and in 1817 he entered a mercantile partnership with his brother-in-law Samuel Veron, as Gardiner, Veron and Company in Philadelphia.

Around the time of Sidney Gardiner's death in 1827, Baldwin Gardiner moved to New York, where he opened a luxury furnishings store at 149 Broadway under his own name. Although he operated his own steam-powered silver manufactory by 1831, Gardiner also retailed silver by other makers, including former Philadelphia colleagues Thomas Fletcher and Edward Lownes. He also imported argand and other lamps and chandeliers from England for sale in his emporium. After 1836, Gardiner moved his store to 39 Nassau Street, where by 1842 he advertised china and glassware as well as lamps and silver. In 1848, around the time Tiffany and Company began retailing silver, Gardiner moved to California. He was in San Francisco during the 1850s before returning to the East Coast, where he died in 1869 in Newark, New Jersey.[1]

Gardiner stamped the Crawford basket with his mark, but whether it indicates that he manufactured as well as sold the basket cannot be definitely established, since both retailers and makers are known to have marked their wares. The profusion of grapes in the cast borders of the basket is related to the cast decoration on the Lownes tea set (see no. 1). Such baskets were especially popular in the 1820s and 1830s. Whether the basket was made in New York or Philadelphia, it shows early evidence of mid-nineteenth-century rococo taste—in its realistic depiction of grapes and scrolling decoration—on an earlier, more classical shape.

NOTE

1. Fennimore 1996, p. 259, presents an account of Gardiner's life and career and illustrates lamps he sold in New York. Dr. Deborah Dependahl Waters, curator of decorative arts, Museum of the City of New York, has researched Baldwin Gardiner for a proposed catalogue of that museum's silver collection and has kindly shared her research, which shows that Gardiner operated a steam-powered silver factory in New York. However, his work as a retailer is better known. Correspondence, Dr. Waters to the High Museum of Art, February 13, 1998, High Museum of Art document files.

4.

Pair of Lamps,
ca. 1835

Manufactured by Thomas Messenger & Sons (1797–1920), London and Birmingham, England; retailed by Jones, Low and Ball (1835–1840), Boston
Gilt brass, glass
Each 25¾ × 19 × 8½ inches
Marks: On metal plaque on each lamp, *MESSENGER & SONS/ LONDON & BIRMINGHAM/MANUFACTURED FOR/JONES, LOWS & BALL/BOSTON*
1982.308.1–.2

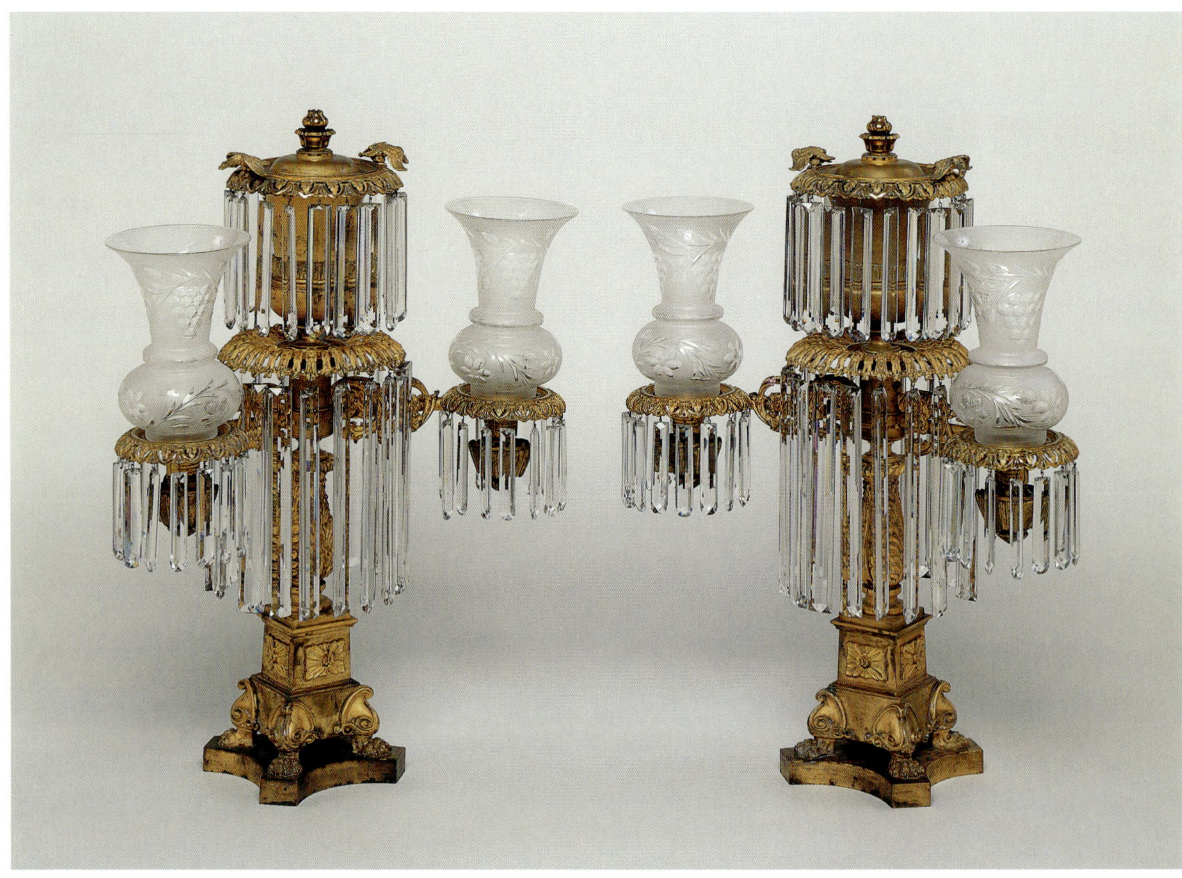

THIS ELEGANT PAIR of monumental classical lamps was part of a revolution in domestic lighting that began in Europe at the end of the eighteenth century and extended through the end of the nineteenth century in the United States. In 1783, François-Pierre Aimé Argand, a Swiss-born scientist working in France, developed an ingenious cylindrical wick for oil-burning lamps that allowed greater circulation of oxygen and produced a much brighter light than customary flat wicks or candles.

Tall narrow glass cylinders, or chimneys (now missing on the Crawford lamps), confined oxygen around the wick and caused air to circulate on both sides of the flame, intensifying the light and dissipating the smoke around the burning wick. The classical gilt urns at the tops of the lamps (now partially obscured by glass prisms, which were added later) held fuel, which in the United States was usually whale oil. Weight and gravity pushed the oil from the urns down the central shaft and out the arms to feed the flames of the ignited wicks.

Although Argand secured an English patent for his cylinder lamps, his innovations were quickly adopted without credit, and cylinder lamps were soon being made in England and France. In 1784, when Thomas Jefferson arrived in Paris as ambassador to France, he greatly admired the new and brighter lamps; the first argand cylinder lamps in America may have been gifts sent by Jefferson.[1] By the end of the century, affluent American parlors were brighter than in colonial days because an industry making these

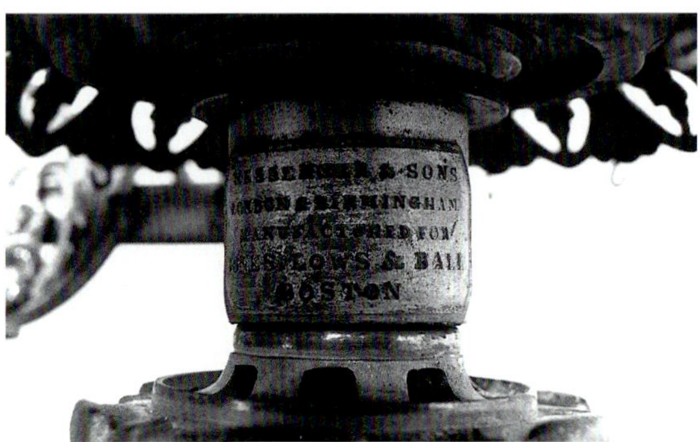

lamps of brass, bronze, and silver plate had developed around the metalsmithing city of Birmingham, England. Soon a luxury trade evolved between Birmingham lamp manufacturers and urban retailers in the new United States. George Washington is known to have owned argand cylinder lamps at Mount Vernon.[2]

Thomas Messenger was a brass founder in Birmingham as early as 1797. A decade later, in 1808, he had specialized in making church candlesticks and patent lamps, probably like Argand's cylinder lamps. By 1825, Messenger's range of products included "chandeliers, candelabra, tripods, lamps of every description, and other ornamental work in bronze and ormolu."[3]

Surviving examples of marked lamps provide evidence that the Messenger firm had an extensive trade with American retailers from the 1820s to at least the 1840s. Whether the names of the English manufacturers appeared on lamps exported to the United States apparently depended on the specific order of each American merchant. The American retailer's name was often put on these lamps as a kind of local advertisement.[4]

Jones, Low and Ball was a luxury goods retailer in Boston dealing in expensive items such as the Crawford lamps and silver (see no. 5). In 1835, the firm advertised that it imported "from the best makers bronze lamps of all kinds." The firm descended from a company established by Boston merchant John McFarlane in 1796, and it eventually evolved into the modern-day Shreve, Crump and Low of Boston.[5]

Gilding was a luxurious finish in American neoclassical interiors in the 1820s and 1830s. The gilding on the lamps would have complemented that on classical furniture of the period. Gold usually decorated contemporary English and French porcelains, which were the preferred decorative tablewares and ornaments for most affluent Americans at that time. These lamps, over two feet tall, would have had an architectural presence on a mantelshelf or table.

Cast animal and plant details, such as the boldly rendered clawed lion feet and acanthus ornament on the Crawford lamps, complemented similar details on American silver and furniture of the 1820s and 1830s. The urn shape of the font at the center top reinforced the classical and architectural effects of the lamps. These details appealed to citizens of the young democracy of the United States, and the spread-winged eagles flanking the tops of the fonts may have been added to appeal to the American market.

Compared to other surviving argand lamps of this period, the Crawford examples seem overendowed with prisms. The middle collars of the central shafts probably had prisms originally. Architectural molding made up the collars around the tops of the urns and the wick sockets on the arms; these collars may have been punched later to hold the prisms. Keeping the prisms clean from the fuel, flame, and smoke around the wick sockets on the arms would have been an enormously time-consuming task, so it is unlikely that all the prisms were with the lamps when they were made. The engraved glass shades around the wick are twentieth-century versions of the missing originals.

NOTES

1. Moss 1988, pp. 75–78.
2. Palmer 1993, pp. 332–333.
3. Fennimore 1996, p. 254.
4. Ibid., p. 259, no. 168.
5. Ibid., p. 254.

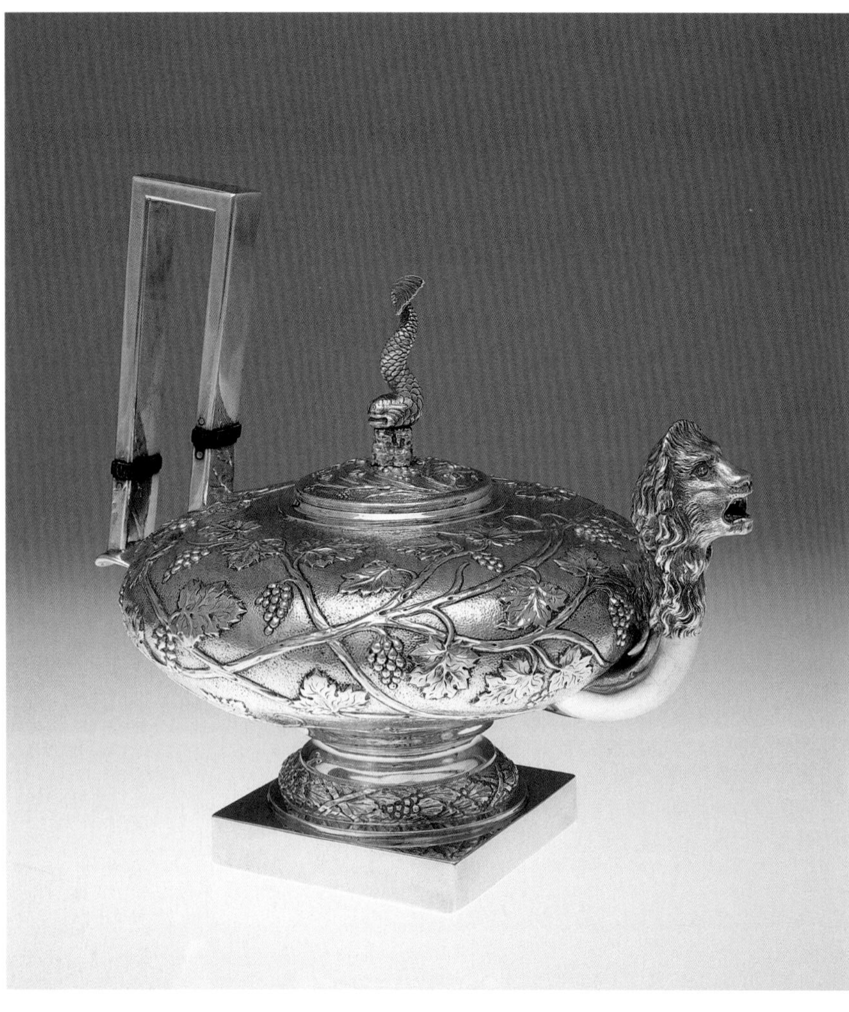

5.

Teapot, 1830s

Obadiah Rich (1809–1888), Boston
Silver and wood
8⅜ × 9 × 6½ inches
Mark: Impressed on bottom, *O. Rich/Boston/fine*
1987.173

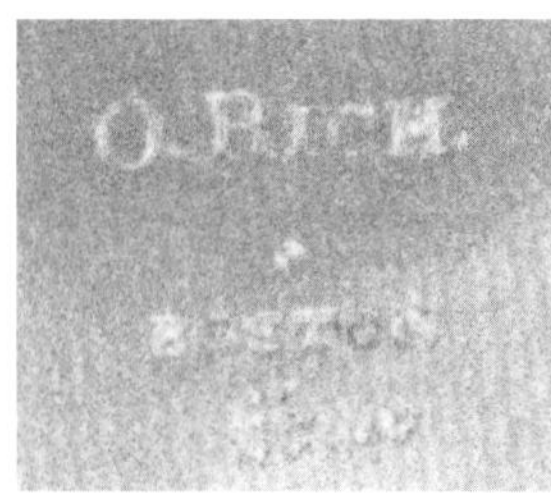

OBADIAH RICH has long been recognized as an important Boston silversmith working in the mature classical and early rococo revival styles during the first half of the nineteenth century (see no. 39).[1] Rich has often been compared to such contemporaries as Thomas Fletcher of Philadelphia, Samuel Kirk of Baltimore (see no. 37), and John Forbes of New York.

Born in Charlestown, Massachusetts, Rich descended from seventeenth-century English settlers of Cape Cod. Rich was apprenticed to Boston silversmith Moses Morse and by 1830 had his own silver shop at 69 Washington Street in Boston. From 1832 to 1835, he worked in partnership with Samuel L. Ward, and the firm operated under both names. Rich then worked under his own name until around 1850, when blindness forced him to retire early, but he continued in the business as a partner in other Boston silver firms, including Bracket and Crosby.[2] During his working years, Rich is known to have supplied silver for the prominent Boston retailer of fancy goods in the late 1830s, Jones, Low and Ball (see no. 4).[3]

The Crawford teapot can be associated with the later classical or Empire style popular between 1825 and 1850, in part because of the archaeological interpretation and adaptation of the classical lamp shape. The pot could date to as early as 1830–1832, but because classical taste continued to be popular until midcentury, the pot could also date to the 1840s. The circular vessel shape set on a contrasting square base was a typical neoclassical convention. The horizontal composition of the teapot is offset by the soaring verticality of the rectangular handle, another element that contrasts with the circular shape of the vessel. The handle is echoed by the elongated dolphin finial of the lid.

Both the roaring lion terminal of the spout and the dolphin finial reflect an interest in animal motifs that was expressed in all areas of decorative art in the earlier classical period of the 1830s.[4] Rich frequently used chasing in ornamenting silver. With the interlaced grapevine on this vessel, he anticipated the scrolling and intertwining natural motifs of the rococo revival of the 1840s and 1850s. Similar rococo details were often evident in earlier classical silver (see no. 1).

NOTES

1. A biography of the silversmith and study of his work is given in Fales 1968, pp. 565–569. Rich is included and his work illustrated in Fales 1973, p. 128, and figs. 34, 106, 116, 220; Hood 1971, p. 197, figs. 220–221; and McClinton 1968, pp. 31, 222. Exhibitions and catalogues that include work by Rich are Newark Museum 1963, no. 116; The Metropolitan Museum of Art 1970, p. xiv and no. 75; and W. Cooper 1993, p. 64, nos. 40–41.

2. Obituary of Obadiah Rich, *Boston Transcript,* July 11, 1888; cited by Fales 1968, p. 566.

3. Ibid., p. 566.

4. Dolphins were popular ornaments on furniture as early as 1815; see The Metropolitan Museum of Art 1970, no. 45. By the 1850s, dolphin-shaped pressed glass candlesticks were being made in New England; see ibid., no. 94. From the late eighteenth century, furniture brasses cast in the shape of lion heads were popular; see ibid., no. 1.

William Ellis Tucker established his porcelain factory in Philadelphia in 1826. The Tucker enterprise—through twelve years and three partnerships—never achieved financial stability or a broad-based patronage outside Philadelphia, although it was commercially successful compared to other American porcelain endeavors. Lack of capital and low tariffs (which permitted imported wares to be sold cheaply) doomed the Tucker factory and many other American ceramic enterprises.

After brief partnerships with John N. Bird and John Hulme, William Tucker was joined by his younger brother Thomas, who signed on as an apprentice and eventually became chief decorator and superintendent of the factory.

Tucker sought federal aid by offering to share his porcelain-making secrets with the government. Although President Andrew Jackson declined Tucker's proposal, he did place orders for porcelain. The Pennsylvania state government also refused to assist, but Tucker's political letter-writing led to a partnership with Alexander Hemphill through the 1831 investment by his father, Judge Joseph Hemphill. Judge Hemphill retained control of his $7,000 investment, which enabled Tucker to move and expand the plant.

After Tucker's death in 1832, Judge Hemphill assumed sole control of the factory with a payment of $10,000 to Tucker's estate. Hemphill retained Thomas Tucker as superintendent until 1837, when bank failures and other financial reversals forced Hemphill to withdraw from the enterprise. Thomas Tucker leased the factory for another six months but was unable to compete with cheaper European goods. Although the ventures were not successful, Tucker wares often won medals at the annual industrial exhibitions at the Franklin Institute in Philadelphia.[1]

The Crawford pitcher was number seven in a pattern book drawn by Thomas Tucker.[2] The vase-shaped pitcher was made from as early as 1828 through the Joseph Hemphill period. The classical pitcher is decorated with a bold polychrome floral design identified with the Tucker firm, which often used classical gilded motifs. Because these wares used animal bone ash instead of kaolin as the hardening agent, they cannot be classified as true, or hard-paste, porcelains.

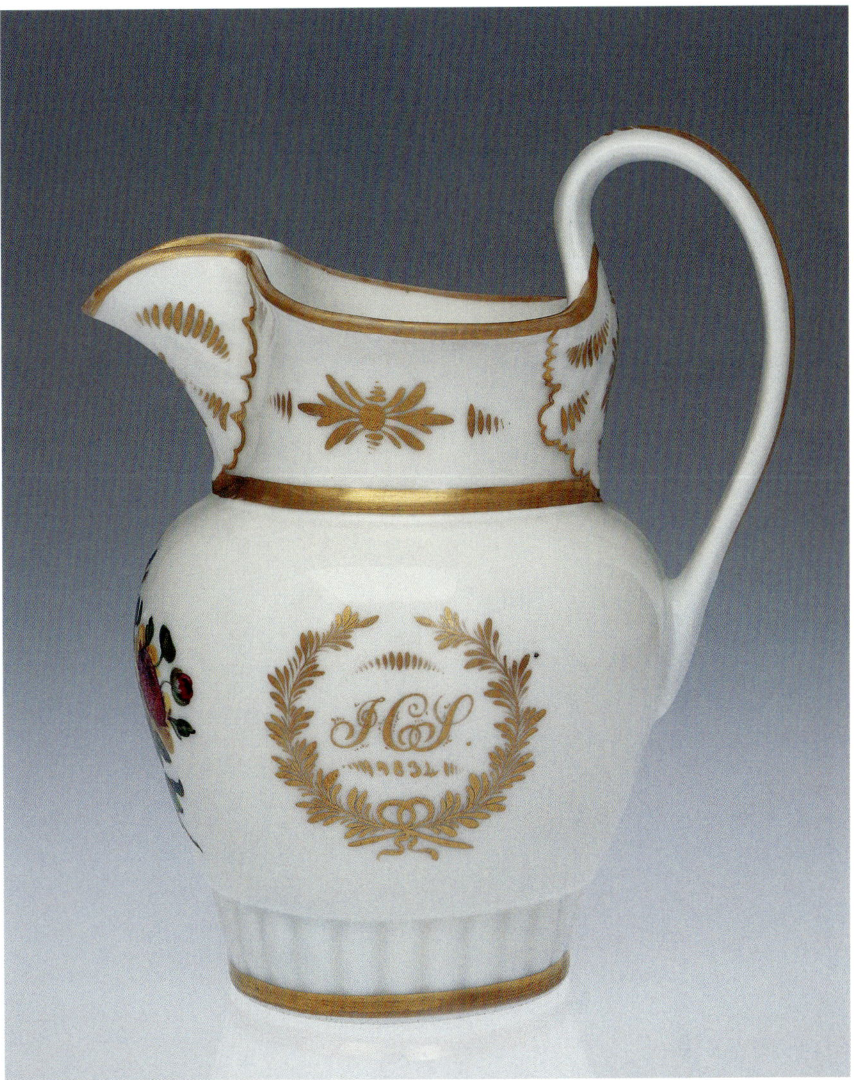

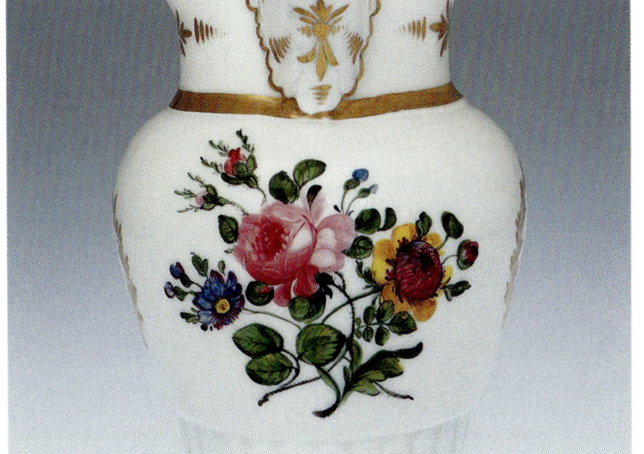

6.

Pitcher, dated 1834

Joseph Hemphill factory, formerly Tucker and Hemphill (1826–1837), Philadelphia
Porcelain with polychrome and gilt decoration
9⅜ × 7⅝ × 5¾ inches
Inscription: In gilt on side, *JCL/1834*
1984.131

NOTES

1. A documented history of the firm is related by P. Curtis 1972 and is recounted in Frelinghuysen 1989, pp. 14–20.

2. Tucker Pattern Book 2, Philadelphia Museum of Art, Library, Rare Book Collection; cited in ibid., p. 90, no. 10.

7.

Pier Table,
ca. 1835

Possibly Philadelphia
Mahogany veneer, marble, and glass
38¼ × 46 × 22½ inches
1986.191

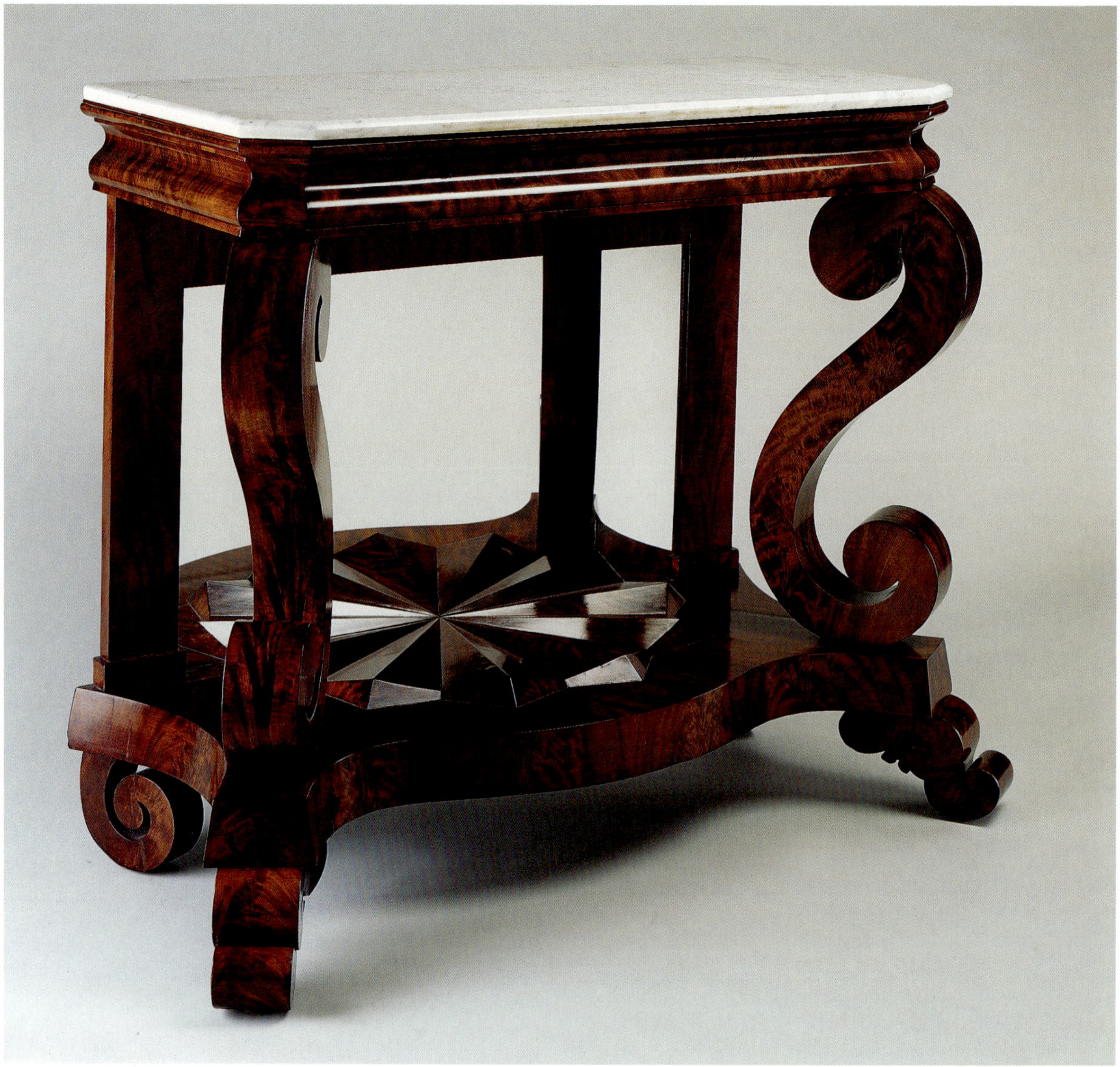

THIS PIER TABLE is in the Grecian, or plain, style prevalent in the United States in the 1830s and 1840s. Andrew Jackson Downing, in his popular 1850 domestic design guide *The Architecture of Country Houses,* noted that Grecian-style furniture was the most widely used in the United States.[1] It was fashionable among both the middle class and the wealthy, as documented in paintings of the period. Furniture historians have attributed this popularity, apparent from the great numbers of surviving examples, both to an American middle class eager for stylish furniture and to an increasingly mechanized industry, which made possible the thinner veneers required to cover the often tight curves.[2] Natural patterns of wood grain in artfully arranged veneers on bold shapes characterize this late phase of the neoclassical taste in European and American furniture, which evolved from the delicate late-eighteenth-century Federal style and the more robust and archaeological French-inspired Empire style of the 1810s and 1820s.

Scrolls and curves appeared in furniture pattern and price books published during the 1830s and 1840s in eastern cities and as far west as Cincinnati, indicating a shift in preference from carved classical to Grecian-style furniture.[3] However, the machinery and the labor required for a skilled artisan to fashion these curving shapes and to apply the veneers made this furniture just as expensive as the classical furniture of the 1820s, with its labor-intensive carving.

Subtle details of the Crawford table indicate the skill of its maker. The S-scrolls supporting the table are canted at the front corners in line with the C-scroll feet at the opposite rear corners. The complex front feet, consisting of an S-scroll on top of a C-scroll, are also parallel to the main supports. This table is more sculptural than most Grecian pier tables, in which such elements were usually set in a straight line from front to back. The vertical ogee shape of the skirt and the angled edge of the plinth above the feet further contribute to the visual interest of the table.

Designs for related tables were published by John Hall in *The Cabinet Makers' Assistant,* 1840. In illustrations of pier tables (pls. 15–17, figs. 81–86), the large scrolls are straight rather than canted. In an 1833 broadside, New York furniture firm Joseph Meeks and Sons (see no. 8, fig. 1) pictured a variant of the Crawford table with a mirrored back. The scrolls between the plinth and the top were also configured in the more typical straight arrangement.[4]

The marble top of the Crawford table was an expensive alternative to wood. The veneered, pie-shaped wedges on the plinth below—arranged in a semicircle that is reflected in the mirror at the back to create a full circle—would have increased the cost and production time. Such semicircles of veneered wedges in ovolo forms appeared on secretaries, sideboards, and other furniture in Philadelphia at the time, suggesting the possible origin of the table.[5] This table was not intended for heavy use but meant to sit against a wall, possibly as a pier between two windows, reflecting light.

NOTES

1. Downing 1969, pp. 412–413. T. G. Smith illustrated the Crawford table as emblematic of furniture in this late Grecian taste in Hall 1996, pp. v–xli, fig. 1. Citing period usage, Smith recommends "Grecian" and "plain style" as appropriate descriptions of furniture of this type.

2. R. Smith 1958, p. 522.

3. T. G. Smith, in Hall 1996, pp. xiv–xvi, figs 5, 6, 7, 23. Lavish use of scrolls and veneers and the unusual composition of elements point not only to an affluent client, but also possibly to a date in the early 1830s for the Crawford table.

4. R. Smith 1958, illustrated p. 523.

5. Two secretaries labeled by Anthony G. Quervelle from Philadelphia are illustrated in R. Smith 1964, pp. 306–307, figs. 6–7. In his design book *The Cabinet Makers' Assistant,* 1840, John Hall illustrated a similar arrangement of veneers on a pedestal or sideboard; see Hall 1996, pl. 41, fig. 187.

8.

Card Table, 1829–1835

Joseph Meeks and Sons (1829–1835), New York
Mahogany
28⅜ × 36 × 35½ inches
Mark: Engraved paper label glued to bottom of interior storage area beneath rotating foldout top, depicting view of five-story wareroom with three signs on facade: between third and fourth floor, *MEEKS & SONS MANUFACTORY;* at the center of the row of windows on the third floor, *of;* between second and third floor, *CABINET FURNITURE;* above central entrance on first floor, *JOSEPH MEEKS & SONS;* printed beneath building facade, *Nos. 43 & 45 Broad Street/NEW-YORK*
1987.180

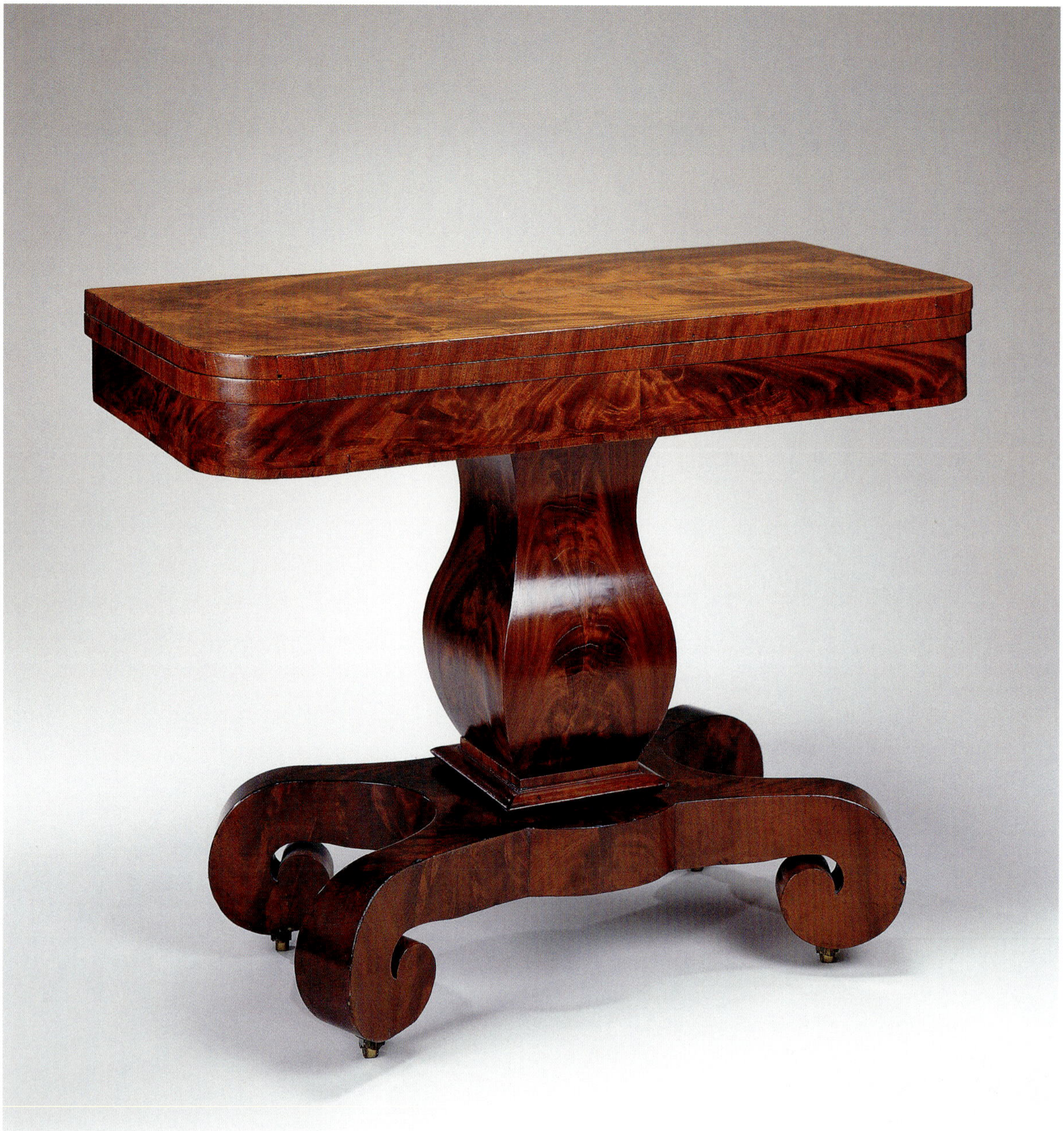

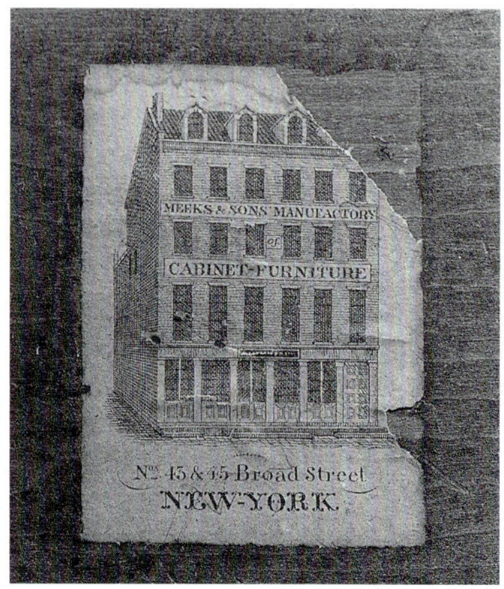

IN 1833, JOSEPH MEEKS and Sons distributed a printed advertisement that showed not only the firm's New York warerooms (the same view as on the label on this table), but also forty-four patterns of draperies, bed hangings, and furniture that the company was offering (fig. 1). Number 34 in the advertisement is a card table that appears identical to this table. Both this card table and another with four S-shaped scrolled feet and a vase-shaped hexagonal center pedestal, shown as number 37, are listed as costing $50.

Joseph Meeks, the founder of the firm, was in business as a cabinetmaker by 1797, when, in partnership with his brother Edward, he first appeared in the New York directory. By 1800, Meeks was working on his own, and when he opened his wareroom and manufactory at 43 and 45 Broad Street in 1829, he had taken his sons into the company. After the elder Meeks withdrew from the firm in 1835, John and Joseph W. Meeks established J. and J. W. Meeks, which lasted until 1855. The company remained briefly at the old Joseph Meeks and Sons stand in Broad Street before moving to 14 Vesey Street by 1836. They were listed in New York directories until 1855, when Joseph Meeks left the partnership. John Meeks and his son, John Meeks Jr., formed John Meeks and Son. The younger Meeks continued to manufacture furniture until 1868.[1]

The 1833 Joseph Meeks and Sons advertisement is the earliest known surviving illustrated public record of the products of an American furniture company. Illustrated catalogues were generally not published by American furniture firms until about the end of the Civil War. The Meeks advertisement documents the Grecian taste in American furniture and its promotion by a firm of national importance seven years before John Hall published his influential *Cabinet Makers' Assistant* in Baltimore in 1840. The range in dates illustrates the long survival of popular styles in nineteenth-century America.[2]

The Meeks broadside used general statements typical of such promotions: "Our establishment being one of the oldest, and now the largest in the United States, we are able to execute orders, to any amount and at the shortest notice." By about 1835, J. and J. W. Meeks had opened a retail outlet in New Orleans. Other American furniture firms followed this precedent and opened branches in other cities by the mid-nineteenth century. The Meeks company was also a leader among American furniture enterprises in producing lines that ranged from the simple to the sophisticated and elaborate.[3]

The Crawford table documents a growing nineteenth-century phenomenon: the development of a widespread and upwardly mobile American middle class. The form itself—a card table—suggests that the owner had leisure time.

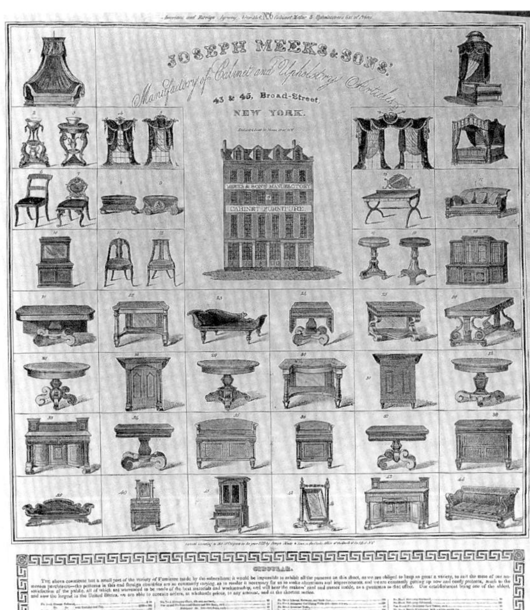

Fig. 1. Advertisement, Joseph Meeks and Sons, *Manufactory of Cabinet and Upholstery Articles,* lithograph, 1833. Department of Drawings and Prints, The Metropolitan Museum of Art, Gift of Mrs. R. W. Hyde, 1943 (43.15.8).

NOTES

1. The history of the various Meeks firms is recounted in Pearce and Pearce 1966, pp. 69–73; and Pearce, Pearce, and Smith 1964, pp. 414–420.

2. See Hall 1996, p. xii.

3. When the Meeks company opened its New Orleans branch, the main outlet was still at 43 and 45 Broad Street in New York, before its move to Vesey Street. A sideboard with a label of J. and J. W. Meeks on Broad Street in New York and Chartres Street in New Orleans is illustrated in Pearce and Pearce 1966, p. 69, fig. 1. The Cincinnati firm of Mitchell and Rammelsberg also opened branches in St. Louis (1855), Memphis (1863), and New Orleans (1866); see Peirce 1979, pp. 211–212, 217–218. See illustrations in Pearce, Pearce, and Smith 1964, pp. 414–420; Pearce and Pearce 1966, pp. 69–73; and Peirce 1979, pp. 209–229.

Industrialization, 1835–1900

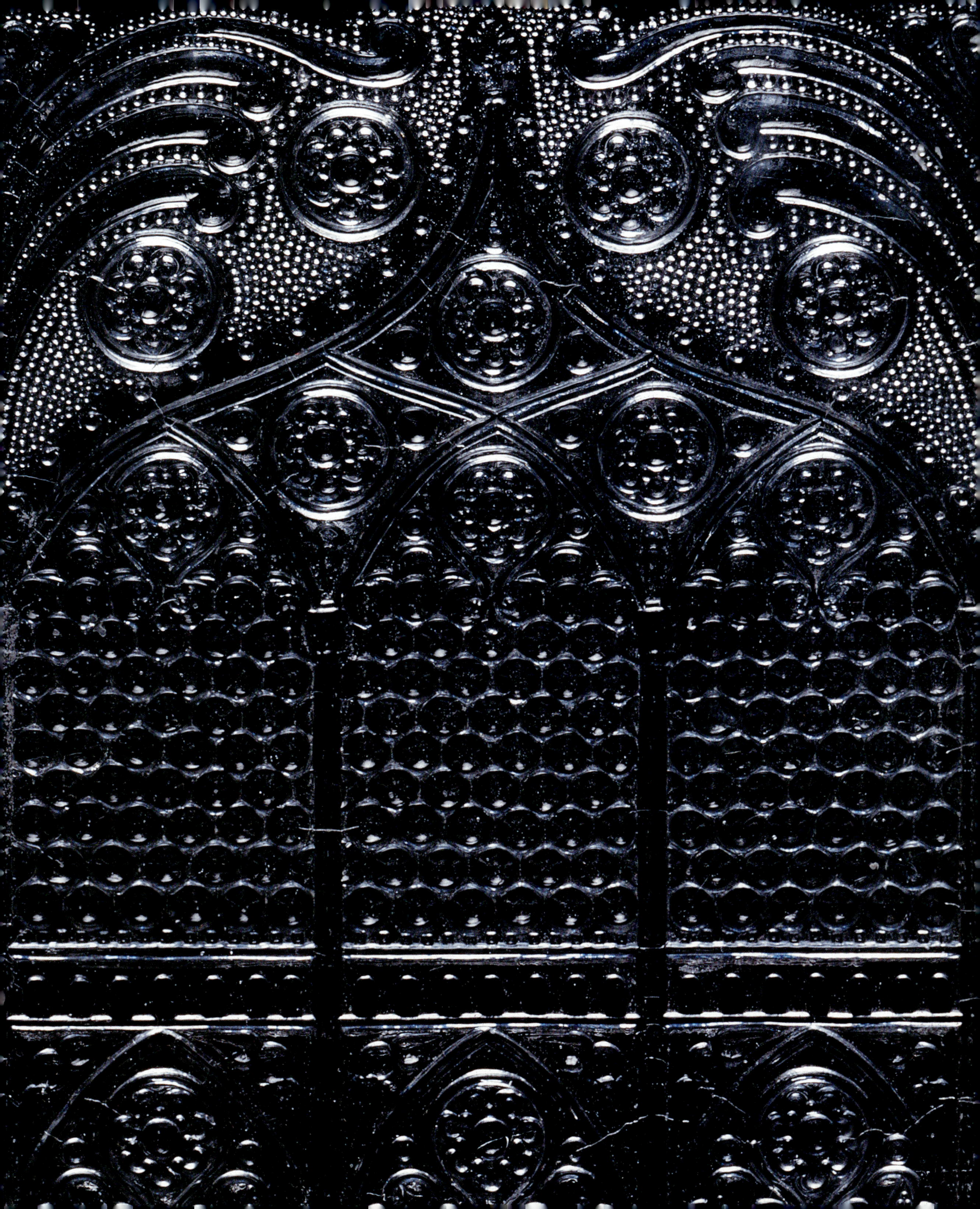

9.

Covered Sugar Bowl,
1831–1833

New England, possibly the Providence Flint Glass Company (1831–1833), Providence, Rhode Island
Press-molded opal glass
5½ × 5 × 5 inches
1984.159

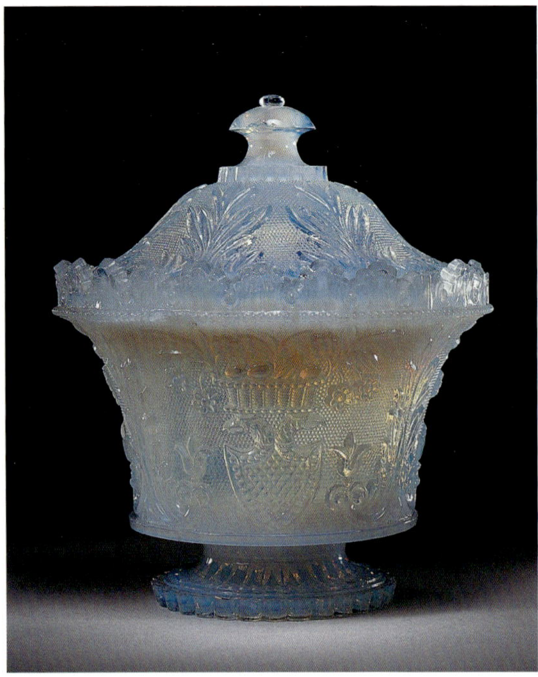

THIS SUGAR BOWL is attributed to the Providence Flint Glass Company because its pattern is similar to a saltcellar that has *PROVIDENCE* imprinted on the bottom. Shields with crossed eagle heads on the saltcellar also appear to be related to the three motifs on the Crawford sugar bowl. The opalescence was achieved by adding bone ash to the glass melt with metallic oxides for color traces. This technique was introduced in the early 1820s at the Baccarat factory in France, and it was used in New England by 1830.[1]

The short-lived Providence Flint Glass Company was established in 1831 on land owned by the Dyer family, which had long been involved in the Phoenix Iron Foundry in Providence. Benjamin Dyer, a druggist, his son Benjamin Dyer Jr., and his nephew Charles Dyer were involved in the new firm. Other partners included George B. Holmes and William Eayers, who was listed as agent for the company in an 1831 advertisement. Eayers would later manage a glasshouse for Luther Russell, who in 1837 became superintendent for Deming Jarves in the new Mount Washington Glass Company (see nos. 136–138).

The 1832 Providence city directory—the only one published during the years of the Providence Flint Glass Company's operation—lists twenty-nine glassworkers who presumably worked there, since there were no other glasshouses in the city. Evidently the company tried to attract experienced workers to compete with the New England Glass Company in East Cambridge, Massachusetts, and the Boston and Sandwich Glass Company in Sandwich, Massachusetts. Financial difficulties overtook the firm soon after its establishment. Apparently, Eayers was no longer the firm's agent by March 14, 1833, when Benjamin Dyer placed an advertisement as treasurer and sole agent of the company in the city newspaper. He was closing the business with "the smallest possible loss to the Stockholders."[2] A public auction to dispose of the Providence Flint Glass Company was announced for May 7, 1833, but was postponed until September 16. By June of 1834, the glasshouse was being used by a Mr. Furbish to house his machine for breaking, cracking, and grinding corn.

While the Crawford sugar bowl cannot be attributed with certainty to the Providence Flint Glass Company, its stippled decoration and opal color are characteristic of the types of wares being produced in New England at the time. By the early 1830s, the eagle was widely accepted as a symbol of the United States, and its use on the sugar bowl was intended to appeal to the American market.

NOTES

1. See Rose 1954, no. 163; Spillman 1981, no. 76; Watkins 1949, pp. 190–191; and K. Wilson 1972, pp. 284–287. There has been some debate as to whether the imprint *PROVIDENCE* worked into the mold of the saltcellar refers to the Rhode Island city or a factory there, or whether it is simply a religious reference; see C. Green 1937, p. 59; and Watkins 1949, p. 190. Although manufacturer-marked press-molded glass is unusual, there are known examples: see no. 11; and Rose 1954, pp. 21–22. A version of the saltcellar, illustrated with views of both the sides and ends, is in McKearin and McKearin 1941, pl. 167. A sugar bowl identical to the Crawford example is also illustrated, pl. 163, but it is attributed to the Boston and Sandwich Glass Company. As a druggist, Benjamin Dyer might have been particularly interested in investing in a glass enterprise because nineteenth-century glasshouses sometimes advertised chemical as well as domestic wares.

2. *Manufacturers' and Farmers Journal and Providence Pawtucket Advertiser,* March 14, 1833; cited in K. Wilson 1972, p. 285.

Pittsburgh Glass

LOCATED AT THE confluence of the Monongahela and Allegheny Rivers (which forms the Ohio River), Pittsburgh was a burgeoning city of 2,500 by the end of the eighteenth century. Isolated by the Allegheny Mountains from the long-settled Atlantic coastal cities, Pittsburgh claimed as its market all the areas along the trade routes of the Ohio and Mississippi River valleys to New Orleans. Materials, access to fuel, the growing western market, location, and industrial enterprise combined to make Pittsburgh a leading glass manufacturing and distribution center for over half of the United States before the Civil War.[1]

This amber bottle (no. 10) was made by blowing molten glass into a twenty-four-rib iron mold. The clear, rich amber hue of the glass and the distinctive globular shape are characteristic of flasks believed to have been made in Zanesville, Ohio, and Pittsburgh. Located along the trade routes of the Muskingum River (a branch of the Ohio River) and the east-west National Road, Zanesville was the westernmost point of what is now called Midwestern glass. The Crawford flask could have been made at the White Glass Works, which operated in Zanesville between 1823 and 1836, or at another glass factory in Zanesville or possibly Pittsburgh.[2]

The development of Pittsburgh as a major glass manufacturing center coincided with a revolution in glassmaking: the introduction of pressed glass and the emergence of a taste for lacy pressed glass. In the first half of the twentieth century, "Sandwich" was a generic term collectors used for lacy pressed glass. While the Massachusetts town of Sandwich on Cape Cod was indeed a major glass manufacturing center (see no. 94), other areas—including the rest of New England (see no. 9), New Jersey, New York, Philadelphia, and Pittsburgh—also manufactured pressed glass. The earliest known American patent for making pressed glass (in the form of furniture knobs) was issued in 1825 to John Palmer Bakewell, a son and partner of the founder of the Bakewell factory.

Bakewell window panes similar to the Crawford example (no. 11) were reportedly found in the mullioned doors of a secretary in either Uniontown, Pennsylvania, or Wheeling, West Virginia. Scholars and collectors have been aware of the production of pressed panes by Bakewell, Pears and Company since at least 1927, when Rhea Mansfield Knittle quoted an 1836 advertisement issued by the firm for "pressed panes for steamboats" in her book *Early American Glass.*[3] Because no steamboats with intact window panes from the period are known to survive, the use of Bakewell pressed glass panes on such vessels cannot be documented except in this advertisement.

Through the 1930s and 1940s, articles and notes in *The Magazine Antiques* described examples of nineteenth-century panes used in exterior and interior door surrounds. Examples of secretary-desks and corner cupboards with pressed panes were also published or noted during that time. Panes marked by makers in Pittsburgh and Wheeling, and others attributed to the area, survive in greater numbers than those made in New England. The Bakewell concern did not

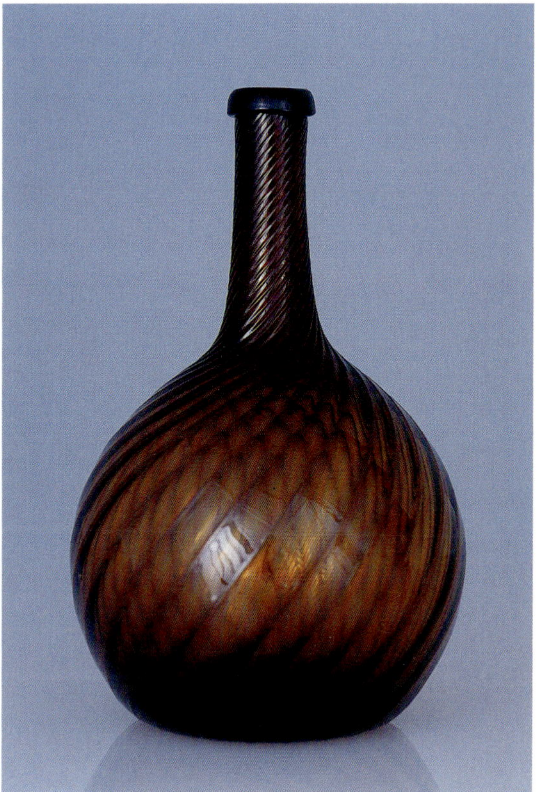

10.

Bottle, ca. 1835

Probably Zanesville, Ohio, area or Pittsburgh
Blown and molded glass
8¾ × 5½ × 5½ inches
1984.164

11.

Window Pane, ca. 1840

Bakewell, Pears and Company (1808–1882), Pittsburgh
Press-molded glass
7 × 5 × ¼ inches
Mark: Printed in raised letters on smooth back of pane in reverse, to be read from the patterned front, BAKEWELL
1990.83

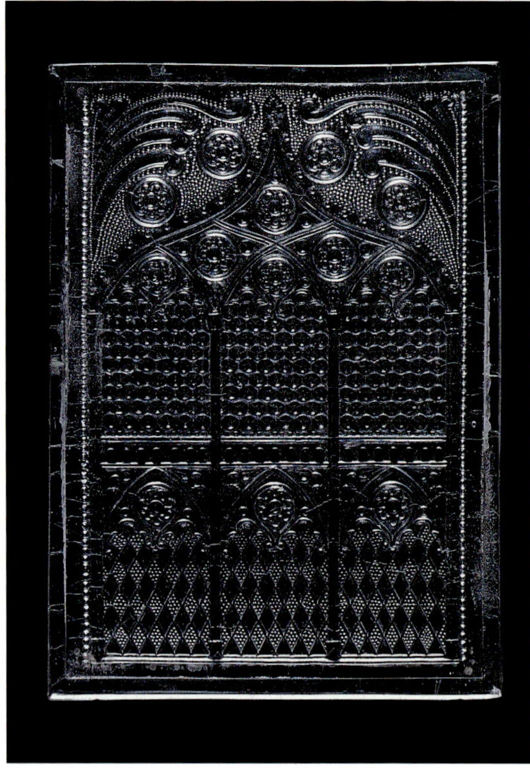

make window glass, so pressed window panes may have been an unusual product for them. This window pane is dominated by a series of Gothic arched forms, while rococo scrolls at the top show the mid-nineteenth-century ease of mixing styles. The overall pressed pattern makes the pane impossible to see through, although it is translucent.[4]

This pair of lamps (no. 12) combines the techniques of press molding, blowing and molding, and engraving. The scalloped and stepped lacy pressed base supports a blown stem and fuel font with engraved decoration. The twelve molded panels around the base of the font beneath the engraving relate the lamps to engraved Pittsburgh sugar bowls. The engraved ornament of grapes and leaves may seem unusual on lamps. A similar pattern was more logically used on a Pittsburgh-attributed decanter from the mid-nineteenth century. The lamps may have been intended for use on a dining table, which would make the grape pattern appropriate.[5]

From the beginning of the glass industry in the Pittsburgh area and throughout the nine-

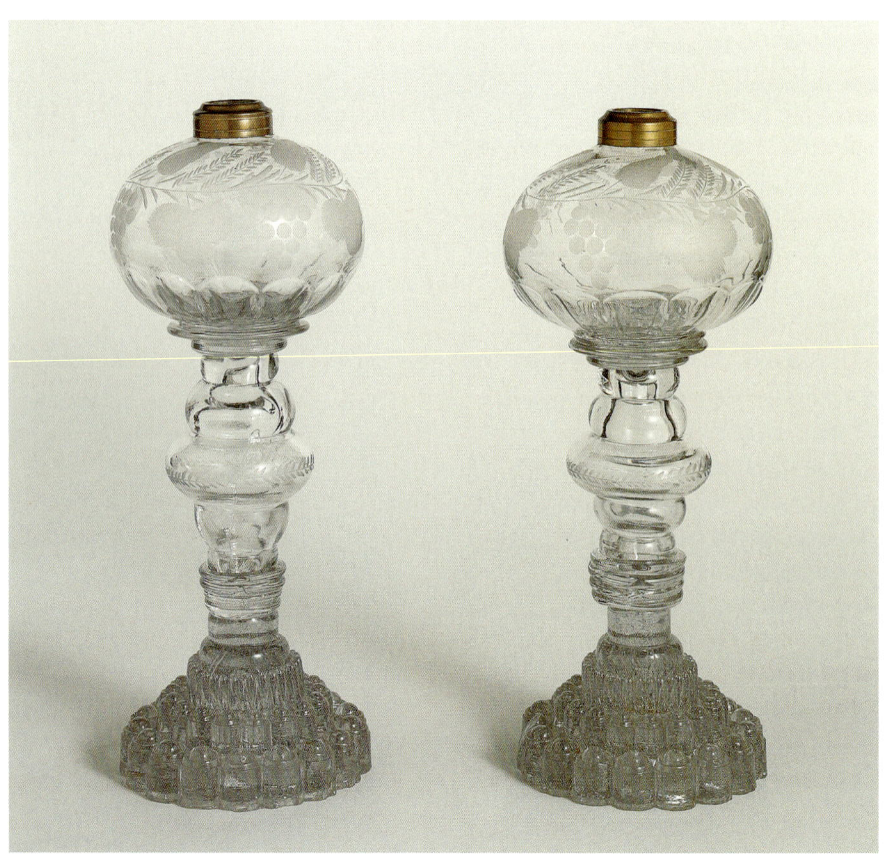

12.

Pair of Whale Oil Lamps, ca. 1850

Pittsburgh area
Press-molded, blown, and engraved glass
Each 11½ × 4¾ × 4¾ inches
1987.167.1–.2

teenth century, many regional manufacturers made free-blown glass. These witch balls on stands (no. 13), likely mantel ornaments, were probably made in Pittsburgh or Wheeling. Opaque white glass looped with brilliant contrasting colors—such as the bold pink of the Crawford ornaments—was typical in the vases that were made in great quantities in both centers in the 1870s.[6] The bright colors on these free-blown ornaments may anticipate the art glass produced in these two cities in the 1880s and 1890s (see nos. 133–134).

All of today's methods of producing and decorating glass tablewares were in use in Pittsburgh before the Civil War: free blowing; blowing and molding; press molding; cutting; and engraving. The early years of the nineteenth century saw virtually continuous growth of the glass industry in Pittsburgh, and by 1876, the city produced half the glass made in the United States.

NOTES

1. For a discussion of the development of Pittsburgh as a glass-making center, see Bining 1936, pp. 255–268; and Innes 1976, pp. 3–11.

2. Innes 1976, p. 193, fig. 175, illustrates a twenty-four-rib bottle believed to have been made in Pittsburgh. A similar but taller bottle is at the Winterthur Museum and is illustrated and discussed in Palmer 1993, p. 355, no. 341.

3. Knittle 1927, p. 307

4. For a complete history of the Bakewell firm, see Innes 1976, pp. 28–33, 49; McKearin and McKearin 1941, pp. 138–139, 589; and Pears 1927, pp. 201–205. Benjamin Bakewell came to Pittsburgh from New York and his native England, where he had been involved in the import trade. By 1810 in Pittsburgh, he had invested in the glass business with Benjamin Page, and their glasshouse was the first successful American factory making flint, or lead, glass. The company descended in the families of the founders until its closure in 1882; see Innes 1976, pp. 184–185. Innes 1976, p. 284, fig. 303; pressed panes are discussed on pp. 283–288. See also Knittle 1927, p. 307; Rose, December, 1938, pp. 294–295; Rose, February, 1938, pp. 81–82; Rose, February, 1947, p. 186. An identical pane in the Winterthur Museum is illustrated and discussed in Palmer 1993, p. 403, no. 389. Palmer notes that identical examples in the Corning Museum of Glass and The Metropolitan Museum of Art came from a secretary found in a home near Wheeling. See also Innes 1976, p. 286; and Kumm 1943, p. 128.

5. Paneled and engraved sugar bowls are shown in Innes 1976, p. 162, fig. 126 and p. 165, fig. 135. A decanter engraved with grapes is shown on p. 156, fig. 118. A lamp with an identical pressed-glass base is illustrated on p. 245, fig. 247.

6. Ibid., p. 184, fig. 164, states that witch balls had been thought to ward off evil spirits and purify the air. By the time the Crawford examples were made, the function was most likely purely decorative. Innes also notes the comparable strengths of Wheeling and Pittsburgh glassmakers in colored glass production; see ibid., p. 101.

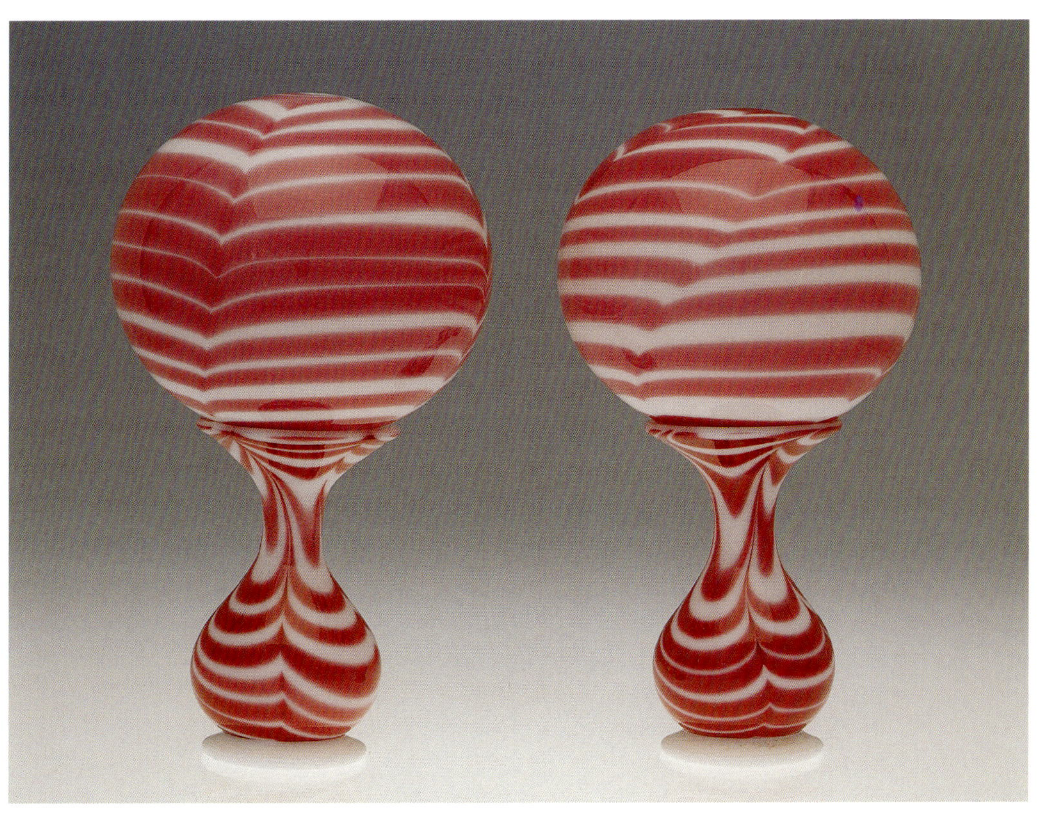

13.

Pair of Ornaments (Witch Balls on Stands), ca. 1870

Probably Pittsburgh or Wheeling, West Virginia, area
Free-blown, looped opaque white and pink glass
Overall: Each 10½ × 6 × 6 inches
Balls: Each approximately 5¼ inches in diameter
Stands: Each 5½ inches in height
1994.156.1–.2

14.

Pitcher, ca. 1845

American Pottery Manufacturing Company (1833–ca. 1852), Jersey City, New Jersey; possibly designed by Daniel Greatbach (working 1839–1866)
Glazed earthenware
8¼ × 9½ × 5⅞ inches
Mark: Molded in raised letters and enclosed in raised circle on bottom, *AMERICAN/POTTERY, CO./JERSEY CITY, N.J.*
1984.132

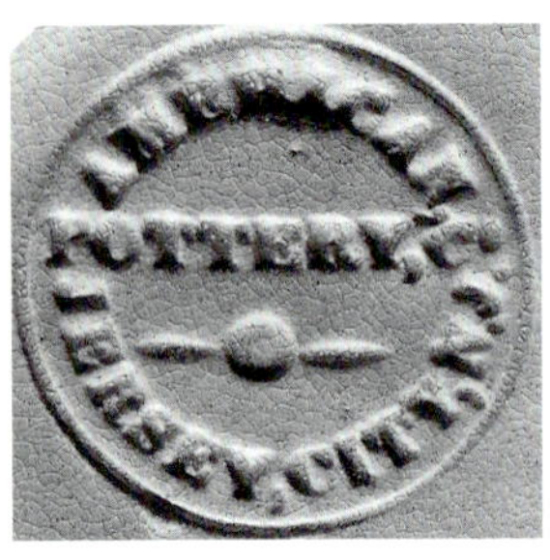

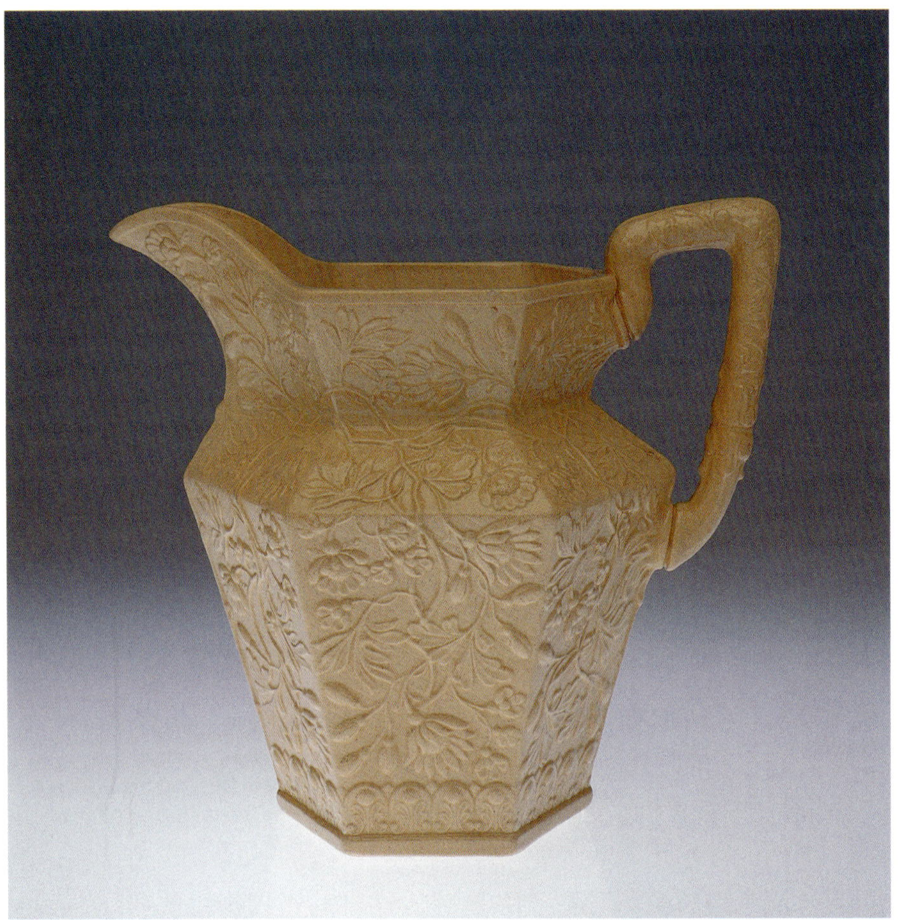

The American Pottery Manufacturing Company capitalized on the popularity of Staffordshire English earthenware molded jugs, which were being imported and sold in great quantities in the United States by the 1830s. Although this pitcher bearing the mark of the company is reminiscent of these imported earthenwares, no exact prototype has been identified. The company was the first American pottery to successfully manufacture on the English system, in which each craftsman focused on one particular task—such as turning, molding, or glazing—to increase quantity and quality of production.[1]

During the Revolutionary War, English potteries lost the colonial market they had dominated, and after the war they were eager to recapture trade in the new United States. The embargo on English goods during the War of 1812, followed by an 1824 protective tariff on imported goods, encouraged the establishment of serious American ceramic and glass enterprises. Technological advances in the United States during the first quarter of the nineteenth century and immigration of experienced European industrialists and artisans further spurred development of such enterprises.

Perhaps as a result of the 1824 tariff, the Jersey Porcelain and Earthenware Company was established in Jersey City, New Jersey, in 1825, a year after the Jersey City Glass Company was founded. Like many early American ceramic manufacturing efforts, this endeavor was short-lived, lasting less than three years. Scottish immigrant David Henderson purchased the manufacturing complex housing the Jersey Porcelain and Earthenware Company in 1828. Initially, Henderson's partner was his brother, James Henderson, and the company mark was *D. and J. Henderson.* In 1833, however, David Henderson incorporated the American Pottery Manufacturing Company, removing the Henderson name from the mark. The Hendersons had begun production in stoneware, but by the time of the name change they were also working in refined earthenware such as the Crawford pitcher. Molded pitchers, tea services, and other hollow forms dominate the surviving output from the 1830s and 1840s.[2]

Henderson's reliance on English molded earthenware prototypes may have resulted from American demand and his hiring of English immigrant ceramic workers, many with experience or family connections in the Staffordshire potteries. For example, James Bennett, brother of successful Baltimore potter Edwin Bennett (see no. 18), was from a family of English potters and worked at the American Pottery Manufacturing Company from 1834 to 1837. In 1838, the English ceramic modeler Daniel Greatbach, who is believed to have worked for Staffordshire's Ridgeway pottery, came to the American Pottery Manufacturing Company. Greatbach remained in Jersey City until 1852, when he entered a partnership with James Carr for a pottery in South Amboy, New Jersey, which lasted until 1854. Greatbach also worked for Christopher Webber Fenton at the United States Pottery Company in Bennington, Vermont (see nos. 15–17). That both Bennett and Greatbach had worked for the American Pottery Manufacturing Company before pursuing other endeavors reflects the intertwining nature of the American ceramic industry and the wandering ways of pottery workers and artisans throughout the nineteenth century.

Scholars believe that American Pottery Manufacturing Company designs made from around 1838 to 1850 or shortly thereafter can be linked to Daniel Greatbach. The overall floral relief decoration of the Crawford pitcher is characteristic of his modeling work.[3] While the pattern on the pitcher suggests the emerging rococo style, which would peak in popularity in the 1850s, the stylized floral images of the bottom border reveal its designer to have an almost classical architectural sensibility.[4]

The American Pottery Manufacturing Company was among the first American ceramic enterprises to attempt competition with the overwhelming production and distribution of the well-established English Staffordshire potteries. The Jersey City enterprise offered the same type of molded earthenwares and was probably the first to make transfer-printed pieces. Around 1852, the pottery was purchased by John Owen Rouse, who had worked at the English Derby factory, and Nathaniel Turner, who had grown up in the Staffordshire pottery business. The name of the company was changed to the Jersey City Pottery, and it continued until 1892, when the original factory buildings were razed.[5]

NOTES

1. Conversation with Diana Stradling, April 24, 1997. D. and J. Henderson and the American Pottery Manufacturing Company have been the focus of Stradling's research for a number of years, and she has kindly shared some of her efforts with the author. Early research on the pottery is found in Barber, *Pottery,* 1976, pp. 118–125; and Watkins 1946. The most comprehensive recent survey is Stradling and Denker 1997.

2. Watkins 1946, p. 389, explains her theory that wares bearing the Crawford pitcher's mark could be dated between 1833 and 1850. Molded wares such as the Crawford pitcher, produced after the 1833 name change, seem not to include the word "Manufacturing" in the marks, possibly due to space limitations.

3. Conversation with Diana Stradling, April 24, 1997.

4. The author is grateful to Diana Stradling for a personal slide presentation and demonstration of the creation of the block to make the molds to produce the pitcher, using small, hand-held press-molds, May 11, 1997. That process of making the molds and producing the pitchers is explained in Stradling and Denker 1997. The Bennington parian pitcher (see no. 15 in this catalogue) was shown at the New York Crystal Palace Exhibition of 1853. The overall molded floral designs of both pitchers seem related.

5. Barber, *Marks,* 1976, p. 44.

Fenton's Works and the United States Pottery Company

Christopher Webber Fenton was born into a New England pottery-making family. His father, Jonathan Fenton Jr., a stoneware potter working as early as 1792 in New Haven, Connecticut, moved in 1801 to Dorset, Vermont, where he operated a stoneware pottery with his sons until 1835. Before 1837, Christopher Fenton moved to Bennington, Vermont, where he married into the Norton family of potters.

Between 1842 and 1847, Fenton was partner with his brother-in-law, Julius Norton, in the Norton and Fenton Pottery. They produced Rockingham stonewares, named for the English factory where the buff-colored wares with mottled brown glazes had been developed.[1] From surviving documents, the firm seems to have specialized in useful rather than decorative objects. However, their experiments with new clay bodies led to a greater interest in producing fancy and decorative wares. By the mid-1840s, English potteries in Staffordshire were producing porcelain figures inspired by marble sculpture, which came to be known as parian ware. Parian, admired for the resemblance of its surface to carved and finished marble, was used in figural ornaments and fancy tablewares. By about 1846, the Bennington partnership was making parian ware with the assistance of John Harrison, an English potter who had worked for the Copeland works in Staffordshire.

At about the same time, the Norton-Fenton partnership was dissolved, and Fenton began to produce both parian porcelain and earthenware goods with innovative glazes. In 1849, he entered into a partnership with businessman Alanson Porter Lyman. During the early 1850s, this venture—the United States Pottery Company—was in full-scale commercial production of parian porcelain and earthenware, and they made an impressive showing at the New York Crystal Palace Exhibition of 1853. However, losses from breakage and competition with cheaper imported goods led to the company's financial ruin. A critically praised showing by the firm at a Boston exhibition held by the Massachusetts Charitable Mechanic Association in 1856 could not forestall the factory's closure two years later.

A pitcher with the same Climbing Rose pattern as the Crawford pitcher (no. 15) was the only example of United States Pottery Company parian ware illustrated in the catalogue of the New York Crystal Palace Exhibition. The company's pitchers particularly impressed Horace Greeley, who wrote, "The Parian Ware of this Company is remarkably fine, especially in the form of pitchers. They are light in material, [and] of graceful outline."[2] Although no English prototype has been identified for this pitcher, the modeling is typical of the natural motifs of midcentury English rococo revival ceramics. The Crawford pitcher bears the mark of Fenton's Works, but other examples of the same form have the mark of the United States Pottery Company, suggesting that the marks may have been used interchangeably between 1847 and 1858. The same mold or a similar one was also used to make earthenware vessels. Because Daniel Greatbach is known to have worked as a modeler for Fenton as early as 1850, it is reasonable to speculate that he may have been responsible for the Climbing Rose parian pitcher design. The original mold for the Fenton's pitcher was made in the same way as the

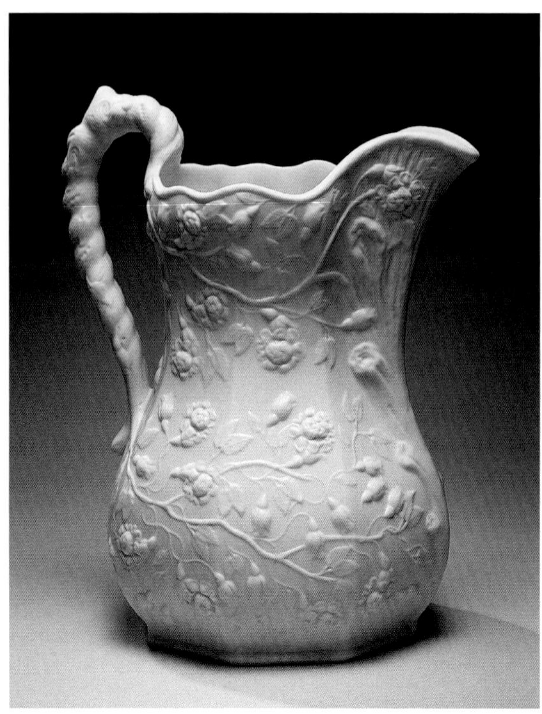

15.

Pitcher, ca. 1850

Made by Fenton's Works (1847–1849) or United States Pottery Company (1849–1858), Bennington, Vermont; possibly designed by Daniel Greatbach (working 1839–1866)
Porcelain
8⅞ × 6⅞ × 10½ inches
Mark: Molded on bottom in rectangular rococo frame, *Fenton's Works/*[abstracted design]*/Bennington,/Vermont*
1984.145

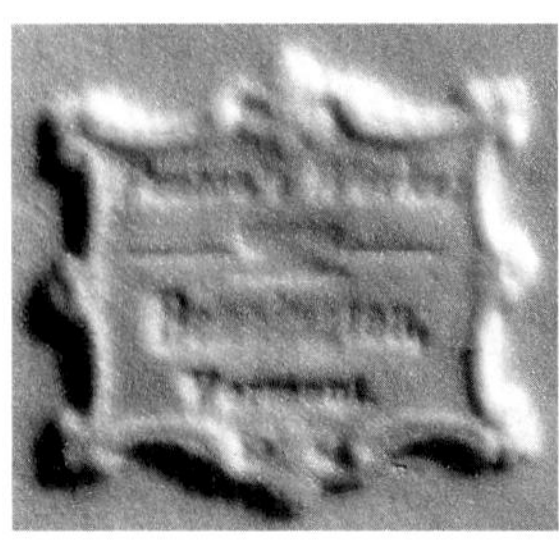

related American Pottery Manufacturing Company's pitcher (see no. 14). Both are hexagonal shapes with overall foliate relief decorations. The rounded shape and the lack of any classical trim make the Fenton pitcher a more full-blown expression of rococo revival.

In addition to parian wares, Fenton introduced various types of earthenware at Bennington. The scroddled ware book-shaped flask in the Crawford Collection (no. 16) bears the same mark as the parian pitcher. Scroddled ware was made by mixing colored clays with a cream-colored clay, producing variegations that went through the entire body of the ceramic, unlike the more common marble wares with surface decoration. Because it was expensive and slow to make, few examples were produced. Most scroddled ware, when it is marked, has the United States Pottery Company label, suggesting that it might date to the 1850s. The Crawford flask is unusual because it bears the Fenton's Works mark. One other flask of this unusually large size and color is known, also with the Fenton mark.[3]

The rococo revival picture frame (no. 17) would have been from the "fancy goods" line at Fenton's Works or the United States Pottery Company. In 1849, Fenton patented his process of flint enamel glazing. Biscuit objects were covered with a transparent glaze and then sprinkled with a metallic oxide. Oxide of manganese was used to create the brown effect. Kiln firing caused the powdered manganese to melt and streak, creating the surface decoration of the frame. Identical frames have been published as Fenton's, and a similar frame is incorporated into the marks on the Crawford parian pitcher and the scroddled book flask.

NOTES

1. A history of Fenton's later firms is recounted in Watkins 1968, pp. 141–153, 211–219.

2. Quoted in Frelinghuysen 1989, p. 138. For the history of the firm see pp. 30–31, 141–142. A matching pitcher with the same mark is in the Bennington Museum, Vermont, and is illustrated and discussed on pp. 138–139, no. 39.

3. Illustrated in Barret 1958, p. 314, pl. 410.

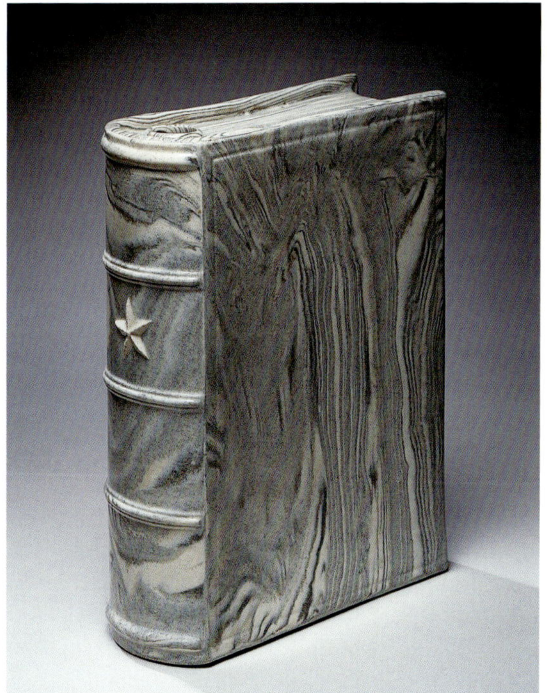

16.

Flask, ca. 1850

Fenton's Works (1847–1849) or United States Pottery Company (1849–1858), Bennington, Vermont
Earthenware (scroddled ware)
10 × 7¾ × 3⅛ inches
Mark: Molded on bottom in rectangular rococo frame, *Fenton's Works*/[abstracted design]/*Bennington,*/*Vermont*
1986.162

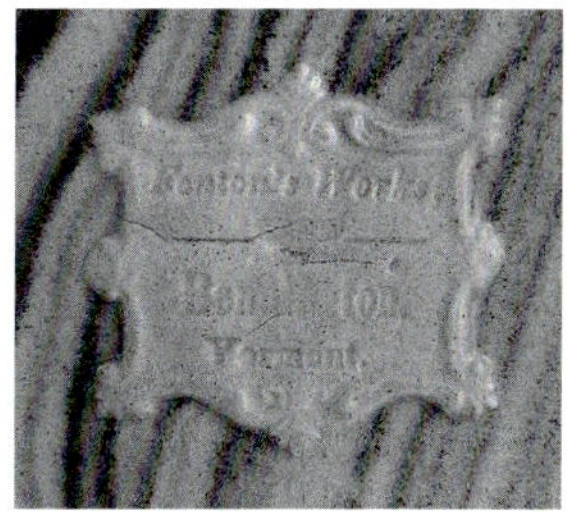

17.

Picture Frame, ca. 1850

Attributed to Fenton's Works (1847–1849) or United States Pottery Company (1849–1858), Bennington, Vermont
Stoneware
12 × 10⅝ × 1⅜ inches
1990.84

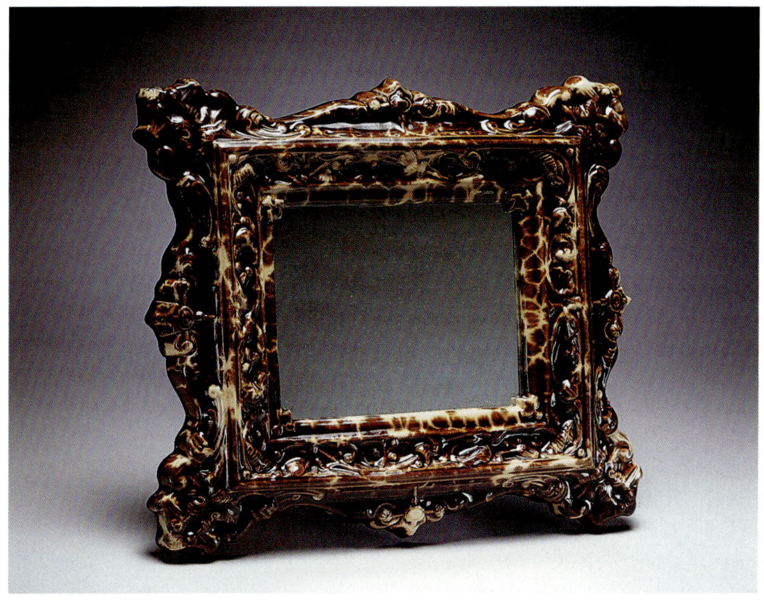

18.

Pitcher, designed ca. 1850

Edwin Bennett Pottery (1846–1936), Baltimore; design attributed to Charles Coxon (1805–1868)
Glazed earthenware
10¼ × 10¾ × 8½ inches
1984.133

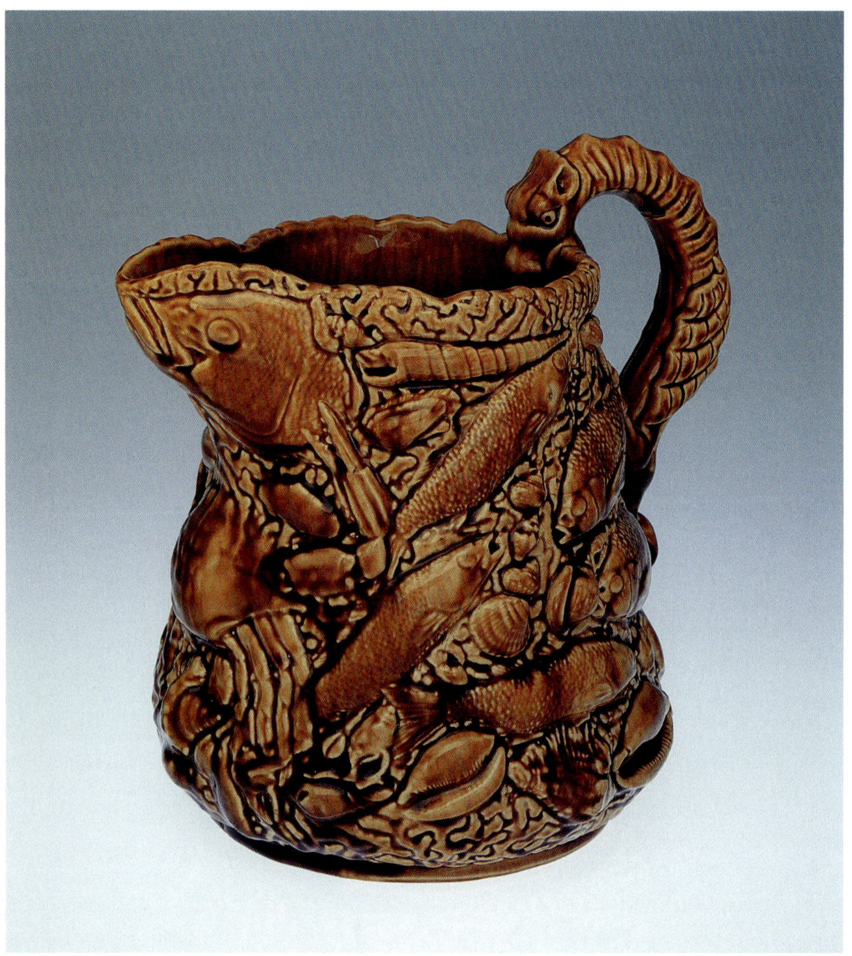

THIS EARTHENWARE PITCHER, molded to depict marine life and shells, may have reflected the importance of the fishing and crabbing industries to the region surrounding Chesapeake Bay, and especially to Baltimore, its major port city. The Edwin Bennett Pottery was one of the most innovative and successful in Baltimore, and with a history spanning ninety years, one of the most enduring American ceramic-manufacturing enterprises of the nineteenth century.[1] Edwin Bennett was one of four sons of the English potter Daniel Bennett of Newhall, Derbyshire. All four Bennett brothers immigrated to the United States and became active in the developing American ceramic industry.

Around 1841, Edwin Bennett followed his eldest brother, James, to the United States. James Bennett had immigrated in 1835 and had first worked at David Henderson's American Pottery Manufacturing Company (see no. 14) in Jersey City, New Jersey. By the time James Bennett sent for his brothers, he had established the first pottery in East Liverpool, Ohio, which later became a major ceramic manufacturing center (see nos. 127–128). When James Bennett decided to move from East Liverpool to Pittsburgh, Edwin Bennett went to Baltimore, apparently to scout business opportunities.[2]

By 1846, Edwin Bennett had established a pottery for the manufacture of cream-colored earthenware in Baltimore, and from about 1850 to 1855, he was joined by his younger brother, William. Rockingham (such as the Crawford pitcher) and yellow earthenwares constituted the output of the firm. Baltimore was a rapidly growing industrial, trading, and railroad center in the 1840s and 1850s, advantageously located for coastal and inland trade. The location also provided clays and easy access to fuel and other raw materials.[3] At midcentury, Baltimore potteries were small concerns, aimed mostly at the local market for simple, utilitarian turned earthenwares and stonewares. The Edwin Bennett Pottery was the first local enterprise to manufacture molded earthenwares, such as the Crawford marine pitcher, which were usually inspired by contemporary English molded wares in pottery and parian. In concept and technical sophistication, these relatively inexpensive Bennett wares were beyond the capabilities of most Baltimore potteries at the time. A modeler and mold-maker with experience in the English industry was essential to their production.[4]

After arriving from England in 1849, Charles Coxon accepted the position of mold-maker at the Edwin Bennett Pottery. Like Bennett, Coxon was born into a family of English potters, although in Staffordshire. Coxon was the only mold-maker on the staff and was probably responsible for introducing molded wares to the Edwin Bennett Pottery and the Baltimore industry. The designs for Bennett molded earthenwares that date to the 1850s (including the Crawford pitcher) have generally been attributed to Coxon. He worked for Bennett until 1857, when he moved on to the New Jersey ceramic industry; he died in Trenton.[5]

In concept, if not in precise form, many of the designs attributed to Coxon can be linked to English prototypes. The marine pitcher, however, has no known English parallel or prototype, nor is it known to have been made at any other American pottery. Examples of this pitcher with blue instead of Rockingham glaze are in the Brooklyn Museum of Art and the National Museum of American History. Although the Crawford pitcher is the only published Rockingham example, others were undoubtedly made and may survive. Because of the expense involved in the manufacture of pottery molds, the Bennett factory surely continued to produce marine pitchers after Coxon left.

Edwin Bennett remained active in the Baltimore industry until his death in 1908. Except for the period of the Civil War, his pottery continued to prosper through two more generations. During the war, Bennett moved his family to Philadelphia, where he joined William T. Gillinder in establishing a glass factory. After the war, he returned to Baltimore, and his pottery began to diversify from the molded earthenwares. They manufactured white tablewares from the 1870s through the end of the century. In 1890 and 1891, Bennett was elected president of the United States Potters Association, which was founded to strengthen and promote the American ceramic industry.[6] His son, Edwin Huston Bennett, expanded the company's interests in 1890, investing in Baltimore's Chesapeake Pottery with David Francis Haynes (see no. 135). In 1895, Edwin AtLee Barber wrote in a profile: "Mr. Edwin Bennett's uninterrupted career as a potter for nearly sixty years entitles him to be called the father of the pottery industry in this country, and at the age of eighty he is still actively pursuing his chosen calling."[7]

NOTES

1. The author is grateful to J. G. and Diana Stradling for information and insights on Edwin Bennett and Charles Coxon. For a history of the Edwin Bennett Pottery, see Barber, *Pottery,* 1976, pp. 196–199, 472–475; Holland 1973; and Myers 1987, pp. 31–35.

2. For information about James Bennett's ceramics career in the United States, see Barber 1898, p. 33. See also Gates and Ormerod 1982, pp. 3–4, for information about the early development of the East Liverpool ceramic industry. James Bennett also worked for the Indiana Pottery Company; see Stefano 1974.

3. Barber, *Marks,* 1976, p. 143; and Myers 1987, p. 32.

4. Myers 1987, p. 32.

5. Barber, *Marks,* 1976, p. 56.

6. Barber, *Pottery,* 1976, p. 198.

7. Barber 1898, p. 38.

19.

Andirons,
1840–1860

Northeastern United States
Cast iron, painted gold
Each 19¾ × 8⅞ × 16 inches
1984.130.1–.2

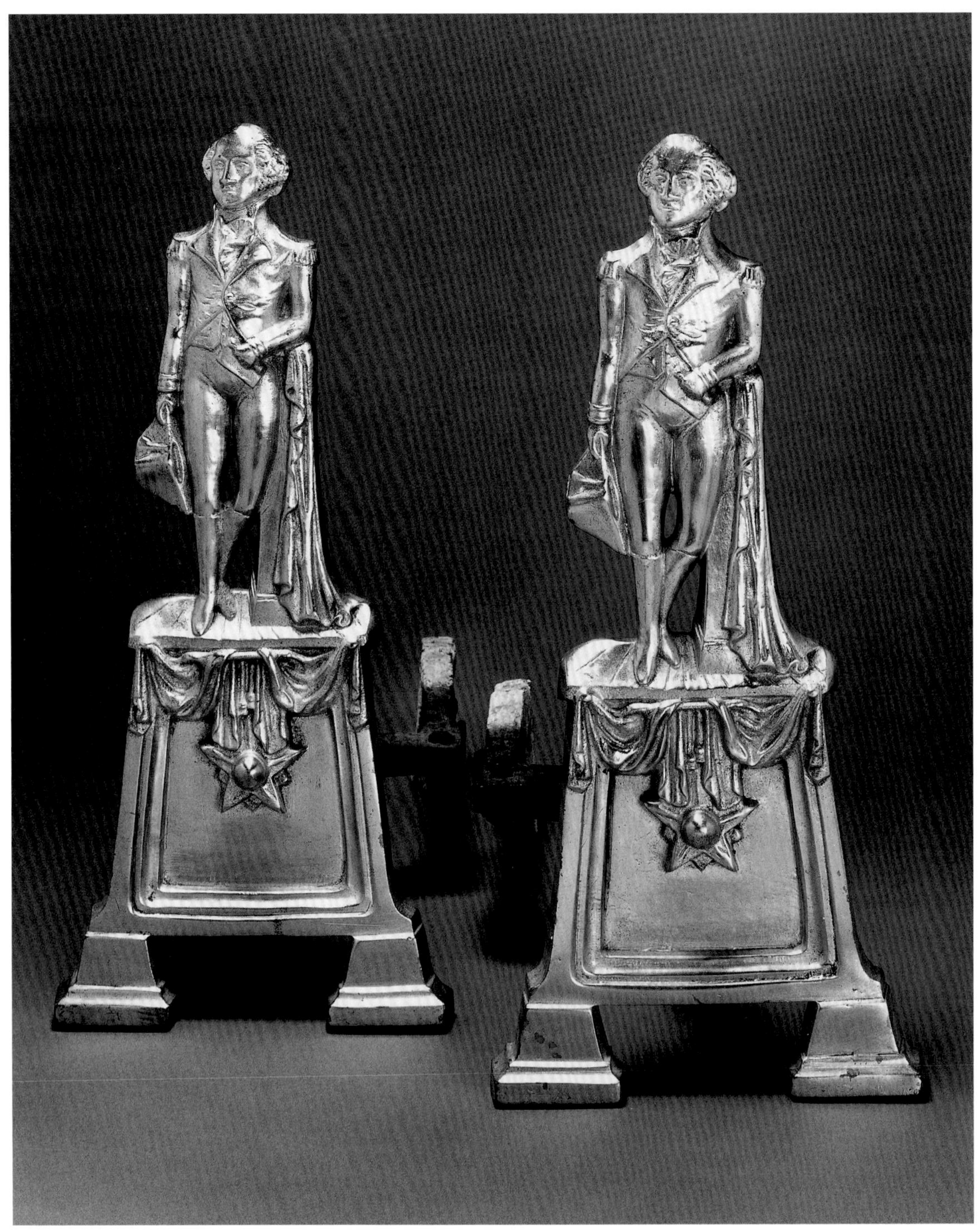

EVEN BEFORE his death in 1799, George Washington had become a powerful icon of American patriotism. Throughout the early nineteenth century, his likeness was incorporated into all manner of decorative arts, both those imported from Europe for the American market and those made in the United States.

The origin of these andirons is not known. They were probably cast in an iron foundry in the northeastern United States. An identical pair was owned by the noted collector Philip Flayderman and is illustrated in his 1930 sale catalogue *Colonial Furniture, Silver and Decorations.*[1] The entry identifies the andirons as from Manchester, Vermont. They may have been made in Boston, in New York, or possibly in Troy, New York, a major center of iron foundries from the 1830s (see no. 20). The Flayderman Collection andirons were dated in the sale catalogue as "early Federal" (1790–1810). Given the broad proportions of the pedestals and the feet on which they stand, an 1830s or 1840s date would be more likely. A later date would also correspond to the development of the cast iron industry in the United States. Although the paint has been renewed, there is still evidence of the original gold paint on the Crawford andirons. An identical set was also painted gold, perhaps in an attempt to simulate brass.[2] The tone of the gold on the Crawford andirons is similar to that on William F. Shaw's 1849 girandole garniture set from Boston (see no. 32).

NOTES

1. Flayderman 1930, p. 274, lot 512.

2. "George Washington" 1982, illustrated p. 20. The same was true of the Flayderman andirons, which were described as brass, but were more likely cast iron painted gold.

20.

Parlor Stove,
ca. 1840

Peter Low (working 1830–1855),
Troy, New York
Cast iron
60 × 33 × 18 inches
Mark: On front step, in raised letters, *P,LOW, & CO, TROY. NY.*
1986.187

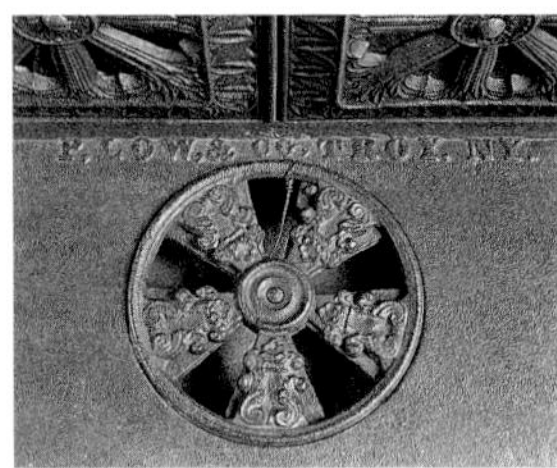

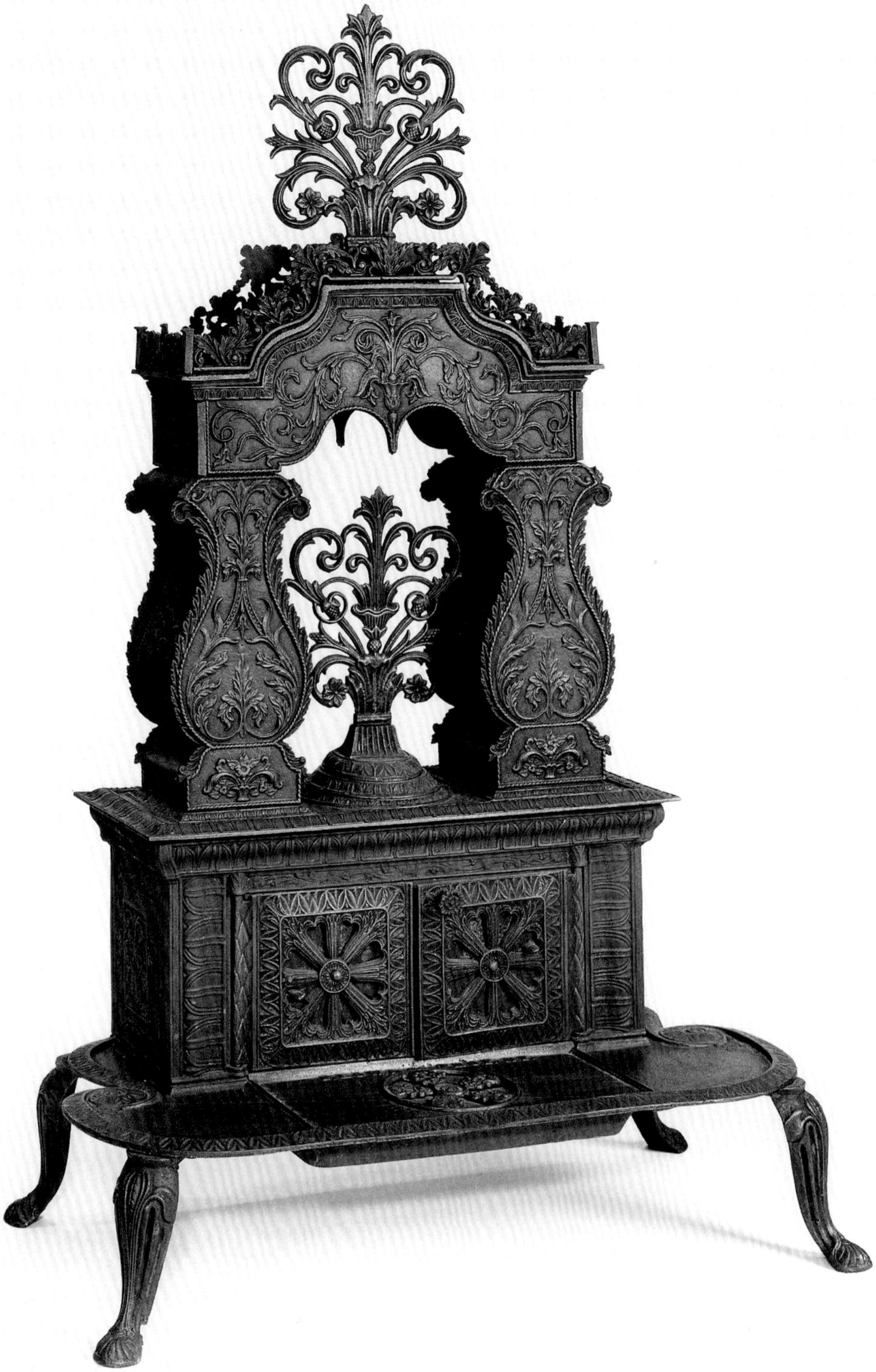

BETWEEN 1825 and 1875, Troy, New York, and its surrounding area was a cast-iron manufacturing center of international significance. While all types of cast-iron products were made there—horseshoes, railroad ties, machine parts, architectural details, building facades, and farming implements—heating and cooking stoves were a mainstay of the regional economy for both Troy and nearby Albany. By the 1830s, the forests of the Northeast were becoming depleted due to heavy settlement and industry. Coal-burning cast-iron stoves were more efficient and cheaper for heating and cooking than the enormous wood-consuming fireplaces of early-American households.

Troy and Albany are located on opposite sides of the Hudson River—the head of navigation for the New York trade artery—and near the western terminus of the Erie Canal, which was completed in 1825 and opened the vast markets to the west and around the Great Lakes. Railroad lines constructed in the 1840s linked Albany and Troy with Boston and the New England markets, as well as the Middle Atlantic states and regions to the south. Key raw materials for cast-iron manufacturing were nearby. Iron ore was mined in the counties along the Hudson River valley. Charcoal was made locally, and coke, which was mined in neighboring Pennsylvania, was brought to the Hudson River on the Delaware and Hudson Canal. Fine molding sand in the immediate area enabled intricate and detailed cast decoration on locally made stoves.[1] In the 1850s, Troy and Albany each had seven foundries, employing 1,700 workers. In 1875, Troy alone boasted seventeen foundries, but in the late 1870s, labor unrest in Troy and discovery of iron ore deposits around the Great Lakes led to cheaper production in that area. By the 1880s, the local industry was in steady decline.[2]

This parlor stove dates from the heyday of Troy's dominance of the cast-iron stove industry in the 1840s. Such innovative column parlor stoves were made in Troy as early as the 1830s. The firebox, fueled by coal, is at the base. The heat from the fire circulated through the vase-shaped columns, which became radiators. The increased area of cast-iron surface provided more efficient radiant circulation and more long-lasting heat than earlier six-sided box stoves did.[3]

The S-shaped scrolls of the columns on the Crawford parlor stove echo Grecian-style furniture (see nos. 7–8). The intricate cast floral decoration relates to the cast and repoussé decoration on contemporary silver (see nos. 2, 37) and to the floral carving on furniture in the emerging modern French style (see no. 44).

Little is known about Peter Low's stove factory, which was listed in the Troy directories from 1830 to 1855.[4] As there were many more listings for stove factories and dealers than for foundries, the various companies probably shared foundry facilities. Troy directories also list pattern makers, who carved intricate designs in mahogany or pine from which iron molds were cast.[5] The designer of the Crawford stove is unknown, but a stove with identical decorative passages in the Albany Institute of History and Art bears the mark of an Albany manufacturer, Low and Leake, and a patent date of August 10, 1844.[6]

NOTES

1. The industry was also encouraged by the establishment in 1824 of Rensselaer Polytechnic Institute, the nation's first engineering school, at Troy. The latest scientific and technological information was available there, and the school must have provided educated manpower to feed the local industries.

2. A history of the development of the stove industry in Troy and a listing of Troy stove manufacturers are found in Waite and Waite 1973. A more comprehensive illustrated survey, together with listings of stove makers in both Troy and Albany, is found in Groft 1981. A photographic survey of stove types, including column parlor stoves, is found in Curtis and Curtis 1974, pp. 16–21. See also no. 83 in this catalogue.

3. See Curtis and Curtis 1974, pp. 16–21; and Groft 1981, pp. 34–49.

4. Between 1830 and 1846, Low operated his stove manufactory and dealership on River Street, the heart of the stove trade in Troy. He was joined in partnership by George W. Hicks between 1847 and 1853. In 1854–1855, Low moved his business to 253 River Street, where he was in partnership with a Mr. Hakes. After that date, Low was no longer listed in local directories. Groft 1981, p. 98; and Waite and Waite 1973, p. 144.

5. See Groft 1981, pp. 20–21, for a discussion of pattern makers.

6. Ibid., p. 43, no. 43.

21.

Ottoman, patented 1854

Manufactured by M. L. Greenwood and Company (1844–ca. 1898), Cincinnati, Ohio; designed by Charles Zeuner
Cast iron with modern upholstery
11½ x 18¾ x 13¾ inches
Mark: Label stenciled in black ink on wooden underside, *M.L. GREENWOOD & CO./CIN. OHIO/ PATENTED JAN. 5, 1854*
1991.354

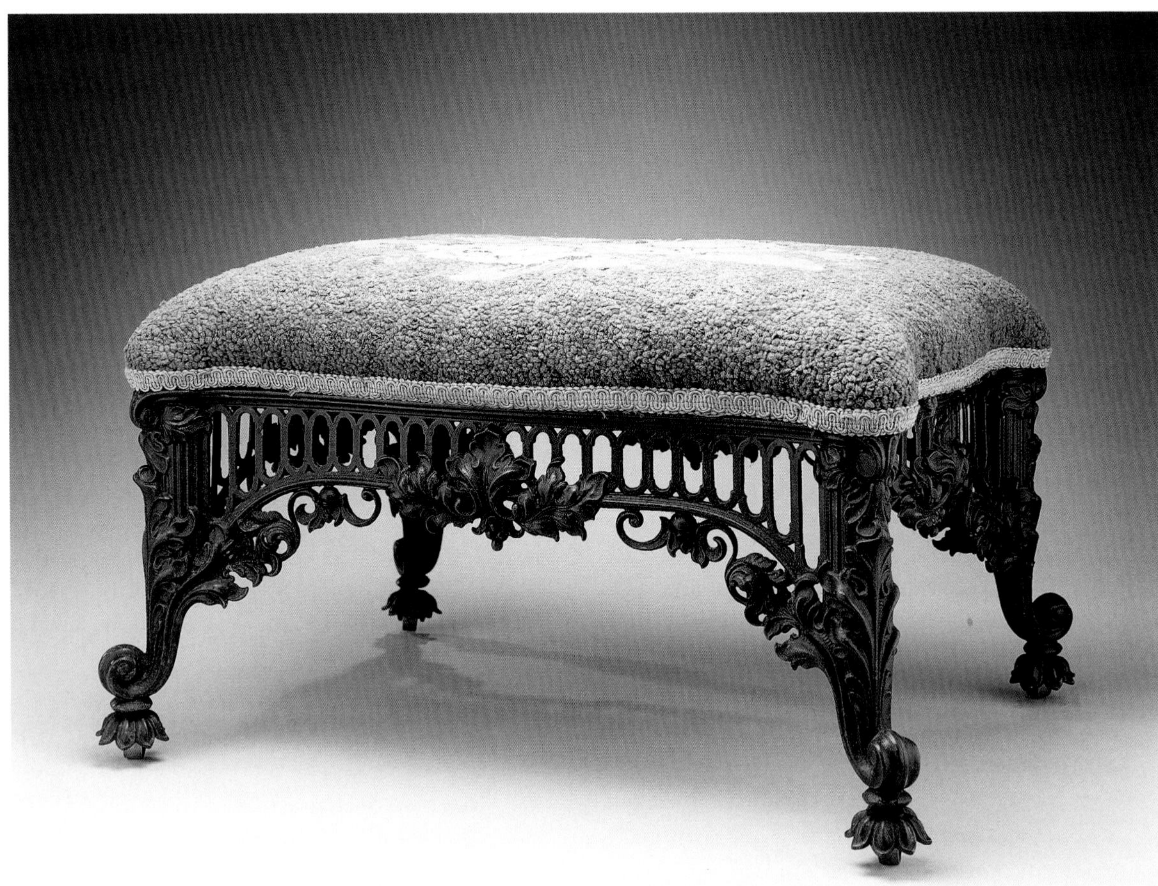

The Greenwood ottoman illustrates that American iron foundries at midcentury were producing a wide variety of products. Between 1800 and 1850, Cincinnati grew from a village settlement to a city of nearly 120,000, and production of iron goods was one of its major industries. Located on the Ohio River about halfway between Pittsburgh and the Mississippi River, the city became a major railroad and steamboat center.[1]

Miles Greenwood's foundry, the Eagle Iron Works, located at the corner of Canal and Walnut Streets, was among Cincinnati's largest iron manufacturers and was active in every type of iron production, including hardware, parlor stoves, and building facades. From 1844, the Eagle Iron Works, under the subsidiary M. L. Greenwood and Company (the name printed on the ottoman), produced many cast-iron products, including "piano stools, store stools, ottomans, shovel and tongs, stands, tables with marble tops, garden seats and chairs, toilet glasses [perhaps similar to no. 22], etc., of beautiful design and finish."[2]

Greenwood was born in New Jersey and moved with his parents to Cincinnati in 1818. He and his father joined Robert Dale Owens's communist colony at New Harmony, Indiana, in 1825, where Greenwood made axes in the village forge. The colony sent him to Pittsburgh to train in the foundry business, and he returned by 1828 to manage their foundry. After the colony failed, Greenwood went to Cincinnati and established the Eagle Iron Works in 1832 with another iron worker, James Webb. In 1840, Greenwood became sole proprietor of the Works, and in the following decades he opened branch operations, including M. L. Greenwood and Company.

During the Civil War, Greenwood sought Union government business as an arms and equipment supplier and received a contract for an iron-clad war vessel. Government bureaucracy and specification changes delayed completion, however, and delivery was not made until after the war. Litigation protracted payment into the 1870s, and the Eagle Iron Works steadily declined in production and profits until the business closed in 1888, three years after Greenwood's death.[3]

Like contemporary cast-iron indoor and garden furniture from eastern foundries, the ottoman embraces the florid French taste, popular in the 1850s. John Henry Belter's rococo-inspired furniture (see no. 44) was known in Cincinnati at the time, and the ottoman was meant to complement that style. Patent records reveal that patent number 616, issued on January 5, 1854, was secured by Charles Zeuner and assigned to M. L. Greenwood and Company. This patent was for the "scroll and leaf" frame of the Crawford ottoman (fig. 1). Charles Zeuner was variously listed in Cincinnati directories between 1851 and 1858 as a machinist and pattern maker, but beyond his authorship of this design, nothing is known about him. The hooked upholstery on the Crawford ottoman is a twentieth-century colonial revival replacement.

NOTES

1. Cist 1859, pp. 164–166, describes Cincinnati's spectacular growth in the first half of the century, its development as a distribution center, and the ready acceptance by its businesses of steam power in factories like the Eagle Iron Works. Cist reported forty-two foundries (a quarter of which were "mainly or entirely in the stove line"), employing more than five thousand. Economic factors in Germany and Ireland in the 1840s brought an unprecedented number of immigrants to the United States, and Cincinnati was a major western destination for them.

2. Ibid., pp. 279–283. Cist outlines the history of the Eagle Iron Works and the evolution of its various operations between 1832 and 1859.

3. Becker 1968, pp. 259–304, provides biographical information about Miles Greenwood and a history of the Eagle Iron Works.

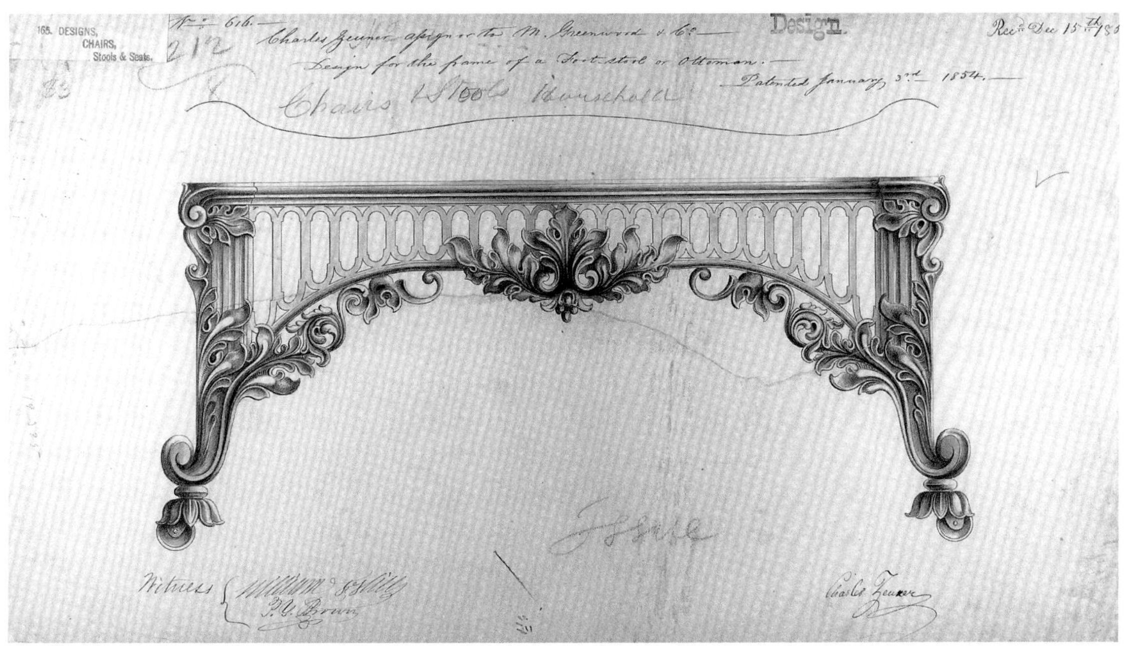

Fig. 1. Patent drawing. U.S. Patent Office. Charles Zeuner, assignor to M. L. Greenwood and Company, Cincinnati. Design patent number 616, issued January 5, 1854.

22.

Table Mirror,
ca. 1860

Probably northeastern
United States
Cast iron and glass
20¾ × 14¼ × 16⅜ inches
1987.171

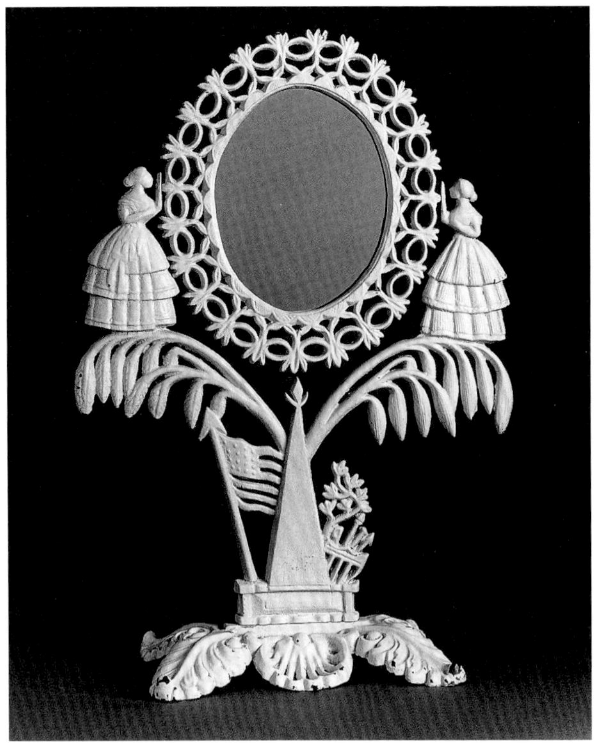

THIS DECORATIVE cast-iron mirror was intended to be placed in a woman's bedchamber on a small table or bureau as a personal vanity. The style of the hoopskirts on the female figures that support and flank the mirror dates it to about the time of the Civil War. The figures stand on olive branches shading the American flag, symbolizing the hope for peace in the years before the conflict.[1]

Many nineteenth-century commentators referred to their era as the age of cast iron. In eighteenth-century England, coke was introduced in the blasting furnace for smelting iron to create a smoother, more liquid iron that was cheaper and better suited for casting in intricate molds. Although iron had for centuries been forged and wrought into tools, military arms, and ornaments, its uses expanded dramatically. In both England and the United States, cast iron began to be used for more than tools, cooking utensils, and weapons, and it became indispensable in the growth of industry and transportation. Architectural details and building facades—such as the United States Capitol dome, constructed during the Civil War—were made of cast iron. Decorative cast-iron garden fencing, furniture, and ornaments were popular from midcentury (see nos. 23, 27).

In the 1860s, Troy, New York, emerged as a major center for iron foundries, producing parlor stoves and other products (see nos. 20, 83). Other cast-iron manufacturing centers in the last half of the nineteenth century included New York, Philadelphia, and—with the discovery of iron deposits in the Great Lakes area—Midwestern cities such as Detroit, St. Louis, and Cincinnati. The enormous foundries emitting great clouds of smoke were seen as evidence of prosperity and progress.[2]

NOTES

1. Sleepy Hollow Restorations, Tarrytown, New York, in Sunnyside, the estate of American author Washington Irving, has a similar vanity mirror. See Otto 1965, p. 312, fig. 312. That example appears to be identical to the Crawford mirror, except for its finial of a pair of putti bound by a floral garland. The Sunnyside mirror's original polychromed decoration also survives. The Crawford mirror has several coats of thick paint, the most recent cream colored. It was found in Alabama, but its provenance is not documented.

2. Snyder 1985, pp. 222–225, discusses the effect of cast iron on the culture and economy and its interpretation by contemporary social observers in the United States.

Cast-Iron Garden Furniture

GARDEN FURNITURE is one of the most familiar survivals of the nineteenth-century American cast-iron industry. Its wide popularity coincided with the publication in 1850 of Andrew Jackson Downing's *The Architecture of Country Houses,* as well as other books and magazines that influenced new suburban tracts, country estates, and urban parks in the last half of the nineteenth century. Downing's promotion of the beautiful American landscape contributed to the demand for cast-iron garden furniture, which, in dismantled form, was distributed nationwide by steamboat and railroad.[1]

In cast-iron furniture, the light that passes through the shapes is as much a part of the pattern as the iron itself, and it gives the pieces a visual airiness that belies their weight. The cast-iron furniture used in outdoor settings such as gardens, cemeteries, and porches was often patterned after contemporary domestic furniture. The Gothic pattern of the Crawford bench and armchairs (no. 23), so named for the horizontal tracery across the back, had been patented in England in 1846 and was made in the United States by 1850. Rococo elements from indoor furniture were included in the floral and scrolled crest rail, C-scrolls and S-scrolls in the arms, and the cabriole legs. The molds for cast-iron furniture were expensive but durable, and popular ones were copied by many foundries and used over long periods. The expense of the molds limited the number of different patterns available; only twenty-three are known throughout the century. Similar Gothic pattern benches were made for the White House grounds in 1852, probably in New York, and a similar bench in a family cemetery was illustrated on the back of a catalogue for Stewart Iron Works in Cincinnati in 1910.[2] The foundry Brown and Owen has not been identified nor its working dates established.

The Grape pattern was one of the most popular made by American foundries between 1850 and World War I. Different foundries introduced slight variations: legs were cast as leaves, vines, or bunches of grapes. This example (no. 24) has legs of grape bunches, which carry out the pattern

23.

Bench and Two Armchairs, 1850–1900

Brown and Owen, probably United States
Cast iron, Gothic pattern
Bench: 36 × 45 × 16½ inches
Armchairs: Each 35½ × 27 × 16½ inches
Mark: Stamped on bench, on back of seat, BROWN & OWEN
1981.1000.90–.92

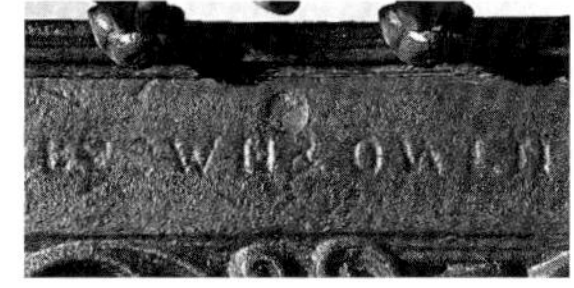

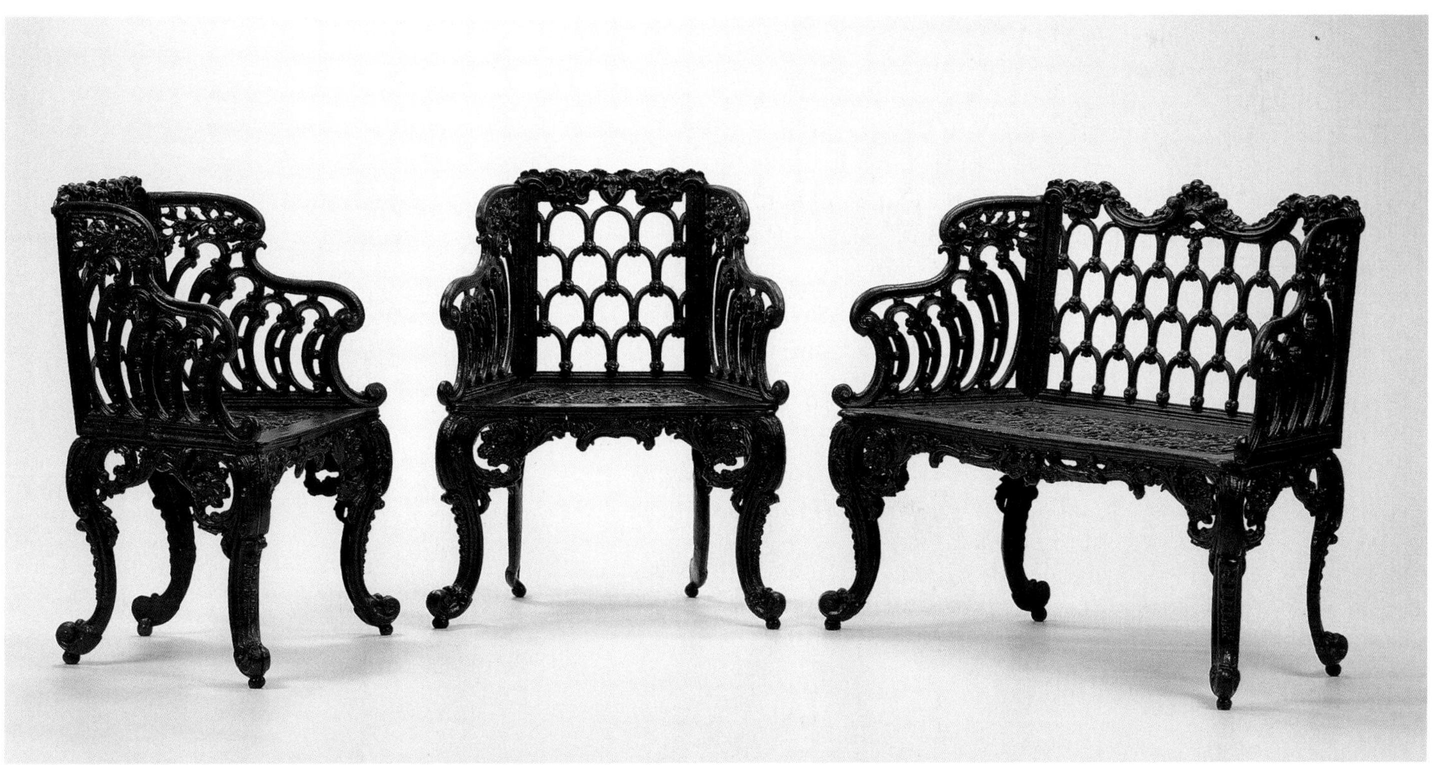

24.

Bench, ca. 1890

John McLean (working 1880–1897), New York
Cast iron, Grape pattern
30¼ × 47 × 28 inches
Mark: Impressed on back of bench at edge of seat, *JOHN MCLEAN/N.Y.*
1984.125

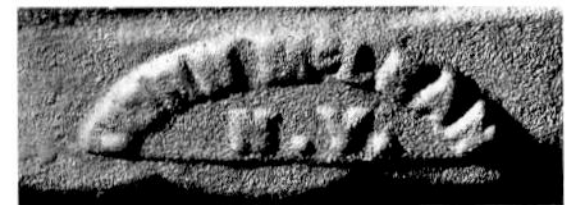

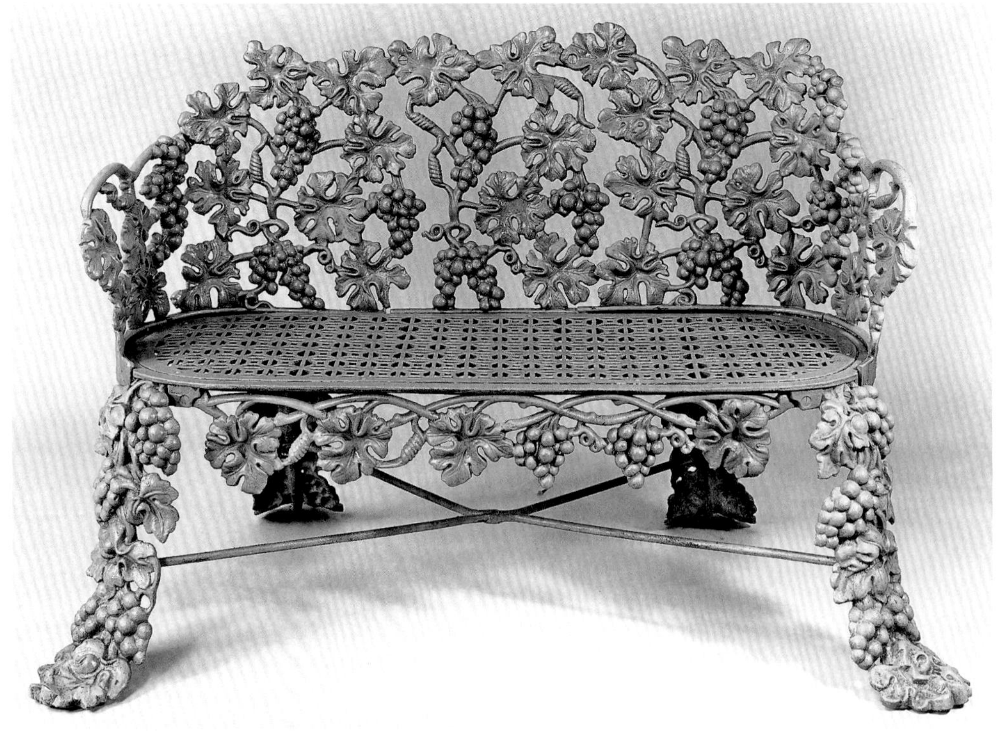

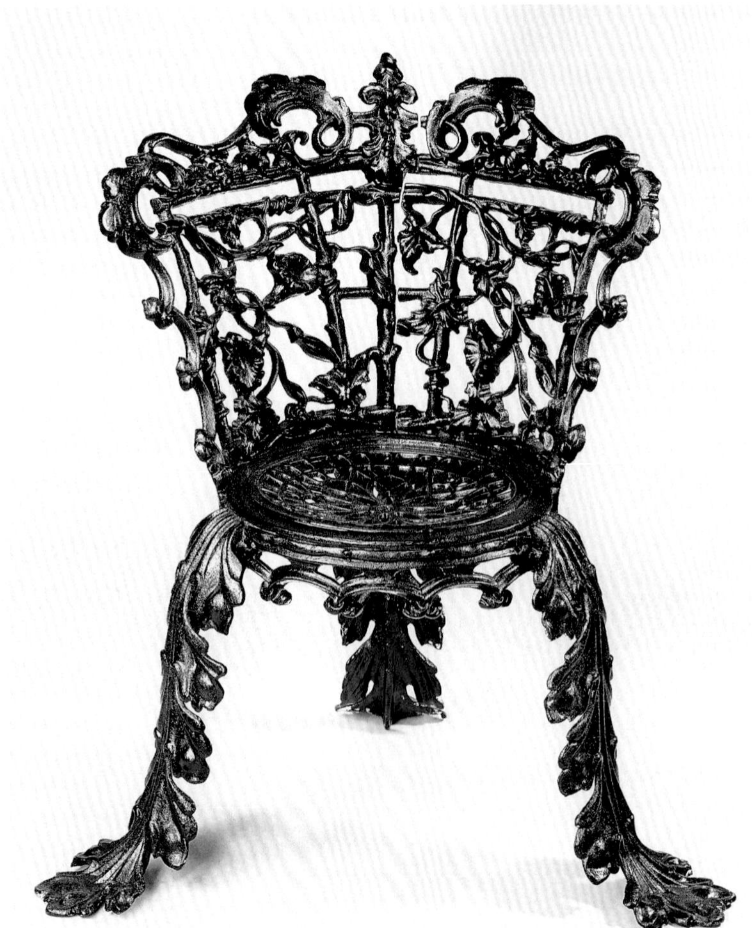

25.

Chair, 1850–1900

United States
Cast iron, Morning Glory pattern
32 × 27½ × 21 inches
1984.123

of the curved back, arm unit, and seat skirt.[3] A Manhattan machinist named John McLean, who listed his shop at 298 Monroe Street in directories between 1880 and 1897, might be the same person whose name is cast in the side of the seat rail.

The popular Morning Glory pattern was made by a number of American foundries and was included in foundry catalogues from the 1850s through the end of the century. An example like the Crawford chair (no. 25) was illustrated in the 1870 catalogue of the New York foundry Janes, Kirtland and Company, which had evolved from the cast-iron stove manufactory Janes, Beebe, and Company in lower Manhattan.[4] The chair does not have a mark, however, and it is not attributed to a specific foundry.

The unmarked bench with a woman's face at the center in a crest (no. 26) is, like the Gothic bench and chairs, related to domestic furniture from the 1850s through the 1870s. In the Crawford Collection, for example, carved wooden female heads are incorporated into the Alexander Roux étagère (see no. 46), the Daniel Pabst cabinet (see no. 54), and the John Jelliff–related sofa (see no. 66). The cabriole legs and the profusion of scrolls also resemble furniture of the 1850s. Flowers in the design suggest gardens, while the acanthus leaves at the center of the skirt and on the scrolled legs provide associations not only with nature but also with classicism, a surviving influence through the 1840s and 1850s, with renewed popularity in the 1860s. The bench was found in Alabama in the mid-1980s, but its maker and history are unknown.

NOTES

1. Snyder 1985, pp. 222–242, discusses nineteenth-century American cast-iron furniture. Mipaas 1979, pp. 34–41, discusses the use of cast-iron furniture and garden ornaments.

2. Snyder 1985, p. 229, accounts for twenty-three different patterns of cast-iron seating furniture. The White House bench is illustrated on p. 232, fig. 8, and the 1910 Stewart catalogue illustration is shown on p. 240, fig. 17.

3. A Grape pattern bench with leaf legs, ca. 1880, by the Detroit foundry Eugene T. Barum is in the collection of the Henry Ford Museum and Greenfield Village in Dearborn, Michigan, and is illustrated in Mipaas 1979, p. 38.

4. Janes, Kirtland and Company 1971, no. 44.

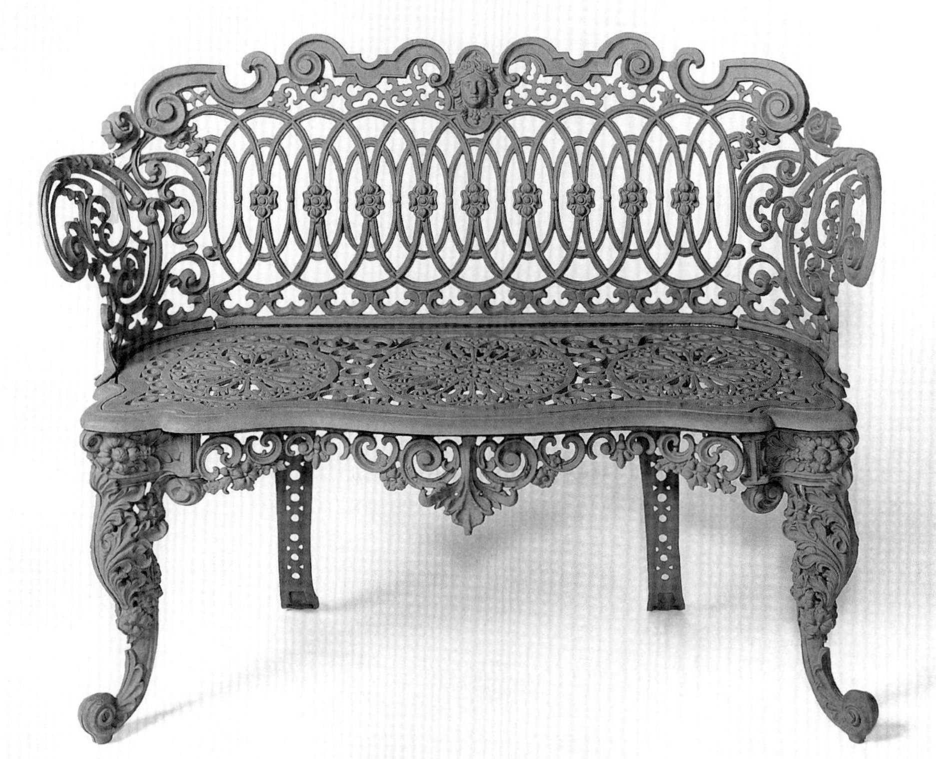

26.

Bench, 1850–1900

United States
Cast iron
32¾ × 44¼ × 16 inches
1987.172

27.

Garden Urn, 1874–1892

J. W. Fiske Ironworks (1864–1934), New York
Cast iron, painted decoration
72 × 56 × 45 inches
Marks: On side of base, *J.W. FISKE/NO. 21 & 23/BARCLAY ST/ N.Y.*; on another side of base, *J.W. FISKE N.Y.*
1984.134.1

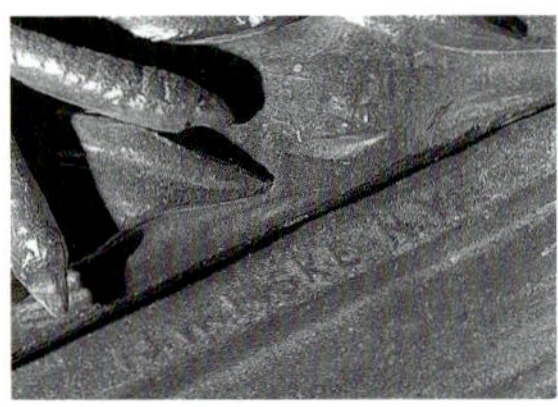

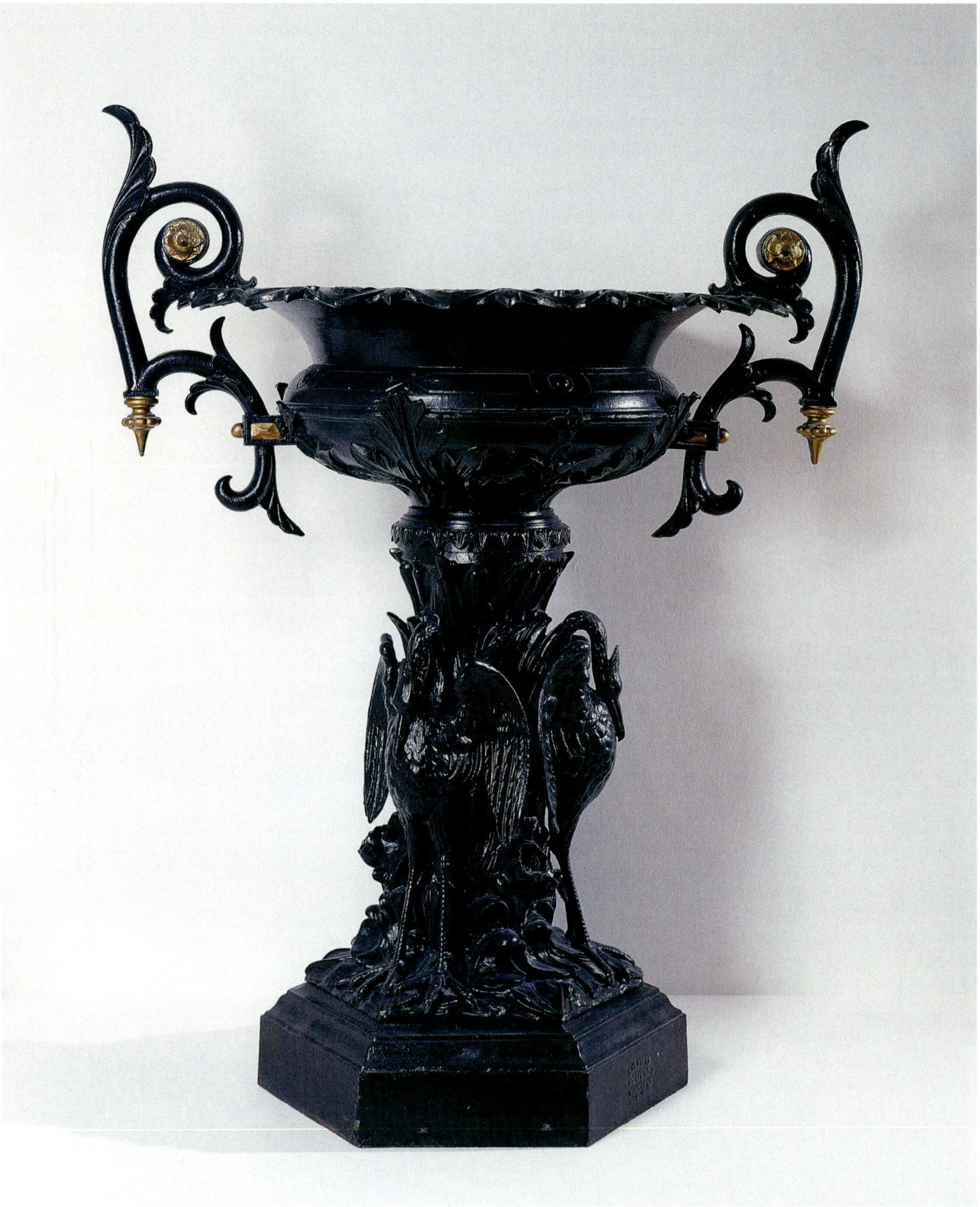

New York directories document the seventy-year survival of the J. W. Fiske Ironworks, maker of this monumental cast-iron garden urn, one of a pair in the Crawford Collection (fig. 1). Founder Joseph W. Fiske was born in Boston and started the business in New York in 1858,[1] but no city directory listing appeared until 1864–1865, when the ironworks were listed at 120 Nassau Street.[2] Although "mostly retired," Fiske was still president of the firm at his death.

J. W. Fiske Ironworks made iron of all kinds, and descriptions in the directories varied only slightly over the years. In 1865–1866, the business was listed simply as "iron," and a year later it was listed as "ornamental iron goods." Fiske must have preferred to be known for its decorative garden cast iron, because from 1883 through

1895–1896, its primary business was listed in directories as "statuary." Even in an early illustrated catalogue from Fiske's 120 Nassau Street address, the firm emphasized its ornamental wares, describing itself as "Manufacturers of Fountains, Vases, Iron and Wire Railings of All Kinds, Iron Stable Furniture, Copper Weather Vanes, Emblematic Signs, and All Kinds of Garden and Cemetery Adornments."[3]

The Crawford urns would have been considered garden adornments, and the pedestals, with their realistically rendered cranes, are highly sculptural. The illustrated catalogue of Fiske vases includes several versions of the Crawford vases of different dimensions and prices. The version closest to the Crawford vases in size was priced at $115 (fig. 2). It was described in the catalogue as a "SHIELD AND LEAF VASE, With Handles on No. 3 Crane Pedestal."[4]

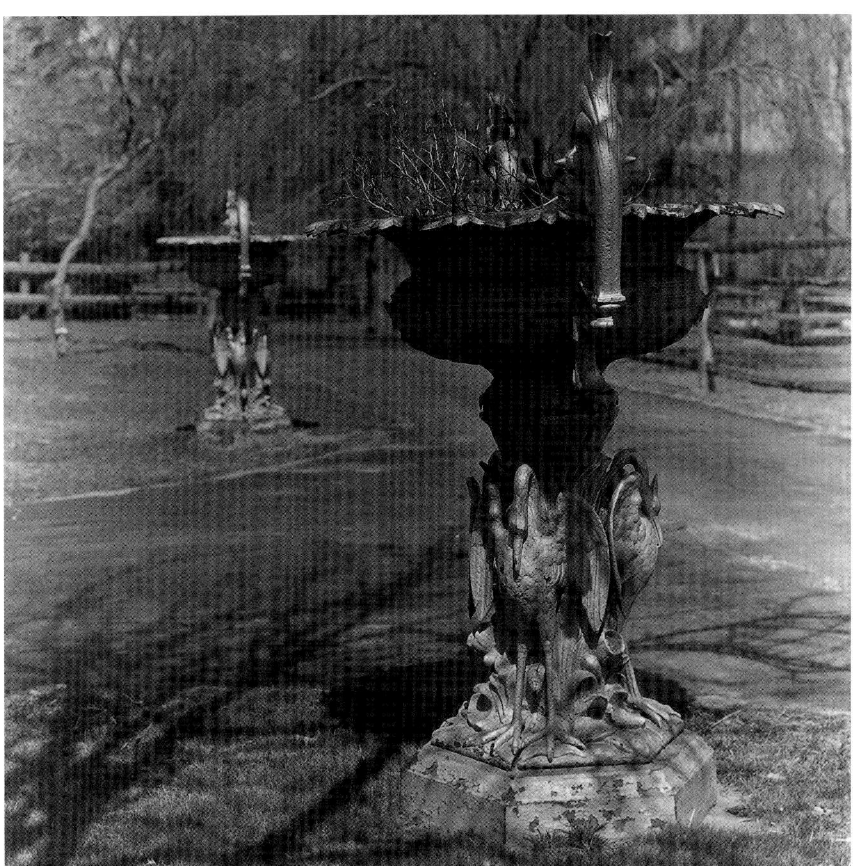

Fig. 1. A view of the urns in what is believed to be their original setting in upstate New York.

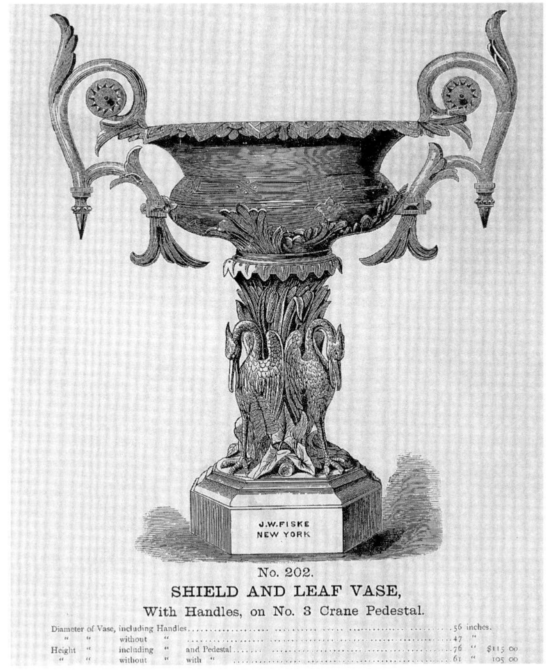

No. 202.

SHIELD AND LEAF VASE,

With Handles, on No. 3 Crane Pedestal.

Diameter of Vase,	including Handles		56 inches.		
" "	without "		47 "		
Height "	including "	and Pedestal	76 "	$115 00
" "	without "	with "	61 "	105 00

Fig. 2. J. W. Fiske, shield and leaf vase, in *Illustrated Price List of Vases,* p. 2, no. 202. New York, late nineteenth century. Department of Drawings and Prints, The Metropolitan Museum of Art, The Elisha Whittelsey Collection, The Elisha Whittelsey Fund, 1950 (50.588.2).

NOTES

1. Obituary of Joseph W. Fiske, *The New York Times,* October 22, 1903, p. 9, col. 6.

2. The J. W. Fiske Ironworks remained at 120 Nassau Street until 1871, when the address changed to 99 Chambers Street. The 1875 directory lists the addresses as 21 Barclay Street and 26 Park Place, addresses also given in an 1874 Fiske catalogue. The earliest date for the Crawford vases, according to the address given on their cast raised labels, would be 1874. Fiske remained at Barclay Street and Park Place locations through 1892, providing a probable latest date, unless the firm continued to make the vases using old labels. In 1892, the firm's listed address changed to 39 Park Place, where it remained through at least 1906. The Barclay Street and Park Place addresses must have been both showrooms and offices. Fiske's 1874 catalogue of zinc statuary listed the office and salesroom at 21 and 23 Barclay Street and 26 and 28 Park Place.

3. Fiske 1864–1870.

4. Fiske 1874–1892, p. 2, no. 202.

Gothic and Elizabethan Revivals, 1845–1865

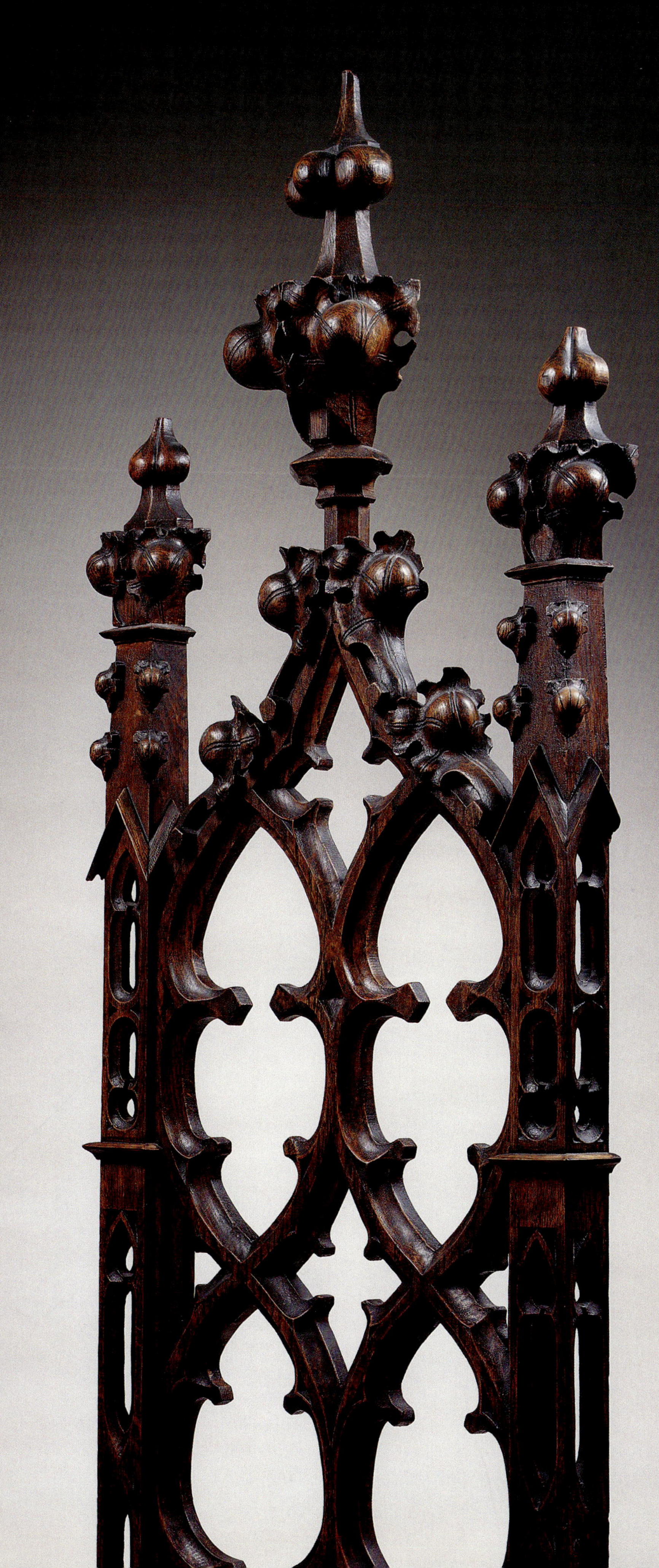

28.

Pitcher and Goblet, 1845

Zalmon Bostwick (working 1846–1852), New York
Silver
Pitcher: 11 × 8½ × 5½ inches
Goblet: 8 × 3⅝ × 3⅞ inches
Mark: Stamped on bottom of pitcher, *Z. Bostwick*
Inscriptions: Engraved on bottom of pitcher, *John W. Livingston/to/Joseph Sampson/1845;* engraved on side of goblet, Sampson crest (lion holding a sword) above *S*
1984.142.1–.2

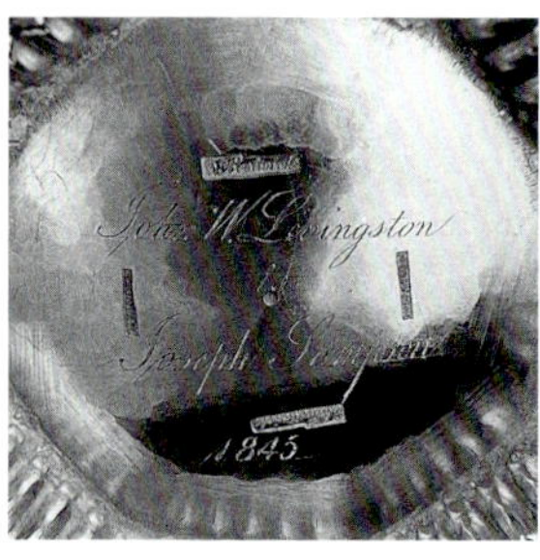

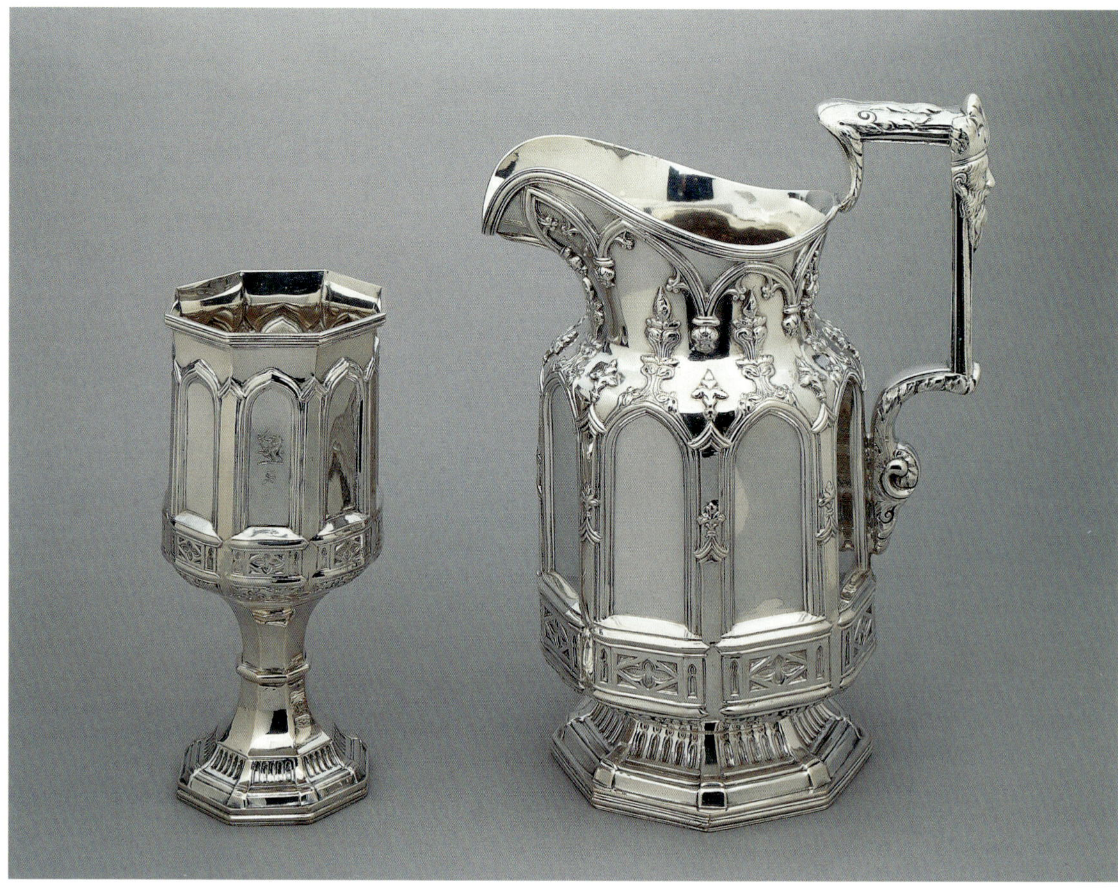

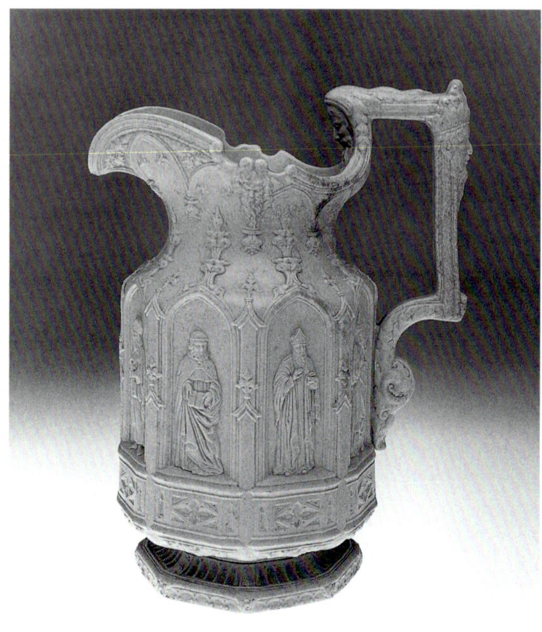

Fig. 1. Pitcher, Staffordshire, England, ca. 1842, High Museum of Art, Gift of Mrs. Martin M. Durrett in memory of Mr. Martin M. Durrett, 69.1000.7.

Few American examples of silver holloware in the Gothic taste of the 1840s have been recorded or published. The Crawford pitcher and goblet match a set (also made by Bostwick with the same inscriptions) in the collection of the Brooklyn Museum of Art.[1] Little is known about Zalmon Bostwick other than his listings as a silversmith in New York directories between 1846 and 1851. He was first listed at 128 William Street, and from 1849 to 1851 he worked at 158 William Street. He died apparently in 1852.[2]

Bostwick's advertisement in the 1848–1849 city directory listed his firm as successor to William Thompson, who was listed as a silvermaker in New York directories between 1810 and 1833 and between 1841 and 1845. Thompson's address between 1841 and 1845 was 129 William Street, near to where Bostwick was listed in 1846. Connections between Thompson and Bostwick, other than the term "successor" in the advertisement, have not been documented; Bostwick may have worked with Thompson before succeeding him. In his advertisement, Bostwick informed the public that he had made "extensive preparations for the manufacture of SILVER WARE, in all its branches; embracing Plain, Chased and Wrought SILVER CUPS, URNS, VASES & C." He also listed a full line of flatware of different patterns.[3]

The prototype for the Bostwick pitcher was an English Staffordshire stoneware pitcher introduced by Charles Meigh at the Old Hall Works at Hanley in 1842 (fig. 1).[4] In form and decorative detail, the Bostwick pitcher closely followed the Meigh example. Major differences between the two are the sculptural figures of apostles in the Gothic arches, modeled masks in scallops on the upper edge of both sides, and a modeled mask on the inside top of the handle on the stoneware pitcher. Bostwick incorporated none of these details into his silver pitcher. The Meigh pitcher must have been popular in the United States in the early 1840s, because it was also the prototype for an earthenware Gothic-style pitcher depicting the apostles, which was made by the American Pottery Manufacturing Company of Jersey City, New Jersey (fig. 2).[5]

John W. Livingston, a descendant of a prominent colonial family that settled the Hudson River valley, presented the Crawford pitcher and goblet to his son-in-law, Joseph Sampson, in 1845. These pieces, along with the set now in The Brooklyn Museum of Art, descended in the Sampson family.

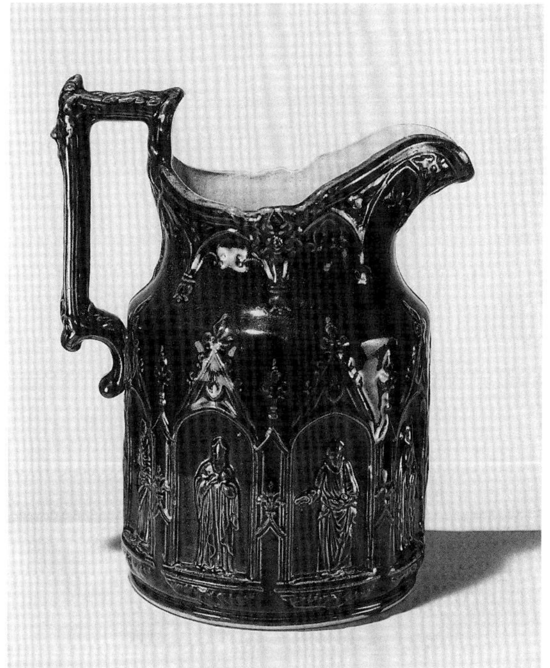

Fig. 2. Pitcher, American Pottery Manufacturing Company, The Brooklyn Museum of Art, Gift of Arthur W. Clement, 43.128.27.

NOTES

1. The Crawford pitcher and goblet are illustrated and discussed in Venable 1994, pp. 55–56, fig. 3.10. The other pitcher and goblet are illustrated and discussed in Brooklyn Museum 1988, p. 160, no. 117.

2. Von Khrum 1978, p. 17.

3. The advertisement is reproduced in R. Green 1972, p. 9. William Thompson is listed in Belden 1980, p. 408.

4. See Mankowitz and Haggar 1957, p. 167.

5. An American Pottery Manufacturing Company apostle-form pitcher in the Brooklyn Museum of Art is discussed and illustrated in Watkins 1946, p. 392, fig. 14.

29.

Pair of Andirons,
patented 1860

Manufactured by Savery and Company (1839–1869), Philadelphia; designed by Theodore W. Lillagore
Cast iron
Each 23½ × 10½ × 18½ inches
Marks: Cast in raised letters on back of each shaft, *SAVERY & CO. PHILADA./3/PATENTED APRIL 2d 1860*
1990.81

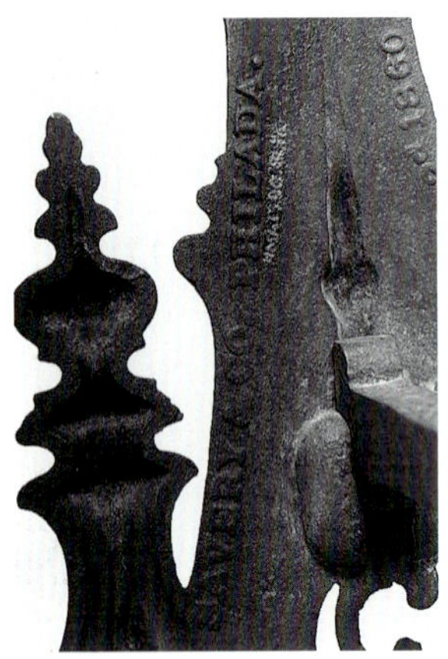

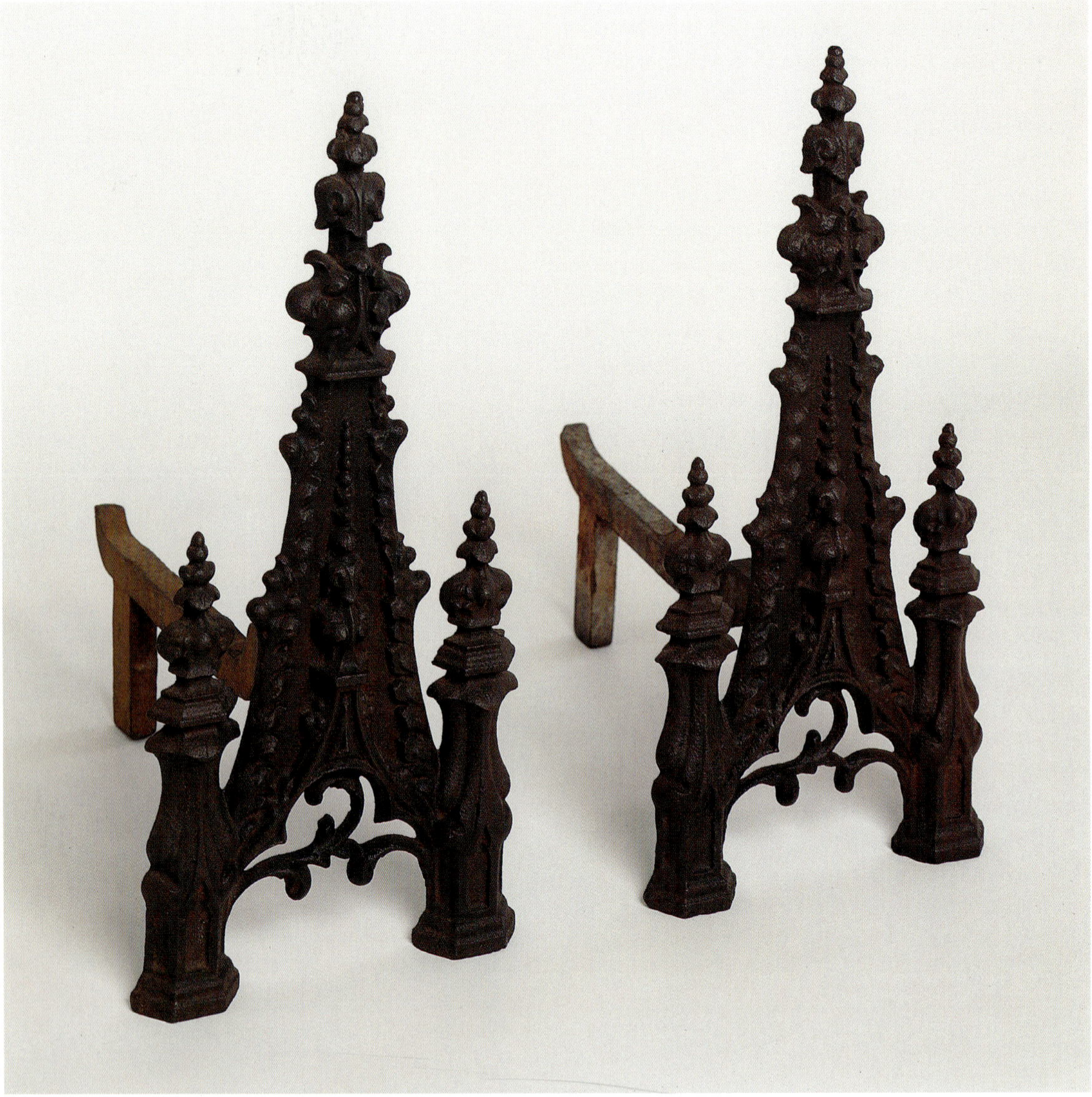

THIS PAIR OF Gothic andirons (called "fire dogs" in patent records), designed by Theodore W. Lillagore of Philadelphia, was patented on April 3, 1860, and the patent assigned to Savery and Company (fig. 1). The Gothic pattern was one of eight designs for fire dogs patented by Lillagore that year, and one of six patents issued to him on April 3.[1] All of Lillagore's patents were assigned to Savery and Company, suggesting that he was employed by them as a designer. The combination of rococo and Gothic revival decoration on the front shafts of these andirons illustrates both the extended survival of styles and their frequent overlapping in nineteenth-century America.

The spire-shaped shafts of the andirons provided appropriate vertical backgrounds for the cast Gothic ornamentation. Trifid arches at the bases, derived from Gothic architectural vocabulary, enclose intertwining rococo scrolls and suggest tracery in Gothic windows. The circular scrolls provide interesting visual contrast with the otherwise vertical Gothic cast decoration. By the time of the 1860 patent, the rococo style was well established in American design, and the incorporation of these scrolls within the dominant Gothic pattern illustrates the eclecticism of the period.

As early as 1845, Savery and Company advertised in Philadelphia's business directory a variety of iron kitchen and cooking hollowares, as well as andirons, suggesting that they specialized in utilitarian wares. In 1869, Savery and Company became Barrow, Savery Company. While the name change might provide a likely latest date for the Crawford andirons, Barrow, Savery Company may have continued to produce andirons with the old mark, since making new molds was expensive.

NOTE

1. *Report* 1861, p. 86; specifications and drawing, pp. 341–342. Note that the date in the mark on the Crawford andirons is a day before the patent was actually issued according to U.S. government records. Other patterns patented by Lillagore at the same time were Eagle, Rose, Shell, Urn, and Globe. An identical pair of Gothic andirons with the same mark is in the collection of the Henry Ford Museum and Greenfield Village in Dearborn, Michigan, and is illustrated and discussed in Howe and Warren 1976, pp. 76–77, no. 161.

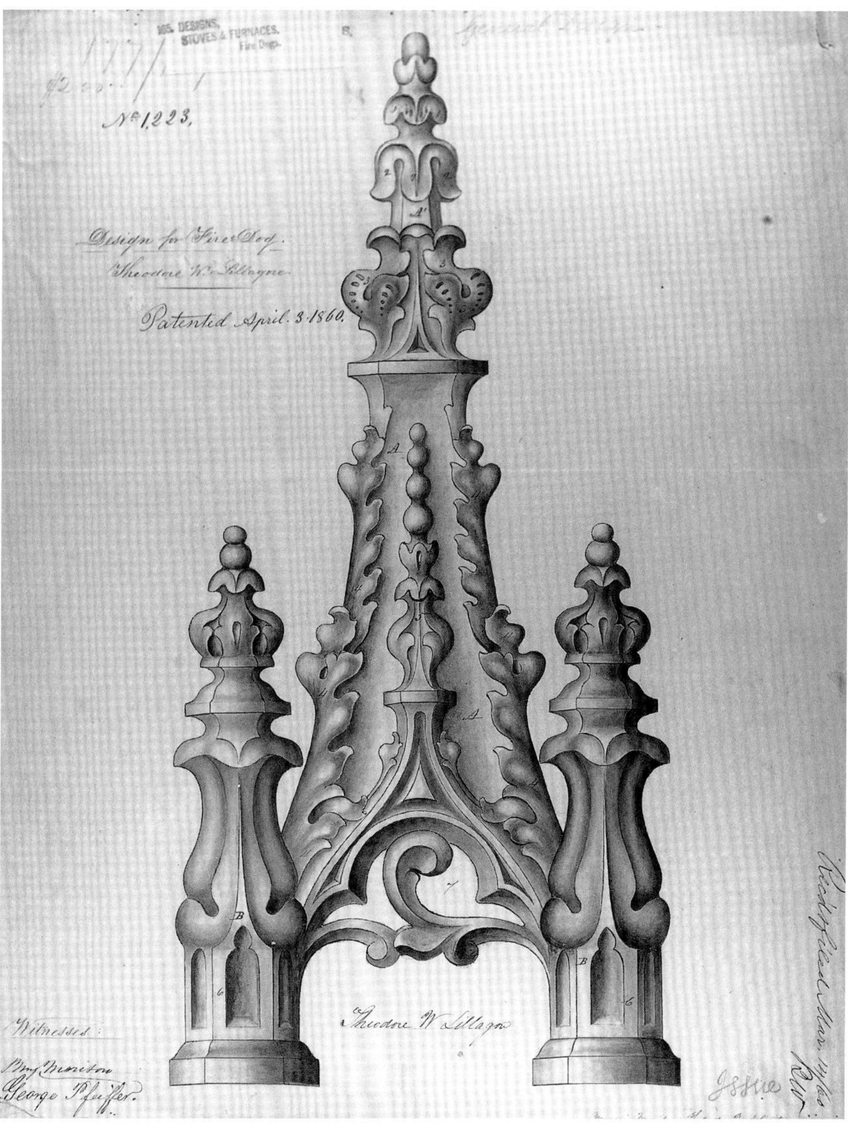

Fig. 1. Patent drawing. U.S. Patent Office, Theodore W. Lillagore of Philadelphia, assigned to Savery and Company. Design for Fire Dog forming part of Letters of Patent Number 1223, dated April 3, 1860.

30.

Center Table, ca. 1850

Probably New York
Rosewood, rosewood veneer, cherry, white marble, and brass casters
30 × 37 × 43 inches
Mark: Label on underside of marble top, *Mr. J. Rathbone/ Kenwood*
Note: Drops on skirt and central finial replaced before 1980.
1983.190

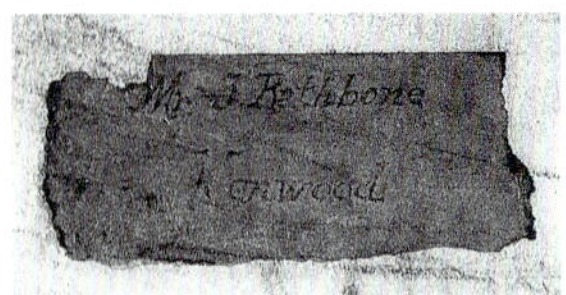

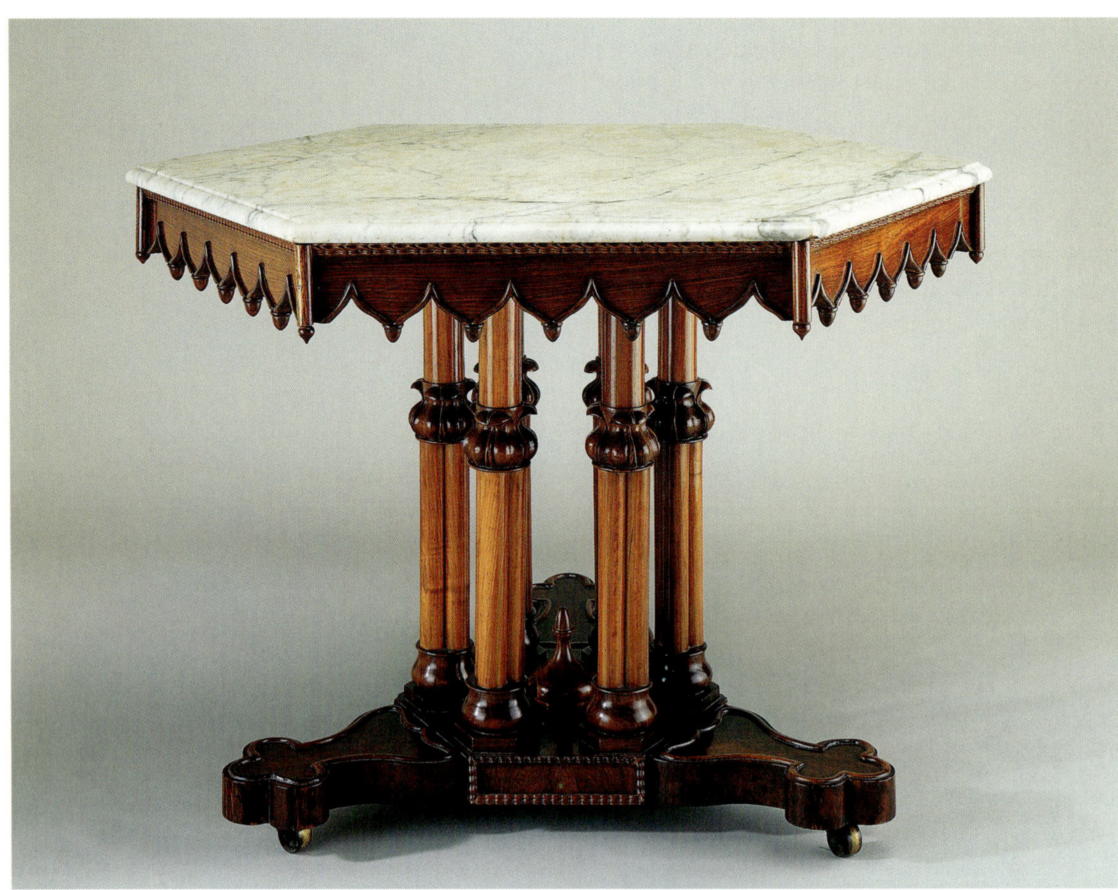

In this piece, Gothic architectural details —six clustered columns, three beaded trefoil terminals on the triangular base, and the ogee-arched scallop skirt—have been imaginatively combined with a hexagonal marble top to create a center table, a quintessential mid-nineteenth-century parlor furniture form. The Crawford table epitomizes the period practice of adapting historical elements into furniture design.[1]

In *The Architecture of Country Houses,* Andrew Jackson Downing wrote: "Centre-tables . . . have long been popular pieces of parlor furniture. In towns, they have given place to sofa-tables—as the latter, scattered here and there in a room, afford various gathering-places for little conversation parties—while the centre-table draws all talkers to a single focus." Downing also suggested that a center table might promote a sense of family unity: "As the centre-table is to us the emblem of the family circle, and the sofa-table that of the evening party, we think the former should hold its place in the country, *par excellence.*"[2]

Downing illustrated a view of the drawing room at Kenwood, Joel Rathbone's estate on the Hudson River south of Albany, New York, in the section of his book titled "Treatment of Interiors" (fig. 1). In the room was a center table similar to the Crawford example. America's leading architect of the Gothic revival in the 1840s and 1850s, Alexander Jackson Davis (see nos. 214–215), designed Kenwood in 1842. In 1844, Rathbone wrote a letter from Albany to Davis at his office in New York: "I am quite anxious you should come; for I want you should help us with the Chairs and Table. . . . I think you had better step into the Boat at once." Davis visited Rathbone at Kenwood, but his records of the visit note only "Gate Lodge and Furniture."[3] No Davis drawing has been located to identify him as the designer of the Crawford table.

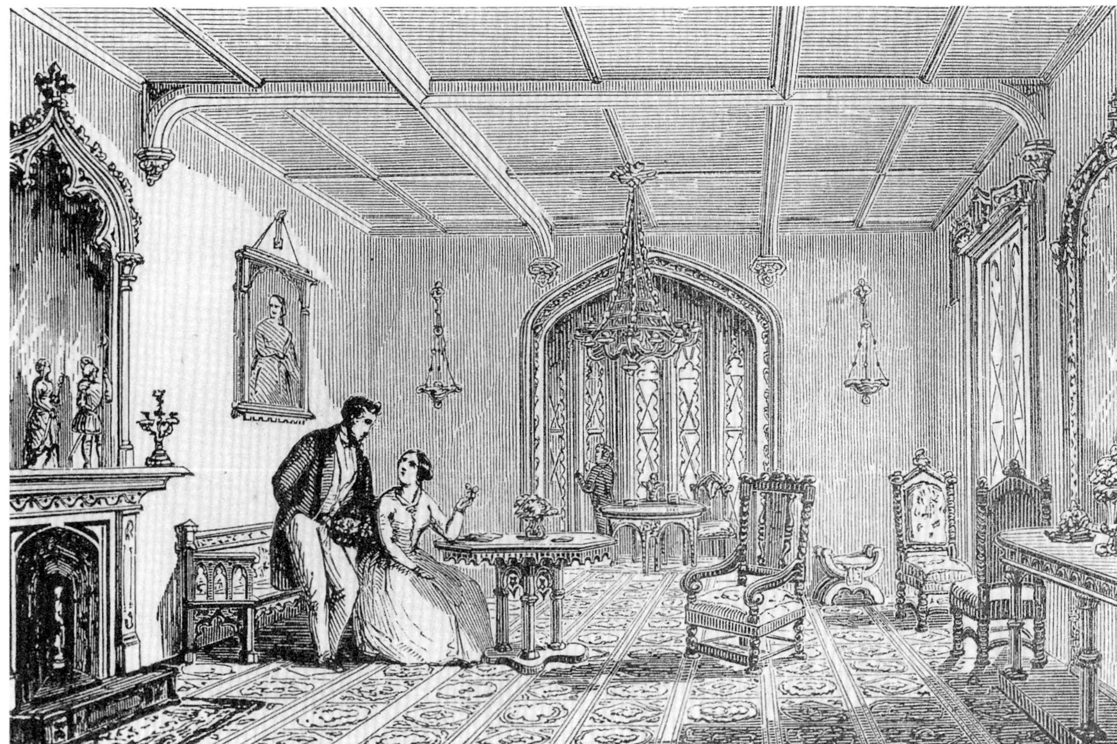

Fig. 1. Drawing room at Kenwood, home of Joel Rathbone, Albany, New York. From Andrew Jackson Downing, *The Architecture of Country Houses* (New York, 1850), fig. 179.

NOTES

1. The Crawford table is discussed and illustrated in Howe 1976, p. 1020, pl. IV; Howe and Warren 1976, p. 41; and Sherrill 1976, p. 1033, fig. 3. The photos of the Crawford table in these sources were taken prior to the restoration of the drops on the skirt and the central finial. The Crawford table is also noted by Davies 1977, p. 1027. A related table, illustrated in Fitzgerald 1982, p. 211, fig. X-4, includes fretwork between the clustered-column legs and has no central finial. Because at least two tables are known and there are differences between this table and the one illustrated in Downing, the authenticity of the label linking it to Kenwood must be questioned.

2. Downing 1969, pp. 428–429. *The Architecture of Country Houses,* one of the earliest American books to provide advice on domestic taste, focused on country (or suburban) homes as opposed to city dwellings. Downing was a native of Newburgh, New York, on the Hudson River, where he operated a nursery business. He published numerous books on gardening as well as the periodical *The Horticulturalist. The Architecture of Country Houses,* published two years before his death in 1852, went through nine printings, and over 16,000 copies had been printed by the end of the Civil War in 1865 (p. vii). The book's influence outlived its author, who, like subsequent nineteenth-century writers, believed that good taste expressed in the home improved family life and promoted domestic tranquility.

3. Rathbone's letter and Davis's record are cited in Davies 1977, p. 1021. Whether Rathbone was referring to the Crawford table is also unknown. Kenwood is discussed in Newton 1942, pp. 222–224.

31.

Solar Lamp, 1850s

Probably Boston area, possibly New England Glass Company (1818–1888), East Cambridge, Massachusetts
Glass, brass, and marble
Base: 15¾ × 5½ × 5½ inches
Globe: 8½ × 8 × 14½ inches
Prisms: Each 7 × 1¼ × ¾ inches
1984.129

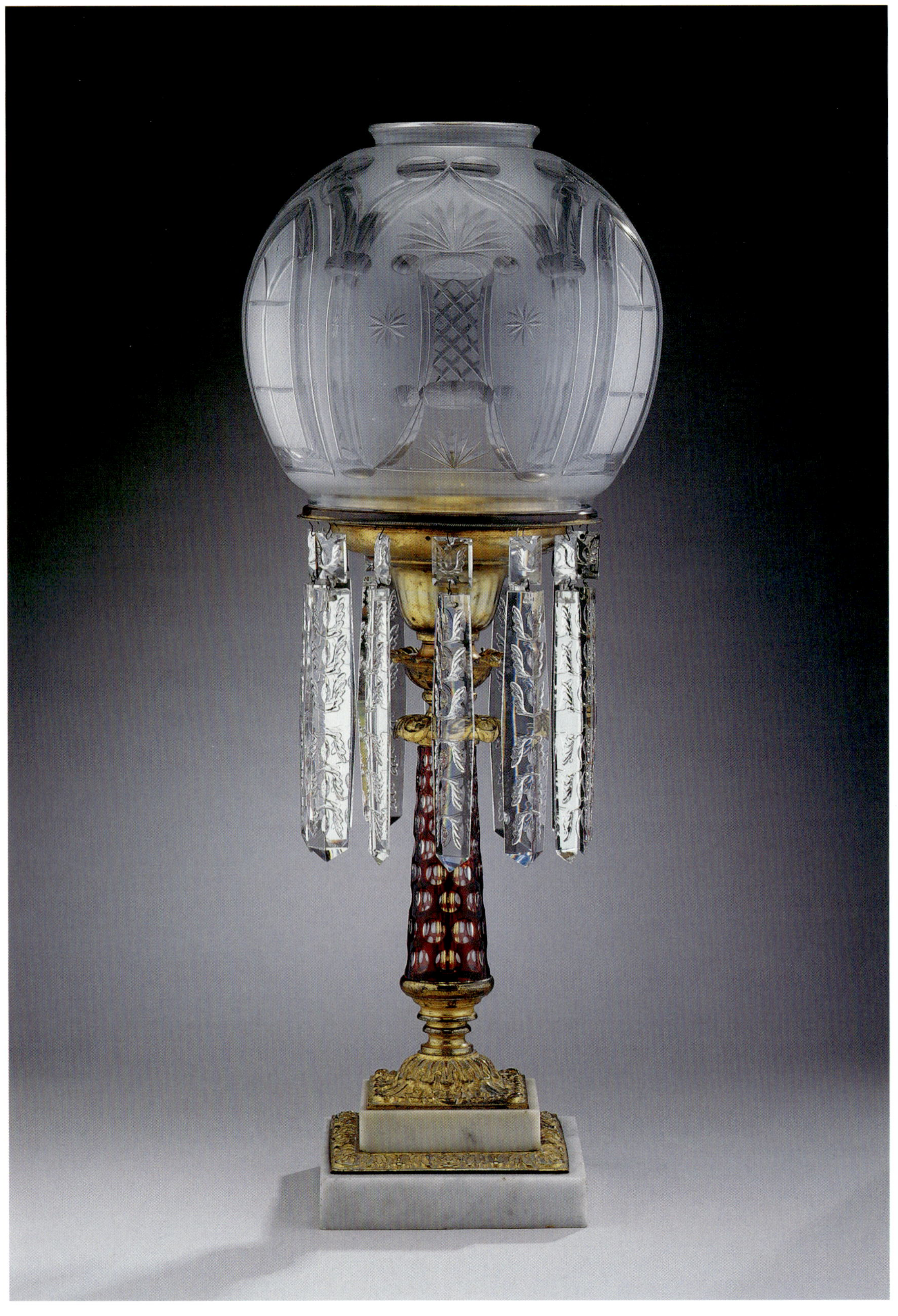

Although the argand lamp (see no. 4) was a tremendous improvement in nineteenth-century lighting, the vertical font above the innovative tubular wick cast a distracting shadow in the radiating light. A lamp introduced in the late 1840s was called a solar lamp because, like the sun, it cast no shadows. The brass font, which held the argand tubular wick, was an inverted pear shape with a circular hole in the top, and it was fixed at its narrow bottom into the glass stem. When the wick was ignited in the font, air drew a column of brilliant white light through the hole in the top. The solar lamp used lard oil, which was less expensive than the whale oil needed for an argand lamp, making better light available to a wider public. On the Crawford lamp, a tall cylindrical glass chimney (now missing) fit over the font's hole and was tapered at the top to ensure a taller air draft and brighter radiating light without casting a shadow from the font. The glass chimney on the Crawford lamp would have extended through the circular hole in the top of the glass shade, adding several inches to the original height of the assembled lamp (fig. 1). The spherical shade rests on a ring around the perimeter of the brass font, concealing its top half.[1]

The original Crawford shade is cut with a pattern of Gothic arches, demonstrating the continuing popularity of that style through the 1850s and 1860s. The clear glass stem was encased in hot liquefied red glass. After it cooled, circles were cut into the red layer to reveal the colorless glass beneath. This technique is the closest to Bohemian-type glass (see no. 45) that has been associated with American glass production in the mid-nineteenth century. The stepped marble base with gilt metal mounts, the cut prisms (which partially obscure the bottom half of the font), and the cut red-to-clear stem enriched the lamp for probable parlor use. These decorative details also added sparkle to the lamp when it was illuminated. The size and weight of the lamp further suggest that it was intended as a permanent, and possibly the only, source of parlor light, and would perhaps have been placed on a characteristic center table (see no. 30). The impact of the bright solar lamp on pre-electrical America was profound, drawing family members and guests around the center table for evening readings and conversations (fig. 2).

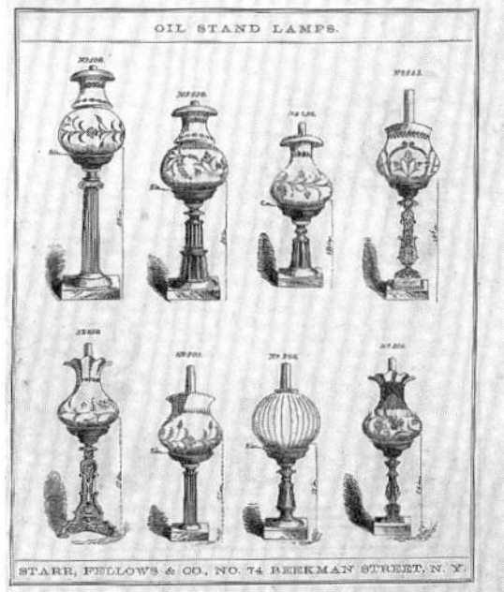

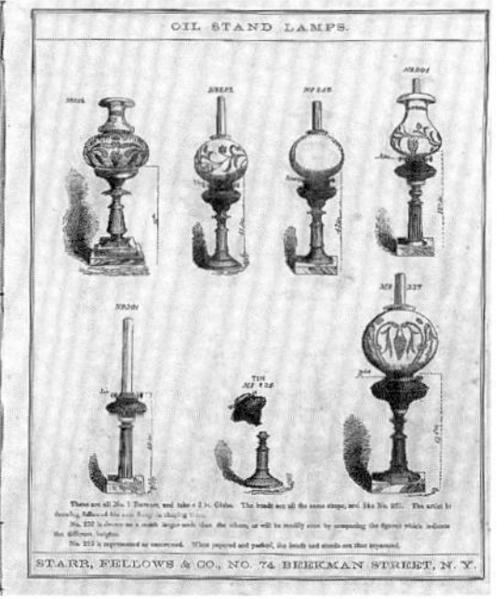

Fig. 1. Solar lamps from a catalogue of Starr, Fellows and Company, New York, 1856.

NOTE

1. Fully assembled solar lamps with metal stems were illustrated in the 1856 catalogue of Starr, Fellows and Company in New York. See Shadel 1970, p. 919, fig. 6. For a description of the working of the solar lamp, see Moss 1988, pp. 80–83.

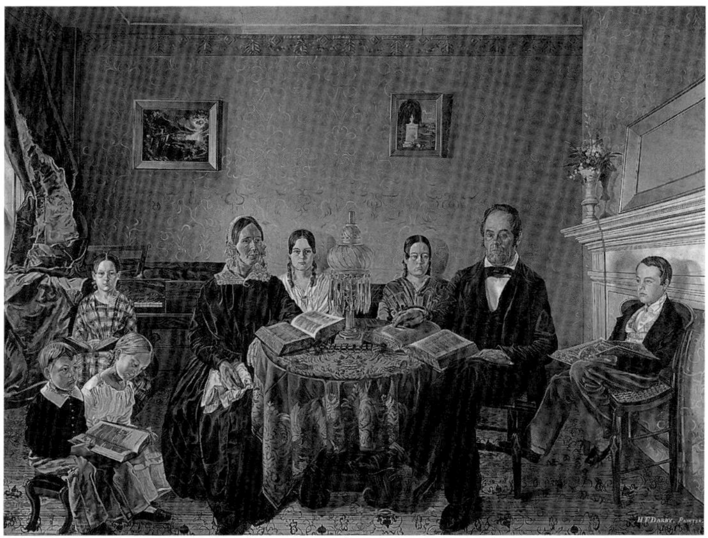

Fig. 2. Henry F. Darby (1829–1897). *The Reverend John Atwood and His Family,* 1845, oil on canvas, 72 × 96¼ inches. Gift of Maxim Karolik for the M. and M. Karolik Collection of American Paintings, 1815–1865. Museum of Fine Arts, Boston.

32.

Girandole Mantel Garniture, patented 1849

William F. Shaw (working 1845–1900), Boston
Gilt brass, marble, and glass
Candelabrum: 16⅛ × 17¼ × 4 inches
Candlesticks: Each 13¾ × 5¾ × 3¼ inches
Marks: Cast in raised block letters on back of chapel of each base, *W. F. SHAW/270 WASH'N ST/BOSTON/PATENT/DEC 18 1849*
1984.120.1–.3

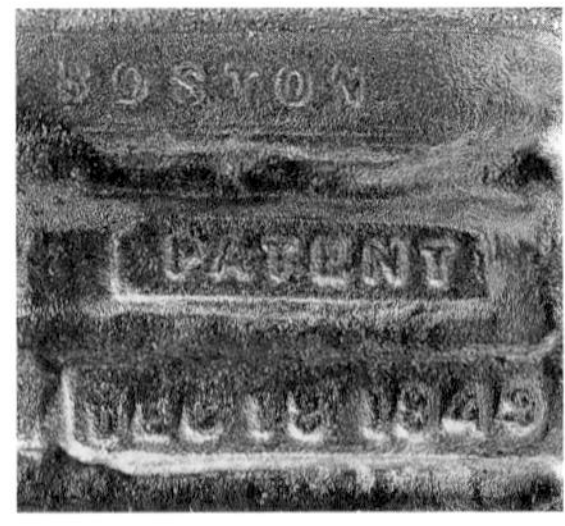

American cast gilt-metal girandole mantel garnitures were manufactured in vast quantities in the 1840s and 1850s, mainly in Philadelphia, New York, and Boston. Girandoles were introduced and became popular during a period of great improvements in oil lamps (see nos. 4, 31), although their luminescent effects relied on traditional candlelight.[1] Elements of girandole garnitures—cast gilt-metal shafts, faceted and cut-glass prisms, and marble bases—reflected the shimmering light from the candles. Their function was not so much to provide useful illumination as to lend a subtle, glittering aura to middle-class American parlors.

Shafts of girandoles, decorated on only one side, were meant to be viewed from the front. The efficient and relatively cheap casting in brass, bronze, and other metals made girandoles reasonably easy to manufacture in the increasingly mechanized American factories of midcentury. Their affordability, as well as improved systems of transportation and distribution, made girandole garnitures available virtually nationwide.

Most surviving girandole garnitures are in the rococo style, which was introduced in the United States in the 1840s and was widely popular in the 1850s. Midcentury eclecticism, however, encouraged the introduction of Gothic details in girandoles, such as William F. Shaw's chapel-patterned shaft for this garniture set, patented in 1849.[2] An advertisement by Shaw in the 1845 Boston directory indicates the breadth of his establishment and provides clues to the general retailing of girandoles and other lighting devices in the United States. Shaw, essentially a general lighting merchant and manufacturer, sold "LAMPS, CHANDELIERS, CANDELABRAS, GIRANDOLES, WICKS, AND GLASSES," as well as oil, supplies, and parts. These included not only his own manufactures but also "those of Messrs. Cornelius and Co.; W. Carleton; Gooding & Co.; Hooper & Co, and a good assortment of RICH ENGLISH LAMPS, of entire *new patterns.*"[3] Shaw also refinished old metal lamps and updated them with new and more efficient mechanisms.

On the Crawford girandoles, Shaw depicted Bigelow Chapel, a Gothic revival structure on the grounds of Mount Auburn Cemetery in

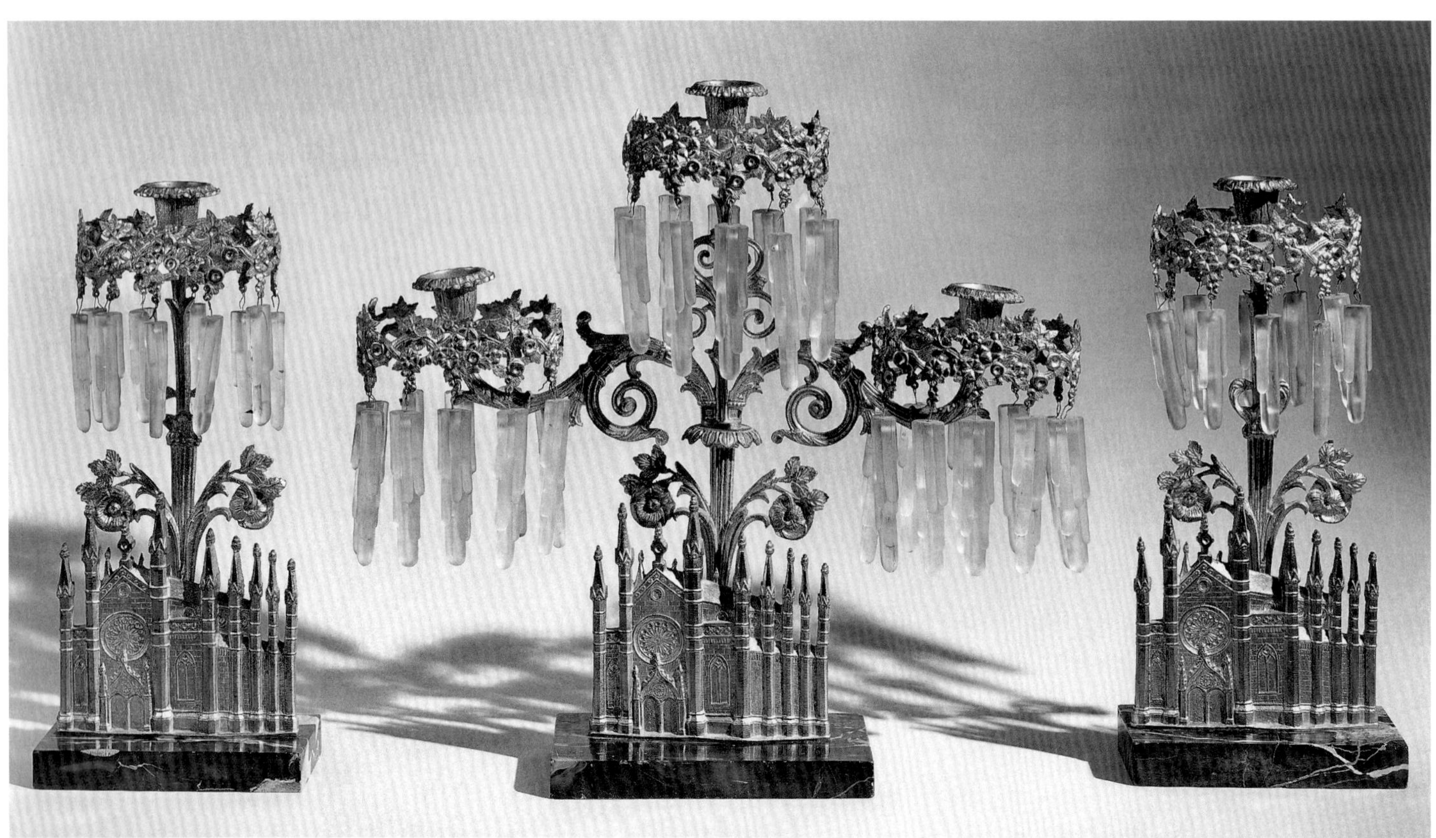

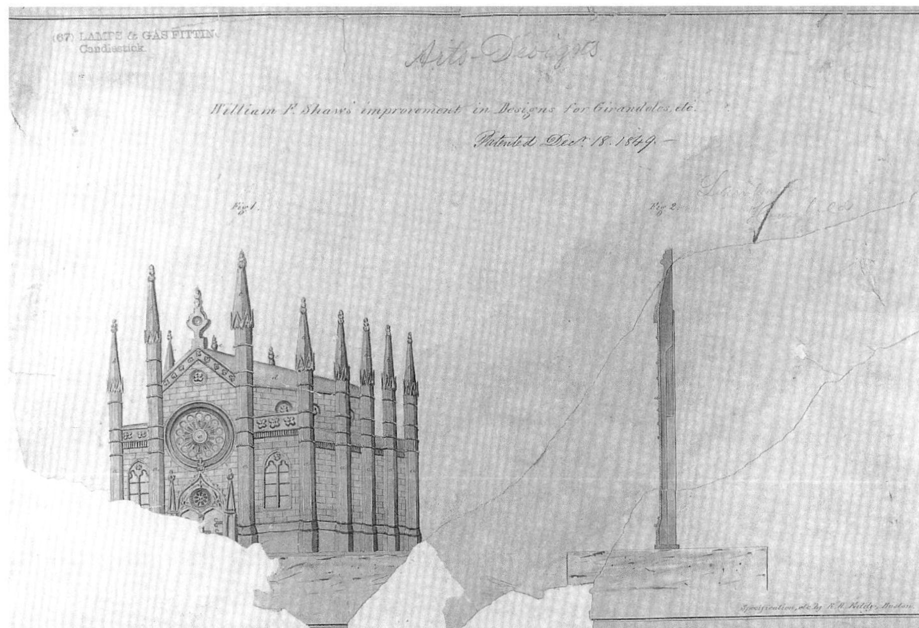

Fig. 1. Patent drawing. U.S. Patent Office, William F. Shaw of Boston. Design for girandoles forming part of Letters of Patent Number 256, dated December 18, 1849.

Cambridge, Massachusetts, just six miles northwest of Boston. One of the earliest planned cemeteries in the United States, Mount Auburn was enjoyed by Boston residents and visitors as a strolling ground, or a kind of public park. The depiction of this early Boston tourist attraction might have given the girandoles a national market. The surviving drawing in the U.S. Patent Office shows that Shaw patented the Bigelow Chapel design for the girandoles (fig. 1). The two individual candlesticks and the three candle sockets in the center candelabrum are set on gilt-metal stalks mounted behind the Bigelow Chapel fronts. In the other two girandole sets in the Crawford Collection (see nos. 50–51), the candelabra stalks are screwed into the shaft figures.

The Shaw girandoles combine the Gothic revival Bigelow Chapel with rococo floral relief rings around the candle sockets and the scrolled arms of the candelabrum. The blue marble of the bases was not commonly used in girandole garnitures and probably would have increased its cost. The original prisms, which were typically coffin-shaped cut glass, were replaced in the 1920s or 1930s with modern cloud-shaped frosted prisms in an attempt to update the girandole set nearly a century after its manufacture.

NOTES

1. For a historical background discussion of girandole mantel garniture sets, see Bacot 1987, pp. 153–156.

2. Howe and Warren 1976, fig. 115a, illustrates and discusses a pair of matching single-socket candlesticks. Bacot 1987, p. 188, no. 201a, illustrates and discusses a central candelabrum from a garniture of the same pattern.

3. The Shaw advertisement in Stimpson's *Boston Directory* 1845, p. 14, is reproduced in Bacot 1987, p. 154.

33.

Side Chair, ca. 1850

American, possibly New York or New Orleans
Oak
69½ × 10½ × 19⅜ inches
Note: The skirt from the back of the chair is mostly intact, but detached.
1987.181

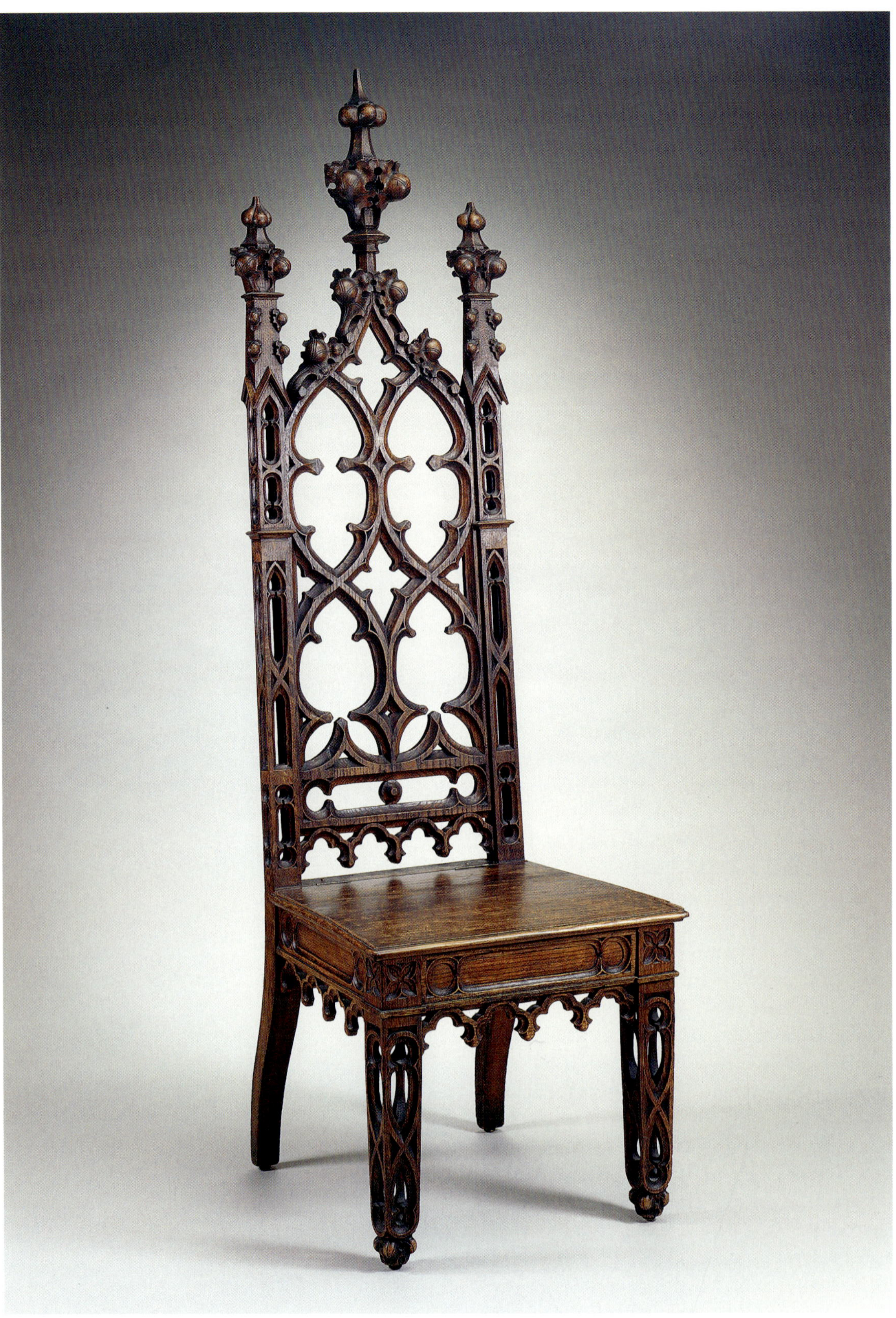

In 1850, Andrew Jackson Downing, America's most widely read advisor on domestic taste at the time, promoted the Gothic in domestic architecture, yet he expressed dissatisfaction with American interpretations of the Gothic style in furniture, preferring restrained and "chaste" designs. He could have been describing this elaborate side chair when he wrote about contemporary American Gothic furniture: "It is too elaborately Gothic—with the same high-pointed arches, crockets, and carving usually seen in the front of some cathedral. Elaborate exhibition of style gives it too ostentatious and stately a character."[1] At almost six feet tall, the Crawford chair is indeed stately and suggests the soaring verticality of Gothic architecture. The chairback is a riot of ornate tracery, echoed in the carved and hollow front legs and rear post side stiles. The central crest ornament of the back and its repetition as terminals for the crocket-decorated steep roof lines of the turret-form side stiles are examples of what Downing criticized in American Gothic furniture.

Ornament and message, rather than comfort or function, seem to have been the primary concerns of the chair's maker and designer. Originally from a set of four, this chair was more a piece of sculpture, intended to create an interior mood, than a practical seat. It probably furnished an entrance hall, where its function would have been primarily decorative, although the seat was hinged to accommodate a storage compartment. A friend waiting in the hall would have had only a brief stay in the uncomfortable chair, but for a stranger (perhaps a salesman), the intimidating scale and lack of comfort might have heightened the anxiety of waiting.[2]

The chair descended in the family of Jared Reese Cook, whose plantation was seven miles east of Vicksburg, Mississippi. A similar set of four chairs was part of the original furnishings of Stanton Hall, built by Frederick Stanton in Natchez, Mississippi, between 1851 and 1856. That two sets, another single chair, and a related settee were found in such proximity suggests that New Orleans may have been the origin for Cook's purchase, and perhaps the manufacture, of these chairs.[3] Certainly by the 1850s the New Orleans furniture industry could have produced them, but large manufacturers in New York, Philadelphia, and Cincinnati also maintained retail outlets and representatives in New Orleans.

NOTES

1. Downing 1969, p. 440.

2. Ames 1992, pp. 32–34.

3. Correspondence, Peter Hill, 1986, High Museum of Art document files. A similar chair was also found in Mississippi (author's telephone conversation with dealer Millie McGehee, April 1997). A chair from the Stanton Hall set is discussed and illustrated in Howe and Warren 1976, pp. 28–29, no. 48. A closely related settee in The Metropolitan Museum of Art was found in New Orleans (records on computer file in the Luce Study Center for American Arts, The Metropolitan Museum of Art) and is illustrated in Davidson and Stillinger 1985, p. 175, no. 271.

34.

Table, ca. 1855

Probably New York
Gilded pine, marble, and gilded composition
35¾ × 29 × 16¾ inches
Marks: Stenciled in black on underside, *G. Platt;* attached to underside, *B. C. Webste . . . / E. Orang . . . /N . . .*
1983.192

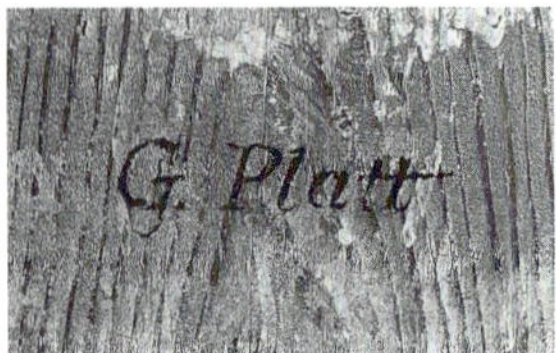

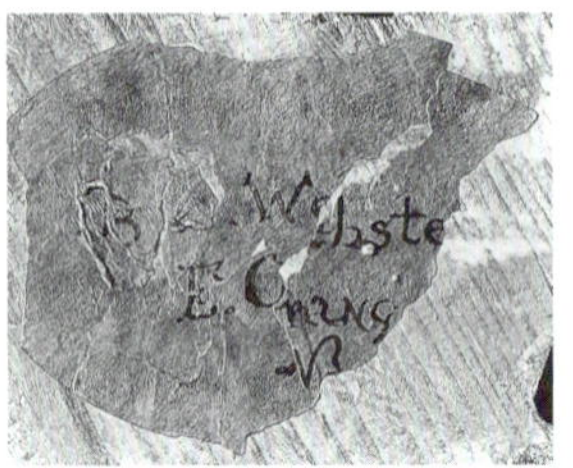

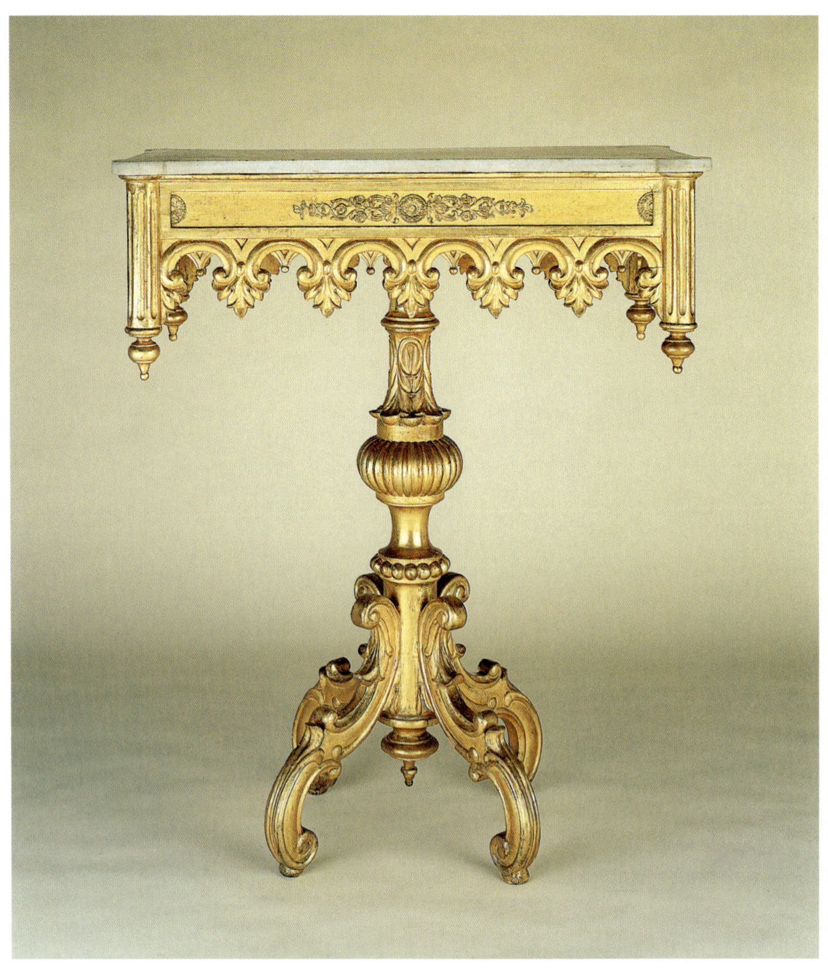

Classical, Gothic, and rococo decorative elements are combined in this small eclectic table, the mate of which is now in the Philadelphia Museum of Art.[1] The scale, materials, and consequent fragility of the table indicate that it was not intended for heavy use but probably served as a kind of ornamental pedestal for decorative objects in a parlor. The finished decoration on all four sides suggests that the table was intended for use in the center of a room rather than against a wall.

The molded composition medallion and the leaf and floral adornments on the inset panels on all four sides recall ormolu mounts or gilt stencil decorations on classical American furniture from the first quarter of the nineteenth century. The central pedestal, with its carved, molded, and gadrooned ball topped by trumpet-shaped leaf carvings and moldings, also relates the table to classical American furniture. The combination of these and other classical elements, such as the gilded surface and white marble top, with the carved Gothic border on the skirt and the four molded, double-scrolled rococo legs supporting the central pedestal places the Crawford table within the context of mid-nineteenth-century eclecticism.

NOTE

1. The mate to the Crawford table is illustrated in Davidson and Stillinger 1985, fig. 207. The paper tags attached to the underside of the Philadelphia and Crawford tables have associated them with the East Orange residence of Benjamin Webster, an affluent New York businessman. Architect Alexander Jackson Davis designed Webster's 1855 Gothic revival villa. Tests conducted on the tag's paper and ink, however, have raised questions about its authenticity and doubts about any association of the tables with Webster and his house. Another inscription, "G. Platt," stenciled on the underside, presumably for New York interior decorator George Platt, must now also be questioned. See Jandl 1975, pp. 1154–1157.

"ELIZABETHAN" WAS A general term applied to furniture with a range of decorative details. The style was introduced in England in the 1820s and quickly became popular in eastern American cities. Interest in such a style evolved out of popular English historical romantic novels by Sir Walter Scott and others. According to furniture historian Robert C. Smith, Elizabethan furniture was adapted from virtually any English historical style from before the mid-eighteenth century. In 1826, English furniture designer George Smith noted that a prominent characteristic of the style was "light, spiral columns in the backs of chairs."[1]

Andrew Jackson Downing devoted whole sections of *The Architecture of Country Houses* to the Elizabethan taste. He defined it as the English interpretation of the fifteenth-century Italian Renaissance. He noted that this furniture combined Gothic and Renaissance details, such as "twisted columns, scroll-work and heavy and quaint carving in wood," providing an effect that was "often grand and somber, always massive, rich, and highly picturesque."[2]

This rosewood armchair has characteristic details: turned columns in the back as well as scrollwork and carving surrounding the upholstered back. Turnings and carving on the front legs and the side and cross stretchers reinforce the decorative qualities. Downing illustrated six chairs related to the Crawford example.

Smith's observation of the looseness of American Elizabethan taste is also reflected in the Crawford chair. Its general configuration and details were inspired by English and northern European prototypes from the last half of the seventeenth century, half a century after Queen Elizabeth's death. The overall proportions—the deep, square seat and shortened back—identify it as a mid-nineteenth-century adaptation of a seventeenth-century form.

Although not original to the chair, the needlework upholstery is probably English, dating to the 1850s.[3] The Crawford chair was reupholstered in 1980 to replace a nonperiod red velvet plush. The application of the upholstery, with the red silk faille around the sides of the seat cushion and its decorative braiding, was based on an Elizabethan chair of the same period by New York's Alexander Roux that retains its original treatment.[4]

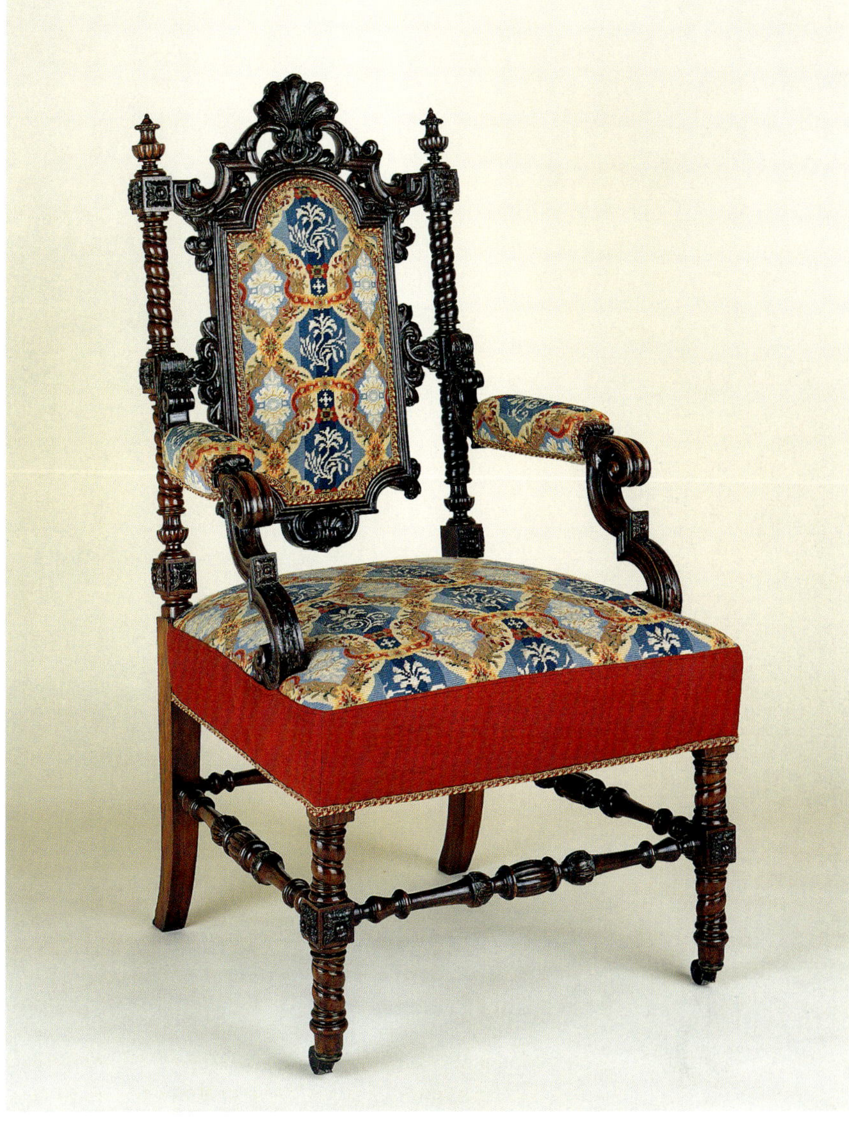

35.

Armchair, ca. 1850

New York
Rosewood, birch, wooden casters, and period needlework cover (replaced)
45⅛ × 23½ × 24 inches
1982.309.1

NOTES

1. Quoted in R. Smith 1959, p. 276.

2. Downing 1969, pp. 390–392.

3. A similar original covering has survived on the seat of an 1850s Gothic revival side chair now in The Metropolitan Museum of Art. The Metropolitan Museum of Art 1970, no. 122.

4. Ibid., no. 120. A side chair that matches the armchair is also in the Crawford Collection, but it is currently upholstered in muslin (1982.309.2). The Crawford chairs were originally part of a set of at least six, including two armchairs and four side chairs; see *Victorian International VIII* (New York: Sotheby Parke Bernet 83, March 26, 1980, lots 495 and 496.)

36.

Parlor Cabinet, 1848–1850

Alexander Roux (1813–1886), New York
Rosewood
90 × 46 × 23½ inches
Mark: Printed paper label glued to underside of top, showing a view of a furniture wareroom in a decorative frame. In shield at top center, *ROUX'S./BROADWAY.;* in shield on left, *MEUBLES/ET/SIEGES/MODERNE;* in shield on right, *FURNITURE/WARE/HOUSE;* across bottom, *NO. 479 NEW YORK. BROADWAY.*
1982.311

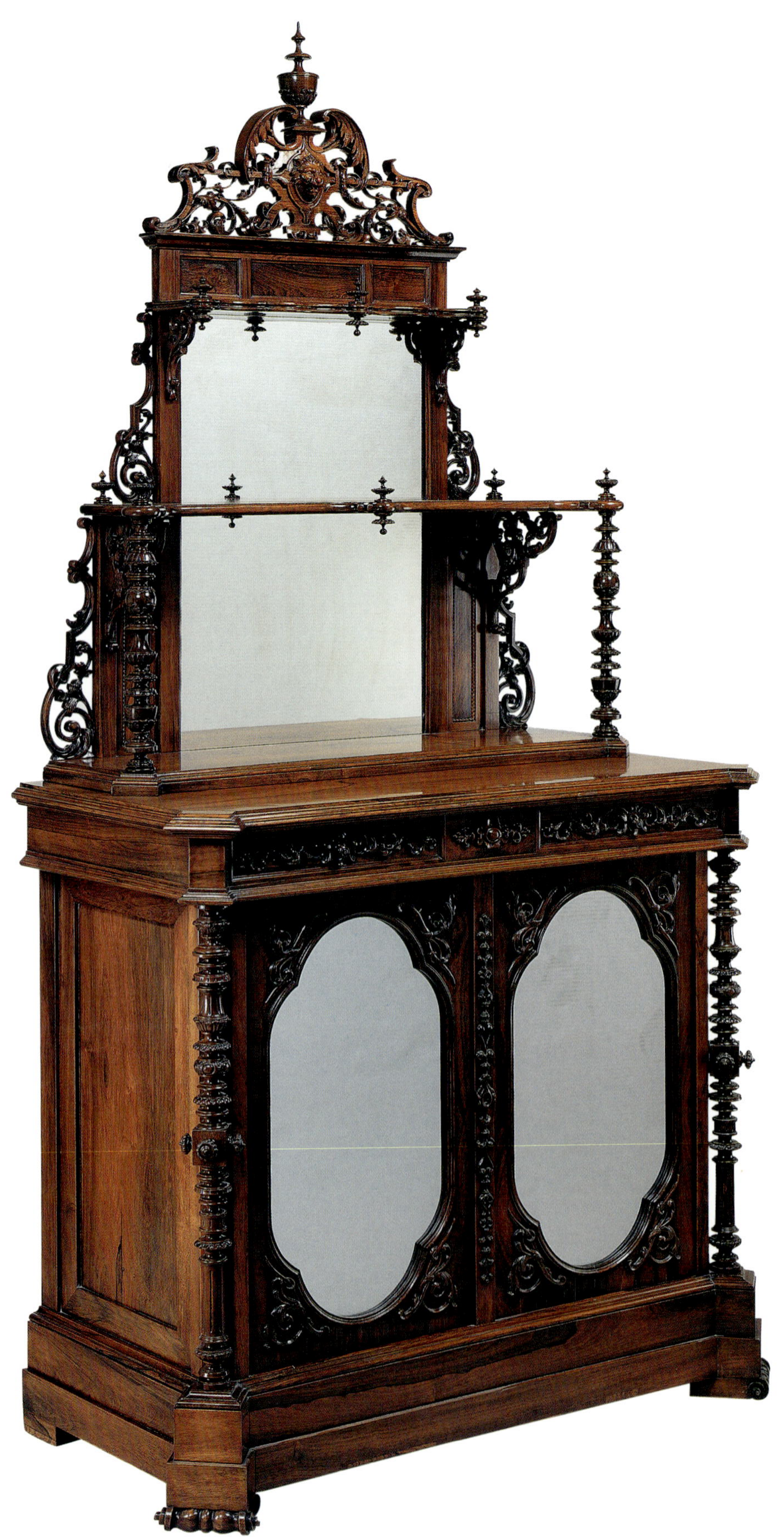

EAGER TO GAIN the patronage of the affluent New York market, Alexander Roux took advantage of a near mania for French furniture. He promoted himself as a "French cabinetmaker" (see no. 61) and used French terms in his labels and advertisements.

The firm advertised the date of its establishment as 1836, although Roux first appears in New York directories in 1837, listed as an upholsterer, at 472½ Broadway. By 1838, Roux had moved to 478 Broadway, where he continued to be listed exclusively as an upholsterer until 1843 (except in 1842, when he was listed also as an importer). In 1847, his brother, Frederick, joined the business. A. and F. Roux moved to 479 Broadway in 1848. A year later, Alexander Roux was working on his own, and in 1850 Roux's furniture warehouse had expanded to include the neighboring premises at 481 as well.[1]

By the 1850s, Roux employed 120 workers in his furniture manufactory, and in the 1870s, the company made annual profits of $250,000 to $500,000 in the nation's largest and most prestigious furniture market. Alexander Roux and Company produced furniture in most of the historical revival styles (see nos. 46, 61). Roux was active in the New York furniture trade until his 1881 retirement, and the firm continued to operate under the direction of his son, Alexander J. Roux, until 1898.

This cabinet combines bold Renaissance designs with more delicate Elizabethan elements, such as the two turned and carved columns supporting the shelf in the upper portion and the engaged columns at the front corners of the base, which echo the turned columns and front legs on the Crawford Elizabethan armchair (see no. 35).

The upper mirror is framed in scrollwork, and the arched crest incorporates a lion's head mask, a characteristic Renaissance motif. The carving on the drawer fronts and around the mirrors on the base repeats the scrolled designs above and contributes to the overall richness of the piece. The cabinet provided storage, but its primary purpose was to reflect light and exhibit small works of art and decorative objects on its shelves.

The printed paper label affixed to the underside of the cabinet top provides documentation of Roux's furniture warehouse at 479 Broadway. It shows a view of a furniture wareroom through tasseled curtains. The paintings on the walls and the drapes surrounding the view suggest that all manner of interior decorations besides furniture were available at Roux's. The printed frame in the label incorporates both Gothic and Renaissance motifs. The label includes the French phrase "meubles et sieges moderne" (modern furniture and seating), indicating that tables, case pieces, and seating furniture were all available.

Dating the Crawford cabinet from the label is imprecise at best. The style of the cabinet and the rococo-inspired furniture on the label suggest a mid-nineteenth-century date. Because the label reads simply "Roux's Broadway," with no first names or initials, it is impossible to determine if the cabinet was made at the time the two brothers were in partnership. The cabinet must date to 1848 or later, after the company moved to 479 Broadway. The labels on a number of documented Roux pieces list 479 and 481 Broadway, the address of the firm after 1850.[2] The Crawford label might indicate a date of 1848–1850, prior to the firm's expansion. However, labels on documented examples known to date to the 1860s list only the 479 Broadway address.[3] Perhaps the most compelling case for the earlier date is that by the 1860s, the Elizabethan style would have been passé to a firm—and a clientele—as sophisticated as Roux's.

NOTES

1. For a history of Roux's firm and a study of his furniture, see Hauserman 1968, pp. 210–217. A number of examples of Roux's furniture are marked with a label listing his address at 479 and 481 Broadway, which dates them to after 1850.

2. Ibid., p. 210. For examples with labels showing the address at 479 and 481 Broadway, see p. 213, figs. 6–6a; p. 215, fig. 9; and pp. 216–217, figs. 14–17a. See also Springer 1980, p. 34.

3. Monkhouse and Michie 1986, pp. 116–118, no. 54.

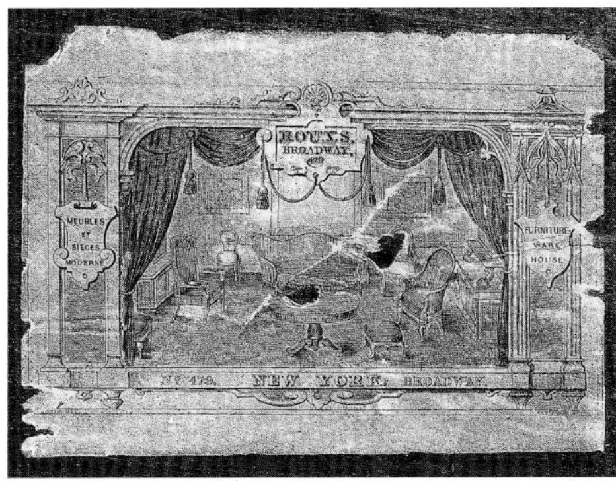

Rococo Revival, 1845–1865

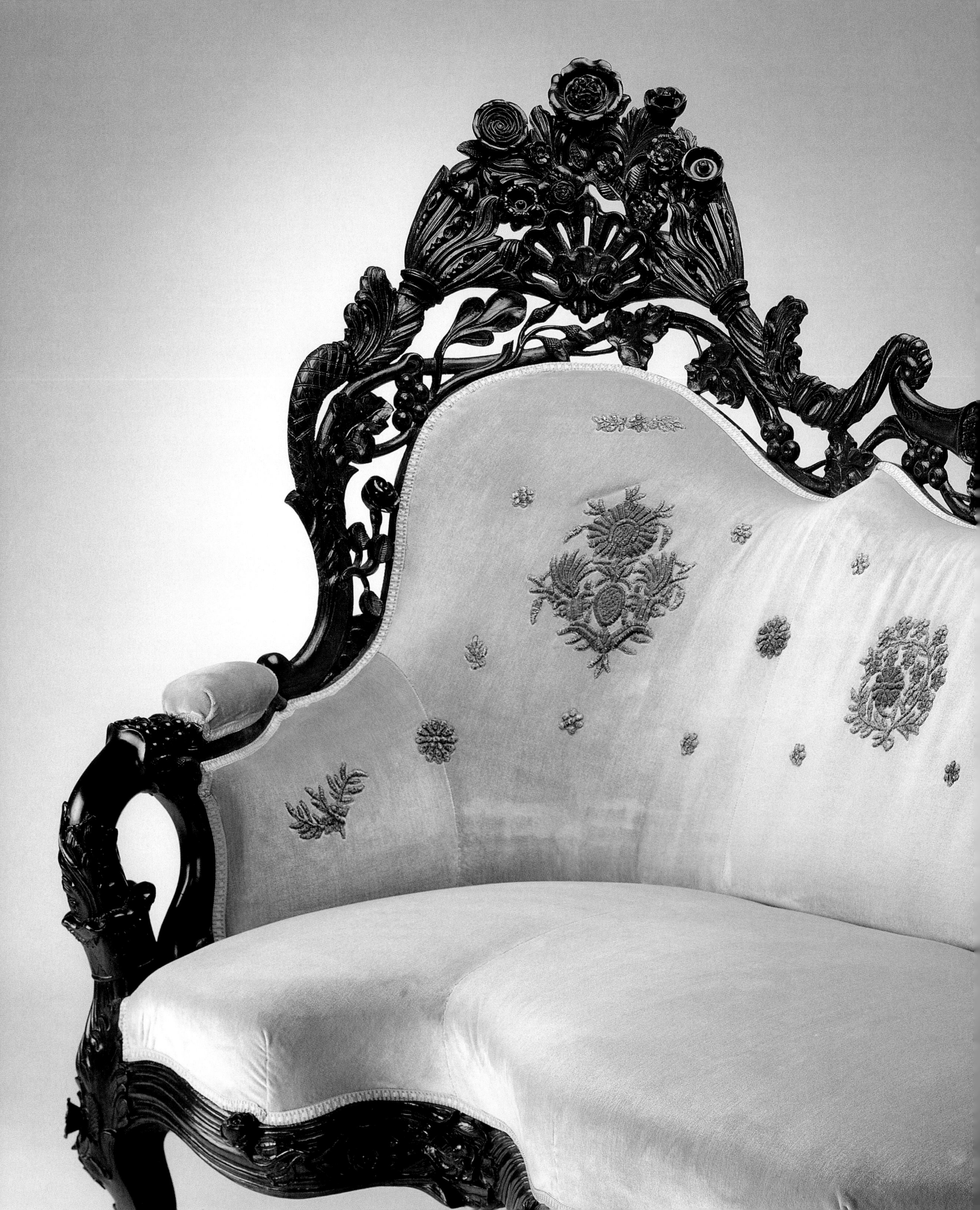

37.

Pair of Pitchers,
ca. 1845

Samuel Kirk (1793–1872),
Baltimore
Silver
Each 16¾ × 9¾ × 6¼ inches
Marks: Stamped on each in separate rectangles, on bottom, *S.Kirk/S.K./11 oz.*
Inscriptions: Engraved in intertwining script on reserve at front of each pitcher beneath spout, *GEA*
1982.302.1–.2

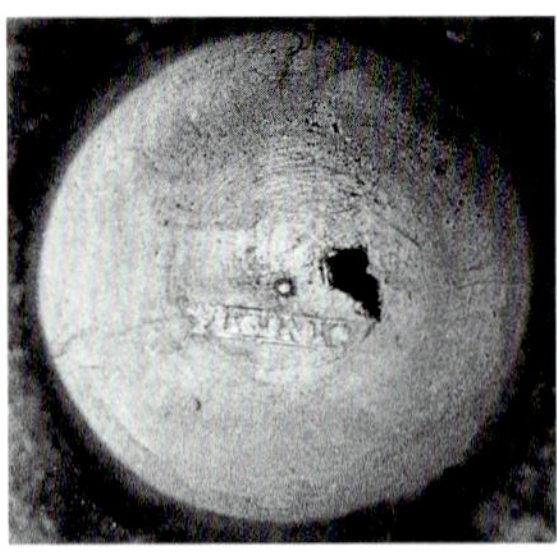

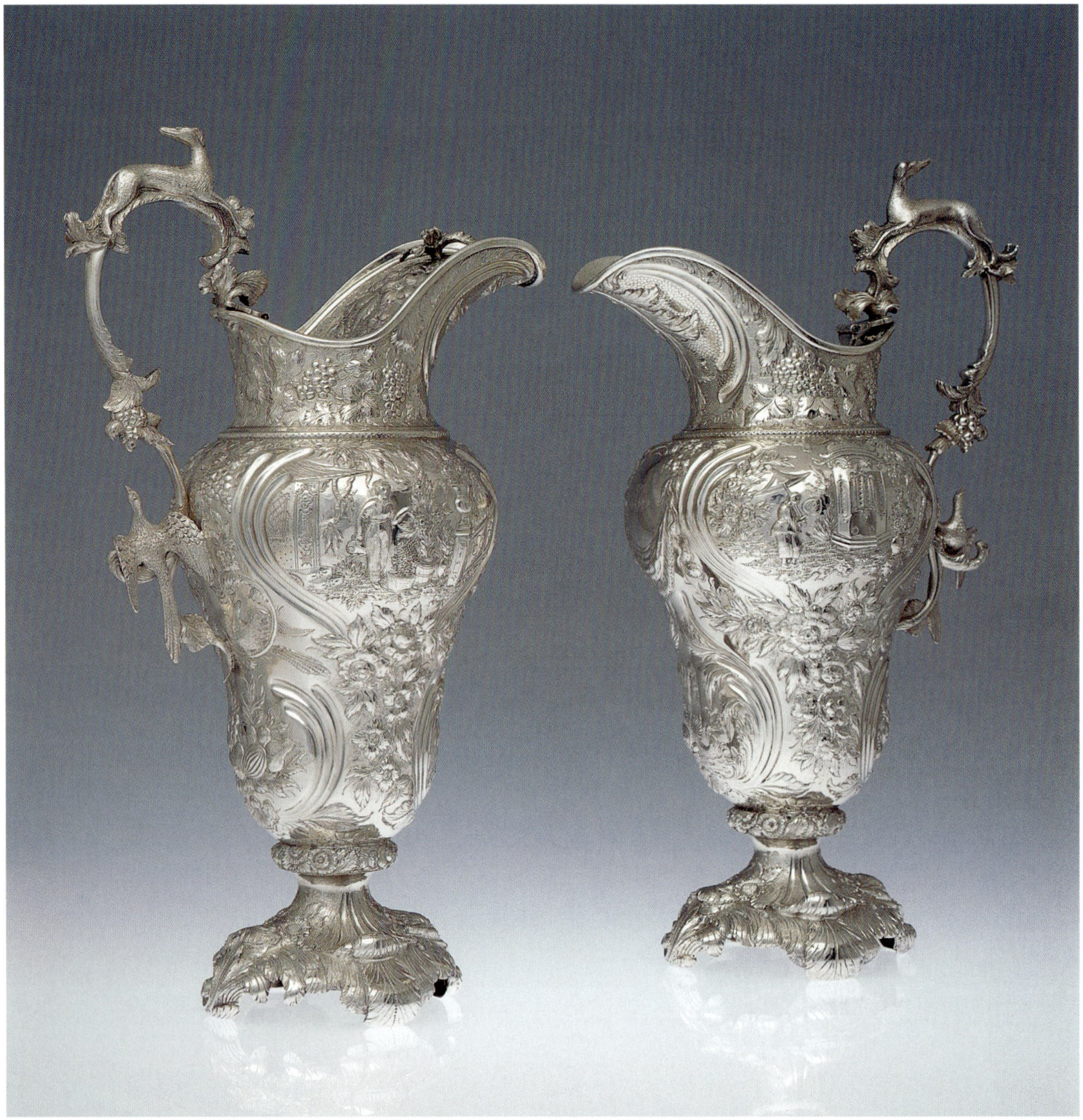

THE FIRM ESTABLISHED by Samuel Kirk dominated the silver industry in Baltimore from the 1820s into the twentieth century. His silver manufactories—Samuel Kirk and Son, later, Samuel Kirk and Sons—were the most enduring, successful, and prolific in nineteenth-century Baltimore. The enterprise operated under the Kirk name until 1979, when it merged with Baltimore's Stieff Company to become Kirk Stieff Company.[1]

Kirk was born in Doylestown, Pennsylvania, and descended through both parents from London silversmiths of the late seventeenth century. Around 1810, Kirk began his apprenticeship with Philadelphia silversmith James Howell, who had worked with the Richardson family dynasty of Philadelphia silver makers.[2] By 1815, Kirk was in Baltimore in partnership with John Smith, another young Philadelphia-trained silversmith, with whom he worked until he began making wares on his own in 1821.[3]

Kirk's career began just after Baltimore established an assay system in 1814, based on the English method of analyzing and weighing silver. Baltimore was the only city in the United States with strict government-supervised regulations for silver. The national standard required that coinage contain 89.2 percent silver; the Baltimore standard for silverwares was 91.7 percent. If coins were melted down to make silver articles, the metal had to be refined to meet the Baltimore standard. In addition to that expense, silver makers were charged five cents per ounce for testing and marking by the Baltimore Assay Office.

Kirk's arrival in Baltimore coincided with a decline in silver making there, as many silversmiths moved outside the city to avoid the new law. In 1818, works by twenty-one firms were approved in the Baltimore Assay Office, and silver tested for Smith and Kirk accounted for 22 percent of this total. In 1828, six firms had silver tested in the Assay Office, and the production of Samuel Kirk accounted for 93 percent.[4]

The Baltimore silver laws were eased in 1830, and during that decade the Assay Office functioned as a public protection agency to settle disputes and to certify silver at the maker's request, even though it was no longer required. Kirk continued to have much of his silver tested by the Assay Office into the early 1840s to assure his customers of the quality of his metal.

Kirk and his firms have come to be most identified with repoussé-decorated silver. In the 1820s, London silversmiths revived mid-eighteenth-century rococo floral and scrolled cast and repoussé decoration. At the same time, Kirk was introducing his early repoussé-decorated wares, which became increasingly popular in the 1830s and 1840s.[5] These silver vessels, hammered from within to form elaborate relief patterns on the exterior, are often called "Baltimore repoussé" or "Baltimore silver," but such wares were also made in Boston, Philadelphia, and New York in the mid-nineteenth century (see nos. 39–41).[6] Nonetheless, the floral repoussé that nearly covers the surface of these and other Baltimore examples was distinctive in American silver.

The inverted pear shapes of these pitchers and their florid repoussé surfaces recall mid-eighteenth-century English and American rococo silver. The floral repoussé surrounds romantic landscapes that depict European youths in front of thatched cottages on one side and Asian youths in gardens on the other. The Asian views also recall eighteenth-century rococo prototypes, but the combination of Asian and European scenes is more characteristic of eclectic nineteenth-century design.

The spirited cast dogs with heads turned back at the handle crests are complemented by exotic cast birds with outstretched wings at the handle bases. Cast scrolls and grapes give the handles an even more flamboyant rococo shape. The bases of the pitchers are composed of beautifully detailed scrolls, completing the rococo effect. The grapes on the handles and engravings of a dolphin spouting water (1982.302.1) and a water fountain flanked by drinking birds (fig. 1, 1982.302.2) follow the nineteenth-century convention of using motifs that suggest the function of an object (see nos. 48, 61, 63). The provenance of the pitchers is unknown, and the initials are unidentified.[7]

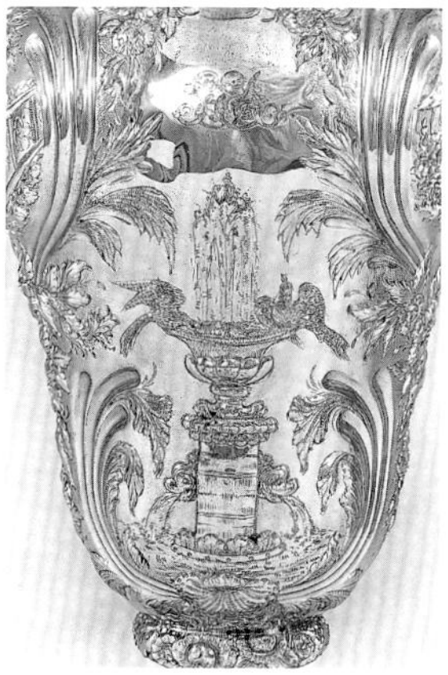

Fig. 1

NOTES

1. For a history of the Kirk firms and various marks, see Rainwater 1986, pp. 100–102. For illustrated surveys of their work and histories of the firms, see Durbin 1968, pp. 868–873; Goldsborough 1975, pp. 135–168; and Goldsborough 1984, pp. 135–162.

2. Belden 1980, p. 236.

3. John Smith moved to Baltimore in 1814 as a partner of Philadelphia silversmith William Hart, who may have made silver in Philadelphia that Smith sold in Baltimore. It is possible that Kirk was responsible for the silver making during his partnership with Smith. The Hart and Smith partnership of 1814 to 1816 overlapped that of Kirk and Smith. See Goldsborough 1984, p. 120. Also overlapping the Kirk and Smith concern was the partnership of John and Thomas Smith in 1817 and 1818. See ibid., p. 282.

4. Baltimore's silver industry and the effect of the Maryland assay law is discussed in Goldsborough 1984, pp. 11–12, 26–37.

5. See Goldsborough 1984, p. 137, nos. 146–147, and p. 139, no. 150, for examples of Kirk's repoussé silver in both classical and rococo styles from the 1820s.

6. Ibid., pp. 12–15; and Venable 1994, p. 59.

7. The Crawford pitchers are illustrated and discussed in Truman 1993, p. 138; and Venable 1994, pp. 59–60, fig. 3.15.

38.

Pitcher, ca. 1850

R. and W. Wilson (1825–1909),
Philadelphia
Silver
11¾ × 7¼ × 5¾ inches
Mark: Stamped on bottom,
R & W WILSON
Inscription: Engraved in reserve on front, *HCW/From/WW*
1989.138

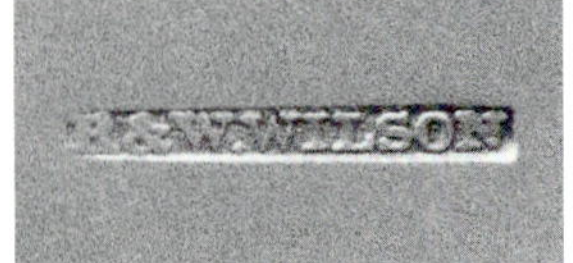

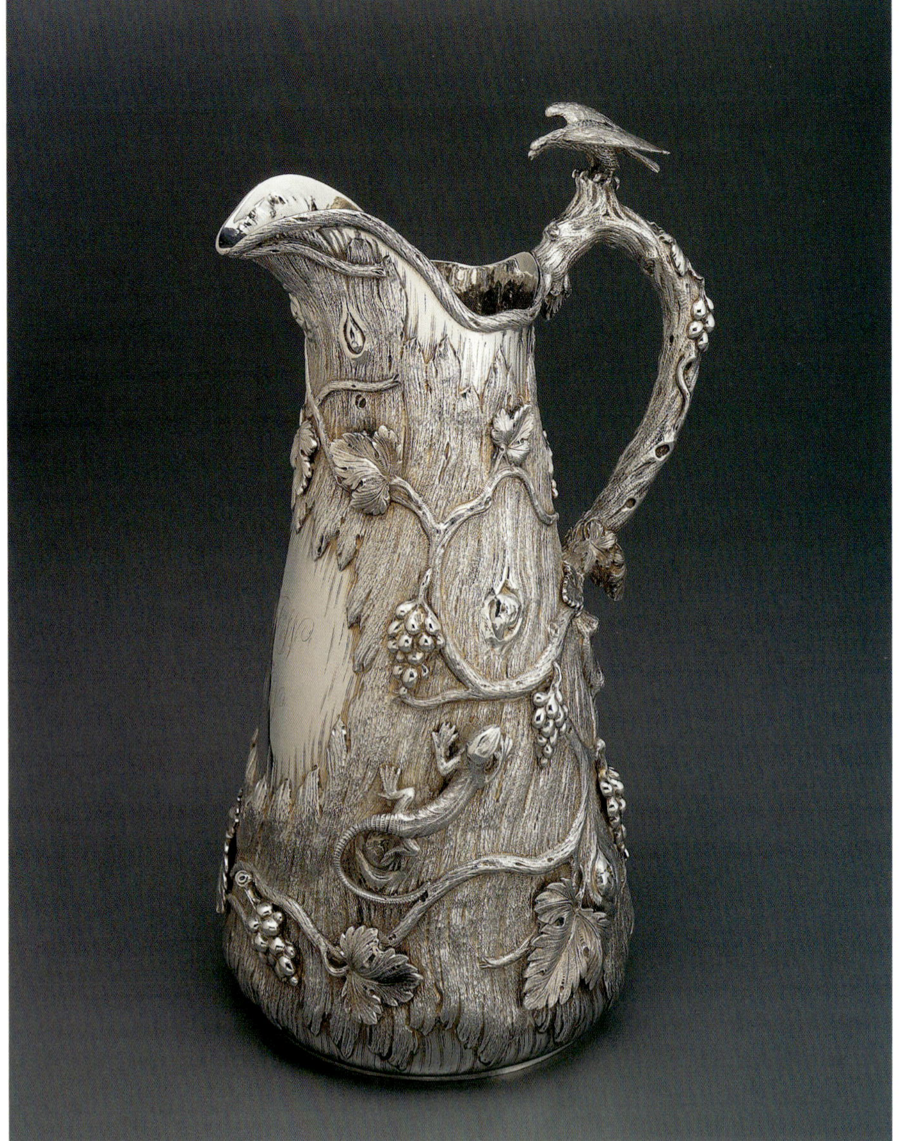

R. AND W. WILSON was an enduring and prolific silver manufacturer and retailer in Philadelphia in the nineteenth century. As early as 1805, a Robert Wilson was listed as a silversmith in the New York directory. He was apparently the father of Robert and William Wilson. Either the elder or the younger Robert Wilson was listed as working on his own in Philadelphia from 1814 to 1824. R. and W. Wilson first appeared in Philadelphia directories in 1825 as a "silver spoon manufactory," at the southwest corner of Fifth and Cherry Streets. The firm and its successors operated at the same location throughout the nineteenth century.[1]

Until 1851, five years after the death of the younger Robert Wilson at age fifty, the firm continued to be listed as R. and W. Wilson, and William Wilson was also listed as a silversmith on his own. After 1851, William Wilson's name appeared alone as a silversmith. William Wilson and Son advertised in an 1856–1857 directory as "Importers and manufacturers of silver and Britannia ware."[2] In an 1859 advertisement, the firm announced the completed "alterations to their store" and invited attention to their stock of "Silverware Which is now unusually large, affording a variety of pattern and design Unsurpassed by any House in the United States, and of finer quality than is manufactured for Table Use in any part of the world."[3] Over twenty years later, in 1880, William Wilson and Son advertised their "Sterling Silver and Electro-Plated Wares." Trading on its longevity, the firm described itself as established in 1812 and "the Largest and Oldest Retail Silverware Manufactory in Philadelphia." By 1909, the business had closed.[4]

The Crawford pitcher combines repoussé and cast decoration. The bark surface and entwining vine were hammered from the interior, while the applied grapes and leaves on the vines, the unusually lifelike lizard on the side, and the eagle on the handle were made of cast silver. Stylistically, the pitcher could date from the late 1840s through the 1850s. The taste for rustic and natural motifs was part of the rococo revival, introduced earlier in American silver by Baltimore's Samuel Kirk (see no. 37). A similarly shaped and marked pitcher with a bark surface and vine, grape, and leaf decoration was presented to John Fritz when he retired as general superintendent of the Cambria Iron Works in 1860, eight years after R. and W. Wilson ceased listings in Philadelphia directories and four years after its successor, William Wilson and Son, began advertising. Both the Fritz and Crawford pitchers (inscribed with unidentified initials) bring to question the marking practices of nineteenth-century Philadelphia silver manufacturers. Fritz also received a repoussé tea service and butter dish marked *R. and W. Wilson,* but whether it was from stock the firm had on hand or William Wilson and Son continued to mark wares with the old firm name is undetermined.[5]

The cast and repoussé decoration on the Crawford pitcher and the Fritz presentation silver is unusually elaborate compared to most known Wilson examples. Apart from presentation pieces and some work in a more florid rococo style, most silver marked by R. and W. Wilson is flatware or simple and conservative holloware.[6]

NOTES

1. Belden 1980, p. 450; Waters 1981, p. 171; T. Wilson 1825, p. 158; Philadelphia directories to 1880.

2. *Public Ledger,* Philadelphia, January 26, 1846. In his will, Robert Wilson bequeathed to his "beloved brother William Wilson all my share of the tools and implements for the manufacture of Silver ware," Philadelphia Register of Wills, 1846, no. 25; Philadelphia directories; *Philadelphia Merchants* 1856, p. 341.

3. *Philadelphia Shopping* 1859, p. 94.

4. Costa 1880, p. 1805; Rainwater 1986, p. 227.

5. The Fritz presentation silver, now in the collection of the State Museum of Pennsylvania, is illustrated and discussed in Getz 1988, pp. 8–11. Given the initials in the Crawford pitcher's inscription, William Wilson might have presented it to a family member, although this has not been documented, and its history is unknown. Undoubtedly, Wilson would have taken the pitcher from stock on hand.

6. Philadelphia Museum of Art 1976, pp. 336–337, 355–356; Ward and Ward 1979, p. 171; Decorative Arts Photographic Collection, Winterthur Museum.

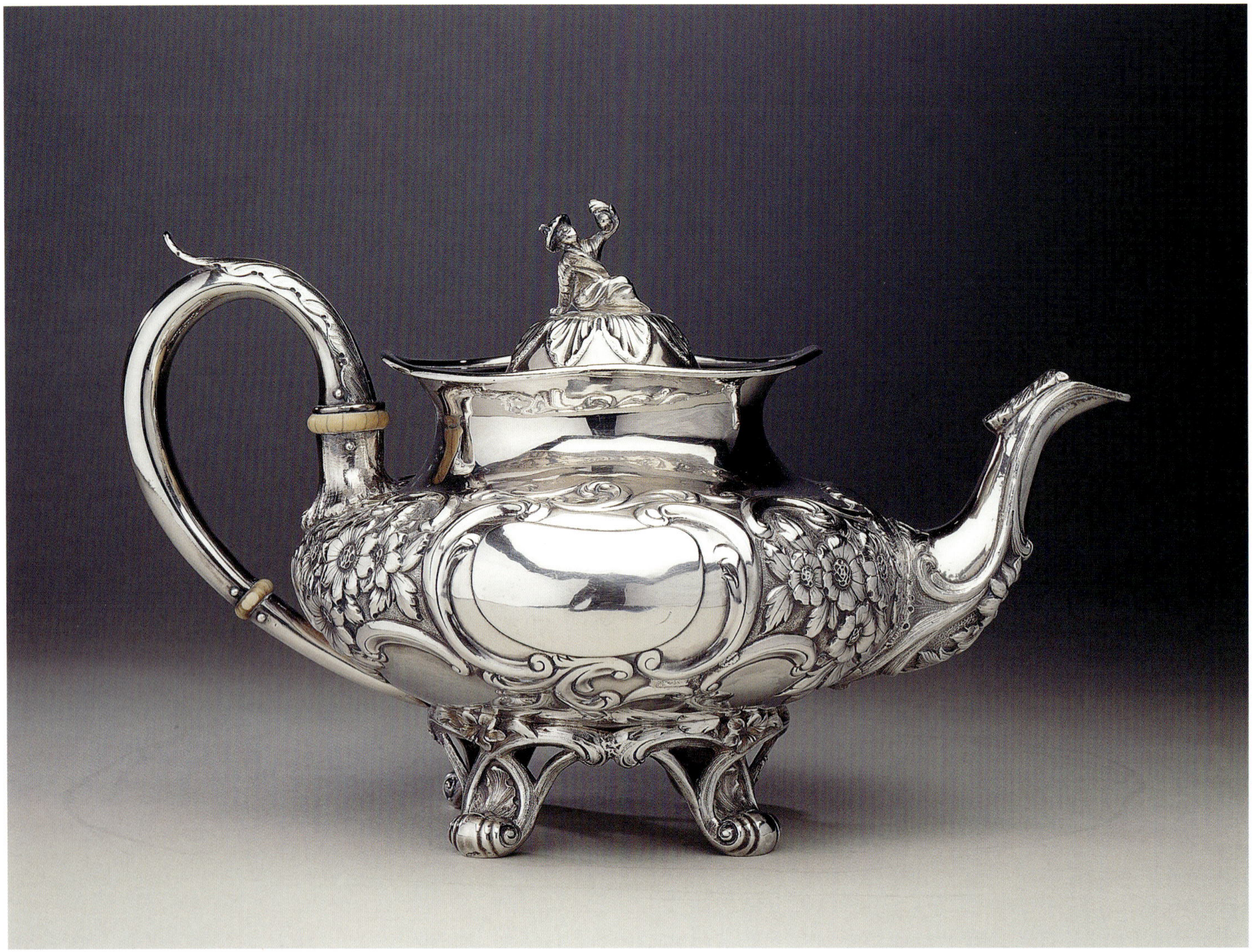

39.

Teapot, 1840s

Obadiah Rich (1809–1888),
Boston
Silver, ivory
7¼ × 10¾ × 6¾ inches
Marks: On bottom: impressed in rectangle, *Pure Silver Coin;* impressed in a shield, *O.Rich/* figure of a griffin facing left/ *BOSTON*
1993.137

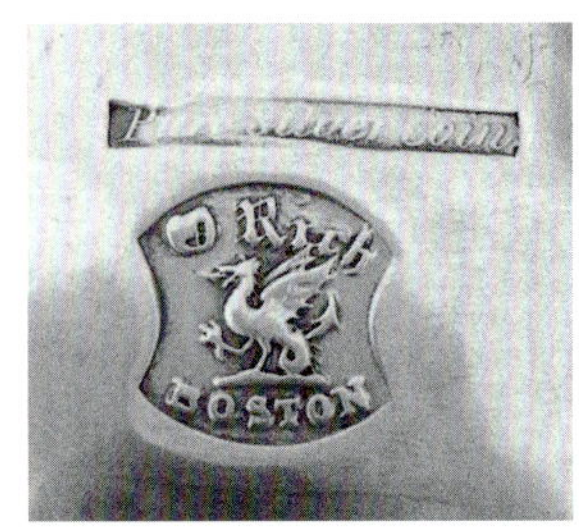

COMPARED TO the more flamboyant designs of contemporary Baltimore silver maker Samuel Kirk (see no. 37), the repoussé and cast decorations on this teapot are understated expressions of the rococo taste (see also no. 5). This style of silver became popular in the 1840s and grew to a near mania in American decorative arts in the 1850s. The Rich teapot is a well-executed early interpretation of conservative nineteenth-century Boston taste and bears the same mark as Obadiah Rich's monumental 1840 Britannia Cup with elaborate rococo repoussé decorations and cast dolphin-shaped handles.[1] Because Rich retired in 1849, it is reasonable to date the pot to the mid- to late 1840s, about the same time as the Kirk pitchers in the Crawford Collection.

Rich may have intended the blank oval cartouche, surrounded by repoussé scrolls and flowers, for an inscription. The ear-shaped handle and the S-shaped spout, both with cast leaves and scrolls, recall eighteenth-century American, English, and French prototypes. The four cast scroll feet, topped by flowers and linked by intertwining scrolls, provide a graceful base for the flattened sphere of the pot.

The domed lid inside the gently undulating collar continues the overall curve of the pot into a pear shape. The cast lid finial, an Asian figure, contributes an exotic chinoiserie effect to the pot. References to China, which were a part of eighteenth-century rococo design and recurred in its mid-nineteenth-century revival, link this Boston teapot with contemporary silver expressions in Baltimore and Philadelphia (see nos. 37, 40).

NOTE

1. See no. 5 in this catalogue for more biographical information about Rich. The Britannia Cup was created to commemorate the sailing of the first steam-powered mail ship between Liverpool and Boston. See Fales 1982, pp. 156–158, for discussion and illustration. The Crawford teapot is illustrated and discussed in Fales 1986, pp. 11–12, fig. 6.

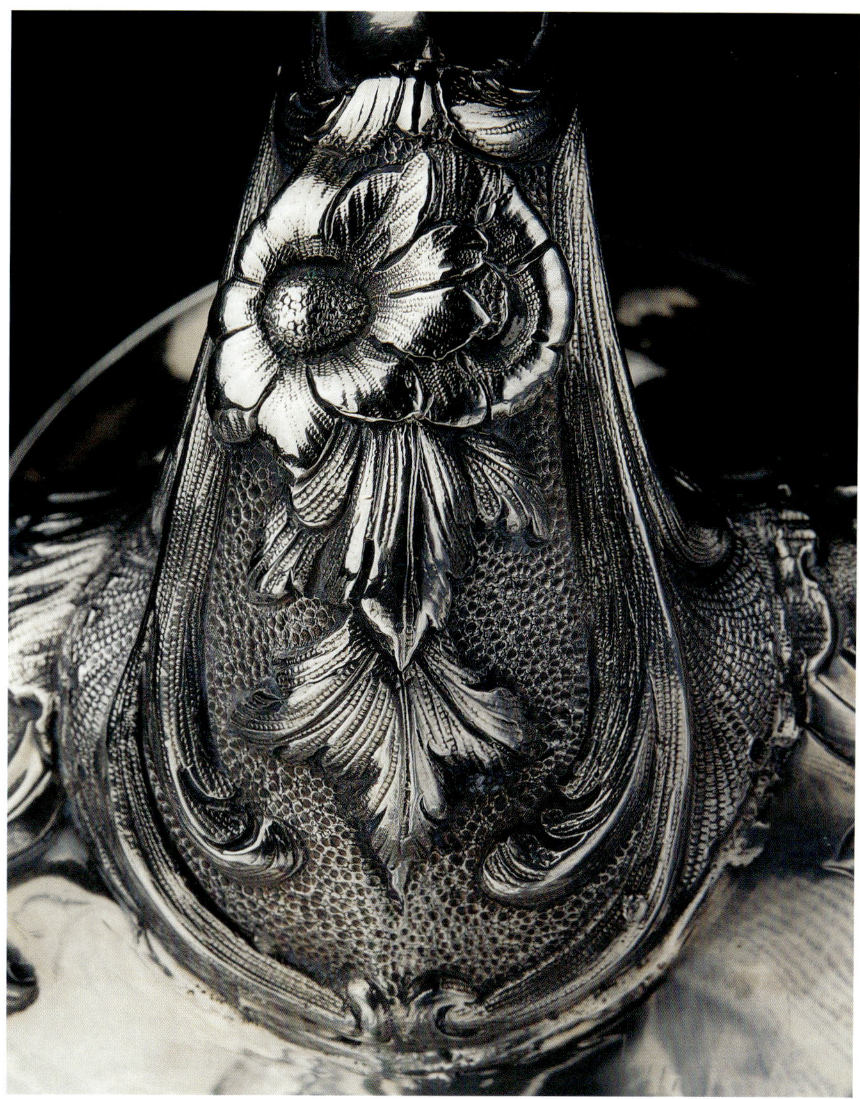

40.

Hot Water Kettle on Stand, ca. 1850

Possibly made by George Sharp (working 1844–ca. 1872); working for Bailey and Company (1846–1878), Philadelphia
Silver
Overall height: 21¼ inches
Kettle: 16½ × 10½ × 8 inches
Stand: 4¾ × 10 × 10 inches
Mark: Impressed on bottom, *BAILEY & CO./136 CHESTNUT ST PHILA/* enclosed in an oval, *S/* a shield and three lions
Inscription: Engraved on side of kettle, *H.T.P.*
1993.138.a–c

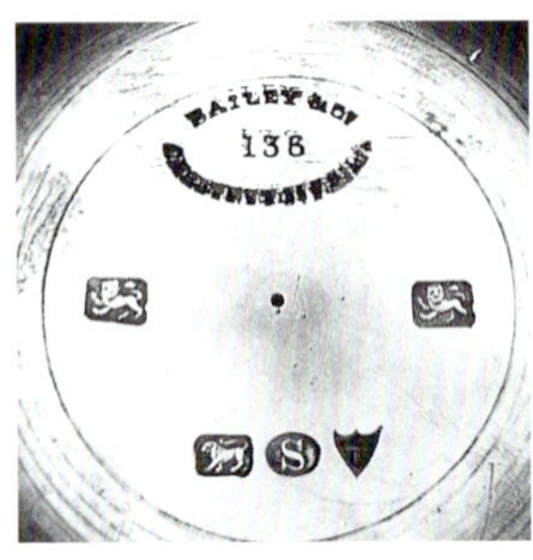

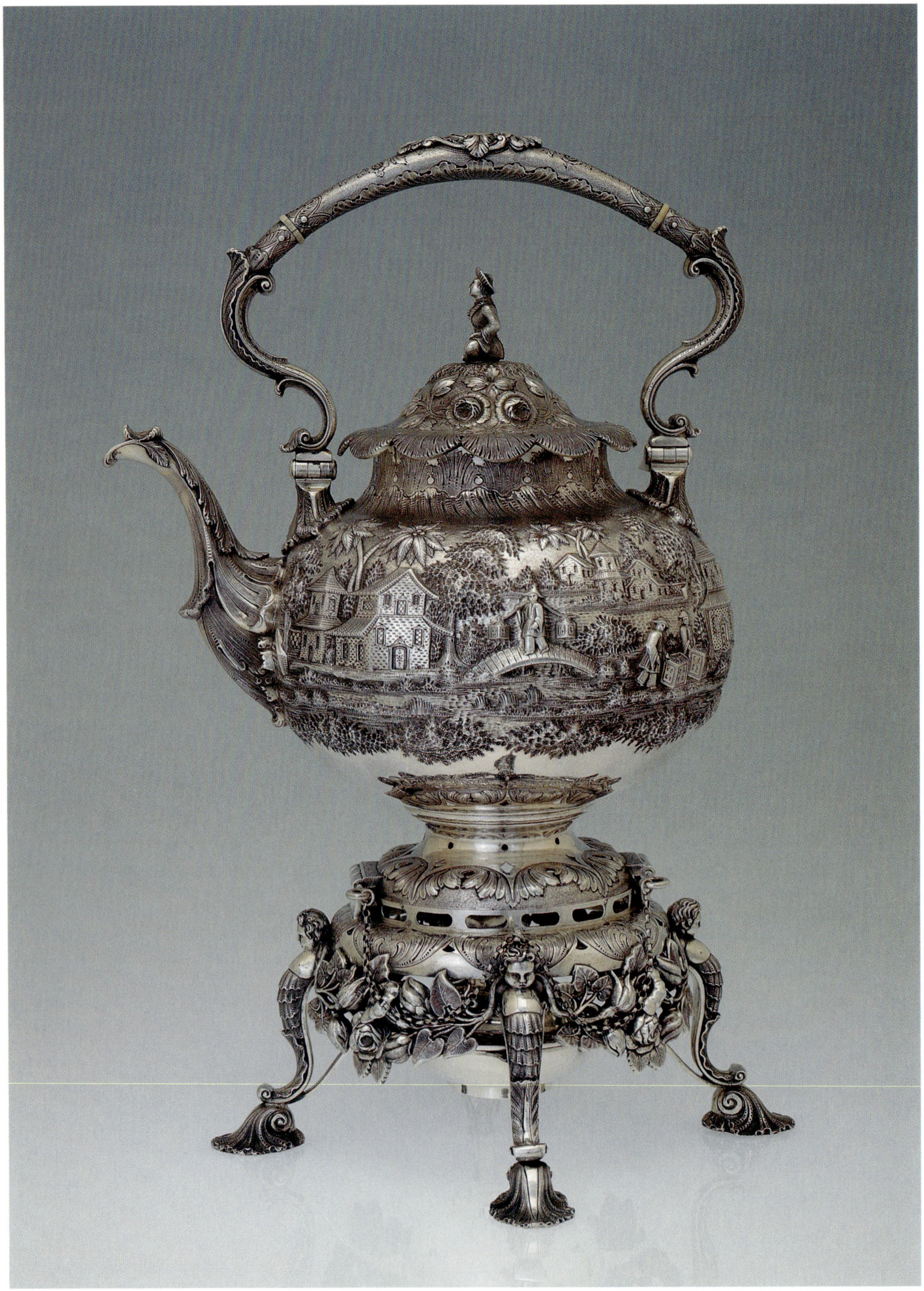

LOCATED ON Chestnut Street, in the heart of Philadelphia's most prestigious commercial district, Bailey and Company was one of the premier jewelry, silver, and luxury goods emporiums in the United States in the 1850s. The firm descended from Bailey and Kitchen, which had been established in 1832 and operated until 1846 (six years after the death of Andrew B. Kitchen) by Joseph Trowbridge Bailey in its original location at 136 Chestnut Street.

In 1846, J. T. Bailey entered a partnership with his brother, Eli W. Bailey, Jeremiah Robbins, and James Gallagher to form Bailey and Company. J. T. Bailey's son, Joseph Trowbridge Bailey, Jr., entered the business in 1851. In 1854, the elder Bailey died, and his son succeeded him as a partner two years later. The company maintained its original headquarters at 136 Chestnut Street until 1859, when a new store at 819 Chestnut Street was completed, and in 1878 the firm became Bailey, Banks and Biddle.[1]

This hot water kettle can be dated between the founding of the company in 1846 and the move to the new building in 1859, according to its mark with the 136 Chestnut Street address. It was part of a large tea service, and a closely related marked set is in the National Museum of American History at the Smithsonian Institution.[2] The Smithsonian set and the Crawford kettle appear to match a service exhibited by Bailey and Company at the Crystal Palace Exposition in New York in 1853.[3]

Bailey and Company maintained a fully equipped silverware factory and completed all aspects of production, from design to melting metal to final engraving. It was on these premises that Philadelphia silversmith George Sharp produced silverware for Bailey and Company. The other mark on the kettle—an *S* enclosed in an oval, a shield, and three lions—is a silver standard.[4] The initials on the Crawford kettle have not been identified.

The kettle—with its round shape, repoussé decoration, ogee spout, and double-ogee handle—and the stand—with its elaborate cast caryatid-figured legs with scroll terminals—closely follow mid-eighteenth-century Philadelphia and London silver prototypes. The chinoiserie repoussé scenes on the sides of the kettle and the Asian figural finial recall the eighteenth-century rococo fascination with Oriental motifs.

Although repoussé rococo silver design was reintroduced as early as the 1830s in the United States (see no. 37) and was popular in the 1840s (see no. 39), the 1850s witnessed its full-blown expression. The fully realized rococo revival style, illustrated in the Crawford kettle, coincided with the popularity of furniture in the style of the New York manufacturer John Henry Belter (see no. 44). Examples of the Philadelphia interpretation of this taste in furniture include the Orem sideboard (see no. 48) and the Henkels desk (see no. 52).

NOTES

1. The history of the firm is recounted in Philadelphia Museum of Art 1976, p. 326; and Rainwater 1986, pp. 15–16. A photograph of the interior of the newly completed Bailey and Company store at 819 Chestnut Street, ca. 1860, appears in Finkel 1980, p. 105.

2. The Smithsonian service is illustrated in Philadelphia Museum of Art 1976, p. 337, no. 291.

3. Silliman and Goodrich 1854, p. 64.

4. For a discussion of the second mark and Sharp's connection with Bailey and Company, see Soeffing 1995, pp. 12–15.

41.

Tea and Coffee Set and Tray, dated 1854

Retailed by Tiffany and Company (1837–present), New York; design attributed to Edward C. Moore (1827–1891); manufactured by John C. Moore and Son Company (1848–1868), New York, for Tiffany and Company
Silver
Kettle on stand: 15 × 10 × 7 inches
Coffeepot: 12⅝ × 9¾ × 6 inches
Teapot: 11⅜ × 9¼ × 5½ inches
Cream pitcher: 8½ × 5 × 4 inches
Sugar bowl: 9 × 7 × 5 inches
Waste bowl: 5¼ × 6 × 6 inches
Tray: 1⅝ × 33 × 20 inches
Marks: Impressed on bottom of kettle on stand, coffeepot, teapot, creamer, sugar bowl, and waste bowl, *76/TIFFANY & CO/M/LATE/M/TIFFANY, YOUNG & ELLIS/550 BROADWAY/502*
Impressed on bottom of tray, *105/TIFFANY & CO/M/LATE/M/TIFFANY, YOUNG & ELLIS/550 BROADWAY/503*
Inscription: On tray, *PRESENTED/CHARLES.F.POND./PRESIDENT OF THE HARTFORD & NW HAVEN./RAILROAD COMPANY./BY UNANIMOUS vote of the Stockholders./at their Annual Meeting./September.20th.1854.*
1985.314.1–7

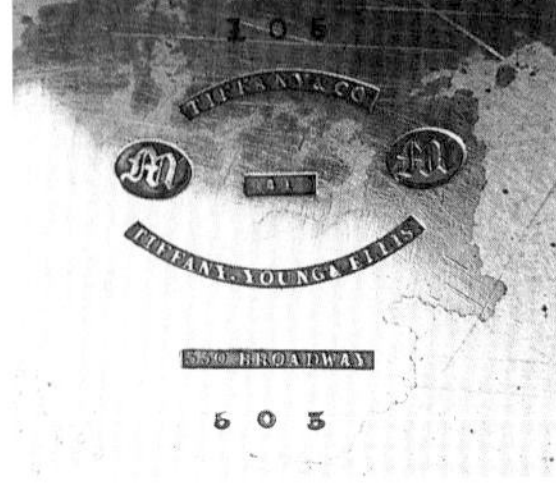

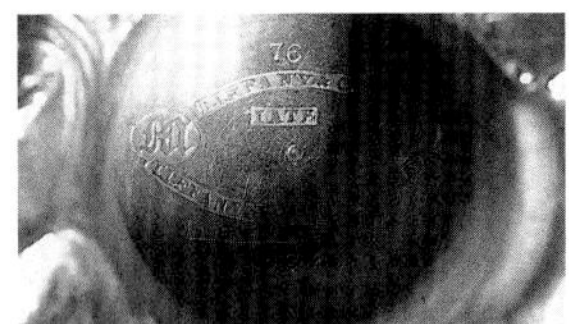

In 1854, the stockholders of the Hartford and New Haven Railroad Company honored the company president with this elaborate silver presentation service. A cast locomotive bell is the finial of each lidded vessel, and views along the line—including trains, stations, tunnels, and a bridge—were executed in repoussé on each. The tray bears an engraved inscription to Charles F. Pond, the presentation date, and engraved views of a locomotive and train car, the railroad stations in Hartford and New Haven, and Yale University, Pond's alma mater.[1] The engraved winged horses symbolize speed, which was associated with trains, and may also refer to the nineteenth-century term for the train, the "iron horse." The border and handles of the tray were cast in the form of a railroad track.

Tiffany and Company of New York was commissioned to design and make the presentation service. The original fancy goods store was established in 1837 by Charles C. Tiffany and John B. Young at 259 Broadway, opposite City Hall, with a $1,000 loan from Tiffany's father. In 1841, J. B. Ellis joined the company and brought substantial capital investment, enabling the firm to expand into diamonds and expensive jewelry in 1845 during an economic panic in Europe. As the store moved uptown—following the city's more affluent residents—to 271 Broadway in 1847, they were retailing silverwares made by a variety of firms, including later rival Gorham Manufacturing Company of Providence, Rhode Island (see nos. 57, 67–68, 72). A Paris branch of the store opened in 1850, as much to provide the New York store with access to European-made goods as to retail abroad.

In 1851, Tiffany, Young and Ellis contracted with New York silver maker John C. Moore to manufacture silver exclusively for the store. At about the same time, Moore's son Edward succeeded him in managing the John C. Moore and Son Company on Prince Street. The younger Moore managed the shop, making silver exclusively for Tiffany, Young and Ellis, and became their chief designer of silver. In 1853, Young and Ellis retired, and Tiffany assumed control. He renamed the business Tiffany and Company and moved to an expanded store farther uptown at 550–553 Broadway, where it remained until moving to Union Square in 1870.[2]

Edward Moore was most likely responsible for the design of the Pond service. In 1850, he made a similar service—with a hot water kettle of the same shape with similar grape and leaf repoussé and cast decoration—for Ball, Tompkins and Black (later Ball, Black and Company) (see no. 56).[3] Around 1855, Tiffany and Company sold another related service by Moore to James E. Birch, a wealthy California stagecoach owner. On the slightly later Birch service, which also has grape and leaf repoussé and cast decoration with slight variations, Moore replaced the railroad themes with motifs celebrating California gold mining.[4] These three related services illustrate Moore's ability to apply his slightly varied "Grape" pattern of holloware to divergent themes. Until his death in 1891, he continued to exert great influence on the design of Tiffany and Company silver (see nos. 96–99, 101–102), including training future Tiffany designers (see nos. 152–156), and possibly even mentoring Louis Comfort Tiffany (see nos. 175–177).[5]

The Tiffany and Company mark appears on the bottom of each piece, with LATE M TIFFANY, YOUNG & ELLIS and the address at 550 Broadway. The 1854 date on the tray, shortly after the dissolution of the partnership, indicates that Tiffany and Company may have been trying to provide a sense of continuity for the firm as it changed names. The *M*s included in the marks stand for Moore. The company's policy of allowing the maker and/or designer to leave his mark did not continue long, and the company's mark soon became the only one used.

NOTES

1. Cochran 1953, pp. 20–21, 450, provides a brief history of the Hartford and New Haven Railroad Company and biographical information about Pond. Additional information about the railroad can be found in Withington 1935, pp. 15–17.

2. For the early history of Tiffany and Company and information about John and Edward Moore, see Carpenter and Carpenter 1997, pp. 6–29; and Venable 1994, pp. 28–31, 35–39.

3. See The Metropolitan Museum of Art 1970, no. 141. Venable 1994, p. 39, states: "Of all Tiffany and Company's competitors in New York, Ball, Black and Company was its retailing arch rival in the 1850s and 1860s."

4. The hot water kettle and tray for the Birch service are illustrated in Carpenter and Carpenter 1997, figs. 23 and 26, and discussed on pp. 19–21.

5. Zapata 1993, pp. 17–20.

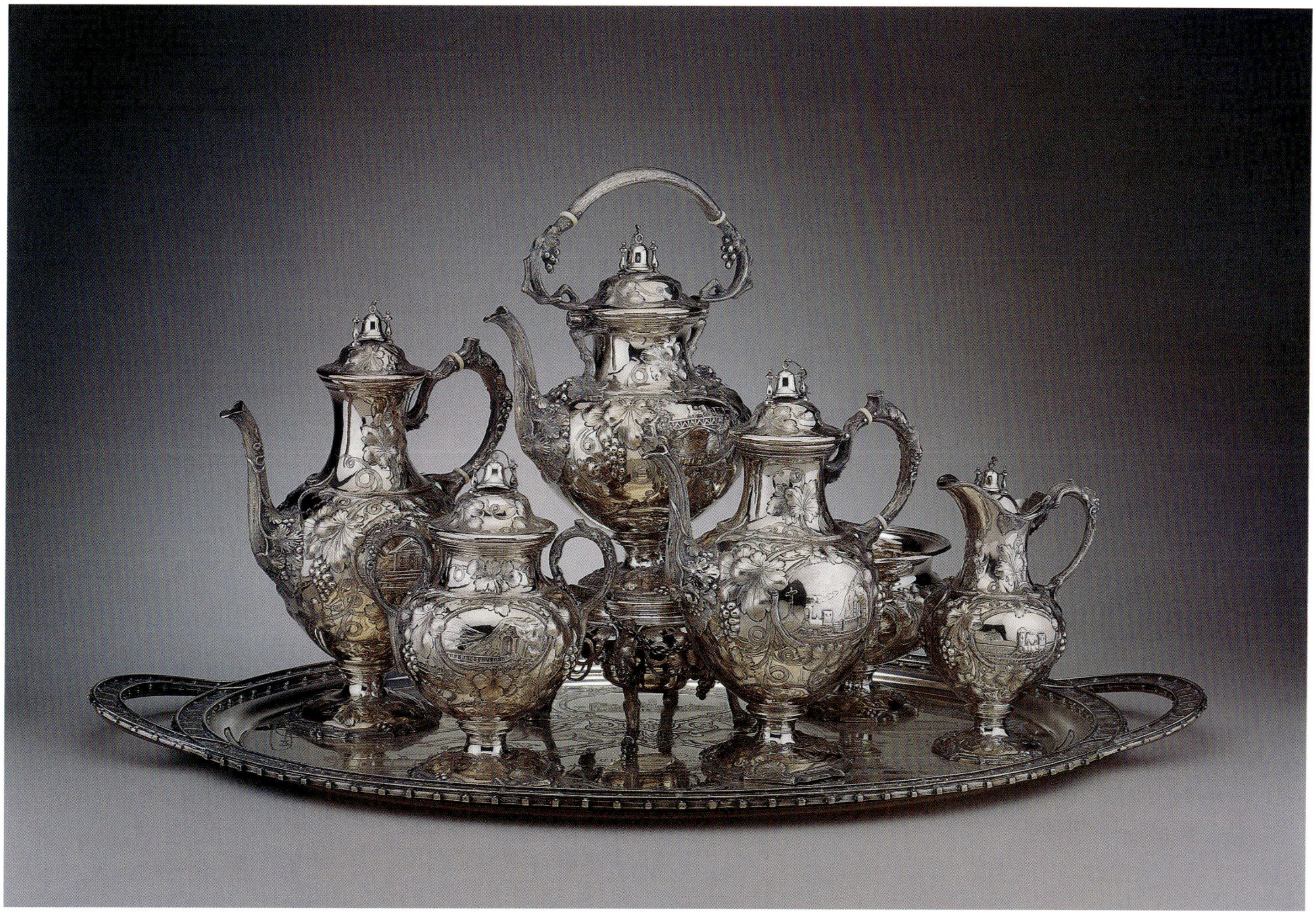

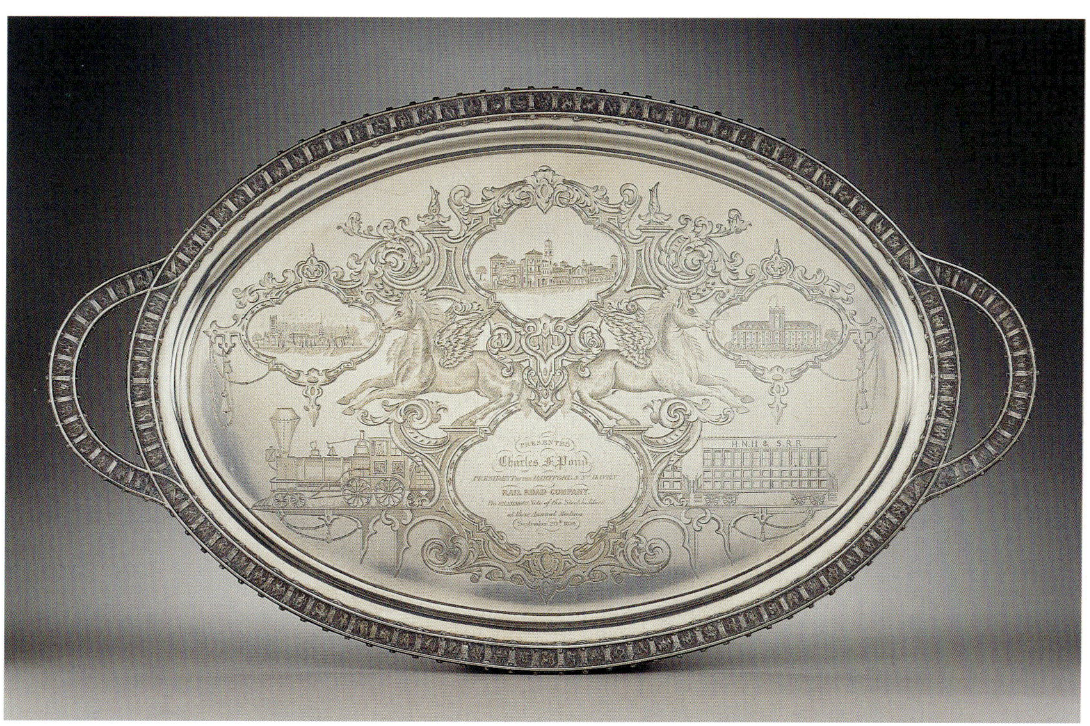
PRESENTED
Charles F. Pond
RAIL ROAD COMPANY.
H.N.H & S.R.R

42.

Pitcher, 1854–1857

William Boch and Brothers (1854–1857), Greenpoint, Brooklyn
Porcelain, gilt decoration
7⅝ × 6½ × 4½ inches
Mark: Impressed on bottom, *WB & BR'S/GREEN POINT L.I.*
Inscription: In gilt on front reserve, *Meine Tochter/Anna/Von/Franz Hoppe* (My daughter/Anna/from/Franz Hoppe)
1982.285

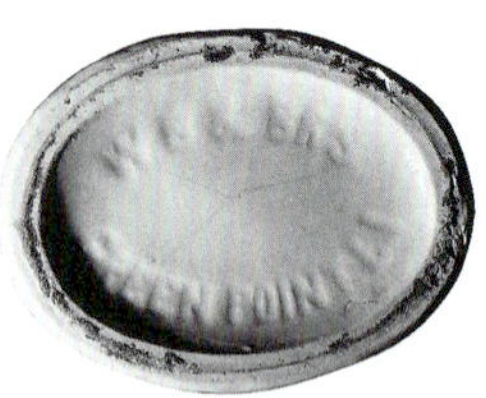

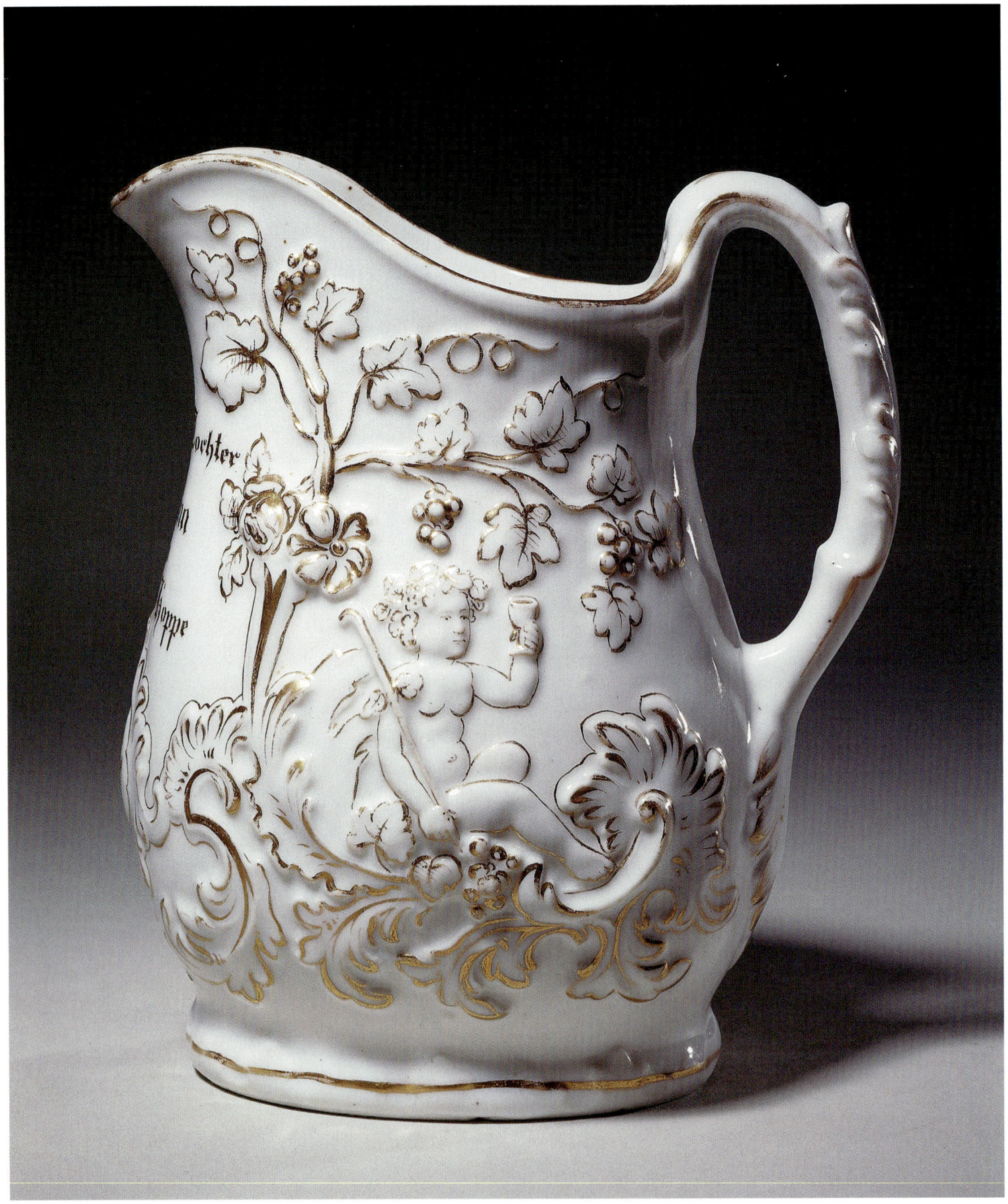

IN THE MID-nineteenth century, Brooklyn (then a separate city from Manhattan) emerged as an American porcelain manufacturing center. In the Greenpoint section, the center of these activities, William, Anthony, and Francis Victor Boch established William Boch and Brothers sometime around 1854. Seven years earlier, Charles Cartlidge and Company had begun porcelain production nearby (see no. 43). Both companies made pitchers and other fancy tablewares, and surviving advertisements and directory listings show that porcelain door hardware, furniture fittings, and trims were production mainstays of both firms.

In 1857, William Boch and Brothers became the Union Porcelain Company, with offices at 82 John Street in Manhattan. Thomas Carll Smith, an architect and entrepreneur, invested in the concern around 1861 and soon assumed ownership. Around 1864, when Smith began producing true hard-paste porcelain instead of the Boch bone china, he renamed the company Union Porcelain Works (see nos. 76–80).[1]

This William Boch and Brothers pitcher contrasts with the earlier porcelain of William Ellis Tucker and Joseph Hemphill in Philadelphia (see no. 6) in both finish and quality of material. Tucker and Hemphill attempted to capture the elite Philadelphia market with fine-quality porcelain bodies and detailed painted decorations after European prototypes. William Boch and Brothers sought a broader and more inclusive market in New York, including hotels, restaurants, and the growing middle class. This pitcher illustrates the increasingly democratized American porcelain business as it evolved from the 1830s through the 1850s, as well as the Bochs's apparently scant interest in competing with finer imported European wares. Although molded in the up-to-date rococo taste of the late 1840s and 1850s, there is little articulation in the modeling of the pitted and heavy porcelain, further blurred by a thick glaze. Gilding, applied quickly to highlight the modeling, provided a showy finish without requiring the painterly skills evident on Tucker wares. The German inscription on the Crawford pitcher implies that the company appealed to recent immigrants, who were eager for prestige goods but had little money for luxuries.

The figure of Bacchus seated amid grapevines suggests that the pitcher was intended for serving wine; it may also have been a pun on the Boch name. An identical pitcher survives that bears the mark of the Union Porcelain Company, indicating that the reorganized Boch concern continued to use the mold after the 1857 name change.[2]

NOTES

1. The histories of the Greenpoint porcelain manufacturers are recounted in Frelinghuysen 1989, pp. 21–26; see also p. 119.

2. Collection of the Henry Ford Museum and Greenfield Village, Dearborn, Michigan. Illustrated in ibid., p. 26, fig. 21.

43.

Pitcher, 1850s

Charles Cartlidge and Company (1848–1856) or American Porcelain Manufacturing Company (1854–1857), Greenpoint, Brooklyn; probably designed by Josiah Jones (1801–1887)
Porcelain
10 × 12¾ × 12¾ inches
Inscription: In gilt on front reserve, *PURSELL*
1993.126

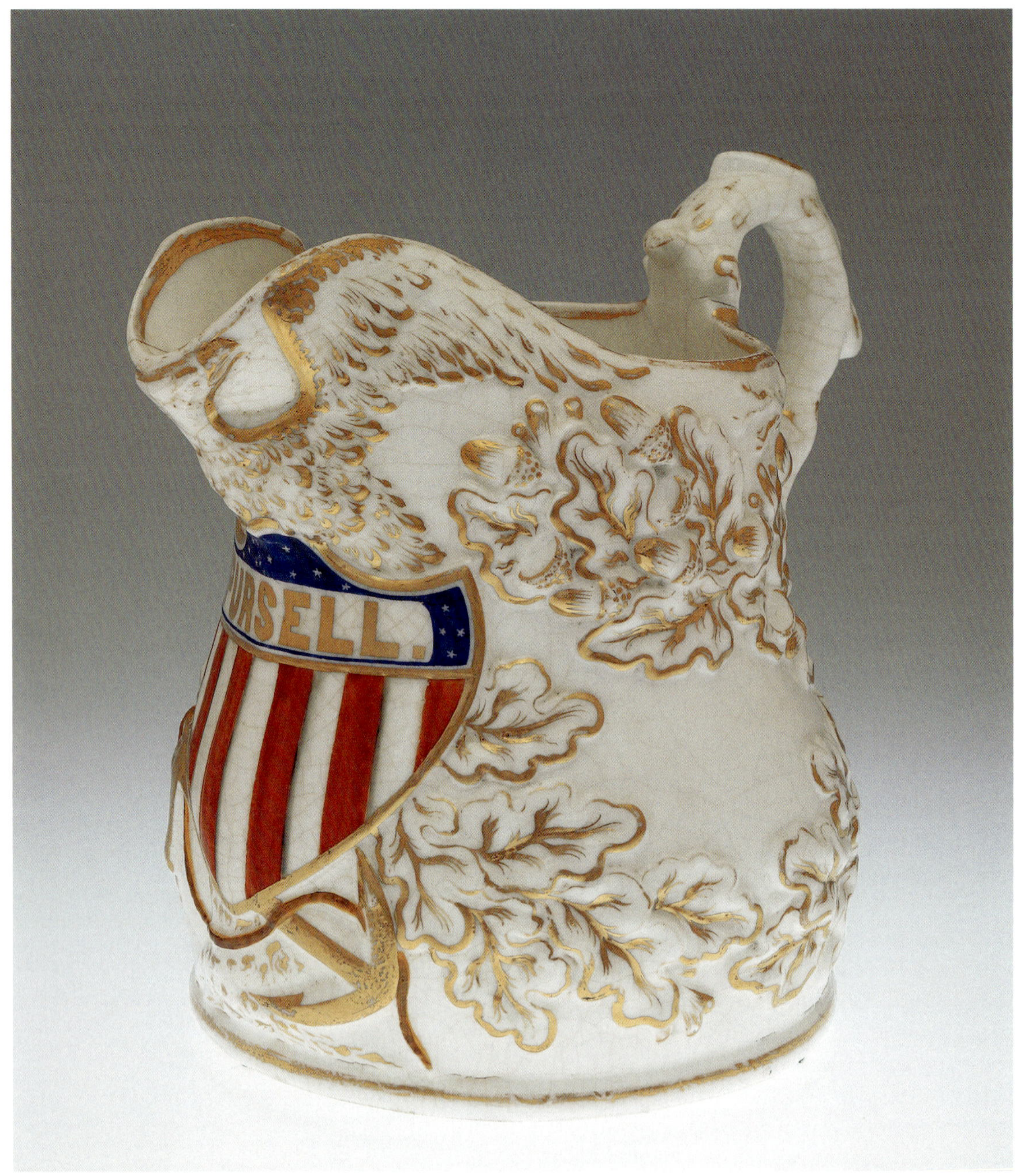

THE AMERICAN porcelain industry was growing by the 1850s, and Charles Cartlidge and Company, together with William Boch and Brothers (see no. 42), made the Greenpoint section of Brooklyn a major porcelain manufacturing center. Charles Cartlidge was born into a family of English potters in Burslem, Staffordshire, where he apprenticed with a friend of his grandfather. After his apprenticeship, Cartlidge worked for Staffordshire potter Joseph Stubbs. Cartlidge not only became a skilled potting technician but also learned all aspects of the business. After visiting the United States, probably on behalf of Stubbs, Cartlidge immigrated to New York in 1832 to become the agent for the Staffordshire potter William Ridgway. In 1841, Cartlidge and his future son-in-law, Herbert Q. Ferguson, expanded Ridgway's trade by opening an agency in New Orleans that Ferguson headed.

Because of Ridgway's unprofitable investments in California and an unsuccessful attempt to establish a pottery in Kentucky, he closed his English business in 1848.[1] That same year, Ferguson returned to Greenpoint and with Cartlidge established Charles Cartlidge and Company. They were joined by Cartlidge's brother-in-law, Josiah Jones, an English sculptor and ceramic modeler, who became the firm's chief designer.[2] Initial productions included porcelain buttons and architectural and furniture fittings. The company also made tablewares, the best known of which were molded acorn and oak leaf pitchers such as the Crawford example. Charles Cartlidge and Company, its neighboring competitor William Boch and Brothers, and the United States Pottery Company of Bennington, Vermont (see nos. 15–17), exhibited porcelains at the New York Crystal Palace Exhibition of 1853.[3]

Like Ridgway, Cartlidge made unwise investments in the early 1850s, and to recoup losses, Charles Cartlidge and Company was reorganized in 1854 as the American Porcelain Manufacturing Company. After shares were sold, Cartlidge lost control of the firm, and it closed in 1857.[4]

The Crawford pitcher is distinctly American in its decorative motifs: an American eagle molded as the spout, and a red, white, and blue shield painted beneath. The base of the handle is shaped like the trunk of an oak tree, with branches of oak leaves and acorns in relief around the sides of the pitcher. These pitchers generally were inscribed. Pursell was the family name of several porterhouse owners around New York at the time, which suggests that the Crawford pitcher may have been used originally in a tavern.[5] Certainly the moderate price and heavy weight of the Cartlidge porcelain made it appropriate for commercial purposes. A listing in a memorandum book left by Cartlidge possibly refers to this form: "large water pitchers with relief figures of eagles and patriotic devices in colors."[6]

NOTES

1. Barber, June, 1895, pp. 688–689, gives biographical information about Cartlidge, including his recollections of his apprenticeship, which introduced him to all aspects of the ceramic business.

2. Barber, September, 1895, pp. 226–227. This article, the fourth in Barber's series on the history of the firm, focuses on Jones.

3. Frelinghuysen 1989, pp. 21–22.

4. Barber, October, 1895, pp. 330–331.

5. Correspondence, Gary and Diana Stradling, April 26, 1992, High Museum of Art document files.

6. Quoted in Barber, *Pottery,* 1976, p. 446.

44.

Sofa and Four Side Chairs, ca. 1855

Probably John Henry Belter (1804–1863), New York
Laminated and carved rosewood with modern silk velvet upholstery and original silver thread embroidered mounts
Sofa: 51½ × 91¾ × 38½ inches
Side chairs: Each 39⅞ × 19⅛ × 27½ inches
1981.1000.61–.65

CABINETMAKER John Henry Belter received a series of patents between 1847 and 1858 for manufacturing sinuous and light, yet durable, furniture.[1] Belter's name has become indelibly associated with the curved and elaborately carved parlor furniture that was popular in the 1850s, like this sofa and four side chairs in the Crawford Collection.[2]

Born in 1804 in southern Germany, Belter may have apprenticed in Württemberg. He is thought to have immigrated to New York around 1840, although his first listing in New York directories was in 1844, when both his shop and his home were at 42½ Chatham Street. By 1853, Belter's shop had moved to 547 Broadway, and a year later his directory listing included a factory at Third Avenue near 76th Street. The 1856 directory noted a move to 552 Broadway and Belter's partnership with his brother-in-law, J. H. Springmeyer. In 1861, two more brothers-in-law, William and Frederick Springmeyer, joined the business, which had moved to 722 Broadway. After Belter's death in 1863, the Springmeyers continued the business under the name J. H. Belter and Company until 1865, when it became Springmeyer Brothers.[3] Despite his innovations, apparent success, and long-term influence, Belter died in poverty.[4]

In his patents, Belter called his lamination process "dishing pressed work." The furniture was essentially made of plywood: layers of wood veneer glued together at cross grains for greater strength. These sheets were pressed together between a metal core mold and a metal outer caul to create a barrel of laminated wood. After the glue between the layers dried, the barrel was cut to create the curved chairbacks, which were then hand carved.

Not all labeled Belter and Springmeyer furniture was laminated, but most seems to have been in the carved rococo style popular in the 1850s and 1860s. While Belter's New York contemporaries like Alexander Roux (see nos. 36, 46, 61) worked in a variety of the styles popular at mid-century, all of the known Belter furniture is related to the Crawford rococo sofa and chairs. Although he identified himself as a "Manufacturer of All Kinds of Fine Furniture" on the printed label of a parlor table in the Museum of the City of New York,[5] no Belter furniture has

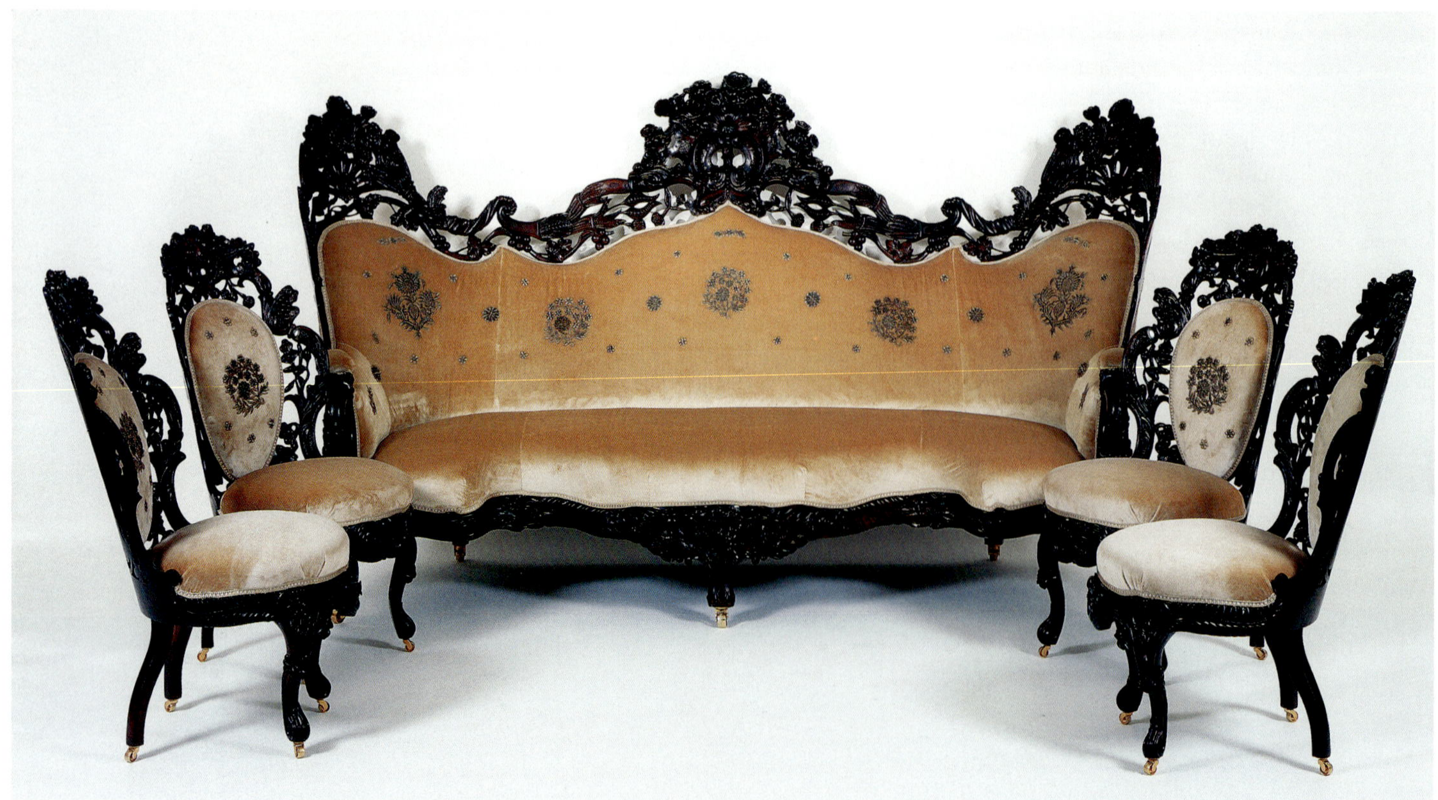

been identified in the mature classical taste of the 1840s (see nos. 7–8), the Elizabethan (see nos. 35–36) or Gothic tastes (see nos. 30, 33–34, 214–215) of the 1850s, or the French classical taste of the 1860s (see nos. 46, 48, 52).

The Crawford furniture is made up of at least seven layers of laminated veneer. Carved rosebuds were applied to the ornate cresting for additional depth. An 1855 bill of sale from Belter described a set that is probably similar as "Arabasket," referring to the carved and open-worked frame. The number of pieces listed in the invoice indicates that the Crawford furniture probably represents only part of the original set. Besides a sofa and four parlor chairs, it listed another sofa, "two Arabasket Rosewood Armchairs," one "Arabasket Rosewood Centre table," and one "Fine Rosewood Étagère."[6]

The Crawford furniture retained its original upholstery, in deteriorated condition, until 1980, when it was replaced with a matching modern silk velvet. The surviving mounts, with the silver thread embroidery somewhat tarnished over the years, were reattached in the original configuration.

The Crawford furniture is carved in a manner consistent with other Belter furniture, with its realistically rendered flowers and grapes and deeply carved shells. Carved openwork in naturalistic motifs, rather than in interlocking C-scrolls, was characteristic of Belter's production.[7] The bold carving of the frames and the cabriole legs was loosely derived from mid-eighteenth-century French and English prototypes. By the 1820s, designs adapted from such sources were being published in England. The English versions, however, were closer to the source in scale and rendering than Belter's bolder and less abstract designs.[8]

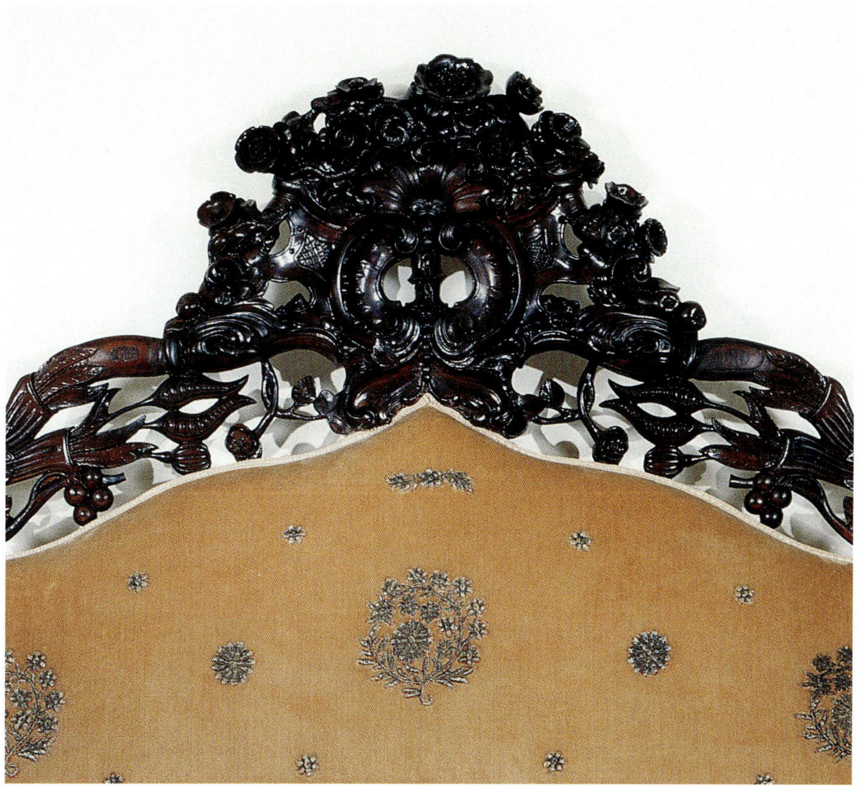

NOTES

1. For a discussion of Belter's patents, see Roth 1977, pp. 1038–1040; and Vincent 1974, pp. 206–234.

2. According to New York cabinetmaker Ernest Hagen, Charles A. Baudouine copied Belter's laminated furniture production with slight variation. As early as 1908, Hagen wrote about "those heavy over decorated parlour suites with rounded perforated backs generally known as 'Belter Furniture' from the original inventor, John H. Belter, 372 Broadway" (Ingerman 1963, pp. 578–579). Some evidence points to the production of curving, laminated furniture in Boston and Philadelphia, but to date no laminated and carved furniture has been documented or labeled by a maker other than Belter. See Schwartz, Stanek, and True 1981, pp. 5–7.

3. The history of the firm was recounted in Downs 1948, pp. 166–168; Schwartz, Stanek, and True 1981, pp. 24–29; and Vincent 1974, p. 209.

4. Ernest Hagen recalled in 1908 that Belter was poor at the time of his death in 1863 (Ingerman 1963, p. 579).

5. Vincent 1974, pp. 207–208, fig. 1.

6. The Metropolitan Museum of Art 1970, no. 126.

7. Schwartz, Stanek, and True 1981, p. 10.

8. George Smith, *The Cabinetmaker's and Upholsterer's Guide* (London: Jones & Co., 1828), pls. CLII and CXLVI; cited and illustrated in Schwartz, Stanek, and True 1981, p. 25.

45.

Covered Goblet,
1850s

Probably Bohemia (now the Czech Republic) for the American market
Ruby stained and cased, engraved non-lead glass
20½ × 7½ × 7½ inches
Inscription: Engraved below image, *THE NEW CAPITOL WASHINGTON*
1984.114

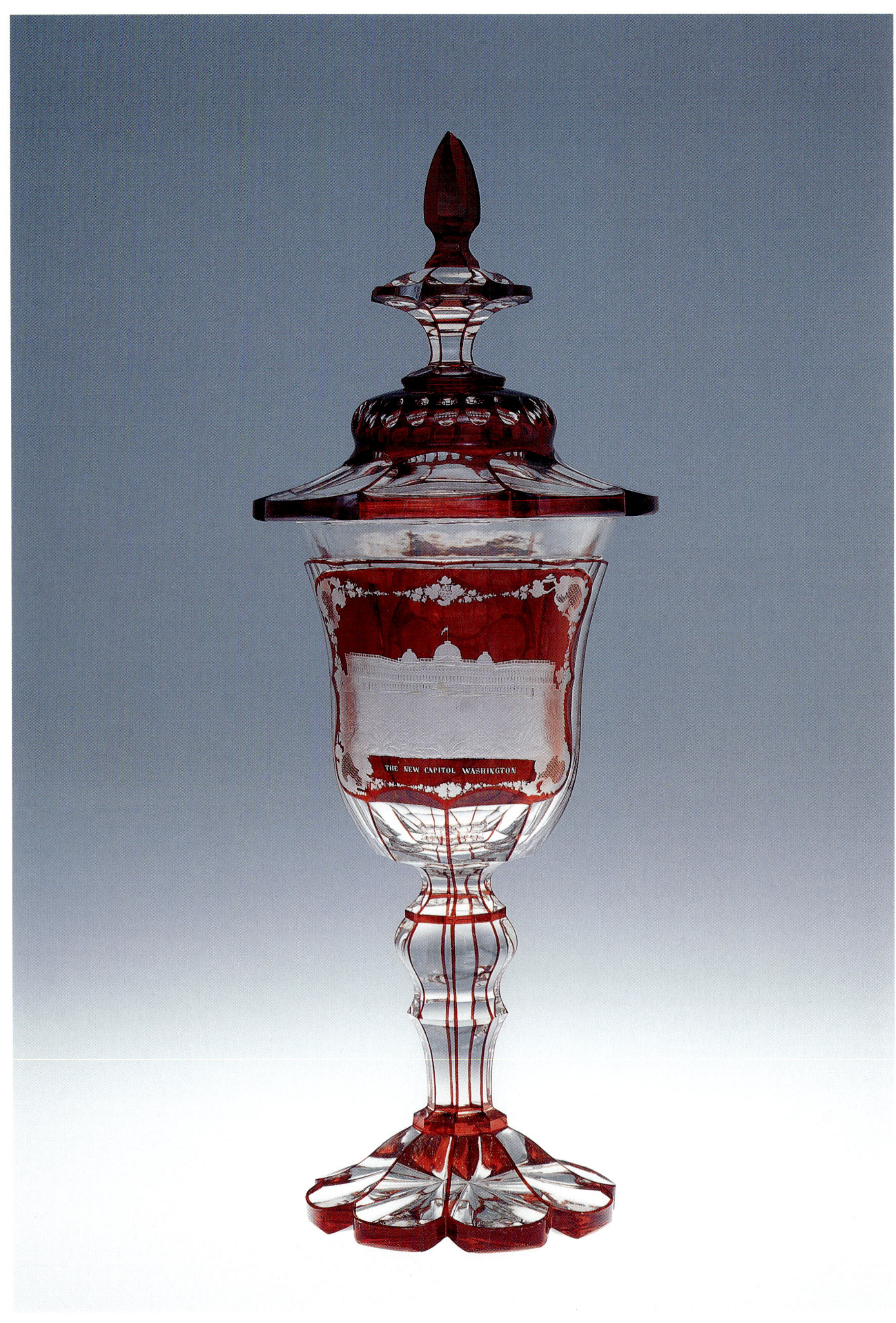

COLOR-CASED OR PLATED and engraved glassware, like this covered goblet decorated with a view of the east facade of the Capitol in Washington, D.C., was probably called Bohemian glass in the mid-nineteenth century.[1] In 1851, the Brooklyn Flint Glass Works reported that "plated or Bohemia Glass Ware is manufactured here in perfection." An 1852 newspaper account of the New England Glass Company described similar wares: "Richly colored and decorated glassware which is so admired under the name 'Bohemian Glass' is manufactured at these works." Colored wares of the nineteenth century with engraved views of notable American buildings and scenery have been described as "Americo-Bohemian" glass. However, no example of this plated or colored cut to clear glass decorated with an American view has been firmly attributed to a mid-nineteenth-century American glass factory, despite claims in period accounts.[2]

The elaborately cut and engraved decoration and the sheer monumentality of the Crawford goblet relate it to contemporary European, rather than American, glassmaking. Lack of lead in the glass further supports a European, and likely Bohemian, attribution. The Capitol decoration confirms that it was intended for the American market.

The view of the Capitol seen on the Crawford goblet never actually existed. Architect Thomas Ustick Walter's two wings—the left housing the House of Representatives and the right housing the Senate—are depicted flanking the original 1820s dome by Charles Bulfinch. The wings were completed in 1857 and 1859, but the Bulfinch dome had already been torn down for construction of a new dome more in scale with the expanded building, which had begun in 1856.[3] Because the view depicts the new wings of the building, the goblet postdates 1851, when President Millard Fillmore approved Walter's proposal, and predates 1855, when the architect envisioned a new dome. An artist who might have seen Walter's initial proposal with the Bulfinch dome depicted an aerial view of the proposed form from the east in an 1852 print.[4] A period print showing the elevation as rendered on the goblet has not been identified.

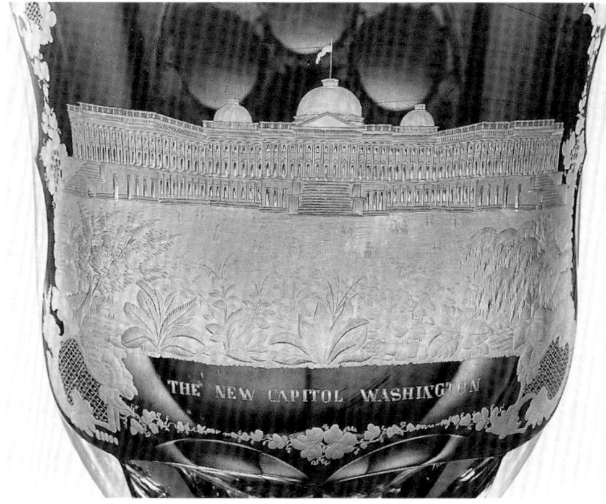

NOTES

1. Silliman and Goodrich 1854, pp. 108–109, 165, describes and illustrates French glass of this type, which had been made in Paris for the New York Crystal Palace Exhibition of 1853, which took place at the present site of the New York Public Library. The text describes this cased French glass as "Bohemian."

2. *Boston Transcript* (June 16, 1852) and *Brooklyn Evening Star* (May 28, 1851), both cited in Spillman 1977, p. 144. The term "Americo-Bohemian" was used to classify mid-nineteenth-century cased glass engraved with American views in two articles describing the wares; see ibid. pp. 134–146; and Spillman 1980, pp. 78–81. See also Spillman 1994, pp. 78–85, pl. XI, which illustrates and discusses a covered goblet identical to the Crawford example in the Corning Museum of Glass.

3. Rosenberger 1948–1950, pp. 301–302, 305.

4. A print by C. Sasche published in Baltimore in 1852 is illustrated in Stokes and Haskell 1932, pl. 81, facing p. 182.

46.

Étagère, 1850–1857

Attributed to Alexander Roux (1813–1886), New York
Rosewood, rosewood veneer, mahogany, mahogany veneer, ash, poplar, and mirrored glass
86½ × 79½ × 29½ inches
1981.1000.66

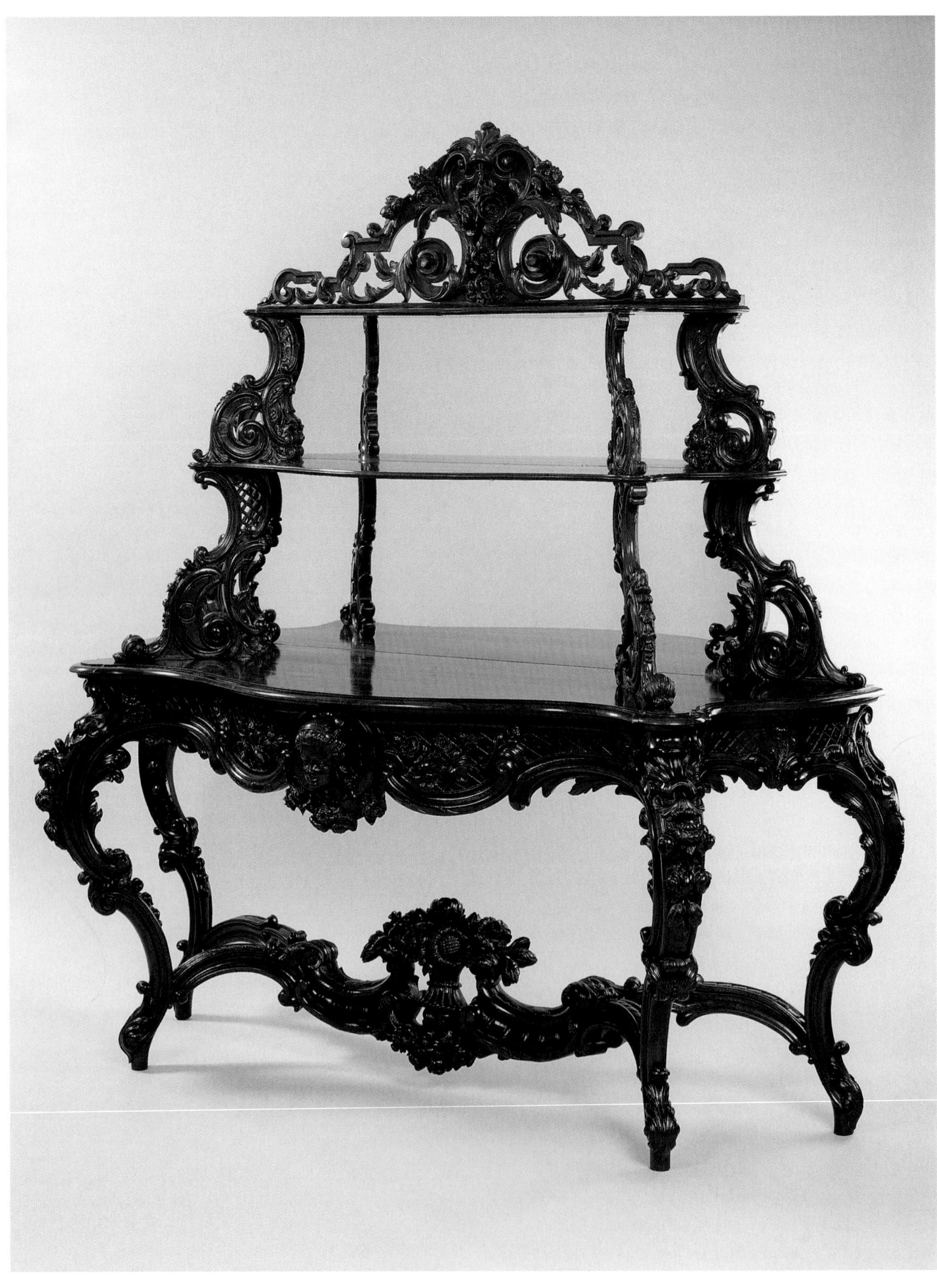

THE MAIN FUNCTION of the sinuously carved Crawford étagère was display. Except for minor carved details, the unmarked étagère appears identical to two other examples that both bear the printed label of Alexander Roux in New York.[1] The label depicts Roux's two warehouses at 479 and 481 Broadway, each with a sign reading *A. Roux* and the addresses. Roux is believed to have used the label between 1850 and 1857, which provides likely dates for the Crawford étagère. In 1850, his wareroom had expanded from 479 Broadway to include the building next door at 481, and the label may have announced his expansion.

Andrew Jackson Downing enthusiastically endorsed Roux's furniture business in *The Architecture of Country Houses:* "In New York, the rarest and most elaborate designs, especially for drawing-room and library use, are to be found at the warehouse of Roux, in Broadway."[2] Downing noted the variety of styles executed at the Roux shop: "At the warehouse of M. A. Roux, Broadway, may be found a large collection of furniture for the drawing-room, library, etc.—the most tasteful designs of Louis Quatorze, Renaissance, Gothic, etc. to be found in the country."[3] Downing identified seven of his illustrations as examples in Roux's inventory, including an étagère, probably considered Louis Quatorze, of a much simpler design than the Crawford example. Another less complex étagère design illustrated his description of its function: "In the centre is a handsome mirror, on either side of which are shelves for articles of *virtu*—bouquets of flowers, scientific curiosities, or whatever else of this kind the owner may indulge his taste in."[4] The advantage of placing a mirror behind the shelves of an étagère was that it allowed the objects to be viewed in the round and reflected light into the drawing room.

New York cabinetmaker Ernest Hagen wrote in 1908 that Roux was well regarded in the furniture industry. After describing his own work at the furniture plant owned by Charles A. Baudouine, Hagen wrote that Roux "was the next best to Baudouine and on good terms with him. Roux's style was rather better than Baudouine's and generally lighter in character, running off in the Louis XVI style. He turned out excellent work for the time. The work even then [1850s] was mostly rosewood with oak for the dining room, but now walnut began to get in fashion."[5]

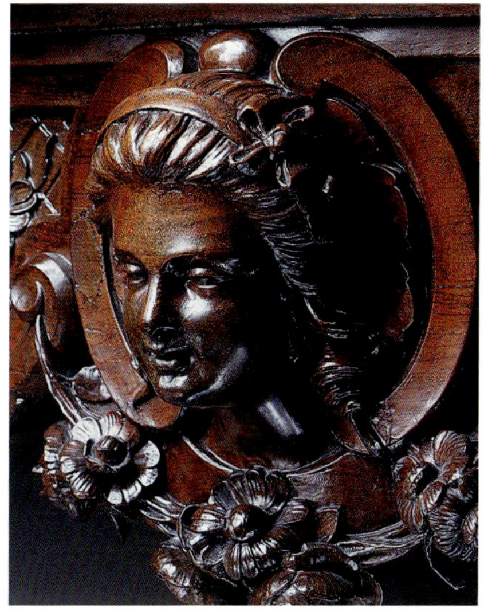

With its intricate sculptural carving, this étagère was undoubtedly expensive. It was made of costly rosewood, which was imported from a tropical climate. The resinous substance of rosewood made it difficult and time-consuming to carve. The amount of floral carving would have complemented even the most florid work of Roux's contemporary John Henry Belter (see no. 44), and the bold convex shape of this étagère resembles Belter's laminated work. In a parlor or drawing room, the étagère would have conveyed the owner's wealth, social status, education, sophistication, and taste for things artistic.

NOTES

1. One étagère is in The Metropolitan Museum of Art (1971.219, 220); see Davidson and Stillinger 1985, pp. 170–171, fig. 263. Another is in the Baltimore Museum of Art (1977.42); see Elder and Stokes 1987, pp. 157–158, no. 119. All three étagères display slight variations. The central scrolled shelf supports on the Metropolitan and Baltimore étagères incorporate open cross-hatching instead of the continuing scrolls on the Crawford example. Each example includes a basket with flowers at the center of the cross stretchers. All three baskets are of the same form, but each bouquet is slightly different. A fourth closely related example, a side table with a marble top and without an étagère, is in the Museum of the City of New York; see The Metropolitan Museum of Art 1970, no. 130. Again, variations occur in the bouquet at the center of the scrolled cross stretchers. For a history of the Roux firm, see no. 36 in this catalogue.

2. Downing 1969, p. 412.

3. Ibid., p. 432.

4. Ibid., p. 456.

5. Ingerman 1963, p. 579.

47.

Mantel, Fireplace Surround, and Cover, ca. 1855

Probably New York
Black walnut, white pine, marble, and cast iron
51 × 56 × 9¼ inches
Mark: Cast on inside top of cover, *WHJ.No*
1983.191

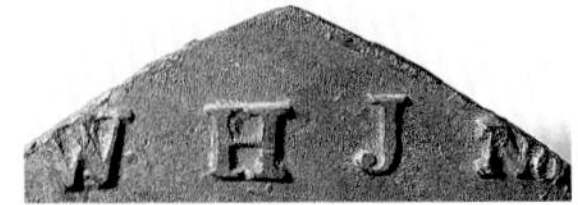

THE EXTRAORDINARY CARVING on this surround combines Gothic architectural elements with rococo scrolls and detailed, lifelike renderings of animals. The centerpiece of the top frieze below the mantel shelf is a pair of birds with a nest and eggs. To the left, a dog in profile scampers away from the nest through a scroll. To the right, a dog snarls at a wolf that looks back over its shoulder as it runs away. The nest appears protected by lush carved foliage and intertwining scrolls.

The carved side columns consist of a tapering hexagonal pedestal wrapped by deep courses of florid scrolling against a background of carved Gothic tracery. Pointed Gothic arches topped with scrolls crown the flanking pedestals. The fireplace opening is fitted with a cast-iron Gothic arch frame and cover plate with perforations that mimic the tracery pattern of a cathedral rose window with a field of scrolls below. The Gothic and rococo details in the cast-iron cover plate echo the similar combination of details in the surround.

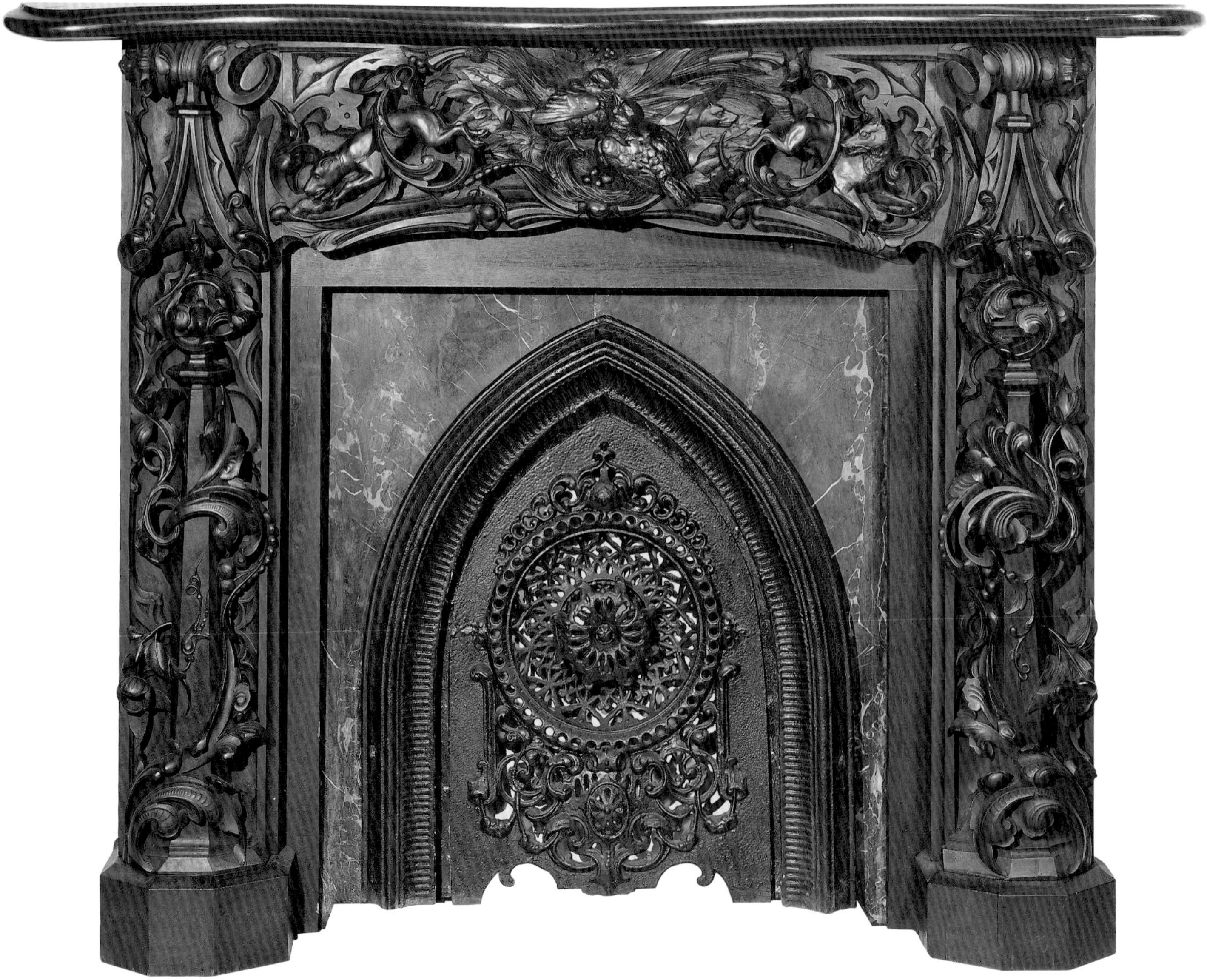

These elements in the fireplace surround and cover plate may have been meant to inspire a sober spiritual and moral environment for the family. The nest motif could be linked with the mythology of the hearth as a source of familial safety, warmth, and togetherness. The top frieze

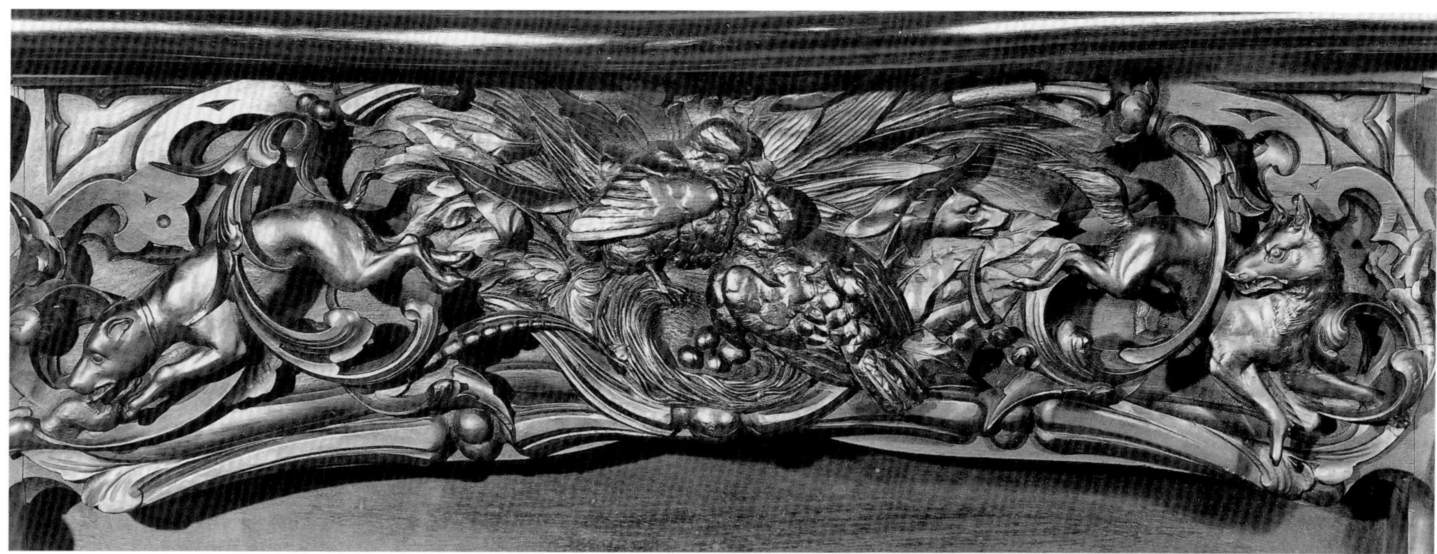

illustrates the notion that family and home are safe havens from the outside world, possibly symbolic of the ruthless business world of nineteenth-century New York.

The detailed sculptural carving of the surround is clearly the work of a highly skilled artisan. The carved details on the fireplace, like those on the attributed John Henry Belter parlor set (see no. 44) and Alexander Roux étagère (see no. 46), attest not only to the skill of the carver but also to the expense of this architectural element. According to an 1859 advertisement, Roux was "prepared to execute all orders for the Furnishing of Houses, such as Wood Mantel-Pieces, Wainscoting, Mirror Frames, Cornices and Cabinet-Work in general, in the best manner at the lowest rates."[1] Walnut was an unusual material for the ornately carved mantels characteristic of the mid-nineteenth century, which were more often made of white marble.

When the fireplace surround was acquired for the Crawford Collection, it was thought to have been removed from a house occupied by William H. Vanderbilt and his family on a Staten Island farm. Although the Staten Island Historical Society has photographs of the exteriors of two of the Vanderbilt houses, no interior photographs have been located to substantiate the provenance.[2]

NOTES

1. In the late 1850s, New York furniture manufacturers apparently were executing interior architectural details such as the Crawford mantel. Roux's advertisement from *Carroll's New York City Directory* is cited by Hauserman 1968, pp. 211–212.

2. Vanderbilt moved his family from Staten Island to a new house on the corner of Fifth Avenue and 40th Street in 1867. Regarding Vanderbilt's Staten Island residences, see correspondence, Richard W. Pollard, Brooklyn, April 27, 1981, High Museum of Art document files.

48.

Sideboard, ca. 1855

Sculptural elements possibly carved by Joseph Alexis Bailly (1825–1883); probably made in Philadelphia
Black walnut, marble, and poplar
108 × 90 × 30 inches
1990.80

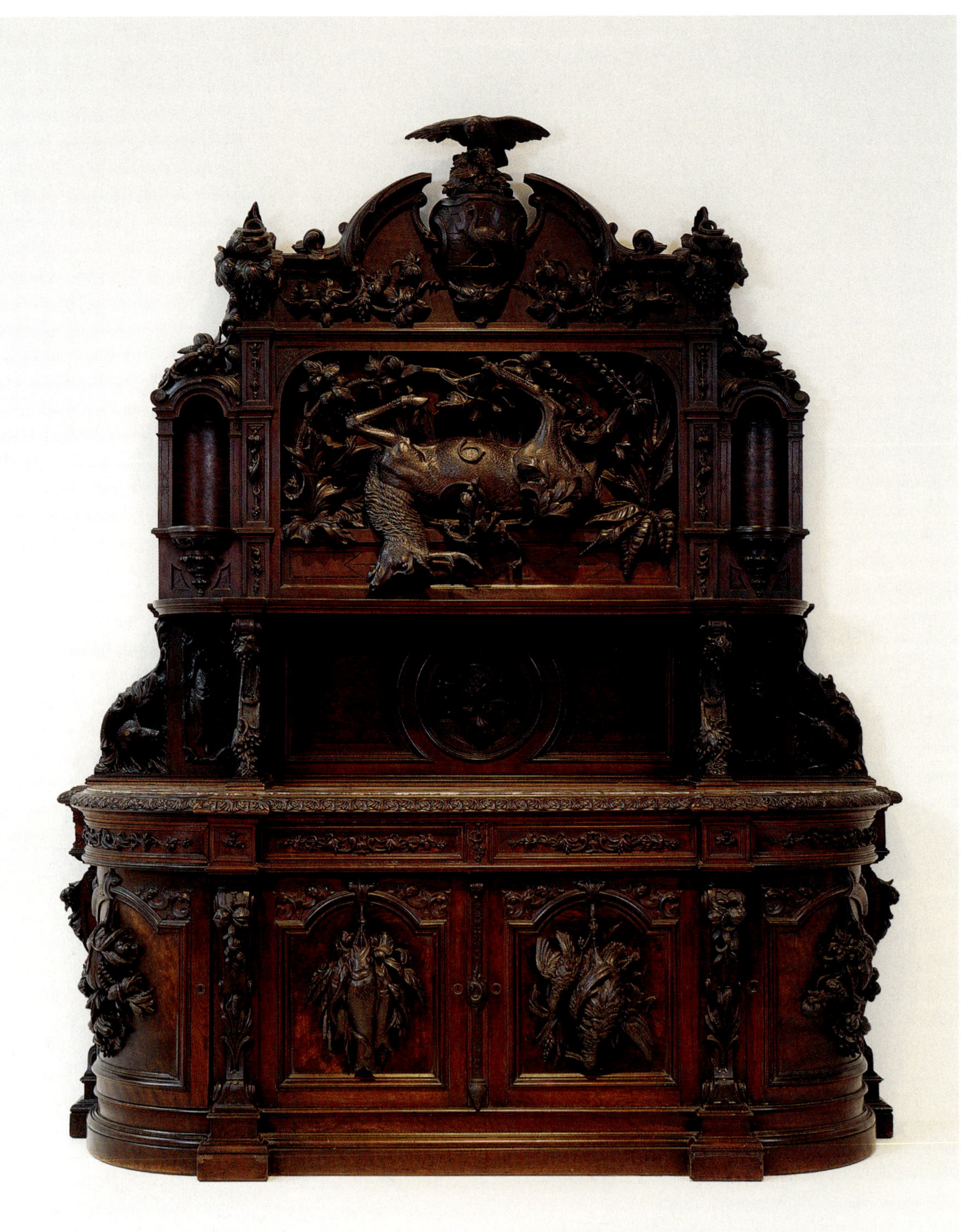

FOLLOWING EUROPEAN royal and aristocratic practices, rooms set aside specifically for dining became more common in American houses during the nineteenth century. In affluent homes, large tables with sets of matching chairs and complementing sideboards furnished these new dining rooms. Before the Civil War, most sideboards (including the Crawford example) were made for wealthy homes and used in the French-inspired rituals of dining, which had become increasingly complex. By the end of the century, middle-class homes also had dining rooms with dining sets, often with matching sideboards.[1]

The Crawford sideboard originally belonged to John Morris Orem, a wealthy Baltimore importer. Orem purchased a tract of land in Baltimore County in 1856, constructed a large Italianate mansion, and gave the eighteenth-century name of Auchentoroly to his estate (fig. 1).[2] The Crawford sideboard was probably commissioned as part of the original furnishings. It incorporates the Orem family coat of arms, evidence of Orem's search for a status similar to that of European aristocracy.

The decorative vocabulary incorporated into this realistically carved and imposing sideboard forthrightly stated its function. The slain stag, a gruesome and detailed rendering, fills the central panel of the back and dominates the sideboard. The finial, a lifelike bird of prey standing on its catch, echoes the dead stag below. Flanking brackets at the base of the back frame depictions of a boar on the left and a hunting dog on the right, facing each other across the marble top. Dead fish and birds are depicted on the lower cabinet doors. Fruits and vegetables are carved in black walnut on the flanking side doors. Realistic depictions of slain animals and harvested crops might be seen to imply the period's understanding of the necessity of embracing death to sustain life.

The tremendous scale and opulent carving of the sideboard indicate its high cost. Its role as a storage piece also demonstrates the owner's wealth. The lower cupboards provided storage for silver and imported porcelain dishes and serving pieces. The flat drawers were intended for storing linens and silver flatware. The shelf beneath the stag, the flanking niches, and the marble serving top were all intended for displaying luxurious serving implements and decorative objects.

Sideboards were among the most impressive objects in mid- to late-nineteenth-century American houses, and they were frequently displayed at international expositions between 1851 and 1876. While exposition furniture often sparked new trends, it was more important for showing the manufacturer's range, design skills, and craftsmanship. The maker of the Crawford sideboard was surely aware of the widely published

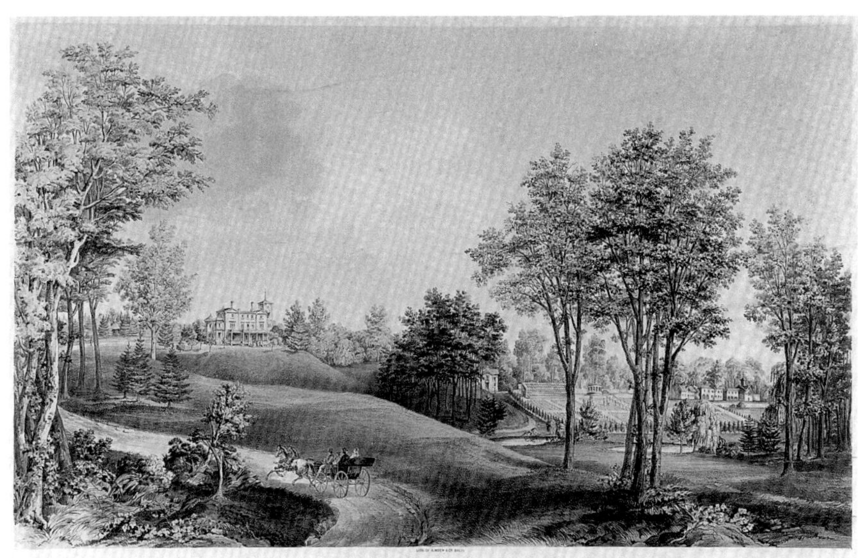

Fig. 1. *Auchentoroly near Baltimore.* Lithograph printed in colors by A. Hoen and Company, Baltimore.

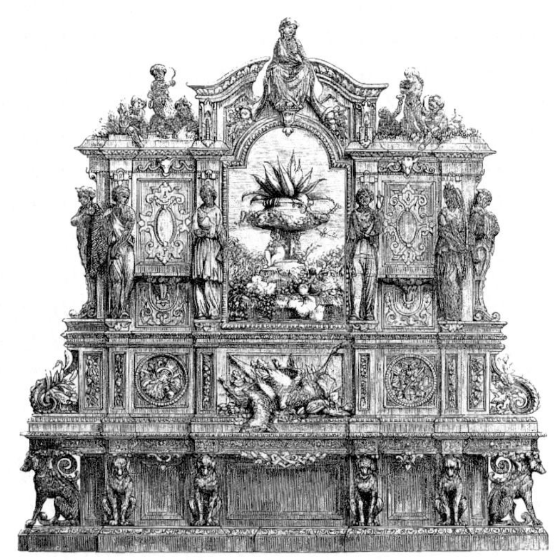

Fig. 2. Sideboard by Fourdinois. *The Art Journal Illustrated Catalogue: The Industry of All Nations* (London, 1851).

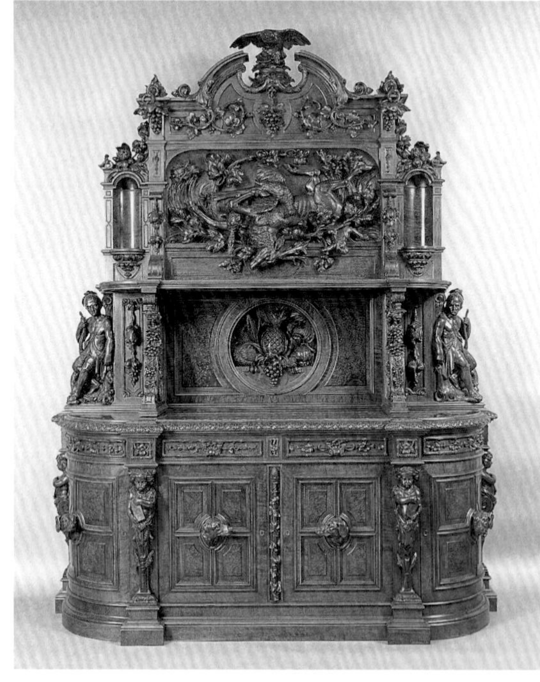

Fig. 3. *Sideboard,* ca. 1855. American, sculptural elements possibly executed by Joseph Alexis Bailly (1825–1883), carved walnut and Groitte d'Italie marble, 114⅜ × 90⅜ × 27½ inches, The Cleveland Museum of Art, Purchase from the J. H. Wade Fund, 1985.72.

sideboard by Parisian cabinetmaker Henri-Auguste Fourdinois for the 1851 Great Exhibition in London's Crystal Palace (fig. 2). The slain stag and other food motifs may have inspired the Crawford sideboard. As early as the 1840s, sideboards incorporating similar themes were being made in France.[3]

A sideboard related to the Crawford example is in the Cleveland Museum of Art (fig. 3). Similarities in scale, detail, and organization point to the same manufacturer as the Crawford sideboard. In an article on the Cleveland sideboard, Henry Hawley provided evidence that it was made in Philadelphia, and this is likely the origin of the Crawford sideboard as well, which was owned in Baltimore, well within the circle of Philadelphia's market at the time. Hawley also suggested Joseph Alexis Bailly, a French sculptor working in Philadelphia in the 1850s, as the possible carver of the Cleveland sideboard. Similarities on both sideboards suggest the same carver.[4]

NOTES

1. Ames 1992, pp. 44, 76–77. Ames discusses the ritual of dining in nineteenth-century America and the evolution of the sideboard from the late eighteenth century, as well as its derivation from fifteenth-century French furniture forms.

2. A description of Auchentoroly is found in McCauley 1975, p. 99. An account of the neighboring Rogers estate, which became Baltimore's Druid Hill Park, can be found in Bevan 1949, pp. 190–199; the sale of Auchentoroly to John Morris Orem in 1856 is described and documented on p. 195. Discussions of Orem and Auchentoroly are in correspondence from Caroline S. Orem to James W. Foster, Director of the Maryland Historical Society, November 20, 1951, in the Vertical File of the Society's library.

3. Ames 1974, pp. 1–27. The Fourdinois sideboard is illustrated and discussed in detail in Ames 1992, pp. 46–51. He also illustrates and discusses an 1844 sideboard made by Parisian cabinetmaker Ringuet-Leprince, who later worked in New York, pp. 48–51, fig. 2.4.

4. Hawley 1987, pp. 202–215.

Cornelius and Company and Cornelius and Baker

For the Great Exhibition at the Crystal Palace in London in 1851, Cornelius and Baker of Philadelphia sent a pair of elaborate fifteen-and-one-half-feet-tall "brass lacquered" chandeliers for display. The description of the pieces in the exhibition catalogue noted: "Messrs. Cornelius and Baker are the most extensive manufacturer of lamps, chandeliers, gas-fixtures, &c., in the United States, employing upwards of seven hundred persons in the several departments of the establishment, which has been in existence for upwards of a quarter of a century."[1] Before establishing his patent lamp manufactory in 1825, Christian Cornelius was listed as a silversmith in the 1810 Philadelphia directory, and then as a silver plater in 1813. In 1831, Robert Cornelius joined his father in the firm, and by 1837 Cornelius and Son was making lamps and chandeliers. The enterprise was ambitious, as well-established foundries in Birmingham, England, had long been supplying the American market with gas lighting fixtures (see no. 4). In 1839 the firm became Cornelius and Company. In 1845, Isaac F. and W. C. Baker joined the firm, and in 1851 the name changed to Cornelius and Baker. Besides gas lamps and chandeliers, Cornelius and Baker manufactured candle-powered lighting devices, including mantel and furniture garnitures and banquet centerpieces.

At the New York Crystal Palace Exhibition

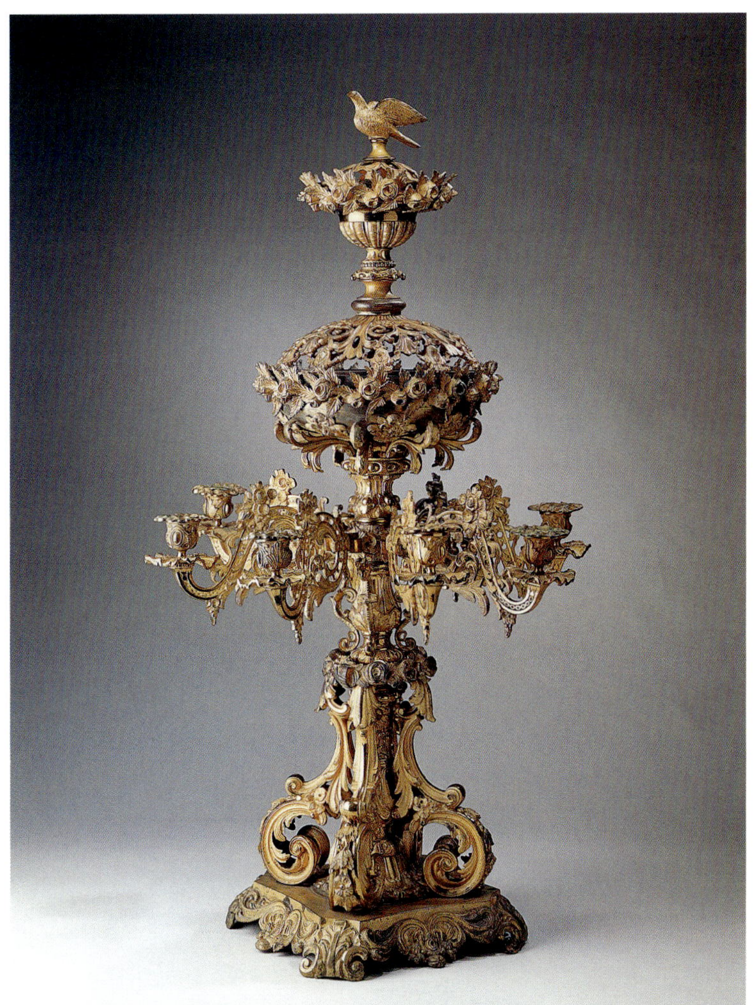

49.

Candelabrum,
designed ca. 1853

Cornelius and Company (1839–1851) or Cornelius and Baker (1851–1869), Philadelphia
Gilded bronze
32 × 18 × 18 inches
Mark: Inscribed on underside of bottom disk, *C & C*
EL 7.1998

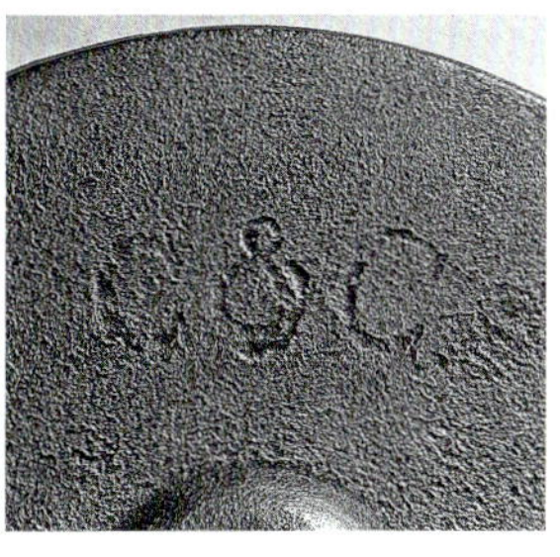

50.

Garniture, 1850s

Possibly Cornelius and Company (1839–1851) or Cornelius and Baker (1851–1869), Philadelphia
Gilded bronze, lead glass, and marble
Candelabrum: 17⅛ × 17½ × 4 inches
Candlesticks: Each 16½ × 5¾ × 3¼ inches
1987.170.1–.3

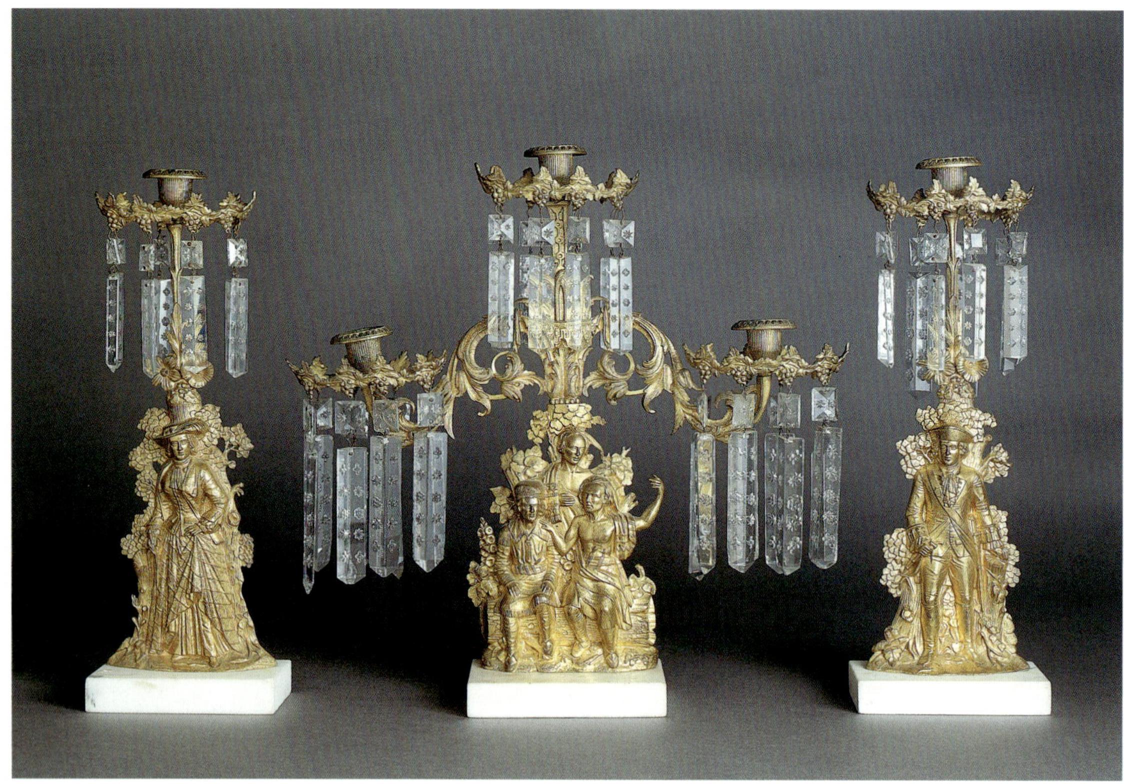

of 1853, Cornelius and Baker (identified as Cornelius and Company) displayed a monumental candelabrum similar in form and ornament to the Crawford example (no. 49).[2] The top section of the gilt bronze candelabrum, crowned by an eagle on an open-worked dome, can be lifted off and replaced with a fitted glass bowl, perhaps to hold flowers. This piece is one of a pair, with its mate now in the Brooklyn Museum of Art.

Girandole garniture sets, introduced in the 1840s, were mass-produced in mechanized factories in Philadelphia, Boston, and New York at least until the Civil War. Considering the many surviving examples, they must have been available throughout the United States as enrichments for tables, cabinet tops, and parlor mantels. Designs for the Crawford gilded garniture set (no. 50) were patented by Isaac F. Baker of Cornelius and Company in 1848 and 1849, around the time William F. Shaw patented his Bigelow Chapel girandole (see no. 32). However, the Cornelius set is more typical of American garnitures because it incorporates figures into the decorative shafts. The uniform deep gold on the Shaw set was characteristic of finishes in Boston, whereas New York and Philadelphia sets were generally lighter in tone with highlighted details, like the Crawford example. An alternative effect, as on the set depicting Paul and Virginie (no. 51), was the less common silvered finish.[3]

On his patent drawings, Baker identified characters from James Fenimore Cooper's widely read novel *The Last of the Mohicans,* published in 1826.[4] The shaft of the centerpiece depicts the heroes of the book, the buckskin-clad Natty Bumppo, or Hawkeye, seated next to his compatriot Chingachgook, chief of the Mohicans, while the chief's son Uncas, the last of the Mohicans, stands behind. The flanking candlestick shafts show Cora Munro and Major Heyward. Because of the patent drawings, the design of *The Last of the Mohicans* garniture is associated with Cornelius and Son and Cornelius and Baker, but the Crawford set is unmarked.

The characters on the shafts of the silvered set (no. 51) are from the 1788 French romance *Paul et Virginie* by Jacques-Henri Bernardin de Saint-Pierre. Paul and Virginie are shown in front of banana and palm trees that evoke the story's tropical setting. Two fatherless children, raised together by their mothers in poverty and innocence on the fictional island of Mauritius, Paul and Virginie were devoted to each other and were miserable when her wealthy and wicked aunt took Virginie to France. Two years later, Virginie joyfully sailed back, but within sight of the eagerly waiting Paul, her ship sank. The heroine modestly chose to drown rather than to disrobe and be rescued by a naked sailor. Paul and the two mothers died of broken hearts soon after, and the wicked aunt suffered horrible guilt for separating the devoted couple.

The romantic tale of *Paul et Virginie* was a popular theme for garnitures. An 1856 advertisement for Starr and Fellows, a New York supplier of garniture sets and other luxury goods, listed Paul and Virginie as one of its patterns.[5] Subtle differences in various models of this set suggest that different firms produced girandoles in this pattern. The portability of girandoles and the proximity of cities where the fixtures were manufactured meant that patterns were easily copied. Most sets were not marked, and marking was inconsistent even at the same firm.

NOTES

1. The 1851 description of Cornelius and Company with an illustration of the exhibited chandelier is in *Crystal Palace* 1970, p. 212. An account of Christian Cornelius and the successive firms descended from his 1825 patent lamp concern—including the later Cornelius and Sons (1870–1886), Cornelius and Hetherington (1886–1888), and Cornelius and Rowland (1888–1900)—is in Fennimore 1996, pp. 226–227, 272. A history of the Cornelius firm is also given in Philadelphia Museum of Art 1976, p. 334, no. 288.

2. Silliman and Goodrich 1854, p. 201.

3. Bacot 1987 provides an illustrated survey of girandole shaft patterns, and he presents issues of connoisseurship in his historical introduction to the girandole chapter (pp. 153–156). Bacot outlines finish variations and warns against attributing unmarked examples to a specific maker. The two Crawford girandoles were found in Mississippi in the 1980s.

4. A *Last of the Mohicans* set at the Winterthur Museum is illustrated and discussed with an illustration of Baker's patent drawings in Fennimore 1996, pp. 226–227. *Last of the Mohicans* garniture sets are also illustrated and discussed in Bacot 1987, pp. 173–176, nos. 243–244, and The Metropolitan Museum of Art 1970, no. 111.

5. The Starr and Fellows advertisement is reproduced in Bacot 1987, p. 165. On p. 177, no. 246 is a five-branch girandole centerpiece in the Paul and Virginie pattern, which Bacot suggests may have been made in Philadelphia because of the fine casting and lemon-yellow gilded finish.

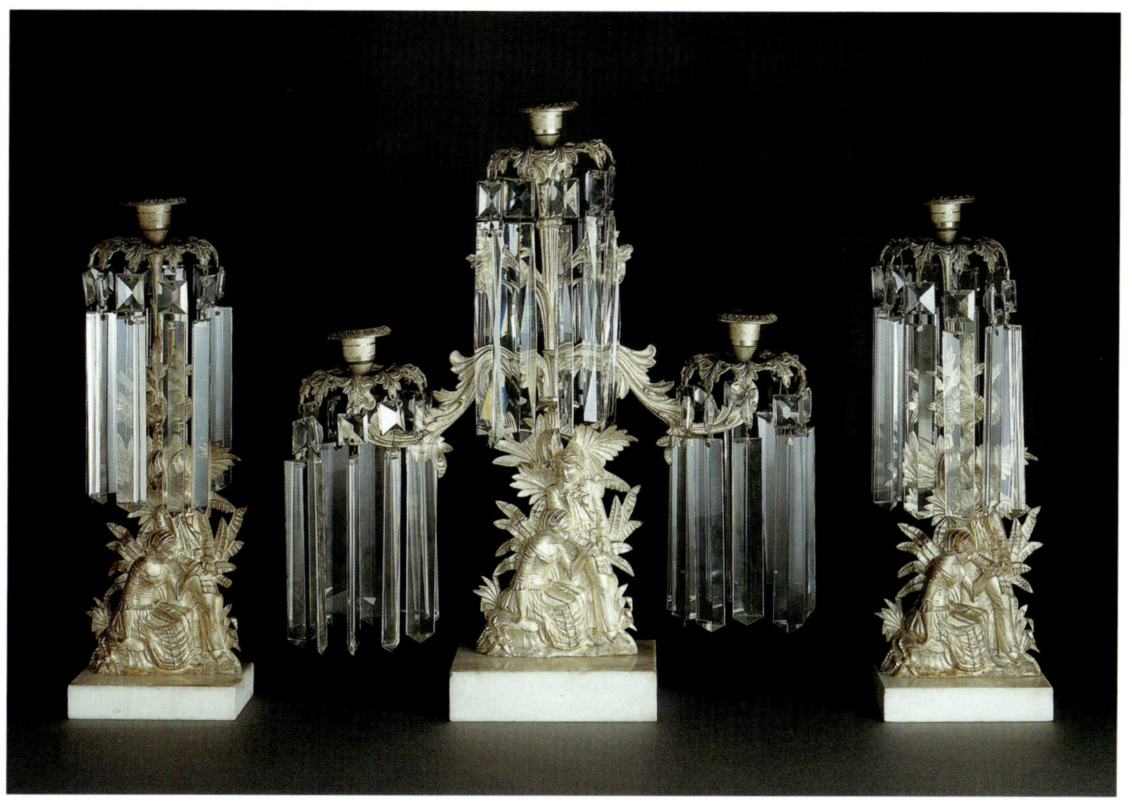

51.

Garniture, 1850s

Possibly Philadelphia or New York
Silvered bronze, lead glass, and marble
Candelabrum: 18¼ × 16 × 15⅝ inches
Candlesticks: Each 15½ × 5 × 3 inches
1987.169.1–.3

52.

Desk, 1860s

George J. Henkels (1819–1883), Philadelphia
Walnut, maple veneer, and leather
56½ × 40 × 24 inches
Mark: Engraved on a lead counterweight of the fall front, *George J. Henkels*
1998.90

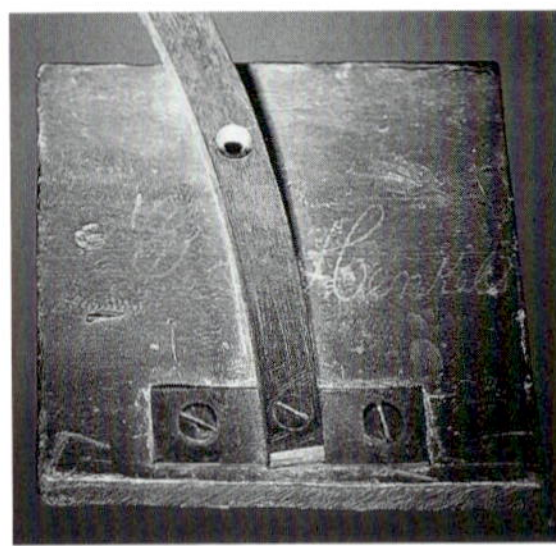

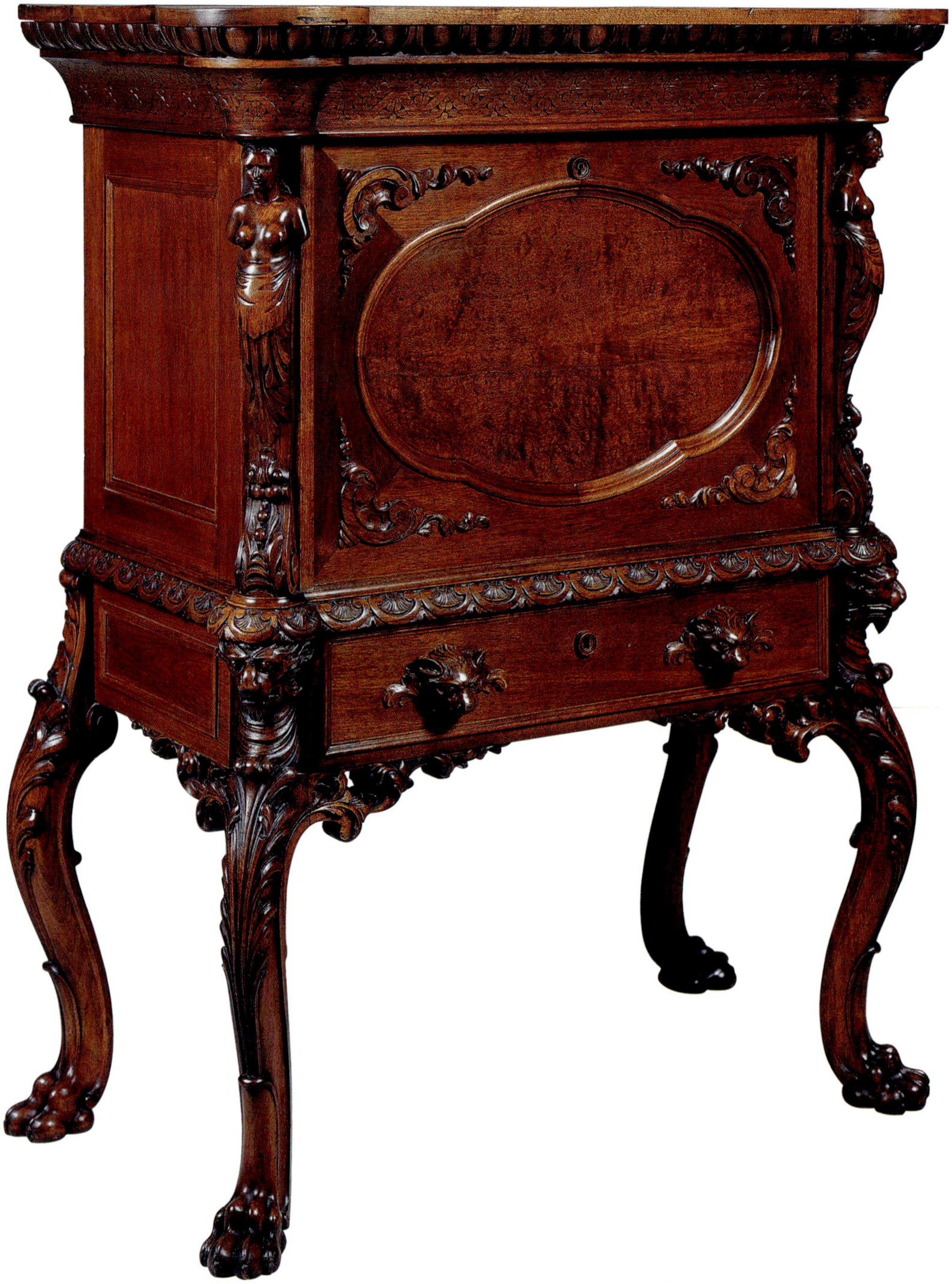

George J. Henkels, whose firm made this fall-front desk, owned and operated one of the largest furniture businesses in Philadelphia in the third quarter of the nineteenth century.[1] After training as a chairmaker, Henkels was first listed in city directories in 1843, and by 1850 he occupied a large furniture-making plant and store on Chestnut Street, Philadelphia's prestigious shopping thoroughfare, just opposite Independence Hall.[2] Henkels's local prominence is indicated not only by his moves westward with fashionable Philadelphians but also by the publication of his furniture in Samuel Sloan's 1867 book, *Homestead Architecture.* Sloan was a well-known Philadelphia architect, and his book brought national attention to Henkels's furniture business.

Kenneth Ames has speculated that Henkels may have been the author of the section on furniture in Sloan's book. Certainly he must have benefited from Sloan's inclusion of twelve wood-engraved illustrations of his furniture. Sloan's book illustrates a suite of library furniture, including a fall-front desk related in form and carved decoration to the Crawford example (fig. 1). The Sloan book described the furniture as "called *Renaissance* in France and *Antique* in this country."[3] Despite the publicity, however, George Henkels was out of business by 1877.

The Crawford desk has cabriole legs and bold carving that relate it to revivals of the rococo in Europe from the 1820s to 1840s and in the United States in the 1840s and 1850s. However, the figural elements and carved roaring lion heads at the front corners are derived from carving on fifteenth- and sixteenth-century European Renaissance furniture. The corner figures are also related to the carved corner decorations on a cabinet by Daniel Pabst of Philadelphia (see no. 54), which also dates to the 1860s, although probably later than the Henkels desk. The cornices and bold scale of the desk's decoration lend the diminutive form a surprising architectural monumentality, which is a characteristic of nineteenth-century Philadelphia furniture.

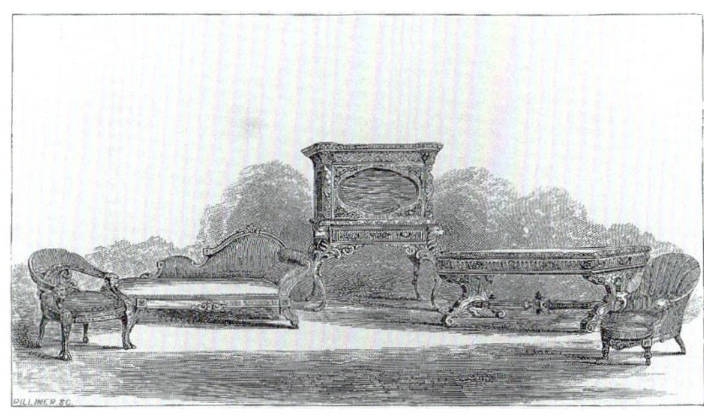

Fig. 1. Samuel Sloan, *Homestead Architecture* (Philadelphia, 1867), fig. 198.

NOTES

1. A similar desk in the Asa Packer Mansion in Jim Thorpe, Pennsylvania, is illustrated in Ames 1973, p. 645, fig. 8. Asa Packer, who had made his fortune in mining, was the wealthiest man in Pennsylvania when he completed his home outside Philadelphia about 1860. That he ordered a desk related to the Crawford example suggests that it was among the more expensive lines that Henkels made.

2. Ibid., pp. 641–650. Henkels moved to 524 Walnut Street in 1857, back to 809–811 Chestnut Street in 1862, and farther west to the corner of Chestnut and 13th Streets in 1867.

3. Cited by ibid., p. 645.

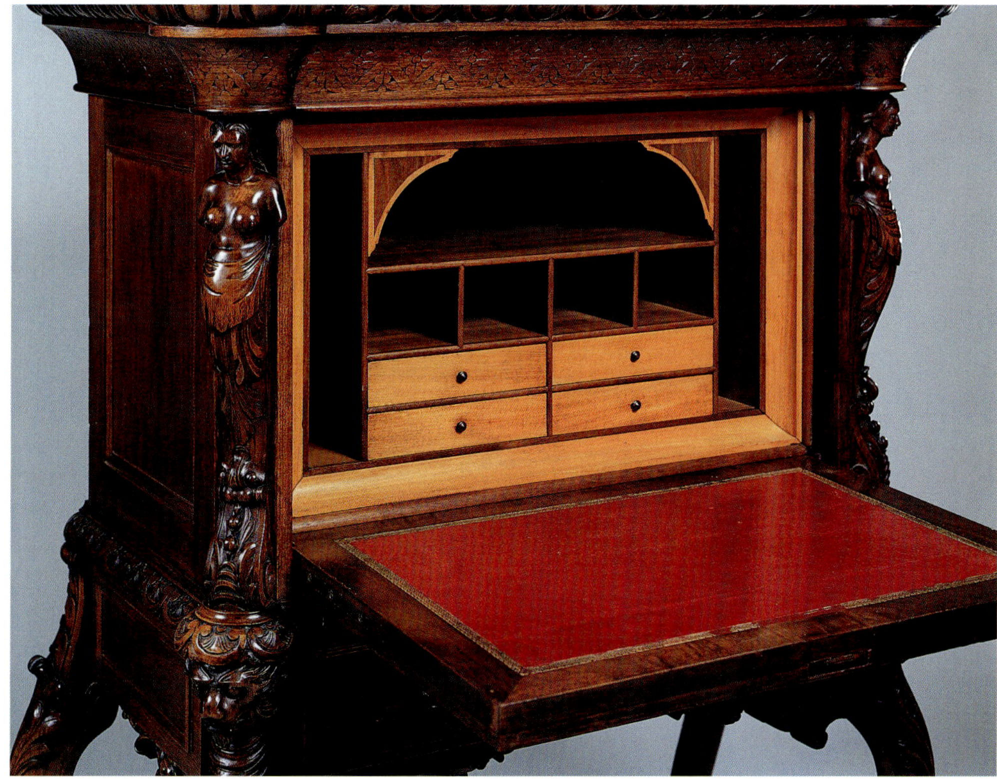

A New Classicism, 1855–1875

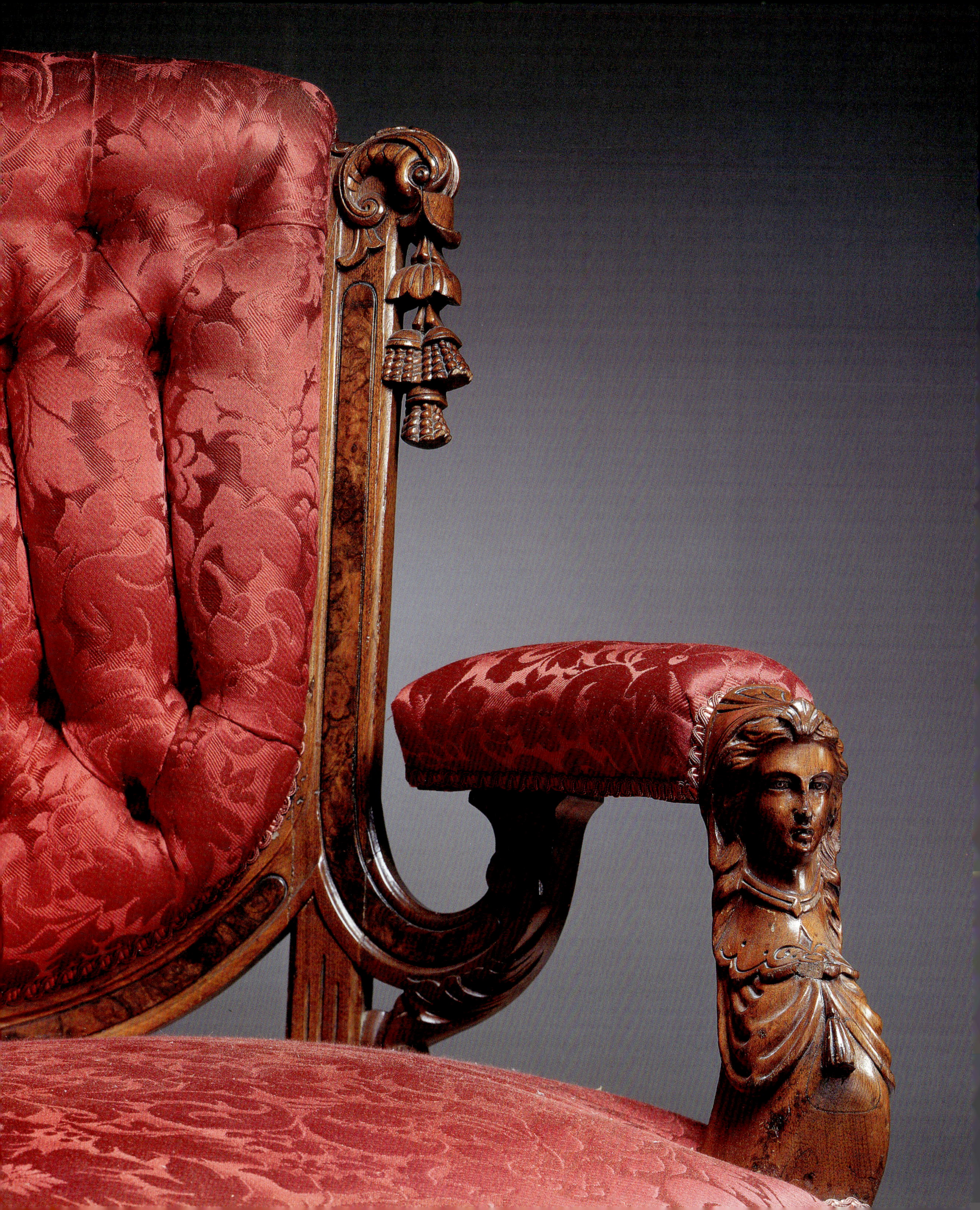

53.

Tall Clock, ca. 1860

Gustave Herter (1830–1898), New York
Walnut, burl walnut veneer, glass, and gilded bronze
70¾ × 26½ × 16¼ inches
Marks: On clock face, *G.HERTER/NEW-YORK;* stamped on back, *G. HERTER/NEW YORK;* stamped on back twice, *22212;* stamped on back of clock mechanism, *14*
1984.143

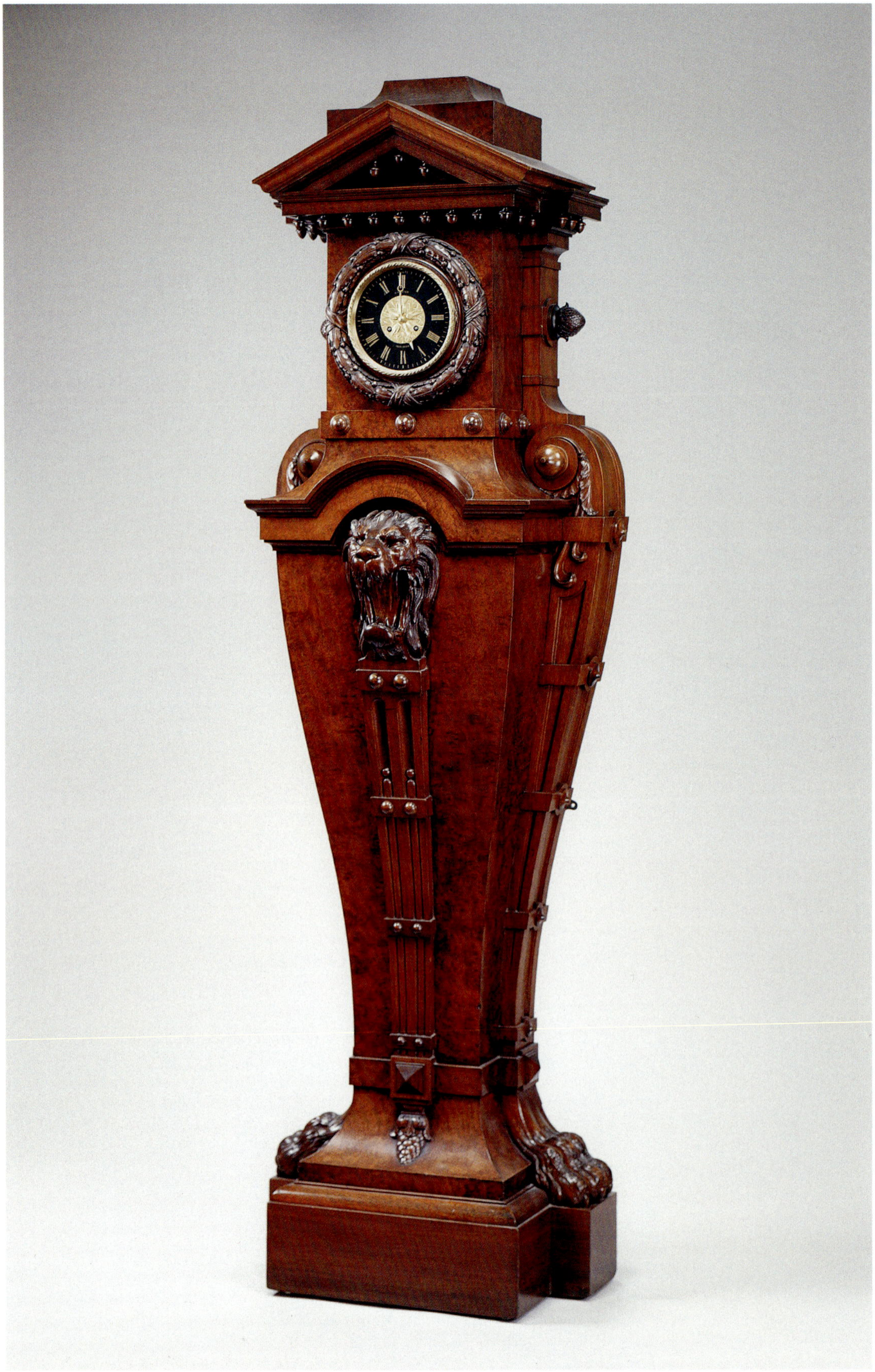

When Gustave Herter signed the renouncement of his German citizenship in 1850, just two years after his arrival in New York, he listed his profession as *Bildhauer* (carver). His background and interest in sculpture is clearly evident in the decoration of the tall clock his company made a decade later. By 1851, Herter, the stepson of a Stuttgart cabinetmaker, was making furniture in New York with Auguste Pottier, who would later become a major rival. In 1853, Herter was in partnership with Erastus Bulkley, and the firm's prominence in the New York furniture industry was demonstrated by its display of a Gothic-style bookcase (now in the Nelson-Atkins Museum in Kansas City) in the New York Crystal Palace Exhibition that year. Herter purchased Bulkley's share in the business five years later and operated it under his own name. It was this firm that made the Crawford clock. Christian Herter followed his brother Gustave to New York in 1859, and in 1864 they formed Herter Brothers (see nos. 107–110).[1]

Below the beautifully carved wreath of bayberries and leaves that surrounds the clock face, a ferociously roaring lion's head forms a central decorative focus for the clock's composition. The overall effect is monumentally architectural in the pedimented crest, which crowns the clock's coffin shape. The lion's head and the wreath recall Renaissance architectural details, and although realistically carved, the lion form is abstracted so that its feet serve as brackets for the base of the piece. The clock is typical of furniture made by Gustave Herter's firm. Similar detail is also evident on other American furniture from the 1850s and early 1860s, such as the Philadelphia sideboard (see no. 48), which suggests that Herter and other makers were well aware of the most fashionable contemporary Parisian furniture.[2]

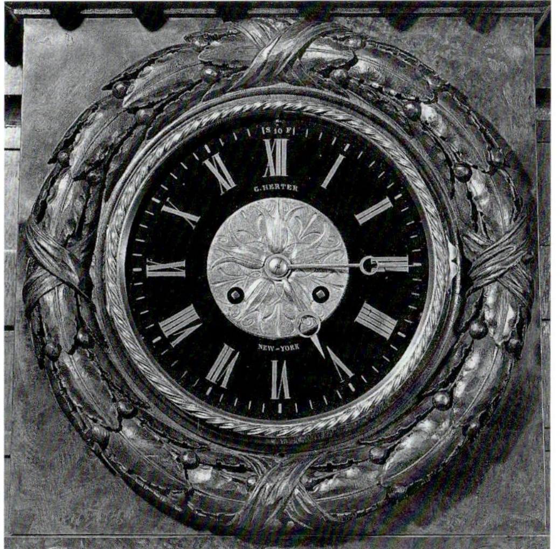

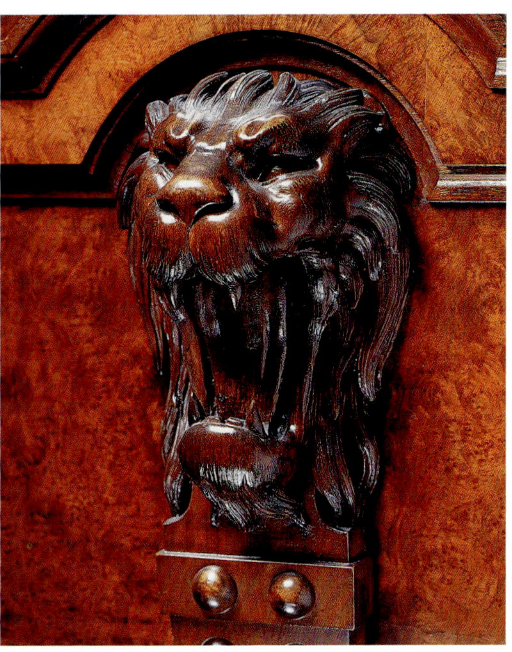

NOTES

1. Gustave Herter's early life and work in New York are recounted in Howe, Frelinghuysen, and Voorsanger 1994, pp. 36–44, 225–228. Works by Herter are discussed and illustrated on pp. 126–138, nos. 1–6. The Crawford clock is illustrated on p. 227. Herter may have worked for Tiffany, Young and Ellis, but his actual role there is unknown; see Carpenter 1997, p. 8. The clock is also illustrated and discussed in Hanks 1986, p. 33, fig. 2.

2. Philadelphia Museum of Art 1978, pp. 107–108, nos. II.26 and II.27, illustrates and discusses a sculptural chair and table incorporating realistic lions and architectural elements designed by Victor-Marie-Charles Ruprich-Robert, and made by Guillaume Grohé of Paris in 1860–1863 for the Château de Fontainebleau. Frelinghuysen cites this parallel in Howe, Frelinghuysen, and Voorsanger 1994, p. 126, no. 1, and includes the clock in a list of three known examples of Herter furniture that rely only on sculpture and monumentality for their decorative effects (p. 248).

54.

Cabinet, 1865–1870

Attributed to Daniel Pabst (1826–1910), Philadelphia
Walnut, maple, poplar, and modern silk curtain
54 × 44 × 23½ inches
1981.1000.52

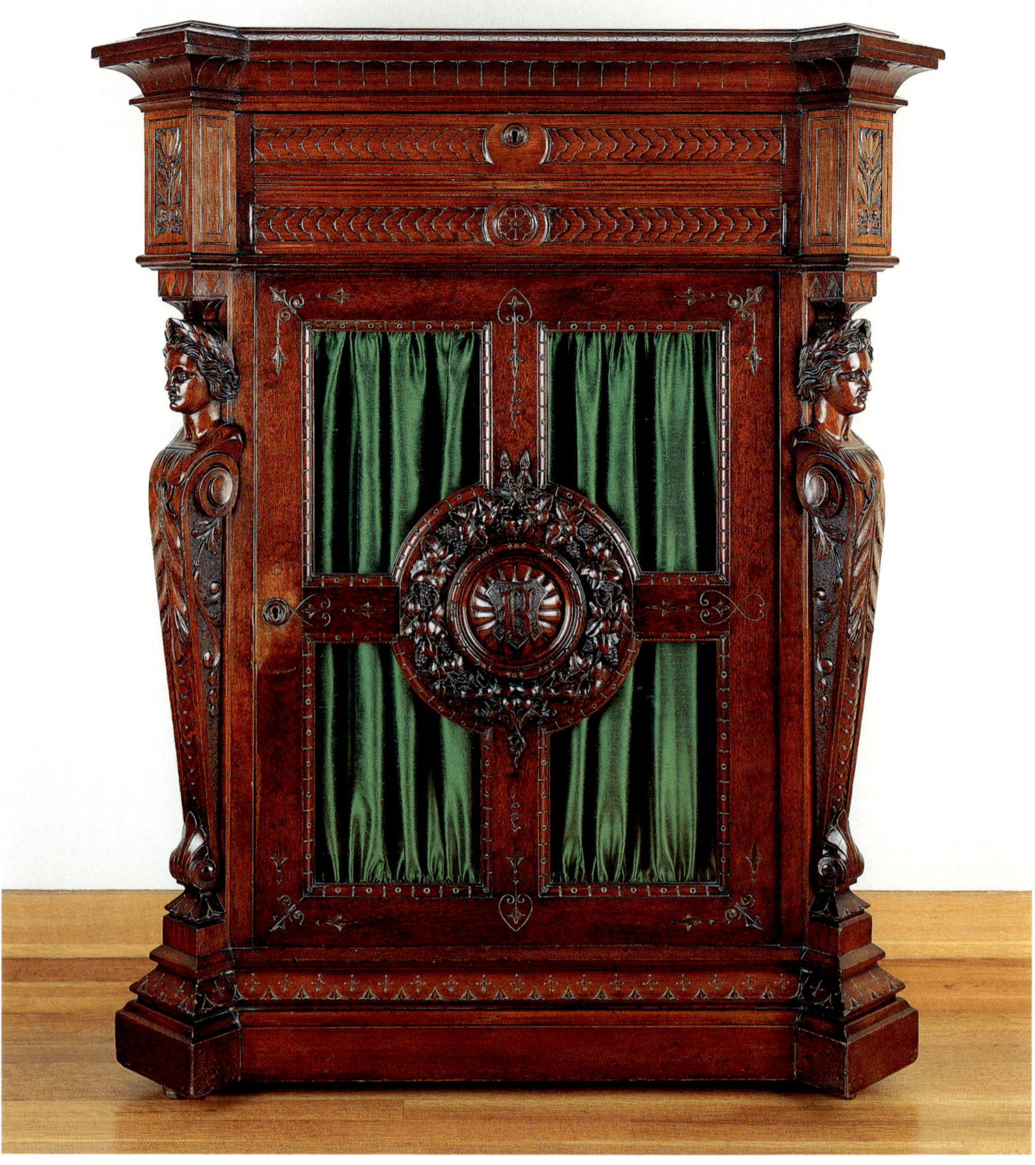

In 1850, almost a third of the nearly 2,200 furniture makers in Philadelphia were German-born, and among the most successful of these was Daniel Pabst.[1] Born in Langenstein, Hesse-Darmstadt, Pabst trained at the local technical school and may have apprenticed with a master craftsman. Because strict guild rules dictated that he work in his native village, where there was little opportunity, Pabst immigrated to Philadelphia at the age of twenty-three and joined the large German community there. Working first as a journeyman cabinetmaker, he opened his own shop at 222 South Fifth Street on July 4, 1854. In 1860, he entered a decade-long partnership with a Francis Krauss, who may have been an investor rather than a cabinetmaker. About 1870, Pabst moved to nearby 269 South Fifth Street, where he worked until he retired in 1896.

Like other Philadelphia shops, Pabst's was much smaller than that of his New York contemporary Alexander Roux (see nos. 36, 46, 61). Pabst, who never employed more than fifty workers (Roux had 120 in the 1850s), was one of a group of conservative, mostly German, cabinetmakers who resisted mechanization, despite the growing number of steam-powered factories in western cities such as Cincinnati. Although Pabst may have used machines in making his furniture, the decoration and finish work was carved by hand. Decoration on Pabst's work, as on this cabinet, often includes the initials of the client, indicating that these were commissioned pieces.[2]

Because no known labeled furniture survives from Pabst's shop, attribution is based on family histories, motifs, methods of construction, and a list of customers Pabst compiled for his daughter shortly before his death. The Crawford cabinet descended in the Beauveau Borie family of Philadelphia and was probably designed for their Italianate house at 1035 Spruce Street. The Bories, whose wealth derived from banking and mercantile interests, were not included in Pabst's list of customers, but family history attributed the cabinet to him.[3]

The Crawford cabinet has stylistic similarities to a cabinet attributed to Pabst since the 1930s, now in the Philadelphia Museum of Art (fig. 1).[4] The same materials were used in both pieces, which share a heavy, massive scale and rectangular shape. The size and design reflect the influence of Renaissance-inspired French and American furniture shown at international expositions from the 1850s. Certain motifs are repeated on the cabinets, particularly the grapevine wreath carved at the center of both doors. The Crawford wreath encloses a "B" for Borie, whereas that on the Philadelphia Museum cabinet encircles a skillfully carved classical female head. The workmanship of the Philadelphia head is similar to that of the carved heads at the tops of the caryatid corner pilasters on the Crawford cabinet. The pilasters on both cabinets have a coiled top scroll, a pattern of overlapping petals, and elongated acanthus leaves at the base, fashioned in the contemporary *néo-grec* taste. The carved moldings around the window panes on the doors and the inset side panels follow the same pattern, and the side panels on both are covered with burl walnut veneer with incised decoration. The overlapping petal motif on the pilasters is repeated horizontally across the fronts and sides of both cabinets.

Writing at about the time the Crawford and Philadelphia Museum cabinets were made, Philadelphia furniture maker George J. Henkels noted, "All cabinet-makers of reputation have their shops and work their own designs, so as to have a pattern exclusively to themselves."[5] Based on their similarities and Henkels's observations on craft practice, as well as the family histories, it would seem that both the Crawford and the Philadelphia Museum cabinets were made in the Pabst shop.

NOTES

1. For accounts of Pabst's career and discussions of attributed furniture, see Philadelphia Museum of Art 1976, p. 378, no. 326, and pp. 401–403, nos. 343–344; Hanks and Talbott 1977, pp. 3–24; Hanks 1980, pp. 94–101; and The Metropolitan Museum of Art 1986, pp. 460–461. See also no. 217 in this catalogue.

2. Hanks and Talbott 1977, p. 10, fig. 4, and p. 14, fig. 9.

3. Furniture from the Beauveau Borie family attributed to Pabst was included in a 1933 exhibition. See ibid., p. 15. The list of Pabst customers is in the curatorial archives of the Philadelphia Museum of Art. See ibid., p. 7.

4. The Philadelphia Museum of Art cabinet is illustrated in ibid., p. 12, fig. 6. That cabinet was first identified and attributed to Pabst by Calvin Hathaway, curator of decorative arts at the Philadelphia Museum of Art, for the 1933 exhibition *Victorian Art.* The cabinet was made for the Philadelphia historian Henry Charles Lea. Lea family history attributed the cabinet to Daniel Pabst as early as 1933, before his name was widely familiar.

5. George J. Henkels, *Household Economy* (Philadelphia: King and Baird, 1867), p. 36; cited in ibid., p. 6. For additional information about Henkels, see no. 52 in this catalogue.

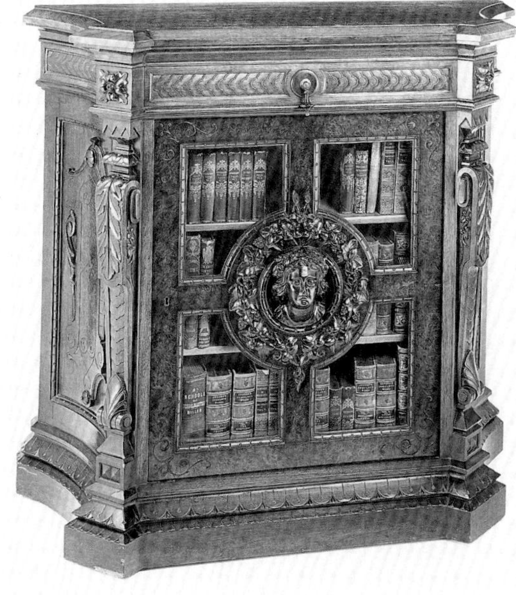

Fig. 1. Cabinet attributed to Daniel Pabst. Philadelphia Museum of Art, Bequest of Arthur H. Lea.

55.

Pitcher, 1860–1865

Retailed and possibly made by Bigelow Brothers and Kennard (1847–1868), Boston
Silver
14⅜ × 7½ × 6⅜ inches
Mark: Stamped on bottom, *BIGELOW BRO. & KENNARD/ BOSTON/ENGLISH STERLING*
1982.303

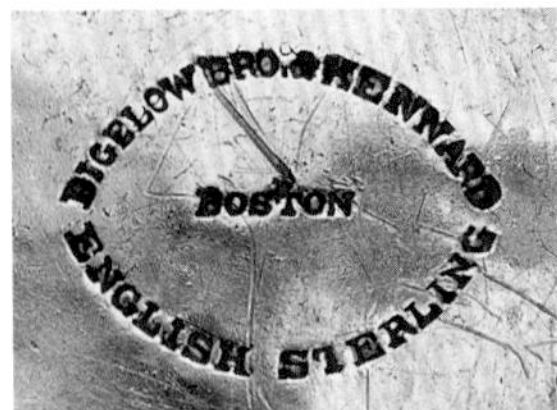

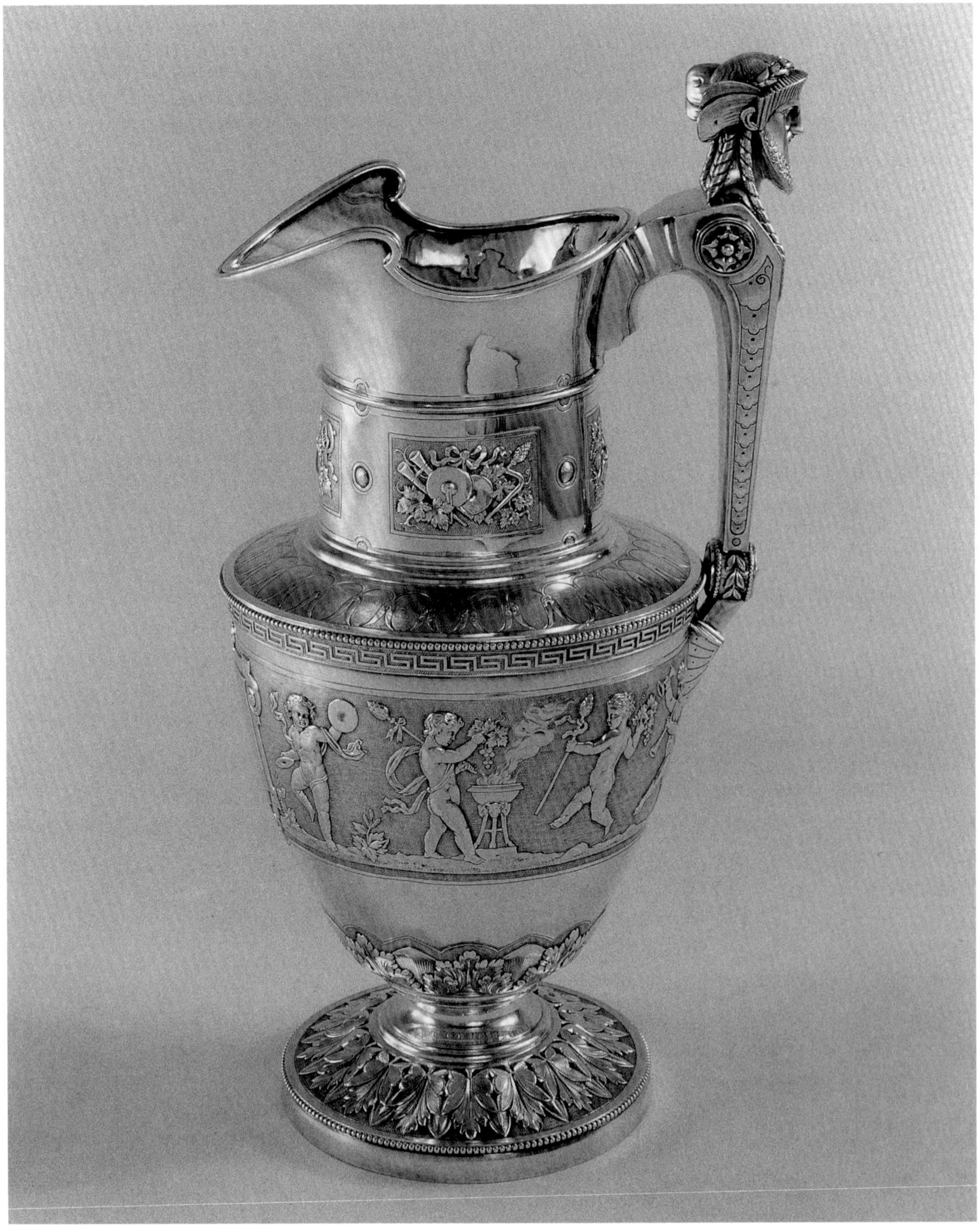

CLASSICAL STYLE dominated design and architecture in the first decades of the nineteenth century. In the 1850s and 1860s, classical elements reintroduced into designs were as much survivals as actual revivals. While increasingly eclectic Americans embraced fashionable new styles, older forms were retained and reinterpreted throughout the century. This Crawford pitcher is a midcentury example of classical expression.

The designer of the pitcher took its shape—an urn on a pedestal with a narrow neck, trefoil spout, and bold angular handle—from classical Greek *oinochoë* forms. The surface decoration was also derived from ancient Greek architectural, sculptural, and decorative sources. The putti in relief on a band around the urn (see detail) resemble sculptures in classical architectural friezes, while the band itself is topped by a Greek-

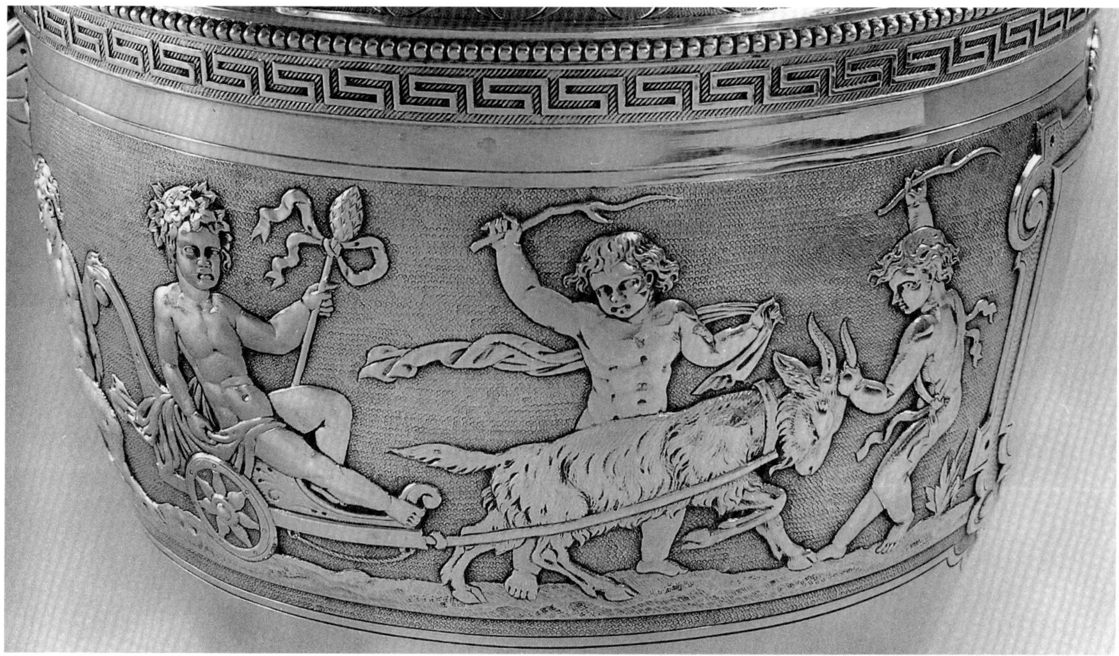

key border and beading. At the front of the pitcher beneath the spout is a classical tablet, possibly intended for an inscription. The base is contrived of chased acanthus leaves and surrounded with cast beading, resembling the molded plaster medallions used on ceilings at the time. At the bottom of the urn is a border of chased acanthus leaves and engraving. The neck has rectangular fields of repoussé musical instruments and leaves. The bold angular handle is crowned with a bearded and helmeted male head and terminates at the bottom with a stylized, elongated acanthus. Cast medallions and engraved leaves on the handle contribute to its monumental and architectural presence. These elements characterize the reinterpretation of classical elements in the 1850s and 1860s.

Inspiration for this pitcher may have been the Etruscan pattern of hollowares introduced by New York's Tiffany and Company in 1858. Similar *oinochoë* forms, decorated with equestrian figures instead of putti, recall architectural friezes. Most of the decorative forms in the Etruscan pattern were derived from Greek rather than Etruscan sources, which is typical of the era's looseness in identifying ancient cultures. Tiffany's Etruscan pattern continued in production until at least 1873.[1]

Bigelow Brothers and Kennard was established in Boston in 1847 and sold silver, watches, and jewelry until at least 1867.[2] In 1869, Bigelow, Kennard and Company was first listed in Boston directories with many of the same partners and was apparently the firm's successor. The company was a luxury goods emporium, supplying the same market in Boston as Tiffany and Company and Ball, Black and Company served in New York. The firm was mainly a retailer, and it is unclear whether they actually made silver. If Bigelow Brothers and Kennard followed the practice of Ball, Black and Company in New York, the firm's mark on the pitcher may have been impressed to identify the retailer rather than the maker.

NOTES

1. The Etruscan pattern is illustrated and discussed in Ward and Ward 1979, p. 174, no. 182.

2. The firm's history is briefly recounted in Belden 1980, pp. 60–61.

56.

Punch Bowl or Fruit Stand, dated 1865

Attributed to John R. Wendt and Company (1860–1871), New York; retailed by Ball, Black and Company (1851–1874), New York
Silver
13¼ × 12¾ × 12¼ inches
Mark: Impressed on bottom, BALL, BLACK & CO./985/1000/ NEW YORK
Inscriptions: Engraved in script on left medallion, *Hon. C. Godfrey/Gunther/New York;* engraved in script on right medallion, *From/his Friends/&/ fellow citizens/April 7th/1865*
1981.1000.57

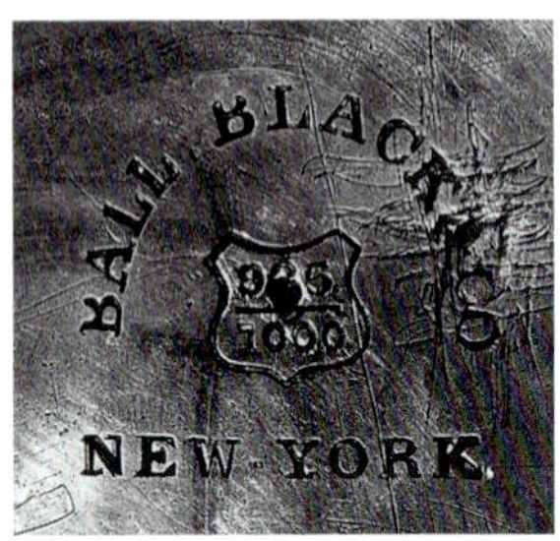

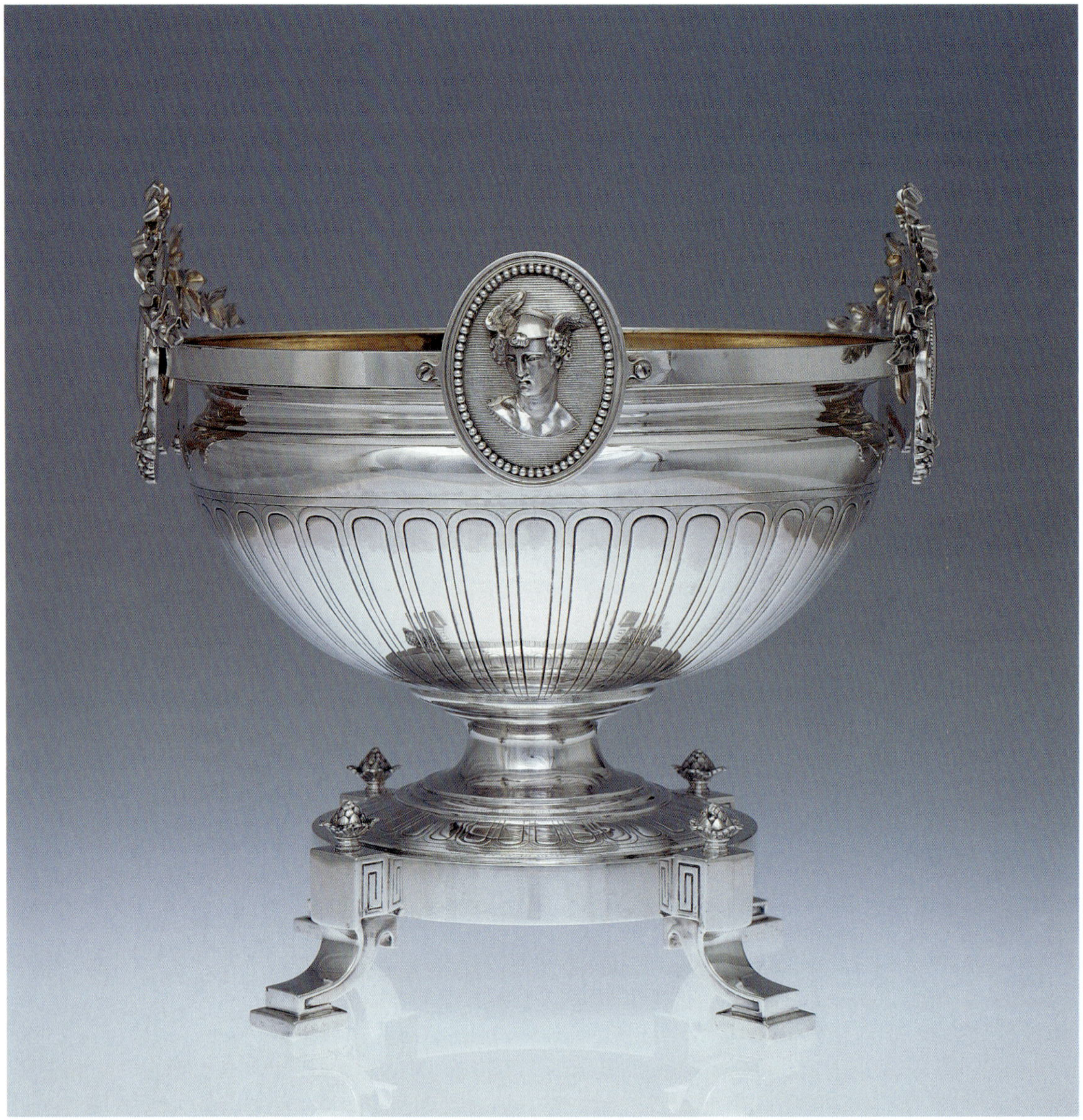

THE *NEW YORK TIMES* announced the presentation of the Crawford punch bowl to Mayor Charles Godfrey Gunther on Saturday, April 8, 1865: "Mayor Gunther was last evening presented by his friends with a very handsome testimonial of their esteem in the shape of a silver punch bowl and fruit stand. The presentation took place at Delmonico's [restaurant] in Fourteenth Street."[1] Political and industrial leaders were often honored with such silver presentations by their supporters or stockholders (see nos. 1, 41). While working as a fur merchant, Gunther became active in politics and, as a member of the Young Men's Democratic General Committee, supported James K. Polk for president as early as 1844. He campaigned for Franklin Pierce in 1852. Gunther lost his first New York mayoral run in 1861 but was elected for a two-year term in 1863. Afterward, he returned to business pursuits until 1878, when he unsuccessfully ran for state senator.[2]

Gunther's bowl was commissioned from Ball, Black and Company at its impressive emporium at 565–567 Broadway, which boasted not only a steam elevator, but also the largest display windows and the first large commercial safe-deposit vault in the United States. The company descended from Frederick Marquand's silver retailing firm, which his associates reorganized as Ball, Tompkins and Black in 1839, and Ball, Black and Company in 1851. The company was New York's greatest rival to Tiffany and Company. Both specialized in silver, jewelry, and other luxury goods and drew the same elite clientele.

Ball, Black and Company participated in international expositions as early as 1851, when it showed a gold floral repoussé tea service at London's Crystal Palace, possibly made by John C. Moore and Company of New York. That same year, Tiffany and Company hired Moore to manufacture silver exclusively for its firm. Neither Ball, Black and Company nor Tiffany and Company actually manufactured silver at that time. Around 1860, Rogers, Wendt, and Wilkinson formed a partnership to create silver for Ball, Black and Company that lasted less than a year. John R. Wendt was a silversmith from Boston, and George Wilkinson was a silver designer at Gorham Manufacturing Company before and after the partnership (see no. 57). After Ball, Black and Company completed its new building at Broadway and Prince Street, John R. Wendt and Company occupied the fourth and fifth floors. While the Wendt Company had a special relationship with Ball, Black and Company (perhaps similar to Moore's contract with Tiffany and Company), John Wendt was never in the retailing partnership, and his silver design and manufacturing company was an independent enterprise housed in the building.[3]

The elegant design of this punch bowl includes classical elements and civic emblems appropriate for a politician. On the double medallions bound by ribbons on one side are engraved the coats of arms of New York State and New York City. On the opposite set of double medallions is an engraved inscription to Gunther (see detail). Over the previous thirty years, the classical had been generally accepted as the architectural style of city, state, and federal government buildings, and the bowl was similarly inspired. The classical motifs on the bowl were not new in 1865, but simply revised to contemporary taste. They not only referred to politics but also expressed the nineteenth-century romantic interest in classical mythology, incorporated throughout the century into American decorative art (see also nos. 55, 79).

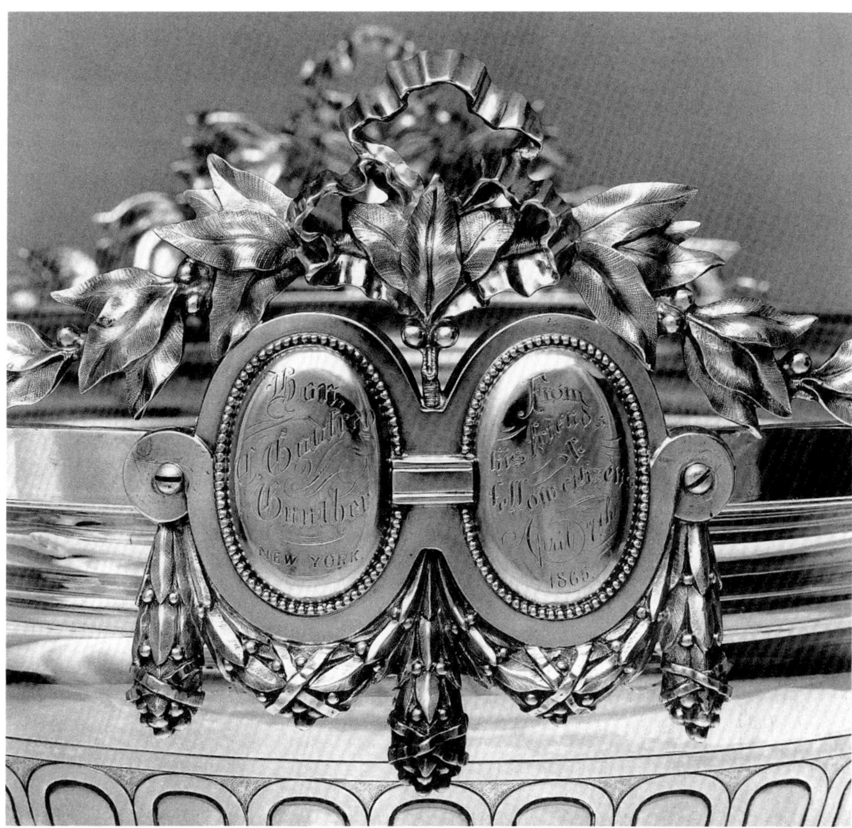

NOTES

1. *New York Times* (April 8, 1865), p. 4, col. 3.

2. A biography of Gunther and an account of his political activities can be found in *National Cyclopaedia* 1893, vol. 3, p. 69.

3. Venable 1994, pp. 40–41, 315, 323, discusses the history of Ball, Black and Company, its rivalry with Tiffany and Company, and its relationship with John R. Wendt and Company.

57.

Chafing Dish, 1863–1867

Gorham Manufacturing Company (1831–present), Providence, Rhode Island; design attributed to George Wilkinson (1819–1894)
Coin silver
7⅝ × 11½ × 10¼ inches
Mark: Impressed on bottom, in shields, rampant lion facing right, anchor, *G/150/S & M*
1982.305

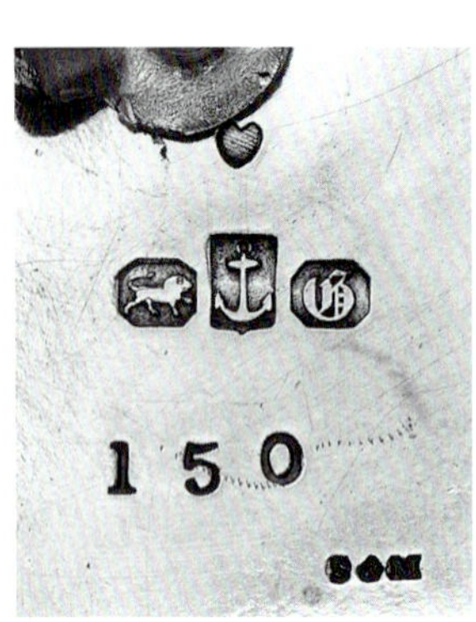

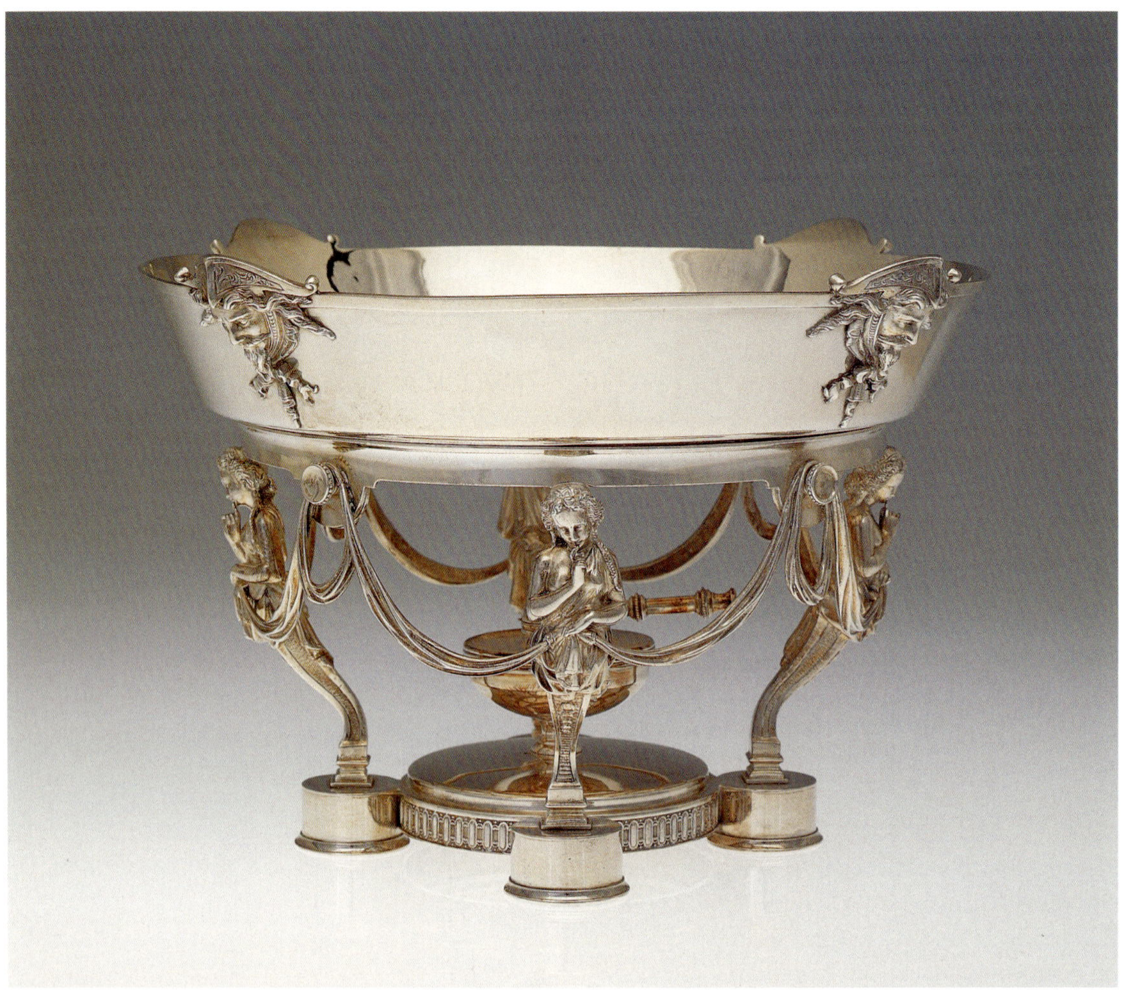

When this chafing dish was made in the 1860s, Gorham Manufacturing Company was the largest producer of silverware in the world. The enterprise began as a small Providence jewelry and spoon-making shop established in 1831 by Jabez Gorham. A decade later, J. Gorham and Son was formed when his son, John, entered the business. Jabez's investment in and withdrawal from the firm in 1848 coincided with a vast expansion envisioned by John. Although the firm had been profitable, the younger Gorham greatly enlarged the shop and introduced new steam-powered machinery that enabled the expansion into holloware production. In less than twenty years, Gorham evolved from a handwork shop into a highly mechanized factory.

Initially, the firm had sold directly to retailers in Boston and New York as well as to itinerant peddlers who carried the wares to the far reaches of New England. During the 1850s, Gorham agents sold nationally to silver retailers. This expansion required additional capital, which John Gorham found by entering an equal partnership with his cousin Gorham Thurber in 1850. In 1852, John Gorham traveled to Europe, where he toured English metal-producing manufactories in Birmingham and Sheffield, examined their machinery and techniques, and studied their products. The expansion of the factory and the introduction of steam-powered machinery resulted in tremendous growth in employment and profits between the early 1850s and 1866, about when the Crawford chafing dish was made. In 1850 Gorham had fourteen employees, and in 1866 it had 312; in 1853 company sales totaled $50,000, and in 1866 they reached $1,093,000.[1]

In 1857, English silversmith George Wilkinson joined the firm as a designer and die cutter.

Wilkinson was among the first of many European-trained designers and artisans Gorham would hire over the next seventy-five years. In 1860, Wilkinson joined a short-lived partnership in New York—Rogers, Wendt and Wilkinson—to manufacture silver for Ball, Black and Company (see no. 56). By December of that year, Wilkinson was back at Gorham, at which time John Gorham promoted him to chief designer and in 1870 to superintendent of the factory. Wilkinson continued at the firm until his death in 1894.[2]

Wilkinson has been credited with the design of the elegant Crawford chafing dish. In the 1850s, rococo repoussé silver dominated American production (see nos. 37, 40–41) and continued to be made throughout the last half of the century. This chafing dish—with its cast caryatid figures supporting the flat round dish decorated with four cast tricorn-hatted male heads—was a radical departure from the textural surfaces and spherical shapes of rococo silver holloware. The graceful cast drapes linking the maidens provide a unified yet airy pattern to the base. The figural columns, taken from classical architecture, are reminiscent of English silver from early in the century. The urn shape of the burner beneath the dish also contributes to the classical effect.

The "150" in the mark was the pattern number for an ice cream stand in the Gorham pattern book and is so designated in their album of product photographs. The dish in the photograph album (fig. 1) is shown without the burner included on the Crawford dish. The rest of the mark consists of a lion facing right (indicating that the dish was made of silver), the anchor (denoting Rhode Island), and the "G" (for Gorham). The company mark was created in the 1850s, but after the mid-1860s, the sometimes left-facing lion consistently faced right. In 1868, Gorham adopted the sterling standard and usually incorporated the word "STERLING" into the mark. Thus, the mark points to a date of between 1863 and 1867 for the Crawford chafing dish.[3]

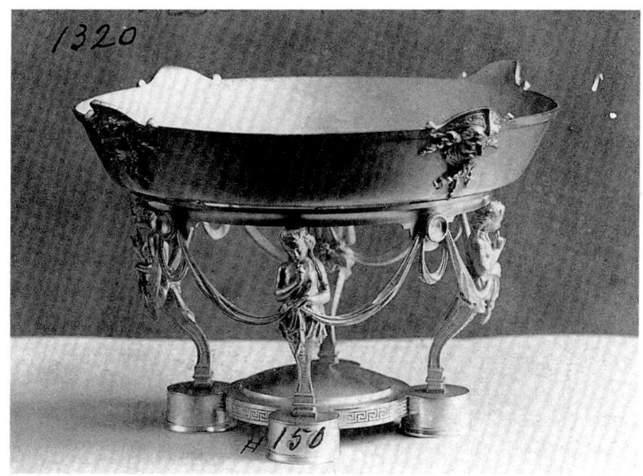

Fig. 1. Ice cream stand. Gorham photographic book of products, vol. I, p. 159.

NOTES

1. Carpenter 1997, pp. 23–52; and Venable 1994, pp. 23–28, are the main published historical accounts of the early Gorham Manufacturing Company.

2. Wilkinson's value to the firm was made clear in 1865, when Gorham and Company incorporated as Gorham Manufacturing Company and he was granted twenty-five shares of company stock and named to the company board of directors. Venable 1994, pp. 49–55, shows a portrait of Wilkinson and discusses his work at Gorham and its national impact. For further biographical information about Wilkinson, see Draper, March–April, 1991, pp. 22–24; and Draper, May–June, 1991, pp. 13–15.

3. Both Venable 1994, p. 50, fig. 3.2; and Carpenter 1997, pp. 50–51, fig. 48, illustrate and discuss the Crawford chafing dish. The ice cream stand from which the chafing dish was adapted was illustrated in the Gorham photographic book of products, assembled between 1865 and 1868. An explanation of marks can be found in Carpenter 1997, pp. 226–237. The firm began using date marks in 1868 with "A," which would indicate that the chafing dish, with no date mark and no "STERLING" mark, predates 1868.

58.

Armchair and Side Chair, ca. 1865

Probably New York
Ebonized, incised, and gilt cherry, gilt-metal mounts, and reproduction upholstery fabric
Armchair: 38 × 30 × 32¾ inches
Side chair: 36¼ × 23¼ × 26½ inches
1981.1000.47–.48

These chairs were part of a large parlor set that included a sofa and other chairs and possibly an *en suite* center table, cabinet, and étagère. The most distinguishing decorations are the gilt-metal putti mounts on the arm supports of the armchair. Carved figural arm supports appeared in American seating furniture as early as 1860. These supports might have been based on armchairs shown by Parisian furniture makers Alexandre-Georges Fourdinois and his son, Henri-Auguste Fourdinois, at the 1855 Exposition Universelle in Paris, which an 1858 account described as "Renaissance chairs carved in rosewood."[1] Whereas the Fourdinois chairs may have been inspired by French Louis XIV furniture, the Crawford chairs have the ebonized finish, gilt and incised decorations, and gilt-metal mounts associated with 1860s and 1870s American interpretations of eighteenth-century French furniture.

The cast- and gilt-metal mounts on the Crawford chairs may have been imported from Europe. The maker or designer might have been aware of the Fourdinois chairs, probably from John Braund's *Illustrations of Furniture, Candelabra, and Musical Instruments from the Great Exhibitions of London and Paris,* published in London in 1858 (fig. 1). That same pattern may have inspired European or possibly American manufacture of cast-metal mounts for arm sup-

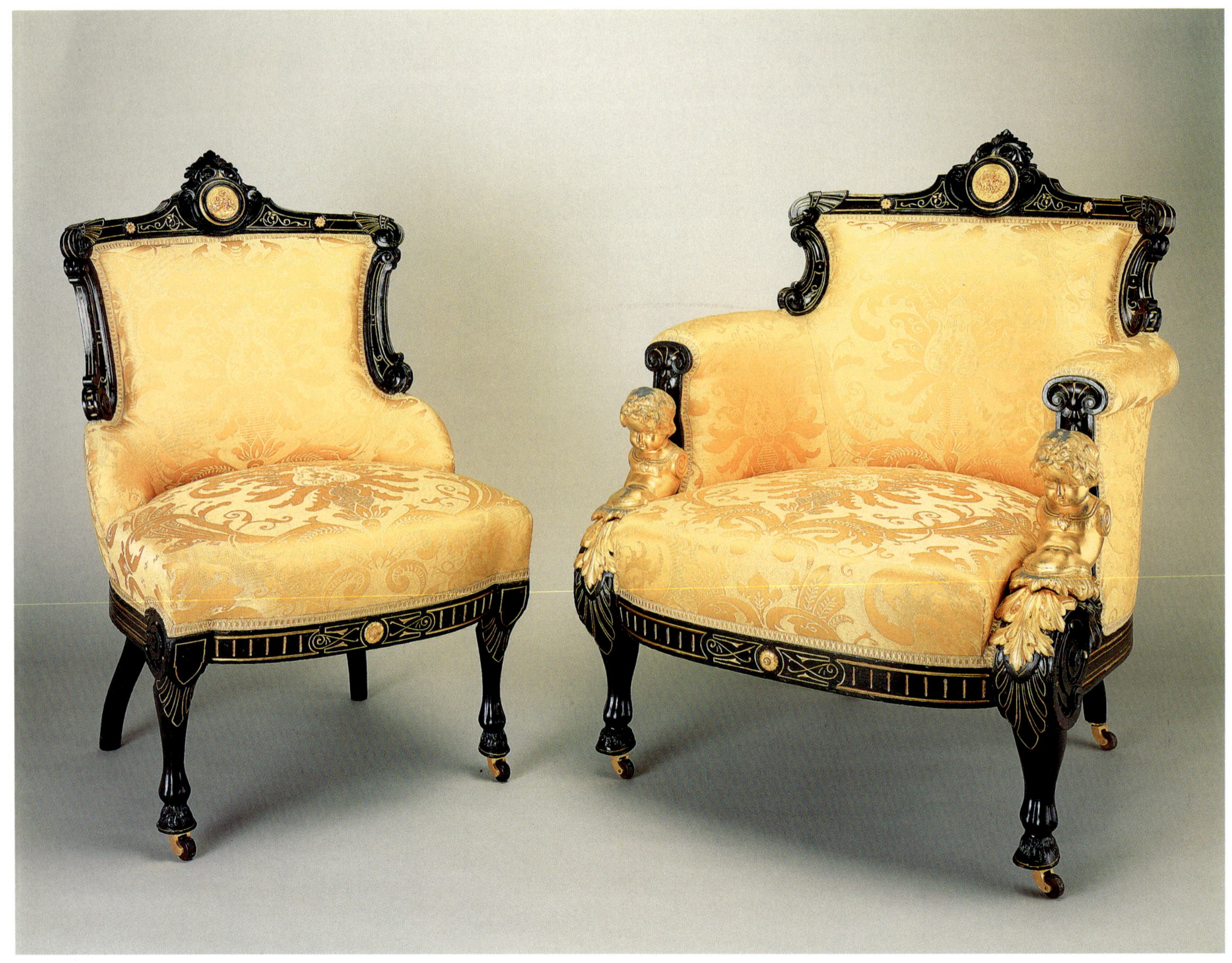

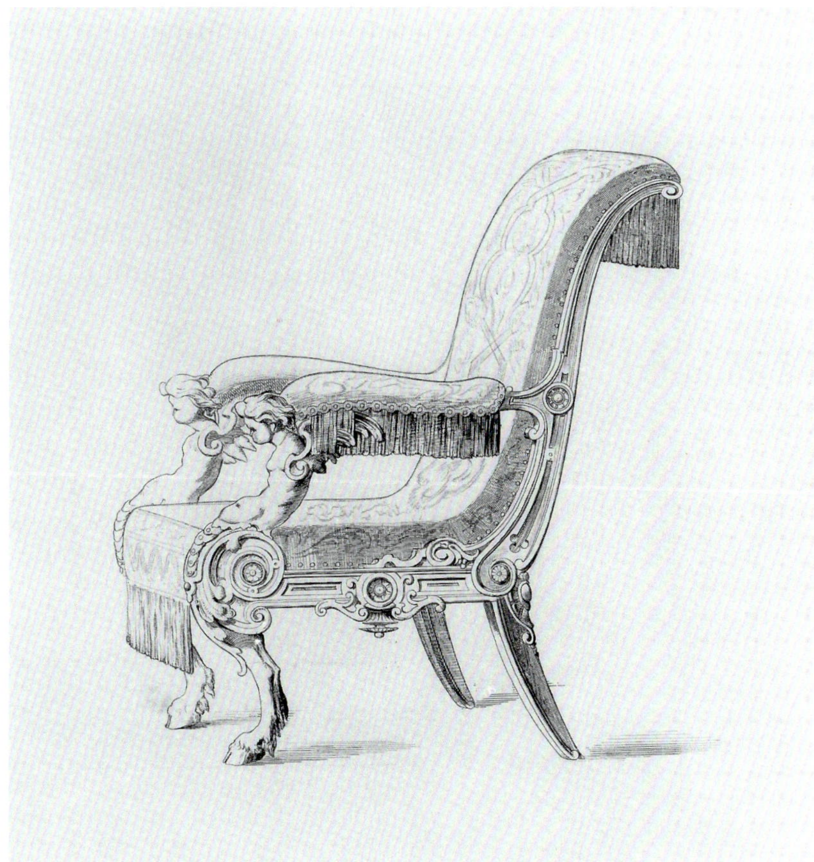

Fig. 1. Alexandre-Georges Fourdinois. *Armchair,* 1856. From J. Braund, *Illustrations of Furniture, Candelabra, and Musical Instruments from the Great Exhibitions of London and Paris* (London, 1858), pl. 23.

ports for seating furniture.[2] The full upholstery on the Crawford armchair allowed a complete cherry frame for support so that the sculptural effect of the Fourdinois chair might be achieved without the cast mount having to bear weight. On both chairs, the animal-leg-shaped front legs, terminating at the bottoms in hooves and at the tops in carved scrolls, further demonstrate the maker's familiarity with the design in Braund's book. The incised and carved decorations highlighted with gilding complement the gilt-metal mounts and provide contrast to the polished ebonized finish of the cherry frame.

NOTES

1. New York furniture maker and interior designer Gustave Herter supplied drawing room furniture for the Portland, Maine, summer residence of New Orleans hotelier Ruggles Sylvester Morse, which he was building in 1859. The Morse sofa and armchair with carved rosewood winged putti arm supports, along with the Fourdinois chair, are illustrated and discussed in Howe, Frelinghuysen, and Voorsanger 1994, pp. 132–133. The term "Renaissance" for these inspirations from eighteenth-century French furniture prototypes is an example of the loose terminology used for describing nineteenth-century furniture styles.

2. Pierre Guerin, a French immigrant, manufactured gilt-metal furniture mounts at the company he established in New York in 1857, which is still operating today. The range and history of his production is yet to be determined. Author's conversations with Catherine H. Voorsanger, associate curator of American decorative arts, The Metropolitan Museum of Art, and Ulysses Dietz, curator of decorative arts, The Newark Museum, July 22–23, 1997.

59.

Desk and Bookcase,
ca. 1865

New York
Ebonized cherry, maple, holly, white pine, poplar, gilt and patinated bronze, glass, and reproduction silk
70 × 52 × 23½ inches
1982.310

Pair of Vases,
ca. 1865

Probably Paris
Porcelain, painted decoration, gilt
Each 14¾ × 8¼ × 8¼ inches
1984.167.1–.2

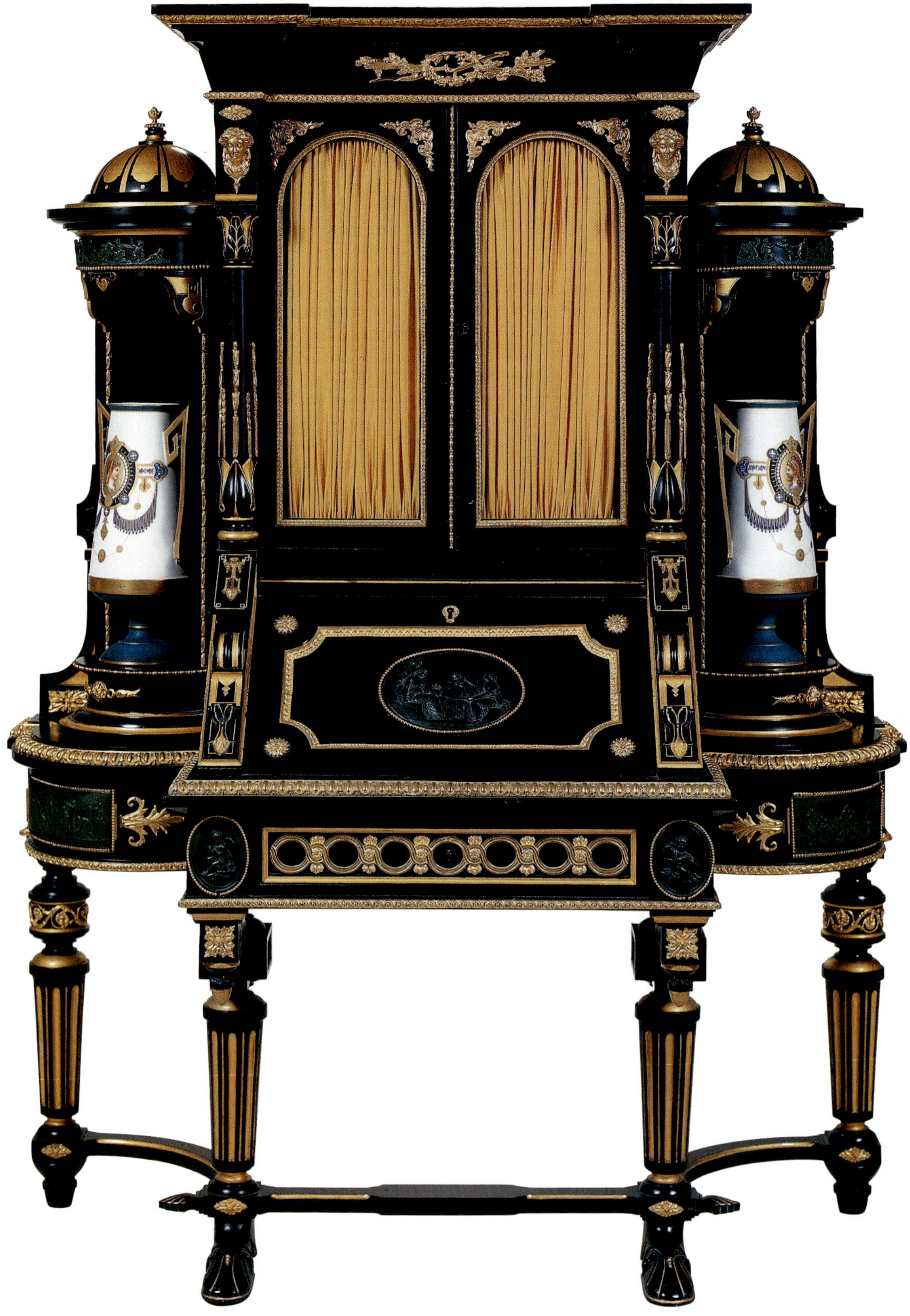

IN 1860, the prominent New York luxury furniture manufacturing and retailing establishment Ringuet-Leprince and L. Marcotte (see no. 60) advertised "rich suites of Black Wood and Gilt . . . Black and Gilt Centre Tables . . . elegant Cabinets to match."[1] Although this Crawford desk and bookcase is not labeled, the advertisement might have described it.

The piece includes architectural elements based on classical and Renaissance sources, such as the turned and reeded pilasters on the sides of the bookcase doors and the tall, narrow niches crowned by domes that flank the upper bookcase section. Domes, integral to Renaissance architecture, were part of the neoclassical public architecture tradition in the United States even as late as the mid-1860s, when the present U.S. Capitol dome was being completed (see nos. 45, 216). A European source for the domes might have been "The Lady's Cabinet and Writing-Table," in the 1793 edition of *The Cabinet-Maker and Upholsterer's Drawing-Book,* by the English furniture designer Thomas Sheraton.[2] The ancient Greek figures on the oval and rectangular cast patinated bronze panels were a further reference to classical sources.[3] The oval panels on the fall front of the desk and its apron provide geometric contrast with the rectangular elements, typical of late-eighteenth-century European neoclassical furniture design. Similarly, the rectangular bronze panels above and beneath the flanking niches contrast with the circular turrets. The vases in the niches reflect the Parisian taste in the 1860s. Paris porcelains were imported throughout the nineteenth century.

The ebonized surface and plethora of gilt and patinated bronze mounts lend the piece a particularly sumptuous appearance. The bookcase and niches for the display of art suggest that the owner had a sense of refinement, which many newly affluent New Yorkers eagerly wanted to convey in the early post–Civil War period.

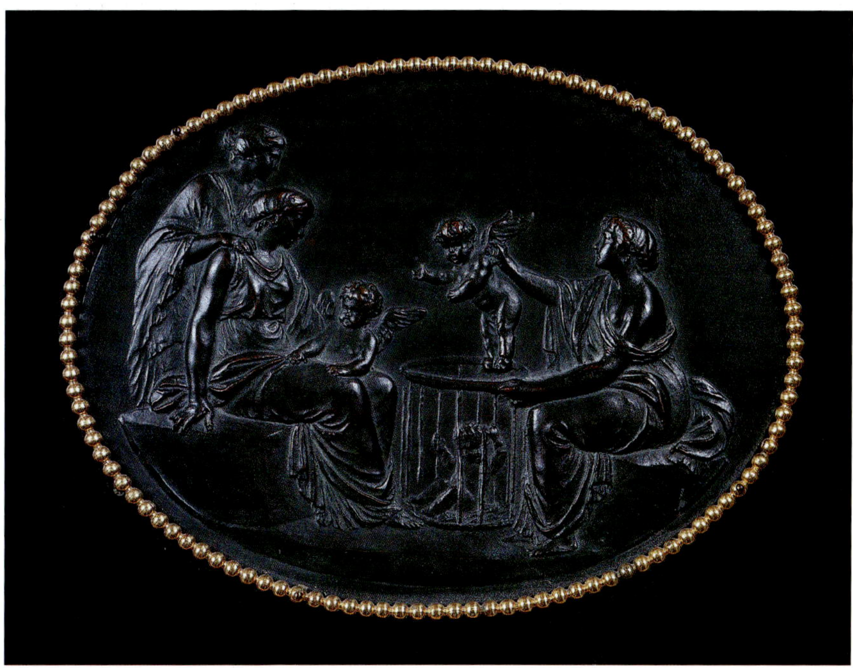

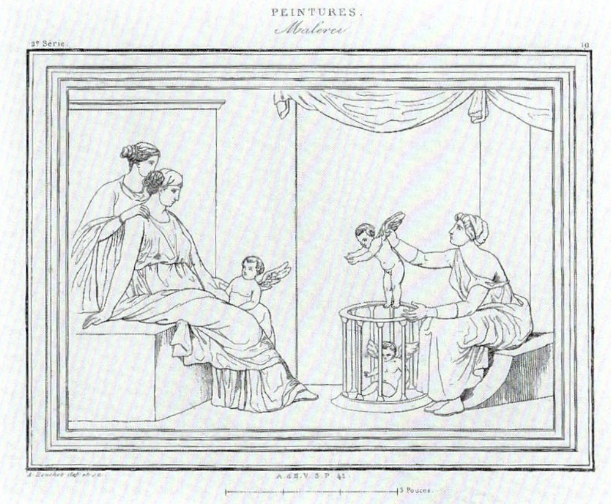

Fig. 1. Louis Barré, *Herculanum et Pompéi,* vol. 2. (Paris: Firmin Didot frères, 1840), pl. 19.

NOTES

1. The advertisement is cited in The Metropolitan Museum of Art 1970, no. 153.

2. Sheraton 1972, pl. L.

3. The relief in the center front of the desk (see detail) is based on an ancient wall painting found at Herculaneum and was also the subject of a well-known painting by Joseph-Marie Vien, *Selling of Cupids,* 1763. The ancient Roman city of Herculaneum was rediscovered in 1709 and excavation of the site began in 1738. The artifacts found there began to be widely known in 1757, when the first of a series of volumes entitled *Le antichità di Ercolano esposte* was published. Subsequent editions with copies after the original plates were widely available and were used as a source by neoclassical artists (fig. 1).

60.

Armchair, 1869

L. Marcotte and Company (1860–1918), New York
Ebonized cherry, beech, and gilt-bronze mounts with original French tapestry upholstery
38⅜ × 25⅛ × 22⅛ inches
1984.172

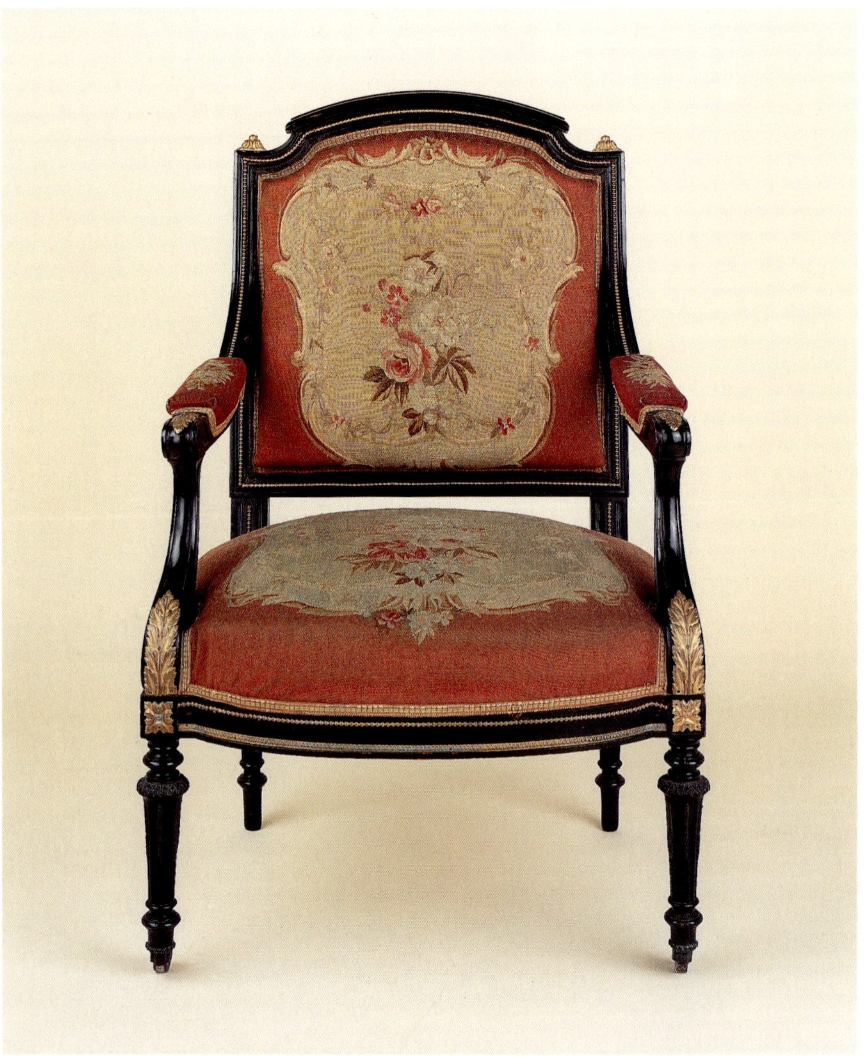

THIS ARMCHAIR was part of a suite of parlor furniture ordered from L. Marcotte and Company in 1869 by Eliphalet Wood for the new stone mansion on his estate, Irving Cliff, overlooking the Hudson River at Irvington, New York. Wood was a merchant in Albany before moving to Chicago in 1854, where he made his fortune in the lumber business in Illinois and Michigan. Returning to New York, Wood commissioned architect Henry C. Dudley to design his new home, which was built in 1868–1869. During the construction of the house, Wood and his family traveled to Europe, where he purchased tapestry upholstery fabric at Aux Genres Gobelins in Paris (fig. 1). Wood purchased a secondhand parlor set by Marcotte, but later decided it was inappropriate for this upholstery and bought the eleven-piece parlor set.[1]

Leon Marcotte was born in France and attended the École des Beaux-Arts, where he trained as an architect. In 1835, his sister married Auguste-Emile Ringuet-Leprince, a successful furniture maker and interior decorator in Paris, who was part of a family of Parisian cabinetmakers active since the late eighteenth century. In Paris during the 1840s, Ringuet-Leprince developed an affluent American clientele, mostly from New York. With the 1848 Revolution in France, Ringuet-Leprince established a New York outlet managed by his brother-in-law, Marcotte. The firm of Ringuet-Leprince and L. Marcotte was listed as furniture maker and also as architect, importer, decorator, and dealer of rugs, textiles, upholstery, bronzes, gas fixtures, chandeliers, looking glass plates, and tapestries. When Ringuet-Leprince retired in 1860, the New York business was renamed L. Marcotte and Company. In 1868, about the time Wood purchased his furniture, the company opened a new wareroom on 17th Street at Union Square.

Like Alexander Roux (see nos. 36, 46, 61), Marcotte relied on his French connections to give him an aura of prestige and to promote his business in New York. The Wood bill of sale (fig. 2) listed the "HOUSE IN PARIS, 15 Avenue de Villars" and the factory at 158 West 32nd Street, as well as the fact that the company manufactured and imported cabinet furniture, looking glass plates and frames, lighting fixtures, carpets, textiles, and "ALL ARTICLES OF ART." The Crawford armchair, with its square seat and back, followed eighteenth-century neoclassical prototypes in scale and form. The *Chapeau de Gendarme* shape of the crest rail (a central arch with reverse curves at either end) was also based on eighteenth-century French design, and it occurs on other documented and attributed Marcotte chairs.[2] But while an eighteenth-century chair might have been painted and gilded, Marcotte ebonized the cherry frame of his chair and decorated it with gilt-bronze mounts rather than carving, a bold and rich nineteenth-century adaptation of the earlier sources.

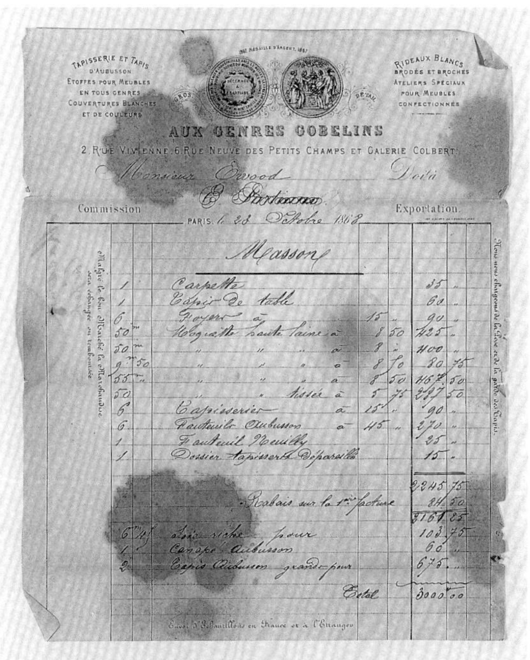

Tapisserie et Tapis d'Aubusson
Etoffes pour Meubles en tous genres
Couvertures blanches et de couleurs

Gros — Détail

Rideaux Blancs brodés et brochés
Ateliers spéciaux pour Meubles confectionnés

AUX GENRES GOBELINS

2, Rue Vivienne, 6, Rue Neuve des Petits Champs et Galerie Colbert.

Monsieur Ewood — Doit à

Commission — Exportation.

PARIS, le 23 Octobre 1868

Masson

1	Carpette		35 ..
1	Tapis de table		60 ..
6	Foyers à	15 ..	90 ..

Fig. 1. Bill of sale from Aux Genres Gobelins to Wood, Paris, 1868.

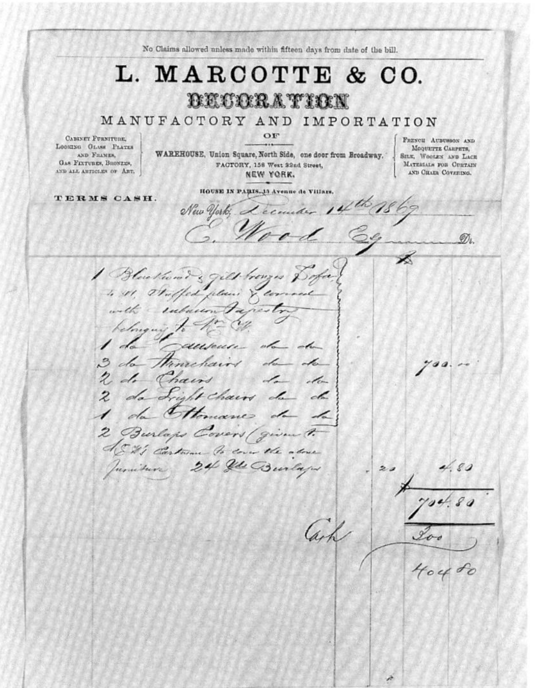

No Claims allowed unless made within fifteen days from date of the bill.

L. MARCOTTE & CO.

DECORATION

MANUFACTORY AND IMPORTATION

OF

Cabinet Furniture, Looking Glass Plates and Frames, Gas Fixtures, Bronzes, and all Articles of Art.

WAREHOUSE, Union Square, North Side, one door from Broadway. FACTORY, 158 West 32nd Street, NEW YORK.

French Aubusson and Moquette Carpets, Silk, Woolen and Lace Materials for Curtain and Chair Covering.

TERMS CASH.

HOUSE IN PARIS, 15 Avenue de Villars.

New York, December 14th 1869

E. Wood Esq. — Dr.

Fig. 2. Bill of sale from L. Marcotte & Co. to Wood, New York, 1869.

NOTES

1. Irving Cliff and its original parlor furniture descended in Wood's family until 1983. A matching armchair from the set is in the Brooklyn Museum of Art, a side chair is in the Smithsonian Institution, and a sofa is in the Detroit Institute of Arts. The set is documented by a bill of sale from Marcotte to Wood, dated December 14, 1869, and the tapestries by a bill of sale from Aux Genres Gobelins to Wood, dated October 23, 1868. The Marcotte bill of sale lists "1 Black wood & gilt bronzes Sofa, Lo. XVI, Stuffed pillow & covered with Aubusson Tapestry belonging to Mr. Wood." The bill of sale and the Smithsonian "Light chair" are illustrated in N. Gray 1994, p. 60, figs. 11 and 12; a comprehensive illustrated study of furniture by Marcotte and an account of his life are found on pp. 49–72. According to a 1983 history of Irving Cliff by Arthur B. Dubois, M.D., great-grandson of Wood, unused tapestry fabric and the marble mantel from the parlor are in the Art Museum, Rhode Island School of Design, in Providence (High Museum of Art document files).

2. N. Gray 1994, pp. 55–57, fig. 7. Often the differences in the suites Marcotte created for his most affluent clients consisted of slight variations in dimensions, mounted gilt-bronze ornaments, and details of legs and arms. Although beautifully executed, the furniture suggests the possible use of interchangeable parts and the wide variety that could be achieved with only incidental changes in detail.

61.

Card Table, 1867–1877

Retailed and probably made by Alexander Roux and Company (1836–1898), New York; possibly made in Paris
Cherry, gilt brass, marquetry of maple, boxwood, hairwood, amboyna burl, African ebony, Macassar ebony, purpleheart, satinwood, and mahogany veneers
30¾ × 34¼ × 18 inches
Mark: Paper label glued to underside of top unit printed in black, *FROM/ALEXANDER ROUX/827 & 829 BROADWAY,/NEW YORK/French Cabinet Maker,/AND IMPORTER OF/FANCY & MOSAIC FURNITURE./ESTABLISHED 1836*
1981.1000.43

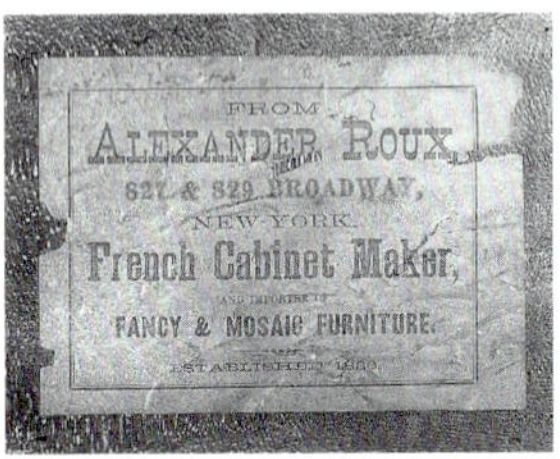

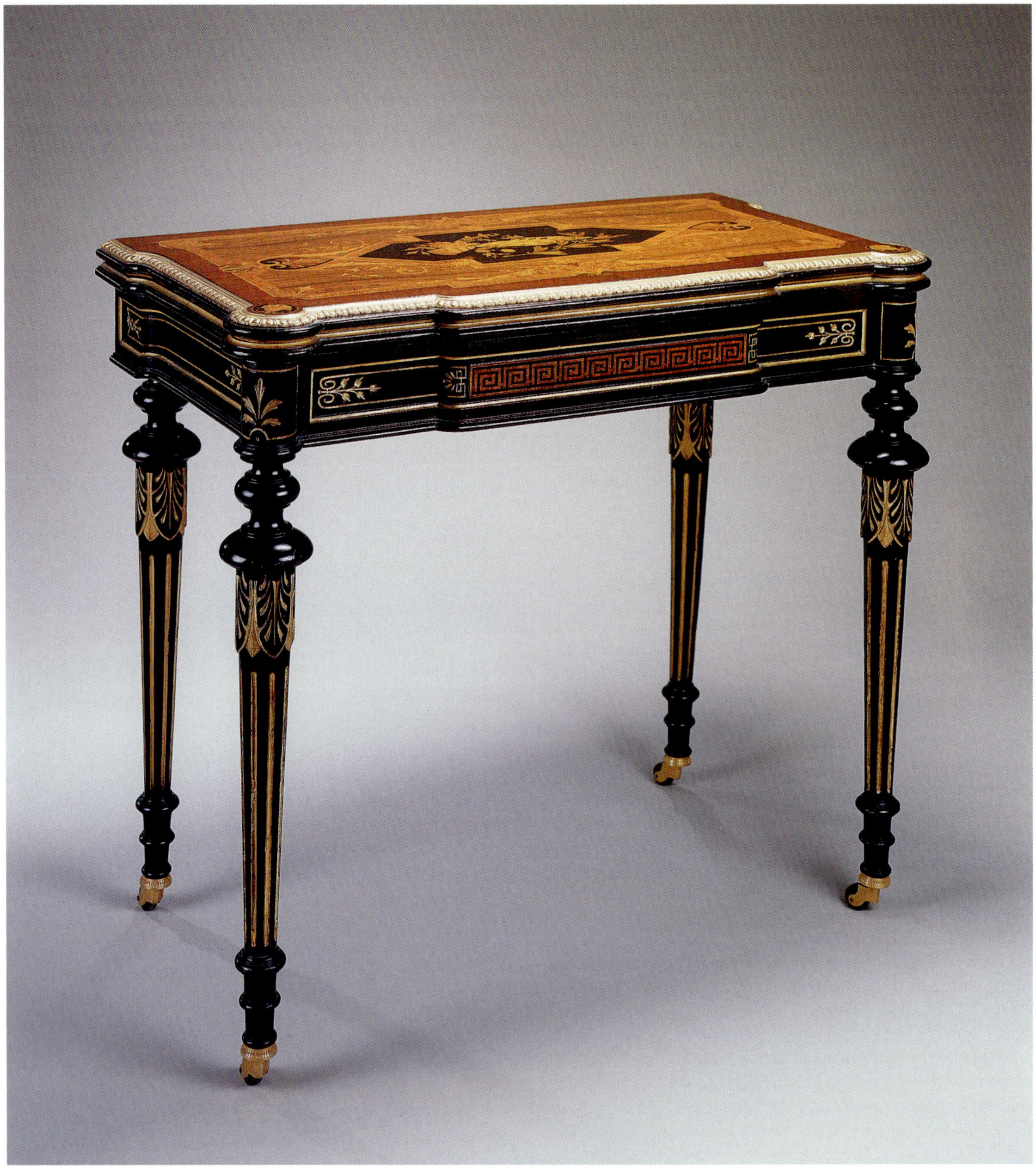

By the time Alexander Roux and Company retailed (and probably made) the Crawford card table, Roux had worked in the New York furniture trade for at least three decades.[1] In 1867, Roux moved uptown from his long-established furniture warerooms at 479–481 Broadway to 827–829 Broadway, the address on the printed label affixed to the underside of the Crawford table. His warerooms remained there for a decade, until the 1877 city directory listed his place of business at 133 Fifth Avenue. These relocations date the table to between 1867 and 1877. It was in the 1870s that Roux enjoyed his greatest success, when his annual business was valued at $250,000 to $500,000.

Throughout his career, Roux was always eager to promote his French heritage and Parisian business connections. In the mid-1850s, the "French Cabinet Maker" announced in an advertisement that he had "just established a new house" in the French capital and had "just received from Paris a large assortment of the latest

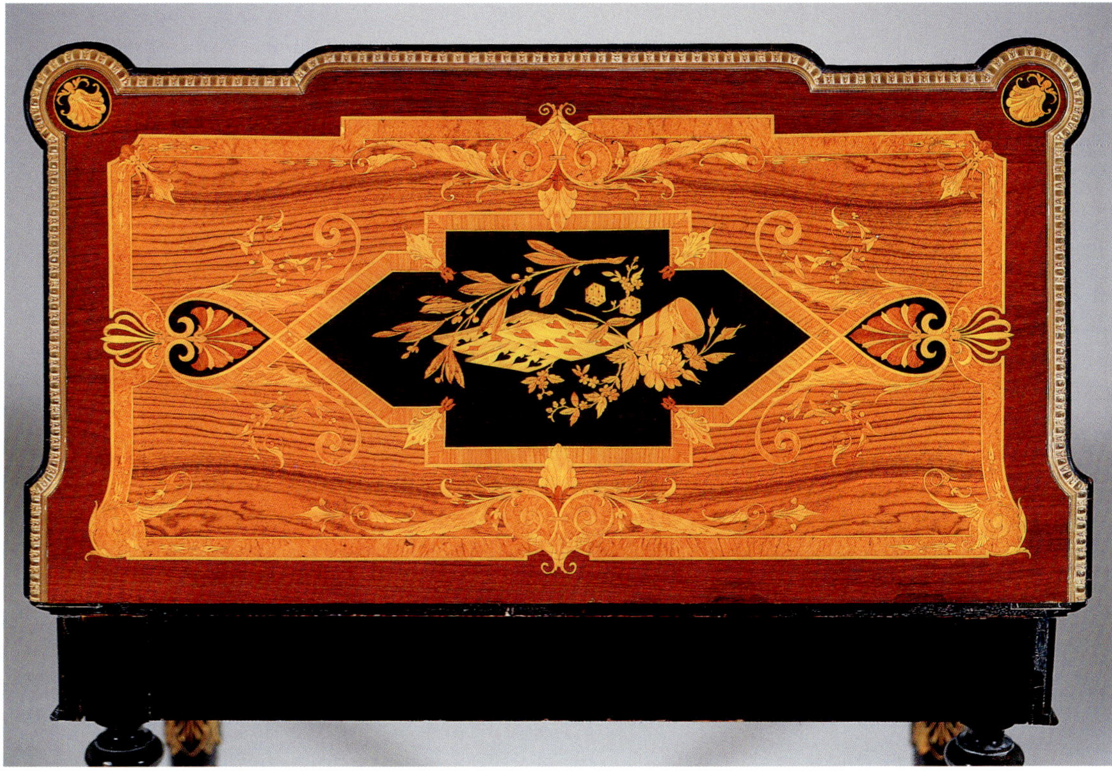

and most fashionable styles of furniture." Roux encouraged buyers to examine "his extensive and splendid stock in Rosewood, Walnut, Oak, Ebony, Mosaic, Margueterie [sic]" and said that he was "prepared to take orders for French fancy inlaid Buhl and Mosaic furniture."[2] According to the label on the Crawford table, Roux continued importing furniture after his 1867 move uptown.

The elaborate marquetry decoration on the Crawford card table—a detailed depiction of card-playing accessories—suggests the table's function. The cast- and gilt-brass trim, the rich marquetry foldout top, and the shapes of the apron and legs of the table were taken from eighteenth-century French Louis XVI furniture. The incised gilt decoration and ebonized surfaces of the cherry legs and apron were standard nineteenth-century finishings for furniture in the earlier French style. The fact that Roux's brother Frederic was a Parisian marquetry worker and that Roux advertised as an importer of furniture from the 1840s suggests that the Crawford table may have been made in Paris rather than in his New York factory. The use of cherry rather than a less expensive secondary wood was unusual in nineteenth-century American furniture production. The expensive materials and high level of craftsmanship further indicate the affluence of Roux's clientele, who had ample wealth to purchase such nonessential decorative furniture forms.

NOTES

1. An unlabeled matching card table is in the Museum of Fine Arts, Houston. The earliest published scholarly research on Roux is Hauserman 1968, pp. 210–217. The article does not illustrate examples of Roux furniture from after the 1850s, which were then largely unknown, but Hauserman chronicles what was known of Roux's life and business, and she describes his roles as a furniture maker, upholsterer, and interior decorator.

2. The Roux advertisement, from an unknown source dated about 1856 in the files of the Department of American Decorative Arts at The Metropolitan Museum of Art, is cited in Howe, Frelinghuysen, and Voorsanger 1994, p. 67. In 1847–1848, Roux was listed in partnership with his brother Frederic. It is unclear whether Frederic Roux lived in New York or Paris during this time.

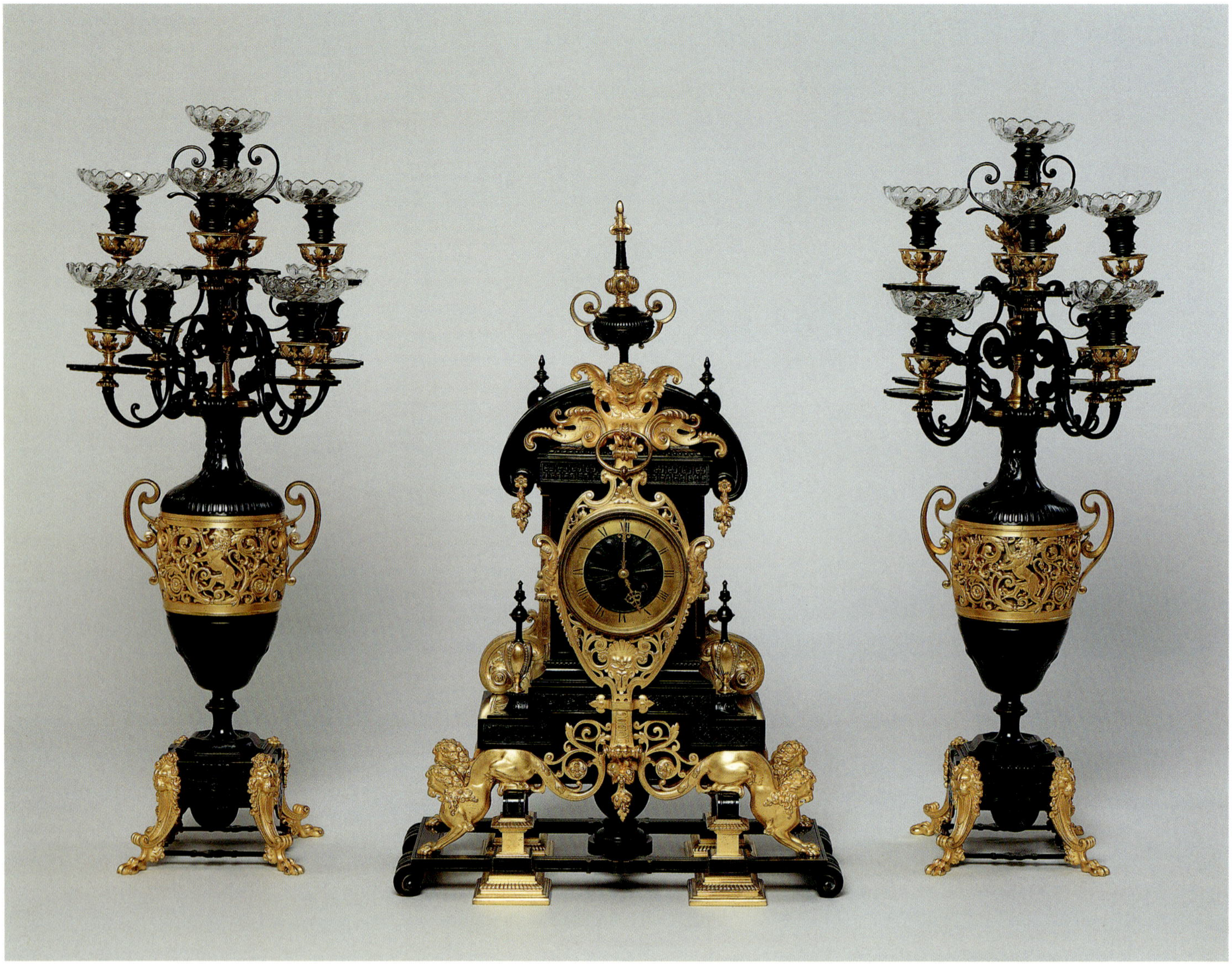

62.

Mantel Garniture,
1865–1875

Retailed by J. E. Caldwell and Company (1848–present), Philadelphia; probably made in France
Bronze, gilt brass, and glass
Clock: 29 × 19 × 9¾ inches
Torchères: Each 35½ × 11¾ × 11¾ inches
Mark: Printed on frame around dial, *J. E. CALDWELL & CO. PHILADELPHIA*
1984.115.1–.3

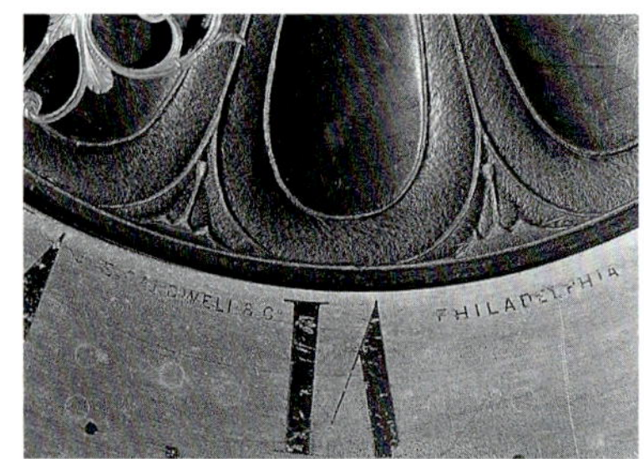

In the type of elaborate and densely furnished parlor that the Crawford garniture probably originally adorned, the fireplace would have been the visual focus. The garniture was useful, with a clock and candelabra for illumination. Richly decorated garnitures of sparkling materials were made in France and exported to the United States for retail by luxury emporiums such as Tilden-Thurber Company in Providence, Rhode Island (see no. 75), Tiffany and Company in New York, and J. E. Caldwell and Company in Philadelphia.

J. E. Caldwell and Company was one of the major luxury goods dealers in nineteenth-century Philadelphia, and it is still in business today.[1]

James E. Caldwell, a watchmaker from Poughkeepsie, New York, was in Philadelphia by 1838, when the firm of Bennett and Caldwell was organized. A decade later, the enterprise became J. E. Caldwell and Company. Caldwell expanded the company through various partnerships and eventually brought his sons into it. In the second half of the century, J. E. Caldwell and Company became one of the premier jewelry and silver retailers in the city. They also stocked art glass, bronze statues, brass goods, paintings, and furniture.

The monumental scale of the clock and urns forming the bases of the candelabra relate the garniture to Renaissance design. Cast- and gilt-brass ornaments, feet, and strapwork contrast with the black bronze in the clock case and the urns of the candelabra, a color scheme that complemented contemporary ebonized furniture. Lions were often incorporated into nineteenth-century Renaissance-inspired furniture design, and the forms on this set are similar to Gustave Herter's tall clock (see no. 53). A winged putto head, also taken from Renaissance design sources, crowns the frame surrounding the clock face, with an additional lion head at its base. With its color scheme of black and gold, derived from eighteenth-century French furniture design, and its large-scale gilt-brass Renaissance-inspired decorations, the Crawford garniture brings together two major design influences prevalent in America in the 1860s and 1870s.

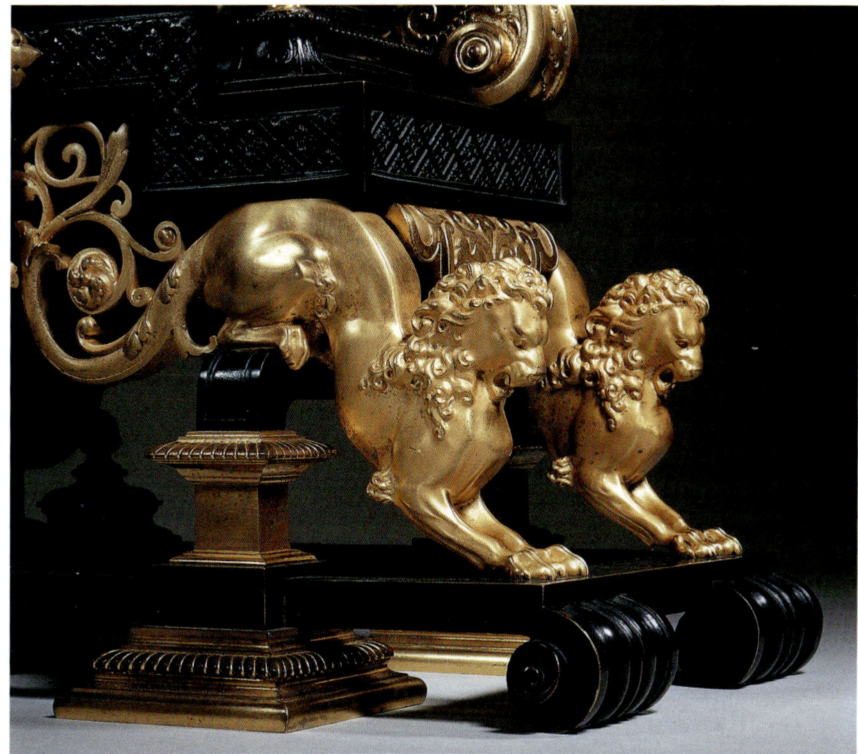

NOTE

1. For a history of J. E. Caldwell and Company and examples of goods they sold, see Philadelphia Museum of Art 1976, p. 356, no. 307, and pp. 384–385, no. 331.

63.

Cabinet, 1867–1872

Thomas Godey (1819–1879), Baltimore
Rosewood, rosewood veneer, maple, bird's eye maple, tiger maple, marquetry of various woods, poplar, cast gilt-bronze decoration, and porcelain
48 × 58 × 17 inches
Mark: Printed card tacked to back of cabinet with view of Godey's warerooms, to the right, *THOMAS GODEY/MANUFACTURER OF/CABINET FURNITURE/NO. 41 Hanover St./BALTIMORE.*
1981.1000.41

Born in Washington, D.C., Thomas Godey moved to Baltimore as a young man, where he worked with successful cabinetmaker John Needles. Godey had been advertising as Needles's successor since 1850, and when Needles retired in 1852, Godey purchased his business, occupying Needles's old stand at 54 Hanover Street. This Godey cabinet in the Crawford Collection was made after 1867, when the Godey enterprise was listed in the Baltimore directory at 41 Hanover Street.[1]

In form and decorative detail, the cabinet illustrates the far-reaching influence of immigrant French cabinetmakers in New York, such as Alexander Roux (see nos. 36, 46, 61) and Leon Marcotte (see no. 60). The elaborate marquetry, incised gilt decoration, ebonized trim, gilt-bronze cast moldings, and porcelain plaque on the Godey cabinet are all associated with such cabinetmakers at the end of the Civil War. The decorative vocabulary and colors were adapted from eighteenth-century Parisian prototypes that were then being revived in Paris and imported to America. New York examples were also being sold to wealthy clients in other American cities. The marquetry panels, gilt-bronze trim, and porcelain plaque may have been imported from France and assembled in Godey's Baltimore manufactory.[2]

The cabinet is characteristic of post–Civil War eclectic American furniture design. It contains eighteenth-century French elements—the

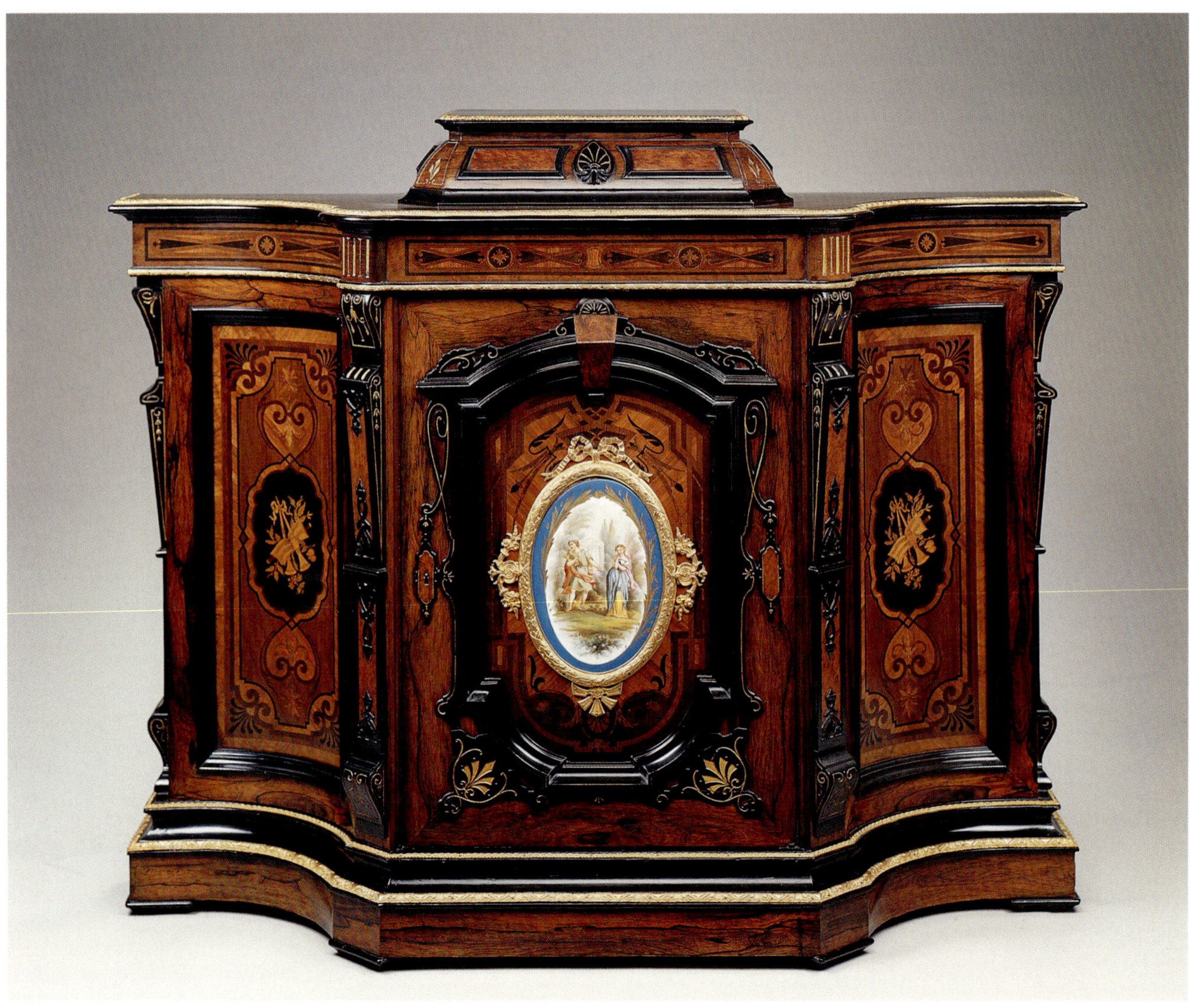

elongated acanthus in the carved and applied decoration and in the marquetry—and also reflects a new larger-proportioned interpretation of classical decoration that evolved in the 1860s and 1870s in furniture and silver. Certain musical motifs—a man holding a harp on the porcelain plaque, and horns and music in the marquetry on the concave side doors—suggest that the cabinet was intended for use in a music room, perhaps for sheet music. Not only did the musical themes indicate a growing awareness of the arts in the post–Civil War American home, but the cabinet itself was intended to be a pedestal for a work of art. A related cabinet, apparently meant as a base for a bronze sculpture, was described as a "Bronze Cabinet" in an 1865 bill of sale from the New York firm Pottier and Stymus.[3]

The printed label tacked to the back of the cabinet (fig. 1) depicts Godey's impressive five-story, five-bay-wide premises at 41 Hanover Street in Baltimore. It was a trade card and advertisement for Godey's thriving business. He received at least two medals in annual exhibitions of products at the Maryland Institute in Baltimore in the 1850s. Godey's eldest son, Harry, joined the firm in 1872, and it became Thomas Godey and Son.[4] The label on the Crawford cabinet would thus seem to date the cabinet between 1867 and 1872. Following the elder Godey's death in 1879, another son, Thomas A. Godey, joined the enterprise in 1883. The name then changed to Thomas Godey and Sons, under which it operated until 1912.

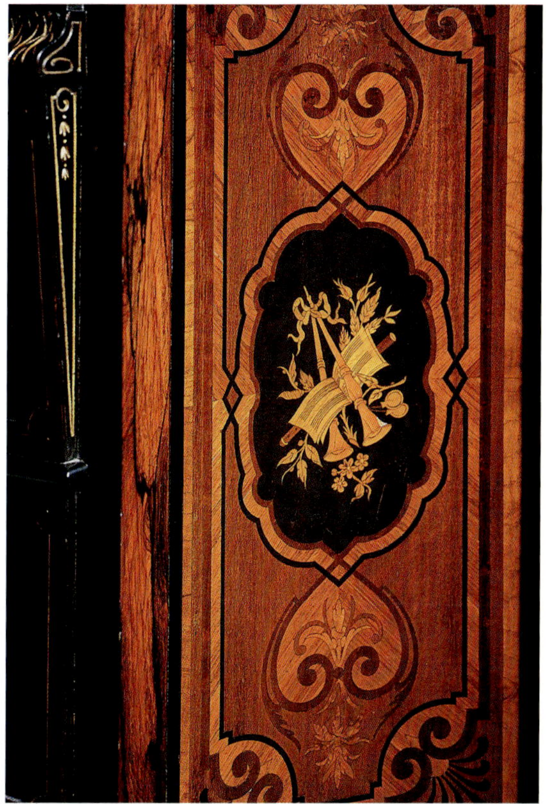

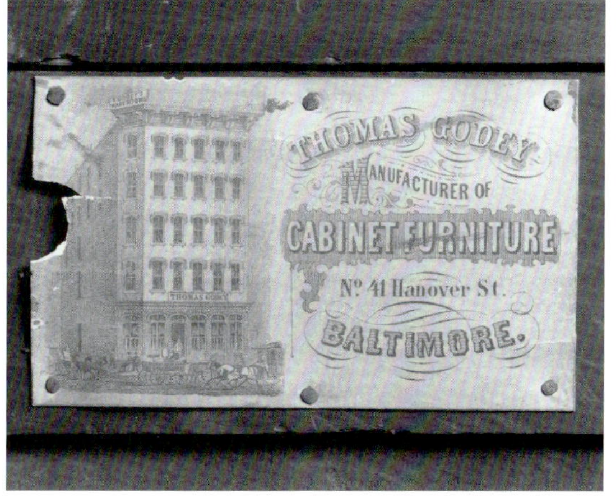

Fig. 1.

NOTES

1. For an account of the Godey firm, see Weidman 1984, pp. 208, 229–230, nos. 207–208. For information about Needles, see pp. 87–88.

2. For information about furniture made in Paris in the 1850s, see Philadelphia Museum of Art 1978, pp. 94–114; and Weidman 1984, p. 205.

3. Monkhouse and Michie 1986, p. 118.

4. Correspondence, Gregory Weidman to David Hanks, June 25, 1982, High Museum of Art document files.

64.

Console with Mirror,
ca. 1870

Probably New York
Rosewood, glass, porcelain, and gilt-brass mounts
106 × 73½ × 20 inches
1985.316

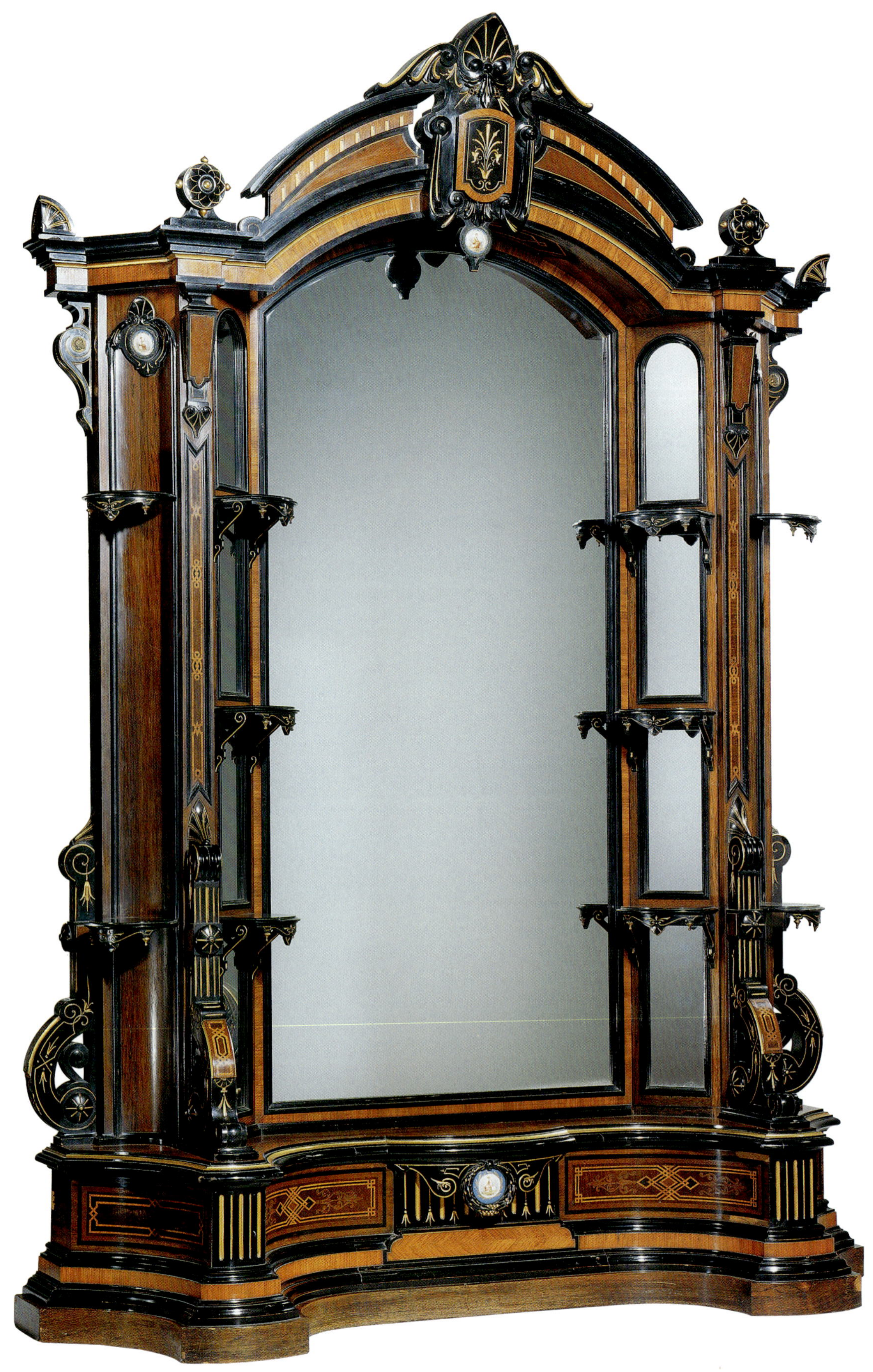

THE CRAWFORD CONSOLE was intended to hold works of art, while the enormous mirror would have reflected the elaborate furniture, light fixtures, and architectural elements of the parlor, drawing room, or salon it originally graced. Thus, the reflected room's furnishings would have contributed to the overall decorative effect of the piece, adding to its powerful statement of the owner's wealth and social position. The rosewood veneered frame is lavishly embellished with ebonized surfaces, incised gilt decoration, marquetry, gilt-metal mounts, and porcelain plaques. This decorative vocabulary was drawn from the richly ornamented Parisian furniture produced in the 1840s and during the French Second Empire, the reign of Napoleon III, which was in turn drawn from eighteenth-century French prototypes. However, the console and mirror were viewed as improvements over earlier examples, made possible by nineteenth-century technological advances, such as the ability to produce the enormous expanse of glass in the mirror and the precise execution of the elaborate and profuse decorations of the frame.

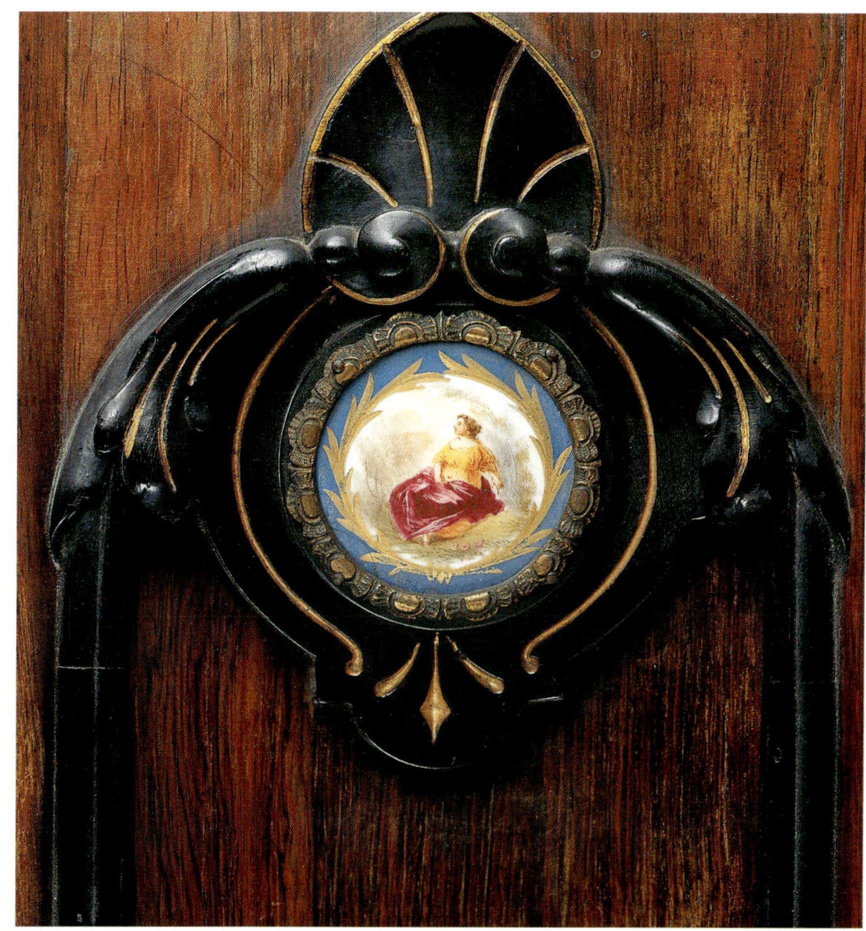

65.

Sofa, ca. 1870

Attributed to A. and H. Lejambre (1865–1907), Philadelphia
Rosewood, upholstered in reproduction silk
47¼ × 73 × 33 inches
1983.194

In the last half of the nineteenth century, Philadelphia's furniture trade, like New York's, was dominated by immigrants from France and Germany. The Lejambre family had been in Philadelphia's furniture business since 1825, when French-born John Peter Alphonse Lejambre opened his upholstery shop. After Lejambre's death, his widow, Anna, operated the shop with her children. By 1853, the company was manufacturing furniture and advertised as a "French Cabinet Maker and Upholsterer." In 1865, Anna Lejambre entered into a partnership with her cousin and son-in-law Henri Lejambre, who had worked as a salesman and an upholsterer in the shop. She ceased to have an active role in the new company, which by 1867 was listed as A. and H. Lejambre. During the 1860s and 1870s, under Henri's leadership, the firm made furniture for some of Philadelphia's leading families.[1] The Crawford sofa, according to family tradition, was made for Henry C. Gibson, an enthusiastic art collector who concentrated on contemporary French and German paintings and sculptures. By the time he died in 1890, Gibson had served on the board of directors and as vice president of the Pennsylvania Academy of Fine Arts in Philadelphia, and he left them his collection of paintings and sculpture.[2]

This sofa is related in form, composition, and decorative detail to a chair made by the Parisian furniture maker Henri-Auguste Fourdinois (fig. 1), which he exhibited at the London Universal Exposition of 1862.[3] Both have rectangular seats and arched rectangular backs, upholstery

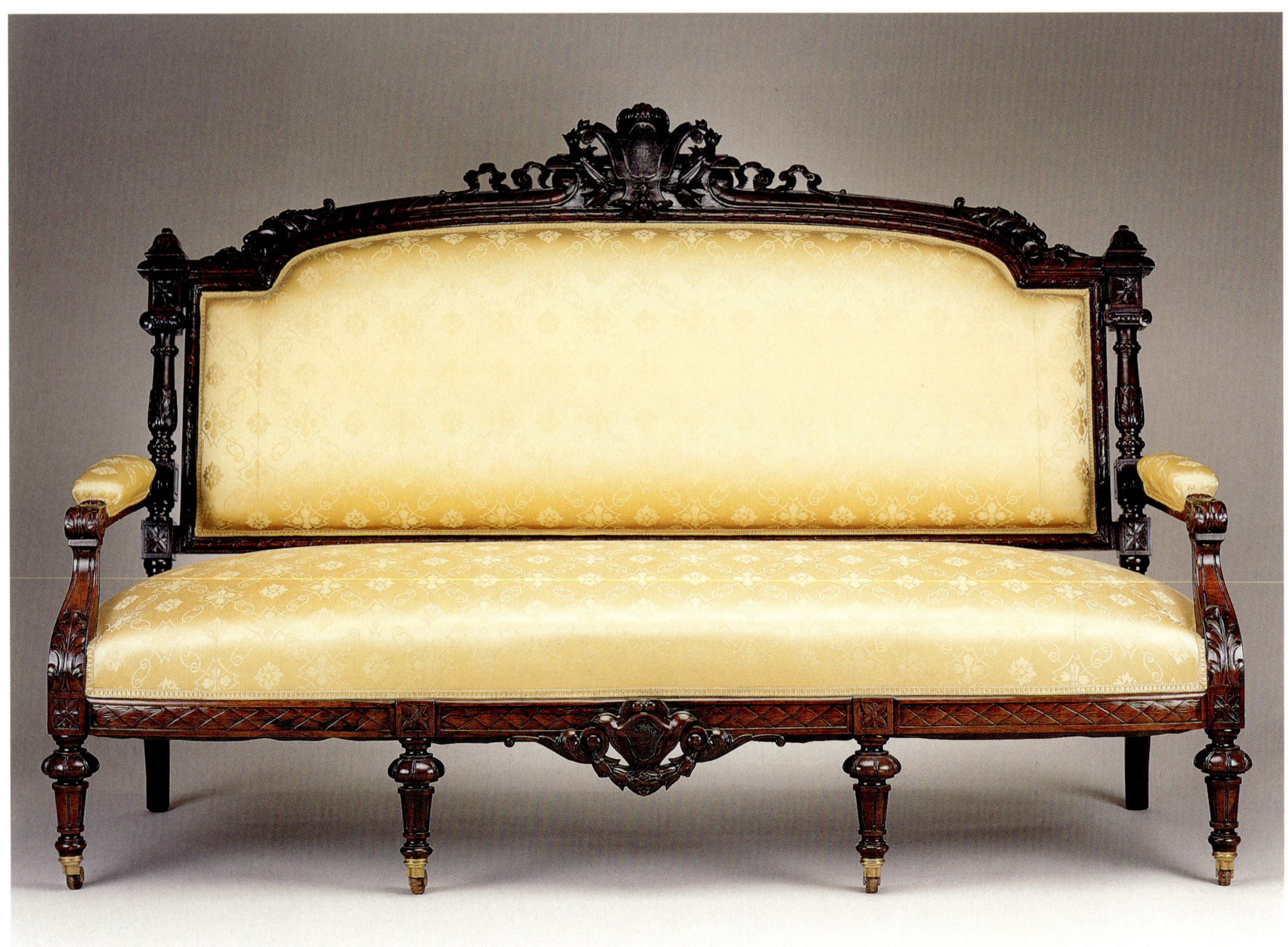

sections framed in wood, trumpet-turned and reeded legs, carving at the center of the front seat apron, and carved cross-foliate devices at the end of the seat frame, where the scrolled arm support continues into the foot. In shape and detail, both the Fourdinois chair and the Lejambre sofa incorporate design vocabulary derived from French Renaissance sources. But while the center of the chair's back crest rail is undecorated, a blank shield on the sofa's crest is flanked by beautifully carved rippling ribbons. This intricate detailing looks to mid-eighteenth-century furniture and gives a delicacy to the unusually large sofa, as does the separation between the back panel and the flanking stiles connected to the arms—an architectural column and stylized capital. This combination of sophisticated ornaments and styles, along with the use of rosewood—the most expensive and fashionable wood available during the third quarter of the nineteenth century—attests to the affluent market for which the sofa was intended.

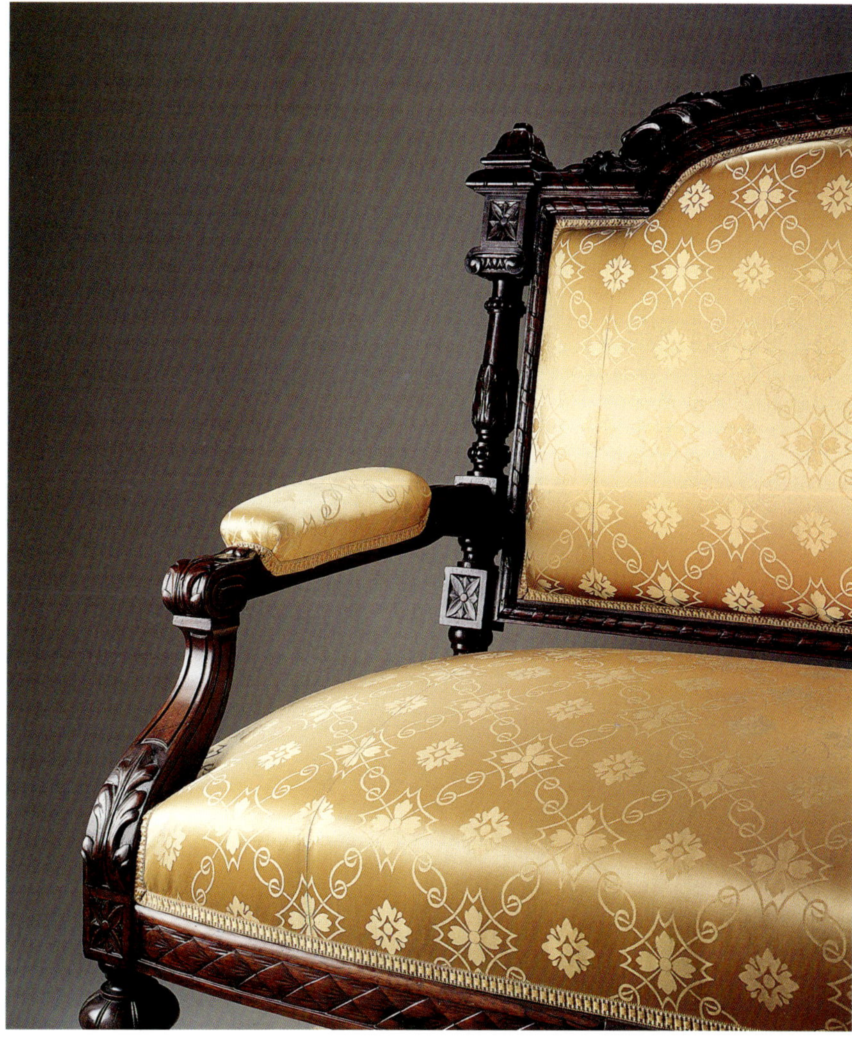

NOTES

1. For a full history of the Lejambre firm and a survey of furniture made by the company for James Dougherty, a successful Philadelphia iron founder and tool manufacturer, see Strickland 1978. The furniture purchased by James Dougherty relates in shape, scale, and ornament to the Crawford sofa. The Gibson, Dougherty, and Ingersoll families were all clients of the Lejambres. For another Lejambre chair, see ibid., p. 604, fig. 10.

2. Correspondence, David A. Hanks, November 18, 1981, High Museum of Art document files. Although no known bill of sale documents the Crawford sofa, family tradition has it that Gibson purchased his furniture from the Lejambre firm. Gibson's collection and his role at the Pennsylvania Academy of Fine Arts is discussed in H. Henderson 1911, pp. 25, 172.

3. Illustrated in Strickland 1978, p. 605, fig. 11. A matching armchair and side chair from the Gibson parlor set were purchased by Peter L. L. Strickland shortly before the sofa was acquired for the Crawford Collection. The Strickland armchair is very close to the Fourdinois illustrated in Strickland.

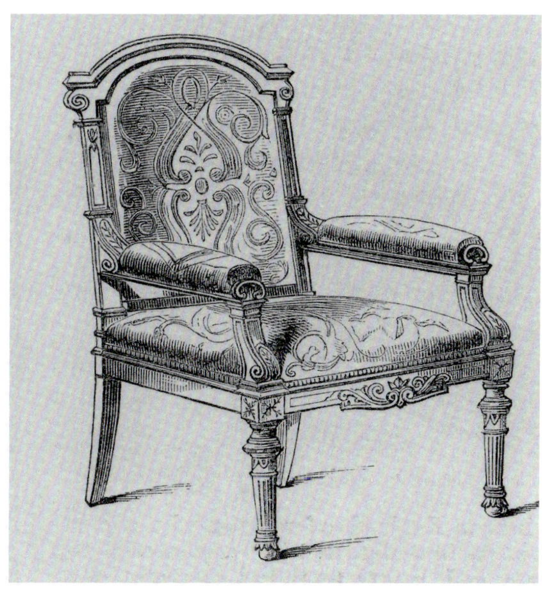

Fig. 1. Chair designed by Henri-Auguste Fourdinois and exhibited at the London Universal Exposition of 1862. *The Art Journal Illustrated Catalogue of the International Exhibition.* (London and New York: J. S. Virtue, 1862), p. 10.

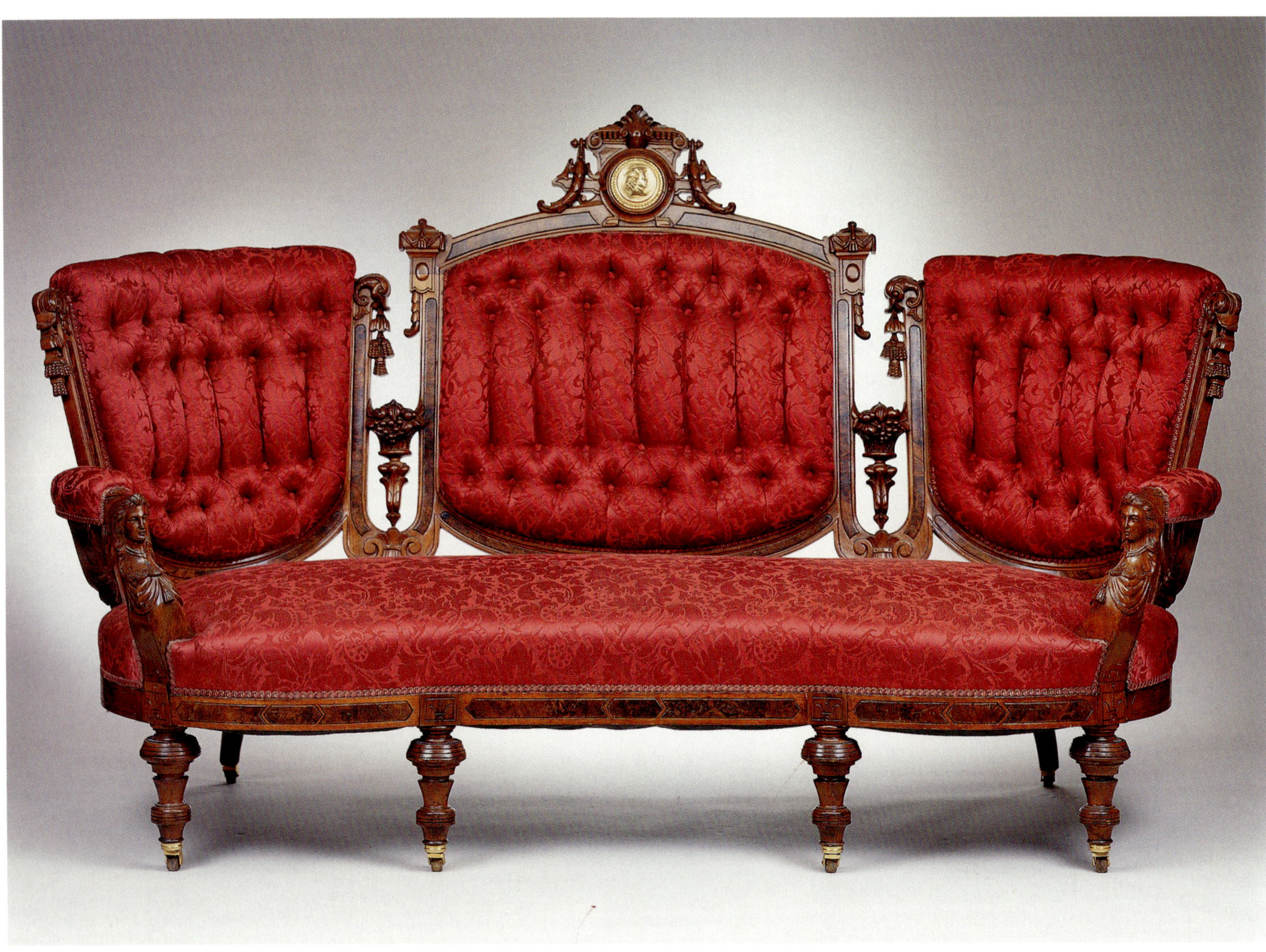

66.

Sofa, 1865–1875

Possibly John Jelliff and Company (1843–1890), Newark, New Jersey
Walnut, walnut veneer, pine, ash, and reproduction silk damask upholstery
46¾ × 78 × 33 inches
1983.193

THIS ELABORATE and deeply tufted sofa is related to two very similar examples in the Newark Museum that have been attributed to John Jelliff and Company.[1] The frames on all three sofas are eclectic combinations of baroque, classical, and Renaissance details, but the Newark sofas are made of rosewood, whereas the Crawford example is walnut.

All three sofas have tripartite, tufted, and overstuffed backs divided by identical carved baskets of fruit on elaborate foliate plinths. The carved frames around the medallions also have details of scrolls topped by stylized, elongated acanthus leaves. On the Crawford sofa, the central crest ornament is a gilt-metal medallion with a female profile. One of the Newark sofas has a central mother-of-pearl cameo medallion; the other has a carved female bust facing forward in the center of the crest. The skirts of the Newark sofas and the frames around the back sections are ornamented with incised decorations; the Crawford sofa is enhanced with burl walnut veneer. All three sofa frames feature carved tassels on the back, characteristic upholstery details of the period. Finally, all three sofas have carved female figural arm supports which, together with the classical details, have been associated with the Jelliff manufactory.[2]

While these similarities suggest that the Crawford example was made at John Jelliff and Company, it seems doubtful that Jelliff himself had anything to do with its design or execution. A stomach ailment caused his early retirement in 1860, before any of the three sofas were designed or made. Born in Norwalk, Connecticut, Jelliff apprenticed at age fourteen to a New York carver and later to Newark furniture makers Lemuel M. and Daniel B. Crane. In 1836, Jelliff entered a cabinetmaking partnership with Thomas L. Vantilburg. From 1843, Jelliff worked on his own in Newark at 301–303 Broad Street. At about that time, he took on an apprentice, Henry H. Miller, who became a workman, salesman, bookkeeper, and ultimately a junior partner in 1853. Miller took over management of the firm after Jelliff's retirement and operated it as John Jelliff and Company until 1890, when the name changed to Henry H. Miller, Successor to John Jelliff and Company. Miller retired in 1898, and by the time he died in 1901, the company had been dissolved.[3]

In 1874, about the time the Crawford sofa was made, John Jelliff and Company occupied a 40,000-square-foot factory in Newark, employed forty-five men, and conducted an annual business of $100,000. According to one account, between 1860 and 1874 business increased threefold due to Mr. Miller's energy and "the counsel of Mr. Jelliff."[4] From surviving examples and a set of drawings by Jelliff now in the Newark Museum, it is clear that the company made furniture in all the styles popular at midcentury, including Gothic, Renaissance, and rococo or modern French taste. An 1874 account stated that "the firm's productions . . . comprise . . . furniture of all descriptions, from medium grades to the most expensive and highly finished products of the art."[5]

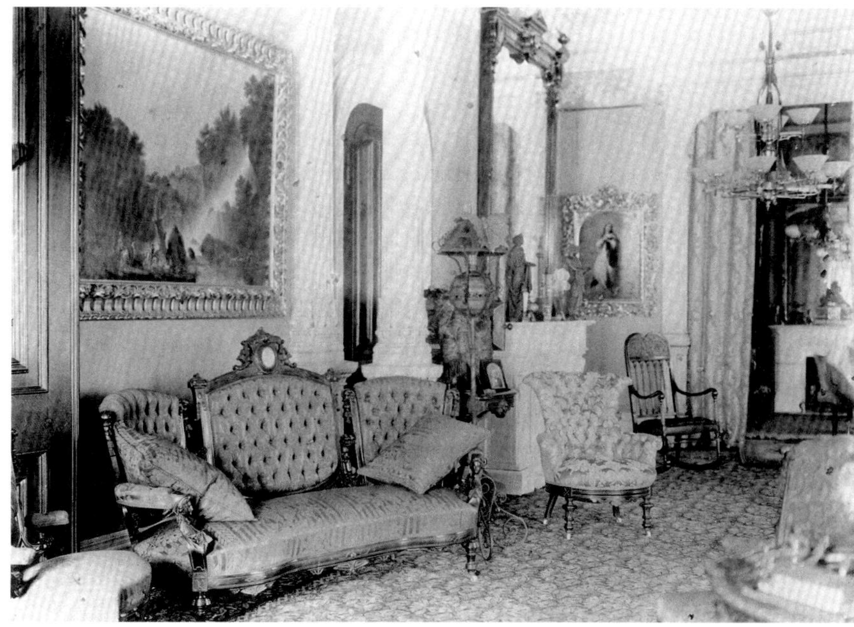

Fig. 1. Interior of the Frederick Tuttle House, 2022 South Michigan Avenue, Chicago, ca. 1880. Built in 1871. Newark Museum. Photo gift of Mrs. Henry Learmonth 1983.

NOTES

1. See Dietz 1980, p. 45, no. 37, and p. 48, no. 40. No. 37 was made by John Jelliff and Company for the Warren Trusdell House in Newark in 1868. No. 40 (fig. 1) is attributed to John Jelliff and Company based on its similarities to no. 37, although it retains a label from its 1871 Chicago retail source, W. W. Strong.

2. See ibid., p. 45. See also The Metropolitan Museum of Art 1970, no. 176; and Springer 1980, p. 38. A sofa in the St. Louis Art Museum with a local history has the same caryatid arm supports and, like the Crawford sofa, is made of walnut. All other details on the St. Louis sofa differ from the Crawford and Newark examples. Although literature in the field has associated the figural arm supports with Jelliff's factory, they were actually incorporated by a number of different makers, including the Phoenix Furniture Company of Grand Rapids, Michigan. See Ames 1975, p. 45, figs. 15 and 16. An armchair possibly made in Baltimore, with a bearded male figural support, is illustrated in Elder and Stokes 1987, pp. 54–55, no. 36.

3. For the history of John Jelliff and Company, see Johnson 1972, pp. 256–261; and Dietz 1986, pp. 1096–1099. For discussions and photographs of the work of Jelliff and Company, see Dietz 1980, nos. 14, 14a, 16, 24, 26, 37–43, and 47.

4. William F. Ford, *The Industrial Interests of Newark, N.J.*, 1874; cited in Johnson 1972, p. 257.

5. Johnson 1972, p. 260.

Gorham Manufacturing Company

As THE WORLD'S LARGEST manufacturer of fine silverwares in the 1860s and 1870s, the Gorham Manufacturing Company maintained a range of production that included virtually every form and style of the time. In the spirit of the period, no particular design seems to have dominated the company's energetic output. Gorham embraced many of the historical revival styles then popular (see no. 57), while at the same time, its designers looked to nature for new ideas. Like contemporary designers of furniture decoration (see no. 61), they were frequently inspired by the intended function of the pieces they were creating. This nut scoop and ice bowl with serving spoon combine natural motifs with those that reflect the function of the objects.

The finial of the nut scoop (no. 67) is a realistic cast squirrel holding a nut, while the pierced and gilded bowl of the scoop is shaped like a walnut shell. The handle suggests a branch, complete with twining leaves to provide a perch for the squirrel and termination for the oversized walnut shell scoop. The scoop is impressed on the back edge of the bowl with the mark adopted by Gorham in the 1850s and a "B" denoting 1869 as the year of manufacture.[1]

Gorham introduced silver ice bowls by the mid-1860s in response to the American preference for serving drinks with ice. The new forms may also have been inspired by the 1867 acquisition of the Alaskan territory. In this period before mechanized refrigeration, ice was harvested during the winter and maintained until consumed, usually with much loss. Nevertheless, the industry provided hefty profits for the New England businesses that exported ice to warmer climates.[2] Ice for the table was a great luxury, and those who could afford it could afford the appropriate silver pieces in which to present it. The form of the Crawford ice bowl (no. 68) was first entered in the Gorham Manufacturing Company cost book on April 15, 1870, and in 1872, the total factory cost, including profit, was $81.96. Gorham made this pattern for over fifteen years.

The silver bowl, cast in a two-part mold in the form of ice chunks, would have suggested the shape of the melting ice in the bowl. Perched on either side is a realistically rendered cast polar bear, each secured with a wing nut, that would seem to be standing on the ice when the bowl was full. As the ice melted, the condensation on the outside of the bowl would have added to the illusion of silver as ice, and suspended silver icicles that might actually drip would have enhanced the theatrical presentation. Underneath the impressed Gorham mark is the number "125," which identified the bowl in its photographic record at the factory. The impressed "D" signifies that the bowl was produced in 1871. Engraved on the side are the initials "G.C.R." in Japanese-style script, evidence of the eclecticism of the period and of the early presence of Japanese taste in American decorative art.[3]

67.

Nut Scoop, 1869

Gorham Manufacturing Company (1831–present), Providence, Rhode Island
Silver, gilt silver
2 × 2¾ × 11 inches
Mark: Inscribed at edge of bowl, rampant lion facing right, anchor, *G* in shield/*STERLING*/*113*/*B*
1991.355

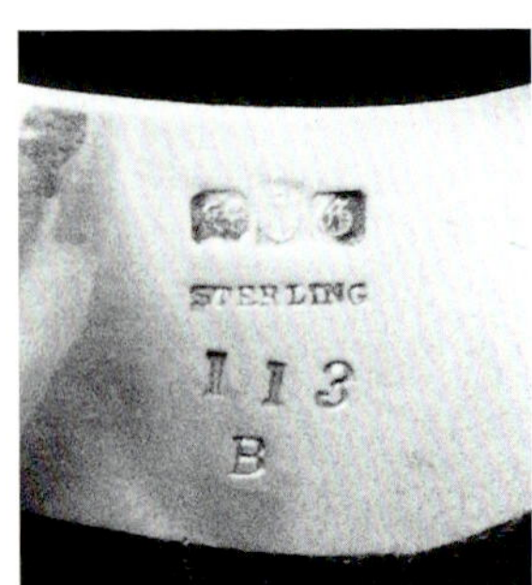

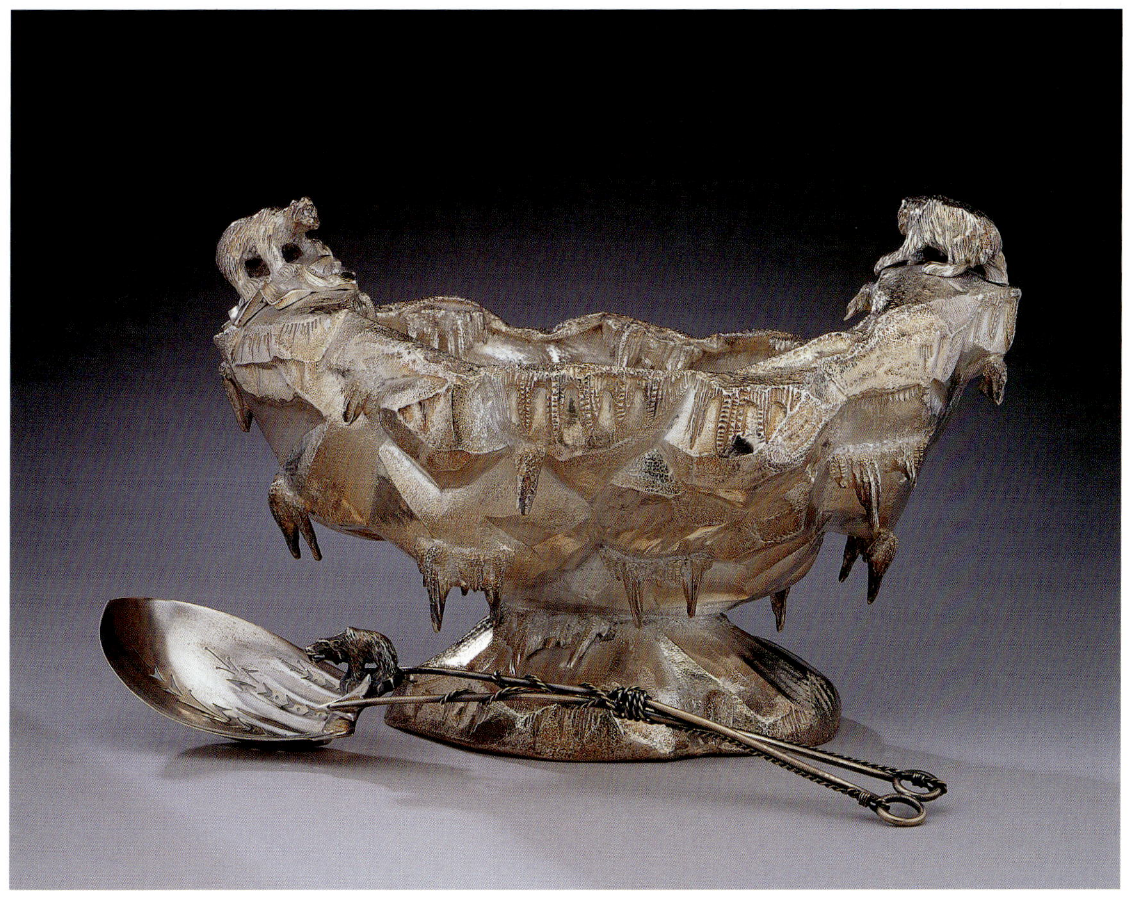

68.

Ice Bowl, 1871, and *Ice Spoon,* 1869

Gorham Manufacturing Company (1831–present), Providence, Rhode Island
Silver
Bowl: 6¾ × 10¾ × 10¾ inches
Spoon: 1¾ × 11¼ × 2½ inches
Marks: Impressed on bottom of bowl, rampant lion facing right, anchor, *G* in shields/*125/STERLING D* over scratched *4131*
Impressed on bottom of spoon bowl, *STERLING/B/* rampant lion facing right, anchor, *G* in shields/*110*
Inscription: Engraved on side of bowl, *G.C.R.*
1990.85, 1994.154

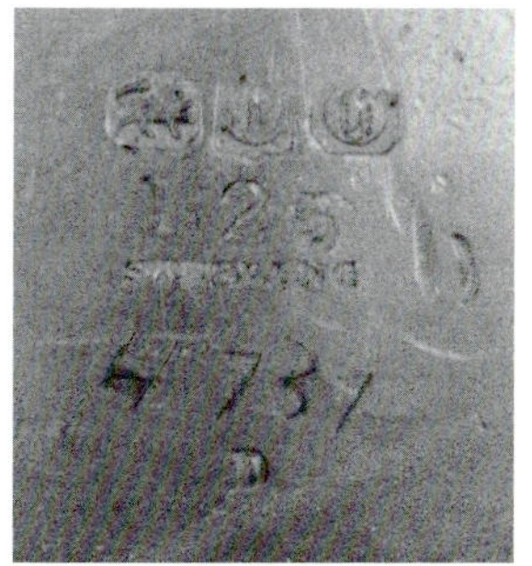

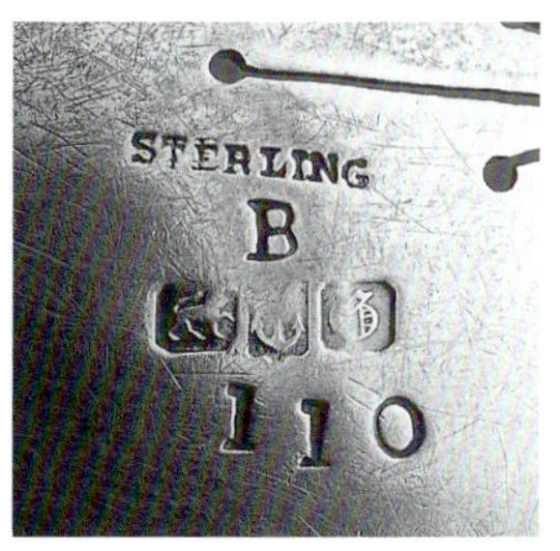

Complementary ice spoons in several variations were introduced in the factory cost book on May 9, 1870. This spoon features a finial cast to match the polar bears on the bowl and a handle formed by a pair of harpoons tied together with rope. The factory cost of the spoon was $8.00. The "B" in the mark indicates 1869 as the date of manufacture, and the number "110" in the mark indicates that the spoon may have been intended to accompany a different Gorham ice bowl.

NOTES

1. See no. 57 in this catalogue for a full explanation of Gorham marks.

2. See Hough 1989, pp. 30–35, for a discussion of the ice harvesting industry as it developed in nineteenth-century New England and of Gorham's production of ice bowls in response to the demand for table ice. Hough's article focuses on ice bowls designed in 1870, a particularly rich year for production.

3. A bowl similar to the Crawford example is illustrated in ibid., p. 30, and reproductions of company file photographs of Gorham ice bowls, including one like the Crawford example, are on p. 31. An identical bowl is illustrated in McClinton 1968, p. 95. An example with its serving spoon in the Dallas Museum of Art is illustrated in Venable 1994, pp. 198–199, fig. 6.69, and the spoon is discussed on p. 347. Like the Crawford examples, the Dallas bowl and spoon have different marks, which may indicate that the bowls and spoons were sold separately.

69.

Cabinet, ca. 1875

Probably Kimbel and Cabus (1863–1882), New York
Rosewood with painted, ebonized, incised gilt, and inlaid decoration
62 × 71 × 22 inches
1985.317

A CABINET IDENTICAL to this one is illustrated in an album of furniture photographs bearing the name of the New York furniture manufacturing firm A. Kimbel and Sons (fig. 1).[1] All of the furniture illustrated is in the French *néo-grec* taste, like this cabinet, or in the English modern Gothic taste, both widely popular in the 1870s in the United States. On the basis of the album, the cabinet in the Crawford Collection has been attributed to the predecessor of A. Kimbel and Sons, Kimbel and Cabus.

Both partners in the firm of Kimbel and Cabus had experience in the New York furniture industry before they affiliated in 1863. Prior to working with Joseph Cabus at 924 Broadway, Anthony Kimbel had worked with Anthony Bembe at 828 Broadway from 1854 to 1863. Bembe and Kimbel had provided furniture for the U.S. Capitol building in 1857 (see no. 216). An account from the 1850s noted that Kimbel had earlier worked as a designer for the prominent mid-nineteenth-century New York furniture manufacturer Charles A. Baudouine on Broadway. A label in another cabinet documents a partnership between Alexander Roux (see nos. 36, 46, 61) and Cabus that is not recorded in any New York business directories and presumably lasted less than a year. By 1862, Cabus was listed as a cabinetmaker working on his own at 924 Broadway, where he was joined a year later by Kimbel.

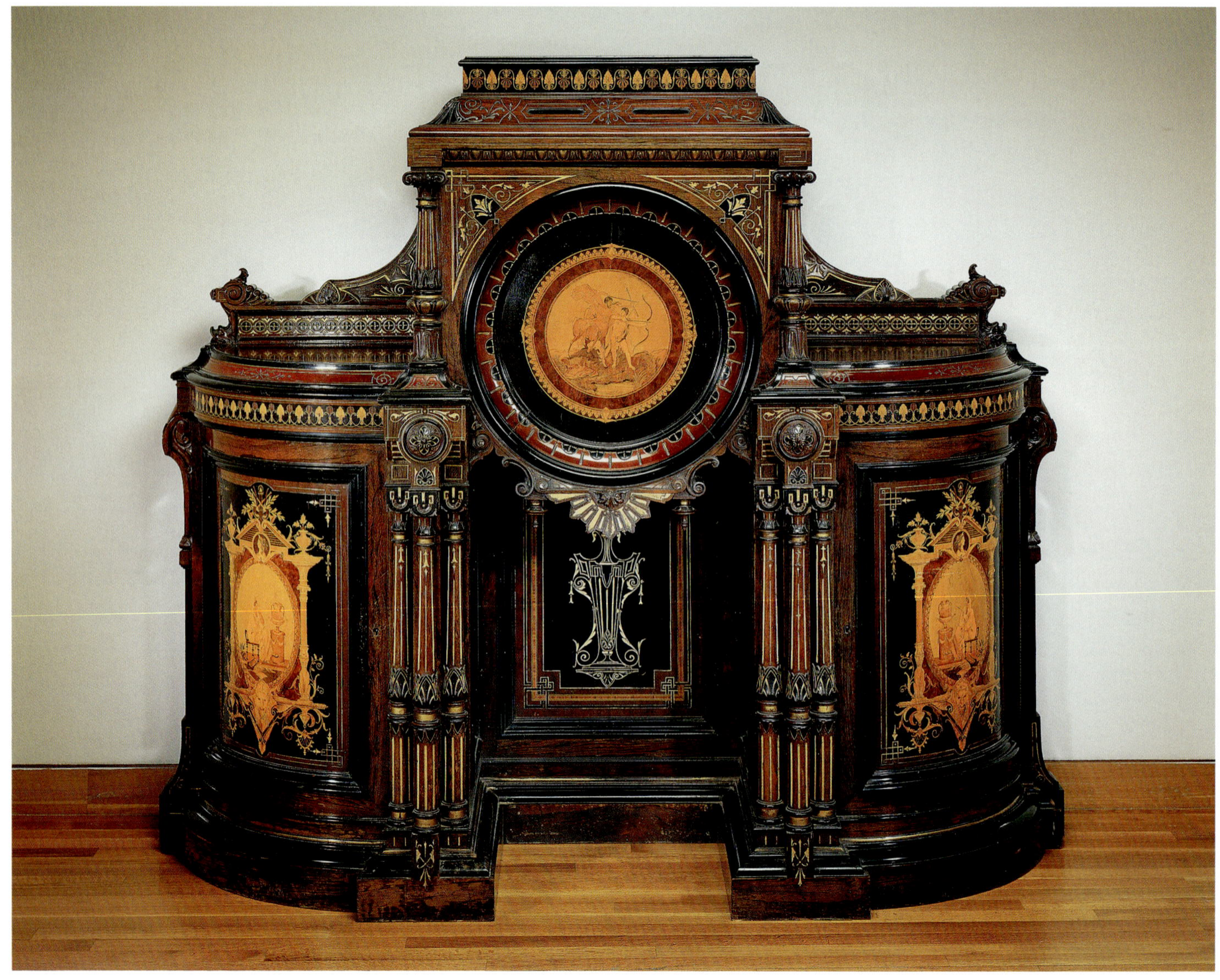

By 1865, the firm's listing in the directory included property at 136 East 18th Street, probably a manufacturing plant. The 1866 directory showed the firm at 928 Broadway, where Kimbel had worked with Bembe. They remained at 928 Broadway until 1874, when the firm was listed at 7 East 20th Street and 458 10th Avenue. In 1882, the partnership was dissolved. Kimbel joined his sons in a furniture business on East 20th Street that continued until 1941 as Kimbel and Sons. Cabus worked as a cabinetmaker on his own at 506 West 41st Street until 1898.[2]

Kenneth Ames has called cabinets such as the Crawford example "key monuments of conspicuous consumption in the Gilded Age."[3] Although equipped with doors and shelves in the sides, the primary function of the cabinet was not storage but display, a lavish pedestal for costly works of art. The cabinet is a polychromed panoply of the type of *néo-grec* furniture decoration popular from the late 1860s to the mid-1870s.

The cabinet, with its curved sides, followed the form of massive Renaissance-inspired furniture introduced and popularized at international exhibitions from the 1850s (see no. 48). It combines painted, carved, marquetried, incised, and gilt decorations representing some of the most costly and time-consuming furniture-craft processes of the 1870s. The three-part arrangement provided space for sculptures or ornaments. No surface, other than that intended to hold sculpture, was left undecorated.

The diverse forms of skillfully executed decoration all rely on classical prototypes. Engaged reeded columns are divided by carved acanthus collars, representing the *néo-grec* interpretations of classical decorations, introduced in the 1860s. The large marquetried central medallion, depicting the instruction of Achilles by the centaur Chiron, reinforces the classical references, as does the marquetry of acanthus blossoms. The space behind the medallion is open and does not give access to storage space. By the 1870s, European-trained craftsmen capable of executing this elaborate marquetry were working in New York (see no. 107), but whether the marquetry on this cabinet was produced locally or purchased from abroad has not been documented.

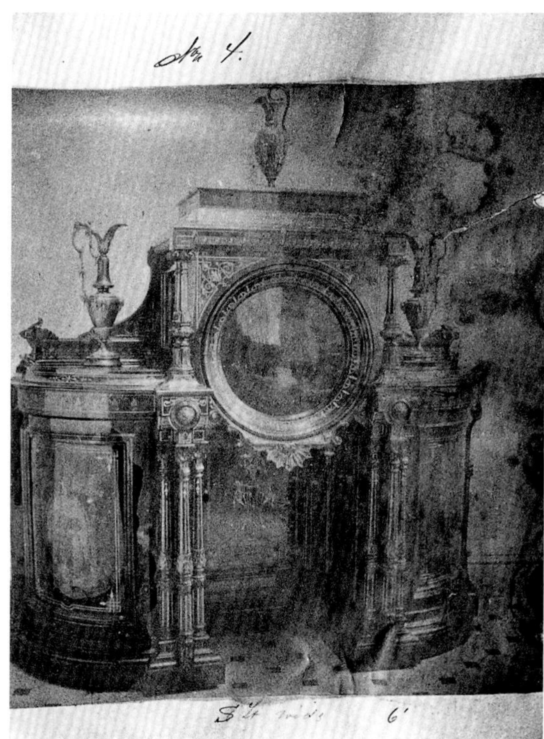

Fig. 1. Cabinet. *A. Kimbel and Sons Album of Furniture I.* (M749.1K49A, p. 6, no. 4). Furniture designed and sold by the New York firm of Kimbel and Cabus between 1875 and 1900.

NOTES

1. *A. Kimbel and Sons Album of Furniture I* (New York, ca. 1875), p. 6, no. 4, in the library of the Cooper-Hewitt National Design Museum, Smithsonian Institution. An identical cabinet is in the Brooklyn Museum of Art. See Peirce, May, 1979, p. 1003, fig. 15.

2. The history of the partnership is outlined by David Hanks in Art and Antiques 1982, pp. 60–69.

3. See Ames 1976, p. 16.

70.

Armchair, ca. 1870

Probably New York
Maple and beech, with mother-of-pearl, ebonized, and marquetry decoration and reproduction silk upholstery
42⅛ × 26 × 22 inches
Gift to the Virginia Carroll Crawford Collection to mark the retirement of Gudmund Vigtel, 1991.348

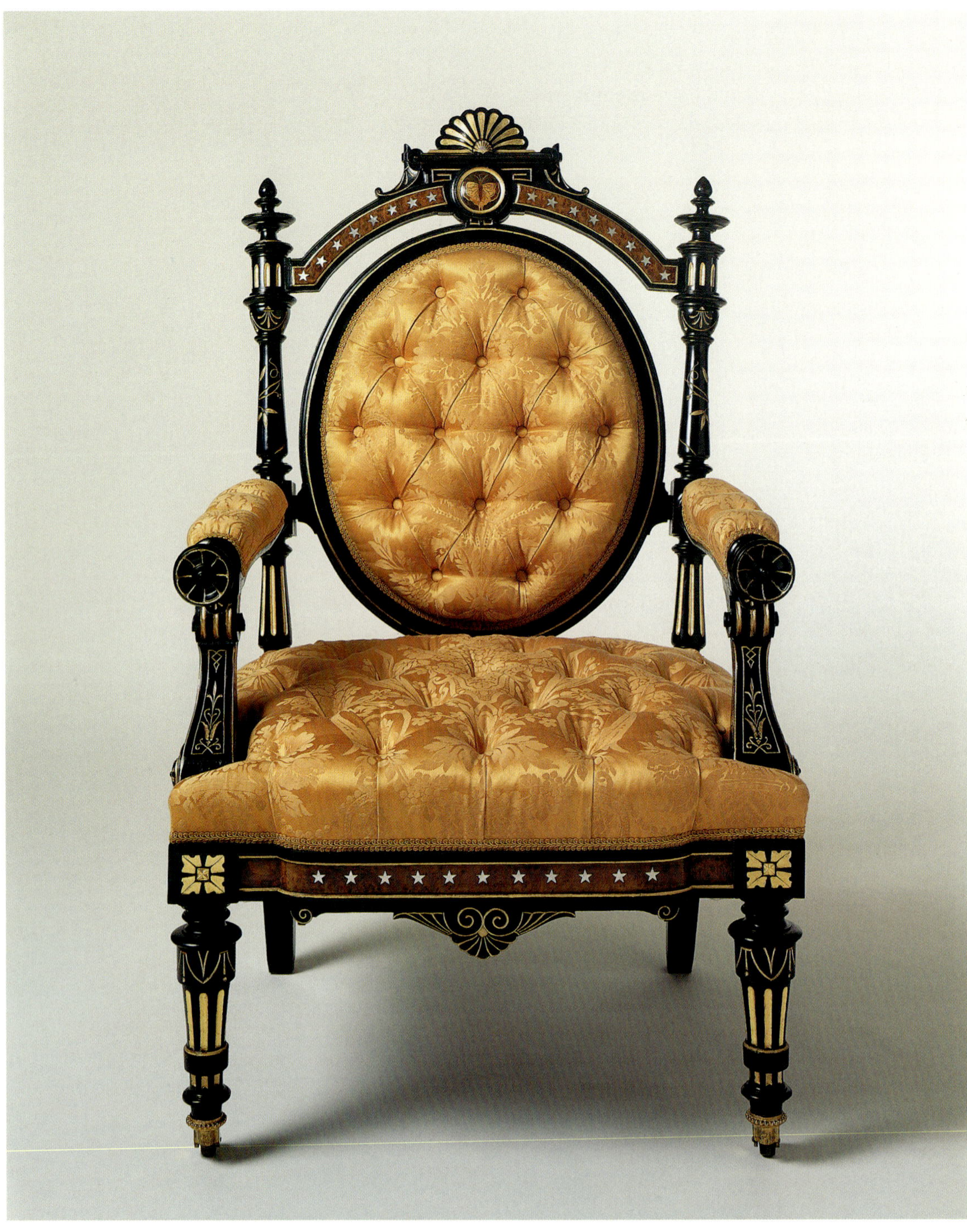

EXCEPT FOR THE marquetry butterfly at its crest, the exuberant Crawford armchair matches a parlor set owned by James Lancaster Morgan, a Manhattan industrialist, for his Brooklyn Heights home (fig. 1). The set descended in his family until it was donated to the Museum of the City of New York in 1927.[1] The Crawford armchair also was undoubtedly part of a parlor set. Family tradition had Morgan purchasing his parlor furniture from a British exhibitor at the Centennial Exposition in Philadelphia in 1876. However, the eclecticism of the Morgan parlor set and the Crawford armchair suggests an American maker. Morgan built his home in 1868–1869, which

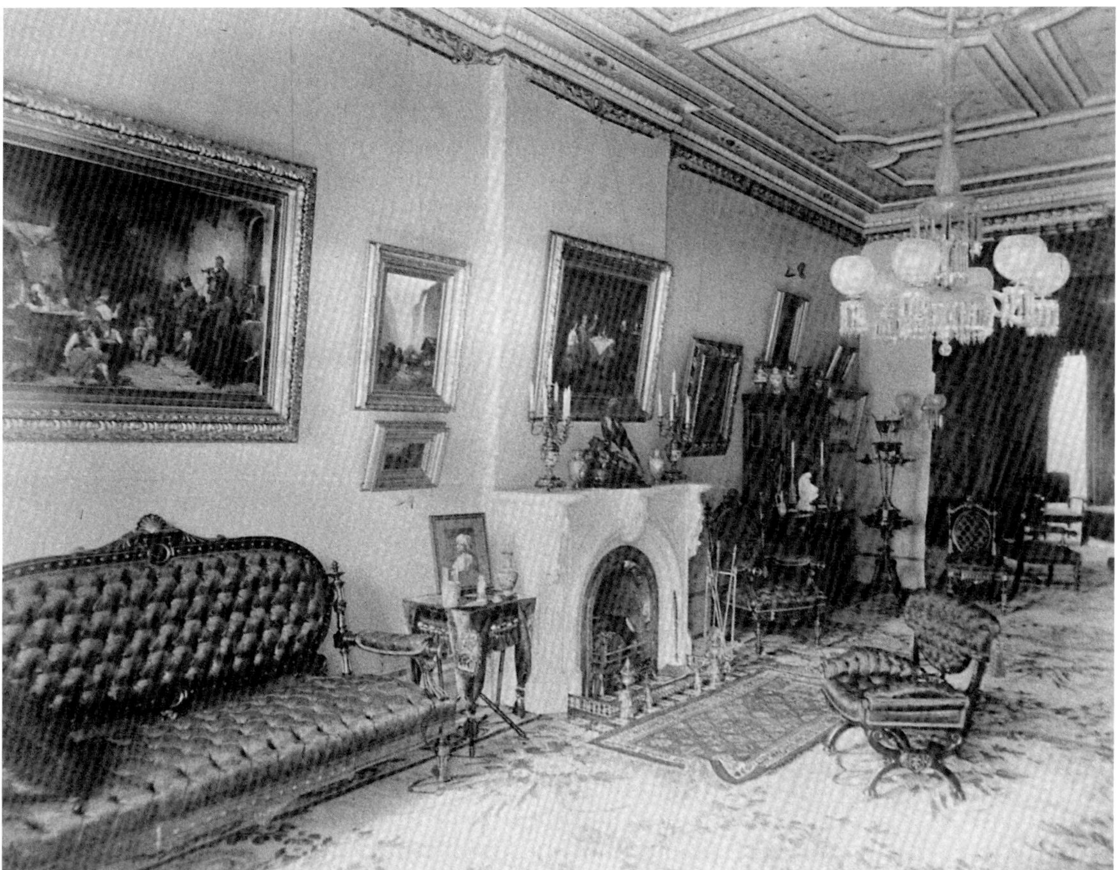

Fig. 1. B. J. Smith. *Front Parlor in the Home of James Lancaster Morgan,* 7 Pierpont Street, Brooklyn, ca. 1879. Museum of the City of New York. Gift of John Hill Morgan and Lancaster Morgan, 27.118.42F.

provides a more likely date for his purchase of the furniture.

The armchair, with its gilt and incised decoration and ebonized surfaces, is comparable to contemporary American furniture by Leon Marcotte (see no. 60), Alexander Roux (see nos. 36, 46, 61), and other European-trained designers and manufacturers in New York who had been influenced by Parisian furniture of the 1850s and 1860s. The maple panels with the mother-of-pearl inlaid stars on the crest and front seat rail, the floating upholstered oval panel in the back, and the open arms create a sense of lightness that contrasts with the ebonized elements. The square seat and rectangular back set off the oval panel and the circular bosses that form the front terminals of the arms, a geometric juxtaposition seen on Louis XVI neoclassical French furniture. Unlike the Marcotte chair in the Crawford Collection, which suggests late-eighteenth-century French furniture as its source, this armchair is an imaginative amalgamation of elements.

NOTE

1. The Morgan furniture has gilt-framed metal medallions at the centers of the crest rails. I am grateful to Dr. Deborah Dependahl Waters, curator of decorative arts, Museum of the City of New York, for showing me the Morgan parlor set in 1994 and calling my attention to photographs of the Morgan interiors in their archives. The tufted upholstery on the set in the photographs was the inspiration for reupholstering the Crawford armchair. A matching armchair without the inlaid stars on the crest and front seat rail is in the Lightner Museum, St. Augustine, Florida.

71.

Armchair, ca. 1875

New York or possibly Europe
Ebony, aspen, and yellow pine, with marquetry of ivory, mother-of-pearl, and light woods, and modern replacement silk
38¾ × 26¾ × 35 inches
Inscription: In a white banner worked in marquetry on back of chair, Kennedy family coat of arms above *AVISE LA FINE*
1983.196

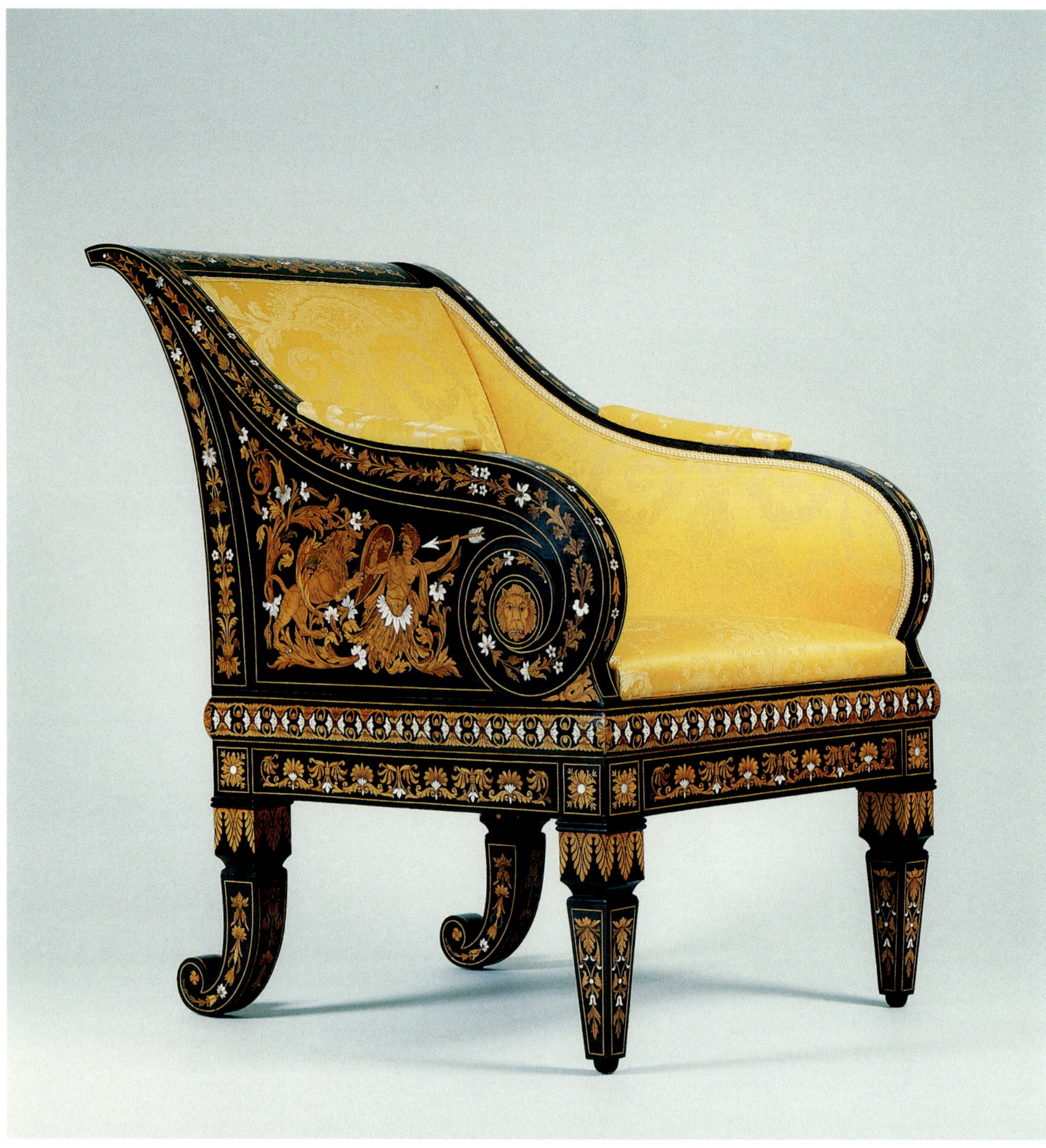

By THE 1870S, elaborate marquetry furniture was the height of fashion in New York, and manufacturers such as Herter Brothers (see nos. 107–110) specialized in this process. The Crawford armchair—with its scrolled crest rail, arms, and rear legs, its straight front legs, generous proportions, and marquetry ornament—is a finely crafted 1870s interpretation of a form generally associated with early-nineteenth-century European and American neoclassical furniture. The line of bell flowers on each arm is typical of neoclassical furniture decoration. The marquetry on the sides complements the classical shape of the chair; it depicts Hercules with his shield and spear in combat with the Nemean lion.

The chair, bearing the Kennedy family coat of arms (see rear view), was possibly first owned by David Sprout Kennedy (fig. 1), the brother-in-law of James Lenox, whose private library ultimately became part of the New York Public Library. Lenox owned at least two related armchairs, also emblazoned with his coat of arms and side marquetry panels depicting mythological creatures: a griffin and Pegasus. Two additional armchairs were owned by Dr. I. Wyman Drummond for his private library in New York. Although nine such armchairs are currently known in museums and private collections, no maker has yet been identified with this distinctive group.[1] However, the affluence of the owners makes it possible that the chairs were purchased in Europe, or perhaps ordered commercially through one of New York's prominent makers and retailers at the time.

NOTE

1. A mate to the Crawford chair, also with the Kennedy family coat of arms, is in The Metropolitan Museum of Art, and another is in a private collection. The Lenox family crest is on similar armchairs in the Museum of the City of New York and the Power House Museum in Ultimo, part of the Museum of Applied Arts and Sciences in Haymarket, New South Wales, Australia. Of four known armchairs without coats of arms, one is in the Brooklyn Museum of Art and one is in the Los Angeles County Museum of Art. A third was sold at Sotheby's Vancouver in 1980, and a fourth, acquired in a San Francisco antiques shop in 1971, is in a private collection.

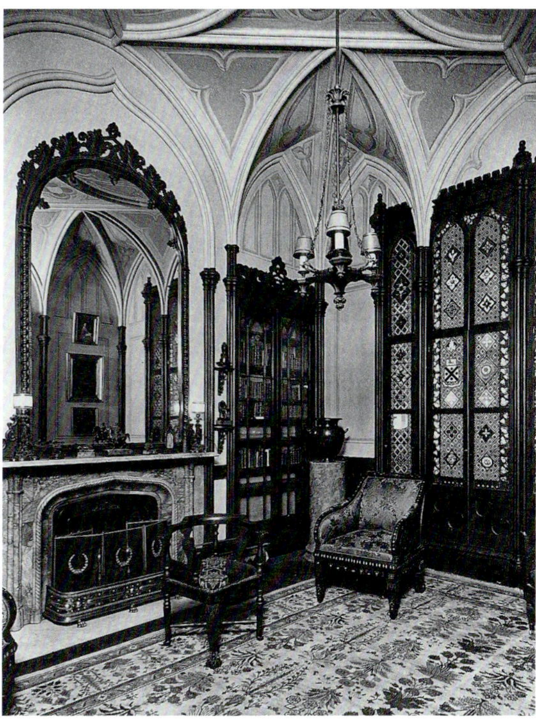

Fig. 1. *Residence of David Sprout Kennedy, Library,* ca. 1920. Museum of the City of New York. Gift of Mrs. Graeme Donald, 32.164.9.

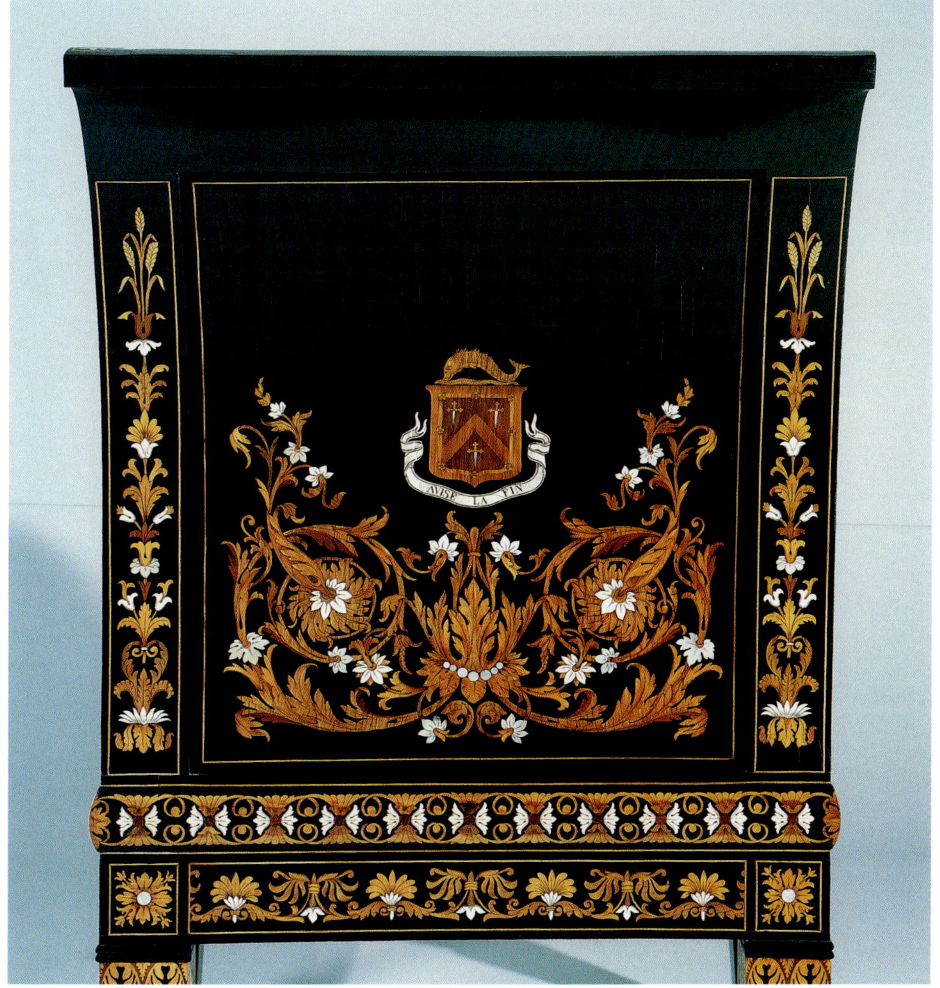

Rear view

Egyptian Taste

A PAIR OF GORHAM silver saltcellars, an armchair from a parlor set, a pair of pedestals, and a colorful mantel garniture are evidence of the American fascination with ancient Egypt in the 1870s and 1880s. Europeans had been intrigued by Egypt since Napoleon's invasion of northern Africa at the turn of the nineteenth century, and designers in London and Paris had incorporated Egyptian elements into their work soon afterward. In the United States, ancient Egyptian forms were introduced into architecture in the first half of the century as part of a general interest in the ancient world that developed out of late neoclassicism. The 1876 Centennial Exposition in Philadelphia, which attracted wide press coverage and ten million visitors, sparked an interest in the remote and exotic cultures represented in many of the exhibits. The temple facade of the Egyptian Court at the Exposition was inscribed "EGYPT-SOUDAN—THE OLDEST PEOPLE OF THE WORLD SENDS ITS MORNING GREETINGS TO THE YOUNGEST NATION" (fig. 1). It drew national attention, reinforcing the widely held nineteenth-century notion of Egypt as the earliest civilization. This fascination with Asia, the Middle East, and historic European cultures had a profound effect on American design during the last quarter of the nineteenth century and well into the twentieth. What is now called the Egyptian revival style of the 1870s and 1880s had its beginnings in the 1860s, and like so many styles in the history of American decorative art, it was introduced in silver a few years earlier than in other media.[1]

By the end of the 1860s, the Gorham Manufacturing Company in Providence, Rhode Island, was the world's largest maker of silverwares. The pair of silver saltcellars (no. 72) in the Crawford Collection was made in 1870, in the Egyptian style Gorham had introduced in the late 1860s. A related saltcellar appears in the Gorham casting

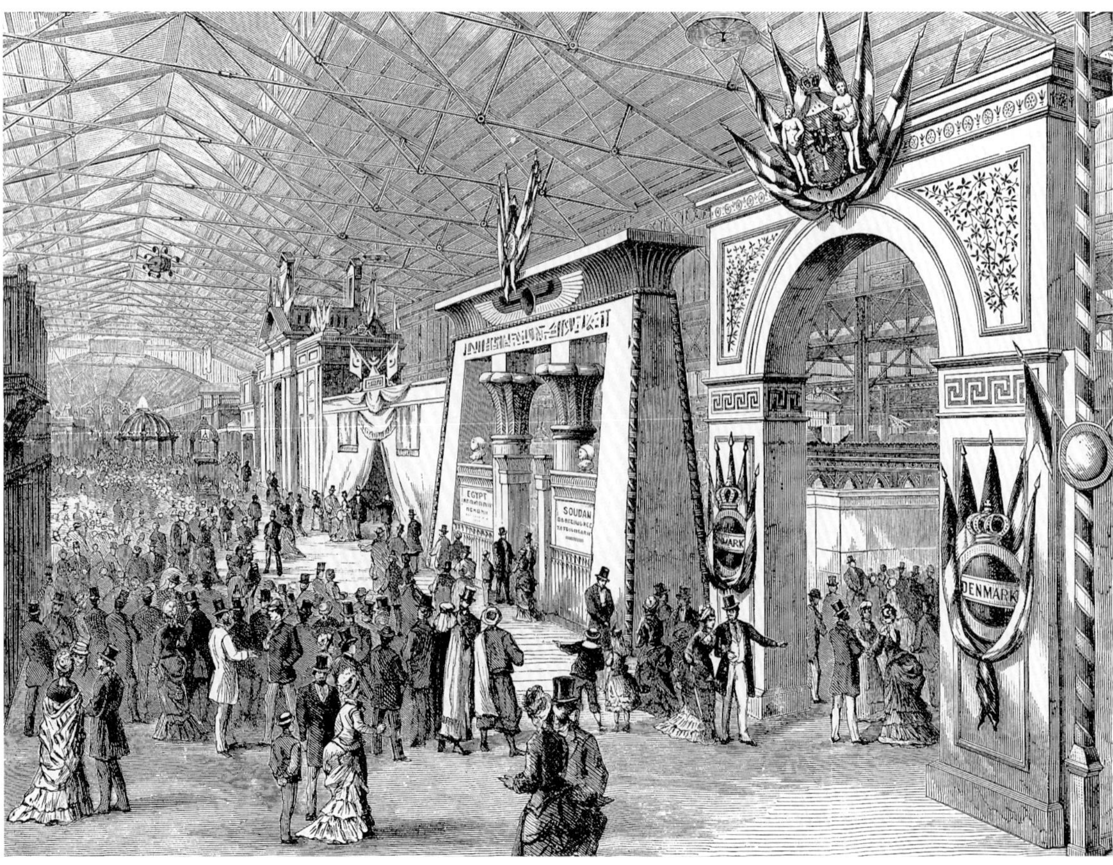

Fig. 1. View inside the Main Building, showing the Spanish, Egyptian, and Danish Courts. From James D. McCabe, *The Illustrated History of the Centennial Exhibition, Held in Commemoration of the One Hundredth Anniversary of American Independence* (Philadelphia: National Publishing Company, 1876).

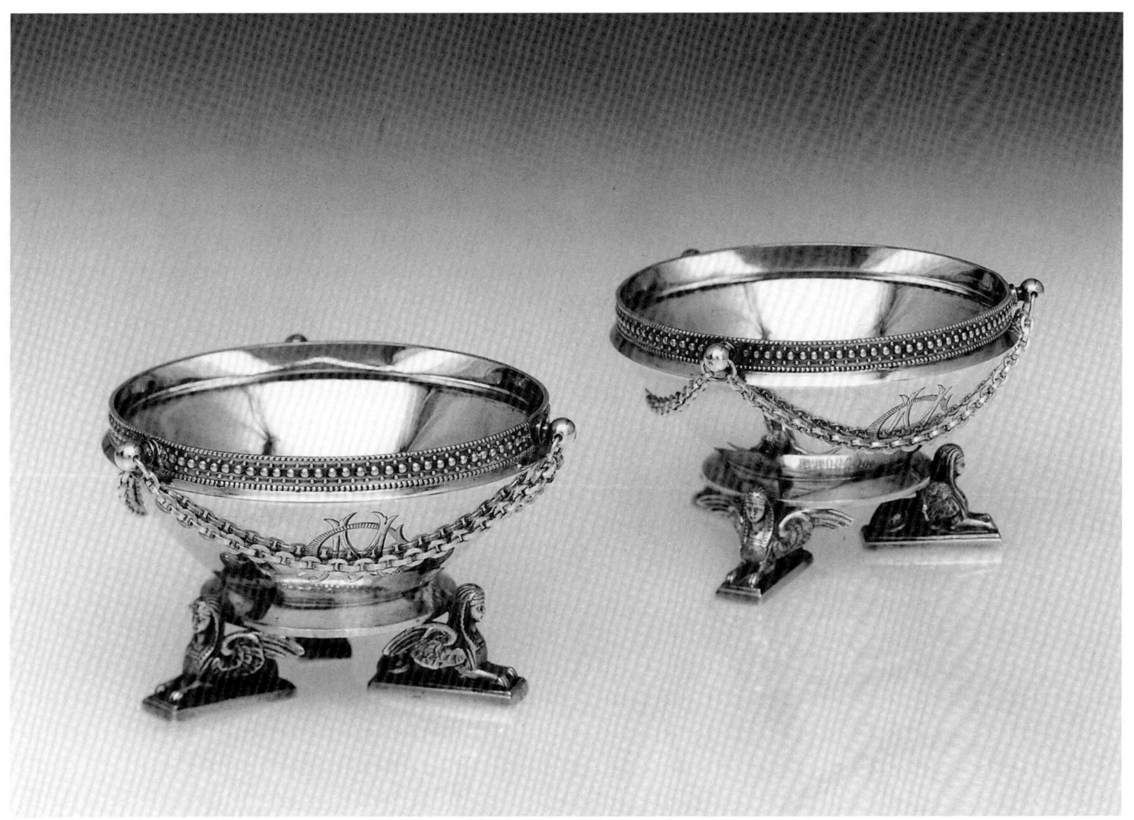

72.

Pair of Saltcellars, 1870

Gorham Manufacturing Company (1831–present), Providence, Rhode Island
Silver
Each 2¼ × 3¾ × 3¾ inches
Marks: Impressed on bottom of each, a rampant lion facing right, an anchor, and a *G* in a shield/ *Sterling/410/C*
Inscriptions: Engraved on sides of each, intertwined *MC*
1991.356.1–.2

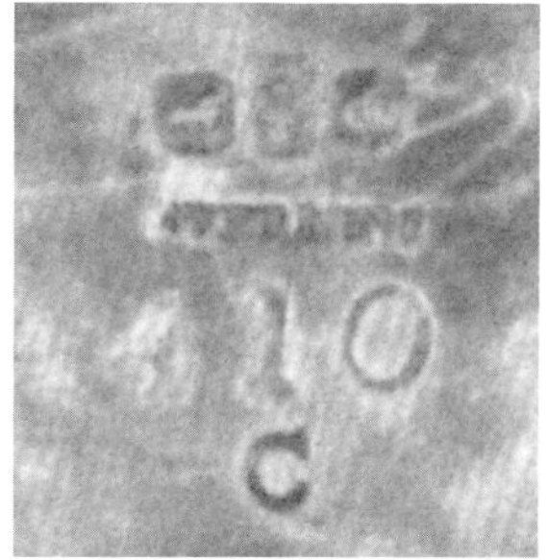

book (fig. 2),[2] and it may have been designed by either George Wilkinson, who became chief designer at Gorham in 1860 (see no. 57), or Thomas J. Pairpoint, who joined the firm in 1868 and designed Gorham's Century Vase for the Centennial Exposition. Saltcellars at the table were a European tradition dating from the Middle Ages, and the lavish use of sterling silver in the production of the Crawford saltcellars suggests how extensively sterling was used for table articles at the time.

By the 1870s, Egyptian taste was expressed in other areas of the decorative arts besides silver. This parlor armchair (no. 73) illustrates the loose and inventive American interpretations of Egyptian themes at the time. The overall form of the chair, with its rectangular back and trumpet-turned legs, may have been drawn from early nineteenth-century French designs based on classical prototypes. The angular details that do resemble the popular notion of Egyptian design are based on Greek and Roman classical sources, particularly the swags in the back of the chair. The winged orb, an ancient Egyptian symbol of

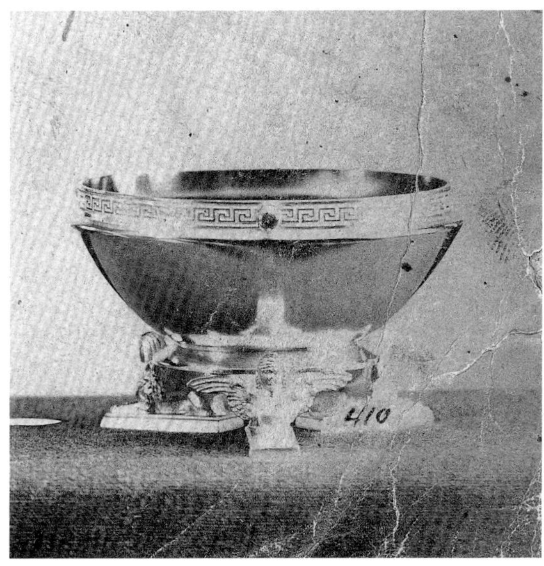

Fig. 2. Saltcellar from the Gorham casting book, vol. 1, p. 24.

73.

Armchair, ca. 1875

Probably New York
Ebonized cherry with gilt decoration and upholstered in replaced nineteenth-century silk
31½ × 28 × 26 inches
1983.195

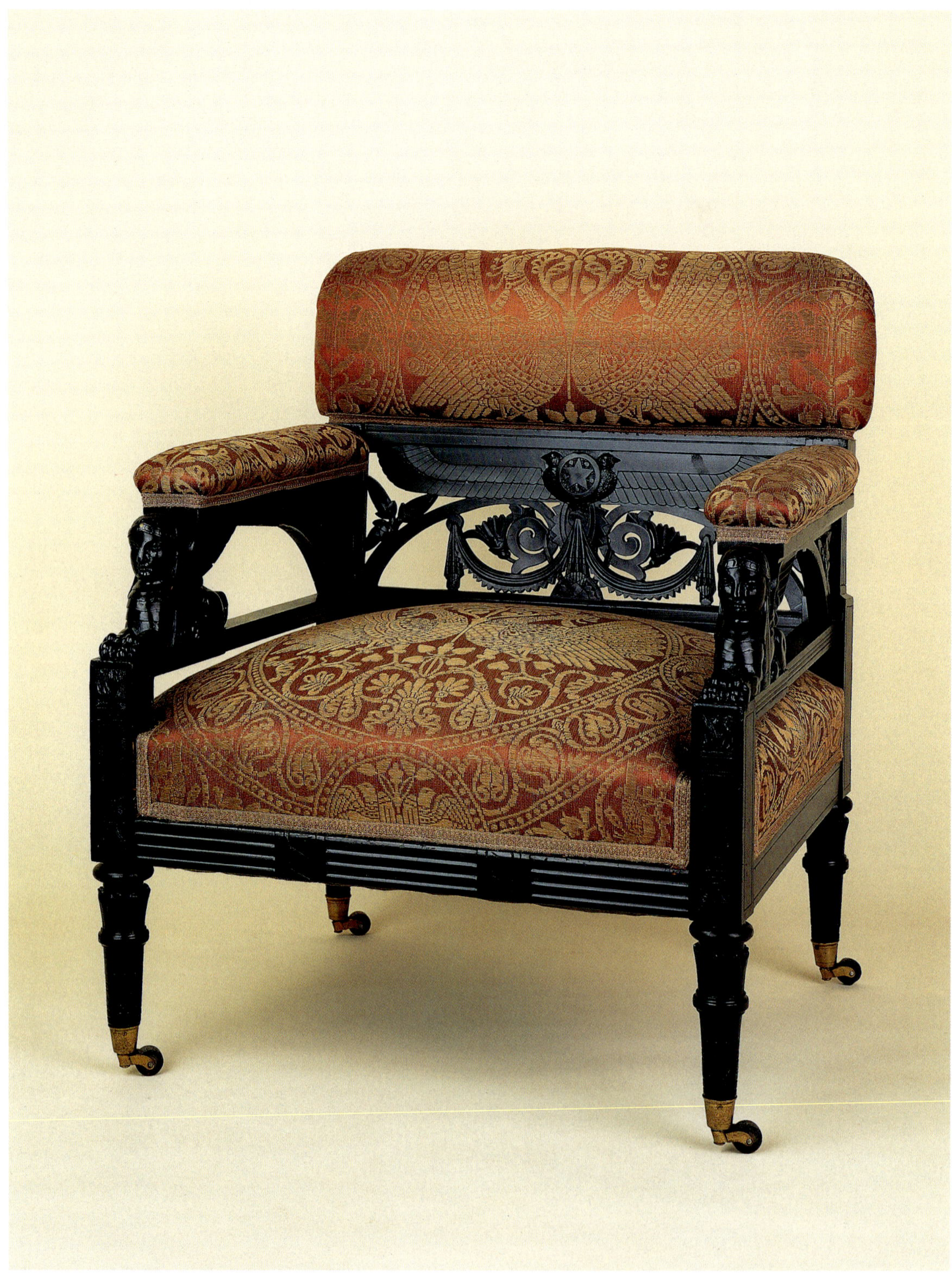

eternity, is incorporated into the back. Lotus blossoms, freely adapted and in various stages of bloom, are included in the back and arm supports. The sphinx arm supports owe their form to the ancient Egyptian monument, but the faces are based on Greek, Roman, and Renaissance sculpture. The chair design was not meant to reproduce an Egyptian artifact, but rather to apply decorations popularly associated with ancient Egypt to a contemporary form.[3]

The pair of pedestals (no. 74) incorporates the sloping, battered shapes, coved moldings, and stylized feather carving seen in the temple facade at the Centennial Exposition's Egyptian Court. The winged orb in the back of the Crawford chair is here adapted to ornament the front corners of the pedestals at the stepped bases. The incised gilt decoration in the inset front panels—simplified papyrus plants—may have been adapted from Owen Jones's influential 1856 illustrated book *The Grammar of Ornament.* Jones admired the stylizations of nature in Egyptian art and was critical of the realistic renderings on furniture in the 1850s, such as those of John Henry Belter (see no. 44). Jones observed that Egyptian motifs like the papyrus and lotus, "symbolizing food for the body and mind," were never "too servile imitation of the type as might be plucked" for design purposes.[4]

This mantel garniture set (no. 75), probably made in France and retailed in Providence, Rhode Island, by Tilden-Thurber Company, is an especially flamboyant late-nineteenth-century interpretation of Egyptian-inspired decoration.

74.

Pair of Pedestals,
ca. 1875

Probably New York
Ebonized cherry with incised and gilt decorations
Each 42 × 25 × 16 inches
1984.150.1–.2

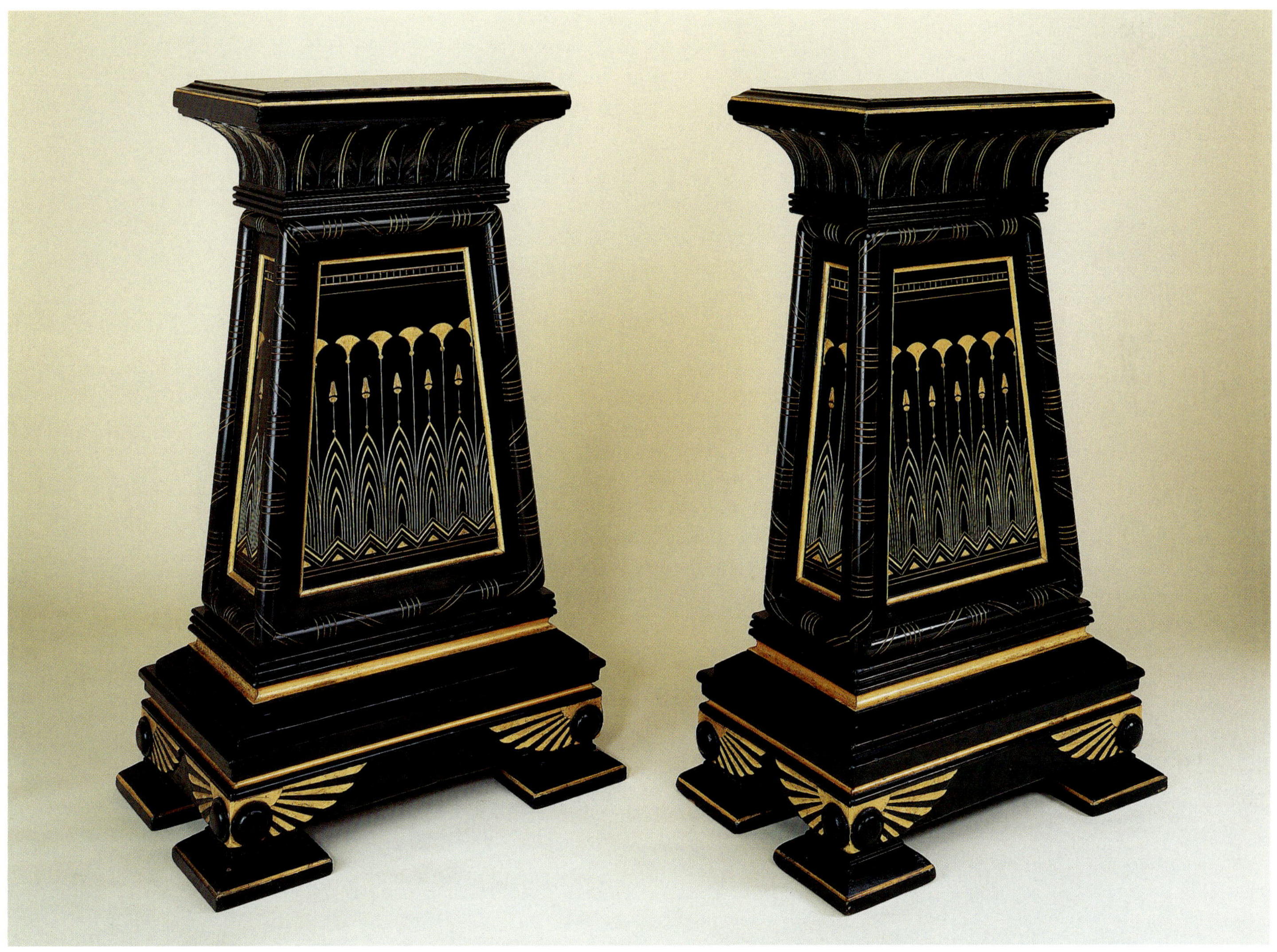

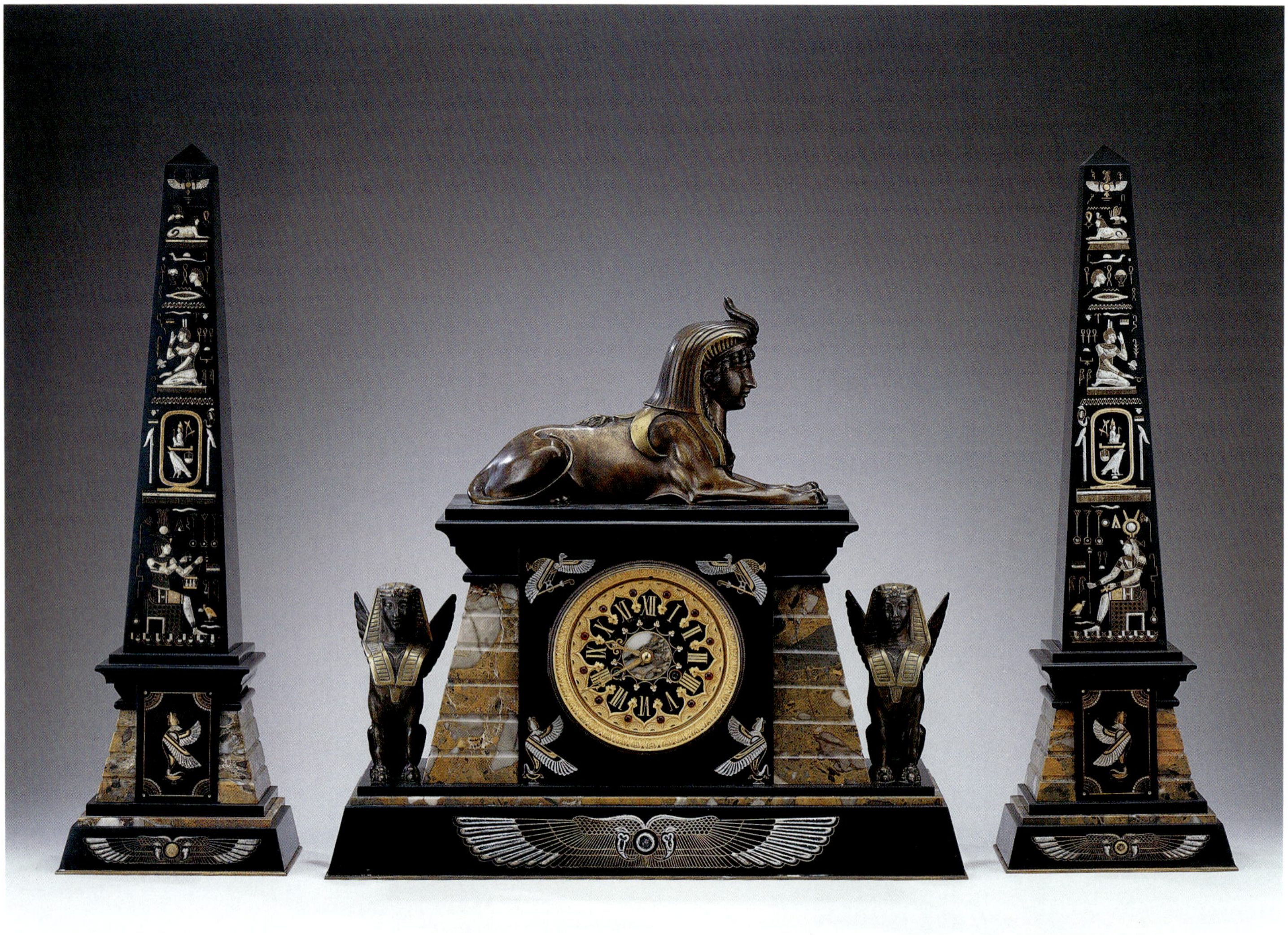

75.

Mantel Garniture,
ca. 1875

Retailed by Tilden-Thurber Company (1856–present), Providence, Rhode Island; probably made in Paris
Marble, gilt-bronze, silver, semiprecious stones, and concrete
Clock: 17½ × 19⅜ × 6¾ inches
Obelisks: Each 27½ × 7 × 5 inches
Mark: Applied in raised letters on clock face, *TILDEN THURBER & CO./Providence*
1984.135.1–.3

Gilt-metal garniture sets were manufactured in New York, Philadelphia, and Boston and were sold wholesale to jewelry and luxury goods emporiums nationally (see nos. 50–51). After the Civil War, mantel garniture sets often included clocks and were increasingly complex combinations of materials with distinctive motifs (fig. 3). These larger and later garnitures were usually made in Paris and imported and sold by American luxury dealers.[5] On this garniture, a variety of European-associated Egyptian elements were freely interpreted and combined to create a decoration strongly linked to contemporary interior design. Both the clock and the matching obelisks were set on battered pedestals, each decoratively incised with a winged orb. As on the arm supports of the parlor armchair, the head of the sphinx crowning the clock owes as much to Ro-

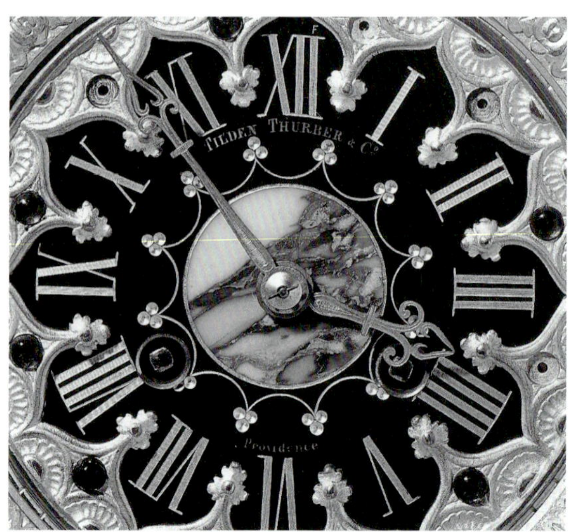

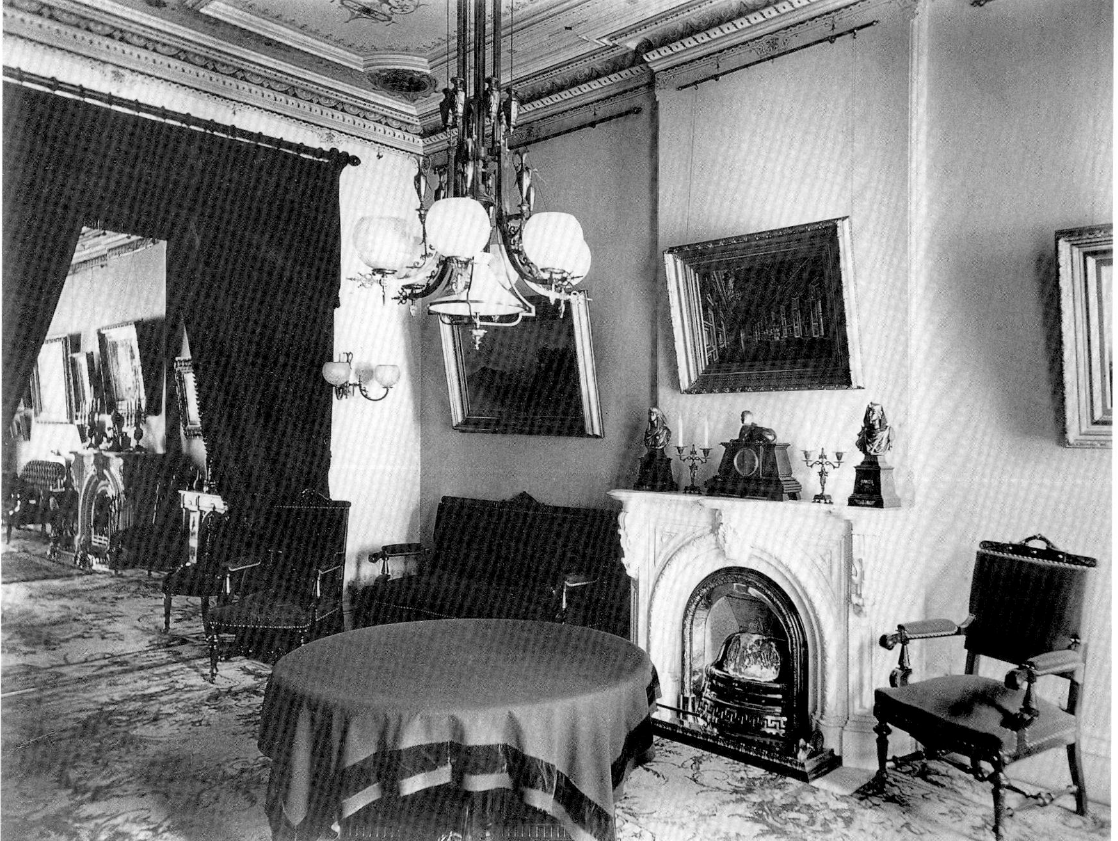

Fig. 3. Butler. *Dining Room Looking West in the Home of James Lancaster Morgan,* 7 Pierpont Street, Brooklyn. 1880–82. Museum of the City of New York, Gift of John Hill Morgan and Lancaster Morgan, 27.228.42H.

man and Greek sources as to Egyptian styles. The ogee arches framing the clock face were drawn from Middle Eastern architectural prototypes. Besides the sphinx, the most recognizable Egyptian forms in the garniture are the flanking obelisks, which may have been inspired by the gift of the obelisk of Alexandria from the government of Egypt to New York. The obelisk, built by Pharaoh Thutmosis III, was dedicated in Central Park behind The Metropolitan Museum of Art on February 22, 1881. The extensive media coverage assured a national awareness of what was popularly called Cleopatra's Needle.[6]

NOTES

1. The nineteenth- and twentieth-century European and American interest in ancient Egypt and its cultural and design consequences is documented in Hudson River Museum 1990, and National Gallery of Canada 1994. For a discussion of Egyptian taste in nineteenth-century American architecture, see Carrott 1978. The Egyptian Court at the Centennial Exposition is discussed in Hudson River Museum 1990, p. 3.

2. Carpenter 1997 is the most comprehensive history of the Gorham Manufacturing Company. A small bowl with the same sphinx supports as the Crawford saltcellar and bearing Gorham's "B" year mark for 1869 is illustrated on p. 69, fig. 80. Additional accounts of Gorham's history can be found in The Metropolitan Museum of Art 1986, pp. 433–434; and Venable 1994, which includes a full bibliography of documentary sources. The Gorham casting books of photographs are now in the John Hay Research Library, Brown University. Gorham Egyptian revival silver is discussed in Cramer 1992. The "C"s in the mark of the Crawford salts stand for the year of manufacture, 1870. Gorham used codes in their marks indicating the year of manufacture, beginning with "A" in 1868, through "Q" in 1884, after which they used symbols. See Carpenter 1997, pp. 230–231, for explanation and code chart.

3. The Crawford armchair nearly matches examples in the Museum of Art, Rhode Island School of Design, and the Philadelphia Museum of Art. See Monkhouse and Michie 1986, pp. 193–194, no. 136. Monkhouse and Michie point to a design for a settee in Percier and Fontaine, *Recueil des decorations et interieures* (Paris, 1801, reissued 1812), pl. 27, as a possible source for these chairs.

4. Jones 1986, pl. IV, no. 17, and p. 22.

5. See National Gallery of Canada 1994, pp. 463–464, no. 309, in which the Crawford garniture is cited. A garniture similar to the Crawford example and inscribed "Tiffany and Company, New York" on the dial is in The Metropolitan Museum of Art; see The Metropolitan Museum of Art 1970, no. 232.

6. The Metropolitan Museum of Art 1993, p. 19.

Union Porcelain Works

SINCE ABOUT 1854, William Boch and Brothers (see no. 42), and later the Union Porcelain Company, produced mostly bone china door and furniture hardware and hotel, restaurant, and fancy wares. Shortly before the Civil War, New York businessman and master builder Thomas Carll Smith invested in the company. He assumed ownership by 1863 in partial payment of debts, when the economic strain of the war caused the company to close. With no real experience in the business, Smith visited the porcelain factories at Sèvres in France and Stoke-on-Trent in England to observe hard-paste porcelain production. Smith renamed his firm Union Porcelain Works, and while continuing to produce staple utilitarian wares, he replaced the company's bone-china clay body with true hard-paste porcelain in 1864 (fig. 1). Union Porcelain Works was the first American concern to successfully apply underglaze polychrome decoration on true porcelain.[1]

By 1874, Smith must have decided that Union Porcelain Works should pursue artistic production, as he hired the German-born sculptor Karl L. H. Müller as chief designer. Müller had trained

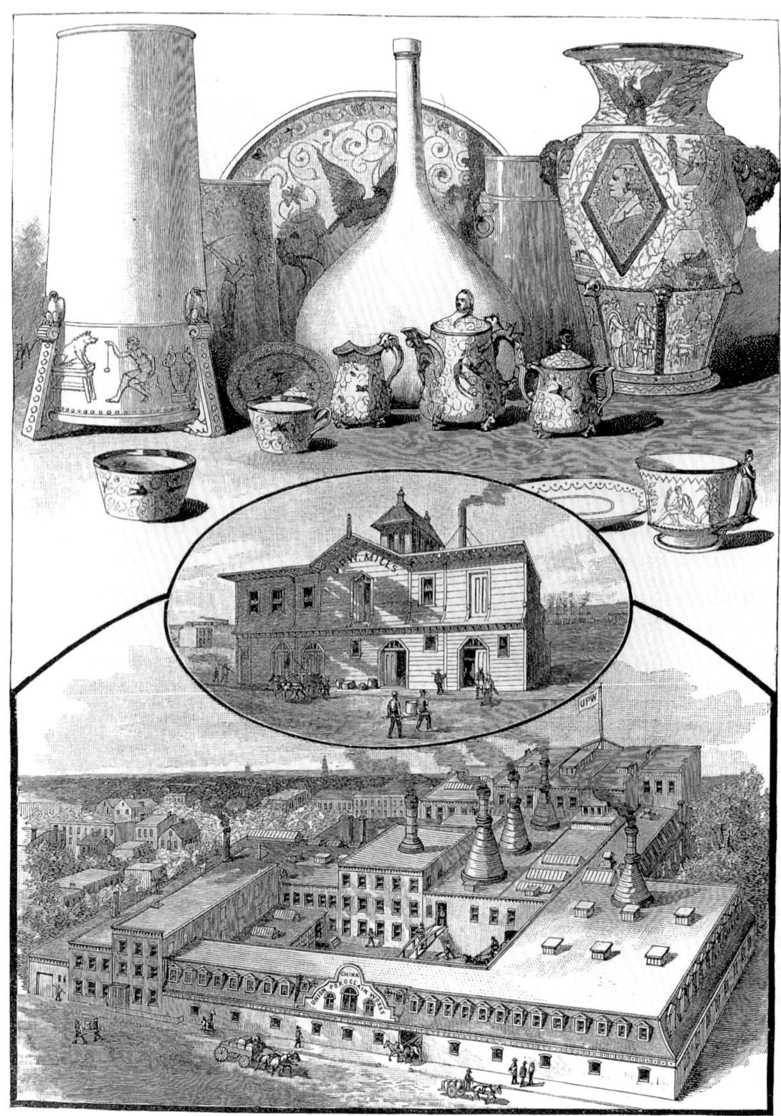

Fig. 1. View of the Union Porcelain Works and wares. From Henry R. Stiles, *The Civil, Political, Professional and Ecclesiastical History and Commercial and Industrial Record of the County of Kings and the City of Brooklyn, N.Y. from 1683 to 1884* (New York: W. W. Munsell and Co., 1884), p. 763.

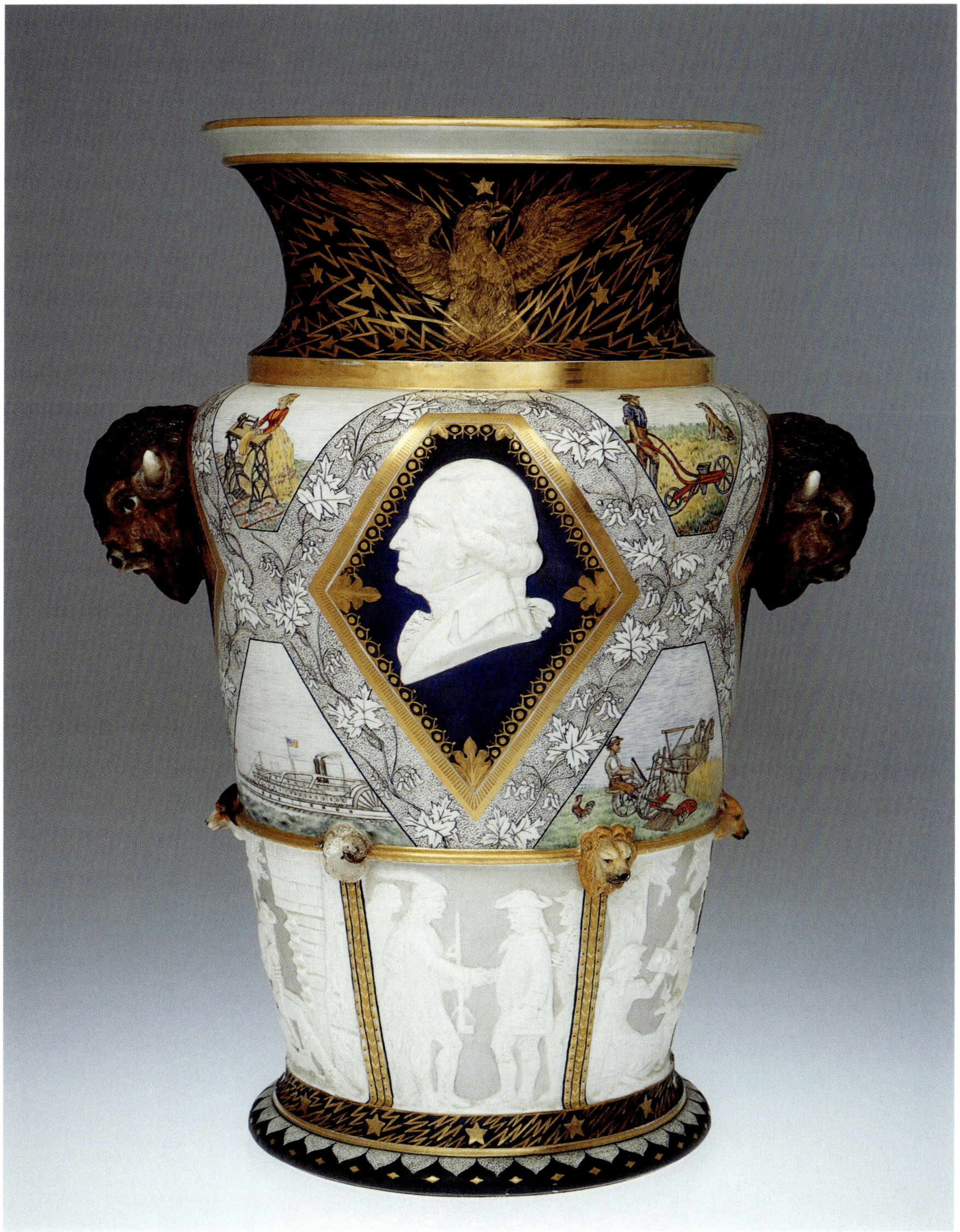

76.

Century Vase, 1876

Manufactured by Union Porcelain Works (1863–ca. 1922), Greenpoint, Brooklyn; designed by Karl L. H. Müller (1820–1887)
Porcelain, gilt decoration
22½ × 12 × 12 inches
Marks: On bottom, *Century Vase/Exhibited at Centennial/Exhibition at Philadelphia/Manufactured 1876/By Union Porcelain Works/Greenpoint; UPW* with an eagle holding an *S* in its beak
1986.163

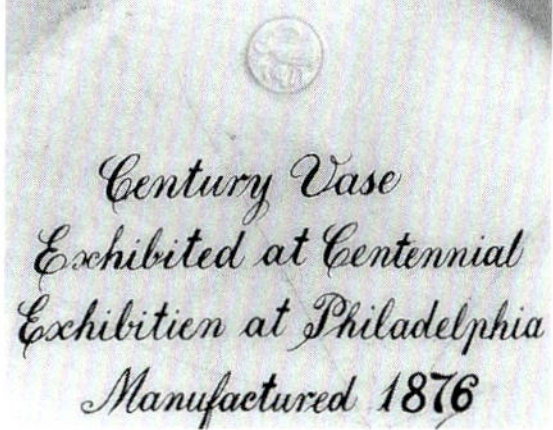

77.

Pedestal, 1876

Union Porcelain Works (1863–ca. 1922), Greenpoint, Brooklyn; designed by Karl L. H. Müller (1820–1887)
Porcelain
45 × 16 × 16 inches
Marks: On side, double-incised circle painted white surrounding incised *K.L./1876/H.M.* around Native American with headdress on horseback; on opposite side, double-incised circle painted white with raised eagle holding an *S* in its beak beneath incised *U.P.W.;* enclosed in a black oval on inside base of pedestal, *MANUFACTURED/BY/UNION/PORCELAIN/WORKS/GREENPOINT, N.Y.*
Inscription: Painted in black, *ELECTRA*
1997.232

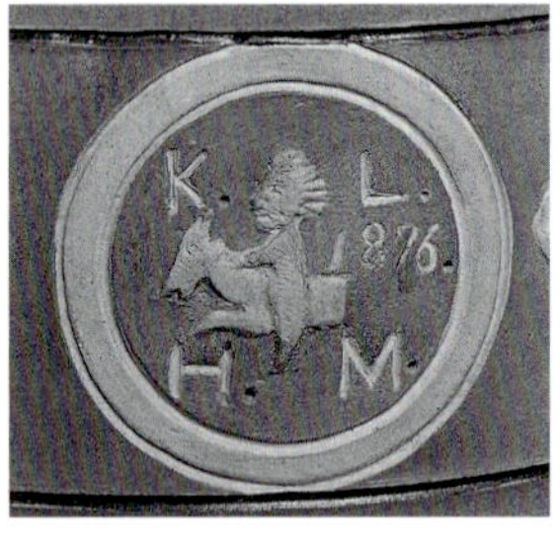

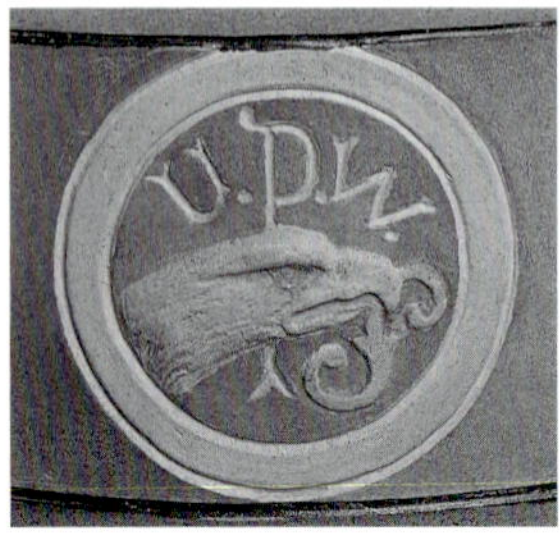

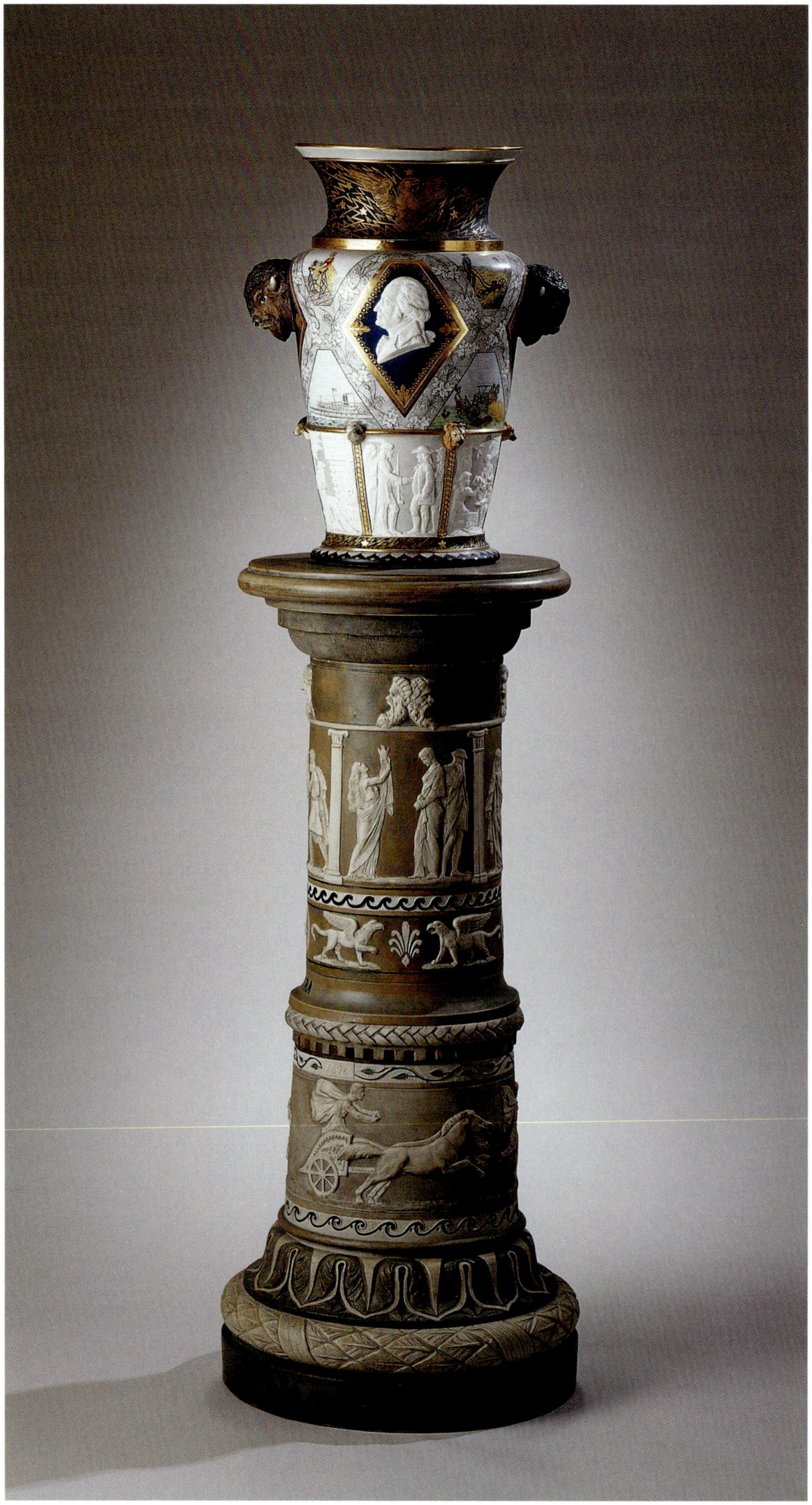

in a German goldsmith's shop, and after studying sculpture in Paris, he came to New York around 1850. Müller studied at the National Academy of Design in New York, and his sculptures were shown in various exhibitions in New York and elsewhere. He and his brother designed and manufactured ornamental sculpture in bronze and other materials for domestic use. After his brother's death, Müller joined the Union Porcelain Works as a modeler and designer.[2]

In January 1875, the United States Potters Association was formed in Philadelphia, with Thomas Carll Smith as treasurer. At the first formal meetings of ceramic industrialists, the member firms of the association decided to stage displays of products expressing a distinctly national character for the 1876 Centennial Exposition in Philadelphia.[3]

The Union Porcelain Works display featured a pair of Century Vases, inspired by Renaissance and classical models. The Century Vase (no. 76) honored America's colonial history in a frieze of white sculptural vignettes around the base. Above this and around George Washington's profile, technological and industrial progress of the nation's first century was celebrated in painted, polychromed vignettes.[4] For many Americans, Washington's image was a powerful patriotic symbol, and it was ubiquitous at the Centennial Exposition and on its souvenirs. Like the Exposition itself, the Century Vase used American history as a point of departure, but it really focused on the industrial progress of the preceding century. The American themes on the vase were complemented by depictions of bison heads as ornamental handles and heads of other native animals mounted as Renaissance-style decorative bosses.

The original pedestals for the Century Vases depicted scenes from the mythological story of Electra in white relief against an apricot background, reminiscent of Josiah Wedgwood's jasper stoneware of the late eighteenth century. The related pedestal in the Crawford Collection (no. 77) has white figures on a grayish green background. Different molds were used to execute the Crawford pedestal, and it may have been a prototype for the Century Vase pedestals. The Crawford pedestal may also have been used in the company's display at the Centennial Exposition and may have held a "finely executed and remarkably life-like bust of Mr. Thos. Smith, which was cast on his own premises." Whether the pedestal supporting the bust was the Crawford pedestal is not known, since no photograph or print of the Union Porcelain Works display has been found. The related pedestals beneath the Century Vases were specifically described at the time: "At two corners of the large glass case are pedestals upon which a classic story is told in bas-relief."[5] The inclusion of classical motifs on the pedestals and other wares from the Union Porcelain Works Centennial display (fig. 2) was typical of the ongoing revival of late-eighteenth-century neoclassical taste in American furniture and silver of the 1860s and 1870s.

Century Vase
Exhibited at Centennial
Exhibitien at Philadelphia
Manufactured 1876
By Union Porcelain Works
Greenpoint

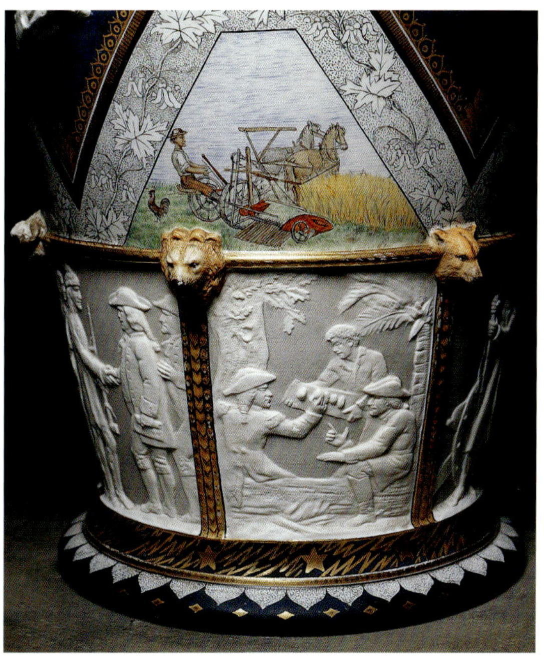

78.

Pitcher, ca. 1876

Union Porcelain Works (1863–ca. 1922), Greenpoint, Brooklyn; designed in 1875 by Karl L. H. Müller (1820–1887)
Bisque porcelain, glazed interior
9 × 6½ × 4½ inches
Mark: Impressed on bottom, eagle head with an *S* in its beak
1984.152

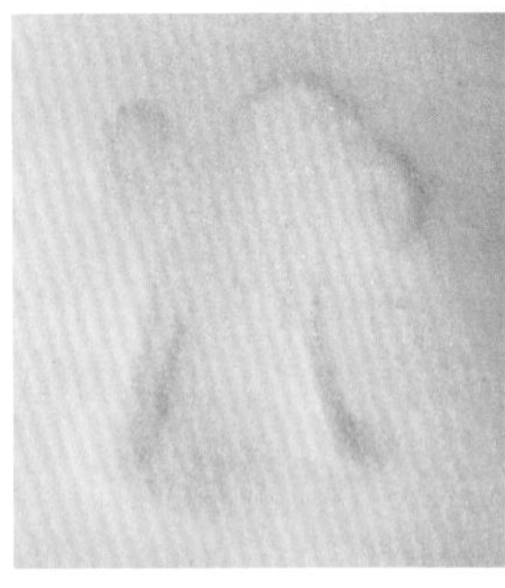

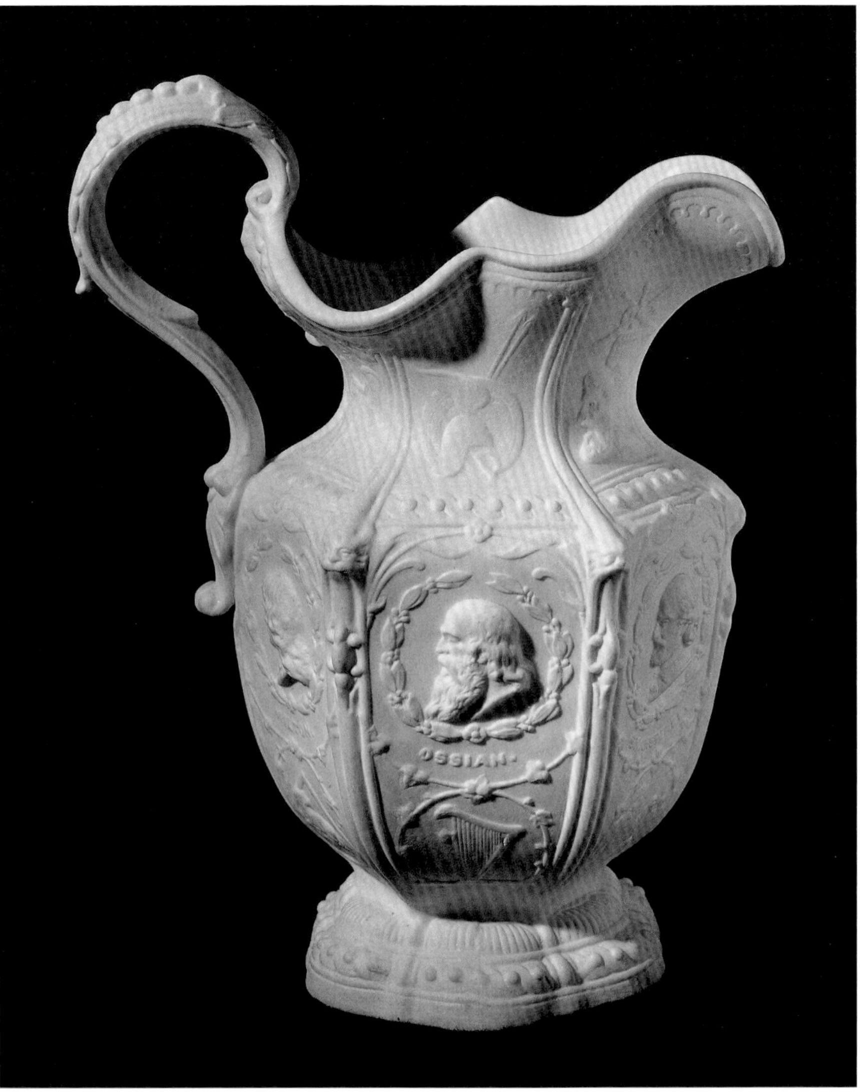

Müller's poets pitcher (no. 78) includes portraits of Homer, Virgil, Ossian, Dante, Shakespeare, and Milton and reflects the nineteenth-century regard for literature that also seems to have been one of Müller's primary interests. A pitcher of this form was included in the Union Porcelain Works display at the Annual American Institute Fair in New York in 1876, where the Century Vases were also exhibited. In his pioneering and comprehensive 1893 book *The Pottery and Porcelain of the United States,* Edwin AtLee Barber described both the Century Vase and the poets pitcher in his section on the Union Porcelain Works. Barber illustrated the poets pitcher and declared it "among the most highly artistic works produced at this factory."[6]

Müller's interests in classical mythology and literature are also seen in a white biscuit porcelain figural group he designed for the Union Porcelain Works in 1877, which depicts a scene from *Oresteia* by Aeschylus (no. 79). Orestes killed his mother and her lover to avenge the murder of his father, Agamemnon, king of Mycenae. The sculptural group shows the shrouded and humiliated Orestes gracefully sprawled over a classical stool at the altar of Athena, Greek goddess of wisdom, where he sought purification from his sin. The presence of the god Apollo, who had ordered Orestes to avenge his father's death, is suggested by the lyre and olive branch beneath Orestes' head and the god's messenger, a raven, perched on Athena's shoulder. In the end,

Athena acquitted Orestes and granted him purification. Because this complex group is the only known example of this model, it has been suggested that it was made in preparation for display at an exposition, possibly the 1878 Exposition Universelle in Paris, but documentation of this is currently lacking.[7]

As early as the Centennial Exposition, Müller was sculpting life-size busts for execution in biscuit, such as this bust of Benjamin Franklin Flanders (no. 80). Born in New Hampshire, by 1842 Flanders was a businessman in New Orleans and later a banker. Having retained his Union sympathies while living in the South, Flanders was appointed mayor of New Orleans after the Civil War and then governor of Louisiana, an office to which he was later elected by popular vote. In 1877, the year Müller created this bust, President Ulysses S. Grant appointed Flanders assistant secretary of the treasury, a position he held until 1886. The history of this bust of Flanders is currently unknown, although Müller was listed as sculptor of a bust of Flanders owned by Thomas Carll Smith in an exhibition at the National Academy of Design in New York in 1878.[8]

In 1884, Henry R. Stiles wrote of the company: "The copying of European designs or patterns is studiously avoided, much originality is displayed and many articles are of such rare artistic beauty, as to excite the wonder and admirations of connoisseurs from all parts of the world." Stiles also noted the obstacles faced by the Union Porcelain Works, not the least of which was "the utter indifference of both the American government, and the people, to efforts and sacrifices for the promotion of our national reputation in industrial art, which in any country of Europe would have been crowned with the highest honors, and have received the most substantial rewards."[9]

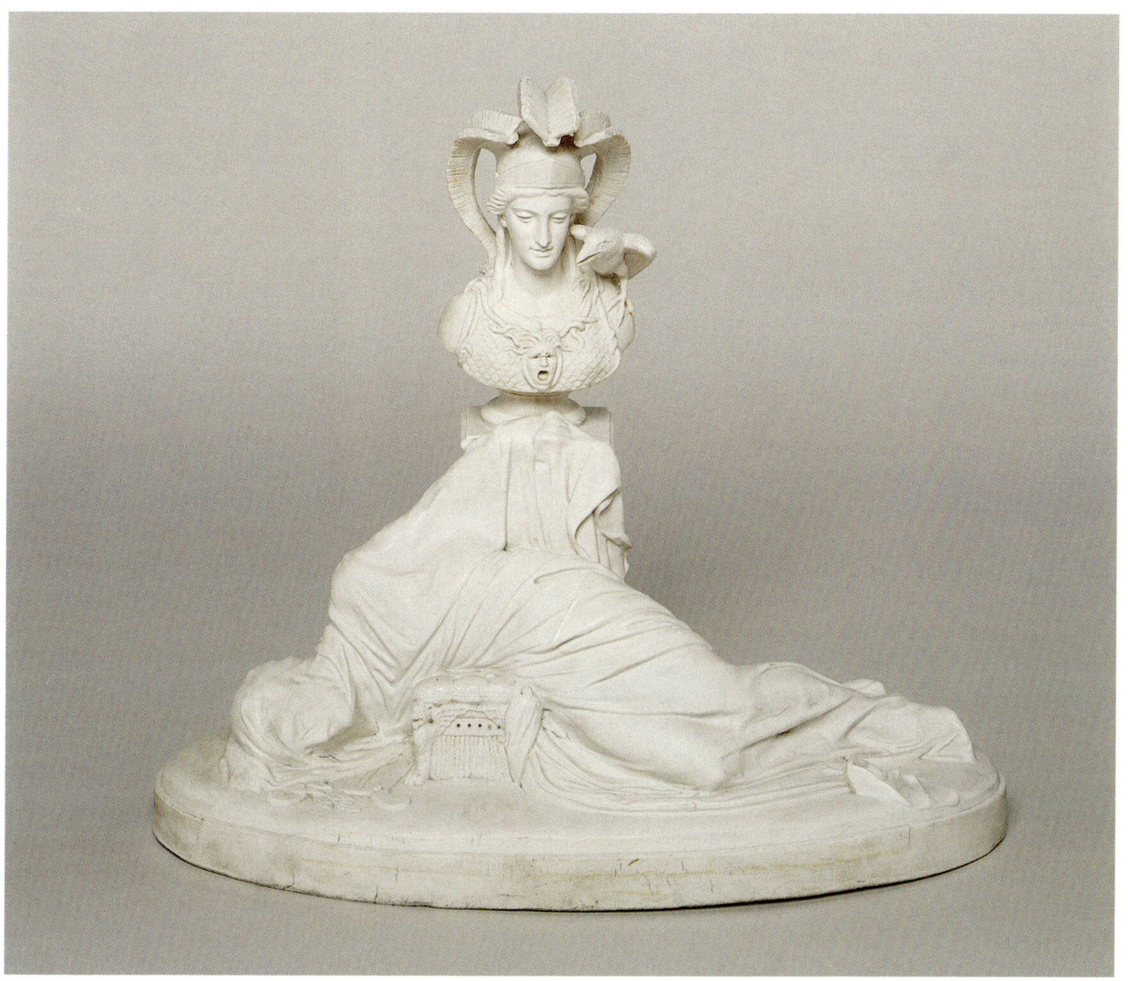

79.

Acquittal of Orestes, 1877

Union Porcelain Works (1863–ca. 1922), Greenpoint, Brooklyn; designed by Karl L. H. Müller (1820–1887)
White biscuit porcelain
18¾ x 22 x 11½ inches
Mark: Incised on lower left side of plinth base, *K.M./U.P.W./1877*
1994.151

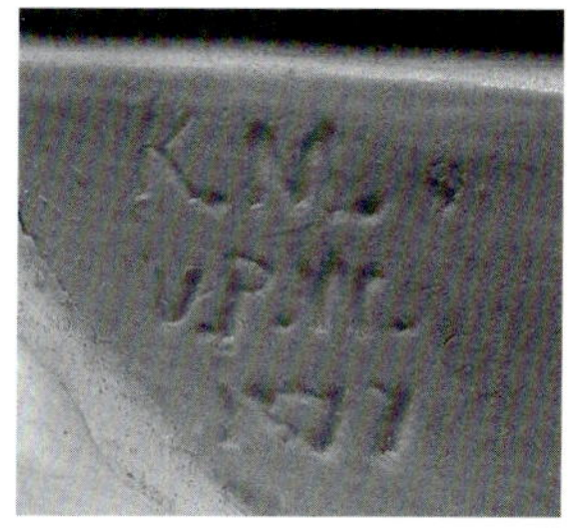

80.

Bust of Benjamin Franklin Flanders, 1877

Union Porcelain Works (1863–ca. 1922), Greenpoint, Brooklyn; designed by Karl L. H. Müller (1820–1887)
Biscuit porcelain
19 × 10½ × 8½ inches
Mark: Incised on back, *U.P.W. 1877.*
1995.180

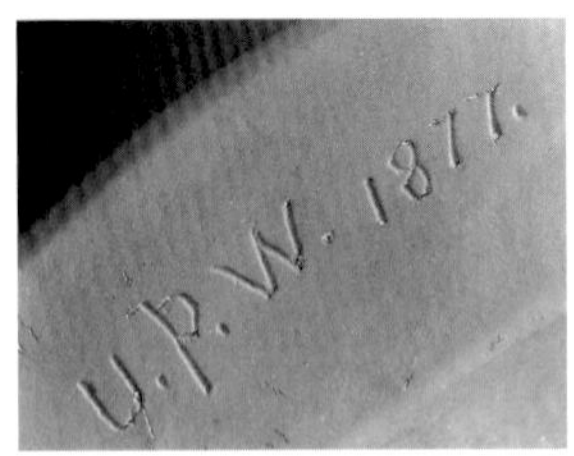

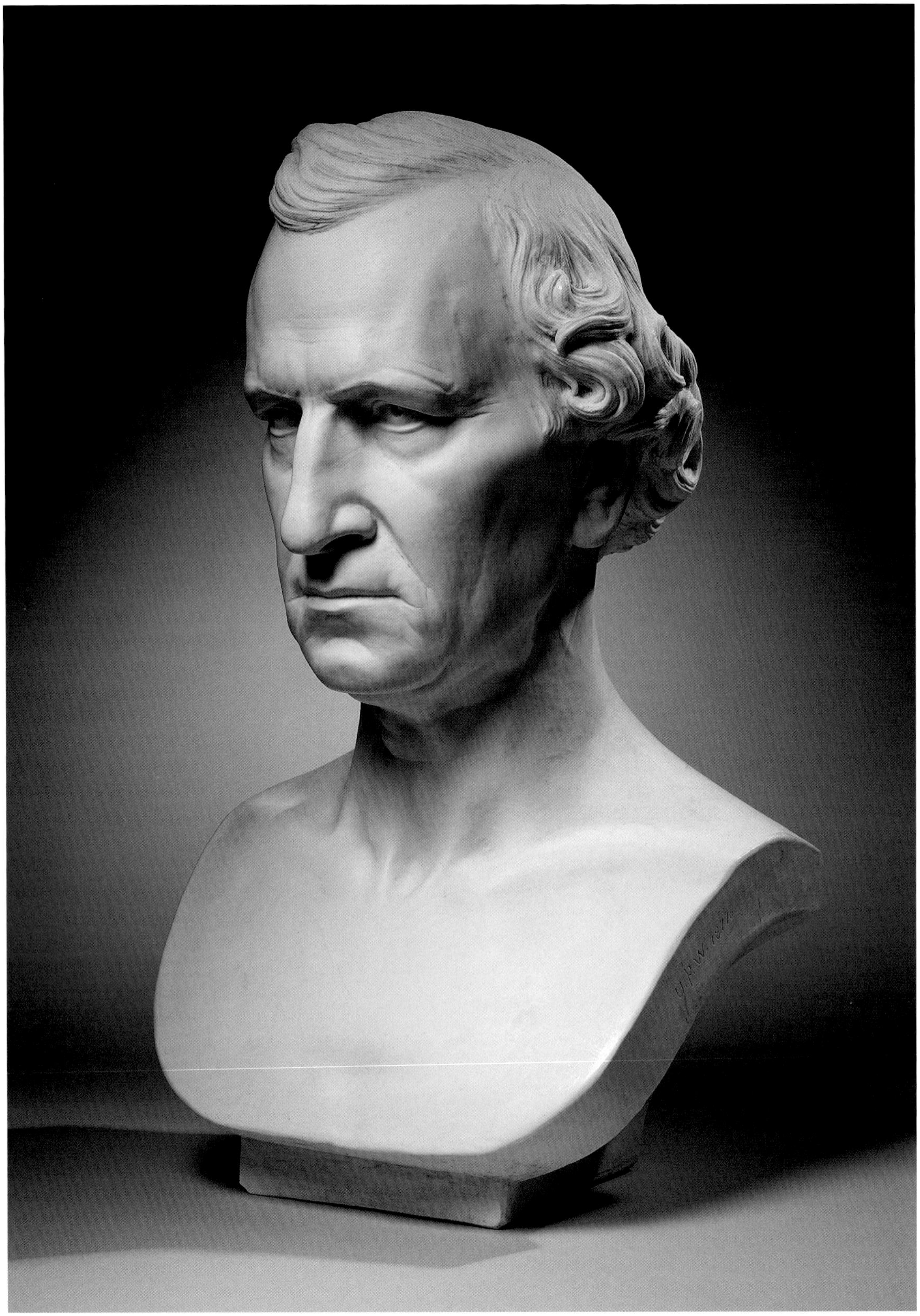

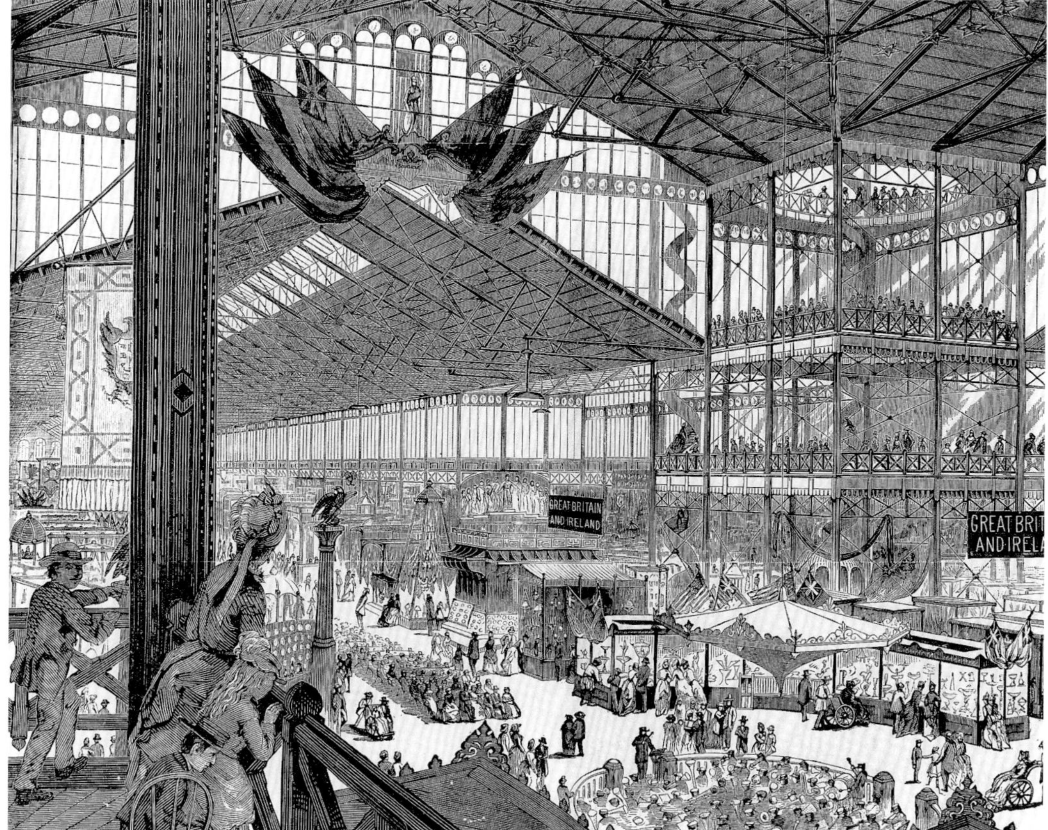

Fig. 2. The Central Aisle of the Main Exhibition Building. From James D. McCabe, *The Illustrated History of the Centennial Exhibition, Held in Commemoration of the One Hundredth Anniversary of American Independence* (Philadelphia: National Publishing Company, 1876).

NOTES

1. The history of the Union Porcelain Works from the time of Smith's ownership of Union Porcelain Company and his travels to European factories is recounted in Stiles 1884, pp. 761–767. Hard-paste porcelain includes kaolin, which allows it to be fired at very high temperatures. Soft-paste, or artificial, porcelain is manufactured with a substitute hardening agent such as bone ash to achieve a higher firing temperature and thus a whiter body, but it is not true porcelain.

2. Müller's career prior to his employment by the Union Porcelain Works is recounted in Frelinghuysen 1989, pp. 157–158.

3. The formation of the United States Potters Association, Smith's role in the organization, and the Centennial Exposition displays are described in J. Stradling 1976, pp. 146–158.

4. The mate to the Crawford Century Vase is in the Brooklyn Museum of Art, a gift of the descendants of Thomas Carll Smith. Other versions of the vase in the same size and smaller also exist, but none have the distinctive decoration of the Brooklyn and Crawford vases. Although Müller actually designed the vase, the concept has been credited to Charles H. L. Smith, son and business associate of the owner of the Union Porcelain Works. See Frelinghuysen 1989, pp. 177–181, nos. 59–60, for illustrations and discussions of the Crawford and Brooklyn vases, as well as a smaller and differently decorated version at The Metropolitan Museum of Art.

5. The Crawford pedestal is illustrated in J. Stradling 1976, p. 149, pl. IV. The pedestals that originally held the Century Vases are now in The Metropolitan Museum of Art and the National Museum of American History, Smithsonian Institution, and they are illustrated and discussed in Frelinghuysen 1989, pp. 174–176. Before its acquisition for the Crawford Collection, this pedestal was owned for many years by a private collector who had purchased it from a dealer on eastern Long Island; the dealer claimed to have acquired it from Nitta Chace, a granddaughter of Thomas Carll Smith. Correspondence, Diana Stradling, September 18, 1995, High Museum of Art document files. The description of the Union Porcelain Works display at the Centennial Exposition is in *Crockery and Glass Journal* 3 (May 25, 1876), p. 15; cited in J. Stradling 1976, pp. 150–151.

6. The probable prototype of the pitcher, dated 1875 and bearing Müller's initials, is illustrated and discussed in Frelinghuysen 1989, pp. 154–155, no. 48. A "Vase in Silver, The Poets" was exhibited by Müller in 1863 at the Fourth Annual Exhibition of the Artists' Fund Society and may have been a predecessor for this design. See ibid., p. 154. Müller also designed the Keramos Vase, inspired by Henry Wadsworth Longfellow's poem "Keramos," for the Centennial Exposition. See ibid., p. 40.

7. Sotheby's, *Fine Americana,* January 23–30, 1993, lot no. 154, suggests that the group might have been made especially for exposition purposes. The Orestes group was formerly in the Walter P. Chrysler Museum in Norfolk, Virginia. Its history before that museum's ownership is unknown.

8. Correspondence, Gary and Diana Stradling, September 2, 1994, High Museum of Art document files; and Dunbar 1935, pp. 291–295. For a general history of the firm, see Barber, *Pottery,* 1976, pp. 252–259.

9. Stiles 1884, pp. 765–766.

81.

Piano, 1876

Hallet, Davis and Company (1843–1890), Boston
Ebonized cherry, spruce, ash, bird's-eye maple, ivory, ebony, and various metals
95 × 82½ × 31¾ inches
Mark: Painted in gold Old English letters at center above keyboard, *Hallet, Davis & Co./ Boston./PATENT*
1983.197

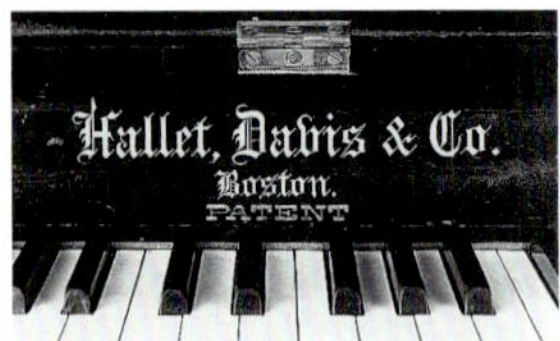

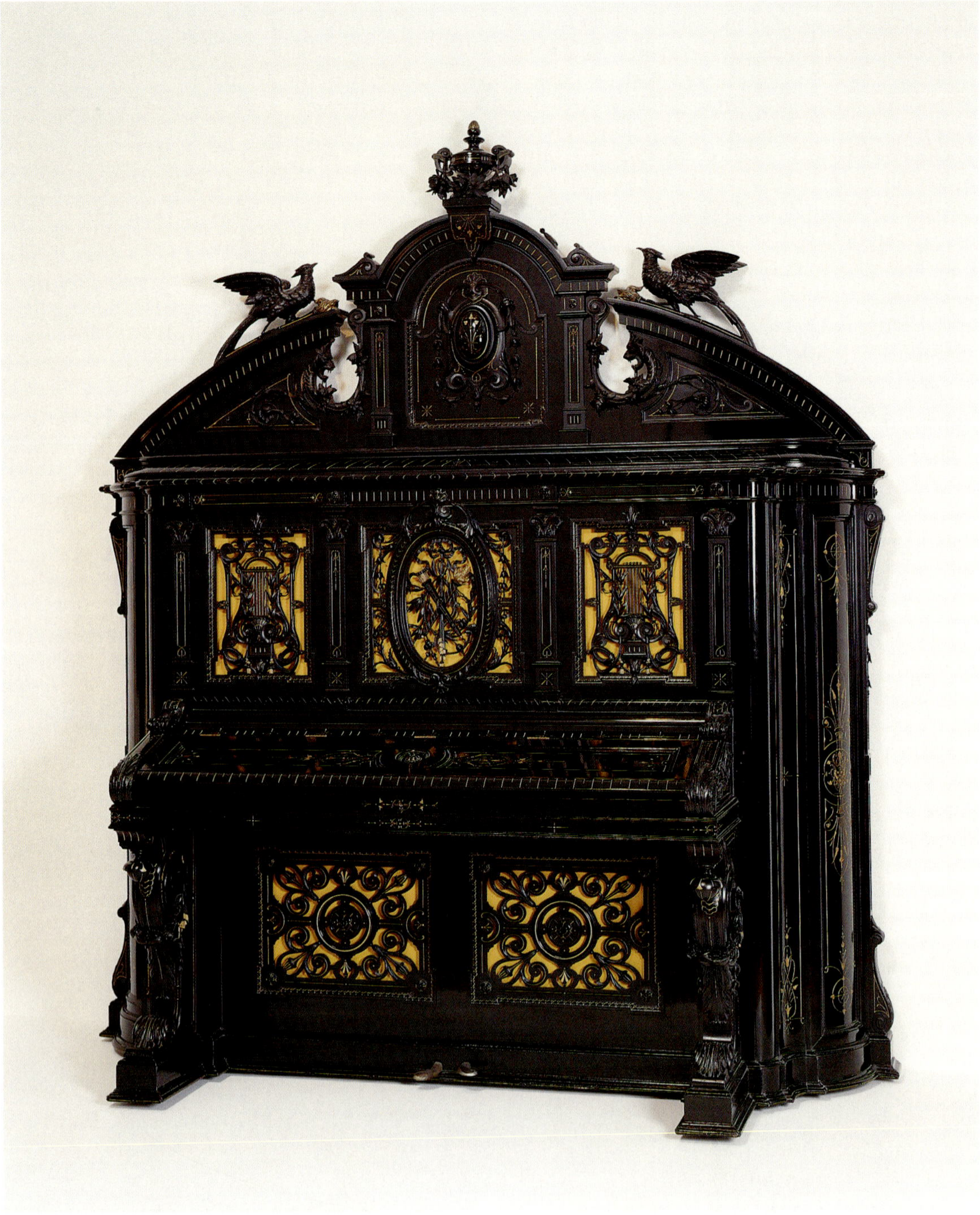

THIS ELABORATE and imposing piano was created for the 1876 Centennial Exposition in Philadelphia. Walter Smith, in the second volume of *The Masterpieces of the Centennial International Exhibition* (1877), described the piano as "the most elaborately constructed instrument of its kind in the exhibition," its "hand-work, the production of skillful carvers . . . the birds and urn on the upper portion and the wreaths at the base, are worked out in full; while the panels, with their wreaths, scrolls, medallions, and symbolic figures, are elaborated with great fidelity of detail" (fig. 1).[1]

In 1876, American industries were still striving to overcome the devastating financial panic of 1873 and the ensuing economic depression that had crippled many businesses. The Centennial Exposition provided an ideal opportunity for firms such as Hallet, Davis and Company to attract national and international recognition. The monumental piano, with its complex carved, gilt, and incised decoration and ebonized surface, epitomized the large-scale and intricately detailed sideboards, cabinets, and other case pieces that European and American furniture manufacturers had been making and exhibiting at expositions since London's Great Exhibition at the Crystal Palace in 1851. The Crawford piano reflected the tastes and aspirations of the American upper and middle classes. Pianos were not only musical instruments, but also major pieces of parlor furniture, acquired as expressions of affluence and symbols of artistic refinement and sophisticated taste. From about 1870 through the first quarter of the twentieth century, pianos were made for a broad market. As Hallet, Davis and Company intended it to demonstrate their full range of technical capabilities, the Crawford piano was certainly among the costliest of those produced in the 1870s.

Along with New York and Baltimore, Boston (which had first made pianos in 1792) was a major center of American piano manufacturing in the last half of the nineteenth century. Hallet, Davis and Company was one of the longest-lived and most innovative of the piano manufacturing firms working in the South End of Boston in 1871.[2] Jones Chickering and Sons emerged by the 1850s as America's largest, most successful, and best-known piano company. Between 1848 and 1853, the Chickering company expanded from one hundred employees to over four hundred, evidence of the growing market. In 1835, Edwin Brown, who had worked for Chickering, and Russel Hallet established Brown and Hallet. Brown retired in 1842, and the following year George H. Davis joined Hallet in a new partnership—Hallet, Davis and Company—which introduced a number of patented and unpatented improvements over the next thirty years. After Davis died in 1879, the company was incorporated under new management, but Hallet must have retained interest, and the firm's name stayed the same. By 1890, neither a Hallet nor a Davis was involved, but Hallet, Davis and Company pianos continued in production. In 1905, the Conway Company was organized and took over Hallet and Davis production. The company changed hands again in 1925, when it was acquired by Winter and Company. In 1959, Winter purchased the Aeolean American Corporation in Memphis, and production of Hallet and Davis pianos was moved south.[3]

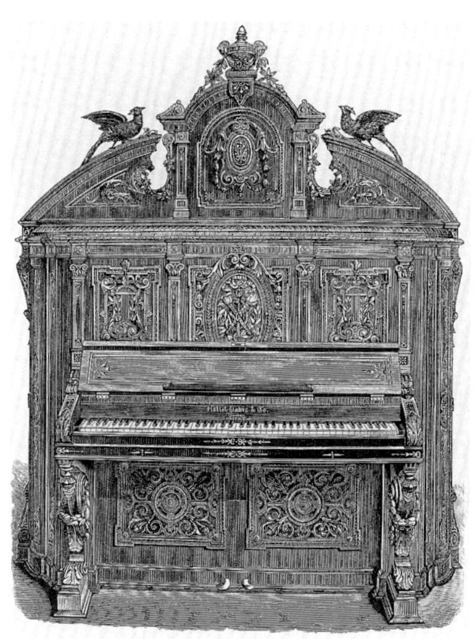

Fig. 1. Walter Smith, *The Masterpieces of the Centennial International Exhibition,* vol. 2 (Philadelphia: Gebbie & Barrie, 1877), p. 120.

The Crawford piano's columns, wreaths, scrolls, bosses, and garlands were derived from classical ornaments filtered through Renaissance architecture and were combined to suggest a fireplace of that period. The projected and garlanded scrolls support the keyboard like a mantel shelf beneath the architectural overmantel of three panels and four pilasters. The piece is topped by an elaborate entablature crest with a pair of pheasants flanking the central top urn. The ebonized surface and gold decoration link the piano with post–Civil War American furniture based on eighteenth-century French prototypes (see nos. 58–59), but the piano's mass and scale, together with its strong architectural sense, embody the popular Renaissance taste of the time.

NOTES

1. W. Smith 1877, p. 119.

2. N. Smith 1978, p. 41. Smith's article discusses the development and evolution of piano manufacturing in Boston from the last half of the nineteenth century until the 1920s. In 1871, there were more than forty piano and related factories in the South End.

3. History of Hallet, Davis and Company is drawn from Dolge 1911, p. 286; Roell 1989, pp. 84–86; and N. Smith 1978, pp. 40–43.

82.

Centerpiece, ca. 1891

Simpson, Hall, Miller and Company (1866–1898), Wallingford, Connecticut
Electroplated silver, probably on britannia metal
18½ × 11½ × 11½ inches
Marks: Impressed on bottom in circle, *SIMPSON, HALL, MILLER & CO.;* enclosed in circle, *QUADRUPLE/PLATE;* below, *1891*
1990.87

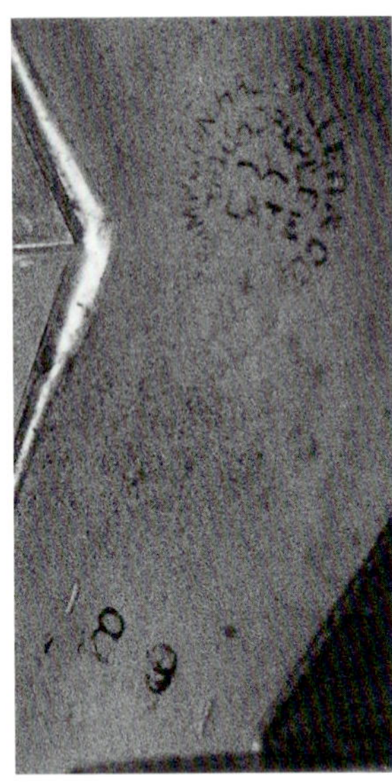

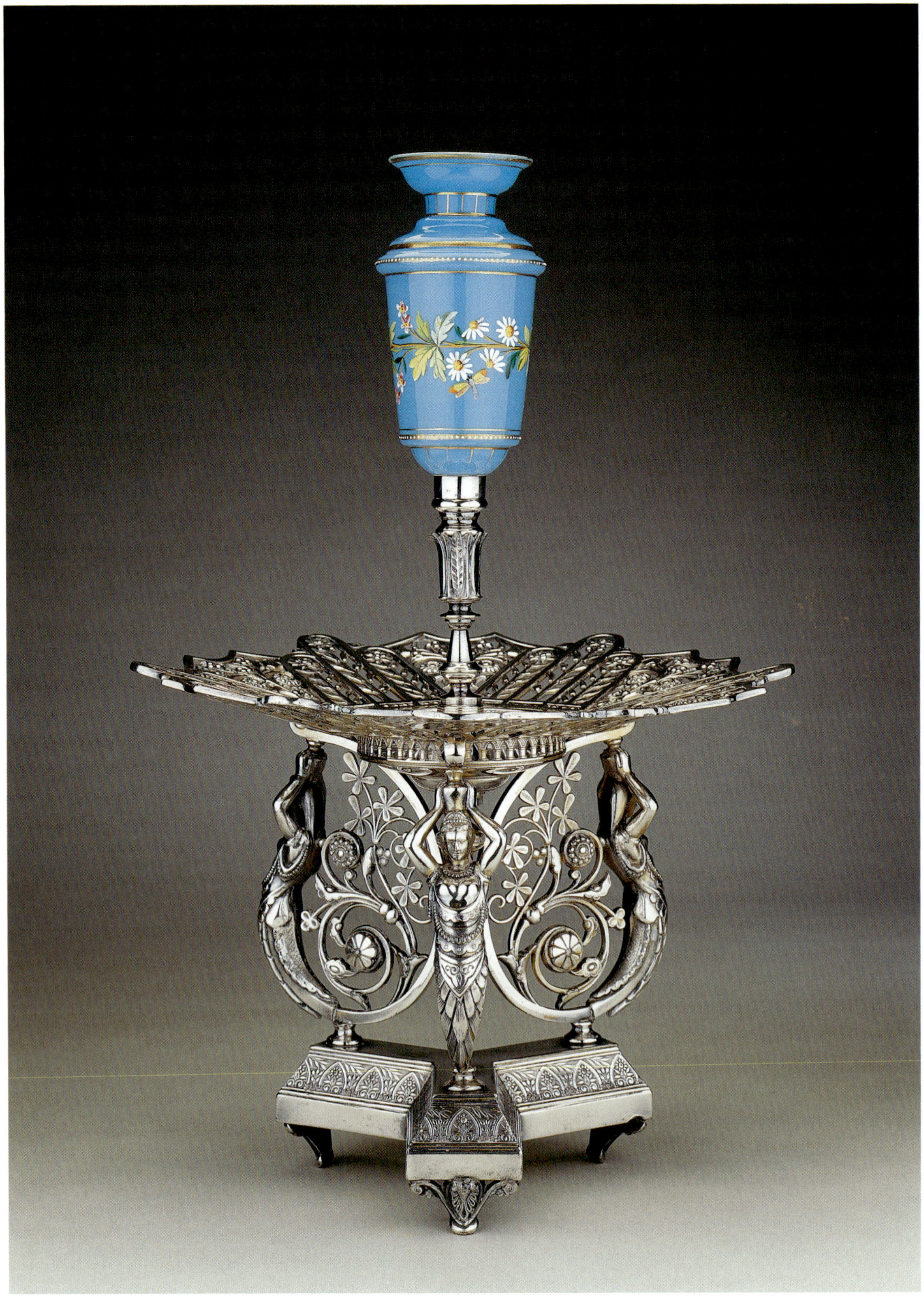

ELECTROPLATING SILVER on base metal—a less expensive alternative to the production of solid silverwares—was introduced in Birmingham, England, by G. R. and H. Elkington, who patented the process in 1840. By the mid-1840s, the area around Hartford, Connecticut, emerged as a center for American experimentation and production of silver-plated tablewares. Among the most successful firms was Simpson, Hall, Miller and Company.

Samuel Simpson had been successfully manufacturing britannia ware in Wallingford, Connecticut, when he helped to establish Simpson, Hall, Miller and Company in 1866. The company flourished, publishing illustrated catalogues and exhibiting at the 1876 Centennial Exposition in Philadelphia and the Australian Exposition in Sydney in 1879. By 1895, Simpson, Hall, Miller and Company expanded into the production of sterling silver. Three years later, the firm was among many incorporated into the new International Silver Company, and its Wallingford factory became the International Silver Company's sterling center.

The Crawford centerpiece is a showy silver-plated table ornament, produced at a fraction of the cost of the same object in solid silver. The influence of silver design on plated wares is immediately apparent. The caryatid figures at the centerpiece's base are related to those on the Gorham chafing dish in the Crawford Collection from the late 1860s (see no. 57). This classical and Renaissance detail was also used on contemporary furniture intended for the same market (see no. 66). The Renaissance details of the centerpiece were combined with stylized and angular interpretations of natural motifs on the fretwork of the circular shelf above the caryatid figures. This mixture of decorative elements was characteristic of American design in the 1870s and 1880s.

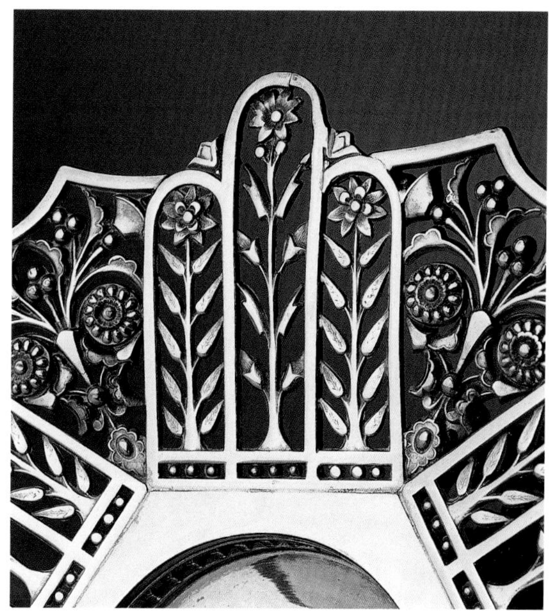

Unlike solid silver, plated wares did not tend to introduce new styles. By the time the New England plated-ware manufacturers fully absorbed and eventually saturated the market for Japanese taste in the 1880s (see no. 106),[1] innovative producers such as Tiffany and Company were looking to other design sources. Nevertheless, the impressive scale and intricate detail of this centerpiece appealed to America's prosperous middle class.

NOTE

1. A brief history of Simpson, Hall, Miller and Company can be found in Rainwater 1986, pp. 183–184; and of the International Silver Company in Rainwater and Rainwater 1988, pp. 26–27. A discussion of the belated adoption and proliferation of the Japanese taste by American silver-plate manufacturers can be found in Hosley 1990, pp. 130–133.

Patent Furniture, 1850s–1880s

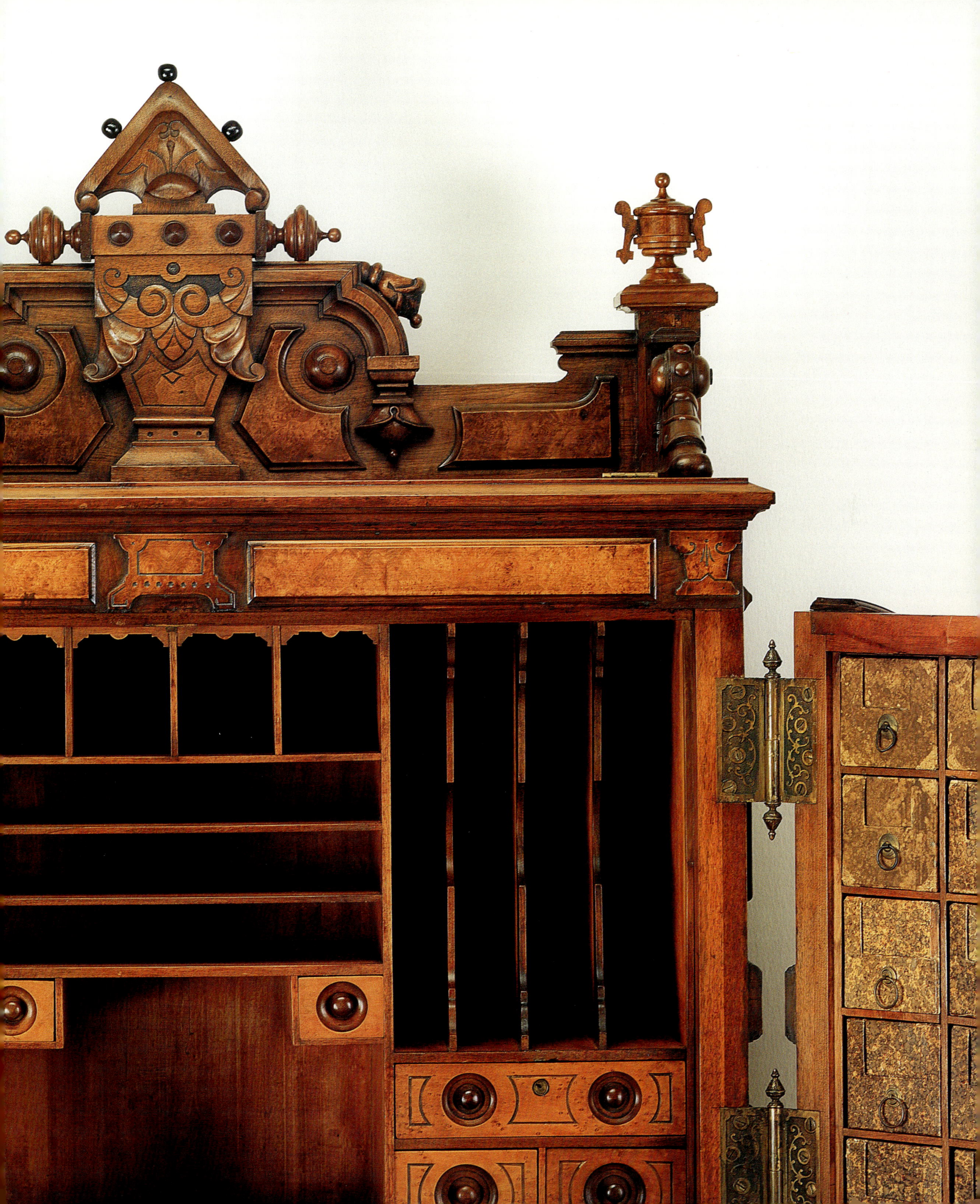

83.

Centripetal Spring Armchair, ca. 1850

American Chair Company (1829–1948), Troy, New York; designed by Thomas E. Warren (working 1849–1852)
Cast iron, steel spring, painted wood, sheet-metal back, reproduction silk upholstery fabric
39¼ x 24½ x 30½ inches
1983.207

THOMAS E. WARREN of Troy, New York, received a patent on September 25, 1849, for a "New and Improved Mode of Constructing Springs." The American Chair Company in Troy produced reclining chairs for trains, and Warren's "centripetal" spring was designed to ease the bumps of train riding. By 1850, a domestic or office chair with a rotating seat mounted on centripetal steel bowed springs was in production at the American Chair Company. The company was located in Troy because the city was a cast-iron production center and a railroad hub (see no. 20).

Warren secured his patent just as John Henry Belter was introducing his elaborately carved and laminated parlor furniture (see no. 44). The curved sheet-metal back of Warren's chairs is similar to the shaped backs of Belter's seating furniture. The cast-iron decoration on the legs, the arm supports, and at the crest is related to the open-carved frames of Belter furniture. In 1850, the American Chair Company's centripetal spring chair was awarded a "second premium" at the Twentieth Annual Exhibition of the Franklin Institute in Philadelphia, one of the few times in the thirty-year history of these exhibitions that a non-Philadelphia firm received recognition. The chair was submitted for the exhibition by the cabinetmaking firm of Stafford and Cookman, the retailing agent for the American Chair Company in Philadelphia. Warren's centripetal spring chairs were also sold by other firms around the country. Versions of Warren's innovative chairs were illustrated, along with the American and English patent dates, in a mid-1850s catalogue of the Iron Manufactory and Warerooms of Chase Brothers and Company in Boston. The catalogue listed the chairs ranging in price from $5 to $65 and described them as "suited to the parlor, boudoir, library, sitting room, or office."[1]

Warren's centripetal spring chair received international recognition when versions were shown at the 1851 Great Exhibition at the Crystal Palace in London. Both an armchair and a side chair version were included in *The Crystal Palace Exhibition Illustrated Catalogue.* Praise in the catalogue was effusive: "The design and fittings of these chairs are equally good and elegant, and certainly we have never tested a more easy and commodious article of household furniture." The centripetal spring chair was a forerunner of the twentieth-century rotating office chair.[2]

A side chair version is in The Metropolitan Museum of Art, and another in the St. Louis Art Museum still has its original upholstery and fringe around the seat. The sheet-metal backs of those chairs have retained polychromed japanned decoration.[3] If the Crawford chair was japanned, that decoration has been lost; the chair back is painted black.

NOTES

1. Chase Brothers and Company, ca. 1855, pp. 35–36. For a discussion of Warren's patent number 6740 and an illustration of the drawing he submitted to the patent office, see Hanks 1981, pp. 126–127 and p. 129, fig. 104. For a discussion of Troy as an industrial and transportation center, see Waite and Waite 1973, p. 136.

2. *Crystal Palace* 1970, p. 152. In a section devoted to the American male's habit of sitting in a tilted chair, Ames 1992, pp. 195–215, illustrates a centripetal armchair at the Wisconsin Historical Society, p. 197, fig. 5.7. In the caption of that photograph, Ames draws parallels between Warren's centripetal spring chair and today's revolving office desk chair.

3. Springer 1980, p. 33; and Davidson and Stillinger 1985, pp. 183–184, fig. 288.

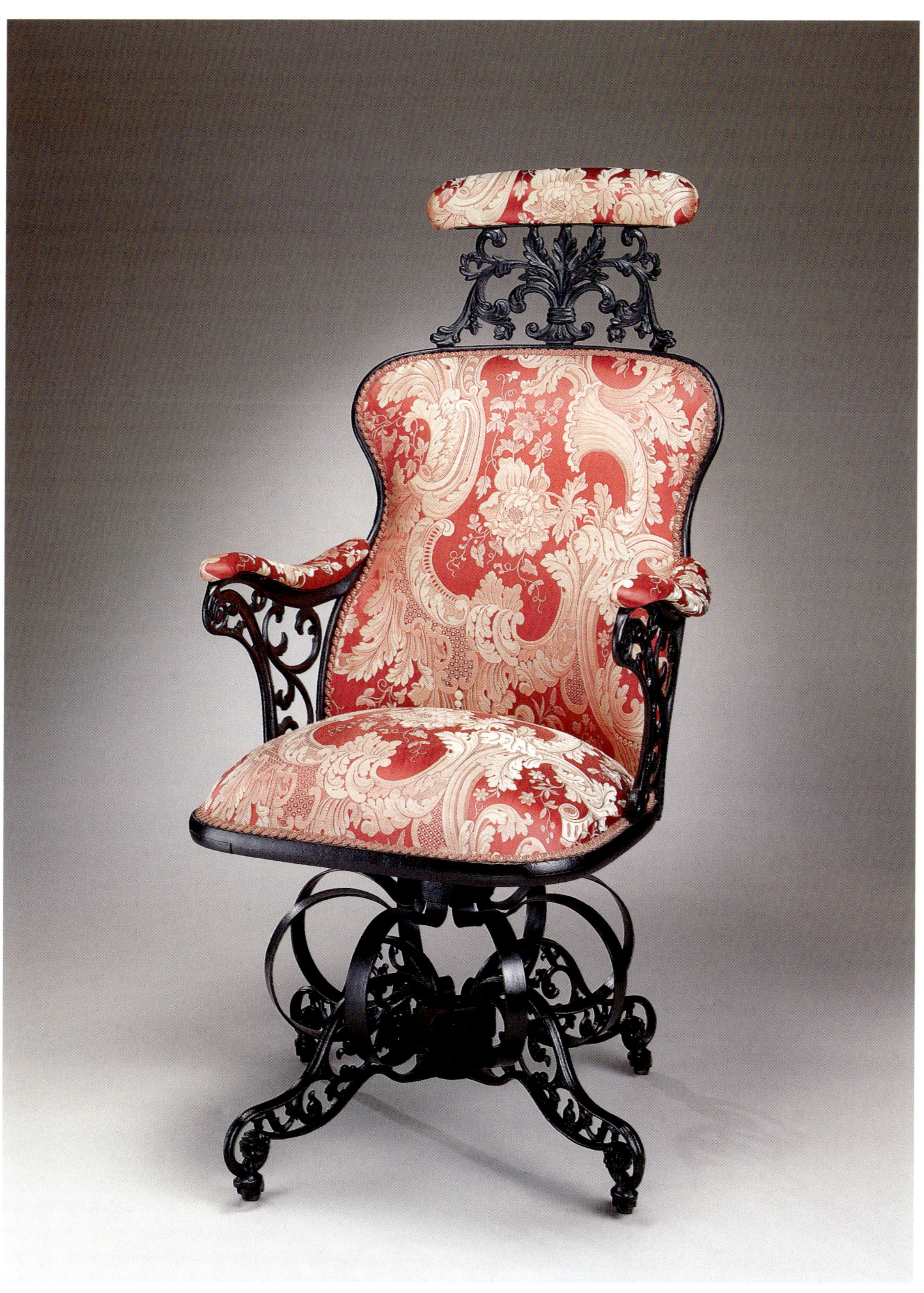

84.

Armchair, patented 1866

Retailed by Lalance and Grosjean (1852–after 1900), New York; designed by François A. Carré, Paris
Steel
34¾ x 19¼ x 29 inches
Mark: Cast in raised letters on brass button at center of top of seat, *LALANCE & GROSJEAN/273/ PEARL ST/N.Y./PATENTED/MAY 15/1866*
1988.220

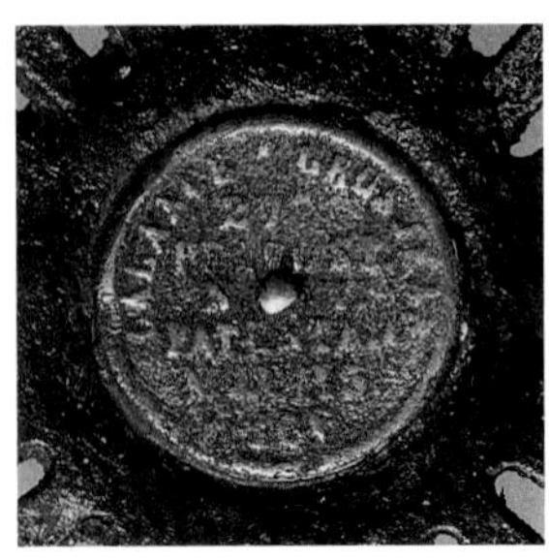

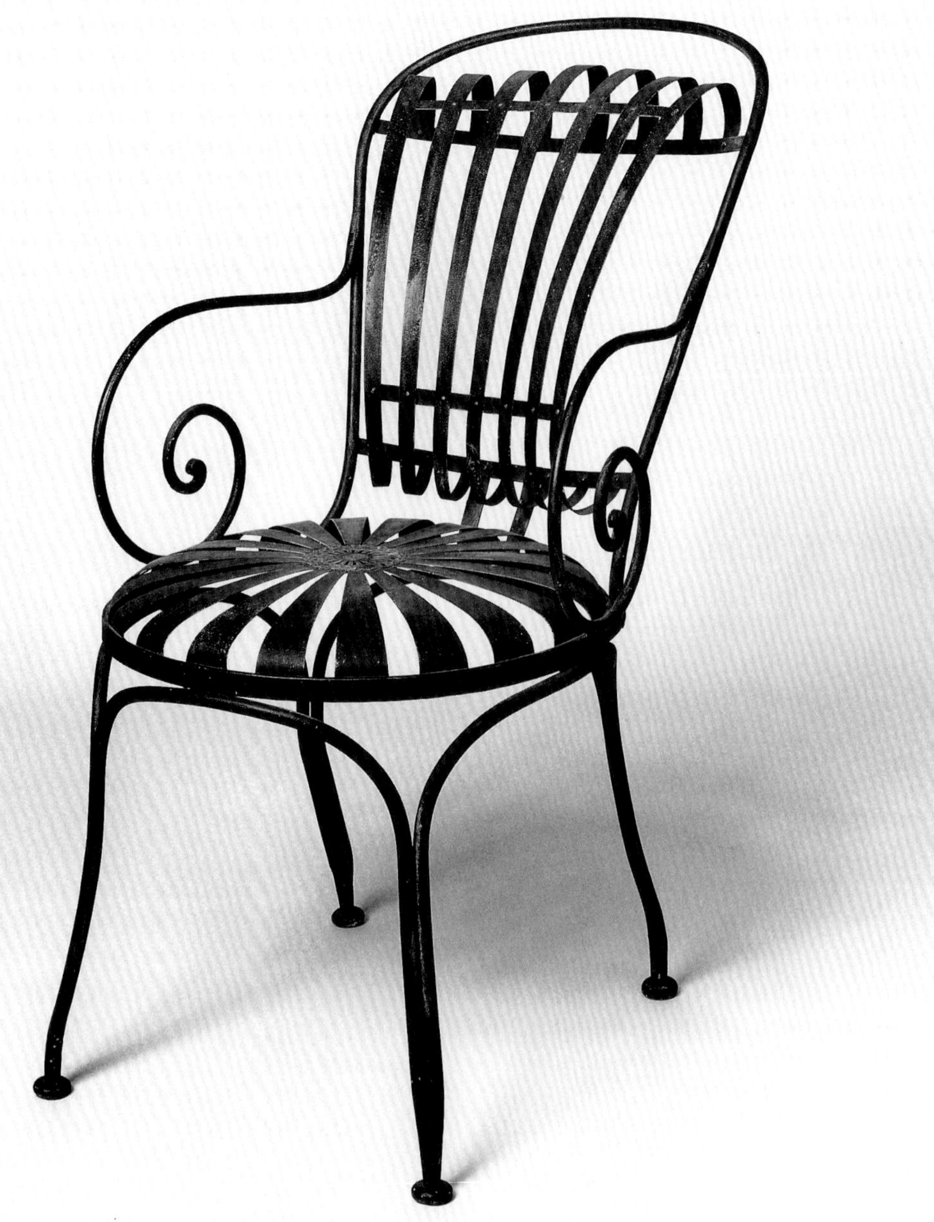

When François A. Carré applied for an American patent for this chair, the benefits he claimed for his new design included a combination of "strength and durability with neatness and convenience."[1] The backs and seats of Carré's outdoor chairs are assembled from strips of sheet steel. In the domed seats, these slats are arranged radially, which provided both a smooth surface and an accommodating flexibility. Carré noted that "common sheet iron seats, either solid or open have little if any elasticity. They are hard, clumsy, and inconvenient." For thirty years, garden furniture in the United States had been made of cast iron (see nos. 23–26), but it was unrelentingly hard, and the cast and raised decoration was often uncomfortable. Carré's steel chair was also much lighter than cast-iron furniture, so it was more easily moved.

Carré's name is not on the brass button mark on the Crawford chair, although the patent date on the mark—May 15, 1866—coincides with that on the patent drawing he submitted (fig. 1). The U.S. patent may have been purchased by a French hardware retailing firm in New York, Lalance and Grosjean, whose name appears on the button. Alfred Lalance was first listed in New York directories in 1852 as an importer of French hardware. The directory the following year listed him in partnership with another Frenchman, Florian Grosjean. Around the time of the chair's patent, the Lalance and Grosjean hardware store was located at 273 Pearl Street, the address on the chair's button. In 1876, the firm produced and displayed metal kitchenwares at the Centennial Exposition in Philadelphia. Lalance and Grosjean continued retailing hardware in New York into the twentieth century.[2]

Whether the Crawford chair was manufactured in the United States or in France and imported by Lalance and Grosjean is not known. An illustrated catalogue of the J. W. Fiske Ironworks in New York (see no. 27), issued around 1870, shows a chair identical to the Crawford example, priced at $7.50. The Fiske catalogue described objects made of iron, but no material is given with the chair's illustration. Carré had stated in his patent application that his technique could be adapted for round and oval shapes, and so could be used for chairs, settees, and stools; the Fiske catalogue illustrates side chairs, rockers, and settees for two or three persons.[3] Lalance and Grosjean also sold a Carré rocker without arms.[4]

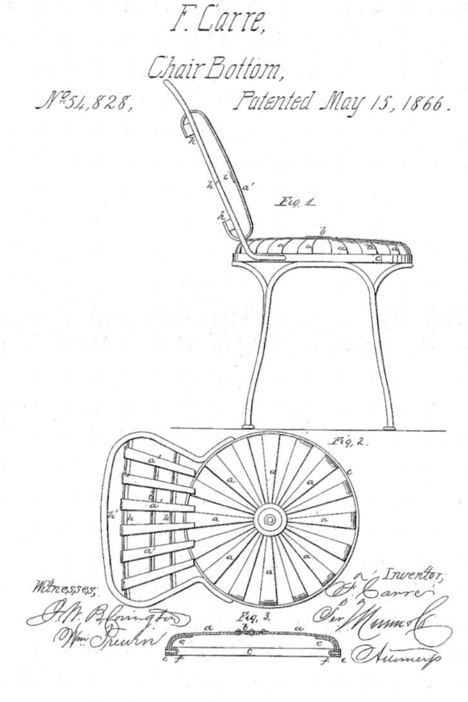

Fig. 1. Patent drawing. U.S. Patent Office. François Carré, of Paris. Improved Seat and Back for Chairs, specifications forming part of Letters Patent Number 54,828, dated May 15, 1866.

NOTES

1. U.S. Patent Office, François Carré, of Paris. Improved Seat and Back for Chairs, specification forming part of Letters Patent No. 54,828, dated May 15, 1866.

2. Another Lalance and Grosjean armchair is illustrated and discussed in Hanks 1981, pp. 80–83; the Carré patent drawing for the side chair appears on p. 82, fig. 62. An illustration from the catalogue of the *Societe Anonymes des Hauts-Fourneaux & Foundries du Val d'Osme* (Paris, ca. 1870) showing an identical armchair appears on p. 83, fig. 63.

3. Fiske, ca. 1864–1870, p. 30. J. W. Fiske was located at 120 Nassau Street from 1864 until 1871.

4. A Lalance and Grosjean–marked rocking chair is illustrated in the unpaginated "Show Section" of *Antiques and the Arts Weekly* (August 5, 1988).

85.

Reclining Armchair,
patented 1866

George Hunzinger (1835–1898), New York
Walnut with ebonized and gilt decoration, reproduction horsehair, and embroidered upholstery with original fringe
38 x 24½ x 35 inches
Mark: Stamped on back of right rear stile, *HUNZINGER/N.Y./PAT.FEB.6/1866*
Needlepoint duplicating the original, gift of Harriet P. Neal.
Modern upholstery duplicating the original, gift of Martha Cade.
1982.312

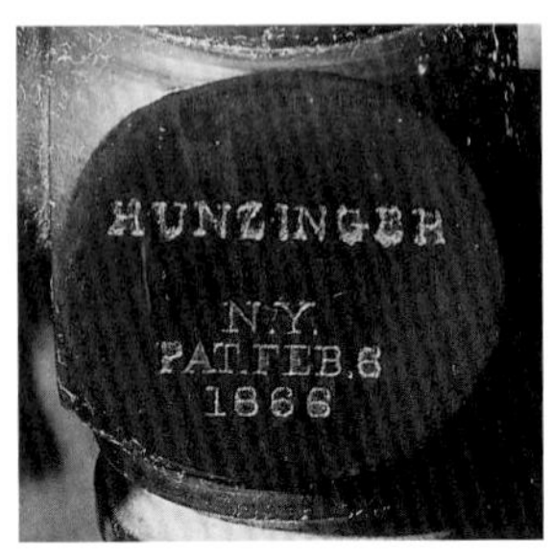

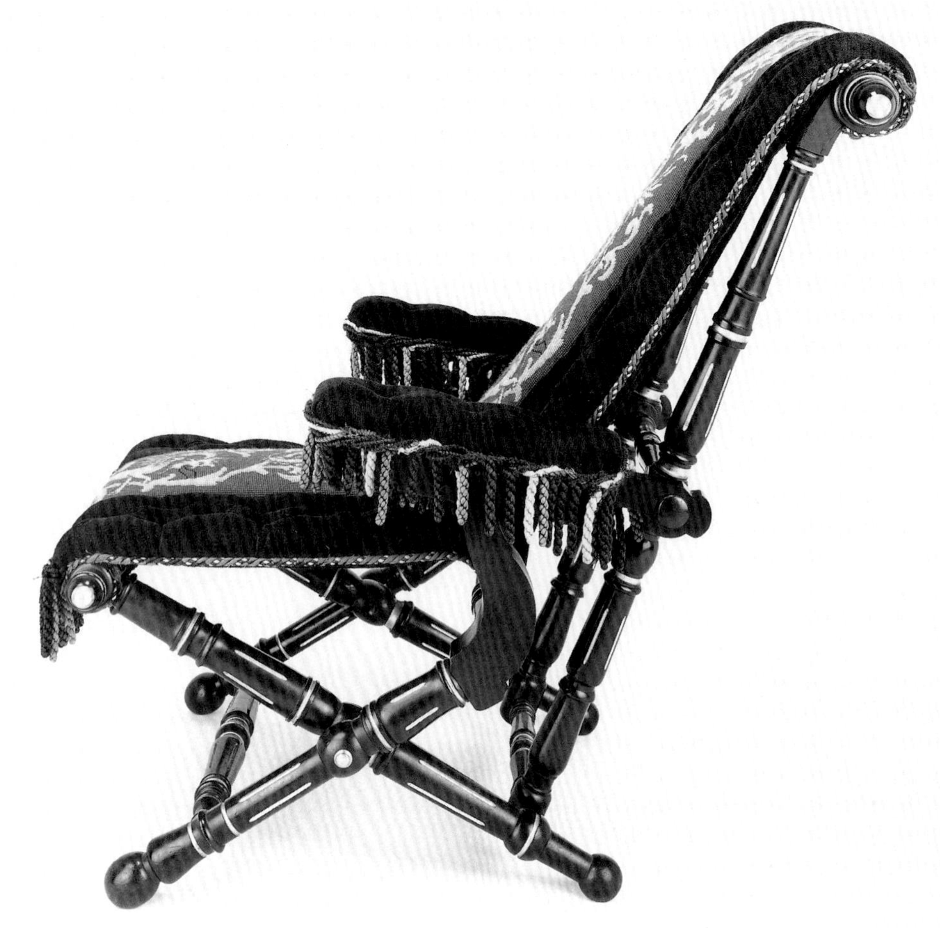

George Jakob Hunzinger's family had made furniture in the German village of Tuttlingen in the Württemberg province on the Swiss border since the early seventeenth century. Württemberg was also the home of Hunzinger's contemporaries John Henry Belter (see no. 44) and Gustave Herter (see no. 53). Hunzinger apprenticed in Germany under his cabinetmaker father and worked as a journeyman cabinetmaker in Geneva. In 1855, he joined a wave of German craftsmen, including Belter and Herter, who immigrated to New York. He received twenty patents for furniture designs, the first of which, in 1861, was for an improved folding and reclining chair with a footboard that could also serve as a table. He assigned an 1864 patent for production to New York furniture maker C. Henry Glinsman, possibly his employer at the time.

In 1865, Hunzinger became a U.S. citizen, and a year later he opened his own furniture business at 192 Laurens Street in Manhattan. Also in 1866 he secured patent number 52,416 for the folding and reclining armchair in the Crawford Collection. The patent was for a ratchet mechanism underneath the arms that enabled the chairback to recline. Hunzinger's patent drawings show turned cross-legs similar to those on the Crawford chair (fig. 1). This was Hunzinger's first commercially successful patent, and the design was made during the remainder of his career. By 1869, Hunzinger's company sold $50,000 in goods annually and employed four or

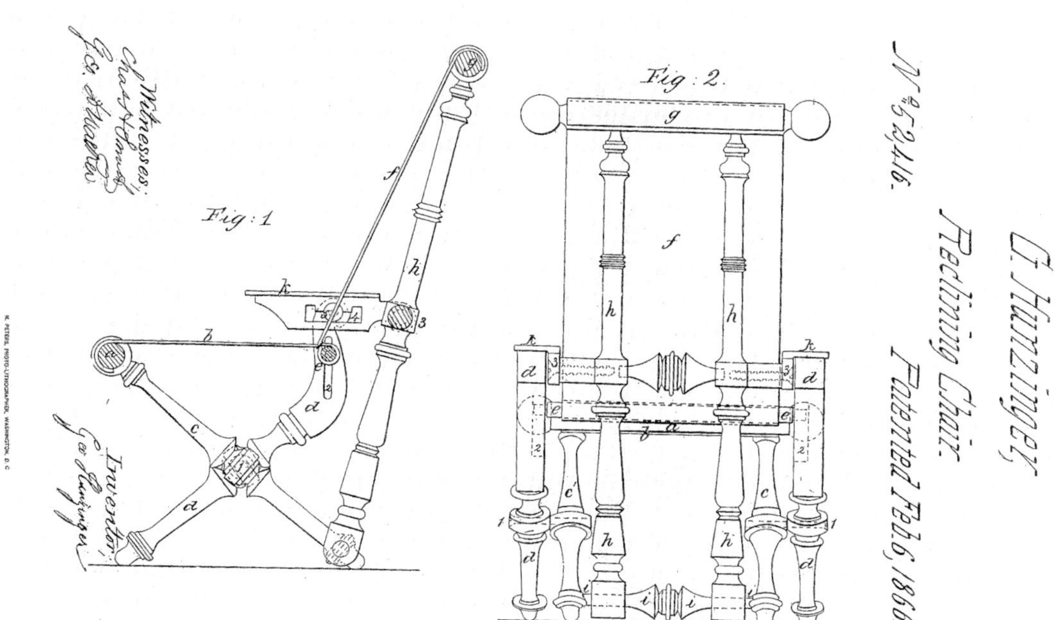

Fig. 1. Patent drawing. U.S. Patent Office, George Hunzinger, of New York. Reclining-Chair, specifications forming part of Letters Patent Number 52,416, dated February 6, 1866.

five men. In 1870, he leased a larger space at 402 Bleecker Street, and two years later he had fifty employees with a business capital of $40,000. Within a year his capital grew to $60,000, and in 1873 he moved his headquarters to a larger facility at 141–143 Seventh Avenue. His 1885 letterhead listed "FANCY CHAIRS" and "ORNAMENTAL FURNITURE." Through the 1870s and 1880s, Hunzinger continued to secure patents for chair springs, platform rockers, and tables with flip-tops.

A fire destroyed Hunzinger's Seventh Avenue factory in 1877 and damaged the neighboring Roux and Company furniture factory on 18th Street (see nos. 36, 46, 61). The two furniture factories, together with a third facing 19th Street, shared a common steam engine, which is believed to have caused the fire. Hunzinger moved his business operation several times after the fire, awaiting completion of his new facility at 323–327 West 16th Street. In the late 1880s, Hunzinger's sons, George Jr. and Alfred, joined the business. After the elder Hunzinger's death in 1898, his six daughters shared the business with their two brothers, and some worked in it. By the early twentieth century, Hunzinger lines had a more restrained look than George Hunzinger's mechanical designs. In the 1920s, attempts to unionize the firm's workforce discouraged the family, and they closed the factory. George Hunzinger and Sons became a real estate and stock holding company.

This Hunzinger folding and reclining chair bears the 1866 patent stamp, and it survived until 1983 with its original upholstery and trim. In order to preserve it, the upholstery and covering fabrics were duplicated and the original trim and fringe reapplied. The arrangement of the needlework stripe down the center of the chair is characteristic of Hunzinger chairs of this patent, as are the bold turnings and X-form of the legs, connecting with the arms and side stiles of the back.[1]

NOTE

1. Harwood 1997, pp. 8–152, provides the most comprehensive account of Hunzinger and his firm, with illustrations of his patents and an extensive photographic survey of his work. The Crawford chair is illustrated and discussed in the appendix, p. 156, fig. E.

86.

Adjustable, Reclining, and Foldable Chair, patented 1876

Marks Adjustable Folding Chair Company (1877–1897), New York; designed by Cevedra B. Sheldon
Enameled cast iron, rattan, walnut, and upholstered arms
46 x 29⅝ x 25½ inches
Mark: Impressed on side of metal frame, *SOLE M'FRS./ MARKS A.F.CHAIR CO. LIMITED 930 B'WAY,/PAT' FEB 1ST, 1876*
1983.208

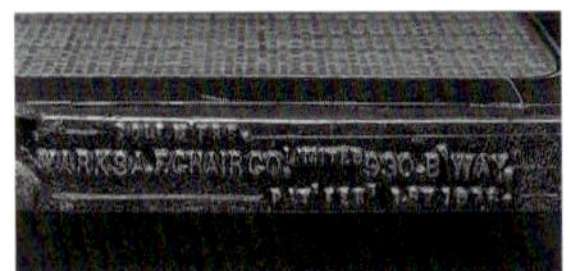

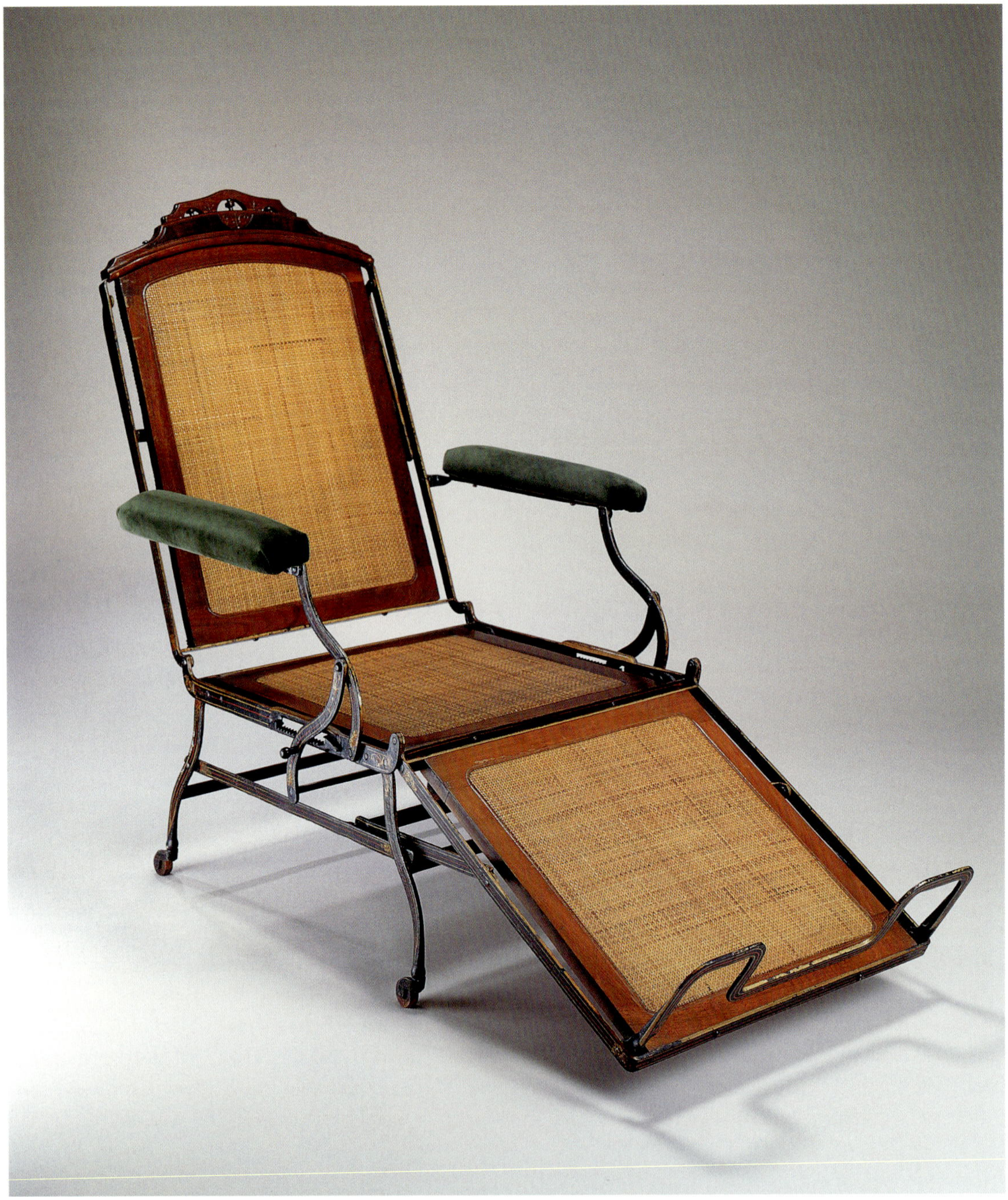

IN 1876, New York businessman, entrepreneur, and inventor Cevedra B. Sheldon designed and patented his adjustable reclining chair, which he called an "invalid-chair" (fig. 1). An 1887 illustrated furniture magazine advertisement for the chair indicated a much broader range of functions: "A Parlor, Library, Smoking, Reclining or Invalid Chair, Lounge, Full Length Bed and Child's Crib Combined, and Adjustable to any Position required for Comfort or Convenience."[1] The hinged rattan-paneled back, footrest, and stationary seat were framed in walnut and set into a floral enamel-decorated cast-iron frame. Two hooked ratchet bars enabled the back and footrest to be locked at various positions from vertical to horizontal. When the back was folded down and the footrest folded up, hinged legs behind each section could be folded down to create a flat bed or lounge with the seat as the center.

Sheldon's design was manufactured and sold by the Marks Adjustable Folding Chair Company, established in New York in 1877 by Pennsylvania-born chair maker Frank R. Marks. Over the next two decades, the company occupied three different locations along Broadway and one in Union Square. By 1895, Marks was also making bicycles, and when the firm was liquidated in 1897, he was no longer involved. Sheldon's participation in the operation of the Marks Adjustable Folding Chair Company has not been determined. In its 1887 advertisement, the company claimed that more than 16,000 chairs had been sold in the United States and England.[2] The firm exhibited in the 1893 Columbian World's Exposition in Chicago, but whether Sheldon's chair was included is unknown.

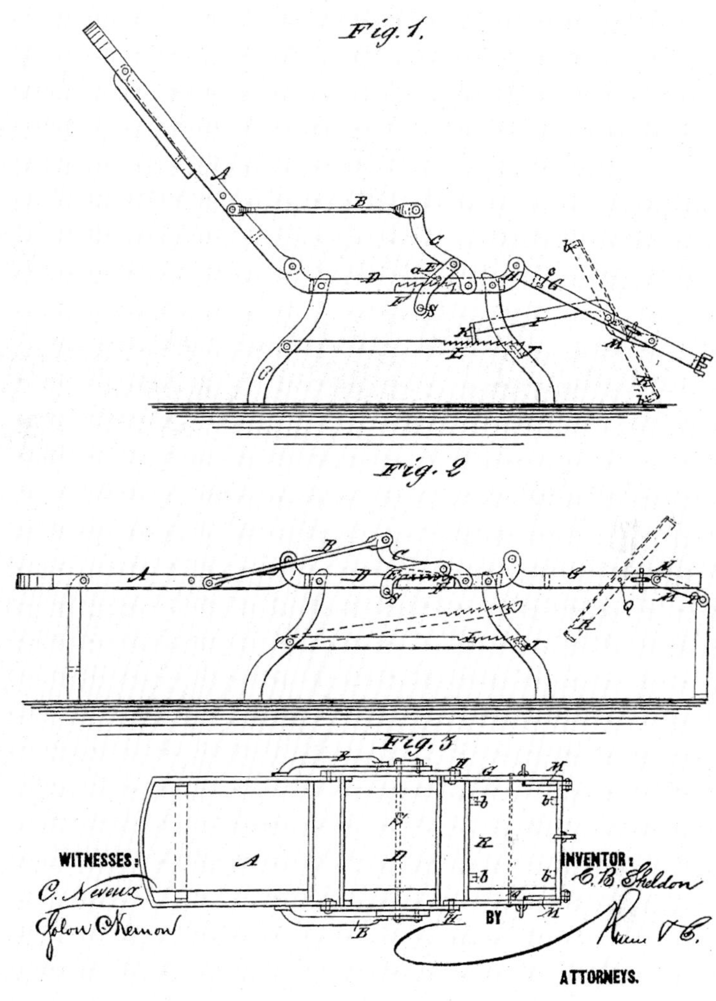

Fig. 1. Patent drawing. U.S. Patent Office. Cevedra B. Sheldon, of New York, Improvement in Invalid-Chairs, specifications forming part of Letters Patent Number 173,071, dated February 1, 1876.

NOTES

1. *The American Furniture Gazette* (August 1, 1887), p. 3; reprinted in Dubrow and Dubrow 1982, p. 246.

2. Another example of the chair is illustrated and discussed in Hanks 1981, pp. 136–139. An additional example of the Marks chair, in The Metropolitan Museum of Art, is discussed and illustrated in Davidson and Stillinger 1985, pp. 184–185, fig. 289.

87.

Wooton Patent Office Cabinet Secretary, 1880–1884

Wooton Desk Manufacturing Company (1874–1884), Indianapolis; designed by William S. Wooton (1835–1907)
Walnut, maple, white pine, cardboard, and bronze
82 x 42½ x 31 inches
Marks: On plaque on left door, *MANUFACTURED BY/WOOTON DESK MANF. CO./INDIANAPOLIS. IND./W.S. WOOTON'S PATENT./OCT.6.1874.*; on right door, *LETTERS*
1987.182

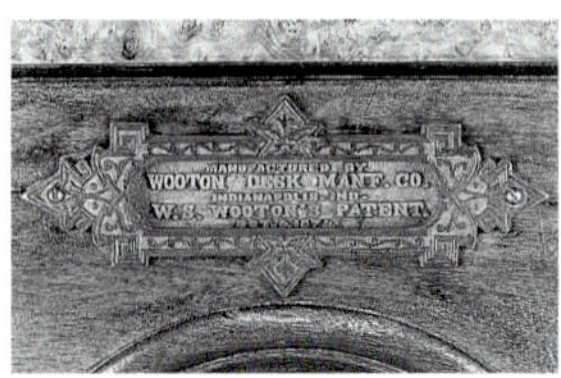

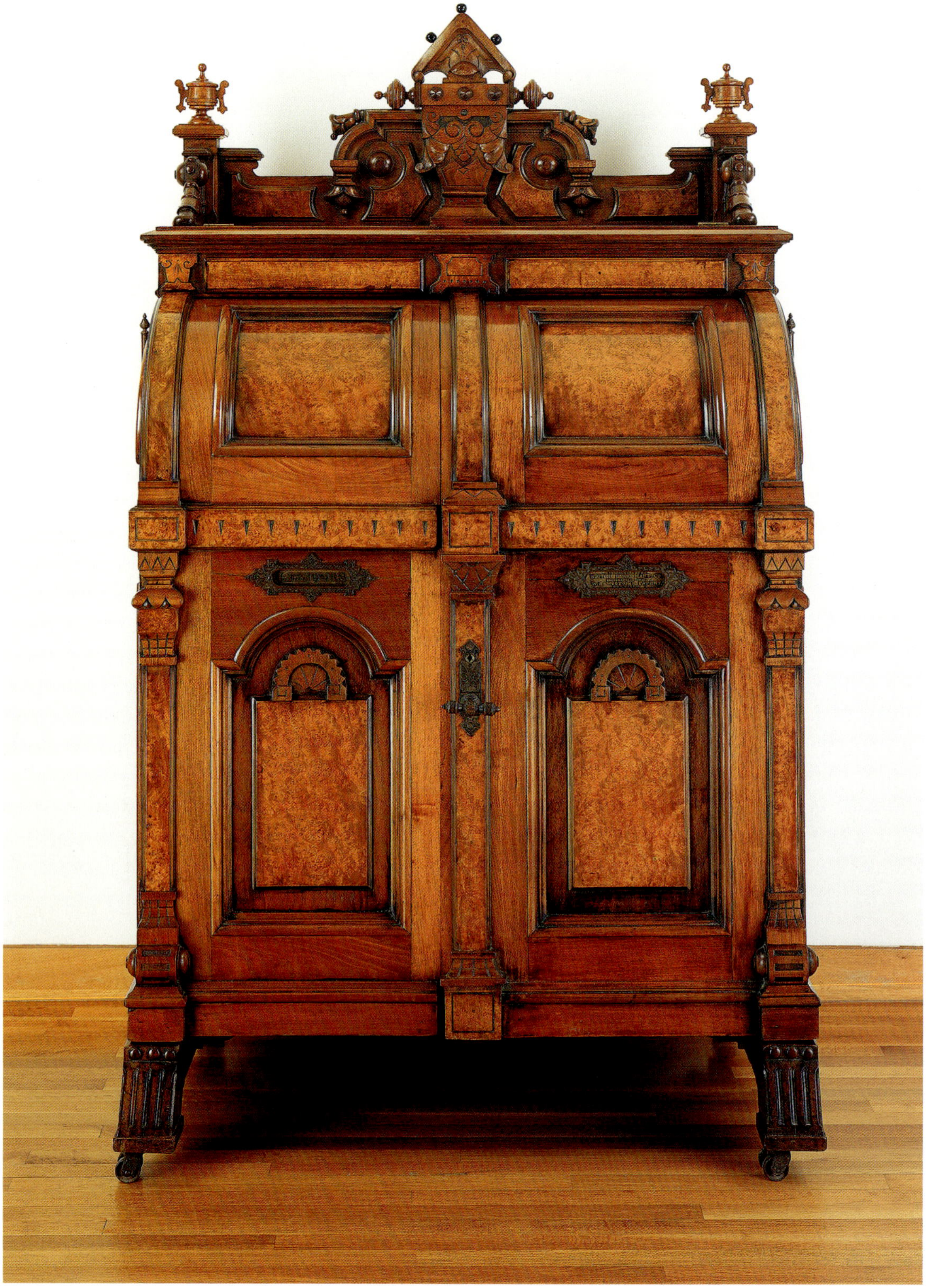

The Wooton patent office cabinet secretary illustrates nineteenth-century revolutions in both industry and business. These desks were constructed using techniques of mass production made possible by interchangeable parts and steam-powered machinery, and their elaborate organization reflects the proliferation of paperwork in post–Civil War commerce. Customers of the Wooton Desk Company included leaders of industry, business, publishing, and politics, such as Jay Gould, John D. Rockefeller, Joseph Pulitzer, Thomas Scribner, Georgia poet Sidney Lanier, President Ulysses S. Grant, Spencer Baird, secretary of the Smithsonian Institution from 1878 to 1887, and William Larrabee, governor of Iowa from 1886 to 1890 (fig. 1).

William S. Wooton was listed as a pattern maker in the Richmond, Indiana, directory as early as 1860. For several months in 1869, he was a partner in a firm that manufactured school, office, and court furnishings. In 1868 and 1869, Wooton patented two designs for school desks, and in 1870 he established William S. Wooton and Company in Indianapolis, which produced school, office, and church furniture. On October 6, 1874, Wooton was issued a patent for his ingenious cabinet secretary (fig. 2). As described in the patent specifications, the secretary consists of "three parts, two of which are together equal in width to the other, each part being provided with compartments or pigeon-holes suitable for storing books, papers, &c., and the two lesser parts

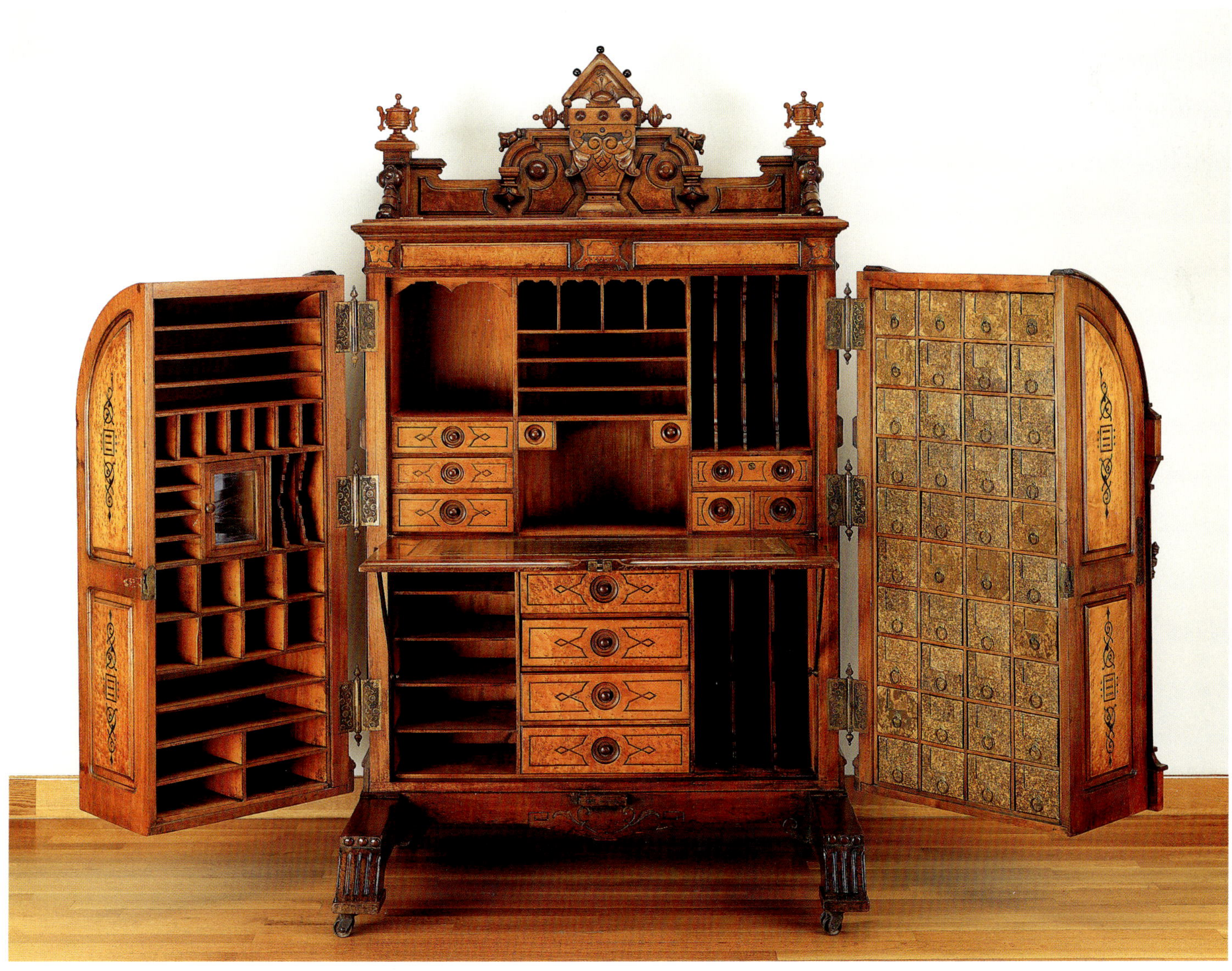

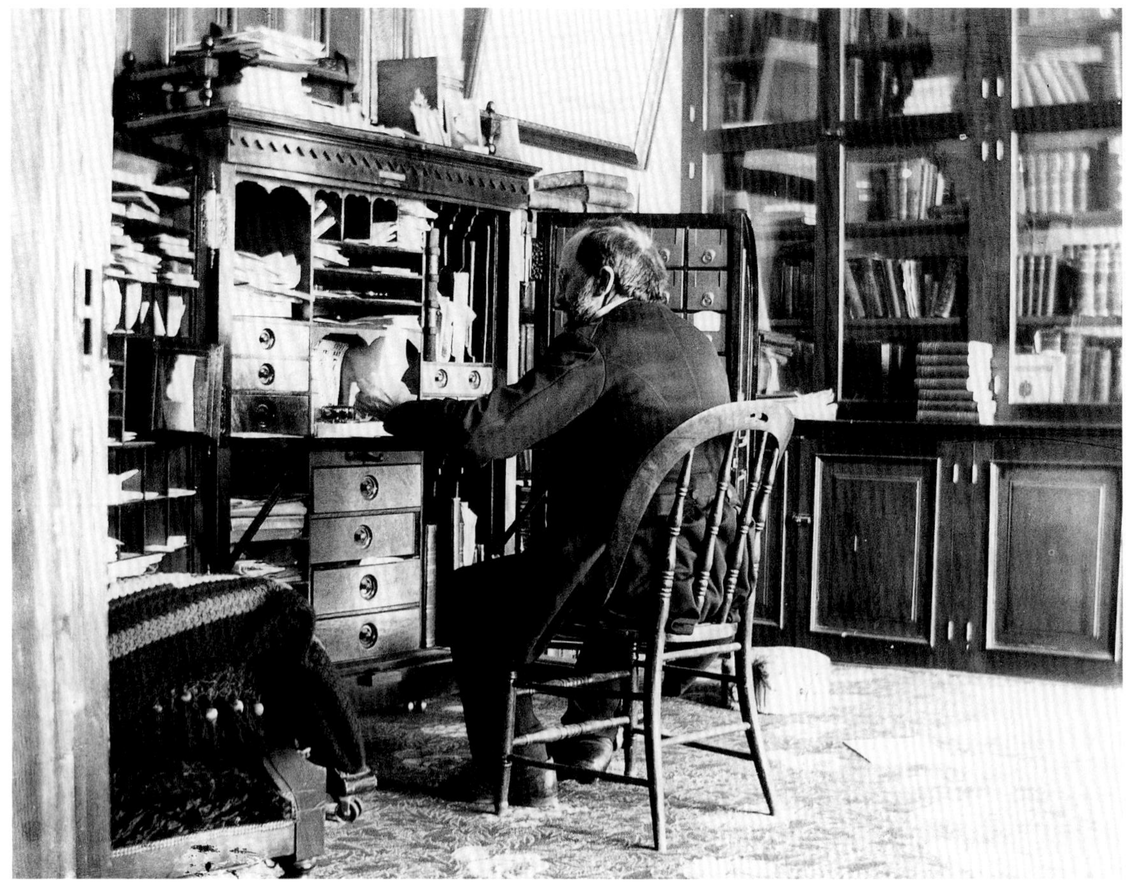

Fig. 1. Governor William Larrabee of Iowa at his Wooton desk.

hinged to the greater part, to serve as doors to the secretary." Shortly after the patent was secured, Wooton entered into a partnership to form the Wooton Desk Company. The venture was highly successful, and by the end of 1875, the value of the company's capital stock had increased from $60,000 to $500,000. A display of Wooton cabinet secretaries at the Centennial Exposition in Philadelphia in 1876 created an international market for the company. The desks were being sold in twelve American cities from Boston to San Francisco, as well as in London, Glasgow, and Rio de Janeiro.

Although early secretaries varied the arrangement of the interior compartments, after 1875 they became more standardized, which enabled the company to use mechanized mass production and interchangeable parts. The Wooton Desk Company introduced four grades of desks: Ordinary, Standard, Extra Grade, and Superior Grade. The Crawford cabinet secretary is an example of the Extra Grade, which often included turned and assembled elements, such as the pair of urns decorating the top gallery and the deep molding surrounding the figured veneer panels. Superior Grade desks had hand-carved elements. The maple interiors of the Extra Grade desks often included incised and gilt decoration, as this example does.

After Wooton's departure in 1880, the Wooton Desk Company became the Wooton Desk Manufacturing Company; therefore the Crawford desk can be dated between 1880 and 1884. From 1884 to 1892, the Wooton Desk Manufacturing Company was a division of Haynes, Spencer, and Company, the reorganized firm in Richmond, Indiana, where Wooton had worked in 1868 and 1869, before he moved to Indianapolis. After that firm closed in 1892, the Wooton Office Desk Company was organized in Indianapolis as a subsidiary of the Indianapolis Cabinet Company, which suffered bankruptcy in 1893, was reorganized in 1894, and apparently continued to manufacture Wooton desks until 1897. No Wooton desks are known to have been made after 1897. While Wooton cabinet secretaries were revolutionary and profitable products in the 1870s, they became victims of advancing technology. The introduction of typewriters and carbon paper created paper storage needs that far exceeded the capacity of the Wooton desk. As American business grew, more efficient and accessible executive desks replaced this type, and the organizational needs of offices were managed by executive assistants and file cabinets.

Wooton served as superintendent of the Wooton Desk Company in 1875, and the following year he was listed as vice president of the firm in the Indianapolis directory. Although Wooton patented a rotary flat-top desk in 1876, he was no longer listed as an officer in the company. In 1880, Wooton moved with his family to Danville, Indiana, and spent the rest of his life ministering in the Society of Friends in various locations. He died in Colorado in 1907.[1]

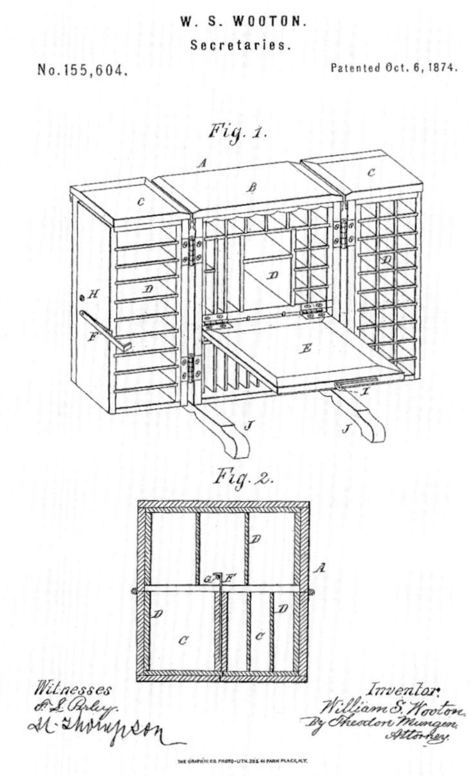

Fig. 2. Patent Drawing. U.S. Patent Office, William S. Wooton, of Indianapolis. Improvement in Secretaries, specifications forming part of Letters Patent Number 155,604, dated October 6, 1874.

NOTE

1. The Wooton patent office cabinet secretary in the Crawford Collection is illustrated in Showalter and Driesbach 1983, p. 68, pl. 6. The history of the firm is given in Betty Lawson Walters, "Makers of the King of Desks," in ibid., pp. 33–42. An examination of the various grades and progressing changes appears in Deborah Cooper, "Evolution of Wooton Patent Desks," in ibid., pp. 45–62. Other accounts are found in D. Cooper 1991, pp. 52–55; Hanks 1981, pp. 182–184; and Lehnert 1991, pp. 54–57.

88.

Reclining Armchair,
patented 1881

Designed and presumably made by Theodore Hofstatter, Jr., New York
Oak and metal, reupholstered with early twentieth-century upholstery
40½ x 27½ x 32 inches
Marks: Stamped twice on back of rear seat rail, *THEO. HOFSTATTER, JR./PATENTED/AUG.30,1881*
1982.314

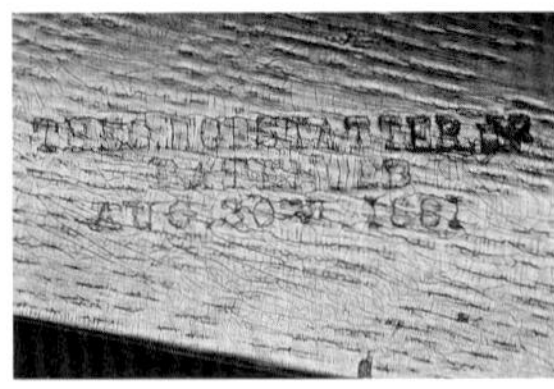

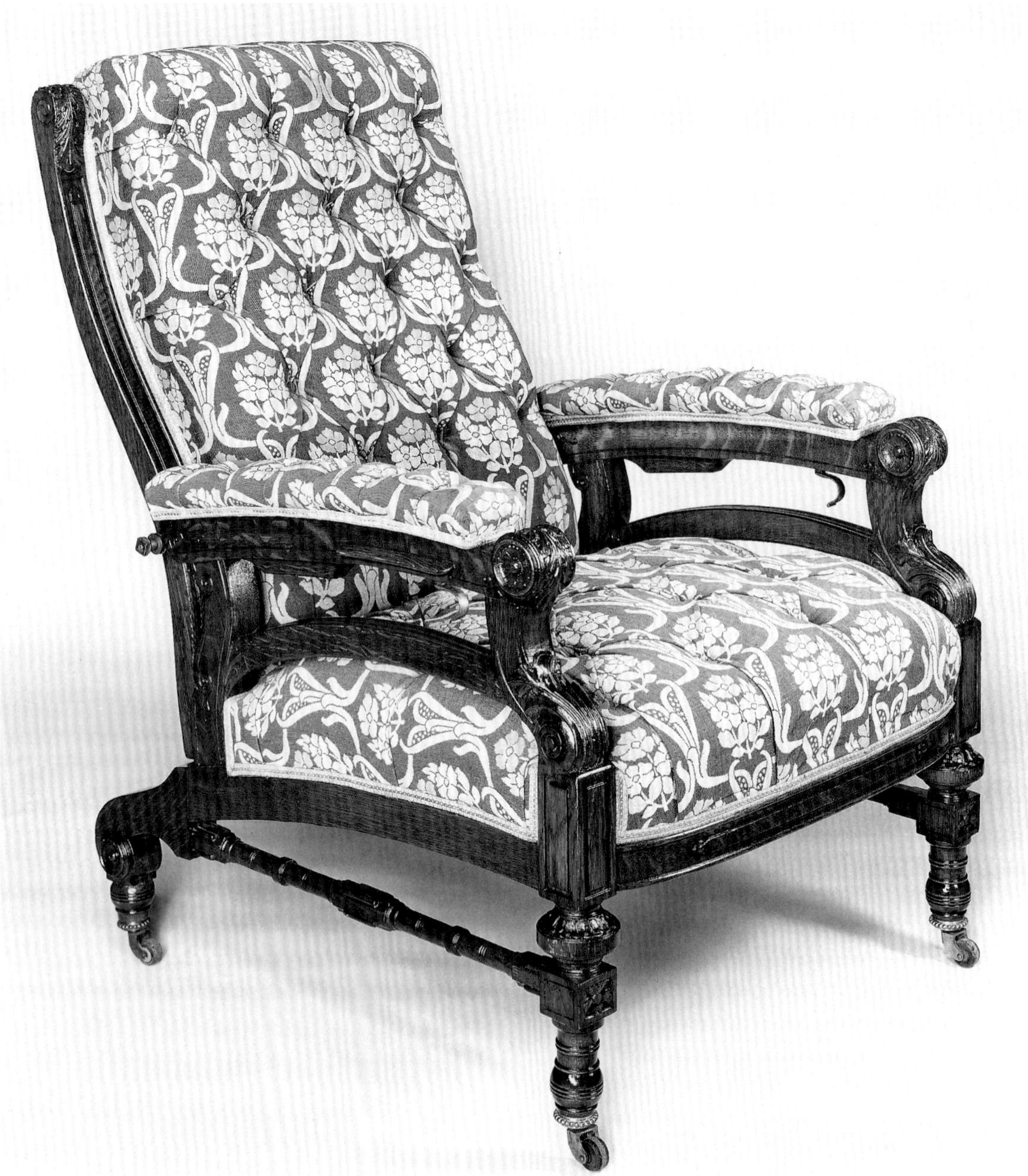

Theodore Hofstatter, Jr., applied for a patent for this reclining armchair on January 16, 1881, and received it on August 30 (fig. 1). A reclining armchair was not a new idea. Many American inventors—such as George Hunzinger (see no. 85) and Cevedra B. Sheldon (see no. 86) —had patented examples with different mechanisms. But according to his patent specifications, Hofstatter improved on previous reclining armchairs. His innovation was a more concealed reclining mechanism, which provided greater convenience because the occupant could control the tilt of the back. The chair arms were hollow, to accommodate ratcheted bars attached to the side stiles of the hinged back. Teeth inside each arm fitted into the ratchet bars and were controlled by hooked handles on the undersides of the arms. When the reclining mechanism was operated, only the hinged back—and not the arms—moved. Hofstatter's specifications and drawings may have been accompanied by a model to demonstrate the mechanism.

Hofstatter noted in his specifications that "the chair-frame may be of any suitable form or style."[1] The Crawford chair closely resembles his drawings, which show the slightly curved shape of the back as well as the raking side rails of the seat that terminate in carved and scrolled feet. The turned side stretchers follow the general shape seen in the drawing, and the arms end in similar scrolls. The carved acanthus-leaf scrolls and incised decorations on the frame relate the Crawford chair to Renaissance-style furniture of the 1870s and 1880s.

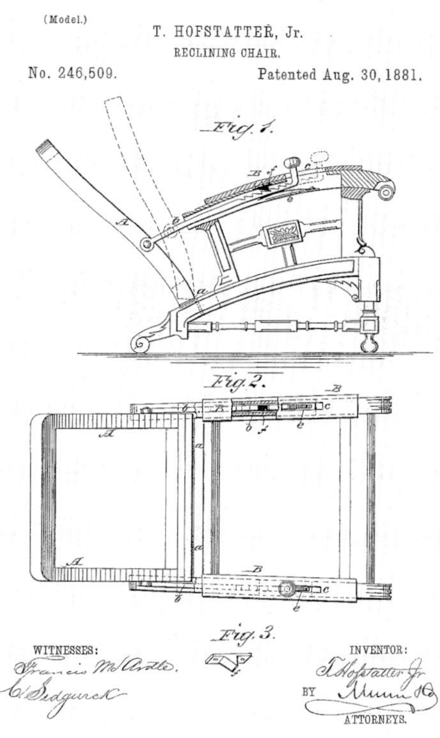

Fig. 1. Patent drawing. U.S. Patent Office, Theodore Hofstatter Jr., of New York. Reclining-Chair, specifications forming part of Letters Patent Number 246,509, dated August 30, 1881.

NOTE

1. Theodore Hofstatter, Jr., "Reclining-Chair. Specification forming part of Letters Patent No. 246,509, dated August 30, 1881." Three weeks later, on September 20, Hofstatter was issued a second patent (no. 247,350) for lounges and sofas "having their head or end portions adjustable for varying the inclination." Hofstatter did not assign his patents to anyone else, which suggests that he manufactured furniture himself. By the early twentieth century, the term "Morris chair" was often associated with the Hofstatter type of upholstered reclining armchair.

Return to Craftsmanship, 1870s

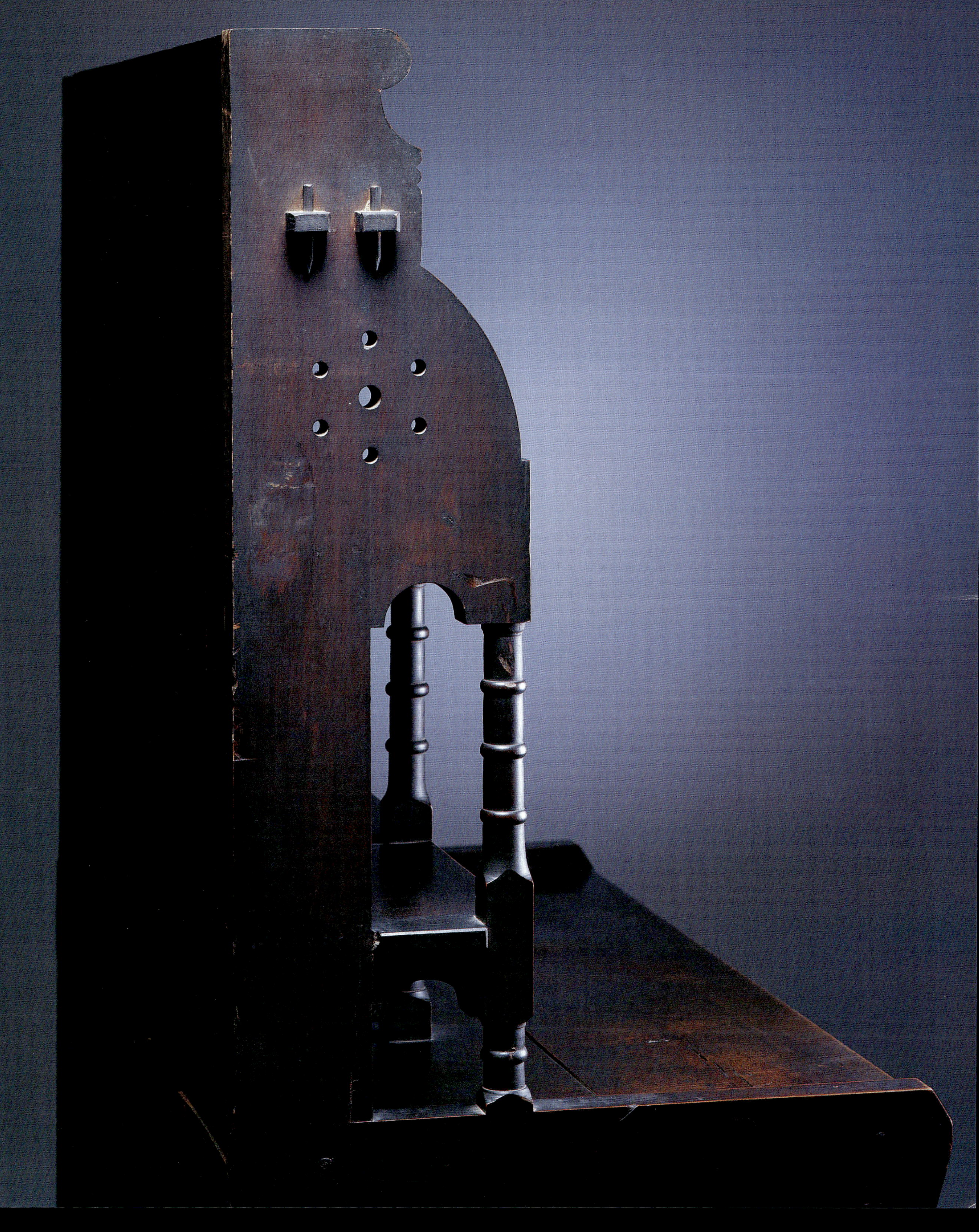

89.

Sideboard, 1875–1885

Probably northeastern urban United States
Walnut, poplar, painted earthenware tiles, and brass mounts
76½ × 54½ × 27⅛ inches
1994.158

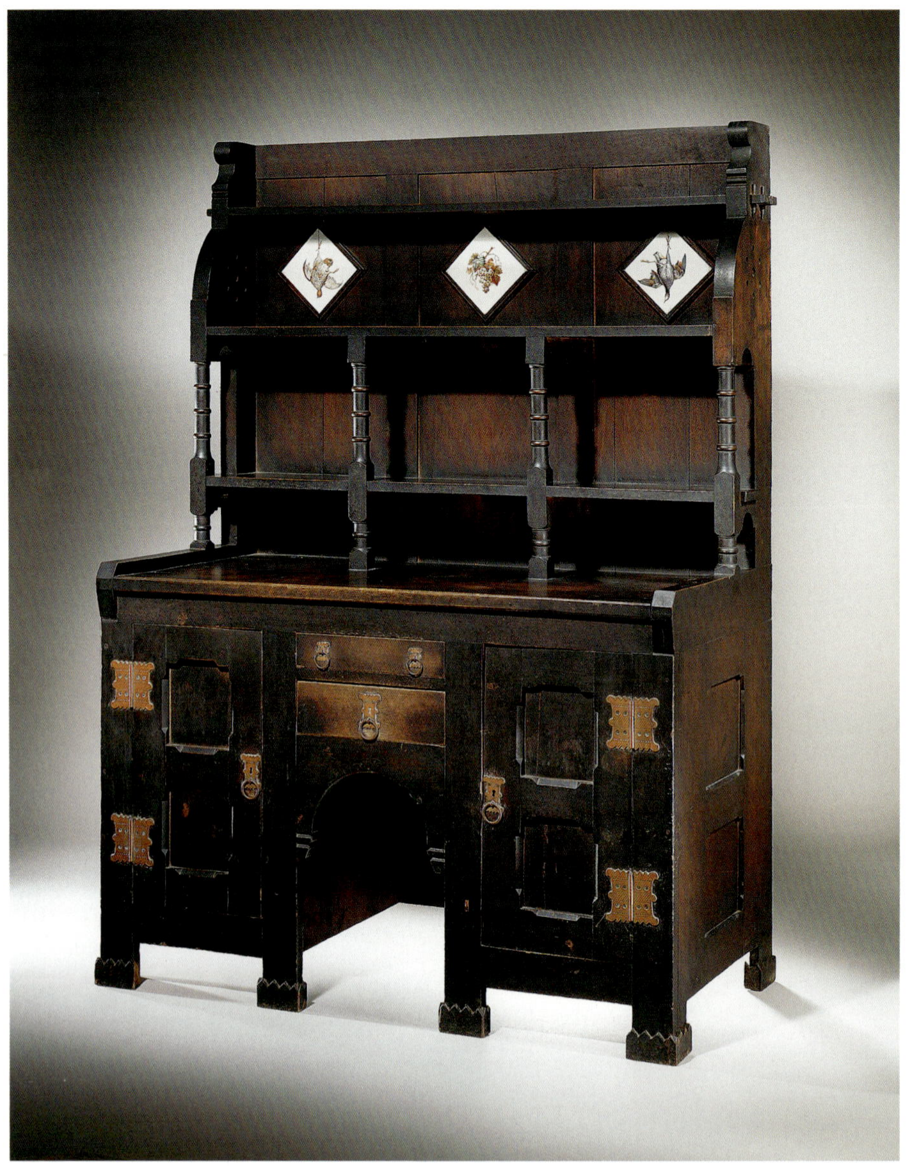

THIS SIDEBOARD'S severe rectangular outline and absence of decoration is in stark contrast to the sinuous curves and sumptuous, often carved, surfaces that had characterized the most stylish and ambitious American furniture since the 1840s. The sideboard was derived from a design by Charles Locke Eastlake in his seminal 1868 book *Hints on Household Taste in Furniture, Upholstery and Other Details.* Eastlake, born into a wealthy family in Plymouth, England, was well educated and trained as an architect. After completing his education, he traveled for three years throughout Europe and became interested in medieval architecture. From 1855 to 1878, Eastlake was secretary of the Royal Institute of British Architects, even though he never practiced. He became keeper of the National Gallery in London in 1878, where he studied and reorganized the collection until his retirement in 1896. In 1872, he wrote *A History of the Gothic Revival,* which was highly respected and remains an important scholarly reference.[1] That same year, an American edition of *Hints on Household Taste* was published in Boston. The popularity of the book was immediate: between 1872 and 1886, it went through seven editions in the United States.

Eastlake, in the preface to the 1869 edition of *Hints on Household Taste,* attempted to diffuse his supposed promotion of medieval- and Gothic-style furniture, stating, "I recommend the re-adoption of no specific type of ancient furniture which is unsuited, whether in detail or general design, to the habits of modern life. It is the spirit and principles of early manufacture which I desire to see revived, and not the absolute forms in which they found embodiment." Despite his denial, Eastlake became indelibly associated with the modern Gothic of the 1870s. Many American publications even referred to an "Eastlake style." He wrote in the preface to the fourth English edition of the book in 1878, "I find American tradesmen continually advertising what they are pleased to call 'Eastlake' furniture, with the production of which I have had nothing whatever to do, and for the taste of which I should be very sorry to be considered responsible."[2]

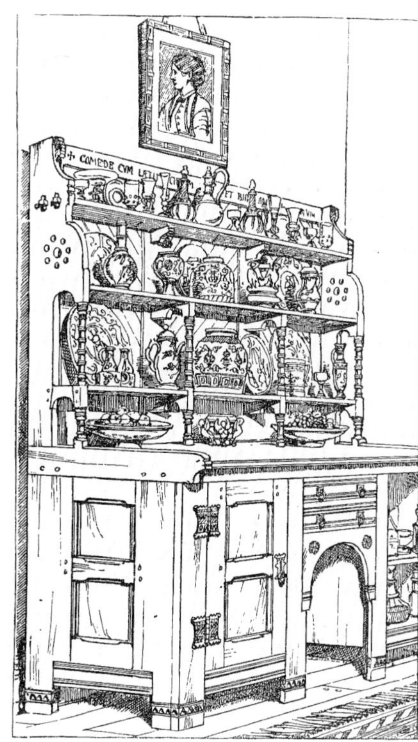

Fig. 1. Sideboard. Charles Locke Eastlake, *Hints on Household Taste in Furniture, Upholstery and Other Details* (Boston: James R. Osgood and Company, 1872), p. 84, pl. XII.

This sideboard is unusual in American Eastlake-influenced furniture in that it is a nearly exact copy of an illustration in *Hints on Household Taste* (fig. 1). Eastlake preferred the turned decoration of the sideboard columns to the carved decoration of much mid-nineteenth century furniture. Furthermore, the construction is clearly evident in the through tenons seen in both the Crawford sideboard and the Eastlake illustration. The sideboard also lacks the highly polished French finish, which Eastlake criticized in furniture dating from the 1850s through the 1870s. In these details, the Crawford sideboard was a harbinger of the art furniture, ceramics, and glass of the Aesthetic movement and the Arts and Crafts movement.

The Crawford sideboard provides interesting contrasts and parallels with the Philadelphia sideboard of the mid-1850s (see no. 48), a design Eastlake would surely have deplored. Except for the fact that Eastlake was describing English furniture, he might have been referring to the earlier Crawford sideboard when he wrote: "Hundreds . . . now following this trade [carving] . . . will imitate in wood, with astonishing precision and delicacy the feathered forms of dead game, or reproduce, line for line and leaf for leaf, a festoon of real flowers." Eastlake found "the carver's skill . . . utterly wasted on such work" and renounced "those trophies of slaughtered hares and partridges which you may occasionally see standing out in bold relief from the backboard of a buffet or the door of a cabinet," and declaring further that "many of them are cleverly executed it is true, but they are in a bad and vicious style of art. Wood-carving applied as a means of decoration in such places should be treated after a thoroughly *abstract* fashion, and made subservient to the general design of the furniture."[3] Despite the later sideboard's straight lines, turned elements, and absence of carving, its three small earthenware tiles were painted with images of dead game. Perhaps the maker and original owner of the sideboard found these tiles acceptable because they were secondary to the overall design and were appropriate to the function of the sideboard, as Eastlake prescribed.

NOTES

1. Charles Locke Eastlake, *A History of the Gothic Revival* (1872. Reprint. Leicester, England: University Press, 1970). For information about Eastlake and his influence in both England and the United States, see the introduction by Mary Jean Smith Madigan to Hudson River Museum 1973, unpaginated; and John Gloag's introduction to Eastlake 1969, pp. v–xix. See also Madigan 1975, pp. 1–22.

2. The preface to the second edition of Eastlake's book is quoted by Gloag in his introduction to the reprint of Eastlake 1969, pp. viii–ix. The quotation regarding American "Eastlake" furniture is from the preface to the fourth edition, in ibid., p. xxiv.

3. Eastlake 1969, pp. 67–69.

90.

Panel, designed 1878–1879

William Morris and Company (1875–1940), London; designed by William Morris (1834–1896)
Woven wool
86½ × 32 inches
1983.209

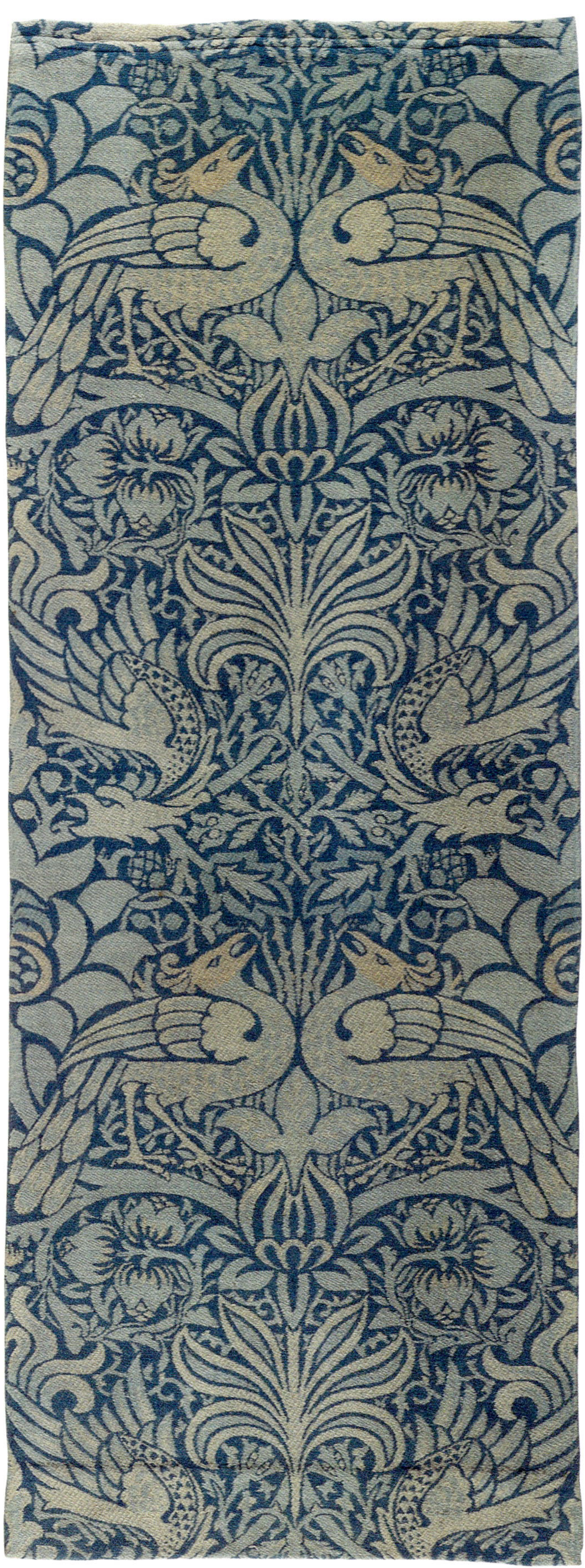

IN THE 1870S, William Morris, along with Charles Locke Eastlake, introduced the United States to a profoundly English taste that combined the decorative and fine arts of the period, leading to the Aesthetic movement in the last two decades of the nineteenth century, and the Arts and Crafts movement in the first decade of the twentieth. Morris was born into an affluent English business family and grew up on his father's estate at Essex outside London. As a child, he was fascinated with medieval and Gothic architecture. Although he attended Oxford University intending to study for the ministry, his friendship with Edward Burne-Jones and the influence of a circle of artistic friends resulted in both men pursuing careers in art: Burne-Jones in painting and Morris in design, after trying architecture. In 1861, Morris established a decorating firm in London with Burne-Jones, the painter Dante Gabriel Rossetti, and other artists.[1]

Morris's firm produced textiles, furniture, stained glass, and all manner of decorations. Eastlake, who was later to write the influential *Hints on Household Taste in Furniture, Upholstery and Other Details,* visited Morris's exhibition at the London Universal Exposition in South Kensington in 1862 and wrote: "As we strolled into the court devoted to messrs Morris and Co.'s medieval furniture, tapestries &c., who could believe that it represented manufactures of the 19th century—the age *par excellence* of cog wheels and steam rams and rifled cannon? Six hundred years have passed since the style of yon cabinet was in vogue."[2] In 1875, Morris bought out the other partners and established Morris and Company. After he took over the firm, agents in continental Europe and the United States began distributing his goods to wider audiences. Morris and Company participated in the 1876 Centennial Exposition in Philadelphia, and Americans, already infatuated with the writings of Eastlake, eagerly bought Morris's products for their homes.

Throughout his career, Morris specialized in textile and embroidery design and production. He served as an advisor to the South Kensington Museum (later the Victoria and Albert Museum) in developing its collections of textiles and tapestries. His familiarity with medieval tapestries is reflected in his woolen, jacquard weave tapestries of the late 1870s and 1880s, such as the Crawford example. Morris used this pattern, *Peacock and Dragon*, for his own drawing room at Kelmscott House in London, and it was also widely marketed in both the United States and Europe. In the United States, the characteristic Morris design of peacocks, dragons, and stylized flowers executed in subtle colors appealed to the art-craving American market.[3] The emphasis on pattern and stylized motifs derived from nature typified not only Morris's textiles, but also American furniture and other decorative arts of the Aesthetic movement (see nos. 107–110).

NOTES

1. For biographical information about Morris, see The Metropolitan Museum of Art 1986, pp. 455–457, and the most recent comprehensive survey, Parry 1996. For a full discussion of the Aesthetic movement in America, see The Metropolitan Museum of Art 1986. For the Arts and Crafts movement in America, see Bowman 1990, and Kaplan 1987.

2. *London Society* (August 1862), p. 106; cited in Parry 1996, p. 358.

3. A curtain with a double panel of the *Peacock and Dragon* design is in the Victoria and Albert Museum and is illustrated and discussed in Parry 1996, p. 271, no. M.80.

91.

Armchair, 1876

Possibly New York
Ebony, ivory, and modern leather upholstery
49½ × 22⅛ × 22 inches
Mark: Brass oval framed in beading, embedded in seat frame at back, with relief decoration of the infant Hercules battling a bear who is standing at a keg, drinking from the spigot; above, *JOHN MATHEW . . ., NE . . . YORK*; below, *K. MULLER F./ 1876*
1985.318

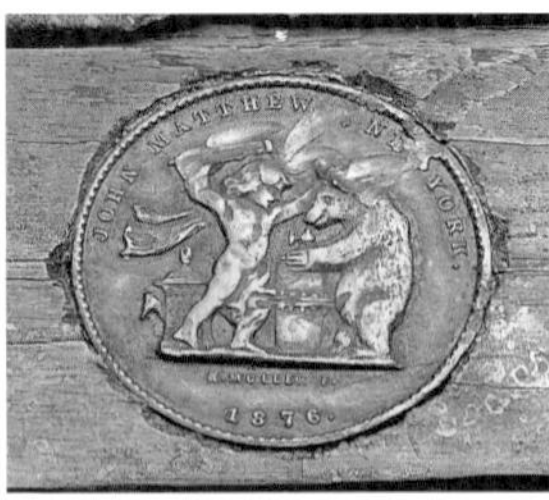

EBONY AND IVORY give an exotic and rich appearance to this armchair, which is related to a design by Charles Locke Eastlake, illustrated in his *Hints on Household Taste in Furniture, Upholstery and Other Details* (fig. 1). The Eastlake design, possibly an inspiration for the Crawford armchair, was manufactured in London by Jackson and Graham. Eastlake contrasted his design with contemporary furniture of the late 1860s and 1870s, noting "how easily a few incised patterns and turned moldings may be substituted for the lumpy carving and 'shaped' legs usually found on such furniture."[1]

The chair illustrated in *Hints on Household Taste* has a square upholstered seat and back like the Crawford chair. Both have spindles—preferred over carving by Eastlake—beneath the arms and between the upholstery and crest rail of the back, although on the Crawford chair the spindles of the back are ivory. The Crawford chair also has spindles on the sides between the stretchers and the seat rails. The finials at the top of the backposts and the circular ivory medallion at the center of the crest further relate this chair to the Eastlake design. The major difference between the chairs is the shorter arm length on the Crawford chair, which makes it seem less confining.

At the time the Crawford chair was made, if the date on the brass label is accurate, the use of ebony and ivory would have evoked cultures considered remote and exotic, such as India or Africa, although the design was thoroughly English. The chair also foreshadowed the artistic use of unexpected materials in American furniture from the 1870s.

The chair may have been made for the office and warerooms of John Matthews, a manufacturer of apparatus for making, bottling, and dispensing soda, mineral waters, and sparkling liquors, at First Avenue between 26th and 27th Streets in New York. The date on the chair's label could also indicate the chair was made for a Matthews display at the Centennial Exposition. Matthews emigrated from England in 1832 and established his business, whose logo appears on the chair's metal label. The creator of the Matthews logo was Karl L. H. Müller, designer for the Union Porcelain Works (see nos. 76–80) and son-in-law of Matthews. In 1882, Union Porcelain Works produced a molded porcelain mug with the same logo, possibly to mark the fiftieth anniversary of the Matthews company.[2]

NOTES

1. Eastlake 1969, p. 165.

2. At least two Union Porcelain Works mugs with the Matthews logo are known, one in the collection of the Brooklyn Museum of Art, and the other in the Museum of the City of New York. The Brooklyn Museum of Art also owns a silver-plated mount designed by Müller for a Matthews soda fountain (1990.155.2). Correspondence, Dr. Barry R. Harwood, associate curator of decorative arts, Brooklyn Museum of Art, August 18, 1998, High Museum of Art document files.

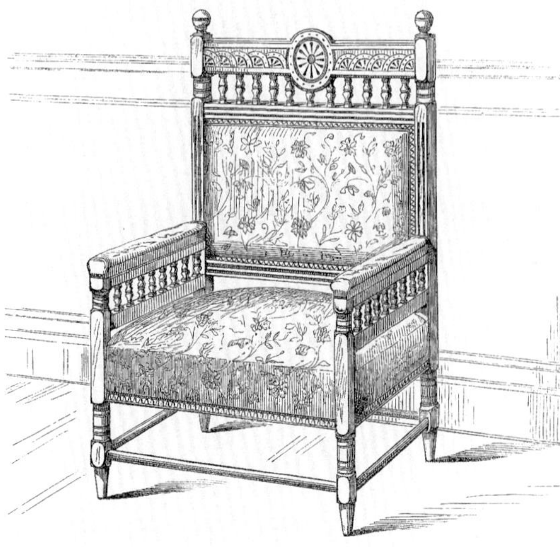

Fig. 1. Armchair. Charles Locke Eastlake, *Hints on Household Taste in Furniture, Upholstery and Other Details* (London: Longmans, Green and Company, 1878), p. 165.

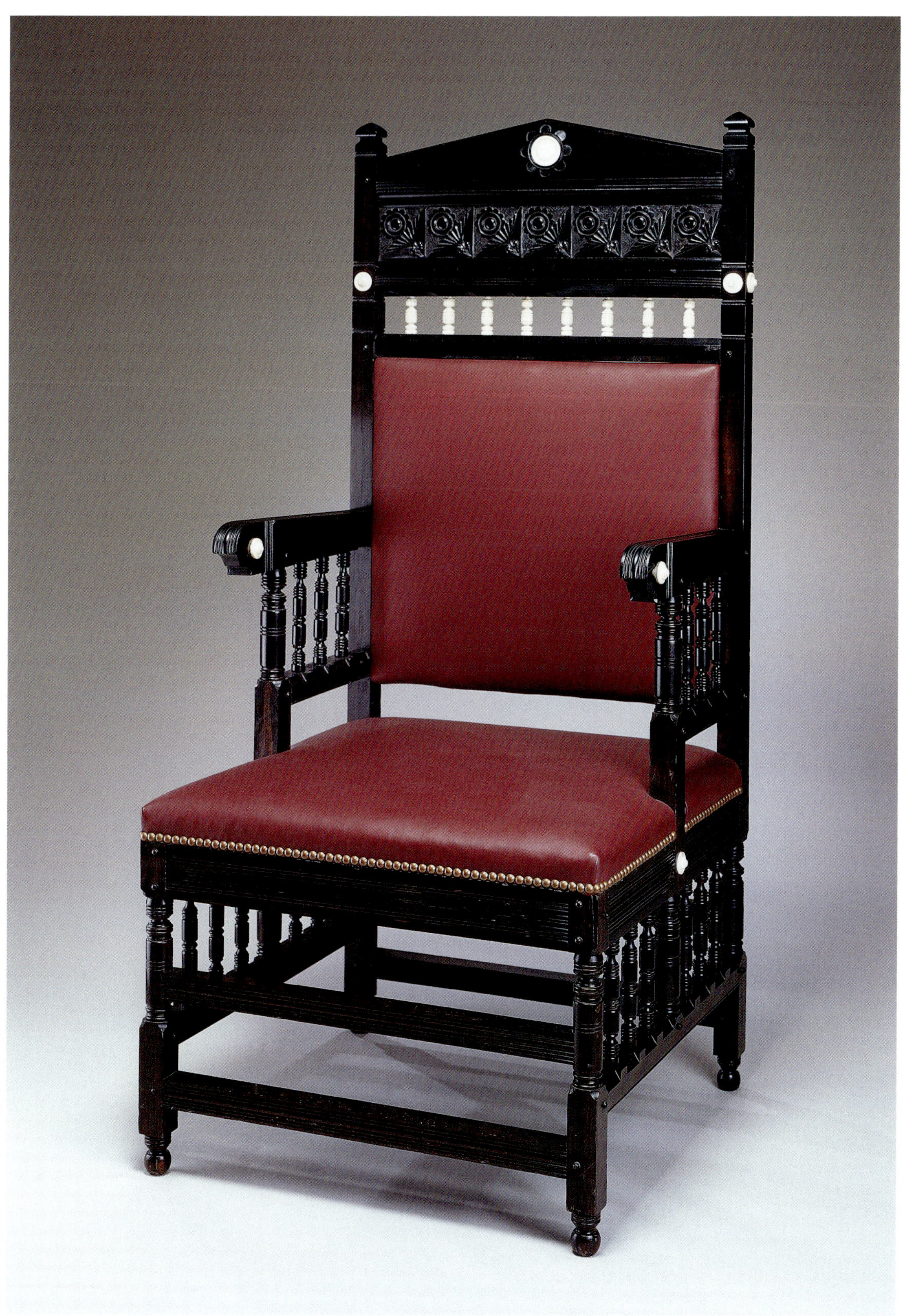

92.

Covered Vase, 1877–1883

John Bennett's American Pottery (1877–1883), New York
Earthenware with polychrome decoration
12¼ × 6¼ × 6¼ inches
Mark: On bottom in green, *J* conjoined with BENNETT/*101 Lex Ave N.Y.*
1982.287

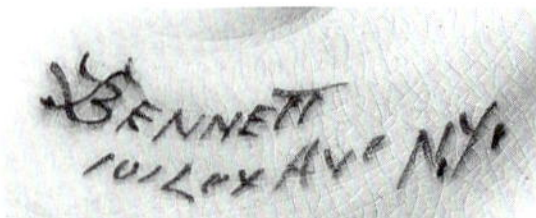

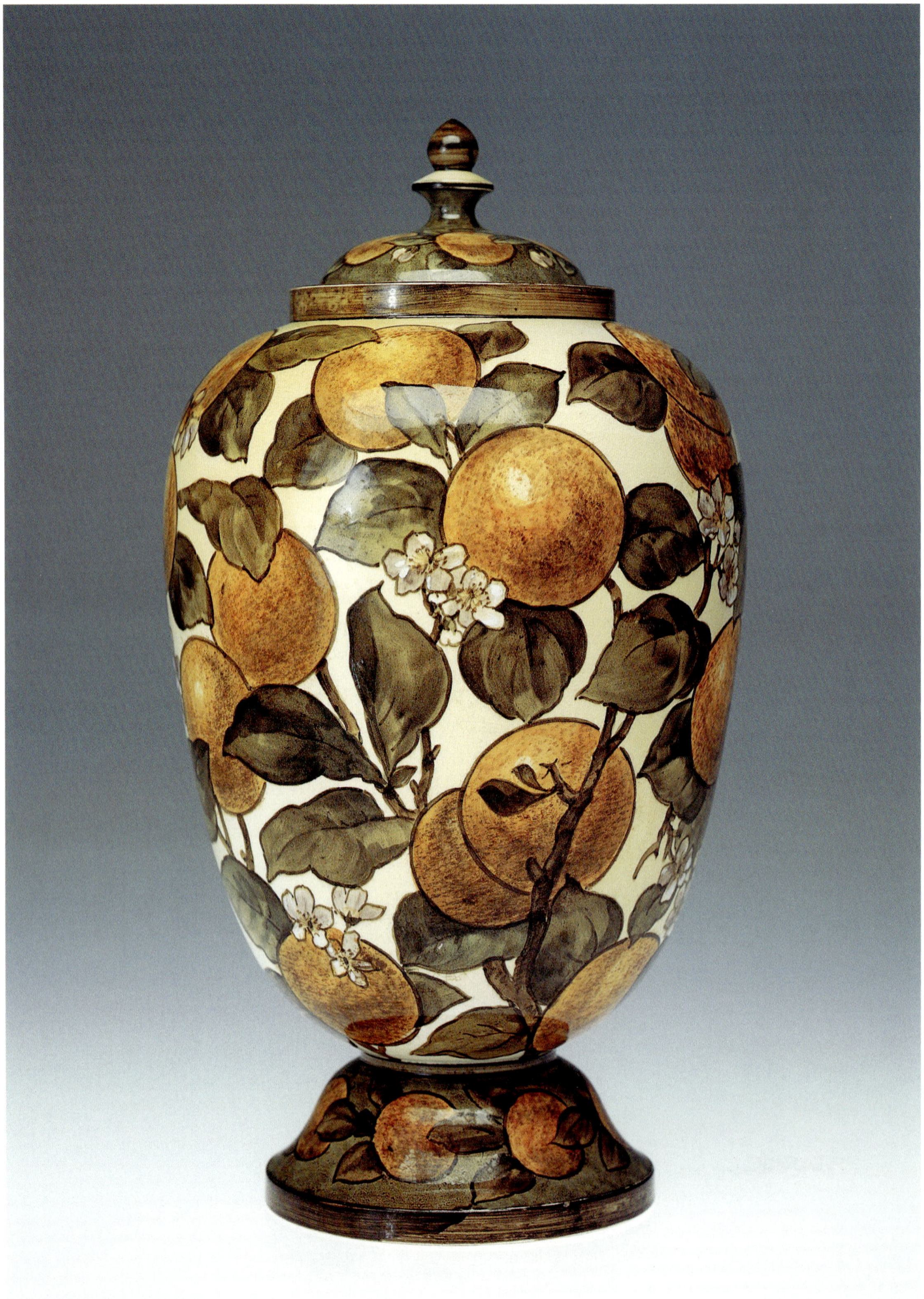

DURING HIS LIFETIME, John Bennett drew widespread acclaim for his painted decoration on pottery. His father was the proprietor of the Sneyd Pottery at Burslem in Staffordshire, England, where the younger Bennett received his initial exposure and training in the pottery business. In 1873, Bennett was hired by Henry Doulton and Company in London, in conjunction with the Lambeth School of Art, to establish a department of painted earthenware underglaze decoration. Designs on Doulton wares were based on the revived interest in European and Middle Eastern tin-glazed earthenwares from the Renaissance to the eighteenth century. Both Doulton's training program and the company's ceramics were influenced by English designer and philosopher William Morris (no. 90).

As a teacher and decorator at Doulton, Bennett was recognized in English ceramic circles, but it was his works in the Doulton display at the 1876 Centennial Exposition in Philadelphia that introduced him to the American market. Encouraged by the response to his work, Bennett immigrated to New York in 1877. He rented a studio at 101 Lexington Avenue, where he gave lessons in ceramic decoration and established John Bennett's American Pottery, the mark and address on the Crawford vase. He also maintained a pottery works where he lived on East 24th Street. Bennett was the first artist to teach pottery decoration for the Society of Decorative Art in New York, which promoted "decorative work of any description done by women."[1] Bennett's work became known nationally when his wares were included in various decorative arts society exhibitions in Boston, Cincinnati, San Francisco, and other cities. Prestigious retailers like Tiffany and Company began selling his work along with English and Continental artistic wares. In spite of his success, however, Bennett retired to a farm in West Orange, New Jersey, in 1883, where he lived quietly for the rest of his life.[2]

Through his teaching and exhibitions, Bennett brought the flat, linear, and stylized decoration associated with Morris and other designers of the English Aesthetic and Arts and Crafts movements to the United States. Bennett probably decorated the Crawford vase during his earliest period here. His muted colors—here olive green and orange on a buff background—and the flat and heavily outlined fruit, leaves, and blossoms owe much to Morris's wallpaper patterns of the period. Bennett's later wares display the more vivid palettes associated with the Japanese taste of the early 1880s. Although Bennett decorated this vase with a natural arrangement of fruits and leaves, he exercised artistic license in unseasonably including both fruit and blossoms in his design. On the base and lid, the oranges and leaves were executed in a more linear, stylized pattern on a green rather than buff background.

NOTES

1. "The New Society of Decorative Art," *New York Times,* June 16, 1877, p. 4; cited in The Metropolitan Museum of Art 1986, p. 218.

2. For an account of Bennett's career, see The Metropolitan Museum of Art 1986, pp. 217–218, 402–403. The Crawford vase is discussed on pp. 217–218 and illustrated on p. 219, fig. 7.20.

93.

Plant Stand, ca. 1875

Probably New York
Wrought iron and marble
34 × 24 × 24 inches
1992.387

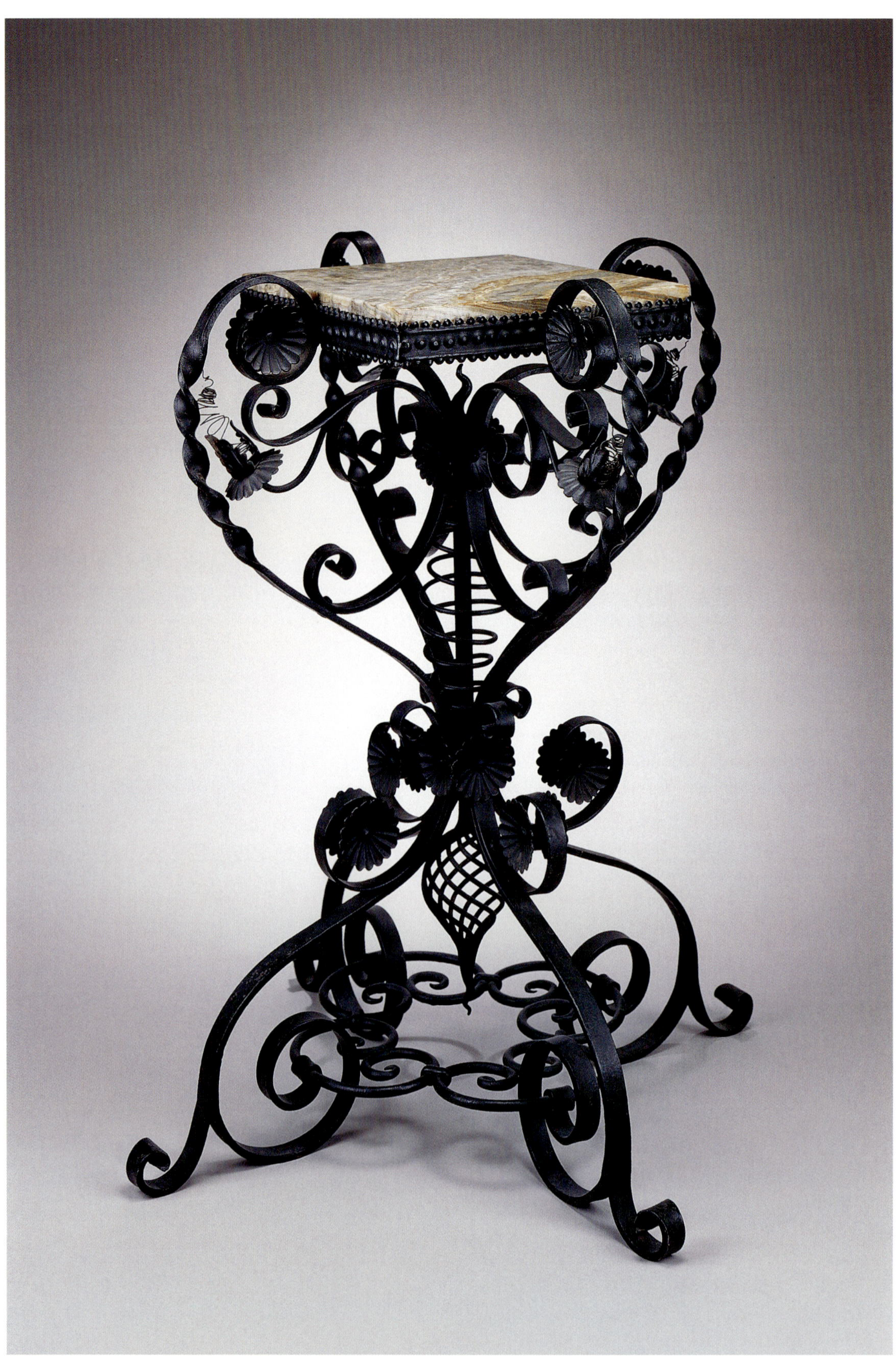

IN THE 1870S AND 1880S, nearly fifty years after cast iron had been introduced on a large scale in America (see nos. 19–27), Charles Locke Eastlake encouraged the production of hand-wrought iron. His book, *Hints on Household Taste in Furniture, Upholstery and Other Details,* illustrated what the author described as an "Old Swiss Iron Candlestick" (fig. 1), possibly an inspiration for this plant stand. Eastlake greatly admired the candlestick's "workmanlike" construction and its "great fertility of invention." Although he did not suggest a reproduction of the candlestick in a time of gas illumination, Eastlake noted that "there are in modern use many objects of decorative metal-work which might be successfully treated with the same spirit of design."[1] Plant stands may have been the kind of products he had in mind.

The unidentified maker of the Crawford plant stand seems to have fulfilled many of Eastlake's preferences in wrought iron, which included "pointed ends . . . twisted into a spiral form," a detail that runs down the center of the stand. The candlestick has a twisted band at the top similar to the four twisted scroll supports of the top of the plant stand. Even the cut border around the marble top of the stand echoes the gallery around the tray base of the candlestick. Although the flowers at the center of the scrolls are stylized, the leaves appear more naturalistically rendered. These floral elements may have been intended to suggest the function of the plant stand. While American manufacturers such as the maker of this plant stand and the Crawford sideboard (see no. 89) adhered closely to Eastlake's principles, they continued to use the associative decoration that had prevailed in American furniture since the 1850s, in spite of Eastlake's criticism of realistically depicted nature in furniture design.

The New York furniture firm Kimbel and Cabus (see no. 69) illustrated similar wrought-iron stands and tables in their furniture catalogue published around 1875, although this stand is not shown. The Kimbel and Cabus examples included twisted iron bands and spirals, stylized flowers, and naturally rendered leaves, much like those on the Crawford stand. Associated Artists, the predecessor to Tiffany Studios (see nos. 175–177), completed the interior decoration of the Seventh Regiment Armory in New York in 1880 using similar wrought iron in the form of chandeliers and fireplace fittings.[2]

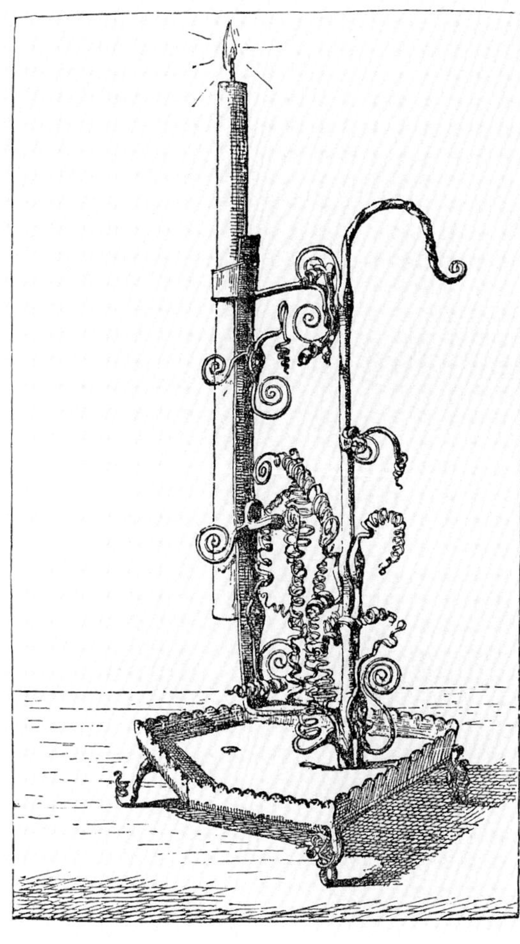

Fig. 1. Candlestick. Charles Locke Eastlake, *Hints on Household Taste in Furniture, Upholstery and Other Details* (London: Longmans, Green and Company, 1878), facing p. 152.

NOTES

1. Eastlake 1969, pp. 152–153.

2. For an account of the decoration of the Seventh Regiment Armory, see Faude 1975.

94.

Pitcher, 1877–1885

Attributed to Boston and Sandwich Glass Company (1825–1888), Sandwich, Massachusetts, and the Gorham Manufacturing Company (1831–present), Providence, Rhode Island
Free-blown and overshot, craquelle, or ice lead glass and silver
12½ × 7¼ × 6¼ inches
Mark: On silver collar, near handle in shields, rampant lion facing left, anchor, and *G*; *STERLING*
1993.136

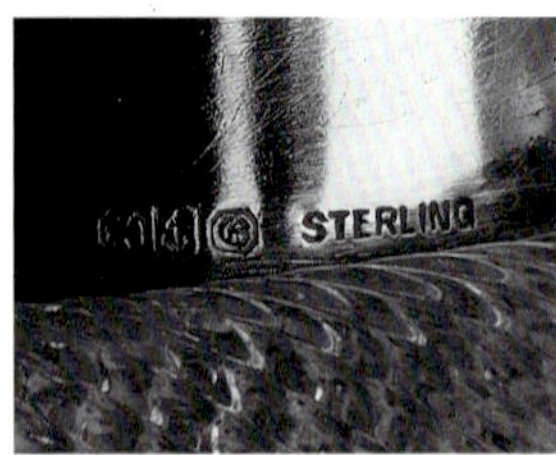

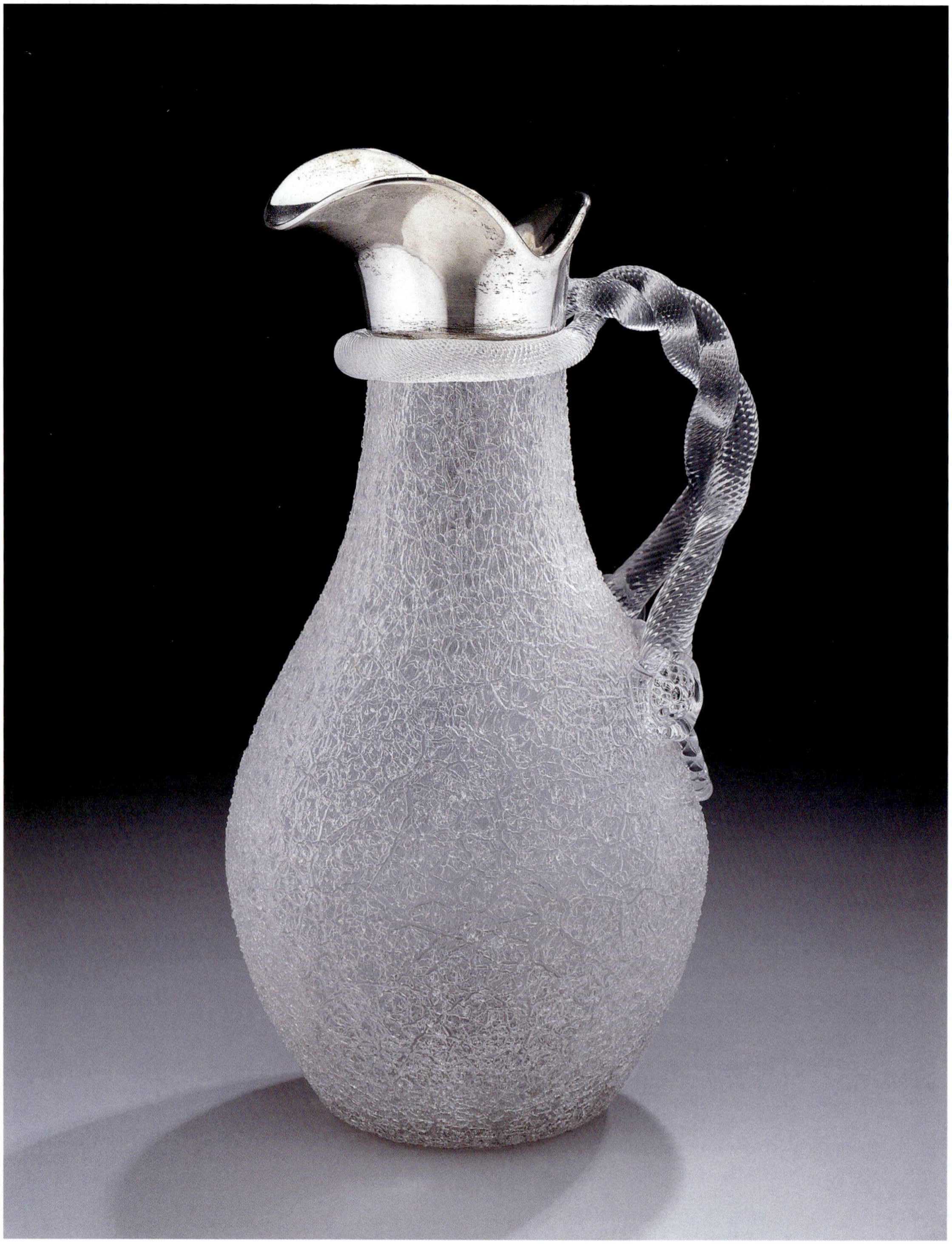

THIS CHAMPAGNE pitcher is attributed to the Boston and Sandwich Glass Company of Sandwich, Massachusetts, but it is not an example of what is generally called "Sandwich glass." That term was used in American glass literature from the 1920s through 1960s to designate pre–Civil War pressed glass rather than the cut and engraved wares that the company had manufactured from its beginning or the art glasswares it produced after the Civil War. The Mount Washington Glass Company (see nos. 136–138) and the New England Glass Company (see nos. 129–132), the major regional competitors of the Boston and Sandwich Glass Company, are today better known than Sandwich for the ornamental art wares of the later period. In a photograph of the 1878 Boston and Sandwich Glass Company exhibition at Mechanics Hall in Boston (fig. 1), examples of the firm's enamel-decorated and opal glasswares are displayed along with a group of ice, or craquelle, glass like the Crawford pitcher, which appears to be very similar in form to a pitcher in this image.[1]

As in every other area of the decorative arts in the nineteenth century, glass artisans and factories looked to historical precedent for inspiration. Sixteenth-century Venetian glass was esteemed as the height of glass artistry, and many of its forms and techniques were re-created in Bohemia, England, and the United States. This pitcher, with its handmade, applied twisted handle and decorations and its distinctive shape, echoes such prototypes. The craquelle technique was inspired by an early Venetian innovation in which a partially blown gather, or quantity of molten glass, was thrust into cold water, which caused the surface of the glass to crack throughout without shattering. The glass gather was then reheated and blown, and it expanded with the crackled effect covering the entire surface. Nineteenth-century American glass manufacturers tried for a similar effect by rolling a lead glass gather over pulverized glass chips spread on a marver (the flat stone surface on which the glass gather was rolled during the blowing process to keep the shape symmetrical). The tiny glass chips adhered to the surface of the glass, giving it a rough texture and a frosted look.[2] The finished surface concealed an ingenious glass pocket blown into the side of the pitcher to hold ice and chill the beverage without diluting it. A craquelle pocketed pitcher in the Corning Museum of Glass, attributed to the Boston and Sandwich Glass Company, is nearly identical to the Crawford example. Even the Gorham silver collar duplicates the glass spout and top shapes of the Corning Museum pitcher.[3]

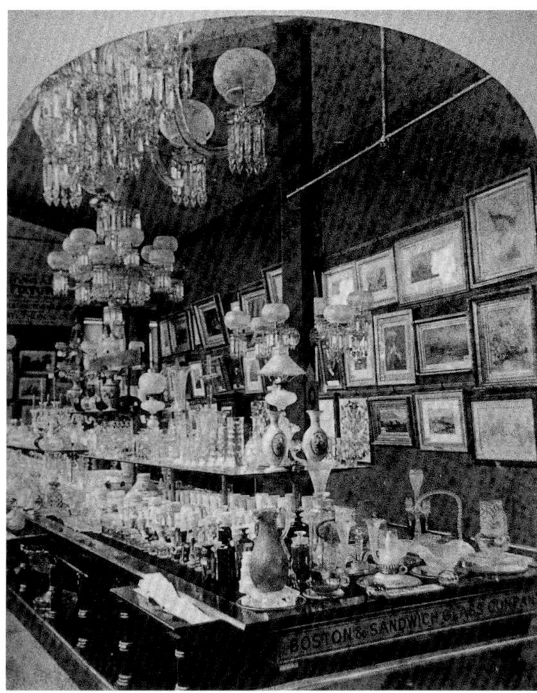

Fig. 1. The 1878 Boston and Sandwich Glass Company display at Mechanics Hall, Boston.

NOTES

1. Illustrated in K. Wilson 1972, p. 358, fig. 332. Overshot, or craquelle, glass was also produced by Hobbs, Brockunier and Company; see The Metropolitan Museum of Art 1986, p. 240.

2. The processes are fully described in Revi 1967, pp. 61–62.

3. The Corning Museum of Glass ice pitcher is illustrated in Frelinghuysen's essay in The Metropolitan Museum of Art 1986, p. 240, fig. 7.44.

95.

Cabinet, 1882

Panels painted by Will Hicok Low (1853–1932)
Ebonized cherry frame, painted wood panels, and glass
52 × 42 × 17½ inches
Marks: In lower right corner of front right panel, lower right corner of left side panel, and lower left corner of right side panel, *1882 Will H. Low;* upper front left panel, *WHL*
1982.320

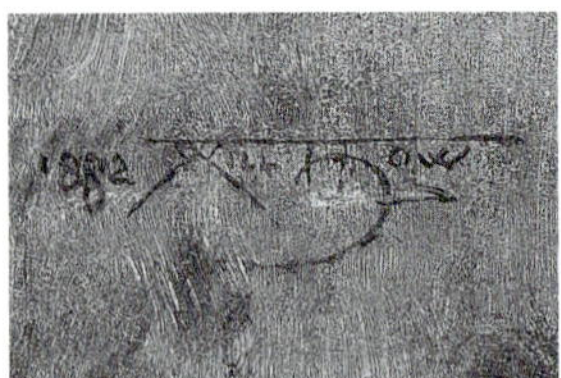

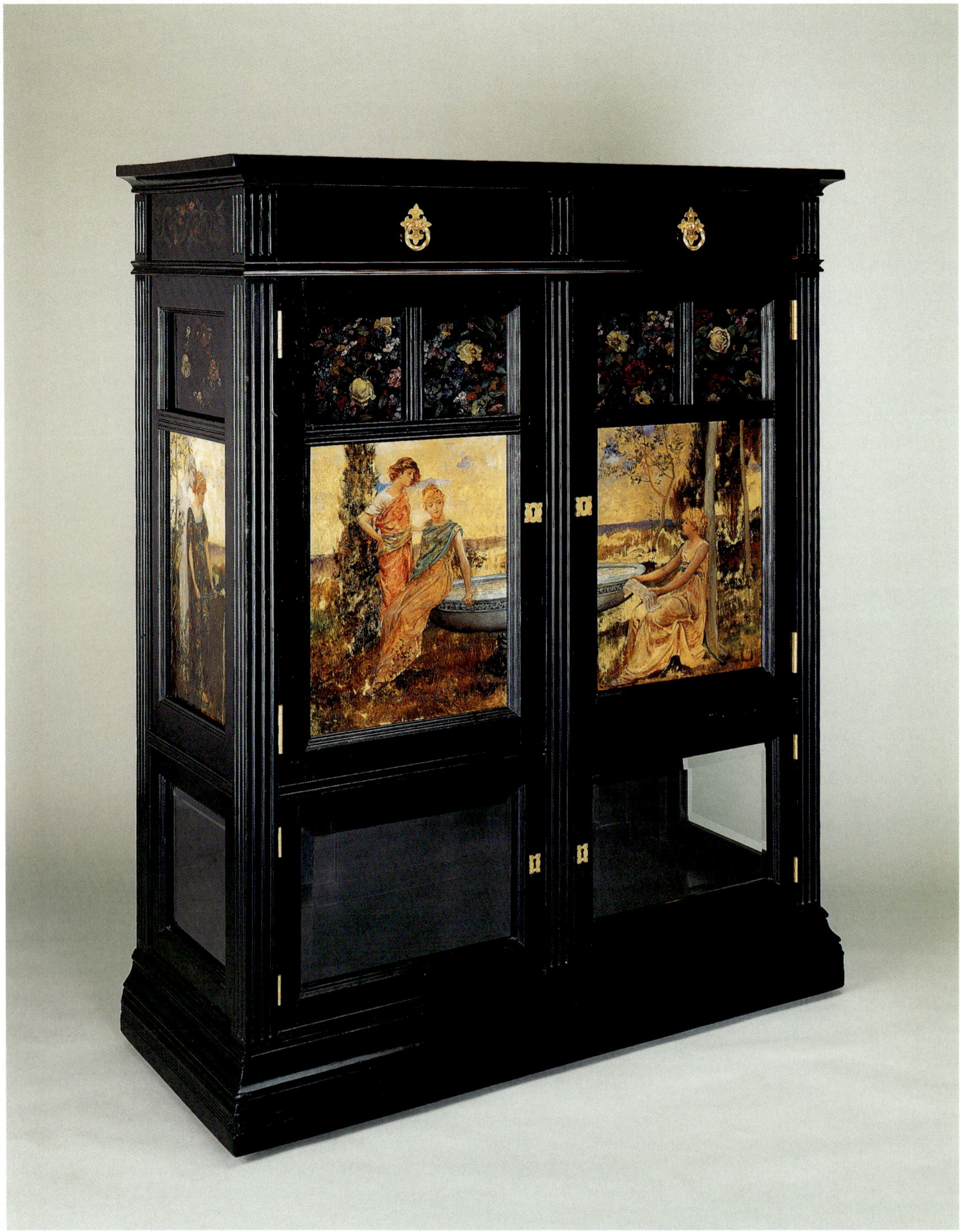

Will Hicok Low, who painted the decorative panels of this cabinet, was born and raised in Albany, New York, where he was inspired to pursue an artistic career after spending time in the studio of sculptor Erastus Dow Palmer, a classmate's father. Low apprenticed at a local manufactory of railroad parlor cars and learned to decorate their interior panels. In 1870–1871, Low moved to New York, where he worked as a magazine illustrator and poster designer and became involved in important art circles. After exhibiting at the National Academy of Design in 1872, Low joined a group of expatriate American art students in Paris, studying with Jean-Léon Gérôme. During his 1873 summer holidays at Barbizon, Low met Jean-François Millet, whose work he admired and who proved to be influential. Millet's decoration of the Chapel of St. Genevieve in the Pantheon in Paris may have encouraged Low to focus on decorative painting after he returned to New York in 1877, although he continued to do easel paintings. Beginning in 1880, Low assisted artist John La Farge in his decorative commissions, which included the Union League Club, the dining room of Cornelius Vanderbilt II, and a program of stained glass windows for William H. Vanderbilt's house on Fifth Avenue (see nos. 109–110).

It was during the time he worked for La Farge that Low painted the panels on the Crawford cabinet.[1] Unfortunately, the identity of the cabinet's maker and its ownership history have been lost. Although it was intended for storage, the cabinet's major function was artistic decoration. The two painted doors and the side panels share a continuing horizon line and can be read as a single narrative. The girl playing violin on the right side panel, whose music is held by the maiden on the right door, has an audience of the two young women on the left door and the maiden on the left side panel, who stands beside a bust of Pan. The vignette on these panels suggests that the cabinet was for sheet music. The flat top and lower cupboard at the base, with its beveled glass panes, are suitable for exhibiting small decorative works of art. The cabinet would have appealed to wealthy Americans in the 1880s, who were eager to demonstrate their artistic sensibilities in home furnishings. Illuminated cabinets such as the Low example are associated with William Morris (see no. 90) in England, who revived them from medieval European furniture as early as the 1870s. However, Low did not paint in the pre-Raphaelite style. Rather, the modeled figures and natural depiction of roses in the smaller upper panels reflect his more Continental background in Paris and Barbizon. Few surviving American examples of these cabinets are known, suggesting that they were not widely made in the United States. The glossy, ebonized surfaces provide a bold contrast to the vivid colors in Low's panels.

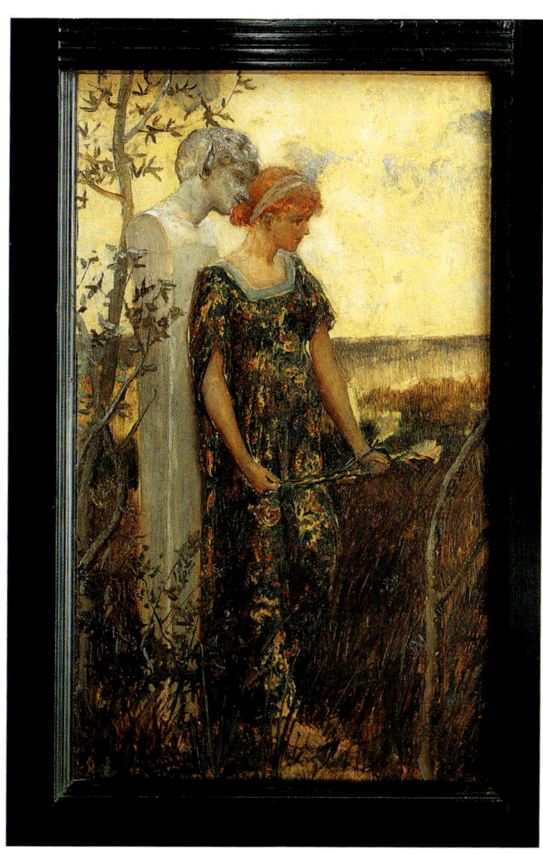

The Crawford cabinet is from Low's early career, before he returned to Europe to further pursue his studies. While he continued to paint canvases in the 1890s and early twentieth century, Low became particularly associated with painted murals in public buildings.

NOTE

1. The Crawford cabinet is illustrated and discussed in the context of the Aesthetic movement in the United States in The Metropolitan Museum of Art 1986, p. 44, fig. I.11. Meixner 1985 gives an account of Low's life, and the Crawford cabinet is illustrated and discussed on pp. 65–66, fig. 19.

Japanese Taste and Exotica, 1870–1910

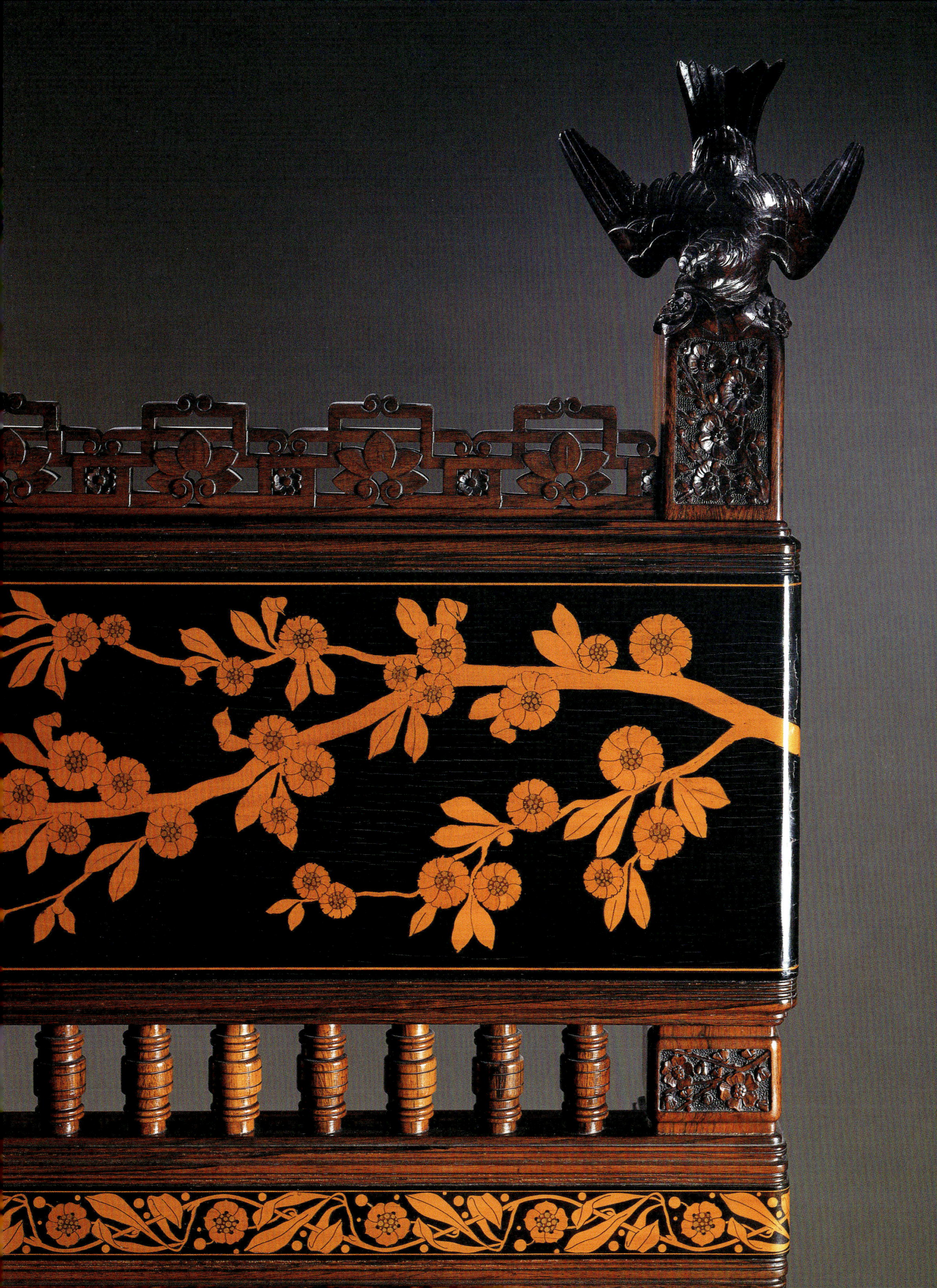

Tiffany and Company Silver in the Exotic Taste

This large comb, with its applied silver-gilt mounts, is an early example of Tiffany silver in the Japanese or exotic taste and a harbinger of the colorful mixed metals with which Tiffany and Company, Gorham Manufacturing Company, and other American silver companies would be identified over the next decade. The stylized flowers and coiled vines on the comb (no. 96) are similar to the Crawford wrought-iron plant stand from the mid-1870s (see no. 93). The "M" in the mark is evidence that Edward C. Moore at least approved the design of the comb.[1]

At the 1878 Exposition Universelle in Paris, two years after the firm's elaborate display at the Centennial Exposition in Philadelphia, Tiffany and Company gained international attention for its mixed-metal silverwares in the Japanese taste. Tiffany's display received the grand prize at the exposition, Moore was awarded a gold medal for his designs, and Charles Louis Tiffany was named a Chevalier in the French Legion of Honor. European royal families and museums purchased Tiffany wares. It was the first time an American firm had elicited such enthusiasm in Europe and an effective endorsement for Tiffany in the United States.

At this time, Tiffany and Company was virtually unrivaled in purveying silver, jewelry, and other luxury goods in New York. After the Civil War, projected peacetime prosperity encouraged Tiffany and Company to purchase Moore's Prince Street manufactory, which had made silver exclusively for the company since 1851 (see no. 41), and Moore was named to the Tiffany board. The 1873 economic depression led to a decline in Tiffany's silver sales by a third, however, and may have prompted Moore to expand beyond the historical styles that had dominated American silver design since the 1840s. At the 1867 Exposition Universelle in Paris, Moore saw the extensive dis-

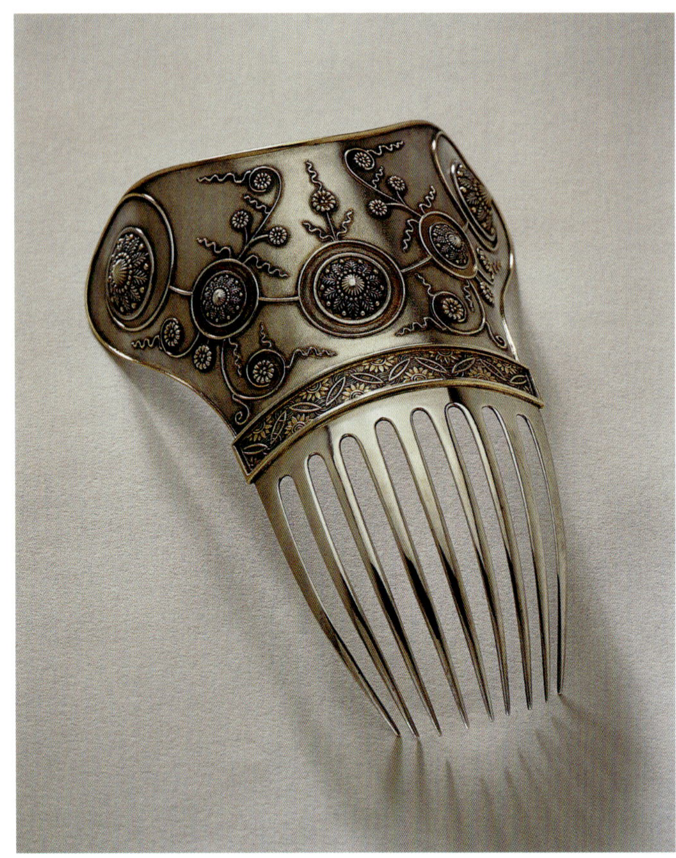

96.

Comb, ca. 1872

Manufactured and retailed by Tiffany and Company (1837–present), New York; designed by Edward C. Moore (1827–1891) or under his supervision
Silver with silver-gilt mounts
7½ × 2¼ × 5½ inches
Marks: Impressed on back, *TIFFANY & CO./3154/STERLING/ UNION SQUARE/M;* scratched on back, *1563*
EL 1.1998

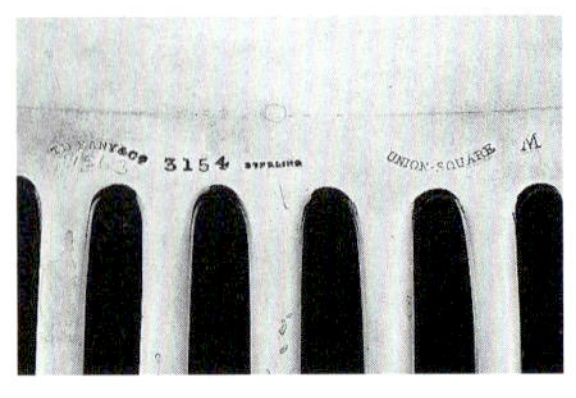

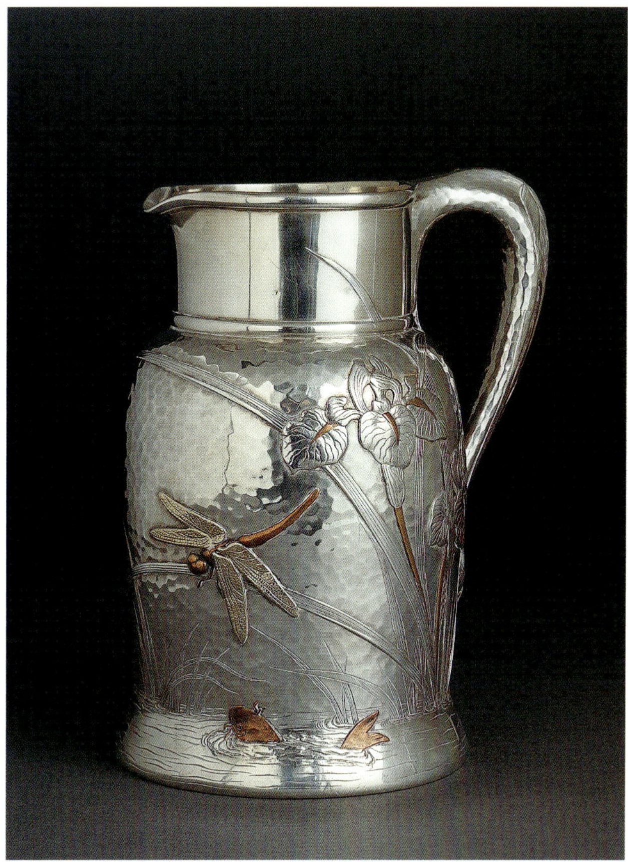

97.

Pitcher, designed ca. 1878

Manufactured and retailed by Tiffany and Company (1837–present), New York; designed by Edward C. Moore (1827–1891) or under his supervision
Silver, copper, brass, and gilt
8⅞ × 7½ × 7½ inches
Mark: Impressed on bottom, *TIFFANY & CO./5051 MAKERS/1641/STERLING SILVER/-AND-/OTHER METALS/144*
1987.175

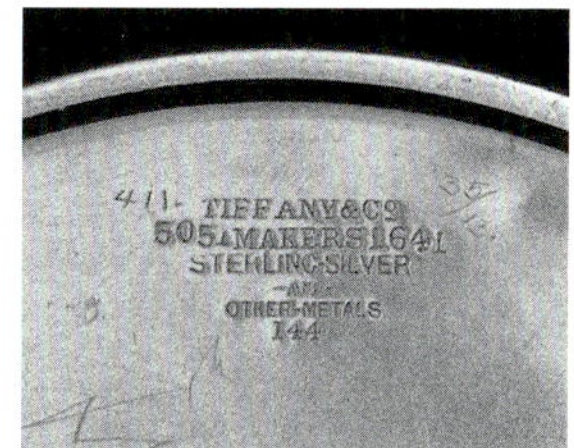

plays of Japanese art and crafts that had a great influence on European artists and designers. Since the 1830s, Tiffany and Company had imported Chinese goods for sale in their New York store, and in 1869, Japanese porcelains, bronzes, and lacquerware were also sold there. Moore began building personal and company collections of Japanese metalwares, textiles, books, and wallpapers as a design resource library. He introduced Tiffany's Japanese pattern flatware in 1871 and began designing silver hollowares and mixed metals in this new taste by the mid-1870s.

The large Japanese display at the Centennial Exposition in Philadelphia attracted major press coverage and provided the initial American exposure to Japanese arts. In 1877, Tiffany and Company hired prominent London industrial designer and ornamentalist Christopher Dresser to tour Japan and buy native wares, but he purchased so extensively that when the wares were

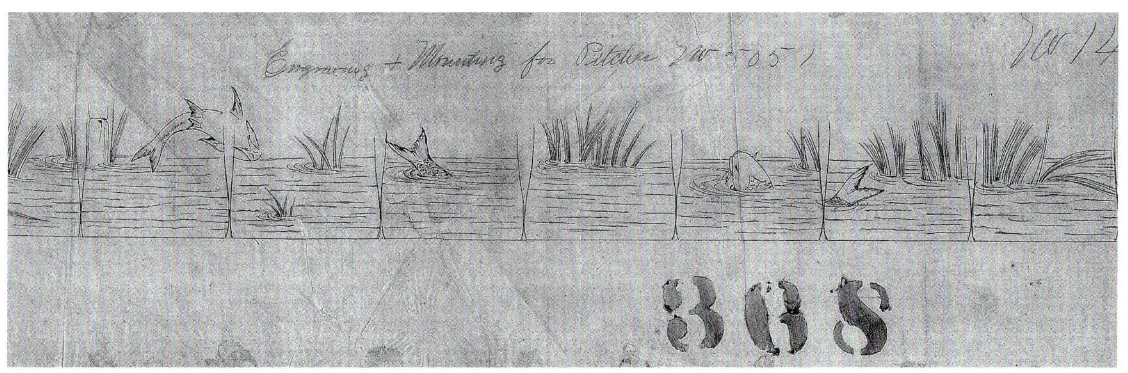

Fig. 1. Tiffany and Company engraving and mounting drawing for pitcher number 5051.

98.

Napkin Clips, ca. 1879

Made by Tiffany and Company (1837–present), New York; designed by Edward C. Moore (1827–1891) or under his supervision
Gilded silver with enamel decoration
Each 2½ × 3½ × ¾ inches
Inscriptions: Cast on front of each, *ET DIEU MON APPUI/MJM*
EL 4.1998.a–.b

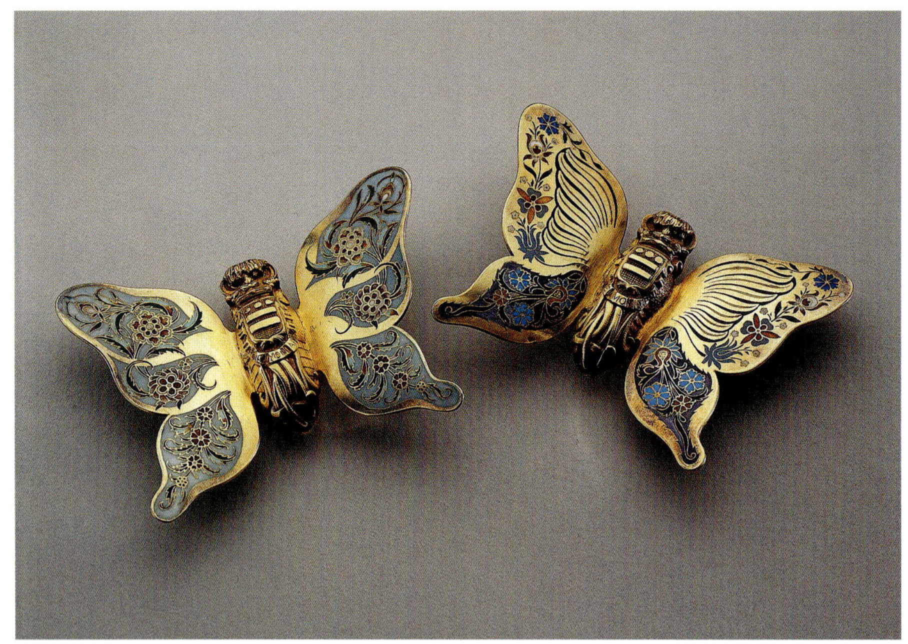

99.

Vase, 1875–1885

Manufactured and retailed by Tiffany and Company (1837–present), New York; designed by Edward C. Moore (1827–1891) or under his supervision
Silver and copper
5 × 2 × 2 inches
Mark: Inscribed on bottom, *TIFFANY & CO/3566 M 6435/ STERLING SILVER*
1988.221

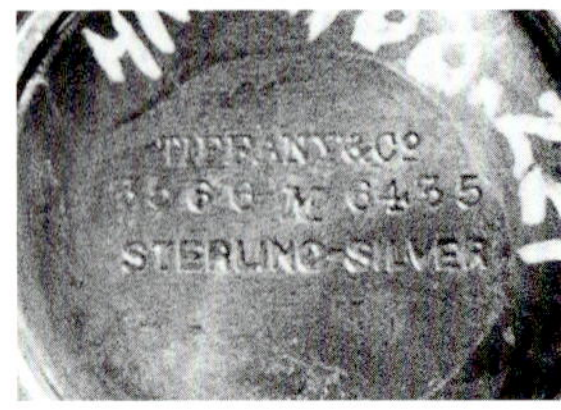

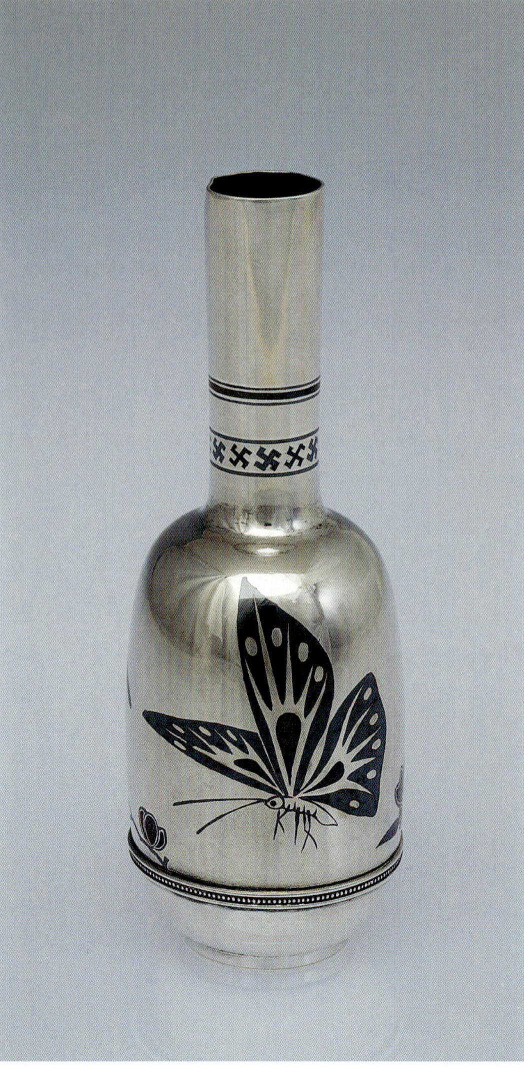

shipped back to New York, they overwhelmed the potential market. An auction of the wares lost money but produced great publicity and identified the firm with Japanese arts.

By 1876, Moore, inspired by Samurai sword guards and other Japanese metalwares, began designing objects such as the Crawford pitcher (no. 97), with cast ornaments in copper, brass, and gilt. Although silversmithing was not a craft rooted in Japanese tradition, Moore was able to suggest Japanese aesthetics in silver. The pitcher design was among the mixed-metal wares Tiffany and Company displayed at the 1878 Exposition Universelle in Paris.[2] Applied decorations in contrasting metal arranged asymmetrically and diagonally suggested Japanese composition to Western eyes. The pond scene and the large scale of the decoration were characteristic of Moore's Japanese designs. The gilt-washed iris blossom with copper stem, the copper carp swimming through the chased rippling pond around the base of the pitcher, and the diagonally set dragonfly with copper body and gilt-washed wings are all realistically depicted (fig. 1). Enhancing the surface of the pitcher below its neck is a hand-hammered background, which Moore introduced in his silver designs around 1876. The hammering complemented the chased rippling and provided a convincing suggestion of water,

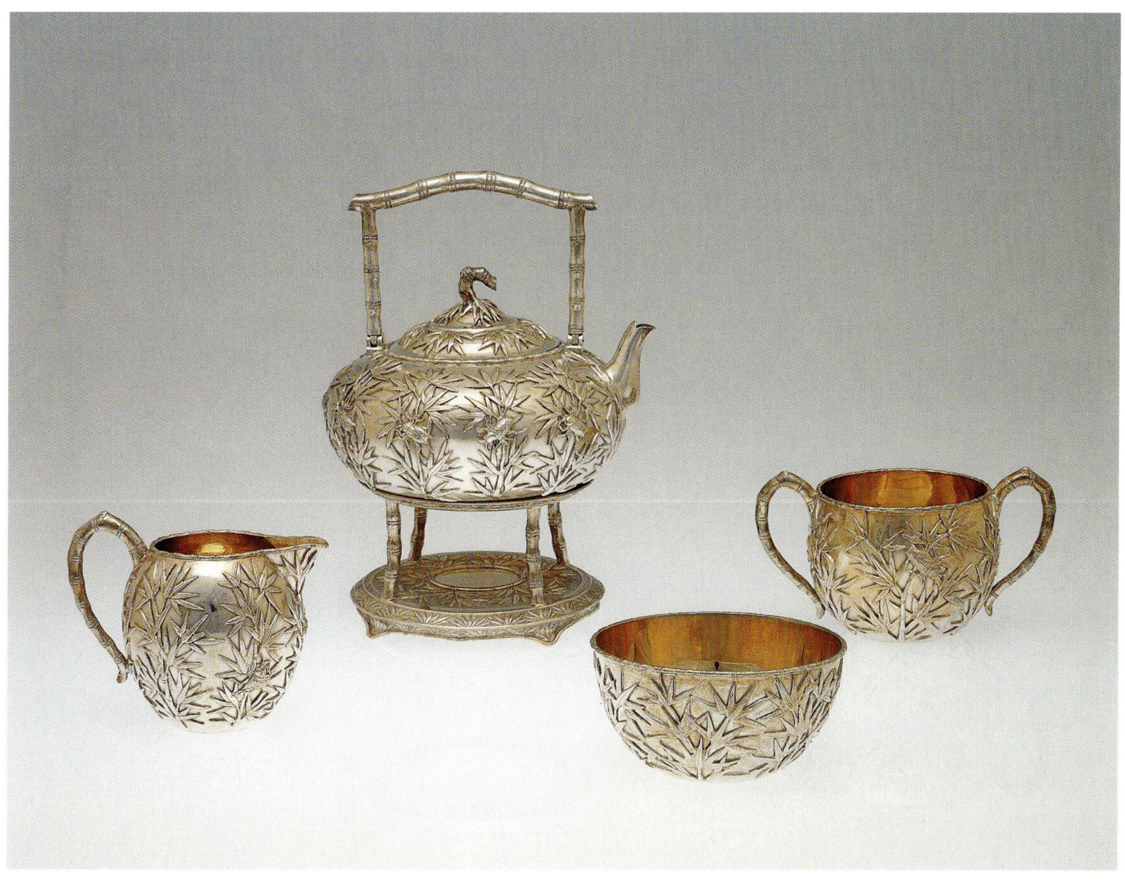

100.

Tea Set, ca. 1880

Made by Wang Hing, Hong Kong; imported and retailed by Tiffany and Company (1837–present), New York
Silver
Kettle with stand: 10¼ × 7½ × 6½ inches
Creamer: 4½ × 5 × 3½ inches
Sugar bowl: 3¼ × 6½ × 3¾ inches
Waste bowl: 2½ × 4¾ × 4¾ inches
Marks: Impressed on bottom of each vessel and kettle stand, *SPECIAL ORDER/FOR/TIFFANY & CO./N.Y.* above square enclosing *WANG/HING/90* and Chinese characters
1986.188.1–.4

reinforced by the spreading shape at the base. The surface also added a handmade effect to the pitcher that, for critics of the period, brought Tiffany's Japanese-taste silver into the realm of art. This combination of utility and art appealed to promoters of the English reform design movement led by Charles Locke Eastlake (see no. 89) and William Morris (see no. 90).

The remarkable workmanship and sheer size of the 1,250-piece Mackay dinner service must have had a dramatic impact at the 1878 Exposition Universelle in Paris. The enormous service, with its Asian-inspired decoration, had been commissioned by John W. Mackay and was used for lavish parties at the Mackay homes in Paris and London. Mackay had made his fortune in the famed Comstock Lode silver mines in Virginia City, Nevada. He provided Tiffany and Company with half a ton of silver from his own mine for production of the service. Although a contemporary newspaper account credited the design of the Mackay service to Charles Grosjean, Moore must have participated in and endorsed the creation of this significant commission.[3] The Crawford butterfly napkin clips (no. 98) were probably made for the Mackay service in 1879, and might not have been shown at the Exposition Universelle. Butterflies were associated with Japanese taste in the 1870s and 1880s.

Moore also looked to other exotic sources for design inspiration. In Russian silver, he discovered the niello technique, which involves inlaying copper or other base metals into silver prepared with an indentation of the proper shape. Moore introduced niello work in 1875–1876, and these wares were included in the displays at the Centennial Exposition in Philadelphia and with the mixed-metal Japanese-taste silver at the 1878 Exposition Universelle in Paris.[4] The small Crawford silver and niello bud vase (no. 99), like the mixed-metal pitcher, incorporates realistic elements into its decoration. Although the niello is inspired by Russian metalwork, the butterfly on the vase relates it to the Japanese taste.

The Crawford tea service (no. 100) by Hong Kong maker Wang Hing was made to order for

101.

Covered Pitcher, 1882

Manufactured and retailed by Tiffany and Company (1837–present), New York; designed by Edward C. Moore (1827–1891) or under his supervision
Silver and gilt
9¾ × 5½ × 4 inches
Mark: Impressed on bottom, *TIFFANY & CO/6654 MAKERS 4165/ STERLING-SILVER/1/2515*
1997.235

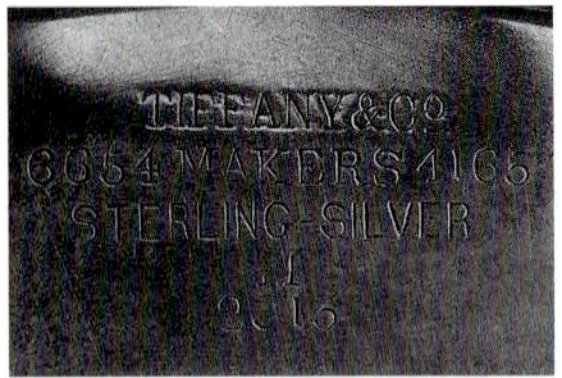

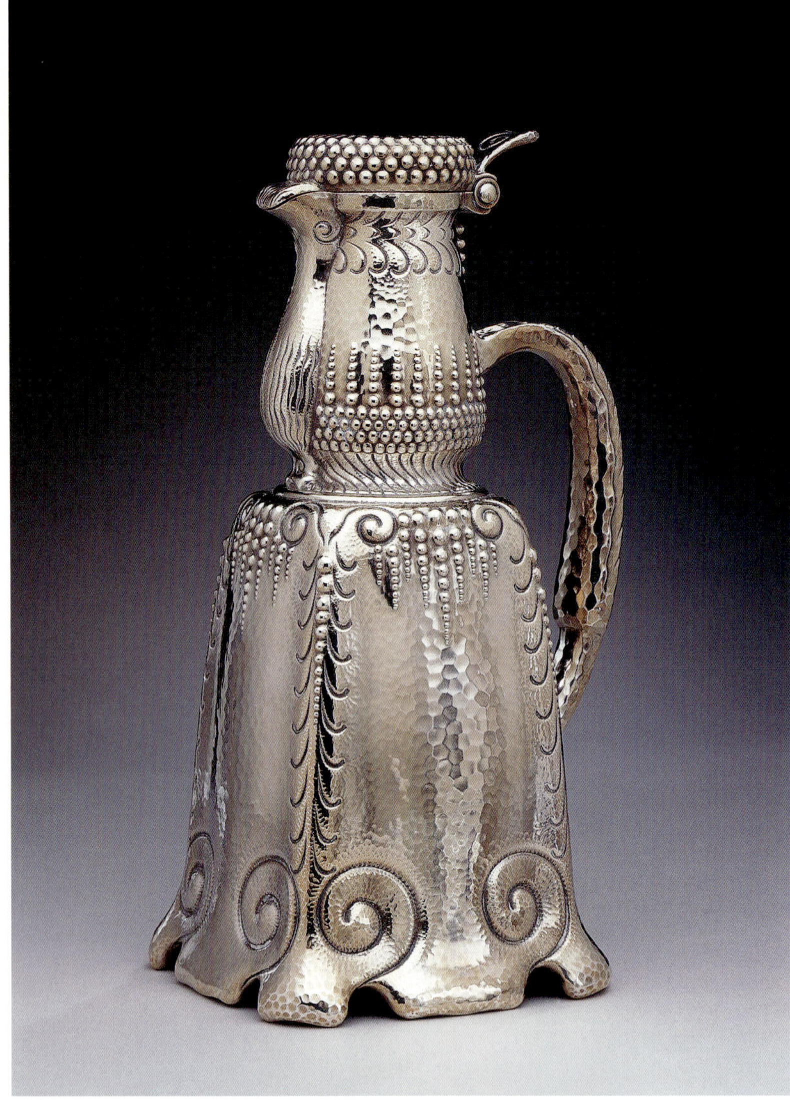

Fig. 2. Tiffany and Company hammered and pearling design for tankard number 6654.

Tiffany for sale in its New York emporium. A typical Asian motif—bamboo shoots—appears in a repoussé pattern covering the surfaces of the vessels, while cast bamboo-reed shapes form the handles. The overall pattern is reminiscent of the bamboo-shoot marquetry background on the Herter Brothers cabinet (see no. 107). Although the decoration on the service is Asian, the forms follow Western prototypes.

Moore looked to the Near East for inspiration for designs such as the Crawford covered pitcher (no. 101). Company records consistently refer to this particular design as a tankard, even though, with its spout, it is obviously a pitcher. The company pattern book lists design number 6654 as "Tankard sq. bottom." A separate Hammered Work ledger lists the decorative design as number 2315 for "Tankard #6654 Pearled & incised."[5] The term "pearl" refers to the relief beading on the top and the graduated beading around the neck and top of the lower section and along the corners of the pitcher (fig. 2). The overall surface of the pitcher is hammered, like the Japanese-taste pitcher, which gives it a similar suggestion of handcraftsmanship.

The initials in the inscription on the pepper mill (no. 102) strongly suggest that it was presented to Louis Comfort Tiffany by Moore. The son of the founder, the younger Tiffany joined Moore on the company's board of directors in 1881 after he had achieved considerable prominence in his own interior decorating business, Louis C. Tiffany and Associated Artists. Moore may have exerted considerable influence on the tastes of Tiffany and may have been a mentor to the young man.[6] Both shared an interest in the Near and Far East. Near Eastern influence is apparent both in the pepper mill's champlevé enamel decoration and its minaret shape. That the company was capable of such beautiful enamelwork has already been seen in the napkin clips from the Mackay service. Tiffany continued enamelwork into the twentieth century, as seen on a coffee service designed by Paulding Farnham (see no. 153). The chased scrolls, floral motifs, and elongated curves in the enamel decoration of the pepper mill are a precursor to the French Art Nouveau.

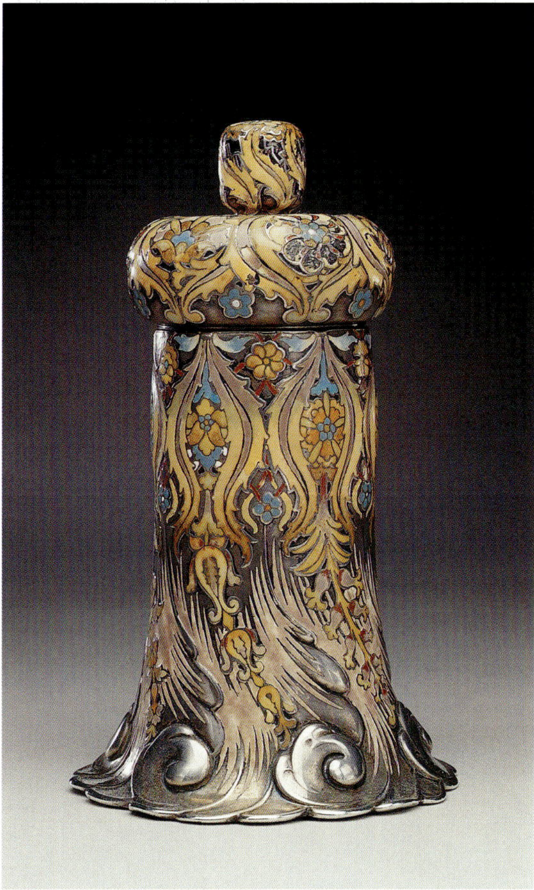

102.

Pepper Mill, 1885

Made by Tiffany and Company (1837–present), New York; designed by Edward C. Moore (1827–1891) or under his supervision; mill mechanism by Peugot Frères, France
Silver with enamel decoration
4¾ × 2¾ × 2¾ inches
Marks: Impressed on bottom, outer rim, *TIFFANY & CO. M STERLING*; on mechanism, *S.G.D.G. PEUGEOT FRERES BREVES*
Inscription: On bottom, outer edge, *L.C.T. from E.C.M.*
EL 5.1998

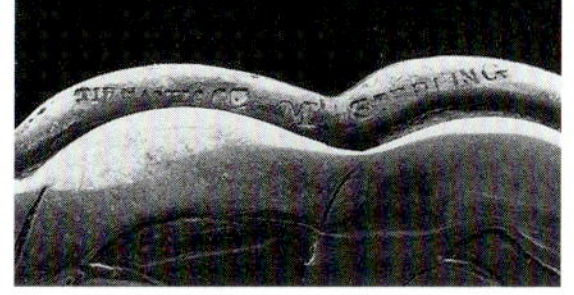

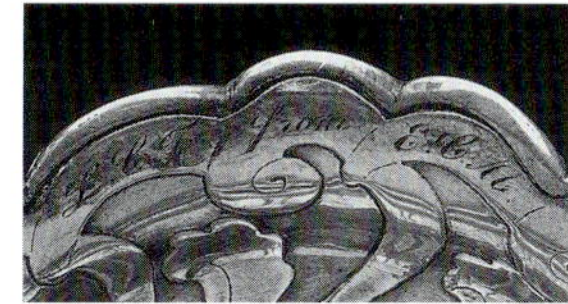

NOTES

1. The comb is described and dated in correspondence, Janet Zapata, April 6, 1998, High Museum of Art document files. For Tiffany and Company's production of Japanese-taste silver, as well as a complete history of the firm under Charles L. Tiffany and Edward C. Moore, see Carpenter and Carpenter 1997, pp. 156–174.

2. Production by Tiffany and other firms in the Japanese taste is discussed in Hosley 1990, pp. 126–131; and Venable 1994, pp. 172–191. Identical pitchers are in the collection of the Art Institute of Chicago and Musee d'Orsay, Paris.

3. Carpenter and Carpenter 1997, pp. 48–58, figs. 54–64, gives biographical information on Mr. and Mrs. Mackay, the commission, and its exhibition at the 1878 Exposition Universelle. A number of the serving pieces are illustrated.

4. Niello is described and illustrated in Venable 1994, pp. 170–172, fig. 6.41.

5. Correspondence, Louisa Bann, Archives Coordinator, Tiffany and Company, April 3, 1997, High Museum of Art document files.

6. Zapata 1993, pp. 20–22, presents a convincing case that Louis C. Tiffany was greatly influenced by Moore, possibly as a mentor.

103.

Pitcher, 1884

Whiting Manufacturing Company (1866–1924), New York
Silver, copper, and gilt
$9\frac{5}{8} \times 6 \times 6$ inches
Mark: Impressed on bottom above inscription, rampant lion facing left with right paw on oval enclosing *W* above *STERLING*/*1008*/*B*
Inscription: On bottom, *EASTERN YACHT CLUB/Annual Cruise/Commodore's Cup/for Sloops/WON IN BUZZARDS BAY/July 1884/by/Cutter "Bedouin"*
1993.139

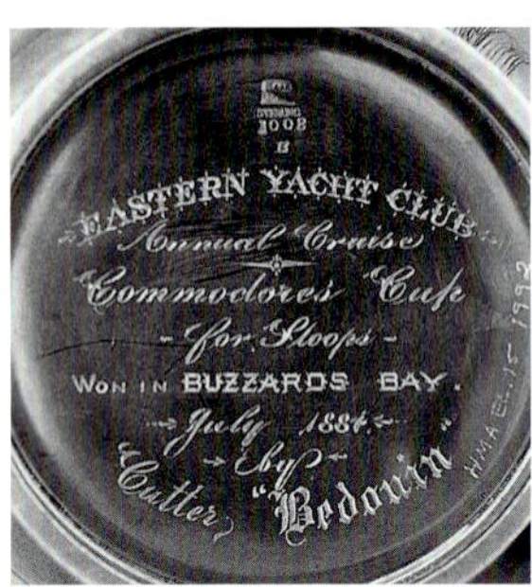

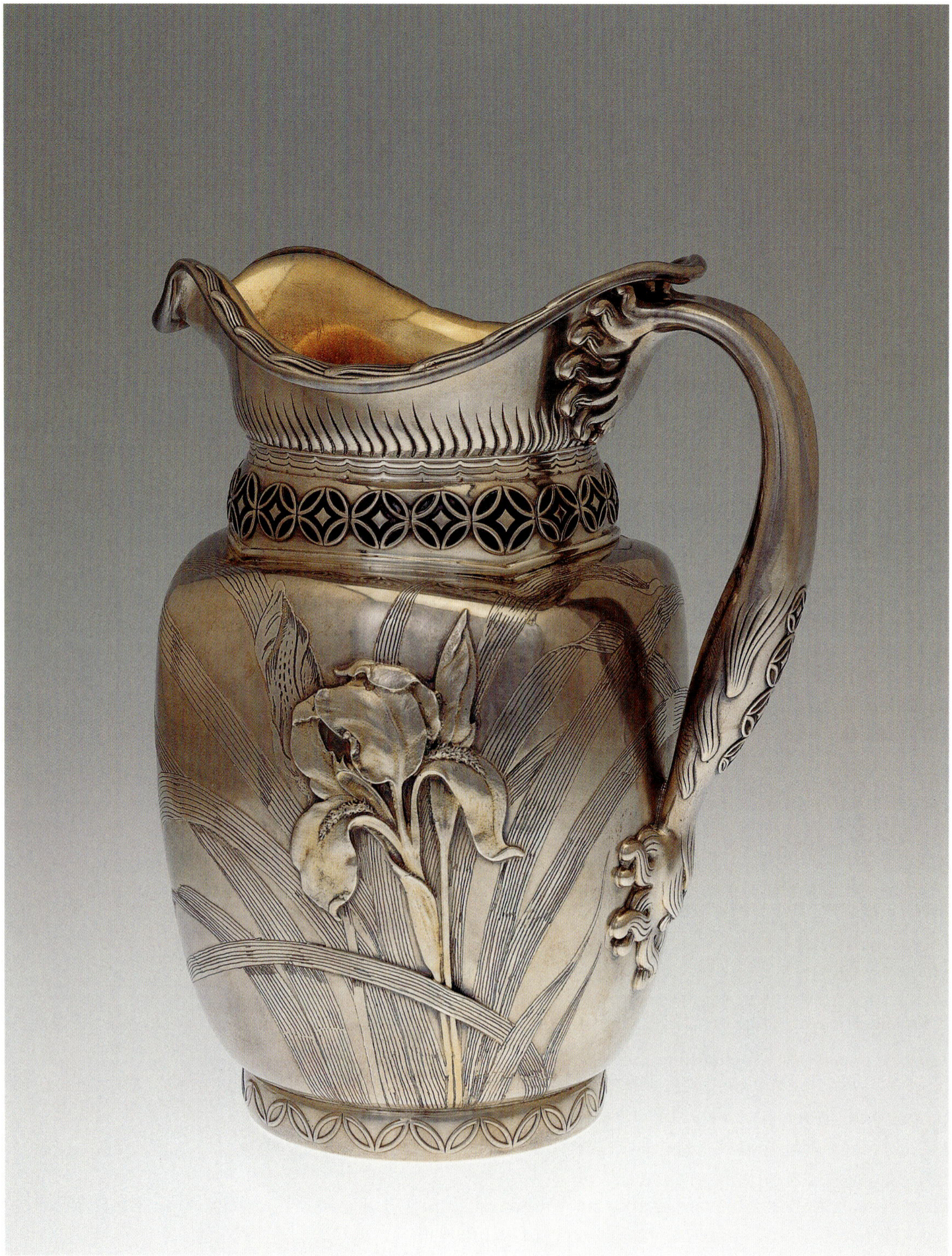

Even before the great success of Tiffany and Company's mixed-metal wares at the 1878 Exposition Universelle in Paris, Tiffany's great rival, Gorham Manufacturing Company, was also making mixed-metal Japanese-style silverwares. Such wares were also made by other manufacturers, including this mixed-metal pitcher by Whiting Manufacturing Company.[1] It is related to the Tiffany and Company mixed-metal pitcher (see no. 97) in both its rounded organic shape and the large scale of its realistic decorative elements. Both pitchers are decorated with gilt iris blossoms and dragonflies, but the surface of the Whiting pitcher is oxidized rather than hand-hammered. Although both handles have distinctive undulating shapes, the Whiting handle has larger terminals that spread over the surface of the pitcher and are mounted with copper coin-like motifs and silver lozenges.

The Tifft and Whiting Company, which had begun producing jewelry in 1840 in North Attleboro, Massachusetts, was succeeded by the Whiting Manufacturing Company, organized in 1866 with William D. Whiting as president. The company manufactured silver in North Attleboro until a fire destroyed the plant in 1875; it then moved to New York, where it maintained manufacturing and commercial departments, although the firm had office and retail operations in the city from as early as 1867. By 1910, production had moved to a factory in Bridgeport, Connecticut. In 1924, Whiting Manufacturing Company was purchased by Gorham, and in 1926 it was moved to Providence, Rhode Island, in the merger.[2]

Charles Osborne began working as a designer for Whiting in North Attleboro in 1871. New York's Dominick and Haff (see no. 104) tried to lure Osborne away, but Edward Moore hired him for Tiffany and Company in 1878, just as the firm was winning accolades for Moore's Japanese-taste silver at the Exposition Universelle. Osborne worked for Tiffany for nine years before returning to Whiting.[3] After losing Osborne to Tiffany, Whiting closely followed Tiffany's products in the late 1870s and 1880s. The related decorations, shapes, and colors on the two Crawford pitchers demonstrate that Whiting was attempting to emulate the success of Tiffany's Japanese-taste silver. Although this pitcher may have been intended for table use, the inscription indicates its function as a racing trophy.

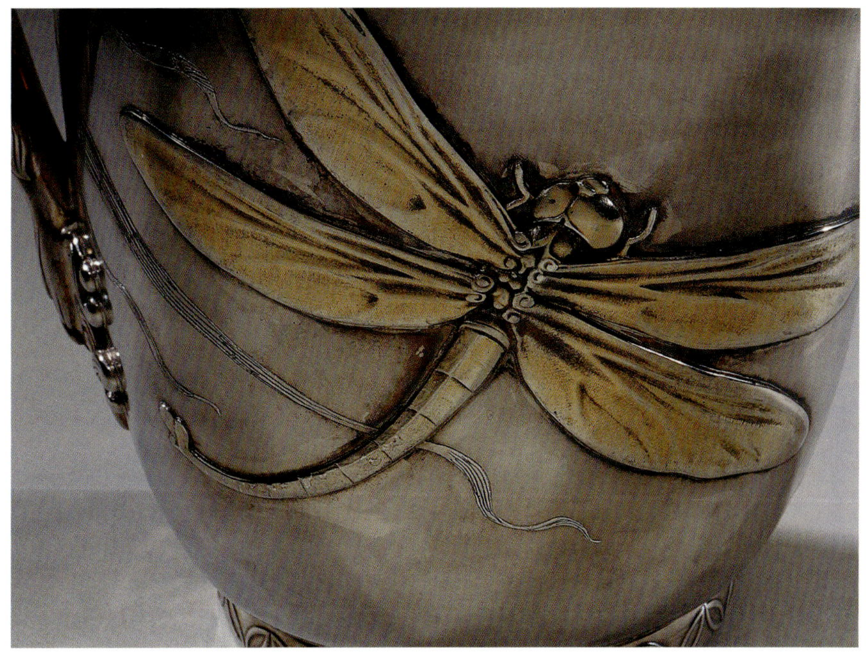

NOTES

1. For discussions of Japanese-taste American silver, the rivalry between Tiffany and Company and Gorham Manufacturing Company, and the products of other firms, see Hosley 1990, pp. 126–131; and Venable 1994, pp. 172–191.

2. For a history of Whiting Manufacturing Company, see Detroit Institute of Arts 1983, pp. 212–213; The Metropolitan Museum of Art 1986, p. 485; Rainwater 1986, p. 224; and Venable 1994, p. 324.

3. Venable 1994, p. 152.

104.

Hot Water Kettle and Stand, ca. 1880

Attributed to Dominick and Haff (1872–1928), New York; retailed by George C. Shreve and Company
Silver
10¼ × 8½ × 9 inches
Marks: Impressed on bottom of stand and kettle, *GEO. C. SHREVE & CO./STERLING;* impressed on bottom of kettle, *96* and oblong enclosing *925* conjoined with empty circle and diamond enclosing *80*
1991.357

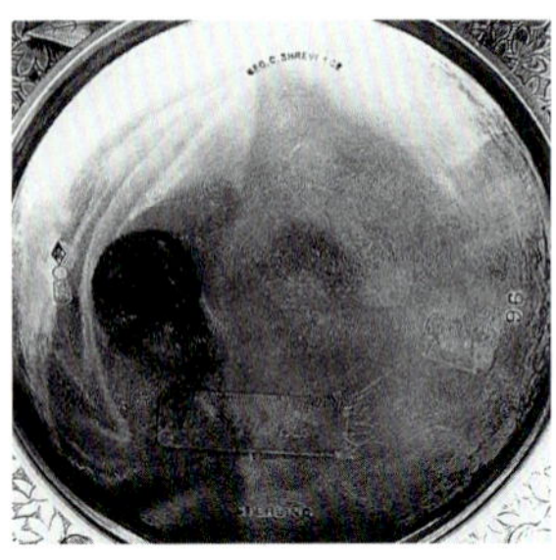

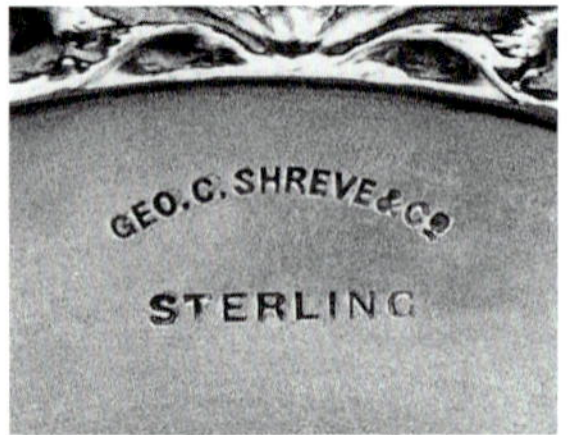

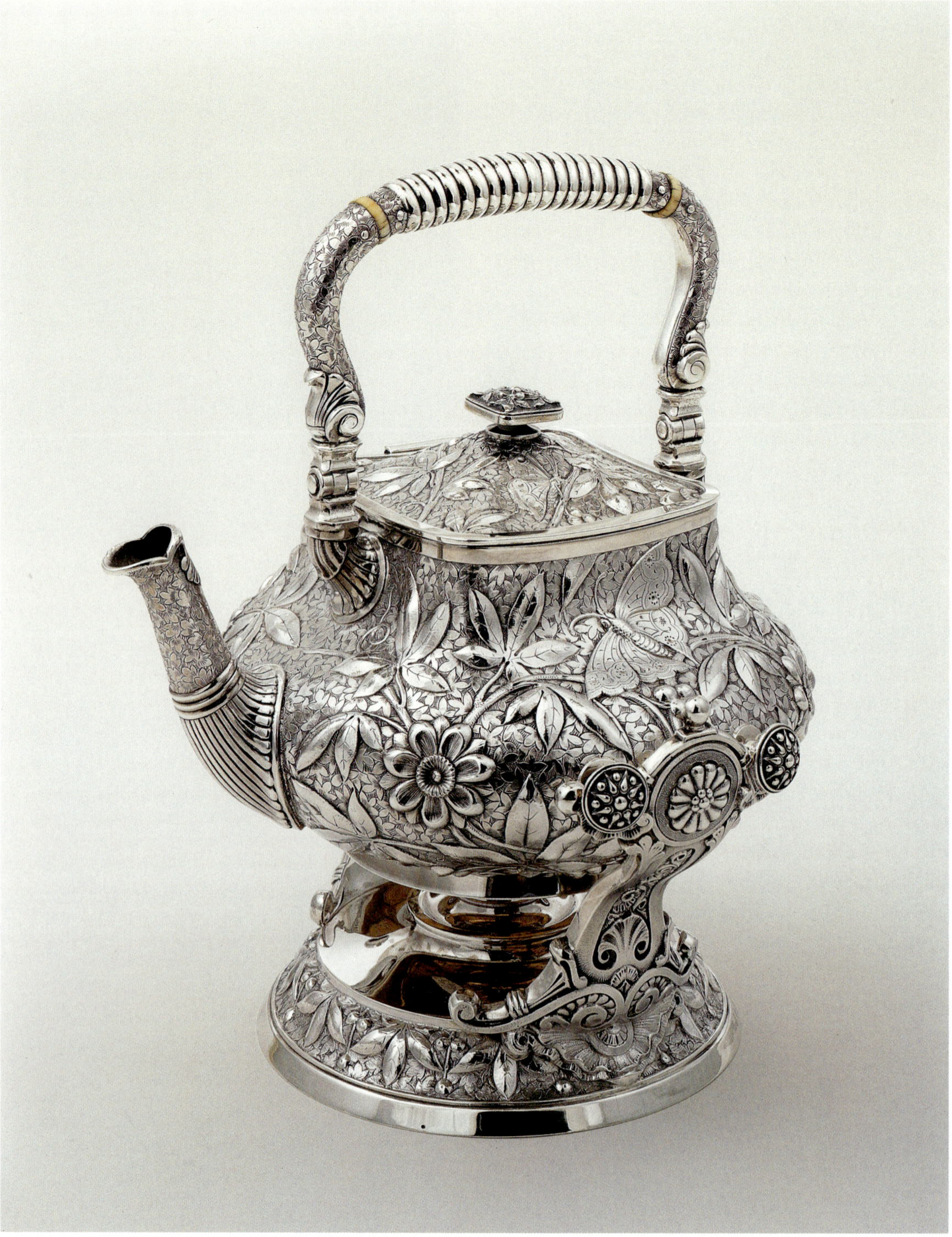

ATTRIBUTION OF this hot water kettle and stand to the prominent New York silver manufacturing firm Dominick and Haff is based on a matching marked set in the Cooper-Hewitt National Design Museum, Smithsonian Institution. The sterling standard and possible date marks in conjoined rectangle, circle, and diamond are consistent with the firm's marks.[1] Beyond the consistently high quality of surviving wares from Dominick and Haff, little has been documented about the history of the company. The few known facts illustrate the complex intermingling of silversmiths and manufacturing firms in the competitive but narrow nineteenth-century American silver industry. Henry Blanchard Dominick descended from George Dominick, a French Huguenot who immigrated to America in 1740. Henry Dominick joined the silver firm of Gale and North to form Gale, North and Dominick in 1868. Leroy B. Haff worked in the retail division of the Gale firm beginning in 1867, and when he became a partner in 1870, the firm was renamed Gale, Dominick and Haff. In 1872–1873, the firm began to be listed as Dominick and Haff.

At the beginning of the partnership, when the firm was listed in directories at 451 Broome Street in New York, Dominick and Haff was known for small fancy wares. A disastrous fire in 1877 led to the construction of a new and larger factory and the production of a wider range of silverwares. The company expanded in 1879, when Dominick and Haff bought out silver manufacturers Adams and Shaw, which had been established in 1873 by Caleb Cushing Adams. From 1875 until 1893, when Haff died, Dominick and Haff operated a retail store on Bond Street in New York. For the next two decades, Dominick and Haff conducted business at 860 Broadway. After 1904, the firm was listed in city directories at various addresses until Dominick died in 1928. At that time, Dominick and Haff was absorbed by silver manufacturer Reed and Barton, of Taunton, Massachusetts.[2]

Around 1880, when the Crawford kettle was probably made, Dominick and Haff, like many American silver manufacturers, was influenced by Japanese-taste wares produced in the 1870s and early 1880s by Tiffany and Company (see no. 97), the Gorham Manufacturing Company, and the Whiting Manufacturing Company (see no. 103). However, the Dominick and Haff kettle has repoussé decorations of insects, leaves, and flowers covering the entire surface, similar to the John T. Vansant Manufacturing Company silver covered dish (see no. 105) and consistent with the marquetry decoration on the contemporary Herter Brothers cabinet (see no. 107). The chased and repoussé pattern of the kettle complements designs cast into the handle, spout, and stand. The overall square shape with rounded corners was a convention of American silver in the Japanese taste, seen also in the Vansant covered dish and Whiting pitcher.

Dominick and Haff sold their wares extensively outside New York. The Crawford kettle and stand bear the retailer's mark of George C. Shreve and Company (now Shreve and Company) of San Francisco. The kettle was undoubtedly part of a large tea service related to the one now in the Cooper-Hewitt, which bears the retailer's mark of Bailey, Banks and Biddle of Philadelphia. A related Dominick and Haff jug now in the British Museum in London is marked by retailers Shreve, Crump and Low of Boston.[3]

NOTES

1. Part of the Cooper-Hewitt service is illustrated and discussed in The Metropolitan Museum of Art 1986, pp. 262 and 271, fig. 8.18. Dominick and Haff marks are discussed in Rainwater 1986, p. 49.

2. The history of Dominick and Haff is related in The Metropolitan Museum of Art 1986, p. 421; Rainwater 1986, pp. 48–49; Rudoe 1991, p. 40; and Venable 1994, p. 318.

3. The jug in the British Museum is discussed in Rudoe 1991, p. 40, no. 81, and is illustrated on pp. 194–195, pls. 49–50.

105.

Covered Dish, 1883

John T. Vansant Manufacturing Company (1881–1884), Philadelphia
Silver
5½ × 10½ × 5¾ inches
Mark: Enclosed in horizontal diamond stamped on bottom of dish, *ENGLISH STERLING* in arch over *925–1000* and *V & Co.*
Inscription: Engraved in script on bottom of dish, *FAS/From Uncle Henry and Aunt Clara/ March 23, 1883*
1981.1000.59 a–b

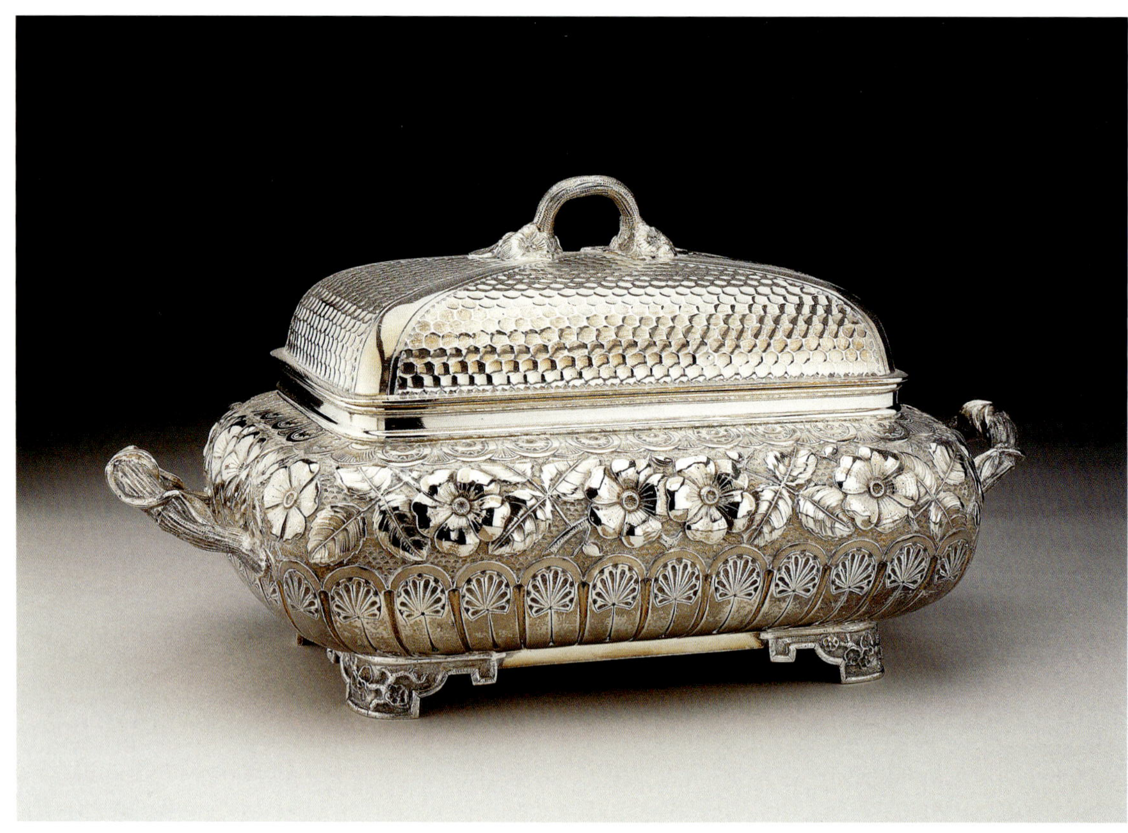

The Japanese taste expressed by silver manufacturers in New York and New England was also apparent in Philadelphia, as evidenced by this entrée dish. Apart from the financial difficulties that plagued the short-lived John T. Vansant Manufacturing Company, little is known about the history of the firm or about John Vansant himself. Financial problems may have led to the various reorganizations and name changes: John T. Vansant Manufacturing Company, John T. Vansant and Brother, and Vansant Silver Company, Ltd. Stephen E. Vansant served as superintendent and manager of Vansant Silver Company, Ltd., but whether he was the brother (as suggested by the 1884–1886 name of the firm) or the son of John Vansant is uncertain. In 1884, the Philadelphia directory noted the residence of John T. Vansant at 724 Spruce Street, with the company at 611 Sansom Street, where the Vansant firm had been located since at least 1882. John T. Vansant and Brother was listed at 618 Chestnut Street in 1885. One indication of business tribulations is an announcement in the trade periodical *Jewelers Weekly,* on August 18, 1886: "John T. Vansant & Brother, manufacturers of silverware, Philadelphia, who have been in financial difficulties recently were sold out by the sheriff."[1] Conditions of the sheriff's sale are unknown, but the firm continued to operate as Vansant Silver Company, Ltd., until 1892, when it was purchased by Simons, Brother and Company, a Philadelphia manufacturer specializing in the production of thimbles, cane heads, and other silver novelties. An undated advertising card, probably from shortly after the absorption

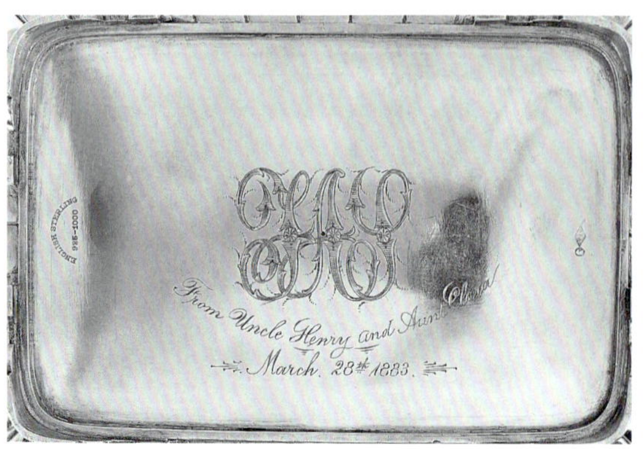

of Vansant, states: "Simons, Bro. & Co. desire to announce the addition to their business of the manufacturing of silver ware—solid & plated—lately carried on by the Vansant Man'f. Co. A large assortment of choice goods on hand and new and original designs constantly added to stock."[2]

Despite business problems, the Vansant firm was clearly skilled in the silver-decorating techniques of the most advanced and popular styles. The Crawford covered dish reflects the Japanese taste of the 1880s, popularized in America by Japan's exhibits at the 1876 Centennial Exposition in Philadelphia. The hammered effect on the cover was derived from Asian metalwares and was first seen on Tiffany and Company silver (see no. 97) and American ceramics (see no. 113) in the late 1870s. The repoussé cherry blossom decorations around the sides of the dish are arranged in a straight horizontal line on a textured field resembling fish scales. At the shoulder of the dish, above the cherry blossoms, the linear aspect is reinforced by a border of fans alternating with radiating circles. Around the base, maple leaves are enclosed in a row of arches. Although the cherry blossoms are realistically rendered, the maple leaves are highly stylized. This combination of realistic and stylized natural elements is also apparent in the decoration on the Herter Brothers bed (see no. 108). The shape of the four cast feet, decorated with asymmetrical cherry branches, is derived from Japanese architectural detail. The engraved inscription indicates that the dish was made while the firm was named the John T. Vansant Manufacturing Company. The initials and inscription have not been identified, and no history of the dish is known. It was originally part of a set of three, each with the same inscription. The matching dishes are now in the Detroit Institute of Arts and The Metropolitan Museum of Art.[3]

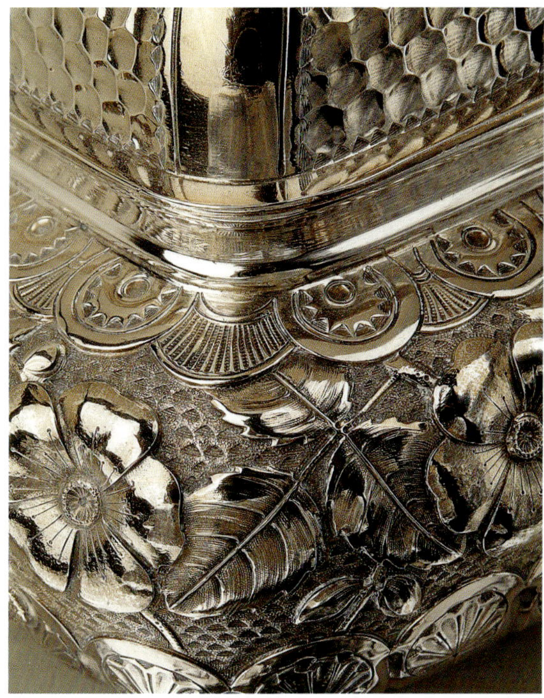

NOTES

1. The announcement of the sheriff's sale is cited in Rainwater 1986, p. 213.

2. Venable 1994, pp. 322–323, relates what little is known about the history of Vansant and cites the advertising card. Another account of the history of the firm is given in Detroit Institute of Arts 1983, p. 209.

3. The Detroit Institute of Arts dish is discussed and illustrated in Detroit Institute of Arts 1983, pp. 209–210. A chocolate pot in a private collection, also made by John T. Vansant Manufacturing Company and retailed by Simons, Brother and Company, is illustrated in Venable 1994, p. 134, fig. 6.11, and discussed on p. 130.

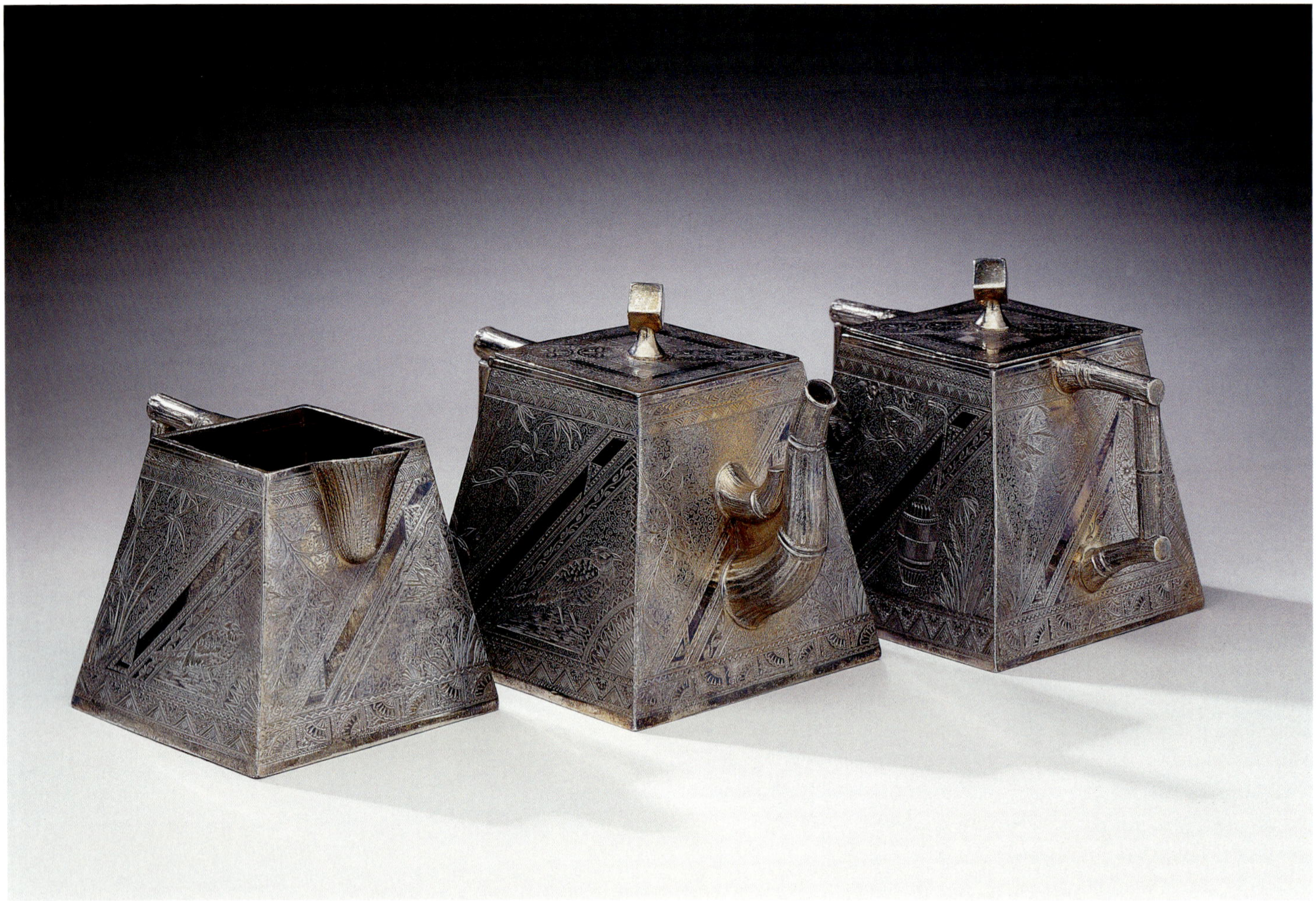

106.

Tea Set, ca. 1885

James W. Tufts Company
(ca. 1875–1891), Boston
Silver plate
Teapot: 4⅛ × 5½ × 3½ inches
Cream pitcher: 3⅜ × 4¼ × 3⅛ inches
Sugar bowl: 4 × 5¼ × 3⅜ inches
Marks: Impressed on bottom of each vessel, in circle surrounding four-pointed star with circle with *T* at center, *JAMES W. TUFTS/ BOSTON/WARRANTED/TRIPLE PLATE/1900*
1995.184 a–d

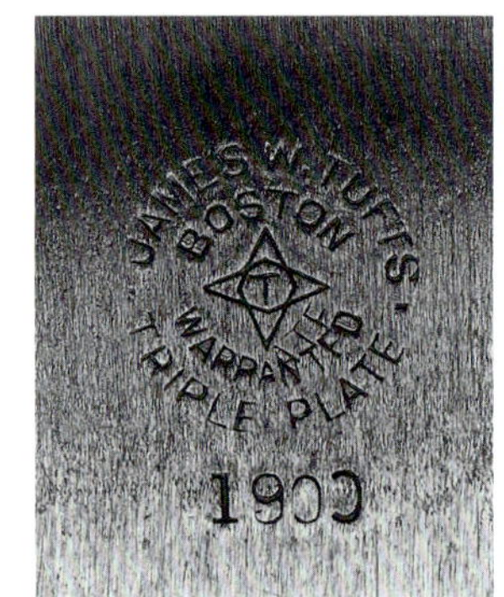

For pioneers like Tiffany and Company, Gorham Manufacturing Company, and Whiting Manufacturing Company, the fascination for silver in the Japanese taste had waned by the late 1880s. However, manufacturers of the less-expensive electroplated silver made Japanese-taste wares available to a much wider and less-affluent market in the 1880s and 1890s. This tea set for two was typical of much American Japanese-taste plated wares, having broad, smooth surfaces covered with angular and diagonal bright-cut decoration.[1]

James W. Tufts began his career as an apprentice in an apothecary store in Charlestown, Massachusetts. Eventually, he owned a chain of three drugstores in the Boston area. His interests included making syrups for the soda fountains in his stores, and he began manufacturing soda fountain equipment with metal parts that were often silver-plated. Tufts also began producing silver-plated tablewares, for which he registered a trademark on February 2, 1875.[2] He constructed an impressive building at the 1876 Centennial Exposition in Philadelphia to display his soda fountain equipment and probably his silver-plated tablewares as well. His company made a silver-plated paperweight as a souvenir of the exhibition.[3]

The Japanese-taste elements of the Tufts tea set include the square forms and the bamboo-shaped handles. The broad, smooth surfaces of the sides of the vessels provide space for intricate, bright-cut patterns, including diagonal bands with exotic birds, flowers, and fans. The stylized effect is reinforced by the square knobs set at angles on the lids of the teapot and sugar bowl. The "1900" in the mark refers to the model number, which is listed in the 1888 Tufts Company catalogue. At that time, the three-piece service cost $10.50 wholesale and $15 with a presentation case.[4] The set probably dates to the mid-1880s, when the Tufts firm was producing silver-plated tablewares as well as manufacturing soda fountain equipment. In 1891, the James W. Tufts Company merged with a number of other firms to create the American Soda Fountain Company.

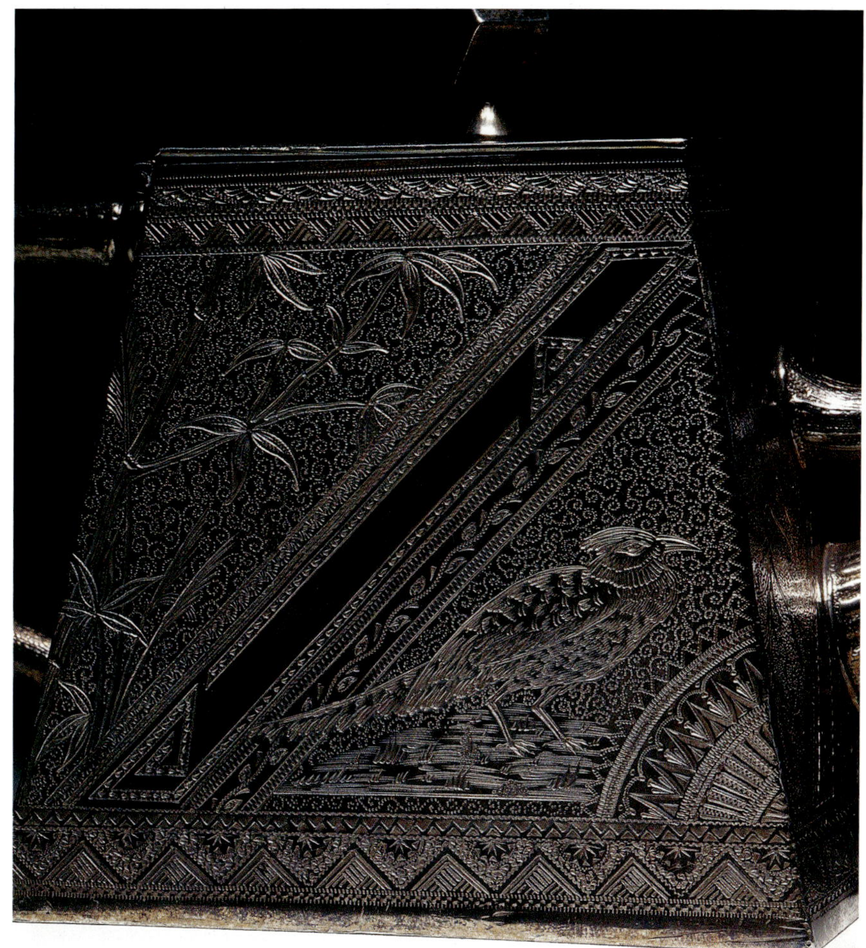

NOTES

1. For a discussion of the Japanese-taste silver plate manufactured in New England at that time, see Hosley 1990, pp. 130–133. See also p. 132, fig. 116, for an illustration of a Tufts tea set in the Wadsworth Athenaeum that is identical to the Crawford example.

2. A discussion of the history of Tufts's firm is found in Rainwater 1986, p. 208. For a discussion of silver plate in nineteenth-century America, see no. 82 in this catalogue.

3. Rainwater and Rainwater 1988, pp. 143–144, figs. 11 and 12.

4. The Tufts Company catalogue of 1888 is cited in Venable 1994, p. 345.

Herter Brothers

IN THE DECADE after his 1848 emigration from Germany, Gustave Herter worked in New York's booming furniture industry and interior design trade, and in 1858 he opened his own firm (see no. 53). In 1859, his younger brother, Christian Herter, signed an "intent for citizenship" in New York City Superior Court, and he probably came to work with his brother at that time. During the Civil War, Gustave Herter's furniture firm made gun stocks. In 1864, Christian became a partner in the company, which was renamed Herter Brothers. Over the next two decades, Herter Brothers made furniture and designed interiors for affluent clients from New York to California. Gustave retired in 1870 and returned to Germany in 1871, at which point Christian assumed control of the company.

The Herter Brothers furniture in the Crawford Collection dates to the mid-1870s and early 1880s, when Christian Herter was directing all aspects of the firm's design and business. The furniture's marquetry decoration, rich and exotic materials, and exacting workmanship reflect Christian Herter's sophistication as a designer. As is often the case with most major nineteenth-century furniture makers, Christian Herter cannot be definitively identified as the maker or designer of specific examples, but his refined eye controlled all of the firm's products. After Christian Herter died in 1883, the firm continued under other managers and investors until 1907.[1]

The Crawford cabinet (no. 107) has been described as "a masterpiece of art furniture"[2] and hailed as "one of the most memorable images of the Aesthetic movement."[3] The beautifully crafted, intricate marquetry panel depicts realistic pairs of cranes and snakes and a trio of butterflies on a lush field of bamboo and sunflowers. The images center around a footed urn at the lower center. The vivid colors and rich texture make the marquetry panel look like embroidery in wood. On the cabinet door, bands of gilt and incised ebonized wood flank a border of low-relief carved bamboo and sunflowers that frames the images on the marquetry panel. The strong rectangular frame is reinforced by the shape of the cabinet. The panel is bordered at the bottom by a perforated fret that includes carved and gilt sunflowers. The ebonized surface, small scale, and rectangular shape of the cabinet, which are related to Japanese furniture, gave the cabinet an exotic look to Western eyes. The graceful saber legs—a striking departure from the tight rectangular shape—also appealed to the American taste for exotic and elegant decoration. The turned fretwork around the top may have suggested Japanese woodwork, but it was also part of English reform design vocabulary. The canine heads at the top four corners are like sentinels guarding the cabinet and its contents.[4]

The Crawford bed (no. 108), like the cabinet, reflects American interpretations of English and Japanese furniture design in the late nineteenth century. The oriental carved fretwork across the top of the headboard looks to Japan, while the row of turned spindles below the marquetry panel reflects English reform design. Realistically carved flying bird finials atop the bedposts complement the birds in the broad marquetry panel below. The central marquetry panel in the footboard depicts a flowering branch, and the same abstracted flowers appear on ebonized fields in the two flanking panels in the footboard and the three panels of the headboard. The two side footboard panels are mirror images.

The bed was part of a large chamber suite that also included a wardrobe (now in the Toledo Museum of Art), a bureau and large mirror (now in the Minneapolis Institute of Arts), and a bedside table (now in the Mark Twain House, Hartford, Connecticut). The suite is believed to have been ordered from Herter Brothers by New York tobacco magnate Pierre Lorillard, possibly for his daughter Emily at the time of her marriage to William Kent in New York on May 1, 1881. Lorillard had constructed the Breakers, a summer mansion in Newport, Rhode Island, which was later owned by the Vanderbilts.[5]

In 1853 and 1854, Gustave Herter was listed in New York directories under "decorator" and "decorations." His early partnership, Bulkley and Herter, focused on specially ordered furniture rather than showroom stock. On his own in 1858–1860, Herter was responsible for the interior

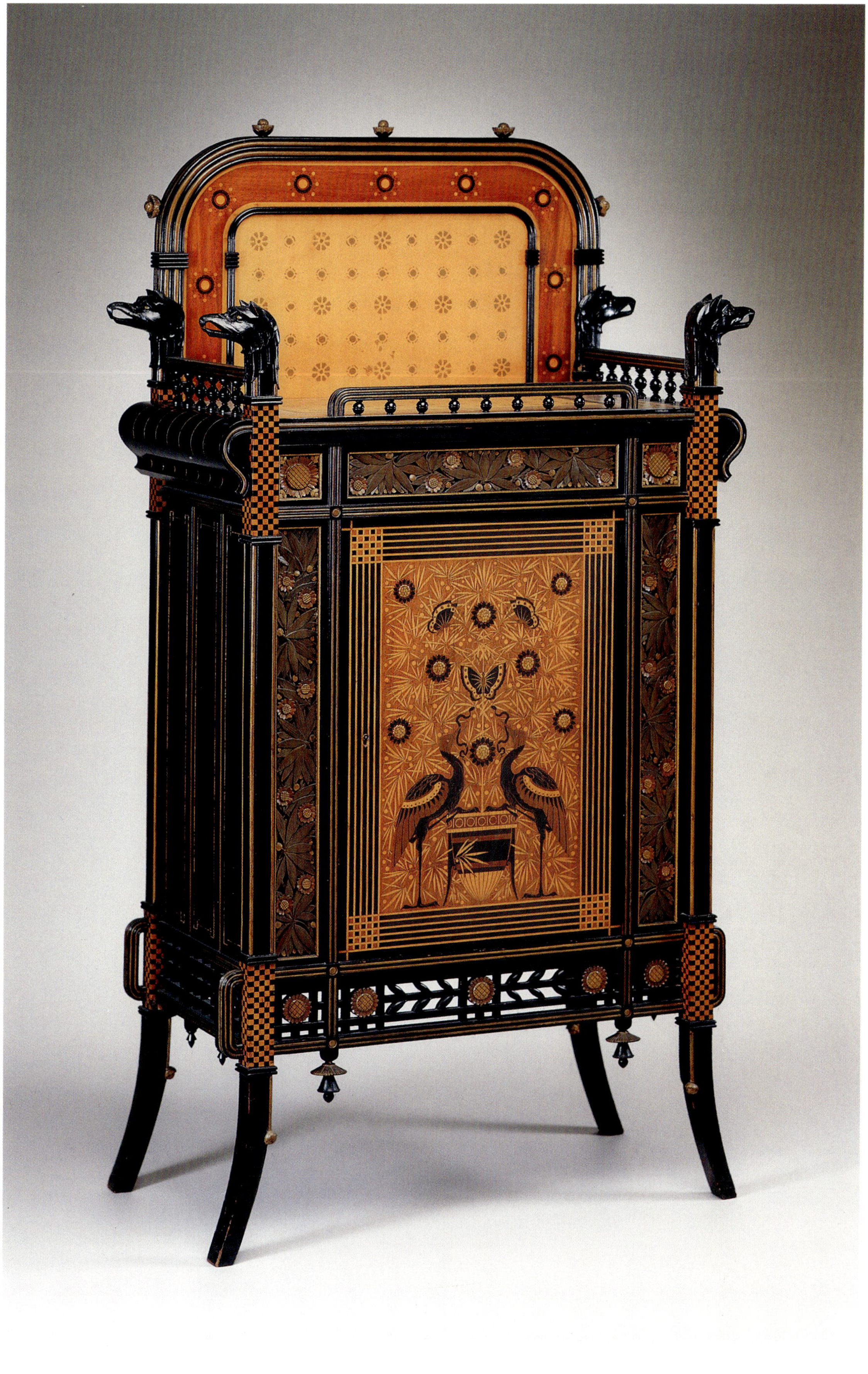

107.

Cabinet, ca. 1875

Herter Brothers (1864–1907), New York
Ebonized cherry, marquetry of various woods, and modern decorative paper
60 × 33 × 16¼ inches
Mark: Branded on back, *HERTER BRO'S*
1981.1000.51

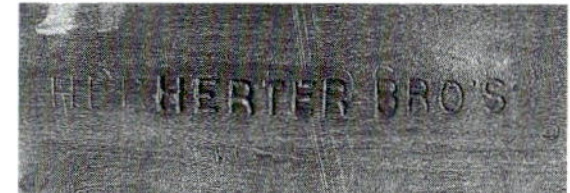

108.

Bed, ca. 1880

Herter Brothers (1864–1907), New York
Ebonized cherry and marquetry of various woods
78 × 66 × 86 inches
Marks: Branded on inside of each side rail, *HERTER BRO'S*
1983.199

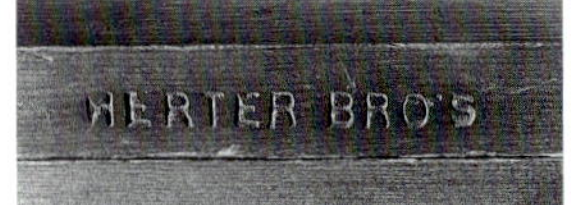

decoration of the summer residence of New Orleans hotelier Ruggles Sylvester Morse in Portland, Maine. Herter Brothers is as well known for their luxurious interiors as for their artistic furniture commissioned in the 1860s and 1870s. They maintained furniture showrooms, first at 547 Broadway and then, in 1870, at 877–879 Broadway along the Ladies Mile shopping district. In 1879, the rooms moved to 18–22 East 18th Street, not far from the Tiffany and Company store on Union Square.

After 1870, Christian Herter continued to receive interior design commissions. In 1879, his firm was hired to supervise the design and furnishing of William H. Vanderbilt's New York mansion on Fifth Avenue between 51st and 52nd Streets (fig. 1). The new mansion was fashionably uptown from Vanderbilt's former residence at Fifth Avenue and 40th Street, which he had built in 1866. As early as 1869, Vanderbilt had purchased furniture from Herter Brothers, and in 1878 the company provided proposals for refurnishing and redecorating a parlor, just before undertaking his new mansion. Herter, in collaboration with architect John B. Snook, supervised the design of both the interior and

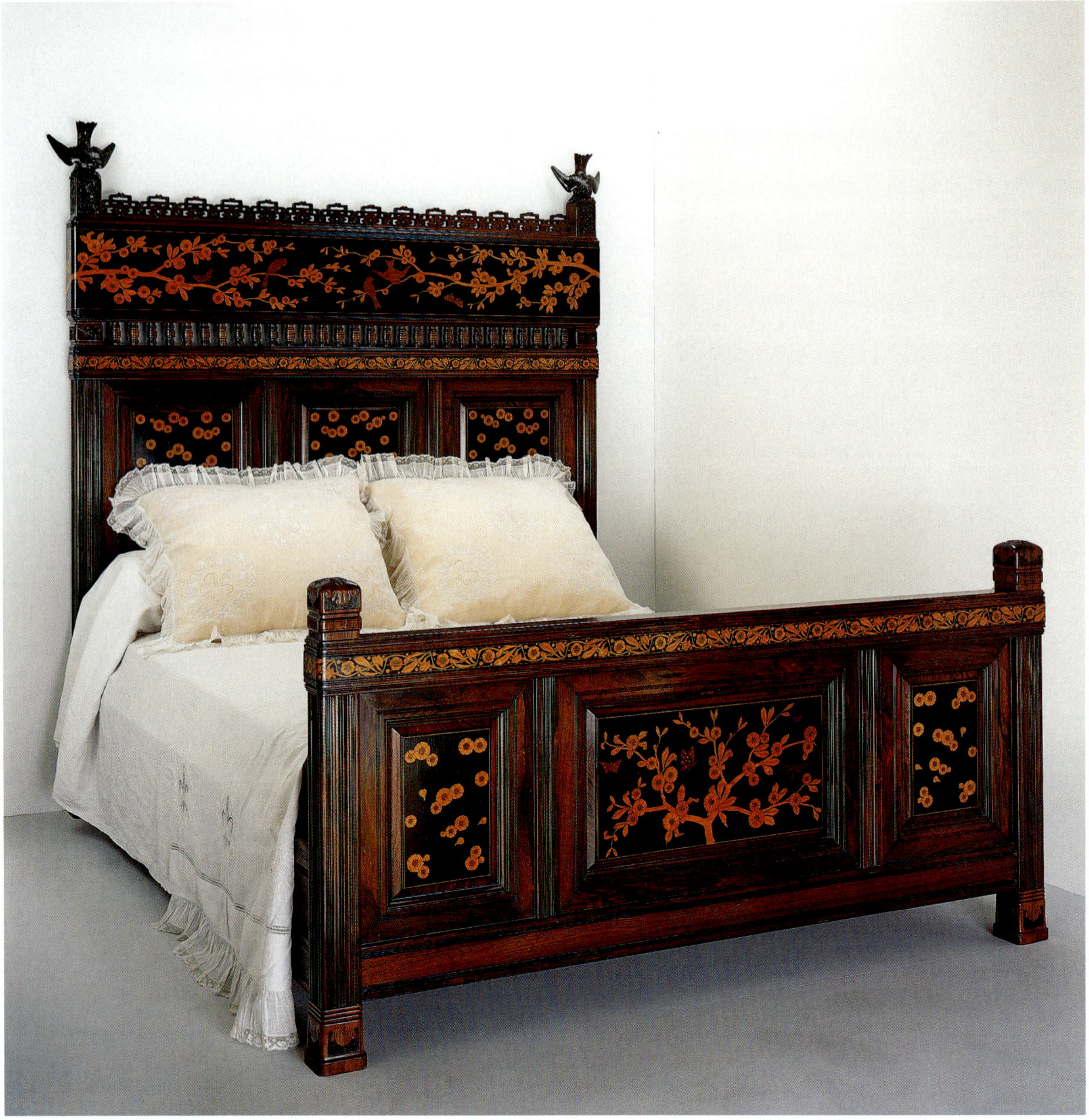

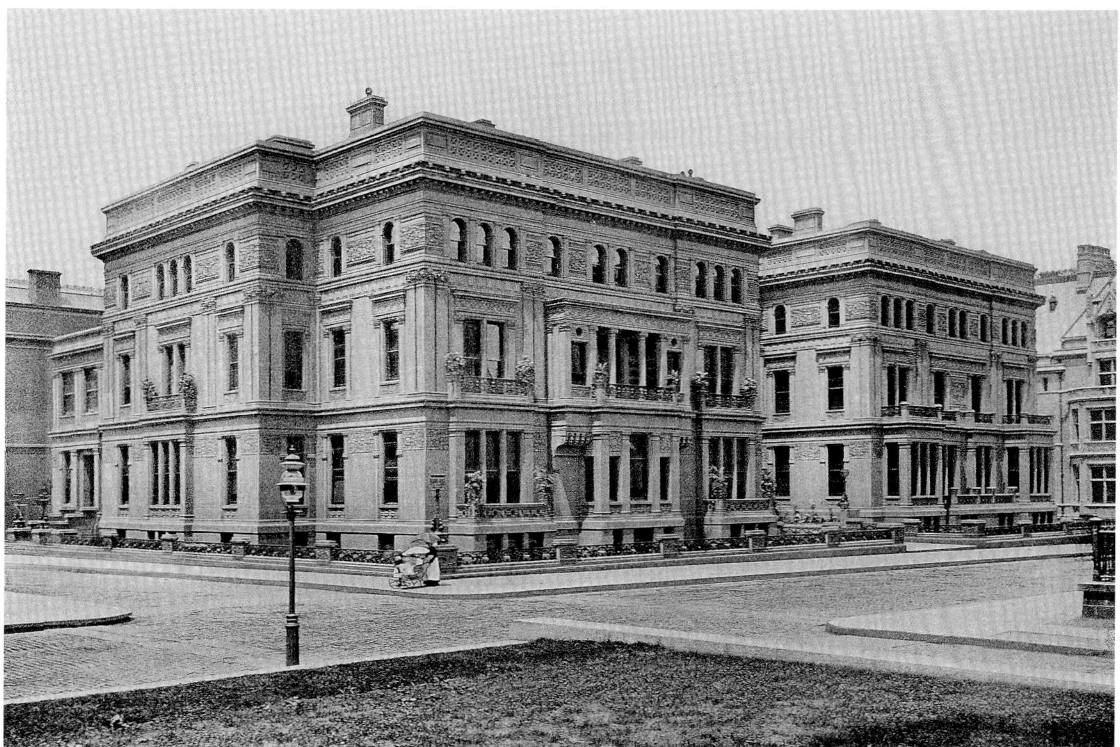

Fig. 1. Vanderbilt house, New York. Photograph from Edward Strahan, *Mr. Vanderbilt's House and Collection* (Boston, 1883–1884).

exterior of Vanderbilt's palace. Plans for the house (fig. 2) were possibly drawn up by Charles Atwood, a Herter staff architect. The sumptuous mansion was completed in just over two years, and Vanderbilt occupied the house in 1882, just a year before Christian Herter's death and three years before his own. A lavishly illustrated four-volume book by Edward Strahan, *Mr. Vanderbilt's House and Collection* (Boston, 1883–1884), reflected the national interest in the Herter commission. Vanderbilt, having inherited and amassed a fortune of two hundred million dollars, was the wealthiest man in America.

The drawing room (fig. 3), with walls lined in glass-jeweled red velvet and beautifully gilded furniture, was one of the grandest of the public spaces in Vanderbilt's mansion. The Crawford side chair (no. 109)—originally upholstered in

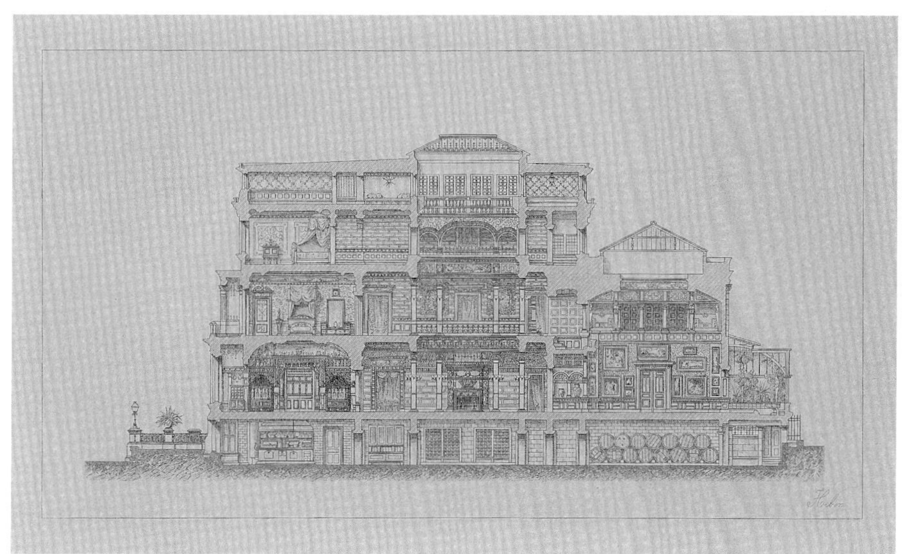

Fig. 2. Vanderbilt house architectural drawing, New York. Photograph from Edward Strahan, *Mr. Vanderbilt's House and Collection* (Boston, 1883–1884).

109.

Side Chair, 1881–1882

Herter Brothers (1864–1907), New York
Gilt maple and mother-of-pearl, reupholstered in nineteenth-century Japanese silk embroidery
34½ × 16 × 16 inches
Marks: Impressed on bottom of back seat rail, *170;* printed on paper label on inside of front rail, *XX DEEP (23K) GOLD LEAF*
1982.316

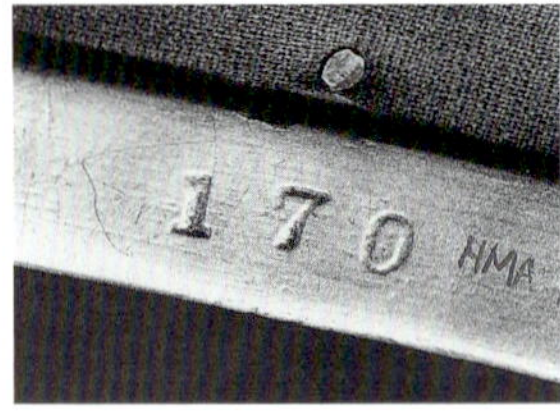

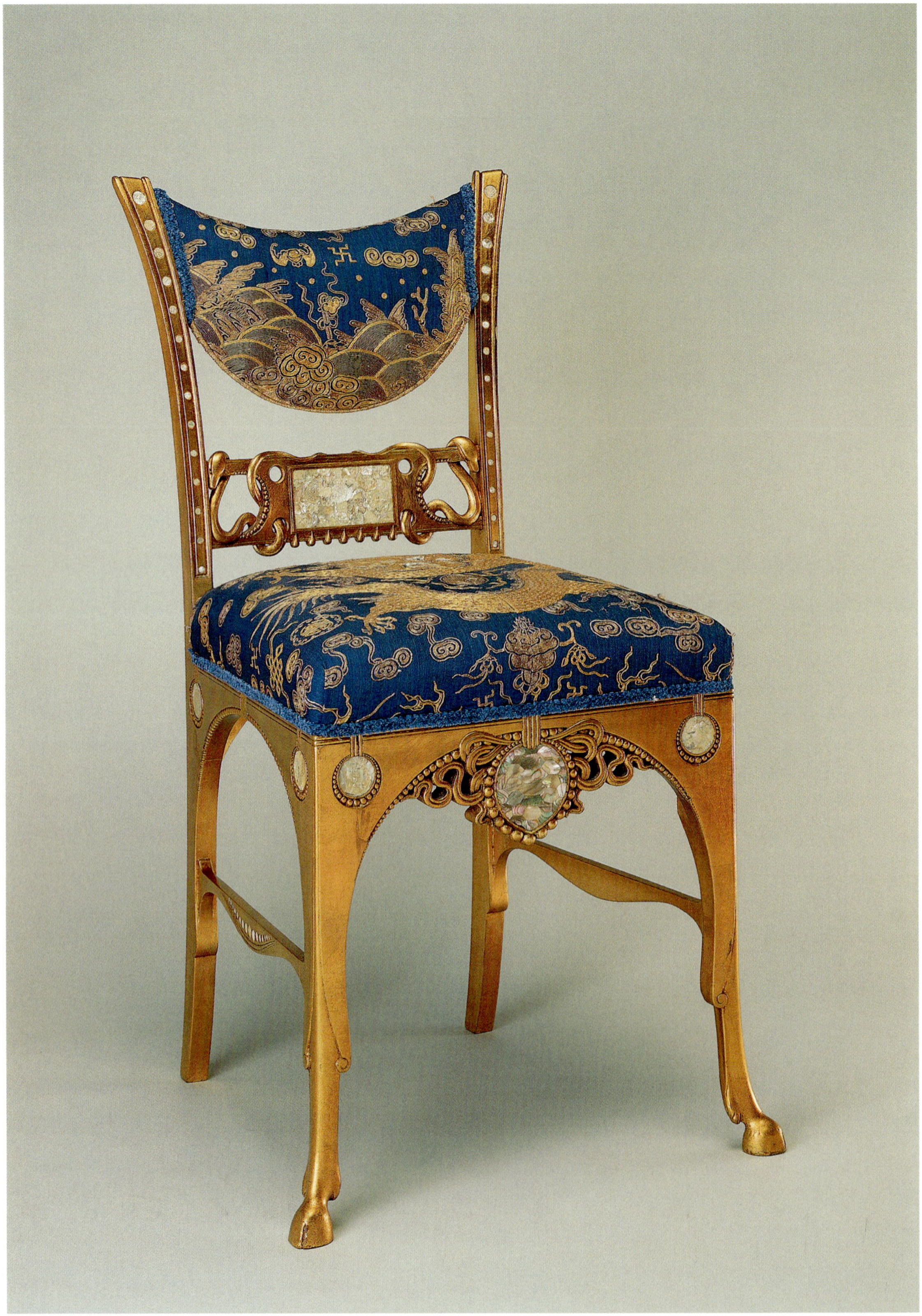

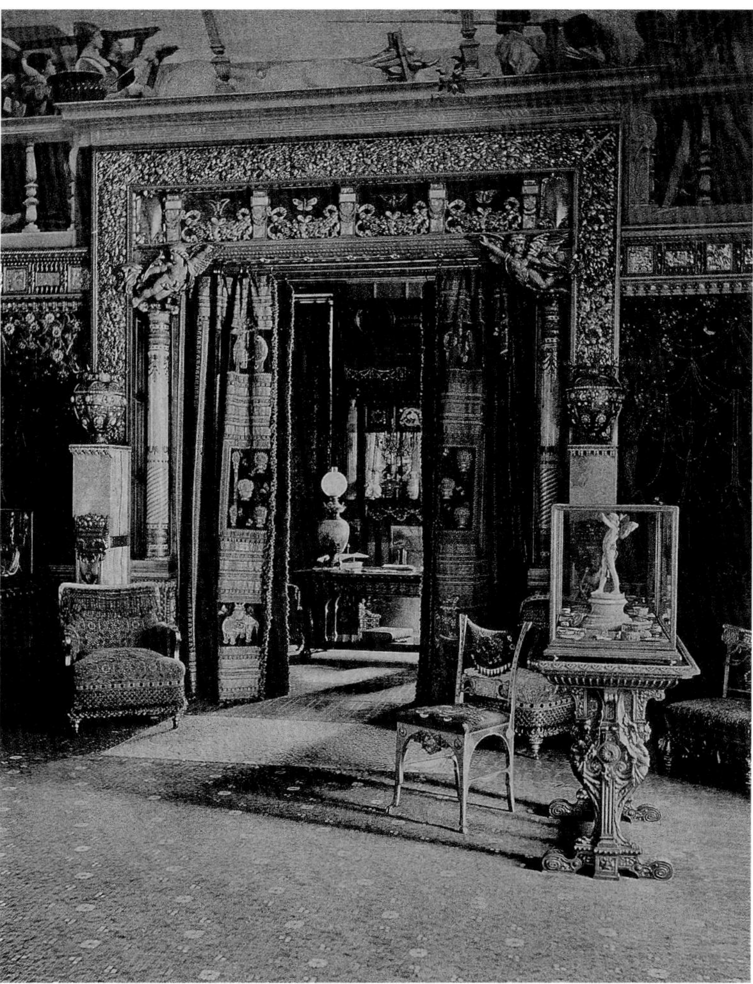

Fig. 3. Vanderbilt house drawing room, New York. Photograph from Edward Strahan, *Mr. Vanderbilt's House and Collection* (Boston, 1883–1884).

red and one of at least a pair made for the drawing room—defies stylistic classification. The exquisite craftsmanship, lush gilding, and sparkling inlaid mother-of-pearl give the effect of glittering jewelry. This is enhanced by the ribboned and reeded carving at the center of the front seat rail around a central brooch-like setting for the largest circular mother-of-pearl inlay. The concave and crescent-shaped upholstered back panel complements the graceful curves of the legs, which extend to the seat rails to create arches on all four sides of the chair. The flaring side stiles of the back, the sensuous swelling of the leg-connecting side rails, and the arches contrast with the square seat. The other straight elements in the composition—the back rail and its rectangular mother-of-pearl panel—are relieved by the pair of sinuous snakes that flank the panel and twine around the rectangular back rail.[6]

The Crawford ottoman (no. 110) descended in the Vanderbilt family, whose tradition holds that it was used in Mrs. Vanderbilt's boudoir on the second floor. A photograph of the boudoir (fig. 4) shows furniture of ebony or ebonized wood rather than rosewood, and no ottoman is visible. The pattern of embroidered upholstery on a settee in the boudoir is similar to the marquetry pattern on the sides of the ottoman. A similar floral embroidered pattern was used for portieres in a Herter Brothers commission of 1882, the library of the John Sloane house at Fifth Avenue and 70th Street. Despite the relationship between the boudoir upholstery and the ottoman marquetry, the ottoman cannot be placed with certainty in the boudoir. Mr. Vanderbilt's bedroom, also on the second floor, was furnished in walnut, but a guest bedroom and dressing room on that floor were furnished in rosewood. Given Christian Herter's preference for furniture of the same wood in a room, the guest bedroom and dressing room seem the most probable original locations for the ottoman. The upholstered top of the ottoman lifts off to reveal a cedar and leather-lined storage box. While the ottoman lacks the glitter of the drawing room chair, rosewood was an exotic and expensive wood for furniture, and the marquetry would have significantly added to its cost. Although the marquetry pattern appears to be random, there is, in fact, a carefully designed repeat on each side. In spite of the relatively simple shape of the ottoman, the multiple moldings around the base and the top, the exotic rosewood, and the elegant marquetry give it a feeling of luxury in keeping with the rest of the Vanderbilt commission. A matching ottoman is in the Museum of Fine Arts, Houston, and an en suite side chair is in the Bowdoin College Museum of Art, Brunswick, Maine.[7]

NOTES

1. Howe, Frelinghuysen, and Voorsanger 1994 provides the most comprehensive illustrated survey of Herter Brothers under the leadership of Gustave and Christian Herter between 1858 and 1882.

2. The Metropolitan Museum of Art 1986, p. 160.

3. Howe, Frelinghuysen, and Voorsanger 1994, p. 178.

4. The Metropolitan Museum of Art 1986, pp. 160 and 169, fig. 5.28, discusses and illustrates the Crawford cabinet. Howe, Frelinghuysen, and Voorsanger 1994, pp. 178–179, no. 26, discusses and illustrates both the Crawford cabinet and the Roosevelt cabinet. The Crawford cabinet is discussed in Hanks 1986, pp. 32–39, and illustrated in fig. 3. The provenance of the Crawford cabinet is undocumented. A contrasting unmarked maple or satinwood cabinet of the same form with only slight variations in its marquetry panel colors is at Sagamore Hill, the Long Island home of President Theodore Roosevelt. The Sagamore Hill cabinet may have been made for Theodore Roosevelt, Sr.'s, home at 6 East 57th Street in New York and might date to the time he hired Philadelphia architect Frank Furness to design his dining room and its furniture, which was executed by Philadelphia maker Daniel Pabst (see no. 217 in this catalogue). No

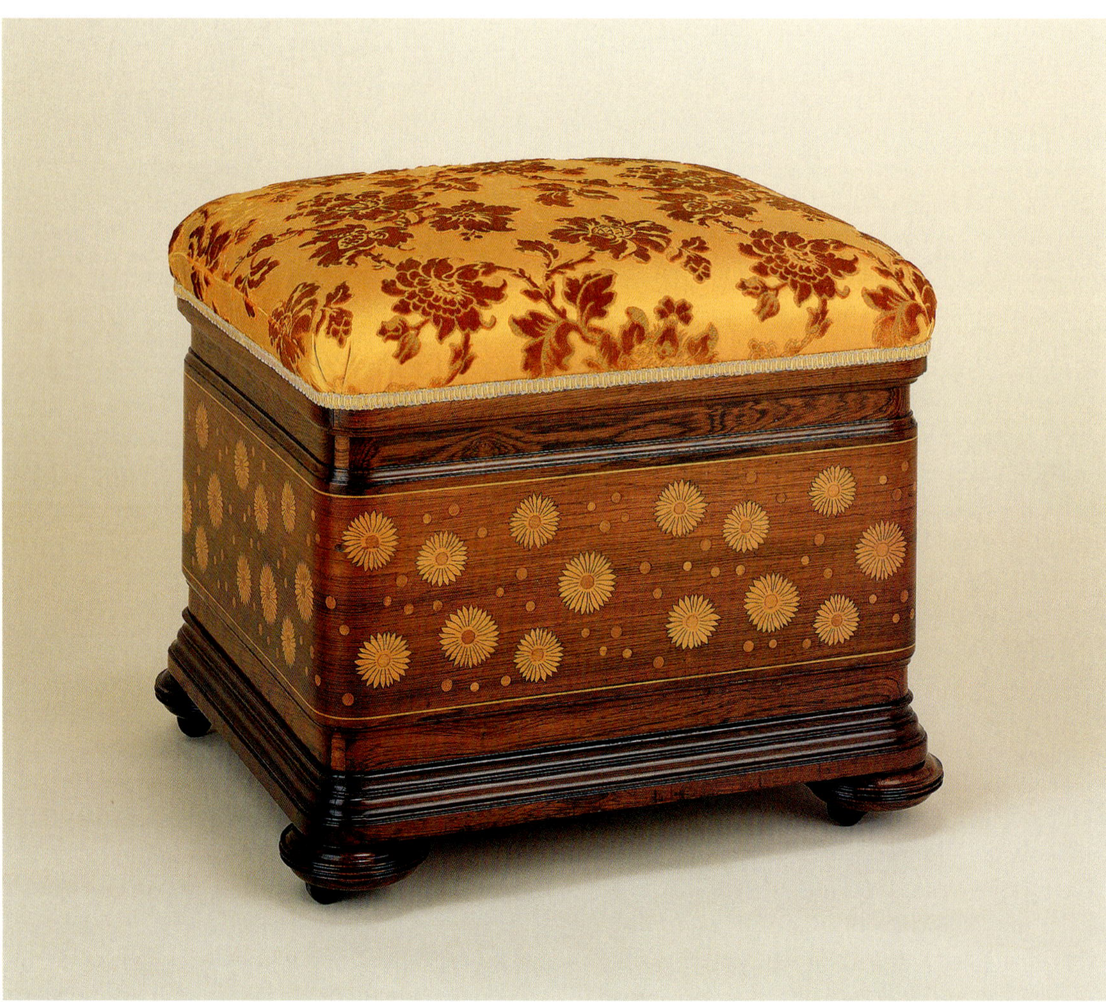

110.

Ottoman, 1881–1882

Herter Brothers (1864–1907), New York
Rosewood with marquetry of various woods, cedar, and leather, reupholstered in nineteenth-century cut-silk velvet
16½ × 19 × 16⅝ inches
Mark: Incised on bottom, *455*
1981.1000.42

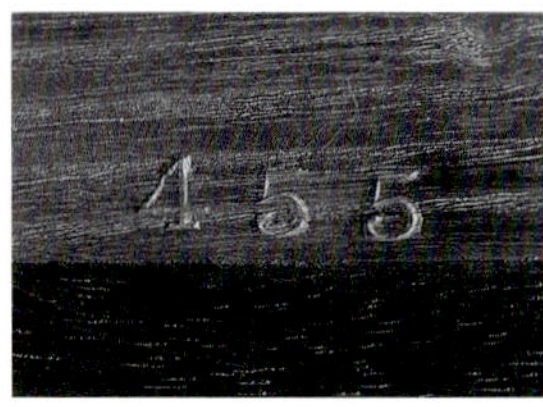

furniture matching the distinctive Herter cabinets is currently known, and it seems likely that they were made to stand alone as art furniture in highly decorated interiors.

5. Correspondence, David A. Hanks to Marilynn Johnson Bordes, November 28, 1982, High Museum of Art document files. The bed and the Toledo Museum of Art wardrobe were sold at Sotheby Parke Bernet, Inc., New York, June 20, 1981, lot 1231. They had been purchased at a sale at White's auction house, Newport, Rhode Island, which reported that they had come from one of the large houses in Newport on "the avenue." Correspondence, Anna Foxen, Administrative Assistant, Decorative Arts and Sculpture, Minneapolis Institute of Arts, to Jody Cohen, Associate Registrar, April 7, 1993, High Museum of Art document files. The Crawford bed is discussed in Hanks 1986, pp. 32–39, and illustrated in fig. 4.

6. The Crawford chair is discussed and illustrated in Howe, Frelinghuysen, and Voorsanger 1994, pp. 202–203, no. 37, and the Vanderbilt commission is outlined on pp. 200–201. The mate to the Crawford chair is in the Carnegie Museum of Art, Pittsburgh. The Crawford chair is discussed in Hanks 1986, pp. 32–39, and illustrated in fig. 5. Herter used this chair form in other commissions. Contemporary photographs show a pair in J. P. Morgan's Madison Avenue mansion in New York, and at least one was in the drawing room of Oliver Ames's Boston mansion. These chairs, however, do not appear to have the detailed articulation in carving apparent in the surviving Vanderbilt chairs.

7. Howe, Frelinghuysen, and Voorsanger 1994, pp. 209–211, discusses and illustrates the Houston ottoman and Bowdoin chair and includes a photograph of the boudoir with the embroidered upholstery. The ottoman sold at Weschler's Auction House, Washington, D.C., February 1975, the property of Gladys Moore Vanderbilt (Countess Szechenyi), daughter of Cornelius Vanderbilt II and granddaughter of William H. Vanderbilt. The Crawford ottoman is discussed in Hanks 1986, pp. 32–39, and illustrated in fig. 6.

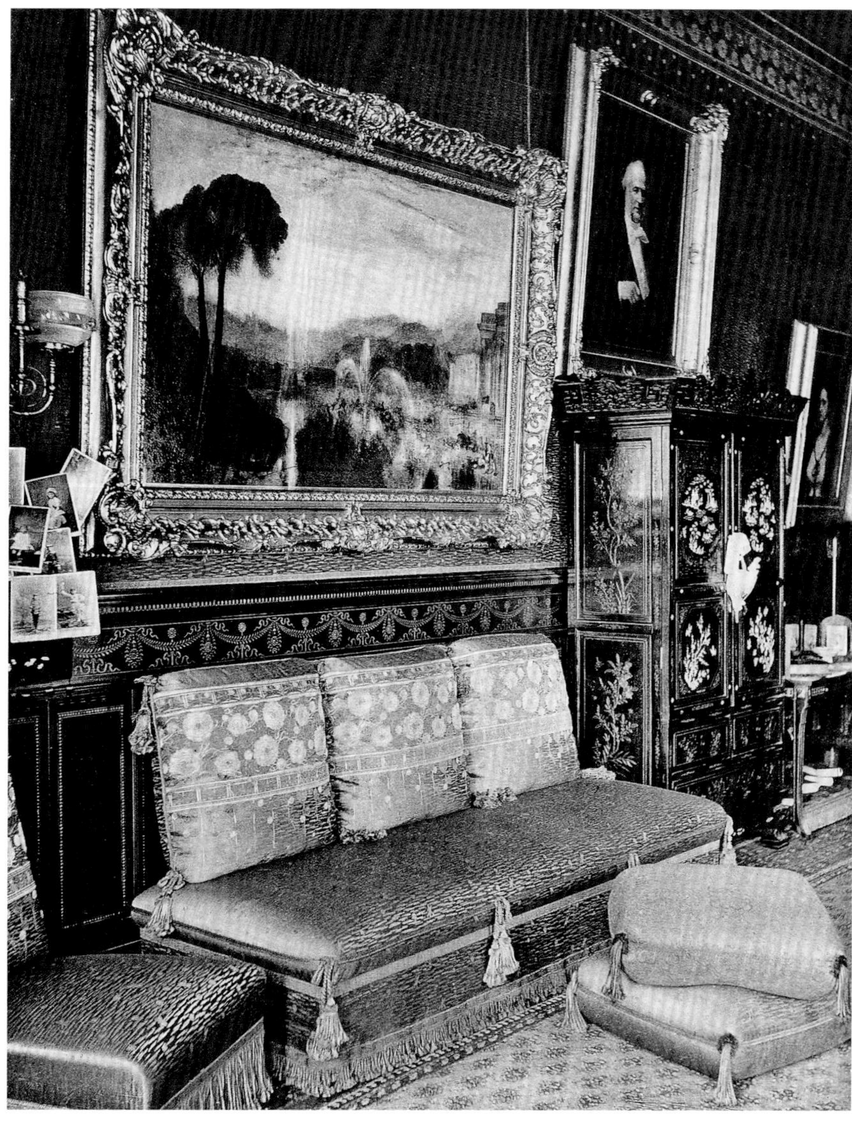

Fig. 4. Vanderbilt house boudoir, New York. Photograph from Edward Strahan, *Mr. Vanderbilt's House and Collection* (Boston, 1883–1884).

Upholstery Treatments of the 1880s

TEXTILES ARE FRAGILE and tend to deteriorate over time. Consequently, the Crawford side chairs and armchair (nos. 111, 112) are rare surviving documents of the virtuosity of the American upholstery trade in the late nineteenth century. The innovation of coil springs greatly improved comfort, influenced the shape of furniture, and contributed significantly to upholstery's importance in interior decoration. Around the time of the Civil War, increasingly mechanized textile production at both American and European mills made a wide variety of fabrics readily available to an affluent American market. At the same time, interior decorating firms such as Herter Brothers (fig. 1) began to appear. The importance of fabrics and trim in expensive nineteenth-century interiors is evident in photographs of opulent homes decorated by Herter Brothers and other firms (see nos. 109–110).

Improved upholstery and springs led to new shapes for chairs, which were determined as much by the emphasis on upholstery as by the traditional wooden frames. Mixtures of different fabrics meant greater variety in color and textures in upholstered furniture. On the Crawford side chair (no. 111), which retains its original upholstery and trim, no wooden frame encloses the square seat cushion, but its shape is defined and emphasized by velvet panels that form its sides.[1] The olive and brown velvets pick up the thread colors used in the ivory silk embroidery panels: brown, olive, red, yellow, and orange. Threads of complementary colors are twisted into a cord to outline the back and seat cushions. The same colored threads are incorporated into the gimp around the bottom of the seat and the bold fringe set against a woven background, which hangs from the bottom of the seat. Velvet provided a

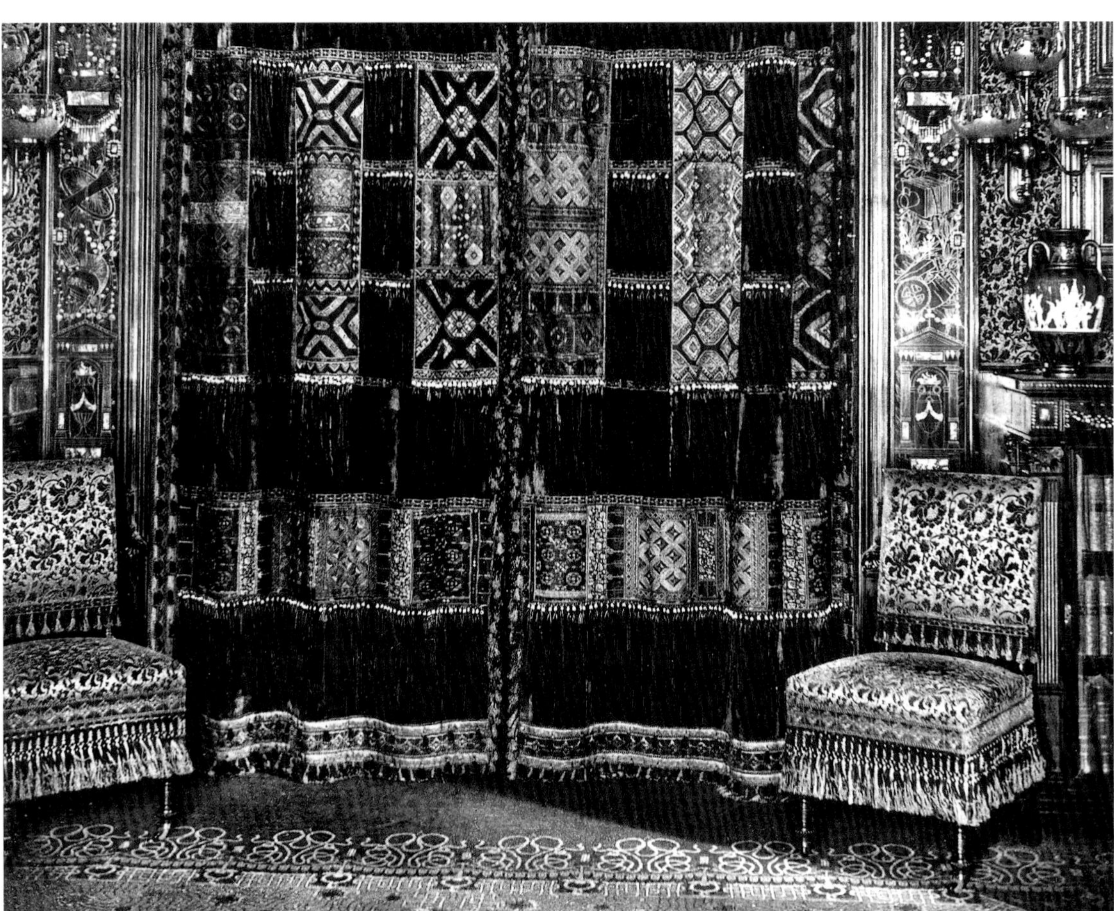

Fig. 1. Upholstered furniture from the William H. Vanderbilt house, New York. Edward Strahan, *Mr. Vanderbilt's House and Collection* (Boston, 1883–84). High Museum of Art, 1984.153.

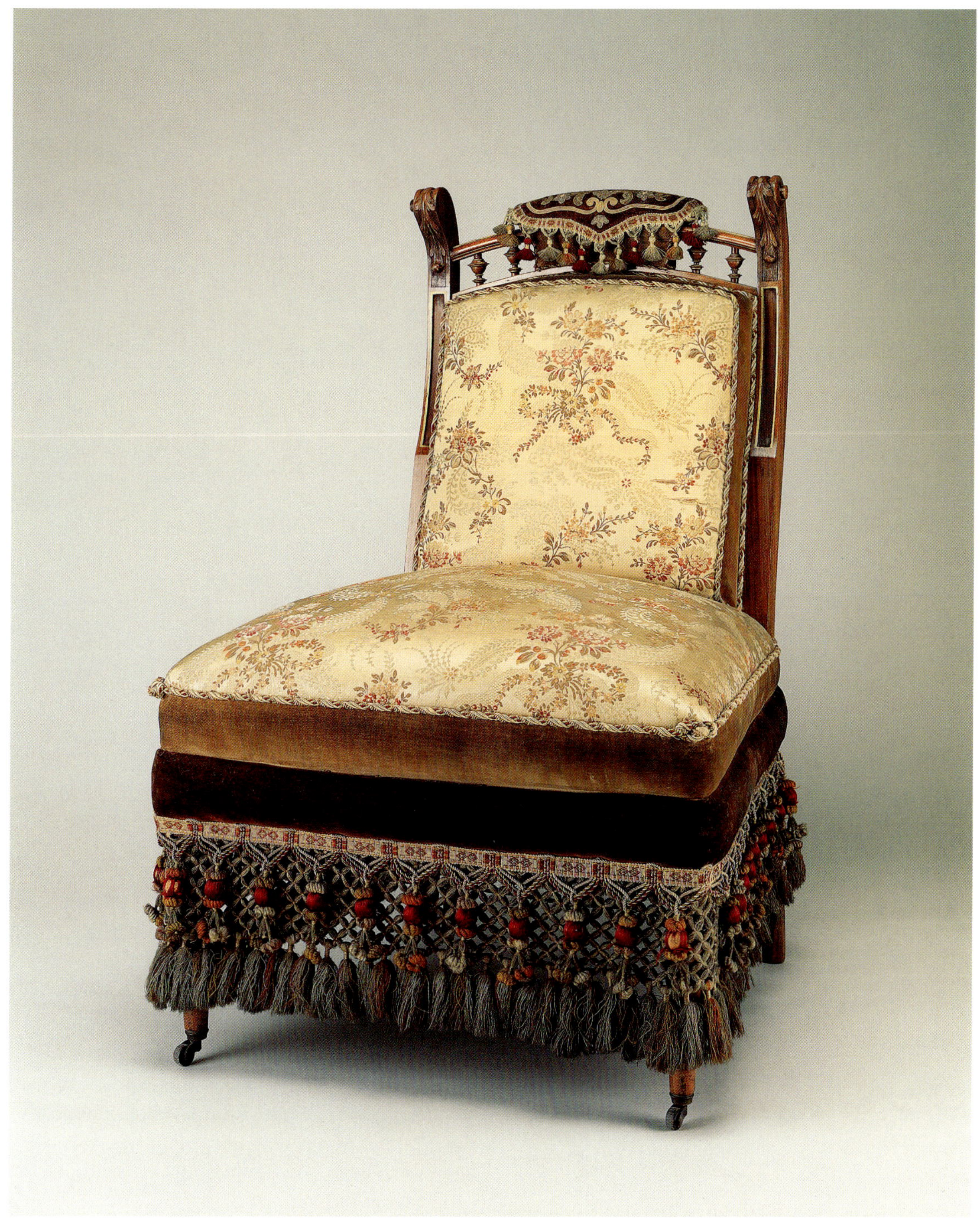

111.

Side Chair, 1880–1885

Probably New York
Walnut with gilded decoration, original upholstery with embroidery on silk, velvet, and silk and wool gimp, cord, and tassels
36 × 24 × 26 inches
1984.117

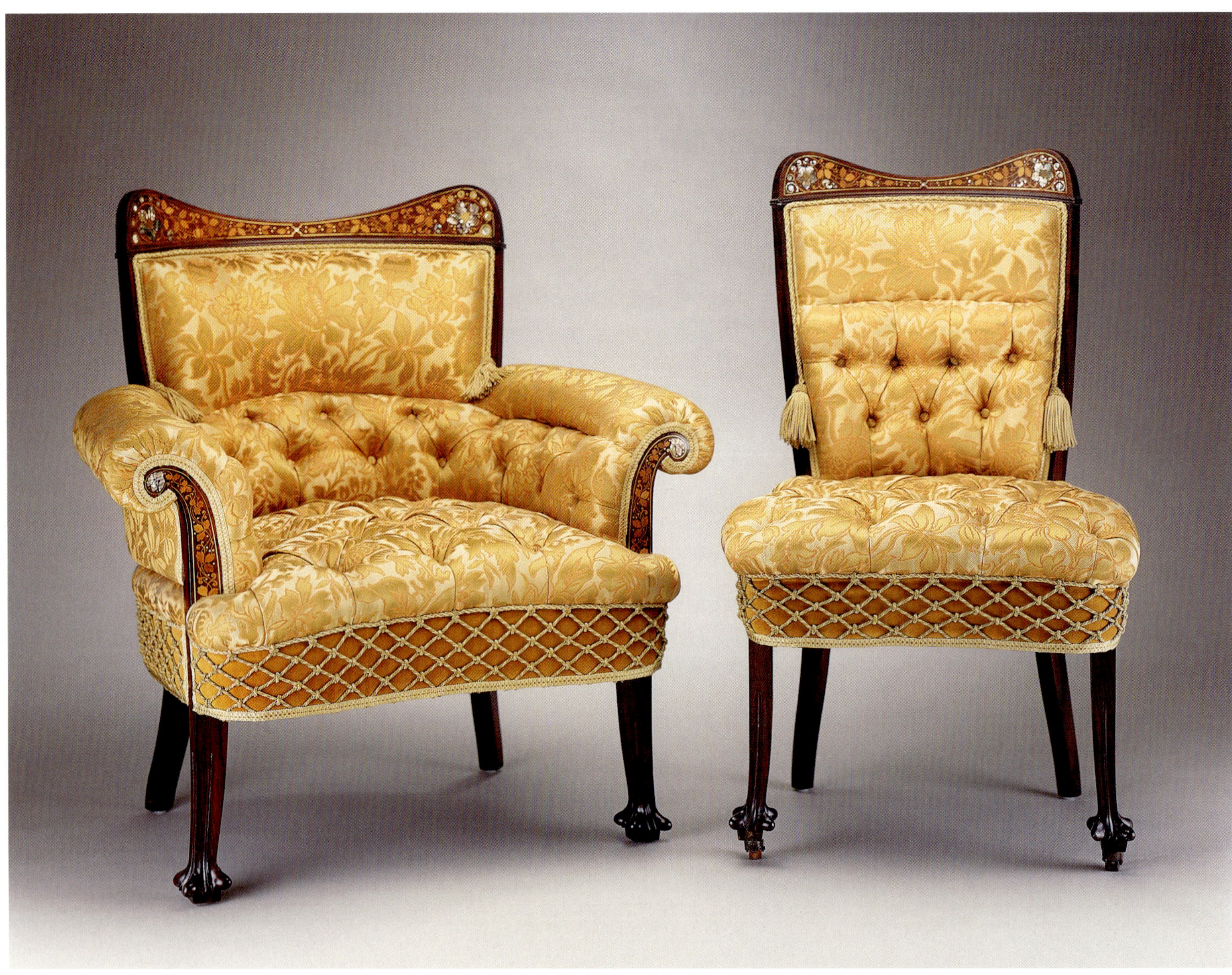

112.

Armchair and Side Chair, 1880–1885

Probably New York
Rosewood and rosewood veneer, marquetry of mother-of-pearl and various lighter woods, brass stringing, ash, chestnut, mostly original upholstery stuffing covered with modern silk damask, modern silk velvet, and modern silk gimp, cord, and tassels
Armchair: 35½ × 32½ × 28 inches
Side chair: 36½ × 19½ × 18½ inches
1981.1000.44–.45

matching background for the headrest on the crest of the chair. The walnut frame, the scroll-shaped, gilded, and carved side-stiles of the back, the crest rail of turned spindles, and the turned legs are secondary to the upholstery treatments for decorative effect.

The exquisitely executed scroll, leaf, and floral marquetry on the graceful matching armchair and side chair (no. 112) relates them to some of the finest American furniture made in the last quarter of the nineteenth century. While the maker and the early history of the chairs remain unknown, the level of workmanship equals that of Herter Brothers and other fine firms who used marquetry. The chairs were purchased at an auction in the Philadelphia area by a local collector in 1979 and kept in as-found condition (figs. 2 and 3).

For the matching armchair and side chair, the High Museum of Art decided to secure related fabrics and trimmings to suggest the original upholstery treatment as closely as possible.[2] Most of the original stuffing was used in the reupholstery, and the deep tufting was retained. A modern silk damask, very close in color and pattern to the original, covers the seats and backs of the chairs. Silk velvet matching the original covers the band around both chairs at seat level, and twisted gold silk was woven in a diamond pattern and applied to the velvet as on the originals. Only a small fragment of the original fringe exists and remains to be reproduced.

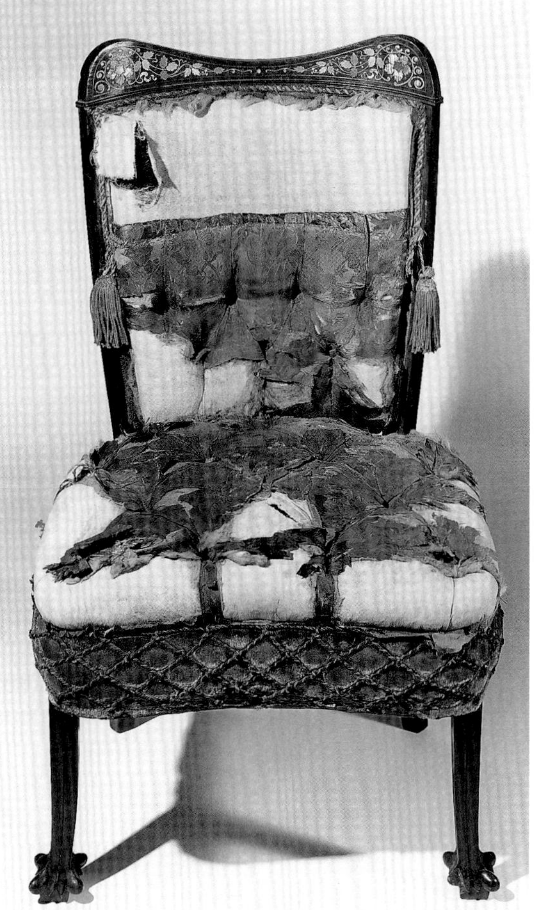

Fig. 2. Side chair before reupholstery. High Museum of Art, 1981.1000.45.

NOTES

1. The practice of framing unpatterned velvet in the decorative, and sometimes silk, tops of cushions dates back at least to the 1850s. See The Metropolitan Museum of Art 1970, no. 120. Other Crawford furniture with upholstery based on the original treatment includes the Belter parlor set (see no. 44) and the Hunzinger chair (see no. 85). Period fabrics are found on the Elizabethan-style armchair (see no. 35) and the Egyptian-style armchair (see no. 73).

2. The decision to reproduce the upholstery treatment was made between 1979 and 1982 and was based on the policy of the High Museum of Art, conservative museum practice, and the most respected scholarly recommendations at the time. Sam Dornsife guided the restoration, which was executed by Henry Urban. Correspondence, High Museum of Art document files.

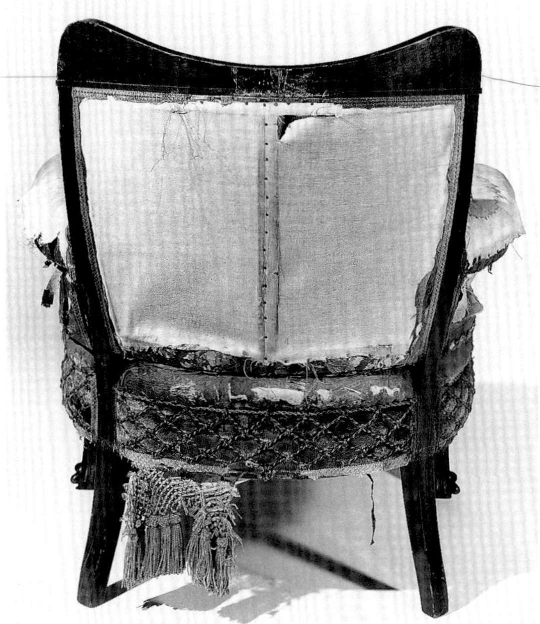

Fig. 3. Armchair before reupholstery. High Museum of Art, 1981.1000.44.

Chelsea Keramic Art Works

CHELSEA KERAMIC Art Works—established in 1872 in Chelsea, Massachusetts, by English potter James Robertson and his three sons, George, Alexander, and Hugh—was among the earliest American potteries to focus on art wares.[1] One of the early decorators at the factory was John Gardner Low. In the 1870s, the factory produced terra-cotta vases with classical shapes and decorations, which were discontinued by 1878 due to poor sales.[2] In 1877, Low established his own pottery in Chelsea, the Low Art Tile Works (see nos. 118–119), and Robertson's oldest son, George, joined Low's firm in 1878. After the departure of Alexander in 1884 to pursue a ceramics career in California, Hugh Robertson became the sole proprietor of the Chelsea Keramic Arts Works.

By the late 1870s, Robertson had become fascinated with the glazes and shapes of Chinese and Japanese ceramics, which he had seen at the 1876 Centennial Exposition in Philadelphia, and also with Middle and Far Eastern ceramics. At the Chelsea pottery, great emphasis was placed on shape, surface decoration, and glaze, as is evident in the green Crawford vase (no. 113), which dates from the late 1870s or early 1880s. The simple form may be based on Asian or Middle Eastern metalwares. The hammered surface decoration, which came to be associated with the Chelsea Keramic Art Works, echoes the Japanese-taste hammered silverwares Tiffany and Company was producing at about the same time (see no. 97). Robertson's process involved hammering the clay while it was in a semi-soft, leathery state. The hammering is visible on both the exterior and interior. The glaze ranges from dark green to yellow, suggesting an aged patina on metalware.

Robertson also admired the rare Oriental *sang-de-boeuf,* or oxblood, glazes he had seen at the Centennial Exposition. From the late 1870s through the 1880s, his quest to achieve this distinctive glaze on Chelsea products became almost obsessive. By 1889, he had succeeded, but the resources of Chelsea Keramic Art Works were exhausted. The Crawford stoneware vase (no. 114) exhibits the *sang-de-boeuf* glaze that Robertson so tirelessly sought and that paved the way to bankruptcy for the Chelsea Keramic Art Works. The classical Chinese shape of this vase, taken from a historical prototype, characterizes *sang-de-boeuf*-glazed Chelsea wares.[3]

In 1891, a group of Boston investors revitalized the pottery and created Chelsea Pottery, U.S.A., with Robertson as manager. In 1895 or 1896, the pottery moved to Dedham, Massachusetts, where it operated as the Dedham Pottery until it closed in 1943. Robertson's son and grandson both directed the Dedham Pottery.

NOTES

1. Histories of the family and firm are recounted in Evans 1987, pp. 46–51; Hawes 1966, pp. 409–413; and The Metropolitan Museum of Art 1986, pp. 407–408.

2. A vase decorated by Low in the classical taste is illustrated in The Metropolitan Museum of Art 1986, p. 202, fig. 7.1.

3. A hammered tea set in The Metropolitan Museum of Art is illustrated and discussed in ibid., p. 214, fig. 7.15, and p. 216. A variety of Chinese-inspired shapes and colors, along with *sang-de-boeuf*-glazed examples, are illustrated on p. 215, figs. 7.16 and 7.17.

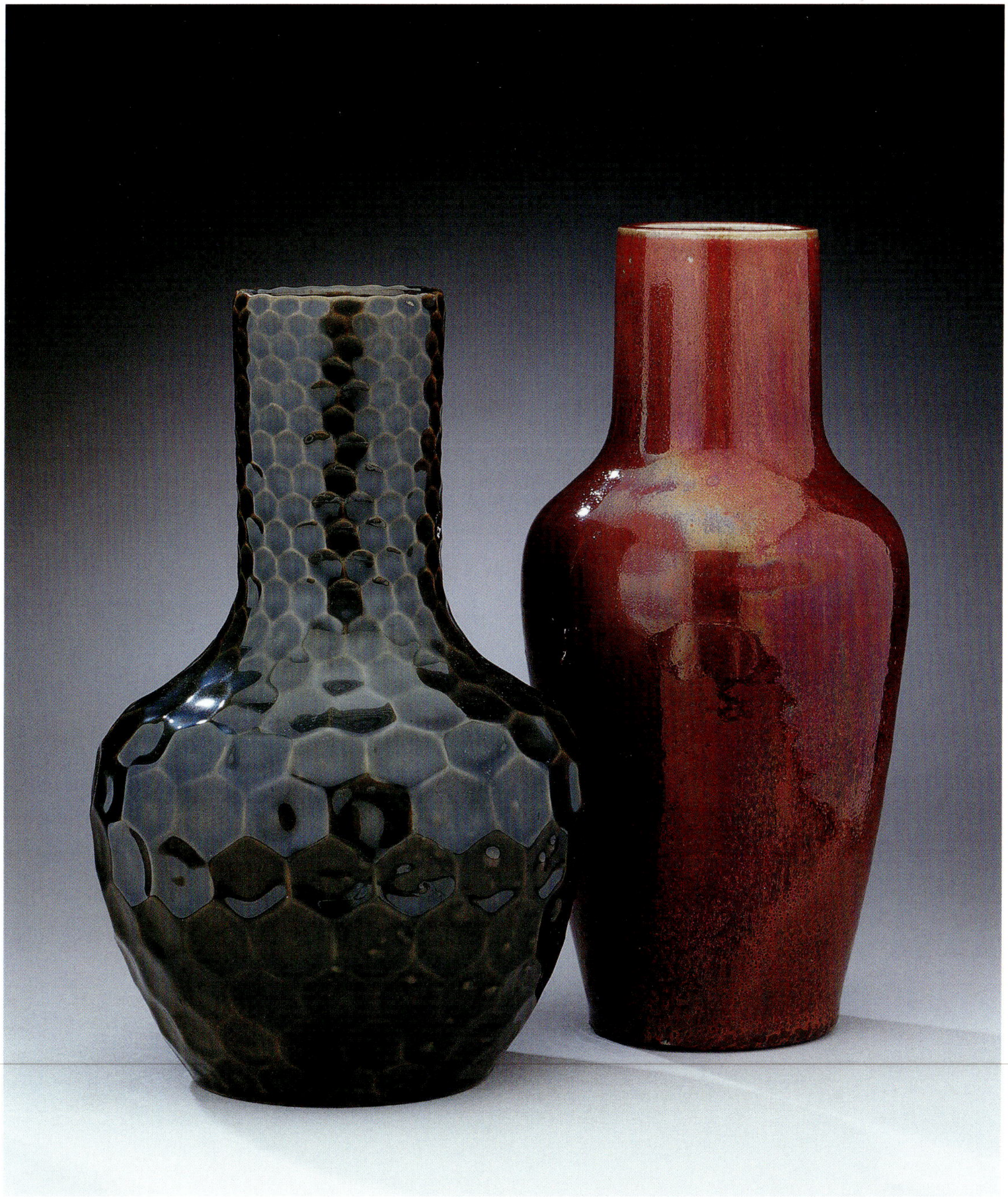

113.

Vase, 1879–1883

Chelsea Keramic Art Works (1872–1889), Chelsea, Massachusetts
Lead-glazed earthenware
7¾ × 4¾ × 4¾ inches
Mark: Impressed on bottom, C/KA/W
1984.160

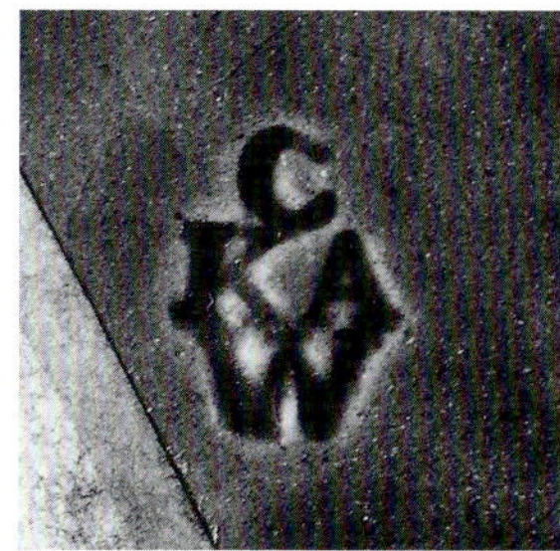

114.

Vase, ca. 1889

Chelsea Keramic Art Works (1872–1889), Chelsea, Massachusetts
Sang-de-boeuf-glazed stoneware
8⅜ × 4 × 4 inches
Mark: Impressed on bottom, C/KA/W
1993.128

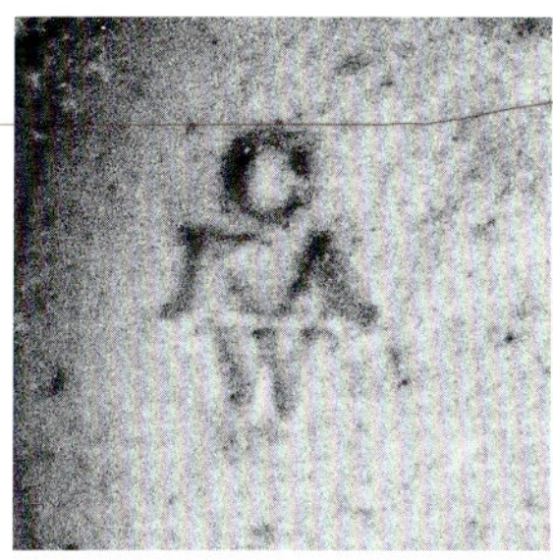

Ott and Brewer

Etruria Pottery—later Ott and Brewer—in Trenton, New Jersey, was named for Josiah Wedgwood's celebrated eighteenth-century English pottery, capitalizing on the American preference for imported European ceramics. Etruria was a partnership between William Bloor, experienced in the potteries of East Liverpool, Ohio; Joseph Ott, a livery stable owner; and Thomas Booth, a stationery businessman. Bloor provided the technical expertise, while Ott and Booth backed the factory with financial investments. Within a year, Booth sold his share, which was later purchased by Ott's nephew, John Hart Brewer. Bloor left the firm in 1871, and Brewer assumed management.[1]

In 1873, Isaac Broome, designer of this vase (no. 115), was hired as artistic director, a new position in American potteries, just before the 1876 Centennial Exposition in Philadelphia. Broome trained at the Pennsylvania Academy of Fine Arts in Philadelphia and, in the late 1850s, traveled through Europe. He worked in the studio of American sculptor Thomas Crawford, who was then completing work for the north pediment of the U.S. Capitol building. Broome returned to the United States as an academician at the Pennsylvania Academy. From 1866 until his employment by Ott and Brewer, Broome operated a terra-cotta works making architectural ornaments, first in Pittsburgh and later in Brooklyn. In hiring Broome, Ott and Brewer made a strong commitment to ornamental wares, an important aspect of the firm's production from the Centennial Exposition until its dissolution. Broome, also an experienced technician, designed the firm's kilns for ceramic production. Perhaps his most important body of work for Ott and Brewer was what he made for the Centennial Exposition, including the Pastoral Vase shape.[2] In 1879, Jennie J. Young celebrated the design in her early historical book *The Ceramic Art: A Compendium of the History and Manufacture of Pottery and Porcelain.* Young described the vase as "partly suggested by mythology, partly original. It carries us back to the golden age of the poets." The combination of mythological figures—including "a female figure which might be that of Flora or Proserpina"—with the Asian fretwork was certainly eclectic. The vase leaned "neither toward scantiness . . . nor overloaded ornamentation . . . The decoration relieves without destroying the fine outline of the vase."[3]

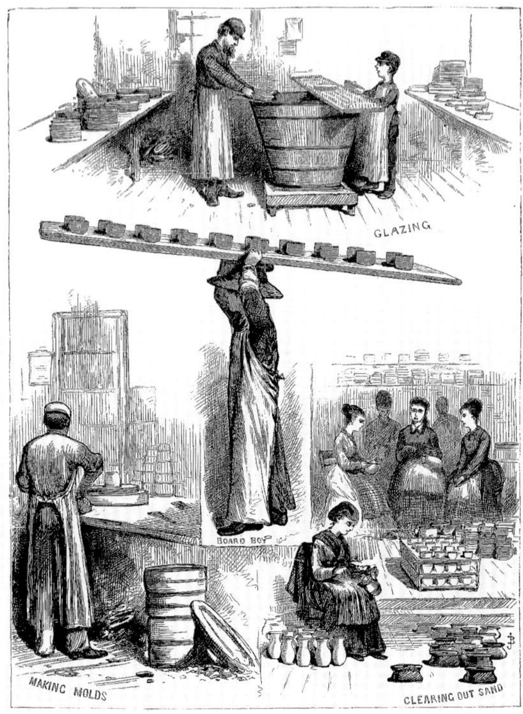

Fig. 1. Workers in a Trenton, New Jersey, pottery. From "In the Potteries—Scenes at Trenton, N. J." *Frank Leslie's Illustrated Newspaper,* New York, vol. 39 (January 9, 1875), p. 293.

Dating the Crawford version of the vase is problematic. Certainly the form was included in the Centennial Exposition, but while surviving accounts list only uncolored parian in the display, this example is modeled of terra-cotta-colored unglazed porcelain. Ceramics molds can be used almost indefinitely, and a Broome family tradition holds that Broome's designs were dated according to the year they were modeled and not the year cast; the date on this piece is 1876. Ownership family tradition states that the vase was purchased at the Centennial Exposition by Bostonians.[4] After the Centennial, in honor of his work, Isaac Broome was named special commissioner on ceramics for the United States and New Jersey to the 1878 Paris Exposition Universelle. For the remainder of his life, Broome worked as a consultant to both tile and porcelain factories.

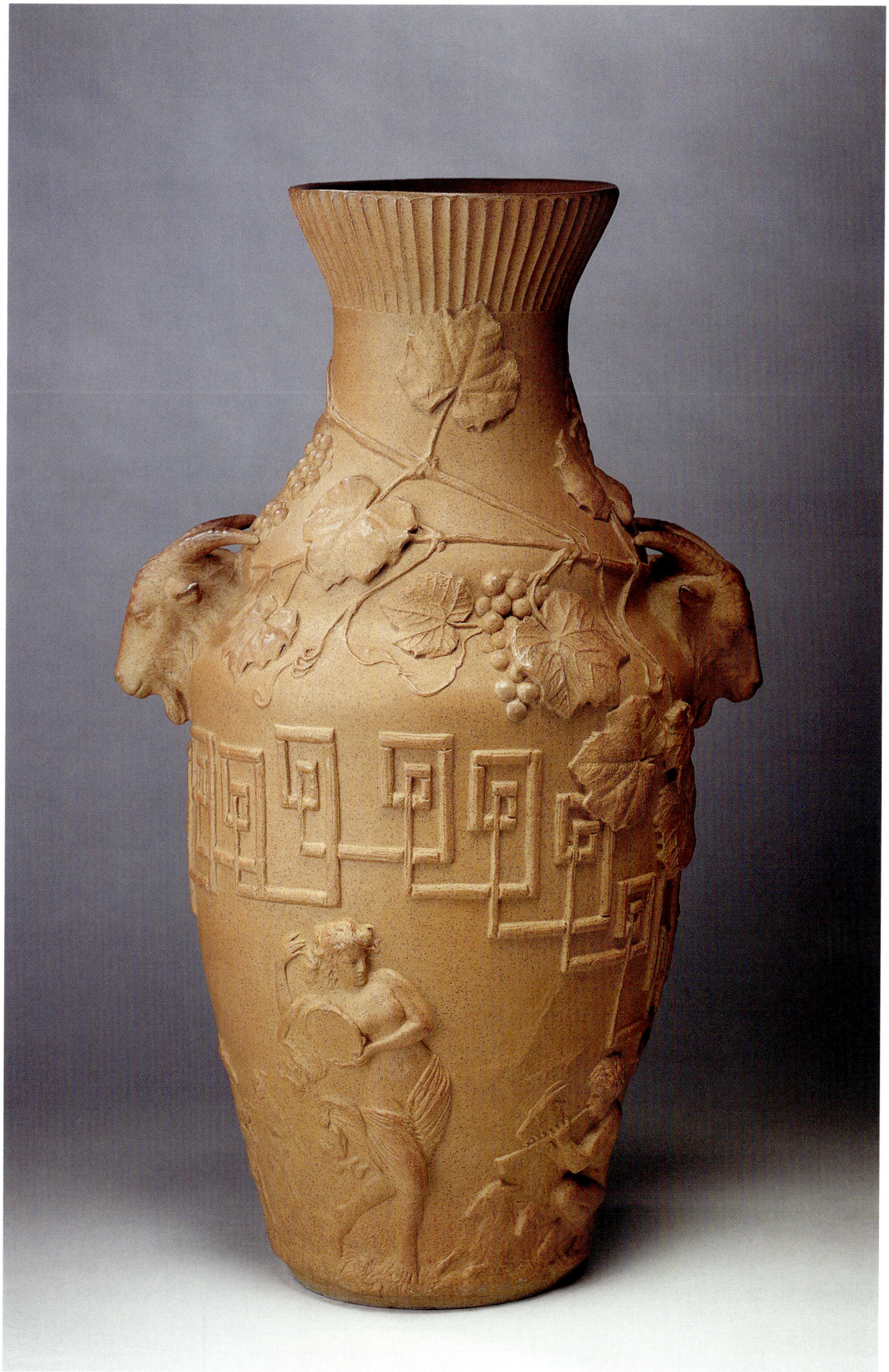

115.

Pastoral Vase, designed 1876

Ott and Brewer (1871–1893), Trenton, New Jersey; designed and modeled by Isaac Broome (1835–1902)
Cast terra-cotta-colored porcelain
17¾ × 10¼ × 10¼ inches
Marks: Incised on side near base, *1876/BROOME.SCULP;* impressed below, *OTT & BREWER*
1981.1000.60

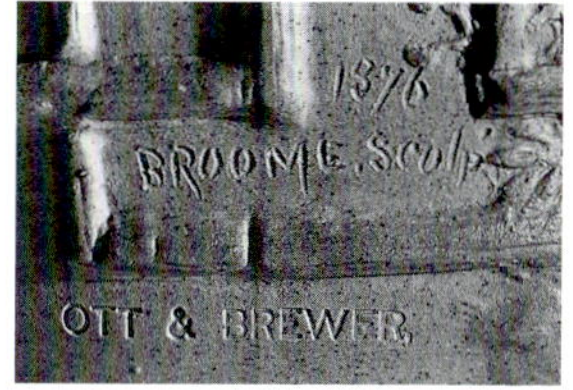

Ott and Brewer also produced wares made of Belleek-type porcelain. Belleek porcelain consists of an exceedingly thin, ivory-colored ceramic body covered with an iridescent glaze, patented in France in 1857, that is reminiscent of seashells. It was first made at McBirney and Company (later Belleek Pottery) in Belleek, Ireland. This accomplishment was supervised by William Bromley Sr. Irish Belleek porcelains were highly regarded: they attracted aristocratic and royal patronage in England in the late 1860s, and by the 1870s, Tiffany and Company and other American retailers were selling Belleek wares.

Although Ott and Brewer experimented with manufacturing Belleek-type porcelains, they were unsuccessful until 1882, when William Bromley Jr. came to work there, followed a year later by his father and brother. These immigrants enabled Ott and Brewer to become the first American enterprise to manufacture Belleek-type wares.[5]

For nearly five years, Ott and Brewer stood alone in making Belleek-type porcelains, and remained a leader in that field of ceramics during

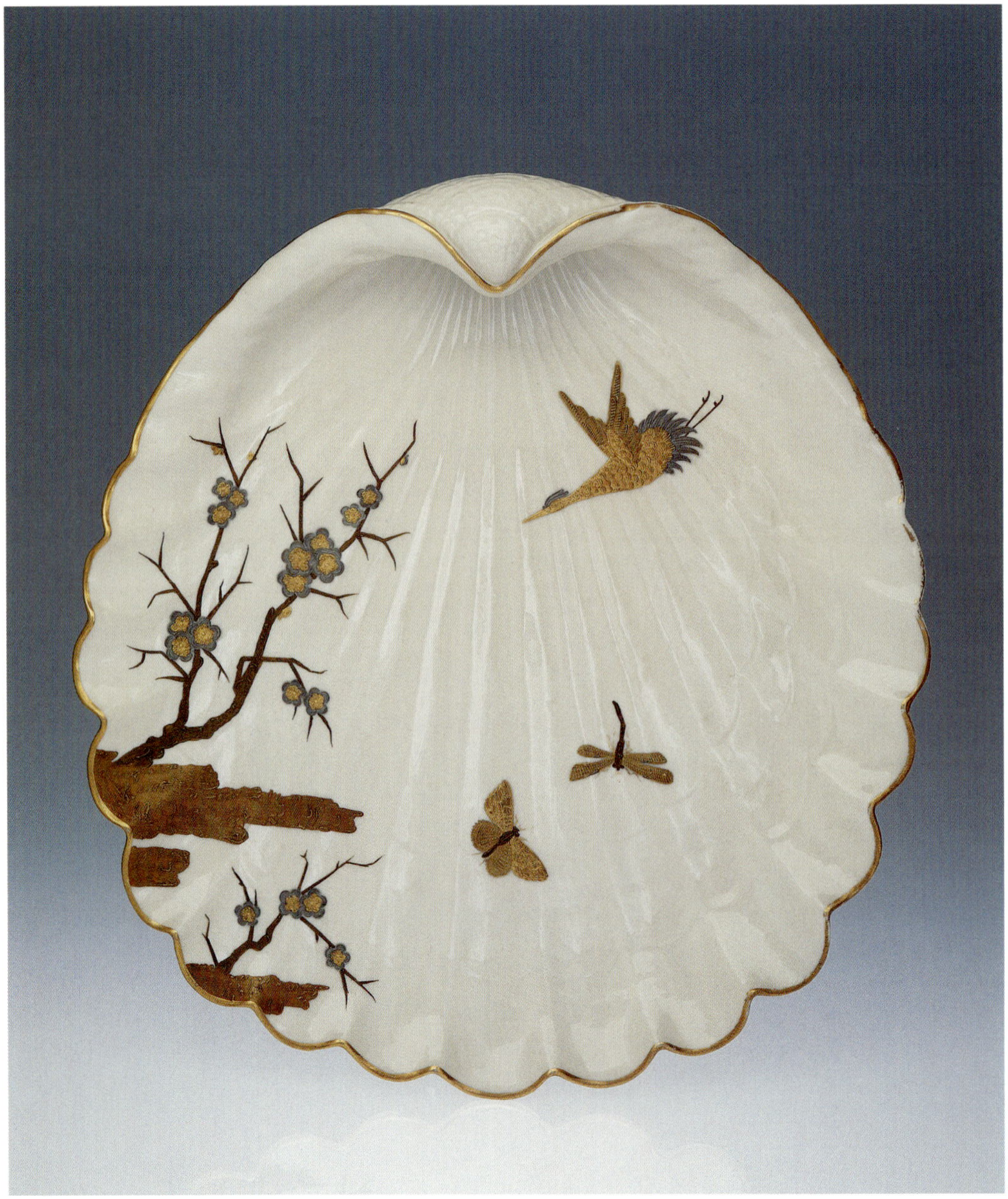

116.

Tray, 1882–1890

Ott and Brewer (1871–1893), Trenton, New Jersey
Belleek-type porcelain with polychrome, silvered, and gilt decoration
15 × 16 × 3¼ inches
Mark: Printed on bottom, script *O & B* with intertwining crescent that encloses *BELLEEK*
1984.137

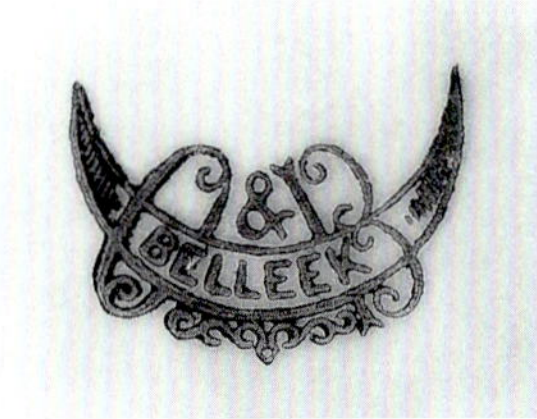

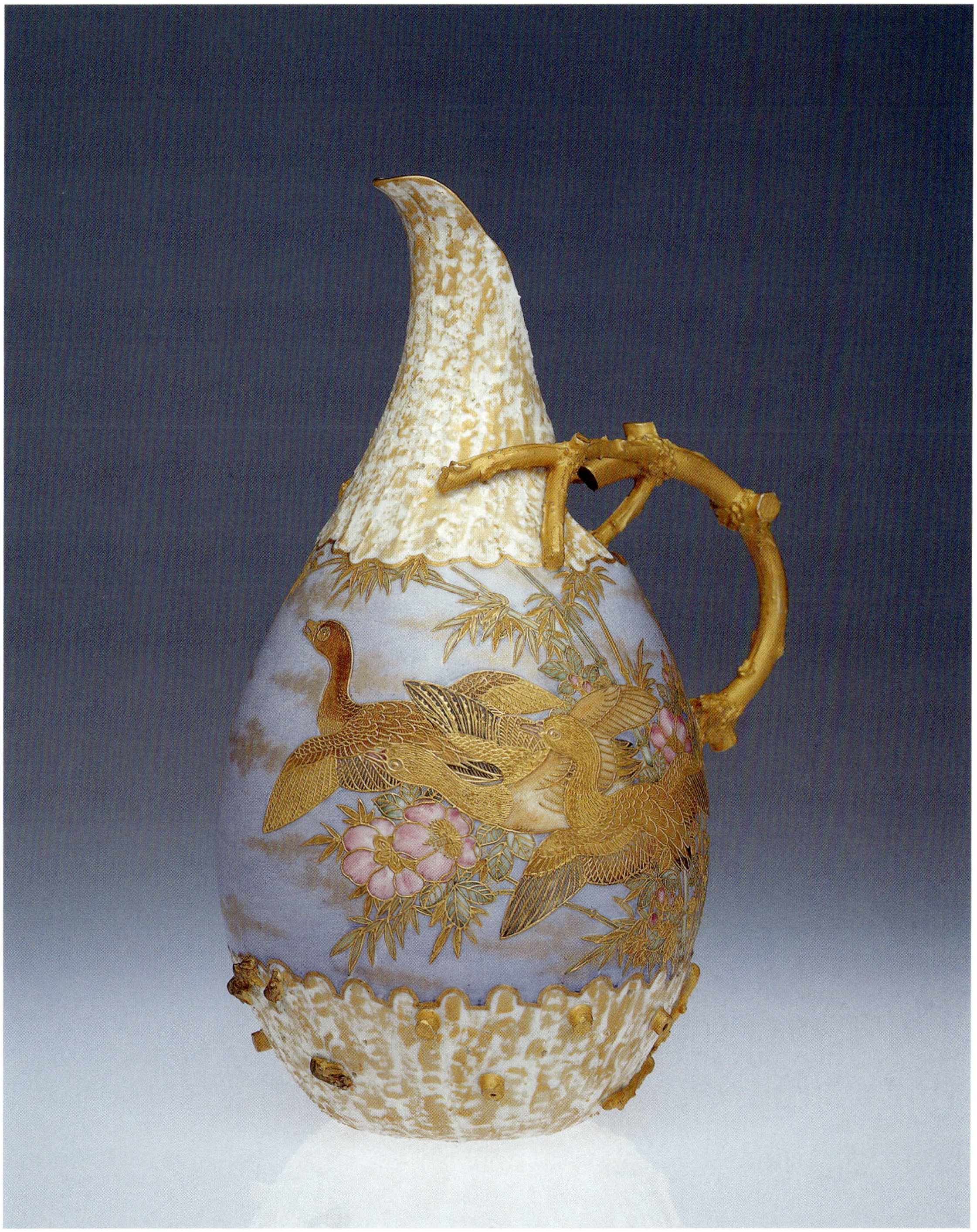

117.

Ewer, 1882–1890

Ott and Brewer (1871–1893), Trenton, New Jersey
Belleek-type porcelain with polychrome and gilt decoration
13¼ × 9 × 6⅝ inches
Mark: Printed on bottom, BELLEEK above a crown and sword with *O & B* below
1984.140

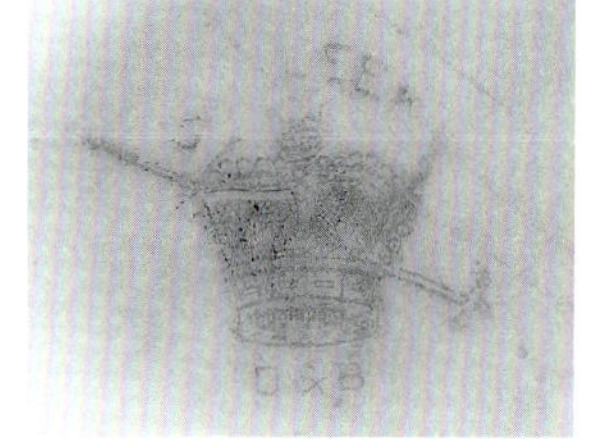

its last decade. The wares were sold in fine retail outlets nationally and were offered alongside imported European porcelains. The company relied heavily on contemporary European ceramics for design, especially the Belleek Pottery in Ireland and the Royal Worcester Company in England. Shell-form trays and dishes were popular in Belleek-type porcelains. Tiffany and Company sold Irish shell-shaped dishes that may have inspired this tray by Ott and Brewer (no. 116). A similar tray in The Metropolitan Museum of Art was part of a tea set, and whether the Crawford example originally accompanied a larger set is unknown.[6]

The diagonal composition of the overglaze enamel decoration with silver and gilt details on the Crawford ewer (no. 117) was associated with the popular Japanese taste of the 1880s. No prototype in Japanese porcelain has been identified, and the ewer seems to be based on European interpretations of Japanese form and decoration. The blue and purple colors and the gilding would have required more than one firing. The birds and plants on the ewer, as on the tray, are in gilt. The ewer, with its delicate gilt twig-shaped handle, was undoubtedly ornamental rather than functional.

Production of expensive decorative wares like the Crawford tray and pitcher lent great prestige to Ott and Brewer. While the firm continued to make utilitarian wares for a broad range of domestic and commercial uses, the Belleek-type ornamental porcelains were intended for a wealthy, elite market. Unlike the earlier Boch Brothers and Bennington porcelains (nos. 15–17), which were made for a broad market, Ott and Brewer Belleek-type porcelains were in the same price range as silver and cut-glass wares.[7]

NOTES

1. Accounts of the firm's history are given in Mitchell 1972, pp. 217–228; and Frelinghuysen 1989, pp. 166–173, 193–201.

2. Mitchell 1972, p. 222. Kaplan 1987, p. 64, discusses and illustrates the Crawford Pastoral Vase. A view of the products exhibited at the Ott and Brewer display at the American Institute Fair in New York includes a number of the firm's Centennial Exposition wares, including a parian version of the Crawford vase, illustrated in Frelinghuysen 1989, p. 42, fig. 34.

3. Jennie J. Young, *The Ceramic Art: A Compendium of the History and Manufacture of Pottery and Porcelain* (New York: Harper and Brothers, 1879), pp. 465–466; cited in J. Stradling 1976, pp. 149–150.

4. High Museum of Art document files.

5. Frelinghuysen 1989, p. 44, recounts the history of Belleek production in Ireland and the emigration of workers from there to the United States to work at Ott and Brewer.

6. Ibid., p. 45, illustrates shell dishes from Tiffany and Company. The tray in The Metropolitan Museum of Art with the same form as the Crawford tray but different decoration is illustrated on p. 197, no. 69. Another example is in the Smithsonian Institution and is illustrated in Patterson 1979, p. 113, pl. 27.

7. Frelinghuysen 1989, p. 198, discusses contemporary prices. The pitcher is illustrated and discussed in The Metropolitan Museum of Art 1986, pp. 207–208, fig. 7.6.

J. and J. G. Low Art Tile Works

John Gardner Low, who had decorated reproductions and adaptations of classical vases at the Chelsea Keramic Art Works (see nos. 113–114), founded J. and J. G. Low Art Tile Works. His father and financial partner, John Low, was a civil engineer. Joining in the enterprise was Arthur Osborne, an English sculptor who had trained at the Graduate School of Design at South Kensington, London, and had also worked at the Chelsea pottery. Another early member of the firm, hired in 1878 as a chemist responsible for glazes, was George W. Robertson, whose family had founded the Chelsea Keramic Art Works. J. and J. G. Low Art Tile Works was one of the most influential and highly regarded American tile factories working in the 1870s and 1880s. The company was awarded a silver medal at the Cincinnati Industrial Exposition in 1879, and a

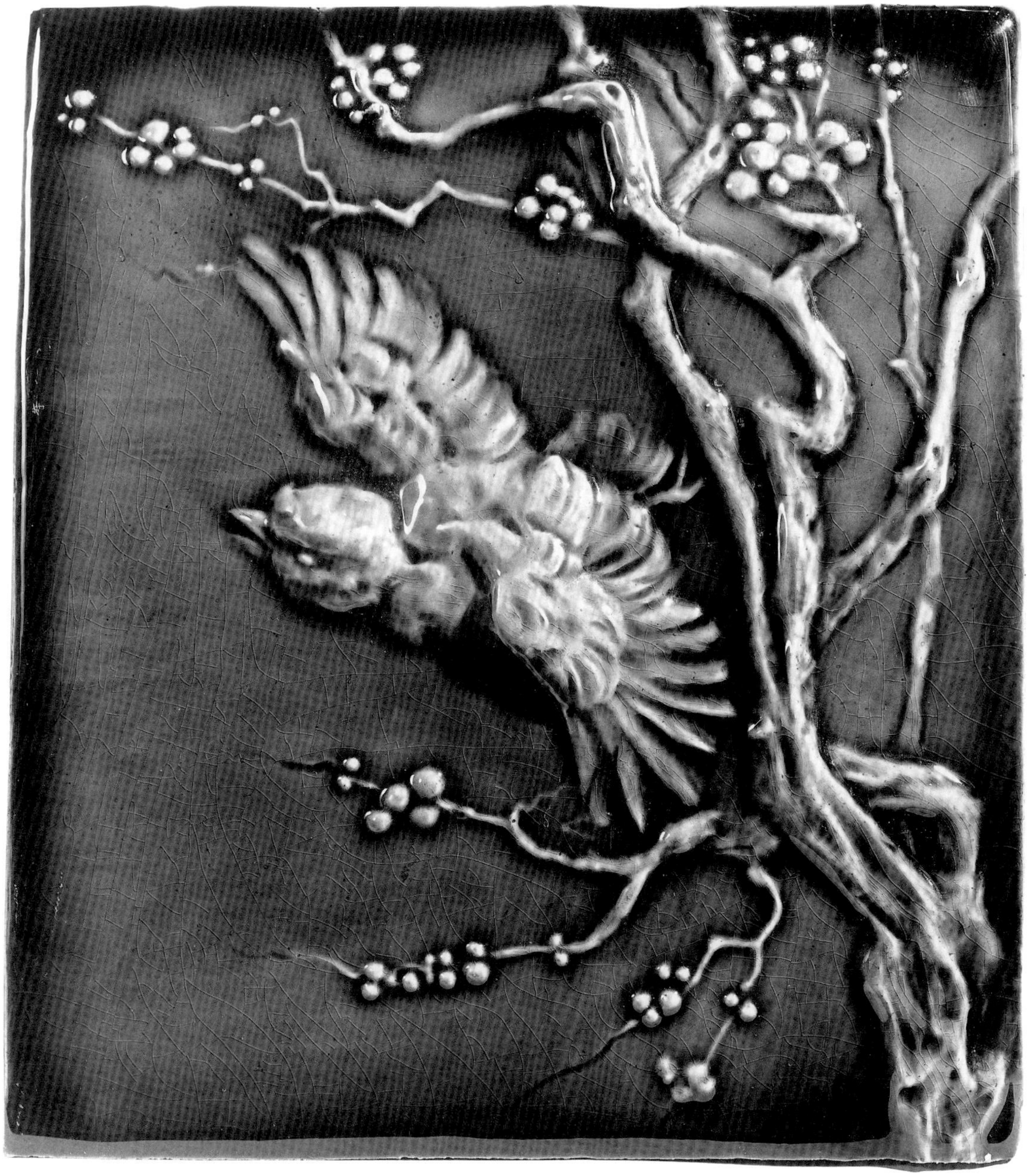

118.

Tile, 1880s

J. and J. G. Low Art Tile Works (1877–1907), Chelsea, Massachusetts; modeled by Arthur Osborne
Glazed earthenware
9½ × 8¼ × 1½ inches
Mark: In lower right corner, under glaze, *AO*
1984.161

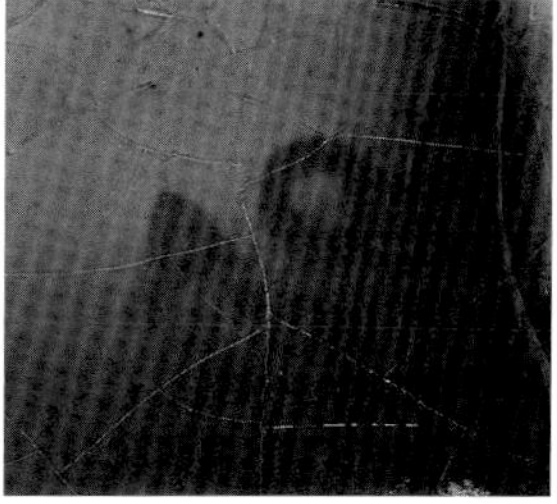

gold medal at an 1880 competition at Stoke-on-Trent, Staffordshire, England, which included leading British tile manufacturers.

In 1883, the name of the firm was changed to J. G. and J. F. Low when John Low retired and was replaced by his grandson, John Farnsworth Low, a chemist educated at the Massachusetts Institute of Technology. The company was best known for its high-gloss tiles with boldly modeled relief decorations. Most of the relief tiles have been attributed to Arthur Osborne, although John G. Low also designed tiles and introduced innovations in tile production.

Through the 1880s and 1890s, Low tiles were produced in the classical, Japanese, and natural styles of the period. High-relief molded tiles were

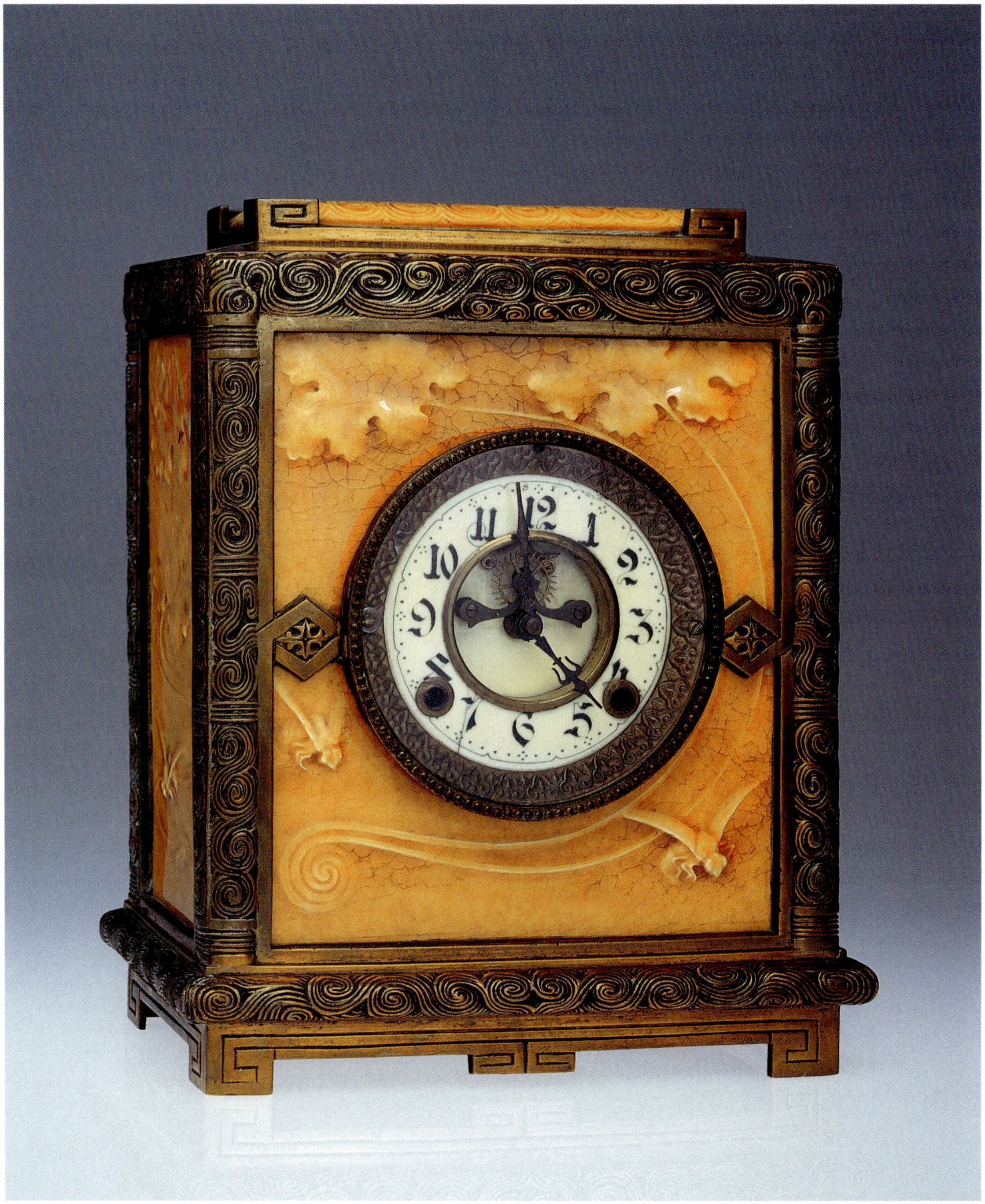

119.

Clock, 1884–1890

Tiles by J. and J. G. Low Art Tile Works (1877–1907), Chelsea, Massachusetts; works by New Haven Clock Company (1853–1956), New Haven, Connecticut
Glazed ceramic tile and bronze
12 × 9¾ × 6 inches
Marks: Impressed on flanking tiles, *J.& J.G.LOW./PATENT/ART TILE WORKS./CHELSEA./MASS.U.S.A./COPYRIGHT 1884 by J.G. & J.F. LOW;* printed in brown on back of front tile, *COPYRIGHT '88;* on clock face, at top, *S F*
1984.146

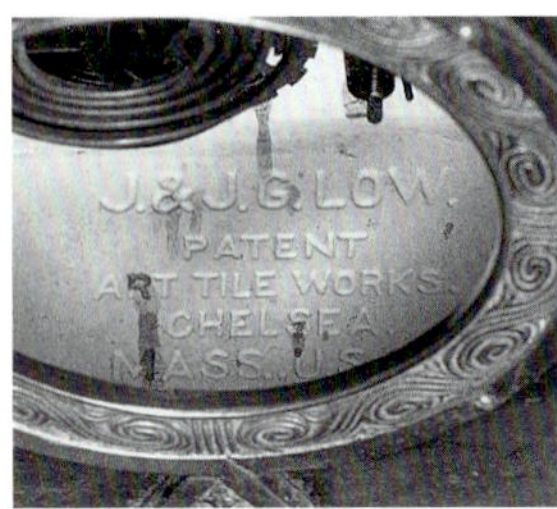

especially popular at the time in America, and the Low Art Tile Works provided competition to the many English imports. At the turn of the century, the popularity of high-relief tiles waned in favor of smoother surface-decorated Arts and Crafts tiles, and Low production ceased in 1902. One year later, the Worcester Art Museum in Massachusetts organized an exhibition to honor the firm's artistic achievements. Although it was no longer in production, the firm was not liquidated until after the death of John G. Low in 1907.[1]

The tile in the Crawford Collection (no. 118), modeled by Arthur Osborne, would have been called a plastic sketch when it was manufactured. The high-relief decoration and glaze are characteristic of Low tiles. The glaze is thinner in the higher sections, revealing the clay body, and pooled in the lower areas, enhancing visual depth. Originally, it may have been sold as an individual tile in a frame, or it may have been part of a larger composition of several tiles.[2] The image of the bird flying on a diagonal in the midst of cherry branches is characteristic of the popular Japanese taste of the period.

The mantel clock (no. 119) is also in the Japanese taste. The works in a related clock at the Museum of Fine Arts, Houston, are attributed to the New Haven Clock Company, which illustrated a similar clock in its 1888 catalogue. Low is known to have contracted with metalware manufacturers in the production of stoves, clock cases, picture frames, and umbrella stands. Clock cases may also have been marketed under the Low name, as a patent for a clock case was granted to them in 1886.[3]

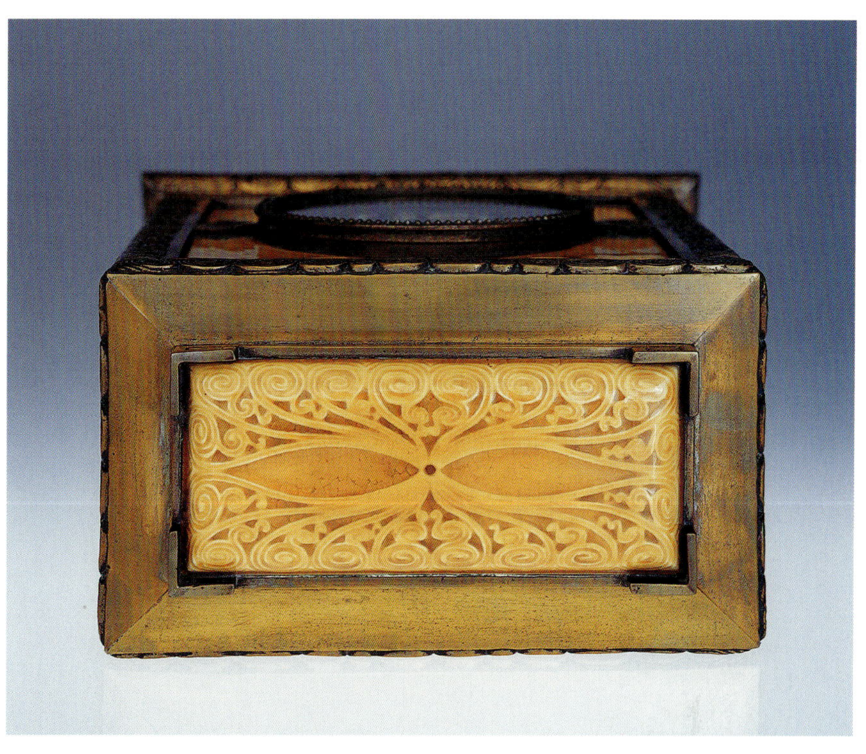

Top view of clock

NOTES

1. For accounts of the history of the Low Art Tile Works, see Evans 1987, pp. 151–153; and The Metropolitan Museum of Art 1986, pp. 449–450. For an illustration of a vase decorated by Low in the classical style, see The Metropolitan Museum of Art 1986, p. 202, fig. 7.1. Awards presented to Low Art Tile Works are outlined in Watkins 1944, p. 251. Low introduced a method of using a screw press with leaves and other natural objects in the molding of tiles; see ibid., pp. 250–251. Low was also a trained artist who studied painting in Paris in the late 1850s; see The Metropolitan Museum 1986, p. 449.

2. The Crawford tile may have been part of a series of tiles for a fireplace surround. See Watkins 1944, p. 252, fig. 7, for a related example.

3. The Metropolitan Museum of Art 1986, p. 289. The related clock at the Museum of Fine Arts, Houston, illustrated on p. 288, fig. 8.30, has a ceramic face. A cast-iron stove decorated with Low tiles is illustrated on p. 287, fig. 8.23.

120.

Desk and Chair,
ca. 1890

R. J. Horner and Company (1886–ca. 1915), New York
Maple, bird's-eye maple, and white pine
Desk: 45¼ × 26¼ × 19½ inches
Chair: 36¼ × 16 × 18¼ inches
Mark: Printed in black on celluloid label tacked to back of desk, *R. J. HORNER & CO.,/ FURNITURE MAKERS,/61-63-65 WEST 23d STREET, N. Y.*
1993.142.1–.2

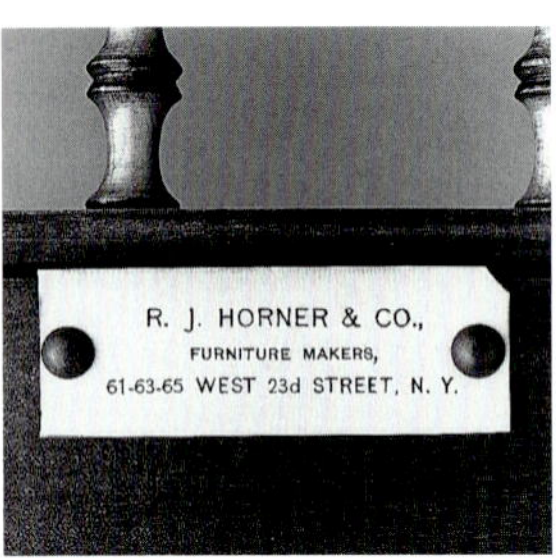

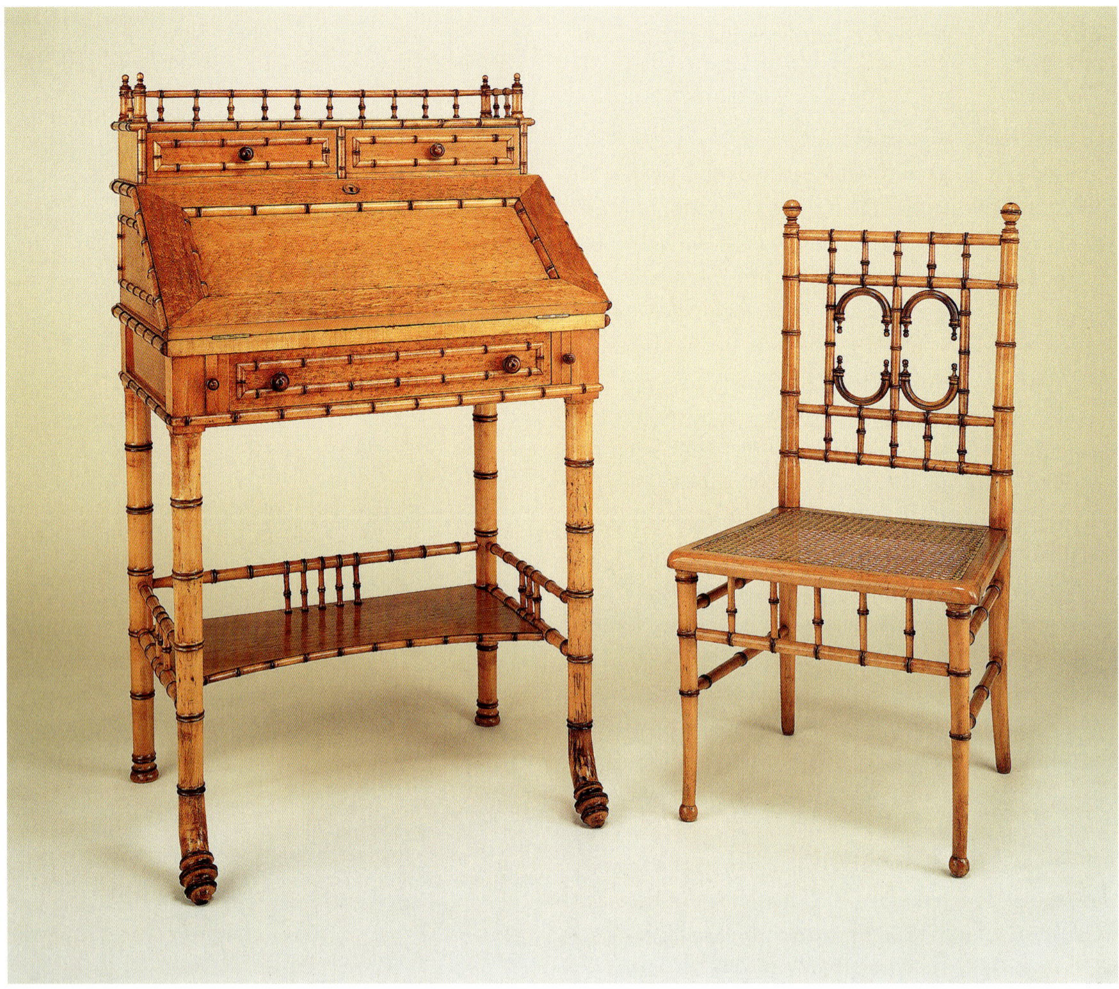

MAPLE THAT WAS stained to a yellowish tone, carved, and turned made this desk and chair resemble bamboo to appeal to the American market for Asian goods in the late nineteenth century. Maple had been used for American imitation bamboo furniture since the late 1860s. American interest in bamboo was stimulated by the natural bamboo furniture in the popular Japanese display at the 1876 Centennial Exposition in Philadelphia, and by its importation by American retailers in the late 1870s.[1]

Advertisements in *The New York Times* indicate that R. J. Horner and Company was retailing furniture at 61–65 East 23rd Street in 1886, with a manufacturing plant in the fifth-story loft of the building. Robert J. Horner entered the New York furniture business after selling curtains at 460 Broadway and working for lace dealer Mills and Gibb. During his years in textiles, Horner may have established important contacts in the furniture business, since New York furniture makers such as Herter Brothers (see nos. 107–110) were expanding into interior decoration at that time. The 1873 financial panic had long passed, and a broad and demanding American middle-class market had evolved. In the 1880s, while New York's established furniture businesses changed management as leaders retired or died, R. J. Horner and Company became one of the most prosperous firms, able to weather another financial panic in 1891. In 1897, a separate factory was listed at 126 West 25th Street. By 1909, the factory address was 147–149 West 25th Street, and the store moved to a more fashionable uptown address at 20 West 36th Street in 1912. By 1915, Horner had merged with George C. Flint and Company, a former neighbor on 23rd Street, to form Horner and Flint. In 1916, neither Flint nor Horner were officers in the company, although both founders had offices at the 36th Street store.[2]

As early as 1887, R. J. Horner and Company displayed its furniture in simulated domestic settings, complete with carpets and draperies. Such displays had been used since the 1870s, and Horner continued using them for at least another twenty years. Horner advertised all types of imported and American furniture. The pieces in the earliest Horner advertisements, which listed bamboo dining sets for gardens and country houses, may have been natural bamboo, but an 1890 advertisement for a "large assortment of BAMBOO MAPLE FURNITURE" could have been describing the Crawford desk and chair.[3] This imitation bamboo furniture was listed by Horner throughout the 1890s. From surviving examples —mostly bedroom furniture and small desks—it seems that imitation bamboo was used mostly in private chambers rather than in more public parlors and reception rooms.

The diminutive scale of the Crawford desk suggests that it was intended for use by a woman. This slant-topped desk and chair incorporate bamboo motifs into traditional Western forms. Drawer fronts with bird's-eye maple veneer are framed by maple bamboo, which is also used for all the support elements and for the gallery fret around the top. Delicately constructed interior pigeonholes are also maple, and are elegant even without additional ornament. The front legs, which flare into projecting feet, are characteristic of a number of American examples. The Crawford desk is one of only a few labeled examples of imitation bamboo furniture.

NOTES

1. An 1869 upholstered chair with imitation bamboo frame by Leon Marcotte is illustrated and discussed in N. Gray 1994, pp. 66–68, fig. 32. Hosley 1990, pp. 141–142, discusses American Japanese-taste furniture, including imitation bamboo. An illustration of an imitation bamboo side chair from New York's Killian Brothers 1876 catalogue is found in Davidson 1969, p. 172, no. 223. Clarence Cook, an influential American arbiter of taste, encouraged the use of Japanese bamboo seating furniture from the New York emporium of importer A. A. Vantine for filling gaps in furnishing summer houses; see Cook 1878, pp. 74–75.

2. R. J. Horner and Company began advertising in *The New York Times* at the end of 1886, before its first city directory listing in 1888. Robert J. Horner's career is recounted in his obituary in *The New York Times* (February 27, 1922), p. 13. R. J. Horner and Company's financial capital was more than $100,000; see Lyon 1889, pp. 19–20.

3. A notice in the *Philadelphia Carpet Trade* (May 1, 1887), p. 382, describes the Horner store's range of available products and its room arrangements: "Everything from the colonial-primitive to the renaissance can be found here, and whole suites of rooms are partitioned off in one of the lofts and arranged complete with carpets, wall-paper, draperies and furniture in a manner to show off the proprieties of bedroom, parlor, dining hall and billiard room furnishings." A Horner advertisement for maple imitation bamboo furniture appears in *The New York Times* (March 19, 1890), p. 16. Examples in museum collections include a dressing bureau in the Munson-Williams-Proctor Institute in Utica, New York; a desk in the Wadsworth Athenaeum in Hartford, Connecticut, illustrated in Hosley 1990, p. 143; and a dressing bureau in The Metropolitan Museum of Art, illustrated in Davidson and Stillinger 1985, p. 192, fig. 300. None of these objects are marked.

121.

Vase, ca. 1880

Probably Rookwood Pottery (1880–1967), Cincinnati; decorated by Maria Longworth Nichols (1849–1912)
Stoneware with painted decoration in colored slip
17¼ × 8½ × 8½ inches
Mark: Signed on outer rim with Japanese characters in vertical sequence and initials *MLN*
1984.127

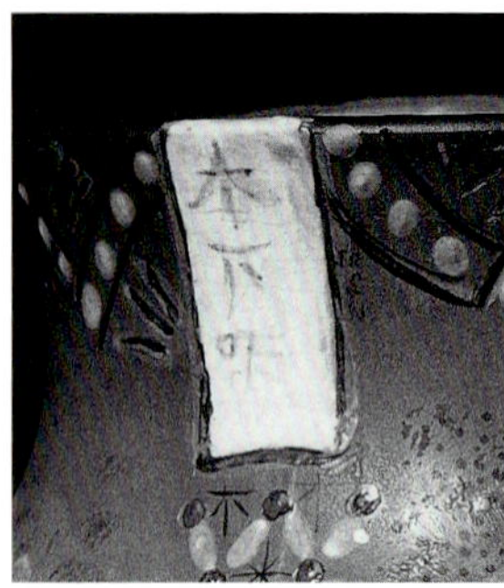

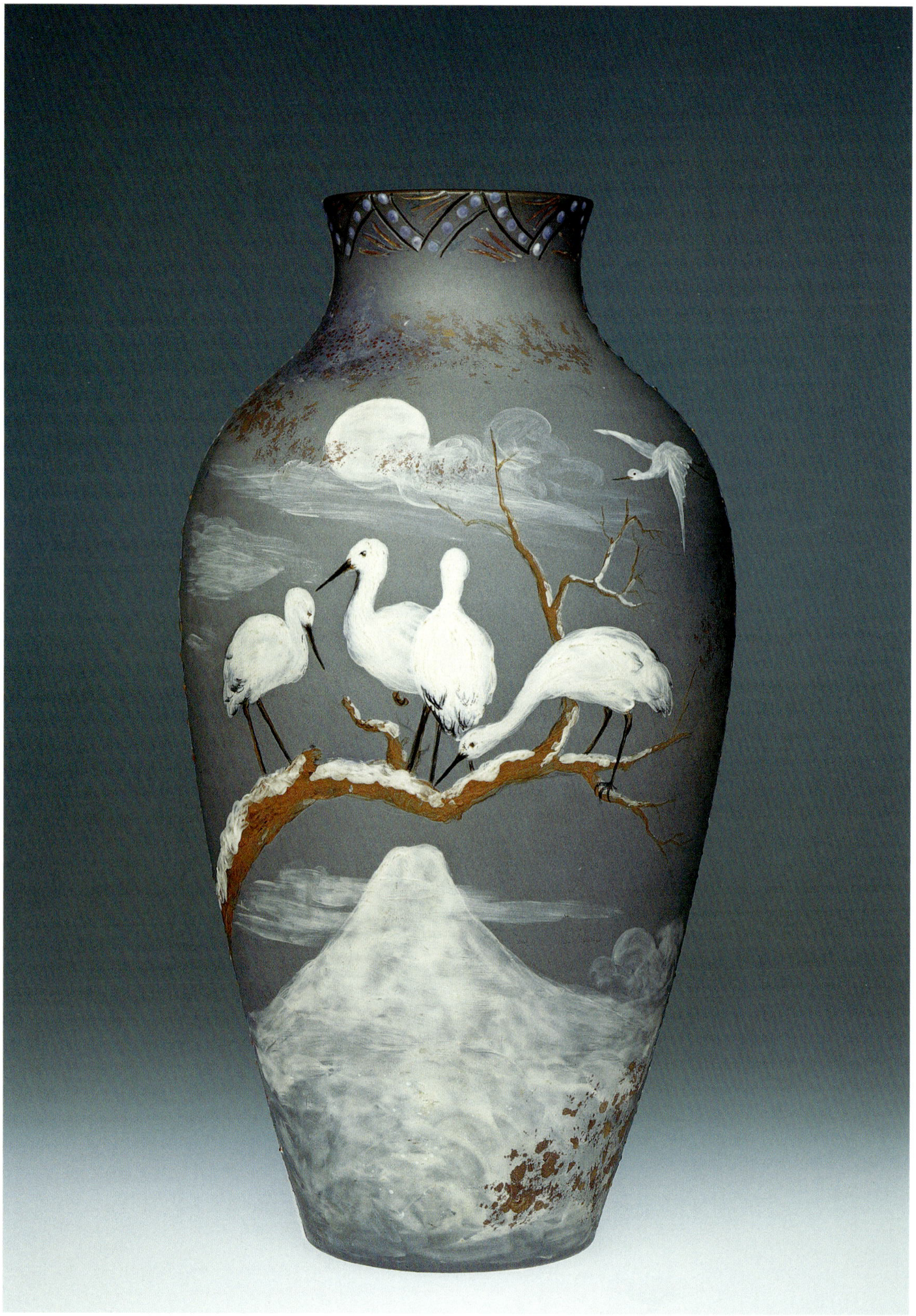

MARIA LONGWORTH NICHOLS decorated this vase in the earliest years of the Rookwood Pottery (see no. 181). She founded Rookwood in Cincinnati with the financial backing of her father, Joseph Longworth. Her family had been prominent in social, cultural, and political affairs in Cincinnati for three generations, and both her father and her grandfather had been art collectors. In 1868, Maria Longworth married George Ward Nichols, who had been an art dealer in New York in the 1850s and had come to Cincinnati to catalogue the Longworth art collections. He later helped to found the Cincinnati Art Museum.[1]

George Nichols shared his wife's interest in the decorative arts and encouraged her pursuits. In 1873, Maria Nichols began painting china on her own, and a year later she enrolled in the first china-painting class at the University of Cincinnati School of Design, where her classmates included other notables in Cincinnati decorative arts, such as Mary Louise McLaughlin (see no. 172), Laura Fry, and Agnes Pittman.[2] In 1875, the Nicholses began collecting Japanese prints, which had a profound influence on Maria Nichols's work. Their collecting increased when they saw the Japanese displays at the 1876 Centennial Exposition in Philadelphia. The couple's interest in ceramics resulted in their publication in 1878 of *Pottery: How It Is Made, Its Shape and Decoration,* which George wrote and Maria illustrated. They extolled the decorations on Japanese and ancient Greek ceramics as the ideals, and the illustrations—suggestions for pottery decoration—were inspired by *Manga,* a multivolume series of Japanese folktales illustrated by Kotushika Hokusai.

Former classmates Maria Longworth Nichols and Mary Louise McLaughlin became rivals in Cincinnati pottery decoration. In 1879, a group of women—former students at the University of Cincinnati School of Design—established the Cincinnati Pottery Club to promote china painting under McLaughlin's leadership. Nichols's invitation to join in organizing the club was purportedly lost, and she took offense, declining subsequent invitations to join. Both Nichols and McLaughlin maintained china-painting studios at Cincinnati's Dallas Pottery, where they each paid to have separate kilns built to fire their work.

Nichols had suggested to her father that he underwrite the cost of moving an operating Japanese pottery—lock, stock, and staff—to the shores of the Ohio River. Although Joseph Longworth did not agree to that venture, he did back her establishment of the Rookwood Pottery. Nichols sought the technical expertise of Joseph Bailey, Sr., superintendent of the Dallas Pottery, in setting up Rookwood. His son, Joseph Bailey, Jr., became superintendent of the new concern, and other members of the Dallas Pottery staff also went to Rookwood. This outraged the management of the older pottery, which closed in 1882. The Cincinnati Pottery Club rented space in the new Rookwood Pottery, but the ladies were evicted, with Nichols's approval, by her new manager, William Watts Taylor. George Nichols died in 1885, and a year later Maria Nichols married Bellamy Storer, Jr., a prominent Cincinnati lawyer. Her interest in the pottery waned as she traveled with her husband and participated in his wide range of political activities. Ultimately, she made a gift of the pottery to Taylor, granting him full management control.

The Crawford vase is a simple Oriental shape, typical of Rookwood's early years. The border decoration may have been inspired by the designs of Emile Gallé, who was also influenced by the Japanese aesthetic in his glass and ceramic studio in France. Gallé may have been the source of the side decorations, which were probably applied to conceal the mold seams. The Japanese symbols near Nichols's initials were used on the earliest Rookwood Pottery. The blue-gray color of the clay was a Nichols creation, and the glazed interior with the matte exterior was characteristic of her early work.[3]

NOTES

1. Maria Longworth Nichols's life and her family are chronicled in Boehle 1990. For a historical survey of the women's art movement in Cincinnati and the founding of the Cincinnati Art Museum, see Carol Macht's introduction in Cincinnati Art Museum 1976, pp. 7–13. The founding and early history of the Rookwood Pottery are discussed in The Metropolitan Museum of Art 1986, pp. 464–465; and in Boehle 1990, pp. 68–79.

2. Nichols's artistic education and background are recounted in The Metropolitan Museum of Art 1986, pp. 464–465.

3. Conversations and correspondence, Anita Ellis, curator of decorative arts, Cincinnati Art Museum, April 26 and 29, 1989, High Museum of Art document files.

122.

Covered Vase, 1884–1890

Faience Manufacturing Company (1880–1892), Greenpoint, Brooklyn; decorated under the supervision of Edward Lycett (1833–1910)
Earthenware with gilt and painted decoration
15¾ × 10¾ × 7½ inches
Marks: On bottom, intertwined initials printed in green, *FMCo*; impressed on bottom, *1121*
1982.286

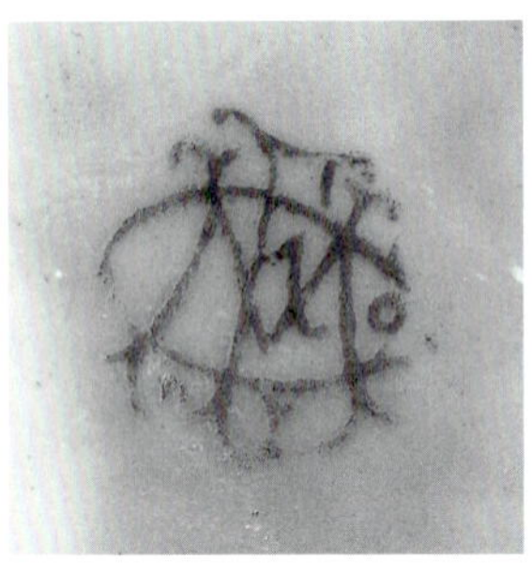

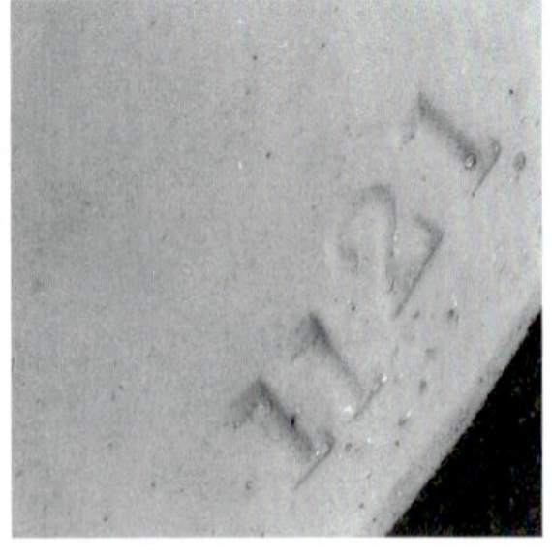

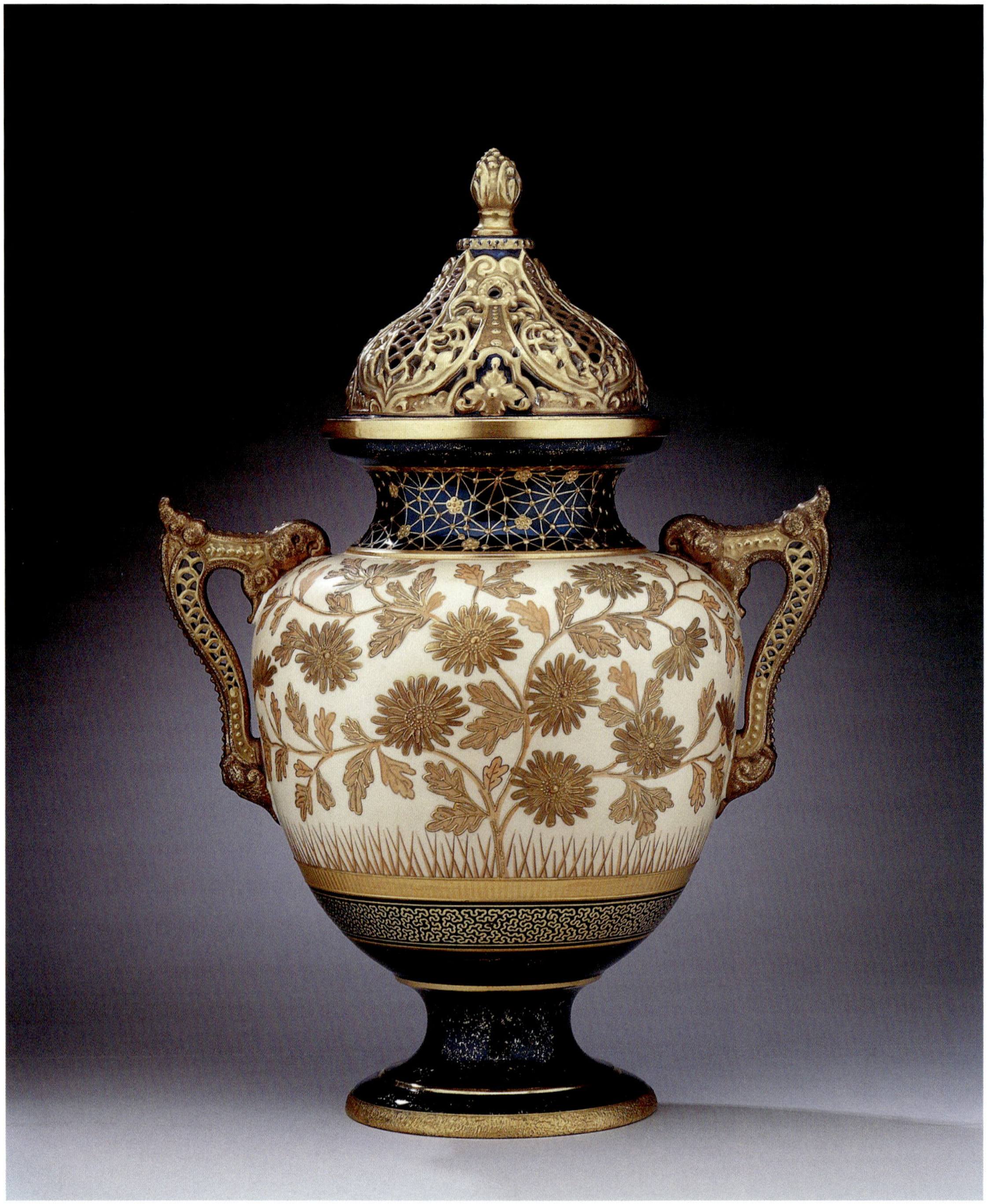

The Faience Manufacturing Company was established in 1880 in the ceramic manufacturing center of Greenpoint, Brooklyn (see nos. 42–43, 76–80). The firm enjoyed its greatest success during the artistic directorship of Edward Lycett, from 1884 to 1890, when this covered vase was decorated. Born in Newcastle-under-Lyme, England, Lycett pursued a china-painting career in nearby Staffordshire potteries and later in London ceramic-decorating studios. In 1861, Lycett and his family immigrated to New York, where he opened a decorating shop on Greene Street in Manhattan. There he established a family dynasty of china painters that lasted four generations and extended to Atlanta, Georgia.[1] At first, Lycett specialized in copying French designs on imported European porcelain blanks and decorating vases of his own design made by the Williamsburgh Terra Cotta Works on Long Island. At the same time, his shop provided painted porcelain panels to furniture makers for decorating cabinets, a practice revived from eighteenth-century France (see no. 63).[2]

After the Civil War, Lycett's shop evolved into a decorating school that instructed ladies in china painting. The shop also fired amateur work, including that of Maria Longworth Nichols, who later established the noted Rookwood Pottery in Cincinnati (see nos. 121, 181). In 1877, Lycett's eldest son, William, assumed management of the New York business when his father traveled to teach china painting at the St. Louis School of Design. Lycett also taught briefly in Cincinnati, where his work was included in an exhibition organized by the Women's Art Museum Association in 1878. He then moved on to the ceramic production center of East Liverpool, Ohio (see nos. 127–128), where he briefly undertook a china-decorating business. By the end of 1879, Lycett had returned to New York, where he formed a brief partnership with another English-trained china decorator, John Bennett (see no. 92).

Lycett worked on his own from 1882 to 1884, when he was appointed artistic director of the Faience Manufacturing Company. There he supervised twenty-five decorators, and he continued to teach. Under Lycett, the Faience Manufacturing Company specialized in large vases decorated with stylized and naturalistic fruits and flowers, often arranged in Japanese-influenced, asymmetrical compositions. Exotic forms with lavish gold decoration provided rich ornaments for the eclectic interiors of the period. The Crawford covered vase, with its perforated gold onion-domed lid and exotic perforated handles, was loosely derived from Near Eastern forms. The stylized gold chrysanthemums on an ivory ground were associated with the Japanese taste then popular in America. The rich blue on the base and neck of the vase came to be identified with Lycett's work and was based on the color of eighteenth-century French Sèvres porcelains.

In 1890, the focus of the Faience Manufacturing Company shifted from manufacturing to importing European ceramics, and Lycett moved to Atlanta. There he joined his son William at the china-painting studio and school that William had begun in 1883. In 1895, Lycett's other sons were also decorating ceramics: Frank in Buffalo, New York, and Joseph in Nashville, Tennessee. In the 1890s and later, Lycett donated a number of his ceramics, including some from the Faience Manufacturing Company period, to the Smithsonian Institution. He continued to decorate china for his own amusement, for his family's use, and for sale in William Lycett's Atlanta studio, where the elder Lycett also taught.

William Lycett attended art school at Cooper Union in New York, where he later taught oil painting and china decorating. He worked with his father from 1877 until he moved to Atlanta. William Lycett died in 1909, and Edward Lycett died a year later. William's son, Edward Cordon Lycett, trained under his father and grandfather and attended the Georgia Institute of Technology in Atlanta. He painted china, watercolor landscapes, and architectural views until his death in 1938. His daughter Lydia and her husband, William A. White, a student of his, operated a small studio and showroom in Atlanta. After White's death in 1956, Lydia Lycett White continued the business until her death, when it was dissolved.

NOTES

1. The history of the Faience Manufacturing Company and Lycett's career are recounted in Barber, "Pioneer of China Painting," 1895, pp. 33–48; Lycett 1941, pp. 201–214, which seems largely based on the Barber article; and The Metropolitan Museum of Art 1986, pp. 426–427. A history of the family, along with illustrations of three generations of their work, is provided in Romeyn 1983.

2. Barber, "Pioneer of China Painting," 1895, pp. 37–38.

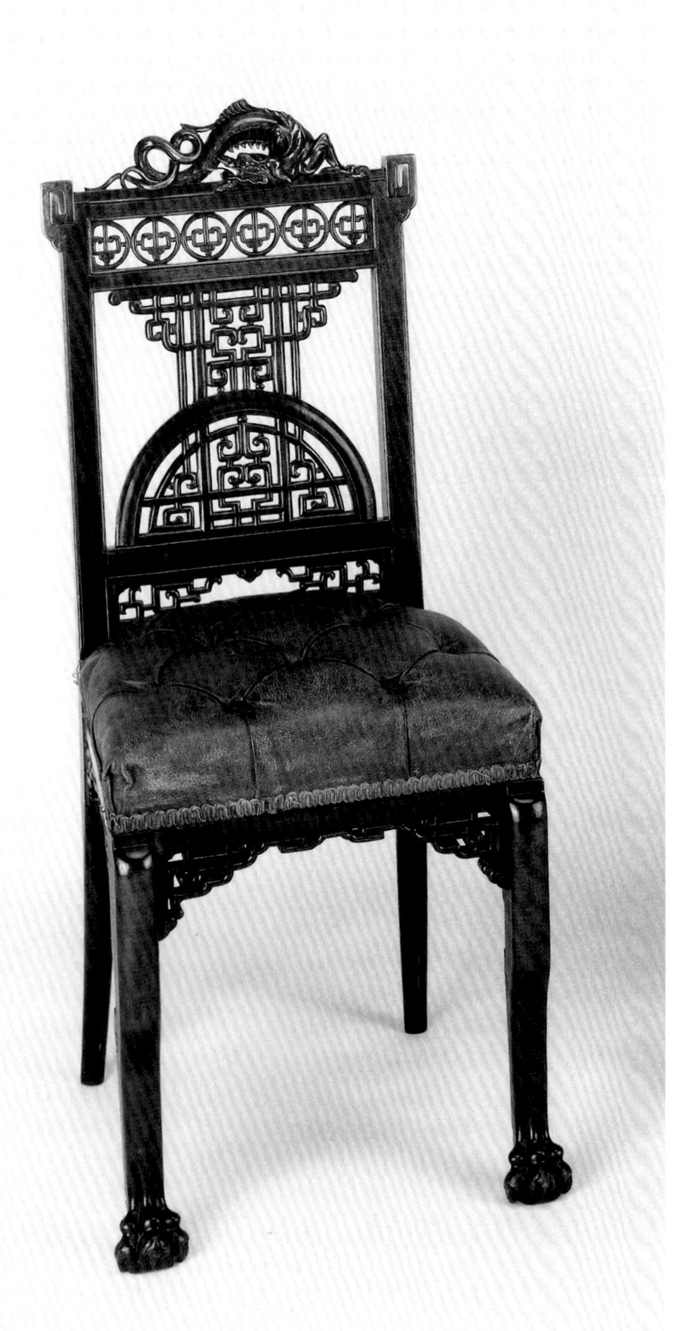

123.

Side Chair, ca. 1890

Gabriel Viardot (working ca. 1860–after 1900), Paris
Sugar maple
36½ × 15 × 18½ inches
Mark: On inside of right front leg in script, *G. Viardot*
1982.318.1

Viardot Furniture

Gabriel Viardot established a furniture business in Paris in 1860, a year before assuming proprietorship of the family firm, Viardot Frères, from his father, Charles. Beginning in 1853, Viardot Frères had a shop in Paris that sold ornamental boxes, writing papers, accessories, jardinieres, wedding presents, and *objets d'art et de fantaisie,* goods similar to those offered by Tiffany and Company (see no. 41). In addition, the firm showed Renaissance-style furniture at the 1855 Exposition Universelle in Paris. Under Gabriel Viardot, the firm exhibited at the Exposition Universelle in Paris in 1867, 1878, and 1889. Today the company is largely remembered for its late-nineteenth-century Asian-style furniture, for which it was highly praised at the 1889 Exposition Universelle. Viardot received a gold medal for his interpretations of *meubles japonais* (Japanese furniture), and the curving of the table top (no. 124)—up at one end and down at the other—derives from Japanese prototypes. However, details such as the legs and fretwork decorations were originally inspired by the furniture then being imported into Paris from Canton, China, and Hanoi, French Indonesia (now Vietnam).[1] The asymmetrical incised decoration, which includes a fan on the tabletop, is reminiscent of engraved decoration on American silver plate in the 1880s (see no. 106). This Crawford table and chair were reportedly acquired from an estate sale in Newport, Rhode Island.[2]

NOTES

1. Victoria and Albert Museum 1987, pp. 134–135, illustrates and discusses a Viardot cabinet in its collection. The legs on the cabinet have an applied gilt-bronze mask mount, but otherwise they are identical to those on the Crawford table. The fretwork skirts on the table and chair are similar in scale and detail to that on the cabinet.

2. High Museum of Art document files.

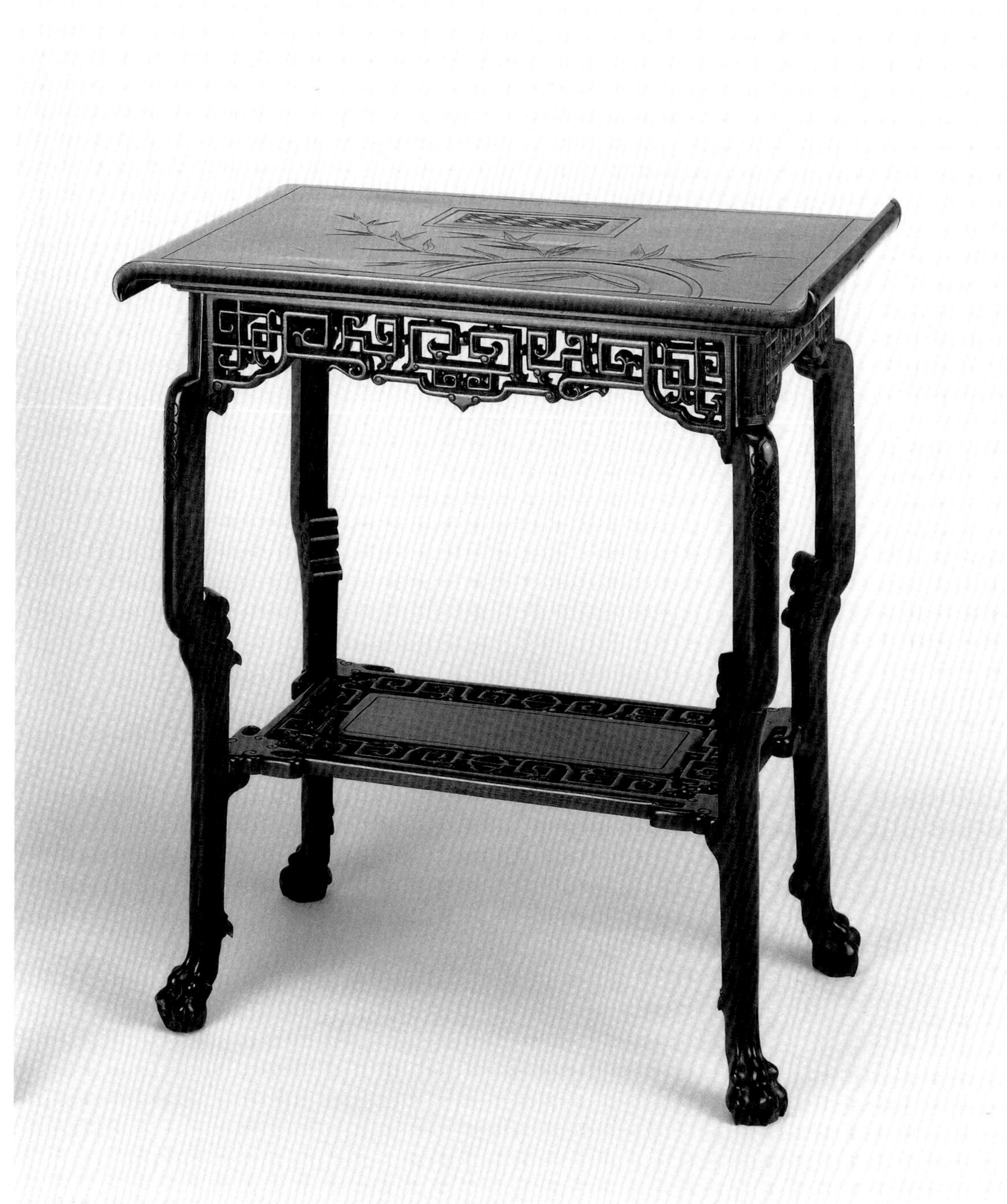

124.

Table, ca. 1890

Gabriel Viardot (working
ca. 1860–after 1900), Paris
Sugar maple
29⅜ × 26¼ × 16¼ inches
Mark: On inside of leg in script,
G. Viardot
1982.318.2

Wicker Furniture

Wicker, which was known in ancient Egypt, classical Greece, and Rome, is not a specific material, but the processes of weaving or tying used in making furniture, baskets, and other objects. Wicker goods have been made from Asian rattan vine, its core (reed), and its outer layer (cane), as well as other natural fibers—including willow, straw, prairie grass, sea grass, and sticks.[1]

The Wakefield Rattan Company has been credited with transforming the wicker craft tradition into a major American industry in the last half of the nineteenth century. Around 1840, company founder Cyrus Wakefield, a Boston grocer, began recycling Asian rattan, which was used for ballast and packing on China trade ships. He stripped the cane from the rattan and sold it to Boston chair makers for weaving into fashionable, resilient chair seats. Wakefield was so successful that he gave up his grocery trade for the rattan business. By the late 1840s, he imported rattan directly from the Far East, and in 1856 he opened a factory making rattan circles for hoop skirts. Baskets were also woven by Irish immigrants at Wakefield's plant in South Reading, Massachusetts, just outside Boston. When iron replaced rattan for use in hoop skirts in the late 1850s, Wakefield expanded his chair-cane manufactory, and throughout the Civil War, his factory produced rattan floor matting, carpets, and railroad seat covers. By the time he died in 1873, the town of South Reading had been renamed Wakefield in his honor, and the newly incorporated Wakefield Rattan Company displayed new lines of wicker rattan furniture, along with chair cane, mats, baskets, baby carriages, cradles, and other household goods in its Boston showroom.

Under the leadership of Cyrus Wakefield II, nephew of the founder, the company increased its line of rattan furniture, opening showrooms in New York in 1875 and San Francisco in 1877, and presenting a display at the 1876 Centennial Exposition in Philadelphia.[2] In 1879, the company began to make furniture from reed, and their strongest competitor, Heywood Brothers and Company in nearby Gardner, Massachusetts, followed suit in 1881. Use of reed quickly spread to smaller wicker furniture makers.

Reed and cane were applied to oak to create the fanciful and highly decorative Crawford wicker table (no. 125). Cane was wrapped around the skirt of the table top and then decorated with swags of applied reed and contrasting stained wooden beads. A bent reed ruffle finishes the skirt. The central pedestal is also wrapped in cane and mounted with vertical reeds bent to suggest a turned wood baluster, a popular motif on wicker furniture in the 1890s. Four decorative scrolls of shaped reed wrapped in cane surround the central pedestal. The four-footed base was also wrapped in cane and ornamented with reed scrolls. The profusion of scrolls, swags, and flowers suggests the decorative possibilities of pliable reed in making wicker furniture. As the prevailing material used for wicker furniture in the 1880s and 1890s, reed became a term used for titles of company catalogues and lines of furniture, as seen on the paper label on this table. The label also indicates that the table was sold in Wakefield's New York store.

The economic panic of 1893 caused a disastrous drop in profits for virtually all American wicker furniture makers. Smaller firms farmed out production to state penitentiaries for cheap labor and provided formidable competition to the large Wakefield and Heywood factories. Their 1897 merger to form Heywood Brothers and Wakefield Company ensured survival of these firms, which reorganized in 1921 under the name Heywood-Wakefield Company.[3]

The Crawford platform rocker (no. 126) was probably made in the first decade after the merger. Like the table, it survives in excellent condition and was undoubtedly used inside rather than on a porch. The factories in both Gardner and Wakefield operated after the merger, but the label on the rocker indicates that it was made at the Wakefield plant. Bent-reed scrollwork is contained in the frame of the chair, with none of the elaborate cresting often seen on earlier wicker. The shaped reed harp in the chairback decorates many American wicker chairs of the era. Coil springs added to the comfort of the chair.

Because of its Asian sources, wicker was part

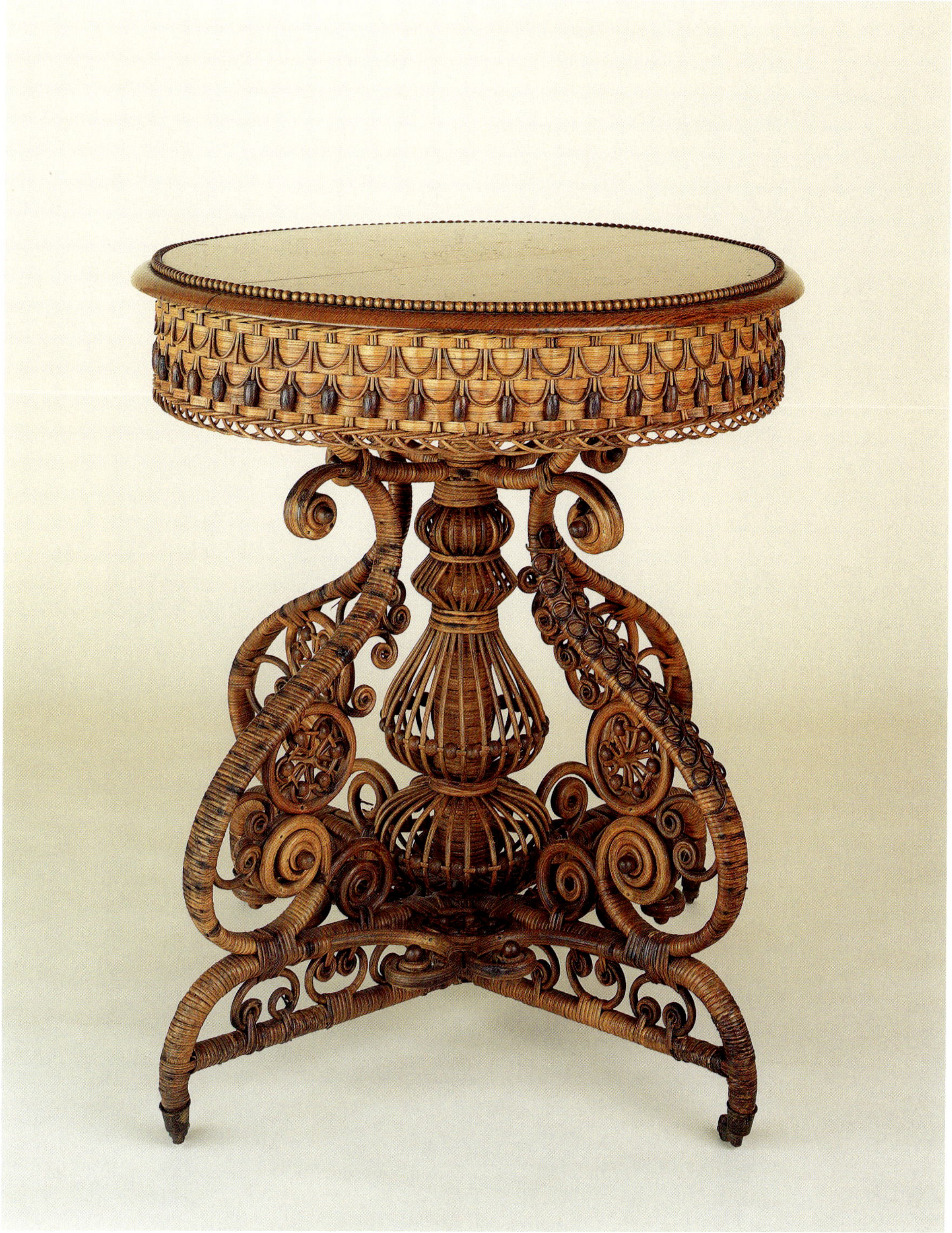

125.

Table, ca. 1895

Wakefield Rattan Company (1873–1897), Wakefield, Massachusetts; retailed by Wakefield Reed Chair Company, New York
Reed, cane, and oak
29¼ × 25 × 25 inches
Mark: Printed in block letters on paper label with printed red border attached to underside of top frame support, *NO. 3557/ MANUFACTURED BY THE/ WAKEFIELD REED CHAIR CO./ NEW YORK.*
1982.313

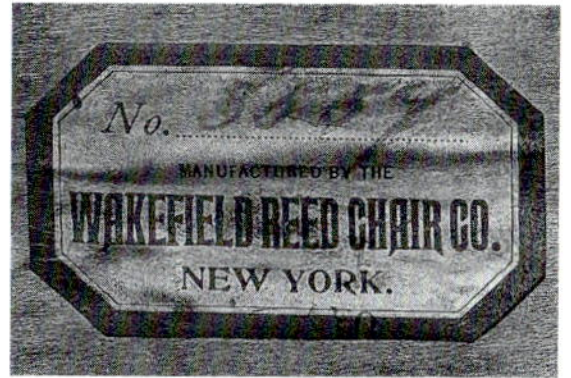

126.

Platform Rocker, 1897–1910

Heywood Brothers and Wakefield Company (1897–1921), Wakefield, Massachusetts
Reed, cane, steel, and oak
42 × 25 × 31½ inches
Marks: Under seat, in red and white on paper label, *HEYWOOD BROTHERS and WAKEFIELD COMPANY/WAKEFIELD, MASS., U.S.A.*; written in wax pencil in white rectangle above, *6068*
1984.171

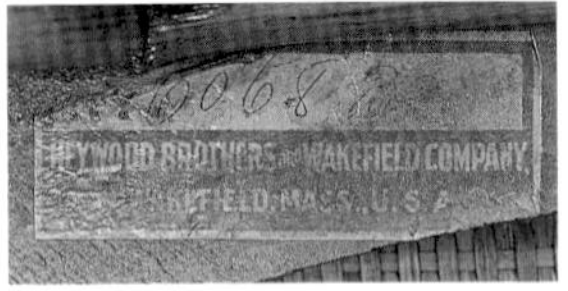

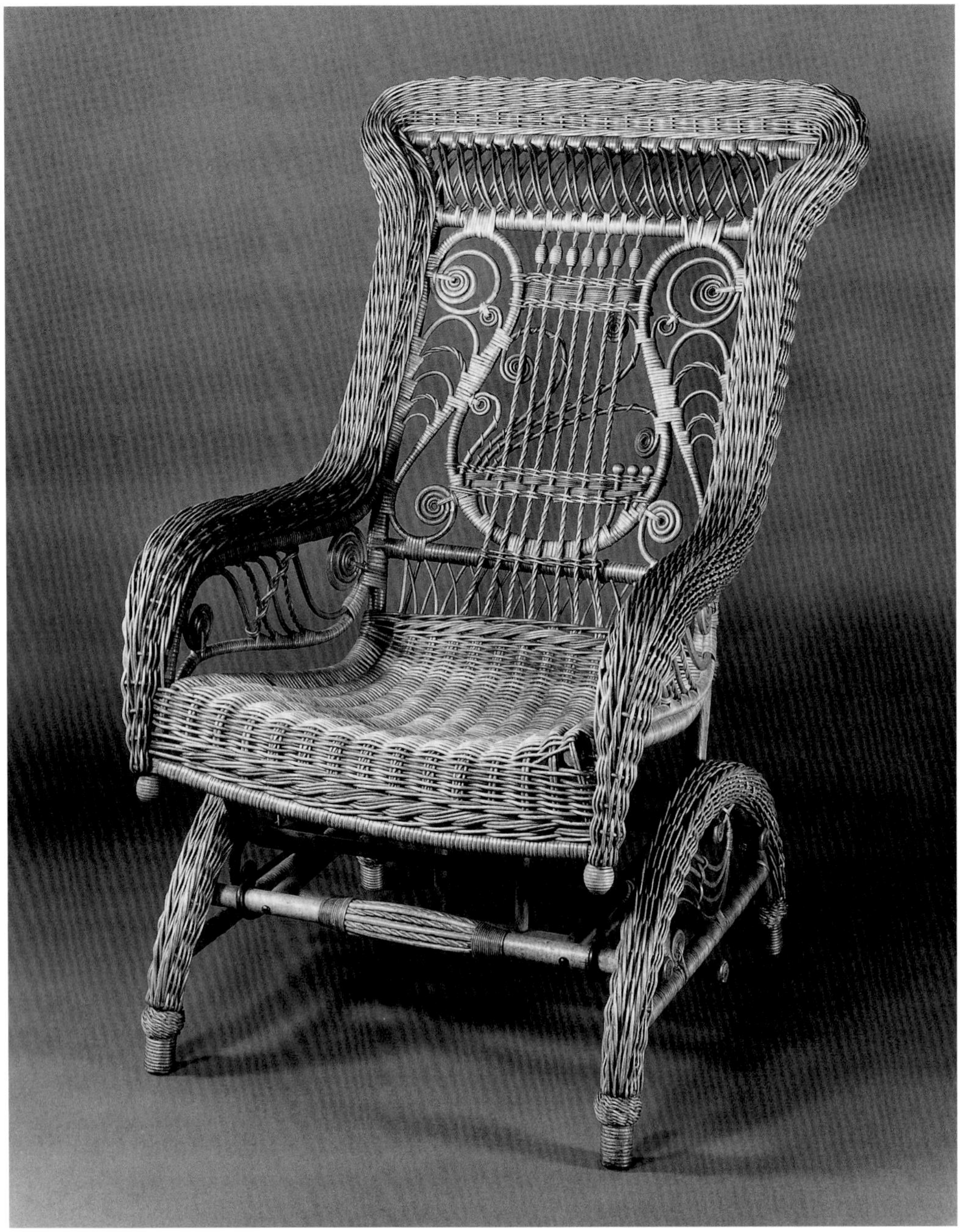

of the Japanese taste in America, and its handmade quality was appealing to those who sought artistic home furnishings. It was also relatively inexpensive, and so it became popular in American interior design. As suites of parlor furniture went out of fashion after the 1870s, one or two wicker accent pieces were often incorporated into American interiors around the turn of the century.

NOTES

1. Katherine Menz, "Wicker," in Art and Antiques 1982, pp. 132–136; and Adamson 1993, pp. 10–21, 25–32, focus on American wicker, but also present broad illustrated histories of wicker in the ancient world, Europe, and America.

2. Adamson 1992, pp. 214–221, provides a complete history of the Wakefield Rattan Company until its merger with Heywood Brothers and Company in 1897, as well as biographical data on Cyrus Wakefield and his successor.

3. The history of Heywood Brothers and Company is recounted in Adamson 1993, pp. 45–48, and the merger of the two firms is described on pp. 61–68.

Knowles, Taylor and Knowles

IN THE LATE nineteenth century, Knowles, Taylor and Knowles was the largest ceramic concern in the pottery center of East Liverpool, Ohio. As early as the 1840s, East Liverpool—with its deposits of clay and coal, and its easy access to the distribution network of the Ohio River valley—attracted potters to settle and work. In 1854, Isaac Watts Knowles established a pottery there, which became a leader in the yellow earthenware trade during the 1860s. In 1870, he expanded with two partners, John N. Taylor and Homer S. Knowles. In 1872, Knowles, Taylor and Knowles added white graniteware, known as hotel china, to its lines of yellow and Rockingham earthenwares. The company produced vast numbers of useful tablewares like those of Ott and Brewer (see nos. 115–117) and other Trenton, New Jersey, potteries.

Perhaps to compete with Ott and Brewer's ornamental Belleek-type porcelain, Knowles, Taylor and Knowles constructed a new porcelain factory in 1888. William Bloor, a founding partner of Ott and Brewer, had manufactured parian ware in East Liverpool in the early 1860s, but no porcelain had been produced there since that time. Knowles, Taylor and Knowles, like Ott and Brewer, had the materials and facilities but required the expertise of skilled immigrants to

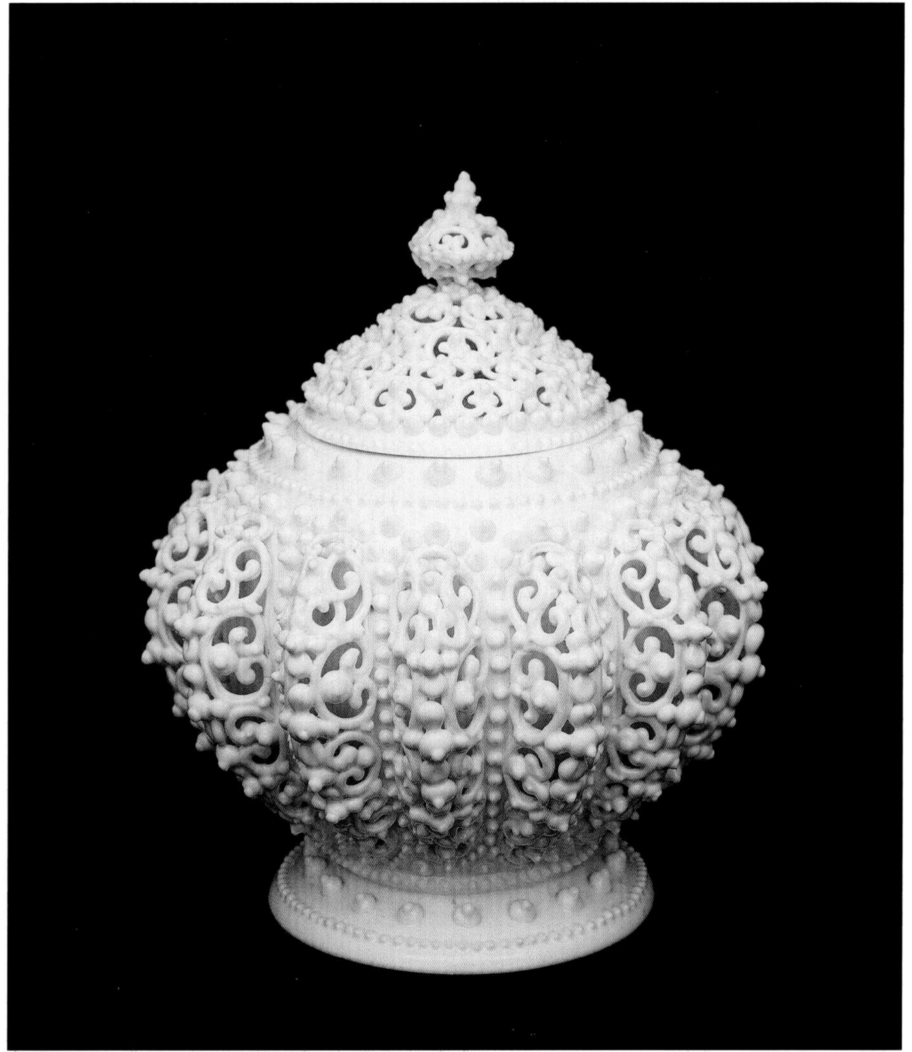

127.

Rose Jar, 1893–1897

Knowles, Taylor and Knowles (1870–1929), East Liverpool, Ohio
Porcelain, Lotus Ware line
7½ × 6¼ × 6¼ inches
Mark: On bottom, stamped in green, K.T.K. CO./crescent moon and star, within a circle surmounted by a crown/LOTUS WARE
1992.383

128.

Vase, 1893–1897

Knowles, Taylor and Knowles (1870–1929), East Liverpool, Ohio
Porcelain, Lotus Ware line
8¼ × 6½ × 5 inches
Mark: On bottom, stamped in purple, *K.T.K. CO.*/crescent moon and star, within a circle surmounted by a crown/*LOTUS WARE*
1984.147

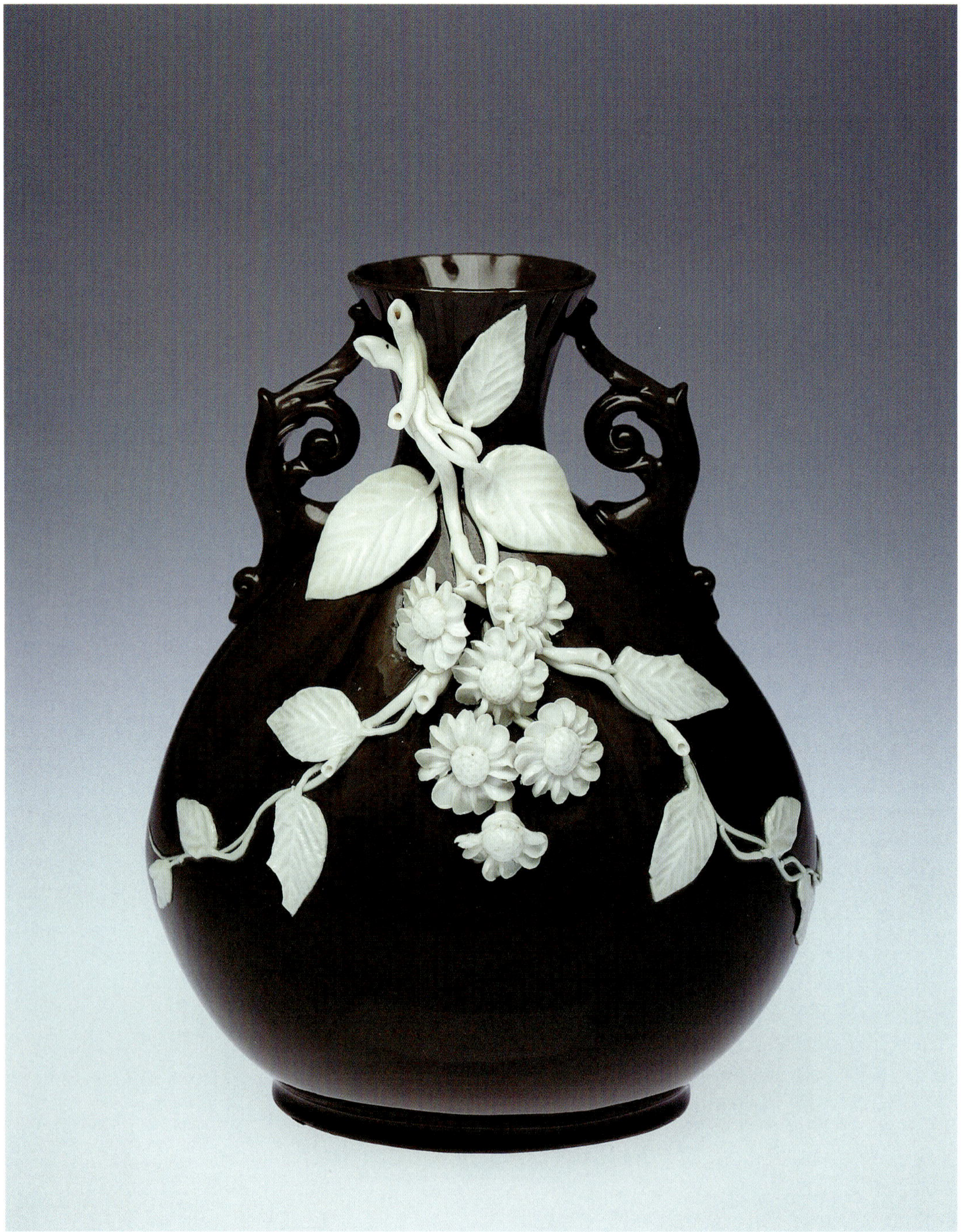

successfully produce Belleek-type porcelain. Joshua Poole, former manager of the Irish Belleek factory, supervised the first Ohio production of Belleek-type porcelain in 1889. Unfortunately, production was cut short when the factory burned the same year, and although it was immediately rebuilt, Knowles, Taylor and Knowles did not resume production of Belleek-type wares. Instead they developed a new line of art porcelains very different from Ott and Brewer's Beleek: Lotus Ware, a bone china, or artificial porcelain.[1]

These examples of Lotus Ware in the Crawford Collection illustrate the variety in the line. Elaborate applied relief decoration characterized the company's art porcelains. The white porcelain rose jar (no. 127) with lacy, jewel-like beading was perhaps inspired by Near Eastern metalwork. Henry Schmidt, a German potter who had worked at Meissen, has been credited with this type of work at Knowles, Taylor and Knowles. The ornament is white porcelain, which was applied while in a gelatin state through a tube, much like decorative cake icing. Edwin AtLee Barber, the pioneer historian of American ceramics, stated that "some of the most artistic ware ever produced in America" came from Knowles, Taylor and Knowles. The firm exhibited Lotus Ware at the 1893 World's Columbian Exposition in Chicago, and Barber illustrated a similar covered jar in his book *The Pottery and Porcelain of the United States.*[2]

The Lotus Ware line included celadon and olive green clay bodies. The olive green clay is represented by a dark green vase (no. 128) in the Crawford Collection. The shape of the vase, probably of Near Eastern inspiration, was called the Umbrian, number 288 in the firm's catalogue.[3] The white of the delicately hand-modeled flowers is in stark contrast to the dark green body. The asymmetrical and diagonal arrangement of the flowers reflects the Japanese taste that continued in the 1890s. The combination of the Near Eastern shape, the Japanese-style ornament, and the unrelated Italian name "Umbrian" illustrates the eclecticism of American design at the end of the nineteenth century. Lotus Ware proved to be an expensive line to produce, and Knowles, Taylor and Knowles retired it in 1897, after just four years of production.

NOTES

1. For the history of Knowles, Taylor and Knowles, see Barber, *Pottery,* 1976, pp. 201–207; and Frelinghuysen 1989, pp. 50–52. Although the porcelain factory was rebuilt immediately after the fire, the Lotus Ware line apparently was not introduced until 1893; see Barber, *Marks,* 1976, p. 108.

2. A letter from Diana Stradling, February 19, 1991, High Museum of Art document files, states that the bowl was number 239 in the Knowles, Taylor and Knowles pattern book. A pitcher with an identically shaped base and decoration in The Metropolitan Museum of Art is illustrated and discussed in Frelinghuysen 1989, pp. 214–215, no. 78. Frelinghuysen explains the decorative process and discusses Henry Schmidt, p. 215. See also Barber, *Pottery,* 1976, p. 206, fig. 88.

3. A vase of the same shape, but all white, is illustrated as number 288 in a Knowles, Taylor and Knowles catalogue shown in Frelinghuysen 1989, p. 219.

New England Glass Works

129.

Decanter, ca. 1882

Attributed to New England Glass Works (1818–1888), East Cambridge, Massachusetts; engraving attributed to Louis Friedrich Vaupel (1824–1899)
Lead glass with wheel-engraved and cut decoration
12½ × 5 × 5 inches
Inscription: Engraved on front for Emelie Vaupel Schuebler, *ES*
1982.290.a–.b

In 1888, after seventy years of leadership in the American glass industry, the New England Glass Company closed its factory as a result of a decade of declining profits. Although the company presented an impressive display at the 1876 Centennial Exposition in Philadelphia, business had suffered substantially from the 1873 financial panic; formidable competition from growing production in Wheeling, West Virginia, and Pittsburgh; and local labor disputes. The company's second-generation factory superintendent, William Leighton, Sr., had gone to Hobbs, Brockunier and Company in Wheeling and in 1864 had perfected a new lime glass that had the same appealing sparkle as lead glass but could be made much less expensively. Although lime glass was quickly adopted by Western manufacturers in the late 1860s and early 1870s, the New England Glass Company continued to make the more expensive lead glass. William Libbey, a veteran manager from the Mount Washington Glass Company, joined the New England Glass Company in 1872, and when it closed in 1877, Libbey leased the facility and continued the operation as the New England Glass Works. Success in the last decade of the factory's operation was due to his tenacity and to that of his son, Edward Drummond Libbey, who succeeded him as proprietor in 1883. During that period, the firm continued to make cut, engraved, blown, and molded clear lead glass.[1]

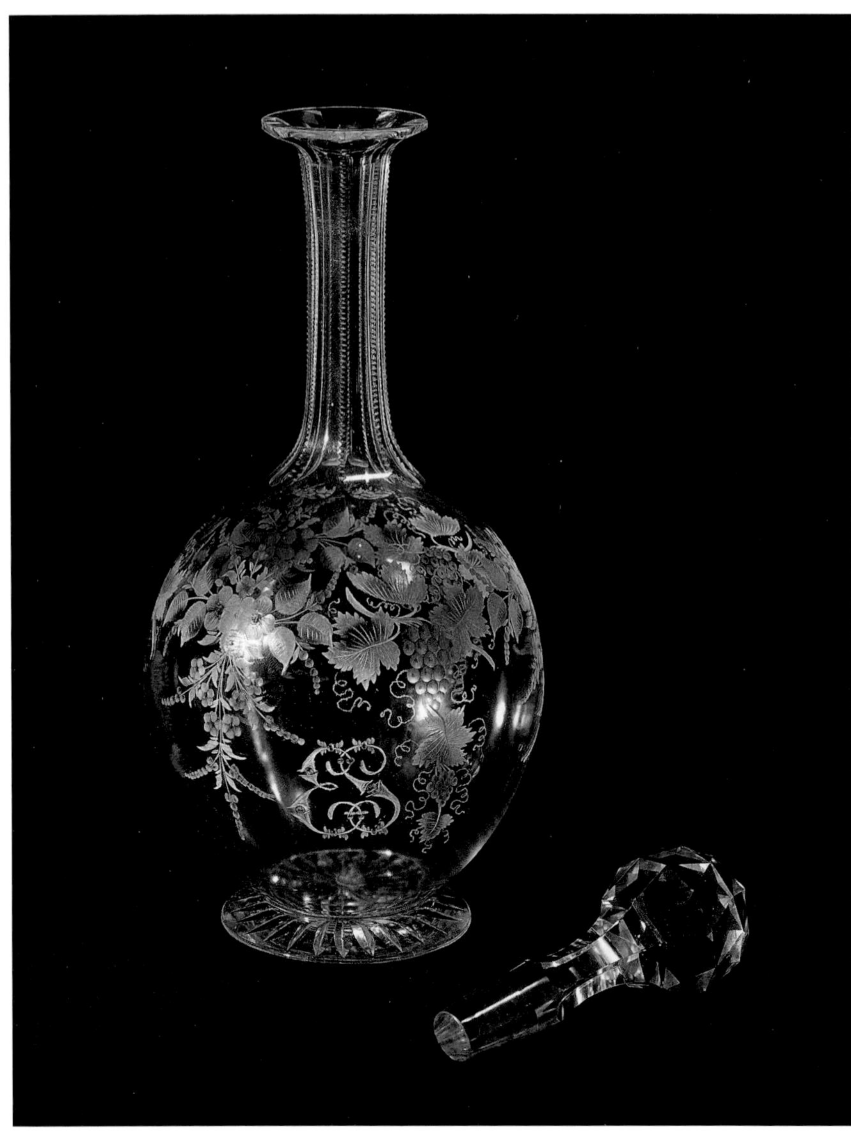

Types of colorless lead glasswares made by the New England Glass Works include this decanter with cut and engraved decoration (no. 129), which is attributed to Louis Friedrich Vaupel, the head of the engraving department from the 1850s into the 1880s. The attribution is based on the decanter's descent from Vaupel's daughter Emelie, for whom it was probably decorated when she married in 1882. Vaupel was born into a glassmaking family in Germany, where he presumably trained. He came to Boston in the 1850s and married a woman from his hometown who was also from a glassmaking family.[2] The engraved grapes and leaves that surround the inscription on the decanter, like the decoration on other glassware attributed to Vaupel, is of high quality and characteristic of much work of this period by German-trained craftsmen.[3]

Under the Libbeys' leadership, the New England Glass Works not only continued production of high-quality lead glass, but, like its regional and Midwestern competitors, it also began producing art, or "fancy," glass. American taste for this fancy glass had been established by imports of colorful English art glass in the late 1870s and early 1880s, and American firms relied on the skills of glassworkers from England. Joseph Locke came to America in 1882 and joined

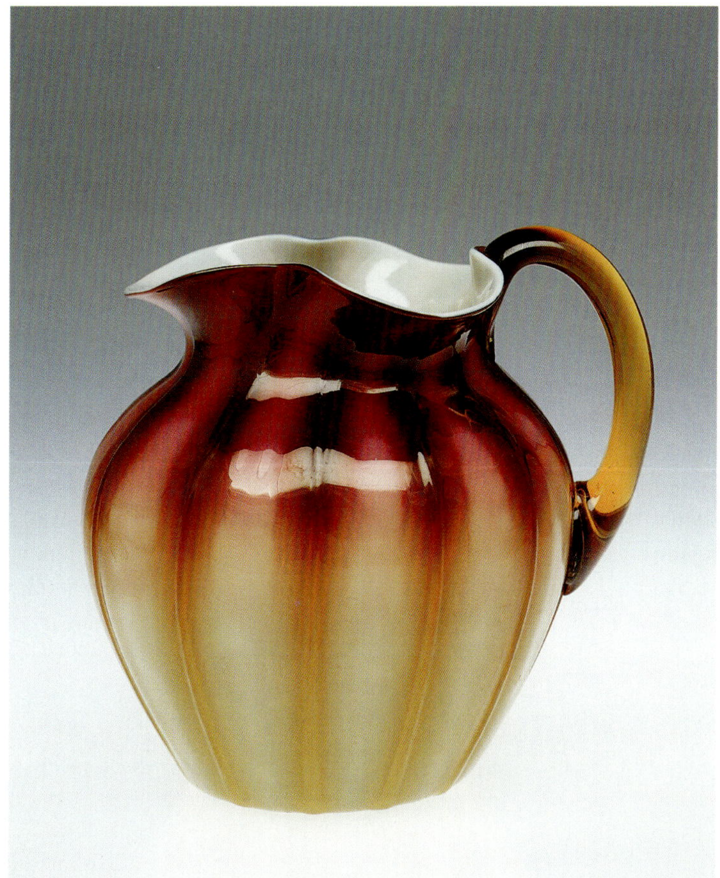

130.

Pitcher, ca. 1886

New England Glass Works (1818–1888), East Cambridge, Massachusetts
Blown and molded glass, Plated Amberina line
7¼ x 7 x 6 inches
1984.158

the New England Glass Works. Born into an English potting family in the ceramic center of Worcester, Locke apprenticed with the Royal Worcester Porcelain Company. He was hired by Guest Brothers—glass engravers and decorators at nearby Stourbridge—to provide designs and decorative work. Later he was employed by another glasshouse, Hodgetts and Richardson, and his work there won a gold medal at the 1878 Exposition Universelle in Paris.

One of Locke's first innovations at the New England Glass Works was the Amberina line of transparent amber art glass, patented in 1883. It was made by adding gold flecks to the molten amber glass and then firing the object at a high temperature, resulting in graduated colors ranging from amber yellow to cherry red. The success of Locke's Amberina line was assured when Tiffany and Company ordered the entire supply for its New York store. With the success of the Hobbs, Brockunier and Company adaptation of the Morgan vase (see no. 133), Locke introduced Plated Amberina about 1886. It was made by covering an opal white glass object in molten Amberina to create a similar opaque porcelain effect. The Crawford Plated Amberina pitcher (no. 130) is similar in shape to the Crawford Hobbs, Brockunier and Company Coral pitcher (see no. 134), but this example has been blown into a ribbed mold, which enhanced the color gradations. Plated Amberina was made only during the firm's final two years.[4]

Another innovation credited to Locke is the Wild Rose line, based on a patent secured by Edward Drummond Libbey, dated March 2, 1886. Within the company, Wild Rose was apparently called "peachblow," and it was intended to compete with Mount Washington Company's Peachblow line and Hobbs, Brockunier and Company's Coral line. In this design, opal and ruby glass were melted and mixed. Firing resulted in color gradations from white to rose pink. Wild Rose was finished either by polishing or by washing in acid to create a matte surface.

The success of the matte finish for receiving gold and polychrome enamel decorations is evident in the Crawford vase bearing Locke's name and the date 1887 (no. 131). The sparkling, jewel-like effect is enhanced by the diminutive size of the vase. The Plated Amberina line demonstrates the influence of porcelain on glass, and Locke must have been inspired by other materials in decorating the vase. The polychrome enamels resemble precious and semiprecious stones, and their framing in gold conveys the sense of overall surface ornament of Asian cloisonné enamels. The asymmetrical and stylized ornamental composition on the small Oriental-inspired vase form would have appealed to the Japanese and artistic tastes of the 1880s.[5]

Another Crawford vase is from Locke's Agata line (no. 132); it illustrates a technique patented on January 18, 1887. Objects were fashioned from the same mixture of glass used in the Wild Rose line, but then the blown and molded object was coated with a mineral or metal oxide stain and spattered with a volatile liquid such as benzine, alcohol, or naphtha, causing the oxide to mottle as the liquid evaporated. The mottled stain adhered to the surface of the vase when it was heated in the muffle (a small oven used to make enamel and gold decoration combine, or fret, with the glass). Colors in the mottled surface of Agata glass include blue, amber, and green, depending on the mineral or metal oxide used. The Crawford vase has a highly polished blue mottled surface over the pink of the glass. Agata could suggest porcelain or metal, but it could also be bathed in acid to give it a matte surface for an entirely different effect.[6]

A year after introducing Agata glass, Libbey moved his business to Toledo, Ohio, which was

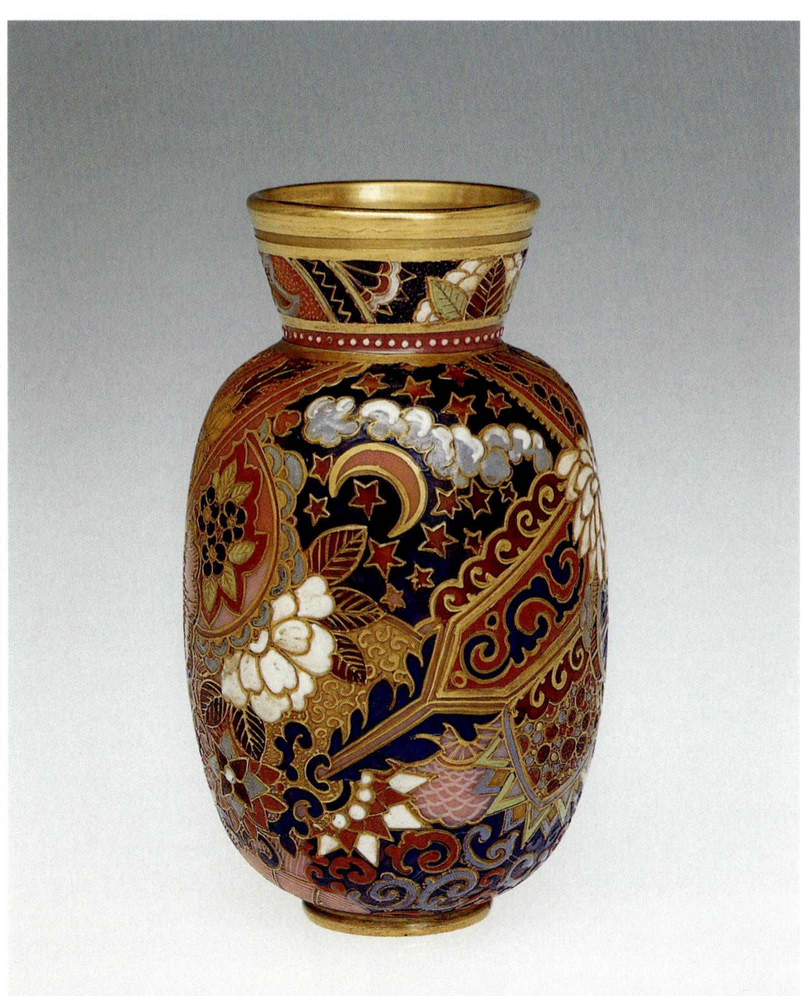

131.

Vase, dated 1887

New England Glass Works (1818–1888), East Cambridge, Massachusetts; decorated by Joseph Locke (1846–1936)
Blown and molded glass with enamel and gilt decoration, Wild Rose line
5¼ × 3 × 3 inches
Mark: Signed in gilt hand-printing on bottom, *BY/J LOCKE/ 1887*
1984.169

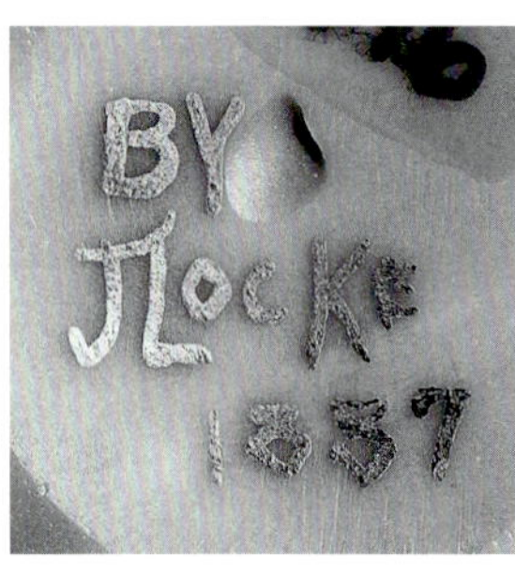

eager for new industry and jobs. Libbey hoped to avoid the labor disputes that had plagued the company by moving, although a number of workers and administrators also moved to Toledo, including Locke. Locke worked for the reorganized and renamed Libbey Glass Company until 1891, when he moved to the glass production center of Pittsburgh to head the design department of the United States Glass Company, which at that time purchased and closed Hobbs, Brockunier and Company. Locke also opened a glass-decorating studio in Pittsburgh that he retained until his death in 1936. Meanwhile, the Libbey Glass Company turned away from art glass to produce increasingly fashionable and profitable rich cut glass (see nos. 157–171).

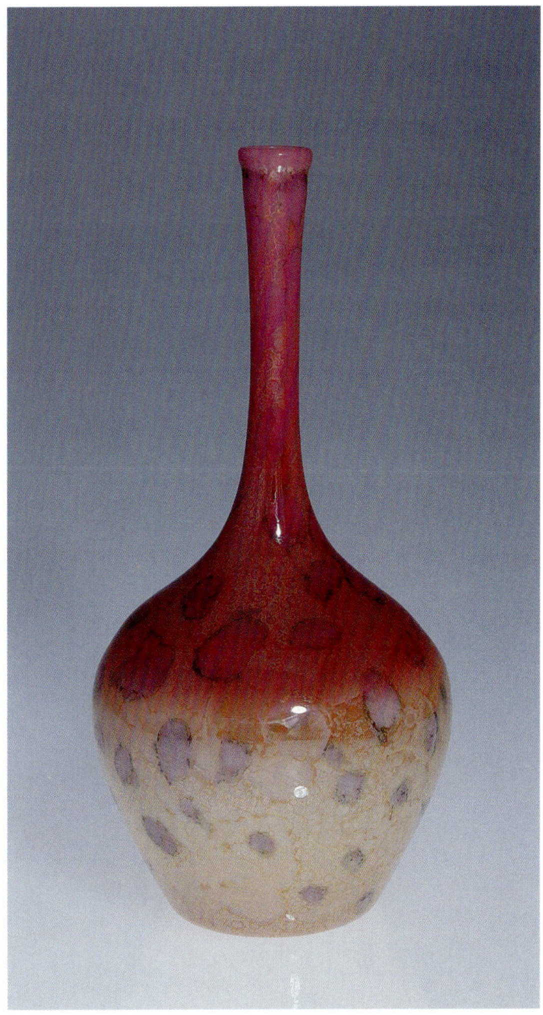

132.

Vase, 1885–1888

New England Glass Works
(1818–1888), East Cambridge,
Massachusetts
Blown and molded glass,
Agata line
8¾ × 3¾ × 3¾ inches
1984.166

NOTES

1. For the history of the New England Glass Company, see The Metropolitan Museum of Art 1986, pp. 458–459. An illustration of the New England Glass Company display at the Centennial Exposition appears in K. Wilson 1972, p. 343, fig. 300, which also outlines the firm's final years in East Cambridge, p. 233. Another illustrated historical account is Toledo Museum of Art 1963. The closing of the company is discussed in Toledo Museum of Art 1968, pp. 9–10.

2. Vaupel's life and career are recounted in Fauster 1971, pp. 669–671. Authorities vary on significant years in Vaupel's life and career, including the date of his immigration and the years he worked for the New England Glass Company. Here the years are rounded off to decades about which all the authorities are in agreement; see ibid.; The Metropolitan Museum of Art 1970, no. 160; Watkins 1930, p. 116; and K. Wilson 1972, p. 33.

3. An unusually large number of Vaupel-attributed engraved glass survives from his family, including a matching decanter, wine glasses, and goblets, also inscribed "ES," in private collections and in the Jones Gallery of Glass and Ceramics, Douglas Hill, Maine. Locations of additional Vaupel-provenance glass are listed in correspondence, Donald Ferland, February 5, 1985, High Museum of Art document files.

4. Locke's biography is recounted in Newman 1987, p. 186; and Revi 1967, pp. 149–151. The processes of making Amberina and Plated Amberina glass are discussed and illustrated in Revi 1967, pp. 16–19; and Toledo Museum of Art 1963, p. 25. Locke's working life at the New England Glass Works is also discussed in The Metropolitan Museum of Art 1986, p. 458.

5. The Wild Rose process is described and illustrated in Revi 1967, pp. 49–51; and Toledo Museum of Art 1963, pp. 25–26. The Crawford Locke vase is discussed and illustrated in The Metropolitan Museum of Art 1986, pp. 244 and 247, fig. 7.54.

6. The Agata line is described and illustrated in Revi 1967, pp. 54–55.

Hobbs, Brockunier and Company

THIS VASE WITH STAND is a glass version of an antique Chinese peachbloom porcelain vase and bronze stand that sold at auction in New York in 1886 for $18,000. The vase had been owned by Mary Morgan, a noted collector, and its sale at such an impressive price for the time generated national press coverage and great public interest, which inspired Hobbs, Brockunier and Company to introduce its adaptation a month later.[1] The firm's catalogue illustrated the glass facsimile with a banner reading "The $18,000 Vase." Production of the glass vase (no. 133) was an early instance of a media-driven market in the United States. Hobbs, Brockunier and Company provided an opportunity for middle-class Americans to own a version of a vase treasured by a millionaire and widely admired by connoisseurs.

The amber pressed glass stand simulated the traditional bronze stand of the Morgan porcelain vase. Hobbs, Brockunier and Company made its version of the vase in its Coral glass line, which was already in production. An 1886 legal battle between the New England Glass Company and the Mount Washington Glass Company awarded use of the name "peachblow" to Mount Washington, but both the Hobbs, Brockunier and Company's Coral and the New England Glass Company's Wild Rose lines (see no. 131) were known by the public and within the trade as peachblow. Coral was made by casing an opal white blown and molded glass form in a transparent amber glass coating with gold salts mixed into the melt. Exposure to heat changed the transparent amber glass coating to a solid cherry red at the top, which turned bright yellow around the base. The colors effectively duplicated those on the glaze of the Morgan vase. The finished shiny glass surface suggested the brilliant glaze on the porcelain vase, although the company also offered an alternative matte surface, achieved by dipping the finished vase in acid.[2]

The Hobbs, Brockunier and Company pitcher (no. 134) was made in the same manner as the vase, and it is related to a similar Plated Amberina example made by the New England Glass Company (see no. 130). The two pitchers illustrate the success of the peachblow process in achieving the colors associated with Chinese porcelains, and they show how leading glass companies copied each others' forms in the 1880s.

Hobbs, Brockunier and Company had connections throughout its history with the New England Glass Company in East Cambridge, Massachusetts. In 1845, John L. Hobbs, superintendent of the cutting department at the New England Glass Company, and James B. Barnes, the engineer who had supervised construction of the furnaces, bought a glasshouse in Wheeling, West Virginia, an emerging glass-manufacturing center, to form Barnes, Hobbs and Company. After

133.

Vase and Stand,
ca. 1886

Hobbs, Brockunier and Company (1845–1891), Wheeling, West Virginia
Blown and molded cased glass and pressed glass, Coral line
Vase: 7⅞ × 3 × 3 inches
Stand: 3⅛ × 3⅜ × 3⅜ inches
1984.163.a–.b

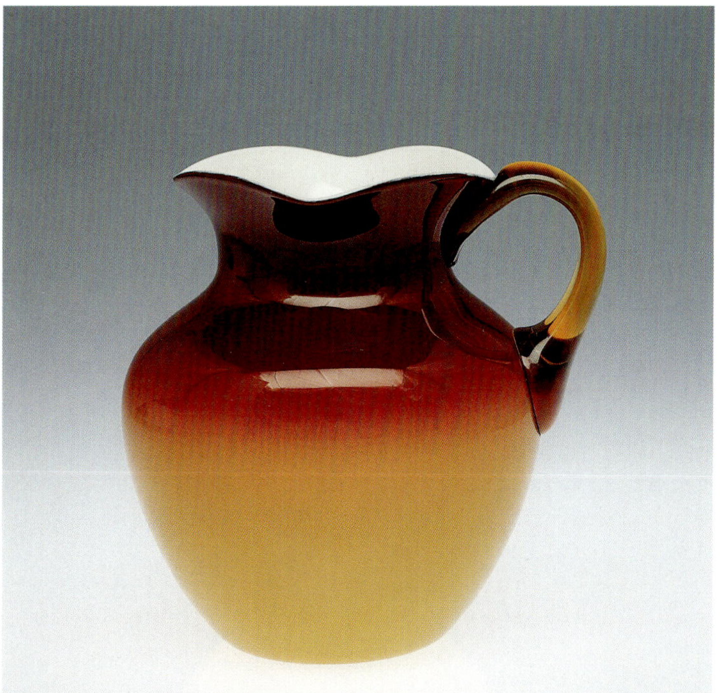

134.

Pitcher, ca. 1886

Hobbs, Brockunier and Company (1845–1891), Wheeling, West Virginia
Blown and molded cased glass, Coral line
7 × 7⅛ × 6 inches
1984.157

the elder Barnes died, his son became a partner in the reorganized firm of Hobbs, Barnes and Company, where he remained until his death in 1863. The Hobbses then took on Charles W. Brockunier, formerly the firm's bookkeeper, and William Leighton, Sr., superintendent at the New England Glass Company, as partners to form Hobbs, Brockunier and Company. The Hobbses brought their knowledge of glassmaking, Brockunier his business acumen, and Leighton his scientific expertise to the firm. Leighton's research resulted in the introduction of lime glass, which simulated the much more expensive lead glass, and this assured success for the new firm. After 1867, William Leighton, Jr. succeeded his father and his experiments led to the firm's production of ruby glass and art glass such as peachblow. Hobbs, Brockunier and Company reached its apogee with its adaptation of the Morgan vase, which remains its best-known product. Just a year later, in 1887, Brockunier and Leighton retired, and the younger Hobbs assumed control of the firm until it was absorbed in 1891 by a conglomerate of Ohio River valley glass factories, the United States Glass Company, which soon closed the factory due to a labor dispute.

At the time of the success of "The $18,000 Vase," similar peachblow lines were made at several Ohio River valley and New England firms, which produced both decorative objects and useful tablewares such as the Crawford pitcher. These art wares—or as Hobbs, Brockunier and Company referred to them in catalogues, "fancy" wares—were inspired by artistic colored glass from England, France, Germany, and Bohemia, which was popular in the United States in the 1880s. These new American glasswares also appealed to readers of Charles Locke Eastlake, who called for artistry in household goods in an age of increasing mass production.

NOTES

1. The American art collector William T. Walters purchased the Morgan vase, which is now in the Walters Art Gallery in Baltimore. The Crawford glass version of the Morgan vase is illustrated and discussed in The Metropolitan Museum of Art 1986, pp. 243–244, fig. 7.49. Historical accounts of Hobbs, Brockunier and Company are given in Di Bartolomeo 1975, pp. 494–501; The Metropolitan Museum of Art 1986, pp. 440–441; and Lee 1933, pp. 48–50, which also includes accounts of the Morgan porcelain vase sale and the publicity surrounding it. Lee shows the illustration of the vase from the firm's catalogue, p. 48.

2. The process of making peachblow-type glass is described in Lee 1933, p. 48. The process was further explained by Gary E. Baker, curator of glass, Chrysler Museum, Norfolk, Virginia, in a conversation with the author, June 9, 1993.

135.

Vase, ca. 1892

Chesapeake Pottery (1882–1914), Baltimore
Semi-porcelain with transfer-printed and gilt decoration
18½ × 12 × 5 inches
1984.126

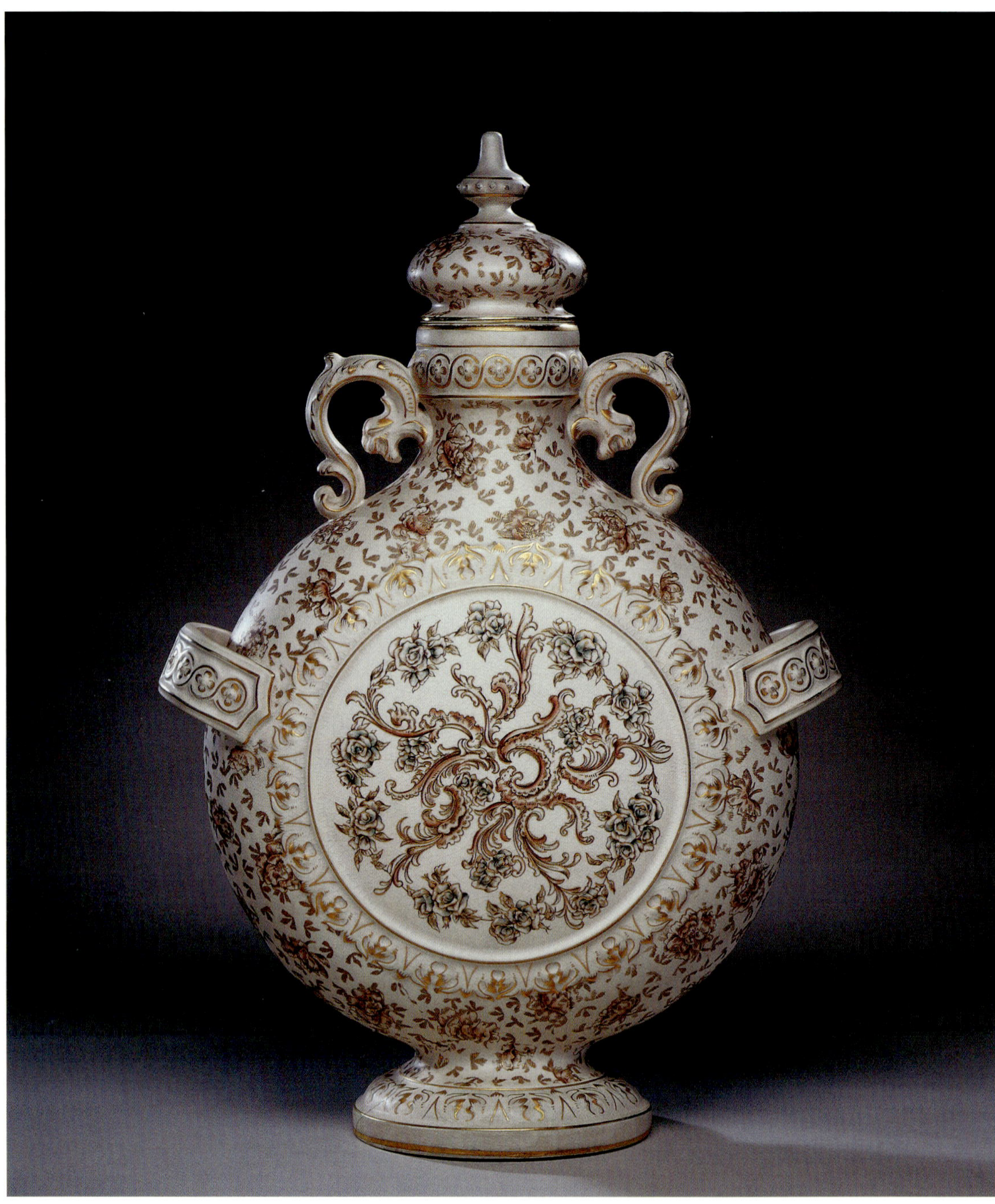

Under the leadership of David Francis Haynes, the Chesapeake Pottery was the leading artistic ceramic company in Baltimore's small pottery industry in the 1880s and 1890s. Although never a concentrated production center on the level of Trenton, New Jersey, or East Liverpool, Ohio, Baltimore provided useful Rockingham and cream-colored earthenwares for a regional market. The Chesapeake Pottery responded to the late-nineteenth-century American fascination with art for the household by incorporating exotic, artistic, and historical elements into mass-produced ornamental wares. Haynes was eager to promote his ideas of art for the masses through the Chesapeake Pottery. According to American ceramic historian Edwin AtLee Barber, Haynes "always held it to be of much greater importance to elevate the quality, as far as possible, of the entire pottery product of the country, than to produce a few fine pieces that should be within the reach of only the wealthy."[1]

Haynes was born and raised in rural Massachusetts. At sixteen, he began working in a crockery store in Lowell, which sent him on business to Europe, where the "art treasures of England and the Continent proved a revelation and education to him."[2] In 1856, Haynes moved to Baltimore, where he was employed by the Abbott Rolling Mills, which manufactured plate iron for ironclad battle vessels during the Civil War. After the war, he mined iron ores and clay in Virginia before returning to Baltimore in 1871 as a partner in Ammidon and Company, merchants in "kerosene oil, lamps, glassware and queensware."[3] In 1877, Haynes took over the firm, renaming it D. F. Haynes and Company. In 1882, he purchased the Chesapeake Pottery from its English founders, Henry and Isaac Brougham and John Tunstall.

Until Haynes's ownership, the pottery had produced utilitarian wares. Haynes undertook an expansion of the pottery that drew skilled labor and management from potteries in Trenton, New Jersey, and England. Frederick Hackney, who had worked for Wedgwood, was put in charge of artistic production. Lewis Taft, who had worked for William Brownfield and Company in England and Ott and Brewer in Trenton (see nos. 115–117), supervised kilns, clay bodies, and glazes.

By 1887, however, Haynes had overextended, and in January of the next year his business was put under trusteeship and the plant auctioned to Edwin Huston Bennett, son of pioneer Baltimore potter Edwin Bennett (see no. 18). Bennett retained Haynes as general manager, and the official name of the company changed to Haynes, Bennett and Company. Semi-porcelain was introduced and thereafter was used in all the company's production.[4] Transfer printing, which had been used in design since Haynes purchased the company, came to dominate the firm's decorative wares of the late 1880s and 1890s.

Haynes was a leader in the American ceramic industry of the 1890s: he was chairman of the Committee on Art and Design of the United States Potters Association and was active on their committee for the 1893 World's Columbian Exposition in Chicago. After Bennett's retirement in 1895, Haynes regained control of the firm with his son, Frank, under the name D. F. Haynes and Son. However, by the time of Haynes's death in 1908, the pottery was again in financial difficulties, and despite a reorganization attempt by Frank Haynes, it closed in 1914.[5]

The Crawford covered vase dates from the Haynes-Bennett management of the Chesapeake Pottery in the early 1890s. The form was evidently a popular one, since several examples survive, each decorated differently.[6] The scale, heft, and lid of this heavy semi-porcelain vase preclude any practical use as a container. The big circular flask form may have been inspired by Near Eastern metals or ceramics, and the molded handles and onion-dome lid contributed to its exotic appeal in the American domestic decorating market of the 1890s. The broad sides provide space for rococo-style transfer-printed floral decoration. The color scheme of muted grays, browns, and rose with gold highlights is typical of Chesapeake wares.

NOTES

1. Barber, *Pottery,* 1976, p. 322. Haynes's early life is outlined on pp. 320–322; and also in FitzPatrick 1957, p. 66.

2. Barber, *Pottery,* 1976, p. 320.

3. Myers 1992, p. 28.

4. Ibid., pp. 38–39.

5. Ibid., pp. 46–49.

6. Illustrated in Barber, *Pottery,* 1976, p. 32, fig. 163; and Myers 1992, fig. 12.

Mount Washington Glass Company

The Mount Washington Glass Company is best remembered for its artistic glassware from the last two decades of the nineteenth century. Its production began in 1837, when it was established by Deming Jarves, the first agent of the New England Glass Company, who later founded the Boston and Sandwich Glass Company. In 1851, William Libbey joined the firm as an accountant; he assumed sole proprietorship in 1866. In 1871, he moved the firm from aging facilities in south Boston to a technically up-to-date factory in New Bedford, Massachusetts, which had been built by dissatisfied workers from the Boston and Sandwich Glass Company. The next year, Libbey sold the Mount Washington Glass Company to become superintendent of the New England Glass Company in East Cambridge, Massachusetts. The severe American economic failure of 1873 forced temporary closure of the factory, but it reopened in 1874 under the management of Frederick S. Shirley.[1]

In 1878, Shirley secured a patent to manufacture his distinctive Sicilian line of glassware (no. 136), which may have been the first line of colored art glass produced in America. With this line, the Mount Washington Glass Company embarked on nearly two decades of leadership in American art glass. Since the 1850s, Charles Locke Eastlake and English art critic John Ruskin had praised the Venetian glass industry, which was then being revived on the adjacent island of Murano. Mount Washington's Sicilian

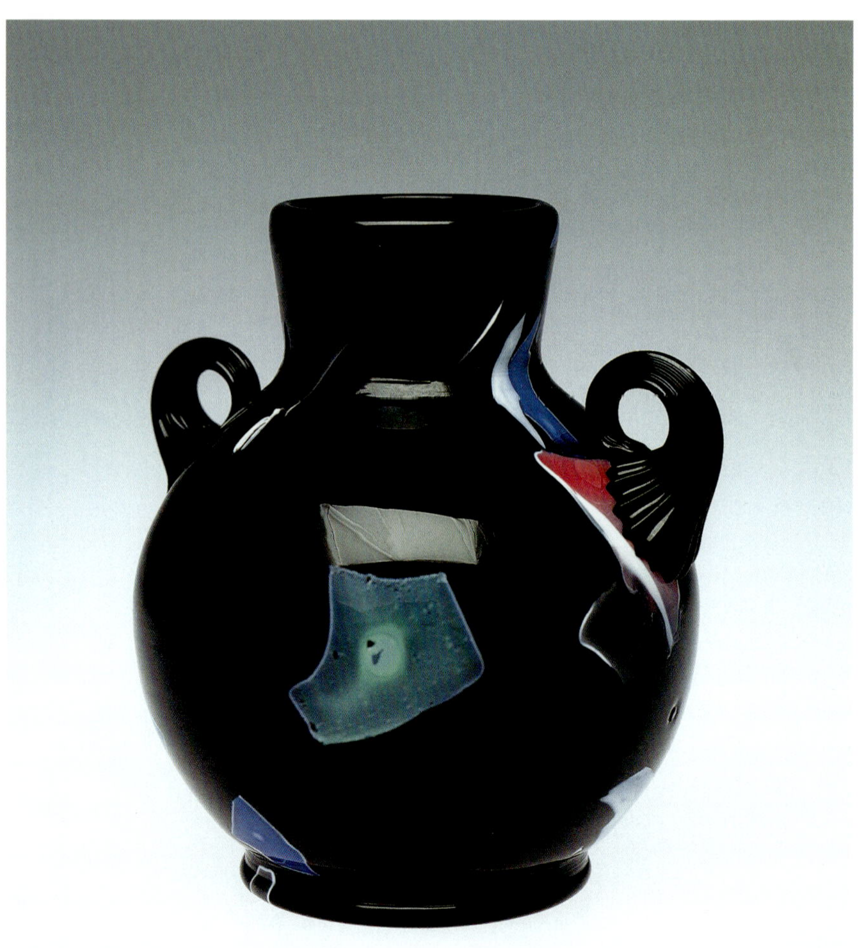

136.

Vase, 1878–1880

Mount Washington Glass Company (1837–1958), New Bedford, Massachusetts; patented by Frederick S. Shirley, 1878
Lead glass containing volcanic lava with inlaid enamel glass decoration; Sicilian line
5¼ × 4¾ × 5½ inches
1987.168

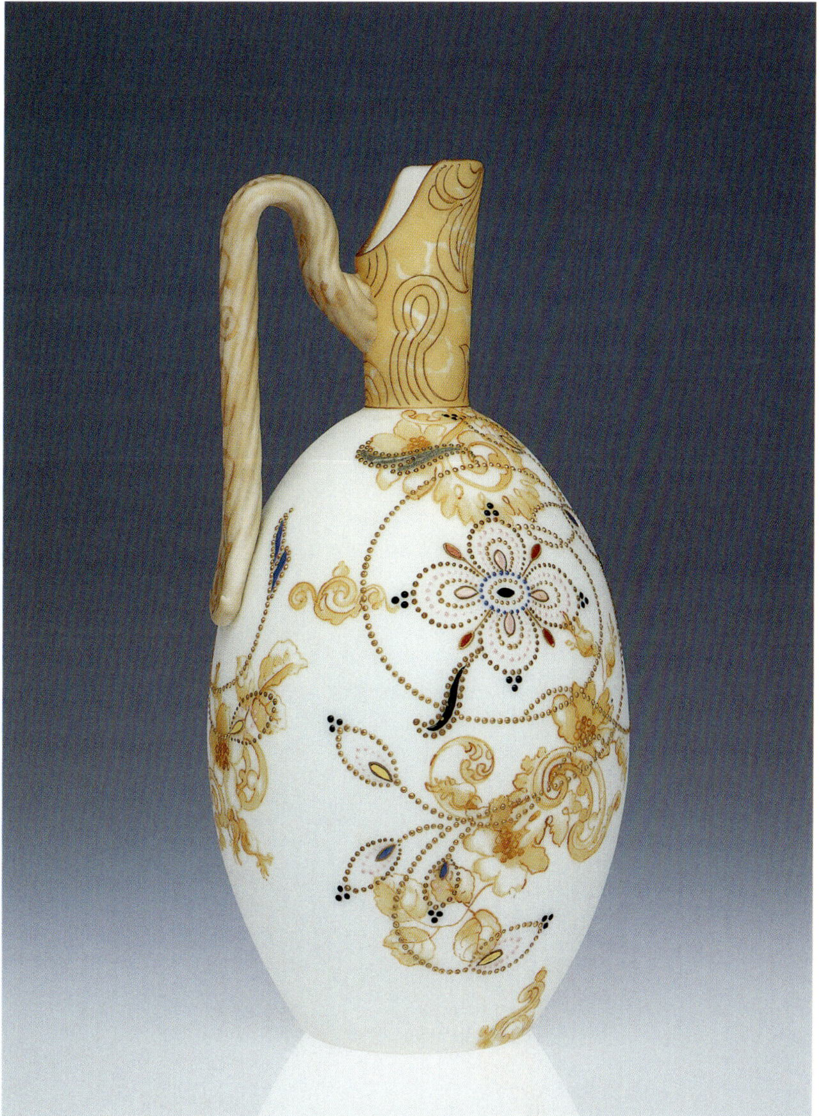

137.

Vase, 1886–1894

Mount Washington Glass Company (1837–1958), New Bedford, Massachusetts; patented by Frederick S. Shirley and Albert Steffin, 1886
Acid-dipped blown and molded opal glass with enamel decoration; Crown Milano line
12 × 5¼ × 5¼ inches
Mark: On circular paper label on bottom of pitcher, printed in green, *CROWN MILANO/MT W G. CO.* surrounding insignia of spread-winged eagle with shield enclosing an *S*
1984.119

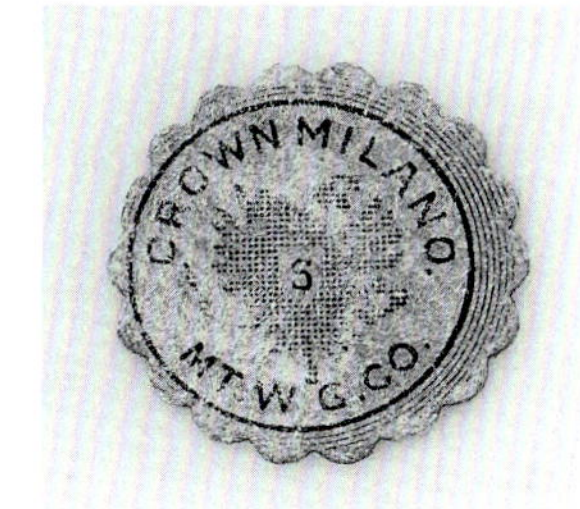

line was made from lead glass combined with volcanic lava ash from Mount Etna on the island of Sicily. The ash gave the finished product its distinctive black color and linked the line with Italy and Venetian glass. The connection with Mount Etna also brought associations with classical Roman glass, which was then being excavated and collected by London's British Museum, adding to the perceived artistic importance of the Sicilian line.

Shirley's patented decorative technique for the Sicilian line involved rolling a molten gather of glass through chips of brightly colored glass and enamels so that after the glass was blown into its shape and reheated, the chips were inlaid in the surface. The variations in each object could not be duplicated or preplanned, which added to the artistic effect, as did the Chinese and classical shapes used in the Sicilian line.[2]

In 1886, Shirley and Albert Steffin, who headed the company's decorating department, were jointly issued a patent for decorating opal white glass, which they introduced commercially as Crown Milano, again suggesting Italian inspirations. In the Crown Milano line, a pattern was stenciled with pulverized carbon, which decorators followed with polychrome enamels. The acid-dipped, matte-finished Crawford vase in the Crown Milano (no. 137) line was made in the shape of a pitcher, although it was intended for ornament rather than table use. Realistic flowers outlined in gold combine with stylized flowers, leaves, and branches applied in enamel beads for a textured effect. Although the shape of the vase and its reeded, twisted handle recall hand-blown Venetian glass, the asymmetrical decoration lends it a Japanese or Near Eastern feel.[3]

The Royal Flemish line was advertised as early as 1889, although it was not patented by Steffin until 1894, when the Mount Washington Glass Company was absorbed by the neighboring Pairpoint Manufacturing Company (see no. 167). Its thick, gilt enamel lines made the glassware resemble the leading of medieval stained glass windows. The Crawford Royal Flemish vase (no. 138) was given an acid bath to create a matte finish. The bulbous base, globular neck, and tall, tapering stem give the vase a Near Eastern shape, while the decoration is inspired by painted Near Eastern glass.[4]

NOTES

1. The history of the Mount Washington Glass Company is recounted in The Metropolitan Museum of Art 1986, p. 457; K. Wilson 1958, pp. 46–48; and K. Wilson 1972, pp. 297–299, 348–357.

2. A related Sicilian vase is in The Metropolitan Museum of Art and is illustrated and discussed in The Metropolitan Museum of Art 1986, pp. 238 and 240, fig. 7.45. The manufacture and decoration of Sicilian glassware are described in Revi 1967, pp. 231–235.

3. The decoration of the Crown Milano line of glassware is described in Revi 1967, pp. 65–68.

4. Royal Flemish decoration is described in ibid., p. 74. A vase similar to the Crawford vase is illustrated on p. 77.

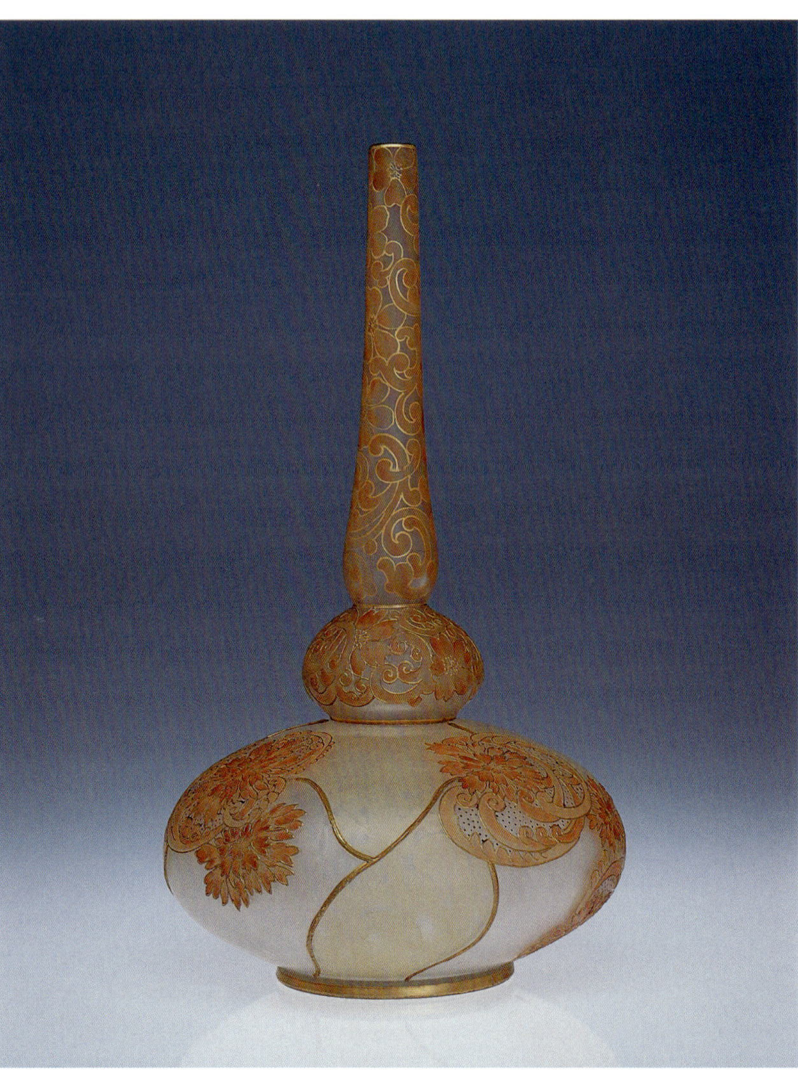

138.

Vase, 1889–1894

Mount Washington Glass Company (1837–1958), New Bedford, Massachusetts; patented by Albert Steffin, 1894
Acid-dipped blown and molded opal glass with enamel decoration; Royal Flemish line
13⅜ × 7 × 7 inches
Marks: Painted in red on bottom, conjoined backward *R* and *F* in diamond; on circular paper label on bottom, *MT W . . . PAT. APPLIED FOR* encircling double headed eagle with shield enclosing an *S*
1984.118

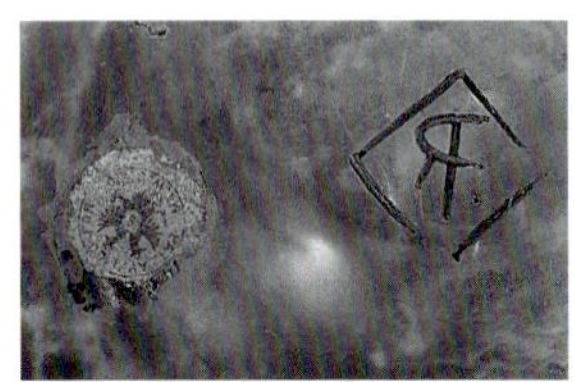

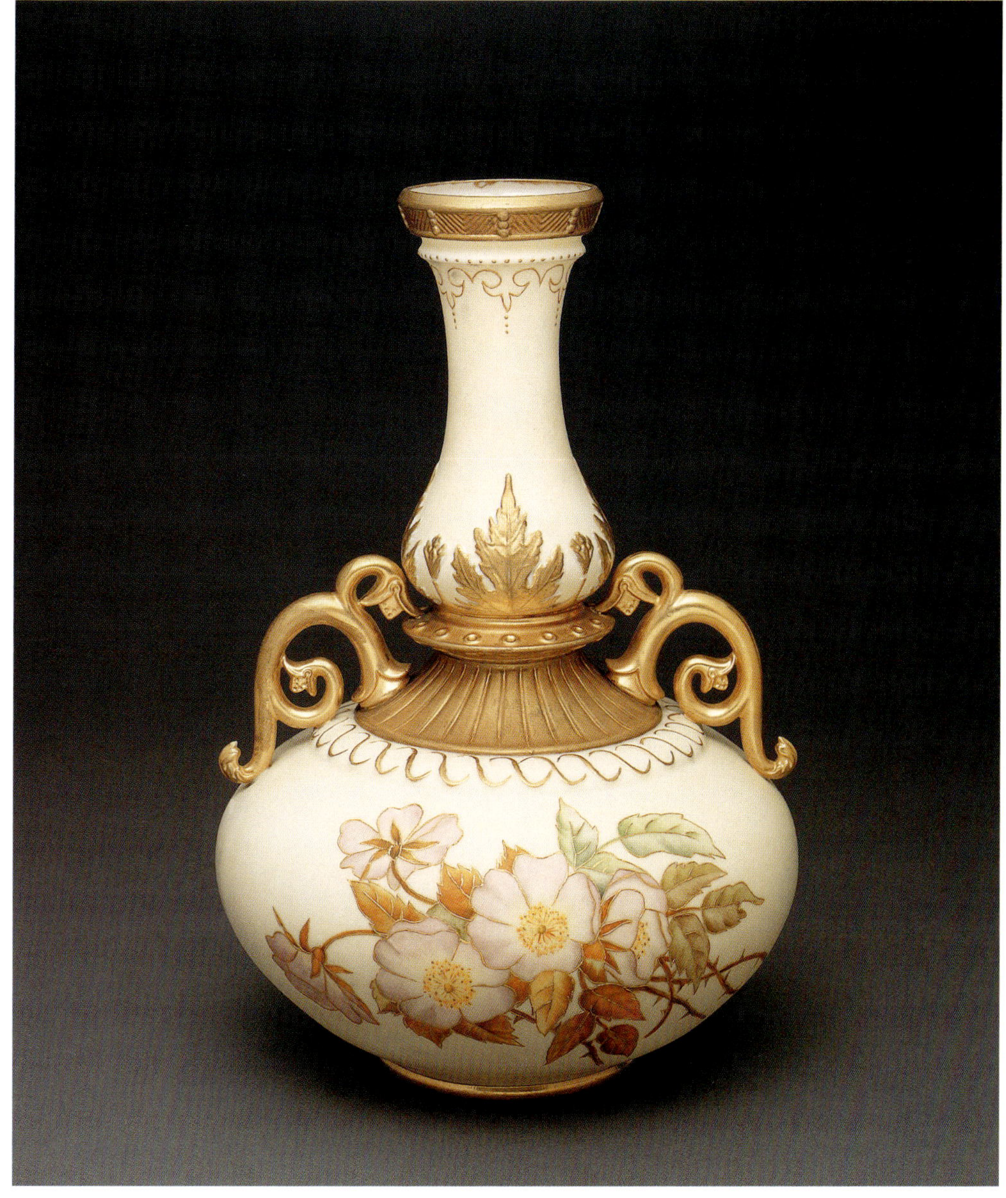

139.

Vase, 1891–1894

American Art China Company (1891–1894), Trenton, New Jersey
Porcelain with gilt and polychrome decoration
12 × 7½ × 7½ inches
Mark: On bottom, in blue, *RE & CO/CHINA*
1985.311

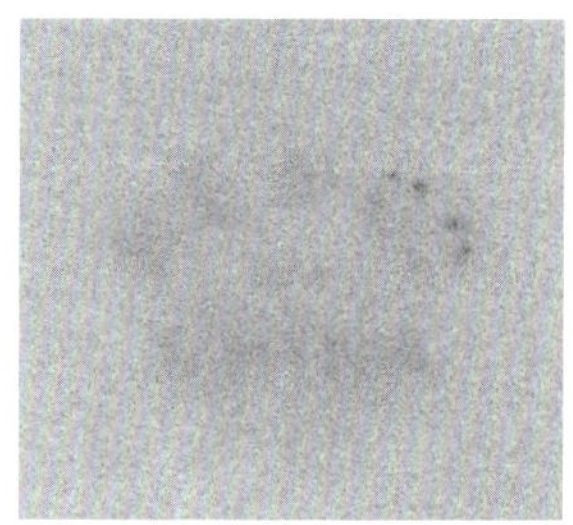

THE AMERICAN ART China Company, established in Trenton, New Jersey, with the partnership of John C. Rittenhouse and George Evans, was a short-lived competitor of Ott and Brewer during the last years of the latter's production of Belleek-type porcelains (see nos. 116–117). From its few known wares, American Art China Company seems to have specialized in highly decorative porcelains with delicately thin, translucent, Belleek-type porcelain bodies and well-executed polychrome overglaze enamel decorations. The Crawford vase reflects late-nineteenth-century eclecticism and interest in the exotic by combining floral decoration from the European ceramic tradition with a Middle Eastern shape. The firm also manufactured white porcelain blanks for decorating. Known marks on American Art China Company wares include the firm's initials or, as in this case, the founders' initials.[1]

NOTE

1. The firm is discussed in Barber, *Pottery,* 1976, p. 241. A three-piece tea set in a late-nineteenth-century elongated rococo style in The Metropolitan Museum of Art, marked with the conjoined initials of the firm's name, is illustrated in Frelinghuysen 1989, pp. 220–221, no. 81.

Late-century Eclecticism, 1876–1905

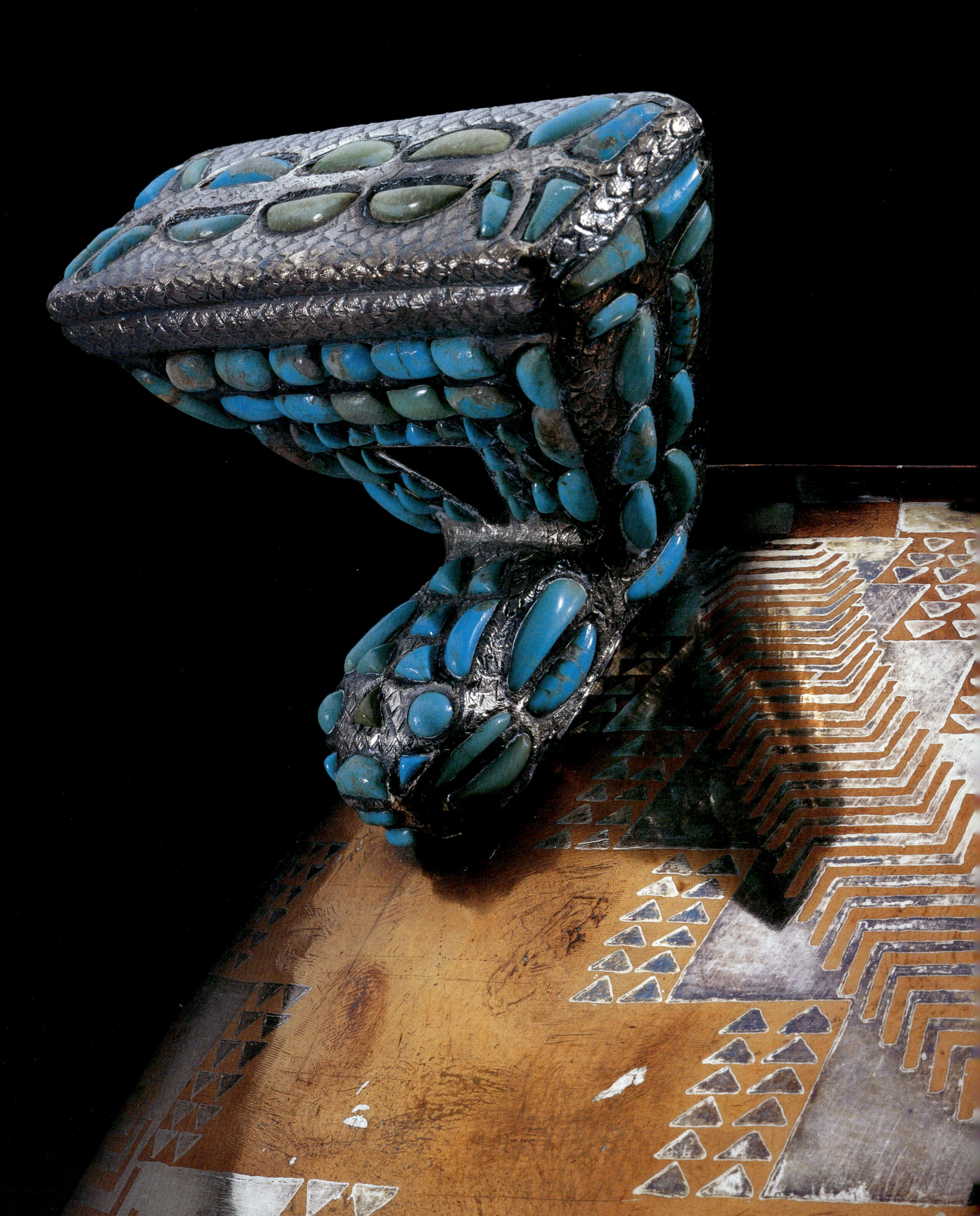

Presidential Porcelain

140.

Soup Bowl, ca. 1880

Manufactured by Haviland and Company (1842–present), Limoges, France; decoration by Theodore R. Davis (1840–1894)
Porcelain with transfer-printed, chromolithographed, painted, and gilt decoration
8¾ × 8¾ × 1¾ inches
Marks: On bottom, printed in red, *FABRIQUÉ PAR/HAVILAND & CO./d'après les dessins/DE;* below, printed in black (replicated signature), *Theo. R. Davis;* printed in green, *H&Co.;* printed in blue, *DESIGN PATENTED/ AUGUST 10TH 1880/NO. 11933;* on side, polychrome eagle with American shield
1986.164.2

141.

Dessert Plate, ca. 1880

Manufactured by Haviland and Company (1842–present), Limoges, France; decoration by Theodore R. Davis (1840–1894)
Porcelain with transfer-printed, chromolithographed, painted, and gilt decoration
8 × 9 × 1⅝ inches
Marks: On bottom, printed in red, *FABRIQUÉ PAR/HAVILAND & CO./d'après les dessins/DE;* below, printed in black (replicated signature), *Theo. R. Davis;* printed in green, *H.&Co.;* printed in blue, *DESIGN PATENTED/ AUGUST 10TH 1880/NO. 11934;* on side, polychrome eagle with American shield
1986.164.1

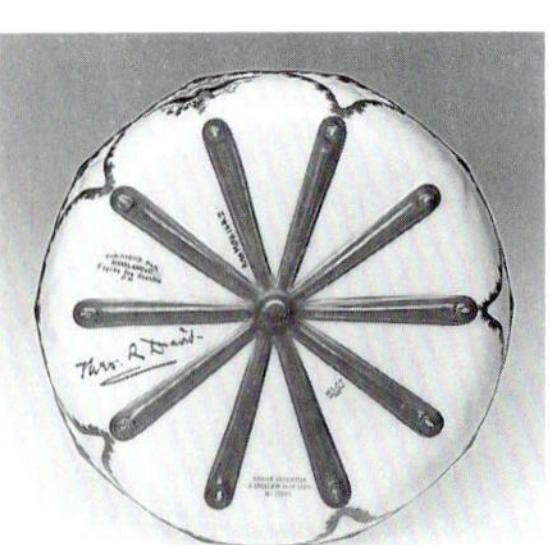

THE DECADENCE associated with the administration of Ulysses S. Grant came to an end when Rutherford B. Hayes was inaugurated in March of 1877. President Hayes and his wife, called "Lemonade Lucy" by historians, established an abstinence policy for state dinners in keeping with their sense of family morality. Instead of the established routine of after-dinner coffee and liqueurs in the Red Room, President and Mrs. Hayes led a promenade through the expanded conservatory adjacent to the State Dining Room before bidding guests farewell.[1]

In 1879, Mrs. Hayes ordered a new state dinner service decorated with plants like those the guests would enjoy during the after-dinner promenade. Haviland and Company of New York, a china-importing company with a porcelain factory in Limoges, France, secured the commission with the lowest price and the shortest promised completion time. Theodore Haviland requested cuttings from the plants in the conservatory for his artists to use in creating the decorations.

In a chance meeting with Mrs. Hayes, American artist Theodore Davis, an illustrator for *Harper's Weekly,* convinced her that appropriate decorations for the state service would be distinctively North American animals, plants, and other subjects. By the end of February, Davis was appointed the designer of the new service to be produced by Haviland and Company.[2]

The state service became a cooperative project between Davis and Theodore Haviland. Davis executed all the designs in watercolor and worked with Haviland on the creation of new shapes specifically for the service. Davis established a studio on the New Jersey shore at Asbury Park because of its relative isolation and proximity to New York, and from there he sent his designs weekly to the Haviland factory in Limoges. Once there, copper engravings were made from the designs and printed onto the porcelain; the colors were then applied to the surface by chromolithography, a technique introduced by Haviland for this commission. Final shadings and gilding were applied by hand, and samples were submitted for Davis's approval before final production began.

The soup bowls in the service, shaped like laurel blossoms, were designed with twelve different scenes.[3] The Crawford example (no. 140) is decorated with the 1776 design, which depicts a New England kitchen fireplace. The 1876

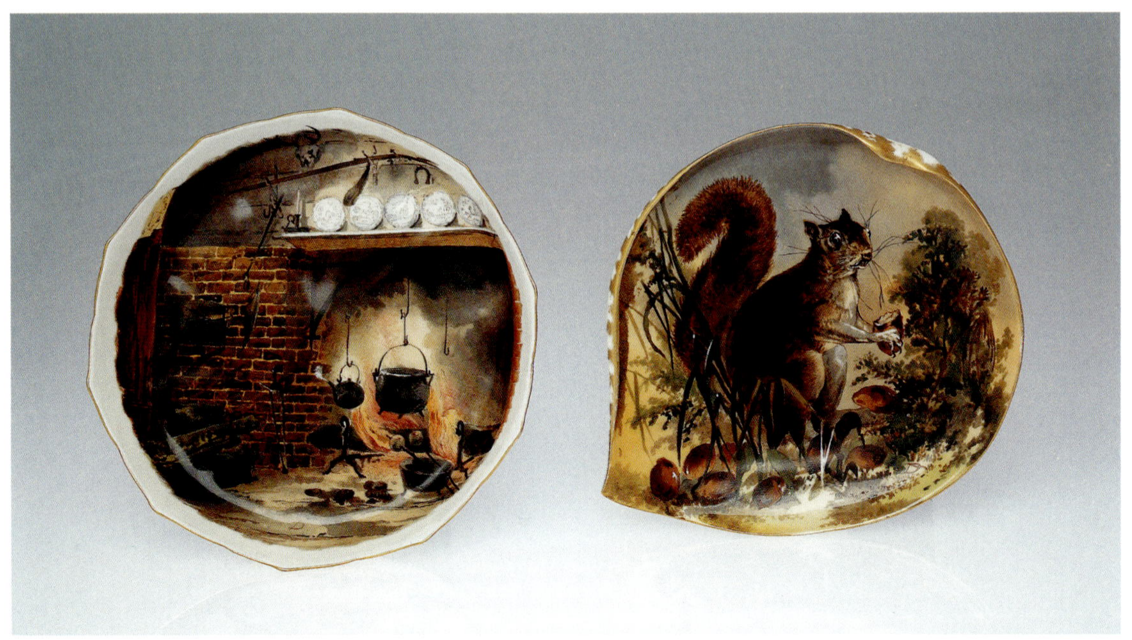

Centennial International Exposition in Philadelphia had popularized America's colonial past, and the design included elements that were popularly but incorrectly associated with colonial days: the flintlock rifle, the grandfather clock, and the "blue willow" plates on the mantel. The suspended stew pot made this design especially fitting for the soup course.

The shape of the dessert (or fruit) plate was based on the leaf of the wild apple tree, and it incorporated related images of native American fruits and nuts in twelve different designs. The pattern of the Crawford plate (no. 141) is the Pecan design and depicts a Texas red squirrel eating a pecan.

Perhaps the most whimsical pieces in the Hayes service were the ice cream trays and dishes (no. 142). The corners were rolled, as they were on all the large platters in the service. Molded onto the surface of the dish was a Canadian snowshoe; as the ice cream melted on the design, it resembled snow.

According to surviving correspondence, Haviland intended to make twenty-five duplicate sets of the Hayes service for public sale. Eight sets were exhibited in stores in cities throughout the United States. The Crawford dishes are from a duplicate set, indicated by the patent date and numbers printed on the bottom, which do not appear on the dishes that were received by the White House in 1880.[4]

NOTES

1. Seale 1986, pp. 487–511. Seale compares the Hayes and Grant administrations. The post-dinner promenade is described on p. 506.

2. The encounter between Davis and Mrs. Hayes is recounted in ibid., pp. 508–510; and Klapthor 1975, p. 100. Klapthor discusses the service and its production at length and illustrates numerous pieces on pp. 97–121. Davis's letter of February 26, 1879, to Webb Hayes, the president's son and private secretary, is quoted on p. 100. According to Haviland publicity at the time, Davis had ample experience to recommend him for the job: "He had fished in the rivers of the East and West and in the sea, hunted fowl and wild game in the forests, the swamps and the mountains; shot the buffalo on the plains, and visited the historic haunts of the Indians in the East; met the Indians in their wigwams, and studied their habits on the prairies of the far West." Cited in Klapthor 1975, p. 187.

3. Klapthor 1975, p. 184 ff.

4. Ibid., pp. 112–113, 116.

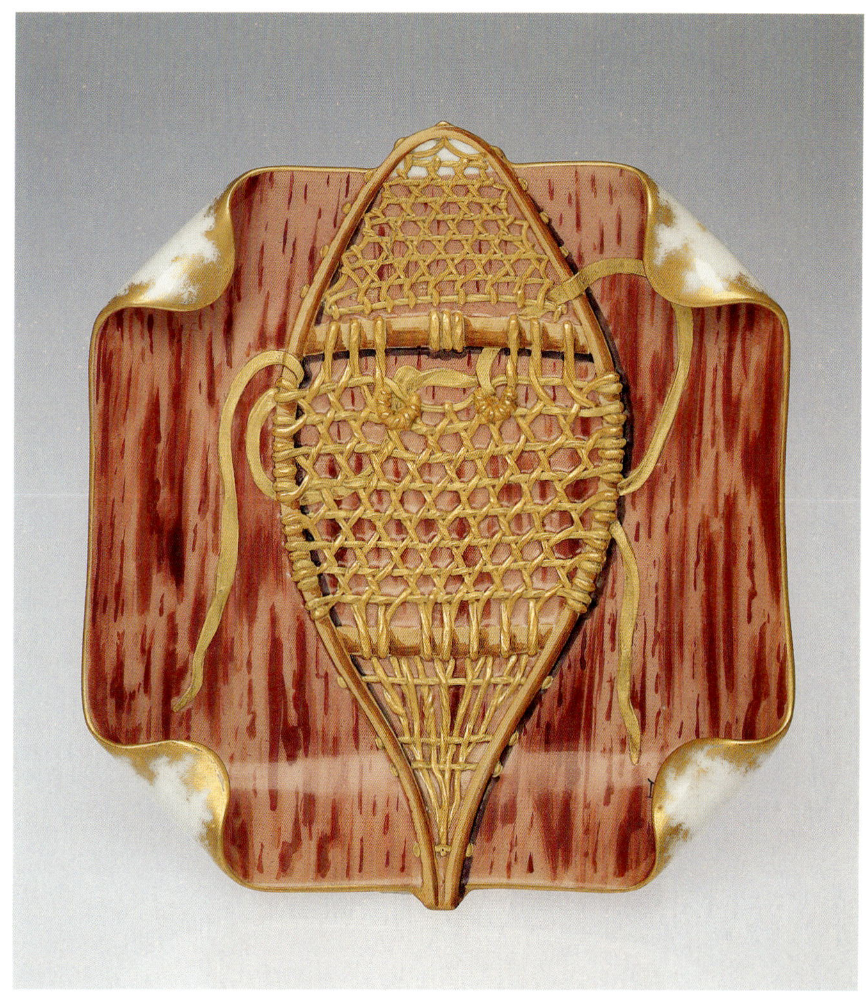

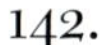

142.

Ice Cream Plate,
ca. 1880

Manufactured by Haviland and Company (1842–present), Limoges, France; decoration by Theodore R. Davis (1840–1894)
Porcelain with transfer-printed, chromolithographed, painted, and gilt decoration
7⅜ × 6⅞ × 1¼ inches
Marks: On bottom, printed in red, FABRIQUÉ PAR/HAVILAND & CO./*d'après les dessins*/DE; below, printed in black (replicated signature), *Theo. R. Davis;* printed in green, *H&Co.;* printed in blue, *DESIGN PATENTED/AUGUST 10TH 1880;* on side, polychrome eagle with American shield
1986.164.3

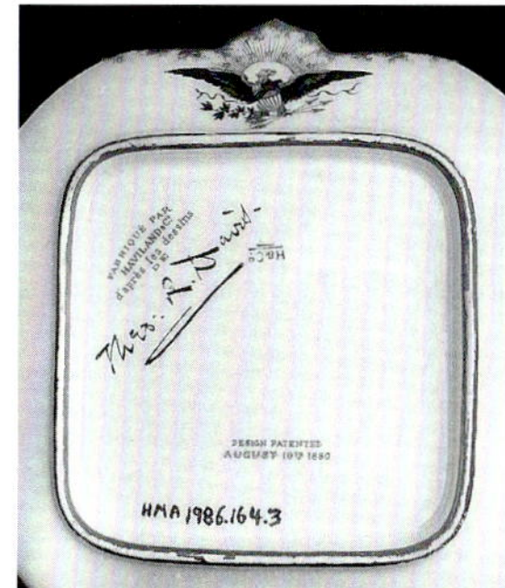

143.

Dressing Table, ca. 1880

New York
Maple, mahogany, white pine, marble, marquetry of mahogany and mother-of-pearl, silver-plated drawer pulls, brass, mirrored glass, and upholstered footrest with replaced velvet
86⅜ × 36 × 18¾ inches
1982.315

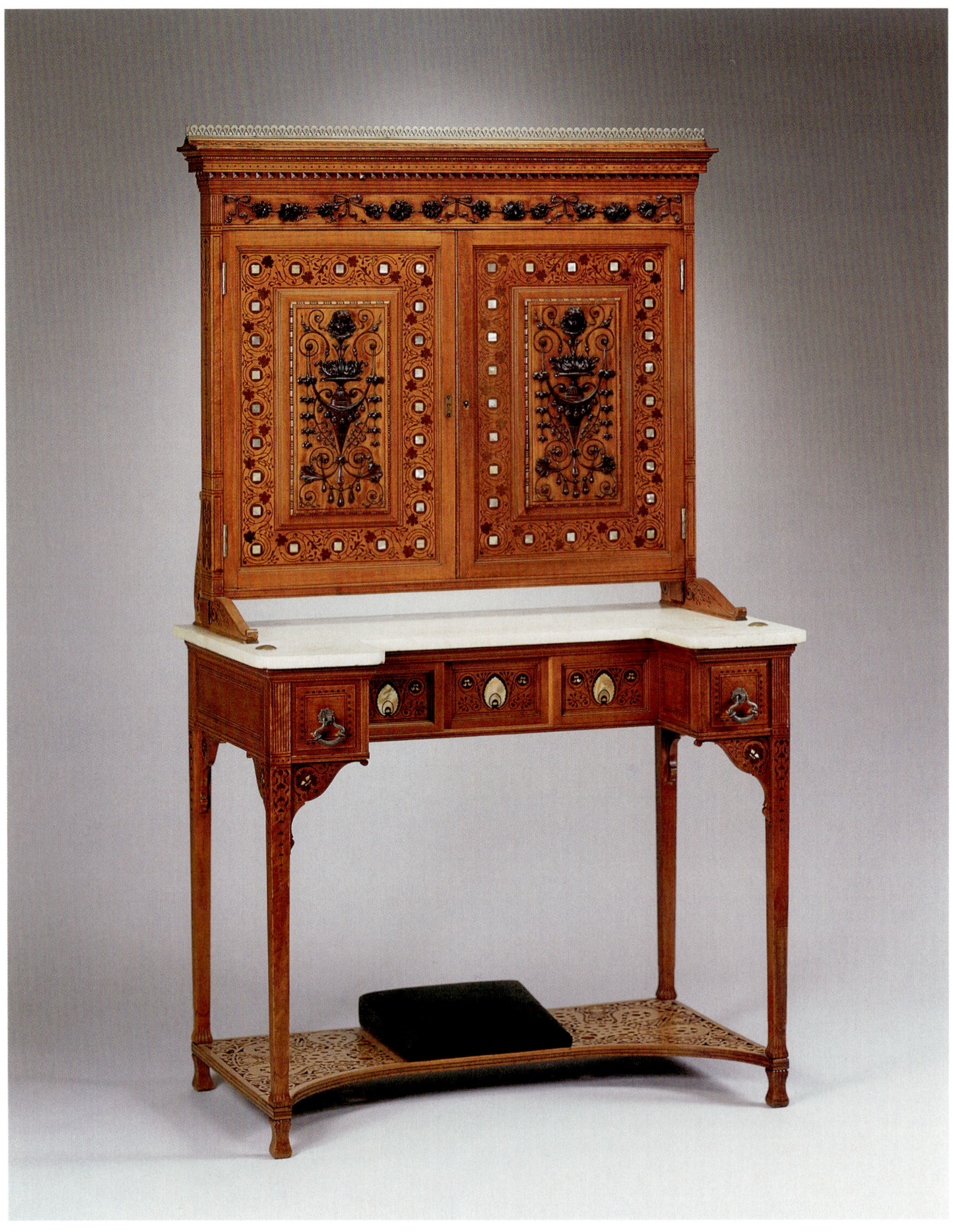

This dressing table matches the woodwork and furniture in a dressing room in the John D. Rockefeller house at 4 East 54th Street, now installed in its entirety in the Museum of the City of New York (fig. 1). Rockefeller purchased the furnished house in 1884 from Arabella Worsham Huntington, who had already remodeled it and had just married railroad magnate Collis P. Huntington. The Rockefeller room includes a full-length dressing mirror flanked by matching cabinets, a side chair, and a small vanity mirror on a table fitted with an upholstered footrest on its stretcher. The room's furnishings appear to be *en suite* with the dressing table, yet there is little space in the existing room that could have accommodated it.[1] The Crawford dressing table may have been commissioned by another client who knew the room.

Mrs. Huntington later told Mitchell Samuels of French and Company in New York that Pottier and Stymus had made furniture for the house. On January 21, 1884, prior to Rockefeller's purchase of the house, furniture maker and interior decorator George Shasty wrote to him, "I have furnished the house [at] 4 West 54th St. and can give you all the information you may desire should you contemplate buying." He wrote him again after the purchase on October 29: "We desire to state that the interior woodwork and decoration of your new residence (#4 West 54th St.) was designed and executed by us. We should be pleased to receive your order for any alteration or addition that you may require."[2] There is no documentation that Shasty did any work for Rockefeller directly. Shasty had earlier worked for Pottier and Stymus, which may further confuse the issue. In addition, Mrs. Huntington may have hired several different furniture and decorating firms for various rooms in the house when she remodeled, so the firm responsible for the dressing room and the Crawford dressing table remains uncertain.

The dressing table, with its beautifully carved and marquetried decoration, is similar in quality to pieces produced by leading New York firms of the time, including Herter Brothers and Herts Brothers. The classical decoration is organized more like that on the Herts cabinet (see no. 144) than the Herter furniture (see nos. 107–110) in the Crawford Collection. Mahogany and maple provide a striking visual contrast, enriched by inlaid mother-of-pearl. Carved mahogany flowers suspended by ribbon bows drape across the crest below the top molding and brass fretwork gallery, and the carved mahogany decoration on the maple door panels depicts a female head above an urn with scrolls, swags, leaves, and drops. The arrangement is symmetrical and delicately classical, and it might have been called Pompeian when it was created.[3] Frames around these panels are marquetried with mahogany scrolls and flowers around circles inlaid with mother-of-pearl squares. When the mirror-backed doors are open, they reveal a third mirror at the back. All of the mirrors are framed in marquetry of maple, mahogany, and mother-of-pearl, an expensive richness that would usually have been hidden. Marquetry drawer fronts with peacock feathers in mother-of-pearl and silver-plated drawer pulls add further opulence to the composition. The complex jigsaw-cut decoration around the upholstered footrest echoes the scroll patterns in the marquetry.

NOTES

1. Maher 1975, pp. 261–274, discusses Collis P. Huntington, Arabella Worsham, the remodeling of the house, and its sale to John D. Rockefeller. He also speculates on the maker of the period rooms from the house now at the Museum of the City of New York and the Brooklyn Museum of Art.

2. Ibid., p. 268.

3. Howe, Frelinghuysen, and Voorsanger 1994, p. 42, discusses the Pompeian influence in American interior decoration between 1860 and 1870. The decorative elements in wall paintings in the ancient city influenced wallpapers and interior design at the end of the eighteenth century and again in the second half of the nineteenth century. The carving on the dressing table is reminiscent of such decorations.

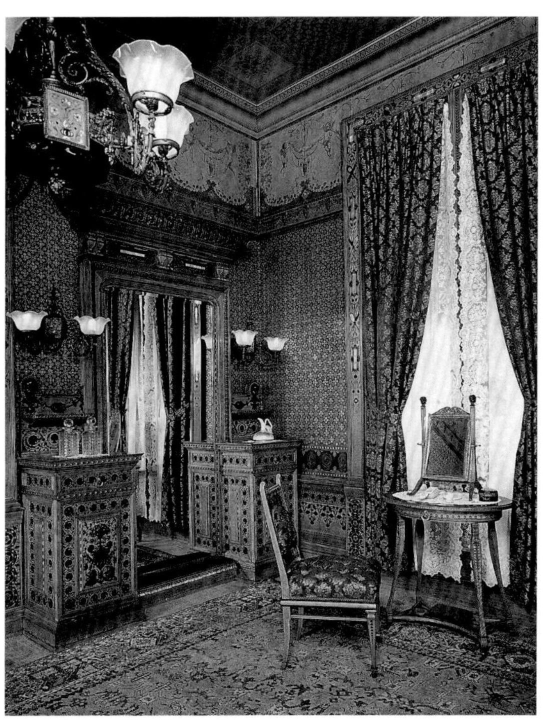

Fig. 1. Dressing room of the John D. Rockefeller, Sr., house, New York, 1880s. Museum of the City of New York.

144.

Cabinet, ca. 1880

Manufactured by Herts Brothers (1872–1937), New York
Rosewood, black walnut, ash, gilt brass, glass, and marquetry of mother-of-pearl, brass, copper, and pewter
59½ × 59¾ × 15¾ inches
Mark: Stamped on back, *HERTS BROTHERS/BROADWAY & 20STNY/ 8127*
1983.201

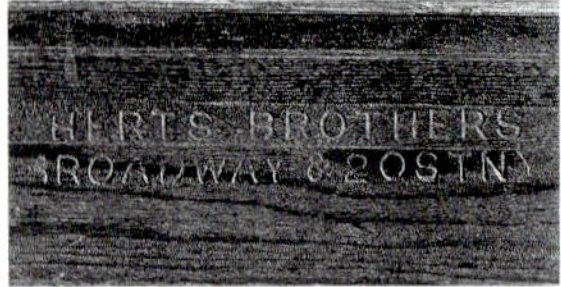

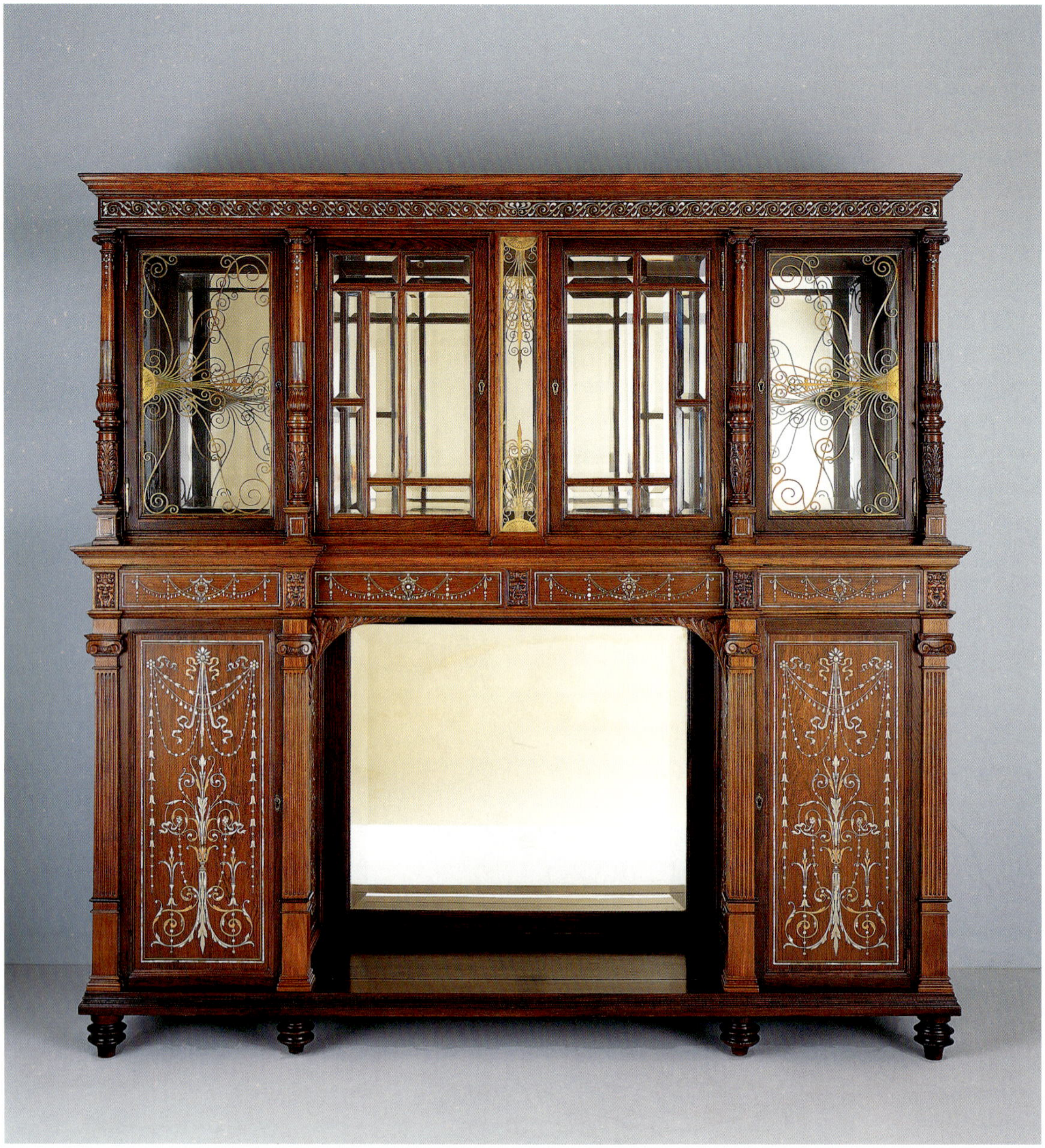

This Herts Brothers cabinet may have been made for the library of the William H. Vanderbilt house in New York, built between 1879 and 1882, although Herter Brothers has been credited with making the Vanderbilt furniture to the designs of Christian Herter, who supervised the project (see nos. 107–110). Swags of mother-of-pearl and metal marquetry across the front and sides of the Crawford cabinet resemble details in photographs of the library woodwork and the library table, which is now in The Metropolitan Museum of Art. To date, however, no photograph of the Vanderbilt library showing the Herts cabinet has been identified, and documentation of its inclusion in the commission is lacking.

The large Herts Brothers emporium at 20th Street and Broadway was near the Herter Brothers showroom at 18 East 22nd Street near Union Square. The enormity of the Vanderbilt commission, in addition to routine production at Herter Brothers, may have encouraged Christian Herter to hire other firms to produce his designs. Herts Brothers, a company with highly skilled craftsmen and a similar German heritage, would have been a likely candidate. Other possibilities are that Vanderbilt later commissioned the Herts Brothers cabinet to coordinate with the library's interior or that another wealthy client, familiar with the room, ordered the cabinet. As the provenance of the Crawford cabinet is unknown, none of these possibilities can be ruled out.[1]

The cabinet's design suggests that it was intended for display; it is a shimmering setting for extraordinary objects. The top section is at eye level and is glazed on three sides for enhanced presentation of its contents. The mirrored back made the cabinet an exhibition vitrine in which precious objects could be studied in the round. Below, shelved cupboards flank a mirrored central niche, possibly intended for an object or simply to reflect light. The cupboards might also have stored additional objects for rotation in the top display area or for study and comparison. The splendid marquetry on the sides and doors makes the cupboards and niche an elegant pedestal for the glazed top section and its contents. The display functions of the Crawford cabinet suggest that its original owner was a collector and connoisseur.

The exotic and extravagant materials used in the superbly crafted cabinet were meant to harmonize with the precious contents on display. The brilliant marquetry in rosewood incorporates lavish mother-of-pearl, copper, brass, and pewter and is a stunning exhibition of the *marqueteur*'s artistry. The pattern of marquetry swags and scrolls on the rosewood cupboard doors is repeated on the lower sides of the cabinet and on the inside panels of the central niche. The architectural elements of engaged columns and pilasters echo European Renaissance cupboards and give the cabinet the effect of a glittering strongbox. Even the scrolled brass screens are protective barriers for valuable objects. The locks, with their brass escutcheons, reinforce the sense of security in the top section.

If Herts Brothers followed the practice of Herter Brothers, the "8127" stamped with the maker's label was probably a factory code for keeping track of a specific commission and its ultimate placement in the house for which it was designed. Herts Brothers had been prominent in the New York furniture trade since it was established in 1872. Four years later, it exhibited at the 1876 Centennial Exposition in Philadelphia. In 1893, when the company displayed at the World's Columbian Exposition in Chicago, it published a brochure that included illustrations of its large store at 20th Street and Broadway and its factory at 104–110 East 32nd Street. The promotion called the company's business "ARTISTIC FURNITURE" and "INTERIOR DECORATIONS." In addition to furniture, Herts Brothers made architectural woodwork for interiors and bank and office fittings. The Herts Brothers store showed a "full and varied stock of RICH FURNITURE of their own special design and manufacture. CHOICE EXAMPLES of Upholstery Materials, Textile Fabrics, Fine Imported Paper Hangings, Fresco Painting and Stained Glass."[2]

NOTES

1. The Crawford cabinet is discussed and illustrated in Howe, Frelinghuysen, and Voorsanger 1994, pp. 77 and 214, fig. 57. The possibility that the Crawford cabinet was part of the Herter Brothers Vanderbilt commission is put forth in Hanks and Peirce 1983, p. 53, and in an unpublished manuscript by Marilyn Johnson, 1983, for a planned expansion of the Hanks and Peirce book, High Museum of Art document files. A marked Herts Brothers cabinet with related scrolled brass screens inside the glazings is in the Newark Museum. The cabinet was in the Ballantine House in Newark as early as 1885 or 1891. It was given to the Newark Museum by a Ballantine family member in 1950; see correspondence, Ulysses Dietz, curator of decorative arts, the Newark Museum, May 14, 1985, High Museum of Art document files.

2. The four-page circular that the firm published for the Columbian Exposition listed the Herts Brothers display in the Manufactures Building and was dated May 1893. The document is in the Winterthur Museum Library.

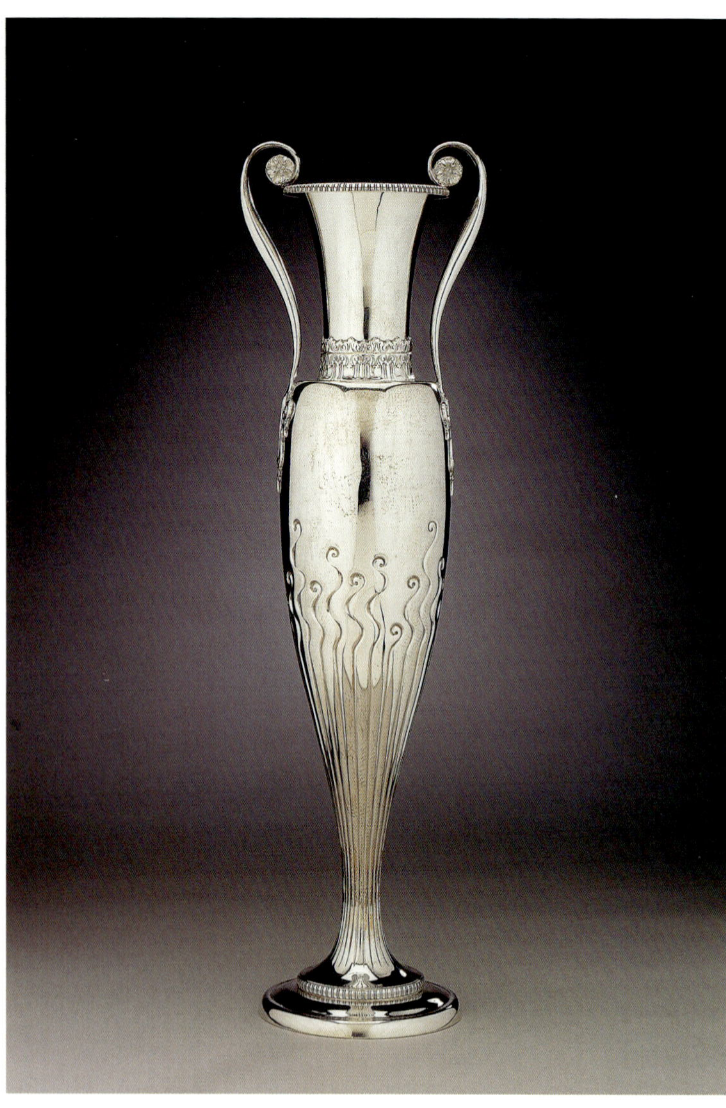

145.

Vase, designed 1891, made 1899

Made and retailed by Tiffany and Company (1837–present), New York
Silver
17¾ × 4¼ × 4¼ inches
Mark: Impressed on bottom, *TIFFANY & CO/11081 MAKERS1445/ STERLING SILVER/925-1000/T*
1984.144

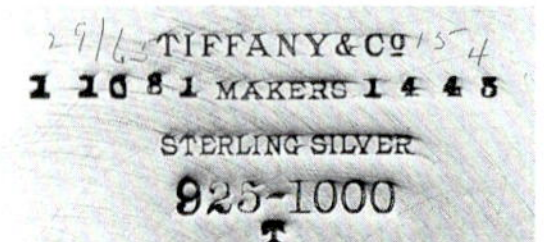

THROUGH ALL the historical revival styles, and even during the artistic and reform movements of the nineteenth century, classicism remained a major influence in design and taste. This Tiffany and Company vase represents an American interpretation of classical ornament toward the end of the century by a firm that was leading affluent American taste in the 1890s.[1]

Edward C. Moore, who supervised the design of Tiffany silver from 1851 until his death in 1891, may have participated in the creation of the Crawford vase. He worked in all of the styles Tiffany produced during that period, and although classicism was part of Moore's repertory, he is perhaps best remembered for his mixed-metal work in the Japanese taste (see nos. 96–99, 101–102). After his death, Moore's students John T. Curran and Paulding Farnham took over silver and jewelry design (see nos. 152–156); either one could have designed the Crawford vase.

The elongated urn shape of the vase, the gadrooning around the top edge, and the pair of ear-shaped handles terminating in scrolled rosettes are all derived from classical sources. The double-stepped base enhances the monumental scale of the vase. The decorative cast band around the neck consists of scrolls beneath classically inspired acanthus leaves. Chasing around the lower portion of the body begins as straight parallel lines to suggest reeding, but each line evolves into a separate sinuous entity that terminates in a scroll. The chased lines are similar both to the decorations on the Tiffany covered pitcher of nearly a decade earlier (see no. 101) and to the French Art Nouveau style, which was significantly influencing American design.[2]

NOTES

1. A pair of related vases is in the Museum of the City of New York, and one is illustrated and discussed in The Metropolitan Museum of Art 1970, no. 274. The vases were made for Harry Harkness Flagler in 1891.

2. The Tiffany and Company pattern books record the Crawford vase form as "Vase—Tall Greek," pattern number 11081 (which is included in the mark), created in 1891. The order number 1445, also in the mark, is recorded in the company order book in 1899, eight years after the design was created, demonstrating the longevity of its appeal. The production cost of the vase in 1899 was $33, while the chasing was an additional $16. Correspondence, Amy N. Northrop, curator, Tiffany and Company Archives, Parsippany, New Jersey, December 27, 1994, High Museum of Art document files.

THIS ORNATE side chair has intricately carved dolphin heads in its crest and colorful scrolled, ribboned, and floral marquetry.[1] The chair's diminutive size, splendid marquetry, and beautifully carved decorations can be compared to the Crawford side chair made by Herter Brothers for the William H. Vanderbilt house (see no. 109).

Besides the dolphin heads, the carving consists mainly of delicate leaves and stylized flowers, with ribbon bows at the top of each back slat. These carved motifs complement those in the marquetry decoration of the back's crest and the front seat rail. Circular holes at the top of the three vertical back slats and the tapering front legs enhance the chair's light and airy appearance, and the motif is repeated on the delicate turned balusters on the front legs, which each have a band of carved relief circles. The back flares slightly as the side stiles reach the carved dolphin-head terminals at the top. These interrelated design motifs contribute to the chair's unity of composition.

The high quality of craftsmanship and rich materials suggest that the Crawford chair was produced by an extremely fine furniture-making firm. In an eighteenth-century chair, the presence of ash as a secondary wood would have suggested a New York origin. However, by the late nineteenth century, improved transportation and wider availability of woods make the geographic origin more difficult to ascertain. The mixed-metal and mother-of-pearl marquetry is similar to that on the Herts Brothers cabinet in the Crawford Collection (see no. 144), and throughout the 1860s and 1870s, marquetry of this quality was executed in New York by Alexander Roux, Kimbel and Cabus, Herter Brothers, and others (see nos. 61, 69, 107–110).

NOTE

1. In 1985, an identical chair was located in Colorado that had belonged to a family "from the east"; see correspondence, Dr. David Curry, curator of American art, Denver Art Museum, October 15, 1985, High Museum of Art document files. The central carved acanthus in the crest is a replacement, according to a conservation report by Rudy Colban at Antique Restoration, Monsey, New York, December 21, 1979, High Museum of Art document files.

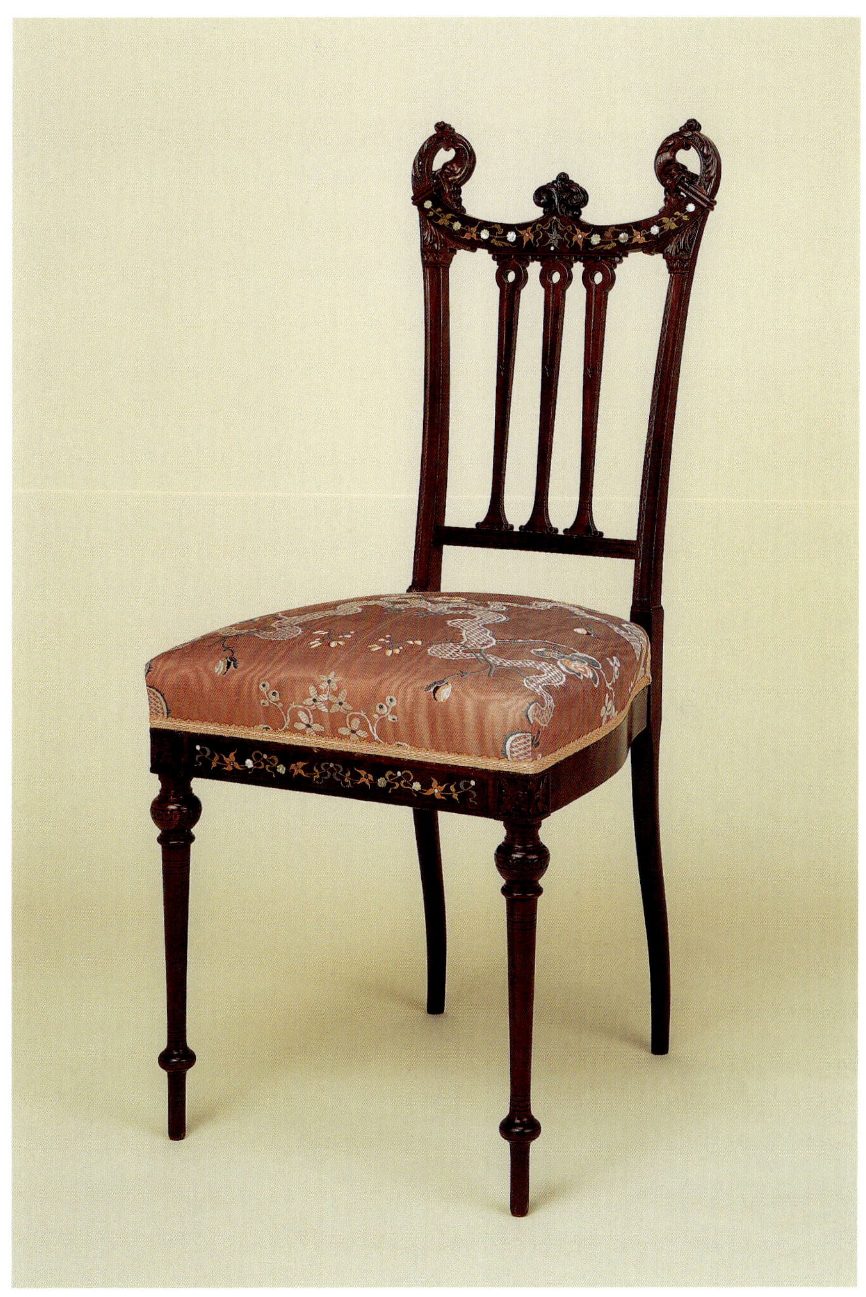

146.

Side Chair, 1885

Probably New York
Mahogany and mahogany veneer on ash with marquetry of mother-of-pearl, brass, copper, pewter, and chestnut; modern replacement silk upholstery
38¾ × 17¼ × 19½ inches
1981.1000.58

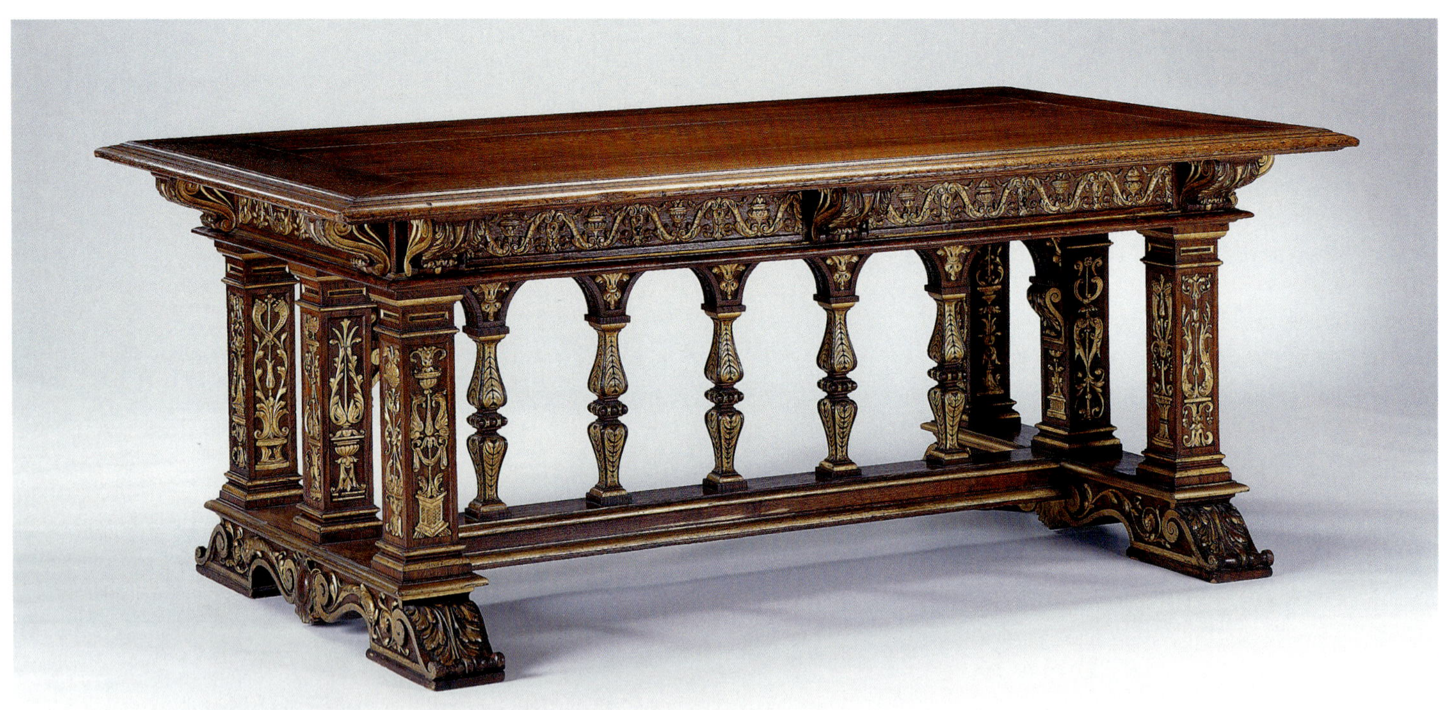

147.

Table, ca. 1890

Probably New York
Oak and aspen with gilt decoration
29 × 41⅜ × 70¾ inches
1983.202

The term "Renaissance" was widely used to describe architecture and furniture during the last third of the nineteenth century. Like other historical revival styles of that period, Renaissance usually referred to classical architectural details that were loosely interpreted to suggest European styles from the fifteenth through the seventeenth centuries. Even as late as the end of the nineteenth century, the word appeared in descriptions of objects and buildings that were completely contemporary in scale, massing, and execution. The Crawford library table, however, was intended to be a more historically accurate recreation. It was part of a larger trend by architects, designers, and their clients, who saw themselves as part of what was called the American Renaissance, beginning after the 1876 Centennial Exposition in Philadelphia and lasting into the first three decades of the twentieth century.

Admiration of genuine Renaissance art and architecture was encouraged by American designers and architects who had studied in Europe. Urban Americans, made wealthy by the Civil War and subsequent industrial development, also traveled to Europe to see international expositions, museums, churches, and palaces in search of worldliness and sophistication. Old Master paintings and antiquities, or copies of them, were often collected by these aspiring Medicis and housed in private palaces along New York's Fifth Avenue, in affluent new suburbs, and at resorts such as Newport, Rhode Island. True to the eclectic decorating style of the period, the taste of collectors was not confined to European Renaissance objects but also included Oriental, Near Eastern, and even American colonial artifacts, which inspired furniture makers to reproduce or more accurately adapt antique styles.[1]

The form and details of the Crawford library table are characteristic of this late-nineteenth-century taste for more rigorous interpretations of historical furniture. It is beautifully constructed, with great attention to detail. The meticulous relief carving is gilded, and the decoration on each side of the square-column legs is completely different. The table, finished on all four sides, was intended to stand impressively in the center of a reception room or library. The designer, maker, and provenance of the table are unknown. It was found in Newport in the early 1980s, where it was reported to have come from a member of the Vanderbilt family.

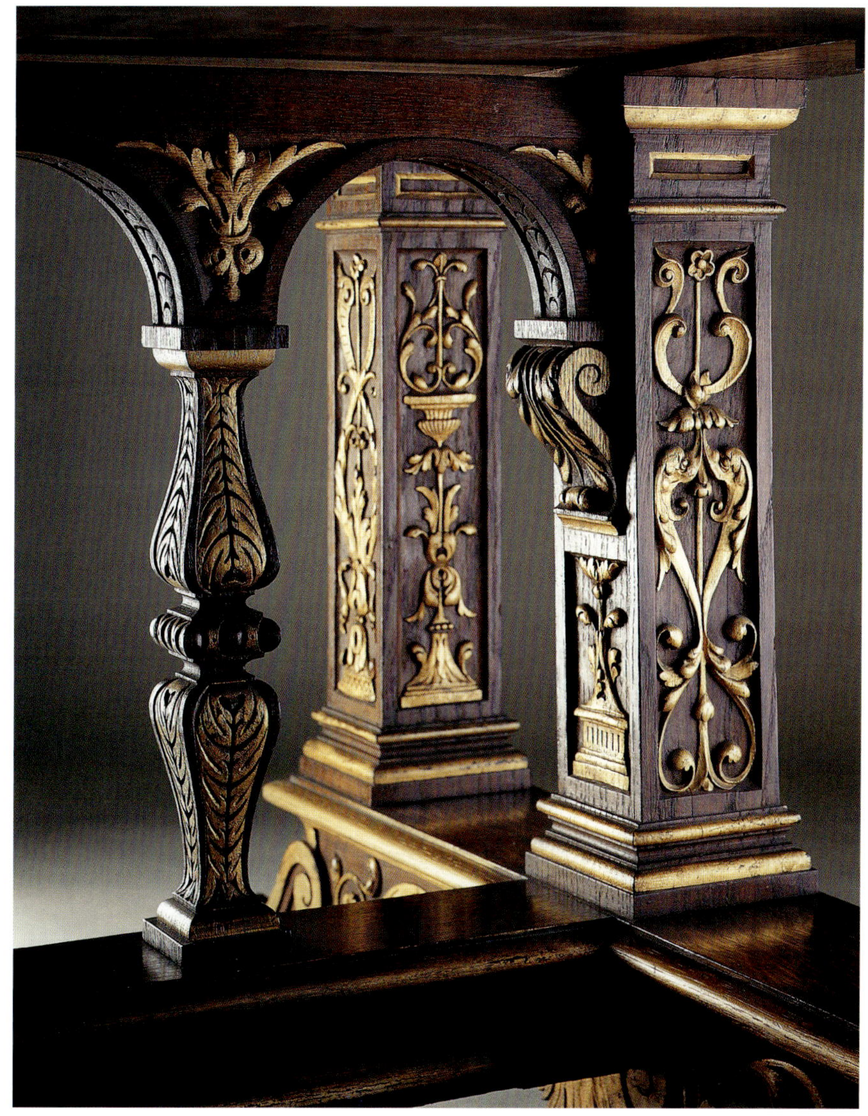

NOTE

1. The eclectic decorating style and more accurate interpretations of historical furniture are discussed and illustrated in Brooklyn Museum 1979, pp. 110–151.

148.

Vase, 1889–1894

Manufactured by Ceramic Art Company (1889–1906), Trenton, New Jersey; decorated by L. S. Harmon
Porcelain
18¼ × 7¾ × 7¾ inches
Marks: On bottom, an artist's palette over a circle enclosing *CAC* over *BELLEEK;* on front of vase, near figure's foot, *L.S.HARMON*
1993.127

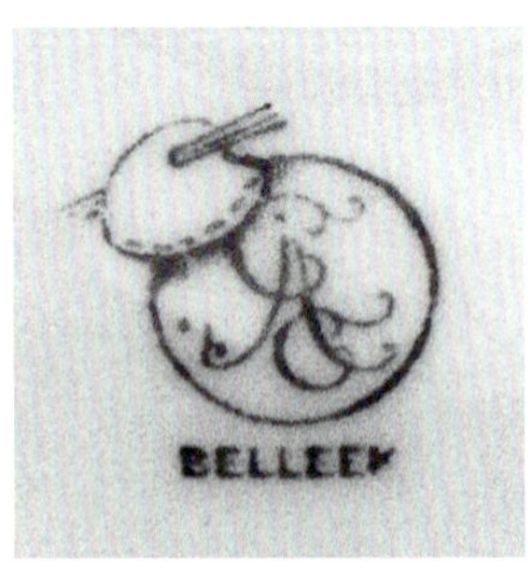

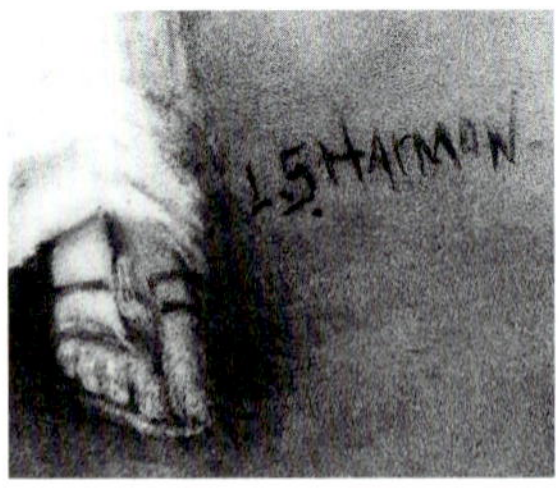

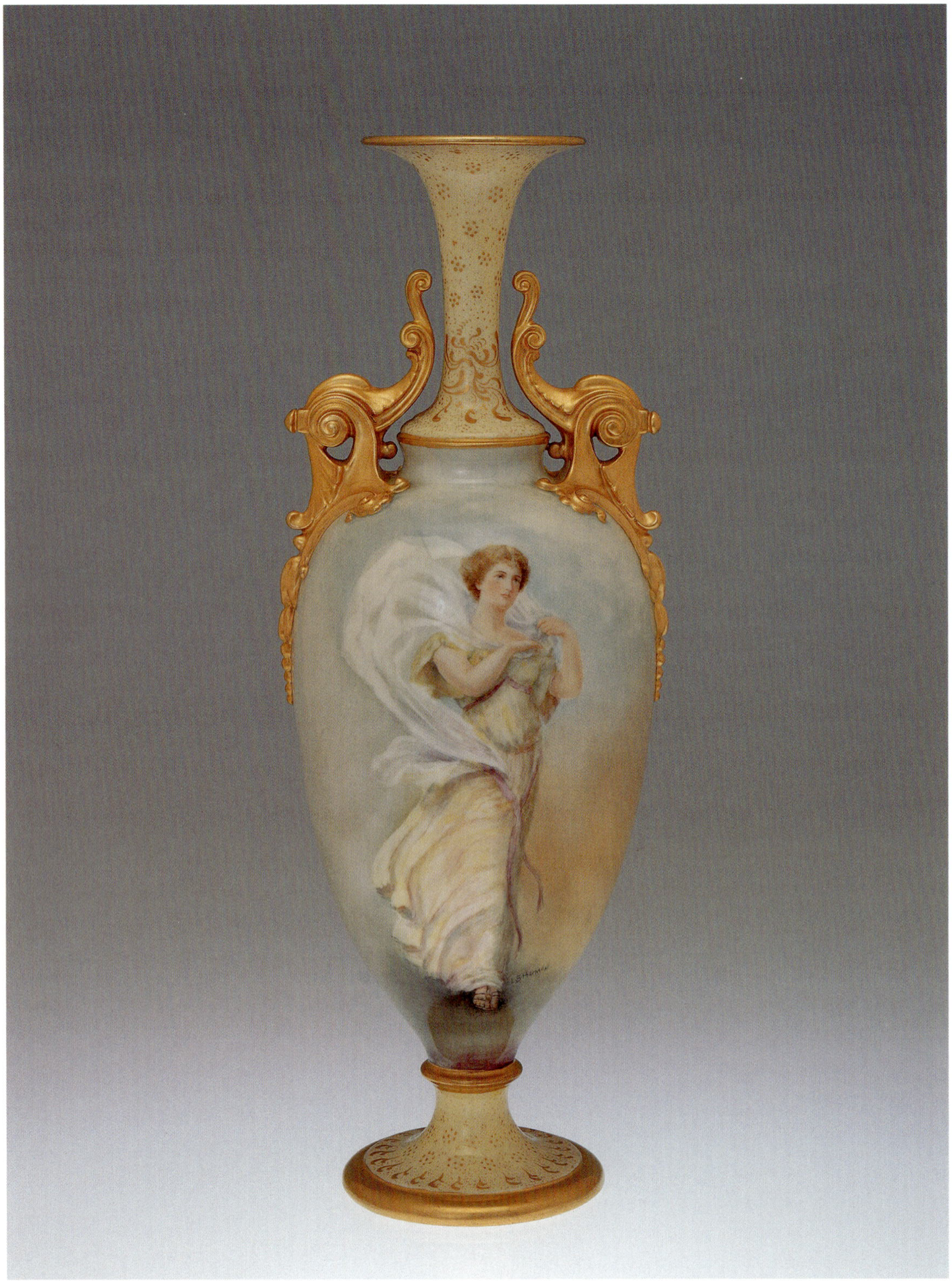

THIS BELLEEK-TYPE porcelain vase was made by the Ceramic Art Company, which its founders envisioned as an art pottery, unlike other Trenton ceramic manufacturers.[1] Walter Scott Lenox had hoped to become an artist, and as a teenager he had sought decorating work in Trenton's ceramic industry, but the field was filled with immigrant workers. While unsuccessful in becoming a decorator, he gained practical experience in ceramic production and business and received some art training. Later, he headed the decorating departments for Trenton's Ott and Brewer (see nos. 115–117) and Willetts Manufacturing Company, and contributed to their introduction of Belleek-type porcelains.

In 1889, Lenox and Jonathan Coxon, Sr., established the Ceramic Art Company. Coxon, who had worked at Ott and Brewer and other Trenton potteries, managed the factory, while Lenox was in charge of decoration. The new firm prospered in the face of adversities that had led to the closings of Ott and Brewer and Willetts Manufacturing Company: the economic depression in the early 1890s; competition from the ceramic industry in East Liverpool, Ohio; labor unrest; and a fuel shortage. By maintaining a small facility and focusing on art wares, the company avoided the labor problems that plagued other Trenton manufacturers.

The Ceramic Art Company's mark, an artist's palette, indicated the founders' dedication to aesthetic pursuits. Retailers showed samples available for order, and the company published a catalogue of its wares in 1892. Only the outlines of the various blanks it produced were shown, since the decoration—whether done by amateurs or by the staff of company artists from England, France, Germany, and Japan—was always unique.

No other work is known by L. S. Harmon, who signed the Crawford vase, but he may have been an independent decorator, since his name has not been otherwise associated with the Ceramic Art Company. The rendering of the classical maiden on the vase suggests that Harmon was a trained artist rather than an amateur. This classical taste in artistic goods, which coincided with the Japanese taste, is evident on the Crawford cabinet decorated by Will Hicok Low in 1884 (see no. 95). Gilding on the European-inspired molded handles became more common on American art porcelains in the 1890s.

By the turn of the century, American taste and the market were changing, and Lenox's failing eyesight made him less involved in decoration of the wares. In 1906, the Ceramic Art Company became Lenox, Incorporated, and its emphasis changed from decorative wares to dinner services.

NOTE

1. The Ceramic Art Company is discussed in Barber, *Pottery,* 1976, pp. 235–238; and Frelinghuysen 1989, pp. 48–50. Denker 1989, pp. 3–32, is the most comprehensive study of Lenox, Incorporated, and the Ceramic Art Company.

149.

Desk, ca. 1895

Retailed and possibly manufactured by Paine's Furniture Company (1835–mid-1980s), Boston
Oak, white pine, and brass
57½ × 30½ × 18 inches
Marks: On oval paper label on back of desk, *PAINE'S/FURNITURE COMPANY./MANUFACTURERS AND IMPORTERS/OF/FINE FURNITURE/48 Canal St. and/141 Friend St./BOSTON./MASS./NO.*; on torn rectangular paper label on back of desk, . . . *N. CO.,/BOSTON./NO. 3228*
1995.187

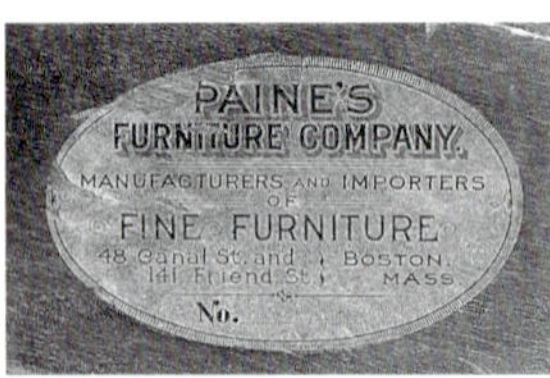

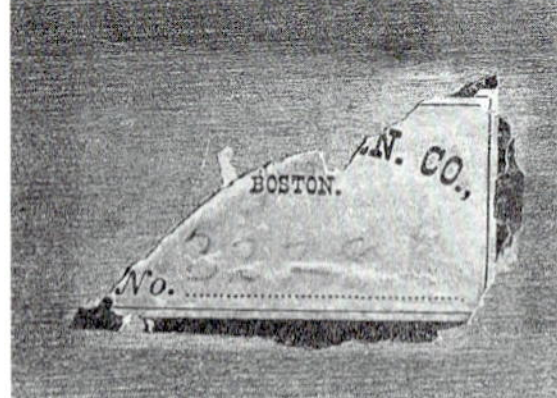

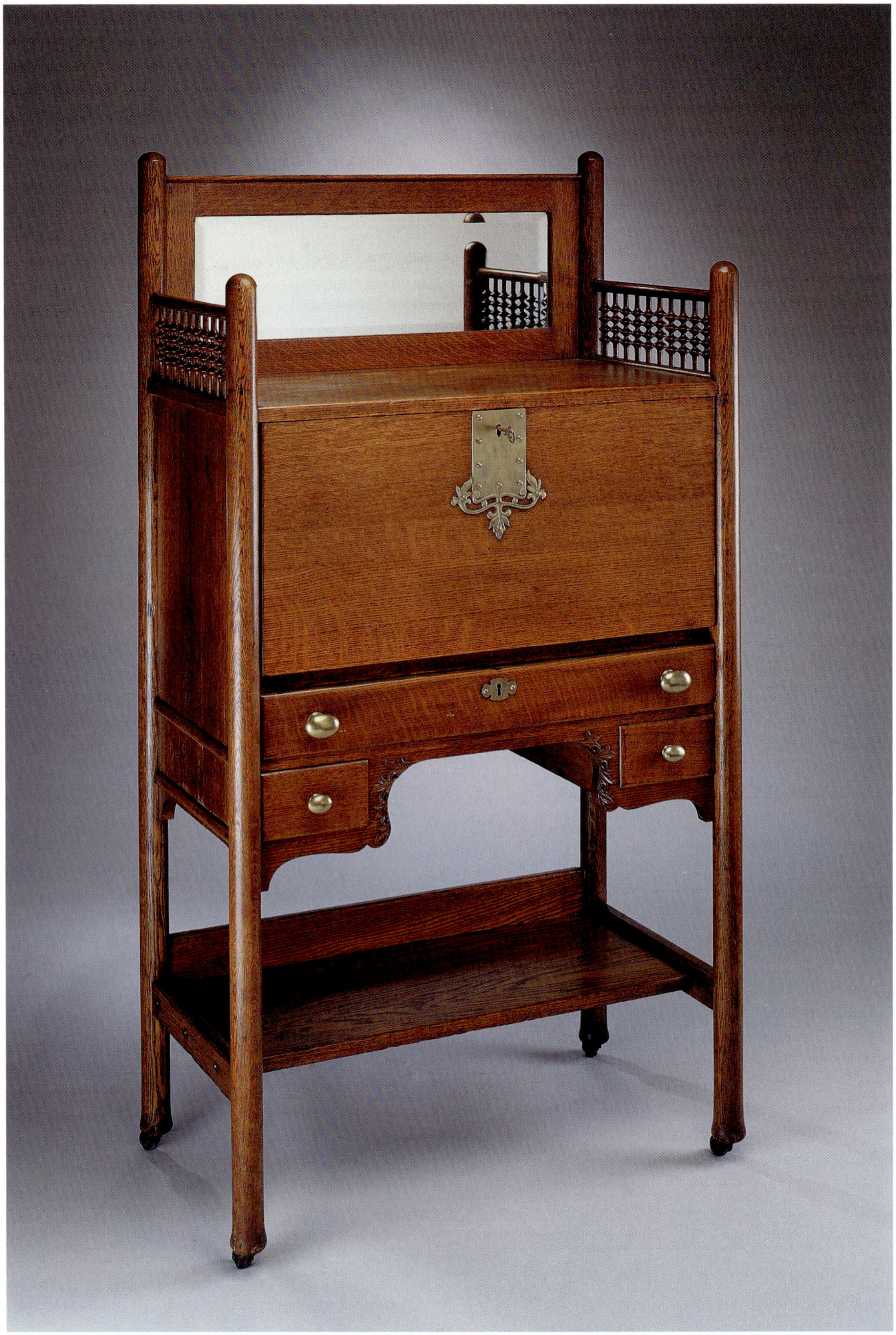

PAINE'S FURNITURE COMPANY was a leader in the Boston furniture trade when it sold, and possibly made, this elegant desk in the Crawford Collection.[1] The company served Boston and much of New England. Leonard B. Shearer began his furniture enterprise in the city, near Blackstone Square, in 1835. At first, he depended on off-season labor from the rural home workshops of New England farmers to supply goods for his Boston store. In 1845, he hired John S. Paine, probably a cabinetmaker, to travel and purchase furniture for the store. Paine then began selling; he traveled both west and south, where he marketed furniture for Shearer and established important contacts for the firm. Around 1852, the firm constructed a factory in Boston so that it could manufacture its own stock rather than purchasing it from farmers and jobbers. The firm greatly expanded, hiring crews and equipping its factory with the latest woodworking machinery.[2] In 1854, Paine married Shearer's sister, and the two men entered a partnership as Shearer and Paine. Soon after, they opened branch houses in New York, Chicago, and New Orleans.

After Shearer was killed in an accident in 1864, Paine assumed control, closed the distant outlets, and consolidated his business in Boston and New England. Leaving his brother George in charge, Paine spent a year in Europe to establish contacts with manufacturers, and in 1870 the company built a new, expanded store at 48 Canal Street.

By the time Paine's Furniture Company sold the Crawford desk, the firm had greatly reduced its manufacturing and had focused on selling furniture, much of it from Grand Rapids, Michigan, and other furniture-making centers outside Boston.[3] Paine's Furniture Company apparently marked furniture it sold as well as furniture it made. A fragment of a label reading "... N. CO., BOSTON." suggests that the Crawford desk may have been made by another Boston firm but sold by Paine's.

The desk demonstrates the popularity of oak in American furniture in the 1890s, which reached its peak in the American Arts and Crafts movement at the turn of the century. The vertical and horizontal rectangles of the desk and the thin legs that extend to form corner posts demonstrate an awareness of the simple and straightforward designs of the English reform movement. The turned spindle railings on either side of the desktop are reminiscent of the English Queen Anne style popular in American domestic architecture at the time, but they also may have been inspired by turned elements on seventeenth-century American oak furniture. Colonial American furniture had been collected at least since the 1876 Centennial Exposition in Philadelphia, especially in New England. By the 1890s, reproductions and adaptations of colonial forms were being incorporated into new furniture and architectural designs.

The elongated, undulating curves of the apron contrast with the overall straight lines of the desk and complement the subtle swelling at the bottoms of the legs and the shapes of the drawer and fall-front brasses. These subtle elements, especially the brass lock plate on the fall-front desk door, indicate the influence of European Art Nouveau. While characteristic of the simpler nineteenth-century Boston taste in furniture, the desk conveys a sophisticated awareness of contemporary European art.

NOTES

1. The history of Paine's Furniture Company is recounted in an unpaginated booklet published by the company to celebrate its centennial in 1935; see Paine's Furniture Company 1935. The firm is also discussed in two articles about furniture in nineteenth-century Boston; see Cooke 1980, pp. 91–93; and Seidler 1982, p. 78.

2. Seidler 1982, p. 78.

3. The centennial brochure records the leaders of the company at about the time the desk was made. Shearer's son, William L. Shearer, worked at Paine's after completing his education. Paine's son, James L. Paine, entered the firm in 1881. In 1885, John S. Paine, William L. Shearer, George Francis Draper Paine, and James L. Paine incorporated as partners under the name Paine's Furniture Company. After the eldest Paine's retirement in 1895, G. F. D. Paine assumed presidency of the firm, with W. L. Shearer as vice president and J. L. Paine as treasurer. Ibid., p. 78.

150.

Armchair and Ottoman, ca. 1895

Possibly Texas
Steer horns and leather
Armchair: 33½ × 42½ × 27 inches
Ottoman: 7½ × 16¼ × 16½ inches
1989.137.1–.2

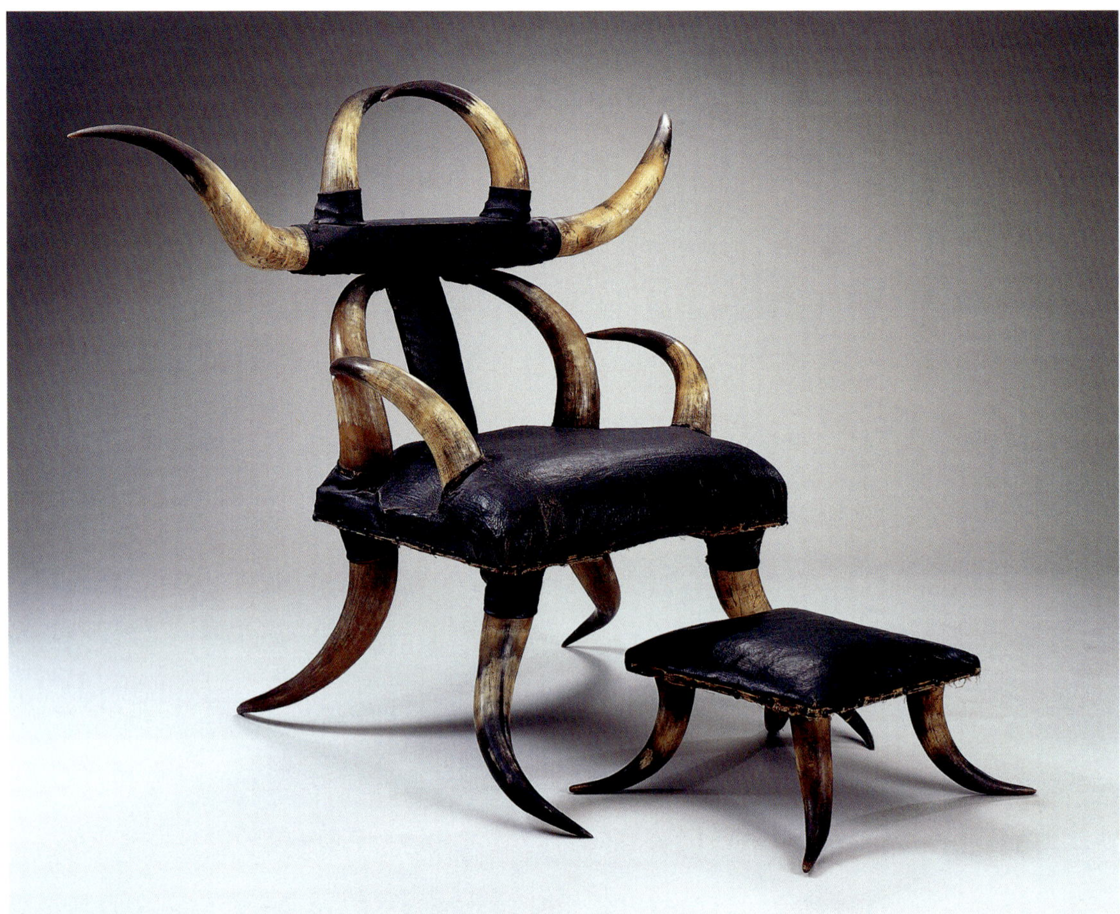

THIS FLAMBOYANT armchair and ottoman were part of a fashion for horn furniture at the turn of the century. The Wild West shows of Buffalo Bill Cody played to large audiences in eastern and midwestern cities, and longhorn furniture evoked the romance of the American cowboy. Even England's Queen Victoria and Kaiser Wilhelm I of Germany owned examples.

Horn furniture dates back to sixteenth-century German hunting lodges. In 1853, a Bohemian cabinetmaker named Wenzel Friedrich immigrated to San Antonio, Texas. His business expanded when he began to make furniture out of Texas steer horns, and by 1889 he had published an illustrated catalogue to meet the widespread demand for his unusual tables and chairs.[1] It is unlikely, however, that the Crawford armchair and ottoman were made by Friedrich. The illustrations in Friedrich's catalogue show designs that were considerably more complex, and his elaborate upholstery was luxurious. With few exceptions, the ends of the horns on Friedrich's furniture were tipped, unlike the Crawford example, to protect clothing. There were other horn furniture makers in San Antonio and elsewhere in Texas, and undoubtedly amateurs were turning out this furniture as well. The Crawford armchair appears more delicate than most Friedrich chairs. This lightness is enhanced by the wide span and upward-turned tips of the pair of horns that make up part of the crest. By the late 1880s, the longhorn steer drives from Texas to Kansas were ending, replaced by railroad transportation. With the end of the drives, longhorn furniture became a nostalgic symbol for a passing way of life in Texas.

NOTE

1. Texas longhorn furniture and Wenzel Friedrich are discussed and illustrated in "Artistry in Horn" 1984, pp. 93–94; and St. John 1981, pp. 60–61. A page from Friedrich's 1890 catalogue is reproduced in Hanks 1981, p. 96, fig. 75.

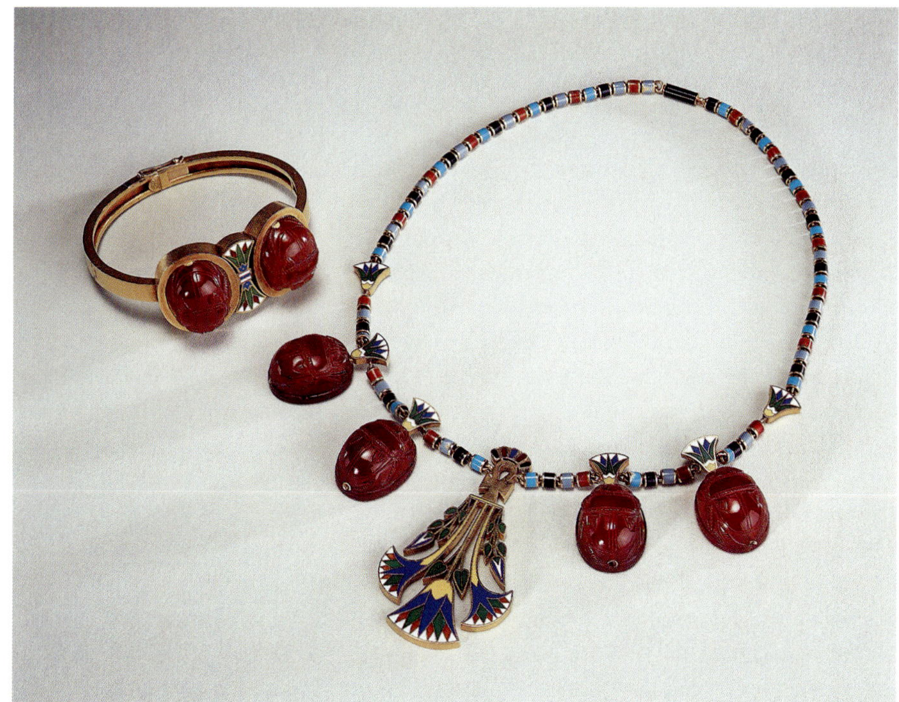

151.

Necklace and Bracelet, ca. 1903

Theodore B. Starr Company (1877–1923), New York
Yellow gold, enameled gold barrel beads, and engraved carnelian scarabs
Necklace: Length 16⅜ inches
Bracelet: 1 × 2⅜ × 2½ inches
Mark: On plaque on bracelet, *T. B. STARR/N.Y.*
EL 8.1998.1–.2

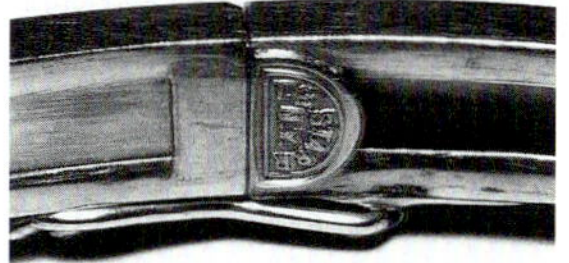

BORN IN New Rochelle, New York, Theodore B. Starr began his long career in New York's elite retail jewelry trade as a messenger boy in 1853. He later worked for the jewelry and watch importers Reed, Taylor and Company and then Peckham, Merrill, Fitch and Company. In 1862, Starr opened his own retailing company. He was joined by Herman Marcus two years later, and the company became Starr and Marcus, a jewelry manufacturing and retailing company. Marcus had trained with the court jeweler in Dresden, before immigrating to New York to work for Tiffany and Company (see no. 41) and Ball, Black and Company (see no. 56) in the 1850s. The Starr and Marcus display at the 1876 Centennial Exposition in Philadelphia received acclaim, especially for its cameos. A year later, Marcus returned to Tiffany and Company, and Starr bought out his partner's share, operating under his own name.

In 1882, the Theodore B. Starr Company opened a large store at 206 Fifth Avenue, which was at the corner of 26th Street and extended through to Broadway. At the time of Starr's death in 1907, his son incorporated the business. In 1918, the company's stock was sold to the silver firm Reed and Barton, although Starr's son continued to operate a retail store at Fifth Avenue and 47th Street until 1923.[1]

The Crawford necklace and bracelet are made of yellow gold with polychromed enamel Egyptian motifs to complement the engraved carnelian scarabs, which the company or client probably imported from Egypt.[2] American romantic interest in Egypt (see nos. 72–75) dates from after the Civil War and continued into the 1920s. This fascination was spurred by archaeological digs supported by such institutions as Boston's Museum of Fine Arts, The Metropolitan Museum of Art, and the Brooklyn Museum of Art, which were collecting and exhibiting Egyptian artifacts at the turn of the century.

NOTES

1. For historical accounts of the Theodore B. Starr Company, see Fales 1995, pp. 282, 421–422. Proddow and Healy 1987, pp. 37, 80–81, and 84, also provides a history with illustrations of the firm's work on pp. 18–19. Janet Zapata refers to the firm in "Two Centuries of American Jewelry," her introduction to Christie's catalogue *American Jewelry,* October 21, 1992, unpaginated.

2. Tiffany and Company had been using colored enamels to decorate jewel-like silver and silver-gilt tablewares since the 1870s, especially in the exotic tastes (see nos. 98, 102, 153 in this catalogue). Proddow and Healy 1987, p. 84, notes that the Theodore B. Starr Company advertised a product line of jewelry in the Egyptian style just prior to their closing in 1923.

Tiffany and Company Silver at the Turn of the Century

These Tiffany and Company objects from the early twentieth century demonstrate the wide range of luxury products made and sold by America's most prestigious emporium at the time. They also illustrate the diverse sources used by Paulding Farnham, the company's head designer from the late 1890s to 1908. After the death of his mentor, longtime chief designer Edward C. Moore (see nos. 96–99, 101–102), Farnham became the firm's head jewelry designer. Typical of his work is the rich decoration on his pieces in the Tiffany display at the 1900 Exposition Universelle in Paris, which included the Crawford bowl (no. 152) based on Native American basket forms and decorations.[1]

Farnham was at the creative center of Tiffany at the turn of the century. He had come to the firm in the late 1870s or early 1880s, scion of an old New York family and nephew of Charles T. Cook, special assistant and successor as president to founder Charles Louis Tiffany. Early in his association with the company, Farnham trained at the so-called "Tiffany School" that Moore had established for promising young designers at the firm's production center on Prince Street. Farnham rose quickly through the ranks, becoming a special assistant by 1885, a member of the board of directors in 1888, and director of the company's jewelry division by 1893. He designed silver and gold presentation pieces in the early 1890s and continued to design jewelry after becoming head designer in the late 1890s.

As head designer for Tiffany, Farnham supervised the design and manufacture of all the firm's displays for the 1900 Exposition Universelle in Paris. A contemporary account described his creations, in which "every race indigenous to the soil has been made to offer tribute in the form of

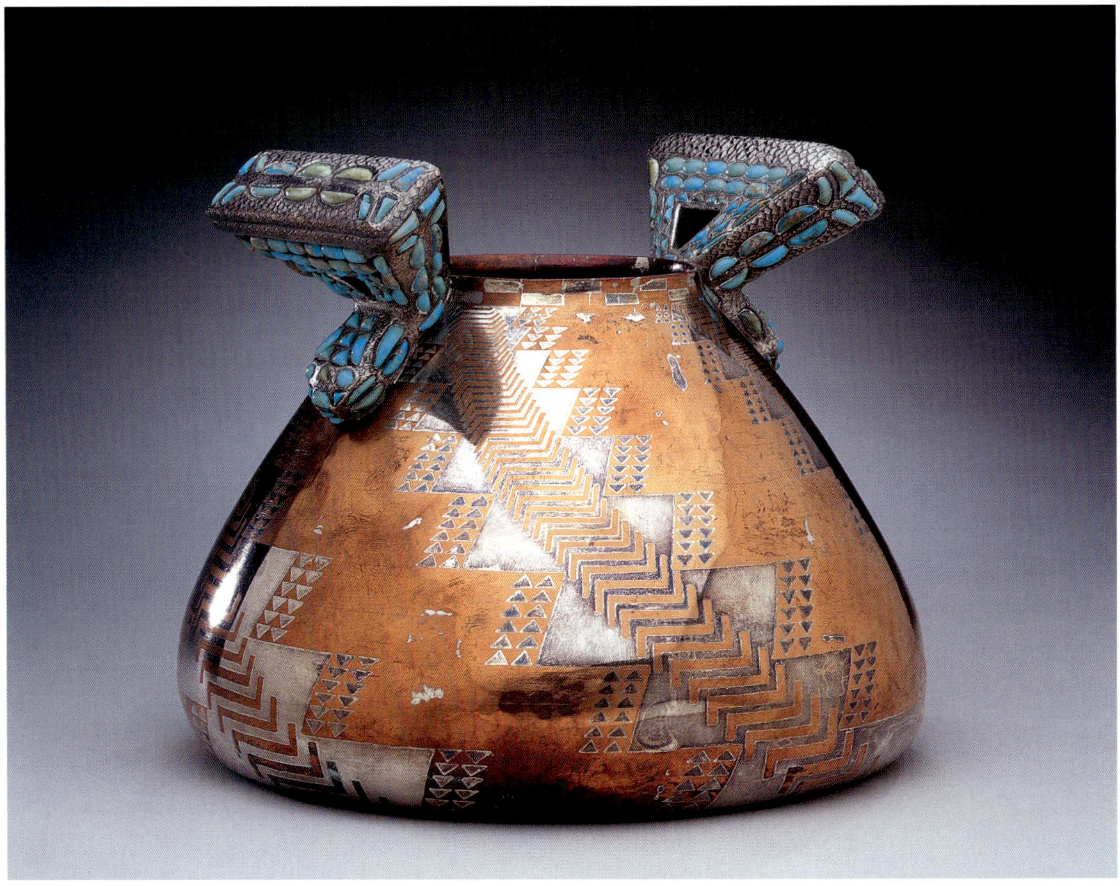

152.

Bowl, 1900

Made by Tiffany and Company (1837–present), New York; designed by Paulding Farnham (1859–1927)
Silver, copper, and turquoise
7½ × 8¾ × 8¾ inches
Mark: Impressed on bottom, *TIFFANY & CO/13362 MAKERS 3/ STERLING SILVER/OTHER METALS/ 8 ½ PINTS* over peacock and feather
1984.170

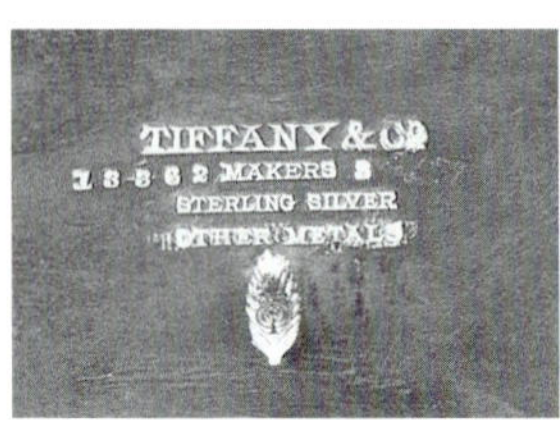

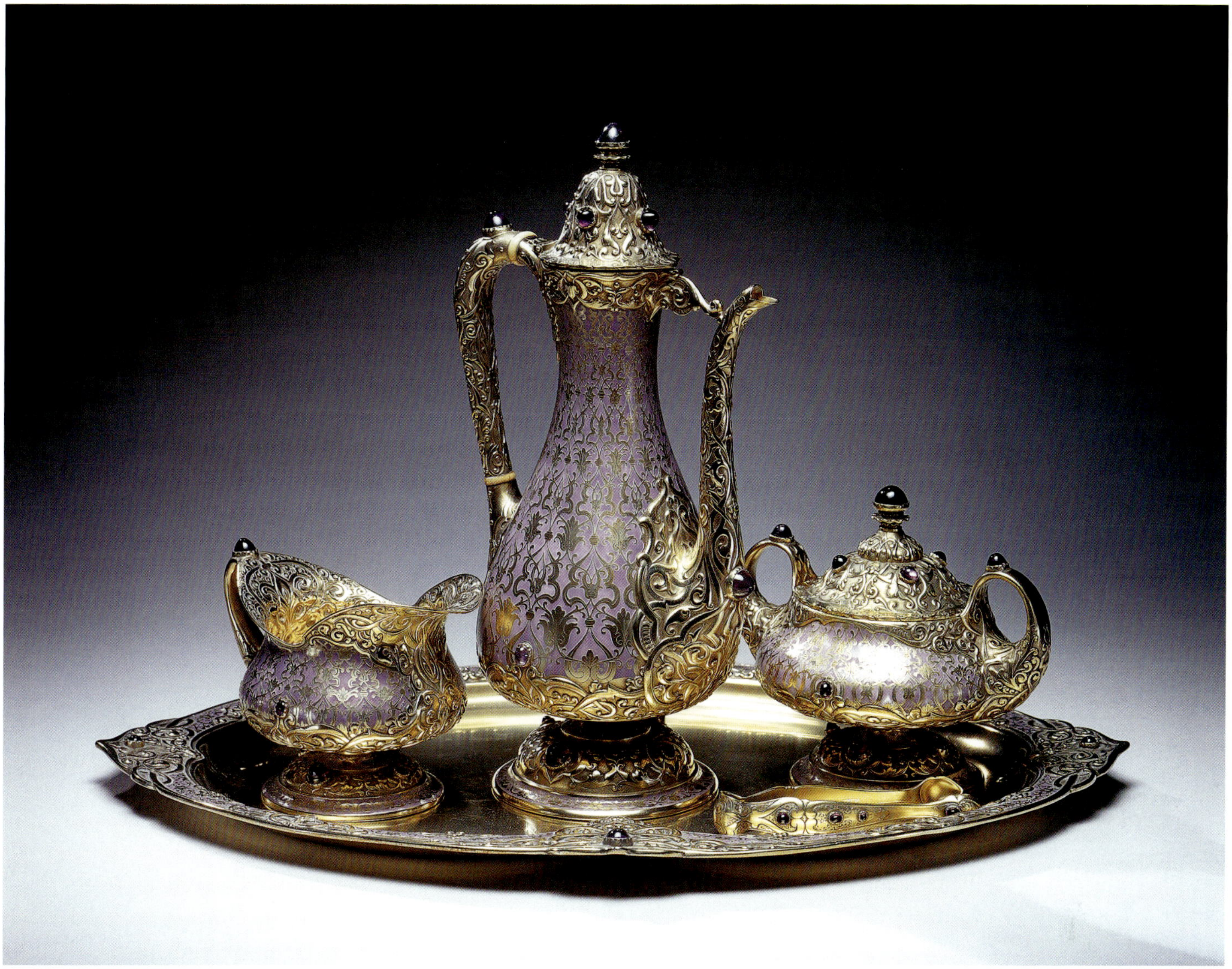

153.

Coffee Set, 1902–1903

Made by Tiffany and Company (1837–present), New York; designed by Paulding Farnham (1859–1927)
Silvergilt (gold-plated silver), enamel, amethysts, and ivory
Coffeepot: 10¾ × 6 × 4¼ inches
Cream pitcher: 3¾ × 4¾ × 3¾ inches
Sugar bowl: 4¾ × 5½ × 4½ inches
Tray: 1 × 11⅝ × 16½ inches
Tongs: ⅝ × 4¼ × 1½ inches

Marks: Coffeepot: Impressed on bottom rim, *TIFFANY & CO MAKERS STERLING SILVER/1 ½ PINTS*
Cream pitcher: Impressed on bottom, *TIFFANY & CO/15311 MAKERS 5180/STERLING SILVER/925-1000/T/2 GILLS*
Sugar bowl: Impressed on bottom, *TIFFANY & CO/15311 MAKERS 516/STERLING/925-1000/2 ½ GILLS*
Tray: Impressed on top, *TIFFANY & CO/15557 MAKERS 5180/STERLING SILVER/925-1000/C*
Tongs: Impressed on inside, *TIFFANY & CO STERLING*
1984.168.1–.5

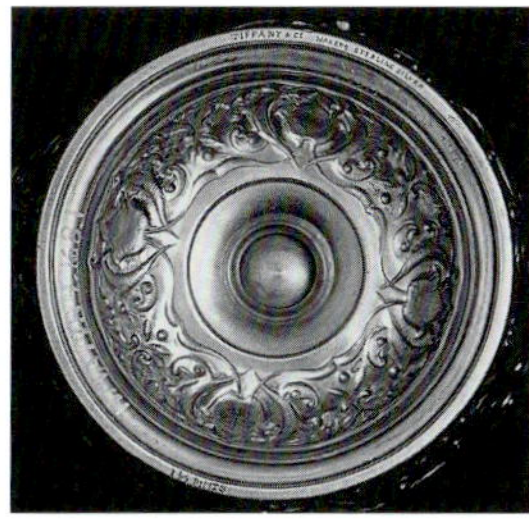

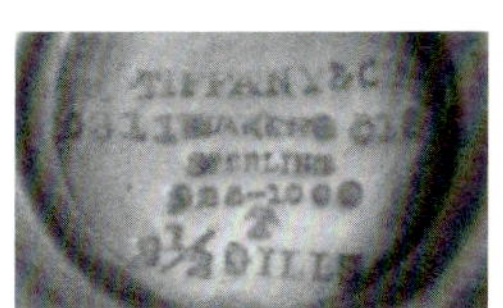

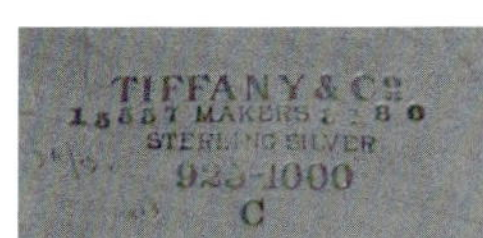

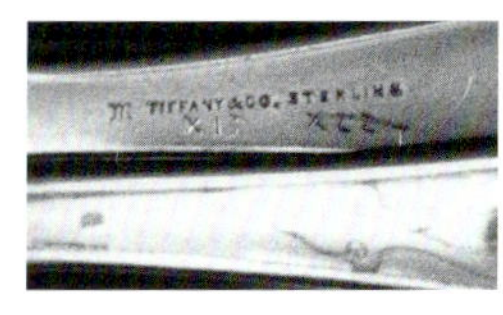

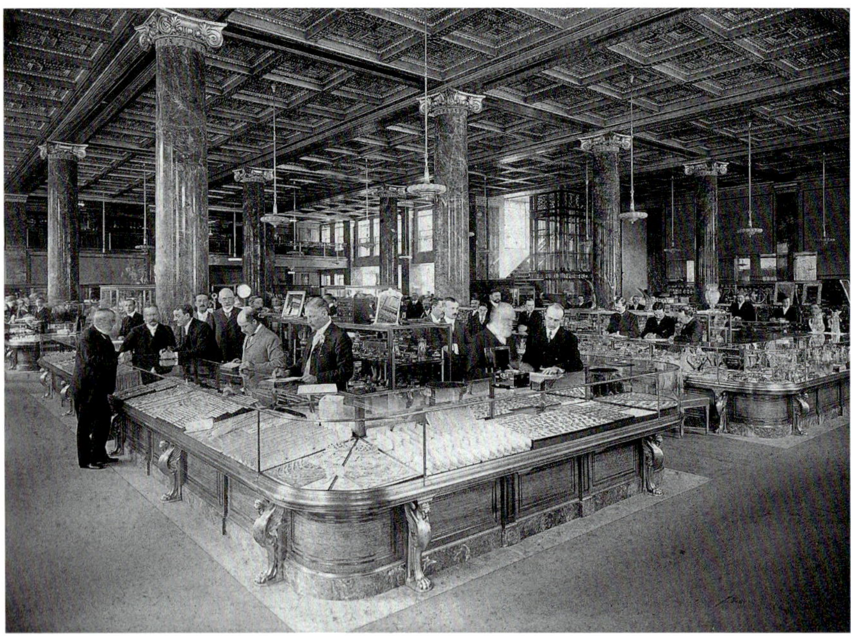

Fig. 1. Interior of the Tiffany and Company Building, ca. 1906. Copyright Tiffany and Company Archives 1999.

models or decorative schemes."[2] The Crawford bowl was one of three in the Paris exhibition that were inspired by Native American forms. A contemporary description accompanying a photograph of the bowl reads, "Large copper bowl: hammered out of one piece, inlaid with silver after some of the Southern Indian basket workers: the ornament represents a flight of birds as is often seen from the waters of the south. The handles are composed of conventional rattlesnake heads, and bodies, set with American turquoise from Arizona."[3]

Farnham was also inspired by classical and Renaissance styles, but this bowl provides another aspect of his design vocabulary. Using Native American art as a source was innovative in 1900; earlier silver from the 1870s had depicted Native American themes, but not art forms.[4] Farnham's jewel-like effect on the bowl, its motif, and handles added new possibilities to European design sensibilities at the Exposition Universelle.

Farnham's background as a jewelry designer is also evident in the Islamic-style coffee service (no. 153). Purple enamel, gold strapwork, silver-gilt (gold-plated sterling silver), and amethysts produce a glittering presence. Farnham's inspira-

154.

Casserole, 1905

Made by Tiffany and Company (1837–present), New York; designed by Paulding Farnham (1859–1927)
Silver
5½ × 13½ × 10 inches
Mark: Inscribed on bottom, *TIFFANY & CO/16175 MAKERS 770/ STERLING SILVER/925-1000/C*
1993.140

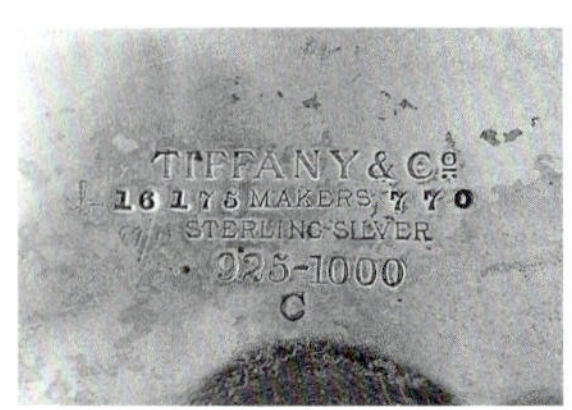

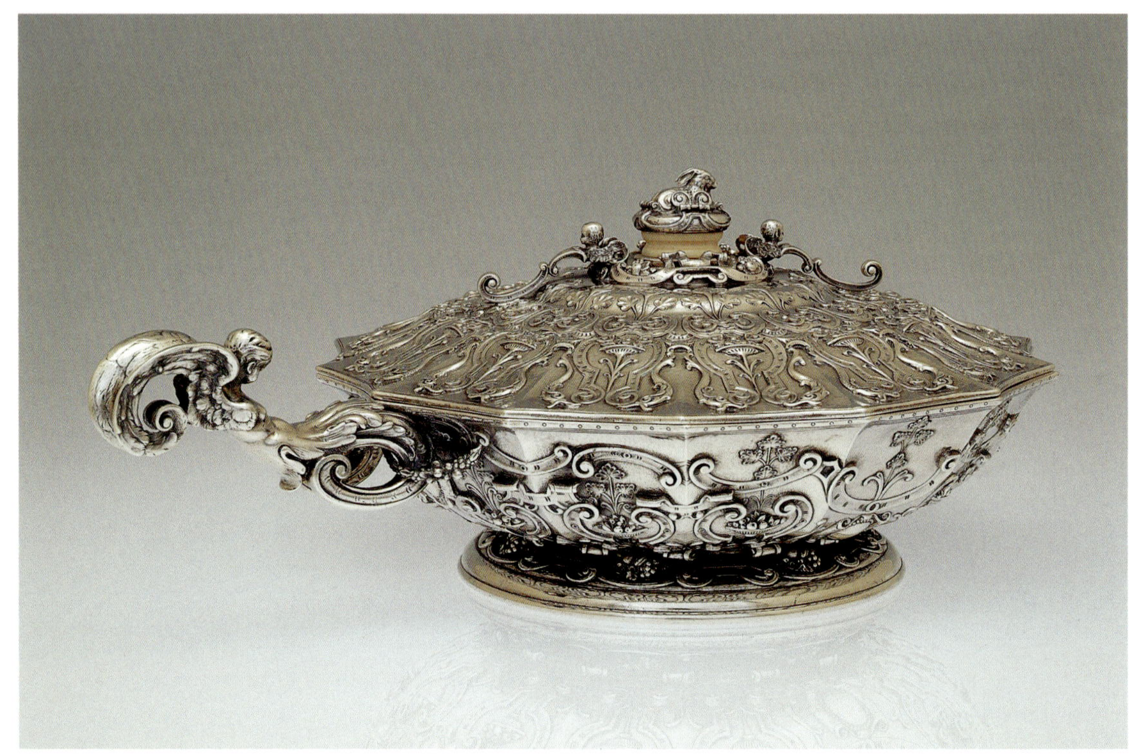

tion was European and Russian jewelry, as well as Near Eastern taste. He had worked in enamel on silver vessels as early as 1889, and with his mentor Moore had created realistic enameled orchids for the 1889 Exposition Universelle in Paris. Farnham may also have been inspired by the Russian enamels imported by Tiffany in the 1890s and by the works created by Russian artist Peter Carl Fabergé for the 1900 Exposition Universelle.[5]

The coffee service was listed in the Tiffany pattern book as "Islamic," and was made in March 1902. The tray was made the following January to match the service. Surviving drawings for the coffee service stipulate chasing in the silvergilt beneath the amethyst knob set in the hinged lid of the coffeepot.[6] The rich purple enamel complements the amethysts mounted throughout the service. Cast silvergilt was used in the spout and the bracket linking it to the pot, and in the handles of the coffeepot, sugar bowl, and cream pitcher. The repoussé strapwork arabesques and the shaped lids of the coffeepot and sugar bowl emulate features in Islamic architecture. The service was intended for coffee, a beverage associated with Turkey, which made the Islamic style an appropriate choice. The intimate scale of the service suggests that it was used for after-dinner coffee in small portions.

The Renaissance silver pattern was introduced by Farnham at the 1904 Louisiana Purchase International Exposition in St. Louis.[7] Farnham expanded on his Renaissance tea service from the World's Fair by creating a casserole and other serving forms in 1905. The Crawford casserole (no. 154) is made completely of silver, and the texture of the bold strapwork brilliantly

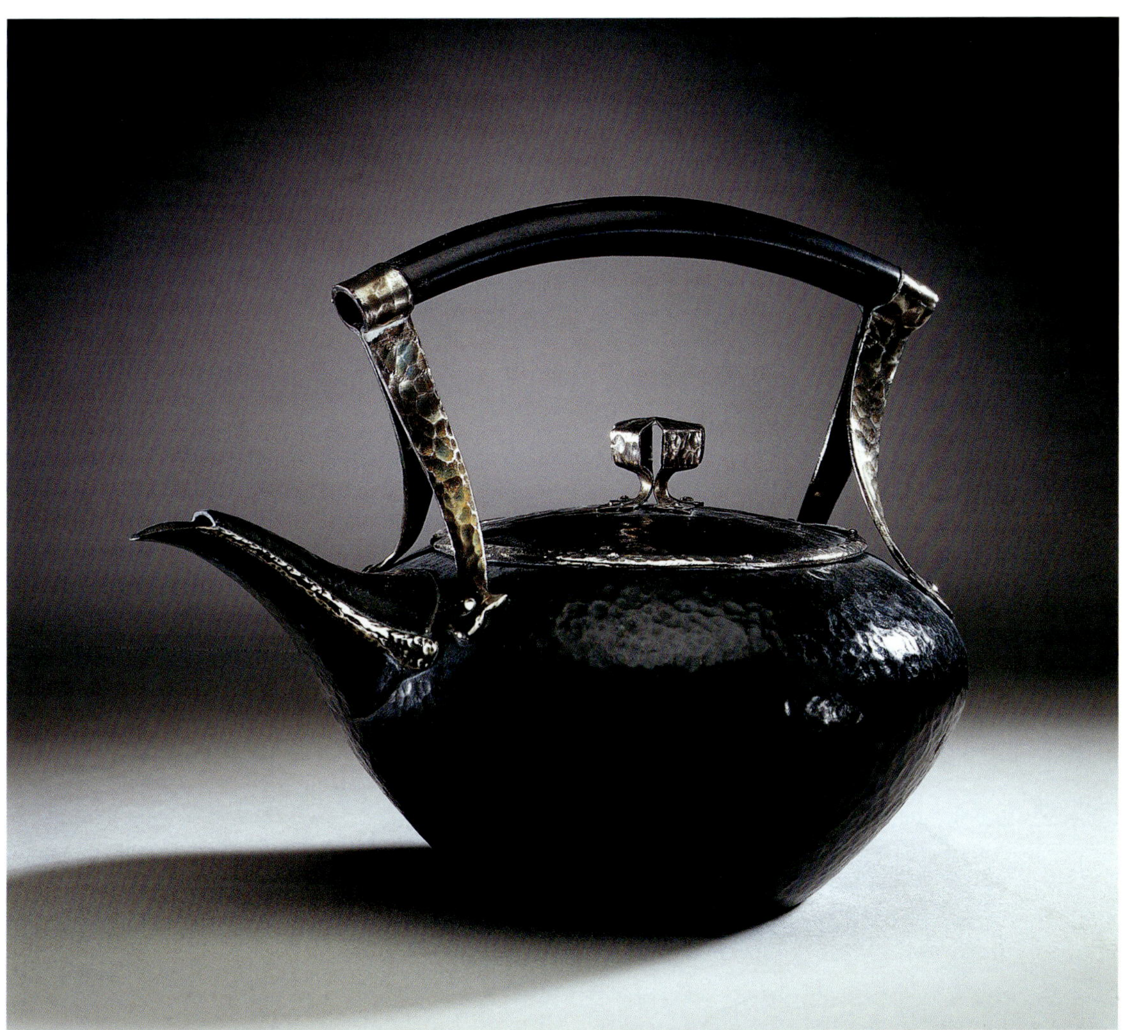

155.

Teapot, 1902–1907

Tiffany and Company (1837–present), New York
Cast iron, silver, and ebonized wood
6 × 7½ × 6 inches
Mark: Impressed on bottom, TIFFANY & CO/MAKERS/SILVER AND/OTHER METALS/C/1 ½ PINTS
1982.307

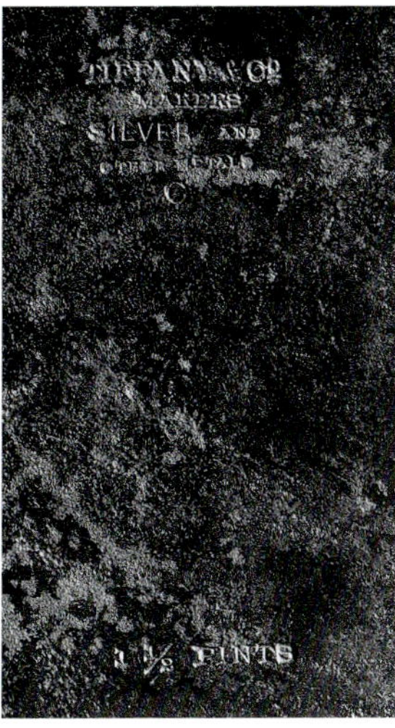

156.

Goblet, 1907

Tiffany and Company (1837–present), New York
Gilt metal
7½ × 4¼ × 4¼ inches
Mark: Stamped on bottom, *TIFFANY & CO*
Inscription: Around foot, *Engineers: Club: December: 9th: 1907*
1988.222

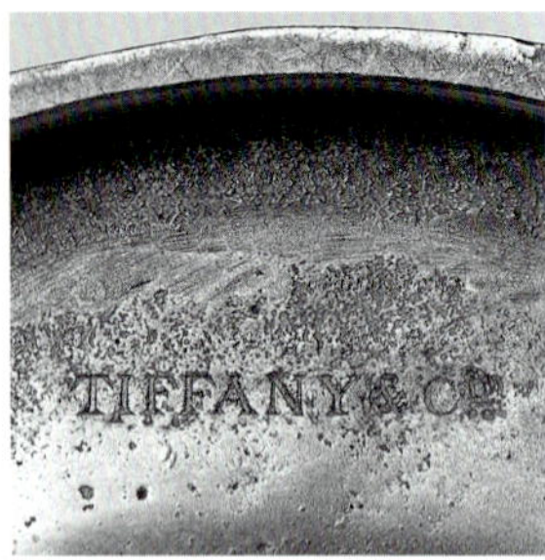

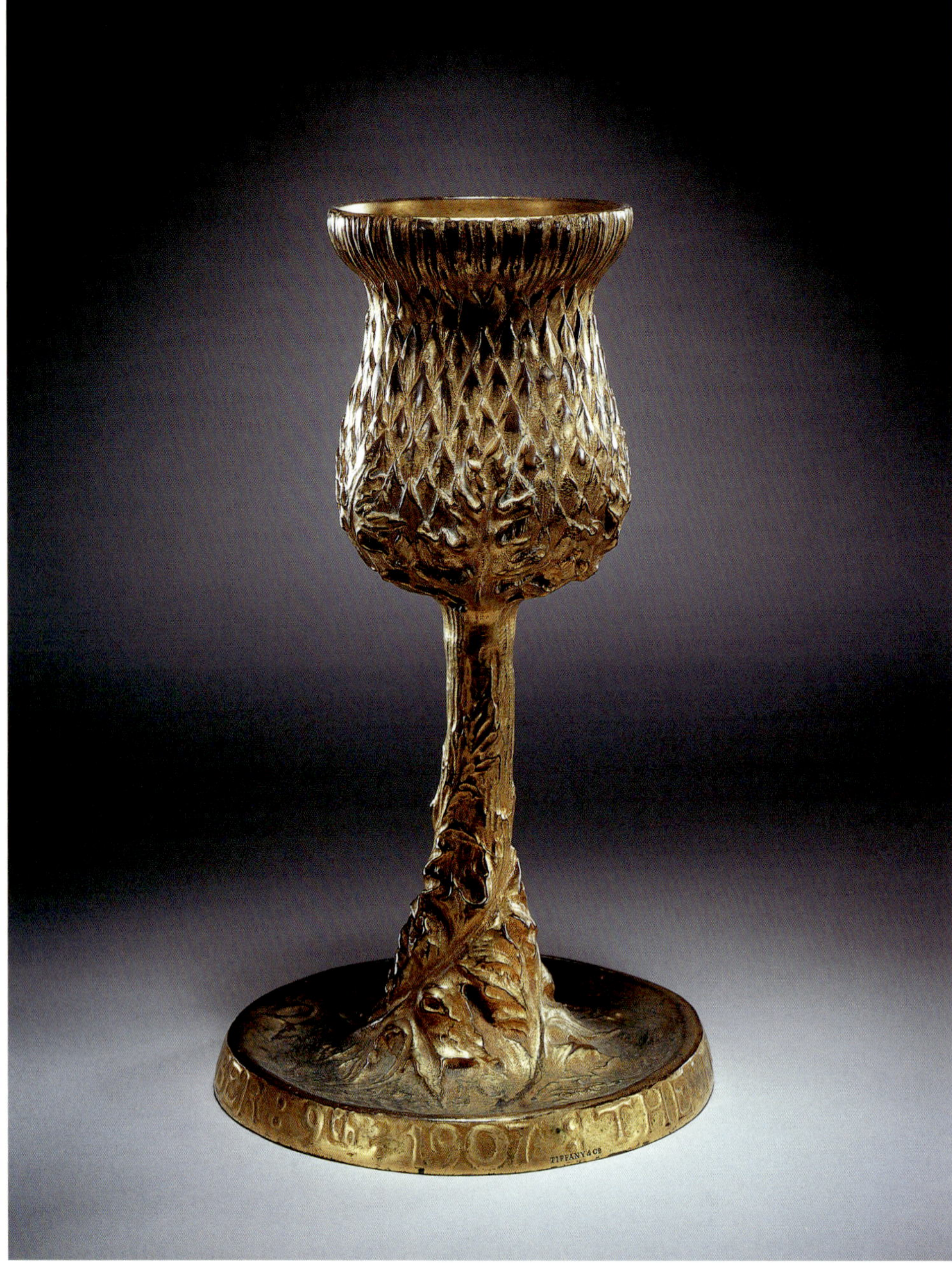

reflects light. Farnham also incorporated winged heads derived from Renaissance art and architecture. The cast silver rabbit finial suggested the possible contents of the casserole.

The Asian form of the cast-iron teapot with silver mounts (no. 155) provides evidence of how long the Japanese taste lasted in America, promoted by Tiffany and Company since the late 1870s (see nos. 96–102). The teapot has the hand-hammered surface of earlier Japanese-taste silver and is made of mixed metals. No pattern number is in the mark, and no designer or specific date of manufacture can be traced. The "C" underneath the company mark is the initial of Charles T. Cook, the firm's president from 1902 to 1907, so the pot can be dated to within a five-year period. The teapot's subtle elegance demonstrates the vast design and production range of the company in the early twentieth century. The simple combination of silver and iron is a counterpoint to the rich mix of silver, copper, and turquoise on the basket bowl and to the gilded silver, amethysts, and enamel of the Islamic coffee service. The rugged, hand-hammered iron and the pot's simple form would have appealed to adherents of the Arts and Crafts movement.

Tiffany and Company created the toasting goblet (no. 156), cast in metal and then gilded, for the opening dinner of the new headquarters of the Engineers' Club at 32 West 40th Street in Manhattan on December 9, 1907. Industrialist Andrew Carnegie had funded the club's new building, and the goblet's thistle-shaped bowl honored him by commemorating his Scottish heritage.[8]

Farnham's involvement in designing the Crawford teapot and goblet cannot be documented. Louis Comfort Tiffany became vice president of the firm after his father's death in 1902, and his strong tastes influenced subsequent output. After the 1907 death of Farnham's uncle, Charles T. Cook, he left the company for independent artistic pursuits.

NOTES

1. Carpenter 1997, pp. 24–26; and Venable 1994, p. 40. The Crawford bowl is illustrated and discussed in Venable 1994, pp. 196–197, fig. 6.66; and in Zapata, April, 1991, p. 724, pl. VII. Zapata, March, 1991, pp. 556–567; and Zapata, April, 1991, pp. 718–729, give a general background on Paulding's work for Tiffany and Company.

2. Zapata, April, 1991, pp. 722–724.

3. Tiffany and Company records refer to the bowl as a "Hupa Indian Basket." The Hupa, or Hoopa, are a tribe in northern California. It is possible that the Hopi, a Southwestern people, were meant, since the piece seems based on a southwestern form and incorporates turquoise from Arizona. Correspondence, Tiffany and Company Archives, December 27, 1994: "The number 3 listed after *MAKERS* in the mark refers to the fact that this bowl was the third in a series of three inlaid bowls of different design made for the Exposition Universelle." The company's pattern book lists the bowl in an entry dated March 16, 1900. Production costs amounted to $613, of which $226 was charged to the jewelry shop, at least partially for setting the turquoise. The Tiffany Archives photographic description lists the bowl as copper inlaid with silver, yet on the record photograph from the archives is a caption reading "silver inlaid with copper." High Museum of Art document files.

4. Venable 1994, pp. 192–197.

5. See Zapata, March, 1991, pp. 560–561. The service is illustrated and discussed in Truman 1993, p. 142. The Near Eastern taste fascinated the affluent in the United States in the years after the 1876 Centennial Exposition in Philadelphia. It began with a craze for Japanese designs, a result of Japan's exhibitions there. This taste for the exotic led to a variety of world influences, including those from the Near and Middle East; see Zapata, April, 1991, pp. 721, 724. For a survey of the works of Peter Carl Fabergé, see Waterfield, n.d.

6. Correspondence with Tiffany and Company Archives, November 15, 1994, High Museum of Art document files.

7. The objects shown in the Louisiana Purchase International Exposition were discussed and illustrated in *The Craftsman* magazine, an unexpected publication to promote Tiffany products. It described the firm's display as a "very noticeable advance in artistic quality of design, and in technique, together with a breadth in choice of subject most agreeable to meet, since it acknowledges the claims of both historical and purely modern art. It shows the exhibitors to be conservative, and yet open to such new ideas as appear legitimate and promise development," *The Craftsman,* November 1904, p. 169. The author praised Farnham for his understanding of "the joyous, exuberant, pagan period which he here treats, as only a poet can do," p. 179. A Renaissance covered dish in a private collection is illustrated in Zapata, April, 1991, p. 728, pl. XIV.

8. The Metropolitan Museum of Art 1970, no. 284, illustrates and discusses a matching goblet in the Museum of the City of New York.

Rich Cut Glass, 1890–1917

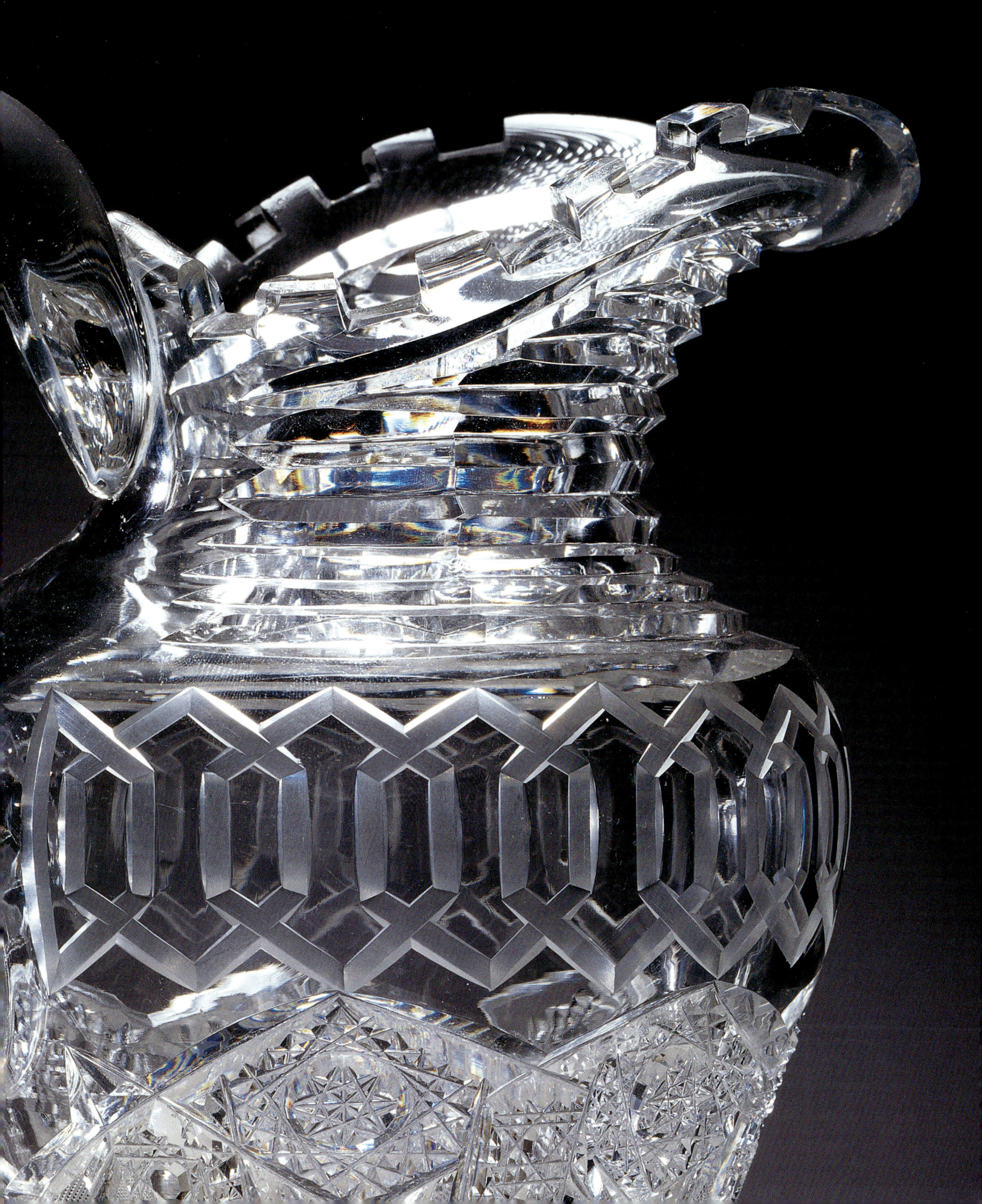

Libbey Glass Company

The Libbey Glass Company evolved out of the New England Glass Works in East Cambridge, Massachusetts (see nos. 129–132), which had been one of the most influential American glass manufacturers since its founding in 1818. In 1872, William L. Libbey left the Mount Washington Glass Works in New Bedford, Massachusetts (see nos. 136–138), to manage the New England Glass Works. Despite a brilliant showing at the 1876 Centennial Exposition in Philadelphia, however, various factors—the economic depression of 1873; the refusal of the New England Glass Works to abandon lead glass for the less expensive lime glass made by its competitors; labor disputes; and lack of cheap fuel—led to the closing of the works in 1878. Libbey then leased the factory and kept it operating, despite continuing financial problems. In 1880, he took his son Edward Drummond Libbey into the firm, which was then called New England Glass Works, W. L. Libbey and Son, Proprietors. In 1883, the younger Libbey inherited the business, which continued manufacturing art glass and cut glass. In 1888, Libbey closed the New England Glass Works and moved the company to Toledo, Ohio. Located on the shores of Lake Erie, Toledo was a developing railroad and steamboat center, enabling easy distribution of the company's products. Eager to attract the company, the city provided land for construction of a new factory and workers' homes and offered natural gas to fuel the new plant. Joseph Locke, who had created art glass for the New England Glass Works (see no. 131), was the first superintendent of the new Toledo factory.

Edward Libbey incorporated the new company as W. L. Libbey and Son, changing the name to Libbey Glass Company in 1892. In that year, a major glassworkers strike in Corning, New York, brought Libbey a contract from Edison General Electric Company to manufacture light bulbs. Between the strike (which eased competition for cut-glass tablewares) and the production of light bulbs, Libbey turned impressive profits. At the 1893 World's Columbian Exposition in Chicago, Libbey constructed an exhibition glass factory that could accommodate five thousand visitors to observe glassmaking and to purchase

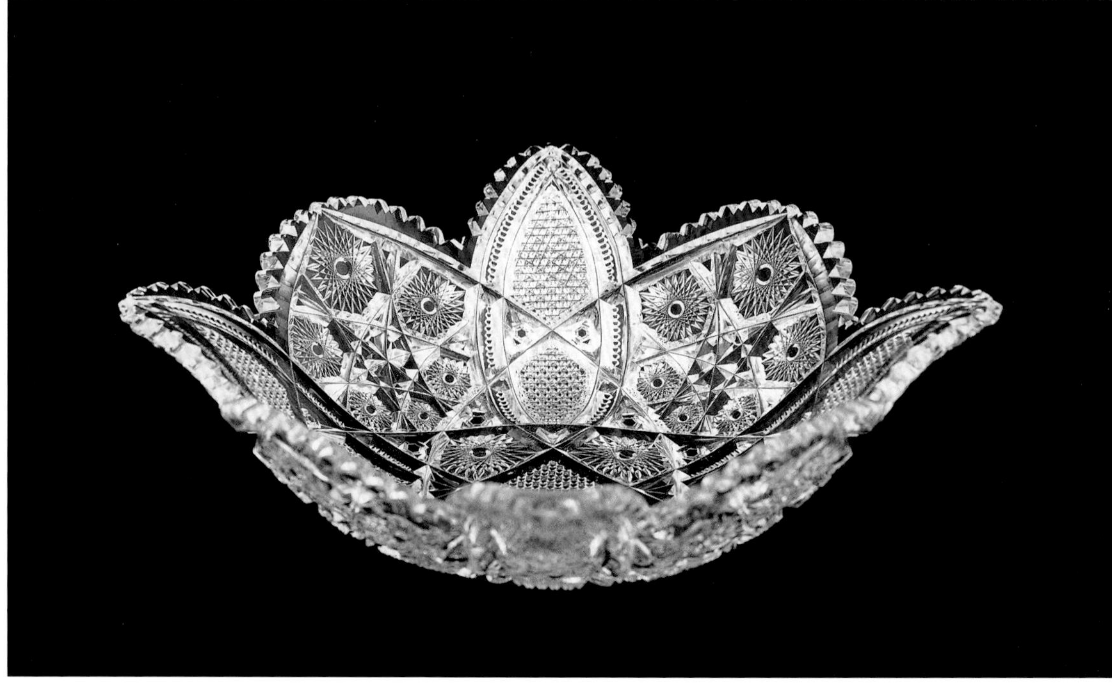

157.

Dish, ca. 1896

Libbey Glass Company (1888–1935), Toledo, Ohio
Cut glass, Marcella pattern
11½ × 14 × 4 inches
Mark: Signed, *Libbey* with sabre
1986.175

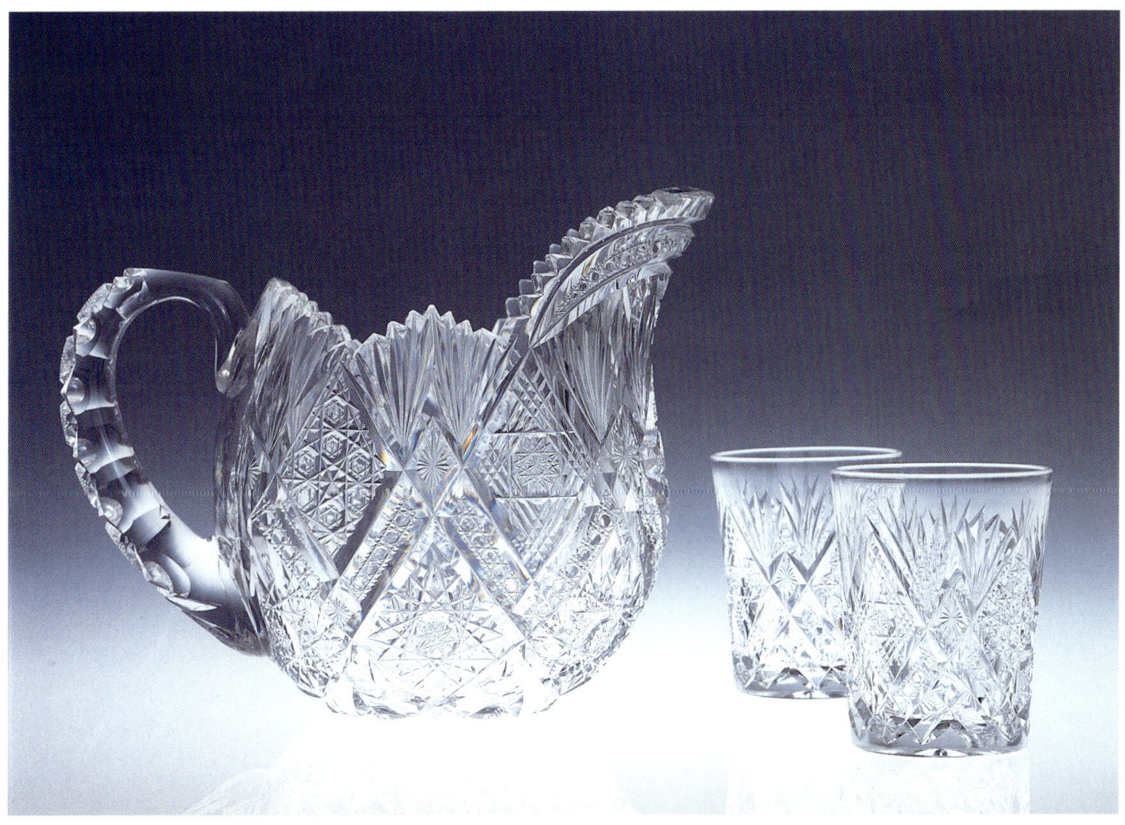

158.

Jug and Two Tumblers, ca. 1896

Libbey Glass Company (1888–1935), Toledo, Ohio
Cut glass, Imperial pattern
Jug: 7¾ × 10½ × 5½ inches
Tumblers: Each 3⅞ × 3 × 3 inches
1986.176.1–.3

products, including cut glass. From the 1890s to World War I, the Libbey Glass Company emerged as a major competitor of the Corning cut-glass manufacturers because it was open to changes in taste, new technology, and innovative promotions and sales methods. Cut glass was only one aspect of the Libbey Glass Company production, but a very important one at the time. By 1900, its glasscutting department employed two hundred workers.[1]

The Marcella and Imperial patterns were both included in a Libbey Glass Company catalogue published in 1896. The catalogue illustrated a nappy, or shallow serving dish, matching the Crawford example (no. 157). Marcella was Libbey's most expensive pattern in dishes and nappies, and its shape of projecting curves and points was unusual. The jug and tumblers in the Crawford Collection (no. 158) are in the Imperial pattern, which was one-third less expensive than Marcella.[2]

NOTES

1. A comprehensive illustrated history of the Libbey Glass Company is presented in Fauster 1979. A history of both the New England Glass Works and the Libbey Glass Company is found in K. Wilson 1994, pp. 825–837.

2. Libbey Glass Company 1968, p. 10, illustrates a Marcella nappy. Sizes ranged from 6 inches across, priced at $30, to 12 by 15 inches, which sold for $52. A dish is also illustrated, but it appears shallower and less articulated than the Crawford example. The blank for the Imperial jug is illustrated in the catalogue but is cut in the Eulalia pattern. The Imperial jug, cut on Libbey blank 374, had a capacity of two quarts and was priced at $32; see p. 18. A tumbler cut in the Imperial pattern, illustrated as no. 286, was priced at $40 per dozen; see p. 25.

T. G. Hawkes and Company

159.

Kerosene Lamp,
ca. 1900

T. G. Hawkes and Company (1880–1962), Corning, New York
Cut glass and electroplated silver lighting device
33⅛ × 9 × 9 inches
Marks: On both knobs of lighting device, in raised letters, *W. H. GLENNY SONS AND CO* in circle around *BUFFALO, N.Y.*
1987.166

T. G. Hawkes and Company was among the most skillful, influential, and longest-surviving of the many glass-cutting companies in the late-nineteenth-century "Crystal City" of Corning, New York. Thomas G. Hawkes was born at his father's estate in Cork, Ireland. After briefly studying engineering at Queens College in Cork, he immigrated to New York in 1863. There he was a draftsman at Hoare and Dailey, a cutting shop in Brooklyn, where he also learned to cut and sell. By 1870, Hawkes was in Corning as foreman at John E. Hoare's cutting shop on the second floor of the Corning Glass Works building. After a decade, Hawkes established his own cutting shop, using blanks from Corning Glass Works, which up to then had restricted its blank business to Hoare.[1]

In 1885, Hawkes received his first order for White House cut-glass tablewares, in the Russian pattern, which his firm had patented in 1882. This pattern was used at the White House until 1938, with replacements supplied by Hawkes and C. Dorflinger and Sons (see no. 169). The company displayed 612 pieces of glass at the 1889 Exposition Universelle in Paris. In 1890, Hawkes incorporated his firm as T. G. Hawkes and Company, and by the end of the decade the firm had twice expanded its facilities.

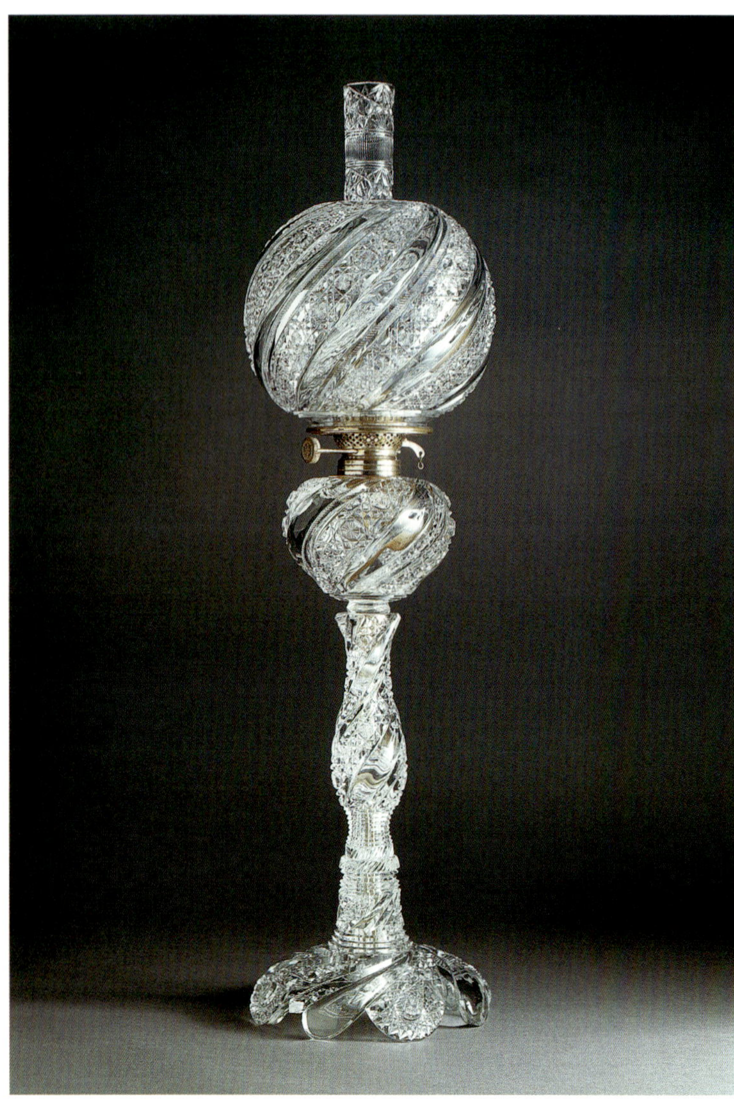

In 1903, Hawkes opened a new factory under the leadership of Frederick Carder, formerly second-in-command at the English factory of Stevens and Williams. The new facility, Steuben Glass Works, was underwritten by Hawkes and ensured a steady supply of glass blanks for his company. By 1904, Steuben Glass Works had nearly replaced C. Dorflinger and Sons and Corning Glass Works as blank suppliers. In 1912, the firm began a department to work with silver mounts supplied by Gorham Manufacturing Company and others, but this was never a major part of their business. The main characteristics of Hawkes wares were thick, sparkling glass and exceedingly deep cutting. The three examples of Hawkes products in the Crawford Collection are remarkable for their craftsmanship and scale.

The lamp (no. 159) is an especially graceful and beautifully cut example of Hawkes's luxury output at the turn of the century. Although composed of several elements, all are visually united by the swirling pattern that begins at the top, spinning around the detachable globe shade, winding around the stem, and continuing down through the base. Without its shade, the lamp and its elegant cut-glass chimney were illustrated in a Hawkes catalogue published around 1900.[2]

"Brilliant Cut glass" is a contemporary term used to describe the heavy, deeply cut lead glass of the turn of the century, although at the time it was called "Rich Cut glass." After 1905, Hawkes introduced two unusual linear patterns that depended largely on deep cuts, nearly halfway through the thick blanks, for visual impact. The Crawford rose bowl (no. 160) is cut in the Panel pattern, which was patented in 1909. This bowl is one of three known of this particularly large scale. The Willow pattern, patented in 1911, was used for the round tray (no. 161). The extraordinary skill of the cutter is evident in the woven effect of the design.[3] However, American taste for Rich Cut glass was dying by the end of the new century's first decade, and World War I contributed significantly to its demise.

After Hawkes's death in 1913, his sons and descendants continued the business, which survived until 1962, largely because it successfully adapted its production to changing American tastes in glass tablewares.

NOTES

1. An early notable Hawkes commission was a pair of "elegant toilet bottles" for prominent local businessman Austin Lathrop, Jr., who presented them to William H. Vanderbilt on his sixtieth birthday in 1881. A history of T. G. Hawkes and Company with photographs and illustrations from published catalogues is found in Farrar and Spillman 1979, pp. 52–123. A more comprehensive study is provided in Spillman 1997, which not only includes Hawkes's biography and a thorough history of the firm, but also presents T. G. Hawkes and Company as a case study of the American cut-glass industry.

2. Illustrated in Farrar and Spillman 1979, p. 79, fig. 204.

3. An 1882 view of the Hawkes plant with a sign reading "Hawkes Rich Cut-Glass Works" is shown in ibid., p. 4, fig. 2. The two patterns are discussed in Spillman 1997, p. 188. A matching rose bowl of the same size and a stand with radiating cuts are illustrated in Wiener and Lipkowitz 1975, p. 193.

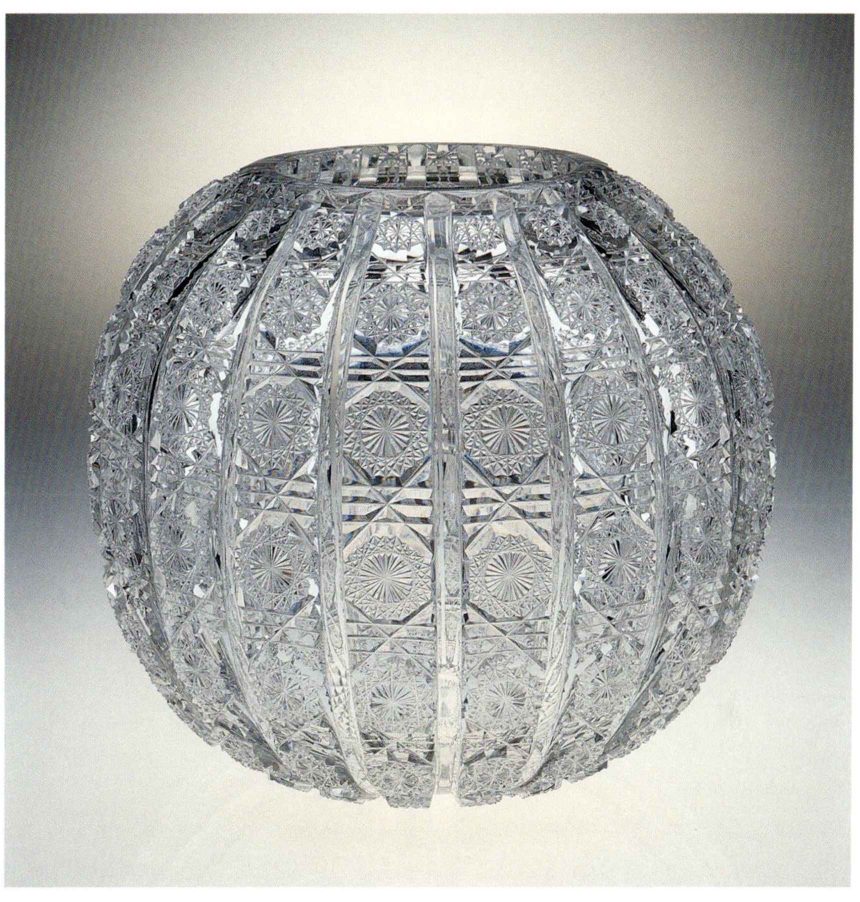

160.

Rose Bowl, ca. 1909

T. G. Hawkes and Company
(1880–1962), Corning, New York
Cut glass, Panel pattern
11 × 12 × 12 inches
1986.184

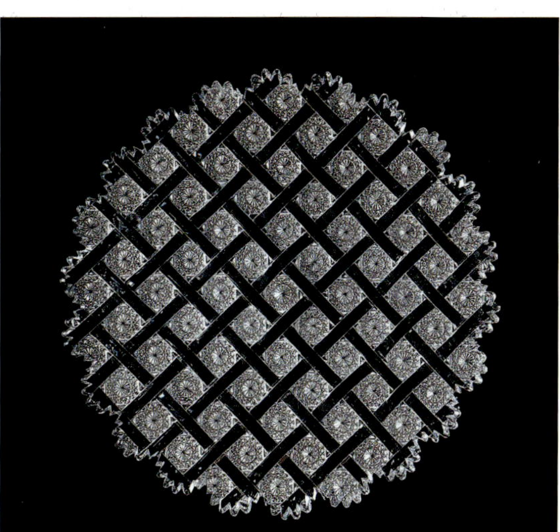

161.

Tray, ca. 1911

T. G. Hawkes and Company
(1880–1962), Corning, New York
Cut glass, Willow pattern
1 × 13¼ × 13¼ inches
1986.185

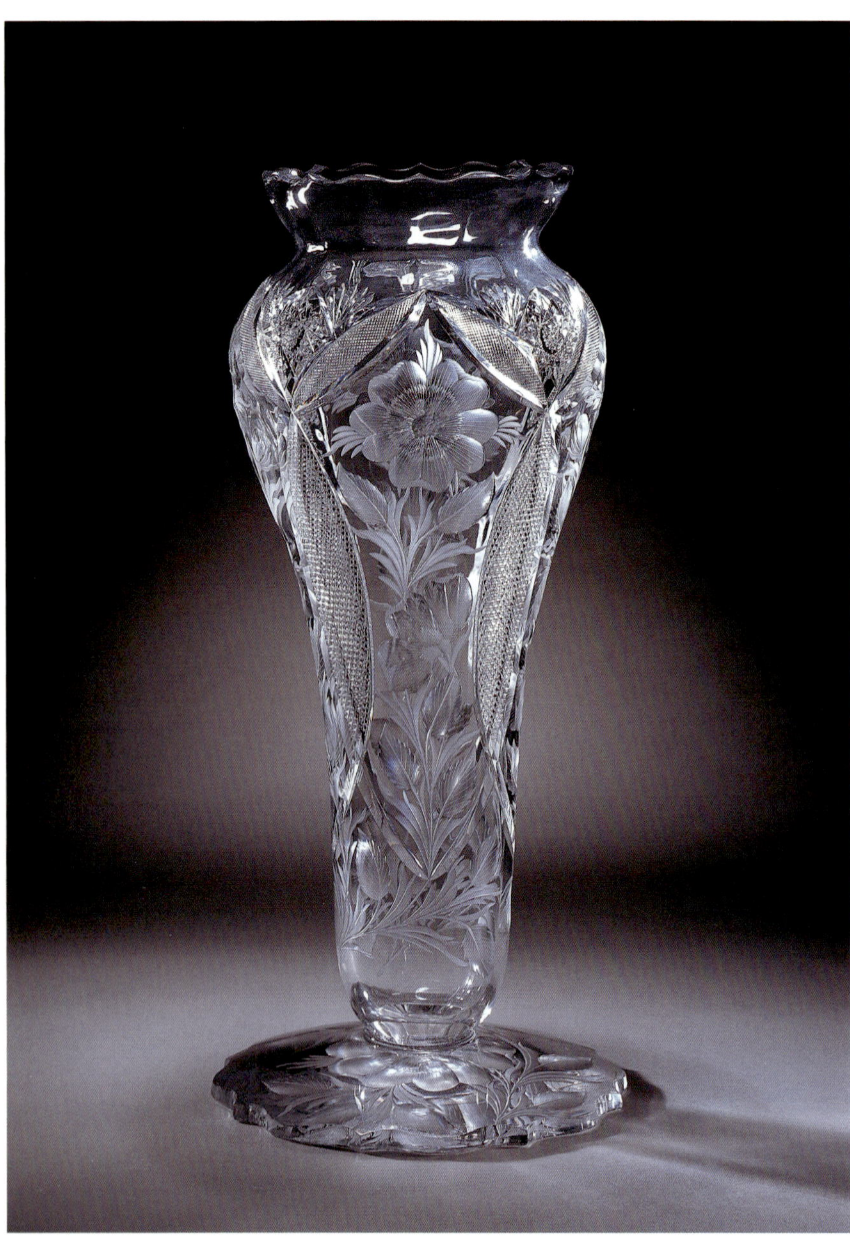

162.

Vase, ca. 1913

Tuthill Cut Glass Company
(1900–1923), Middletown,
New York
Cut and engraved lead glass
18¼ × 8¼ × 8¼ inches
Mark: Signed on bottom, *Tuthill*
1986.179

The Tuthill Cut Glass Company specialized in cutting and engraving tablewares, such as goblets, plates, and smaller serving pieces. The firm's founder, Charles G. Tuthill, had trained and worked as a cutter at T. G. Hawkes and Company (see nos. 159–161) before establishing a small glasscutting shop in Corning, New York, in 1895. In 1900, Tuthill moved to Middletown, New York, and started another small glasscutting house; when his brother and sister-in-law joined two years later, the firm became the Tuthill Cut Glass Company. Rather than manufacturing their own glass, Tuthill decorated blanks made by other companies, including C. Dorflinger and Sons and the Pairpoint Corporation.

Charles Tuthill created most of the designs for the company, and also cut and engraved them, while his brother, James, is credited with some designing and with improving an acid polish for cut glass. James's wife, Susan, managed the plant and inspected the products. Tom Mortenson, who had worked at Niland Cut Glass Company in Deep River, Connecticut, was superintendent at the firm for ten years and also created designs. The firm employed twelve to fifteen engravers and cutters, including American, Austrian, and Danish workers.[1]

While the Crawford vase is unusually large, it is characteristic of the Tuthill Cut Glass Company's wares in its combination of rich cutting and beautifully rendered and realistic floral engraving.

NOTE

1. Historical accounts of the Tuthill Cut Glass Company and illustrations of its wares are presented in Farrar and Spillman 1979, pp. 287–288; and Swan 1986, pp. 224–228.

FOUNDED IN CHICAGO in 1871 by Edward Hand Pitkin and Jonathan William Brooks, Pitkin and Brooks became one of the largest wholesale and retail china and glassware dealers in the Midwest. They began cutting and engraving glassware in the 1880s, and by 1906 they were producing much of their own cut glass in three factories in Chicago and Chicago Heights. They used blanks from the firm's subsidiary, the Chicago Flint and Lime Glass Company, in Chesterton, Indiana.

Pitkin and Brooks exhibited at the 1893 World's Columbian Exposition in Chicago, where American cut glass received international acclaim. The company advertised three grades of glasswares: P&B, the highest grade, with elaborate patterns and deep cutting on pure lead-glass blanks; Standard grade; and Imported grade, which was made abroad according to Pitkin and Brooks's specifications. Only the finest grade, such as the Crawford punch bowl, was signed with an acid-etched P&B inside a diamond.

The firm prospered by supplying its large glass and china store in Chicago through its manufacturing expansions in Chicago; Chesterton; Valparaiso, Indiana; and Bowling Green, Ohio. With the onset of World War I, however, the government's requirement for lead, essential for cut-glass production, together with changing American taste, caused the business to decline quickly. By 1923, the Chicago directory no longer listed Pitkin and Brooks.[1]

Punch bowls were expensive, large, and impressive forms in cut glass. This example is unusual in its cutting, which consists mainly of curved and mitred lines without floral and hobstar decorations, and relates to late-nineteenth-century pressed-glass patterns. The thick, clear lead glass and the deep wheel-cutting are characteristic of better American tablewares at the turn of the century. The form was blown and molded in two separate sections with a knob at the bottom of the bowl that fits securely into a cap at the top of the pedestal. A matching bowl is in the Lightner Museum in St. Augustine, Florida.

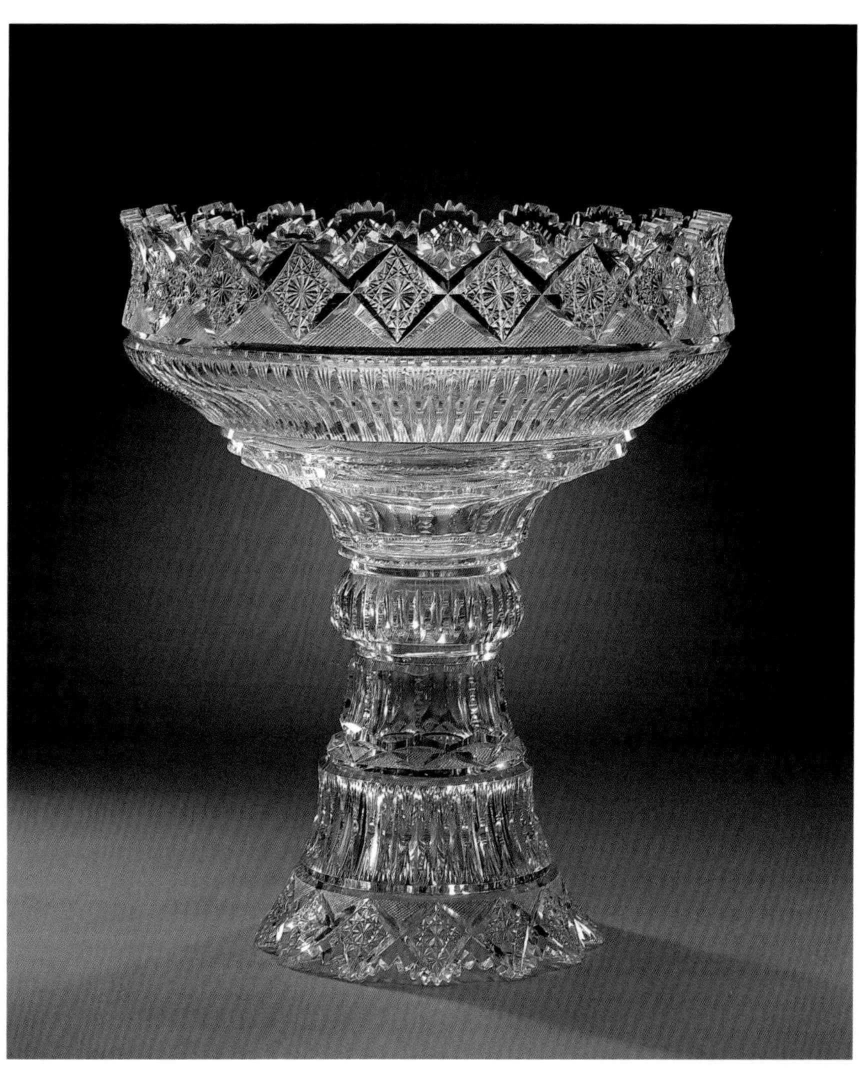

163.

Punch Bowl on Stand,
ca. 1900

Pitkin and Brooks (1871–ca. 1923), Chicago
Cut glass, Derby pattern
16⅛ x 13¾ x 13¾ inches
Marks: On both bowl and base, in a diamond, *P&B*
1986.183.a–.b

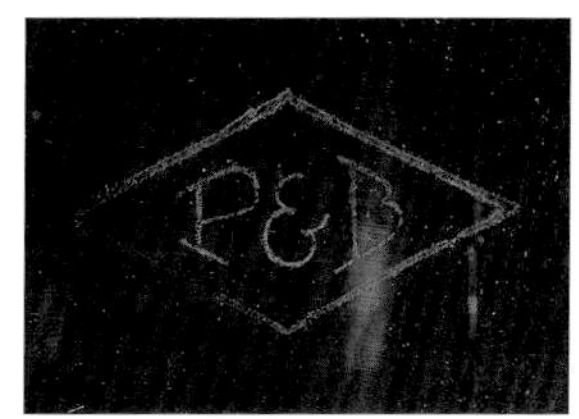

NOTE

1. The history of Pitkin and Brooks is recounted in Darling 1979, pp. 85–87.

H. P. Sinclaire and Company

Henry Purdon Sinclaire, Jr., founder of H. P. Sinclaire and Company, descended from leaders in the late-nineteenth-century American glass industry. Sinclaire studied at the Rochester Business University and joined T. G. Hawkes and Company (see nos. 159–161) in Corning as a bookkeeper. There his money-management skills led to quick advancement while he learned the glass business under Thomas Hawkes. At that time, the Hawkes firm specialized in Rich Cut glass, but because European engraved glass was so popular in America, Hawkes included engraved wares designed by Sinclaire in the company's display at the 1889 Exposition Universelle in Paris. In addition to his skills in money management, Sinclaire was also successful in selling to retailers, and by the late 1890s he traveled regularly on behalf of the firm. Disagreements with Hawkes led Sinclaire to become a shareholder in the Corning Glass Works, where his brother was secretary, and ultimately to establish his own cutting and engraving business. In 1904, with investor backing, H. P. Sinclaire and Company erected a new cutting and engraving plant in Corning to compete with Hawkes.[1]

Sinclaire's business sense overcame his personal preference for engraved glass, and the firm produced both Rich Cut glass and engraved wares. With the impending closure of C. Dorflinger and Sons (see no. 169), which had supplied his firm with blanks, Sinclaire established a glassblowing factory in 1920 in Bath, New York, with workers from the Dorflinger factory. He also expanded his commercial lines to support the firm's cut and engraved glass and to meet competition from cheaper European wares. He even introduced a line of baking glassware just before his death in 1927. Upon Sinclaire's death, branch factories closed at once, but cutting and engraving on in-stock blanks continued for about a year at the Corning facility.

Early in its history, the company did not issue catalogues, as Sinclaire believed that high-quality wares would find customers. However, with America's entry into World War I, and the ensuing economic scare and lack of raw materials, the

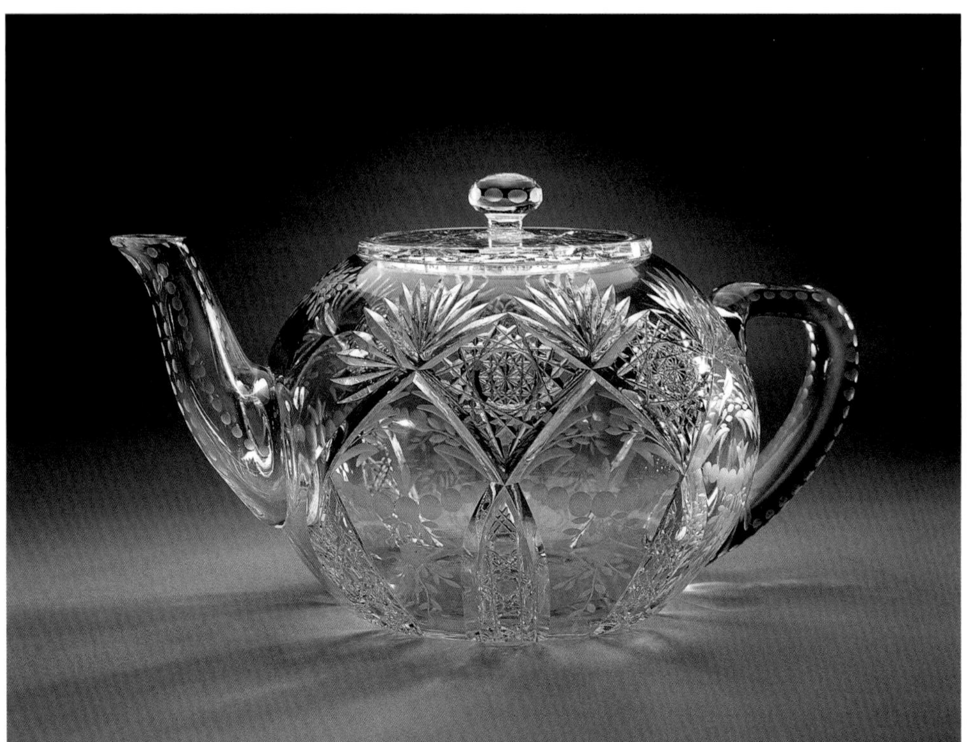

164.

Teapot, ca. 1917

Cut by H. P. Sinclaire and Company (1904–1928), Corning, New York
Cut glass
4⅜ × 9¼ × 5¾ inches
Mark: Beneath handle, in circle *S*
1986.180.a–.b

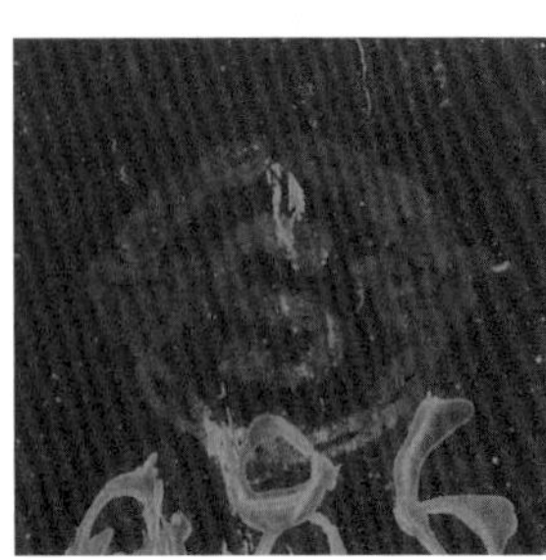

company assembled a photographic inventory in 1917 for a stock-reduction sale. Blanks for all three of the Sinclaire pieces in the Crawford Collection were included in the inventory, but these forms may have been in production for several years. The teapot (no. 164) is primarily decorative; its untempered glass is unsuitable for boiling water. The pot has both cut and engraved decorations, characteristic of many Sinclaire wares. The gracefully undulating oval compote (no. 165) has been called an orange bowl by modern collectors, although the 1917 inventory described it simply as a bowl. The illustrated inventory example is completely engraved, whereas the Crawford bowl is both cut in hobstars and geometric patterns and engraved in a floral and leaf band around the top edge. A compote identical to the round Crawford compote (no. 166) is illustrated in the photographic inventory.[2] The Crawford examples of Sinclaire glass demonstrate the firm's brilliant cutting as well as its engraving, for which it was most distinguished among Corning's glass companies.

NOTES

1. Sinclaire's father, Henry P. Sinclaire, Sr., was secretary of the Corning Glass Works, and his uncle, Amory Houghton, was its founder. See Farrar 1974, pp. 1–20; and Farrar and Spillman 1979, pp. 203–223, for the history of H. P. Sinclaire and Company.

2. The same style blank, cut in a similar pattern as the Crawford teapot, is illustrated as no. 1896, pl. 99, of the 1917 inventory, reproduced in Farrar and Spillman 1979, p. 256. The oval compote, or orange bowl, blank is no. 309, pl. 13, in the 1917 inventory and is reproduced in Farrar 1974, p. 58. The invoice describes the Crawford form as an orange bowl with standard, High Museum of Art document files. The round compote is illustrated as no. 284, pl. 11, in the 1917 inventory, illustrated in Farrar 1974, p. 56. The price list records the pattern as Vendome, with a price of $23.

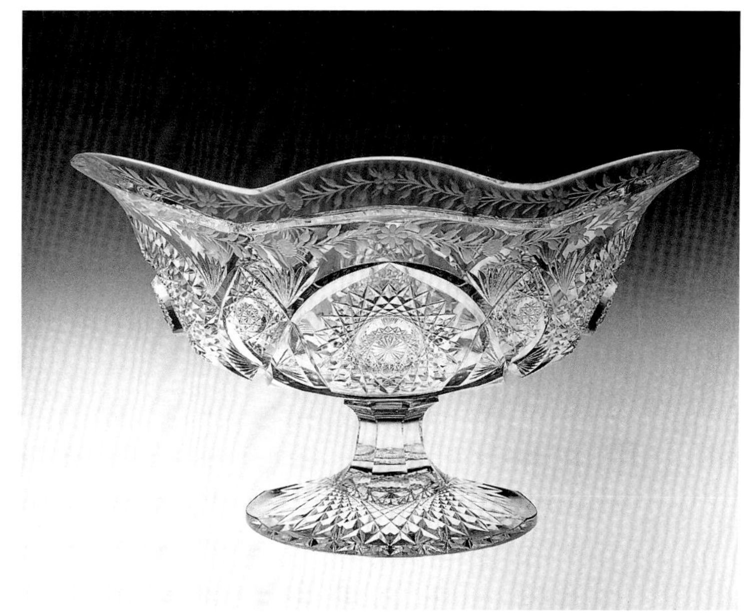

165.

Compote, ca. 1917

Cut by H. P. Sinclaire and Company (1904–1928), Corning, New York
Cut glass
$7\frac{1}{8} \times 12\frac{3}{4} \times 8\frac{3}{8}$ inches
Mark: On side, *S*
1986.182

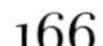

166.

Compote, ca. 1917

Cut by H. P. Sinclaire and Company (1904–1928), Corning, New York
Cut glass, Vendome pattern
$6\frac{5}{8} \times 10 \times 10$ inches
Mark: On bottom of top piece, in circle *S*
1986.181.a–.b

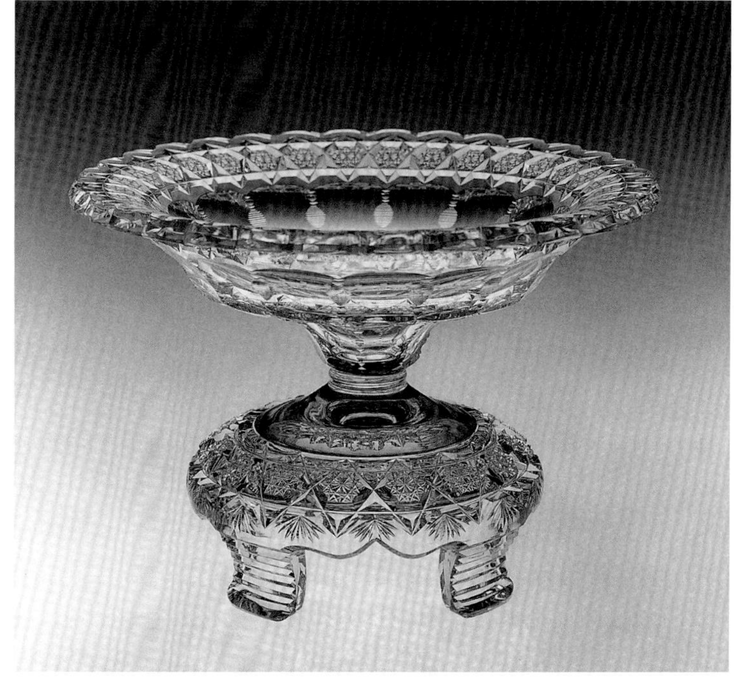

167.

Plate, 1900–1910

Attributed to Pairpoint Corporation (1900–1938), New Bedford, Massachusetts
Cut glass, Berwick pattern
1⅜ × 11¾ × 11¾ inches
1986.178

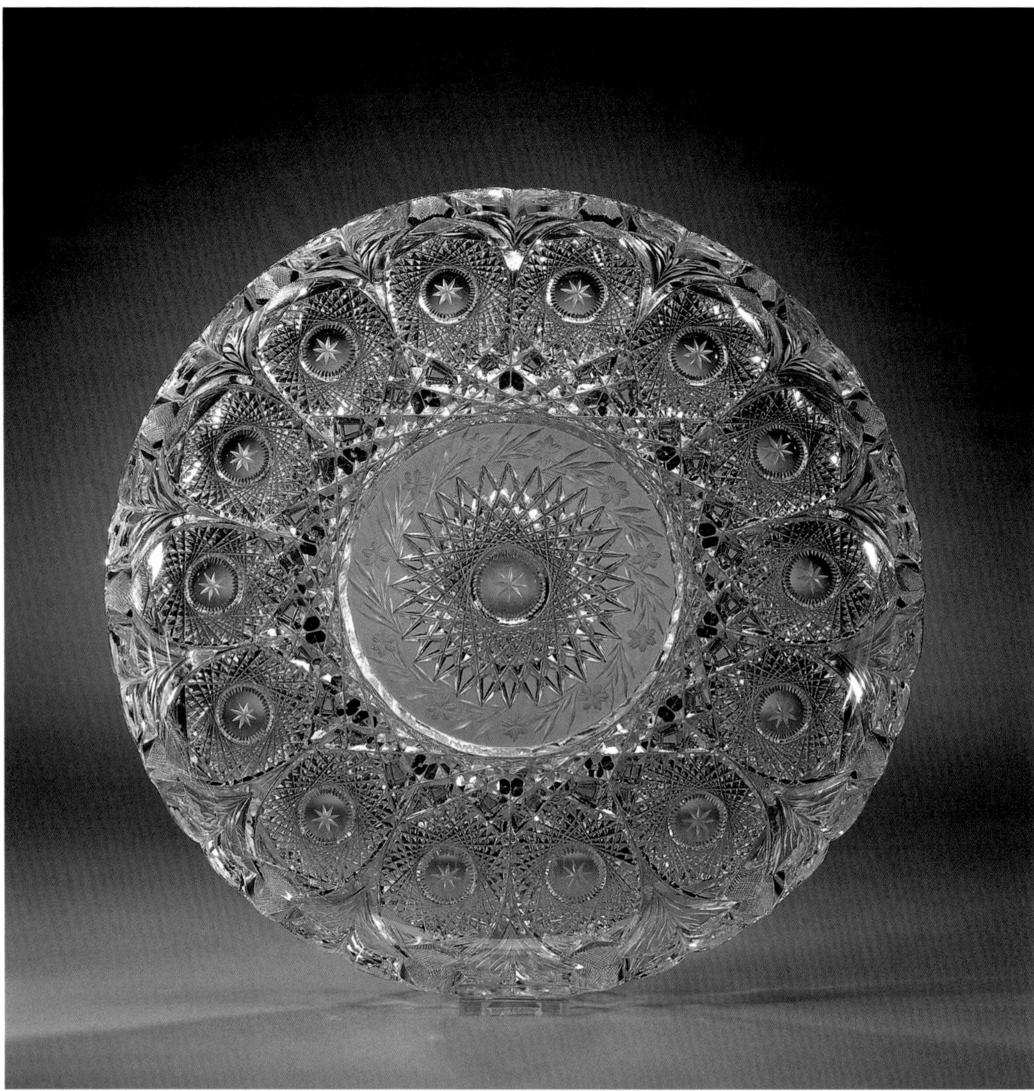

The Pairpoint Manufacturing Company, established in 1880, made silver-plated britannia wares in New Bedford, Massachusetts, adjacent to the Mount Washington Glass Company (see nos. 136–138).[1] The company was named for Thomas J. Pairpoint, first superintendent of the firm from 1880 to 1885. Even before the Pairpoint Manufacturing Company purchased the Mount Washington Glass Company in 1894, the two firms cooperated in producing art glass with silver-plated mounts. By 1897, a diversified Pairpoint Manufacturing Company employed twelve hundred workers, including one hundred glassblowers and three hundred glasscutters. The firm's other employees worked in the company's paper goods and silver-plating divisions. In 1900, the company was reorganized as the Pairpoint Corporation, which not only cut and engraved glass, but also manufactured and distributed glass blanks to cutting and engraving shops around the country.

The Berwick pattern included both straight and curved cuts, as well as floral engraving. The Crawford plate may have been intended for use as a serving tray, although its recessed circular center suggests that it could have been a stand for a compote, pitcher, or vase.

NOTE

1. The history of the Pairpoint Corporation is recounted in Swan 1986, pp. 89–98. An identical plate is illustrated in Boggess and Boggess 1977, p. 102.

WHEN THE MERIDEN Silver Plate Company was established in 1869, it made silver plate and small cut-glass items. Around 1895, it expanded into cut-glass tablewares under the name Meriden Cut Glass Company. The firm never actually manufactured glass; instead it cut blanks made by other companies, including the local Meriden Flint Glass Company, which closed in 1896. Meriden later purchased blanks from the Mount Washington Glass Works/Pairpoint Corporation (see nos. 136–138, 167), which had merged in New Bedford, Massachusetts.[1] In 1898, the area between New Haven and Hartford, Connecticut, was the manufacturing headquarters for silver, silver-plate, and glasscutting firms, many of which formed a loose conglomeration named the International Silver Company. Each company maintained its identity, but the overall business was administered collectively. The Meriden Cut Glass Company merged with the cut-glass divisions of Wilcox Silver Plate Company, another member of the International Silver Company.

The pattern on the Crawford pitcher, unusually complex for rich cut glass, was called Alhambra, although collectors have subsequently referred to it as Greek Key because of its encircling engraved chain. Thomas A. Shanley, superintendent of the Meriden Cut Glass Company, was granted the patent for this elaborate design, which includes the castellated top edge and the vertical series of hobstars enclosed in cross-cut hexagons, on January 17, 1911 (fig. 1). Meriden used paper labels rather than acid-etching its name or insignia into the glass, and no label survives on the Crawford pitcher.

The Meriden Cut Glass Company, like most American cutting houses, suffered not only from changing fashion but also from the sudden scarcity of lead due to World War I. The effect of the war on the company was severe; by 1919, Shanley was working in a laundry. In 1923, when the Meriden Cut Glass Company closed, lead-glass blanks were no longer being made.

NOTE

1. The history of the Meriden Cut Glass Company is recounted in Swan 1986, pp. 228–235. Other forms by Meriden in the Alhambra pattern are illustrated in figs. 339–345. Patent papers show that Shanley assigned the rights to patent number 41,091 to the International Silver Company.

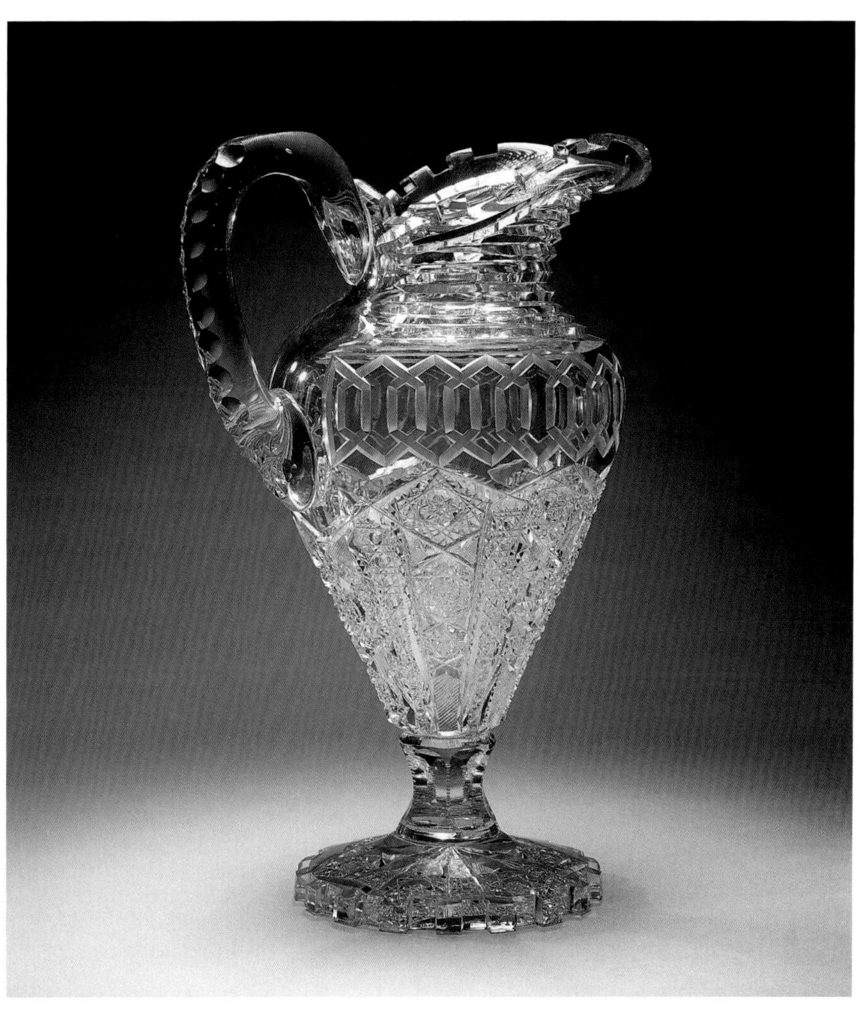

168.

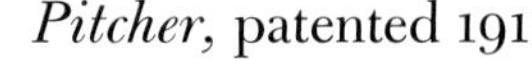

Pitcher, patented 1911

Meriden Cut Glass Company (ca. 1895–1923), Meriden, Connecticut; designed by Thomas A. Shanley (working 1904–1918)
Cut lead glass, Alhambra pattern
11½ × 8 × 5½ inches
1986.186

DESIGN.
T. A. SHANLEY.
CUT GLASS VESSEL OR SIMILAR ARTICLE.
APPLICATION FILED NOV. 14, 1910.

41,091. Patented Jan. 17, 1911.

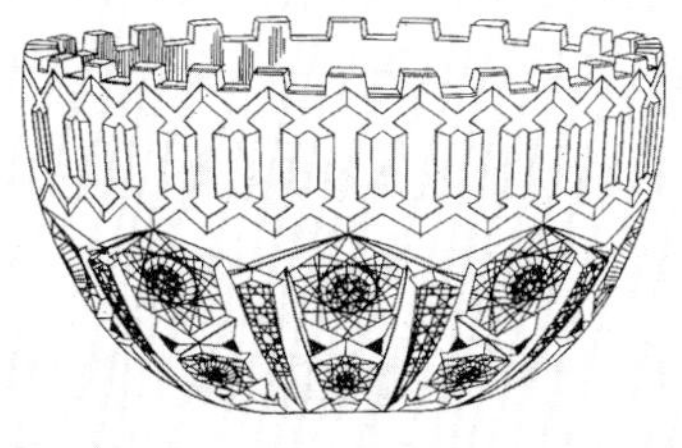

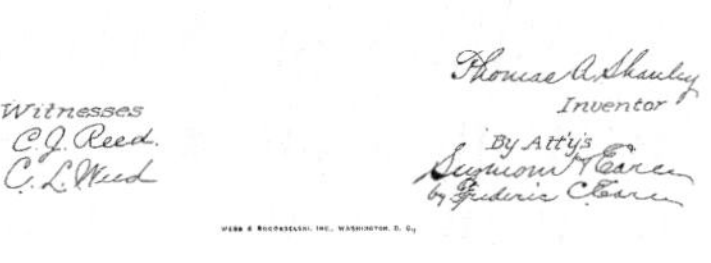

Fig. 1. Patent drawing. U.S. Patent Office. Thomas A. Shanley, assignor to International Silver Company of Meriden, Connecticut. Design for a cut-glass vessel or similar article, number 41,091, dated January 17, 1911.

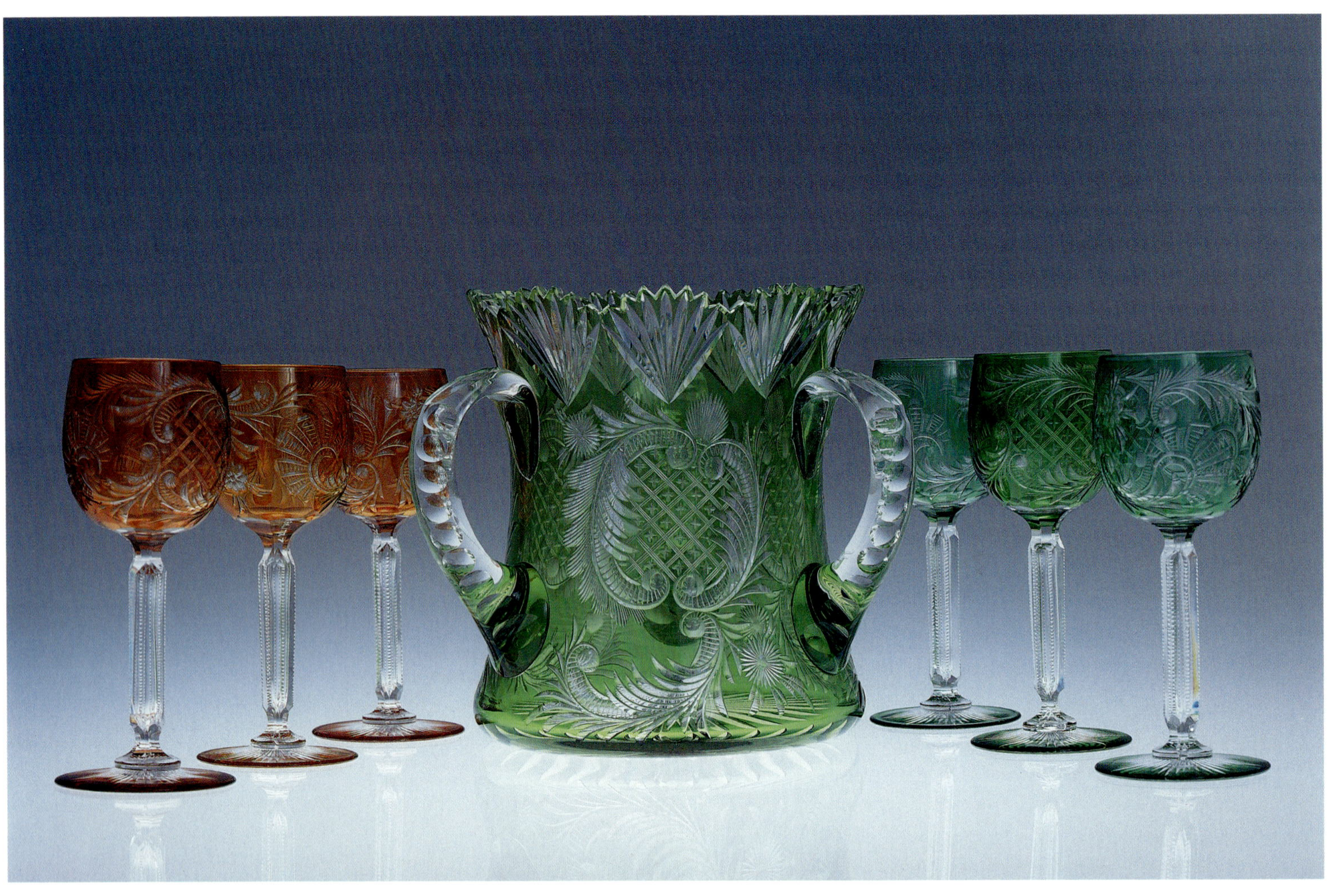

169.

Wine Cooler and Six Wine Glasses, 1900–1915

C. Dorflinger and Sons (1892–1921), White Mills, Pennsylvania; probably designed by Walter J. Graham
Colored cut to clear glass, Rococo pattern
Cooler: 7¾ × 8⅝ × 8⅝ inches
Glasses: Each 6½ × 2⅝ × 2⅝ inches
1986.177.1–.7

THIS SET OF ROCOCO pattern wine cooler and goblets was made by C. Dorflinger and Sons, one of the leading American glassmaking, cutting, and engraving companies in the last half of the nineteenth century. Christian Dorflinger was born in France and trained at the Cristalleries de Saint-Louis in Lorraine. In 1847, after an eight-year apprenticeship, he immigrated with his family to Philadelphia. He and his brother Edward worked at a glass factory in Camden, New Jersey, where they gained experience in the American glass trade, and in 1851 they moved to Brooklyn. One year later, with investors' backing, Dorflinger established the Long Island Flint Glass Works in Brooklyn. After steady growth through the 1850s, his business interests expanded with the 1860 opening of the Greenpoint Flint Glass Works in the Greenpoint section of Brooklyn, already a porcelain-making center (see nos. 42–43). Dorflinger lured French-trained craftsmen from Lorraine to his Brooklyn factories, where he produced fine cut-glass tablewares. In 1861, he received an order from the Lincoln White House. However, poor health forced Dorflinger into early retirement, and he moved his family to rural White Mills, Pennsylvania.[1]

As Dorflinger began to recover his health, he established a glasshouse in White Mills in 1865. He was soon bringing experienced, European-born glassworkers from his Brooklyn enterprise to White Mills and shipping glass blanks back to Brooklyn for cutting and engraving. By 1867, he had opened a cutting and engraving department at White Mills, and less than ten years later, the company won a certificate for its display at the 1876 Centennial Exposition in Philadelphia. In 1880, the introduction of a cutting wheel that could make curved and mitered cuts brought a radical change in style. No longer limited to straight lines, designers and cutters developed Brilliant Cut glass. As a result, cut glass grew in popularity and began to compete with silver as a standard wedding gift. Dorflinger, along with competitors in Corning, Toledo, Chicago, New England, and elsewhere, became a major wholesale source for this fashionable glassware. Beginning in the 1870s, he took his sons into the business, and in 1892, the company name changed to C. Dorflinger and Sons. The company flourished until nearly the time of Dorflinger's death in 1915, when taste shifted away from Brilliant Cut glass. World War I brought shortages of manpower and lead, which, along with increasing labor problems, caused the company to close in 1921, when many American glasscutting shops that were unable to adapt to changing tastes also went out of business.

The Rococo pattern was introduced during the period of Dorflinger's greatest success, around 1900. Walter J. Graham, the longtime head of the factory's engraving department, has been credited with designing the pattern.[2] C. Dorflinger and Sons provided colored and cased blanks to many cutting shops, and made a specialty of these highly decorative wares. The engraved cased glass was made and decorated as it had been since the mid-nineteenth century in Bohemia (see no. 45). A clear blank was encased in colored glass so that when the outside colored layer was cut through, the clear glass was exposed. The flat wafer bases of these glasses, each cut with a radiating star, are seen on many examples of Dorflinger stemware from the early twentieth century. The Crawford wine set illustrates the richness that color added to American cut and engraved glass in the brilliant period and the continuing influence of imported Bohemian colored glass.

NOTES

1. A detailed and well-illustrated biography of Christian Dorflinger and the history of Dorflinger's factories is presented in Feller 1988, pp. 1–60.

2. Ibid., p. 178, pl. 48, illustrates an identical green wine glass, which Feller credits to Graham.

170.

Pitcher, ca. 1905

Probably northeastern United States
Engraved lead glass mounted in silver
13⅝ × 10¾ × 7¾ inches
Mark: Stamped on underside of silver mount, *STERLING*
1986.174

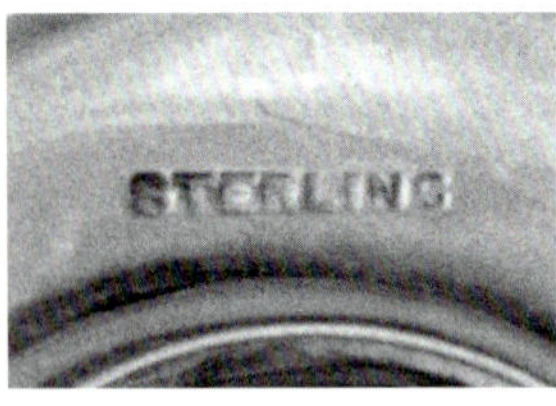

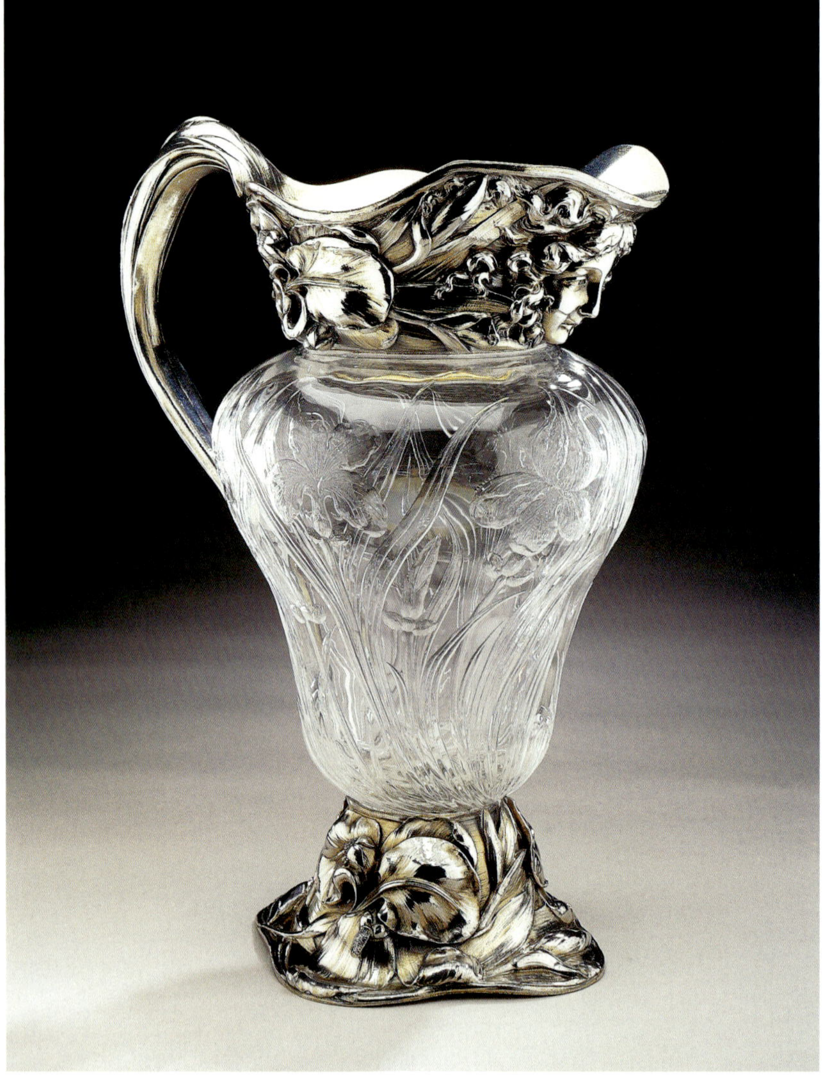

No marks are evident on the Crawford pitcher except for "STERLING" stamped on the underside of the base, which suggests an American manufacturer for at least the silver base, collar, and handle, since the American standard for silver was sterling (silver that is 925–1000 fine, with copper as the alloy) and "sterling" was used by American manufacturers in their marks. The superior quality of the glass engraving indicates that the vase may have been made in one of the best American glasscutting houses at the turn of the century, such as J. Hoare and Company, which worked with Gorham Manufacturing Company (see nos. 173–174) on its Martelé line, or T. G. Hawkes and Company (see nos. 159–161), both in Corning, New York. Although American glass-engraving and glasscutting shops often did not sign decorated wares, it was less common for silver manufacturers of the period to not sign or trademark their work.

The Crawford pitcher's undulating curves of silver complement the inverted pear shape of the engraved glass vessel. Realistically rendered iris blossoms and stems are engraved into the glass and cast into the silver mounts, unifying the work of separate manufacturers. Iris is personified as a woman's face in the silver collar just beneath the spout of the pitcher. The pitcher's overall design shows the influence of French Art Nouveau, suggesting a date of around 1905, as well as a designer of sophistication at an accomplished silver manufactory.

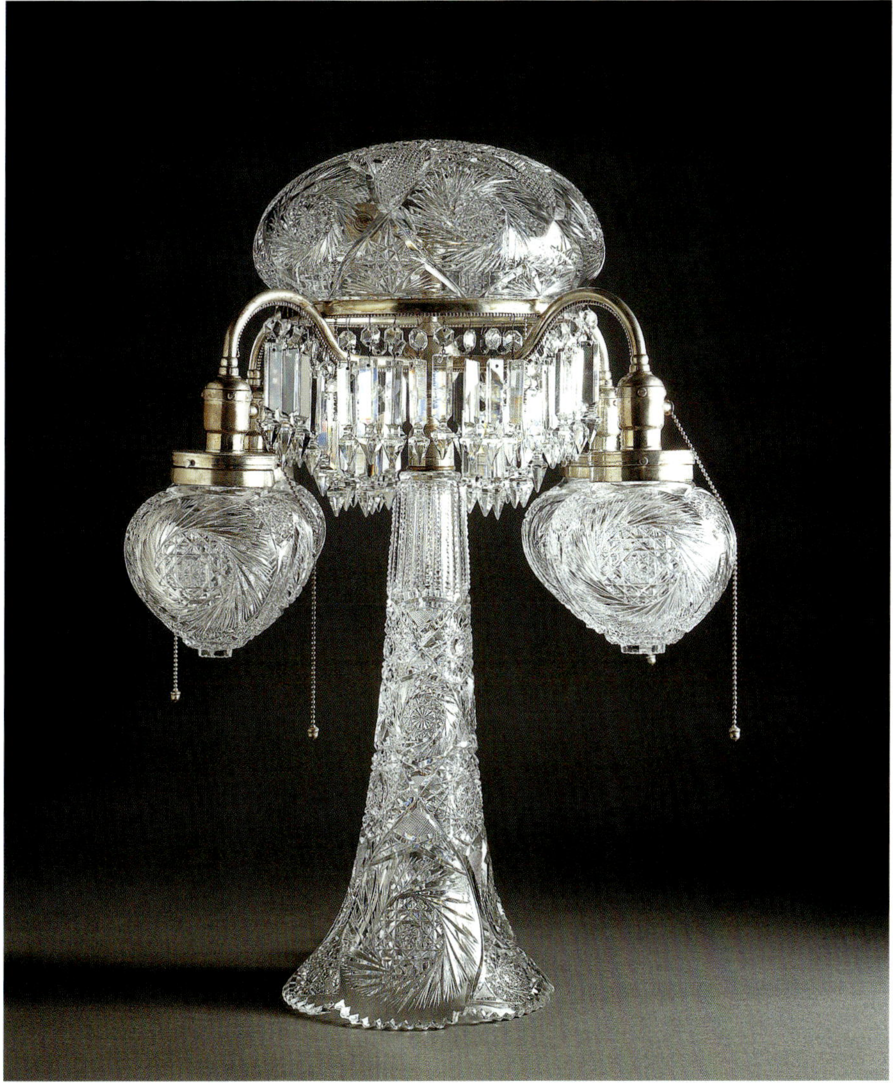

171.

Lamp, ca. 1910

United States
Cut glass and electroplated silver
30 × 24 × 24 inches
1987.165

TABLE LAMPS WERE uncommonly large forms in early-twentieth-century American Rich Cut glass. They usually consisted of several separate pieces of glass, each individually cut, and were especially expensive because they required so much time in production and decoration.

The grand scale of the Crawford lamp suggests that it was intended for a spacious salon of a turn-of-the-century mansion or a public space such as a hotel lobby. The design combines plated silver with a cut-glass pattern of pinwheels on the base, the crowning shade, and four hanging globes. Although pinwheels appeared in cut-glass patterns as early as 1896, they were increasingly used after 1900. The profusion of pinwheels on the lamp, as well as its electrification, date it between about 1905 and 1915. Identical lamps are in the Lightner Museum in St. Augustine, Florida, and the Corning Museum of Glass. The Corning Museum attributes its lamp to either the Quaker City Cut Glass Company in Philadelphia or J. D. Bergen and Company, in Meriden, Connecticut, because of the close relationship of cut details, particularly pinwheels, to other examples.[1]

NOTE

1. The Corning Museum lamp is discussed and illustrated in Corning Museum of Glass 1996, pp. 10, 12. The Lightner Museum lamp is illustrated in Pearson 1975, p. 178. A total of six of these lamps are known, and three are in private collections. John C. Roesel, a collector and researcher, provided research and advice in the preparation of this essay.

Art Nouveau and Arts and Crafts, 1900–1915

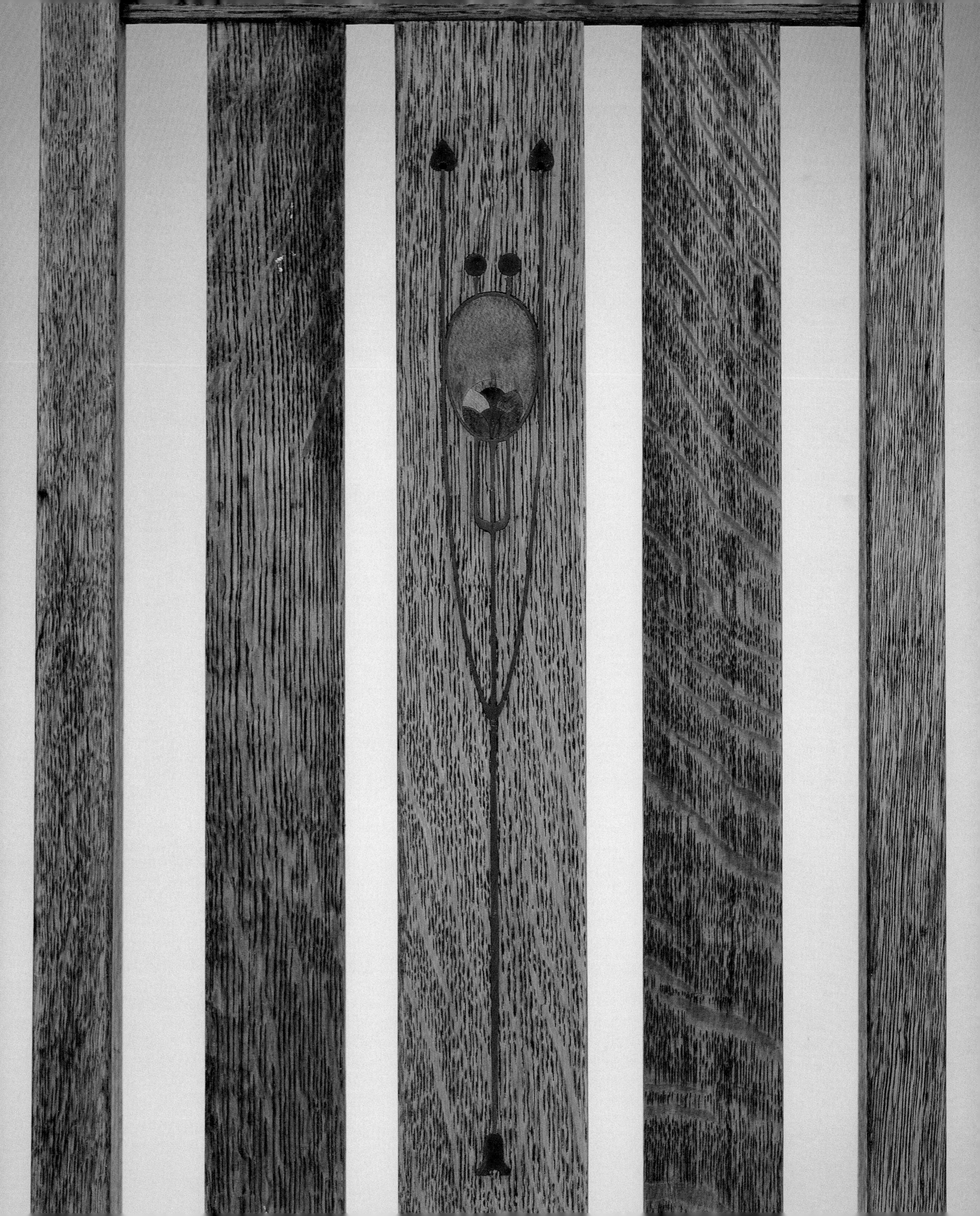

172.

Vase, 1889–1901

Mary Louise McLaughlin (1847–1939), Cincinnati
Porcelain
4¾ × 4 × 4 inches
Marks: Inscribed on bottom, *MCL/II/281;* painted in underglaze blue, *Losanti*
1991.346

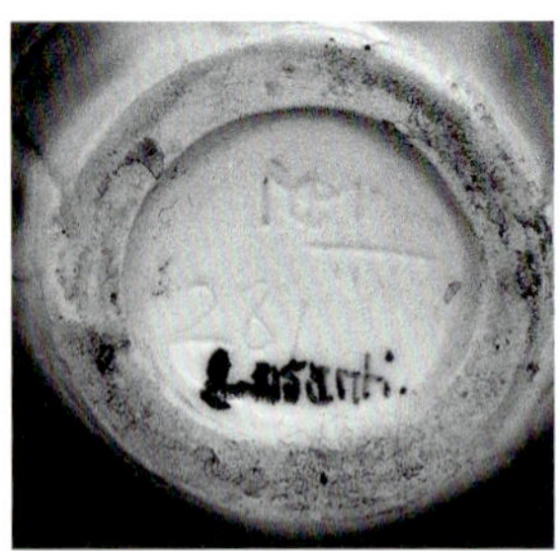

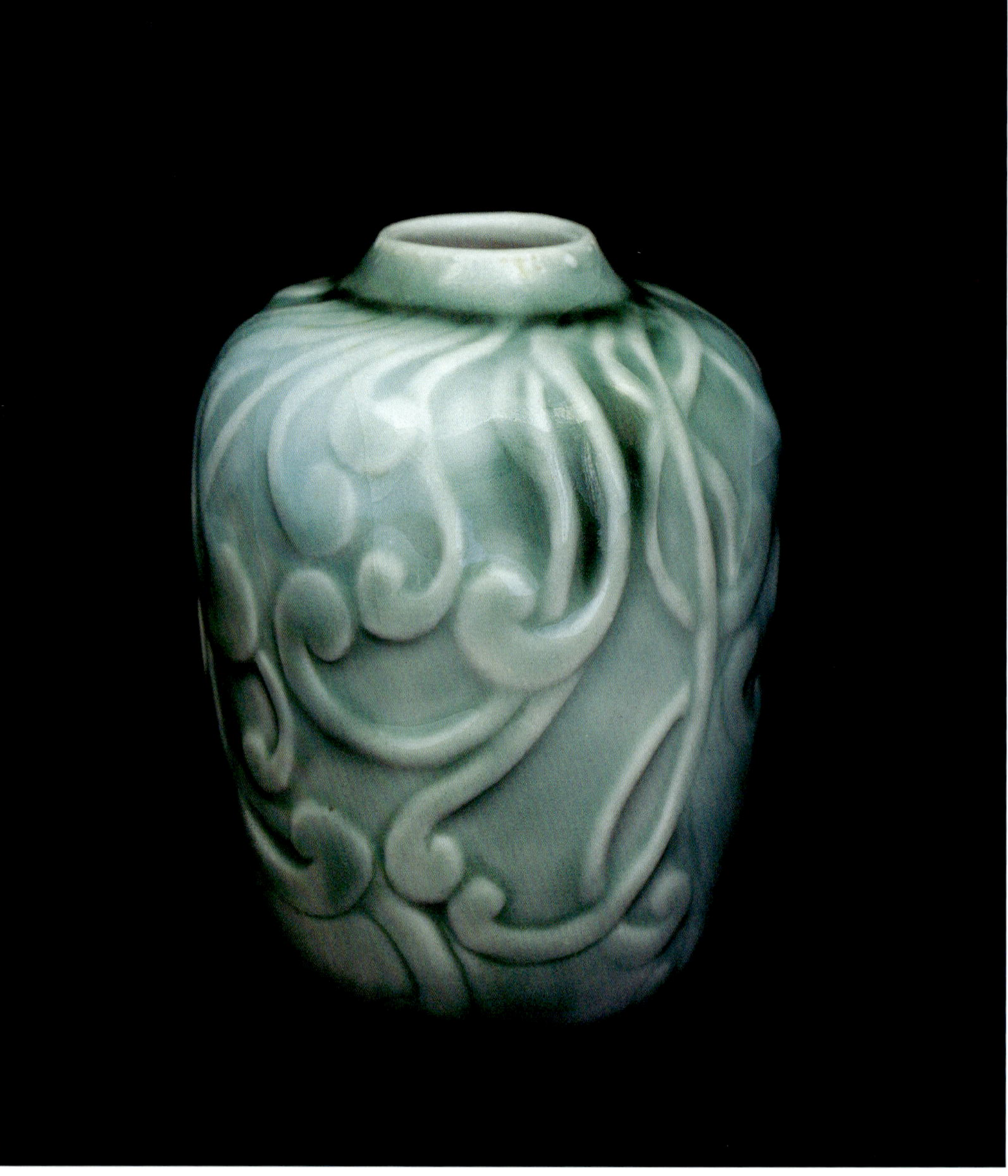

Mary Louise McLaughlin was among the first Americans to successfully manufacture porcelain outside a factory setting. By the time she fired her first wares in the backyard kiln of her Cincinnati home in 1898, McLaughlin was already a skilled artisan with extensive training and widespread recognition in a variety of media.[1] She had studied at the University of Cincinnati School of Design from 1873 to 1877, taking courses in wood carving with Benn Pitman, and independently with Henry Lindley Fry and his son, William. In the Cincinnati section of the Women's Pavilion at the 1876 Centennial Exposition in Philadelphia, McLaughlin exhibited a desk that she had designed and carved under the tutelage of the Frys.[2]

McLaughlin began her work in ceramics in 1874, when she enrolled in a china-painting course at the university. She had seen the underglaze slip-decorated faience from Haviland and Company of Limoges, France (see nos. 140–142), displayed at the Centennial Exposition, and sought to emulate the style. Within a year she had achieved the same effect, and her slip-decorated wares were exhibited in Cincinnati and New York and at the 1878 Exposition

Universelle in Paris, where her work won an honorable mention. In 1879, McLaughlin founded the Cincinnati Pottery Club with eleven other women and served as its president. The club was more interested in decorating pottery than turning or molding it, and began firing its wares at the Frederick Dallas Pottery in Cincinnati, moving on to the Rookwood Pottery in 1880. An ongoing misunderstanding with Rookwood's founder, Maria Longworth Nichols (see no. 121), may have contributed to the Cincinnati Pottery Club leaving Rookwood in 1883.[3]

McLaughlin abandoned her work in ceramics for over a decade while she pursued decorative metalwork and writing. In 1898, however, she began experimenting in porcelain production, being "unable to resist entering what appeared to be an unoccupied field."[4] Porcelain production had been attempted in American factories as early as 1770, but McLaughlin doggedly pursued individual manufacture, following a published account of methods used at Sèvres. More wares were lost than produced, and profits proved elusive even in the two most successful years of 1901 and 1902. The expense of McLaughlin's experiments and her lack of commercial success may have led her to abandon porcelain making around 1904.

Although McLaughlin painted much of her work, carved decoration seems to have been a specialty in her porcelain endeavors. She derived the scrollwork on the Crawford vase from Chinese celadon wares. After making this carved example, McLaughlin put it through several firings and reglazings until she achieved this rich green glaze. She finished the vase in time for the 1901 Pan-American Exposition in Buffalo, where her work was awarded a bronze medal; that year, the vase was also included in the exhibition of the Keramic Society of New York. It was later shown in Chicago and at the 1904 Louisiana Purchase International Exposition in St. Louis.[5]

NOTES

1. See the biography of McLaughlin in Kaplan 1987, pp. 249–250. Besides ceramics, wood carving, and metalwork, McLaughlin worked in stained glass, needlework, painting, and sculpture. She also wrote several books on ceramics and European history.

2. The desk is illustrated in ibid., p. 8, no. 14. For biographies of Pitman and the Frys, see The Metropolitan Museum of Art 1986, pp. 428, 462–463.

3. For an account of the feud between two leaders of the women's art movement in Cincinnati, see Cincinnati Art Museum 1976, pp. 10–12.

4. Frelinghuysen 1989, p. 60.

5. The Crawford vase is illustrated and discussed in ibid., pp. 268–269, no. 105.

Gorham Manufacturing Company: Martelé

THIS SILVER-COVERED wine pitcher from Gorham Manufacturing Company is a combination of English Arts and Crafts techniques and French Art Nouveau forms and decorations. In 1890, when the firm completed its new plant at Elmwood near Providence, Rhode Island, it was the largest and most highly mechanized silver factory in the world. English-trained designer William Christmas Codman arrived in Providence just in time to supervise designs for the company's large display at the 1893 World's Columbian Exposition in Chicago. Codman was an experienced, somewhat conservative designer who looked to history for inspiration, and the silver in Gorham's display reflected the classical grandeur of the Exposition's "White City" of buildings and canals. After the Exposition, however, Codman's work changed direction, turning to England's Arts and Crafts movement and the current art of France and Belgium. The handwork and contemporary forms were a departure from Gorham's pioneering mechanized production and more historical styles and decorations.

Gorham's president, Edward Holbrook, supported these changes. In 1876, Holbrook became head agent in charge of New York sales, and by

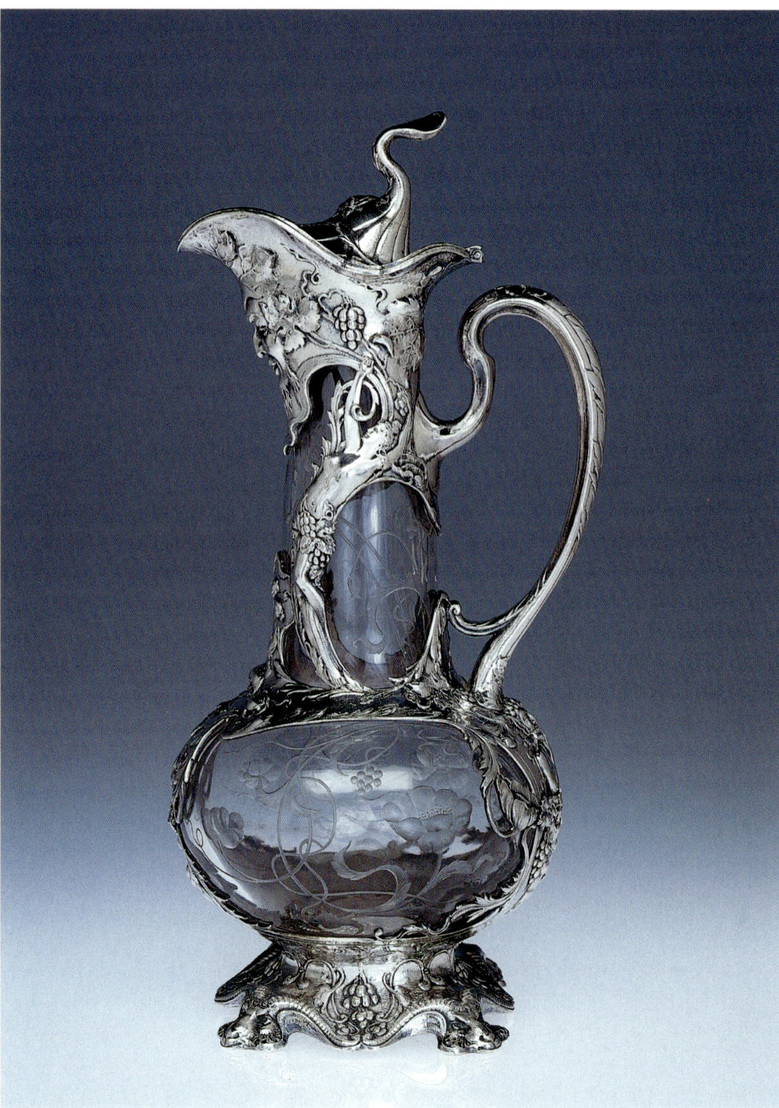

173.

Wine Pitcher, 1900

Silver by Gorham Manufacturing Company (1831–present), Providence, Rhode Island; designed by or under the supervision of William Christmas Codman (1839–1921); silver chased by Edward Zior (1868–1927); glass engraved by J. Hoare and Company (1868–1920), Corning, New York; retailed by Shreve, Crump and Low (1869–present), Boston
Silver and engraved lead glass; Martelé line
13⅞ × 7 × 5⅞ inches
Marks: Impressed on bottom, *SHREVE, CRUMP & LOW CO.*; impressed inside lid at hinge, *950.1000 FINE*
1982.306

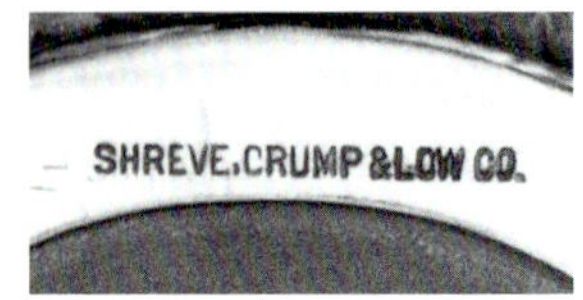

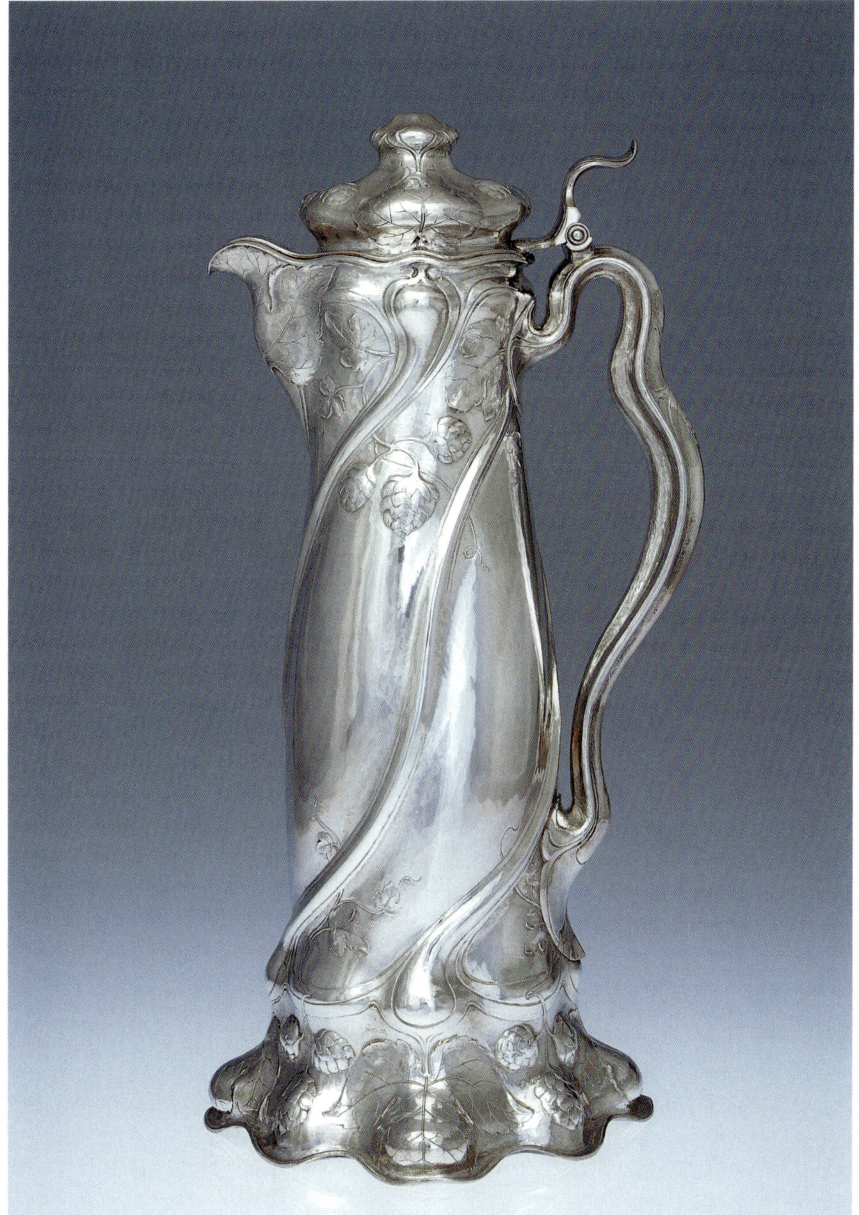

174.

Covered Pitcher, 1904

Gorham Manufacturing Company (1831–present), Providence, Rhode Island; designed by or under the supervision of William Christmas Codman (1839–1921); chased by William E. Jordan (1861–1947); retailed by Spaulding and Company, Chicago (1888–present)
Silver and engraved lead glass; Martelé line
17 × 8¼ × 7⅞ inches
Marks: Impressed on bottom, SPAULDING & CO./CHICAGO/*Martelé*/spread-winged eagle, over rampant lion, anchor, and *G*, in shields/*950–1000 FINE*; scratched on bottom, *230*
1982.304

1877 he was the company's highest paid executive. His steady acquisition of company shares increased his power, and by 1888, when he was made the firm's treasurer, he had a controlling interest. From 1878 to 1890, Gorham's annual business increased from $521,000 to $3 million.

At the enormous Elmwood factory, a school was created to train workers in raising silver vessels from flat metal sheets, reviving traditional methods that had been abandoned at Gorham for mechanization. In 1897, samples of Codman's new designs were included in a Boston exhibition that led to the establishment of the Society of Arts and Crafts, Boston. Later that year, the company—probably due to the efforts of Holbrook—organized a viewing of the new wares at the Waldorf Astoria Hotel in New York. In 1899, Gorham registered Martelé, the French term for hand-hammered, as the trademark name for its new line of handcrafted silver. The French name may have been intended to arouse interest at the upcoming 1900 Exposition Universelle in Paris, where Gorham introduced Martelé to international acclaim. Not only did Gorham receive five gold medals for its silver, but Holbrook was inducted as a Chevalier into the French Legion of Honor.[1]

The Crawford silver and glass wine pitcher (no. 173) was shown at the 1900 Exposition Universelle. It is marked with the impressed name of Shreve, Crump and Low Company, leading Boston merchants of jewelry, silver, and other luxury goods. That neither the Gorham mark nor the Martelé name was included was characteristic of these early experimental wares prior to the Exposition. Gorham records show that the engraved glass jug was provided by J. Hoare and Company, one of the earliest and longest-surviving of the Corning, New York, cut-glass manufacturers. Gorham chaser Edward Zior was responsible for the decoration, which was atypical of Martelé in its graceful depiction of a semi-nude female and the face of Bacchus, the Roman god of wine, underneath the spout. Plants and flowers were the more usual decorations on Martelé silver. The cost of labor, materials, administrative costs, and profit allowance totaled $274.67, and the net price, or the price to Shreve, Crump and Low, was $300. The wine pitcher combined silver and engraved lead glass, the two most expensive and desirable materials for tablewares in the United States at the turn of the century.[2]

Gorham records describe the Crawford covered pitcher (no. 174) as a tankard and indicate that it was made for the leading Chicago retailer, Spaulding and Company, in 1904 for a net price of $300. Henry A. Spaulding had managed European operations for Tiffany and Company, but in 1888 he moved to Chicago and formed Spaulding and Company with L. J. Leiter. The company's major silent partner was Holbrook, who financially controlled Gorham Manufacturing Company. Spaulding and Company retailed imported wares and Gorham silver, introducing Martelé to the American market in its Chicago store. The important Chicago Arts and Crafts Society had been established in 1897, which meant that there were potential buyers for Martelé silver there. The form of the covered pitcher is closely related to one made for the 1900 Exposition Universelle, with different floral decoration, a hammered knob on the lid, and distinctive shapes in the spout and handle; such variations characterize Martelé silver. William E. Jordan, a Gorham employee from 1878 to 1927, chased the decoration on the Crawford pitcher.[3]

NOTES

1. Carpenter 1997, pp. 179–203, gives an illustrated discussion and history of the Martelé line.

2. Samuel J. Hough, Cranston, Rhode Island, has researched the Gorham records for data related to the Crawford wine pitcher, and his outline regarding the making and chasing of the jug is in the High Museum of Art document files. A similar pitcher without the detailed repoussé ornament is pictured in Gorham records with a matching tray and glasses. The Gorham photograph is reproduced in McClinton 1968, p. 115.

3. Hough also researched Gorham records on the tankard-shaped covered pitcher, and his outline and letter of October 21, 1994, are in the High Museum of Art document files. The tankard shown at the Exposition Universelle is illustrated in Carpenter 1997, p. 194, no. 255.

Tiffany Studios

Louis Comfort Tiffany is one of the most familiar names in decorative art, and is widely associated with the American interpretation of French Art Nouveau. The son of wealthy New York luxury merchant Charles Louis Tiffany (see nos. 41, 96–102, 145, 152–156), the younger Tiffany was interested in art from childhood, when he sketched wildflowers at his father's summer estate, Tiffany Hall, near Irvington-on-Hudson, New York. While attending Eagleswood Military Academy at Perth Amboy, New Jersey, between 1863 and 1865, he may have studied with landscape artist George Inness, who lived nearby. It also has been suggested that Tiffany studied art under Edward C. Moore, chief designer for Tiffany and Company, at the firm's factory on Prince Street.[1] After graduating, Tiffany toured Europe before studying briefly at the National Academy of Design in New York, where he may have first become acquainted with the painter Samuel Colman. He studied art in Paris for a year in 1868 and then returned to New York, where he opened a studio. In 1869, he toured North Africa and Spain with Colman and was fascinated with the art, architecture, and vibrant colors he saw there.

By 1876, Tiffany was creating ornamental glass windows and had working access to a glasshouse in Brooklyn.[2] In 1879, with Colman and others, he established Louis C. Tiffany and Associated

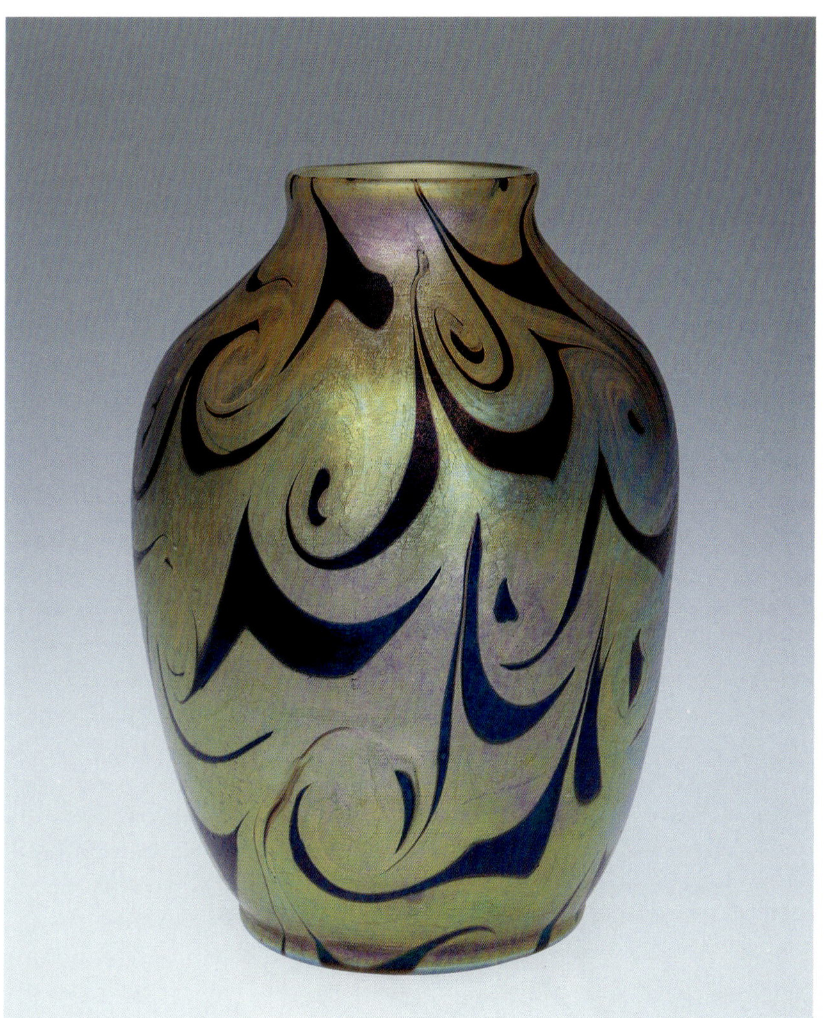

175.

Vase, ca. 1905

Tiffany Studios (1900–1932), New York; designed by Louis Comfort Tiffany (1848–1933)
Blown Favrile glass
7⅞ × 5½ × 5½ inches
Mark: Circular paper label printed in black, attached to bottom, - *TIFFANY FAVRILE GLASS - REGISTERED TRADE MARK* -, surrounding stylized circular initials, *LCT*
1984.124

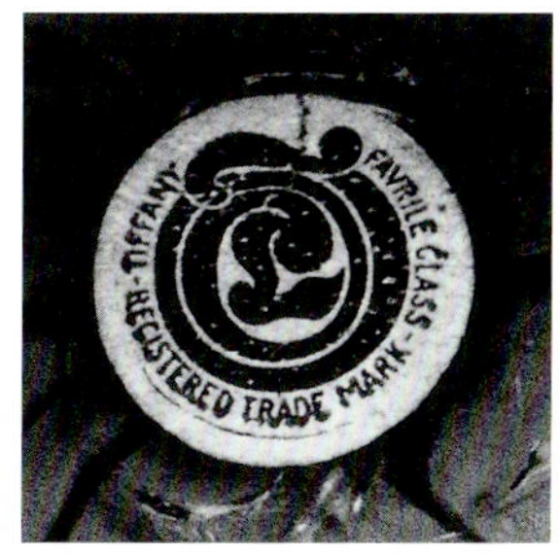

176.

Box and Cover,
1898–1900

Tiffany Glass and Decorating Company (1892–1900), Corona, Long Island; designed by or under the supervision of Louis Comfort Tiffany (1848–1933)
Enamel on copper
1¾ × 4¼ × 4¼ inches
Marks: Impressed on bottom, Tiffany Glass and Decorating Company logo over *9041/10,* with incised *Louis C. Tiffany* signature beneath; inscribed to right of logo, *590/26*
1984.128.a–.b

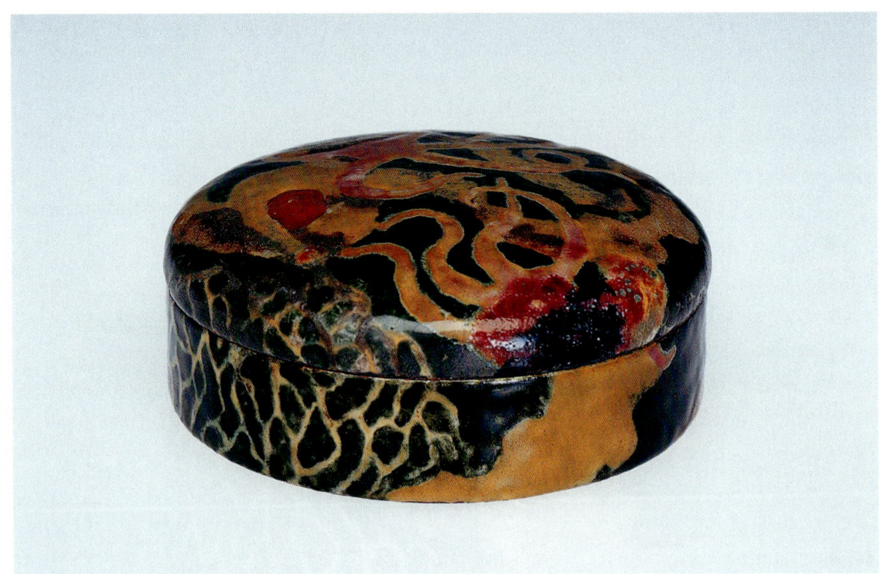

Artists, an interior decorating firm. Early commissions included the Seventh Regiment Armory on Park Avenue in New York and the Mark Twain residence in Hartford, Connecticut. By 1881, Tiffany had registered a patent for opalescent window glass, and Associated Artists had gained national recognition. It was around this time that Tiffany joined the board of his father's firm, Tiffany and Company; the elder Tiffany continued to control his company's production and also supported his son's artistic endeavors. In 1882–1883, President Chester A. Arthur commissioned Tiffany and Associated Artists to renovate the White House, a commission awarded probably in part because of Tiffany's family, business, and social connections. Associated Artists disbanded in 1883, and Tiffany's interest in glass led him to establish the Tiffany Glass Company in 1885. He attended the 1889 Exposition Universelle in Paris, where he saw the most recent French art glass, including the work of Emile Gallé, and even traveled to Nancy to visit Gallé's factory later that year.

In 1892, Tiffany Glass Company became Tiffany Glass and Decorating Company, and glass furnaces were soon constructed at Corona, Long Island. In 1894, Tiffany registered the trademark "Favrile" for use on all of the firm's glasswares. Around 1895, Tiffany divided his enterprise into the Stourbridge Glass Company for glass production and the Allied Arts Company for production in other areas. At the 1900 Exposition Universelle in Paris, Tiffany and Company and Louis Comfort Tiffany had neighboring displays. Also in 1900, Tiffany Glass and Decorating Company became Tiffany Studios to more effectively market the younger Tiffany's artistic enterprises outside of Tiffany and Company.

The trademark on the richly colored gold and purple Crawford vase (no. 175) was registered in 1904 by Tiffany, incorporating his stylized initials. The shimmering hues on the vase are a result of Tiffany's endless experiments with color and reflect his artistic achievements in glass. The gold is composed of yellow and blue glass filaments that are convoluted by the glassblower into a swirling pattern set against an iridescent purple background. The interior is cased in white opaque and turquoise glass. The vase's graceful, asymmetrical form and the pontil mark from the blower's pipe must have made Tiffany's glass especially appealing to American Arts and Crafts critics.[3]

Tiffany established an enameling division in 1898 as part of the Allied Arts Company. In his enamelwares, Tiffany looked to nature, especially flowers, plants, and sea life for inspiration. The colors on this enamel-on-copper box (no. 176) have a marine quality, and the top is decorated with an octopus-like animal. Tiffany's great interest in color is apparent on the box, and his attention to detail is shown by the continuity of the decoration between the top and bottom. The mark of the Tiffany Glass and Decorating Company indicates that the box was probably made before the name change to Tiffany Studios in 1900.[4]

At about the time Tiffany was beginning to produce enamelware, he also began experimenting in pottery. He showed the enamels at the 1900 Exposition Universelle in Paris and the 1901 Pan-American Exposition in Buffalo, but he did not exhibit pottery until the 1904 Louisiana Purchase International Exposition in St. Louis. Most of Tiffany's pottery incorporates flowers, and this vase is modeled after the hollyhock (no. 177). The glaze enabled the whiteness of the highly fired semi-porcelain clay to show through in areas of greatest relief, and it pooled in recessed areas, where its color ranged from green to nearly black. Because the pooling of the glaze varied in the firing, each of the vases was different even though they were made using molds. Clearly not intended to hold water, the hollyhock vase was conceived as sculptural ornament, even without flowers. Wares made using the ivory glaze on this vase were shown in St. Louis and the following year in the New York Keramic Society exhibition. Ceramics were also shown in 1905 in the new Tiffany and Company store on Fifth Avenue at 37th Street in New York.[5]

NOTES

1. A chronology of Tiffany's life is presented in Duncan, Eidelberg, and Harris 1989, pp. 156–158. Zapata 1993, pp. 7–40, outlines Tiffany's life until his father's death in 1902 and describes the father-son relationship as close and supportive. The probability of a mentor relationship between Moore and Tiffany is discussed on pp. 19–24. See also no. 102 in this catalogue.

2. Eidelberg 1990, pp. 504–505.

3. The asymmetrical shape of the Crawford vase is characteristic of Tiffany's early glasswares. See ibid., pp. 503–515.

4. Zapata convincingly argues that the "9041" in the mark represents a form and the second number, here "10," distinguishes the decorative motif. The Crawford box is illustrated in Zapata 1993, p. 50, fig. 10, and described on pp. 69–70. Zapata notes that an identical box enameled with a frog seated on lily pad is marked "9041/3."

5. Early production and exhibition of Tiffany pottery is documented in Eidelberg 1968, pp. 57–61. By 1914, Louis Comfort Tiffany had apparently ended his work in pottery. Eidelberg notes that when Charles de Kay wrote the biography *The Art of Louis Comfort Tiffany* (New York, 1914), with his subject's cooperation, he discussed the pottery in the past tense.

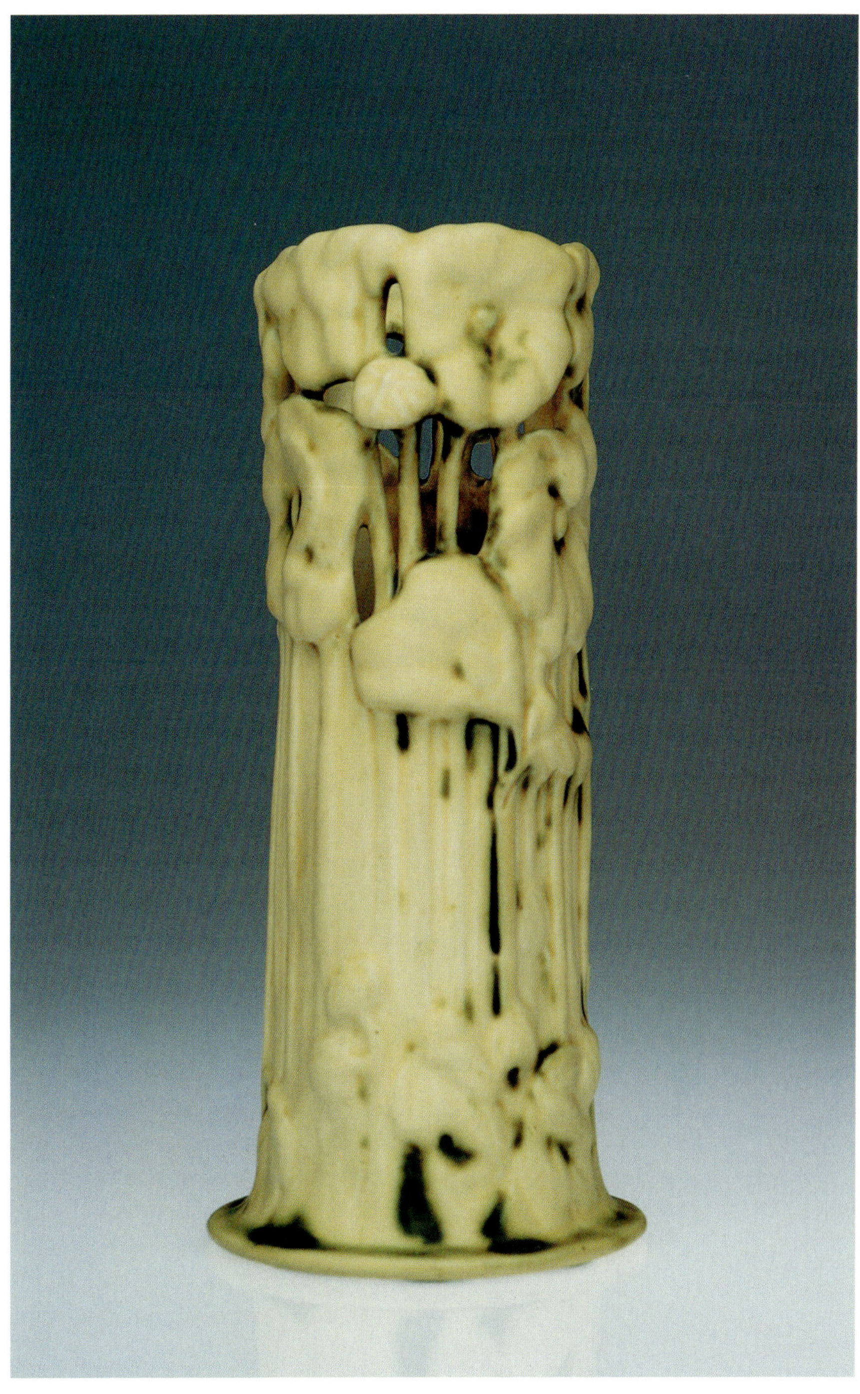

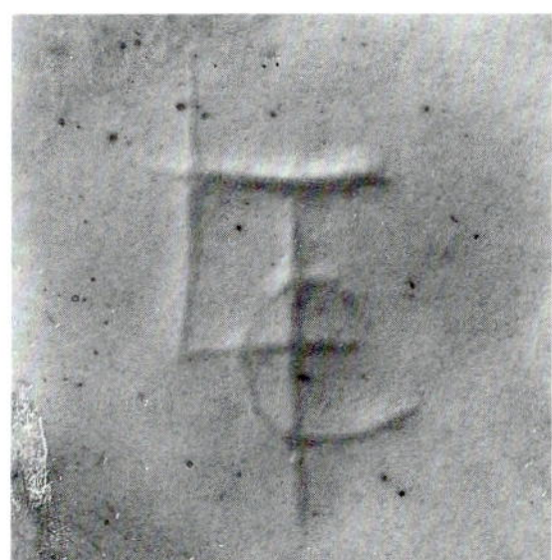

177.

Vase, ca. 1905

Tiffany Studios (1900–1932), New York; designed by Louis Comfort Tiffany (1848–1933)
Glazed semi-porcelain
10 × 4½ × 4½ inches
Mark: Incised on bottom, *LCT*
1984.136

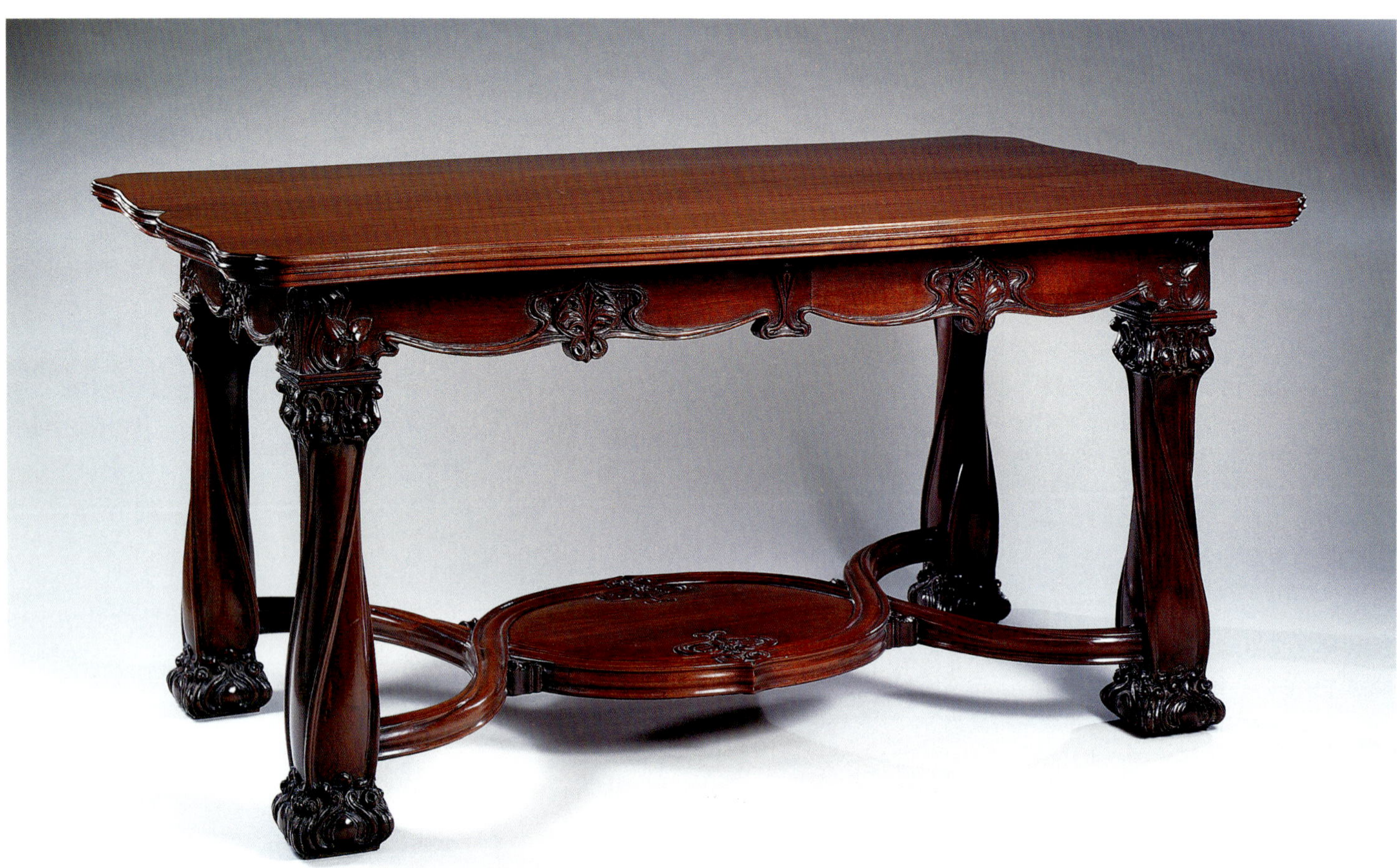

178.

Table, ca. 1905

Northeastern United States
Mahogany, birch, yellow poplar, and beech
30¾ × 60 × 35½ inches
1982.319

This large table is an American expression of the new European taste at the end of the nineteenth century.[1] S. Bing's L'Art Nouveau, the Parisian art and furnishings emporium, erected a large pavilion at the 1900 Exposition Universelle in Paris, and the store's name came to denote a broad European design style characterized by graceful, elongated curves twined into organic compositions.

Art Nouveau decoration was not often seen in American design, except for William Christmas Codman's Martelé silver by the Gorham Manufacturing Company (see nos. 173–174), the creations of Louis Comfort Tiffany and his Tiffany Studios (see nos. 175–177), and other single instances. The Crawford table represents a rather naive American interpretation of this sophisticated and subtle European expression. Curves in the legs, along the apron, and in the stretcher were simply applied to a traditional table rather than integrated into the form, while the top, apron, legs, and stretcher are treated as isolated elements and do not flow together to create a unified whole. Nonetheless, the table is significant because of the awareness it shows of this advanced European style.

NOTE

1. The table is illustrated and discussed in Whitney Museum of American Art 1985, pp. 10 and 12, fig. 1.11.

Charles Rohlfs

Some of the most distinctive and idiosyncratic American furniture of the late nineteenth and early twentieth centuries was produced by the Charles Rohlfs Workshop in Buffalo, New York. Although often associated with the Arts and Crafts movement in America because of his use of oak and traditional construction techniques, Rohlfs's work defies categorization.[1] He shunned the term "mission" to describe his designs; indeed, his influences were diverse, including medieval woodwork, French Art Nouveau, traditional Norwegian furniture, and Chinese, Moorish, and other exotic sources.

Rohlfs's workshop must have resembled an artist's studio more than a furniture factory, such as those of Stickley (see nos. 188–193), the Roycrofters (see nos. 198–199), or Charles P. Limbert and Company (see no. 202). It was considerably

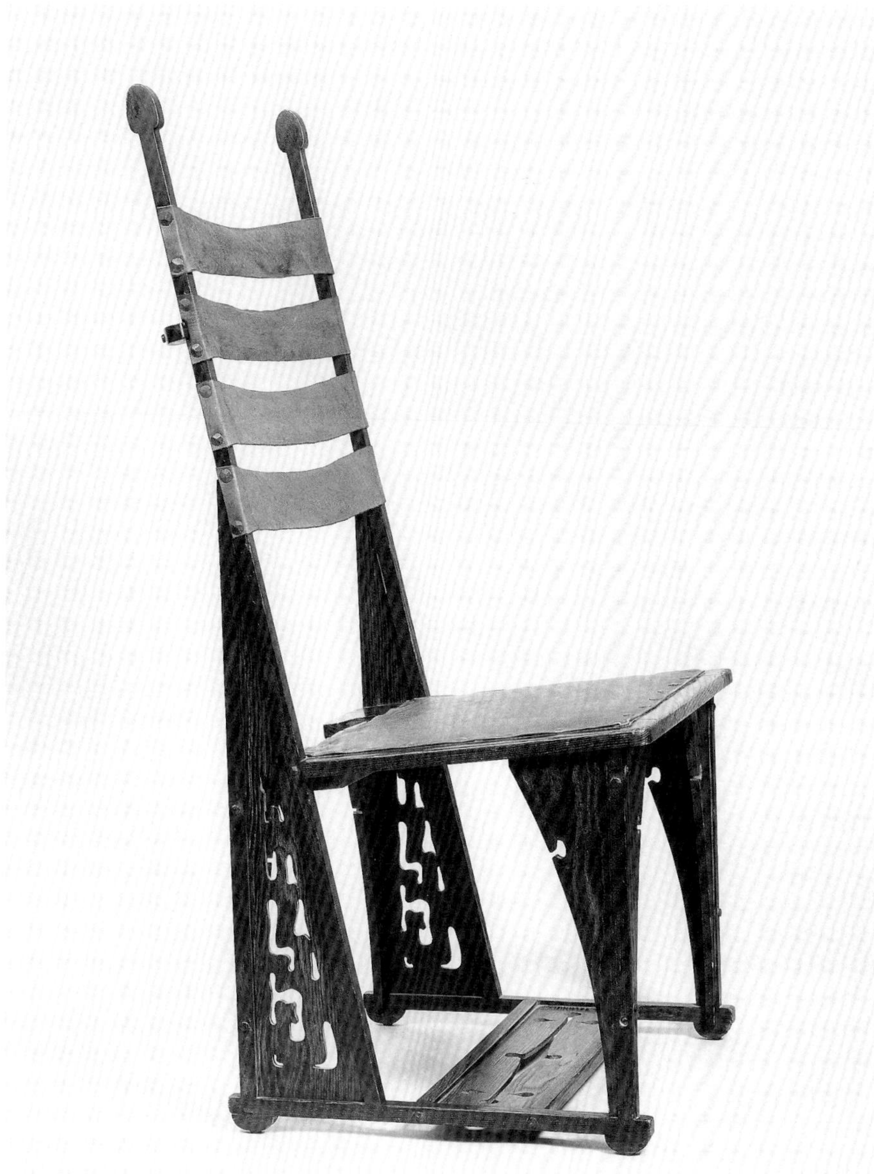

179.

Side Chair, dated 1905

Charles Rohlfs Workshop (1898–1928), Buffalo, New York; designed by Charles Rohlfs (1853–1936)
Oak with replaced padded leather seat and four ladder-back splats
46¼ × 22½ × 20 inches
Mark: Carved on back of proper right leg, *R* enclosed in stylized Chinese rectangle above *19/05*
1983.96

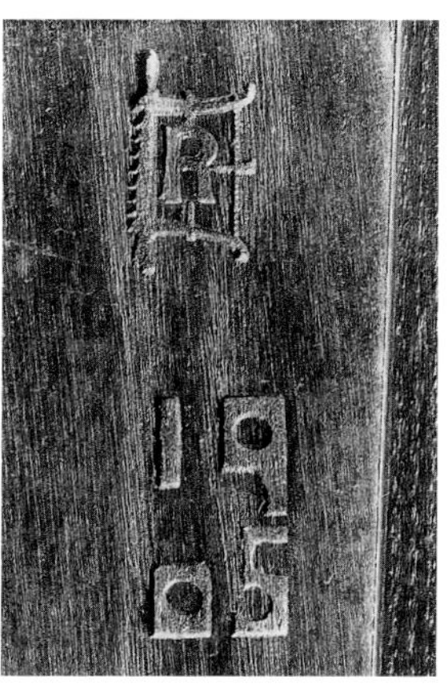

180.

Folding Screen,
dated 1900

Charles Rohlfs Workshop (1898–1928), Buffalo, New York; designed by Charles Rohlfs (1853–1936)
Oak with replaced leather hinges
72 × 22¼ × ½ inches
Mark: Carved on lower left corner of left panel frame, *1900* above *R* enclosed in stylized Chinese rectangle
1981.1000.53

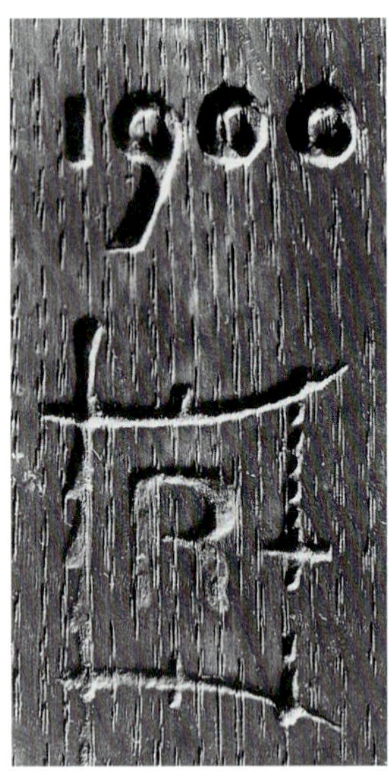

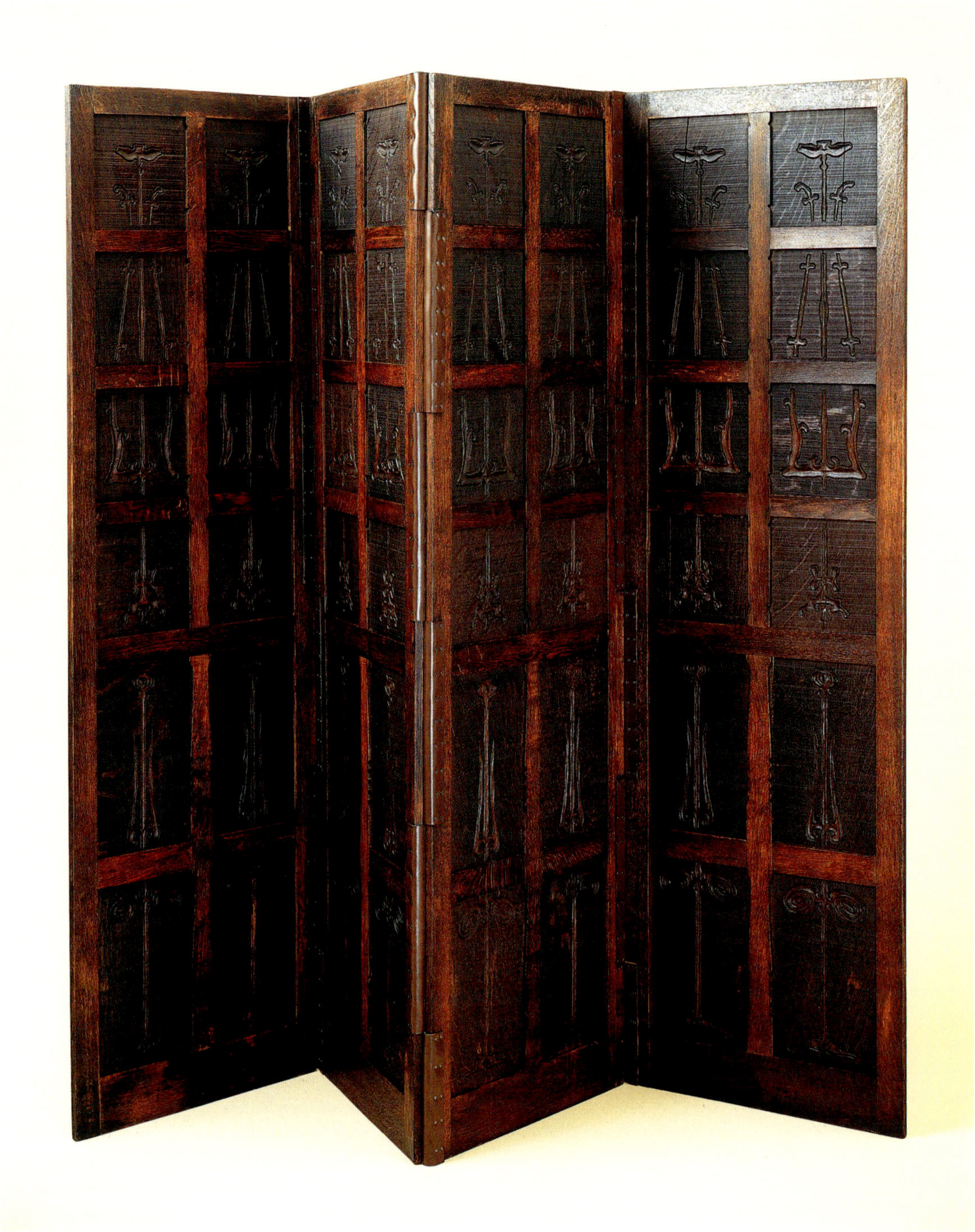

smaller than most American Arts and Crafts furniture-making facilities; Rohlfs never employed more than eight craftsmen, with whom he worked very closely.[2] The workshop specialized in commissioned, one-of-a-kind pieces and ensembles, and its output was quite varied.

Furniture making was Rohlfs's third career. Born in New York, he was forced to seek employment at age twelve after the death of his cabinetmaker father in 1865. At sixteen, he entered the foundry business, and by 1872 he was designing cast-iron stoves and furnaces. While attending courses at Cooper Union in New York, Rohlfs also worked in the professional theater and achieved recognition as a Shakespearean actor and scholar. He finally submitted to pressures exerted by his fiancee's family, however, and gave up the theater when he married in 1884. He then moved to Buffalo to manage a foundry business. There, his furniture making evolved out of the need to furnish his family's home. He made furniture from his own designs in his attic workshop and his creations attracted the attention of friends and outside clients, who began commissioning pieces.

In 1898, Rohlfs opened his art furniture workshop in downtown Buffalo. The workshop achieved national recognition in 1900 when Chicago's Marshall Field's department store exhibited his furniture. Rohlfs's furniture was also shown the following year at the Pan-American Exposition in Buffalo, and in 1902, Rohlfs was the only American furniture maker invited to participate at the International Exhibition of Modern Decorative Arts in Turin, Italy. After the Turin exhibition, Rohlfs was elected to the Royal Society of Arts in London. A further distinction was the commission of a set of chairs for Buckingham Palace, awarded by King Edward VII. In 1904, the Charles Rohlfs Workshop exhibited at the Louisiana Purchase International Exposition in St. Louis.

This chair and folding screen were made for Rohlfs's home and descended through his son, Roland Rohlfs. The dark oak frame, brown leather seat, and ladder-back slats of this chair (no. 179) are similar to Stickley's furniture. However, the jig-cut shaping of the finials of the side stiles and the stylized cutouts in the triangular-shaped legs and cross stretcher distinguish Rohlfs's work from the more linear American Arts and Crafts furniture. The Crawford screen (no. 180) is one of two designed by Rohlfs (the location of the other is unknown) shown in an early twentieth-century photograph of the Rohlfs house interior.[3] As a part of the late-nineteenth-century craze for the Japanese style, folding screens became popular in American interiors. They were made by a number of American firms, including Tiffany Studios and Stickley's Craftsman Workshops.[4]

The dark brown oak and leather hinges of the screen relate it to other American Arts and Crafts furniture. The general construction—a framework of stiles and cross stretchers enclosing carved panels—follows the medieval construction technique of wainscoting. The distinctive notches in the framework are characteristic of the Charles Rohlfs Workshop. The elongated carving of stylized floral motifs on the inset panels suggests an awareness of contemporary French Art Nouveau design.

NOTES

1. For illustrations of Rohlfs's works and discussions of his career, see Bowman 1990, pp. 58–61; Clark 1972, p. 28; Kaplan 1987, p. 240; Ludwig 1983, pp. 87–88; and Volpe and Cathers 1988, pp. 40–44.

2. Interview by Robert Judson Clark with Roland Rohlfs, August 1, 1971; cited in Kaplan 1987, p. 240.

3. Correspondence, Robert Judson Clark, Princeton University, New Jersey, November 4, 1979, High Museum of Art document files.

4. The Crawford screen is illustrated and discussed in Komanecky and Butera 1984, pp. 106–107, fig. 119. A Stickley screen is illustrated on p. 107, fig. 118, along with a Tiffany Studios screen on p. 101, fig. 113. In his essay, pp. 41–119, Michael Komanecky discusses the history of European and American screens in the late nineteenth century.

181.

Vase, dated 1901

Rookwood Pottery (1880–1967), Cincinnati; decorated by Grace Young (1869–1947)
Earthenware
14½ × 6¼ × 6¼ inches
Marks: Impressed on bottom, *GY/RP* monogram surrounded by fourteen flame points/*I*/*907C*/—*Pablino Diaz/(Kiowa)* in script
1993.129

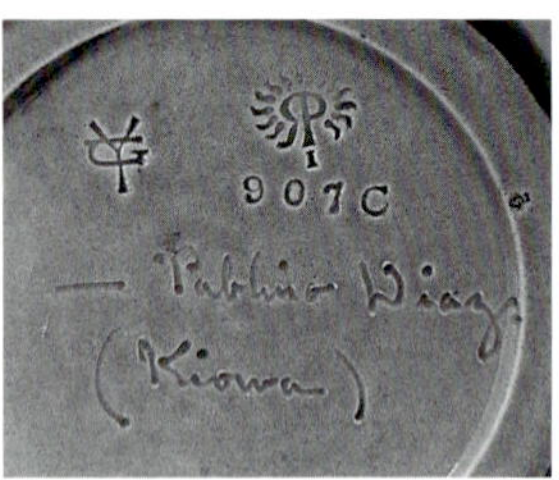

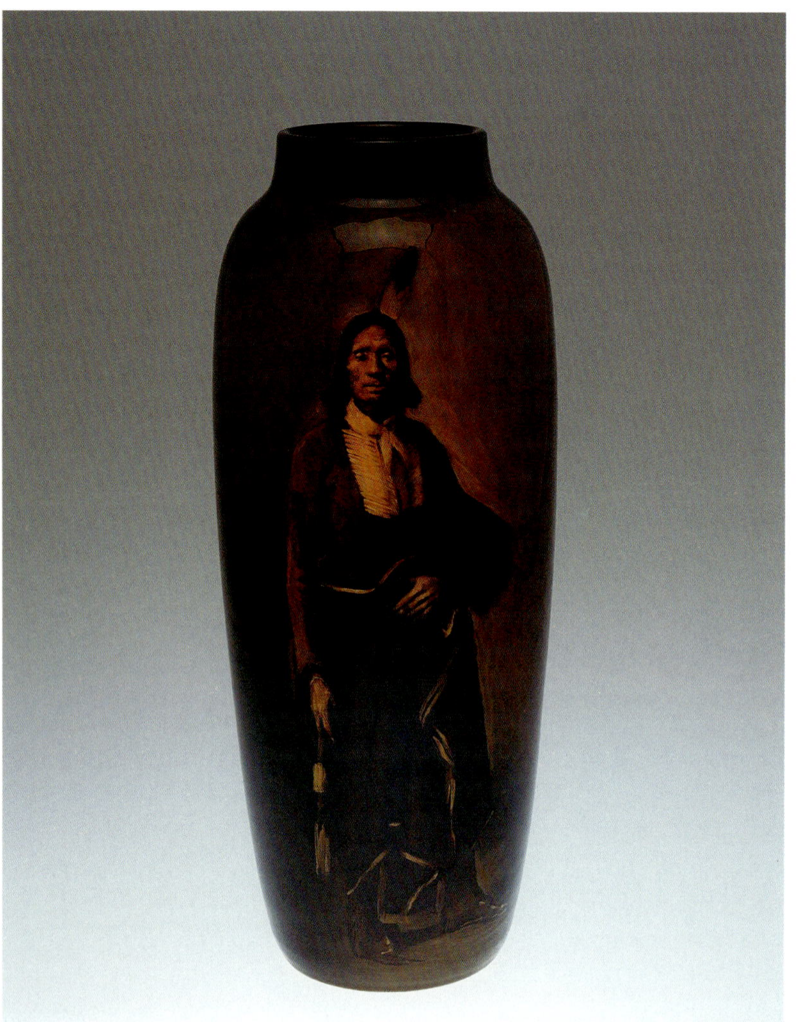

The Rookwood Pottery was the best known and longest flourishing American art pottery. Its establishment in 1880 predated the American Arts and Crafts movement, and it survived for eighty-seven years, long after the movement had ended. This vase was painted by Grace Young, who was among the first of Rookwood's artists to depart from floral decorations in favor of portraits. Many portrait vases were executed at Rookwood in the 1890s, and subjects included African Americans, Native Americans, and adaptations from Old Master and modern German portraits. The Crawford vase is a relatively late example.[1]

Maria Longworth Nichols, who founded the Rookwood Pottery, was fascinated by the Japanese ceramics at the 1876 Centennial Exposition in Philadelphia (see no. 121). The earliest Rookwood wares reflected the Japanese influence that was permeating American decorative arts at the time. Nichols hired professional ceramicists and artists, many of whom had trained at the Cincinnati Art Academy. By 1883, she employed seven artists to decorate pottery, and the firm's experiments had led to what would later be called Rookwood's Standard glaze, seen on the Crawford vase. Standard glaze involved decoration painted in liquid clay on a dark background and covered with yellow-tinted glaze. The effect was a hard and shiny finish with deep, rich colors. Rookwood artists explored various subjects, and by the late 1880s, flowers were replacing the early Japanese-inspired decoration. Nichols hired William Watts Taylor to manage the pottery in 1883. Although Taylor's concern for profits led to a greater standardization of forms, experiments in glazing and new ceramic bodies continued, even after Nichols remarried and gave the pottery to Taylor in 1890.

Taylor actively merchandised and publicized Rookwood Pottery, which received medals and recognition at the Exposition Universelle in Paris in 1889 and in 1900, and at the World's Columbian Exposition in Chicago in 1893. In 1881, the year it opened, the Cincinnati Art Museum received a collection of twenty-nine pieces of Rookwood from the Women's Art Museum Association. European museums began acquiring pieces from the Exposition Universelle in 1889, and by the early 1890s, over one hundred retailers nationwide were selling Rookwood's art ware.[2]

Among the decorative themes at Rookwood in the 1890s, portraiture vied with floral decoration as the favorite subject. Portrait vases, however, did not have the same broad appeal as those decorated with flowers and were never as commercially viable. In the first few years of the twentieth century, portraits were eased out as a major form of decoration. This coincided with Rookwood's introduction of matte glazes, which soon superseded the Standard glaze as a result of competition from another art pottery, the Grueby Faience Company of Boston (see nos. 195–196). American taste in Arts and Crafts was shifting away from highly reflective glazes, which were thought of as too industrial.[3]

Grace Young was born just across the Ohio River from Cincinnati in Covington, Kentucky, and attended the Cincinnati Art Academy, where she later taught. In 1886, Young joined the decorating staff of Rookwood Pottery and worked there until 1904, when she returned to teaching at the Academy. Young was known for her portrait decorations at Rookwood, particularly those of Native Americans.[4]

This portrait depicts Pablino Diaz of the Kiowa tribe of Plains people, then living in Oklahoma. It is based on a photograph (fig. 1), probably taken in 1898 at the Trans-Mississippi Exposition in Omaha by the fair's official photographer, Frank A. Rinehart, who photographed a number of Plains people that summer.[5] The vase was unusual among Rookwood's Native American portraits, which were usually executed on shorter, broader vases and showed only a face or bust. Here, on a tall and thin vase, the Diaz

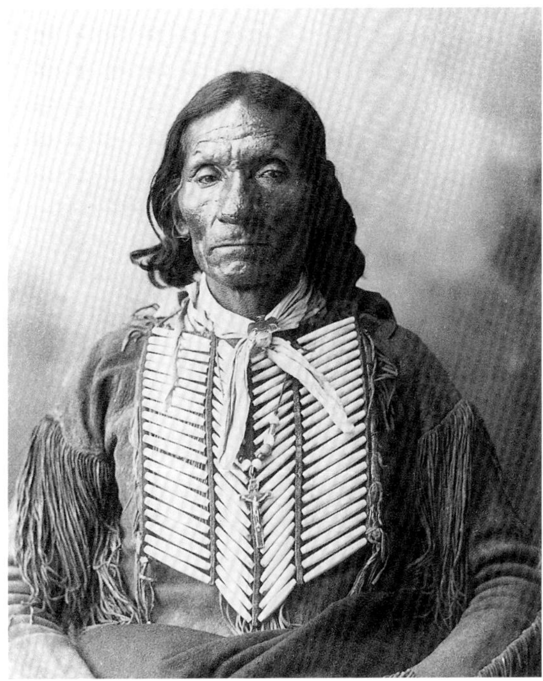

Fig. 1. Pablo Diaz—Kiowa. Photographed by Frank Rinehart, 1898.

portrait is one of only a few that showed the full figure. Rinehart's photograph shows Diaz's jacket and chest ornaments as Young rendered them. However, the Rookwood artist took liberties, expanding the half-length photograph into a full-length portrait. In the 1909 edition of his pioneering study on American ceramics, Edwin AtLee Barber included an illustration of this vase. Young reportedly selected the Pablino Diaz vase for Barber's collection, but research has yet to prove that he actually owned it.[6]

NOTES

1. For a general history of the Rookwood Pottery, see Peck 1991. A historical overview by Kenneth R. Trapp appears in Ellis 1992, pp. 10–41, and a discussion of portraits on Rookwood vases, especially those of Native Americans, is on pp. 19–20.

2. See Peck 1991, pp. 155–160; and Ellis 1992, p. 17.

3. Ellis 1992, pp. 27–32.

4. Peck 1991, p. 148.

5. Correspondence from Paula Fleming at the Smithsonian Institution's National Museum of Natural History, Anthropological Archives, May 7, 1997, identifies Young's source as a Rinehart photograph from the archives there, High Museum of Art document files. A biography of Frank A. Rinehart is provided in the introduction to Sutton 1972, n.p.

6. Barber, *Pottery,* 1976, p. 479, fig. 247. Correspondence, Gary and Diana Stradling, February 18, 1992, High Museum of Art document files.

Arthur J. Stone

A 1919 MAGAZINE article characterized Arthur J. Stone as the successor to Paul Revere, the best-known early American silversmith, a comparison based on Stone's handmade silver and his training of apprentices.[1] Although Stone is associated with the Arts and Crafts movement, he had broad experience in the mechanized English and American silver industries in the nineteenth century.

Born in Sheffield, England, Stone apprenticed with a local silversmith, Edwin Eagle, for seven years while taking evening courses at the National School of Design. After working for a year as a chaser and designer in Edinburgh, Scotland, he returned to Sheffield to do repoussé and fluting work. From 1875 to 1884, Stone worked for James Dixon and Sons of Sheffield as a designer, modeler, and chaser of silverware. In 1884, attracted by the generous salaries offered to English-trained workers in the American silver industry, Stone immigrated to Concord, New Hampshire, where he worked for the William B. Durgin Silver Company. He moved in 1887 to Gardner, Massachusetts, where for six years he was a designer and head of the holloware department at the Frank W. Smith Silver Company. After working for the P. J. Howard Company in New York in 1895, Stone returned to Gardner to marry Elizabeth Bent Eaton, the wealthy widow of a furniture manufacturer, and to work as an independent silver designer.

In 1901, Stone established his own silver studio in Gardner and joined the Society of Arts and Crafts, Boston, at the "Craftsman" level. He won the Society's "Master" level in 1903 and his designs garnered a silver medal at the 1904 Louisiana Purchase International Exposition in St. Louis. He practiced independently for about five years, and in 1906 began hiring assistants and apprentices to train as silversmiths. Also in that year, he was awarded his second "Master" level from the Society. In 1913, Stone was the first recipient of the Society's "Medalist" award, their highest honor for metalwork.[2]

Stone's membership in the prestigious Society of Arts and Crafts brought him customers and commissions. His shop made wares for domestic table use, for presentation, and for religious purposes. His clients included socially prominent families, churches, and architects in the

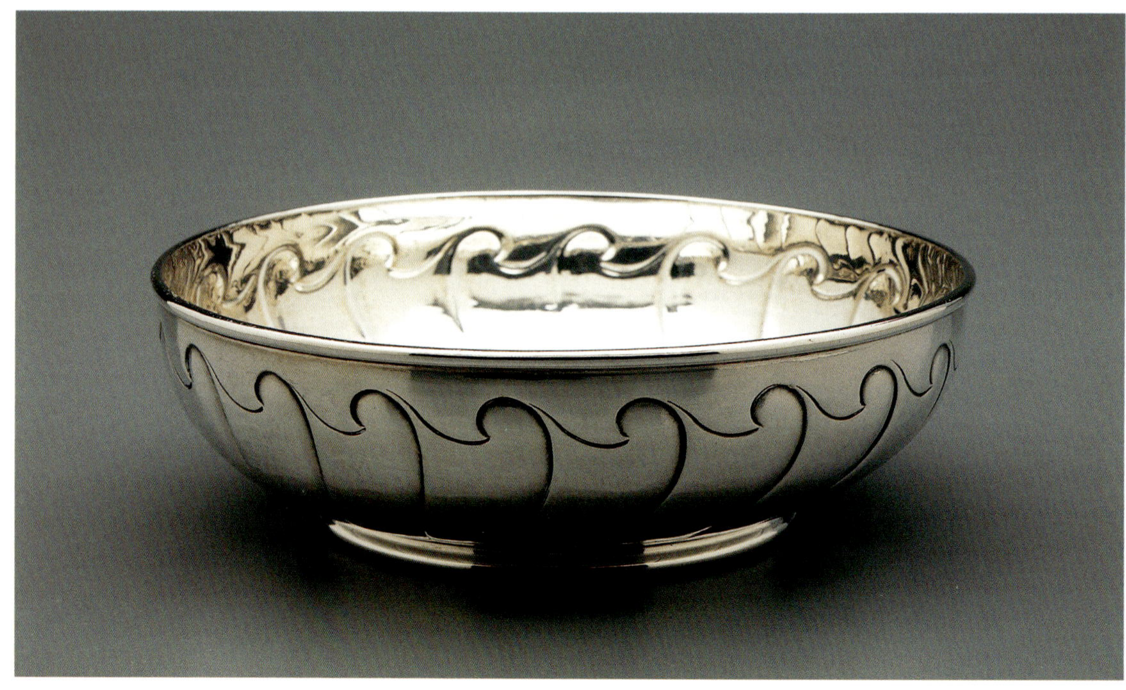

182.

Bowl, 1901–1906

Arthur J. Stone (1847–1937),
Gardner, Massachusetts
Silver
1¾ × 5½ × 5½ inches
Mark: Impressed on bottom, *STERLING*/hammer
1989.139

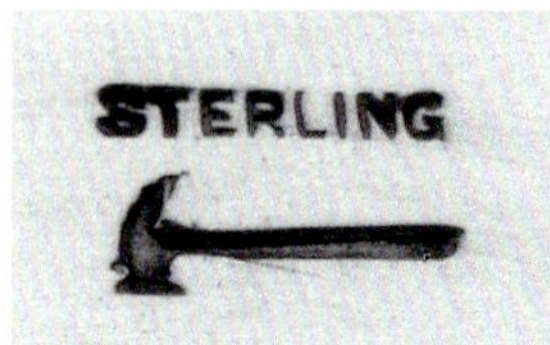

East and Midwest, and he produced a number of commemorative presentation pieces for Harvard and Yale Universities.[3]

Stone's shop operated under an apprenticeship system, and of the more than twenty-five apprentices he trained, many went on to earn "Craftsman" and "Master" designations from the Society of Arts and Crafts. While most specialized in particular disciplines and processes of silversmithing, they were trained in all aspects of the craft. Stone's mark was on every piece because he was involved in the design and decoration of all of the shop's output, but when an assistant's work met Stone's standards, he was also allowed to impress his initial under Stone's mark.[4]

Stone was involved in all processes of silversmithing, particularly his specialties of chasing and repoussé work, until he suffered a mild stroke in 1926. Although the stroke limited his participation, he remained involved with the design process until he officially retired on his ninetieth birthday in 1937. He sold the studio, and his former assistants and new apprentices continued to work at Stone Associates until it closed its doors in 1957.

This repoussé bowl (no. 182) probably dates to the first five years of Stone's independent shop, between 1901 and 1906, although Stone's mark alone on the bowl suggests an early date. The small circular shape, scalloped repoussé decoration, and hand-hammered surface are characteristic of Stone's early work. Stone seems to have been looking at late-seventeenth and early-eighteenth-century American chased work for inspiration.

A later example from the Stone shop is the small mustard pot (no. 183) with hinged lid and miniature spoon. Rather than making reproductions of colonial American or early English silver, Stone created new designs based on historical decorations and forms. The pot and spoon are early-twentieth-century adaptations of American Federal silver prototypes. The mustard pot is lined with cobalt glass, which shows through the perforations in its silver reticulated sides.

Besides Stone's touchmark, the pot is marked with a "B," indicating that Stone was assisted by William Blair, a "Craftsman" level member of the Society of Arts and Crafts who worked in Stone's holloware shop from 1908 to 1909. The assistants hammered the shapes, and Stone was responsible for the design and decoration. The spoon is marked with an "L" for Sylvanus E. Lamphrey, who worked in Stone's flatware shop from 1909 to 1912. The overlapping working dates of these two craftsmen provide the specific date of 1909 for the manufacture of the mustard pot.[5]

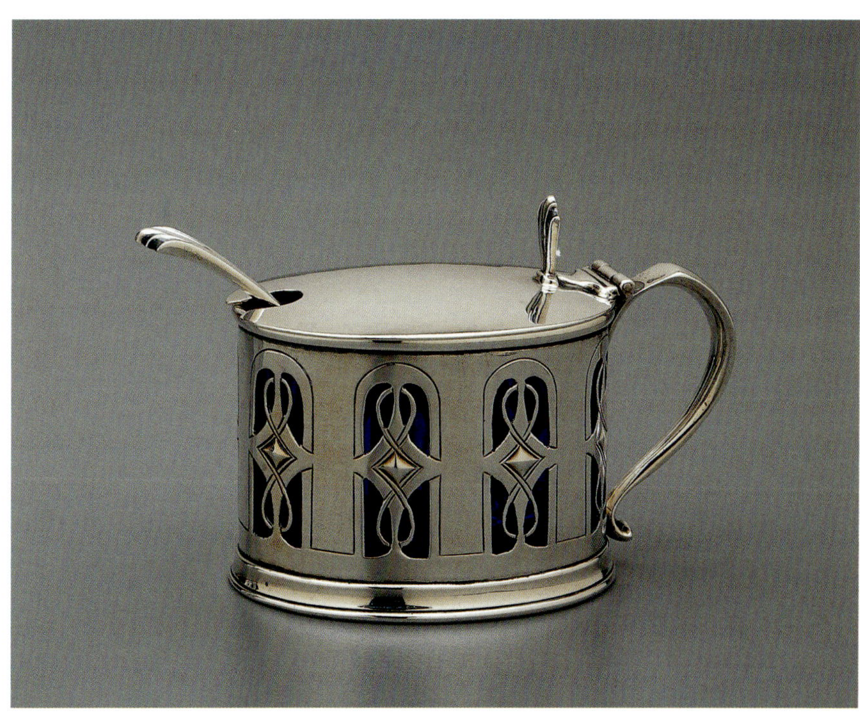

183.

Mustard Pot and Spoon, 1909

Arthur J. Stone (1847–1937), assisted by William Blair and Sylvanus E. Lamphrey, Gardner, Massachusetts
Silver and glass
Pot: 2½ × 3¼ × 1⅞ inches
Spoon: 3¼ × ⅞ inches
Marks: Pot: Impressed on bottom, *STERLING A. STONE* and hammer/*B*
Spoon: Impressed on handle, *STERLING A. STONE* and hammer/*L*
1989.140.a–b

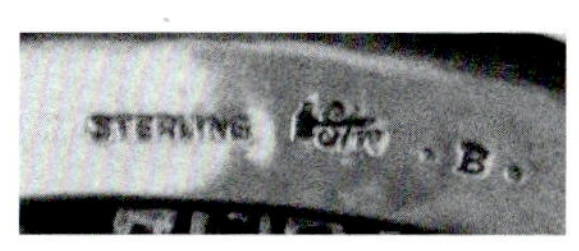

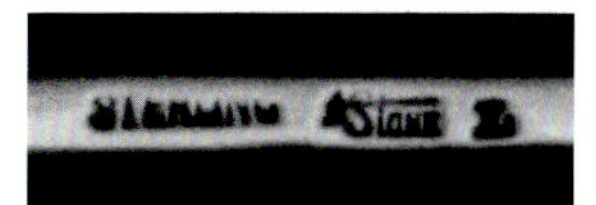

NOTES

1. Sargent 1919, pp. 121–125.

2. For biographical information about Stone, see Boston Athenaeum 1981, pp. 5–9. Stone's apprenticeship and early training are discussed in Stone 1902, pp. 169–189. The levels of membership in the Society of Arts and Crafts, Boston "Craftsman," "Master," and "Patron" (later "Associate")—are discussed in Meyer 1997, p. 34.

3. See Boston Athenaeum 1981, pp. 10–19; and Sargent 1906, p. 34.

4. See Boston Athenaeum 1981, pp. 9, 20–21; and Gardner Museum 1991, pp. 10–11.

5. Boston Athenaeum 1981, p. 21.

The Van Briggle Pottery Company

From his childhood in Felicity, Ohio, Artus Van Briggle was determined to become a painter, following in the footsteps of his ancestor Pieter Brueghel the Elder. At the age of seventeen, Van Briggle enrolled at the Cincinnati Art Academy, and the following year he went to work for Rookwood Pottery (see no. 181), painting slip floral decorations on vases. He was a highly regarded decorator at Rookwood, and when a new pottery facility was completed in 1891, he was one of the few assigned a private studio. Van Briggle also continued his painting, and one of his canvases was exhibited at the 1893 World's Columbian Exposition in Chicago.

Because of his promise as a decorator and his success in Chicago, the Rookwood Pottery granted Van Briggle a leave of absence with financial support to study in Paris. During his three-year stay, he studied at the Académie Julian, where he won prizes for painting and drawing and took courses in sculpture and clay modeling. He admired the "dead" or matte glazes on Chinese Ming porcelains at the Musée des Arts Decoratifs and the Sèvres Museum. In 1896, he returned to Cincinnati and the Rookwood Pottery. Maria Longworth Nichols Storer, founder of the Rookwood Pottery, provided Van Briggle with a small kiln for ceramic experiments in his home studio, and by 1898 he was able to approximate the matte glazes he had so admired in France. Rookwood continued his work with matte glazes after his departure.

Van Briggle had suffered from chronic tuberculosis since childhood, and early in 1899 he resigned from Rookwood and moved to the healthier climate of Colorado Springs. He continued to pursue both painting and ceramics and experimented with local and imported clays in the laboratories of Colorado College. Here Van Briggle achieved the matte glaze he had been seeking. With further patronage from Storer, Van Briggle opened his own pottery in Colorado Springs, and by the end of 1901, the first Van Briggle pottery was offered for sale.[1] With the subtle tones of the matte glazes and the stylized, low-relief modeling in elongated Art Nouveau curves, the pottery met with immediate success. In 1902, the Van Briggle Pottery Company was made a joint stock company. Van Briggle's small personal studio was expanded and by 1904 had fourteen employees.

Also in 1902, Van Briggle married Anne Gregory, an American artist he had met in Paris. Because of her artistic interests and talents, as well as the continuing poor health of her husband, Anne assumed a major role in the business, including management and design. The mark of the new pottery was incised with conjoined "A"s for Anne and Artus. Van Briggle pottery received high praise at the Paris Salon exhibition in 1903 and at the 1904 Louisiana Purchase International Exposition in St. Louis, where it was awarded numerous medals. Van Briggle died of tuberculosis during that exhibition, on July 4, 1904.

Anne Van Briggle assumed the presidency of the company, and in 1907–1908 she built an expanded pottery plant in memory of Artus. She remarried in 1908 but continued her work at the pottery until 1912, when she sold it and moved with her husband to Denver. The Van Briggle Pottery Company was subsequently sold and reorganized a number of times, but it continued producing the early designs of Van Briggle in addition to new lines.

Designs for the Crawford vase (no. 184) and plate (no. 185) are attributed to Artus Van Briggle.[2] The pottery's designs often included plants indigenous to Colorado; stylized poppies, a favorite flower of Anne Van Briggle, were used on both these examples.[3] Van Briggle incorporated low-relief modeling into the structure rather than applying it to the surface, illustrating his departure from the flat, painted-slip decorations he had executed for Rookwood. During the early years of production, molds were made from Van Briggle's designs intended for limited issue. After the wares were molded, they were finished by hand, causing slight variations. They were then fired, glazed, and refired.

Marks on these pieces provide clues to their date of manufacture. Both the vase and plate were designed by Van Briggle in 1902, with the date hand-inscribed beneath the Van Briggle name and mark. The vase marks include the

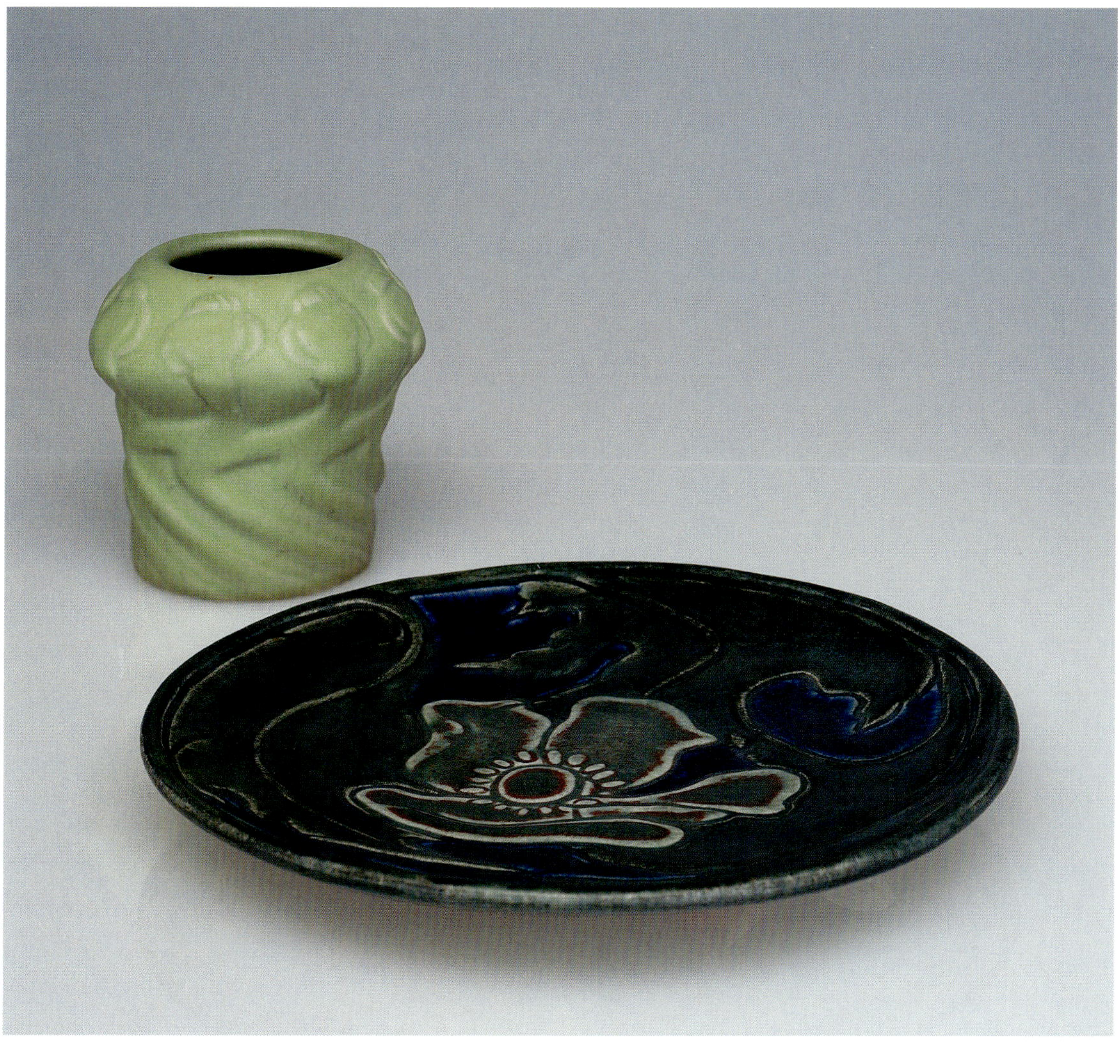

184.

Vase, designed 1902

Van Briggle Pottery Company (1901–ca. 1920), Colorado Springs, Colorado; designed by Artus Van Briggle (1869–1904)
Earthenware with matte glaze
3¾ × 4 × 4 inches
Mark: Incised on bottom, conjoined *A*s within a rectangle/*VAN BRIGGLE /1902/85–15 70*
1984.139

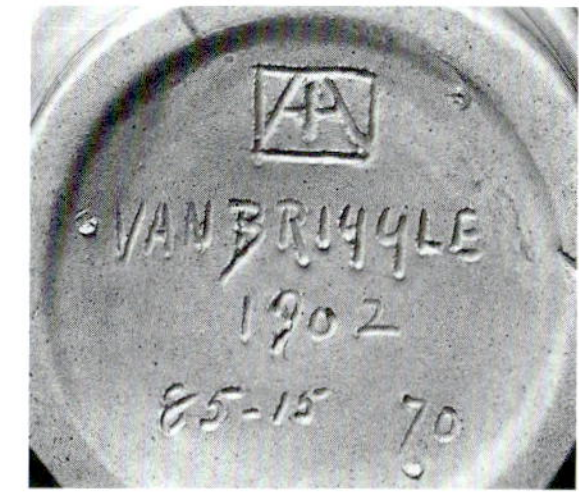

185.

Plate, designed 1902

Van Briggle Pottery Company (1901–ca. 1920), Colorado Springs, Colorado; designed by Artus Van Briggle (1869–1904)
Earthenware with matte glaze
1 × 8½ × 8½ inches
Marks: Incised on bottom, conjoined *A*s within a rectangle/*VAN BRIGGLE/1902/III/*impressed *20*
1985.312

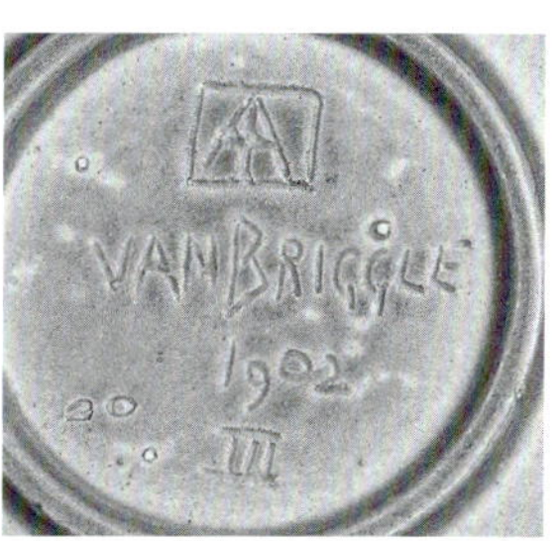

pottery logo, the name, and the date of the design. The inscribed "85–15" suggests that this example was produced in 1915, long after the artist had died and his widow had sold the pottery. The "70" may identify the finisher. The same logo, name, and date of the design are inscribed on the plate. The impressed pattern number, "20," and the inscribed "III," indicating clay type, were customary markings at the pottery in 1902 and 1903.[4]

NOTES

1. Accounts of Van Briggle's biography and the history of the pottery are presented in Arnest 1975, pp. 9–19; Bogue 1968, pp. 1–49; Evans 1987, pp. 297–301; and Kovel and Kovel 1993, pp. 229–238.

2. See Newton Robert Wyman's "Catalogue of Van Briggle Designs," in Arnest 1975, p. 38, nos. 20–21.

3. Arnest 1975, p. 11.

4. Marks are discussed and dated in ibid., pp. 21–22; Evans 1987, p. 301; and Kovel and Kovel 1993, pp. 236–238.

186.

Vase, designed 1902

American Terra Cotta and Ceramic Company (ca. 1885–1941), Terra Cotta, Illinois; designed by Hugh M. G. Garden (1873–1961)
Earthenware with matte glaze
11⅞ × 6¼ × 6¼ inches
Mark: Impressed on bottom, *TECO*
1993.130

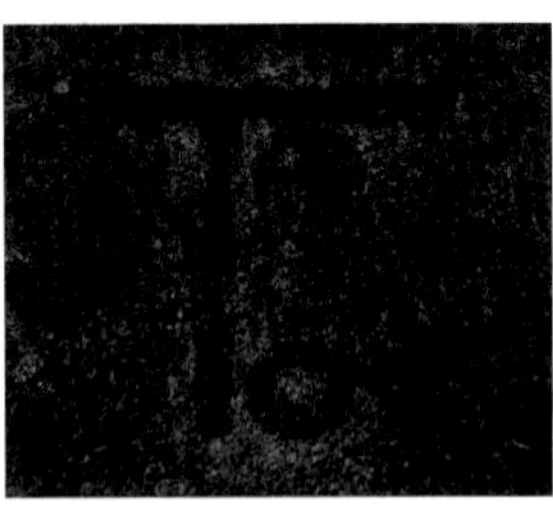

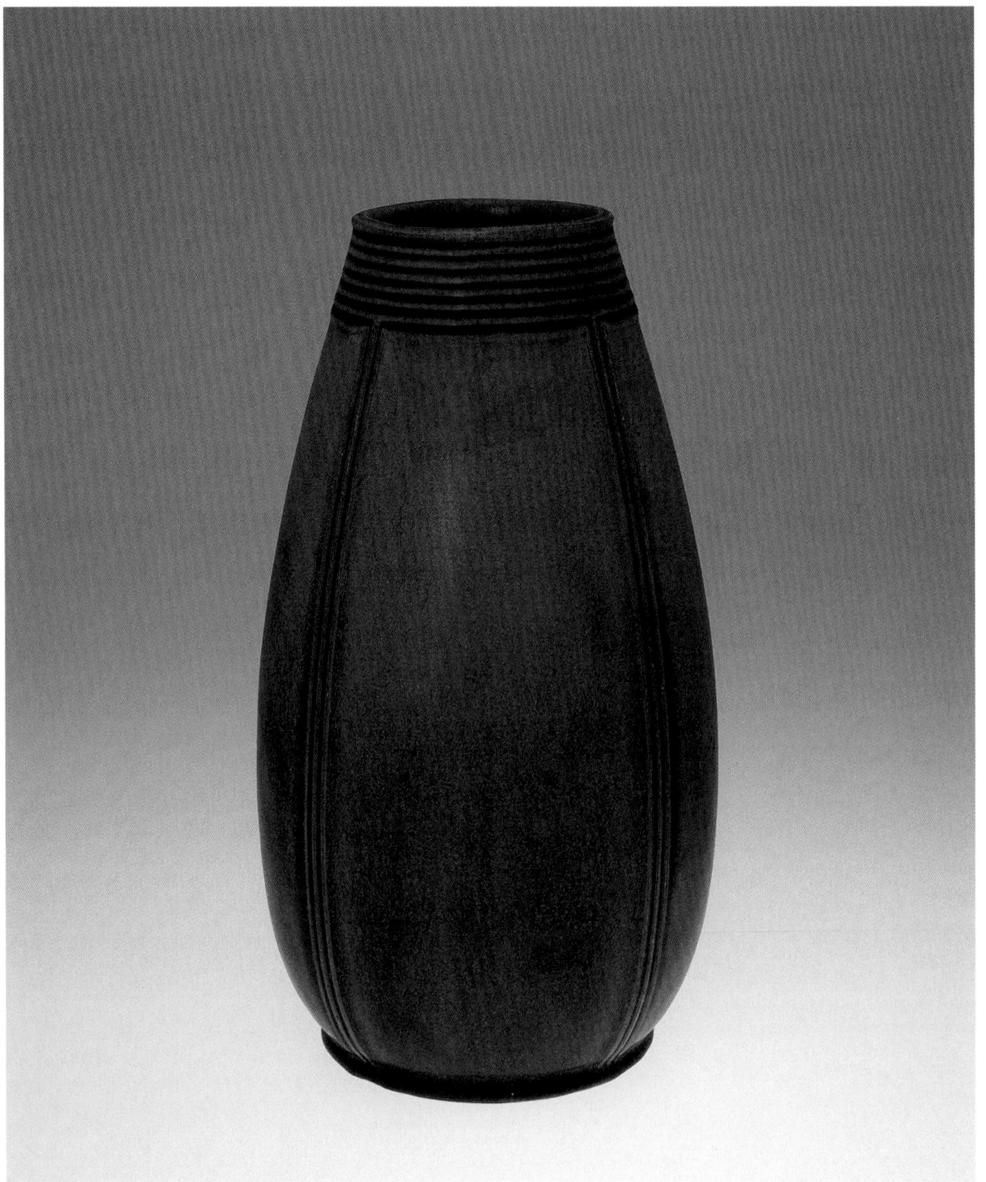

William Day Gates discovered clay deposits on his land forty-five miles northwest of Chicago, and in 1881, he established the Spring Valley Tile Works, which sold drain tile, brick, and architectural terra-cotta. In 1887, the firm was reincorporated as the American Terra Cotta and Ceramic Company, and their expanded line of architectural decorations included chimney tops and roof finials, along with garden urns and other landscape ornaments.

The development of the company coincided with the tremendous rebuilding of Chicago after the devastating fire of 1871. The search for nonflammable building materials created a ready market for terra-cotta architectural elements. Terra-cotta also suited architects and builders because it was less expensive to mold clay ornaments than to carve stone architectural details.

Gates, a Chicago lawyer, was also an amateur potter and experimented in kiln work. The success of his terra-cotta business, which continued to prosper into the 1920s, enabled him to establish an art pottery, Gates Potteries, which at first produced work of his own design. Because of his contacts in the Chicago building community, Gates persuaded local architects to submit pottery designs for his new venture. He named the art pottery line Teco, from the Latin words "terra" and "cotta," and experimented with glazes so that the art pottery could be baked in the same kilns as the architectural ornaments.[1]

The involvement of architects in the design of Teco ware distinguished the firm's output among its contemporaries. Gates was a supporter of the Chicago Architectural Sketch Club, which sponsored talks, design competitions, and annual exhibitions at the Art Institute of Chicago. He exhibited giant terra-cotta garden vases in the club's annual exhibitions in 1894 and 1895, and the Teco art pottery line debuted there in 1900. By 1901, Gates had produced over 150 shapes for the Teco line in collaboration with architects. By 1904, when the company exhibited at the Louisiana Purchase International Exposition in St. Louis, nearly 300 different forms were in production.[2]

One of Gates's primary concerns was providing quality pottery inexpensively. Unlike other Arts and Crafts wares at the turn of the century, Teco ware was not turned on a potter's wheel but was instead made in molds, substantially cutting the cost of production. The decorative effect of Teco ware was derived largely from its shape and sculptural qualities rather than from painted decoration or expensive experimental glazes. The so-called Teco green, seen on this example, was the most extensively used color.[3]

The Crawford vase has a barrel shape with linear-relief molded decoration, and the form may have been used as a lamp base. It was designed by Chicago architect Hugh M. G. Garden and was among the Teco forms shown at the first Annual Exhibition of Applied Arts at the Art Institute of Chicago in 1902. The simple, elegant design apparently appealed to Frank Lloyd Wright (see nos. 223–224), as the vase appears on a shelf above a bookcase in a photograph of the living room of the Isabel Roberts house, which he designed in 1908 (fig. 1).

Garden was born in Canada and received no academic architectural training. As a young man he apprenticed with Minneapolis architect William Channing Whitney, and by 1892 he had joined the Chicago Architectural Sketch Club. In the early 1890s, Garden was working as a freelance draftsman for architects, including Louis H. Sullivan (see no. 221) and Wright, whose work influenced him deeply. He later became a partner with architect Richard E. Schmidt, a venture that lasted nearly the rest of his career. Garden's best-known building is the 1907 Montgomery Ward warehouse.[4]

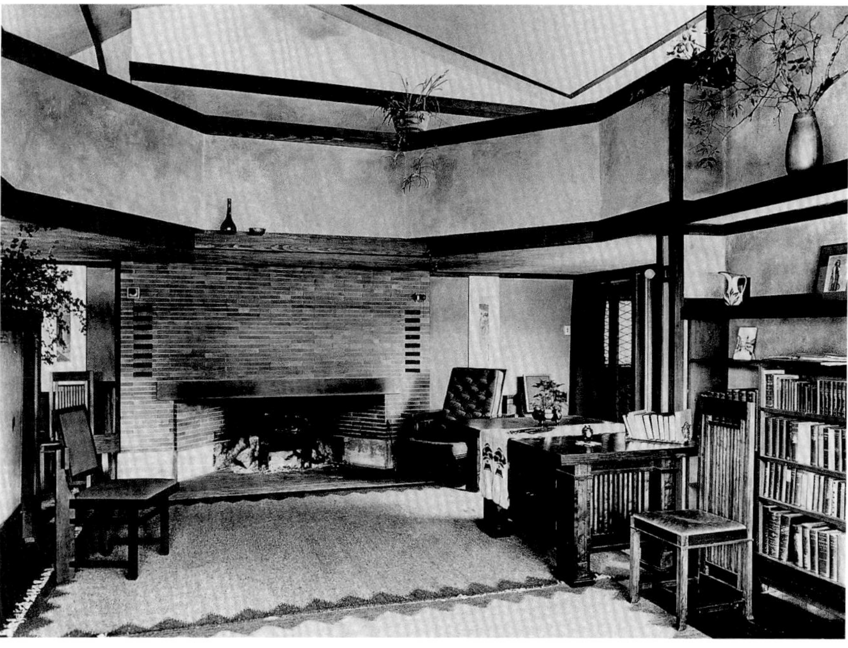

Fig. 1. Isabel Roberts house. Designed by Frank Lloyd Wright, 1908.

The onset of the Great Depression in 1929 brought a halt to construction in Chicago, resulting in the rapid decline of the American Terra Cotta and Ceramic Company and the end of the Teco line. In 1930, ownership passed out of the Gates family. The plant continued to produce garden pottery until 1941, when it was taken over by industries necessary to the war effort.

NOTES

1. An illustrated history of Gates Potteries and Teco ware appears in Darling 1989, pp. 14–74. The firm is also discussed in Darling 1979, pp. 54–70; and Evans 1987, pp. 278–281.

2. For an illustration of the Teco exhibit at the Louisiana Purchase International Exposition in St. Louis, see Darling 1989, p. 40, fig. 38. Gates was also a member of the Cliff Dwellers, a Chicago social club composed of prominent local architects, artists, writers, and musicians. In 1909, the club decorated its new headquarters with Teco wares. For a discussion of the Cliff Dwellers Club and photographs of its rooms, see ibid., pp. 30–32, fig. 24.

3. For a discussion of Teco green, see D. Stradling 1983, pp. 9–36.

4. For a biography and survey of the work of Hugh M. G. Garden, see Greengard 1966. The Montgomery Ward warehouse is illustrated on p. 5. For Garden's obituary, see "Architects Weed" 1961.

187.

Vase, ca. 1904

Weller Pottery (1872–1949), Zanesville, Ohio; designed by Frederick Hurten Rhead (1880–1942)
Earthenware
14½ × 7⅞ × 7⅞ inches
Marks: Impressed on bottom, *Weller Faience Rhead/C345/5;* on body of vase, beneath standing figure, *E. J.*
1993.131

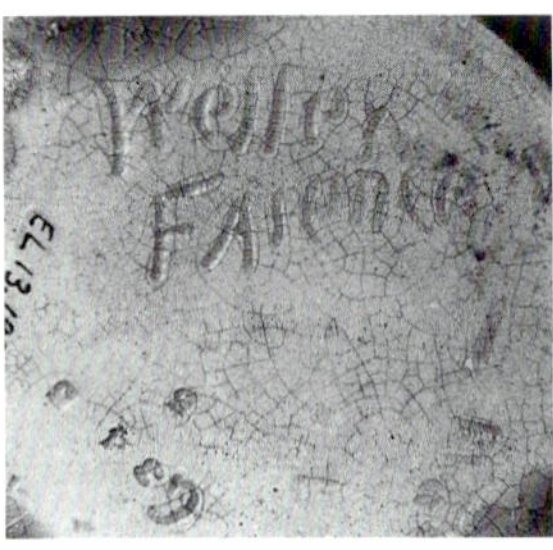

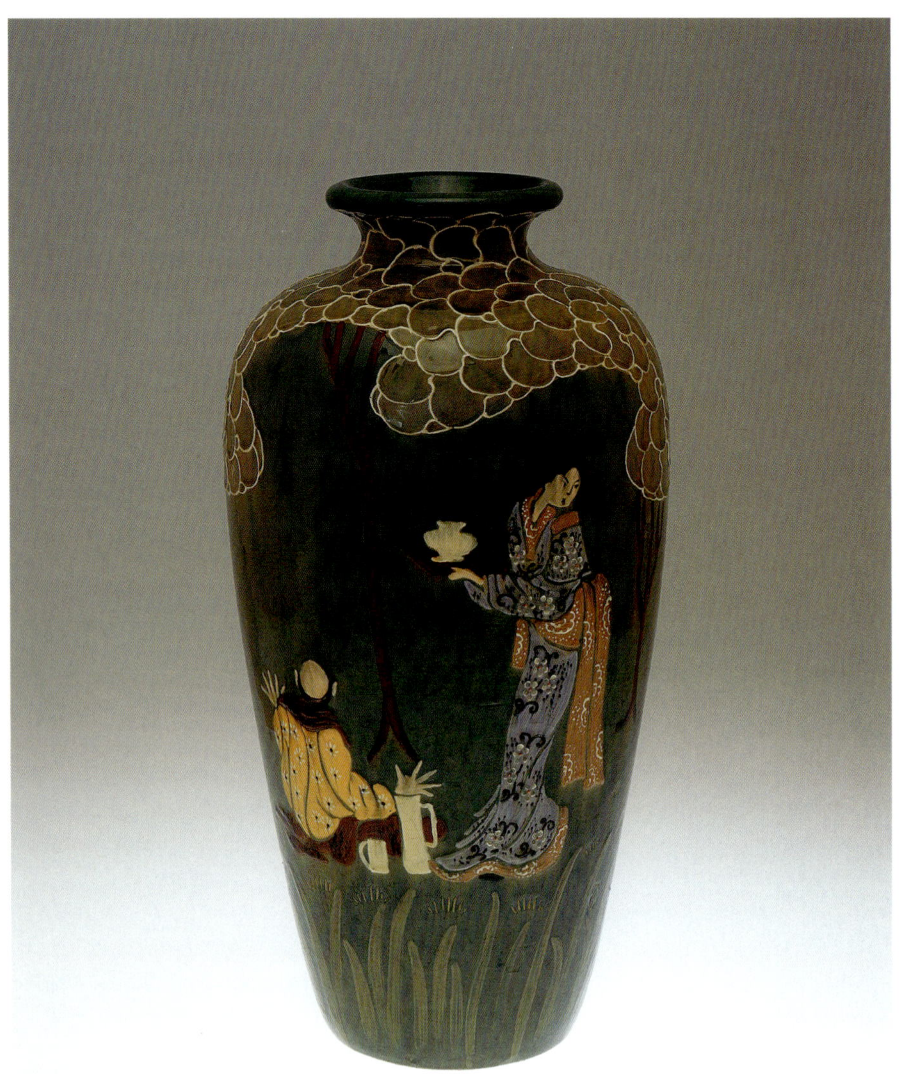

Frederick Hurten Rhead was born into a family of English potters in Staffordshire, where he was educated at the Wedgwood Institute in Burslem and the Stoke-on-Trent Government Art School. He served an apprenticeship with his father at Brownfield's Guild Pottery in Cobridge before becoming art director of the Wardle Pottery in Staffordshire and an instructor at the Government Art School in Longton. At this time, he also assisted his father in establishing an art pottery for Wileman and Company at Longton.[1]

In 1902, Rhead immigrated to the United States and joined the Vance/Avon Faience Company in Tiltonville, Ohio, a small six-kiln art pottery. Two years later, Rhead moved to Zanesville, Ohio—widely known as "Clay City"—where he became a designer for the large and prosperous Weller Pottery. He stayed at Weller for less than a year, moving on to its major Zanesville rival, the Roseville Pottery Company. Although both Weller and Roseville manufactured art pottery, they were large, commercial firms that followed the design leadership of smaller potteries such as the Rookwood Pottery in Cincinnati (see nos. 121, 181).[2]

The intense colors and the distinctive white trailed slip that outlines the foliage of the trees on this vase are distinctive to the designs of Rhead.[3] The Crawford vase was in Weller's Jap-Birdimal line, but Rhead had used trailed slip decoration at Vance/Avon Faience Company as early as 1902. The white slip, or liquid clay, was squeezed from a bag through a fine nozzle to give an outline effect. Rhead continued to use the trailed slip technique when he went on to Roseville Pottery and at his other pottery jobs at least until the 1920s. The trailed slip technique had been used in England to decorate pottery from the late nineteenth century, and Rhead must have been aware of the technique there. This shiny green vase was derived from an Asian form, and the figures with their colorful costumes reflect the Japanese influence in late-nineteenth-century English art pottery. The mark identifies Rhead's design of the vase and its decoration, and the initials "E. J." refer to the artist at Weller who executed the decoration.

In 1909, Rhead began working with potters Adelaide Alsop Robineau and Taxile Doat (see nos. 210–211) at the University City Pottery, part of the People's University, where he was head pottery instructor. People's University underwent a federal investigation for questionable fund management, and both Robineau and Rhead had departed the University City Pottery by 1911.[4]

Next, Rhead embarked on a lecture tour of California and worked for several California ceramic enterprises and on his own before returning in 1917 to Zanesville as head of design and decoration at the American Encaustic Tiling Company. In 1927, he moved to East Liverpool, Ohio, where he worked as art director for the Homer Laughlin China Company until his death in 1942. He was best known there for his creation of the popular, colorful, and inexpensive Fiesta ware, developed in 1935.[5]

Rhead worked in virtually every aspect of the American ceramic industry during the first four decades of the twentieth century. He designed and made pottery, provided instruction, and wrote articles for pottery and art journals throughout his career. Coming out of the long-established and well-organized English industrial ceramic tradition, Rhead was a key figure in the development of the twentieth-century American ceramic industry.

NOTES

1. Dale 1986, pp. 10–23, summarizes Rhead's early life and family background in Staffordshire and his American career, and provides a photographic survey of Rhead's work.

2. Rhead's work at Vance/Avon Faience, Weller Pottery, and Roseville Pottery is discussed and illustrated in ibid., pp. 24–59. For histories of these firms, see Evans 1987, pp. 303–306, 323–329, and 264–268, respectively.

3. The Crawford vase is illustrated and discussed in Dale 1986, pp. 36–39, fig. 41B. The English companies W. Moorcroft, Ltd., and Doulton and Company, Ltd., used trailed slip decoration extensively; examples are shown on p. 12, fig. 3, and p. 35, fig. 36.

4. For information about Rhead at the University City Pottery, see ibid., pp. 62–67. See nos. 210–211 in this catalogue for additional information about Edward Gardner Lewis, the People's University, and the University City Pottery.

5. For Rhead's California years, see Dale 1986, pp. 80–107. For his years at the American Encaustic Tiling Company and the Homer Laughlin China Company, see ibid., pp. 108–123.

Gustav Stickley's Craftsman Workshops

GUSTAV STICKLEY is indelibly associated with the Arts and Crafts movement in the United States. Although both Charles Rohlfs in Buffalo (see nos. 179–180) and the Roycrofter community in East Aurora, New York (see nos. 198–199), preceded him in making furniture following the tenets of the British Arts and Crafts movement in the 1890s, Stickley was the most successful promoter of Arts and Crafts in the United States in the first decade of the twentieth century. His monthly magazine *The Craftsman* had a wide circulation, bringing attention to his furniture and to Arts and Crafts designs in metalwork, ceramics, and textiles, as well as promoting related architecture and relevant social and aesthetic ideas.

Born Gustave Stoeckel in rural Wisconsin, Stickley was the eldest of thirteen children. After his father deserted the family, they moved to Brandt, Pennsylvania, where his mother had relatives operating a chair factory. From the mid-1870s, Stickley and his younger brothers worked in the factory, and Stickley found his career in the manufacture of furniture. In various partnerships, often with family members, he sold and manufactured furniture until 1916.

In the early 1890s, Stickley moved to Syracuse, New York, where he established a chair factory with a partner in suburban Eastwood. An 1898 trip to Europe gave him firsthand contact with products of the British Arts and Crafts movement and French Art Nouveau. By 1899, Stickley had bought out his partner and was operating the enterprise on his own under the name United Crafts. He began experimenting with new structural designs, inspired by European prototypes, that clearly showed the construction of the furniture. In the summer of 1900, Stickley premiered his *New Furniture* to the industry at the semiannual Grand Rapids, Michigan, furniture fair. The response was immediate and enthusiastic. By exhibiting his furniture to the American trade in Grand Rapids, Stickley was exposing his radical new ideas about design not only to powerful retailers who might distribute his goods, but also to his competitors. His subsequent successful showing at the 1901 Pan-American Exposition in Buffalo encouraged manufacturers in Chicago, Cincinnati (see no. 201), and Grand Rapids (see no. 202) to introduce their own lines of mission and Arts and Crafts furniture.[1]

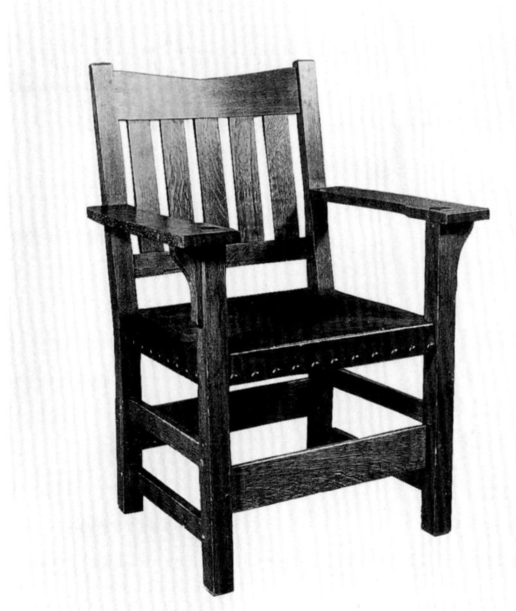

Fig. 1. Armchair, designed ca. 1901, manufactured ca. 1904–1907. Made by Gustav Stickley's Craftsman Workshops, Eastwood, New York. High Museum of Art, Gift of Roy Frangiamore, 1978.1000.14

An armchair in the High Museum of Art (fig. 1) is similar to one Stickley exhibited at the Pan-American Exposition. It epitomizes Stickley's ideas and style with its emphasis on material, construction, and function. Made entirely of oak, the chair has continuous square legs and posts, flat stretchers, through tenons, pegged construction, and severe straight lines, relieved by the V-shape of the crest rail and curved arm brackets. Writing in 1901, Stickley provided his own definition of the term "mission":

> The sole consideration at the basis of the design must be the thing itself and not its ornamentation. It must be a chair, a table, a bookcase, or a bed that fills its mission of usefulness as well as it possibly can, it must be well-proportioned and honestly constructed, as beautifully finished as possible for the wood of which it is made, and as stable as would be required in a perfect thing of its kind.[2]

In 1903, Stickley organized the first exhibition of Arts and Crafts decorative art in upstate New York at his Craftsman Building in Syracuse.

The exhibition traveled to neighboring Rochester, where it was shown at the Mechanics Institute. The Rochester exhibition arrangements were made by Harvey Ellis, an innovative local architect who had been working in Rochester after dropping out of West Point Academy. Ellis came under the influence of Henry Hobson Richardson during his work on the New York State Capitol in Albany in the 1870s (see no. 218). After working for several Midwestern architects, Ellis returned to his native Rochester to pursue his interest in painting and Arts and Crafts design. In 1903, Ellis's house plans and designs were published in *The Craftsman,* and after the Rochester exhibition, he joined Stickley's growing Craftsman Workshops in Syracuse.[3]

Ellis died at the beginning of January 1904, but during his nine months at the Craftsman Workshops, he had a profound impact on the furniture designs there. At the beginning of that year, a group of furniture he had designed, including a side chair similar to the Crawford example (no. 188), was introduced in an article in *The Craftsman,* "Structure and Ornament in the Craftsman Workshops." Made of the oak favored by Stickley, the furniture was distinguished from

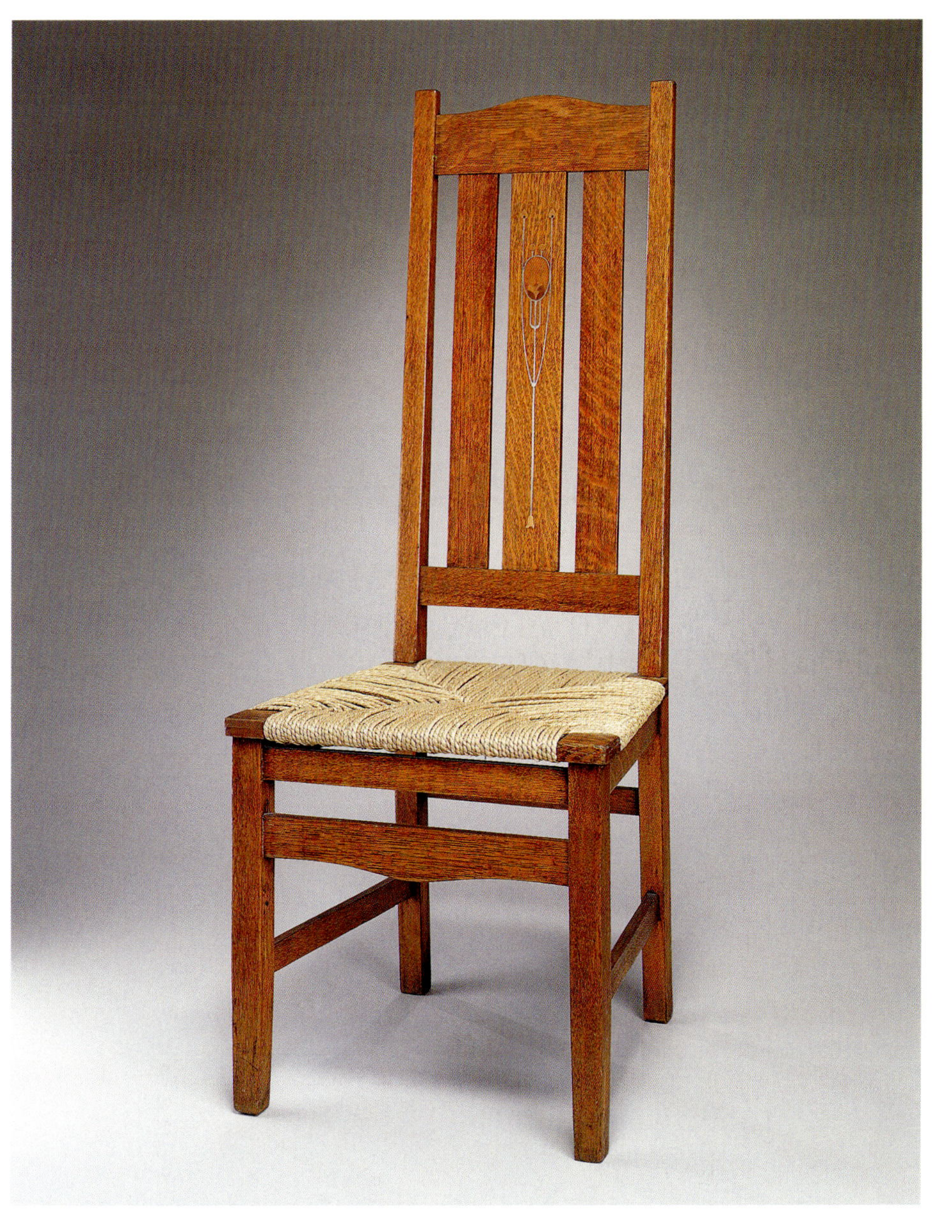

188.

Side Chair, designed 1903

Made by Gustav Stickley's Craftsman Workshops (1899–1916), Eastwood, New York; design attributed to Harvey Ellis (1852–1904)
Oak, mahogany, copper, and pewter, with replaced rush seat
47¾ × 18¼ × 16½ inches
Note: The chair appears to have been refinished and any evidence of a label has been lost.
1986.193

previous designs by a lightness and verticality more closely resembling innovative contemporary British furniture, such as that designed by Glasgow architect Charles Rennie Mackintosh.

The Ellis side chair design is delicate and spare, with a soaring attenuation. Ellis's furniture was also ornamented with inlaid mahogany, copper, and pewter, which was atypical of Stickley products but further linked the Ellis designs with English and European prototypes. According to *The Craftsman* article:

> [The decoration is used] to relieve and make interesting what otherwise would have been a too large area of plain, flat surface. It, in every case, emphasizes the structural lines; accenting in most instances the vertical elements, and so giving a certain slenderness of effect to a whole which were otherwise too solid and heavy. . . . Further, this ornament . . . appears to proceed from within outward. It bears no trace of having been applied. It consists of fine markings, discs, and other figures of pewter and copper, which, like the stems of plants and obscured, simplified floral forms, seem to pierce the surface of the wood from beneath.

The article goes on to place the inlay work in a context with the standard Stickley oak:

> The silvery lines with their expanded terminals of bright bronze or colored woods, contrast well with the gray-brown of the oak. . . . Under the action of fuming and of other chemical processes, which might be compared to the experiences and trials of an individual, it discloses unsuspected qualities of beauty previously lying concealed within its heart.[4]

The materials and labor required for the metal inlay added considerable expense to furniture that had been intended primarily for a middle-class market. As a result, few examples like the Crawford chair were made. According to Stickley's daughter, those made were primarily for exhibition to the furniture trade and to show in some retail stores but were not commercially manufactured.[5]

In an article in *The Craftsman* the month after Ellis died, Stickley paid tribute to him: "Mr. Ellis was a man of unusual gifts; possessing an accurate and exquisite sense of color, a great facility in design and a sound judgment of effect. . . .

189.

Planter, ca. 1905

Gustav Stickley's Craftsman Workshops (1899–1916), Eastwood, New York
Copper
7 × 11 × 5¼ inches
Mark: Stamped on bottom center enclosed in double circle, *-THE-CRAFTSMAN-WORKSHOPS-GUSTAV-STICKLEY*, around joiner's compass enclosing motto *Als/ik/kan*
1986.189

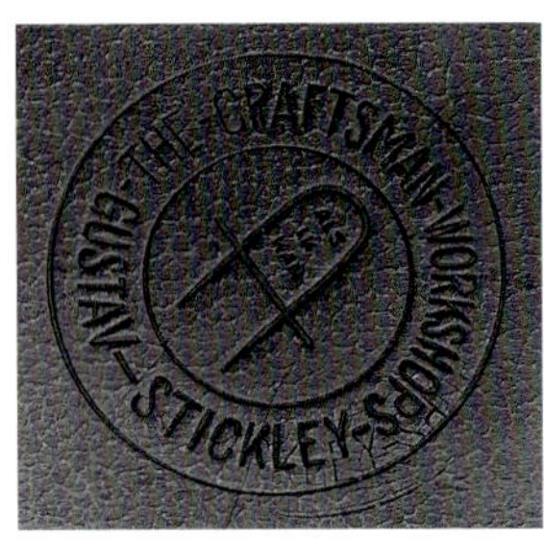

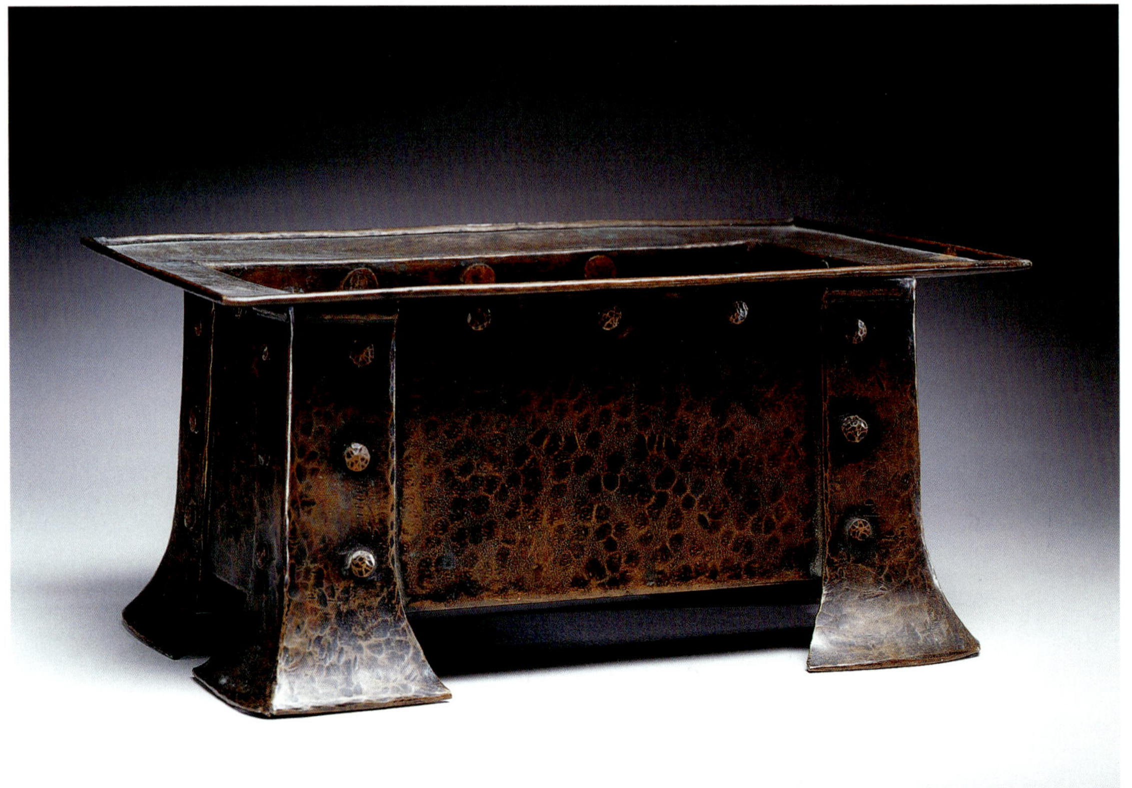

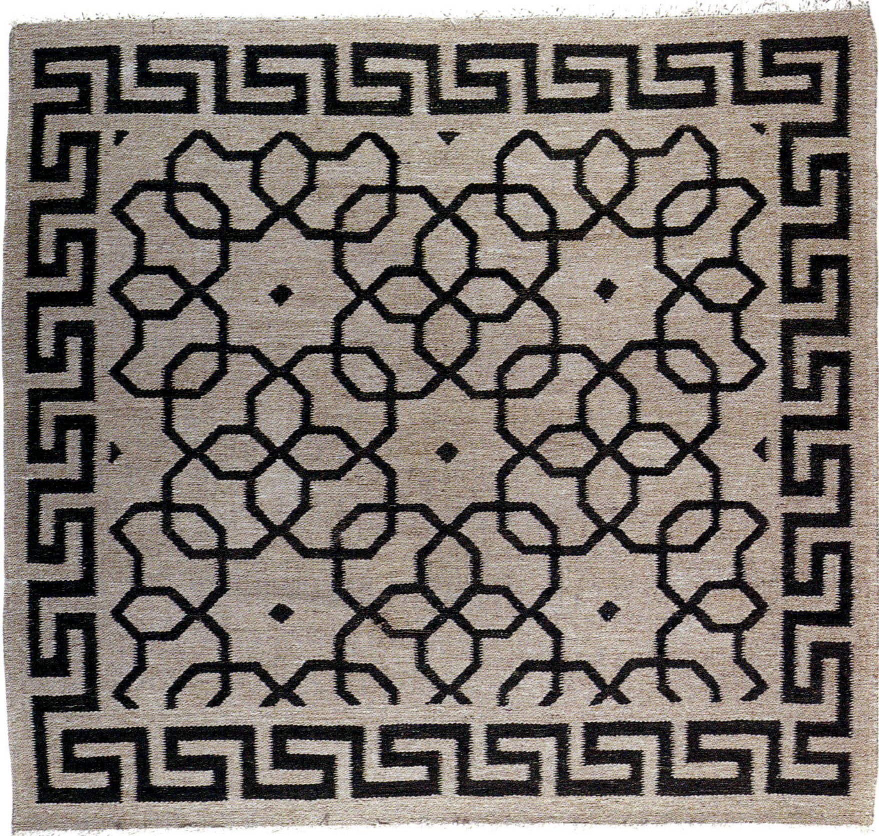

190.

Rug, ca. 1910

Retailed by Gustav Stickley's Craftsman Workshops (1899–1916), New York; probably made in India
Wool
73 × 76 inches including fringe
1983.210

Altogether, he is to be regretted as one who possessed the sacred fire of genius."[6] One of Ellis's long-lasting influences on Stickley was an interest in all aspects of interior design.

Sometime before 1905, Stickley added a metal workshop to his Craftsman Workshops, feeling that the stamped, light metal drawer pulls and furniture hinges that were being mass-produced for furniture were inappropriate for the sturdy Craftsman Workshops pieces. Shortly after it opened, the metal workshop was also manufacturing accessories in copper and wrought iron.

A wrought-copper planter (no. 189) in the Crawford Collection, marked with the insignia of the Craftsman Workshops, is characteristic of its copper accessories. Its entire surface was hammered to reflect the handcrafted techniques involved in its construction. The rivets and straps holding the planter together expose the means of construction just as the mortise and tenon and peg construction of Stickley's furniture made visible its joinery. The broad and low rectangular shape with its deep overhang relates the planter to the bungalow houses illustrated in *The Craftsman.* From the residue and wear on its interior, it appears to have been used as a planter for some time. A catalogue from around 1905 shows an illustration of a cigar box of the same form, fitted with a lid and a bail handle.[7]

In 1906, Stickley moved his showrooms and business headquarters to Manhattan. Two years later, he purchased property in rural New Jersey, where he intended to build the Craftsman Farms. He hoped to establish a boys' school—the Craftsman Farms School of Citizenship—and a community of craftspeople. The increasing financial strains of a growing business, however, never allowed him to go beyond building his own home and several buildings at Craftsman Farms.

In 1913, Stickley moved all the Craftsman Workshops enterprises except the furniture-manufacturing plant into a single twelve-story facility in Manhattan at 6 East 39th Street. The Craftsman Workshops occupied the entire building and consisted of furniture showrooms; accessory, carpet, and textile showrooms; exhibition areas leased to home and garden businesses; lecture and meeting rooms; editorial offices for *The Craftsman;* and a restaurant on the top floor. Stickley's hope was for Craftsman Farms to provide the fresh produce for the restaurant.

The two Crawford carpets, an area rug (no. 190) and an extended hall runner (no. 191), are characteristic of the types of rugs Stickley sold. The rugs were probably woven in India and were undoubtedly selected for the subtle, muted tones in their flat, geometric designs. Stickley wrote in his 1910 *Catalogue of Craftsman Furniture Made by Gustav Stickley at the Craftsman Workshops:*

> As all Craftsman furniture is made of oak, and as the interior woodwork of a Craftsman room corresponds in character to the furniture, it follows that so important a part of the furnishing as a rug would naturally show coloring based for the most part upon the wood and leaf tones and a texture that is in keeping with the sturdy fibre and dull mellow surface of the wood.[8]

The type of labels used on the sideboard and settle in the Crawford Collection indicate that they were made in the company's last period between 1912 and 1916. Although they are fabricated from Stickley's preferred wood, quartered white oak, and follow the straight structural lines he introduced in 1900, there are, nonetheless, elements in each piece that suggest later production.

This sideboard form (no. 192)—three central drawers flanked by cupboards with a long drawer across the bottom and a plate rack at the back—was introduced early in the century and continued in production for most of the firm's history.[9] The frame was fastened together with wooden pegs in a straightforward attempt to show its construction. Earlier examples of the same form have through tenons on the front and side stretchers of the frame extending through the front legs. The lack of through tenons on the Crawford example is characteristic of Stickley's more mature designs. The change in the construction of the sideboard may have been due to cost, but it was also in keeping with the evolving simplification all of Stickley's original designs underwent. The paper label on the Crawford sideboard confirms that it was made between 1912 and 1915.

House designs in *The Craftsman* often featured built-in benches in stair halls and fireplace inglenooks. Although settles, like the Crawford example (no. 193), were not common Stickley products, he seems to have thought of them as part of the Craftsman interior, especially where there was a fireplace:

> The settle was a seat and chest combined. It was placed near the old chimney, while we use it for hall furniture. Settles were usually of hard wood, though sometimes of soft wood painted. Few re-

191.

Runner, ca. 1910

Retailed by Gustav Stickley's Craftsman Workshops (1899–1916), New York; probably made in India
Wool
38¼ × 209 inches
1983.211

main to us today and these are mostly in collections. The settles of New England were ornamented with panels or carvings. We rarely find them veneered. The settle was not merely a luxury, but a convenience. It served as a chest and as a seat [on] which two or three people might be accommodated. It was probably an evolution from the old chest, some tired person wishing a back for his seat.[10]

This article also pointed to the growing interest in colonial furniture, which had been stirred in 1876 with the Centennial Exposition in Philadelphia's Fairmont Park. The Arts and Crafts movement furthered this interest with its use of oak and a kind of romantic association of craftsmanship with preindustrial or colonial and Federal America. Such interest was further encouraged by the publication of new reference books on colonial furniture, which often emphasized forms of the seventeenth century. These furniture styles related to Arts and Crafts furniture in their frequent use of oak, straight lines, and evidence of construction with exposed wooden pins and through tenons.

Although not illustrated in any known catalogue, the settle, or hall bench, in the Crawford Collection can be dated between 1912 and 1916, based on the decal label. A settle of the same general shape and construction, but with a tall back, was shown in the 1912 Stickley catalogue.[11] The seat lifted to reveal storage space, as in this example. Brass buttons on the back of the Crawford settle may have held cords to secure cushions. The flat back of the settle suggests that it was intended to be set against a wall.

The year 1913 marked a downward turn for Stickley. Elsie de Wolfe had published her widely popular interior decoration book, *The House in Good Taste* (New York, 1911). She shunned the somber, dark oak furniture and muted colors of Craftsman interiors for more delicate eighteenth-

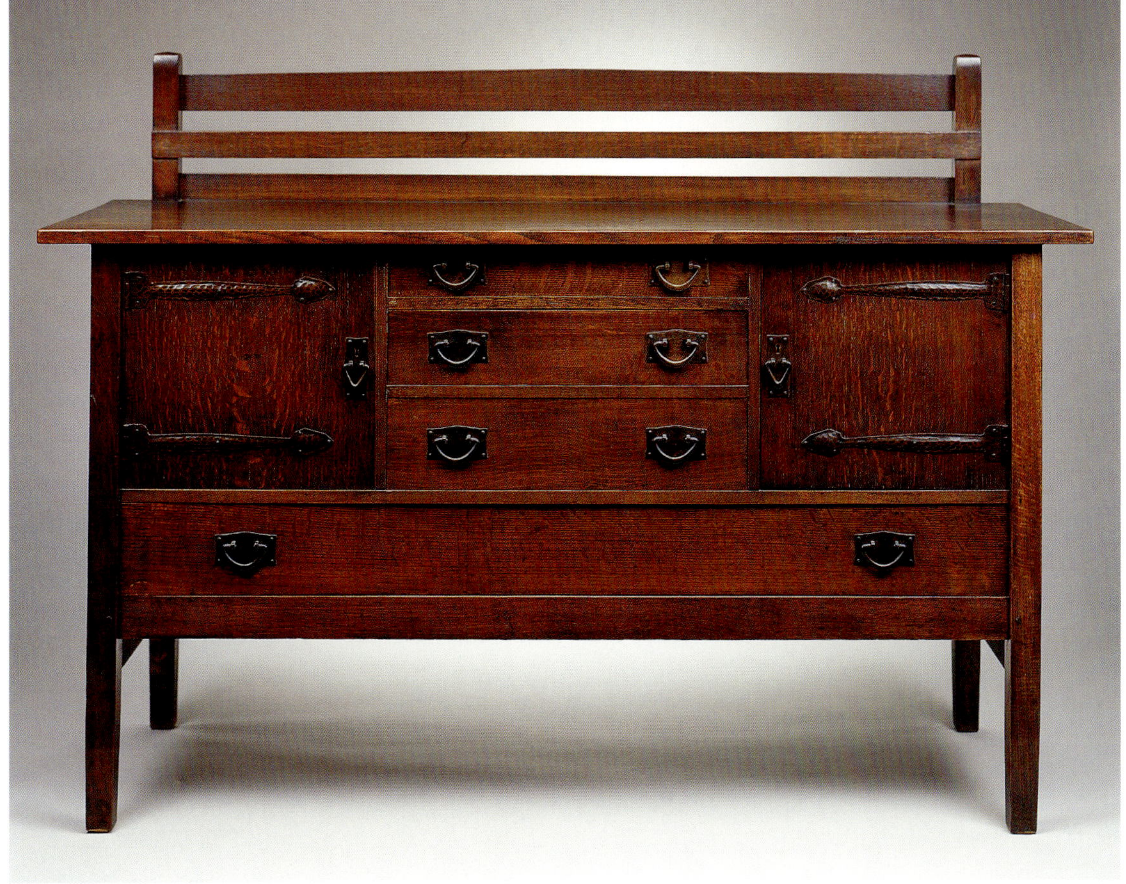

192.

Sideboard, 1912–1915

Gustav Stickley's Craftsman Workshops (1899–1916), Eastwood, New York
White oak, oak veneer, and copper mounts
48¾ × 66 × 23¾ inches
Mark: Printed paper label affixed to bottom of central top drawer, *CRAFTSMAN/TRADE/MARKS/ REG'D/IN U.S./PATENT OFFICE,* over and around joiner's compass enclosing motto *Als/ik/kan,* above facsimile of Stickley surname signature, above *THIS PASTER TOGETHER WITH MY DE-/VICES AND SIGNATURE (BRANDED) ON A/PIECE OF FURNITURE STANDS AS MY/GUARANTEE TO THE PURCHASER THAT/THE PIECE IS MADE WITH THE SAME/CARE AND EARNESTNESS THAT HAS/ CHARACTERIZED ALL MY EFFORTS/ FROM THE BEGINNING, AND IS MEANT/TO IMPLY THAT I HOLD MYSELF RE-/SPONSIBLE FOR ANY DEFECTS IN MATE-/RIAL, WORKMANSHIP OR FINISH THAT/MAY BE DISCOVERED BY THE PUR-/CHASER EVEN AFTER THE PIECE HAS/BEEN IN USE FOR A REASONABLE/ LENGTH OF TIME, AND THAT I WILL/EITHER MAKE GOOD ANY DEFECTS OR/TAKE BACK THE PIECE AND REFUND/THE PURCHASE PRICE./THIS PIECE WAS MADE IN MY/CABINET SHOPS AT EASTWOOD, N.Y./GUSTAV STICKLEY*
1984.141

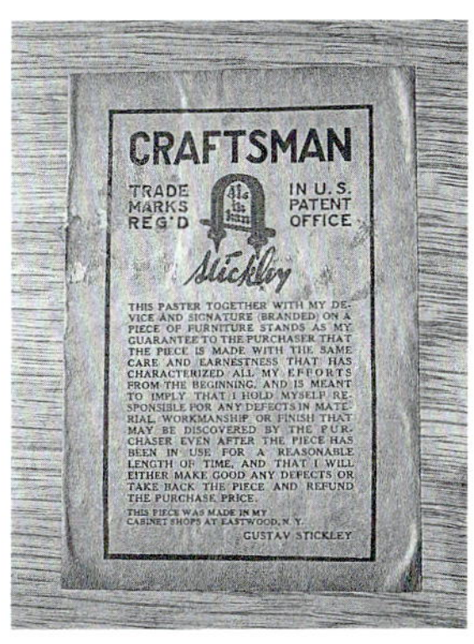

century historical furniture styles and a lighter palette, and her vision soon overcame Stickley's in the popular taste. At the same time, Stickley found himself overextended by his investment in the Manhattan facility. Within three years, the nation was gearing up for war in Europe and had more crucial issues than furniture on its mind. From the time the new Craftsman Building was occupied, profits from Stickley's Craftsman Workshops began to decline. In March of 1915, he filed for bankruptcy. *The Craftsman* continued publication for one more year.

In 1918, after closing the Craftsman Workshops in Eastwood and the Craftsman Building in Manhattan, Stickley returned to Syracuse, where he lived in an apartment in the home of his daughter and son-in-law. The Craftsman Workshops were absorbed into the company of Stickley's brothers and longtime competitors, J. G. and L. Stickley in Syracuse. Stickley died in 1942, leaving no will and no estate.

NOTES

1. Two biographies have provided accounts of Stickley's life and career: see Freeman 1966; and M. Smith 1983. Abbreviated accounts are presented in Bowman 1990, pp. 70–91; Clark 1972, p. 38; and Kaplan 1987, pp. 216–218.

2. Cited in Ludwig 1983, p. 63.

3. Memorial Art Gallery 1972, pp. 44–49.

4. *Craftsman* 5, 1904.

5. Cathers 1981, p. 49.

6. Stickley 1904, p. 520.

7. Illustrated in Bowman 1990, p. 118.

8. *Catalogue of Craftsman Furniture Made by Gustav Stickley at the Craftsman Workshops* 1910; reprinted in *Stickley Craftsman* 1979, p. 125. The area rug is discussed and illustrated in Whitney Museum of American Art 1985, p. 18, fig. 117. A 1909 view of Stickley's own living room at Craftsman Farms in Morris Plains, New Jersey, showed a rug similar in pattern to the Crawford area rug; see Freeman 1966, pp. 56–57.

9. The sideboard was illustrated in the 1909 catalogue as number 814, and again in 1910 and 1912. By the 1915 catalogue, it was apparently no longer in production. Springer 1980, p. 46, illustrates an earlier version of the same sideboard.

10. J. Curtis 1902, p. 299.

11. Stickley 1991, p. 17.

193.

Settle, 1912–1916

Gustav Stickley's Craftsman Workshops (1899–1916), Eastwood, New York
White oak with metal buttons on back that may have held cords for cushions
31 × 47½ × 25¼ inches
Mark: On lower back panel, red decal consisting of joiner's compass enclosing motto *Als/ik/kan* over facsimile of Stickley surname signature
1983.203

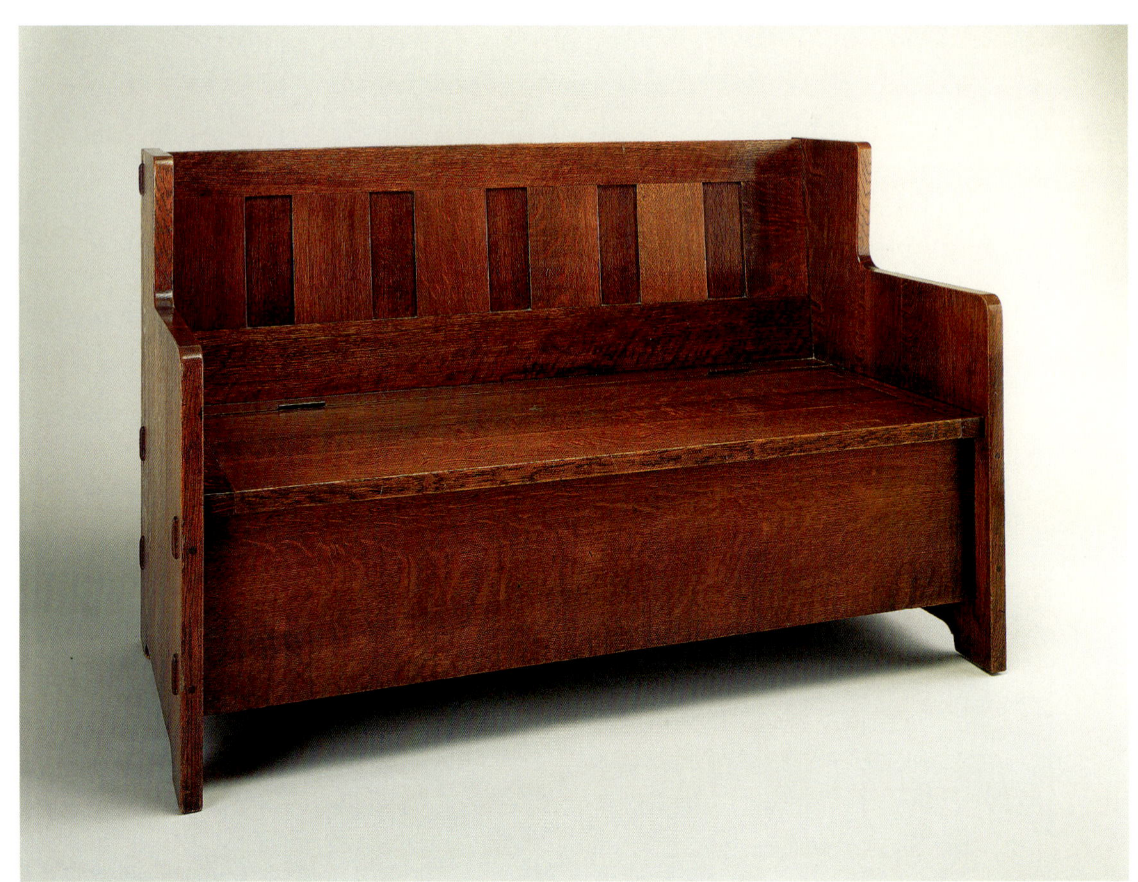

IN 1894, Theopholis Anthony Brouwer established the Middle Lane Pottery, named for its location on Middle Lane in East Hampton, New York. He had been a student at New York College and at the National Academy of Design, where he exhibited his paintings. Brouwer's move from the city to the seaside of East Hampton in 1893 coincided with his new interest in ceramics, which he pursued for the following two decades.[1]

Untrained in chemistry or ceramic production, Brouwer developed his own techniques through extensive experimentation and was involved in every aspect of production at the pottery, from design and concept to throwing, turning, molding, glazing, and decorating. Brouwer's direct, hands-on approach, strikingly unlike conventional manufacturing processes of the time, presaged American mid- and late-twentieth-century studio pottery production.

Brouwer's major innovations were in firing and glazing. Rather than use a long firing process in the kiln, he subjected his glazed wares to the intense heat of near-direct flame for as little as seventeen minutes. Then, instead of slowly cooling the baked pottery in the kiln, he removed it immediately and allowed it to cool outside the kiln chamber. The Crawford vase is an example of Brouwer's high luster "Fire Painting," the result of his heating and cooling innovations and his learning to anticipate and manipulate the intense heat in his kiln. The fiery, multicolored iridescence, typical of Brouwer's Fire Painted wares, is due to the intensity of the fire exposure and the natural reaction of the glaze rather than to brushwork.

Brouwer operated the Middle Lane Pottery in East Hampton from 1894 to 1902. In 1903, he moved the enterprise to West Hampton, where it became known as the Brouwer Pottery, but he continued to use the whale jawbone with the incised *M* for his mark, often adding his incised signature, as on this vase. Brouwer remained interested in ceramics for the remainder of his life, but other interests were absorbing his attention by 1911, including carving statues from an especially hard concrete he had developed. Because of the promise of his Fire Painting, Brouwer incorporated the Ceramic Flame Company in New York in 1925. The corporation was listed as an art pottery, but no marked examples are known. The company was not dissolved until 1946, long after Brouwer's death.

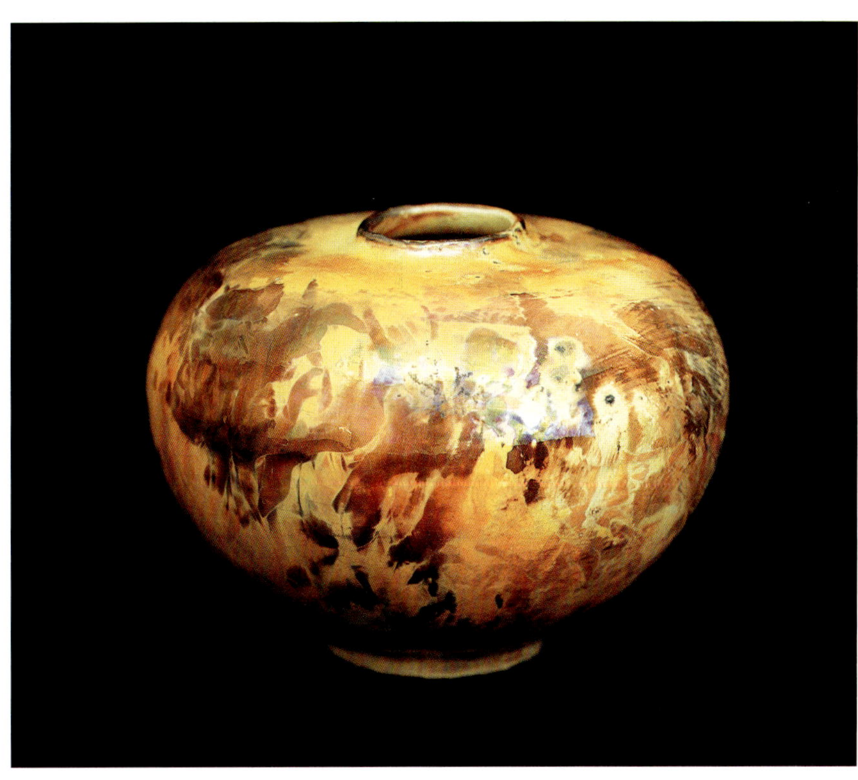

194.

Vase, 1903–1910

Middle Lane Pottery or Brouwer Pottery (1894–1911), East Hampton or West Hampton, New York; designed by Theopholis Anthony Brouwer (1864–1932)
Earthenware with luster glaze
3½ × 4¾ × 4¾ inches
Mark: In script incised on bottom of vase, whale jawbone enclosing *M* above *Brouwer*
1984.155

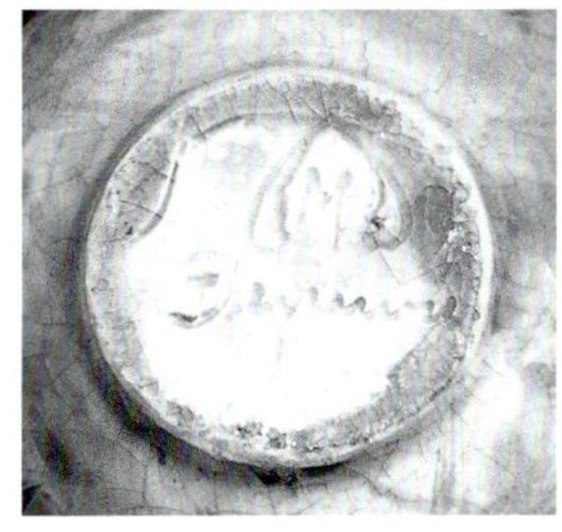

NOTE

1. For a history of the Middle Lane Pottery and a description of the types of wares produced by Brouwer, see Evans 1987, pp. 173–176; Ludwig 1983, p. 98; and Volpe and Cathers 1988, pp. 104–106. The Crawford vase is illustrated and discussed in High Museum of Art 1980, p. 27, no. C.32.

Grueby Faience Company

The Crawford lamp (no. 195) combines a Tiffany Studios leaded and stained glass shade in the Dogwood pattern with a green earthenware vase by the Grueby Faience Company of Boston, probably made between 1902 and 1906, when the two enterprises are known to have collaborated. Both the lamp base and the yellow vase (no. 196) in the Crawford Collection are made up of organic shapes, suggesting growing plant life, in the natural colors associated with the Grueby Faience Company.

As a teenager, William Henry Grueby worked for the Low Art Tile Works in Chelsea, Massachusetts (see nos. 118–119). Throughout his ceramics career, he made architectural faience for interior and exterior decoration. Grueby left Low in 1890 and formed an architectural terra-cotta company in 1891 with Eugene Atwood, who had also worked for Low Art Tile Works. Atwood and Grueby was a subsidiary of Fiske, Homes and Company, a manufacturer of brick, terracotta, and masonry products. They sent Grueby to view the World's Columbian Exposition in Chicago in 1893, where he saw the matte glazes and natural shapes used by French art potters that later characterized the pottery of the Grueby Faience Company.

Grueby dissolved his partnership with Atwood in 1894 and formed the Grueby Faience Company.[1] Grueby's partners were George Prentiss Kendrick and William Hagerman Graves. Grueby brought the value of his well-known name and his knowledge of glazes to the venture, and he assumed the managerial duties of the company. Kendrick, a founding member of the Society of Arts and Crafts, Boston, and an architectural draftsman, became chief designer for the enterprise. Graves, who had taken architectural courses at the Massachusetts Institute of Technology, was in charge of sales and public relations, arranging for the firm's work to be shown in group and solo exhibitions.

For at least the first decade after its incorporation, the Grueby Faience Company produced vessels designed by Kendrick and employed young women graduates of local art schools to execute his designs. Although they used designs by Kendrick and others, the hand-throwing of the pots and the individual modeling assured variations in each piece of Grueby pottery.

The pottery's wares were highly acclaimed in the exhibitions Graves arranged. From 1900, when 100 examples were shown at the Exposition Universelle in Paris, the wares were recognized internationally and compared with the matte-glazed wares of French avant-garde potters. That same year, the revolutionary Parisian gallery of S. Bing, L'Art Nouveau, began to show Grueby pottery.[2]

Although pottery had been a mainstay of the operation since 1897, the Grueby Pottery Company did not incorporate as a separate entity until 1907. When declining profits caused both the Grueby Faience and Grueby Pottery Companies to go into receivership in 1909, they reorganized as the Grueby Faience and Tile Company. They continued producing pottery designed by Kendrick and others, but because Grueby adhered to the slow and expensive practice of individually turning and hand-modeling each piece, the pottery line at the Grueby Faience Company was closed down in 1913. The Grueby Faience and Tile Company was sold to C. Pardee, a New Jersey tile manufacturer in 1919. Grueby managed the faience line until his death in 1925.[3]

Grueby pursued the same sort of cooperative ventures between companies he had seen at Low Art Tile Works (see no. 119). The Grueby Faience Company provided tiles to Gustav Stickley's Craftsman Workshops for mounting in furniture and to Tiffany Studios for setting into bronze mounts. This relatively simple Dogwood pattern lampshade is characteristic of the shades Tiffany Studios provided for Grueby vase bases. The broad mouth of Kendrick's 1897 vase design gave ample opening for the necessary oil tank. After electricity replaced oil in 1906, Tiffany no longer needed Grueby's broad-mouthed ceramic vase bases.

The green of this lamp base was the most familiar color associated with Grueby wares and was widely copied by other potteries, yet Grueby worked in a variety of colors, including the matte yellow of the Crawford vase.[4] The mark on the

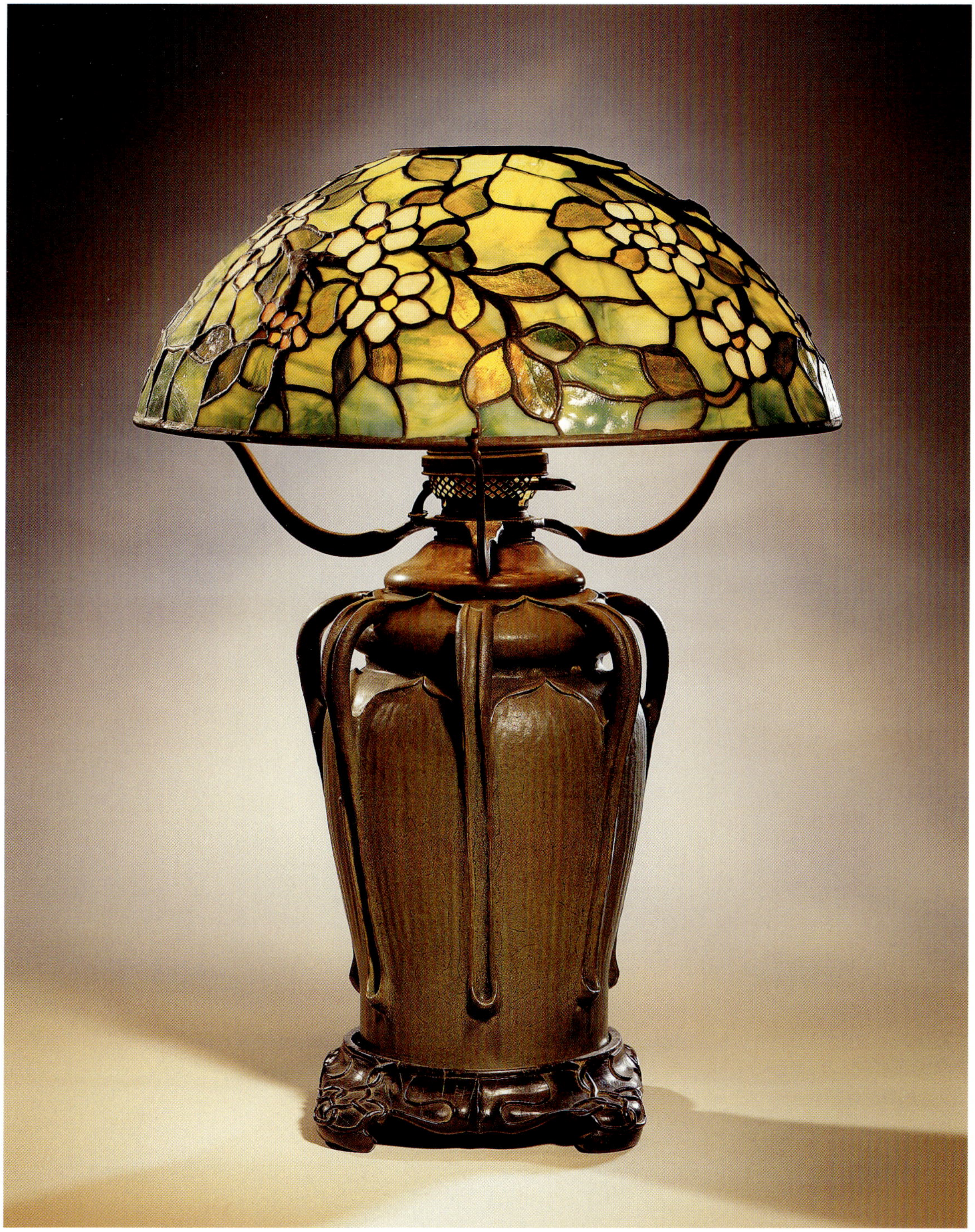

195.

Lamp, 1902–1906

Base by Grueby Faience Company (1894–1919), Boston; designed by George Prentiss Kendrick (1850–1919). Shade by Tiffany Studios (1900–1932), Corona, Long Island, New York
Glazed earthenware, leaded glass, bronze, and teak
Base: 10¾ × 8¼ × 8¼ inches
Shade: 6⅝ × 15 × 15 inches
Marks: Paper label on bottom of base, *GRUEBY·POTTERY/·BOSTON·U·S·A·/REGISTERED/TRADE MARK,* in a circle around a double tulip; paper label on bottom of base, *GRUEBY POTTERY·/PRICE $ 35.00/CON. NO. 8253;* impressed in circle on bottom, *GRUEBY·POTTERY/·BOSTON·U·S·A·;* impressed on bottom, *35;* paper label on oil font, *GRUEBY POTTERY./PRICE $60.00/CON. NO. 5335*
1984.148

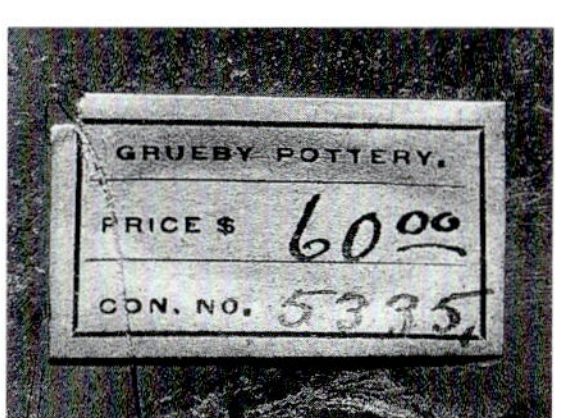

vase was used prior to the independent incorporation of the Grueby Pottery Company. The vase was designed either by Kendrick or by someone adapting his ideas.

NOTES

1. Montgomery 1993, the most recent and comprehensive study of Grueby, recounts his early life prior to the 1894 formation of Grueby Faience Company; see pp. 5–18. A vase marked "Atwood and Grueby" is illustrated in pl. IV. See also Bowman 1990, pp. 152–155; Clark 1972, pp. 136–143; Evans 1987, pp. 118–121; Kaplan 1987, pp. 258–259; and Keen 1978, pp. 31–33.

2. In 1901, the Grueby Faience Company showed its pottery at the International Artistic and Industrial Exhibition of Ceramics and Glass in St. Petersburg, Russia. That same year, they received a gold medal at the Pan-American Exposition in Buffalo. A year later, they showed at the First International Exhibition of Modern Decorative Art at Turin, Italy. The company was awarded the *Grand Prix* at the 1904 Louisiana Purchase Exposition in St. Louis. As early as 1899, museums were showing Grueby Faience Company pottery in exhibitions organized at the Museum of Fine Arts, Boston, and the Art Museum of the Rhode Island School of Design in Providence. Montgomery 1993, pp. 29–30, 41–54.

3. Ibid., pp. 69–70.

4. Ibid., p. 110. The Crawford lamp is illustrated on p. 49, fig. 69. The vase form on a carved wooden base is shown in a photograph published in *House Beautiful,* December 1898, reproduced in ibid., p. 29, fig. 37. The vase form was included in a photograph titled "Specimens of Grueby Pottery exhibited in the Palace of Varied Industries Exposition Universelle, Paris, 1900," reproduced in ibid., p. 41, fig. 52. A yellow version of the lamp base is illustrated in pl. XLV. Another green vase is illustrated in Clark 1972, p. 137, no. 185. American imitators of Grueby pottery are described in Montgomery 1993, pp. 82–86.

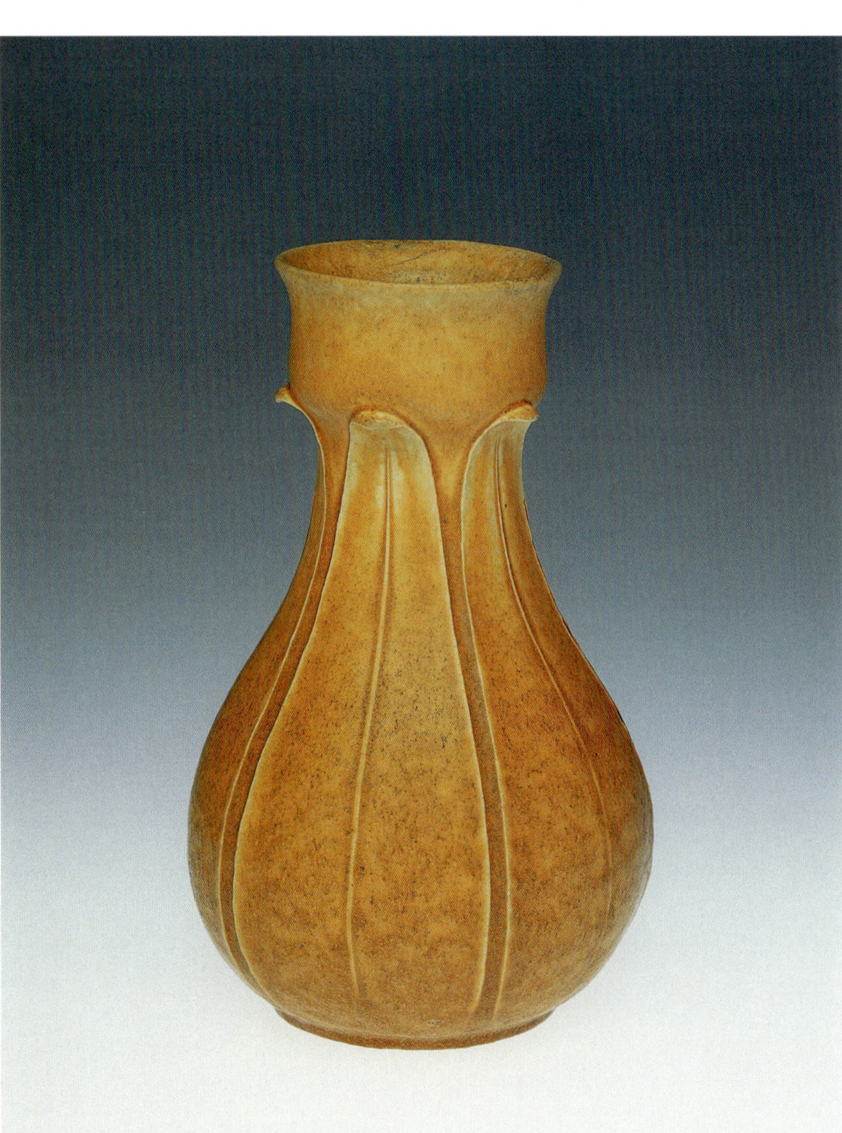

196.

Vase, 1897–1907

Grueby Faience Company (1894–1919), Boston; possibly designed by George Prentiss Kendrick (1850–1919)
Glazed earthenware
7⅝ × 4¾ × 4¾ inches
Mark: On bottom, impressed in a circle around a stylized lotus flower, *GRUEBY POTTERY/BOSTON, U.S.A.*
1982.289

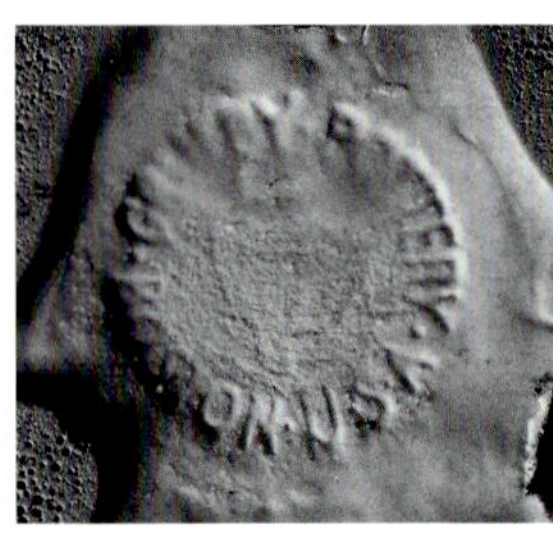

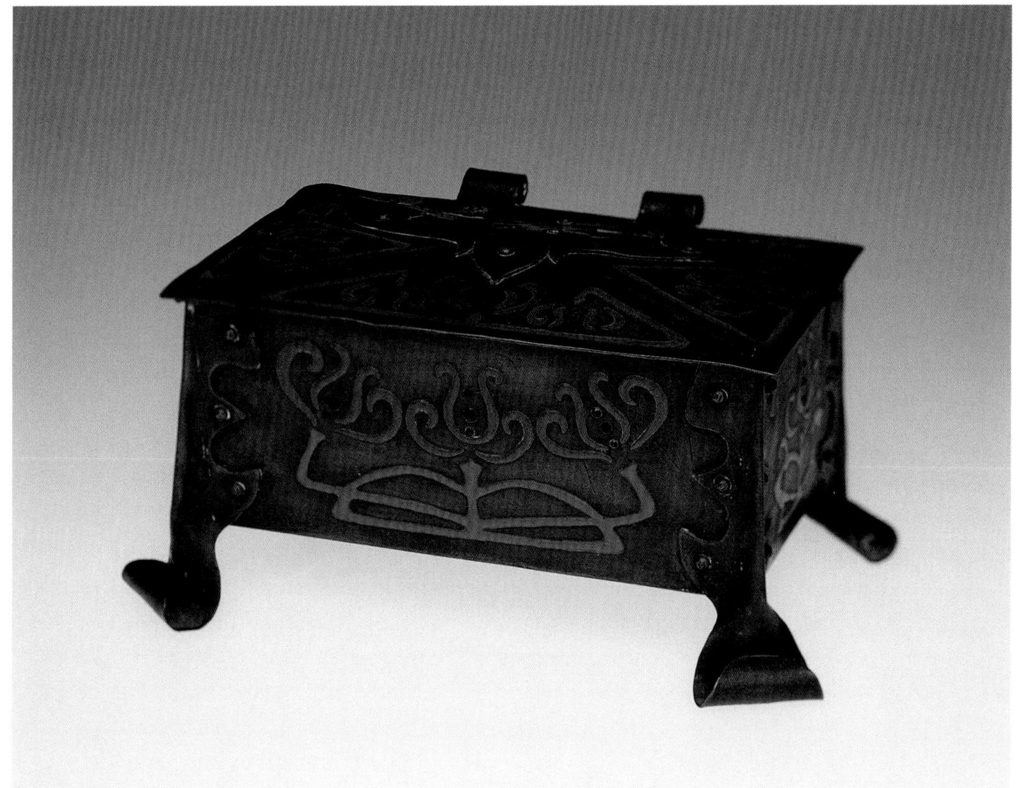

197.

Jewel Casket, ca. 1905

Art Crafts Shop (1905–1906), Buffalo, New York
Hammered copper with enamel decoration and felt lining
4½ x 9⅛ x 6⅛ inches
Mark: Impressed on bottom, enclosed in oval with sprig of three cherries and leaves, *THE/ART/CRAFTS/SHOP*
1984.165

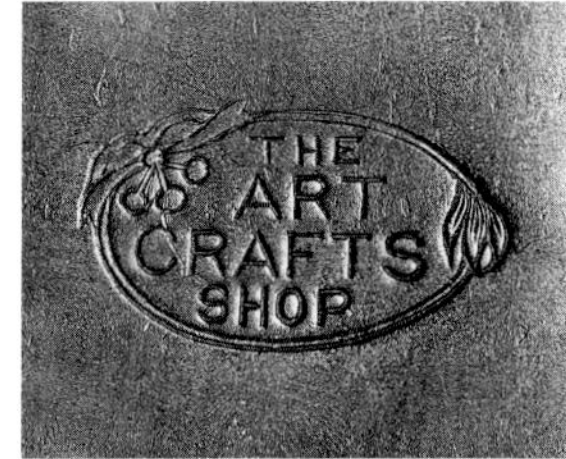

The Arts and Crafts Company was listed in Buffalo city directories in 1902. By 1903, the company had moved, and the listing included Otto L. Heintz as proprietor. Heintz was also listed as a principal in the nearby Heintz Brothers, a jewelry manufacturing firm established around 1876. By 1905, the Arts and Crafts Company had become the Art Crafts Shop, and in 1906 the name changed again to the Heintz Art Metal Shop.[1] The firm advertised in Gustav Stickley's periodical *The Craftsman,* and exhibited at Stickley's Permanent Home Exposition in the Craftsman Building in New York (see nos. 188–193). They also briefly operated a shop in Manhattan, but closed at the beginning of the Great Depression in 1930.[2]

The Crawford jewel casket is marked with the name of the firm used in 1905–1906, providing the date for its production.[3] The shape, with its canted sides, scrolled feet, and overhanging lid, is similar to a copper planter made by Stickley's Craftsman Workshops around 1905 (see no. 189). Both were constructed with a hammered surface finish and exposed rivets as part of the decoration.

The Art Crafts Shop departed from Stickley convention by applying bright red and green enamel over the patinated copper surface. The symmetrical Art Nouveau floral enamel decoration on the top, front, and sides complements the cut-metal corner elements terminating in scrolled feet and the shaped and cut escutcheon plate of the lid hinges. The scrolled feet are related to the exaggerated scroll forms of the hinges.

NOTES

1. Dave White, "A Nearly Forgotten Maker of Memories," *Buffalo News Magazine* (April 11, 1982): 15–16; cited in Ludwig 1983, p. 90.

2. Ibid., p. 90.

3. The Crawford jewel casket is illustrated and discussed in Whitney Museum of American Art 1985, p. 25, fig. 1.25.

Roycrofters

Elbert Green Hubbard was a flamboyant, colorful, and charismatic promoter of the Arts and Crafts movement in America at the turn of the twentieth century. A salesman and advertising executive, Hubbard achieved success as a junior partner in his brother-in-law's firm, J. D. Larkin and Company, a soap manufacturer in Buffalo, New York. By 1892, feeling unfulfilled in his business career, Hubbard sold his shares in Larkin to pursue his education and a literary career. After a brief special enrollment at Harvard University, Hubbard traveled to England in 1894. There he met his intellectual idol, William Morris, the leader of the early Arts and Crafts movement in England. In addition to Morris and Company, which manufactured decorative art, textiles (see no. 90), and wallpaper, Morris had also established the Kelmscott Press, devoted to the production of books as works of art.[1]

By 1895, Hubbard was determined to establish an American press like Morris's. A social idealist as well as a businessman, he wanted to publish his own writings and promote his own ideology. Hubbard set up the Roycroft Press near his home in the small town of East Aurora, outside Buffalo. According to Hubbard, the name meant "king's craft," but it more likely referred to the seventeenth-century English printers Thomas and Samuel Roycroft, whose works Hubbard collected. Hubbard adapted the symbol used by Cassiodorus (a medieval French monk and manuscript illuminator) of a stylized cross over a circle enclosing an "R," for use on printed material published at the Roycroft Press and at the various craft shops Hubbard later established. The circle was divided into three segments, symbolizing faith, hope, and love.

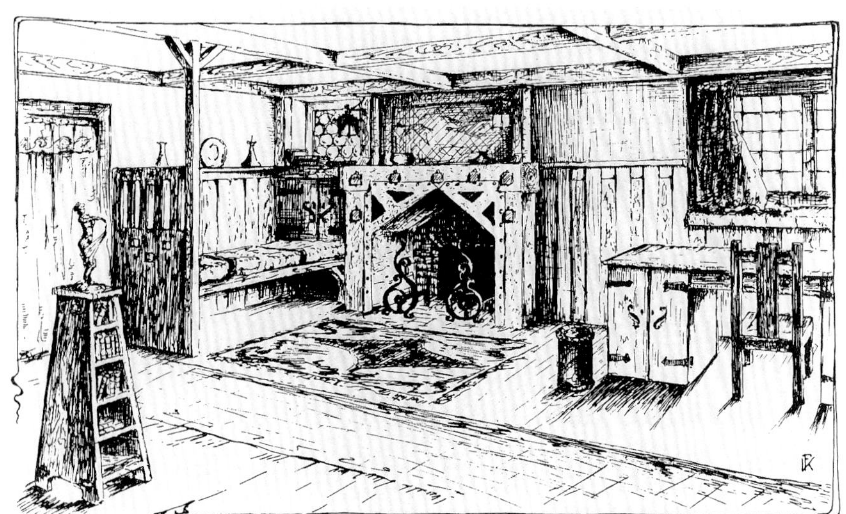

Fig. 1. A Roycroft interior from a 1904 Roycroft furniture catalogue.

At the same time, Hubbard began publishing a monthly magazine, *The Philistine.* It included stories by George Bernard Shaw, Stephen Crane, and others, but served mainly as a dais for Hubbard's own writings and philosophies. *The Philistine* met with immediate success and quickly achieved a wide circulation. Hubbard also became a popular speaker on the lecture circuit and on a vaudeville tour. Ever the promoter, he encouraged visitors to come to East Aurora, and there his complex grew steadily. By 1903, the Roycroft Press had been substantially enlarged and the Roycroft Inn had been constructed to accommodate visitors. At first, Hubbard hired local craftsmen to construct new buildings on his Roycroft campus, but he soon established the Furniture Shop and the Copper Shop of the Roycrofters to finish and furnish them. The shops drew aspiring artisans from colleges and universities as well as the business world, idealists attracted by Hubbard's lectures and writings.

The initial furniture makers were the local carpenters who built the Roycroft buildings, and by 1897 the furniture was being sold to visitors. Like all of the products made in the Roycroft Shops, the works were not signed by the artisan, nor were the designers recorded; either the cross and circle or "Roycroft" printed in old English was incised on the furniture. Based on general forms of American Arts and Crafts furniture, Roycroft furniture was largely unadorned and relied for decoration on the form of the piece and on pins and joints used in construction. Proportion, simplicity, and strength were major concerns of Roycroft designers.[2]

Hubbard was not a career furniture man like Gustav Stickley, and his passion remained the Press. Nonetheless, furniture was included in Roycroft catalogues as early as 1904, and by 1906 a catalogue devoted to the furniture was

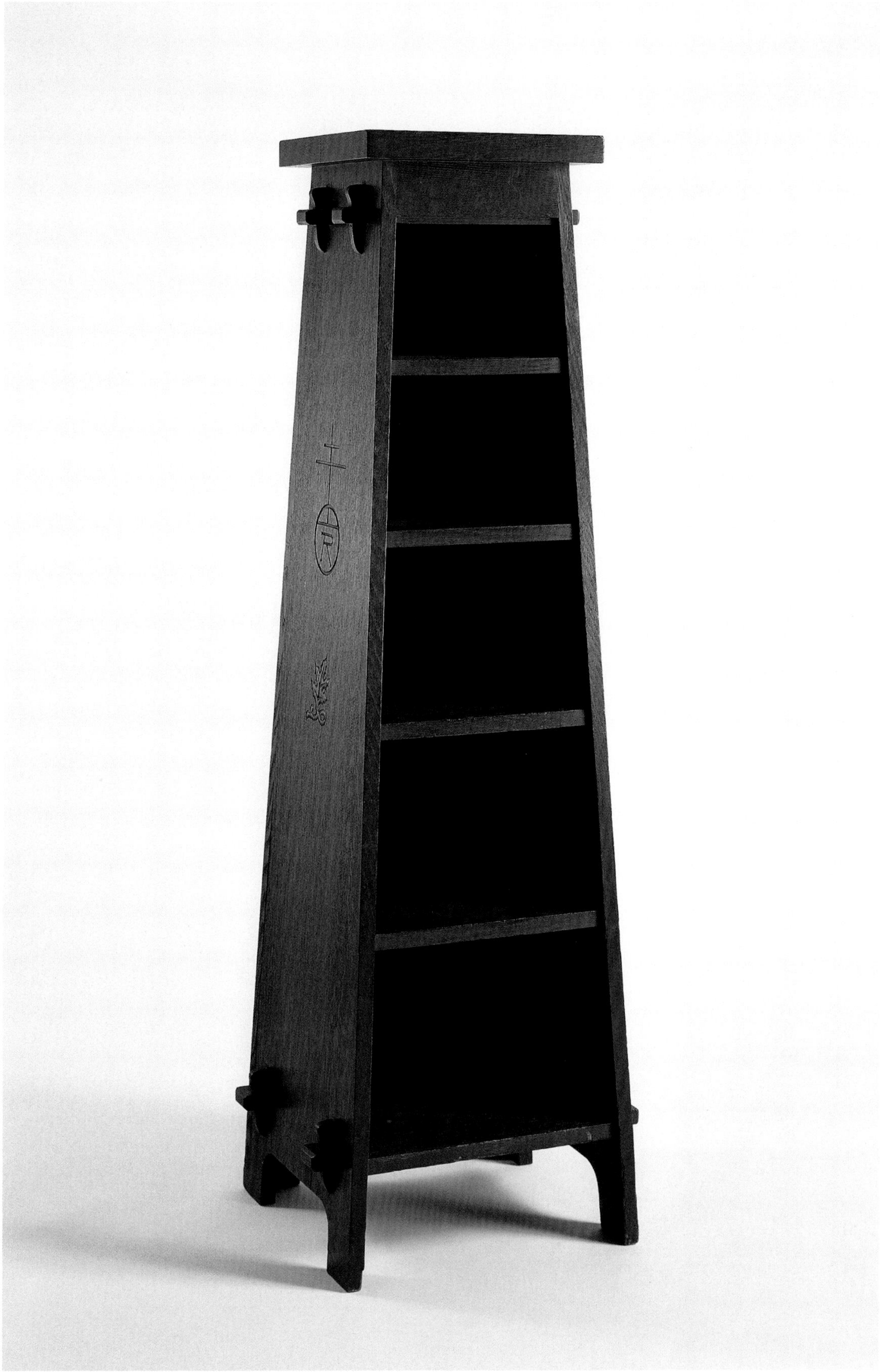

198.

Magazine Pedestal,
ca. 1906

Furniture Shop of the Roycrofters (1896–1938), East Aurora, New York
Oak
63½ × 21 × 18 inches
Marks: On side, incised stylized cross over a circle enclosing an *R;* maple leaf below
1990.82

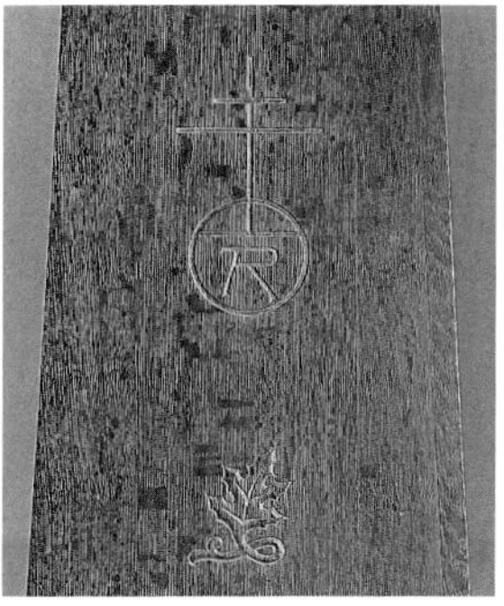

published. Although it never produced on the large scale of Gustav Stickley's Craftsman Workshops (see nos. 188–193), the Furniture Shop of the Roycrofters was important as an early expression of the American Arts and Crafts movement.

The form of the magazine pedestal (no. 198) in the Crawford Collection first appeared in Roycroft catalogues as early as 1904 (fig. 1). The design of the pedestal relies on the bold vertical proportions and sloping sides, the quarter-sawn oak with the secret Roycroft finish, and the construction pins that hold it together. Its shape is unique to the Furniture Shop of the Roycrofters. Versions of the design appeared as early as 1904 in illustrations of proposed Roycroft interiors by illustrator Victor Toothaker.[3] Whether he was actually responsible for the design of the pedestal remains unknown. The Roycroft symbol incised on both sides of the pedestal is the only adornment. Another example has incised leaf and floral ornaments on the sides.

The Furniture Shop continued to produce furniture as late as the 1930s, but by the end of World War I, the rage for Arts and Crafts furniture was passing and production diminished. Between 1903 and 1909, the Furniture Shop included ten full-time employees. At its height, between 1912 and 1919, it employed 80 to 100 craftspeople, both full-time and part-time, out of a total 500 Roycrofters employed in all of the shops. The popularity of Roycroft furniture—which required metal handles, hinges, and locks—led to the opening and development of the Copper Shop (see no. 200).

When Elbert Hubbard supervised advertising and promotion for J. D. Larkin and Company in the 1880s and 1890s, he set up a premium program for customers. To produce the prizes, the

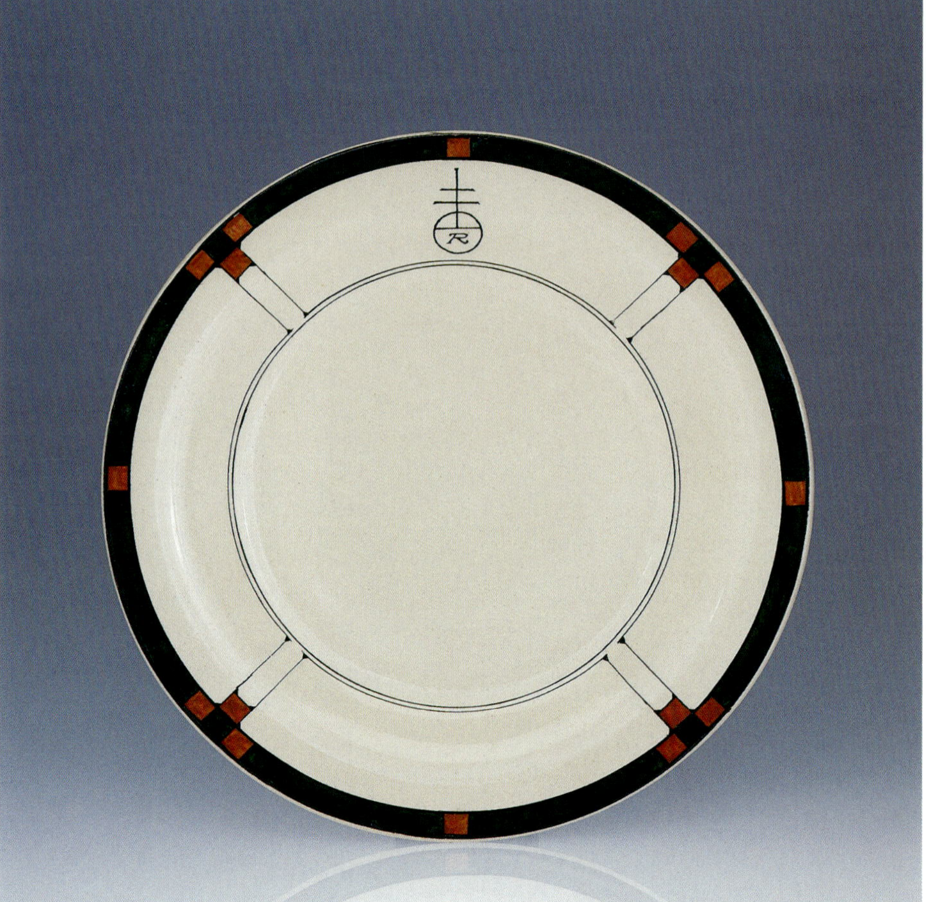

199.

Plate, ca. 1910

Buffalo Pottery Company (1901–1956), Buffalo, New York; possibly designed by Dard Hunter (1883–1966)
Glazed earthenware
1⅛ x 10 x 10 inches
Mark: Stamped on bottom, *SEMI-VITREOUS*/figure of a standing buffalo facing left/ *BUFFALO POTTERY*
1984.121

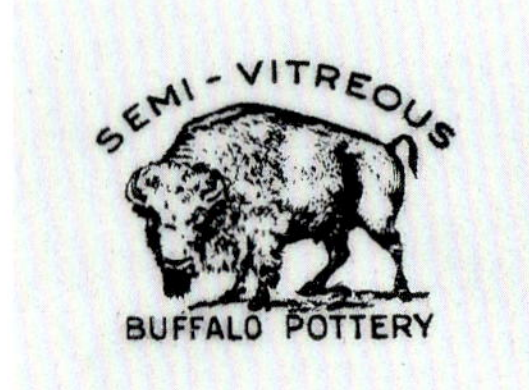

Buffalo Pottery Company, with J. D. Larkin as president, was chartered in 1901 and began producing chinaware in 1903. In spite of the paternalistic socialism practiced at East Aurora, Hubbard did not abandon the practicalities of business or his admiration of successful enterprise. He maintained his links with the business world and his family connections with J. D. Larkin and Company. When the Roycroft Inn opened, china was needed for the hotel dining rooms. Because the Shops of the Roycrofters never included a major ceramic studio, Hubbard's family and former business connections led to commissioning Roycroft china from the Buffalo Pottery.[4]

The small plate in the Crawford Collection (no. 199) is from the china commissioned for the Roycroft Inn, probably in the first decade of the twentieth century. The ivory earthenware plate has a linear border of brown and dark green as well as the familiar Roycroft symbol. The muted colors and geometric design are related to those on ceramic accessories made by the Buffalo Pottery for the Larkin Administration Building designed by Frank Lloyd Wright in 1904.[5] Dard Hunter may have designed the china. Hunter came to East Aurora in 1903 and designed stained glass, metalwares, and illustrations for Roycroft publications, and the china may reflect his interest in Viennese Secessionist design.[6]

NOTES

1. For a biography of Elbert Hubbard, see Champney 1968. Sketches of Hubbard's life and career are also found in Bowman 1990, pp. 64–65; and Hamilton 1992, pp. 7–109.

2. For a history of the Furniture Shop of the Roycrofters, see Cathers 1981, pp. 85–98.

3. Toothaker's illustration of a Roycroft interior from a 1904 catalogue, which included a form similar to the Crawford magazine pedestal, is shown in Hamilton 1992, p. 43. The pedestal is illustrated in the 1906 *Catalog of Roycroft,* 1981, p. 12, no. 80. The pedestal was offered in oak at $22, mahogany at $27.50, and ash at $20. Six years later, in the 1912 catalogue, it appears on p. 18, offered in oak and mahogany at the same prices.

4. For the history of the Buffalo Pottery, see Altman and Altman 1987, pp. 19–32; and Kovel and Kovel 1993, pp. 14–17. The Crawford plate is illustrated and discussed in Whitney Museum of American Art 1985, p. 23, fig. 1.21.

5. A cuspidor from the Larkin Administration Building is illustrated in Altman and Altman 1987, p. 17, fig. 8.

6. Whitney Museum of American Art 1985, p. 23. Hunter went to East Aurora from Ohio State University in Columbus. He designed the stained glass windows for the Roycroft Inn, then under construction, and was involved in a variety of other Roycroft pursuits, including setting up the Copper Shop of the Roycrofters with Karl Kipp; see McConnell 1990, pp. 17–22. For a discussion of Hunter's Secessionist influence, see Koch 1967, pp. 80–82. See Dard Hunter, *My Life with Paper* (New York: Knopf, 1958), pp. 29–43; cited in Koch 1967, p. 80, for a discussion of foreign periodicals at Roycroft. Commercial Buffalo Pottery china is discussed in Altman and Altman 1987, pp. 140–155.

200.

Pair of Lanterns, ca. 1912

Tookay Shop (1911–1920s), East Aurora, New York
Copper and leaded glass
11½ × 5½ × 5½ inches
Marks: In leading on sides of lanterns, facing double *K*s in circle
1984.122.1–.2

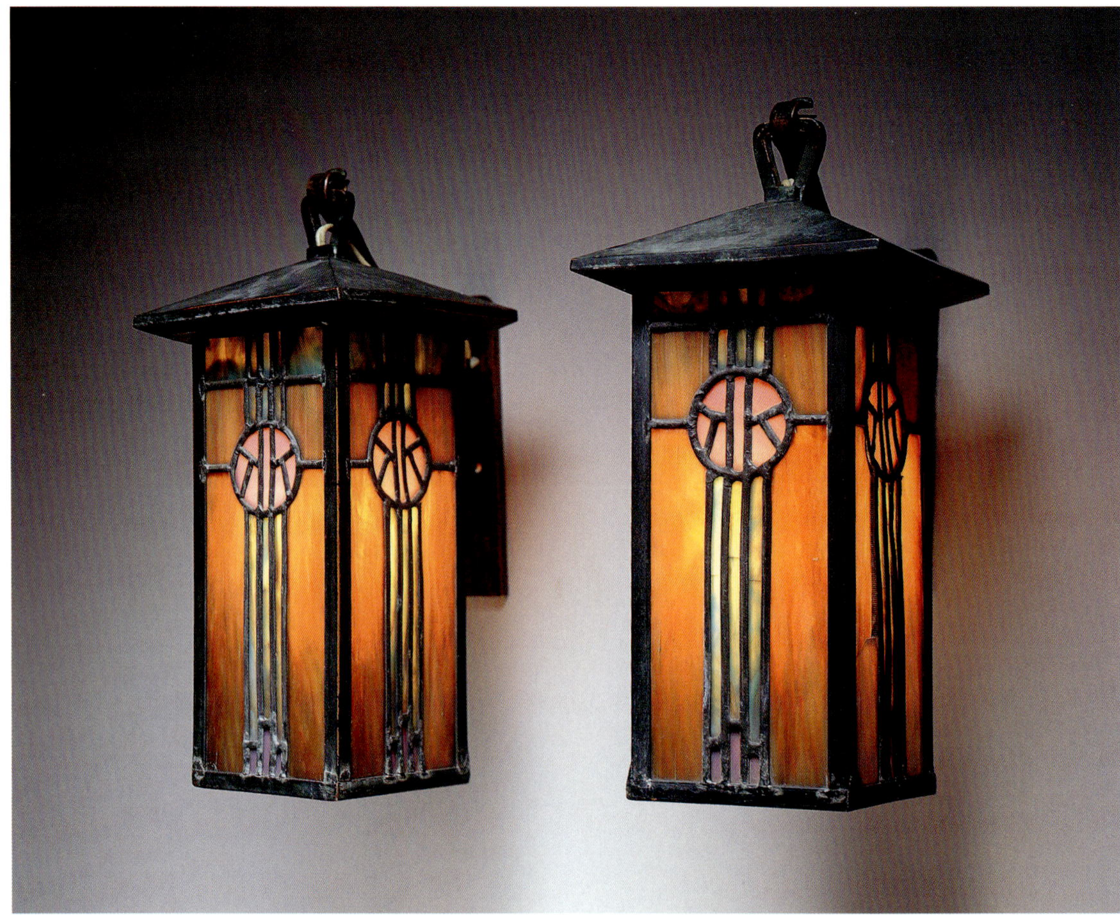

THIS PAIR OF hanging lanterns incorporates the insignia of the Tookay Shop—reverse double-"K"s enclosed in a circle—in the design of their leading. Tookay was a play on the initials of the shop's founder, Karl Kipp. The square shape of the lanterns is related to the Roycroft magazine pedestal also in the Crawford Collection (see no. 198), and the insignia is similar to that used in the Roycroft community.

The Tookay Shop evolved out of Elbert Hubbard's Roycroft Shops in East Aurora, New York. Kipp, formerly a banker, joined the Roycrofters in 1908, drawn by the charismatic Hubbard to pursue a life in the Arts and Crafts movement. Hubbard, who encouraged artisans to explore different crafts, at first assigned Kipp to the Roycroft bindery shop to work in leather. He soon recognized Kipp's expertise and organizational abilities, and placed him in charge of the Copper Shop of the Roycrofters later that same year.[1]

When the Roycroft campus began to expand after 1900, local craftsmen and Roycrofters were hired to provide furniture and metal accessories, such as door hinges, hardware, and andirons, for the new buildings. Hubbard added handmade copper decorative accessories to the Roycroft output as early as 1903.

Under Kipp's leadership, with the assistance of Walter U. Jennings, also from the bindery, the Copper Shop introduced a wide array of products, from desk and smoking items to candlesticks and decorative accessories. Kipp became an adept designer of metalwares and created prototypes for the shop craftsmen to execute. The shop's products reflect Kipp's awareness of contemporary European design through the English and Continental design periodicals that Hubbard made available to the artisans. Fellow Roycrofter Dard Hunter returned from design studies in Vienna in 1908 and became a lifelong friend and influence to Kipp (see no. 199). The play of straight lines and circles in the lanterns shows the influences of Hunter, Viennese Secessionist design at the turn of the century, and the designs of Scottish architect Charles Rennie Mackintosh.[2]

After Kipp and Jennings left the Copper Shop in 1911, they established the independent Tookay Shop in East Aurora, where they could capitalize on the flow of tourists to the Roycroft campus. Before leaving Roycroft, Kipp had become a member of the Society of Arts and Crafts, Boston, at the "Master Craftsman" level, and had been selling copper and sterling silver jewelry under his own name. The Tookay Shop operated on Church Street in East Aurora, with a showroom on Main Street.

By 1912, advertisements for the Tookay Shop appeared in *The Craftsman* magazine, and work from the shop was shown in Stickley's Permanent Home Exposition in the Craftsman Building in New York. Also in 1912, the Tookay Shop published a retail catalogue based on the Roycroft prototype. Kipp's prose echoes Hubbard's effusive style:

> Pottery, Glassware and China beautiful as may be found will last only as long as it is tenderly cared for and protected but Metal-Work is made to endure always. Time will mellow its tones, and the hands of many generations may leave their marks on its surface—but the thing itself is indestructible. It is, therefore, my desire to make—and direct in my workshop the making of—only such things as will be worthy to be a permanent part of the home wherein they may be placed. I would also have each piece seem good enough to look at more than once, each day, beautiful enough to live with all the years—and then significant enough to pass on to other generations who will treasure it for these same reasons. To this work and these ideals I have dedicated my life.[3]

After Hubbard died in the sinking of the *Lusitania* in 1915, the Roycroft community was led by his son, Elbert Hubbard, Jr. One of the younger Hubbard's first innovations was to open Roycroft departments in stores across the country, and he persuaded both Kipp and Jennings to return to Roycroft to help meet the increased demand. While working for Roycroft, Kipp continued to operate the Tookay Shop into the 1920s, expanding into pewter and experimenting in new Art Deco shapes. With the onset of the Great Depression in 1929, demand for Roycroft products diminished. Prior to the closing of the Roycroft community in 1938, Kipp moved to Olean, New York, where he became head designer for Daystrom Corporation, a manufacturer of metal furniture.

NOTES

1. The Tookay Shop is discussed in Bowman 1990, p. 112; Clark 1972, p. 49; and Kaplan 1987, pp. 385–386.

2. See Schweiger 1984; Kaplan 1987, pp. 83–85; and Roycroft Art Museum 1992, "Karl Kipp Chronology," inside back cover.

3. Roycroft Art Museum 1992, p. 2.

201.

Magazine Stand,
ca. 1906

Shop of the Crafters at Cincinnati (1904–1920), Cincinnati
Oak, various inlaid woods, glass, and brass
58 × 28 × 12 inches
1984.149

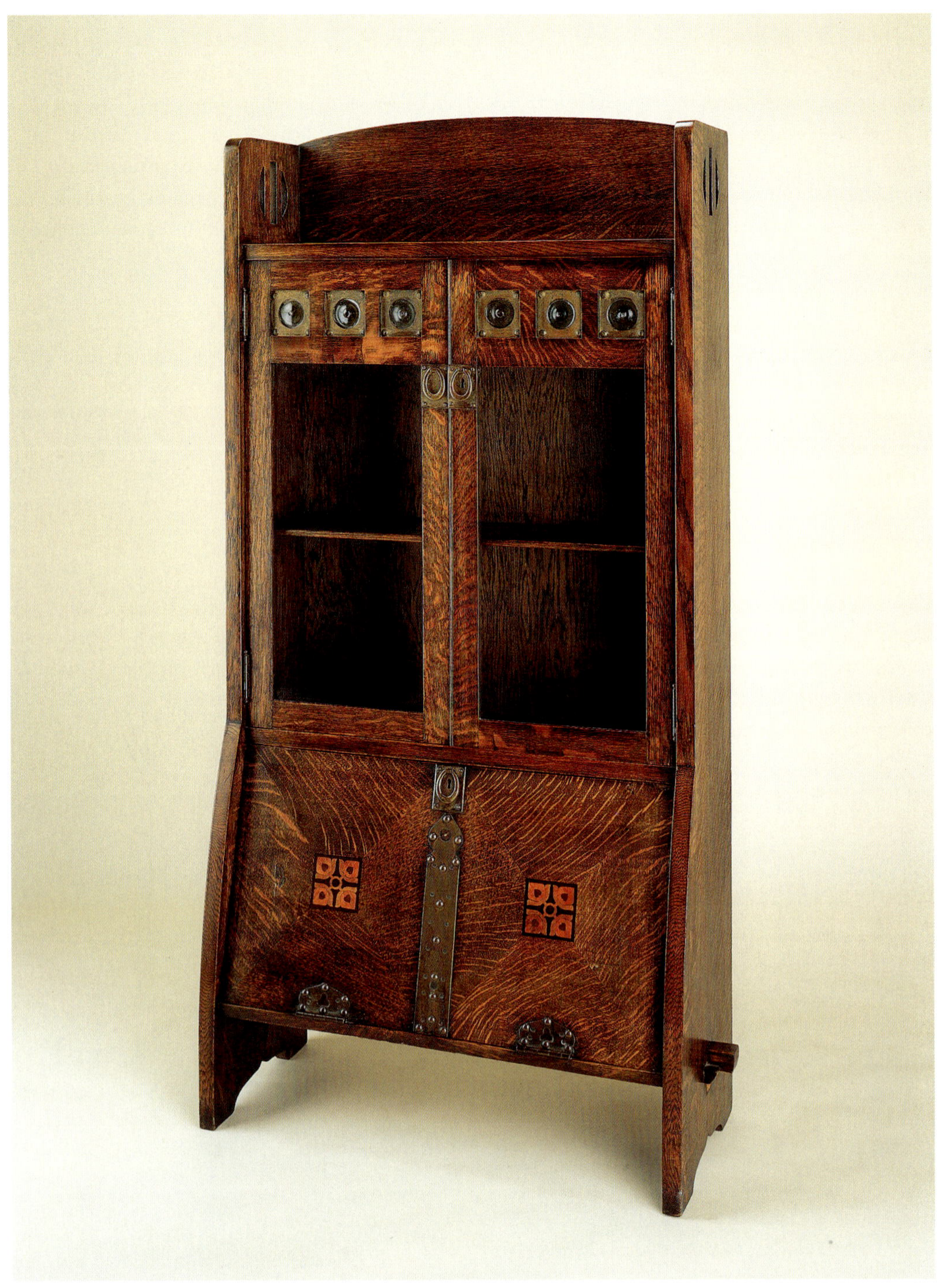

Diverse cultural influences and marketing contributed to the distinctive furniture lines produced by the Shop of the Crafters at Cincinnati. Its founder, Oscar Onken, was a shrewd businessman who had two decades of experience manufacturing picture frames, moldings, and mirrors and dealing in etchings, engravings, and "art goods." In 1903, he established the Oscar Onken Company with his brother Robert and investors and expanded his business to include "furniture novelties." Gustav Stickley had already introduced his line of Craftsman furniture, and the growing American market for Arts and Crafts furniture may have encouraged Onken to name the furniture division of his business Shop of the Crafters.

As early as 1904, the Shop of the Crafters at Cincinnati was advertising in national magazines. The 1905–1906 Cincinnati directory listed the Shop of the Crafters as "Manufacturers of Arts and Crafts Furniture" and the Oscar Onken Company as "Manufacturers of Mission Furniture."[1] The Oscar Onken Company was in business until 1931, eleven years after the Shop of the Crafters closed.

Cincinnati had been a leading American furniture-manufacturing center from the mid-nineteenth century until it was surpassed by Grand Rapids, Michigan, in the late nineteenth century. Many of the workers in Cincinnati's furniture industry were Germans who had immigrated to the United States beginning in the 1840s. When Onken began manufacturing furniture in 1903, he had a local resource of experienced woodworkers to produce his Arts and Crafts lines. The local furniture industry had been highly mechanized, and although the company's 1906 catalogue states that "the Crafters turn out only hand-made things,"[2] Onken in fact maintained a factory in Cincinnati and distributed goods nationally and to Canada and Mexico. While there was handwork on the objects produced by the Crafters, methods of mass production made the broad distribution possible.

The use of oak and through tenons on this stand are hallmarks of American Arts and Crafts furniture, but certain elements of the stand reflect Continental influence beyond the English Arts and Crafts movement that so dominated most American Arts and Crafts furniture design. The use of exotic wood inlays and the cutouts in the side panels relate the stand to turn-of-the-century Viennese Secessionist design. Viennese and German furniture was known to American furniture makers from European design periodicals and was exhibited to great acclaim at the 1904 Louisiana Purchase International Exposition in St. Louis.

The introduction to the 1906 Shop of the Crafters catalogue praised the work of Budapest designer Paul Horti at the St. Louis exposition and gave credit to Horti for "his work with the Shop of the Crafters of Cincinnati [which] has contributed to the distinction it enjoys for productions that are pure in style and of artistic beauty." Horti, who also worked for Charles P. Limbert and Company (see no. 202), is credited with introducing "a touch of inlay work of colored woods or metal, that enlivens the strong simple lines of Mission furniture." Inlay work was unusual on American Arts and Crafts furniture, and the figured and slightly convex quartered oak panels on the lower doors around the marquetry squares of the Crawford magazine stand were distinctive to Crafters furniture. Specifications for the stand in the 1906 catalogue listed its European elements, including "Marquetry Panels of Imported Colored Austrian Woods" and "Imported Green [glass] Roundels in Upper Door" (fig. 1).[3]

NOTES

1. Extant labels on furniture from the Shop of the Crafters at Cincinnati list "OSCAR ONKEN CO. SOLE OWNERS," and the shop seems to have been a division of that company. S. Gray 1983 is a reprint of the Shop of the Crafters at Cincinnati 1906 catalogue. The magazine stand is illustrated on p. 10, no. 336, and was priced at $36. The history of the Shop of the Crafters is recounted in Trapp 1986. Trapp cites the 1889 Cincinnati directory as listing Onken and Vance as "Manufacturers of mouldings, frames, mirrors and Dealers in Etchings, Engravings and Art Goods," p. 9. Trapp cites the 1905–1906 directory for Shop of the Crafters and Oscar Onken Company listings, p. 10. Bowman 1990, p. 67, fig. 37a–b, illustrates a marked desk and chair, and its paper label is illustrated on p. 235.

2. S. Gray 1983, p. 68.

3. The introduction to the catalogue appears in S. Gray 1983, pp. 4–5. See also Kaplan 1987, p. 248. The specifications for the magazine stand are given in S. Gray 1983, p. 10.

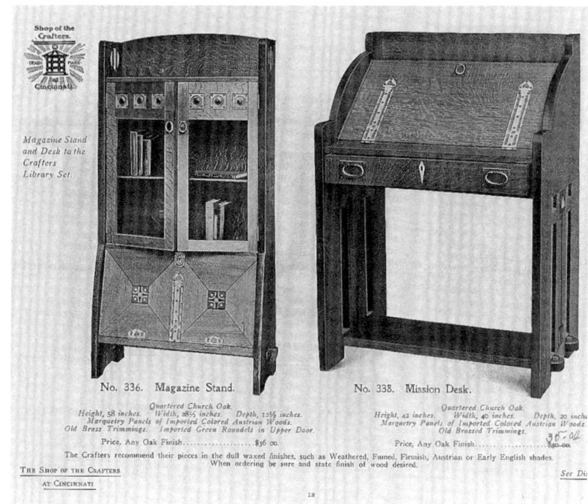
Shop of the Crafters.
TRADE MARK
at Cincinnati.

Magazine Stand and Desk to the Crafters Library Set.

No. 336. Magazine Stand.

Quartered Church Oak.
Height, 58 inches. Width, 28½ inches. Depth, 12½ inches.
Marquetry Panels of Imported Colored Austrian Woods.
Old Brass Trimmings. Imported Green Roundels in Upper Door.

Price, Any Oak Finish.................... $36 00.

No. 338. Mission Desk.

Quartered Church Oak.
Height, 42 inches. Width, 40 inches. Depth, 20 inch
Marquetry Panels of Imported Colored Austrian Woods.
Old Brassed Trimmings.

Price, Any Oak Finish.................... ~~$40.00~~ 35.00

The Crafters recommend their pieces in the dull waxed finishes, such as Weathered, Fumed, Flemish, Austrian or Early English shades. When ordering be sure and state finish of wood desired.

THE SHOP OF THE CRAFTERS AT CINCINNATI

See Di

12

Fig. 1. *Shop of the Crafters at Cincinnati,* 1906, p. 12. The Metropolitan Museum of Art, The Elisha Whittelsey Collection, The Elisha Whittelsey Fund. 1960. (60.565.6)

202.

Taboret, designed ca. 1906

Charles P. Limbert and Company (1902–1944), Grand Rapids and Holland, Michigan
White oak
18 × 16 × 16 inches
Marks: Branded under top edge, rectangle enclosing an outline of a craftsman planing wood on a workbench superimposed on text, *LIMBERTS/ARTS CRAFTS/FURNITURE/TRADE MARK/MADE IN/GRAND RAPIDS/AND HOLLAND;* under top edge, *234*
1986.195

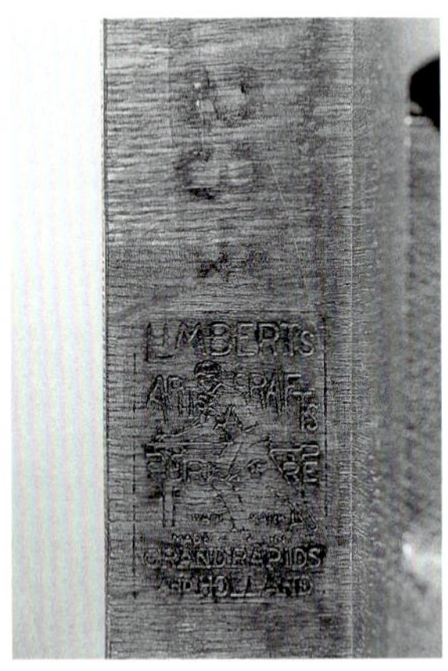

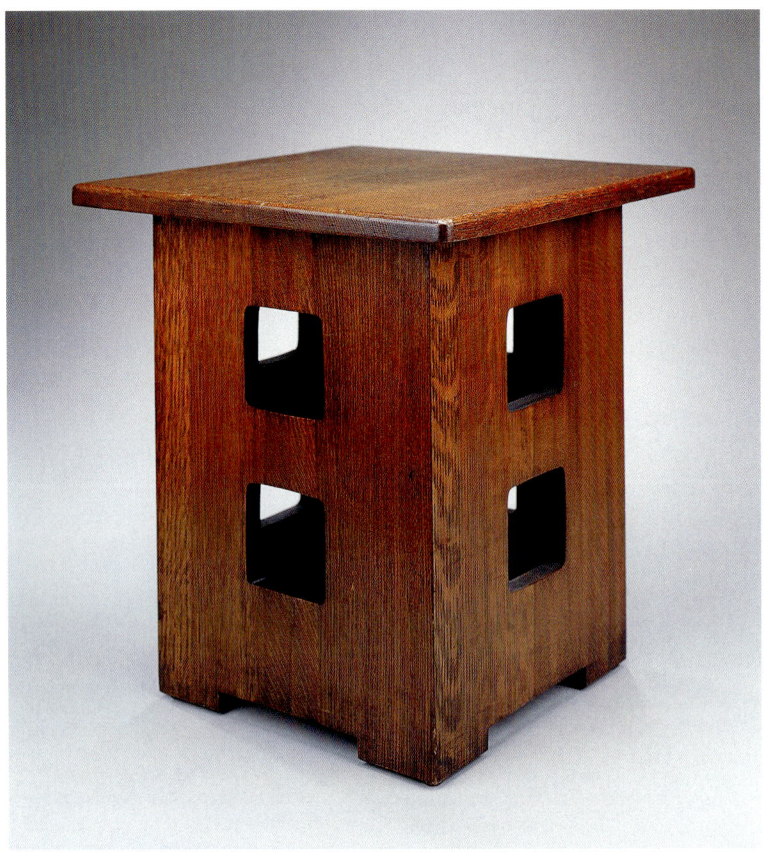

Following in his father's trade, Charles P. Limbert became a furniture salesman representing various Midwestern factories in the 1870s and 1880s. He moved to the expanding furniture-making center of Grand Rapids, Michigan, in 1889. After a brief stint as a partner in a furniture showroom, Limbert started his own firm in 1894, manufacturing chairs.[1]

In the summer of 1900, Gustav Stickley's new designs introduced at the Grand Rapids furniture trade show (see nos. 188–193) began to influence the products of the Grand Rapids furniture trade.[2] Two years later, Charles P. Limbert and Company launched its Holland Dutch Arts and Crafts line of furniture, and the next year it published an illustrated catalogue. The 1903 catalogue contained sketches that emphasized the elements of construction, such as pegs and through tenons, reinforcing the Arts and Crafts qualities of the furniture. Limbert's designs focused on square and rectangular shapes, but the straight lines were relieved with curving aprons, rectangular panels with heart-shaped cutouts, and splayed legs, all suggesting northern European peasant furniture.

By 1905, when this taboret was in production, Limbert's furniture line had been substantially altered and expanded.[3] At first, Limbert furniture had been made in ash and oak in a variety of finishes, but by 1905 the company was mainly using solid white oak with no veneers and placing less emphasis on European peasant motifs. The furniture in the 1905 catalogue still had the occasional heart-shaped cutouts and splayed legs, but it featured square and rectangular forms and simpler—often square—cutouts in the panels. These elements, featured in this taboret, show the growing influence of designers like Charles Rennie Mackintosh in Glasgow, and Viennese Secessionist design.[4] A regional influence may have been Chicago's Prairie School architects such as Frank Lloyd Wright (see nos. 223–224). Some of these qualities may also have been the result of Limbert's hiring the Austrian designer Louis Gohlke, his son William Gohlke, and Hungarian architect Paul Horti. During this period,

Limbert himself traveled extensively in Europe, studying both contemporary furniture and historical examples.[5] The 1905 catalogue acknowledged an awareness of European design: "We have made a careful study of this distinctive school of design, which is much cultivated by European artists. In England by the Arts and Crafts societies—in France it is known as the new art [Art Nouveau]—in Germany and Austria as Kunst Handwerk—and in America it is a revival of the Old Mission Furniture found in the Missions in California and Mexico."[6]

In subsequent publications, the company gave its interpretation of what it called the "Spanish influence" in American Arts and Crafts and attempted to reconcile the name of the Holland Dutch Arts and Crafts line with the term "Mission furniture":

> Spain, not being a manufacturing nation, depended largely upon the Holland Dutch importations for their fabrics, furniture, plate and other manufactured articles. . . . The Spanish missionaries and monks, who settled the western coast of America and established the missions of Mexico and California, were familiar with styles of furniture made in the Netherlands, and patterned after it as well as they could with the crude material and inadequate tools they had at hand.[7]

This fanciful explanation of Limbert furniture design distanced the term "mission" from philosophical reform sources.

Concern for the workers' health and welfare was an ideal of the Arts and Crafts movement, and when Charles P. Limbert and Company moved its factory and headquarters from the increasingly congested and industrial Grand Rapids to the more bucolic Holland, Michigan, it gave the following explanation:

> An environment more conducive to artistic effort and a higher quality of craftsmanship was sought and eventually discovered in the little town of Holland, Michigan, . . . the most typically Dutch settlement in America . . . extraordinarily prosperous, attractive and quaint.[8]

The company made much of the supposed Dutch ethnicity of the workers, a clever sales ploy that appealed to popular notions of the Arts and Crafts movement.

The branded mark showing a craftsman planing wood reinforced the idea that Limbert furniture was handmade. Although hand-techniques were employed for joining and finishing, the furniture was made in a factory mostly by machinery. The top of the Crawford taboret is secured to the base with eight screws rather than a traditional furniture joint, demonstrating that although Limbert was committed to Arts and Crafts appearances, he was willing to use time-saving technology.

Gustav Stickley's Craftsman Workshops entered bankruptcy proceedings in 1915 as the Arts and Crafts rage was fading, but Charles P. Limbert and Company continued to produce its Holland Dutch Arts and Crafts line. Production continued for another year but was supplemented by furniture in Chinese, Italian, Queen Anne, William and Mary, and Federal styles. In 1917, Limbert was producing only colonial revival furniture. Limbert sold the business in 1922, a year before his death. Furniture production under the Limbert name continued until 1944.

NOTES

1. In his introduction to the reprint of the 1903 catalogue *Limbert Arts and Crafts Furniture,* 1992, pp. v–vii, C. G. Carron provides biographical information about Limbert, the history of the firm, and background on the Grand Rapids furniture trade; see Carron 1992, pp. v–vii. The early history of Grand Rapids as a furniture-making center is outlined in Ames 1975, pp. 23–50.

2. Kaplan 1987, p. 243.

3. The form, Limbert number 234, is illustrated in the facsimile of the 1905 catalogue reprinted in S. Gray 1990, p. 23, with a group of twelve other taborets. The same form is illustrated and discussed in Clark 1972, p. 78, no. 106.

4. Architectural elements such as doors with series of square windows, as well as tables and chairs with square cutouts, were part of the Mackintosh design vocabulary. See the illustration of the entrance hall and furniture with related cutouts in the 1901–1904 Walter W. Blackie House, designed by Mackintosh, outside Glasgow, in Kaplan 1987, p. 84, fig. 13. For an illustrated survey of Viennese Secessionist design, see Schweiger 1984. A work table with a square lattice designed by the Austrian architect Josef Hoffman may have inspired the square cutouts on the Crawford taboret and other Limbert designs; that table is illustrated in Noever 1992, p. 69, no. 86.

5. S. Gray 1990, p. 5. Paul Horti also worked for the Shop of the Crafters at Cincinnati (see no. 201 in this catalogue); see Carron 1992, p. vi.

6. S. Gray 1990, p. 14.

7. "Charles P. Limbert Company Cabinet Makers," Booklet No. 112, n.d.; reproduced in S. Gray 1990, p. 70.

8. Ibid., p. 139.

203.

Vase, 1908–1915

Marblehead Pottery (1904–1936), Marblehead, Massachusetts
Pottery with glazed decoration
6¾ × 3¾ × 3¾ inches
Marks: Painted on bottom, *T*; impressed on bottom, inside circle, *M P* flanking emblem of a sailing ship
1984.116

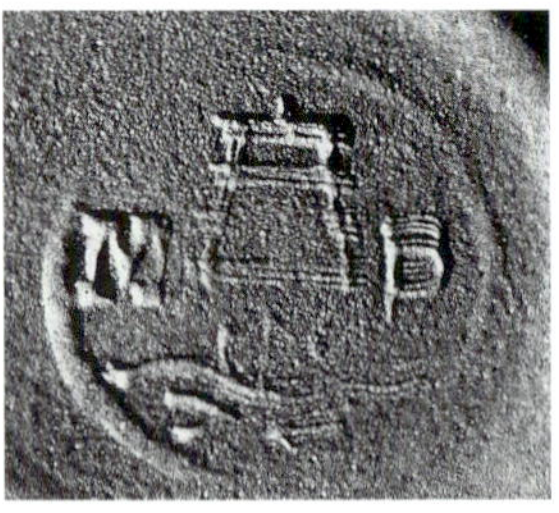

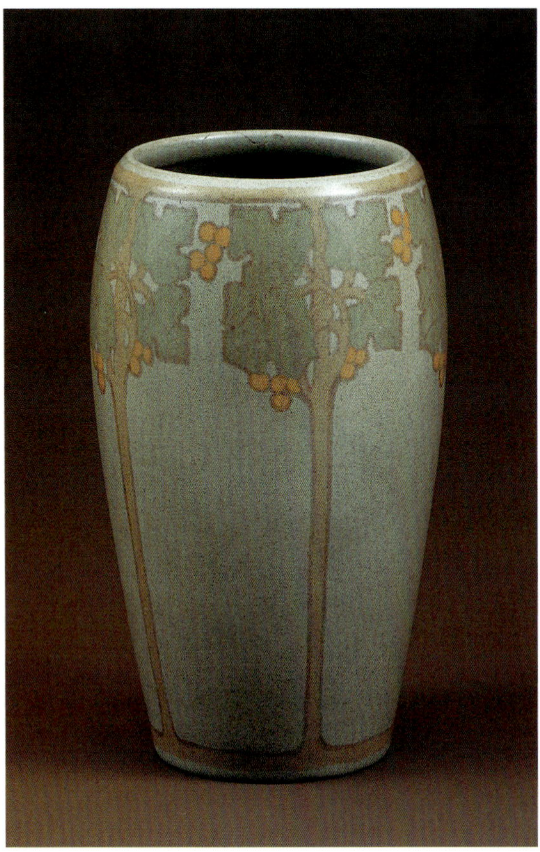

In 1904, Dr. Herbert J. Hall, a Marblehead physician, established the Handcraft Workshops, with programs in pottery, handweaving, woodcarving, and metalwork. Dr. Hall hoped his workshops would provide therapeutic benefit to his patients who were "nervously worn out."[1] Alfred Eugene Baggs, a professionally trained ceramicist, was taken on to assist in the pottery program.[2] Between 1905 and 1908, experiments led Baggs to change from using clay from the Marblehead area to a new recipe combining New Jersey stoneware clays and Massachusetts brick clays.

By 1908, under Baggs's supervision, the pottery had evolved from a therapeutic program to a successful commercial pottery with a small professional staff capable of standardized production. The pottery moved from workrooms in Dr. Hall's Devereux Mansion to a building on Front Street in Marblehead, where summer tourists became a major source of revenue. Most of the wares were thrown on a wheel by the English potter John Swallow. Hannah Tutt was chief decorator, and the "T" painted on the bottom of the Crawford vase may mean that the decoration is hers. By 1919, the pottery had published a catalogue from which customers could choose shapes and background colors, but the specific color schemes and patterns were selected by the designers and decorators. Wares in the muted, matte background colors without decoration were sold for substantially less than the decorated wares. Despite the catalogue merchandising, the hand-thrown and hand-painted production assured the singularity of each Marblehead product.

In 1915, Baggs took over ownership of the pottery from Dr. Hall. After 1928, Baggs taught at other schools but continued to guide the Marblehead Pottery and spent his summers working there until it closed in 1936. The pottery won awards at exhibitions at the Art Institute of Chicago, the Cleveland Museum of Art, the Syracuse Museum of Fine Arts, and from the Society of Arts and Crafts, Boston.

The simple shape and muted colors of the Crawford vase are characteristic of Marblehead Pottery, and the repetitive, tree-like motif is typical of Marblehead's painted style.

NOTES

1. From Herbert J. Hall, M.D., "Marblehead Pottery," *Keramics Studio* 10 (June 1908): 31; cited in Kaplan 1987, p. 256.

2. Baggs was a student of Charles F. Binns at the New York School of Clayworking and Ceramics in Alfred, New York. For information about Binns and his influence on American ceramics, see Bowman 1990, p. 140. The Marblehead Pottery history is recounted in ibid., pp. 156–157; Cooper-Hewitt 1987, p. 124; Evans 1987, pp. 157–160; and Kaplan 1987, pp. 256–257.

204.

Vase, ca. 1910

Paul Revere Pottery (1906–1942), Boston or Brighton, Massachusetts
Pottery with glazed decoration
5⅝ × 4¼ × 4¼ inches
Marks: Painted on bottom, A over M/S.E.G.
1982.288

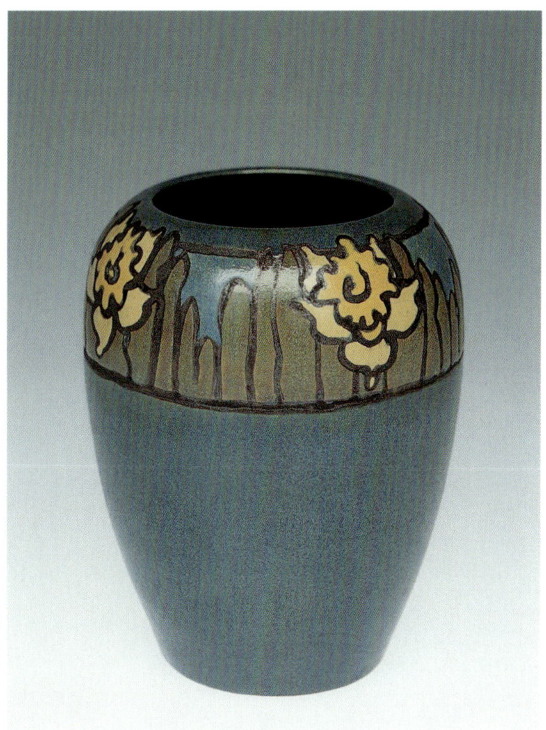

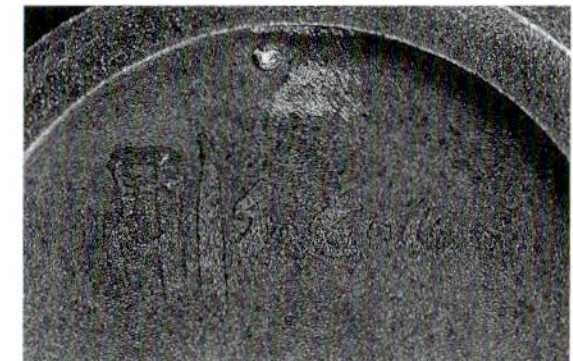

At the turn of the twentieth century, the Saturday Evening Girls' Club was organized to benefit the daughters of immigrant Italian and Jewish families in Boston's inner city. The group met for weekly readings and craft workshops at the North End branch of the Boston Public Library. They established the Paul Revere Pottery as part of the social and practical improvement programs at the suggestion of Edith Guerrier, a librarian at the branch and supervisor of the club, and her friend Edith Brown, who became director and chief designer.[1]

Through the generosity of the club's patron, Mrs. James J. Storrow, the group acquired a kiln in 1906. Two years later, the pottery began regular production in a building in the North End of Boston near the historic Old North Church, and the name was selected because of Revere's association with the neighborhood. The pottery's intent was to provide young women with occupational preparation, experience, and income for further education. After a year's training, the girls were employed to decorate the wares. Before 1915, the staff included ten girls undergoing a year of training and decorating the work, the designer, and the kiln-man, who fired the wares. Through its Bowl Shop, the pottery sold vases, children's sets, breakfast sets, electrical lamp bases, tea sets, and dinner services. Special orders with monograms, initials, and inscriptions were also accepted.

The pottery was expanded in 1915, when Mrs. Storrow built a colonial-style structure designed by Edith Brown in Brighton, a streetcar suburb of Boston. On the landscaped grounds, readings provided diversion and cultural growth for the girls as they worked. Brown continued as director of the pottery until her death in 1932. Although production continued for another decade, the venture never became an independent profit-making enterprise. Mrs. Storrow and others supported the pottery throughout its thirty-eight years of operation.

The Crawford vase is decorated with incised outlines filled in with solid, mineral-based colors characteristic of Paul Revere Pottery decorations. Animals and stylized flowers were commonly used motifs, and shapes tended to be simple. The "S.E.G." painted on the base is the initials of the club, and the decorator signed with her initials, "A.M." The identity of this decorator is currently unknown and records have not been located to identify the more than two hundred girls who decorated wares at the pottery.

NOTE

1. Accounts of the history and goals of the Paul Revere Pottery are found in Bowman 1990, p. 173; Evans 1987, pp. 213–216; Kaplan 1987, pp. 312–313; and Keen 1978, p. 55.

205.

Vase, 1910

Newcomb Pottery (1894–1940), New Orleans; thrown and fired by Joseph F. Meyer (1848–1931); decorated by Anna Frances Simpson (1880–1930)
Earthenware
12¼ × 7¼ × 7¼ inches
Marks: On bottom: impressed, *JM;* impressed, *C* enclosing *N;* written in blue, *DI* [unclear]; written in blue, *DO-15;* impressed, *K;* written in blue, *AFS*
1981.1000.56

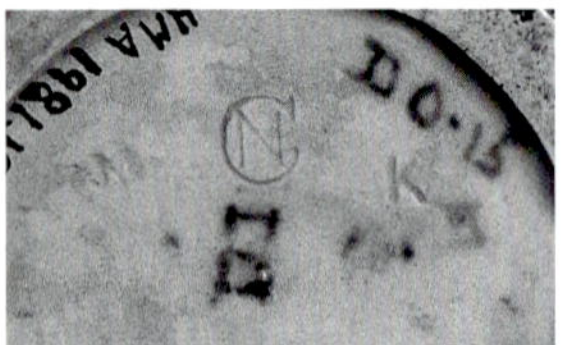

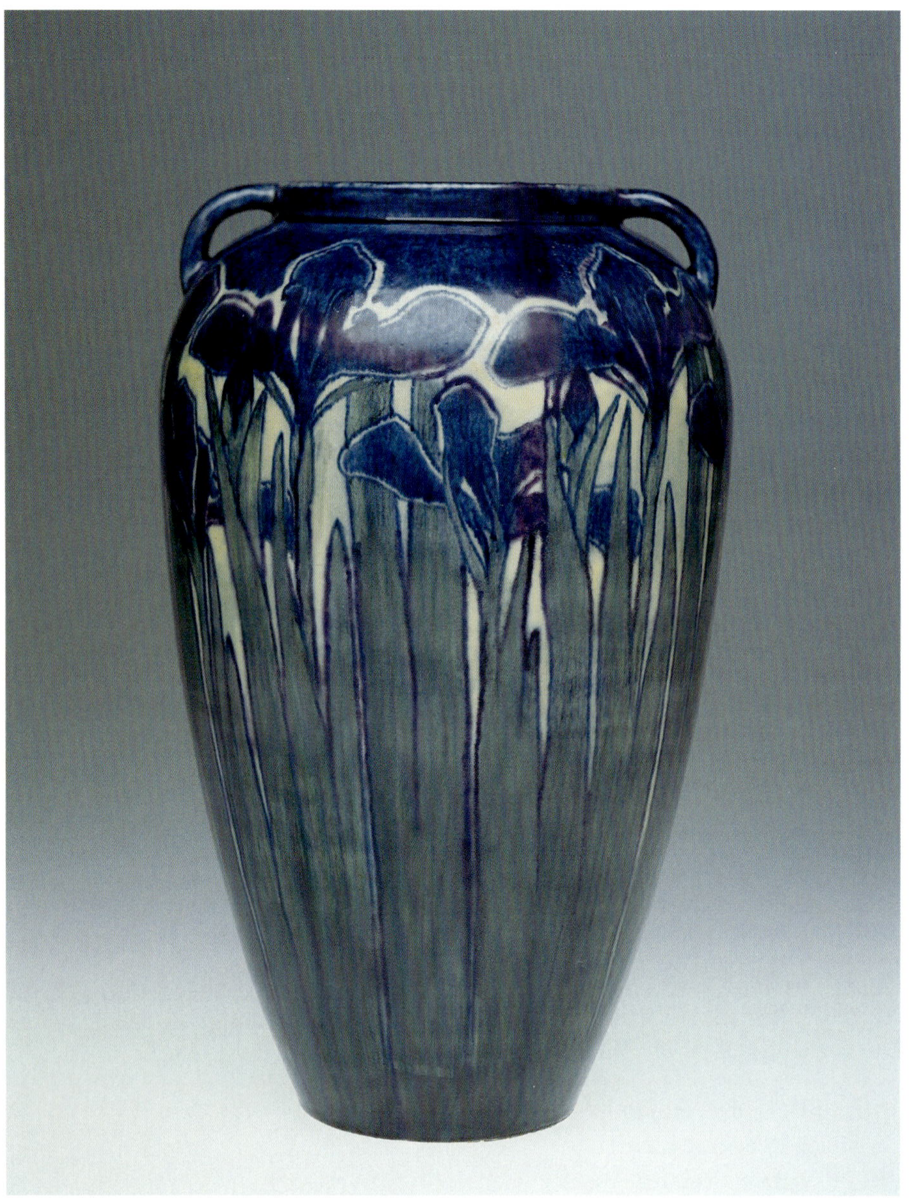

The Newcomb Pottery was an educational enterprise affiliated with Sophie Newcomb Memorial College in New Orleans. It was the earliest, most successful, and longest-surviving Arts and Crafts pottery in the Deep South. In 1899, founding director Mary Sheerer wrote, "The whole thing was to be a southern product, made of southern clays, by southern artists, decorated with southern subjects."[1] Such specific focus led to wares decorated with stylized plants and animals indigenous to the region and romanticized moonlit landscapes suggested by the swampy bayou country around New Orleans. Southern motifs remained a constant theme throughout the nearly half century the Newcomb Pottery was in operation.

As it had in Cincinnati in the 1870s and 1880s (see nos. 121, 172), interest in ceramics in New Orleans began with a women's club. The women decorated ceramics made at the New Orleans Art Pottery, thrown and fired by Joseph Fortune Meyer and George Ohr. Also, classes were offered in china-decorating at the 1884 Cotton Centennial Exposition in New Orleans by members of the art faculty at Tulane University.

The women's club became associated with

Newcomb College around 1894 through the efforts of the Newcomb College art instructor Ellsworth Woodward, who was part of a new generation of professionally trained artisans. He had studied at two recently established New England institutions: the Massachusetts Normal Art School and the Rhode Island School of Design. At the new pottery, Mary Sheerer supervised the decorators, who were selected from art classes at Newcomb College. Sheerer had trained at the Art Students League in New York and at the Cincinnati Art Academy, where she had worked with pioneering women china decorators.

Like the Paul Revere Pottery in Boston (see no. 204), the Newcomb Pottery provided young women with instruction that enabled them to earn a living in an honorable, satisfying, and creative profession. For the first twenty-five years of the pottery, training was limited to design and decoration, while the actual throwing and firing remained the responsibility of professional male potters. Joseph Meyer, who had made pots for the early women's decorating club at the New Orleans Art Pottery, worked at the Newcomb Pottery from 1896 until 1925, when blindness forced him to retire. He has been credited with throwing and firing most of the pottery's wares during its first thirty years.

The Crawford vase is characteristic of the wares produced by the Newcomb Pottery during its first fifteen years.[2] Blue, black, and green were colors associated with the pottery throughout its existence, and the high-gloss, transparent lead glaze was used exclusively until 1911.[3] The vase is typical of the simple shapes made by Meyer, with broad smooth surfaces designed to enhance the characteristic decoration derived from native southern plants and painted in elongated, curved lines associated with European Art Nouveau.

The vase has the "C" enclosing the "N" mark of the Newcomb Pottery and the impressed initials of Joseph Meyer. The impressed "K" was used after 1895 on wares having a white clay body with high-gloss glazes. The different letters used may indicate experimental varieties of clay or glaze. The painted registration number "DO-15" indicates that the piece was made in 1910.[4] Also written in blue are the initials of the decorator, Anna Frances Simpson, who had a long and prolific association with the Newcomb Pottery. She entered the college as a "normal" art student in 1902, graduated in 1906, and was registered as a graduate art student until 1908. From 1908 to 1929, she was listed in Newcomb College catalogues as an "arts craftsman." Besides decorating pottery, she was also a needleworker and a printmaker. Her pottery was shown in the Education Palace at the 1915 Panama-Pacific Exposition in San Francisco.[5]

The Newcomb Pottery was an educational experiment that met with surprising commercial success. Widely admired and marketed, the pottery received medals at a number of expositions in the early twentieth century: Paris in 1900; Buffalo in 1901; Charleston, South Carolina, in 1902; St. Louis in 1904; and Portland, Oregon, in 1905. The pottery at Newcomb College survived the Great Depression and continued to operate, but on a reduced scale, until 1940.

NOTES

1. Quoted in Poesch 1984, p. 18. This catalogue of a traveling exhibition is the most comprehensive published study of the Newcomb Pottery. Other accounts are Bowman 1990, pp. 160–164; M. Eidelberg, "Art Pottery," in Clark 1972, pp. 144–149; Evans 1987, pp. 182–186; and Kaplan 1987, pp. 324–325.

2. The vase is illustrated and discussed by M. Eidelberg in Clark 1972, p. 148, no. 210.

3. Paul Cox, a ceramic chemist trained at New York's Alfred University, joined the Newcomb staff in 1910. By 1911, he had introduced a matte glaze in response to waning consumer interest in high-gloss glazes. The new matte glaze quickly became the standard at Newcomb Pottery. See Evans 1987, p. 183.

4. W. Bob, "Basic Marks and Dating," in Poesch 1984, p. 91.

5. Ibid., p. 105.

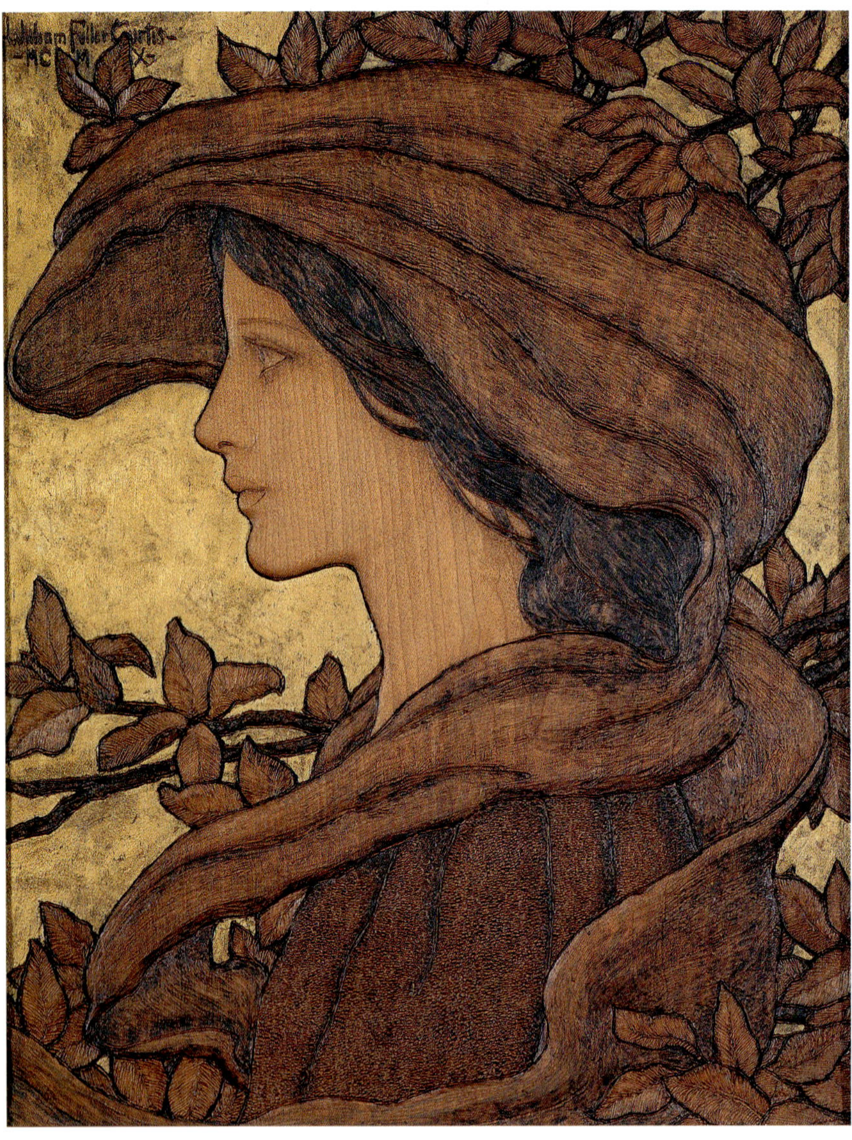

206.

Profile of a Young Woman, dated 1910

William Fuller Curtis (born 1873), probably New York
Carved, burned, and painted tulipwood with gold background
18 × 13⅝ inches
Mark: Signed in upper left corner of front, *William Fuller Curtis-/-MC M X-*
1988.226

Born in Staten Island, New York, William Fuller Curtis studied art in Paris, and he was creating dramatic profiles of idealized young women like this example by 1902. He was awarded a silver medal for a panel at the 1904 Louisiana Purchase International Exposition in St. Louis. Curtis also created wood panels to decorate the altar of the Church of St. Michael and All Angels in Geneseo, New York, and the interior of the Cosmos Club in Washington, D.C. Although listed in *Mantle Fielding's Dictionary of American Painters, Sculptors and Engravers* as a "painter, sculptor, and worker in applied arts," he seems to have been most highly regarded for his carved panels.[1]

Gustav Stickley's periodical *The Craftsman* celebrated Curtis and his work in two illustrated articles published in 1911 and 1912, just after he created the Crawford panel. The authors found his panels well-suited as a focus for an Arts and Crafts interior, having seen a number of rooms where "all the wall decorations, the carpets, heavy draperies, the ceilings . . . [are] related back to Mr. Curtis's study in gold and brown."[2] The 1911 article also described the process used by Curtis. Beginning with a pencil sketch on the wood, the surface was carved to create the bas relief image; and "over this carved surface he uses the usual pyrographic [wood-burning] tools, by which he secures many different tones and suggestions of colors. . . . There is no color in these burned carvings, beyond the use of gold, which seems to fit in most harmoniously with the tones of the burned wood and the natural color and brings about an effect of original beauty, which while definitely modern, is Medieval in sumptuousness."[3] The title and specific subject of the Crawford panel is unknown, but the *Craftsman* article noted that Curtis worked from live models and created their costumes. While the colors and techniques in Curtis's panels are in accord with the Arts and Crafts aesthetic vision, the idealized young women he depicted are similar to decorations on the earlier Ceramic Art Company vase (see no. 148) and the Will Low painted cabinet (see no. 95).

NOTES

1. Abbreviated biographies of William Fuller Curtis and accounts of his career are in McGlauflin 1935, p. 108; and Opitz 1986, p. 196.

2. *Craftsman* 21, 1911, pp. 258–259.

3. Ibid., p. 259. For the second *Craftsman* article on Curtis's work, see *Craftsman* 22, 1912.

The Kalo Shop

IN THE EARLY twentieth century, when Arthur J. Stone was emerging as the most prominent Arts and Crafts silversmith in New England (see nos. 182–183), the Kalo Shop, under the design leadership of the dynamic Clara Barck Welles, was the leading handwrought-silver studio in Chicago. Clara Barck left her Oregon home at the age of thirty-two to attend design classes at the Art Institute of Chicago. In September 1900, she opened the Kalo Shop (after the Greek word for beauty) at 175 Dearborne Street in Chicago.

With a staff composed mostly of young women called the "Kalo Girls," Barck's shop specialized in decorative burnt-leather objects, weaving, and simple jewelry. In 1905, she married George S. Welles, a coal businessman and an enthusiastic amateur metalworker. After her marriage, the artist's interests shifted to metalware production. At their home in suburban Park Ridge, the Welleses established the Kalo Art-Craft Community to stock an expanded Kalo Shop, then located in the Fine Arts Building on Michigan Avenue in downtown Chicago.

The early Kalo Art-Craft Community consisted of chief designer Clara Barck Welles, a silversmith to execute her designs, and the Kalo Girls to provide assistance. The School of the Art Institute of Chicago no longer offered instruction in metalworking, so Welles began intensive metalwork apprentice instruction and supervision, envisioning the Kalo Art-Craft Community as a school within a workshop. The success of her instruction and her designs drew the attention of trained silversmiths, mostly Scandinavian, seeking work. Ultimately, the Kalo Shop employed as many as twenty-five silversmiths.

After the Welleses divorced in 1914, the Kalo

207.

Tray, ca. 1910

Made and retailed by the Kalo Shop (1900–1970), Park Ridge and Chicago, Illinois; design attributed to Clara Barck Welles (1868–1965)
Silver, mounted with a rose quartz cabochon
¾ × 7¼ × 12 inches
Mark: Stamped on back, *STERLING/HAND BEATEN/AT/KALO SHOPS/PARK RIDGE/ILLS./4151*
1986.190

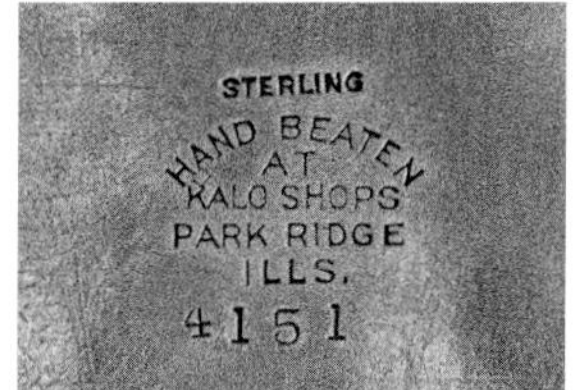

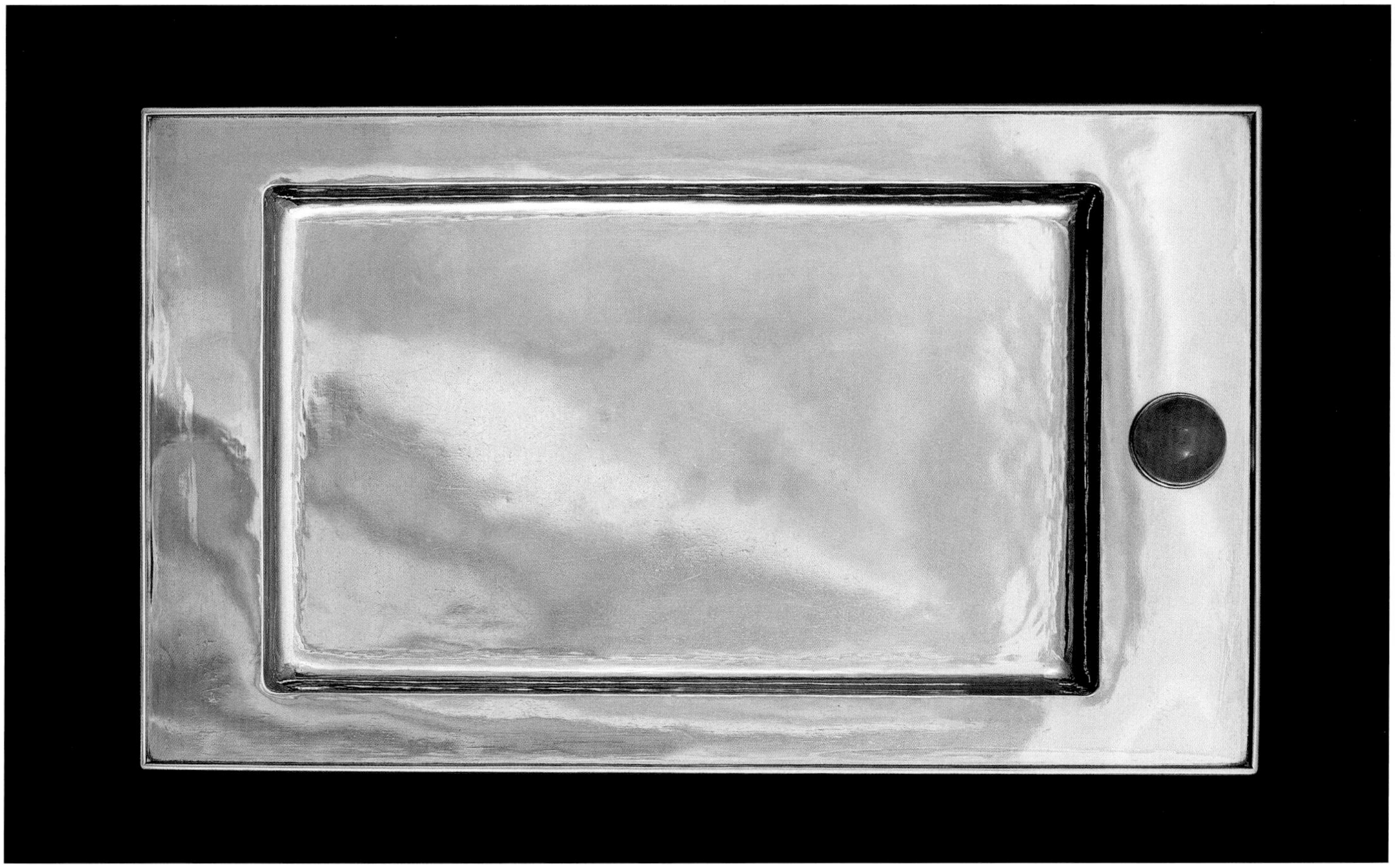

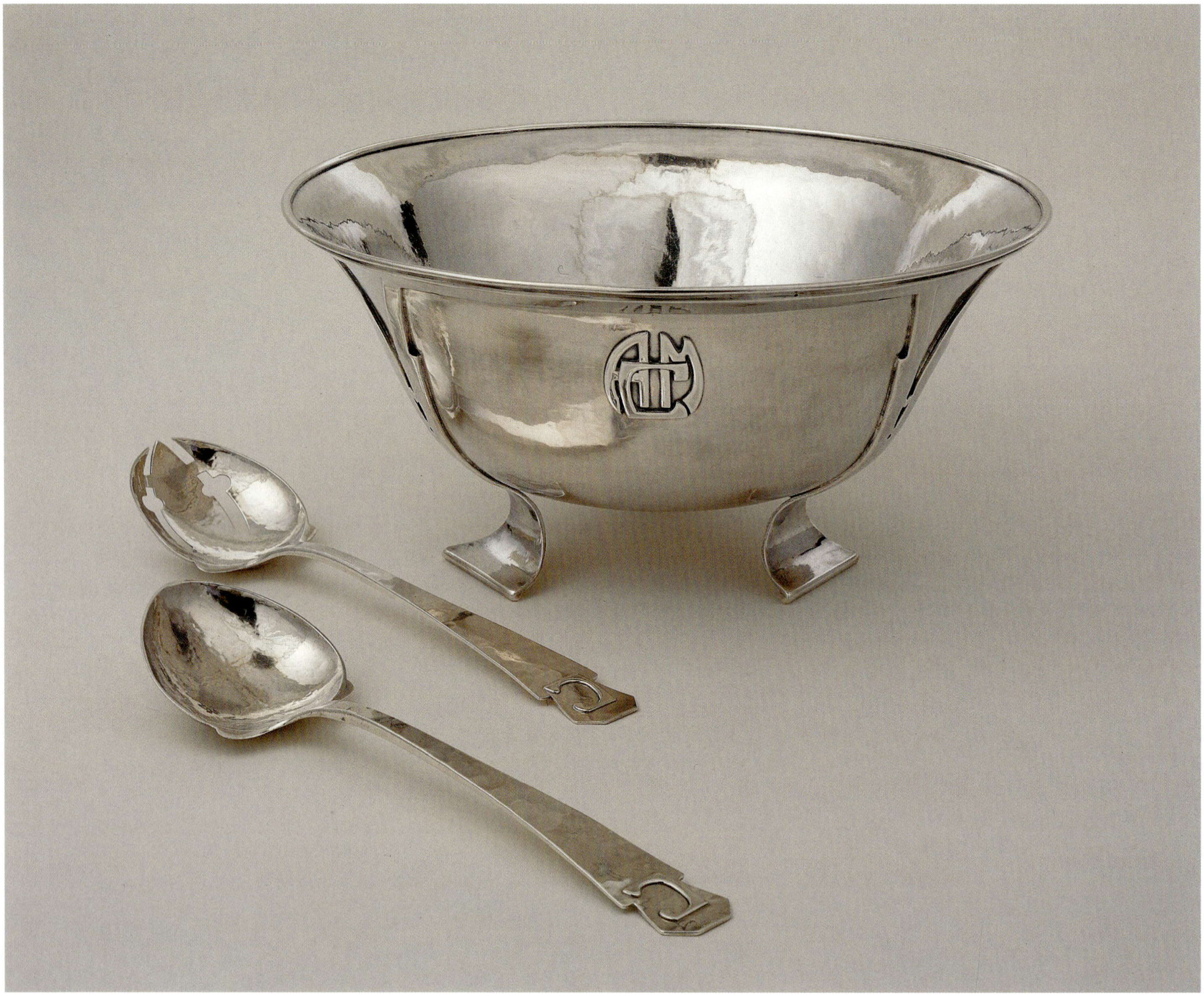

208.

Salad Set, dated 1911

Made and retailed by the Kalo Shop (1900–1970), Park Ridge and Chicago, Illinois; design attributed to Clara Barck Welles (1868–1965)
Silver
Bowl: 5⅝ × 11¼ × 11¼ inches
Spoons: Each 9⅝ × 2⅝ × ⅝ inches

Marks: Bowl: Stamped on bottom, *STERLING/HAND BEATEN/AT/KALO SHOPS/PARK RIDGE, ILLS./8144.*
Spoons: Stamped on back of handles, *STERLING KALO 5*
Inscriptions: Bowl: Applied conjoined silver initials, *AMC;* engraved in script on bottom of bowl, *Harry H. Lobdell/to Allan M. Clement/October 31, 1911*
Spoons: Applied in silver on handles, *C*
1990.86.1–.3

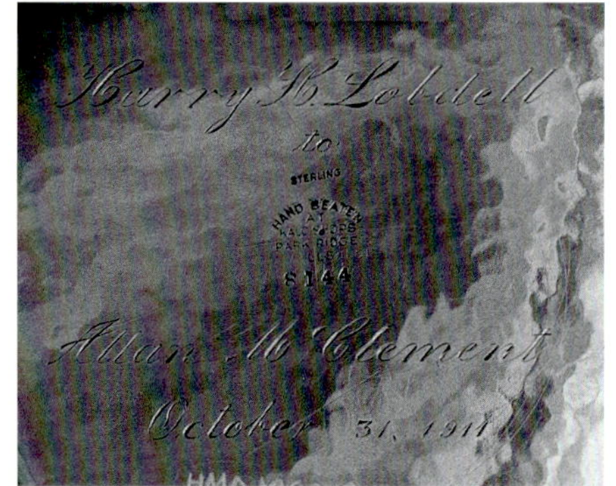

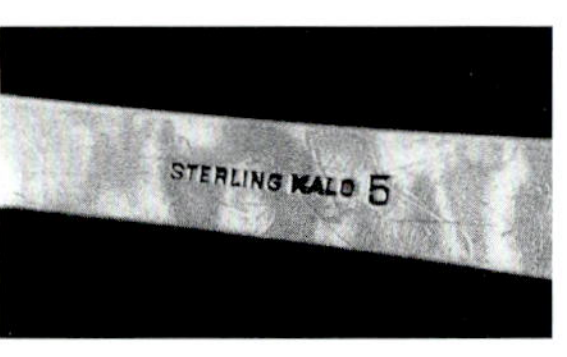

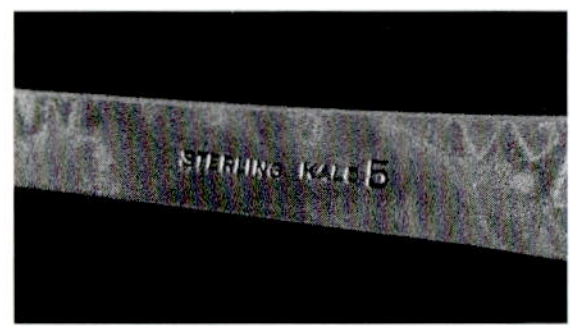

Art-Craft Community closed and the suburban workshop and retail outlet store were consolidated and expanded in larger downtown quarters on North Michigan Avenue. From 1914 to 1918, a retail outlet also operated at 130 West 54th Street in New York. Between 1920 and her 1940 retirement to California, Welles moved the Kalo Shop several times around downtown Chicago. The Metropolitan Museum of Art invited her participation in a major exhibition of contemporary design in 1937.

During her forty years in business, Welles became well known not only for her innovative silver designs, but also for her management skills. She was an advocate for women's rights and encouraged women to participate in all of the arts, especially metalwork. After her retirement, Welles continued to own the shop until 1959, when she turned it over to the four remaining employees, who kept the shop open until 1970.[1]

The silver tray and salad set in the Crawford Collection were produced during the years of the Park Ridge Kalo Art-Craft Community, between 1905 and 1914. Presumably designed by Clara Barck Welles, both have the characteristic hand-hammered surface of Kalo Shop wares, which was associated with Arts and Crafts silver as evidence of its handmade production. The finish had first gained popularity in Japanese-taste American silver in the 1870s and 1880s (see nos. 97, 155) and remained a staple of silver production and ornament in handwrought and industrially made wares styled after the Arts and Crafts silver during the first third of the twentieth century.

Welles's earliest designs were heavily influenced by British Arts and Crafts silver from the late nineteenth century. Especially influential was the work of Charles R. Ashbee, a colleague of the Scottish reform designer, Charles Rennie Mackintosh. Ashbee's designs were well known in Chicago after being included in the first exhibition of the Chicago Arts and Crafts Society at the Art Institute of Chicago in 1898. The simple rectangular tray (no. 207), made asymmetrical by a mounted rose quartz cabochon, or convex-cut stone, clearly reflects the tendencies of designers like Ashbee.

The tight rectangular composition of the tray, which Welles favored in her early designs, was soon abandoned for the soft curves seen in the salad set (no. 208). The round shapes were initially adopted to provide additional strength for holloware pieces, but they soon became integral to the Kalo Shop's designs, as did the intertwining initials on the bowl. The use of semiprecious stones to ornament the silver, a convention adapted from British Arts and Crafts prototypes, was abandoned by the Kalo Shop in the 1910s.

For the most part, hand processes dominated production at the Kalo Shop. Welles's designs were hammered up from heavy rolled plates of silver by the shop's silversmiths. The shop did little advertising but it maintained a large and loyal following both locally and nationally.[2]

NOTES

1. For a history of the Kalo Shop and biographical information about Clara Barck Welles, see Darling 1977, pp. 45–55; and Kaplan 1987, pp. 279–280, nos. 141–142.

2. As the location of the workshop changed over the years, the mark changed as well. The term "HAND BEATEN" was added to the mark around 1910 to emphasize the craft aspect of the production. "HAND WROUGHT" replaced "HAND BEATEN" in 1914.

209.

Tapestry Portiere, 1913

Made by Herter Looms (1908–1934), New York; designed by Albert Herter (1871–1959)
Dyed wool
117 × 58½ inches
Mark: Woven into lower right corner, *1913 HL* with flower
1996.135

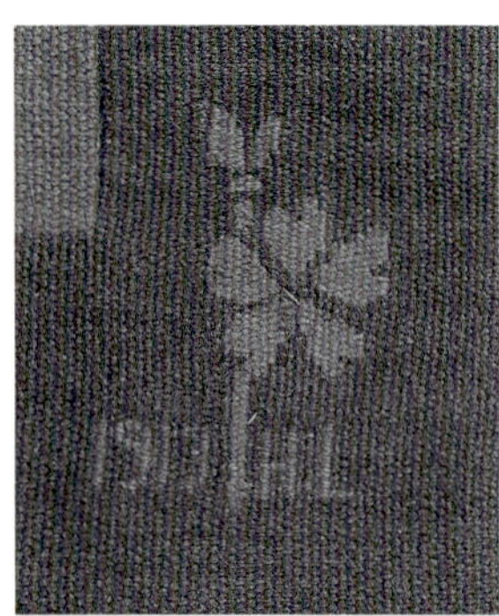

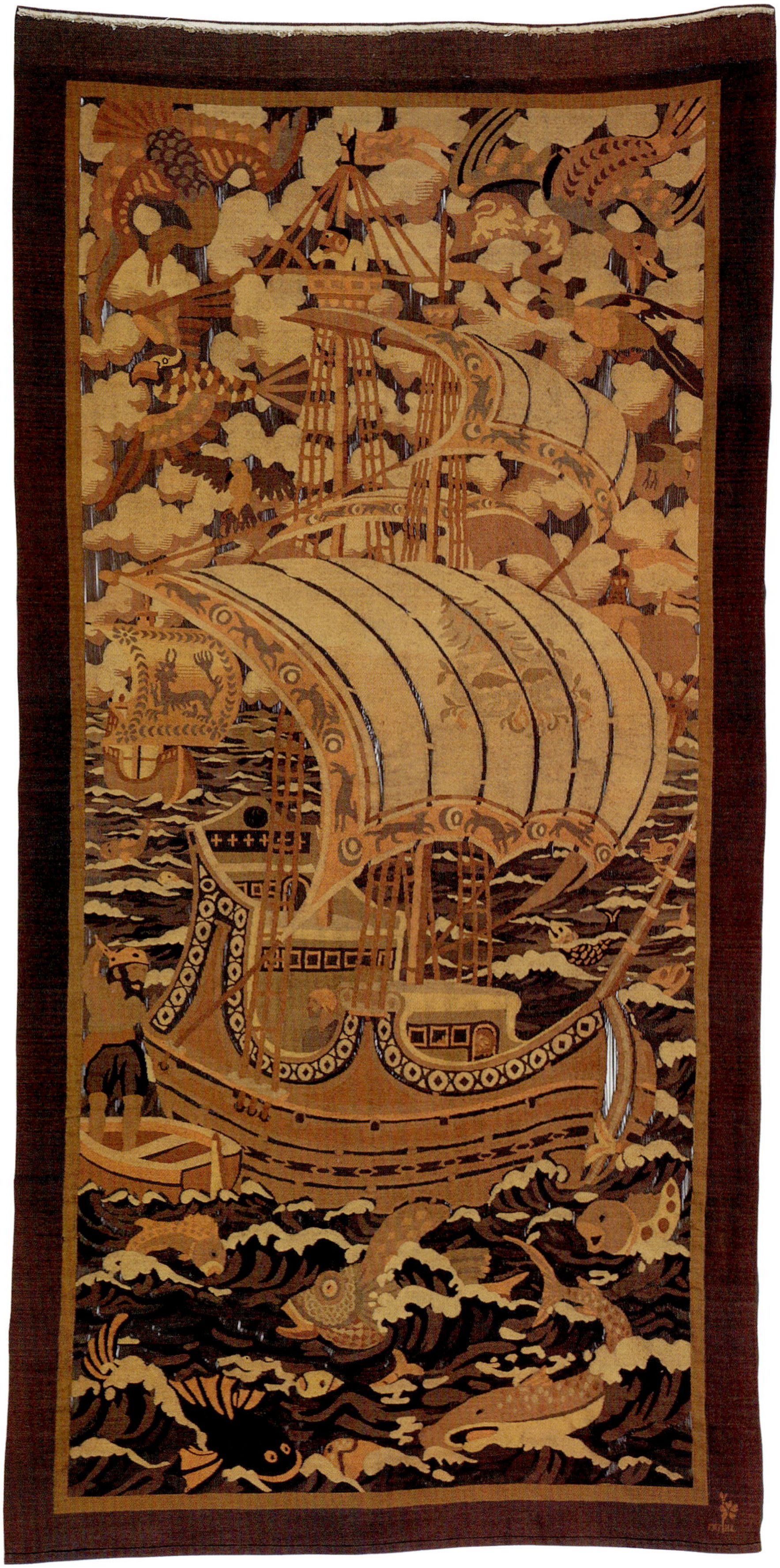

Albert Herter, son of interior decorator and furniture maker Christian Herter (see nos. 107–110), had already won several awards for painting at international expositions when he established Aubusson Looms in New York in 1908, which became Herter Looms the following year.[1] Herter studied at the Gobelins tapestry manufactory in France and promoted the taste for tapestries in the United States in the 1910s, bringing French weavers to New York from Aubusson, the French weaving center, to execute his tapestry designs. Herter Looms made hanging tapestries, furniture and floor coverings, and portieres for hanging in interior doors, like this example, and produced reproductions and adaptations of historic weavings as well as new designs by Herter. A studio of artists developed cartoons from Herter's designs for the French weavers to follow. Charles C. Pillow, Viscount Exmouth, was a dye chemist at the firm who helped develop the Herter Looms' distinctive palette.[2]

Herter's technological innovations are evident in this portiere decorated with Herter's design, which received acclaim for its innovative "transparent" weave.[3] The dyed vertical warp threads were left exposed and unwoven to allow light to shine through when the portiere was hanging in a doorway. The transparent weave enhances the sky section so that light passing through resembles sunlight shimmering through clouds. The Crawford portiere is dated 1913, when it was first exhibited at the Art Institute of Chicago. Together with its mate, now in the Fine Arts Museums of San Francisco, it decorated the Herter Looms booth at the 1915 Panama-Pacific Exposition in San Francisco where the firm received a Gold Medal (fig. 1).[4]

Herter Looms was one of three major tapestry manufactories in the United States in the late nineteenth and early twentieth centuries, all in the New York area.[5] The taste for tapestries in the United States stemmed from a variety of sources. English reform designer William Morris introduced woven wall hangings in England in the 1870s and 1880s; these hangings were also popular in the United States (see no. 90). Also, a mania in the 1890s for Renaissance and eighteenth-century furnishings spurred interest in antique and reproduction tapestries. The

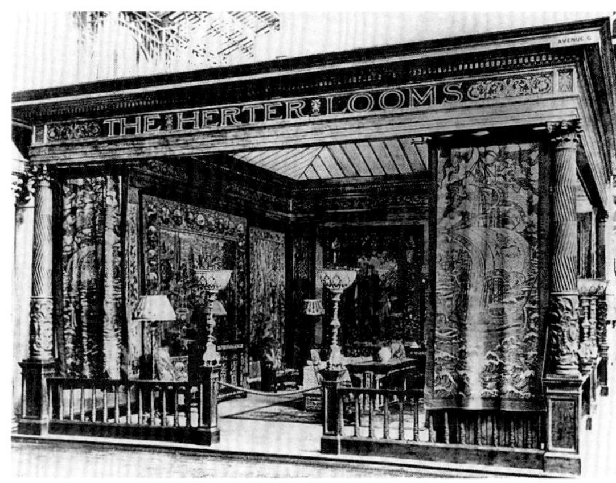

Fig. 1. Herter Looms booth, Varied Industries Building, 1915 Panama-Pacific Exposition, San Francisco.

Arts and Crafts movement fostered a fascination with handwoven textiles, and while Herter was not identified with the Arts and Crafts movement, he was interested in traditional methods of hand-production.

The interest in tapestries continued into the 1920s, and inexpensive, mass-produced hangings were imported from Europe, usually loosely based on historical prototypes and decorated with historical and mythological subjects. In 1921, Herter disassociated himself from Herter Looms, and pursued his painting in Santa Barbara, California. Herter Looms continued making tapestries until the Great Depression forced its closing in 1934.[6]

NOTES

1. Opitz 1986, p. 399. Herter received honorable mention at the Paris Salon in 1890, a medal at the 1895 Atlanta Exposition, honorable mention at the 1897 Nashville Exposition, a bronze medal at the 1900 Exposition Universelle in Paris, and a silver medal at the 1901 Buffalo Pan-American Exposition.

2. Turner 1996, p. 659.

3. Bennett 1992, p. 310.

4. Ibid.

5. Hunter 1925, pp. 274–275. Herter Looms, Baumgartens, and the Edgewater Factory in Edgewater, New Jersey, were making tapestries through the 1920s and into the 1930s.

6. Turner 1996, p. 659.

University City Pottery and Porcelain Works

UNUSUAL IN THE history of ceramics in the United States, the pottery and porcelain enterprises at University City, Missouri, between 1910 and 1915 were blessed with unlimited financial resources, the most modern, specialized facilities, and some of the best-known talent in the field. Nevertheless, the project was short-lived and never profitable. The pottery's founder, Edward Gardner Lewis, overestimated the power of financial backing in artistic enterprise and underestimated the impact of human disagreements and conflicts among artists and technicians.[1]

Lewis, a salesman who found women to be his best customers, established the American Woman's League in 1907. The high cost of advertising his business lured him to what he hoped would be the profitable business of publishing. He founded University City at the western edge of St. Louis, near Washington University, to serve as the national headquarters for his activities in publishing and education. The focus of the American Woman's League was the People's University, centered in an elaborate complex of exposition-style edifices around his publishing headquarters.[2] Most of the education provided was by correspondence, and the initial public response was indeed encouraging: in 1910, the first year of operation, fifty thousand students were enrolled. Lewis's profits from publications, along with student tuition, supported the development of the University's Art Institute.

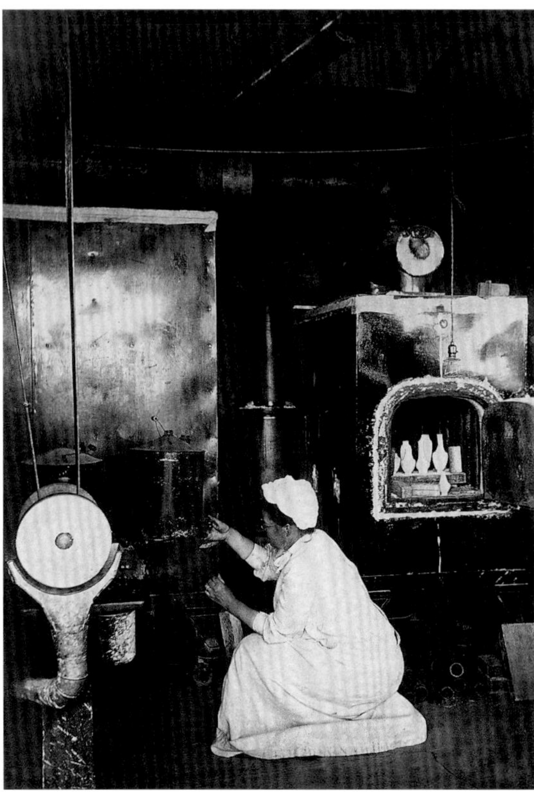

Fig. 1. Adelaide Alsop Robineau at the kilns, 1911.

Special attention was lavished on the School of Ceramic Art. Lewis hired the world-renowned French ceramic artist Taxile Doat as head of the school. Lewis and his wife were both amateur potters who had worked with Doat's published methods, which may account for Lewis's intense interest in establishing the School of Ceramic Art. He had brought Doat to St. Louis as a consultant in 1909 while planning the University pottery. Doat had enjoyed international accolades for his work, particularly for his *pâte-sur-pâte* decorations at the National Manufactory at Sèvres, where he had the honor and convenience of a private studio.

Doat was well known among ceramicists in the United States for a series of articles on porcelain production that were translated and published in 1903 by Samuel Robineau in his periodical *Keramic Studio,* which was edited by his wife, the celebrated ceramic artist Adelaide Alsop Robineau (fig. 1). In addition to Doat, Lewis hired the Robineaus to join in the enterprise, and the Robineaus in turn recommended Frederick Hurten Rhead (see no. 187), an English potter with extensive experience in the American pottery business. Rhead was to manage the details of setting up facilities to the specifications of the artists. He also wrote a ceramic textbook and organized kits for students taking the University's correspondence courses in ceramics.

Unprecedented salaries of $10,000, modern equipment, and freedom from commercial considerations and teaching responsibilities must have lured both the Robineaus and Doat to University City. A master of contracts, Doat arranged for a staff of French assistants, his own equipment and materials from France, and all expenses.

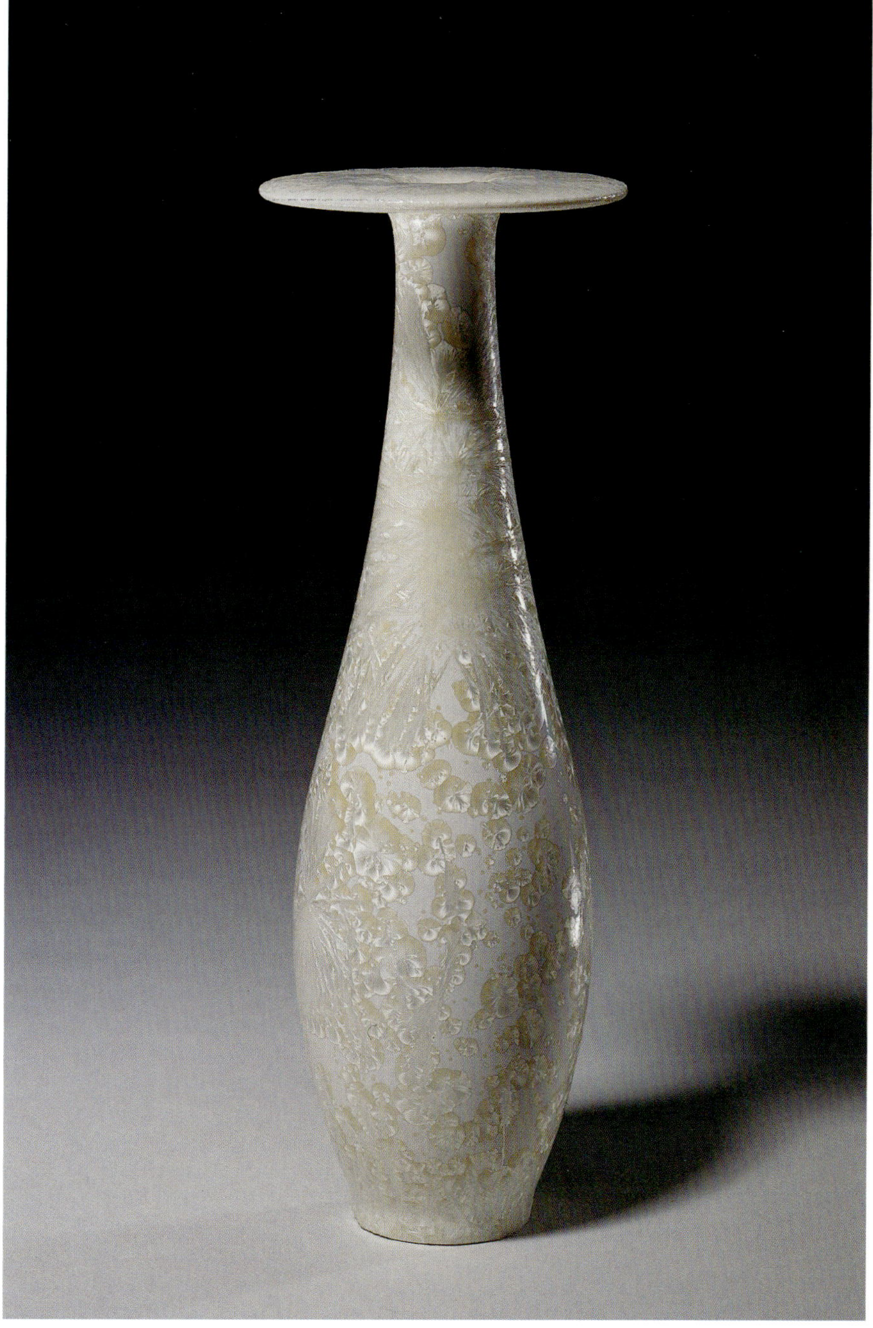

210.

Vase, 1910

University City Pottery (1910–1912), University City, Missouri; Adelaide Alsop Robineau (1865–1929)
Porcelain with crystalline glaze
8⅝ × 3 × 3 inches
Mark: Excised on bottom, conjoined monogram *AR* in circle surrounded by incised *1910/123/UC*
1984.151

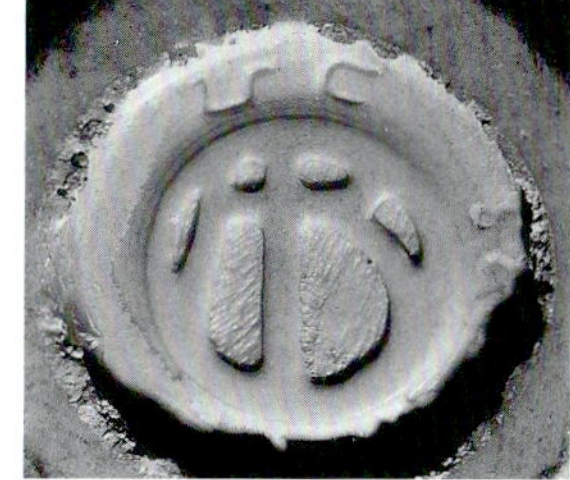

In addition, the University purchased a collection of Doat's ceramics, which he had been unable to sell in France.[3] Adelaide Robineau, a trained china painter who had moved on to porcelain and glaze production using Doat's methods, was also drawn to University City by the prospect of working with Doat.

The dreams of both the founder and the artists were short-lived, however. When the artists were not involved in the creation of monumental exposition vases to establish the reputation of the school, they were subjected to countless visitors and crowded social functions celebrating Lewis's genius in hiring them. Robineau was an enthusiastic student and an ardent experimenter, eager to discuss glazes and clay bodies with Doat and his staff. Although Doat showed interest in Robineau's overtures, his jealous assistant for bodies and glazes, Emile Diffloth, furnished only the finished mixtures and offered neither discussion nor recipes.[4]

In 1911, Lewis's irregular business practices, as well as a charge of mail fraud, led to a government investigation of the American Woman's League, while plummeting profits and growing disappointments forced the departures of Rhead and the Robineaus. Lewis managed to retain Doat and reorganized the ceramic enterprise as the University City Porcelain Works in 1912. While Lewis left to establish a new town, Atascadero, California, headquarters of the American Woman's Republic, Doat continued to operate the porcelain works until it closed.

Despite the enormous financial investment in the University City ceramic undertakings, Lewis never envisioned a commercial ceramic enterprise. The products of the University City Pottery and the later University City Porcelain Works were never marketed. Lewis's goal was rather to provide ideal working conditions for the most celebrated ceramic artists he could find.

The small Crawford vase (no. 210) from Adelaide Robineau's time at University City has a crystalline glaze, which she adapted from Doat's published formulas and used through most of her career. The simple shape was characteristic of Robineau's work, even in her elaborately carved large-scale pieces.[5] While Robineau may have been disappointed with the lack of collaboration at the school, she was, nonetheless,

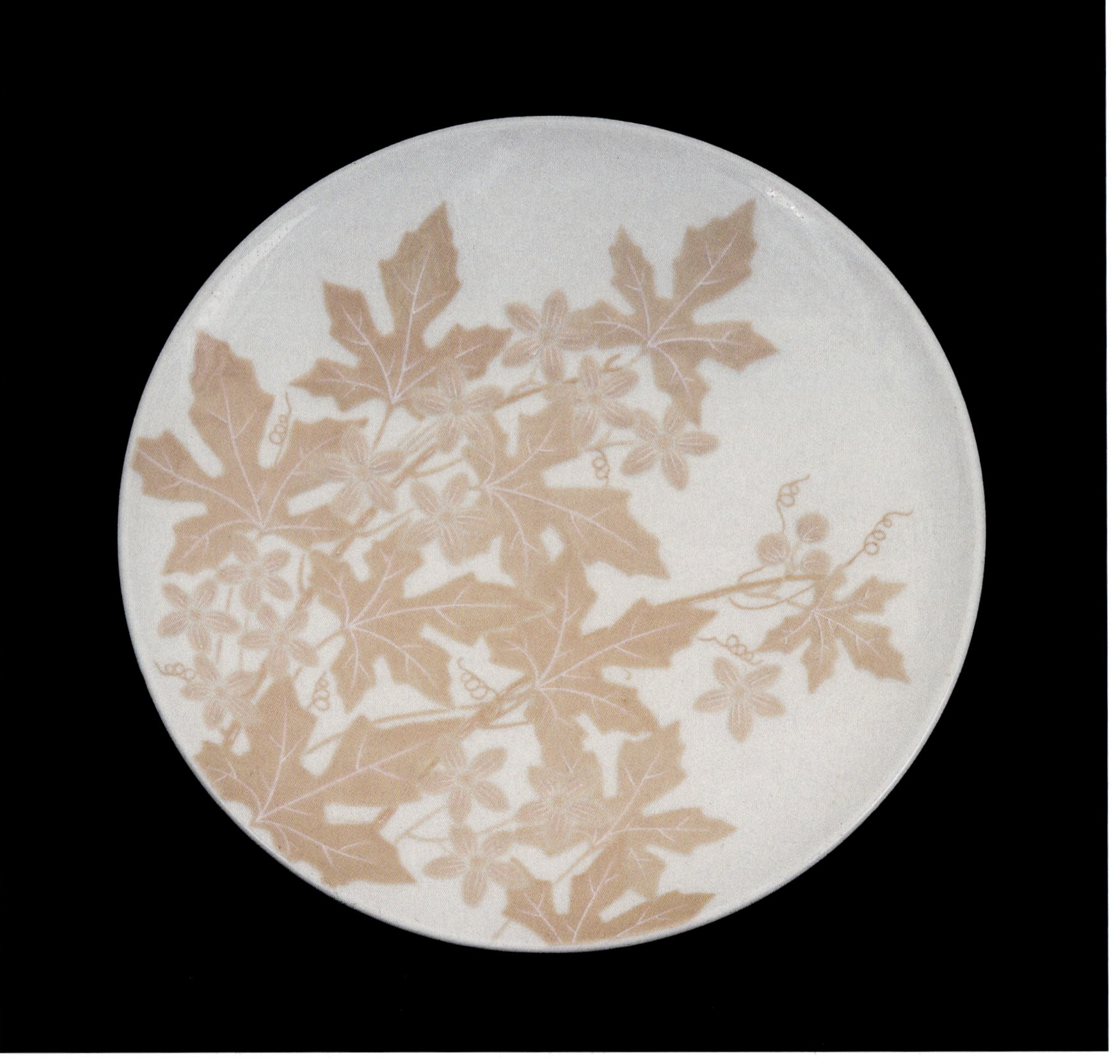

211.

Plate, 1914

University City Porcelain Works (1912–1915), University City, Missouri; designed by Taxile Doat (1851–1938)
Porcelain
9¼ × 9¼ × 1⅛ inches
Mark: On bottom in double circle, *UNIVERSITY CITY·MO·* surrounding *1914/PORCELAIN/ WORKS/ DT* monogram
1984.138

accustomed to working on her own. In the years before and after her time in University City, Robineau worked in Syracuse, New York, with the sole technical assistance of her husband. In 1916, the Syracuse Museum of Fine Arts (later the Everson Museum of Art) purchased a collection of Robineau porcelains from the artist. At her death in 1929, Robineau's career was celebrated in a memorial retrospective exhibition at The Metropolitan Museum of Art.

The Crawford plate (no. 211), designed by Taxile Doat (fig. 2), is from the final full year of the University City Porcelain Works production, in 1914. Much of the activity at the porcelain works in that year focused on a proposed exhibition of wares at the 1915 Panama-Pacific International Exposition in San Francisco, although no evidence survives that the works were actually shown.[6] The Virginia creeper decoration on the plate shows the *pâte-sur-pâte* technique Doat perfected at Sèvres. The cameo effect was achieved by applying layers of pink liquid porcelain clay, or slip, on the contrasting white background. After the closure of the porcelain works in 1915, Doat returned to France and lived the remainder of his life at his Villa Kaolin in Sèvres.

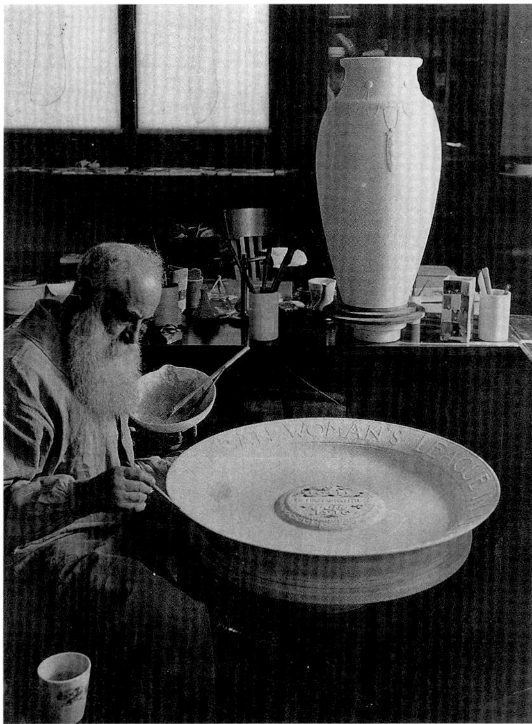

Fig. 2. Taxile Doat, working at University City, Missouri, ca. 1910. University City Public Library Archives.

NOTES

1. For a history of the pottery, see Evans 1987, pp. 286–291; and Frelinghuysen 1989, pp. 62–64. An account of the enterprise written by Frederick Hurten Rhead and edited by Paul Evans has been reprinted in Weiss 1981, pp. 93–115.

2. Only a few of the University City Pottery buildings were actually constructed. Since 1930, the high-rise domed headquarters building has served as City Hall for University City. A model of the proposed campus is exhibited there; see Fifield 1987, pp. 123–125.

3. Weiss 1981, pp. 96, 99–100. The Doat porcelains from France were eventually acquired by the St. Louis Art Museum.

4. Ibid., pp. 100–101. A vase made by Diffloth at University City is illustrated and discussed in Frelinghuysen 1989, pp. 282–283.

5. Perhaps Robineau's best-known work is the carved Scarab Vase now in the Everson Museum of Art; see Frelinghuysen 1989, p. 63, fig. 51. The most comprehensive study of Robineau and her work is found in Weiss 1981.

6. Evans 1987, p. 289.

212.

Vase, ca. 1915

Fulper Pottery Company
(ca. 1860–ca. 1945), Flemington,
New Jersey
Stoneware with flambé glaze,
Vasekraft line
13¼ × 11 × 11 inches
Mark: Stamped vertically in
block letters in blue ink enclosed
in rectangle on bottom of vase,
FULPER
1984.154

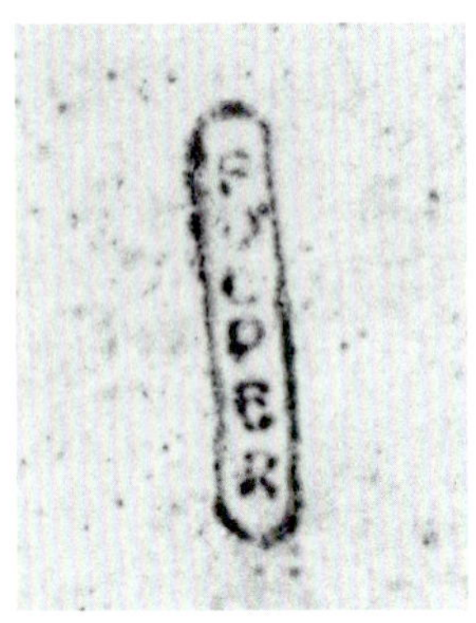

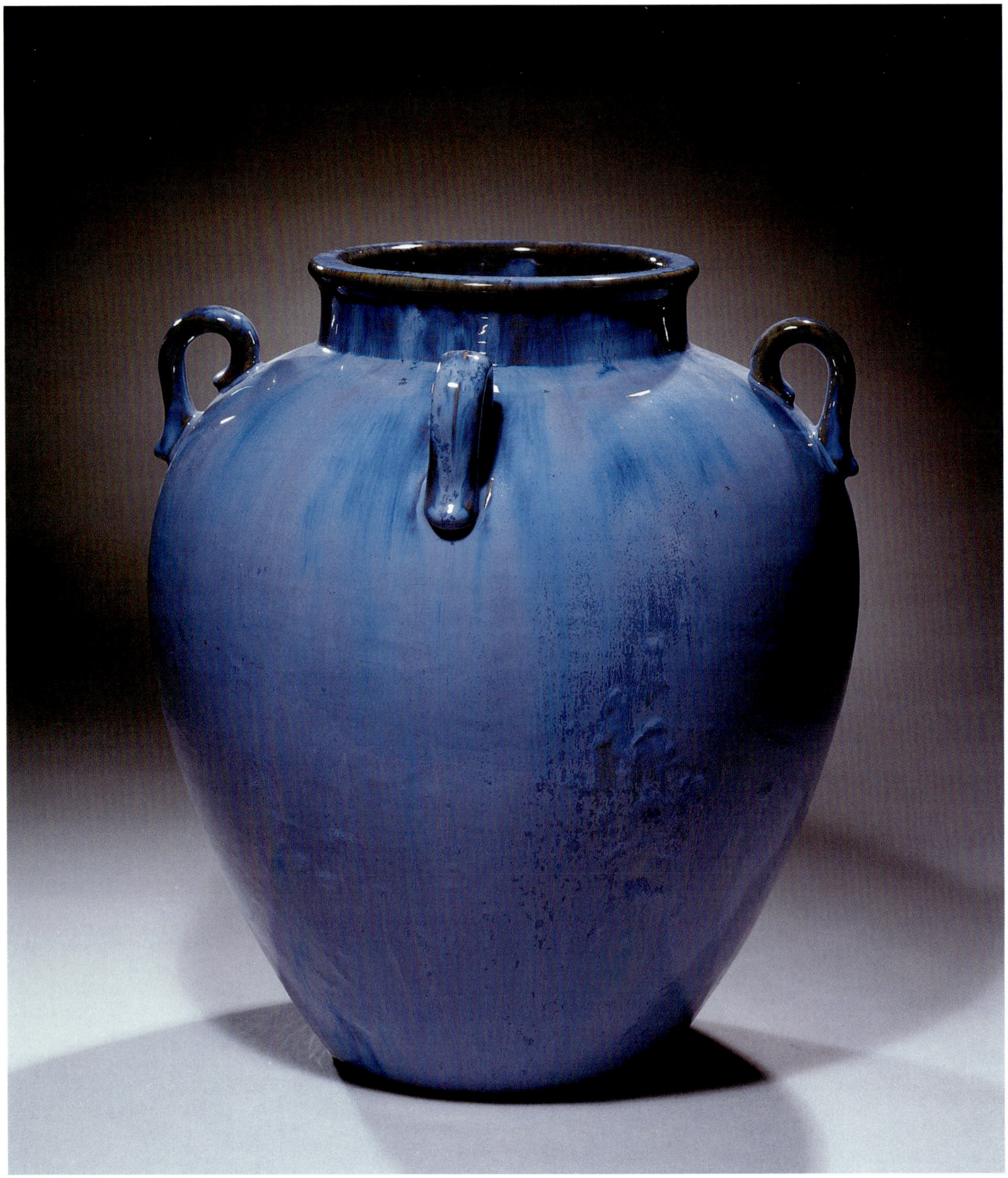

As early as 1814, the Samuel Hill Pottery was operating in Flemington, New Jersey. After the death of Samuel Hill, the pottery was purchased by Dutch immigrant Abraham Fulper, who had worked with Hill for a number of years and who later passed on the pottery to his four sons and grandchildren. The company manufactured utilitarian stonewares under various names, including G. W. Fulper & Brothers and Fulper Brothers, until 1899, when it was incorporated as the Fulper Pottery Company. When it introduced its art ware line Vasekraft in 1909, the company was nearly a century old.[1]

Abraham Fulper's grandson William Hill Fulper II joined the family company in 1898 and helped lead the firm's expansion into art pottery. In 1911, J. Martin Stangl joined the company as superintendent of the technical division, and Stangl and Fulper worked together closely over the next four years, introducing new shapes and glazes to the Vasekraft line. In 1915, the company received a gold medal for its exhibition of art pottery at the Panama-Pacific International Exposition in San Francisco. The company shared exhibition space with Gustav Stickley (see nos. 188–193) and displayed its pottery on Stickley's oak furniture.[2]

An art pottery meant for domestic display, Vasekraft was also a practical addition to the company's productions. The same stoneware bodies and the same kilns were used for both the utilitarian wares and the art pottery.[3] The major investment Vasekraft required was for experimentation with glazes, which became a company specialty. Most Fulper vessels were made in molds, although some were hand-turned. Fulper's inexpensive art pottery was aimed at a broad and growing middle-class market, and the Vasekraft enterprise was commercially successful for two decades.

The large Vasekraft vase in the Crawford Collection bears the blue stamped mark associated with the earliest products in the line, made between 1909 and 1915. Its simple shape, thick clay, and scale are all characteristic of the Vasekraft line, designed to emphasize the glaze with its broad, smooth surfaces. The flambé glaze with subtle striations of blue and hints of lavender may have been the "Blue of the Sky" listed in Fulper catalogues. The Fulper Pottery Company derived its shapes from classical and Chinese prototypes. Unlike its predecessors and many of its contemporaries, including Cincinnati's Rookwood Pottery (see no. 181), the Fulper art wares relied solely on basic forms and glazes rather than on painted decoration or modeling for visual impact. The Crawford vase seems classical in shape, whereas the glaze seems Oriental in inspiration.[4]

The Vasekraft line, one of the last American Arts and Crafts potteries introduced, was also one of the few art pottery lines to survive World War I. The death of William Hill Fulper II in 1928 and the purchase of the plant by Stangl in 1930 spelled the end of the Vasekraft line. Under Stangl's leadership, the pottery shifted its production to dinnerware, figurines, and gift wares. In 1955, the name of the pottery was officially changed to Stangl, although it had already been known by that name for at least a decade. The pottery closed shortly after Stangl's death in 1972.

NOTES

1. For a history of the Fulper Pottery Company, see Blasberg 1979; and Evans 1987, pp. 109–112.

2. Blasberg 1979, p. 37.

3. In its catalogues and advertising, Fulper consistently referred to the clay it used as "earthenware" rather than "stoneware," perhaps to disassociate the Vasekraft line from the utilitarian wares; see ibid., p. 34.

4. For a discussion of marks, see ibid., pp. 68–73. For a discussion of glazes and colors, see pp. 13–33. The cover shows a vase of the same form as the Crawford example with a different blue glaze.

213.

Table Lamp, ca. 1915

Possibly Chicago
Bronze, leaded and colored glass, replaced brass finial from the 1950s or 1960s
22½ × 24 × 24 inches
1984.156

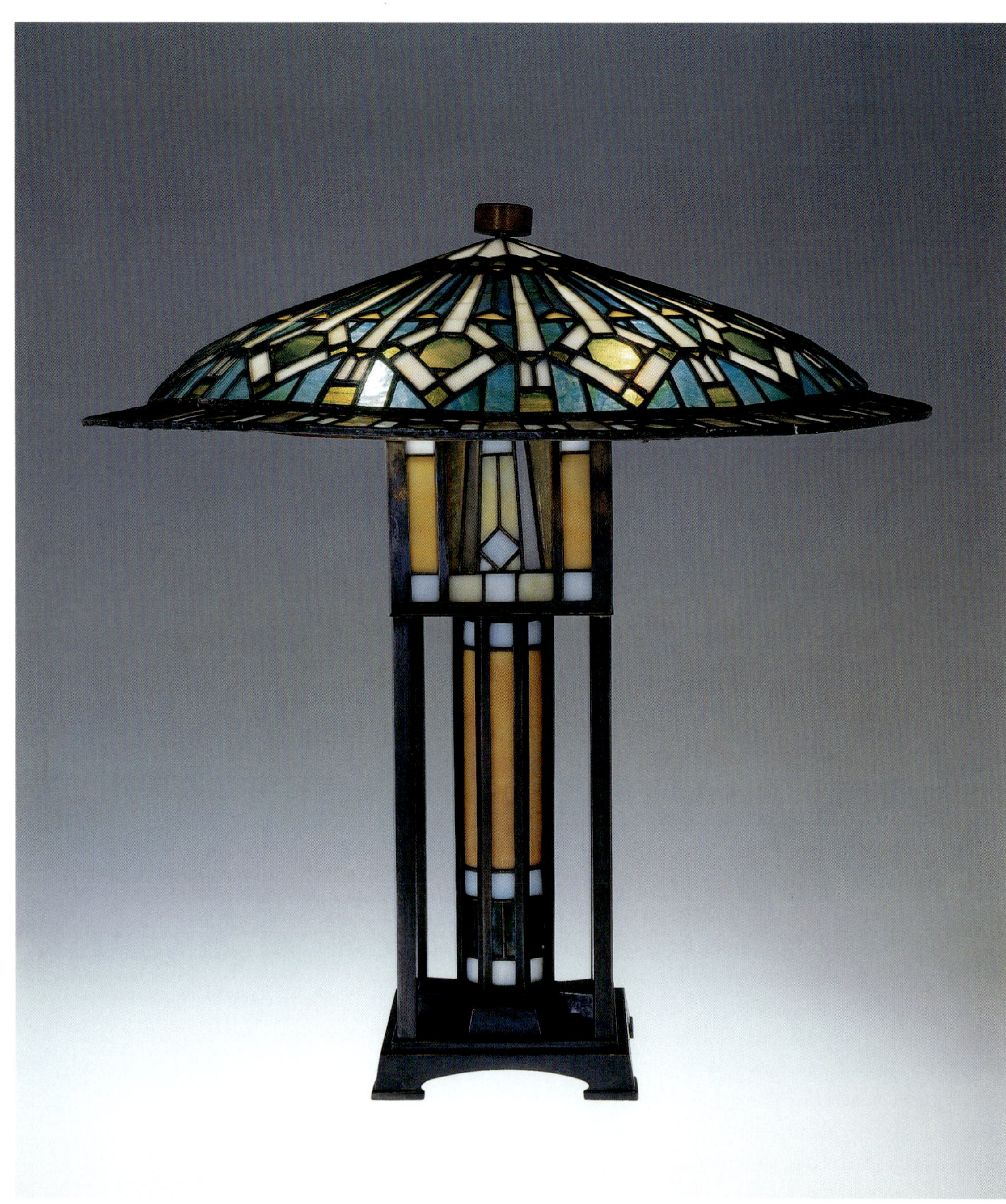

ALTHOUGH THE maker and designer of this table lamp is unknown, the subtle hues of the colored glass, the angular leading, and the overall shape are related to the designs of Chicago's Prairie School architects, such as Frank Lloyd Wright and George Elmslie (see nos. 223–225). The colored-glass lampshade may have been inspired by Louis Comfort Tiffany, but the naturally rendered flowers and sensuous, curved leading on Tiffany's shades contrasts with the geometric shapes in this lamp. When illuminated, the electrical lamp provided a subtle atmosphere in what was most likely a Prairie School or an Arts and Crafts interior. The distracting and ill-fitting terminal on the shade is a replacement, probably from the 1950s or 1960s, and the form of the original is unknown.

Designs by Architects

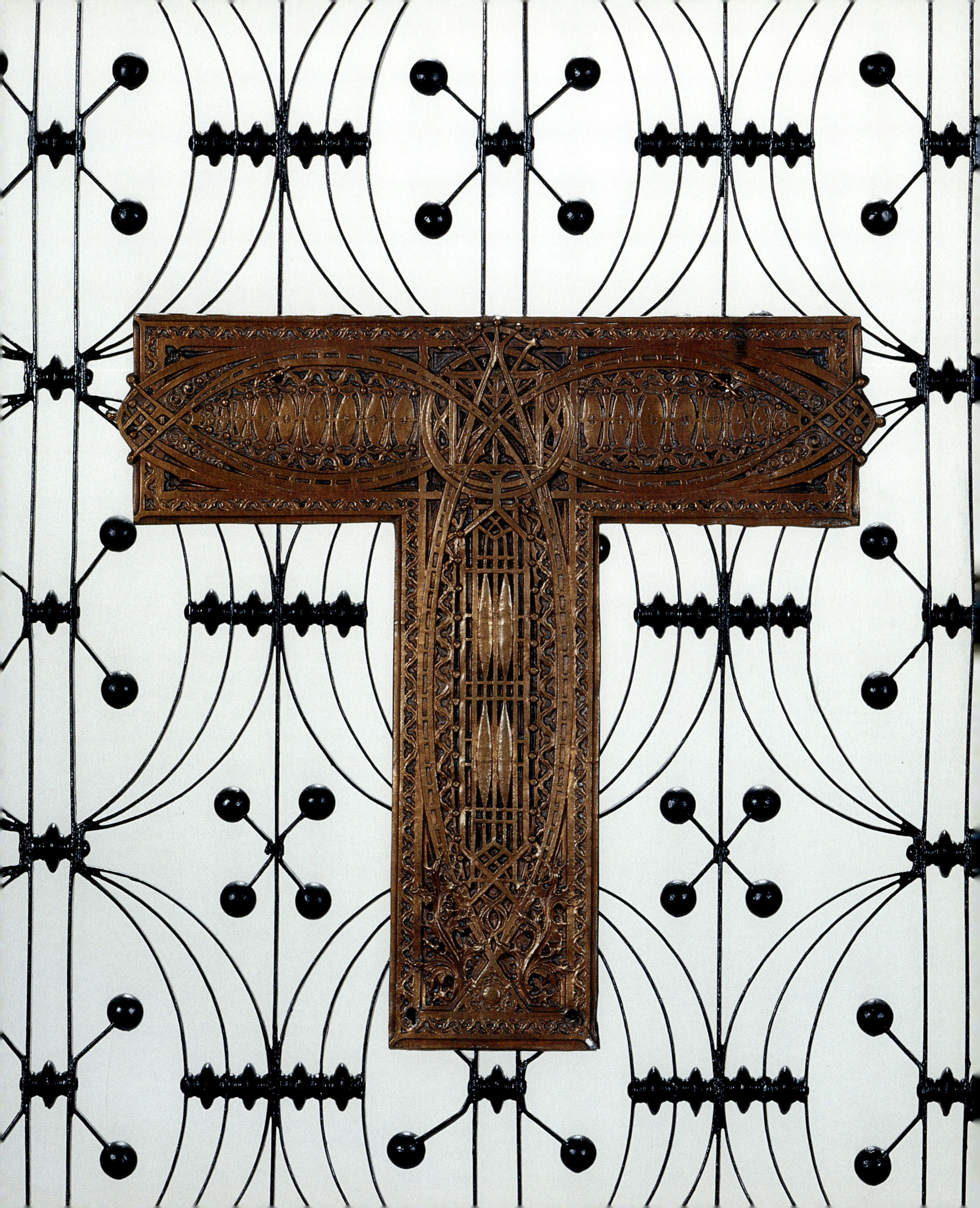

Alexander Jackson Davis

Alexander Jackson Davis was among the first American architects to gain national recognition. Although in partnership with Ithiel Town from 1829 to 1835 and again briefly in 1842–1843, Davis spent most of his half-century career practicing alone in New York. He designed all types of buildings: state capitols, hotels, university structures, commercial buildings, and private residences. Davis, Town, and Philadelphia architect Thomas Ustick Walter (see no. 216) attempted to establish an American Institution of Architects in 1837, but it lasted less than a year. In 1857, however, both Davis and Walter were leaders in organizing the American Institute of Architects, which still functions today. Davis's work began in the prevailing Greek revival style with Town, but by the 1830s and 1840s he was designing in the romantic Gothic revival style, influenced by English designers and tastemakers Augustus Pugin and John Claudius Loudon.[1]

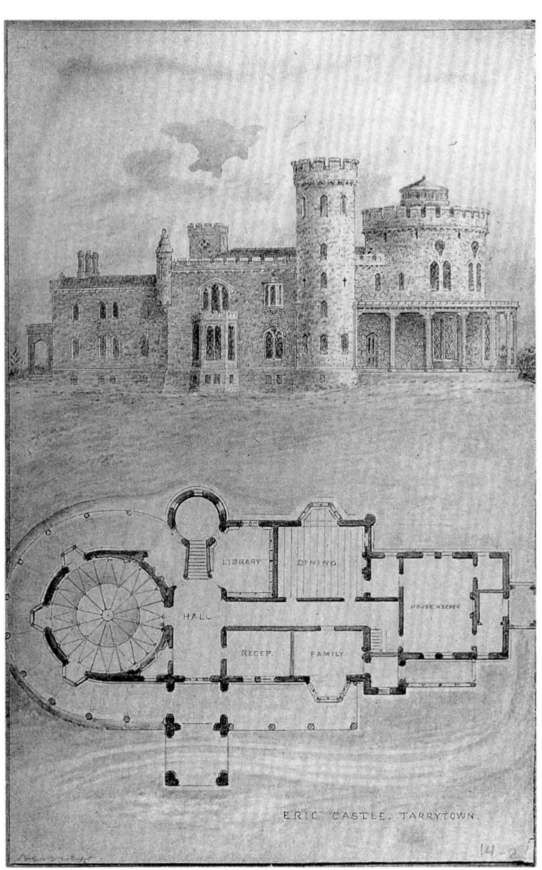

Fig. 1. Rear elevation and plan for Ericstan by Alexander Jackson Davis.

Both Davis and Walter designed furniture for the interiors they created. As early as 1850, Andrew Jackson Downing promoted the architect's overall involvement in planning a house: "The province of the architect does not cease with designing the general plan and exterior of any building, but . . . he should carry out the same spirit and style in all parts of the edifice." Downing felt that this involvement would provide "an intelligent unity reigning over the whole."[2] Davis worked with Andrew Jackson Downing for over a decade, providing architectural illustrations for his periodical, *The Horticulturalist,* and his books. Publication of Davis's plans and houses in Downing's widely circulated book *The Architecture of Country Houses* ensured a broad public awareness of his designs.

In the early 1840s, Davis developed over fifty designs for furniture in the Gothic style to complement his design for a house at Tarrytown, New York, for William Paulding and his son Philip.[3] Davis apparently designed the two chairs in the Crawford Collection for another major Tarrytown commission, Ericstan, the John J. Herrick house on a hill overlooking the Hudson River, built between 1855 and 1859 (fig. 1). One of Davis's most castle-like villas, the stone house consisted of a large circular crenelated tower on the river facade with two additional towers and a corner turret.

A drawing in The Metropolitan Museum of Art of a chair (possibly the walnut chair now in the Museum of the City of New York), which is similar to the Crawford side chair (no. 214), was sketched by the architect's son, Joseph B. Davis, and labeled as having been designed for Herrick. Davis adapted Gothic window tracery for the back of the innovative and delicate chair. The canted front legs and straight rear legs terminate in feet resembling deer hooves. Leaf carvings in the back enriched the Gothic character of Davis's design.[4]

The monumental Crawford armchair (no. 215) descended in the family of a later owner of Ericstan and may have been part of the furniture Davis designed for Herrick.[5] Of deeper and broader proportions and more heavily

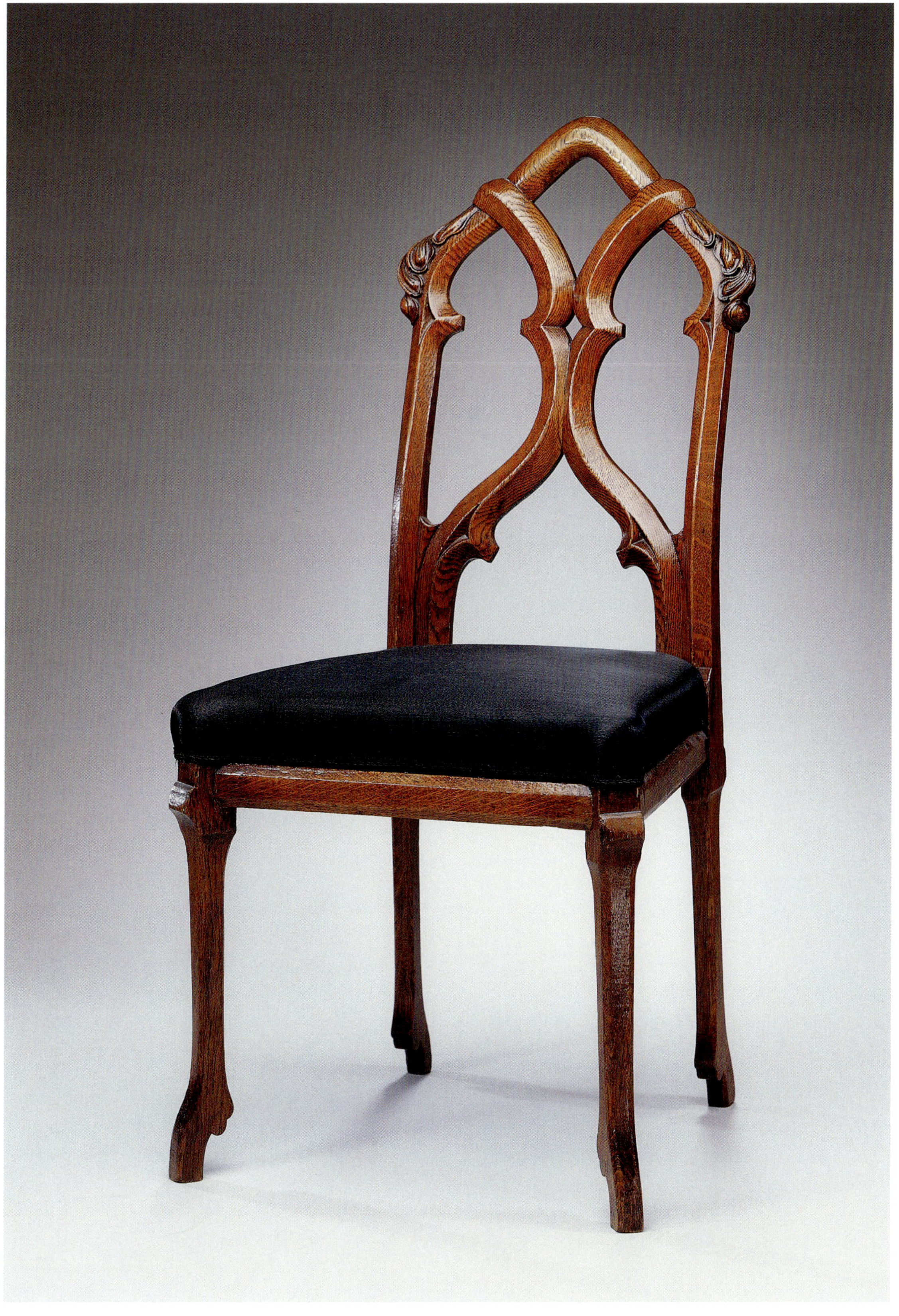

214.

Side Chair, ca. 1857

Designed by Alexander Jackson Davis (1803–1892); manufacture attributed to Burns and Brother (1857–1859), New York
Oak with modern horsehair upholstery
39 × 18¼ × 20 inches
1981.1000.46

215.

Armchair, ca. 1857

Design attributed to Alexander Jackson Davis (1803–1892); manufacture attributed to Burns and Brother (1857–1859), New York
Oak with modern leather upholstery
62¾ × 30⅜ × 34 inches
1982.317

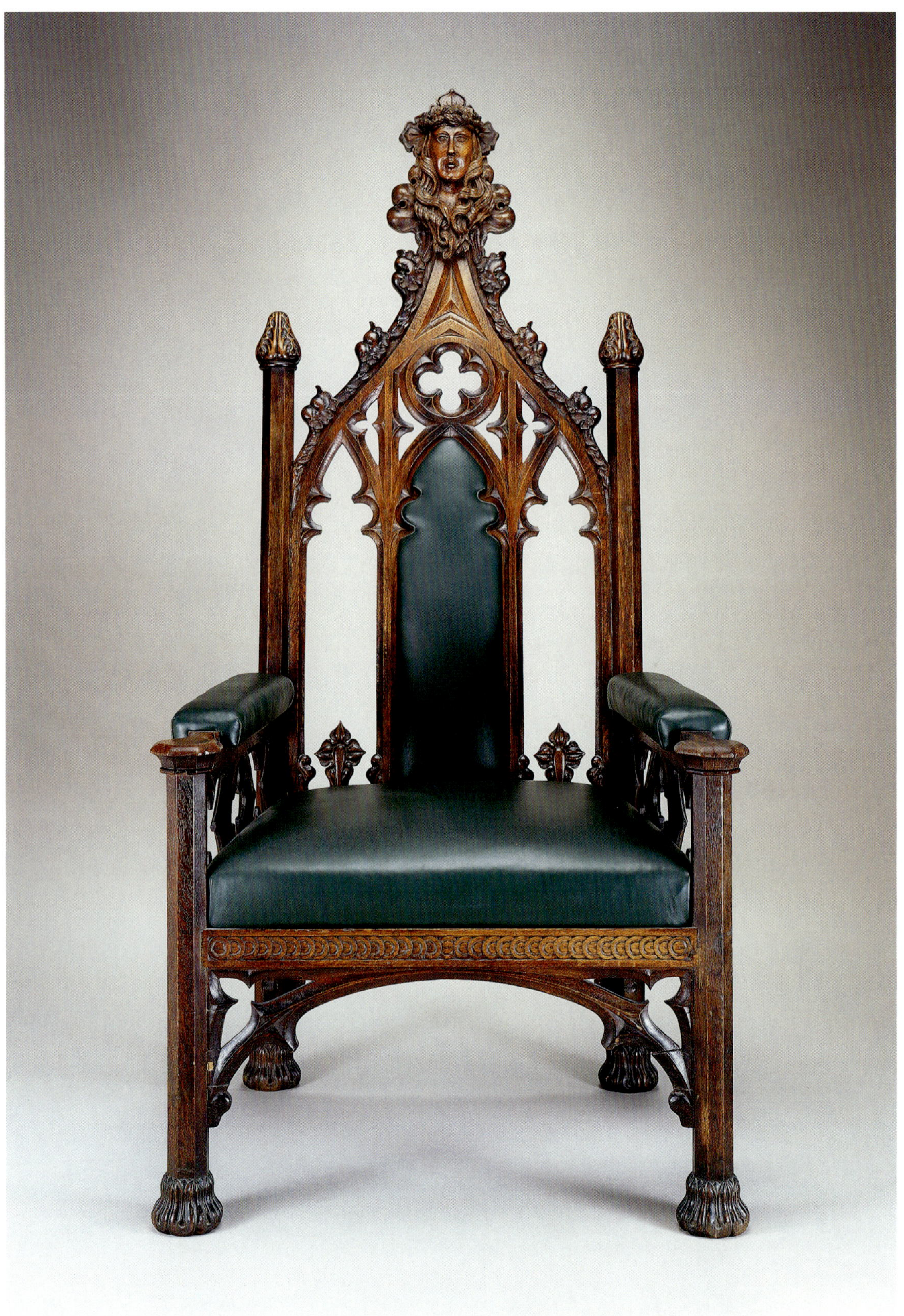

ornamented with carving than the side chair, the armchair may have been part of the furnishings of Herrick's library. A carved head of a nymph is the central terminal for the Gothic-arched crest of the armchair. Foliate terminals of the rear hexagonal side posts and the crocketed detailing of the back, arm supports, and the seat skirt combine for a heavily Gothic design.

William Burns, a furniture maker, probably fabricated Davis's furniture designs for Ericstan. Burns came to New York from Scotland in 1833 and worked in partnership with Peter Trainque from 1842 to 1856. Downing praised the New York firm for "the most correct Gothic furniture that we have yet seen executed in this country." Burns was in partnership with his brother Thomas between 1857 and 1859, when the Crawford chairs were possibly made, and he worked on his own from 1860 until his death in 1867.[6]

John Herrick, the wealthy flour merchant who commissioned Ericstan, waited four years for its completion in 1859 at a cost of $60,000. The volatile economy during the Civil War and the enormous cost of Ericstan forced him to sell it to Dr. Edward Maynard in 1865 for $150,000. Later the estate was sold to Alfredrick Smith Hatch, in whose family the Crawford armchair descended. The house was demolished in 1944.[7]

Davis's furniture designs were a small aspect of his overall architectural practice, and his day books indicate that it was limited to major domestic commissions. He seems to have worked with a limited number of furniture makers, and his actual involvement in the production of his designs remains undocumented. Nonetheless, Davis appears to have been among the first American architects to design furniture for his commissions.[8]

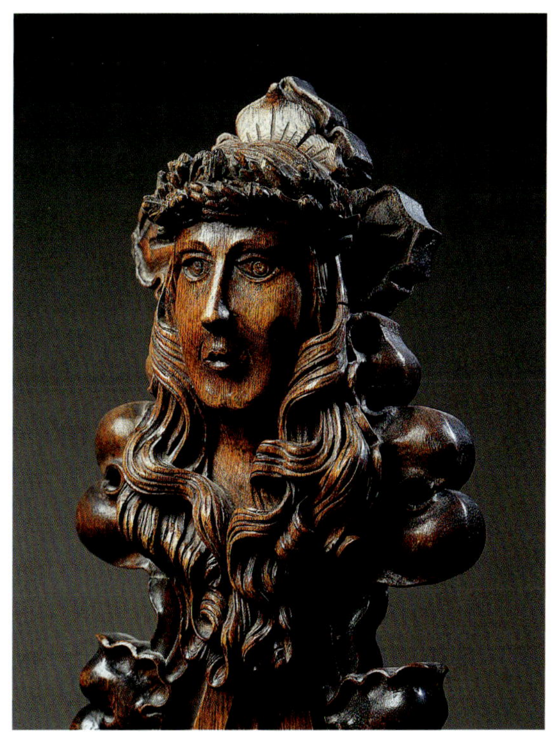

NOTES

1. The most comprehensive biographies and accounts of Davis's career are found in Donnell 1936; The Metropolitan Museum of Art 1992; and Newton 1942.

2. Downing 1969, p. 365.

3. Davis's work with Downing is described in The Metropolitan Museum of Art 1992, pp. 20–21. For illustrations and a discussion of the Paulding commission, see Davies 1977.

4. Similar chairs are illustrated in Davies 1977, p. 1018, pl. III; and Howe and Warren 1976, p. 16. Another example is in The Metropolitan Museum of Art; see Davies 1977, p. 1027, no. 48. A mahogany or walnut version of the chair is in the Cleveland Museum of Art; see Hawley 1987, pp. 186–193.

5. Davies 1977, p. 1022.

6. Downing 1969, p. 440, footnote. See Davies 1977, p. 1020, for a discussion of the Davis and Burns collaboration.

7. The Metropolitan Museum of Art 1992, pp. 77, 116.

8. See Mallach 1966, pp. 44, 51, 86; and Page 1980, pp. 34–45.

216.

Armchair, 1857

Designed by Thomas Ustick Walter (1804–1887); manufactured by Bembe and Kimbel (1854–1863), New York
Oak and leather
39 × 24 × 27 inches
Marks: In ink on bottom of caned slip seat, *Wister H. Brother;* label stenciled on inside of back seat rail, *A. BEMBE A. KIMBEL/928/BROADWAY/NEW YORK*
1981.1000.50

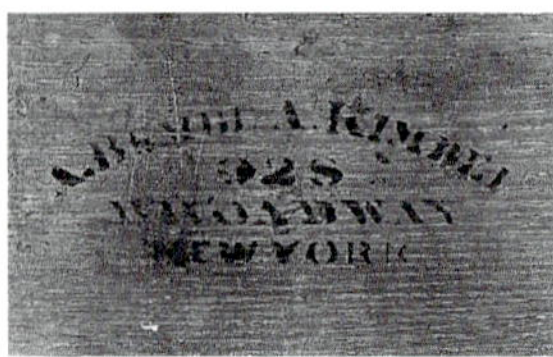

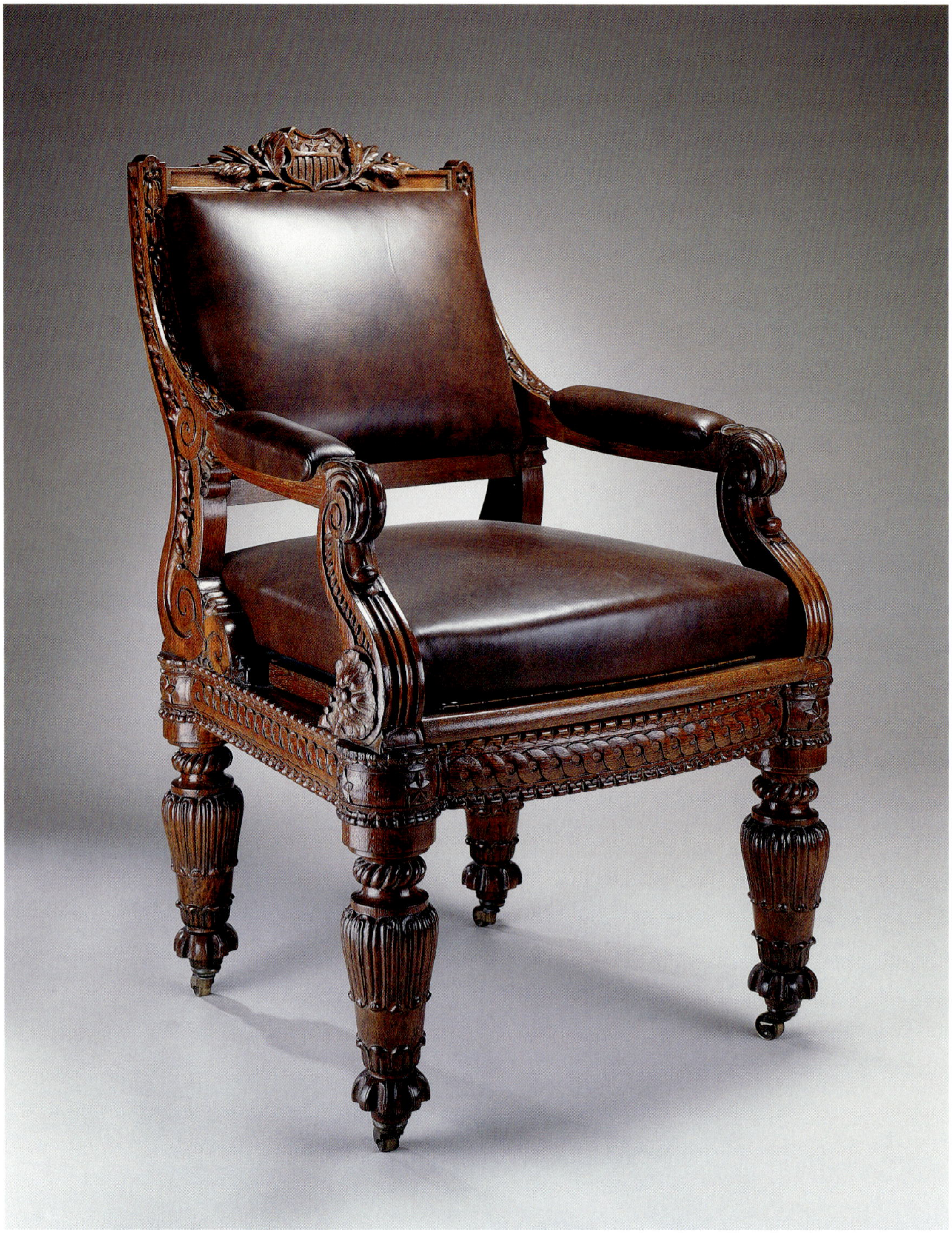

Thomas Ustick Walter was the son and grandson of masons and became a master bricklayer while studying in a Philadelphia architect's office in the 1820s. Walter opened his own architectural office in 1830 and soon received a commission for the Greek revival plan for Girard College in Philadelphia in 1833.[1] In 1850, when a contest for expanding the overcrowded Capitol Building in Washington, D.C., opened, Walter's design was one of five accepted by the government. He was named architect of the Capitol expansion by President Millard Fillmore and given the job of combining the plans and overseeing the building's expansion.[2] Walter held this position until 1865, and during his tenure two wings, one at either end, were completed for the Senate and House of Representatives. Moreover, Walter was responsible for the design and construction of the present cast-iron dome on the structure, which was completed during the Civil War—while Walter was the architect of the Capitol, the building assumed its present form.

In addition to his other duties as architect of the Capitol expansion, Walter designed furniture for the House and Senate Chambers, including Congressional desks and chairs (fig. 1). The Crawford armchair was created by Walter and used in the Hall of Representatives between 1857 and 1873. The initial oak chairs were ordered from Bembe and Kimbel, a furniture manufacturer in New York.[3] The 1857 chairs were monumental in scale and rich in both classical and Renaissance architectural details. The heavily scrolled front arm supports and side stiles of the back, together with the massive acanthus-carved legs gave the chairs an imposing architectural presence that complemented the classical details Walter had incorporated throughout the expanded Capitol. The generous proportions of the chairs were a consideration for comfort in drawn-out Congressional sessions, while the carved U.S. shield at the center of the crest spoke of the serious business of government. The noted Civil War photographer Mathew B. Brady posed President Abraham Lincoln in one of the chairs for an official presidential portrait taken in 1860. An 1873 refurnishing resulted in the sale and dispersal of the Walter chairs.[4]

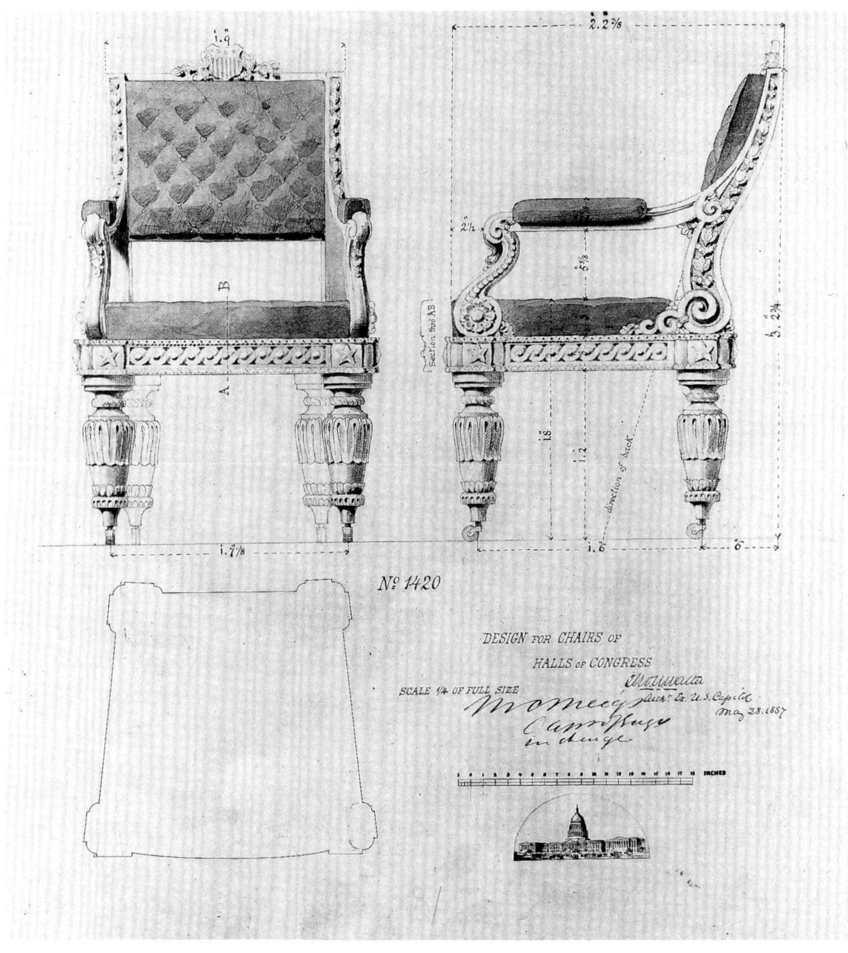

Fig. 1. Design for Chairs of Halls of Congress, by Thomas Ustick Walter. From the collection of the Architect of the Capitol.

NOTES

1. Aikman 1963, p. 51. For illustrations and discussion of Girard College, see Hamlin 1964, p. 83 and pl. XXI, opposite p. 88.

2. Maroon 1993, pp. 38–39.

3. Other examples of the Walter Congressional chair are in the Massachusetts Historical Society, Kane 1976, p. 969; the Maryland Historical Society, Weidman 1984, p. 229, no. 206; and the Henry Ford Museum, Bishop 1972, p. 395, no. 690. Walter's original drawing for the chair, dated May 28, 1857, survives in the office of the Architect of the Capitol. The furniture-making partnership of Anthony Bembe and Anthony Kimbel was first listed in the New York directory for 1854–1855 when they were working at 56 Walker Street. The 1858 directory listed the firm at 928 Broadway, the address on the mark of the Crawford chair. They continued to be listed at 928 Broadway until the 1864 directory. In that directory, Kimbel was listed in partnership with Joseph Cabus at 924 Broadway (see also no. 69 in this catalogue), while Bembe was not mentioned; however, a Carl Bembe was listed as working at the old Bembe and Kimbel stand at 928 Broadway.

4. Weidman 1984, p. 229.

217.

Dining Table, ca. 1875

Designed by Frank Furness (1839–1912); manufacture attributed to Daniel Pabst (1826–1910), Philadelphia
Oak, chestnut, butternut, and ash
26¼ × 66 × 66 inches
1983.198

This dining table combines the carving skill of Daniel Pabst's shop with the idiosyncratic designs of architect Frank Furness. The dining table was part of the original furnishings of the residence of Theodore Roosevelt, Sr., at 6 West 57th Street in Manhattan. Furness provided designs for the dining room of the mansion, built around 1875 by architect Russell Sturgis (fig. 1).[1]

Frank Furness began his architectural training in the New York offices of Richard Morris Hunt in 1859. Hunt was one of the most prominent American architects of his time and the first American to study in Paris at the École des Beaux-Arts. In Hunt's office, Furness was exposed to the latest English and French architectural theories, while also learning the rudiments of architectural work and draftsmanship. After serving in the Union army during the Civil War, Furness briefly returned to Hunt's office before opening his own firm in his native Philadelphia in 1867. Influenced by the English design reformers and educators Owen Jones and Christopher Dresser, Furness used extensive decoration and pattern in his designs for both buildings and furniture. His commissions included the Pennsylvania Academy of Fine Arts in 1871, banks and other commercial buildings, railroad stations, and houses throughout Philadelphia, its suburbs, and neighboring towns. Louis Sullivan (see no. 221) worked briefly with Furness in 1873 and recalled his office as "a true workshop savoring of the guild where craftsmanship was paramount and personal."[2]

In the 1850s, carved animal and hunt motifs were popular in dining rooms (see no. 48); Pabst and Furness used a related image, a heron eating a frog, for the Crawford table. A Furness drawing for the pedestal base survives, with the frog facing away from the heron's beak instead of facing in as it appears on the table (fig. 2).[3] Apart from

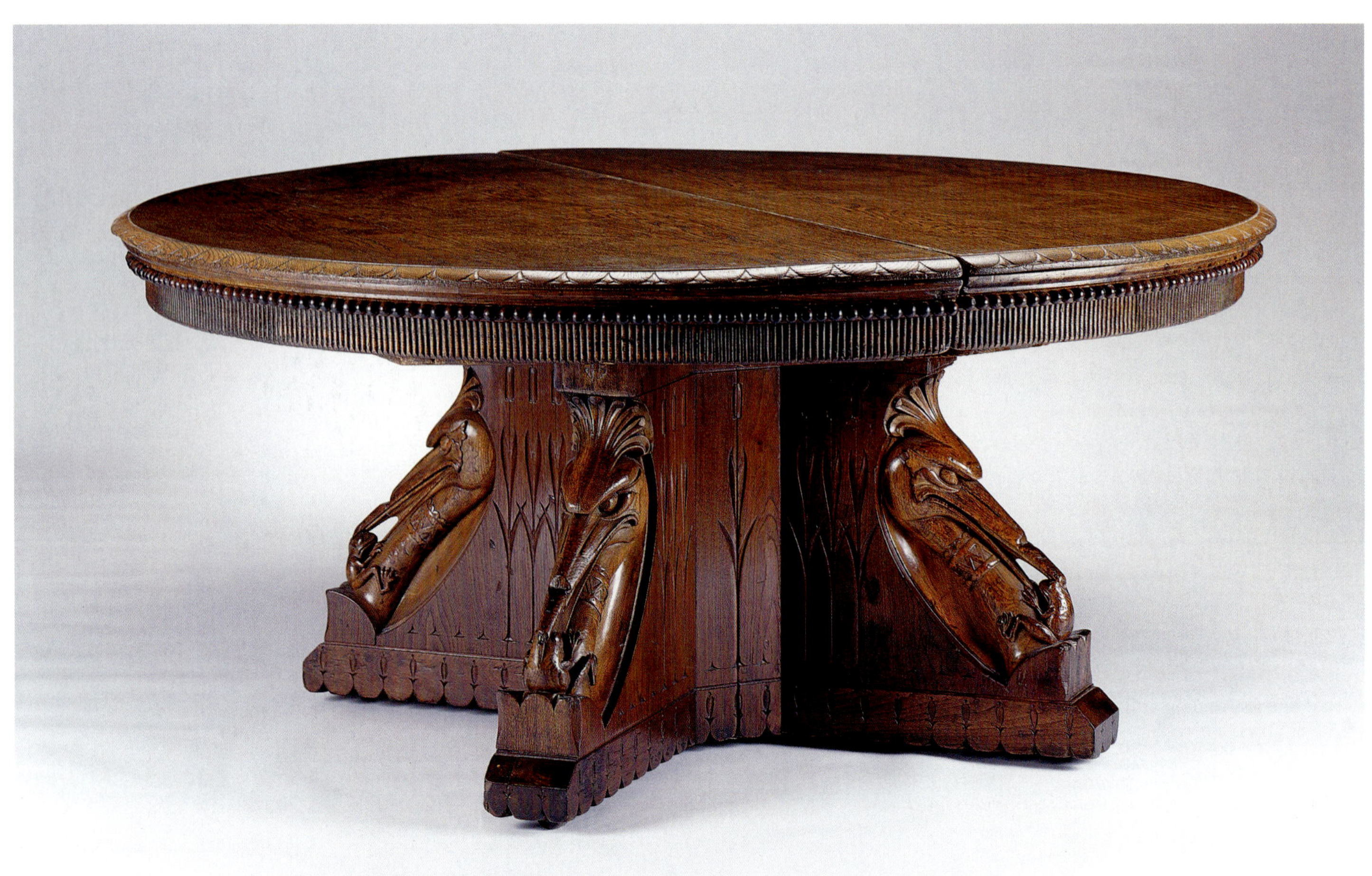

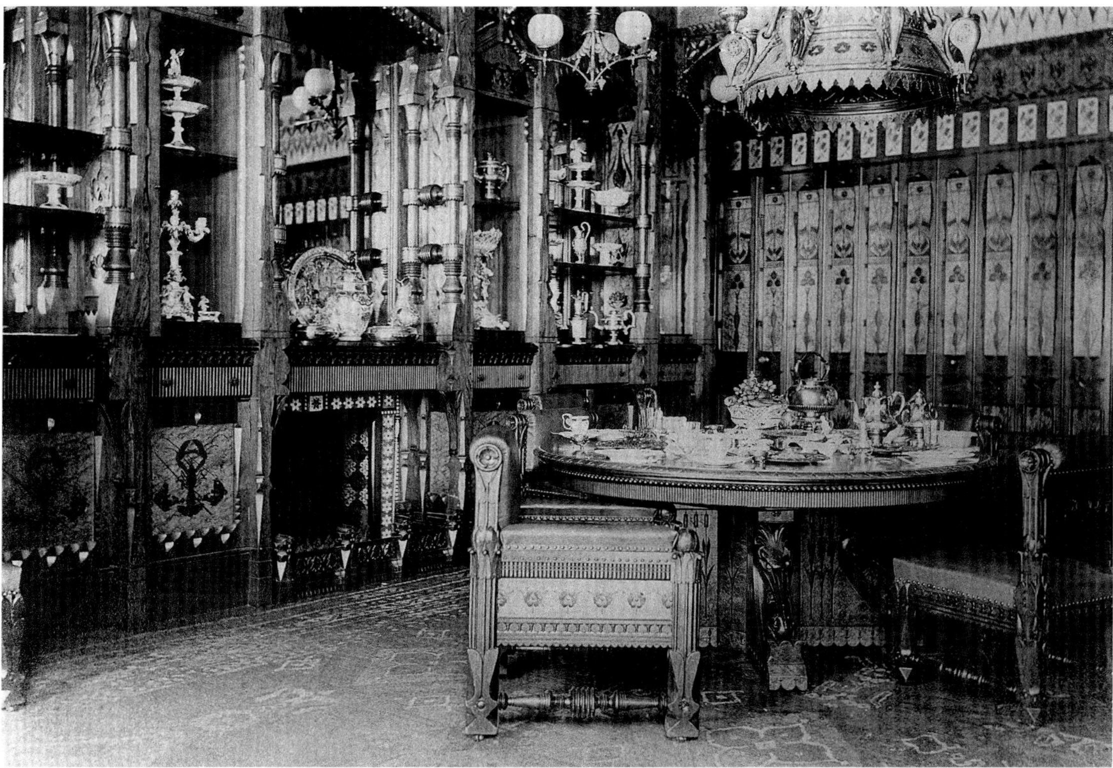

Fig. 1. Dining room, Theodore Roosevelt, Sr., house, ca. 1880.

the sculptural heron and frog motif, the rest of the decoration on the table is relatively flat. The incised carving on the pedestal, the reeding on the table skirt, and the beading under the table top recall Pabst's earlier carving (see no. 54) and reflect Furness's love of pattern.

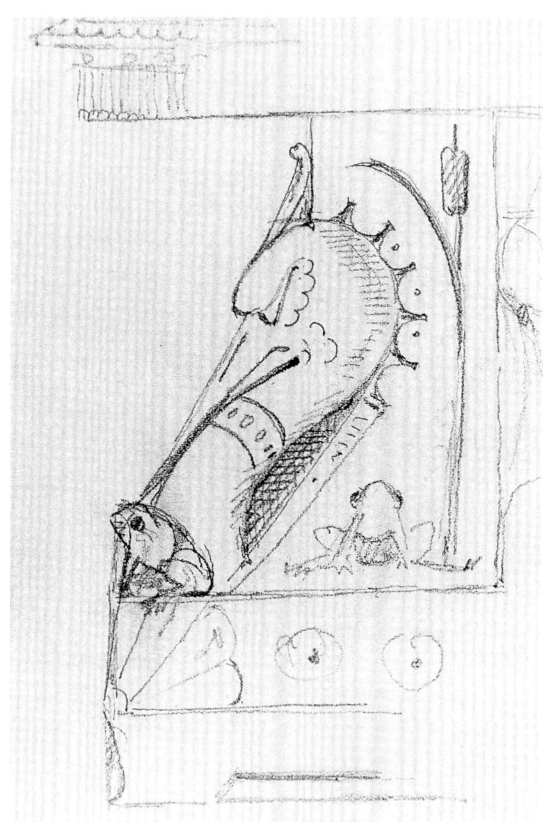

Fig. 2. Frank Furness. Pencil study for table base, ca. 1875. Dining room, Theodore Roosevelt, Sr., house.

NOTES

1. Both Theodore Roosevelt, Sr., and the Furness family were on Pabst's list of clients, hence the attribution of the table to the Pabst shop. Furniture designed by Furness, much of it presumably executed in the shop of Daniel Pabst, is illustrated and discussed in Kaplan, May, 1987. The Crawford table is illustrated and discussed on pp. 1094–1095, pl. I. A letter now in the Philadelphia Museum of Art curatorial archives recalls that Furness's designs were executed by a "German carver" for the Roosevelt commission; see Hanks and Talbott 1977, p. 20.

2. Louis Sullivan, *The Autobiography of an Idea* (New York, 1924; reprinted 1956), pp. 193–194; cited in Kaplan, May 1987, p. 1089.

3. Furness's drawing is shown in Thomas, Lewis, and Cohen 1991, p. 181, fig. 46c.

218.

Desk, 1877–1878

Probably designed by Leopold Eidlitz (1823–1908); made by Weller, Brown and Mesmer (1872–1884), Buffalo, New York
Mahogany, leather, and brass
29⅛ × 26½ × 23¾ inches
Mark: Applied brass numbers on back, under top, *67*
Inscriptions: Various penciled inscriptions and dates inside drawer
1983.200

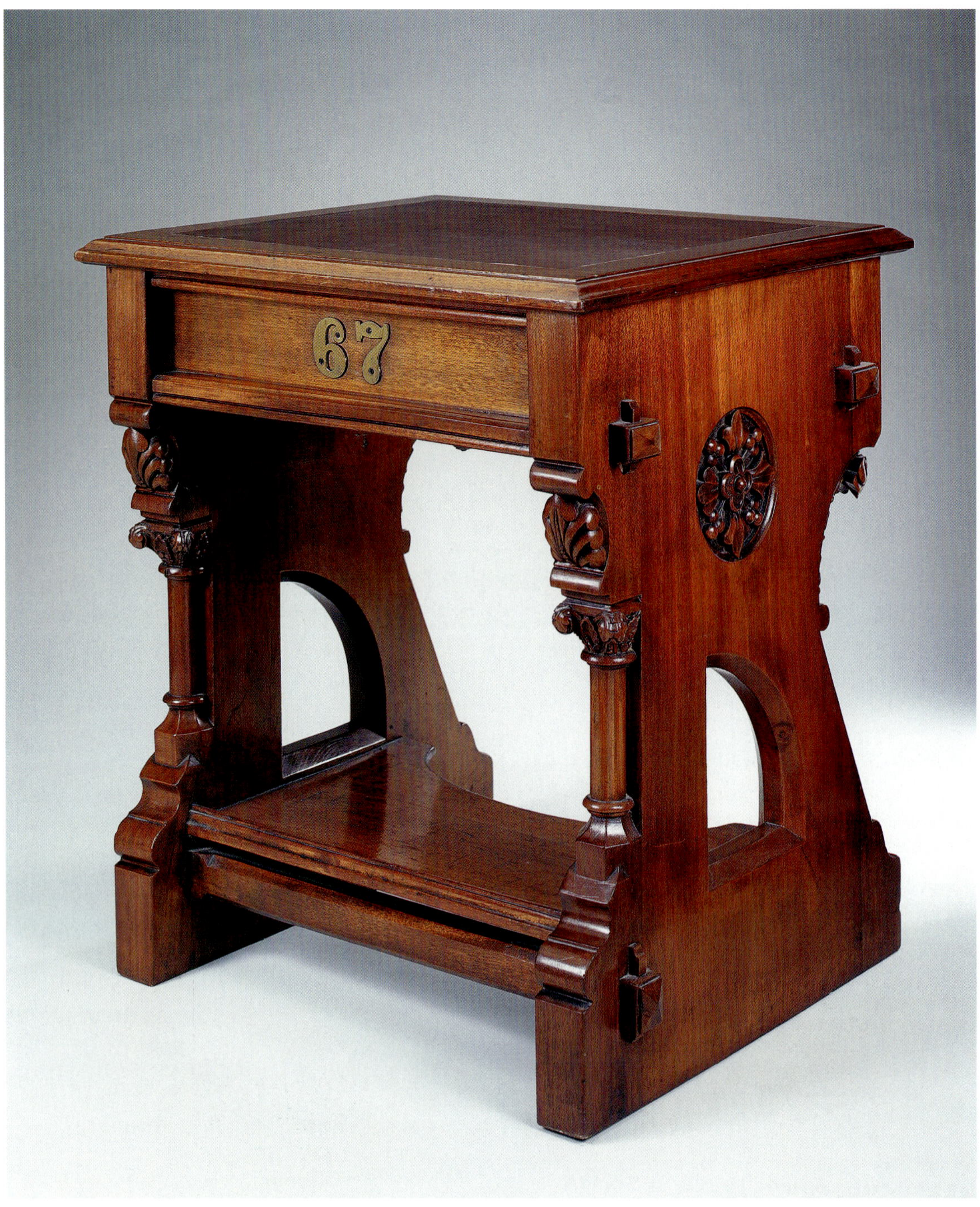

This desk was one of 128 produced from a design probably by Leopold Eidlitz for his Assembly Chamber in the New York State Capitol in Albany in 1877 or 1878 (fig. 1). Born in Prague, Eidlitz studied at Vienna Polytechnic to be a land steward to construct estate administration buildings. In 1843, at age twenty, Eidlitz immigrated to New York, where he found work as a draftsman for Richard Upjohn, a leading American architect of the Gothic revival style. While never formally trained as an architect, Eidlitz was a great admirer of the engineering of Gothic architecture, and he incorporated various Gothic and Romanesque forms in his buildings.

By 1846, Eidlitz had formed a partnership with Charles Blesch, a Bavarian with the formal architectural background Eidlitz lacked. Later, and on his own, Eidlitz designed a number of Gothic churches as well as commercial buildings. Together with Alexander Jackson Davis (see nos. 214–215) and Thomas U. Walter (see no. 216), Eidlitz was a founding member of the American Institute of Architects in 1857.

By 1875, when Eidlitz was called in to evaluate the troubled New York State Capitol in tenuous progress in Albany, he had achieved recognition for buildings in New York, New England, and the Midwest.[1] The Capitol had originally been designed by Canadian architect Thomas Fuller in 1867. Fuller remained on the Capitol project until 1876, when he was replaced by a firm specifically created to complete the building: Eidlitz, Richardson and Company, consisting of Eidlitz, Henry Hobson Richardson, and Frederick Law Olmsted. Eidlitz and Richardson divided the Capitol, and each assumed responsibility for large sections of the building's interior.[2] Eidlitz planned the Assembly Chamber, the Court of Appeals courtroom beneath, and the Assembly and Senate staircases in the north wing of the building, while Richardson took responsibility for the Senate, or south wing, of the Capitol and Olmsted supervised the landscaping.

Eidlitz's monumental Gothic Assembly Chamber was dominated by a soaring groined-vault ceiling, with its three-ton center stone fifty-six feet above the floor—the widest known span ever attempted in Gothic groined-vault architecture.[3] Eidlitz selected architectural elements from his Assembly Chamber to ornament the desks, which were manufactured by Weller, Brown and Mesmer of Buffalo, a firm hired to complete the woodwork in the chamber. Eidlitz believed in organic architecture and exposed the supporting arches of the groined-vault ceiling and their massive supporting columns. The mortise and tenon joints of the Crawford desk reflect this belief. Foliate capitals on the two engaged columns of the desk and the foliate medallions on either side followed the forms of the four granite support columns and their capitals in the chamber. The quarter-round pierced sections on each side of the desk reflect the curves of the arches of the room.

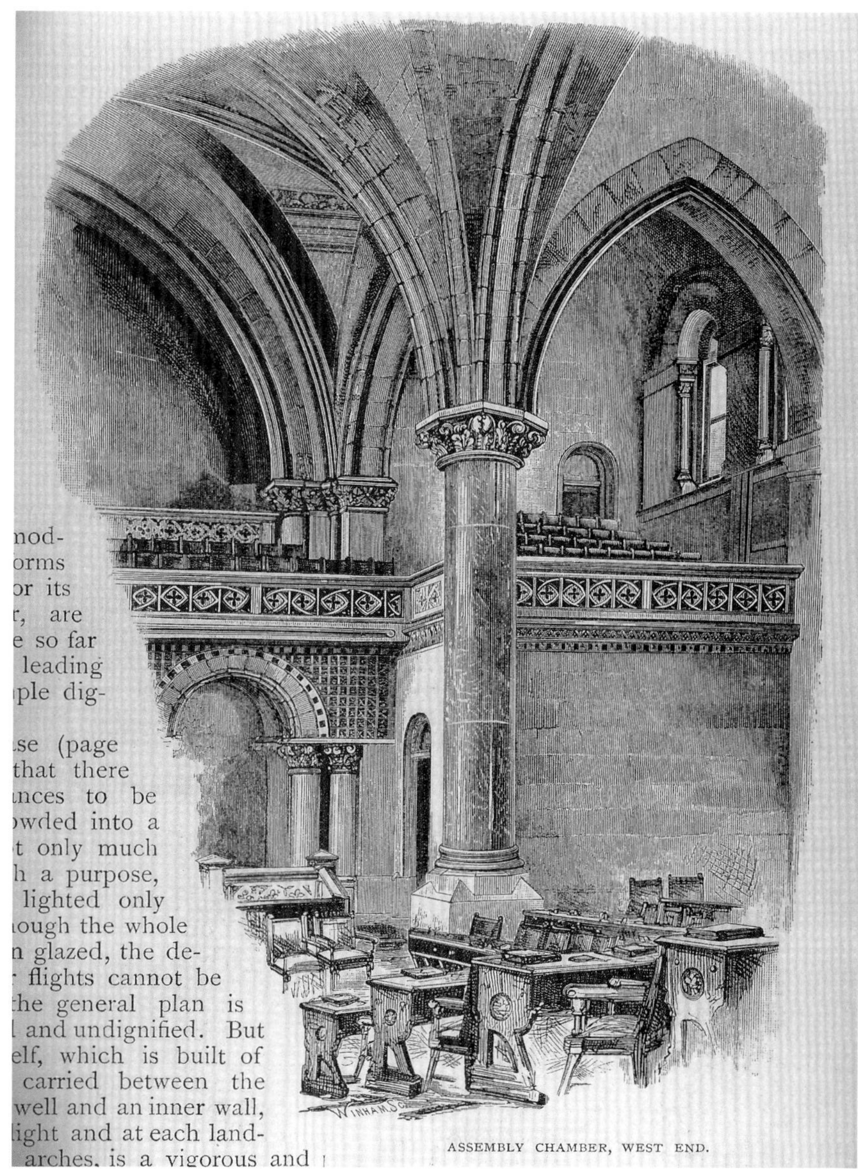

Fig. 1. Assembly Chamber, west end. *Scribner's Monthly* 19 (December 1879), p. 171.

NOTES

1. For a biography of Eidlitz and a list of his commissions, see Placzek 1982, pp. 13–16.

2. For an account of the history of the construction of the New York State Capitol, see Roseberry 1964.

3. Disturbing cracks began appearing shortly after the ceiling was completed. The state political bureaucracy, however, took nearly a decade to demolish the ceiling and replace it with a flat, carved and beamed oak and papier-mâché ceiling, which also provided better acoustics for the chamber. Ibid., pp. 42–61, 82–89, gives the checkered history of the Assembly Chamber.

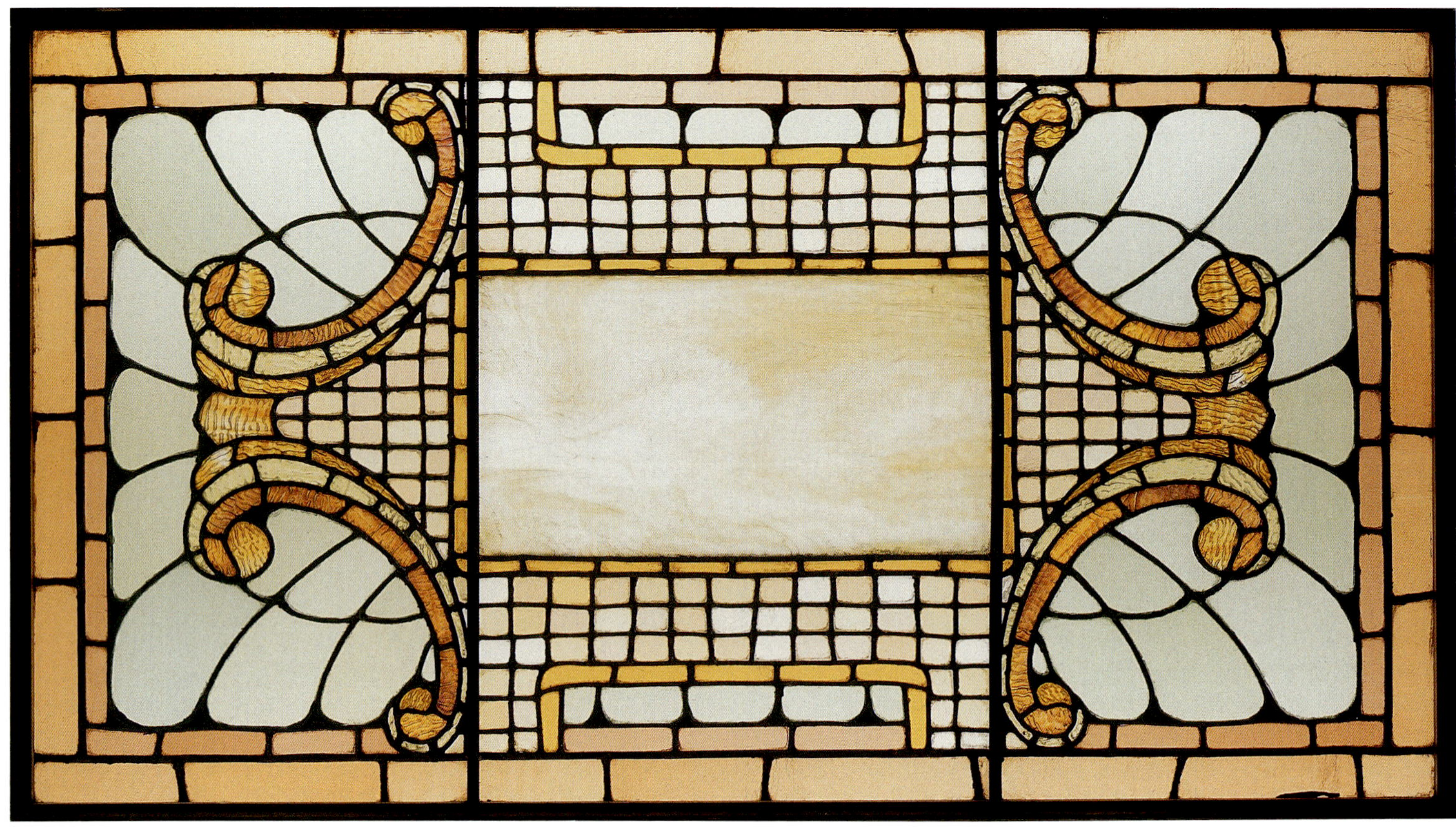

219.

Window, ca. 1890

Colored glass with leading in wood frame
Designed by Edward Colonna (1862–1948); probably made in Montreal, Canada
19½ × 35¼ inches
1992.385

Edward Colonna was born outside Cologne, Germany, and may have trained in architecture in Brussels before immigrating to New York in 1882. There he worked briefly for Louis Comfort Tiffany, possibly on some interior design commissions, and later for prominent New York architect Bruce Price. The precise nature of his work for them is unknown, but it does suggest that Colonna was exposed to leading New York designers and had an awareness of European sources. In 1885, Colonna was hired as a designer by Barney and Smith Manufacturing Company of Dayton, Ohio, where he soon became part of the artistic community. In 1888, he married Louise McLaughlin, daughter of a leading Cincinnati architect and niece of Mary Louise McLaughlin, a major force in Cincinnati's artistic pottery movement (see no. 172). Barney and Smith supplied cars to the Canadian Pacific Railway, and the railroad's major expansions may have encouraged Colonna to open an architectural office in Montreal from 1890 to 1893. While Colonna was designing railroad stations for Canadian Pacific, William Van Horne commissioned him to expand and redecorate his Montreal mansion around 1890.

Van Horne, president of Canadian Pacific Railway, was a Montreal business leader, as well as an avid art collector, and he had purchased a large older house in an affluent residential neighborhood along one of the city's major boulevards, Sherbrook Street. The Crawford window was an upper pane in one of the large vertical windows in the redecorated salon. In such a high location, it did not need to be transparent; rather, its function was to provide decoration and subtle light. Made of colored glass—rather than more deeply hued stained glass—the window design may have been related to architectural elements and patterns in the salon's woodwork and plaster ceiling decorations. The gold and white of the window complemented the color scheme of the room.

Van Horne's art collection consisted of paintings and Chinese objects purchased from L'Art Nouveau, the Paris shop of S. Bing. A letter of reference from Van Horne may have enabled Colonna to meet Bing on a trip to Paris in 1897, two years after he had opened his store. Bing combined painting and sculpture with decorative art in his shop, and he carried the work of contemporary European designers, as well as the Favrile glass of Louis Comfort Tiffany (see no. 175). Colonna was a principal designer for Bing between 1897 and 1903, and he gained something of an international reputation. He also worked as a painter, interior decorator, and antiques dealer, but it was only briefly at L'Art Nouveau that Colonna found the attention he had been seeking for his work. With the closing of Bing's shop in 1903, Colonna returned to Montreal to work in architecture.[1]

NOTE

1. A comprehensive illustrated study of Edward Colonna and his work is presented in Dayton Art Institute 1983, with an essay by Martin Eidelberg, pp. 6–81. The exhibition catalogue presents work from Colonna's years in Dayton and Montreal and his work in Paris for L'Art Nouveau. The Van Horne commission is discussed on pp. 24–27. A window identical to the Crawford window in the Lillian Nassau, Ltd., collection is illustrated on p. 25, fig. 44, and is no. 68 in the exhibition catalogue.

220.

Grill, 1883

Possibly J. B. and J. M. Cornell (ca. 1860–after 1905), New York; possibly designed by Hubert, Pirsson and Company (1880–1888), New York
Cast iron
37 × 18 inches
1995.183

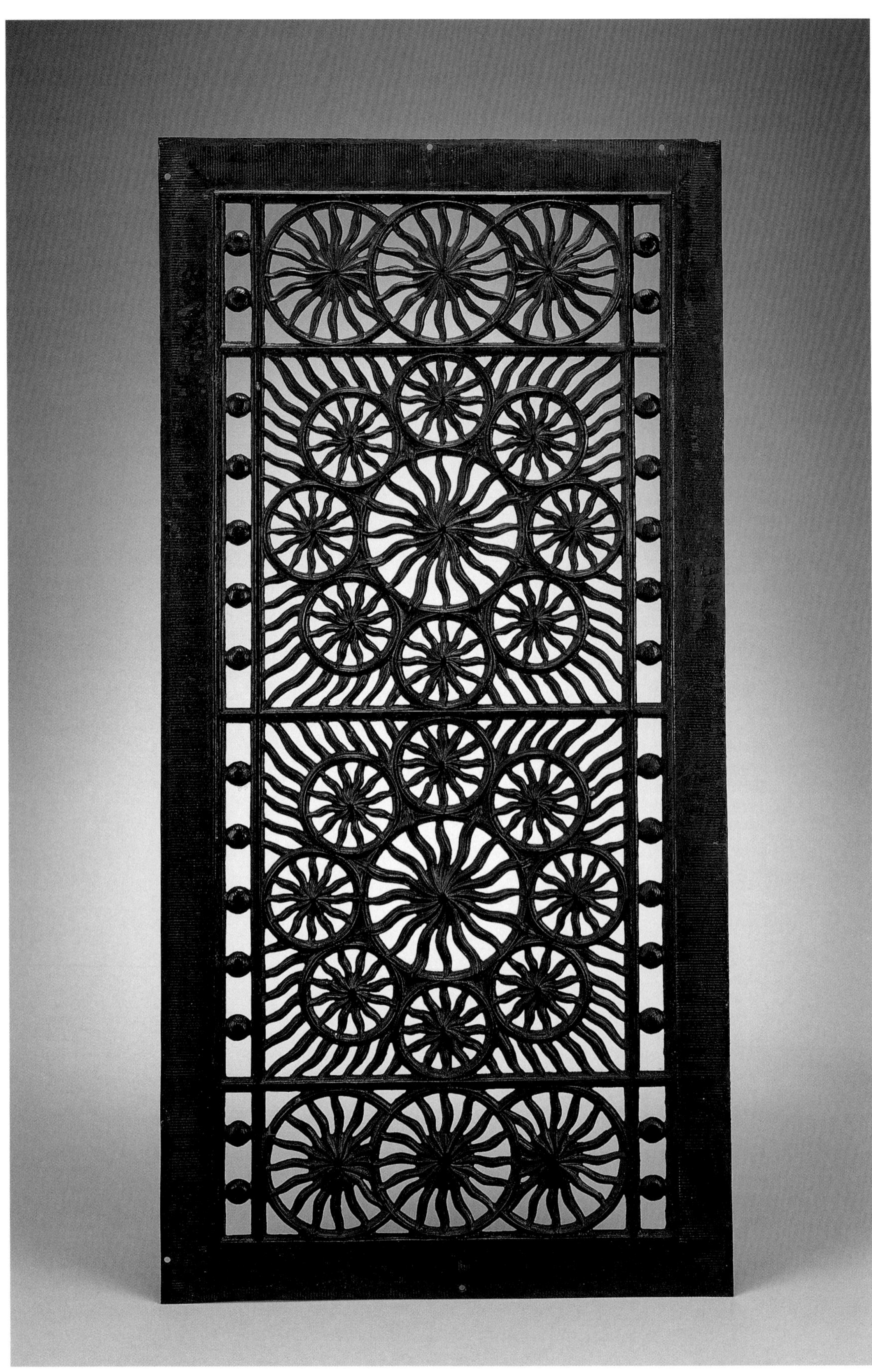

This cast-iron register grill was part of the original interior fittings of the Hotel Chelsea at 222 West 23rd Street in New York, which was designed by the architectural firm of Hubert, Pirsson and Company in 1883.[1] Philip Hubert and James Pirsson maintained an office at 54 West 33rd Street in Manhattan, and the partnership specialized in the large apartment buildings that were replacing single family houses in the city. After Pirsson's death, Hubert practiced on his own in New York until he retired to California in 1895.[2]

The irregular roofline and facade of the brick hotel were the result of chimneys, dormers, recesses, and projections that characterized large-scale American urban architecture built in the 1880s. At eleven stories, the building was one of the tallest in Manhattan at the time of its completion. Built as a cooperative apartment house, it became a hotel in 1905 and appealed especially to authors and artists, including Mark Twain, Sarah Bernhardt, Lillian Russell, O. Henry, Tennessee Williams, John Sloan, and Jackson Pollock. The J. B. and J. M. Cornell foundry manufactured the elaborate and sculptural cast-iron balconies on the exterior of the building and may also have made this unmarked interior grill.[3] The nearly abstract floral motifs consisting of circular sunbursts are a stylized rendering of nature of the type that was fashionable in the 1880s. Hubert, Pirsson and Company either designed the grill or participated in its selection.

NOTES

1. The Hotel Chelsea is discussed in White and Willensky 1988, pp. 278–279.

2. Hubert, Pirsson and Company is discussed in Withey and Withey 1956, p. 305.

3. One of the cast-iron balconies is illustrated and the Cornell foundry is discussed in Gayle 1974, p. 181. The foundry was first listed in city directories in 1860 as J. B. and W. W. Cornell, for brothers John B. and William W. The firm continued at 135–143 Centre Street in New York after 1867, when it opened a large foundry at 524 West 26th Street. The Centre Street address was used for offices and showroom. After William Cornell died in 1870 and John Cornell's son became a partner in 1873, the firm's name changed to J. B. and J. M. Cornell. By 1895, the Cornell foundry office was listed as the estate of J. B. Cornell at 143 Centre Street and 240 11th Avenue. In 1905, Cornell was still in city directories, but only the foundry site on 11th Avenue was listed.

221.

Elevator Grill with Decorative Plate, 1893–1894

Designed by Louis H. Sullivan (1856–1924); made by Winslow Brothers Company, Chicago
Painted cast and wrought iron and bronze
73 × 31 inches
1982.291

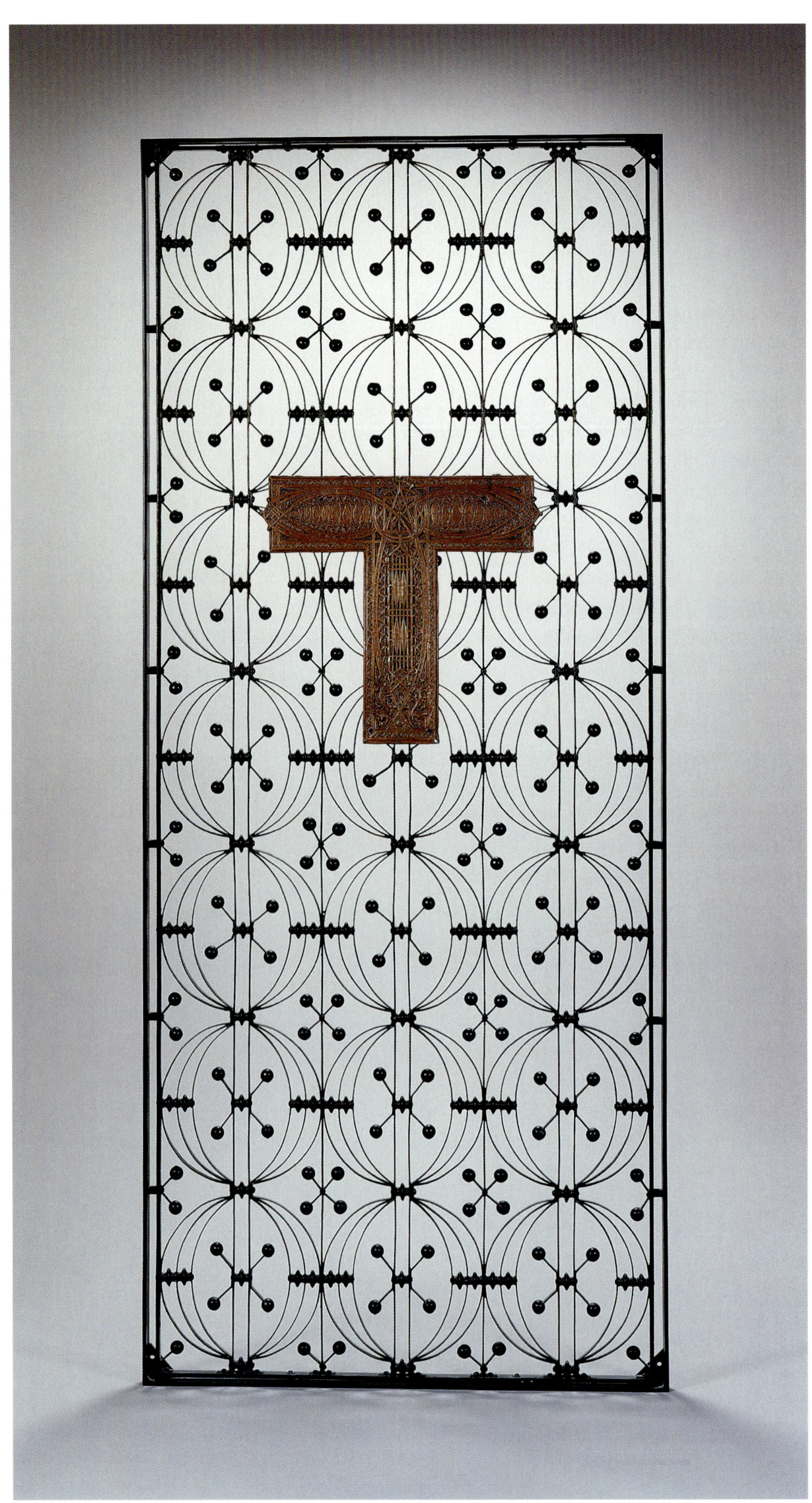

THE ELEVATOR grill and its decorative bronze T-shaped plate designed by Louis Sullivan was taken from one of the upper floors of the Chicago Stock Exchange Building (fig. 1).[1] Born in Boston, Sullivan attended the Massachusetts Institute of Technology for a year and then moved to Philadelphia in 1873, where he was a draftsman briefly for Frank Furness (see no. 217). He finished his apprenticeship in Chicago under engineer-architect William Le Baron Jenney, who helped develop skyscraper skeleton construction. In 1880, Sullivan began working for Chicago architect Dankmar Adler, and the two were partners from 1883 to 1895. Their firm was commissioned to design the Chicago Stock Exchange Building in 1893; it was one of two hundred buildings they designed. Just as construction of the Stock Exchange began, Frank Lloyd Wright (see nos. 223–224) resigned from Adler and Sullivan as head draftsman to establish his own office, and he was succeeded by George Grant Elmslie (see no. 225), who worked with Sullivan until 1909.

The screen's geometric circles and spheres are stylized interpretations of seed germs—an appropriate motif for the nation's largest agricultural stock exchange—and reflected the ideas of British designer Owen Jones, who had promoted the abstraction of nature in design in the 1850s. Circular elements with leaves in the cast-bronze T-shaped plate detail (see page 361) echo the elements in the screen and reinforce agricultural associations. The open design of the Stock Exchange elevator screens revealed the mechanical workings and construction of the elevator shaft. While more conservative eastern architects tended to mask a building's mechanics with elaborate classical details, Sullivan felt that design should celebrate rather than conceal them.

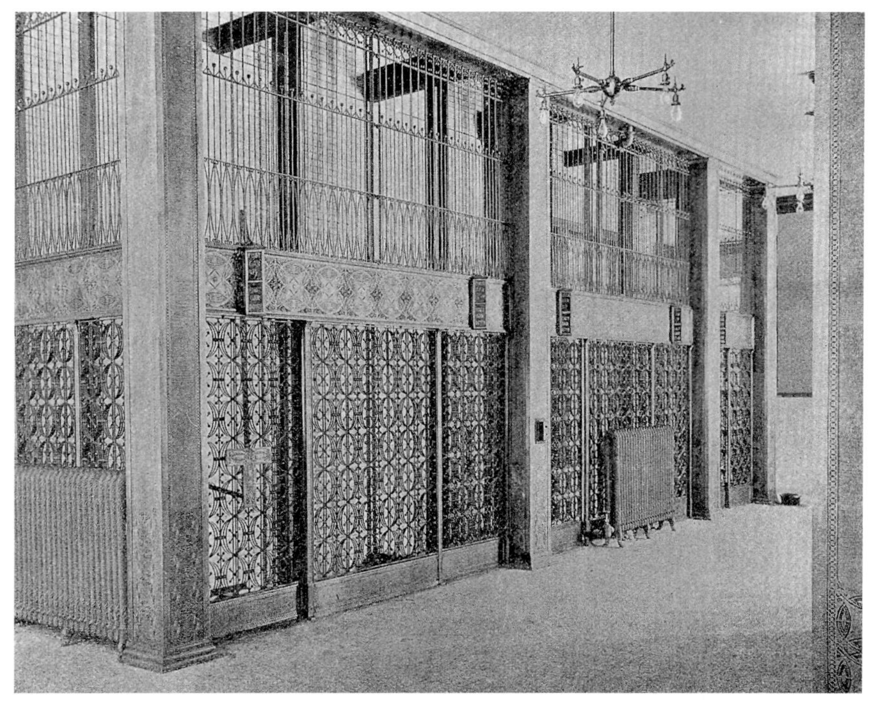

Fig. 1. Elevator enclosures, main floor, Stock Exchange Building, Chicago. Louis H. Sullivan, architect. *Ornamental Iron* (Chicago: Winslow Brothers Company, 1894).

NOTE

1. The ground floor grills and a similar T-shaped plate are illustrated and discussed in Saliga 1990, p. 139. The Trading Room was installed in the Art Institute of Chicago after the building's controversial demolition in 1972. The room and history of the building are discussed in Vinci 1979. The cast-iron staircase of the Chicago Stock Exchange Building is now in The Metropolitan Museum of Art; see Davidson and Stillinger 1985, pp. 16–17, figs. 9–10.

222.

Armchair, ca. 1903

Probably designed by Herts and Tallant (1900–1911) or F. Richards Anderson (born 1875); possibly made by Herts Brothers (1872–1937), New York
Oak with original leather upholstery
45½ × 30 × 24¼ inches
1986.192

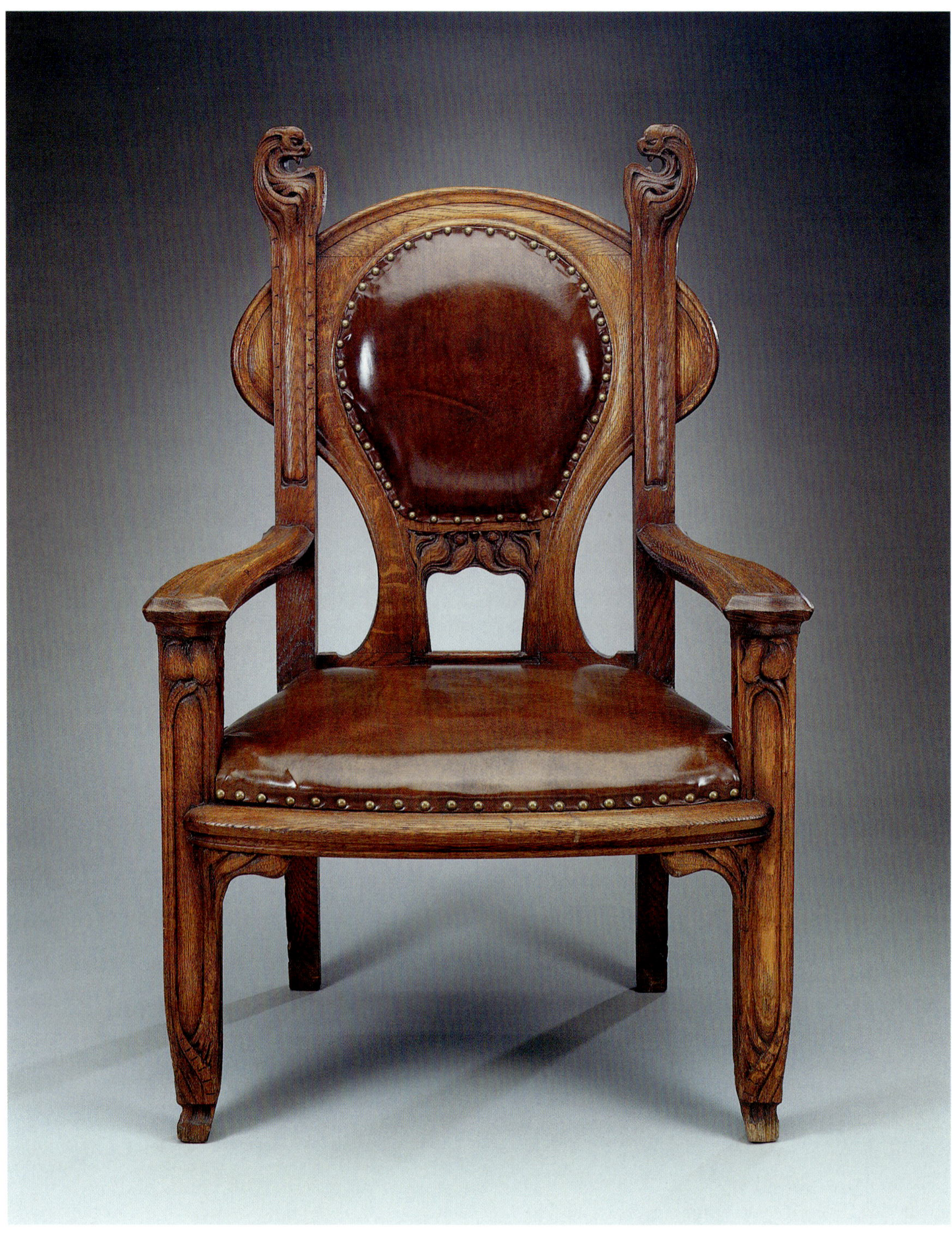

While the identities of the designer and maker of the Crawford armchair are uncertain, it was clearly part of the colorful and dynamic Art Nouveau interior of the 1903 New Amsterdam Theater on New York's 42nd Street. A period photograph shows at least ten of these chairs in the theater's New Amsterdam Room, a gentleman's smoking lounge (fig. 1). Eight matching armchairs surround a massive rectangular center table, with two additional chairs in the background. The New York architectural firm of Herts and Tallant was awarded the 1902 commission for the theater's overall design by the owners, the highly successful theatrical producers Marc Klaw and Abraham Lincoln Erlanger.[1]

Henry Beaumont Herts and Hugh Tallant met at the École des Beaux-Arts in Paris in the 1890s. Herts was the son of a founder of Herts Brothers, the prominent New York interior decorators and furniture manufacturers (see no. 144). He attended the architectural program at Columbia University and studied at the École des Beaux-Arts. Tallant was there on a fellowship from Harvard University, where he had already completed bachelor's and master's degrees in mathematics and engineering. The two returned to New York in 1900 to establish their architectural firm. Tallant largely took responsibility for design and decoration, while Herts was in charge of engineering and business aspects.

During their partnership, Herts and Tallant established a reputation in New York for the design of theaters; Herts's new technique for cantilevered balcony construction was used in the New Amsterdam Theater. Erlanger's assistant F. Richards Anderson had also studied design in Paris, and his involvement in the theater's planning included coordinating the artists and craftspeople who decorated it. Although Anderson's contributions to the theater's design are not clear, he was credited with its interior design in the opening night program. He may have designed the Crawford armchair, although he was known mainly as a costume designer. If Anderson did not design the chair, Tallant was more likely than Herts to have designed it. Because of Herts's family connections, Herts Brothers probably manufactured the chair. The firm did provide specially ordered furniture for the theater's ladies lounge.[2]

The form of the chair and its suite of furniture complemented the many curved elements of the domed and colonnaded smoking room, and its throne-like scale was intended to flatter the male clientele. The chair's languid curves were associated with the very modern Art Nouveau, although the large scale and rather nonorganic form were more in keeping with Germanic interpretations of that style. The elongated curves appropriately suggest wafting cigar smoke.

Over the eleven years of their partnership, Herts and Tallant designed other theater buildings around Times Square as well as the Brooklyn Academy of Music. After the firm was dissolved in 1911, Tallant joined the firm of Lord and Hewlitt to form Lord, Hewlitt, and Tallant, and in 1931 moved to Savannah, Georgia. Herts practiced architecture on his own and contributed to some thirty other theater designs in New York during the remainder of his career.

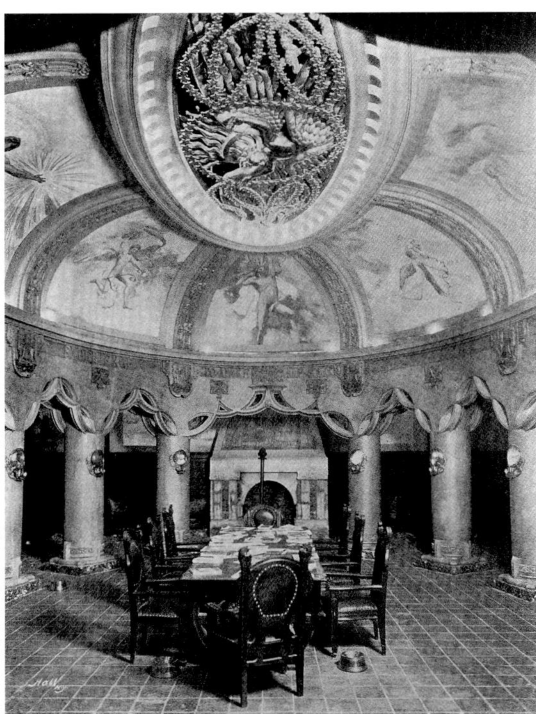

Fig. 1. New Amsterdam Theater smoking lounge, 1903.

NOTES

1. The Crawford armchair is illustrated and discussed in Whitney Museum of American Art 1985, pp. 12–14, fig. 12. Background on the New Amsterdam Theater, its impact, and its design are recounted in M. Henderson 1997, pp. 10–33. This source also describes the full theatrical and cinematic history of the New Amsterdam Theater and its 1996–1997 restoration by Disney Development Corporation, which retained architect Hugh Hardy. Before and after photographs and descriptions of the theater and its restoration are found in Gladstone 1997. The theater is also discussed in Stern, Gilmartin, and Massengale 1983, pp. 209–212; and Young 1973, pp. 4–5.

2. For background on Herts and Tallant and on Anderson's involvement, see M. Henderson 1997, pp. 22–31.

Frank Lloyd Wright

FRANK LLOYD WRIGHT was central to the evolution of the distinctively Midwestern Prairie style of architecture. After leaving Adler and Sullivan in Chicago (see no. 221), Wright opened his own office in 1893 at his suburban Oak Park home, attracting young architects with his radical new ideas. Within ten years, Wright had completed one of his early Prairie-style masterpieces, the 1902 house for Chicago businessman Ward W. Willits in Highland Park.

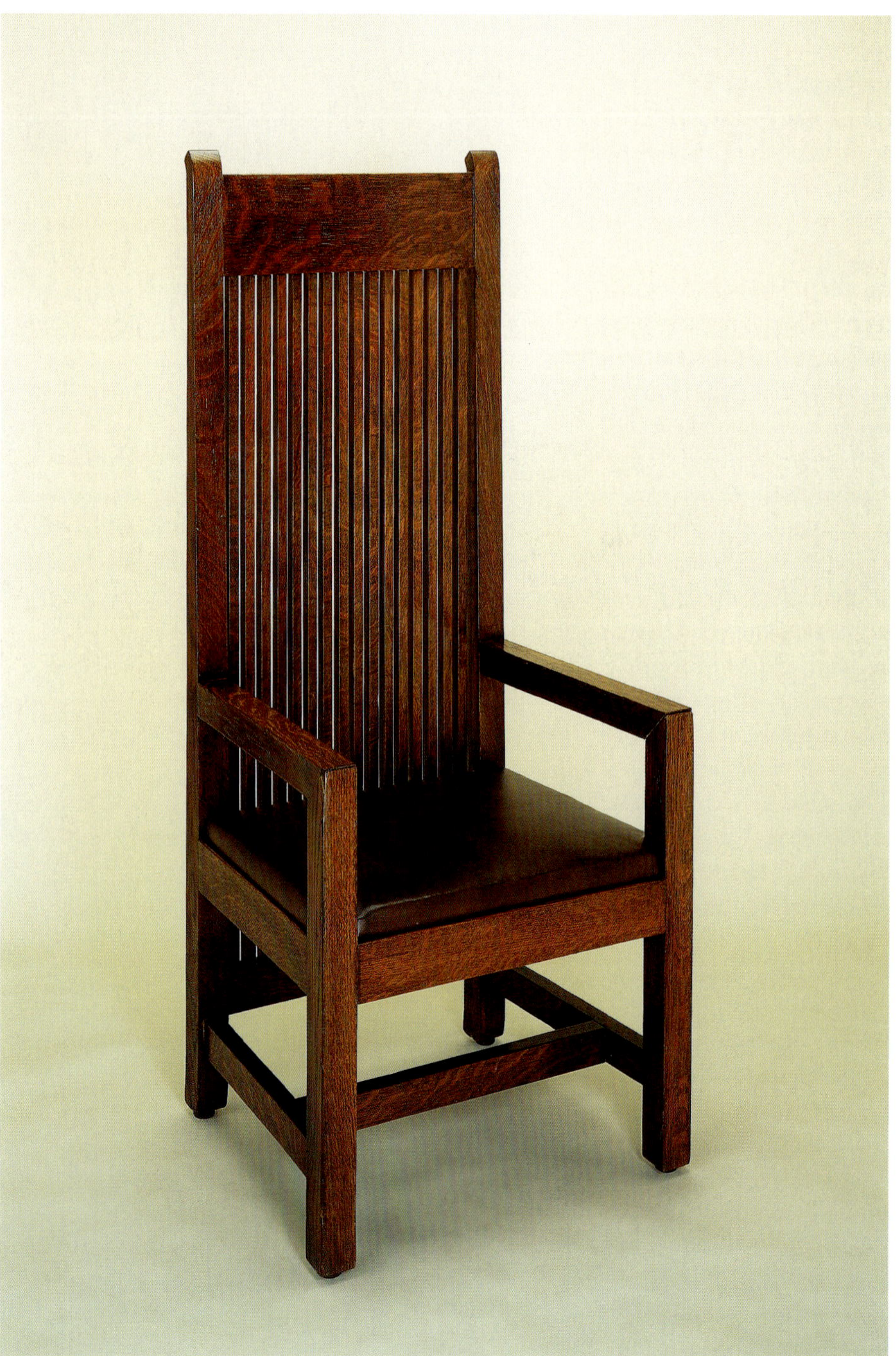

223.

Armchair, ca. 1902

Designed by Frank Lloyd Wright (1867–1959); made by John W. Ayers (1850–1914)
Design Copyright © The Frank Lloyd Wright Foundation, Taliesin West, Scottsdale, Arizona
Oak with replaced leather upholstery, based on original surviving fragments
56¼ x 23 x 20 inches
Marks: Inscribed inside top of seat rail and on bottom of front rail slip seat, *XII;* in pencil on top of rear rail of slip seat, *W*
1981.1000.49

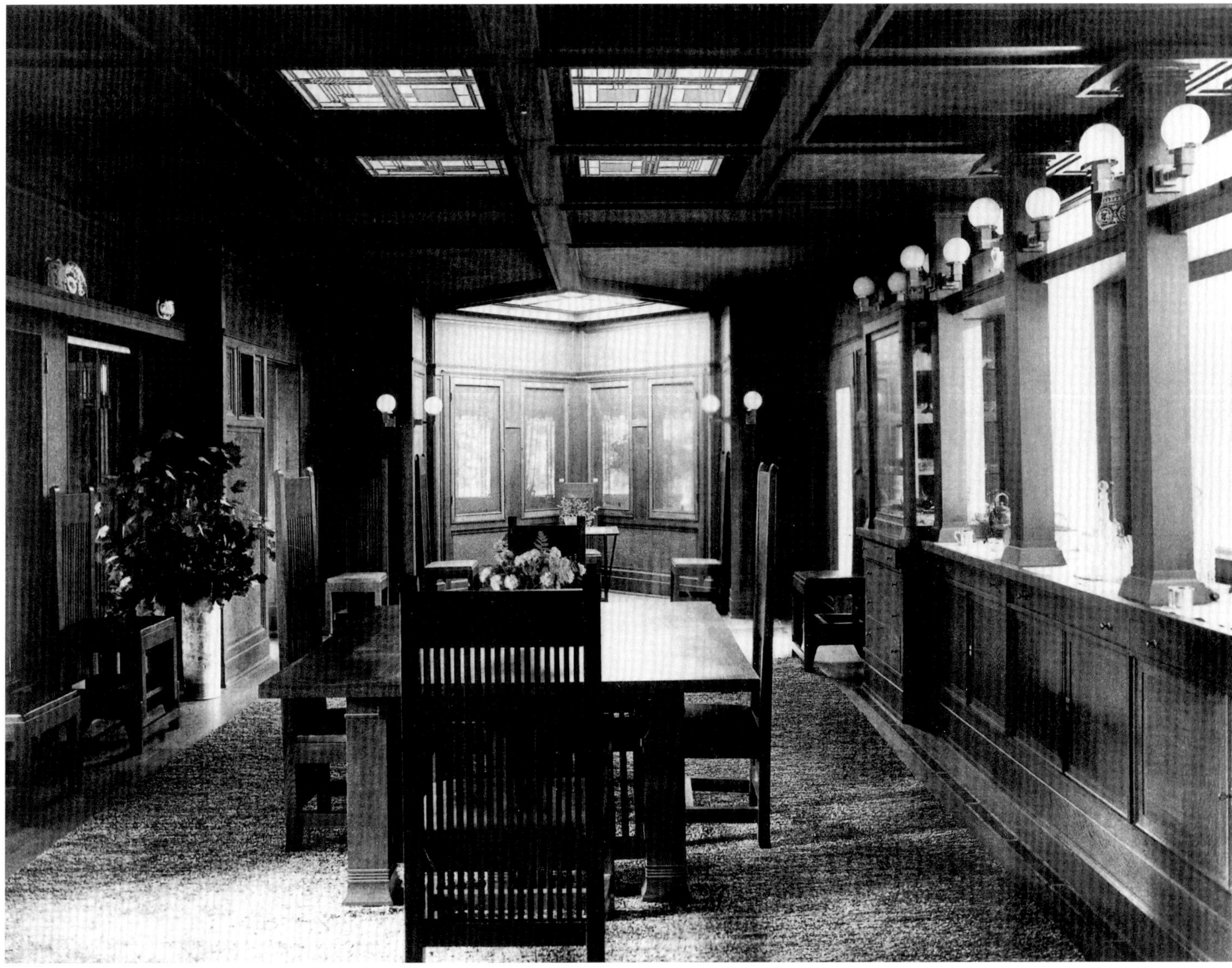

Fig. 1. Dining room, Ward W. Willits house.

The Willits house is a sprawling, low-eaved, cruciform-shaped villa with strong horizontal lines that parallel the flat prairie landscape.[1] Wright typically designed the furniture for his houses, and the Crawford armchair (no. 223) is from the Willits dining room set (fig. 1).[2] The simple, squared elements of the chair—the spindles, stiles, legs, arms, and seat—suited the architecture of the room. When the chairs were arranged around the table, the tall chairbacks acted as screens, providing the privacy of an inner court while admitting light through the spindles. When set around the walls, the chairs reinforced the strong square and rectangular elements composing the room. Unlike contemporary Arts and Crafts artisans who valued individual creativity, Wright desired complete aesthetic control over his projects. Some Prairie School architects tolerated their clients' use of Arts and Crafts furniture, but they generally preferred to design their own. Wright felt that machine-made furniture by trained and skilled cabinetmakers most appropriately conveyed his designs. He found a willing maker in John W. Ayers, who strictly followed Wright's designs.[3]

Wright designed chairs similar to the Willits example for his own dining room as early as 1895, and he used similar designs through the first decade of the twentieth century.[4] In his 1932 autobiography, Wright admitted the difficulties he had in designing furniture: "to design it as architecture and make it 'human' at the same time—fit for human use. I have been black and blue in some spot, somewhere almost my entire life from too intimate contact with my own early furniture."[5]

Wright's windows for the J. Avery Coonley playhouse, like the Willits chair, were important elements in the overall aesthetic vision of the building. Wright had already designed a residence for the Chicago businessman in 1909. In 1912, Coonley commissioned a children's playhouse for an innovative kindergarten organized by his wife for family and neighborhood children. The building, on the Coonley estate grounds in suburban Riverside, was called a playhouse because of a small stage at one end. Wright designed not only the furnishings for the kindergarten, but also a series of colored glass windows with motifs based on balloons, confetti, and parade flags (fig. 2).[6] The Crawford window (no. 224) was one of many that lined both sides of a clerestory running the width of the playhouse. These small windows complemented large vertical windows in the building with similar designs. The lead lines in the windows emphasized the strong horizontal elements of the building's facade and admitted additional light into the main classroom-theater area. The extended horizontal arrangement of the windows suggested a long, passing parade.

224.

Window, 1912

Designed by Frank Lloyd Wright (1867–1959)
Design Copyright © The Frank Lloyd Wright Foundation, Taliesin West, Scottsdale, Arizona
Oak, colored glass, and leading
24 × 38⅜ inches
1995.182

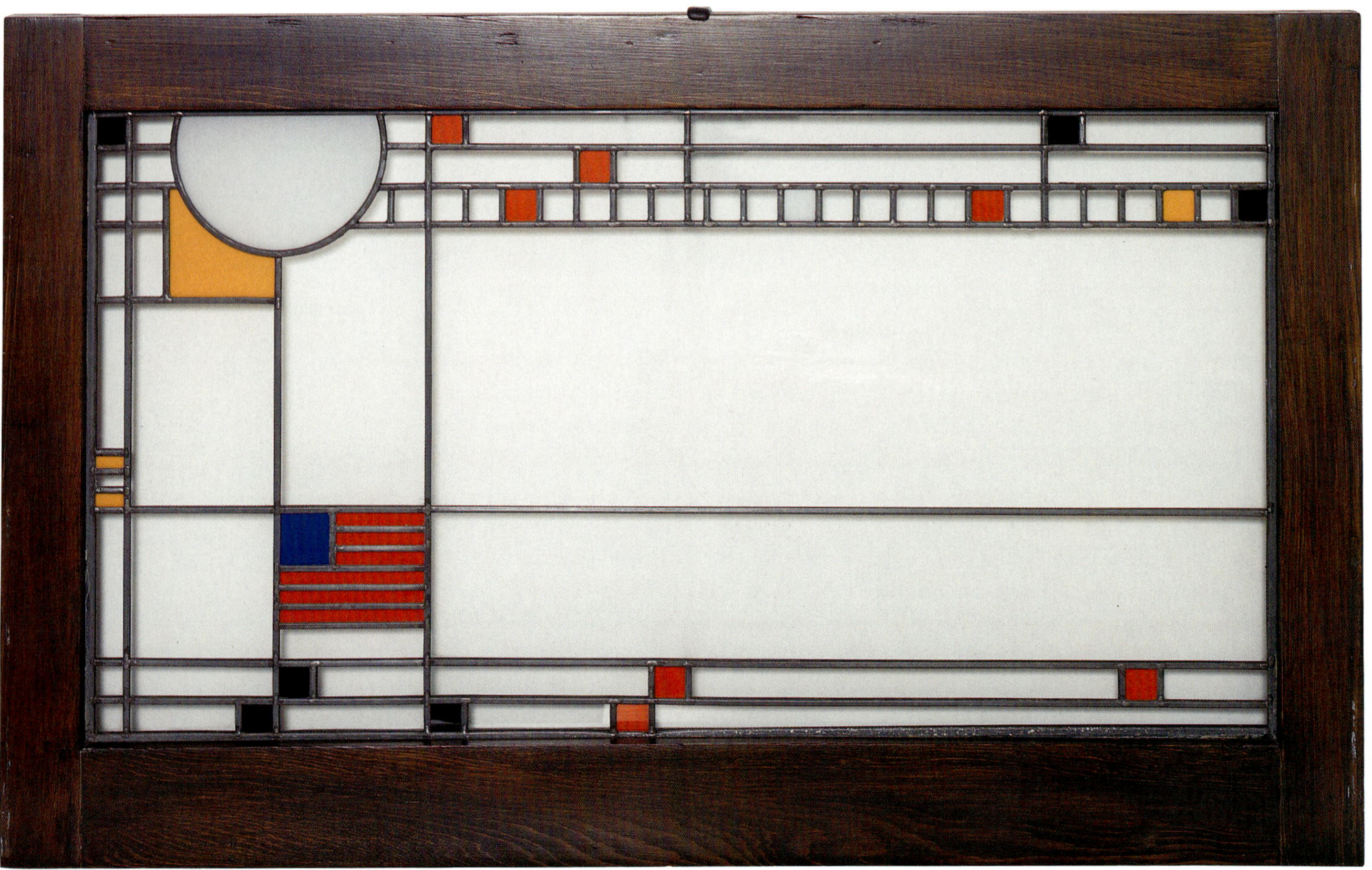

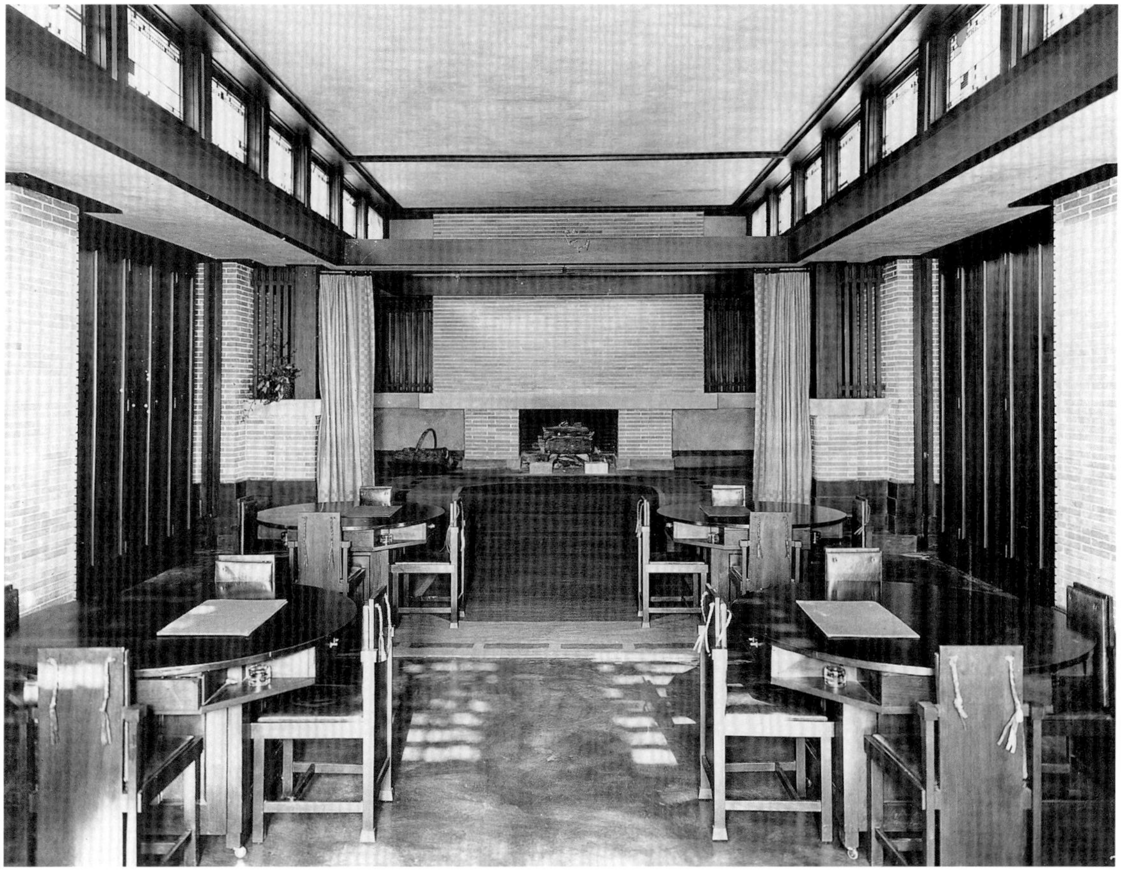

Fig. 2. Interior, J. Avery Coonley playhouse.

NOTES

1. Whitney Museum of American Art 1982, p. 8, discusses the house and its furniture. The Ward Willits house and its setting are discussed in Hitchcock 1942, pp. 42–43; the house and plans are illustrated in figs. 73–76.

2. Other chairs from the Willits dining room are in the St. Louis Art Museum, Springer 1980, p. 4; The Metropolitan Museum of Art, Davidson and Stillinger 1985, p. 195, figs. 308–309; and the Victoria and Albert Museum.

3. After operating a small factory in Salem, Massachusetts, Ayers moved to Chicago in 1887. He worked in Chicago on his own and in several partnerships until retiring in 1913; see Darling 1984, pp. 265, 358.

4. Ibid., p. 258.

5. Wright 1932, p. 145.

6. The Coonley playhouse and kindergarten is discussed in Hanks 1989, pp. 74–81. Six of the clerestory windows, including the Crawford example, are illustrated on pp. 78–79.

225.

Armchair, ca. 1914

Designed by Purcell and Elmslie (1912–1922), Minneapolis and Chicago; possibly made by George Niedecken and Company, Milwaukee
Oak, with modern corduroy upholstery
37¼ × 27⅞ × 26½ inches
1987.183

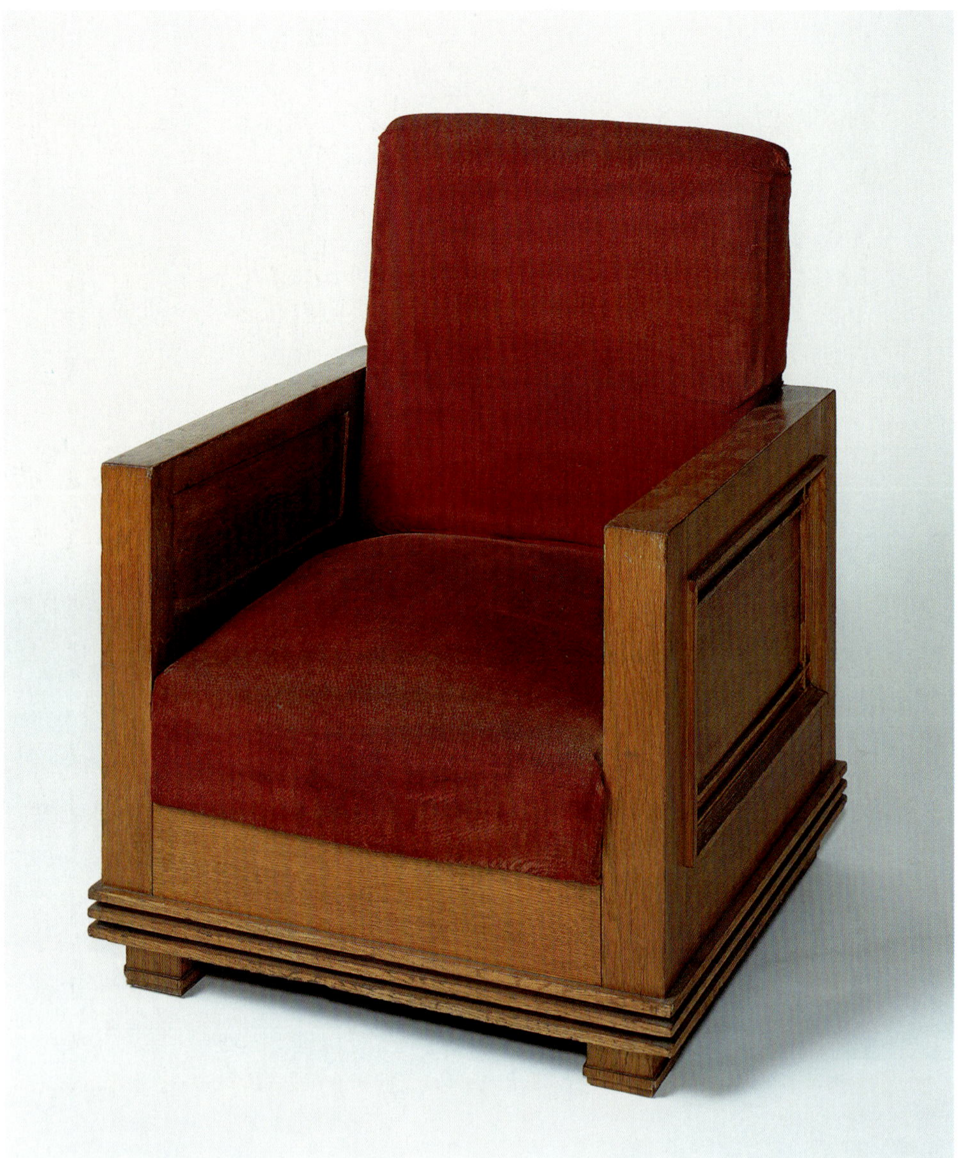

THE SQUARE ARMCHAIR in the Crawford Collection was part of an interior by Purcell and Elmslie for a Minneapolis store the firm designed in 1914. Evolving out of the earlier Minneapolis firm of Purcell and Feick, and later Purcell, Feick and Elmslie, Purcell and Elmslie was one of the more successful Midwestern architectural firms working in the Prairie style in the early twentieth century. George Grant Elmslie was born in Scotland and immigrated to Chicago with his family in 1884. By 1887, he was in the office of prominent Chicago architect Joseph Lyman Silsbee, where he worked with Frank Lloyd Wright. When Wright moved to Chicago's Adler and Sullivan firm in 1889, he encouraged Elmslie to join him there. Elmslie became chief draftsman at Adler and Sullivan in 1894 and remained with Sullivan until his firm was dissolved.

Like Elmslie, William Gray Purcell was of Scottish ancestry. Raised in suburban Oak Park, Illinois, Purcell was inspired by the work of local architects in Chicago and attended architectural school at Cornell University, graduating in 1899. He worked briefly at Sullivan's office in 1903, where he and Elmslie formed a lasting friendship. Subsequently, Purcell toured Europe with classmate George Feick, Jr. After their return in 1907, the two Cornell graduates established the firm Purcell and Feick in Feick's native Minneapolis. Elmslie joined Purcell and Feick after he left Sullivan's office in 1909. By the end of 1912, Feick, who had become progressively less central to the firm's work, withdrew from the partnership. The firm became Purcell and Elmslie, and George Elmslie returned to Chicago, where he opened a branch office.[1]

Like Wright and many of the Prairie School architects, Purcell and Elmslie designed total and interrelated environments, feeling that architecture should serve the function of the building. Elmslie's work as Sullivan's draftsman prepared him for providing decorative graphics that could be incorporated into patterns for walls and stained glass, furniture, and other three-dimensional objects. The focus behind these Prairie School firms was the creation of unified and organic environments: machines where the function of the building could be carried out.

Many of Purcell and Elmslie's commissions were residential, although they also secured public, church, and commercial projects. The armchair in the Crawford Collection was an integral element in the decorative scheme designed by the firm for Lawrence H. Lucker's Minnesota Phonograph Company, a retail store in downtown Minneapolis (fig. 1).[2] The firm had previously designed other phonograph and record stores in Chicago, San Francisco, and Kansas City.[3]

In the Prairie School manner, the firm used the square as the basic compositional theme in their designs for the company (fig. 2). This is reflected in the seat, back, and sides of the Crawford chair and in the double moldings on each side. The firm's repeated use of the square lent the chair a unified and organic appearance that related it to other furnishings and decorative elements in the salesroom.[4] The scheme extended to the exterior of the store in the illuminated stained-glass sign over the show window and entrance, which was framed by double-molded lines forming squares at each corner.

Despite Elmslie's return to Chicago and Purcell's removal to Philadelphia for a brief period in 1918, the firm survived until 1922, when illness forced Purcell to withdraw. The two architects worked independently from that time on.

Purcell and Elmslie frequently used George

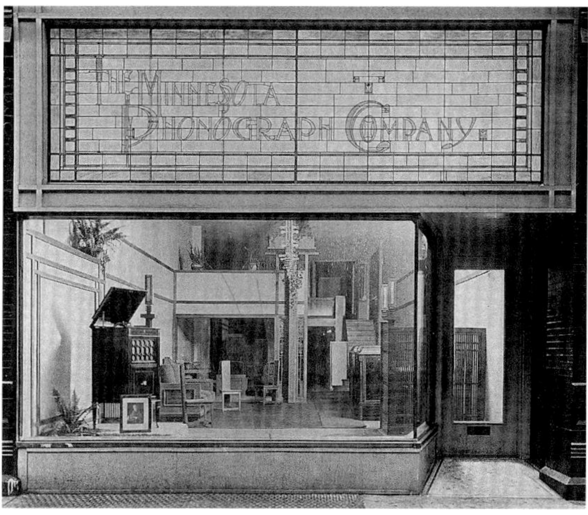

Fig. 1. Exterior of the Minnesota Phonograph Company. Photograph originally published in *The Western Architect* (January 1915).

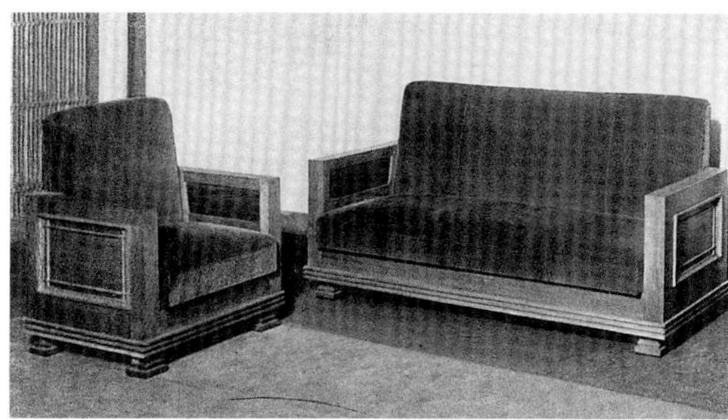

Fig. 2. Furniture for the Minnesota Phonograph Company. Photograph originally published in *The Western Architect* (January 1915).

Niedecken and Company of Milwaukee to execute their furniture designs. Since Niedecken had made the furniture for the phonograph store Purcell and Elmslie had designed in Chicago, it is likely that it also made the furniture for the Minnesota Phonograph Company.[5]

NOTES

1. For a discussion of the history and commissions of Purcell and Elmslie, see Gebhard 1965; and Hammons 1994, pp. 214–298. For a statement by the architects, see Purcell and Elmslie 1912, pp. 430–435. A photographic survey of the firm's work was published in *Western Architect;* see Purcell and Elmslie 1975, pp. 80–129.

2. Hammons 1994, p. 285, no. 42.

3. Ibid., pp. 239, 262–265. The Kansas City shop is illustrated in Purcell and Elmslie 1975, pp. 96 and 102, pls. 12 and 18. The exterior of the Chicago store is shown on p. 98, pl. 14.

4. A leaded glass lamp from the Minnesota Phonograph Company is illustrated and discussed in Hammons 1994, pp. 264 and 285, no. 42. The same lamp form is illustrated in Purcell and Elmslie 1975, p. 102, pl. 18.

5. Hammons 1994, p. 265.

Greene and Greene

MUCH OF THE well-known work by the Pasadena architectural firm of brothers Charles Sumner Greene and Henry Mather Greene was contemporary with—and related to—the Prairie-style houses of Frank Lloyd Wright (see nos. 223–224).[1] Both Wright and Greene and Greene either designed or selected the furniture and accessories for their houses and were strongly influenced by Japanese design: Wright from trips to Japan, and the Greenes from viewing the extraordinary open-frame Japanese temple at the 1893 World's Columbian Exposition in Chicago.

Pasadena, just outside flourishing Los Angeles, developed as a resort community of expensive second homes. With their fine materials and exquisite craftsmanship, Greene and Greene furnishings, executed under the close supervision of Charles Greene, reflect the interest in high-quality artisanry encouraged by Louis Comfort Tiffany, while the designs were influenced by the simple lines and honest construction promoted by Gustav Stickley and the American Arts and Crafts movement.

James A. Culbertson, a benefactor of the California Institute of Technology, commissioned a house by Greene and Greene in 1903. It began as an adaptation of an English Tudor country home furnished with Craftsman furniture and Rookwood pottery. With later additions by Greene and Greene, the Culbertson house and its furnishings evolved into an eclectic assemblage. This wall lantern (no. 226) was one of a pair designed by Greene and Greene for a 1906 expansion of the house. The elegant Japanese-style corner brackets reflect the exacting workmanship of Peter Hall, who began collaborating with Charles Greene on furniture and interior woodwork designs as early as 1903. Peter and John Hall had established their woodworking company in Pasadena to cater to the design standards established by the Greenes. The Asian look of the lamp's frame is enhanced by the elegant asymmetrical floral leading of its amber glass panes, which were crafted by Emil Lange, maker of a number of lamps and windows for Greene and Greene.[2]

The Crawford sideboard table (no. 227) was designed for the home of Charles M. Pratt.[3] Its rectangular shape and exposed construction express the Arts and Crafts furniture aesthetic, but this is softened by the graceful lobed ends of its top, the "rising cloud"-shaped stretcher characteristic of Greene and Greene, and the luxurious materials of walnut and ebony. The refined drawer handles —simple walnut bars with inlaid square pegs and a central rectangle of ebony—are seen on other examples of Greene and Greene case-design work. The overhanging table top suggests the low, wide eaves of Greene and Greene bungalow rooflines, while the table's small scale, rich materials, and exacting craftsmanship suggest its Asian design inspiration. The Pratt house (fig. 1) was relatively small, with a simple and easy-circulating floor plan that suited the wealthy Pratts, who were winter residents in Nordhoff (now Ojai), California. Because the Pratts entertained guests at a nearby hotel, the dining room of the house was small, and they did not require a

226.

Wall Lantern, ca. 1907

Designed by Greene and Greene (1893–1922); glass by Emil Lange; woodwork by Peter Hall Manufacturing Company (1906–1923), Pasadena, California
Leaded glass, mahogany, and ebony
17¾ × 8 × 7¼ inches
1985.320

large sideboard with spacious storage cabinets, but rather drawers fitted to store silver flatware. The small sideboard table reflects the informal southern California lifestyle.

NOTES

1. Bowman 1990, p. 46, provides a general history of Greene and Greene.

2. The mate to the Crawford wall lantern is in the Museum of Fine Arts, Houston. Descriptions, discussions, floor plans, and illustrations of the James A. Culbertson house are presented in Makinson 1977, pp. 65–69, 122–125. Furnishings are described, discussed, and illustrated in Makinson 1979, pp. 17, 52–55, 103.

3. The Pratt table is illustrated in Trapp 1993, p. 168, fig. 123. The Pratt house is discussed in Hirschl and Adler Galleries 1989, p. 107.

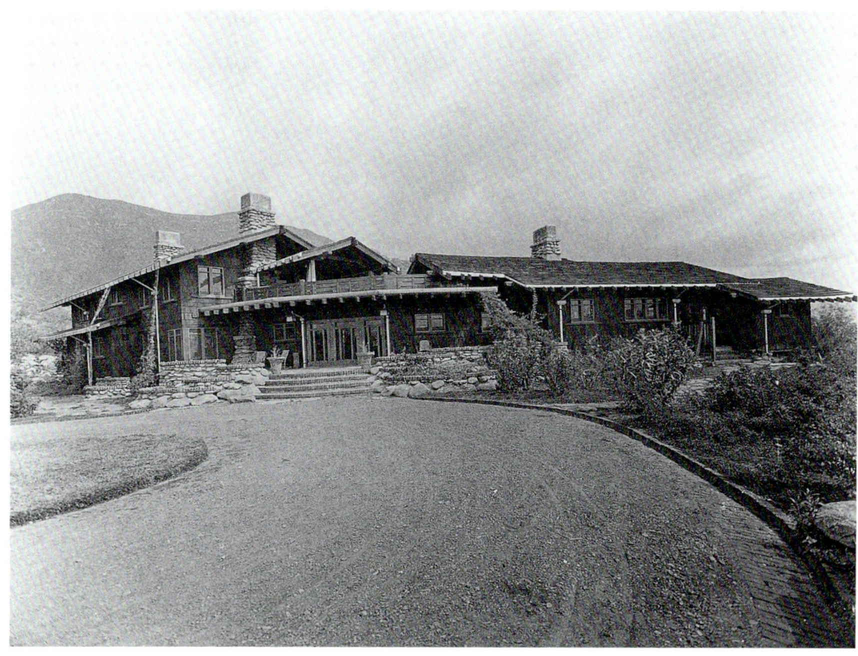

Fig. 1. Pratt house. Photograph by Leroy Hulbert.

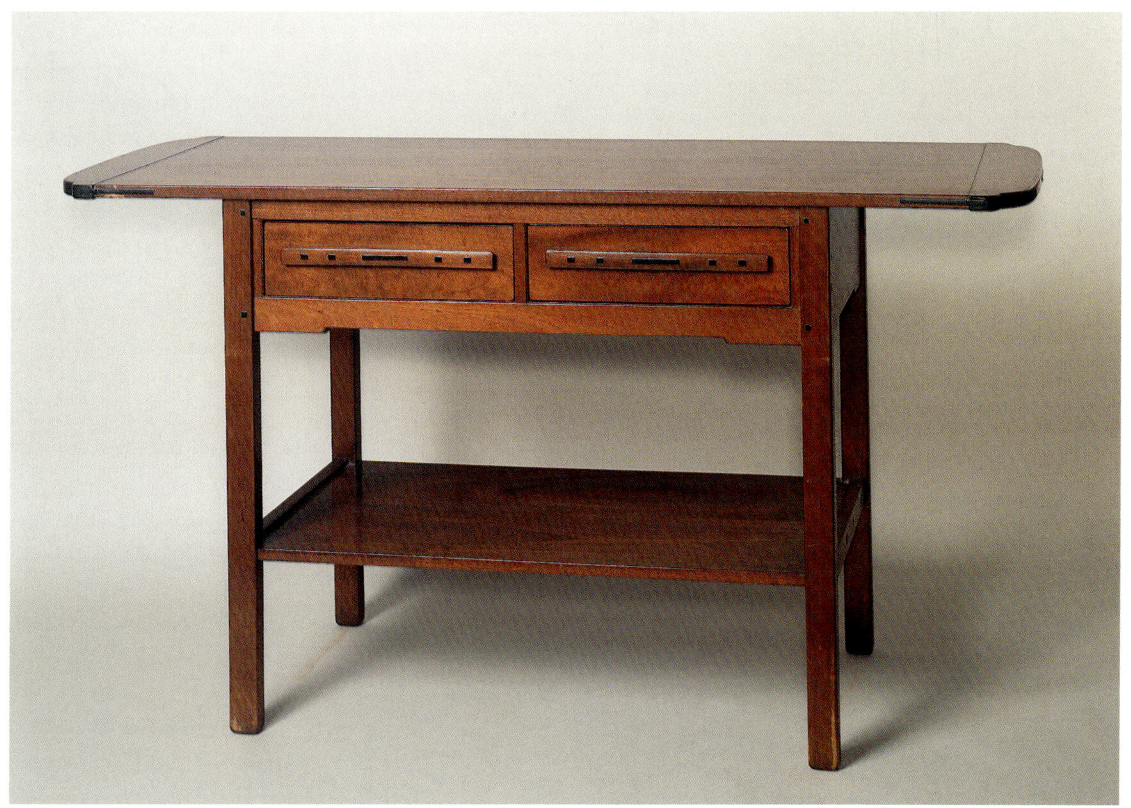

227.

Sideboard Table,
ca. 1909

Designed by Greene and Greene (1893–1922); made by Peter Hall Manufacturing Company, Pasadena, California
Walnut and ebony
36 × 64½ × 21¼ inches
Mark: Branded beneath lower shelf and beneath sides of top, *His/Sumner/True/Greene/Mark*
1986.194

Glossary

art glass A term introduced by manufacturers in the 1870s for colored glassware, generally decorated and sometimes free-blown, that was popular in the late nineteenth century.

beading In metal, wood, or ceramics, a series of small carved beads used for edges, rims, and surface decorations.

Belleek Thinly potted, ivory-colored porcelain with an iridescent glaze. The glaze was introduced by McBirney and Company in Belleek, Ireland, and the town's name has become a generic term for this type of ware.

biscuit ware Ceramic ware that has been fired once but is not yet glazed.

blown glass Glassware created by blowing air into a quantity of molten glass, either by mouth with a blowpipe or by machine.

boss In furniture, ceramics, metals, and other materials, an applied ornamental stud or knob, sometimes used to hide a structural element.

bright-cut A type of decoration on silver in which the designs, usually geometric, are sharply engraved, producing a sparkling effect. First became popular in the late eighteenth century, and again in the 1880s with American Japanese-taste silver and silver plate.

Brilliant Cut glass A term applied by collectors and historians to the popular, deeply cut lead glass tablewares produced from the Centennial to the beginning of World War I; popularly called Rich Cut glass.

britannia metal An alloy of tin with copper and antimony having the appearance of pewter and often used as a cheap substitute for it.

cabochon In jewelry or metalwork, a precious or semiprecious stone with a smooth domed surface rather than facets.

cabriole leg A furniture leg with an S-shaped curve, convex at the top and concave at the bottom. This type of leg came into general use in the early eighteenth century.

cartoon A full-scale preparatory drawing for a tapestry or painting.

caryatid A draped female figure used as a column to support an entablature.

cased glass Glass covered with a thin layer of differently colored glass; the outer layer may be cut through to show the color underneath. A clear blank covered with colored glass and then cut with a design is called colored cut-to-clear glass.

case furniture Furniture designed to contain something; for example, bookcases, cupboards, and bureaus.

celadon In ceramics, a translucent green glaze originally developed in China and later used in Europe and America.

champlevé Enamelware in which patterns are grooved out and filled in with colored enamels. The resulting thin raised lines are similar to cloisonné.

chasing In metalwork, decoration made with a hammer and small punches.

chinoiserie A European style of decoration that reflects Chinese art or decorative motifs, particularly referring to the intricate style popular in late seventeenth- and eighteenth-century Europe.

chromolithography In ceramics, color lithographic transfer printing.

clay body The type or mixture of clays used in making a ceramic piece.

crocket In architecture or furniture, an ornament on the inclined sides of pinnacles or finials, or projecting from spires, gables, etc., usually in the form of buds or curled leaves.

en suite In ceramics, glass, silver, or furniture, a matching set.

escutcheon A protective or ornamental shield or border around a keyhole on a piece of furniture or door.

étagère A parlor furniture form with shelves to hold small decorative objects backed by a mirror.

faience Tin-glazed earthenware; or in France, a term for earthenware.

flambé glaze In ceramics, a Chinese glaze of a copper-red color with gray, purple, lavender, and opalescent blue streaks.

flint glass Glass with a high lead oxide content; lead glass. Rich Cut glass is generally made with lead; the metal in the glass gives it a brilliant, sparkling quality.

gadroon In furniture and silver, decorative fluting or reeding that approaches an oval form.

garniture An ornament or decoration, usually used on a mantel or cabinet top.

gimp A flat, narrow braid used as a decorative finish for upholstery.

girandole A candlestick or candelabrum hung with prisms, or a wall-hung lighting fixture.

glass blank A piece of lead glass that has been formed by blowing or molding, but has not yet been decorated by cutting or engraving.

hard-paste porcelain True porcelain with kaolin added to harden and whiten the porcelain, as opposed to artificial or soft-paste porcelain, which relies on other materials, like soapstone, as whitening and hardening agents.

hobstar In Rich Cut glass, a star pattern that was characteristic of American glass beginning in the 1880s.

holloware Vessels that have significant depth and volume, such as cups, bowls, and vases, as distinguished from flatware, which includes plates, platters, and eating and serving utensils.

jacquard weave A variegated weave made on a jacquard loom; used for brocade, tapestry, and damask.

japanning Covering wood or metal furniture with a highly varnished surface in imitation of the Japanese lacquerwork that was introduced in England in the 1650s.

jardiniere A large vase for displaying flowers.

lacy pressed glass A twentieth-century term for pressed glass with a stippled background surrounding the pattern. The earliest pressed glass generally imitated the geometric patterns of cut glass, while lacy pressed glass might include elements such as eagles, flowers, or fruit in the design.

lime glass Glass containing a substantial amount of lime, used in most commercial glass products.

marquetry Patterns of various woods and other materials which are formed into veneers then applied to the surfaces of furniture.

niello A method of decorating metal using incised designs filled with a deep black metallic alloy of sulfur with silver, copper, or lead.

ogee In furniture and architecture, an S-shaped curve, or a molding with an S-shaped profile.

oinochoë A classical Greek jug resembling a pitcher, with a handle attached at the lip rim and the shoulder.

ormolu Brass made to look like gold.

ovolo A rounded convex molding or quarter-round molding.

parian ware A white or ivory porcelain body that has a smoother unglazed surface and lower firing temperature than regular porcelain; the marble-like surface was used primarily for statuary and ornamental pieces. The name is derived from the Greek island of Paros, which provided marble for classical sculptures.

pâte-sur-pâte In ceramics, low-relief decoration built up of slip. Usually white slip is applied with a brush to a colored or dark body.

plinth In the display of sculpture, a square block used as a base.

pontil mark When handworking glass, a round hollow mark left after breaking off the pontil or iron rod by which the glass is handled during its shaping.

pressed glass Glass formed by machine pressing rather than blowing, a process invented around 1825. Pressed glass required less skill, was more consistent, and was substantially cheaper than blown glass.

Queen's ware A generic term for cream-colored or white earthenware.

repoussé In metalwork, a type of chasing in which relief decoration is made by hammering on the reverse side.

scroddled ware Different colors of earthenware clay combined to form a marbleized body.

silvergilt Gilded silver.

slip Liquefied clay, often applied in a contrasting color as decoration on pottery.

slip-casting When slip, or liquefied clay, is poured into a plaster-of-paris mold, the mold absorbs the water from the slip so that the clay can be removed at a leather-hard consistency and then dried and fired.

strapwork A decorative design of crossing and interlacing bands.

taboret French term for stool; also tabouret or taborette.

through tenons Construction rails that extend through the sides or fronts of case-furniture forms.

tracery In architecture or on decorative objects, decoration of branching or interweaving lines.

trifid Divided into three lobes.

wainscotting Wood paneling; or in furniture, solid panels enclosed in framing.

Bibliography

Adamson 1992
Adamson, Jeremy. "Wakefield Rattan Company." *The Magazine Antiques* 142 (August 1992): 214–221.

Adamson 1993
———. *American Wicker: Woven Furniture from 1850 to 1930.* Washington, D.C., and New York: National Museum of American Art with Rizzoli International Publications, 1993.

Aikman 1963
Aikman, Lonelle. *We, the People; the Story of the United States Capitol, Its Past and Its Promise.* Washington, D.C.: United States Capitol Historical Society, 1963.

Altman and Altman 1987
Altman, Seymour, and Violet Altman. *The Book of Buffalo Pottery.* West Chester, Pa.: Schiffer Publishing, 1987.

Ames 1973
Ames, Kenneth L. "George Henkels, Nineteenth-Century Philadelphia Cabinetmaker." *The Magazine Antiques* 104 (October 1973): 641–650.

Ames 1974
———. "The Battle of the Sideboards." *Winterthur Portfolio* 9 (1974): 1–27.

Ames 1975
———. "Grand Rapids Furniture at the Time of the Centennial." *Winterthur Portfolio* 10 (1975): 23–50.

Ames 1976
———. "What is the Neo-Grec?" *Nineteenth Century* 2 (summer 1976): 12–21.

Ames 1992
———. *Death in the Dining Room & Other Tales of Victorian Culture.* Philadelphia: Temple University Press, 1992.

"Architects Weed" 1961
"Architects Weed, Garden Die." *Architectural Forum* 115 (November 1961): 16.

Arnest 1975
Arnest, Barbara M., ed. *The Van Briggle Story.* Colorado Springs, Colo.: Colorado Springs Fine Arts Center, 1975.

Art and Antiques 1982
Art and Antiques. *Nineteenth Century Furniture: Innovation, Revival and Reform.* New York: Art and Antiques, 1982.

"Artistry in Horn" 1984
"Artistry in Horn." *Americana* 12 (September/October 1984): 93–94.

Bacot 1987
Bacot, H. Parrott. *Nineteenth Century Lighting: Candle-powered Devices, 1783–1883.* West Chester, Pa.: Schiffer Publishing, 1987.

Barber, "Pioneer of China Painting," 1895
Barber, Edwin Atlee. "The Pioneer of China Painting in America." *New England Magazine* (September 1895): 33–48.

Barber, June, 1895
———. "Historical Sketch of the Green Point Porcelain Works. I. Charles Cartlidge and William Ridgway." *The Clay Worker* 23 (June 1895): 688–689.

Barber, July, 1895
———. "Historical Sketch of the Green Point Porcelain Works. II. Establishment of Works and First Products." *The Clay Worker* 24 (July 1895): 23–25.

Barber, August, 1895
———. "Historical Sketch of the Green Point Porcelain Works. III. Decorators and their Work." *The Clay Worker* 24 (August 1895): 120–122.

Barber, September, 1895
———. "Historical Sketch of the Green Point Porcelain Works. IV. Josiah Jones, Modeler." *The Clay Worker* 24 (September 1895): 226–227.

Barber, October, 1895
———. "Historical Sketch of the Green Point Porcelain Works. V. Portrait Modeling." *The Clay Worker* 24 (October 1895): 330–332.

Barber 1898
———. "Pioneers in American Pottery, III: James Bennett, Edwin Bennett, Rockingham Ware." *China Glass & Pottery Review* 2 (April 1, 1898): 33–38.

Barber, *Marks,* 1976/Barber, *Pottery,* 1976
———. *Marks of American Potters.* 1904. With *The Pottery and Porcelain of the United States.* 1909. Reprint. New York: Feingold and Lewis, 1976.

Barret 1958
Barret, Richard Carter. *Bennington Pottery and Porcelain: A Guide to Identification.* New York: Bonanza Books, 1958.

Becker 1968
Becker, Carl M. "Miles Greenwood." In *For the Union: Ohio Leaders in the Civil War.* Edited by Kenneth W. Wheeler. Columbus, Ohio: Ohio State University Press, 1968, pp. 259–319.

Becker 1969
———. "The Ironmaster and the Sculptor." *Bulletin,* Cincinnati Historical Society 27 (1969): 123–137.

Belden 1980
Belden, Louise Conway. *Marks of American Silversmiths in the Ineson-Bissell Collection.* Charlottesville, Va.: University Press of Virginia, 1980.

Bennett 1992
Bennett, Anna Gray. *Five Centuries of Tapestry from the Fine Arts Museums of San Francisco.* San Francisco: Fine Arts Museums of San Francisco and Chronicle Books, 1992.

Bevan 1949
Bevan, Edith Rossiter. "Druid Hill, Country Seat of the Rogers and Buchanan Families." *Maryland Historical Magazine* 64 (September 1949): 190–199.

Bining 1936
Bining, William. "The Glass Industry in Western Pennsylvania, 1797–1857." *Western Pennsylvania Historical Magazine* 19 (December 1936): 255–268.

Bishop 1972
Bishop, Robert Charles. *Centuries and Styles of the American Chair, 1640–1970.* New York: Dutton, 1972.

Blasberg 1979
Blasberg, Robert W., with Carol L. Bohdan. *Fulper Art Pottery: An Aesthetic Appreciation, 1909–1929.* New York: Jordan-Volpe Gallery, 1979.

Boehle 1990
Boehle, Rose Angela. *Maria Longworth Nichols.* Dayton, Ohio: Landfall Press, 1990.

Boggess and Boggess 1977
Boggess, Bill, and Louise Boggess. *American Brilliant Cut Glass.* New York: Crown Publishers, 1977.

Bogue 1968
Bogue, Dorothy McGraw. *The Van Briggle Story.* Colorado Springs, Colo.: Dentan-Berkeland Print Co., 1968.

Boston Athenaeum 1981
Boston Athenaeum. *Arthur J. Stone Handwrought Silver, 1901–1937.* Boston: Library of the Boston Athenaeum, 1981.

Bowman 1990
Bowman, Leslie Greene. *American Arts & Crafts: Virtue in Design.* Los Angeles: Los Angeles County Museum of Art, 1990.

Brooklyn Museum 1979
Brooklyn Museum. *The American Renaissance: 1876–1917.* Brooklyn: Brooklyn Museum, 1979.

Brooklyn Museum 1988
———. *Masterpieces in the Brooklyn Museum.* New York: Harry N. Abrams and the Brooklyn Museum, 1988.

Bruhn 1979
Bruhn, Thomas P. *American Decorative Tiles, 1870–1930.* Storrs, Conn.: University of Connecticut, William Benton Museum of Art, 1979.

Carpenter 1997
Carpenter, Charles H., Jr. *Gorham Silver.* San Francisco: Alan Wofsy Fine Arts, 1997.

Carpenter and Carpenter 1997
Carpenter, Charles H., Jr., with Mary Grace Carpenter. *Tiffany Silver.* San Francisco: Alan Wofsy Fine Arts, 1997.

Carron 1992
Carron, Christian G. Introduction to *Limbert Arts and Crafts Furniture: The Complete 1903 Catalog.* New York: Dover Publications, 1992.

Carrott 1978
Carrott, Richard G. *The Egyptian Revival: Its Sources, Monuments and Meaning, 1808–1858.* Berkeley and Los Angeles: University of California Press, 1978.

Catalog of Roycroft 1981
Catalog of Roycroft Furniture and Other Things. 1906. Reprint. New York: Turn of the Century Editions, 1981.

Cathers 1981
Cathers, David. *Furniture of the American Arts and Crafts Movement: Stickley and Roycroft Mission Oak.* New York: New American Library, 1981.

Champney 1968
Champney, Freeman. *Art and Glory: The Story of Elbert Hubbard.* New York: Crown Publishers, 1968.

Chase Brothers and Company, ca. 1855
Chase Brothers and Company. *Illustrated Catalogue of Chase Brothers & Co.'s Useful and Ornamental Bronzed Iron Goods, Iron Railings & C. Manufactory and Ware Rooms, No. 22 Congress Street corner of Post Office Avenue.* Boston: [ca. 1855].

Cincinnati Art Museum 1976
Cincinnati Art Museum. *The Ladies, God Bless 'Em: The Woman's Art Movement in Cincinnati in the Nineteenth Century.* Cincinnati: Cincinnati Art Museum, 1976.

Cist 1859
Cist, Charles. *Sketches and Statistics of Cincinnati in 1859.* Cincinnati: Moore, Wilstach, Keys & Co., 1859.

Clark 1972
Clark, Robert Judson, ed. *The Arts and Crafts Movement in America, 1876–1916.* Princeton, N.J. and Chicago: The Art Museum, Princeton University, and the Art Institute of Chicago, distributed by Princeton University Press, 1972.

Cochran 1953
Cochran, Thomas C. *Railroad Leaders, 1845–1890: The Business Mind in Action.* Cambridge, Mass.: Harvard University Press, 1953.

Cook 1878
Cook, Clarence. *The House Beautiful: Essays on Beds and Tables, Stools and Candlesticks.* New York: Scribner, Armstrong and Company, 1878.

Cooke 1980
Cooke, Edward S., Jr. "The Boston Furniture Industry in 1880." *Old-Time New England* 70 (1980): 82–98.

D. Cooper 1991
Cooper, Deborah. "Wooton Patent Desks." *Woodworking* (March–April 1991): 52–55.

W. Cooper 1993
Cooper, Wendy A. *Classical Taste in America 1800–1840.* Baltimore and New York: Baltimore Museum of Art and Abbeville Press, 1993.

Cooper-Hewitt 1987
Cooper-Hewitt, National Design Museum. *American Art Pottery.* New York: Cooper-Hewitt, National Design Museum, Smithsonian Institution, 1987.

Corning Museum of Glass 1996
Corning Museum of Glass. *Annual Report.* Corning, N.Y.: Corning Museum of Glass, 1996.

Costa 1880
Costa, Isaac, comp. *Gopsill's Philadelphia City Directory for 1880.* Philadelphia: James Gopsill, 1880.

Craftsman 5, 1904
"Structure and Ornament in the Craftsman Workshops." *The Craftsman* 5 (January 1904): 395–396.

Craftsman 21, 1911
"A New Idea in Interior Decoration: Illustrated by W. F. Curtis." *Craftsman* 21 (December 1911): 252–259.

Craftsman 22, 1912
"Color Decoration for Wood." *Craftsman* 22 (September 1912): 672–675.

Cramer 1992
Cramer, Diana. "Egyptian Revival Style by Gorham." *Silver* 25 (March–April 1992): 7–9.

Crystal Palace 1970
The Crystal Palace Exhibition Illustrated Catalogue London 1851. 1851. Reprint. New York: Dover Publications, 1970.

J. Curtis 1902
Curtis, Jessie Kingsley. "Chests, Chairs and Settles." *The Craftsman* 2 (September 1902): 296–303.

P. Curtis 1972
Curtis, Phillip H. "The Production of Tucker Porcelain, 1826–1838: A Re-evaluation." In *Ceramics in America.* Winterthur Conference Report, 1972. Edited by Ian M. G. Quimby. Charlottesville, Va.: University Press of Virginia, for The Henry Francis du Pont Winterthur Museum, pp. 339–374.

Curtis and Curtis 1974
Curtis, Will, and Jane Curtis. *Antique Wood Stoves: Artistry in Iron.* Ashville, Maine: Cobblesmith, 1974.

Dale 1986
Dale, Sharon. *Frederick Hurten Rhead: An English Potter in America.* Erie, Pa.: Erie Art Museum, 1986.

Darling 1977
Darling, Sharon S. *Chicago Metalsmiths.* Chicago: Chicago Historical Society, 1977.

Darling 1979
———. *Chicago Ceramics and Glass.* Chicago: Chicago Historical Society, 1979.

Darling 1984
———. *Chicago Furniture: Art, Craft and Industry, 1833–1983.* Chicago, New York, and London: Chicago Historical Society with W. W. Norton and Company, 1984.

Darling 1989
———. *Teco: Art Pottery of the Prairie School.* Erie, Pa.: Erie Art Museum, 1989.

Davidson 1969
Davidson, Marshall B. *The American Heritage History of Antiques from the Civil War to World War I.* New York: American Heritage Publishing Co., 1969.

Davidson and Stillinger 1985
Davidson, Marshall B., and Elizabeth Stillinger. *The American Wing at The Metropolitan Museum of Art.* New York: The Metropolitan Museum of Art and Alfred A. Knopf, 1985.

Davies 1977
Davies, Jane B. "Gothic Revival Furniture of Alexander J. Davis." *The Magazine Antiques* 111 (May 1977): 1014–1027.

Dayton Art Institute 1983
Dayton Art Institute. *E. Colonna.* Dayton, Ohio: Dayton Art Institute, 1983.

Denker 1989
Denker, Ellen Paul. *Lenox China: Celebrating a Century of Quality, 1889–1989.* Trenton, N.J.: Lenox China and the New Jersey State Museum, 1989.

Detroit Institute of Arts 1983
Detroit Institute of Arts. *The Quest for Unity: American Art Between the World's Fairs, 1876–1893.* Detroit, Mich.: Detroit Institute of Arts, 1983.

Di Bartolomeo 1975
Di Bartolomeo, Robert E. "Hobbs Brockunier's Fancy Glass." *The Magazine Antiques* 107 (March 1975): 494–501.

Dietz 1980
Dietz, Ulysses. "Century of Revivals: Nineteenth-Century American Furniture from the Collection of the Newark Museum." *Newark Museum Quarterly* 31 (spring–summer 1980, published 1983).

Dietz 1986
———. "A Major New Piece in the Jelliff Puzzle." *The Magazine Antiques* 129 (May 1986): 1096–1099.

Dolge 1911
Dolge, Alfred. *Pianos and their Makers.* Covina, Calif.: Covina Publishing Company, 1911.

Donnell 1936
Donnell, Edna. "A. J. Davis and the Gothic Revival." *Metropolitan Museum Studies* 5, part 2 (1936): 183–233.

Downing 1969
Downing, A. J. *The Architecture of Country Houses.* 1850. Reprint. New York: Dover Publications, 1969.

Downs 1948
Downs, Joseph. "John Henry Belter and Company." *The Magazine Antiques* 54 (September 1948): 166–168.

Draper, March–April, 1991
Draper, Elaine. "The Gorham Years." *Silver* 24 (March–April 1991): 22–24.

Draper, May–June, 1991
———. "The Wilkinson Influence." *Silver* 24 (May–June 1991): 13–15.

Dubrow and Dubrow 1982
Dubrow, Elaine, and Richard Dubrow. *Furniture Made in America, 1875–1905.* Exton, Pa.: Schiffer Publishing, 1982.

Dunbar 1935
Dunbar, Edith Flanders. *The Flanders Family from Europe to America.* Rutland, Vt.: Tuttle Publishing Co., 1935

Duncan, Eidelberg, and Harris 1989
Duncan, Alastair, Martin Eidelberg, and Neil Harris. *Masterworks of Louis Comfort Tiffany.* New York: Harry N. Abrams, 1989.

Durbin 1968
Durbin, Louise. "Samuel Kirk, Nineteenth-Century Silversmith." *The Magazine Antiques* 94 (December 1968): 868–873.

Eastlake 1969
Eastlake, Charles L. *Hints on Household Taste In Furniture, Upholstery and Other Details.* 1878. Reprint. New York: Dover Publications, 1969.

Eidelberg 1968
Eidelberg, Martin. "Tiffany Favrile Pottery: A New Study of a Few Known Facts." *Connoisseur* 169 (September 1968): 57–61.

Eidelberg 1990
———. "Tiffany's Early Glass Vessels." *The Magazine Antiques* 137 (February 1990): 502–515.

Elder and Stokes 1987
Elder, William Voss III, and Jayne E. Stokes, *American Furniture, 1680–1880, from the Collection of the Baltimore Museum of Art.* Baltimore: Baltimore Museum of Art, 1987.

Ellis 1992
Ellis, Anita J. *Rookwood Pottery: The Glorious Gamble.* New York: Rizzoli International and Cincinnati Art Museum, 1992.

Evans 1987
Evans, Paul. *Art Pottery of the United States.* New York: Feingold & Lewis Publishing, 1987.

Fales 1968
Fales, Martha Gandy. "Obadiah Rich, Boston Silversmith," *The Magazine Antiques* 94 (October 1968): 565–569.

Fales 1973
———. *Early American Silver.* Rev. ed. New York: E. P. Dutton & Co., 1973.

Fales 1982
———. "The Brittania Cup." *The Magazine Antiques* 122 (July 1982): 156–158.

Fales 1986
———. "Rich Silver." *Silver* 19 (July–August 1986): 8–13.

Fales 1995
———. *Jewelry in America: 1600–1900.* Woodbridge: Antique Collectors' Club, 1995.

Farrar 1974
Farrar, Estelle Sinclaire. *H. P. Sinclaire, Jr., Glassmaker, Vol. I.* Garden City, N.Y.: Farrar Books, 1974.

Farrar and Spillman 1979
Farrar, Estelle Sinclaire, and Jane Shadel Spillman. *The Complete Cut and Engraved Glass of Corning.* New York: Crown Publishers, 1979.

Faude 1975
Faude, Wilson H. "Associated Artists and the American Renaissance in the Decorative Arts." *Winterthur Portfolio* 10 (1975): 101–130.

Fauster 1971
Fauster, Carl U. "Louis Vaupel, Master Glass Engraver." *The Magazine Antiques* 99 (May 1971): 696–701.

Fauster 1979
———. *Libbey Glass Since 1818.* Toledo, Ohio: Len Beach Press, 1979.

Feller 1988
Feller, John Quentin. *Dorflinger: America's Finest Glass, 1852–1921.* Marietta, Ohio: Antique Publications, 1988.

Fennimore 1996
Fennimore, Donald L. *Metalwork in Early America: Copper and its Alloys from the Winterthur Collection.* Winterthur, Del.: The Henry Francis du Pont Winterthur Museum, 1996.

Fifield 1987
Fifield, Barringer. *Seeing St. Louis.* St. Louis: Washington University, 1987.

Finkel 1980
Finkel, Kenneth. *Nineteenth-Century Photography in Philadelphia.* New York: Dover Publications, with the Library Company of Philadelphia, 1980.

Fiske, ca. 1864–1870
Fiske, J. W. *Manufacturers of Fountains, Vases, Iron and Wire Railings of All Kinds, Iron Stable Furniture, Copper Weather Vanes, Emblematic Signs and All Kinds of Garden and Cemetery Ornaments.* New York: J. W. Fiske, [ca. 1864–1870].

Fiske 1874
———. *Illustrated Catalogue of Zinc Statuary Manufactured by J. W. Fiske.* New York: J. W. Fiske, 1874.

Fiske, ca. 1874–1892
———. *Illustrated Price List of Vases manufactured by J. W. Fiske, 21 and 23 Barclay Street and 26 and 28 Park Place, Cor. Church St., New York.* New York: J. W. Fiske, [ca. 1874–1892].

Fitzgerald 1982
Fitzgerald, Oscar P. *Three Centuries of American Furniture.* Englewood Cliffs, N.J.: Prentice-Hall, 1982.

FitzPatrick 1957
FitzPatrick, Nancy R. "The Chesapeake Pottery Company." *Maryland Historical Magazine* 52 (March 1957): 65–71.

Flayderman 1930
Flayderman, Philip. *Colonial Furniture, Silver and Decorations.* New York: American Art Association, Anderson Galleries, 1930.

Freeman 1966
Freeman, John Crosby. *The Forgotten Rebel: Gustav Stickley and His Craftsman Mission Furniture.* Watkins Glen, N.Y.: Century House, 1966.

Frelinghuysen 1989
Frelinghuysen, Alice Cooney. *American Porcelain, 1770–1920.* New York: The Metropolitan Museum of Art, 1989.

Gardner Museum 1991
Gardner Museum. *A Century of Gardner Sterling Silver.* Gardner, Mass.: Gardner Museum, 1991.

Gates and Ormerod 1982
Gates, William C., Jr., and Dana E. Ormerod. "The East Liverpool Pottery District: Identification of Manufacturers and Marks." *Historical Archaeology* 16 (1982): 1–11 and 115–127.

Gayle 1974
Gayle, Margot. *Cast-Iron Architecture in New York: A Photographic Survey.* New York: Dover Publications, 1974.

Gebhard 1965
Gebhard, David. "Purcell and Elmslie, Architects." *Prairie School Review* 2 (First Quarter, 1965): 5–15.

"George Washington" 1982
"George Washington: American Superhero." *Antiques and The Arts Weekly* (January 1, 1982): 20.

Getz 1988
Getz, Gail M. "John Fritz Ironmaster: A Testimonial in Silver." *Silver* 21 (January–February 1988): 8–11.

Gladstone 1977
Gladstone, Valerie. "Design." *Art News* 96 (June 1997): 92–94.

Glazier and Filley 1989
Glazier, Ira A. and William P. Filley. *Germans to America: Lists of Passengers Arriving at U.S. Ports. Vol. 5 May 1853–Oct. 1853.* Wilmington, Del.: Scholarly Resource, 1989.

Goldsborough 1975
Goldsborough, Jennifer Faulds. *Maryland Silver in the Collection of the Baltimore Museum of Art.* Baltimore: Baltimore Museum of Art, 1975.

Goldsborough 1984
———. *Silver in Maryland.* Baltimore: Maryland Historical Society, 1984.

Gowans 1976
Gowans, Alan. *Images of American Living: Four Centuries of Architecture and Furniture as Cultural Expression.* New York: Harper & Row, 1976.

N. Gray 1994
Gray, Nina. "Leon Marcotte: Cabinetmaker and Interior Decorator." *American Furniture* (1994): 49–72.

S. Gray 1983
Gray, Stephen, ed. *Arts and Crafts Furniture: Shop of the Crafters at Cincinnati.* 1906. Reprint. New York: Turn of the Century Editions, 1983.

S. Gray 1990
———. *Charles P. Limbert Company, Cabinet Makers, Grand Rapids, Michigan.* Rev. ed. New York: Turn of the Century Editions, 1990.

C. Green 1937
Green, Charles W. "A Most Important Discovery at Sandwich." *The Magazine Antiques* 32 (August 1937): 58–60.

R. Green 1972
Green, Robert Alan. "The Silversmiths of the City of New York (1841–1851)." *Silver* 5 (November–December 1972): 8–11.

Greengard 1966
Greengard, Bernard C. "Hugh M. G. Garden." *Prairie School Review* 3 (First Quarter, 1966): 5–18.

Groft 1981
Groft, Tammis Kane. *Cast with Style: Nineteenth Century Cast-Iron Stoves from the Albany Area.* Albany, N.Y.: Albany Institute of History and Art, 1981.

Hall 1996
Hall, John. *John Hall and the Grecian Style in America: The Cabinet Makers' Assistant; A Series of Select and Original Modern Designs for Dwelling Houses; and A New and Concise Method of Hand-Railing.* 1840. Reprint, with an essay by Thomas Gordon Smith. New York: Acanthus Press, 1996.

Hamilton 1992
Hamilton, Charles F. *Roycroft Collectibles.* Tavares, Fla.: SPS Publications, 1992.

Hamlin 1964
Hamlin, Talbot. *Greek Revival Architecture in America.* 1944. Reprint. New York: Dover Publications, 1964.

Hammons 1994
Hammons, Mark. "Purcell and Elmslie, Architects." In *Art and Life on the Upper Mississippi, 1890–1915.* Ed. by Michael Conforti. Newark, Del.: University of Delaware Press; London and Toronto: Associated University Presses in association with Minneapolis Institute of Arts, 1994.

Hanks 1980
Hanks, David A. "Daniel Pabst: Philadelphia Cabinetmaker." *Art and Antiques* 3 (January–February 1980): 94–101.

Hanks 1981
———. *Innovative Furniture in America from 1800 to the Present.* New York: Horizon Press, 1981.

Hanks 1986
———. "Herter Brothers: Art in Furniture Design." *Journal of Decorative and Propaganda Arts* 1 (Spring 1986): 32–39.

Hanks 1989
———. *Frank Lloyd Wright, Preserving an Architectural Heritage: Decorative Designs from the Domino's Pizza Collection.* New York: E. P. Dutton, 1989.

Hanks and Peirce 1983
Hanks, David A., and Donald C. Peirce. *The Virginia Carroll Crawford Collection of American Decorative Arts, 1825–1917.* Atlanta: High Museum of Art, 1983.

Hanks and Talbott 1977
Hanks, David A., and Page Talbott. "Daniel Pabst-Philadelphia Cabinetmaker." *Bulletin* (Philadelphia Museum of Art) 73 (April 1977): 3–24.

Harwood 1997
Harwood, Barry, R. *The Furniture of George Hunzinger: Invention and Innovation in Nineteenth-Century America.* Brooklyn: Brooklyn Museum of Art, 1997.

Hauserman 1968
Hauserman, Dianne D. "Alexander Roux and his 'Plain and Artistic Furniture.'" *The Magazine Antiques* 93 (February 1968): 210–217.

Hawes 1966
Hawes, Lloyd E. "Hugh Cornwall Robertson and the Chelsea Period." *The Magazine Antiques* 89 (March 1966): 409–413.

Hawley 1987
Hawley, Henry. "American Furniture of the Mid-Nineteenth Century." *Bulletin of the Cleveland Museum of Art* 74 (May 1987): 185–215.

H. Henderson 1911
Henderson, Helen W. *The Pennsylvania Academy of Fine Arts and other Collections of Philadelphia.* Boston: L. C. Page & Co., 1911.

M. Henderson 1997
Henderson, Mary C. *The New Amsterdam: The Biography of a Broadway Theater.* New York: A Round Table Press Book, Hyperion, 1997.

High Museum of Art 1980
High Museum of Art. *A Thing of Beauty.* Atlanta: High Museum of Art, 1980.

Hirschl & Adler Galleries 1989
Hirschl & Adler Galleries. *From Architecture to Object: Masterworks of the American Arts and Crafts Movement.* New York: Hirschl & Adler Galleries, 1989.

Hirschl & Adler Galleries 1991
———. *Neo-Classicism in America: Inspiration and Innovation, 1810–1840.* New York: Hirschl & Adler Galleries, 1991.

Hitchcock 1942
Hitchcock, Henry-Russell. *In the Nature of Materials, 1887–1941: The Buildings of Frank Lloyd Wright.* New York: Duell, Sloan and Pearce, 1942.

Holland 1973
Holland, Eugenia Calvert. *Edwin Bennett, 1818–1908, and the Products of His Baltimore Pottery.* Baltimore: Maryland Historical Society, 1973.

Hood 1971
Hood, Graham. *American Silver: A History of Style, 1650–1900.* New York: Praeger Publishers, 1971.

Hosley 1990
Hosley, William. *The Japan Idea: Art and Life in Victorian America.* Hartford, Conn.: Wadsworth Athenaeum, 1990.

Hough 1989
Hough, Samuel J. "The Class of 1870 Gorham Sterling Ice Bowls." *Silver* 22 (September–October 1989): 30–35.

Howe 1976
Howe, Katherine Susman. "The Gothic Revival Style in America, 1830–1870." *The Magazine Antiques* 109 (May 1976): 1014–1023.

Howe and Warren 1976
Howe, Katherine Susman, and David B. Warren. *The Gothic Revival Style in America, 1830–1870.* Houston, Tex.: Museum of Fine Arts, Houston, 1976.

Howe, Frelinghuysen, and Voorsanger 1994
Howe, Katherine Susman, Alice Cooney Frelinghuysen, and Catherine Hoover Voorsanger. *Herter Brothers: Furniture and Interiors for a Gilded Age.* New York: Harry N. Abrams with the Museum of Fine Arts, Houston, 1994.

Hudson River Museum 1973
Hudson River Museum. *Eastlake-Influenced American Furniture, 1875–1890.* Yonkers, N.Y.: Hudson River Museum, 1973.

Hudson River Museum 1990
———. *The Sphinx and the Lotus: The Egyptian Movement in American Decorative Arts, 1865–1935.* Yonkers, N.Y.: Hudson River Museum, 1990.

Hunter 1925
Hunter, George Leland. *The Practical Book of Tapestries.* Philadelphia and London: J. B. Lippincott Company, 1925.

Ingerman 1963
Ingerman, Elizabeth A. "Personal Experiences of an Old New York Cabinetmaker." *The Magazine Antiques* 84 (November 1963): 576–580.

Innes 1976
Innes, Lowell. *Pittsburgh Glass, 1797–1891: A History and Guide for Collectors.* Boston: Houghton Mifflin Company, 1976.

Jandl 1975
Jandl, H. Ward. "George Platt, interior decorator (1812–1873)." *The Magazine Antiques* 107 (June 1975): 1154–1157.

Janes, Kirtland and Company 1971
Janes, Kirtland and Company. *Ornamental Ironwork.* 1870. Reprint. Princeton, N.J.: Pyne Press, 1971.

Johnson 1972
Johnson, J. Stewart. "John Jelliff, Cabinetmaker." *The Magazine Antiques* 102 (August 1972): 256–261.

Jones 1986
Jones, Owen. *The Grammar of Ornament.* 1856. Reprint. New York: Portland House, 1986.

Kane 1976
Kane, Patricia E. "Furniture Owned by the Massachusetts Historical Society." *The Magazine Antiques* 109 (May 1976): 960–969.

Kaplan 1987
Kaplan, Wendy. *"The Art that is Life": The Arts and Crafts Movement in America, 1875–1920.* Boston: Museum of Fine Arts, Boston, 1987.

Kaplan, May, 1987
———. "The Furniture of Frank Furness." *The Magazine Antiques* 131 (May 1987): 1088–1095.

Keen 1978
Keen, Kirsten Hoving. *American Art Pottery 1875–1930.* Wilmington, Del.: Delaware Art Museum, 1978.

Klapthor 1975
Klapthor, Margaret Brown. *Official White House China, 1789 to the Present.* Washington, D.C.: Smithsonian Institution Press, 1975.

Knittle 1927
Knittle, Rhea Mansfield. *Early American Glass.* New York: The Century Company, 1927.

Koch 1967
Koch, Robert. "Elbert Hubbard's Roycrofters as Artist-Craftsmen." *Winterthur Portfolio* 3 (1967): 67–82.

Komanecky and Butera 1984
Komanecky, Michael, and Virginia Fabbri Butera. *The Folding Image: Screens by Western Artists of the Nineteenth and Twentieth Centuries.* New Haven, Conn.: Yale University Art Gallery, 1984.

Kovel and Kovel 1993
Kovel, Ralph, and Terry Kovel. *Kovels' American Art Pottery: The Collector's Guide to Makers, Marks and Factory Histories.* New York: Crown Publishers, 1993.

Kumm 1943
Kumm, Marguerite. "The Glass and China Cupboard." *The Magazine Antiques* 44 (September 1943): 127–128.

Lee 1933
Lee, Ruth Webb. "Peachblow Glass." *The Magazine Antiques* 24 (August 1933): 48–50.

Lehnert 1991
Lehnert, Gene. "Building the king of desks." *Woodworking* (March–April 1991): 54–57

Libbey Glass Company 1968
Libbey Glass Company. *Cut Glass.* 1896. Reprint, Toledo, Ohio: Antique and Historic Glass Foundation, 1968.

Ludwig 1983
Ludwig, Coy L. *The Arts and Crafts Movement in New York State: 1890s–1920s.* Hamilton, N.Y. : Gallery Association of New York State, 1983.

Lycett 1941
Lycett, Lydia. "China Painting by the Lycetts." *Atlanta Historical Bulletin* 6 (July 1941): 201–214.

Lyon 1889
Lyon, Robert P. *The Official Reference Book of the Furniture Trade Giving the Names, Addresses and Credit Ratings of the Furniture, Carpet, Upholstery, Undertaking, Wall Paper, Picture Frame, Looking Glass, Bedding and Cabinet Wood Trades.* [New York]: 1889.

Madigan 1975
Madigan, Mary Jean Smith. "The Influence of Charles Locke Eastlake on American Furniture Manufacture, 1870–90." *Winterthur Portfolio* 10 (1975): 1–22.

Maher 1975
Maher, James T. *The Twilight of Splendor: Chronicles of the Age of American Palaces.* Boston: Little, Brown and Company, 1975.

Makinson 1977
Makinson, Randell L. *Greene & Greene: Architecture as Fine Art.* Salt Lake City, Utah; Santa Barbara, Calif.: Perigrine Smith, Inc., 1977.

Makinson 1979
———. *Greene and Greene: Furniture and Related Designs.* Salt Lake City, Utah, and Santa Barbara, Calif.: Perigrine Smith, Inc., 1979.

Mallach 1966
Mallach, Stanley. "Gothic Furniture Designs by Alexander Jackson Davis." Master's thesis, University of Delaware, 1966.

Mankowitz and Haggar 1957
Mankowitz, Wolf, and Reginal G. Haggar. *The Concise Encyclopedia of English Pottery and Porcelain.* New York: Hawthorn Books, [1957].

Maroon 1993
Maroon, Fred J. *The United States Capitol.* New York: Stewart, Tabori and Chang, 1993.

McCauley 1975
McCauley, Lois B. *Maryland Historical Prints, 1752–1889.* Baltimore: Maryland Historical Society, 1975.

McClinton 1968
McClinton, Katharine Morrison. *Collecting American 19th Century Silver.* New York: Bonanza Books, 1968.

McConnell 1990
McConnell, Kevin. *Roycroft Art Metal.* West Chester, Pa.: Schiffer Publishing, 1990.

McGlauflin 1935
McGlauflin, Alice Coe, ed. *Who's Who in American Art.* Washington, D.C.: American Federation of Arts, 1935.

McKearin 1946
McKearin, Helen. "Early Nineteenth-Century Glassmaking in Ohio." *The Magazine Antiques* 49 (January 1946): 52–55.

McKearin and McKearin 1941
McKearin, George S., and Helen McKearin. *American Glass.* New York: Crown Publishers, 1941.

Meixner 1985
Meixner, Laura L. "Will Hicok Low (1853–1932): His Early Career and Barbizon Experience." *American Art Journal* 17 (autumn 1985): 51–70.

Memorial Art Gallery 1972
Memorial Art Gallery. *A Rediscovery—Harvey Ellis: Artist, Architect.* Rochester, N.Y.: Memorial Art Gallery, University of Rochester, 1972.

The Metropolitan Museum of Art 1970
Metropolitan Museum of Art. *19th Century America: Furniture and Other Decorative Arts.* New York: The Metropolitan Museum of Art, 1970.

The Metropolitan Museum of Art 1986
———. *In Pursuit of Beauty: Americans and the Aesthetic Movement.* New York: The Metropolitan Museum of Art, 1986.

The Metropolitan Museum of Art 1992
———. *Alexander Jackson Davis: American Architect, 1803–1892.* New York: Rizzoli International Publications, 1992.

The Metropolitan Museum of Art 1993
———. *The New York Obelisk or How Cleopatra's Needle Came to New York and What Happened When It Got Here.* New York: The Metropolitan Museum of Art and Abrams, 1993.

Meyer 1997
Meyer, Marilee Boyd. *Inspiring Reform: Boston's Arts and Crafts Movement.* Wellesley, Mass.: Davis Museum and Cultural Center, 1997.

Mipaas 1979
Mipaas, Esther. "Cast-Iron Furnishings: Sitting Pretty in the Garden." *American Art and Antiques* 2 (May–June 1979): 34–41.

Mitchell 1972
Mitchell, James. "Ott & Brewer: Etruria in America." *Winterthur Portfolio* 7 (1972:) 217–228.

Monkhouse and Michie 1986
Monkhouse, Christopher P., and Thomas S. Michie. *American Furniture in Pendleton House.* Providence, R. I.: Museum of Art, Rhode Island School of Design, 1986.

Montgomery 1993
Montgomery, Susan J. *The Ceramics of William H. Grueby.* Lambertville, N.J.: Arts and Crafts Quarterly Press, 1993.

Moss 1988
Moss, Roger W. *Lighting for Historic Buildings.* Washington, D.C.: Preservation Press, 1988.

Myers 1987
Myers, Susan H. "Edwin Bennett: An English Potter in Baltimore." *Ars Ceramica* 4 (1987): 31–35.

Myers 1992
———. "Aesthetic Inspirations: Baltimore Potters and the Art Craze." *American Ceramic Circle Journal* 8 (1992): 25–54.

National Cyclopaedia 1893
The National Cyclopaedia of American Biography. Vol. 3. New York: James T. White and Company, 1893.

National Gallery of Canada 1994
National Gallery of Canada. *Egyptomania: Egypt in Western Art, 1730–1930.* Ottawa: National Gallery of Canada, 1994.

Newark Museum 1963
Newark Museum. *Classical America 1815–1845.* Newark, N.J.: Newark Museum, 1963.

Newman 1987
Newman, Harold. *An Illustrated Dictionary of Glass.* New York and London: Thames and Hudson, 1987.

Newton 1942
Newton, Roger Hale. *Town and Davis Architects.* New York: Columbia University Press, 1942.

Noever 1992
Noever, Peter. *Josef Hoffman Designs.* Vienna and Munich: Austrian Museum of Applied Arts and Prestel-Verlag, 1992.

Optiz 1986
Opitz, Glenn B., ed. *Mantle Fielding's Dictionary of American Painters, Sculptors, and Engravers.* Poughkeepsie, N.Y.: Apollo, 1986.

Otto 1965
Otto, Celia Jackson. *American Furniture of the Nineteenth Century.* New York: Viking Press, 1965.

Page 1980
Page, Marian. *Furniture Designed by Architects.* New York: Whitney Library of Design, 1980.

Paine's Furniture Company 1935
Paine's Furniture Company. *One Hundred Years at Paine's: 1835–1935.* 1935.

Palmer 1993
Palmer, Arlene. *Glass in Early America: Selections from the Henry Francis du Pont Winterthur Museum.* Winterthur, Del.: The Henry Francis du Pont Winterthur Museum, 1993.

Parry 1996
Parry, Linda, ed. *William Morris.* London: Philip Wilson Publishers with The Victoria and Albert Museum, 1996.

Patterson 1979
Patterson, Jerry E. *Porcelain.* Smithsonian Illustrated Library of Antiques. New York: Cooper-Hewitt, National Design Museum, Smithsonian Institution, 1979.

Pearce and Pearce 1966
Pearce, John N., and Lorraine W. Pearce. "More on the Meeks Cabinetmakers." *The Magazine Antiques* 90 (July 1966): 69–73.

Pearce, Pearce, and Smith 1964
Pearce, John N., Lorraine W. Pearce, and Robert C. Smith. "The Meeks Family of Cabinetmakers." *The Magazine Antiques* 85 (April 1964): 414–420.

Pears 1927
Pears, Thomas Clinton, Jr. "The First Successful Flint Glass Factory in America." *The Magazine Antiques* 11 (March 1927): 201–205.

Pearson 1975
Pearson, J. Michael. *Encyclopedia of American Cut and Engraved Glass, 1880–1917*. Vol. 1. Miami Beach, Fla.: J. Michael Pearson, 1975.

Peck 1991
Peck, Herbert. *The Book of Rookwood Pottery*. Cincinnati: Cincinnati Art Galleries, 1991.

Peirce 1979
Peirce, Donald C. "Mitchell and Rammelsberg, Cincinnati Furniture Manufacturers, 1847–1881." *Winterthur Portfolio* 13 (1979): 209–229.

Peirce, May, 1979
———. "New York Furniture at the Brooklyn Museum." *The Magazine Antiques* 115 (May 1979): 994–1003.

Philadelphia Merchants 1856
The Philadelphia Merchants' and Manufacturers' Business Directory for 1856–57. Philadelphia: Griswold & Co., 1856.

Philadelphia Museum of Art 1976
Philadelphia Museum of Art. *Philadelphia: Three Centuries of American Art*. Philadelphia: Philadelphia Museum of Art, 1976.

Philadelphia Museum of Art 1978
———. *The Second Empire: Art in France under Napoleon III*. Philadelphia: Philadelphia Museum of Art, 1978.

Philadelphia Shopping 1859
The Philadelphia Shopping Guide and Housekeeper's Companion for 1859. Philadelphia: S. E. Cohen, 1859.

Placzek 1982
Placzek, Adolph K., ed. *Macmillan Encyclopedia of Architects*. Vol. 2. New York: Macmillan Publishing Co., Free Press, 1982.

Poesch 1984
Poesch, Jessie. *Newcomb Pottery: An Enterprise for Southern Women, 1895–1940*. Exton, Pa.: Schiffer Publishing, 1984.

Proddow and Healy 1987
Proddow, Penny, and Debra Healy. *American Jewelry: Glamour and Tradition*. New York: Rizzoli, 1987.

Purcell and Elmslie 1912
Purcell, William Gray and George G. Elmslie. "The American Renaissance?" *Craftsman* 21 (January 1912): 430–435.

Purcell and Elmslie 1975
———. "The Work of Purcell and Elmslie." In *Prairie School Architecture, Studies from 'The Western Architect.'* 1915. Reprint. Ed. by H. Allen Brooks. Toronto: University of Toronto Press, 1975.

Quimby 1995
Quimby, Ian M. G., with Dianne Johnson. *American Silver at Winterthur*. Winterthur, Del.: Henry Francis du Pont Winterthur Museum, 1995, distributed by the University Press of Virginia.

Rainwater 1986
Rainwater, Dorothy T. *Encyclopedia of American Silver Manufacturers*. West Chester, Pa.: Schiffer Publishing, 1986.

Rainwater and Rainwater 1988
Rainwater, Dorothy T., and H. Ivan Rainwater. *American Silverplate*. West Chester, Pa.: Schiffer Publishing, 1988.

Report 1861
Report of the Commissioner of Patents for the Year 1860. Washington: George W. Bowman, Printer, 1861.

Revi 1967
Revi, Albert Christian. *Nineteenth-Century Glass: Its Genesis and Development*. Rev. ed. London and Camden, N.J.: Nelson, 1967.

Roell 1989
Roell, Craig H. *Pianos in America: 1890–1940*. Chapel Hill, N.C.; London: University of North Carolina Press, 1989.

Romeyn 1983
Romeyn, Carlyn Crannell. *The Lycetts*. [Oklahoma City]: International Porcelain Art Teachers, Inc., 1983.

Rose, February, 1938
Rose, James H. "Fresh Reflections on American Glass." *The Magazine Antiques* 33 (February 1938): 81–82.

Rose, December, 1938
———. "The Editor's Attic, Again Pressed Window Panes." *The Magazine Antiques* 34 (December 1938): 294–295.

Rose, February, 1947
———. "Lacy Glass Window Panes, Their Use, Process and Origin." *The Magazine Antiques* 51 (February 1947): 120–121.

Rose, September, 1947
———. "More Lacy Glass Window Panes: An Editorial Footnote." *The Magazine Antiques* 52 (September 1947): 186.

Rose 1954
———. *The Story of American Pressed Glass of the Lacy Period, 1825–1850*. Corning, N.Y.: Corning Museum of Glass, 1954.

Roseberry 1964
Roseberry, Cecil R. *Capitol Story*. Albany, N.Y.: State of New York, 1964.

Rosenberger 1948–50
Rosenberger, Homer T. "Thomas Ustick Walter and the Completion of the United States Capitol." *Records of the Columbia Historical Society of Washington, D.C.*, 50 (1948–1950): 273–322.

Roth 1977
Roth, Rodris. "A Patent Model by John Henry Belter." *The Magazine Antiques* 111 (May 1977): 1038–1040.

Roycroft Art Museum 1992
Roycroft Art Museum. *Karl Kipp and His Work at the Tookay Shop, East Aurora, New York*. Ca. 1914. Reprint. East Aurora, N.Y.: Roycroft Art Museum, 1992.

Rudoe 1991
Rudoe, Judy. *Decorative Arts, 1850–1950: A Catalogue of the British Museum Collection.* London: British Museum Press, 1991.

Saliga 1990
Saliga, Pauline, ed. *Fragments of Chicago's Past. The Collection of Architectural Fragments at The Art Institute of Chicago.* Chicago: The Art Institute of Chicago, 1990.

Sargent 1906
Sargent, Irene. "The Work of Arthur J. Stone, Silversmith." *Keystone* 27 (January 1906): 33–36.

Sargent 1919
———. "Arthur Stone, Silversmith, Successor to Paul Revere." *Keystone* 47 (September 1919): 121–125.

Scharf and Westcott 1884
Scharf, J. Thomas, and Thompson Westcott. *History of Philadelphia, 1609–1884.* Philadelphia: L. H. Everts & Co., 1884.

Schuyler 1879
Schuyler, Montgomery. "The Capitol of New York." *Scribner's Monthly* 19, no. 2 (December 1879): 161–178.

Schwartz, Stanek, and True 1981
Schwartz, Marvin D., Edward J. Stanek, and Douglas K. True. *The Furniture of John Henry Belter and the Rococo Revival: An Inquiry into Nineteenth-Century Furniture Design Through a Study of the Gloria and Richard Manney Collection.* New York: E. P. Dutton, 1981.

Schweiger 1984
Schweiger, Werner J. *Wiener Werkstätte: Design in Vienna, 1903–1932.* New York: Abbeville Press, 1984.

Seale 1986
Seale, William. *The President's House.* Washington, D.C.: White House Historical Association with the cooperation of the National Geographic Society and Harry N. Abrams, 1986.

Seidler 1982
Seidler, Jan M. "A Tradition in Transition: The Boston Furniture Industry, 1840–1880." *Nineteenth Century* 8, nos. 3–4 (1982): 65–84.

Shadel 1970
Shadel, Jane. "Glass Lighting Devices." *The Magazine Antiques* 98 (December 1970), pp. 916–921.

Sheraton 1972
Sheraton, Thomas. *The Cabinet-Maker and Upholsterer's Drawing-Book.* 1793. Reprint. New York: Dover Publications, 1972.

Sherrill 1976
Sherrill, Sarah B. "Living with Antiques: Lee B. Anderson's Collection of American Gothic Revival Furniture and Paintings." *The Magazine Antiques* 109 (May 1976): 1032–1041.

Showalter and Driesbach 1983
Showalter, J. Camille, and Janice Driesbach, eds. *Wooton Patent Desks: A Place for Everything and Everything in Its Place.* Indianapolis, Ind., and Oakland, Calif.: Indiana State Museum and the Oakland Museum, 1983.

Silliman and Goodrich 1854
Silliman, B., and C. R. Goodrich. *The World of Science, Art, and Industry Illustrated from Examples in the New York Exhibition, 1853–54.* New York: G. P. Putnam and Company, 1854.

M. Smith 1983
Smith, Mary Ann. *Gustav Stickley: The Craftsman.* Syracuse, N.Y.: Syracuse University Press, 1983.

N. Smith 1978
Smith, Nancy A. "Piano-forte Manufacturing in Boston." *Old-Time New England* 69 (summer–fall 1978): 37–47.

R. Smith 1958
Smith, Robert C. "Late Classical Furniture in the United States, 1820–1850." *The Magazine Antiques* 74 (December 1958): 519–523.

R. Smith 1959
———. "Gothic and Elizabethan Revival furniture, 1800–1850." *The Magazine Antiques* 75 (March 1959): 272–276.

R. Smith 1964
———. "Philadelphia Empire Furniture by Antoine Gabriel Quervelle." *The Magazine Antiques* 86 (September 1964): 304–309.

W. Smith 1877
Smith, Walter. *The Masterpieces of the Centennial International Exhibition.* Vol. 2, *Industrial Art.* Philadelphia: Gebbie and Barrie, 1877.

Snyder 1985
Snyder, Ellen Marie. "Victory over Nature, Victorian Cast-Iron Seating Furniture." *Winterthur Portfolio* 20 (winter 1985): 221–242.

Soeffing 1995
Soeffing, D. Albert. "Some Bailey & Co. Marks and Their Significance." *Silver* 28 (November–December, 1995): pp. 12–15.

Spillman 1977
Spillman, Jane Shadel. "Glasses with American Views." *Journal of Glass Studies* 19 (1977): 134–146.

Spillman 1980
———. "Glasses with American Views—Addenda." *Journal of Glass Studies* 22 (1980): 78–81.

Spillman 1981
———. *American and European Pressed Glass in the Corning Museum of Glass.* Corning, N.Y.: Corning Museum of Glass, 1981.

Spillman 1994
———. "Glasses engraved with American views." *The Magazine Antiques* 146 (July 1994): 78–85.

Spillman 1997
———. *The American Cut Glass Industry: T. G. Hawkes and his Competitors.* Woodbridge, England: The Antique Collectors' Club with The Corning Museum of Glass, 1997.

Springer 1980
Springer, Lynn E. "American Furniture." *St. Louis Art Museum Bulletin,* n.s., 15, no. 3 (summer 1980): 1–48.

Stefano 1974
Stefano, Frank, Jr. "James Clewes, Nineteenth-Century Potter, Part II: The American Experience." *The Magazine Antiques* 105 (March 1974): 553–555.

Stern, Gilmartin, and Massengale 1983
Stern, Robert A. M., Gregory Gilmartin, and John Montague Massengale. *New York, 1900: Metropolitan Architecture and Urbanism 1890–1915.* New York: Rizzoli International Publications, 1983.

St. John 1981
St. John, Richard. "Horned Furniture: A Hit in the 1800s." *Texas Longhorn Journal* 6 (November–December 1981): 60–61.

Stickley 1904
Stickley, Gustav. "Chips from the Craftsman Workshop." *Craftsman* 5 (February 1904): 518–520.

Stickley 1909
———. *Craftsman Homes, Second Series.* New York: Craftsman Publishing Company, 1909.

Stickley 1991
———. *The 1912 and 1915 Gustav Stickley Craftsman Furniture Catalogs.* New York and Philadelphia: The Athenaeum of Philadelphia and Dover Publications, 1991.

Stickley Craftsman 1979
Stickley Craftsman Furniture Catalogues: Unabridged Reprints of Two Mission Furniture Catalogs: "Craftsman Furniture Made by Gustav Stickley" and "The Work of L. & J. G. Stickley." New York: Dover Publications, 1979.

Stiles 1884
Stiles, Henry R., ed. *The Civil, Political, Professional and Ecclesiastical History and Commercial and Industrial Record of the County of Kings and the City of Brooklyn, N.Y. from 1683 to 1884.* New York: W. W. Munsell & Co., 1884.

Stokes and Haskell 1932
Stokes, I. N. Phelps, and Daniel Haskell. *American Historical Prints: Early Views of American Cities from the Phelps Stokes and Other Collections.* New York: New York Public Library, 1932.

Stone 1902
Stone, Mrs. Arthur J. "Byways Among Craftsmen." *Handicraft* I (November 1902): 169–189.

D. Stradling 1983
Stradling, Diana. "Teco Pottery and the Green Phenomenon." *Tiller* 1 (March–April 1983): 9–36.

Stradling and Denker 1997
Stradling, Diana, and Ellen Paul Denker. *Jersey City: Shaping America's Pottery Industry, 1825–1892.* Jersey City, N.J.: Jersey City Museum, 1997.

J. Stradling 1976
Stradling, J. G. "American Ceramics and the Philadelphia Centennial." *The Magazine Antiques* 110 (July 1976): 146–158.

Strickland 1978
Strickland, Peter L. L. "Furniture by the Lejambre family of Philadelphia." *The Magazine Antiques* 113 (March 1978): 600–613.

Sutton 1972
Sutton, Royal. *The Face of Courage: The Indian Photographs of Frank A. Rinehart.* Fort Collins, Colo.: Old Army Press, 1972.

Swan 1986
Swan, Martha Louise. *American Cut and Engraved Glass of the Brilliant Period in Historical Perspective.* Radnor, Pa.: Wallace-Homestead Book Company, 1986.

Teeters 1963
Teeters, Negley K. "Caleb Lownes of Philadelphia: 1754–1828." *Prison Journal* XLIII (autumn 1963): 1–12.

Thomas, Lewis, and Cohen 1991
Thomas, George C., Michael J. Lewis, and Jeffrey A. Cohen. *Frank Furness: The Complete Works.* New York: Princeton Architectural Press, 1991.

Toledo Museum of Art 1963
Toledo Museum of Art. *The New England Glass Company, 1818–1888.* Toledo, Ohio: Toledo Museum of Art, 1963.

Toledo Museum of Art 1968
———. *Libbey Glass, A Tradition of 150 Years.* Toledo, Ohio: Toledo Museum of Art, 1968.

Trapp 1986
Trapp, Kenneth R. "The Shop of the Crafters at Cincinnati, 1904–1920." *Tiller* 2 (January 1986): 8–25.

Trapp 1993
———. *The Arts and Crafts Movement in California: Living the Good Life.* New York, London, and Paris: Abbeville Press, 1993.

Truman 1993
Truman, Charles, ed. *Sotheby's Concise Encyclopedia of Silver.* London: Conran Octopus Limited, 1993.

Turner 1996
Turner, Jane, ed. *The Dictionary of Art, Vol. 31.* London: Macmillan Publishers, 1996.

Venable 1994
Venable, Charles L. *Silver in America, 1840–1940: A Century of Splendor.* Dallas: Dallas Museum of Art, 1994.

Victoria and Albert Museum 1987
Victoria and Albert Museum. *Art and Design in Europe and America 1800–1900.* New York: E. P. Dutton, 1987.

Vincent 1974
Vincent, Clare. "John Henry Belter: Manufacturer of All Kinds of Fine Furniture." In *Technological Innovation and the Decorative Arts.* Winterthur Conference Report, 1973. Ed. by Ian M. G. Quimby and Polly Anne Earl. Charlottesville, Va.: University Press of Virginia, 1974, pp. 206–234.

Vinci 1979
Vinci, John. *The Art Institute of Chicago: The Stock Exchange Trading Room.* Chicago: The Art Institute of Chicago, 1979.

Volpe and Cathers 1988
Volpe, Tod M., and Beth Cathers. *Treasures of the Arts and Crafts Movement, 1890–1920.* Text by Alistair Duncan. New York: Harry N. Abrams, 1988.

Von Khrum 1978
Von Khrum, Paul. *Silversmiths of New York City, 1684–1850.* New York: Paul Von Khrum, 1978.

Waite and Waite 1973
Waite, John J., and Diana S. Waite. "Stovemakers of Troy, New York." *The Magazine Antiques* 103 (January 1973): 136–144.

Ward and Ward 1979
Ward, Barbara McLean, and Gerald W. R. Ward. *Silver in American Life.* New York: American Federation of Arts, 1979.

Waterfield
Waterfield, Hermione. *Fabergé: The Forbes Magazine Collection.* N.p., n.d.

Waters 1981
Waters, Deborah Dependahl. "The Workmanship of an American Artist: Philadelphia's Precious Metals and Craftsmen, 1788–1832." Ph.D. diss., University of Delaware, 1981.

Watkins 1930
Watkins, Lura Woodside. *Cambridge Glass, 1818 to 1888.* New York: Bramhall House, 1930.

Watkins 1944
———. "Low Art Tiles." *The Magazine Antiques* 45 (May 1944): 250–252.

Watkins 1946
———. "Henderson of Jersey City and His Pitchers." *The Magazine Antiques* 50 (December 1946): 388–392.

Watkins 1949
———. "The Providence Flint Glass Company," *The Magazine Antiques* 55 (March 1949): 190–191.

Watkins 1968
———. *Early New England Potters and their Wares.* 1950. Reprint. Hamden, Conn.: Archon Books, 1968.

Weidman 1984
Weidman, Gregory R. *Furniture in Maryland, 1740–1940: The Collections of the Maryland Historical Society.* Baltimore: Maryland Historical Society, 1984.

Weiss 1981
Weiss, Peg, ed. *Adelaide Alsop Robineau: Glory in Porcelain.* Syracuse, N.Y.: Syracuse University Press and the Everson Museum of Art, 1981.

White and Willensky 1988
White, Norval, and Elliot Willensky, eds. *AIA Guide to New York City.* San Diego: Harcourt Brace Jovanovich, 1988.

Whitney Museum of American Art 1982
Whitney Museum of American Art, Fairfield County. *Shape and Environment: Furniture by American Architects.* New York: Whitney Museum of American Art, Fairfield County, 1982.

Whitney Museum of American Art 1985
Whitney Museum of American Art. *High Styles: 20th Century American Design.* New York: Whitney Museum of American Art and Summit Books, 1985.

Wiener and Lipkowitz 1975
Wiener, Herbert, and Freda Lipkowitz. *Rarities in American Cut Glass.* Houston, Tex.: Collectors House of Books, 1975.

K. Wilson 1958
Wilson, Kenneth M. "The Mount Washington Glass Works and Its Successors, 1837–1958." *The Magazine Antiques* 74 (July 1958): 46–48.

K. Wilson 1972
———. *New England Glass and Glassmakers.* New York: Thomas Y. Crowell Company, 1972.

K. Wilson 1994
———. *American Glass: 1760–1930.* New York: Hudson Hills Press with the Toledo Museum of Art, 1994.

T. Wilson 1825
Wilson, Thomas. *The Philadelphia Directory and Stranger's Guide for 1825.* Philadelphia: Thomas Wilson and William D. Vandau, 1825.

Withey and Withey 1956
Withey, Henry F., and Elsie Rathburn Withey. *Dictionary of American Architects (Deceased).* Los Angeles: New Age Publishing Company, 1956.

Withington 1935
Withington, Sidney. *The First Twenty Years of Railroads in Connecticut.* New Haven, Conn.: Published for the Tercentenary Commission of the State of Connecticut by Yale University Press, no. XLV, 1935.

Wright 1932
Wright, Frank Lloyd. *An Autobiography.* New York, London, and Toronto: Longmans, Green and Co., 1932.

Young 1973
Young, William C. *Documents of American Theater History. Vol. 2, Famous American Playhouses, 1900–1971.* Chicago: American Library Association, 1973.

Zapata, March, 1991
Zapata, Janet. "The Rediscovery of Paulding Farnham: Tiffany's Designer *Extraordinaire,* Part I: Jewelry." *The Magazine Antiques* 139 (March 1991): 556–567.

Zapata, April, 1991
———. "The Rediscovery of Paulding Farnham, Tiffany's Designer *Extraordinaire,* Part II: Silver." *The Magazine Antiques* 139 (April 1991): 718–729.

Zapata 1993
———. *The Jewelry and Enamels of Louis Comfort Tiffany.* New York: Harry N. Abrams, 1993.

Index

Photo Credits

COLOR PLATES

Peter Harholdt: 3, 12, 18, 20, 21, 28, 31, 32, 34, 38, 39, 46, 49, 52, 55, 62, 66, 70, 73, 78, 83, 84, 92, 96, 99, 102, 105, 106, 118, 122, 126, 128, 130, 132, 135, 146, 150, 154, 156, 158, 163, 168, 177, 178, 180, 183, 186, 188, 193, 194, 196, 198, 199, 204, 206, 209, 218, 221, 223, 234, 250, 257, 260, 264, 266, 270, 272, 273, 274, 275, 277, 278, 281, 285, 286, 287, 288, 290, 291, 294, 297, 303, 306, 321, 322, 323, 324, 325, 329, 336, 340, 350, 353, 356, 361, 363, 364, 366, 368, 370, 374, 376, 378, 386

Michael McKelvey: 17, 24, 34, 42, 44, 48, 51, 76, 100, 101, 138, 140, 164, 195, 202, 240, 255, 284, 295, 312, 313, 333, 346, 348, 387

David Zeiger: 25, 40, 56, 74, 80, 86, 90, 110, 112, 134, 143, 184, 196, 197, 200, 224, 225, 227, 228, 232, 241, 242, 244, 245, 246, 247, 248, 249, 252, 253, 254, 258, 259, 268, 276, 282, 283, 285, 289, 292, 298, 300, 301, 175, 305, 306, 310, 315, 316, 318, 327, 330, 331, 334, 343, 344, 347, 354

Robert Wells: 26, 60, 68, 69, 88, 108, 116, 120, 136, 144, 145, 161, 166, 170, 190, 210, 212, 214, 217, 230, 236, 237, 239, 262, 265, 326, 338, 380, 384

Helga Photo Studio: 50, 64, 94, 174

Mary Carolyn Pindar: 382

Unless noted below, illustration photos were provided by the lending institution.

FIGURES (PAGE NO., FIG. NO.)

The Metropolitan Museum of Art: 29, fig. 1; 53, fig. 2; 117, fig. 1; 339, fig. 1

United States Patent Office: 47, fig. 1; 59, fig. 1; 65, fig. 1; 165, fig. 1; 167, fig.1; 169, fig. 1; 173, fig. 2; 175, fig. 1; 291, fig. 1

Peter Hill: 53, fig. 1

High Museum of Art: 56, fig. 1; 320, fig. 1; Peter Harholdt, 211, figs. 1-2; 213, fig. 3; 215, fig. 4; 216, fig. 1; Helga Photo Studio, 219, fig. 2-3

The Brooklyn Museum of Art: 57, fig. 2

The Winterthur Library. Printed Book and Periodical Collection: 61, fig. 1; 98, fig. 2; 157, fig. 1; 179, fig. 1; 187, fig. 1

Old Sturbridge Village. Photograph by Thomas Neill: 63, fig. 1

Museum of Fine Arts, Boston: 63, fig. 2

Maryland Historical Society, Baltimore; 97, fig. 1

© The Cleveland Museum of Art, 1997: 98, fig. 3

Hagley Museum and Library: 103, fig. 1

Philadelphia Museum of Art: 109, fig. 1

Brown University Library: 115, fig. 1; 143, fig. 2

Woodruff Library, Emory University: 119, fig. 1

Nina Gray: 121, figs. 1-2

Cooper-Hewitt, National Design Museum Branch, Smithsonian Institution Libraries: 137, fig. 1

Museum of the City of New York: 139, fig. 1; John Wallace Gillies, 141, fig. 1; 147, fig. 3; 261, fig. 1; 379, fig. 1;

Atlanta History Center: 131, fig. 1; 142, fig. 1; 148, fig. 1; 155, fig. 2

Newark Museum: 133, fig. 1

State Historical Society of Iowa: 172, fig. 1

Sterling and Francine Clark Art Institute Library: 182, fig. 1

Sandwich Glass Museum: 189, fig. 1

Copyright Tiffany & Co. Archives 1999. Not to be published or reproduced without prior permission. No permission for commercial use will be granted excepted by written license agreement: 195, fig. 1; 198, fig. 2; 279, fig. 1

J. Garrison and Diana Stradling: 222, fig. 1

Smithsonian Museum, National Museum of Natural History, Anthropological Archives: 311, fig. 1

The Frank Lloyd Wright Foundation, Taliesin West, Scottsdale, Arizona: 317, fig. 1; 381, fig. 1; 383, fig. 2

Design Copyright © The Frank Lloyd Wright Foundation, Taliesin West, Scottsdale, Arizona: 380, 382

Charles Hamilton: 332, fig. 1

The Fine Arts Museums of San Francisco: 351, fig. 1

Everson Museum of Art, Syracuse, New York: 352, fig. 1

University City Public Library Archives: 355, fig. 2

Avery Architectural and Fine Arts Library, Columbia University in the City of New York: 362, fig. 1; 387, fig. 1

Library of Congress: 367, fig. 1

Theodore Roosevelt Birthplace National Monument: 369, fig. 1

Architectural Archives of the University of Pennsylvania, photograph by George Thomas: 369, fig. 2

Georgia Institute of Technology Library: 371, fig. 1

Art Institute of Chicago: 377, fig. 1

William Gray Purcell Papers, Northwest Architectural Archives, University of Minnesota Libraries: 385, figs. 1–2

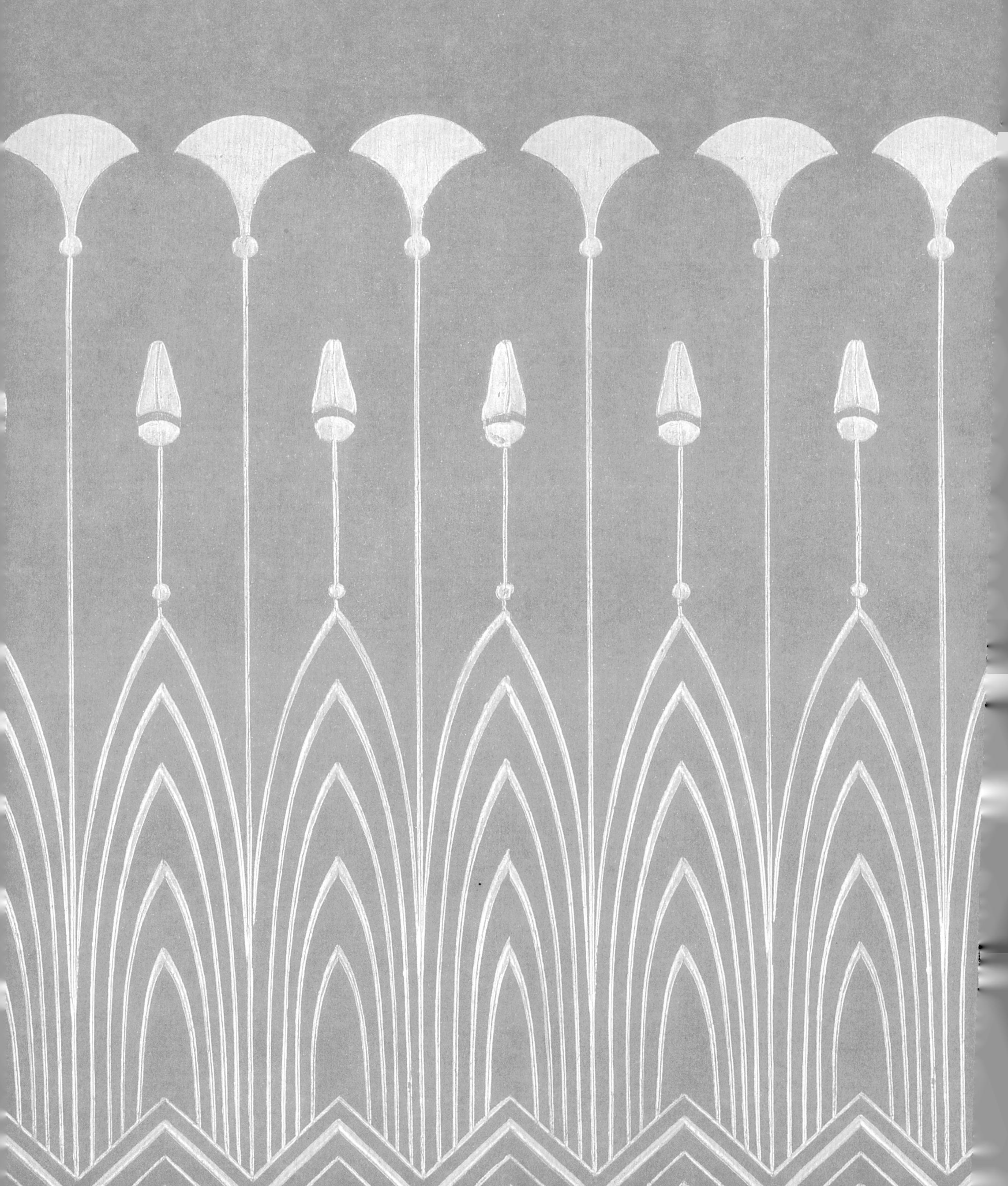